CHAMBERS
Quick
Facts

D0173768

CHAMBERS
Quick
Facts

Editor

MIN LEE

Chambers

Published 1991 by W & R Chambers Ltd
43-45 Annandale Street, Edinburgh EH7 4AZ

British Library Cataloguing in Publication Data

A catalogue record for this book is available from the
British Library

ISBN 0-550-17252 1

Compilers

      Antonia Dodds
      Thérèse Duriez
      Melanie Hanbury
      Jo Hargreaves
      Kieran Lee
      David Whyte

Cover design by John Marshall

Typeset by Charlesworth & Co Ltd
Printed in England by Clays, St Ives, plc

CONTENTS

HUMAN LIFE

HISTORY

COMMUNICATION *continued*

SCIENCE, TECHNOLOGY AND ENGINEERING

ARTS AND CULTURE

SPORTS AND GAMES

THOUGHT AND BELIEF

ALPHABETICAL CONTENTS

AN INTRODUCTION TO QUICK FACTS

This book is a collection of compelling and useful facts presented in an accessible and friendly way.

The facts are grouped thematically, so that the lists and tables follow a logical progression, from **Space** to **Earth**, through **Natural History, Human Life, History, Social Structure, Communication, Science and Technology, Arts and Culture, Sports and Games,** completing the view of human knowledge with a section on **Thought and Belief.** A thematic **Contents** lists each table under its section heading; a second, **Alphabetical Contents** ensures that the user will be able to find any topic even if (s)he is not sure to which category it belongs.

This wealth of information incorporates the latest information compiled from Chambers' own databases and many specialized sources. A proportion of the material in this book is adapted from the Ready Reference section of *The Cambridge Encyclopedia* which was edited and produced jointly by Chambers and Cambridge University Press.

The ground covered is so vast that lists and tables must be selective rather than totally comprehensive, but both coverage and treatment are exceptional for a work of this size.

ABBREVIATIONS USED IN QUICK FACTS

AD Anno Domini	F Fahrenheiht	K Kelvin
admin. administration	fl oz fluid ounce(s)	kg kilogram(s)
BC Before Christ	fl flourished (floruit)	kJ kilojoules
c century	Fr French	km kilometre(s)
c. circa	Ft foot (feet)	l litre(s)
C Celsius (Centigrade)	g gram(s)	L Lake
C central	gall gallons	Lat Latin
cc cubic centimetre(s)	Ger German	lb pound(s)
Chin Chinese	Gr Greek	l y light year(s)
cm centimetre(s)	h hour(s)	m metre(s)
Co County	ha hectare(s)	min minute(s)
cont. continued	Hung Hungarian	ml mile(s)
cu cubic	I(s) Island(s)	mm millimetre(s)
cwt hundredweight(s)	ie that is (id est)	Mt Mount(ain)
e estimate	in inch(es)	Mts Mountains
E east(ern)	Ir Irish	N north(ern)
eg for example	Ital Italian	no. number
Eng English	Jap Japanese	oz ounce(s)

ABBREVIATIONS USED IN QUICK FACTS *continued*

p(p)   page(s)
pop   population
Port   Portuguese
pt   pint(s)
r.   reigned
R   River
Russ   Russian

S   South(ern)
sec   second(s)
Span   Spanish
sq   square
St   Saint
Sta   Santa
Ste   Sainte

Swed   Swedish
TV   Television
v.   versus
vols. volumes
W   west(ern)
yd   yard(s)
Z   zodiac

Other conventions

Months in parenthesis are abbreviated to the first three letters (3 Jan 1817)

National holiday abbreviations   p 250
Currency abbreviations   p 241
Chemistry abbreviations   pp 322-3
International organizations   pp 259 and 261

SPACE

PLANETARY DATA

Planet	Distance from sun (million km/ml)				Sidereal period	Axial rotation (equatorial)	Diameter (equatorial)	
	Maximum		Minimum				km	ml
Mercury	69.4	43.0	46.8	29.0	88 d	58 d 16 h	4878	3031
Venus	109.0	67.6	107.6	66.7	224.7 d	243 d	12104	7521
Earth	152.6	94.6	147.4	91.4	365.26 [1]	23 h 56 m	12756	7927
Mars	249.2	154.5	207.3	128.5	687 d	24 h 37 m 23 s	6794	4222
Jupiter	817.4	506.8	741.6	459.8	11.86 y	9 h 50 m 30 s	142800	88700
Saturn	1512	937.6	1346	834.6	29.46 y	10 h 14 m	120000	74600
Uranus	3011	1867	2740	1699	84.01 y	16–28 h [2]	52000	32300
Neptune	4543	2817	4466	2769	164.79 y	18–20 h [2]	48400	30000
Pluto	7364	4566	4461	2766	247.7 y	6 d 9 h	1145	711

[1] 365 d 5 h 48 m 46 s   [2] Different latitudes rotate at different speeds.
y: years   d: days   h: hours   m: minutes   s: seconds   km: kilometres   ml: miles

PLANETARY SATELLITES

	Year discovered	Distance from planet		Diameter	
		km	ml	km	ml
Earth					
Moon	–	384000	238000	3476	2155
Mars					
Phobos	1877	938000	583000	27	17
Deimos	1877	2346000	1458000	15	9
Jupiter					
Metis	1979	128000	79000	40	25
Adrastea	1979	129000	80000	24	15
Amalthea	1892	181000	112000	270	168
Thebe	1979	222000	138000	100	60
Io	1610	422000	262000	3650	5850
Europa	1610	671000	417000	3400	1925
Ganymede	1610	1070000	665000	5260	3270
Callisto	1610	1883000	1170000	4800	3000
Leda	1974	11110000	6904000	20	12
Himalia	1904	11480000	7134000	180	110
Lysithea	1938	11720000	7283000	40	25
Elara	1905	11740000	7295000	80	50
Ananke	1951	21200000	13174000	30	19
Carme	1938	22600000	14044000	40	25
Pasiphae	1908	23500000	14603000	50	30
Sinope	1914	23700000	14727000	40	25

PLANETARY SATELLITES (cont.)

	Year discovered	Distance from planet km	ml	Diameter km	ml
Saturn					
Atlas	1980	138 000	86 000	40	25
1980 S27	1980	139 000	86 000	100	60
1980 S26	1980	142 000	88 000	100	60
Epimetheus	1980	151 000	94 000	140	90
Janus	1980	151 000	94 000	200	120
Mimas	1789	186 000	116 000	390	240
Enceladus	1789	238 000	148 000	500	310
Calypso	1980	295 000	183 000	30	19
Telesto	1980	295 000	183 000	24	15
Tethys	1684	295 000	183 000	1 050	650
Dione	1684	377 000	234 000	1 120	700
Dione B	1982	378 000	235 000	15	9
Rhea	1672	527 000	327 000	1 530	950
Titan	1655	1 222 000	759 000	5 150	3200
Hyperion	1848	1 481 000	920 000	400	250
Iapetus	1671	3 560 000	2 212 000	1 440	900
Phoebe	1898	12 965 000	8 047 000	160	100
1990S18	1990	~135 000		~10	
Uranus					
Miranda	1948	130 000	81 000	400	250
Ariel	1851	191 000	119 000	1 300	800
Umbriel	1851	266 000	165 000	1 100	700
Titania	1787	436 000	271 000	1 600	1000
Oberon	1787	583 000	362 000	1 600	1000
Cordelia	1986	49 300	31 000	15	9
Ophelia	1986	53 300	33 000	20	12
Bianca	1986	59 100	37 000	50	30
Cressida	1986	61 750	38 000	70	40
Desdemona	1986	62 700	39 000	50	30
Juliet	1986	64 350	40 000	70	40
Portia	1986	66 090	41 000	90	55
Rosalind	1986	69 920	43 000	50	30
Belinda	1986	75 100	47 000	50	30
Puck	1986	85 890	53 000	170	105
Neptune					
Triton	1846	355 000	221 000	3 800	2 400
Nereid	1949	5 510 000	3 424 000	300	190
1989 N6	1989	48 200	30 000	50	30
1989 N5	1989	50 000	31 000	90	55
1989 N3	1989	52 500	33 000	140	90
1989 N4	1989	62 000	39 000	160	100
1989 N2	1989	73 600	46 000	200	125
1989 N1	1989	117 600	73 000	420	260
Pluto					
Charon	1978	20 000 000	12 500 000	1 000	620

ANNUAL METEOR SHOWERS

Meteors appear to radiate from named star region

Name	Dates	Star region	Name	Dates	Star region
Quadrantids	1–6 January	Beta Boötis	Leonids	14–20 November	Zeta Leonis
Lyrids	19–22 April	Nu Herculis	Andromedids	26 November–	Gamma
Eta Aquarids	1–8 May	Eta Aquarii		4 December	Andromedae
Delta Aquarids	15 July–10 August	Delta Aquarii	Geminids	9–13 December	Castor
Perseids	27 July–17 August	Eta Persei	Ursids	20–22 December	Kocab
Orionids	15–25 October	Nu Orionis			

TOTAL & ANNULAR SOLAR ECLIPSES 1991–2007

Date	Extent of eclipse	Visible from parts of[1]
15 January 1991	Annular[2]	S Pacific, New Zealand, S Australia
11 July 1991	Total	Mid-Pacific, C & S America
4–5 January 1992	Annular	N American coast, Mid-Pacific
30 June 1992	Total	S American coast, S Atlantic Ocean
10 May 1994	Annular	Mid-Pacific, N America, N Africa
3 November 1994	Total	Indian Ocean, S Atlantic, S America, Mid-Pacific
29 April 1995	Annular	S Pacific, S America
24 October 1995	Total	Middle East, S Asia, S Pacific
9 March 1997	Total	C & N Asia, Arctic
26 February 1998	Total	Mid-Pacific, C America, N Atlantic
22 August 1998	Annular	Indonesia, S Pacific, Indian Ocean
16 February 1999	Annular	Indian Ocean, Australia
11 August 1999	Total	N Atlantic, N Europe, Middle East, N India
21 June 2001	Total	S Atlantic, S Africa, Madagascar
14 December 2001	Annular	Pacific, C America
10 June 2002	Annular	Indonesia, Pacific, Mexico
4 December 2002	Total	S Africa, Indian Ocean, Australia
31 May 2003	Annular	Iceland, Greenland
23 November 2003	Total	Antarctic
8 April 2005	Annular/ Total	Pacific, Panama, Venezuela
3 October 2005	Annular	Atlantic, Spain, Libya, Indian Ocean
29 March 2006	Total	Atlantic, Libya, Turkey, Russia
22 September 2006	Annular	Guyana, Atlantic, Indian Ocean

[1] The eclipse begins in the first country named.
[2] In an annular eclipse a ring-shaped part of the sun remains visible.

LUNAR ECLIPSES 1991–2008

Date	Percentage eclipsed	Time of mid-eclipse	Where visible
21 December 1991	Partial	10.34	Pacific, N America (W Coast), Japan, Australia
15 June 1992	Partial	04.58	N, C and S America, W Africa
9–10 December 1992	Total	23.45	Africa, Europe, Middle East, part of S. America
4 June 1993	Total	13.02	Pacific, Australia, SE Asia
29 November 1993	Total	06.26	N and S America
25 May 1994	Partial	03.32	C and S America, part of N America, W Africa
15 April 1995	Partial	12.19	Pacific, Australia, SE Asia
4 April 1996	Total	00.11	Africa, SE Europe, S America
27 September 1996	Total	02.55	C and S America, part of N America, W Africa
24 March 1997	Partial	04.41	C and S America, part of N America, W Africa
16 September 1997	Total	18.47	S Africa, E Africa, Australia
28 July 1999	Partial	11.34	Pacific, Australia, SE Asia
21 January 2000	Total	04.45	N America, part of S America, SW Europe, W Africa
16 July 2000	Total	13.57	Pacific, Australia, SE Asia
9 January 2001	Total	20.22	Europe, Asia, Africa
5 July 2001	Partial	14.57	Asia, Australia, Pacific
16 May 2003	Total	03.41	Americas, Europe, Africa
9 November 2003	Total	01.20	Americas, Europe, Africa, W Asia
4 May 2004	Total	20.32	Europe, Africa, Asia
28 October 2004	Total	03.05	Americas, Europe, Africa
17 October 2005	Partial	12.05	E Asia, Pacific, N America
7 September 2006	Partial	18.53	Australia, Asia, E Africa
3 March 2007	Total	23.22	Europe, Asia, Africa
28 August 2007	Total	10.39	Australia, Pacific, part of N America
21 February 2008	Total	03.27	Americas, Europe, Africa
16 August 2008	Partial	21.12	Europe, Africa, W Asia

THE LUNAR 'SEAS'

Latin name	English name	Latin name	English name
Lacus Somniorum	Lake of Dreams	Mare Serenitatis	Sea of Serenity
Mare Australe	Southern Sea	Mare Smythii	Smyth's Sea
Mare Crisium	Sea of Crises	Mare Spumans	Foaming Sea
Mare Fecunditatis	Sea of Fertility	Mare Tranquillitatis	Sea of Tranquillity
Mare Frigoris	Sea of Cold	Mare Undarum	Sea of Waves
Mare Humboldtianum	Humboldt's Sea	Mare Vaporum	Sea of Vapours
Mare Humorum	Sea of Humours	Oceanus Procellarum	Ocean of Storms
Mare Imbrium	Sea of Showers	Palus Epidemiarum	Marsh of Epidemics
Mare Ingenii	Sea of Geniuses	Palus Putredinis	Marsh of Decay
Mare Marginis	Marginal Sea	Palus Somnii	Marsh of Sleep
Mare Moscoviense	Moscow Sea	Sinus Adstuum	Bay of Heats
Mare Nectaris	Sea of Nectar	Sinus Iridum	Bay of Rainbows
Mare Nubium	Sea of Clouds	Sinus Medii	Central Bay
Mare Orientale	Eastern Sea	Sinus Roris	Bay of Dew

THE CONSTELLATIONS

Latin name	English name	Latin name	English name	Latin name	English name
Andromeda	Andromeda	Cygnus	Swan	Pavo	Peacock
Antlia	Air Pump	Delphinus	Dolphin	Pegasus	Winged Horse
Apus	Bird of Paradise	Dorado	Swordfish	Perseus	Perseus
Aquarius (Z)	Water Bearer	Draco	Dragon	Phoenix	Phoenix
Aquila	Eagle	Equuleus	Little Horse	Pictor	Easel
Ara	Altar	Eridanus	River Eridanus	Pisces (Z)	Fishes
Aries (Z)	Ram	Fornax	Furnace	Piscis Austrinus	Southern Fish
Auriga	Charioteer	Gemini (Z)	Twins	Puppis	Ship's Stern
Boötes	Herdsman	Grus	Crane	Pyxis	Mariner's Compass
Caelum	Chisel	Hercules	Hercules	Reticulum	Net
Camelopardalis	Giraffe	Horologium	Clock	Sagitta	Arrow
Cancer (Z)	Crab	Hydra	Sea Serpent	Sagittarius (Z)	Archer
Canes Venatici	Hunting Dogs	Hydrus	Water Snake	Scorpius (Z)	Scorpion
Canis Major	Great Dog	Indus	Indian	Sculptor	Sculptor
Canis Minor	Little Dog	Lacerta	Lizard	Scutum	Shield
Capricornus (Z)	Sea Goat	Leo (Z)	Lion	Serpens	Serpent
Carina	Keel	Leo Minor	Little Lion	Sextans	Sextant
Cassiopeia	Cassiopeia	Lepus	Hare	Taurus (Z)	Bull
Centaurus	Centaur	Libra (Z)	Scales	Telescopium	Telescope
Cepheus	Cepheus	Lupus	Wolf	Triangulum	Triangle
Cetus	Whale	Lynx	Lynx	Triangulum	
Chamaeleon	Chameleon	Lyra	Harp	Australe	Southern Triangle
Circinus	Compasses	Mensa	Table	Tucana	Toucan
Columba	Dove	Microscopium	Microscope	Ursa Major	Great Bear
Coma Berenices	Berenice's Hair	Monoceros	Unicorn	Ursa Minor	Little Bear
Corona Australis	Southern Crown	Musca	Fly	Vela	Sails
Corona Borealis	Northern Crown	Norma	Level	Virgo (Z)	Virgin
Corvus	Crow	Octans	Octant	Volans	Flying Fish
Crater	Cup	Ophiuchus	Serpent Bearer	Vulpecula	Fox
Crux	Southern Cross	Orion	Orion		

[Z]. Found on the Zodiac

LARGEST GROUND-BASED OPTICAL, INFRARED, AND SUBMILLIMETRE TELESCOPES

Telescope name	Type	Observatory	Site (altitude m/ft)	Mirror size m	Founded
Anglo-Australian Telescope (AAT)	optical	Anglo-Australian Observatory	Siding Spring Mountain NSW, Australia (1 165m/ 3 820 ft)	3.9	1974
Bol'shoi Teleskop Azimutal'nyi	optical	Special Astrophysical Observatory	Mt Pastukhov, Zehenshuskaia, USSR (2 100 m/6 900 ft)	6.0	1976

LARGEST GROUND-BASED OPTICAL, INFRARED, AND SUBMILLIMETRE TELESCOPES (cont.)

Telescope name	Type	Observatory	Site (altitude m/ft)	Mirror size m	Founded
—	optical	Byurakan Astrophysical Observatory	Mt Aragatz, Armenia (1 500 m/ 5 000 ft)	2.6	1976
C Donald Shane Telescope	optical	Lick Observatory	Mt Hamilton California, USA (1 277 m/ 4 190 ft)	3.05	1959
California Submillimetre Observatory	submillimetre	California Institute of Technology	Mauna Kea, Hawaii, USA (4 160 m/ 13 650 ft)	10.4	1986
Canada-France-Hawaii Telescope (CFHT)	optical	Canada-France-Hawaii Telescope Corporation	Mauna Kea, Hawaii, USA (4 180 m/ 13 720 ft)	3.6	1979
—	optical	Cerro Tololo Inter-American Observatory	Cerro Tololo, Chile (2 160 m/ 7 100 ft)	4.0	1976
ESO New Technology Telescope	optical	European Southern Observatory	Cerro Tololo, Chile (2 160 m/ 7 100 ft)	3.6	1990
ESO 3.6m	optical	European Southern Observatory	Cerro La Silla, Chile (2 400 m/ 7 850 ft)	3.6	1976
—	optical	German-Spanish Astronomical Centre	Calar Alto, Spain (2 160 m/ 7 100 ft)	3.5	1985
George Ellery Hale Telescope	optical	Palomar Observatory	Palomar Mountain, California, USA (1 700 m/ 5 600 ft)	5.08	1948
Ire'ne'e du Pont Telescope	optical	Mount Wilson and Las Campanas Observatories	Cerro Las Campanas, Chile (2 510 m/ 8 235 ft)	2.57	1977
Isaac Newton Telescope	optical	Observatory Roque de los Muchachos	La Palma, Canary Islands (2 336 m/ 7 660 ft)	2.54	1984
James Clerk Maxwell Telescope (JCMT)	submillimetre	Royal Observatory, Edinburgh, UK	Mauna Kea, Hawaii, USA (4 160 m/ 13 650 ft)	15.0	1987
Keck Telescope	optical/ infrared	California Association for Research and Astronomy (CARA)	Mauna Kea, Hawaii, USA (4 160m/ 13 650 ft)	10.0	1990

LARGEST GROUND-BASED OPTICAL, INFRARED, AND SUBMILLIMETRE TELESCOPES (cont.)

Telescope name	Type	Observatory	Site (altitude m/ft)	Mirror size m	Founded
—	optical	McDonald Observatory	Mt Locke, Texas, USA (2 070 m/ 6 791 ft)	2.7	1968
Multiple Mirror Telescope	optical	Whipple Observatory	Mt Hopkins, Arizona, USA (2 606 m/ 8 550 ft)	4.5	197?
NASA Infrared Telescope Facility (IRTF)	infrared	NASA	Mauna Kea, Hawaii, USA (4 160 m/ 13 650 ft)	3.0	1979
Nicholas U Mayall Telescope	optical	Kitt Peak National Observatory	Kitt Peak, Arizona, USA (2 100 m/ 6 900 ft)	3.8	1973
Shajin Telescope	optical	Crimean Astrophysical Observatory	Simeis, Ukraine, USSR (680 m/ 2 230 ft)	2.6	1961
Swedish/ European Submillimetre Telescope	submillimetre	European Southern Observatory	Cerro Tololo, Chile (2 160 m/ 7 100 ft)		1987
United Kingdom Infrared Telescope (UKIRT)	infrared	Royal Observatory, Edinburgh	Mauna Kea, Hawaii, USA (4 180 m/ 13 720 ft)	3.6	1979
William Herschel Telescope	optical	Observatory Roque de los Muchachos	La Palma, Canary Islands (2 332 m/ 7 650 ft)	4.2	1987

MAJOR SPACE 'FIRSTS'

Mission	USA/ USSR	Launch date	Event date	Event description
Sputnik 1	USSR	4 Oct 57	4 Oct 57	Earth satellite
Sputnik 2	USSR	3 Nov 57	3 Nov 57	Dog Laika
Explorer 1	USA	1 Feb 58	1 Feb 58	Discovered radiation belt (Van Allen)
Luna 1	USSR	2 Jan 59	2 Jan 59	Escaped earth gravity
Vanguard 2	USA	17 Feb 59	17 Feb 59	Earth photo
Luna 2	USSR	12 Sep 59	14 Sep 59	Lunar impact
Luna 3	USSR	4 Oct 59	7 Oct 59	Lunar photo (dark side)
TIROS 1	USA	1 Apr 60	1 Apr 60	Weather satellite
Transit 1B	USA	13 Apr 60	13 Apr 60	Navigation satellite
ECHO 1	USA	12 Aug 60	12 Aug 60	Communications satellite
Sputnik 5	USSR	19 Aug 60	20 Aug 60	Two dogs recovered alive

MAJOR SPACE 'FIRSTS' (cont.)

Mission	USA/ USSR	Launch date	Event date	Event description
Vostok 1	USSR	12 Apr 61	12 Apr 61	Manned orbital flight
Mariner 2	USA	26 Aug 62	14 Dec 62	Venus flyby
Vostok 6	USSR	16 Jun 63	16 Jun 63	Woman in orbit
Mariner 4	USA	28 Nov 64	15 Jul 65	Mars flyby pictures
Early Bird	USA	6 Apr 65	6 Apr 65	Commercial geostationary communications satellite
Venera 3	USSR	16 Nov 65	1 Mar 66	Venus impact
A-1 Asterix	France	26 Nov 65	26 Nov 65	French launched satellite
Gemini 7	USA	4 Dec 65	} 15 Dec 65	Manned rendevous
Gemini 6	USA	15 Dec 65		
Luna 9	USSR	31 Jan 66	3 Feb 66	Lunar soft landing
Gemini 8	USA	16 Mar 66	16 Mar 66	Manned docking
Luna 10	USSR	31 Mar 66	3 Apr 66	Lunar orbiter
Cosmos 186/188	USA	22 Oct 67– 28 Oct 67	27 Oct 67– 29 Oct 67	Automatic docking
Zond 5	USSR	14 Sep 68	21 Sep 68	Animals moon orbit
Apollo 8	USA	21 Dec 68	24 Dec 68	Manned lunar orbit
Soyuz 4	USSR	14 Jan 69	} 16 Jan 69	Transfer of crews
Soyuz 5	USSR	15 Jan 69		
Apollo 11	USA	16 Jul 69	20 Jul 69	Manned lunar landing
Oshumi	Japan	11 Feb 70	11 Feb 70	Japanese launched satellite
Long March	China	24 Apr 70	24 Apr 70	Chinese launched satellite
Venera 7	USSR	17 Aug 70	15 Dec 70	Venus soft landing
Luna 16	USSR	12 Sep 70	21 Sep 70	Unmanned sample return
Luna 17	USSR	10 Nov 70	17 Nov 70	Unmanned Moon rover
Mars 2	USSR	19 May 71	27 Nov 71	Mars orbit
Mars 3	USSR	28 May 71	2 Dec 71	Mars soft landing
Mariner 9	USA	30 May 71	13 Nov 71	Mars orbit
Prospero	UK	28 Oct 71	28 Oct 71	UK launched satellite
Pioneer 10	USA	3 Mar 72	3 Dec 73	Jupiter flyby
			Apr 83	Crossed Pluto orbit
			14 Jun 83	Escaped solar system
Pioneer 11	USA	6 Apr 73	Apr 74	Jupiter flyby
			Sep 79	Saturn flyby
Mariner 10	USA	3 Nov 73	5 Feb 74	Venus flyby
			Mar 74– Mar 75	Mercury flyby
Venera 9	USSR	8 Jun 75	22 Oct 75	Venus orbit
Apollo/Soyuz	USA/ USSR	15 Jul 75	17 Jul 75	Manned international co-operative mission
Viking 1	USA	20 Aug 75	20 Jul 76	Spacecraft operations on Mars surface
Viking 2	USA	9 Sep 75	3 Sep 76	
Voyager 2	USA	20 Aug 77	9 Jul 79	Jupiter flyby
			26 Aug 81	Saturn flyby
			24 Jan 86	Uranus flyby
			24 Aug 89	Neptune flyby
Voyager 1	USA	5 Sep 77	5 Mar 79	Jupiter flyby
			13 Nov 80	Saturn flyby
ISEE-C	USA	12 Aug 78	Sep 85	Comet intercept
Ariane/CAT	ESA	24 Dec 79	24 Dec 79	European launcher
Rohini	India	18 Jul 80	18 Jul 80	Indian launched satellite

MAJOR SPACE 'FIRSTS' (cont.)

Mission	USA/ USSR	Launch date	Event date	Event description
STS1	USA	12 Apr 81	12 Apr 81	Space shuttle flight
STS2	USA	12 Nov 81	12 Nov 81	Launch vehicle re-use
Soyuz T9	USSR	27 Jun 83	27 Jun 83	Construction in space
STS 51A	USA	8 Nov 84	16 Nov 84	Satellite retrieval
Vega 1	USSR	15 Dec 84	6 Mar 85	Halley flyby
Giotto	ESA	2 Jul 85	13 Mar 86	Close up of comet Halley
Soyuz T15	USSR	13 Mar 86	13 Mar 86	Ferry between space stations
Soyuz TM4/6	USSR	21 Dec 87	21 Dec 88	Year-long flight
Phobos 2	USSR	12 Jan 88	Apr 89	Phobos rendezvous
Buran	USSR	15 Nov 88	15 Nov 88	Unmanned space shuttle
Muses-A	Japan	24 Jan 90	21 Apr 90	Moon orbiter
HST	USA/ ESA	24 Apr 90	25 Apr 90	Large space telescope
Soyuz TM-11	USSR	2 Dec 90	12 Dec 90	Paying passenger flight

NASA MAJOR LAUNCHES

Mission	Launch	Duration (h:min)	Crew	Comment
Mercury (Freedom 7)	5 May 61	00:15	Shepard	First US manned suborbital flight
Liberty Bell 7	21 Jul 61	00:16	Grissom	Suborbital flight
Mercury (Friendship 7)	20 Feb 62	04:55	Glenn	First US manned orbital flight
Aurora 7	24 May 62	04:56	Carpenter	Orbital flight; manual reentry
Sigma 7	3 Oct 62	09:13	Schirra	6 orbits
Mercury (Faith 7)	15 May 62– 16 May 62	34:20	Cooper	22 orbits; last Mercury flight
Ranger VII	28 Jul 64– 31 Jul 64	68:36		First close-up TV pictures of lunar surface
Gemini II	19 Jan 65			Unmanned suborbital test flight
Gemini III	23 Mar 65	04:53	Grissom Young	First manned Gemini flight
Gemini IV	3 Jun 65– 7 Jun 65	97:56	McDivitt White	First spacewalk (by White, 36 min)
Gemini V	21 Aug 65– 29 Aug 65	190:56	Cooper Conrad	Simulated rendezvous manoeuvres
Gemini VI	25 Oct 65			Orbit not achieved
Gemini VII	4 Dec 65– 18 Dec 65	330:35	Borman Lovell	Part of mission with-out spacesuits
Gemini VII-A	15 Dec 65– 16 Dec 65	25:51	Schirra Stafford	First space rendezvous (with Gemini VII)
Gemini VIII	16 Mar 66– 17 Mar 66	10:42	Armstrong Scott	Rendezvous/docking with Agena target vehicle
Surveyor I	30 May 66– 2 Jun 66			First soft lunar landing, Ocean of Storms
Gemini IX-A	3 Jun 66– 6 Jun 66	72:21	Stafford Cernan	Docking not achieved

NASA MAJOR LAUNCHES (cont.)

Mission	Launch	Duration (h:min)	Crew	Comment
Gemini X	18 Jul 66– 21 Jul 66	70:47	Young Collins	First docked vehicle manoeuvres and spacewalks
Lunar Orbiter I	10 Aug 66– 29 Oct 66			First US craft to orbit moon
Gemini XI	12 Sep 66– 15 Sep 66	71:17	Conrad Gordon	Rendezvous/docking and spacewalks
Gemini XII	11 Nov 66– 15 Nov 66	94:35	Lovell Aldrin	Rendezvous/docking and spacewalks
Apollo I	Jan 67		Grissom White Chaffee	Astronauts killed in command module at launch site
Apollo IV	9 Nov 67			Successful launch of unmanned module
Apollo V	22 Jan 68– 24 Jan 68			Flight test of lunar module in earth orbit
Apollo VII	11 Oct 68– 22 Oct 68	260:09	Schirra Eisele Cunningham	First manned Apollo flight in earth orbit
Apollo VIII	21 Dec 68– 27 Dec 68	147:01	Borman Lovell Anders	First manned orbit of moon (10 orbits)
Apollo IX	3 Mar 69– 13 Mar 69	241:01	McDivitt Scott Schweickart	First manned lunar module flight in earth orbit
Apollo X	18 May 69– 26 May 69	192:03	Stafford Young Cernan	First lunar module orbit of moon
Apollo XI	16 Jul 69– 24 Jul 69	195:18	Armstrong* Aldrin* Collins	First men on moon 20 Jul, Sea of Tranquillity
Apollo 12	14 Nov 69– 24 Nov 69	244:36	Conrad* Bean* Gordon	Moon landing, 19 Nov, Ocean of Storms
Apollo 13	11 Apr 70– 17 Apr 70	142:54	Lovell Swigert Haise	Mission aborted, ruptured oxygen tank
Apollo 14	31 Jan 71– 9 Feb 71 9 Feb 71	216:02	Shepard* Mitchell* Roosa	Moon landing 5 Feb, Fra Mauro area
Apollo 15	26 Jul 71– 7 Aug 71	295:12	Scott* Irwin* Worden	Moon landing, 30 Jul, Hadley Rille; Lunar Roving Vehicle used
Apollo 16	16 Apr 72– 27 Apr 72	265:51	Young* Duke* Mattingly	Moon landing, 20 Apr, Descartes
Apollo 17	7 Dec 72– 19 Dec 72	301:52	Cernan* Schmitt* Evans	Longest Apollo mission, 11 Dec, Taurus-Littrow
Apollo-Soyuz (Test project)	15 Jul 75– 24 Jul 75	217:28	Stafford Brand Slayton	Rendezvous/docking with Soyuz 19 (cf. facing page)

*Astronauts who landed on the moon; the remaining astronaut was the pilot of the command module.

SHUTTLE FLIGHTS 1981–90

Flight/Name	Launch	Landing	Commander/Pilot/Number of other crew	Payload
STS-1 (C)	12 Apr 81	14 Apr 81	Young/Crippen/none	Test flight
STS-2 (C)	12 Nov 81	14 Nov 81	Engle/Truly/none	Test flight
STS-3 (C)	22 Mar 82	30 Mar 82	Lousma/Fullerton/none	OSS 1* (PDP*)
STS-4 (C)	27 Jun 82	4 Jul 82	Mattingly/Hartsfield/none	CIRRIS 1*
STS-5 (C)	11 Nov 82	16 Nov 82	Brand/Overmyer/2	SBS 3, Telesat 6
STS-6 (Ch)	4 Apr 83	9 Apr 83	Weitz/Bobko/2	TDRS 1
STS-7 (Ch)	18 Jun 83	24 Jun 83	Crippen/Hauck/3	Telesat 7, Palapa 3
STS-8 (Ch)	30 Aug 83	5 Sep 83	Truly/Brandenstein/3	Insat 1B
STS-9 (C)	28 Nov 83	8 Dec 83	Young/Shaw/4	Spacelab 1*
STS 41-B (Ch)	3 Feb 84	11 Feb 84	Brand/Gibson/3	Westar 6, IRT, Palapa 4, MMU1
STS 41-C (Ch)	6 Apr 84	13 Apr 84	Crippen/Scobee/3	LDEF 1, MMU 2
STS 41-D (D)	30 Aug 84	5 Sept 84	Hartsfield/Coats/4	SBS 4, Leasat 2, Telstar 3C
STS 41-G (Ch)	5 Oct 84	13 Oct 84	Crippen/McBride/5	ERBS
STS 51-A (D)	8 Nov 84	16 Nov 84	Hauck/Walker/3	Telesat 8, Leasat 1
STS 51-C (D)	24 Jan 85	27 Jan 85	Mattingly/Shriver/3	USA 8
STS 51-D (D)	12 Apr 85	19 Apr 85	Bobko/Williams/5	Telesat 9, Leasat 3
STS 51-B (D)	29 Apr 85	6 May 85	Overmyer/Gregory/5	Nusat, Spacelab 3*
STS 51-G (D)	17 Jun 85	24 Jun 85	Brandenstein/Creighton/5	Morelos 1, Arabsat 1B, Telstar 3D, Spartan 1
STS 51-F (Ch)	29 Jul 85	6 Aug 85	Fullerton/Bridges/5	PDP
STS 51-I (D)	27 Aug 85	3 Sep 85	Engle/Covey/5	Aussat 1, ASC 1, Leasat 4
STS 51-J (A)	3 Oct 85	7 Oct 85	Bobko/Grabe/3	USA 11, USA 12
STS 61-A (Ch)	30 Oct 85	6 Nov 85	Hartsfield/Nagel/6	GLOMR, Spacelab D1*
STS 61-B (A)	26 Nov 85	3 Dec 85	Shaw/O'Connor/5	Morelos 2, Aussat 2, OEX, RCA Satcom K2
STS 61-C (C)	12 Jan 86	18 Jan 86	Gibson/Bolden/5	RCA Satcom K1, Hitchhiker G1*
STS 51-L (Ch)	28 Jan 86	exploded	Scobee/Smith/5	TDRS
STS 26 (D)	29 Sept 88	3 Oct 88	Hauck/Covey/3	TDRS 3
STS 27 (A)	2 Dec 88	6 Dec 88	Gibson/Gardner/3	USA 34 (Lacrosse 1)
STS 29 (D)	13 Mar 89	18 Mar 89	Coates/Blaha/3	TDRS
STS 30 (A)	4 May 89	8 May 89	Walker/Grabe/3	Magellan
STS 28 (C)	8 Aug 89	13 Aug 89	Shaw/Richards/3	DoD
STS 34 (A)	18 Oct 89	23 Oct 89	Williams/McCulley/3	Galileo
STS 33 (D)	23 Nov 89	28 Nov 89	Gregory/Blaha/3	DoD
STS 32 (C)	9 Jan 90	20 Jan 90	Brandenstein/Wetherbee/3	LDEF
STS 36 (A)	28 Feb 90	4 Mar 90	Creighton/Casper/3	DoD
STS 31 (D)	25 Apr 90	29 Apr 90	Shriver/Bolden/3	HST
STS 41 (D)	6 Oct 90	10 Oct 90	Richards/Cabana/3	Ulysses
STS 38 (A)	16 Nov 90	20 Nov 90	Covey/Culbertson/3	DoD
STS 35 (C)	3 Dec 90	10 Dec 90	Brand/Gardner/3	Astro-1

A: Atlantis   Ch: Challenger   C: Columbia   D: Discovery
*not separated from shuttle

SKYLAB MISSIONS

Mission	Launch	Splashdown	Crew
1	14 May 73	–	Unmanned
2	25 May 73	22 Jun 73	Conrad, Kerwin, Weitz
3	28 Jul 73	25 Sep 73	Bean, Garriott, Lousma
4	16 Nov 73	8 Feb 74	Carr, Gibson, Pogue

MAJOR USSR MAN-RELATED LAUNCHES

Mission	Launch	Duration (h:min)	Crew	Comment
Vostok 1	12 Apr 61	01:48	Gagarin	First space flight
Vostok 2	6 Aug 61	25:18	Titov	Earth orbits
Vostok 3	11 Aug 62	94:22	Nikolayev	First dual mission
Vostok 4	12 Aug 62	71:00	Popovich	First dual mission
Vostok 6	16 Jun 63	70:50	Tereshkova	First woman in space
Voshkod 1	12 Oct 64	24:17	Komarov/Feoktistov/Yegorov	Three man flight
Voshkod 2	18 Mar 65	26:02	Belyayev/Leonov	First spacewalk (EVA)
Soyuz 1	23 Apr 67	27:00	Komarov	Cosmonaut killed at re-entry
Soyuz 4	14 Jan 69	71:14	Shatalov	Khrunov and Yeliseyev transferred from Soyuz 5
Soyuz 5	15 Jan 69	72:46	Volynov/Khrunov/Yeliseyev	Docked with Soyuz 4
Soyuz 6	11 Oct 69	118:42	Shonin/Kubasov	First mission with multiple crews
Soyuz 10	22 Apr 71	48:00	Shatalov/Yeliseyev/Rukavishnikov	Docked with Salyut 1 space station
Soyuz 11	6 Jun 71	552:00	Dobrovolsky/Volkov/Patsayev	Docked with Salyut 1; crew killed on re-entry
Salyut 3	25 Jun 74	214 days	Soyuz 14	Operational military space station
Soyuz 14	4 Jul 74	16 days	Popovich/Artyukhin	Docked with Salyut 3
Salyut 4	26 Dec 74	769 days	Soyuz 17/Soyuz 18/Soyuz 20	Space station; re-entered 2 Feb 1977
Soyuz 17	9 Jan 75	30 days	Gubarev/Grechko	Docked with Salyut 4
Soyuz 19 (Apollo-Soyuz Test Project)	15 Jul 75	6 days	Kubasov/Leonov	First international space mission with USA; crew transfer
Salyut 5	22 Jun 76	412 days	Soyuz 21/Soyuz 24	Space station; re-entered 8 Aug 1977
Soyuz 21	6 Jul 76	49 days	Volynov/Zholobov	Docked with Salyut 5
Soyuz 23	14 Oct 76	2 days	Zudov/Rozhdestivensky	Attempted docking with Salyut 5
Soyuz 24	7 Feb 77	18 days	Gorbatko/Glazkov	Docked with Salyut 5
Salyut 6	29 Sep 77	1764 days	Soyuz 25 through Soyuz 40	Space station; re-entered 29 July 82
Soyuz 26	10 Dec 77	96 days	Romanenko/Grechko	First prime crew Salyut 6; broke endurance record
Soyuz 27	10 Jan 78	65 days	Dzhanibekov/Makarov	First visiting crew to Salyut 6
Soyuz 28	2 Mar 78	8 days	Gubarev/Remek	Second visiting crew to Salyut 6
Soyuz 29	15 Jun 78	140 days	Kovalenok/Ivanchenko	Second prime crew of Salyut 6
Soyuz 32	25 Feb 79	108 days	Lyakhov/Ryumin	Third prime crew of Salyut 6, broke endurance record
Soyuz T1	16 Dec 79	100 days		Redesigned Soyuz craft
Soyuz T4	12 Mar 81	75 days	Kovalenok/Savinykh	Last prime crew of Salyut 6
Soyuz 39	22 Mar 81	8 days	Dzhanibekov/Gurragcha	Mongolian cosmonaut
Soyuz 40	14 May 81	8 days	Popov/Prunariu	Last visiting crew to Salyut
Salyut 7	19 April 82	9 years	Soyuz T5 through Soyuz T15	Space station; re-entered 7 Feb 91
Soyuz T5	14 May 82	106 days	Berezovoy/Ledebev	Crew broke endurance record
Soyuz T7	19 Aug 82	113 days	Popov/Serebrov/Savitskaya	Savitskaya, second woman in space
Soyuz T9	27 June 83	149 days	Lyakhov/Alexandrov	Docked with Salyut 7
Soyuz T10-1	27 Sep 83		Titov/Strekalov	Exploded on launch-pad; crew safe

MAJOR USSR MAN-RELATED LAUNCHES (cont.)

Mission	Launch	Duration (h:min)	Crew	Comment
Soyuz T10	8 Feb 84	263 days	Kizim/Solovyev/Atkov	Crew broke endurance record
Soyuz T12	17 Jul 84	12 days	Dzhanibekov/Savitskaya/Volk	Docked with Salyut 7; first female EVA
Soyuz T14	17 Sep 85	65 days	Vasyutin/Volkov/Grechko	Docked with Salyut 7; mission terminated when Vasyutin fell ill
MIR 1	19 Feb 86	Projected orbit 10 years	Soyuz T15 onwards	Space station; designed for modular construction
Soyuz T15	13 Mar 86	125 days	Kizim/Solovyov	Docked with both MIR 1 and Salyut 7
Soyuz TMI	21 May 86	9 days		Redesigned Soyuz T craft
Kvant 1	31 Mar 87	in orbit		Astrophysical module attached to MIR 1
Soyuz TM3	22 Jul 87	160 days	Viktorenko/Alexandrov/Faris	Docked with MIR 1
Soyuz TM4	21 Dec 87	179 days	Titov/Manarov/Levchenko	Docked with MIR 1; Titov and Manarov completed 365 day flight
Kvant 2	26 Nov 89	in orbit		Module added to MIR 1 station on 6 Dec 89
Kristall	31 May 90	in orbit		Material processing module added to MIR 1
Soyuz TM11	2 Dec 90	175 days	Afanasyev/Manarov/Akiyama	Docked with MIR 1; Japanese journalist on board
Soyuz TM12	18 May 91		Artsebarski/Krikalyev/Sharman	Docked with MIR 1; First British cosmonaut

SOME SATELLITES IN GEOSTATIONARY ORBIT

Communications

Business

SBS 1	1980
SBS 2	1981
SBS 3	1982
SBS 4	1984
SBS 5	1988
SBS 6	1990

International

Intelsat 2 F-2	1967
Intelsat 2 F-3	1967
Intelsat 2 F-4	1967
Intelsat 3 F-2	1968
Intelsat 3 F-3	1969
Intelsat 3 F-4	1969
Intelsat 3 F-6	1970
Intelsat 3 F-7	1970
Intelsat 4 F-1	1975
Intelsat 4 F-2	1971
Intelsat 4 F-3	1971
Intelsat 4 F-4	1972
Intelsat 4 F-5	1972
Intelsat 4 F-7	1973
Intelsat 4 F-8	1974
Intelsat 4A F-1	1975
Intelsat 4A F-2	1976
Intelsat 4A F-3	1978
Intelsat 4A F-4	1977
Intelsat 4A F-6	1978
Intelsat 5 F-1	1981
Intelsat 5 F-2	1980
Intelsat 5 F-3	1981
Intelsat 5 F-4	1982
Intelsat 5 F-5	1982
Intelsat 5 F-6	1983
Intelsat 5 F-7	1983
Intelsat 5 F-8	1984
Intelsat 5 F-9	1984
Intelsat 5A F-10	1985
Intelsat 5A F-11	1985
Intelsat 5A F-12	1985
Intelsat 5A F-13	1988
Intelsat 5A F-15	1989
Intelsat 6 F-2	1989
Intelsat 6 F-4	1990

Arabian

Arabsat 1A	1985
Arabsat 1B	1985

Asian

Asiasat 1	1990

Australian

Aussat 1	1985
Aussat 2	1985
Aussat 3	1987

Brazilian

Brasilsat 1	1985
Brasilsat 2	1986

Canadian

Anik	1978
Anik 1	1972

SOME SATELLITES IN GEOSTATIONARY ORBIT (cont.)

Anik 2	1973	TV-Sat 2	1989	Cosmos 2054	1989
Anik 3	1975	DFS Copernicus 2	1990	Cosmos 2085	1990
Anik C1	1985	***Indian***		Ekran 1	1976
Anik C2	1983	Apple	1981	Ekran 2	1977
Anik C3	1982	Insat 1A	1982	Ekran 3	1979
Anik D1	1982	Insat 1B	1983	Ekran 4	1979
Anik D2	1984	Insat 1C	1988	Ekran 5	1980
Anik E2	1991	Insat 1D	1990	Ekran 6	1980
Telesat 1	1972			Ekran 7	1981
Telesat 2	1973	***Indonesian***		Ekran 8	1982
Telesat 3	1975	Palapa 1	1976	Ekran 9	1982
Telesat 4	1978	Palapa 2	1977	Ekran 10	1983
Telesat 5	1982	Palapa 3	1983	Ekran 11	1983
Telesat 6	1982	Palapa 5	1987	Ekran 12	1984
Telesat 7	1983	Palapa B-2R	1990	Ekran 13	1984
Telesat 8	1984			Ekran 14	1985
Telesat 9	1985	***Italian***		Ekran 15	1986
		Sirio 1	1977	Ekran 16	1987
Chinese		Italsat	1991	Ekran 17	1987
China 15	1984			Ekran 18	1988
China 18	1986	***Japanese***		Ekran 19	1988
China 22	1988	Ayama 1	1979	Gorizont 1	1978
China 25	1988	Ayama 2	1980	Gorizont 2	1979
China 26	1990	CS-2A	1983	Gorizont 3	1979
		CS-2B	1983	Gorizont 4	1980
European		CS-3A	1988	Gorizont 5	1982
Astra 1A	1988	CS-3B	1988	Gorizont 6	1982
Astra 1B	1991	ECS 1	1979	Gorizont 7	1983
ECS 1	1983	ECS 2	1980	Gorizont 8	1983
ECS 2	1984	ETS 2	1977	Gorizont 9	1984
ECS 4	1987	ETS 3	1982	Gorizont 10	1984
ECS 5	1988	ETS 5	1987	Gorizont 11	1985
ESA GEOS 2	1978	JCSat 1	1989	Gorizont 12	1986
Marcopolo 1	1989	JCSat 2	1990	Gorizont 13	1986
Olympus	1989	Sakura 2A	1983	Gorizont 14	1987
Eutelsat 2	1990	Sakura 2B	1983	Gorizont 15	1988
Eutelsat 2	1991	Sakura 3A	1988	Gorizont 16	1988
Astra 1B	1991	Sakura 3B	1988	Gorizont 17	1989
		Superbird 1	1989	Gorizont 18	1989
French		Yuri 3A	1990	Gorizont 19	1989
TDF 1	1988			Gorizont 20	1990
Telecom 1A	1984	***Mexican***		Gorizont 21	1990
Telecom 1B	1985	Morelos 1	1985	Gorizont 22	1990
Telecom 1C	1988	Morelos 2	1985	Gorizont 23	1991
TDF 2	1990	***Pan-American***		Raduga 1	1975
		Panamsat (PAS 1)	1988	Raduga 2	1976
French/German				Raduga 3	1977
Symphonie 1	1974	***Soviet***		Raduga 4	1978
Symphonie 2	1975	Cosmos 1888	1987	Raduga 5	1979
		Cosmos 1894	1987	Raduga 6	1980
German		Cosmos 1897	1987	Raduga 7	1980
DFS-Kopernicus 1	1989	Cosmos 1940	1988		
TV-Sat 1	1987	Cosmos 1961	1988		

SOME SATELLITES IN GEOSTATIONARY ORBIT (cont.)

Raduga 8	1981	RCA Satcom 3R	1981	GOES 5	1981
Raduga 9	1981	RCA Satcom 4	1982	GOES 6	1983
Raduga 10	1981	RCA Satcom 5	1982	GOES 7	1987
Raduga 11	1982	RCA Satcom 6	1983	SMS 1	1974
Raduga 12	1983	RCA Satcom 7	1983	SMS 2	1975
Raduga 13	1983	RCA Satcom K1	1986	SMS 3	1975
Raduga 14	1984	RCA Satcom K2	1985		

Military Communications

Raduga 15	1984	RCA Satcom C1	1990	NATO 1	1970
Raduga 16	1985	TDRS 1	1983	NATO 2	1971
Raduga 17	1985	TDRS 3	1988	NATO 3A	1976
Raduga 18	1986	TDRS 4	1989	NATO 3B	1977
Raduga 19	1986	Telstar 3A	1983	NATO 3C	1978
Raduga 20	1987	Telstar 3C	1983	NATO 3D	1984
Raduga 21	1987	Telstar 3D	1985	NATO 4A	1991
Raduga 22	1988	Westar 1	1974		
Raduga 23	1989	Westar 2	1974	***Soviet***	
Raduga 24	1989	Westar 3	1979	Cosmos 2133	1991
Raduga 25	1989	Westar 4	1982		
Raduga 26	1990	Westar 5	1982	***UK***	
Raduga 27	1991			Skynet 1A	1969

Swedish

Maritime Communications

Tele-X	1989			Skynet 2A	1974
		Marecs 1	1981	Skynet 2B	1974
US		Marecs 2	1984	Skynet 4A	1990
ASC 1	1985	Marisat 1	1976	Skynet 4B	1988
Aurora 2	1991	Marisat 2	1976	Skynet 4C	1990
Comstar 1A	1976	Marisat 3	1976		
Comstar 1B	1976	Inmarsat 2	1990	***US***	
Comstar 1C	1978	Inmarsat 2	1991	DSCS 1	1971
Comstar 1D	1981			DSCS 2	1971
Early Bird	1965	**Meteorology**		DSCS 3	1973
Galaxy 1	1983	***Japanese***		DSCS 4	1973
Galaxy 2	1983	GMS 1	1977	DSCS 5	1975
Galaxy 3	1984	GMS 2	1981	DSCS 6	1975
Galaxy 6	1990	GMS 3	1984	DSCS 7	1977
Gstar 1	1985	GMS 4	1989	DSCS 8	1977
Gstar 2	1986	Himawari 1	1977	DSCS 11	1978
Gstar 3	1988	Himawari 2	1981	DSCS 12	1978
Gstar 4	1990	Himawari 3	1984	DSCS 13	1979
Intelsat 1 F-1	1965			DSCS 14	1979
Leasat 1	1984	***European***		DSCS 15	1982
Leasat 2	1984	Meteosat 1	1977	DSCS 16	1982
Leasat 3	1985	Meteosat 2	1981	DSCS TYPE 3	1985
Leasat 4	1985	Meteosat P2	1988	Fleetsatcom 1	1978
Leasat 5	1990	MOP 1	1989	Fleetsatcom 2	1979
LES 6	1968	MOP 2	1991	Fleetsatcom 3	1980
LES 8	1976			Fleetsatcom 4	1980
LES 9	1976	***US***		Fleetsatcom 5	1981
RCA Satcom 1	1975	GOES 1	1975	Fleetsatcom 7	1986
RCA Satcom 2	1976	GOES 2	1977	Fleetsatcom 8	1989
RCA Satcom 3	1979	GOES 3	1978	IMEWS	1987
		GOES 4	1980		

SOME SATELLITES IN GEOSTATIONARY ORBIT (cont.)

IMEWS 1	1970	IMEWS 9	1979	USA 12	1985
IMEWS 2	1971	IMEWS 10	1979	USA 20	1986
IMEWS 3	1972	IMEWS 11	1981	USA 28	1987
IMEWS 4	1973	IMEWS 12	1981	USA 48	1989
IMEWS 5	1975	IMEWS 13	1982	DSP	1990
IMEWS 6	1976	Tactical comsat	1969		
IMEWS 7	1977	USA 7	1984	**Research**	
IMEWS 8	1978	USA 11	1985	IUE 1978 Ultra-violet Obs	

THE EARTH

There are no universally agreed estimates of the natural phenomena given in this section. Surveys make use of different criteria for identifying natural boundaries, and use different techniques of measurement. The sizes of continents, oceans, seas, deserts, and rivers are particularly subject to variation.

Age 4 500 000 000 years (accurate to within a very small percentage of possible error)
Area 509 600 000 sq km/197 000 000 sq ml
Mass 5976 $\times$ 10^{27} grams
Land surface 148 000 000 sq km/57 000 000 sq ml (c.29% of total area)

Water surface 361 600 000 sq km/140 000 000 sq ml (c.71% of total area)
Circumference at equator 40 076 km/24 902 ml
Circumference of meridian 40 000 km/24 860 ml

CONTINENTS

Name	Area sq km	sq ml	Lowest point below sea level	m	ft	Highest elevation	m	ft
Africa	30 293 000	11 696 000 (20.2%)	Lake Assal, Djibouti	156	512	Mt Kilimanjaro, Tanzania	5895	19 340
Antarctica	13 975 000	5 396 000 (9.3%)	Bently subglacial trench	2538	8327	Vinson Massif	5140	16 864
Asia	44 493 000	17 179 000 (29.6%)	Dead Sea, Israel/Jordan	400	1312	Mt Everest, China-Nepal	8848	29 028
Oceania	8 945 000	3 454 000 (6%)	Lake Eyre, S Australia	15	49	Puncak Jaya (Ngga Pulu)	5030	16 500
Europe*	10 245 000	3 956 000 (6.8%)	Caspian Sea, USSR	29	94	Mt El'brus, USSR	5642	18 510
North America	24 454 000	9 442 000 (16.3%)	Death Valley, California	86	282	Mt McKinley, Alaska	6194	20 320
South America	17 838 000	6 887 000 (11.9%)	Peninsular Valdez, Argentina	40	131	Aconcagua, Argentina	6960	22 831

*Including western USSR.

MAJOR ISLAND GROUPS

Name	Country	Sea/Ocean	Constituent Islands
Aeolian	Italy	Mediterranean	Stromboli, Lipari, Vulcano, Salina
Åland	Finland	Gulf of Bothnia	Ahvenanmaa, Eckero, Lemland, Lumparland, Vardo
Aleutian	Alaska	Pacific	Andreanof, Adak, Atka, Fox, Umnak, Unalaska, Unimak, Near, Attu, Rat, Kiska, Amchitka
Alexander	Canada	Pacific	Baranof, Prince of Wales
Antilles, Greater	—	Caribbean	Cuba, Jamaica, Haiti and the Dominican Republic, Puerto Rico
Antilles, Lesser	—	Caribbean	Windward, Leeward, Netherlands Antilles

MAJOR ISLAND GROUPS (cont.)

Name	Country	Sea/Ocean	Constituent Islands
Andaman	India	Bay of Bengal	over 300 islands including N Andaman, S Andaman, Middle Andaman, Little Andaman
Azores	Portugal	Atlantic	nine main islands: Flores, Corvo, Terceira, Graciosa, São Jorge, Faial, Pico, Santa Maria, Formigar, São Miguel
Bahamas	UK	Atlantic	700 islands including Great Abaco, Acklins, Andros, Berry, Cay, Cat Crooked, Exuma, Grand Bahama, Inagua, Long, Mayaguana, New Providence, Ragged
Balearic	Spain	Mediterranean	Ibiza, Mallorca, Menorca, Formentera, Cabrera
Bay Islands	Honduras	Caribbean	Utila, Roatan, Guanja
Bismarck Archipelago	Papua New Guinea	Pacific	c.200 islands including New Britain, New Ireland, Admiralty, Lavonga, New Hanover
Bissagos	Guinea-Bissau	Atlantic	15 islands including Orango, Formosa, Caravela, Roxa
Canadian Arctic Archipelago	Canada	Arctic	main islands: Baffin, Victoria, Queen Elizabeth, Banks
Canaries	Spain	Atlantic	Tenerife, Gomera, Las Palmas, Hierro, Lanzarote, Fuerteventura, Gran Canaria
Cape Verde	Cape Verde	Atlantic	10 islands divided into 1. Barlavento (windward) group: Santo Antão, São Vicente, Santa Luzia, São Nicolau, Boa Vista, Sal and 2. Sotavento (leeward) group: São Tiago, Maio Fogo, Brava
Caroline	USA	Pacific	c.680 islands including Yop, Ponape, Truk, Kusac, Belau
Chagos	UK	Indian	Diego Garcia, Peros, Banhos, Salomon
Channel	UK	English	Jersey, Guernsey, Alderney, Sark
Chonos Archipelago	Chile	Pacific	main islands: Chaffers, Benjamin, James, Melchior, Victoria, Luz
Commander	USSR	Bering Sea	main islands: Bering, Medny
Comoros	Republic of the Comoros (excluding French Mayotte)	Mozambique Channel	Grande Comore, Anjouan, Moheli, Mayotte
Cook	New Zealand	Pacific	main islands: Rarotonga, Palmerston, Mangaia
Cyclades	Greece	Aegean	c.220 islands including Andros, Mikonos, Milos, Naxos, Paros, Kithnos, Sérifos, Tinos, Siros
Denmark	Denmark	Baltic	main islands: Zealand, Fyn, Lolland, Falster, Bornholm

MAJOR ISLAND GROUPS (cont.)

Name	Country	Sea/Ocean	Constituent Islands
Desolation	France	Indian	Kerguélen, Grande Terre, and 300 islets
Dodecanese	Greece	Aegean	12 islands including Kásos, Kárpathos, Rhodes, Sámos, Khalki, Tilos, Simi, Astipalaia, Kós, Kálimnos, Léros, Pátmos
Ellice	Tuvalu	Pacific	main islands: Funafuti, Nukefetau, Nukulailai, Nanumea
Falkland	UK	Atlantic	over 200 islands including W Falkland, E Falkland, S Georgia, S Sandwich
Faroe	Denmark	Atlantic	22 islands including Stromo, Ostero
Fiji	Fiji	Pacific	main islands: Viti Levu, Vanua Levu
Frisian, North	Germany and Denmark	North Sea	main islands: (German) Sylt, Föhr, Nordstrand, Pellworm, Amrum; (Danish) Rømø, Fanø, Mandø
Frisian, East	Germany and Denmark	North Sea	main islands: Borkum, Juist, Norderney, Langeoog, Spiekeroog, Wangerooge
Frisian, West	Germany and Denmark	North Sea	main islands: Texel, Vlieland, Terschelling, Ameland, Schiermonnikoog
Galapagos	Ecuador	Pacific	main islands: San Cristobal, Santa Cruz, Isabela, Floreana, Santiago, Fernandina
Gilbert	Kiribati	Pacific	main islands: Tarawa, Makin, Abaiang, Abemama, Tabiteuea, Nonouti, Beru
Gotland	Sweden	Baltic	main islands: Gotland, Fårö, Karlsö
Greenland	Denmark	N Atlantic/Arctic	main islands: Greenland, Disko
Hawaiian	USA	Pacific	8 main islands: Hawaii, Oahu, Maui, Lanai, Kauai, Molokai, Kahoolawe, Niihau
Hebrides, Inner	UK	Atlantic	main islands: Skye, Eigg, Coll, Tiree, Mull, Iona, Staffa, Jura, Islay
Hebrides, Outer	UK	Atlantic	Lewis, N and S Uist, Benbecula, Barra
Indonesia	Republic of Indonesia	Pacific	13 677 islets and islands including Java, Sumatra, Kalimantau, Celebes, Lesser Sundas, Moluccas, Irian Jaya
Ionian	Greece	Aegean	Kerkira, Kefalliniá, Zakinthos, Levkas
Japan	Japan	Pacific	main islands: Hokkaido, Honshu, Shikoku, Kyushu, Ryuku
Juan Fernandez	Chile	Pacific	Más a Tierra, Más Afuera, Santa Clara
Kuril	USSR	Pacific	56 islands including Shumsu, Iturup, Urup, Paramushir, Onekotan, Shiaskhotan, Shikotan-to, Kunashir, Shimushir

MAJOR ISLAND GROUPS (cont.)

Name	Country	Sea/Ocean	Constituent Islands
Laccadive	India	Arabian Sea	27 islands including Amindivi, Laccadive, Minicoy, Androth, Kavaratti
Line	Kiribati	Pacific	main islands: Christmas, Fanning, Washington
Lofoton	Norway	Norwegian Sea	main islands: Hinnøy, Austvågøy, Vestvågøy, Moskenes
Madeira	Portugal	Atlantic	Madeira, Ilha do Porto Santo, Ilhas Desertas, Ilhas Selvagens
Malay Archipelago	Federation of Malay	Pacific/Indian	main islands: Borneo, Celebes, Java, Luzon, Mindanao, New Guinea, Sumatra
Maldives	Republic of Maldives	Indian	19 clusters, main island: Male
Malta	Republic of Malta	Mediterranean	main islands: Malta, Gozo, Comino
Mariana	Commonwealth of the Northern Mariana Islands	Pacific	14 islands including Saipan, Tinian, Rota, Pagan, Guguan
Marquesas	France	Pacific	10 islands including Nukultiva, Ua Pu, Ua Huka, Hiva Oa, Tahuata, Fatu Hiva, Eiao, Hatutu
Marshall	Marshall Islands	Pacific	main islands: Bikini, Wotha, Kwajalein, Eniwetok, Maiura, Jalut, Rogelap
Mascarenes	France	Indian	main islands: Réunion, Mauritius, Rodrigues
Melanesia	–	Pacific	main groups of islands: Solomon Islands, Bismarck Archipelago, New Caledonia,Papua New Guinea, Fiji, Vanuatu
Micronesia	–	Pacific	main groups of islands: Caroline, Gilberts, Marianas, Marshalls, Guam, Kiribati, Nauru
New Hebrides	Republic of Vanuatu	Pacific	main islands: Espíritu Santo, Malekula, Efate, Ambrim, Eromanga, Tanna, Epi, Pentecost, Aurora
New Siberian	USSR	Arctic	main islands: Kotelny, Faddeyevski
Newfoundland	Canada	Atlantic	Prince Edward, Anticosti
Nicobar	India	Bay of Bengal	main islands: Great Nicobar, Camorta with Nancowry, Car Nicobar, Teressa, Little Nicobar
Northern Land	USSR	Arctic	main islands: Komsomolets, Bolshevik, October Revolution
Novaya Zemlya	USSR	Arctic	2 main islands: North, South
Orkney	UK	North Sea	main islands: Mainland, South and North Ronaldsay, Sanday, Westray, Hoy, Stronsay, Shapinsay, Rousay
Pelagian	Italy	Mediterranean	Lampedusa, Linosa, Lampione

MAJOR ISLAND GROUPS (cont.)

Name	Country	Sea/Ocean	Constituent Islands
Philippines	Republic of the Philippines	Pacific	over 7100 islands and islets including Luzon, Mindanao, Samar, Palawan, Mindoro, Panay, Negros, Cebu, Leyte, Masbate, Bohol
Polynesia	–	Pacific	main groups of islands: New Zealand, French Polynesia, Phoenix islands, Hawaii, Line, Cook islands, Pitcairn, Tokelau, Tonga, Society, Easter, Samoa, Kiribati, Ellice
Queen Charlotte	Canada	Pacific	150 islands including Prince Rupert, Graham, Moresby, Louise, Lyell, Kunghit
São Tomé and Príncipe	Republic of São Tomé and Príncipe	Atlantic	main islands: São Tomé, Príncipe
Scilly	UK	English Channel	c.150 islands including St Mary's, St Martin's, Tresco, St Agnes, Bryher
Seychelles	Republic of Seychelles	Indian	115 islands including Praslin, La Digue, Silhouette, Mahé, Bird
Shetland	UK	North Sea	100 islands including Mainland, Unst, Yell, Fetlar, Whalsay
Society	France	Pacific	island groups: Windward, Leeward; main island: Tahiti.
Solomon	Solomon Islands	Pacific	main islands: Choiseul, Guadalcanal, Malaita, New Georgia, San Cristobal, Santa Isabel
South Orkney	UK	Atlantic	main islands: Coronation, Signy, Laurie, Inaccessible
South Shetland	UK	Atlantic	main islands: King George, Elephant, Clarence, Gibbs, Nelson, Livingstone, Greenwich, Snow, Deception, Smith
Sri Lanka	Republic of Sri Lanka	Indian	main islands: Sri Lanka, Mannar
Taiwan	Republic of China	China Sea/Pacific	main islands: Taiwan, Lan Hsü, Lü Tao, Quemoy, the Pescadores
Tasmania	Australia	Tasman Sea	main islands: Tasmania, King, Flinders, Bruny
Tierra del Fuego	Argentina/Chile	Pacific	main islands: Tierra del Fuego, Isla de los Estados, Hoste, Navarino, Wallaston, Diego Ramirez, Desolacion, Santa Ines, Clarence, Dawson
Tres Marias	Mexico	Pacific	Maria Madre, Maria Magdalena, Maria Cleofas, San Juanito
Tristan da Cunha	UK	Atlantic	5 islands including Tristan da Cunha, Gough, Inaccessible, Nightingale

MAJOR ISLAND GROUPS (cont.)

Name	Country	Sea/Ocean	Constituent Islands
Tuamotu Archipelago	France	Pacific	c.80 islands including Makatea, Fakarava, Rangiroa, Anaa, Hao, Reao, Gambiev, Duke of Gloucester
Vesterålen	Norway	Norwegian Sea	main islands: Hinnøy, Langøya, Andøya, Hadseløy
Virgin	USA	Caribbean	over 50 islands including St Croix, St Thomas, St John
Virgin	UK	Caribbean	main islands: Tortola, Virgin Gorda, Anegada, Jost Van Dyke.
Zanzibar	Tanzania	Indian	main islands: Zanzibar, Tumbatu, Kwale
Zemlya Frantsa-Iosifa	USSR	Arctic	c.167 islands, including Graham Bell, Wilczekland, Georgeland, Hooker, Zemlya Alexsandry, Ostrov Rudol'fa

OCEANS

Name	Area sq km	sq ml		Greatest depth	m	ft	Average depth	m	ft
Arctic	13 986 000	5 400 000	(3%)	Eurasia Basin	5122	16 804	Arctic	1 330	4 300
Atlantic	82 217 000	31 700 000	(24%)	Puerto Rico Trench	8 648	28 372	Atlantic	3 700	12 100
Indian	73 426 000	28 350 000	(20%)	Java Trench	7 725	25 344	Indian	3 900	12 800
Pacific	181 300 000	70 000 000	(46%)	Mariana Trench	11 040	36 220	Pacific	4 300	14 100

LARGEST SEAS

Name	Area* sq km	sq ml	Name	Area* sq km	sq ml
Coral Sea	4 791 000	1 850 200	Arafura Sea	1 037 000	400 000
Arabian Sea	3 863 000	1 492 000	Philippine Sea	1 036 000	400 000
S China (Nan) Sea	3 685 000	1 423 000	Sea of Japan	978 000	378 000
Mediterranean Sea	2 516 000	971 000	E Siberian Sea	901 000	348 000
Bering Sea	2 304 000	890 000	Kara Sea	883 000	341 000
Bay of Bengal	2 172 000	839 000	E China Sea	664 000	256 000
Sea of Okhotsk	1 590 000	614 000	Andaman Sea	565 000	218 000
Gulf of Mexico	1 543 000	596 000	North Sea	520 000	201 000
Gulf of Guinea	1 533 000	592 000	Black Sea	508 000	196 000
Barents Sea	1 405 000	542 000	Red Sea	453 000	175 000
Norwegian Sea	1 383 000	534 000	Baltic Sea	414 000	160 000
Gulf of Alaska	1 327 000	512 000	Arabian Gulf	238 000	92 200
Hudson Bay	1 232 000	476 000	St Lawrence Gulf	238 300	92 000
Greenland Sea	1 205 000	465 000			

Oceans are excluded.
*Areas are rounded to the nearest 1 000 sq km/sq ml.

LARGEST ISLANDS

Name	Area* sq km	sq ml	Name	Area* sq km	sq ml
Australia	7 892 300	3 046 500	North I, New Zealand	114 000	44 200
Greenland	2 131 600	823 800	Newfoundland	109 000	42 000
New Guinea	790 000	305 000	Cuba	105 000	40 500
Borneo	737 000	285 000	Luzon	105 000	40 400
Madagascar	587 000	227 600	Iceland	103 000	39 700
Baffin	507 000	196 000	Mindanao	94 600	36 500
Sumatra	425 000	164 900	Novaya Zemlya (two islands)	90 600	35 000
Honshu (Hondo)	228 000	88 000	Ireland	84 100	32 500
Great Britain	219 000	84 400	Hokkaido	78 500	30 300
Victoria, Canada	217 300	83 900	Hispaniola	77 200	29 800
Ellesmere, Canada	196 000	75 800	Sakhalin	75 100	29 000
Celebes	174 000	67 400	Tierra del Fuego	71 200	27 500
South I, New Zealand	151 000	58 200	Tasmania	67 900	26 200
Java	129 000	50 000			

*Areas are rounded to the nearest three significant digits.

LARGEST LAKES

Name/Location	Area* sq km	sq ml	Name/Location	Area* sq km	sq ml
Caspian Sea, Iran/USSR	371 000	143 240[1]	Balkhash, USSR	17 000–	6 500 –
Superior, USA/Canada	82 260	31 760[2]		22 000	8 500[1]
Aral Sea, USSR	64 500	24 900[1]	Ontario, Canada	19 270	7 440[2]
Victoria, E Africa	62 940	24 300	Ladoga, USSR	18 130	7 000
Huron, USA/Canada	59 580	23 000[2]	Chad, W Africa	10 000–	4 000 –
Michigan, USA	58 020	22 400		26 000	10 000
Tanganyika, E Africa	32 000	12 350	Maracaibo, Venezuela	13 010	5 020[3]
Baikal, USSR	31 500	12 160	Patos, Brazil	10 140	3 920[3]
Great Bear, Canada	31 330	12 100	Onega, USSR	9 800	3 800
Great Slave, Canada	28 570	11 030	Rudolf, E Africa	9 100	3 500
Erie, USA/Canada	25 710	9 920[2]	Eyre, Australia	8 800	3 400[3]
Winnipeg, Canada	24 390	9 420	Titicaca, Peru	8 300	3 200
Malawi/Nyasa, E Africa	22 490	8 680			

[1] salt lakes
[2] average of areas given by Canada and USA
[3] salt lagoons
*Areas are given to the nearest 10 sq km/sq ml.
The Caspian and Aral Seas, being entirely surrounded by land, are classified as lakes.

HIGHEST MOUNTAINS

Name	Height* m	ft	Location
Everest	8 850	29 030	China-Nepal
K2	8 610	28 250	Kashmir-Jammu
Kangchenjunga	8 590	28 170	India-Nepal
Lhotse	8 500	27 890	China-Nepal
Kangchenjunga S Peak	8 470	27 800	India-Nepal
Makalu I	8 470	27 800	China-Nepal

HIGHEST MOUNTAINS (cont.)

Name	Height* m	ft	Location
Kangchenjunga W Peak	8420	27620	India-Nepal
Llotse E Peak	8380	27500	China-Nepal
Dhaulagiri	8170	26810	Nepal
Cho Oyu	8150	26750	China-Nepal
Manaslu	8130	26660	Nepal
Nanga Parbat	8130	26660	Kashmir-Jammu
Annapurna I	8080	26500	Nepal
Gasherbrum I	8070	26470	Kashmir-Jammu
Broad-highest	8050	26400	Kashmir-Jammu
Gasherbrum II	8030	26360	Kashmir-Jammu
Gosainthan	8010	26290	China
Broad-middle	8000	26250	Kashmir-Jammu
Gasherbrum III	7950	26090	Kashmir-Jammu
Annapurna II	7940	26040	Nepal
Nanda Devi	7820	25660	India
Rakaposhi	7790	25560	Kashmir
Kamet	7760	25450	India
Ulugh Muztagh	7720	25340	Tibet
Tirich Mir	7690	25230	Pakistan
Muz Tag Ata	7550	24760	China
Communism Peak	7490	24590	USSR
Pobedy Peak	7440	24410	China-USSR
Aconcagua	6960	22830	Argentina
Ojos del Salado	6910	22660	Argentina-Chile

*Heights are given to the nearest 10 m/ft.

LARGEST DESERTS

Name/Location	Area* sq km	sq ml
Sahara, N Africa	8600000	3320000
Arabian, SW Asia	2330000	900000
Gobi, Mongolia and NE China	1166000	450000
Patagonian, Argentina	673000	260000
Great Victoria, SW Australia	647000	250000
Great Basin, SW USA	492000	190000
Chihuahuan, Mexico	450000	175000
Great Sandy, NW Australia	400000	150000
Sonoran, SW USA	310000	120000
Kyzyl Kum, SW USSR	300000	115000
Takla Makan, N China	270000	105000
Kalahari, SW Africa	260000	100000
Kara Kum, SW USSR	260000	100000
Kavir, Iran	260000	100000
Syrian, Saudi Arabia/Jordan/Syria/Iraq	260000	100000
Nubian, Sudan	260000	100000
Thar, India/Pakistan	200000	77000
Ust'-Urt, SW USSR	160000	62000

LARGEST DESERTS (cont.)

Name/Location	Area* sq km	sq ml
Bet-Pak-Dala, S USSR	155 000	60 000
Simpson, C Australia	145 000	56 000
Dzungaria, China	142 000	55 000
Atacama, Chile	140 000	54 000
Namib, SE Africa	134 000	52 000
Sturt, SE Australia	130 000	50 000
Bolson de Mapimi, Mexico	130 000	50 000
Ordos, China	130 000	50 000
Alashan, China	116 000	45 000

*Desert areas are very approximate, because clear physical boundaries may not occur.

LONGEST RIVERS

Name	Outflow	Length* km	ml
Nile-Kagera-Ruvuvu-Ruvusu-Luvironza	Mediterranean Sea (Egypt)	6 690	4 160
Amazon-Ucayali-Tambo-Ene-Apurimac	Atlantic Ocean (Brazil)	6 570	4 080
Mississippi-Missouri-Jefferson-Beaverhead-Red Rock	Gulf of Mexico (USA)	6 020	3 740
Chang Jiang (Yangtze)	E China Sea (China)	5 980	3 720
Yenisey-Angara-Selenga-Ider	Kara Sea (USSR)	5 870	3 650
Amur-Argun-Kerulen	Tartar Strait (USSR)	5 780	3 590
Ob-Irtysh, Asia	Gulf of Ob, Kara Sea (USSR)	5 410	3 360
Plata-Parana-Grande	Atlantic Ocean (Argentina/Uruguay)	4 880	3 030
Huang Ho (Yellow)	Yellow Sea (China)	4 840	3 010
Congo (Zaire)-Lualaba	Atlantic Ocean (Angola-Zaire)	4 630	2 880
Lena	Laptev Sea (USSR)	4 400	2 730
Mackenzie-Slave-Peace-Finlay	Beaufort Sea (Canada)	4 240	2 630
Mekong	S China Sea (Vietnam)	4 180	2 600
Niger	Gulf of Guinea (Nigeria)	4 100	2 550

*Lengths are given to the nearest 10 km/ml, and include the river plus tributaries comprising the longest watercourse.

HIGHEST WATERFALLS

Name	Height m	ft	Name	Height m	ft
Angel (upper fall), Venezuela	807	2 648	Pilao, Brazil	524	1 719
Itatinga, Brazil	628	2 060	Ribbon, USA	491	1 612
Cuquenan, Guyana-Venezuela	610	2 000	Vestre Mardola, Norway	468	1 535
			Roraima, Guyana	457?	1 500?
Ormeli, Norway	563	1 847	Cleve-Garth, New Zealand	450?	1 476?
Tysse, Norway	533	1 749			

Distances are given for individual leaps.

DEEPEST CAVES

Name/Location	Depth m	ft	Name/Location	Depth m	ft
Jean Bernard, France	1494	4900	Dachstein-Mammuthöhle, Austria	1174	3852
Snezhnaya, USSR	1340	4397	Zitu, Spain	1139	3737
Puertas de Illamina, Spain	1338	4390	Badalona, Spain	1130	3707
Pierre-Saint-Martin, France	1321	4334	Batmanhöhle, Austria	1105	3626
Sistema Huautla, Mexico	1240	4067	Schneeloch, Austria	1101	3612
Berger, France	1198	3930	G E S Malaga, Spain	1070	3510
Vqerdi, Spain	1195	3921	Lamprechtsofen, Austria	1024	3360

MAJOR VOLCANOES

Name	Height m	ft	Major eruptions (years)	Last eruption (year)
Aconcagua (Argentina)	6960	22831	extinct	
Ararat (Turkey)	5198	18350	extinct	Holocene
Awu (Sangihe Is)	1327	4355	1711,1856,1892	1968
Bezymianny (USSR)	2800	9186	1955–6	1984
Coseguina (Nicaragua)	847	1598	1835	1835
El Chichón (Mexico)	1349	4430	1982	1982
Erebus (Antarctica)	4023	13200	1947,1972	1986
Etna (Italy)	3236	10625	122,1169,1329,1536, 1669,1928,1964,1971	1986
Fuji (Japan)	3776	12388	1707	1707
Galunggung (Java)	2180	7155	1822,1918	1982
Hekla (Iceland)	1491	4920	1693,1845,1947–8, 1970	1981
Helgafell (Iceland)	215	706	1973	1973
Jurullo (Mexico)	1330	4255	1759–74	1774
Katmai (Alaska)	2298	7540	1912,1920,1921	1931
Kilauea (Hawaii)	1247	4100	1823–1924,1952, 1955,1960,1967–8, 1968–74,1983–7	1991
Kilimanjaro (Tanzania)	5930	19450	extinct	Pleistocene
Klyuchevskoy (USSR)	4850	15910	1700–1966,1984	1985
Krakatoa (Sumatra)	818	2685	1680,1883,1927, 1952–3,1969	1980
La Soufrière (St Vincent)	1232	4048	1718,1812,1902, 1971–2	1979
Laki (Iceland)	500	1642	1783	1784
Lamington (Papua New Guinea)	1780	5844	1951	1956
Lassen Peak (USA)	3186	10453	1914–5	1921
Mauna Loa (Hawaii)	4172	13685	1859,1880,1887,1919, 1950	1984
Mayon (Philippines)	2462	8084	1616,1766,1814,1897, 1968	1978
Nyamuragira (Zaire)	3056	10026	1921–38,1971,1980	1984
Paricutin (Mexico)	3188	10460	1943–52	1952
Pelée, Mont (Martinique)	1397	4584	1902,1929–32	1932
Pinatubo, Mt (Philippines)	1462	4795	1391,1991	1991
Popocatepetl (Mexico)	5483	17990	1920	1943
Rainier, Mt (USA)	4392	14416	1st-c BC, 1820	1882
Ruapehu (New Zealand)	2796	9175	1945,1953,1969,1975	1986
St Helens, Mt (USA)	2549	8364	1800,1831,1835, 1842–3,1857,1980–	1987
Santorini/Thira (Greece)	1315?	4316?	1470 BC, 197 BC, AD 46, 1570–3,1707–11,1866–70	1950
Stromboli (Italy)	931	3055	1768,1882,1889,1907,1930, 1936,1941,1950,1952	1986
Surtsey (Iceland)	174	570	1963–7	1967

MAJOR VOLCANOES (cont.)

Name	Height m	ft	Major eruptions (years)	Last eruption (year)
Taal (Philippines)	1 448	4 752	1911, 1965, 1969	1977
Tambora (Sumbawa)	2 868	9 410	1815	1880
Tarawera (New Zealand)	1 149	3 770	1886	1973
Unzen (Japan)	1 360	4 461	1360, 1791	1991
Vesuvius (Italy)	1 289	4 230	79, 472, 1036, 1631, 1779, 1906	1944
Vulcano (Italy)	502	1 650	antiquity, 1444, 1730–40, 1786, 1873, 1888–90	1890

MAJOR EARTHQUAKES

All magnitudes on the Richter scale.

The energy released by earthquakes is measured on the logarithmic Richter scale. Thus

2	Barely perceptible
5	Destructive
7+	Major earthquake

Location	Year	Magnitude	Deaths	Location	Year	Magnitude	Deaths
Cabanatuan City	1990	7.7	1653	Chillan (Chile)	1939	7.8	30 000
NW Iran	1990	7.5	36 000	Quetta (India)	1935	7.5	60 000
N Peru	1990	5.8	200	Gansu (China)	1932	7.6	70 000
Romania	1990	6.6	70	Nan-shan (China)	1927	8.3	200 000
Philippines	1990	7.7	40	Kwanto (Japan)	1923	8.3	143 000
San Francisco	1989	6.9	100	Gansu (China)	1920	8.6	180 000
Armenia (USSR)	1988	7.0	25 000	Avezzano (Italy)	1915	7.5	30 000
Mexico City	1985	8.1	7 200	Messina (Italy)	1908	7.5	120 000
N Yemen	1982	6.0	2 800	Valparaiso (Chile)	1900	8.0	20 000
S Italy	1980	7.2	4 500	San Francisco (USA)	1906	8.3	500
El Asnam (Algeria)	1980	7.3	5 000	Ecuador/Colombia	1868	*	70 000
NE Iran	1978	7.7	25 000	Calabria (Italy)	1783	*	50 000
Tangshan (China)	1976	8.2	242 000	Lisbon (Portugal)	1755	*	70 000
Guatemala City	1976	7.5	22 778	Calcutta (India)	1737	*	300 000
Kashmir	1974	6.3	5 200	Hokkaido (Japan)	1730	*	137 000
Managua (Nicaragua)	1972	6.2	5 000	Catania (Italy)	1693	*	60 000
S Iran	1972	6.9	5 000	Caucasia (USSR)	1667	*	80 000
Chimbote (Peru)	1970	7.7	66 000	Shensi (China)	1556	*	830 000
NE Iran	1968	7.4	11 600	Chihli (China)	1290	*	100 000
Anchorage (USA)	1964	8.5	131	Silicia (Asia Minor)	1268	*	60 000
NW Iran	1962	7.1	12 000	Corinth (Greece)	856	*	45 000
Agadir (Morocco)	1960	5.8	12 000	Antioch (Turkey)	526	*	250 000
Erzincan (Turkey)	1939	7.9	23 000				

*Magnitude not available.

EARTHQUAKE SEVERITY MEASUREMENT

Modified Mercalli intensity scale (1956 Revision)

Intensity value	Description
I	Not felt; marginal and long-period effects of large earthquakes.
II	Felt by persons at rest, on upper floors or favourably placed.
III	Felt indoors; hanging objects swing; vibration like passing of light trucks; duration estimated; may not be recognized as an earthquake.
IV	Hanging objects swing; vibration like passing of heavy trucks, or sensation of a jolt like a heavy ball striking the walls; standing cars rock; windows, dishes, doors rattle; glasses clink; crockery clashes; in the upper range of IV, wooden walls and frames creak.
V	Felt outdoors; direction estimated; sleepers wakened; liquids disturbed, some spilled; small unstable objects displaced or upset; doors swing, close, open; shutters, pictures move; pendulum clocks stop, start, change rate.
VI	Felt by all; many frightened and run outdoors; persons walk unsteadily; windows, dishes, glassware break; knickknacks, books, etc, fall off shelves; pictures off walls; furniture moves or overturns; weak plaster and masonry D crack; small bells ring (church, school); trees, bushes shake visibly, or heard to rustle.
VII	Difficult to stand; noticed by drivers; hanging objects quiver; furniture breaks; damage to masonry D, including cracks; weak chimneys broken at roof line; fall of plaster, loose bricks, stones, tiles, cornices, also unbraced parapets and architectural ornaments; some cracks in masonry C; waves on ponds, water turbid with mud; small slides and caving in along sand or gravel banks; large bells ring; concrete irrigation ditches damaged.
VIII	Steering of cars affected; damage to masonry C and partial collapse; some damage to masonry B; none to masonry A; fall of stucco and some masonry walls; twisting, fall of chimneys, factory stacks, monuments, towers, elevated tanks; frame houses move on foundations if not bolted down; loose panel walls thrown out; decayed piling broken off; branches broken from trees; changes in flow or temperature of springs and wells; cracks in wet ground and on steep slopes.
IX	General panic; masonry D destroyed; masonry C heavily damaged, sometimes with complete collapse; masonry B seriously damaged; general damage to foundations; frame structures, if not bolted, shift off foundations; frames racked; serious damage to reservoirs; underground pipes break; conspicuous cracks in ground; in alluviated areas sand and mud ejected, earthquake fountains, sand craters.
X	Most masonry and frame structures destroyed with their foundations; some well-built wooden structures and bridges destroyed; serious damage to dams, dikes, embankments; large landslides; water thrown on banks of canals, rivers, lakes, etc; sand and mud shifted horizontally on beaches and flat land; rails bent slightly.
XI	Rails bent greatly; underground pipelines completely out of service.
XII	Damage nearly total; large rock masses displaced; lines of sight and level distorted; objects thrown into the air.

Note

Masonry A. Good workmanship, mortar and design; reinforced, especially laterally, and bound together by using steel, concrete etc; designed to resist lateral forces.

Masonry B. Good workmanship and mortar; reinforced, but not designed in detail to resist lateral forces.

Masonry C. Ordinary workmanship and mortar; no extreme weakness like failing to tie in at corners, but neither reinforced nor designed against horizontal forces.

Masonry D. Weak materials, such as adobe; poor mortar; low standards of workmanship; weak horizontally.

MAJOR TSUNAMIS

Tsunamis are long-period ocean waves associated with earthquakes, volcanic explosions, or landslides. They are also referred to as *seismic sea waves* and popularly, but incorrectly, as *tidal waves*.

Location of source	Year	Height m	ft	Location of deaths/damage	Deaths
Sea of Japan	1983	15	49	Japan, Korea	107
Indonesia	1979	10	32	Indonesia	187
Celebes Sea	1976	30	98	Philippine Is	5 000
Alaska	1964	32	105	Alaska, Aleutian Is, California	122
Chile	1960	25	82	Chile, Hawaii, Japan	1 260
Aleutian Is	1957	16	52	Hawaii, Japan	0
Kamchatka	1952	18.4	60	Kamchatka, Kuril Is, Hawaii	many
Aleutian Is	1946	32	105	Aleutian Is, Hawaii, California	165
Nankaido (Japan)	1946	6.1	20	Japan	1 997
Kii (Japan)	1944	7.5	25	Japan	998
Sanriku (Japan)	1933	28.2	93	Japan, Hawaii	3 000
E Kamchatka	1923	20	66	Kamchatka, Hawaii	3
S Kuril Is	1918	12	39	Kuril Is, USSR, Japan, Hawaii	23
Sanriku (Japan)	1896	30	98	Japan	27 122
Sunda Strait	1883	35	115	Java, Sumatra	36 000
Chile	1877	23	75	Chile, Hawaii	many
Chile	1868	21	69	Chile, Hawaii	25 000
Hawaii Is	1868	20	66	Hawaii Is	81
Japan	1854	6	20	Japan	3 000
Flores Sea	1800	24	79	Indonesia	4–500
Ariake Sea	1792	9	30	Japan	9 745
Italy	1783	?	?	Italy	30 000
Ryukyu Is	1771	12	39	Ryukyu Is	11 941
Portugal	1775	16	52	W Europe, Morocco, W Indies	60 000
Peru	1746	24	79	Peru	5 000
Japan	1741	9	30	Japan	1 000 +
SE Kamchatka	1737	30	98	Kamchatka, Kuril Is	?
Peru	1724	24	79	Peru	?
Japan	1707	11.5	38	Japan	30 000
W Indies	1692	?	?	Jamaica	2 000
Banda Is	1629	15	49	Indonesia	?
Sanriku (Japan)	1611	25	82	Japan	5 000
Japan	1605	?	?	Japan	4 000
Kii (Japan)	1498	?	?	Japan	5 000

WIND FORCE AND SEA DISTURBANCE

Beaufort number	Wind speed m/sec	Wind speed kph	Wind speed mph	Wind name	Observable wind characteristics	Sea disturbance number	Average wave ht. m	Average wave ht. ft	Observable sea characteristics
0	1	<1	<1	Calm	Smoke rises vertically	0	0	0	Sea like a mirror
1	1	1–5	1–3	Light air	Wind direction shown by smoke drift, but not by wind vanes	0	0	0	Ripples like scales, without foam crests
2	2	6–11	4–7	Light breeze	Wind felt on face; leaves rustle; vanes moved by wind	1	0.3	0–1	More definite wavelets, but crests do not break
3	4	12–19	8–12	Gentle breeze	Leaves and small twigs in constant motion; wind extends light flag	2	0.3–0.6	1–2	Large wavelets; crests beginning to break; scattered white horses
4	7	20–28	13–18	Moderate	Raises dust, loose paper; small branches moved	3	0.6–1.2	2–4	Small waves becoming longer; fairly frequent white horses
5	10	29–38	19–24	Fresh	Small trees in leaf begin to sway; crested wavelets on inland waters	4	1.2–2.4	4–8	Moderate waves with a more definite long form; many white horses; some spray possible
6	12	39–49	25–31	Strong	Large branches in motion; difficult to use umbrellas; whistling heard in telegraph wires	5	2.4–4	8–13	Large waves forming; more extensive white foam crests; some spray probable
7	15	50–61	32–38	Near gale	Whole trees in motion; inconvenience walking against wind	6	4–6	13–20	Sea heaps up; streaks of white foam blown along
8	18	62–74	39–46	Gale	Breaks twigs off trees; impedes progress	6	4–6	13–20	Moderately high waves of greater length; well-marked streaks of foam
9	20	75–88	47–54	Strong gale	Slight structural damage occurs	6	4–6	13–20	High waves; dense streaks of foam; sea begins to roll; spray affects visibility
10	26	89–102	55–63	Storm	Trees uprooted; considerable damage occurs	7	6–9	20–30	Very high waves with long overhanging crests; dense streaks of foam blown along; generally white appearance of surface; heavy rolling
11	30	103–17	64–72	Violent storm	Widespread damage	8	9–14	30–45	Exceptionally high waves; long white patches of foam; poor visibility; ships lost to view behind waves
12–17	≥33	≥118	≥73	Hurricane		9	14	>45	Air filled with foam and spray; sea completely white; very poor visibility

CLIMATIC ZONES

The earth may be divided into zones, approximating to zones of latitude, such that each zone possesses a distinct type of climate.

The principal zones are:

Tropical One zone of wet climate near the equator (either constantly wet or monsoonal with wet and dry seasons, tropical savannah with dry winters); the average temperature is not below 18°C;

Amazon forest	Congo Basin
Malaysia	Indonesia
S Vietnam	S E Asia
India	Australia
Africa	

Subtropical Two zones of steppe and desert climate (transition through semi-arid to arid);

Sahara	Australia
Central Asia	Kalahari
Mexico	

Mediterranean Zones of rainy climates with mild winters; coolest month above 0°C but below 18°C;

California	parts of Chile
S Africa	SW Australia
S Europe	

Temperate Rainy climate (includes areas of temperate woodland, mountain forests, and plains with no dry season; influenced by seas – rainfall all year, small temperature changes); average temperature between 3°C and 18°C;

Most of Europe	New Zealand
Eastern Asia	Southern Chile
NW/NE USA	

Boreal Climate with a great range of temperature in the northern hemisphere (in some areas the most humid month is in summer and there is ten times more precipitation than the driest part of winter. In other areas the most humid month is in winter and there is ten times more precipitation than in the driest part of summer); in the coldest period temperatures do not exceed 3°C and in the hottest do not go below 10°C;

Prairies of USA	N USSR
parts of S Africa	parts of Australia

Polar caps (2) of arctic snow climate (tundra and ice-cap) with little or no precipitation. There is permafrost in the tundra and vegetation includes lichen and moss all year and grass in the summer; the highest annual temperature in the polar region is below 0°C and in the tundra the average temperature is 10°C.

Arctic regions of USSR	Antartica
and N America	

GREAT ICE AGES

Precambrian era	Early Proterozoic
Precambrian era	Upper Proterozoic
Paleozoic era	Upper Carboniferous
Cenozoic era	Pleistocene*
	(Last 4 periods of glaciation)
	Gunz (Nebraskan or Jerseyan) 520 000–490 000 years ago
	Mindel (Kansan) 430 000–370 000 years ago
	Riss (Illinoian) 130 000–100 000 years ago
	Wurm (Wisconsan and Iowan) 40 000–18 000 years ago

*The Pleistocene era is synonymous with 'The Ice Age'

GEOLOGICAL TIME SCALE

Eon	Era	Period	Epoch	Million years before present	Geological events	Sea life	Land life
		Quaternary	Holocene		Glaciers recede. Sea level rises. Climate becomes more equable.	As now.	Forests flourish again. Humans acquire agriculture and technology.
				0.01			
			Pleistocene		Widespread glaciers melt periodically causing seas to rise and fall.	As now.	Many plant forms perish. Small mammals abundant. Primitive humans established.
		Tertiary		2.0			
			Pliocene	5.1	Continents and oceans adopting their present form. Present climatic distribution established. Ice caps develop.	Giant sharks extinct. Many fish varieties.	Some plants and mammals die out. Primates flourish.
			Miocene	24.6	Seas recede further. European and Asian land masses join. Heavy rain causes massive erosion. Red Sea opens.	Bony fish common. Giant sharks.	Grasses widespread. Grazing mammals become common.
			Oligocene	38.0	Seas recede. Extensive movements of earth's crust produce new mountains (eg Alpine-Himalayan chain).	Crabs, mussels, and snails evolve.	Forests diminish. Grasses appear. Pachyderms, canines and felines develop.
			Eocene	54.9	Mountain formation continues. Glaciers common in high mountain ranges. Greenland separates. Australia separates.	Whales adapt to sea.	Large tropical jungles. Primitive forms of modern mammals established.
			Paleocene		Widespread subsidence of land. Seas advance again. Considerable volcanic activity. Europe emerges.	Many reptiles become extinct.	Flowering plants widespread. First primates. Giant reptiles extinct.
		Cretaceous	Late	65	Swamps widespread. Massive alluvial deposition. Continuing limestone formation. S America separates from Africa. India, Africa and Antarctica separate.	Turtles, rays, and now-common fish appear.	Flowering plants established. Dinosaurs become extinct.
			Early	97.5			
		Jurassic	Malm	144	Seas advance. Much river formation. High mountains eroded. Limestone formation. N America separates from Africa. Central Atlantic begins to open.	Reptiles dominant.	Early flowers. Dinosaurs dominant. Mammals still primitive. First birds.
			Dogger	163			
			Lias	188			
		Triassic	Late	213	Desert conditions widespread. Hot climate gradually becomes warm and wet. Break up of Gondwanaland into continents.	Icthyosaurs, flying fish, and crustaceans appear.	Ferns and conifers thrive. First mammals, dinosaurs, and flies.
			Middle	231			
			Early	243			

Eon	Era	Period	Epoch/Series	Age (Ma)	Geology	Animal life	Plant/insect life
Phanerozoic	Palaeozoic	Permian	Late / Early	248 / 258	Some sea areas cut off to form lakes. Earth movements form mountains. Glaciation in southern hemisphere.	Some shelled fish become extinct.	Deciduous plants. Reptiles dominant. Many insect varieties.
Phanerozoic	Palaeozoic	Carboniferous	Pennsylvanian / Mississippian	286 / 320	Sea-beds rise to form new land areas. Enormous swamps. Partly-rotted vegetation forms coal.	Amphibians and sharks abundant.	Extensive evergreen forests. Reptiles breed on land. Some insects develop wings.
Phanerozoic	Palaeozoic	Devonian	Late / Middle / Early	360 / 374 / 387	Collision of continents causing mountain formation (Appalachians, Caledonides and Urals) Sea deeper but narrower. Climatic zones forming. Iapetus ocean closed.	Fish abundant. Primitive sharks. First amphibians.	Leafy plants. Some invertebrates adapt to land. First insects.
Phanerozoic	Palaeozoic	Silurian	Pridoli / Ludlow / Wenlock / Llandovery	408 / 414 / 421 / 428	New mountain ranges form. Sea level varies periodically. Extensive shallow sea over the Sahara.	Large vertebrates.	First leafless land plants.
Phanerozoic	Palaeozoic	Ordovician	Ashgill / Caradoc / Llandeilo / Llanvirn / Arenig / Tremadoc	438 / 448 / 458 / 468 / 478 / 488	Shore lines still quite variable. Increasing sedimentation. Europe and N America moving together.	First vertebrates. Coral reefs develop.	None.
Phanerozoic	Palaeozoic	Cambrian	Merioneth / St David's / Caerfai	505 / 525 / 540	Much volcanic activity, and long periods of marine sedimentation.	Shelled invertebrates. Trilobites.	None.
Proterozoic	Precambrian	Vendian		590	Shallow seas advance and retreat over land areas. Atmosphere uniformly warm.	Seaweed. Algae and invertebrates.	None.
Proterozoic	Precambrian	Riphean	Late / Middle / Early	650 / 900 / 1300	Intense deformation and metamorphism.	Earliest marine life and fossils.	None.
Proterozoic	Precambrian	Early Proterozoic		1600 / 2500	Shallow shelf seas. Formation of carbonate sediments and 'red beds'.	First appearance of stromatolites.	None.
Archaean	Precambrian	Archaean (Azoic)		4600	Banded iron formations. Formation of the earth's crust and oceans.	None.	None.

CHINESE ANIMAL YEARS AND TIMES 1984–2007

Chinese	English	Years		Time of day (hours)	Chinese	English	Years		Time of day (hours)
Shu	Rat	1984	1996	2300–0100	Ma	Horse	1990	2002	1100–1300
Niu	Ox	1985	1997	0100–0300	Yang	Sheep	1991	2003	1300–1500
Hu	Tiger	1986	1998	0300–0500	Hou	Monkey	1992	2004	1500–1700
T'u	Hare	1987	1999	0500–0700	Chi	Cock	1993	2005	1700–1900
Lung	Dragon	1988	2000	0700–0900	Kou	Dog	1994	2006	1900–2100
She	Serpent	1989	2001	0900–1100	Chu	Boar	1995	2007	2100–2300

YEAR EQUIVALENTS

Jewish[1] (AM)

5750	(30 Sep	1989—19 Sep	1990)
5751	(20 Sep	1990— 8 Sep	1991)
5752	(9 Sep	1991—27 Sep	1992)
5753	(28 Sep	1992—15 Sep	1993)
5754	(16 Sep	1993— 5 Sep	1994)
5755	(6 Sep	1994—24 Sep	1995)
5756	(25 Sep	1995—13 Sep	1996)
5757	(14 Sep	1996— 1 Oct	1997)
5758	(2 Oct	1997—20 Sep	1998)
5759	(21 Sep	1998—10 Sep	1999)
5760	(11 Sep	1999—29 Sep	2000)

Islamic[2] (H)

1410	(4 Aug	1989—23 Jul	1990)
1411	(24 Jul	1990—12 Jul	1991)
1412	(13 Jul	1991— 1 Jul	1992)
1413	(2 Jul	1992—20 Jun	1993)
1414	(21 Jun	1993— 9 Jun	1994)

Islamic (cont.)

1415	(10 Jun	1994—30 May	1995)
1416	(31 May	1995—18 May	1996)
1417	(19 May	1996— 8 May	1997)
1418	(9 May	1997—27 Apr	1998)
1419	(28 Apr	1998—16 Apr	1999)
1420	(17 Apr	1999— 5 Apr	2000)

Hindu[3] (SE)

1911	(22 Mar	1989—21 Mar	1990)
1912	(22 Mar	1990—21 Mar	1991)
1913	(22 Mar	1991—20 Mar	1992)
1914	(21 Mar	1992—21 Mar	1993)
1915	(22 Mar	1993—21 Mar	1994)
1916	(22 Mar	1994—21 Mar	1995)
1917	(22 Mar	1995—20 Mar	1996)
1918	(21 Mar	1996—21 Mar	1997)
1919	(22 Mar	1997—21 Mar	1998)
1920	(22 Mar	1998—21 Mar	1999)
1921	(22 Mar	1999—21 Mar	2000)

Gregorian equivalents are given in parentheses and are AD (= Anno Domini).

[1] Calculated from 3761 BC, said to be the year of the creation of the world. AM = Anno Mundi.

[2] Calculated from AD 622, the year in which the Prophet went from Mecca to Medina. H = Hegira.

[3] Calculated from AD 78, the beginning of the Saka era (SE), used alongside Gregorian dates in Government of India publications since 22 Mar 1957. Other important Hindu eras include: Vikrama era (58 BC), Kalacuri era (AD 248), Gupta era (AD 320), and Harsa era (AD 606).

PERPETUAL CALENDAR 1801–2000

The calendar for each year is given under the corresponding letter overpage.

1801	I	1821	C	1841	K	1861	E	1881	M
1802	K	1822	E	1842	M	1862	G	1882	A
1803	M	1823	G	1843	A	1863	I	1883	C
1804	B	1824	J	1844	D	1864	L	1884	F
1805	E	1825	M	1845	G	1865	A	1885	I
1806	G	1826	A	1846	I	1866	C	1886	K
1807	I	1827	C	1847	K	1867	E	1887	M
1808	L	1828	F	1848	N	1868	H	1888	B
1809	A	1829	I	1849	C	1869	K	1889	E
1810	C	1830	K	1850	E	1870	M	1890	G
1811	E	1831	M	1851	G	1871	A	1891	I
1812	H	1832	B	1852	J	1872	D	1892	L
1813	K	1833	E	1853	M	1873	G	1893	A
1814	M	1834	G	1854	A	1874	I	1894	C
1815	A	1835	I	1855	C	1875	K	1895	E
1816	D	1836	L	1856	F	1876	N	1896	H
1817	G	1837	A	1857	I	1877	C	1897	K
1818	I	1838	C	1858	K	1878	E	1898	M
1819	K	1839	E	1859	M	1879	G	1899	A
1820	N	1840	H	1860	B	1880	J	1900	C
1901	E	1921	M	1941	G	1961	A	1981	I
1902	G	1922	A	1942	I	1962	C	1982	K
1903	I	1923	C	1943	K	1963	E	1983	M
1904	L	1924	F	1944	N	1964	H	1984	B
1905	A	1925	I	1945	C	1965	K	1985	E
1906	C	1926	K	1946	E	1966	M	1986	G
1907	E	1927	M	1947	G	1967	A	1987	I
1908	H	1928	B	1948	J	1968	D	1988	L
1909	K	1929	E	1949	M	1969	G	1989	A
1910	M	1930	G	1950	A	1970	I	1990	C
1911	A	1931	I	1951	C	1971	K	1991	E
1912	D	1932	L	1952	F	1972	N	1992	H
1913	G	1933	A	1953	I	1973	C	1993	K
1914	I	1934	C	1954	K	1974	E	1994	M
1915	K	1935	E	1955	M	1975	G	1995	A
1916	N	1936	H	1956	B	1976	J	1996	D
1917	C	1937	K	1957	E	1977	M	1997	G
1918	E	1938	M	1958	G	1978	A	1998	I
1919	G	1939	A	1959	I	1979	C	1999	K
1920	J	1940	D	1960	L	1980	F	2000	N

PERPETUAL CALENDAR 1801–2000 (cont.)

A

January	February	March	April

January
S	M	T	W	T	F	S
1	2	3	4	5	6	7
8	9	10	11	12	13	14
15	16	17	18	19	20	21
22	23	24	25	26	27	28
29	30	31				

February
S	M	T	W	T	F	S
				1	2	3	4
5	6	7	8	9	10	11
12	13	14	15	16	17	18
19	20	21	22	23	24	25
26	27	28				

March
S	M	T	W	T	F	S
				1	2	3	4
5	6	7	8	9	10	11
12	13	14	15	16	17	18
19	20	21	22	23	24	25
26	27	28	29	30	31	

April
S	M	T	W	T	F	S
						1
2	3	4	5	6	7	8
9	10	11	12	13	14	15
16	17	18	19	20	21	22
23	24	25	26	27	28	29
30						

May
S	M	T	W	T	F	S
	1	2	3	4	5	6
7	8	9	10	11	12	13
14	15	16	17	18	19	20
21	22	23	24	25	26	27
28	29	30	31			

June
S	M	T	W	T	F	S
				1	2	3
4	5	6	7	8	9	10
11	12	13	14	15	16	17
18	19	20	21	22	23	24
25	26	27	28	29	30	

July
S	M	T	W	T	F	S
						1
2	3	4	5	6	7	8
9	10	11	12	13	14	15
16	17	18	19	20	21	22
23	24	25	26	27	28	29
30	31					

August
S	M	T	W	T	F	S
		1	2	3	4	5
6	7	8	9	10	11	12
13	14	15	16	17	18	19
20	21	22	23	24	25	26
27	28	29	30	31		

September
S	M	T	W	T	F	S
					1	2
3	4	5	6	7	8	9
10	11	12	13	14	15	16
17	18	19	20	21	22	23
24	25	26	27	28	29	30

October
S	M	T	W	T	F	S
1	2	3	4	5	6	7
8	9	10	11	12	13	14
15	16	17	18	19	20	21
22	23	24	25	26	27	28
29	30	31				

November
S	M	T	W	T	F	S
			1	2	3	4
5	6	7	8	9	10	11
12	13	14	15	16	17	18
19	20	21	22	23	24	25
26	27	28	29	30		

December
S	M	T	W	T	F	S
					1	2
3	4	5	6	7	8	9
10	11	12	13	14	15	16
17	18	19	20	21	22	23
24	25	26	27	28	29	30
31						

B (leap year)

January
S	M	T	W	T	F	S
1	2	3	4	5	6	7
8	9	10	11	12	13	14
15	16	17	18	19	20	21
22	23	24	25	26	27	28
29	30	31				

February
S	M	T	W	T	F	S
				1	2	3	4
5	6	7	8	9	10	11
12	13	14	15	16	17	18
19	20	21	22	23	24	25
26	27	28	29			

March
S	M	T	W	T	F	S
				1	2	3
4	5	6	7	8	9	10
11	12	13	14	15	16	17
18	19	20	21	22	23	24
25	26	27	28	29	30	31

April
S	M	T	W	T	F	S
1	2	3	4	5	6	7
8	9	10	11	12	13	14
15	16	17	18	19	20	21
22	23	24	25	26	27	28
29	30					

May
S	M	T	W	T	F	S
	1	2	3	4	5		
6	7	8	9	10	11	12
13	14	15	16	17	18	19
20	21	22	23	24	25	26
27	28	29	30	31		

June
S	M	T	W	T	F	S
					1	2
3	4	5	6	7	8	9
10	11	12	13	14	15	16
17	18	19	20	21	22	23
24	25	26	27	28	29	30

July
S	M	T	W	T	F	S
1	2	3	4	5	6	7
8	9	10	11	12	13	14
15	16	17	18	19	20	21
22	23	24	25	26	27	28
29	30	31				

August
S	M	T	W	T	F	S
			1	2	3	4
5	6	7	8	9	10	11
12	13	14	15	16	17	18
19	20	21	22	23	24	25
26	27	28	29	30	31	

September
S	M	T	W	T	F	S
						1
2	3	4	5	6	7	8
9	10	11	12	13	14	15
16	17	18	19	20	21	22
23	24	25	26	27	28	29
30						

October
S	M	T	W	T	F	S
	1	2	3	4	5	6
7	8	9	10	11	12	13
14	15	16	17	18	19	20
21	22	23	24	25	26	27
28	29	30	31			

November
S	M	T	W	T	F	S
				1	2	3
4	5	6	7	8	9	10
11	12	13	14	15	16	17
18	19	20	21	22	23	24
25	26	27	28	29	30	

December
S	M	T	W	T	F	S
						1
2	3	4	5	6	7	8
9	10	11	12	13	14	15
16	17	18	19	20	21	22
23	24	25	26	27	28	29
30	31					

PERPETUAL CALENDAR 1801–2000 (cont.)

C

January
S	M	T	W	T	F	S
	1	2	3	4	5	6
7	8	9	10	11	12	13
14	15	16	17	18	19	20
21	22	23	24	25	26	27
28	29	30	31			

February
S	M	T	W	T	F	S
					1	2	3
4	5	6	7	8	9	10
11	12	13	14	15	16	17
18	19	20	21	22	23	24
25	26	27	28			

March
S	M	T	W	T	F	S
					1	2	3
4	5	6	7	8	9	10
11	12	13	14	15	16	17
18	19	20	21	22	23	24
25	26	27	28	29	30	31

April
S	M	T	W	T	F	S
1	2	3	4	5	6	7
8	9	10	11	12	13	14
15	16	17	18	19	20	21
22	23	24	25	26	27	28
29	30					

May
S	M	T	W	T	F	S
		1	2	3	4	5
6	7	8	9	10	11	12
13	14	15	16	17	18	19
20	21	22	23	24	25	26
27	28	29	30	31		

June
S	M	T	W	T	F	S
					1	2
3	4	5	6	7	8	9
10	11	12	13	14	15	16
17	18	19	20	21	22	23
24	25	26	27	28	29	30

July
S	M	T	W	T	F	S
1	2	3	4	5	6	7
8	9	10	11	12	13	14
15	16	17	18	19	20	21
22	23	24	25	26	27	28
29	30	31				

August
S	M	T	W	T	F	S
				1	2	3	4
5	6	7	8	9	10	11
12	13	14	15	16	17	18
19	20	21	22	23	24	25
26	27	28	29	30	31	

September
S	M	T	W	T	F	S
						1
2	3	4	5	6	7	8
9	10	11	12	13	14	15
16	17	18	19	20	21	22
23	24	25	26	27	28	29
30						

October
S	M	T	W	T	F	S
	1	2	3	4	5	6
7	8	9	10	11	12	13
14	15	16	17	18	19	20
21	22	23	24	25	26	27
28	29	30	31			

November
S	M	T	W	T	F	S
				1	2	3
4	5	6	7	8	9	10
11	12	13	14	15	16	17
18	19	20	21	22	23	24
25	26	27	28	29	30	

December
S	M	T	W	T	F	S
						1
2	3	4	5	6	7	8
9	10	11	12	13	14	15
16	17	18	19	20	21	22
23	24	25	26	27	28	29
30	31					

D (leap year)

January
S	M	T	W	T	F	S
	1	2	3	4	5	6
7	8	9	10	11	12	13
14	15	16	17	18	19	20
21	22	23	24	25	26	27
28	29	30	31			

February
S	M	T	W	T	F	S
					1	2	3
4	5	6	7	8	9	10
11	12	13	14	15	16	17
18	19	20	21	22	23	24
25	26	27	28	29		

March
S	M	T	W	T	F	S
						1	2
3	4	5	6	7	8	9
10	11	12	13	14	15	16
17	18	19	20	21	22	23
24	25	26	27	28	29	30
31						

April
S	M	T	W	T	F	S
	1	2	3	4	5	6
7	8	9	10	11	12	13
14	15	16	17	18	19	20
21	22	23	24	25	26	27
28	29	30				

May
S	M	T	W	T	F	S
			1	2	3	4
5	6	7	8	9	10	11
12	13	14	15	16	17	18
19	20	21	22	23	24	25
26	27	28	29	30	31	

June
S	M	T	W	T	F	S
						1
2	3	4	5	6	7	8
9	10	11	12	13	14	15
16	17	18	19	20	21	22
23	24	25	26	27	28	29
30						

July
S	M	T	W	T	F	S
	1	2	3	4	5	6
7	8	9	10	11	12	13
14	15	16	17	18	19	20
21	22	23	24	25	26	27
28	29	30	31			

August
S	M	T	W	T	F	S
					1	2	3
4	5	6	7	8	9	10
11	12	13	14	15	16	17
18	19	20	21	22	23	24
25	26	27	28	29	30	31

September
S	M	T	W	T	F	S
1	2	3	4	5	6	7
8	9	10	11	12	13	14
15	16	17	18	19	20	21
22	23	24	25	26	27	28
29	30					

October
S	M	T	W	T	F	S
		1	2	3	4	5
6	7	8	9	10	11	12
13	14	15	16	17	18	19
20	21	22	23	24	25	26
27	28	29	30	31		

November
S	M	T	W	T	F	S
					1	2
3	4	5	6	7	8	9
10	11	12	13	14	15	16
17	18	19	20	21	22	23
24	25	26	27	28	29	30

December
S	M	T	W	T	F	S
1	2	3	4	5	6	7
8	9	10	11	12	13	14
15	16	17	18	19	20	21
22	23	24	25	26	27	28
29	30	31				

PERPETUAL CALENDAR 1801–2000 (cont.)

E

January
S	M	T	W	T	F	S
		1	2	3	4	5
6	7	8	9	10	11	12
13	14	15	16	17	18	19
20	21	22	23	24	25	26
27	28	29	30	31		

February
S	M	T	W	T	F	S
					1	2
3	4	5	6	7	8	9
10	11	12	13	14	15	16
17	18	19	20	21	22	23
24	25	26	27	28		

March
S	M	T	W	T	F	S
					1	2
3	4	5	6	7	8	9
10	11	12	13	14	15	16
17	18	19	20	21	22	23
24	25	26	27	28	29	30
31						

April
S	M	T	W	T	F	S
	1	2	3	4	5	6
7	8	9	10	11	12	13
14	15	16	17	18	19	20
21	22	23	24	25	26	27
28	29	30				

May
S	M	T	W	T	F	S
			1	2	3	4
5	6	7	8	9	10	11
12	13	14	15	16	17	18
19	20	21	22	23	24	25
26	27	28	29	30	31	

June
S	M	T	W	T	F	S
						1
2	3	4	5	6	7	8
9	10	11	12	13	14	15
16	17	18	19	20	21	22
23	24	25	26	27	28	29
30						

July
S	M	T	W	T	F	S
	1	2	3	4	5	6
7	8	9	10	11	12	13
14	15	16	17	18	19	20
21	22	23	24	25	26	27
28	29	30	31			

August
S	M	T	W	T	F	S
				1	2	3
4	5	6	7	8	9	10
11	12	13	14	15	16	17
18	19	20	21	22	23	24
25	26	27	28	29	30	31

September
S	M	T	W	T	F	S
1	2	3	4	5	6	7
8	9	10	11	12	13	14
15	16	17	18	19	20	21
22	23	24	25	26	27	28
29	30					

October
S	M	T	W	T	F	S
		1	2	3	4	5
6	7	8	9	10	11	12
13	14	15	16	17	18	19
20	21	22	23	24	25	26
27	28	29	30	31		

November
S	M	T	W	T	F	S
					1	2
3	4	5	6	7	8	9
10	11	12	13	14	15	16
17	18	19	20	21	22	23
24	25	26	27	28	29	30

December
S	M	T	W	T	F	S
1	2	3	4	5	6	7
8	9	10	11	12	13	14
15	16	17	18	19	20	21
22	23	24	25	26	27	28
29	30	31				

F (leap year)

January
S	M	T	W	T	F	S
		1	2	3	4	5
6	7	8	9	10	11	12
13	14	15	16	17	18	19
20	21	22	23	24	25	26
27	28	29	30	31		

February
S	M	T	W	T	F	S
					1	2
3	4	5	6	7	8	9
10	11	12	13	14	15	16
17	18	19	20	21	22	23
24	25	26	27	28	29	

March
S	M	T	W	T	F	S
						1
2	3	4	5	6	7	8
9	10	11	12	13	14	15
16	17	18	19	20	21	22
23	24	25	26	27	28	29
30	31					

April
S	M	T	W	T	F	S
	1	2	3	4	5	
6	7	8	9	10	11	12
13	14	15	16	17	18	19
20	21	22	23	24	25	26
27	28	29	30			

May
S	M	T	W	T	F	S
				1	2	3
4	5	6	7	8	9	10
11	12	13	14	15	16	17
18	19	20	21	22	23	24
25	26	27	28	29	30	31

June
S	M	T	W	T	F	S
1	2	3	4	5	6	7
8	9	10	11	12	13	14
15	16	17	18	19	20	21
22	23	24	25	26	27	28
29	30					

July
S	M	T	W	T	F	S
		1	2	3	4	5
6	7	8	9	10	11	12
13	14	15	16	17	18	19
20	21	22	23	24	25	26
27	28	29	30	31		

August
S	M	T	W	T	F	S
					1	2
3	4	5	6	7	8	9
10	11	12	13	14	15	16
17	18	19	20	21	22	23
24	25	26	27	28	29	30
31						

September
S	M	T	W	T	F	S
	1	2	3	4	5	6
7	8	9	10	11	12	13
14	15	16	17	18	19	20
21	22	23	24	25	26	27
28	29	30				

October
S	M	T	W	T	F	S
			1	2	3	4
5	6	7	8	9	10	11
12	13	14	15	16	17	18
19	20	21	22	23	24	25
26	27	28	29	30	31	

November
S	M	T	W	T	F	S
						1
2	3	4	5	6	7	8
9	10	11	12	13	14	15
16	17	18	19	20	21	22
23	24	25	26	27	28	29
30						

December
S	M	T	W	T	F	S
	1	2	3	4	5	6
7	8	9	10	11	12	13
14	15	16	17	18	19	20
21	22	23	24	25	26	27
28	29	30	31			

PERPETUAL CALENDAR 1801–2000 (cont.)

G

January
```
 S  M  T  W  T  F  S
          1  2  3  4
 5  6  7  8  9 10 11
12 13 14 15 16 17 18
19 20 21 22 23 24 25
26 27 28 29 30 31
```

February
```
 S  M  T  W  T  F  S
                   1
 2  3  4  5  6  7  8
 9 10 11 12 13 14 15
16 17 18 19 20 21 22
23 24 25 26 27 28
```

March
```
 S  M  T  W  T  F  S
                   1
 2  3  4  5  6  7  8
 9 10 11 12 13 14 15
16 17 18 19 20 21 22
23 24 25 26 27 28 29
30 31
```

April
```
 S  M  T  W  T  F  S
          1  2  3  4  5
 6  7  8  9 10 11 12
13 14 15 16 17 18 19
20 21 22 23 24 25 26
27 28 29 30
```

May
```
 S  M  T  W  T  F  S
             1  2  3
 4  5  6  7  8  9 10
11 12 13 14 15 16 17
18 19 20 21 22 23 24
25 26 27 28 29 30 31
```

June
```
 S  M  T  W  T  F  S
 1  2  3  4  5  6  7
 8  9 10 11 12 13 14
15 16 17 18 19 20 21
22 23 24 25 26 27 28
29 30
```

July
```
 S  M  T  W  T  F  S
          1  2  3  4  5
 6  7  8  9 10 11 12
13 14 15 16 17 18 19
20 21 22 23 24 25 26
27 28 29 30 31
```

August
```
 S  M  T  W  T  F  S
                1  2
 3  4  5  6  7  8  9
10 11 12 13 14 15 16
17 18 19 20 21 22 23
24 25 26 27 28 29 30
31
```

September
```
 S  M  T  W  T  F  S
    1  2  3  4  5  6
 7  8  9 10 11 12 13
14 15 16 17 18 19 20
21 22 23 24 25 26 27
28 29 30
```

October
```
 S  M  T  W  T  F  S
             1  2  3  4
 5  6  7  8  9 10 11
12 13 14 15 16 17 18
19 20 21 22 23 24 25
26 27 28 29 30 31
```

November
```
 S  M  T  W  T  F  S
                   1
 2  3  4  5  6  7  8
 9 10 11 12 13 14 15
16 17 18 19 20 21 22
23 24 25 26 27 28 29
30
```

December
```
 S  M  T  W  T  F  S
    1  2  3  4  5  6
 7  8  9 10 11 12 13
14 15 16 17 18 19 20
21 22 23 24 25 26 27
28 29 30 31
```

H (leap year)

January
```
 S  M  T  W  T  F  S
          1  2  3  4
 5  6  7  8  9 10 11
12 13 14 15 16 17 18
19 20 21 22 23 24 25
26 27 28 29 30 31
```

February
```
 S  M  T  W  T  F  S
                   1
 2  3  4  5  6  7  8
 9 10 11 12 13 14 15
16 17 18 19 20 21 22
23 24 25 26 27 28 29
```

March
```
 S  M  T  W  T  F  S
 1  2  3  4  5  6  7
 8  9 10 11 12 13 14
15 16 17 18 19 20 21
22 23 24 25 26 27 28
29 30 31
```

April
```
 S  M  T  W  T  F  S
             1  2  3  4
 5  6  7  8  9 10 11
12 13 14 15 16 17 18
19 20 21 22 23 24 25
26 27 28 29 30
```

May
```
 S  M  T  W  T  F  S
                1  2
 3  4  5  6  7  8  9
10 11 12 13 14 15 16
17 18 19 20 21 22 23
24 25 26 27 28 29 30
31
```

June
```
 S  M  T  W  T  F  S
    1  2  3  4  5  6
 7  8  9 10 11 12 13
14 15 16 17 18 19 20
21 22 23 24 25 26 27
28 29 30
```

July
```
 S  M  T  W  T  F  S
          1  2  3  4
 5  6  7  8  9 10 11
12 13 14 15 16 17 18
19 20 21 22 23 24 25
26 27 28 29 30 31
```

August
```
 S  M  T  W  T  F  S
                   1
 2  3  4  5  6  7  8
 9 10 11 12 13 14 15
16 17 18 19 20 21 22
23 24 25 26 27 28 29
30 31
```

September
```
 S  M  T  W  T  F  S
       1  2  3  4  5
 6  7  8  9 10 11 12
13 14 15 16 17 18 19
20 21 22 23 24 25 26
27 28 29 30
```

October
```
 S  M  T  W  T  F  S
                1  2  3
 4  5  6  7  8  9 10
11 12 13 14 15 16 17
18 19 20 21 22 23 24
25 26 27 28 29 30 31
```

November
```
 S  M  T  W  T  F  S
 1  2  3  4  5  6  7
 8  9 10 11 12 13 14
15 16 17 18 19 20 21
22 23 24 25 26 27 28
29 30
```

December
```
 S  M  T  W  T  F  S
       1  2  3  4  5
 6  7  8  9 10 11 12
13 14 15 16 17 18 19
20 21 22 23 24 25 26
27 28 29 30 31
```

PERPETUAL CALENDAR 1801–2000 (cont.)

I

January

S	M	T	W	T	F	S
				1	2	3
4	5	6	7	8	9	10
11	12	13	14	15	16	17
18	19	20	21	22	23	24
25	26	27	28	29	30	31

February

S	M	T	W	T	F	S
1	2	3	4	5	6	7
8	9	10	11	12	13	14
15	16	17	18	19	20	21
22	23	24	25	26	27	28

March

S	M	T	W	T	F	S
1	2	3	4	5	6	7
8	9	10	11	12	13	14
15	16	17	18	19	20	21
22	23	24	25	26	27	28
29	30	31				

April

S	M	T	W	T	F	S
				1	2	3	4
5	6	7	8	9	10	11
12	13	14	15	16	17	18
19	20	21	22	23	24	25
26	27	28	29	30		

May

S	M	T	W	T	F	S
					1	2
3	4	5	6	7	8	9
10	11	12	13	14	15	16
17	18	19	20	21	22	23
24	25	26	27	28	29	30
31						

June

S	M	T	W	T	F	S
	1	2	3	4	5	6
7	8	9	10	11	12	13
14	15	16	17	18	19	20
21	22	23	24	25	26	27
28	29	30				

July

S	M	T	W	T	F	S
			1	2	3	4
5	6	7	8	9	10	11
12	13	14	15	16	17	18
19	20	21	22	23	24	25
26	27	28	29	30	31	

August

S	M	T	W	T	F	S
						1
2	3	4	5	6	7	8
9	10	11	12	13	14	15
16	17	18	19	20	21	22
23	24	25	26	27	28	29
30	31					

September

S	M	T	W	T	F	S
		1	2	3	4	5
6	7	8	9	10	11	12
13	14	15	16	17	18	19
20	21	22	23	24	25	26
27	28	29	30			

October

S	M	T	W	T	F	S
				1	2	3
4	5	6	7	8	9	10
11	12	13	14	15	16	17
18	19	20	21	22	23	24
25	26	27	28	29	30	31

November

S	M	T	W	T	F	S
1	2	3	4	5	6	7
8	9	10	11	12	13	14
15	16	17	18	19	20	21
22	23	24	25	26	27	28
29	30					

December

S	M	T	W	T	F	S
		1	2	3	4	5
6	7	8	9	10	11	12
13	14	15	16	17	18	19
20	21	22	23	24	25	26
27	28	29	30	31		

J (leap year)

January

S	M	T	W	T	F	S
				1	2	3
4	5	6	7	8	9	10
11	12	13	14	15	16	17
18	19	20	21	22	23	24
25	26	27	28	29	30	31

February

S	M	T	W	T	F	S
1	2	3	4	5	6	7
8	9	10	11	12	13	14
15	16	17	18	19	20	21
22	23	24	25	26	27	28
29						

March

S	M	T	W	T	F	S
	1	2	3	4	5	6
7	8	9	10	11	12	13
14	15	16	17	18	19	20
21	22	23	24	25	26	27
28	29	30	31			

April

S	M	T	W	T	F	S
				1	2	3
4	5	6	7	8	9	10
11	12	13	14	15	16	17
18	19	20	21	22	23	24
25	26	27	28	29	30	

May

S	M	T	W	T	F	S
						1
2	3	4	5	6	7	8
9	10	11	12	13	14	15
16	17	18	19	20	21	22
23	24	25	26	27	28	29
30	31					

June

S	M	T	W	T	F	S
		1	2	3	4	5
6	7	8	9	10	11	12
13	14	15	16	17	18	19
20	21	22	23	24	25	26
27	28	29	30			

July

S	M	T	W	T	F	S
				1	2	3
4	5	6	7	8	9	10
11	12	13	14	15	16	17
18	19	20	21	22	23	24
25	26	27	28	29	30	31

August

S	M	T	W	T	F	S
1	2	3	4	5	6	7
8	9	10	11	12	13	14
15	16	17	18	19	20	21
22	23	24	25	26	27	28
29	30	31				

September

S	M	T	W	T	F	S
		1	2	3	4
5	6	7	8	9	10	11
12	13	14	15	16	17	18
19	20	21	22	23	24	25
26	27	28	29	30		

October

S	M	T	W	T	F	S
					1	2
3	4	5	6	7	8	9
10	11	12	13	14	15	16
17	18	19	20	21	22	23
24	25	26	27	28	29	30
31						

November

S	M	T	W	T	F	S
	1	2	3	4	5	6
7	8	9	10	11	12	13
14	15	16	17	18	19	20
21	22	23	24	25	26	27
28	29	30				

December

S	M	T	W	T	F	S
		1	2	3	4
5	6	7	8	9	10	11
12	13	14	15	16	17	18
19	20	21	22	23	24	25
26	27	28	29	30	31	

PERPETUAL CALENDAR 1801–2000 (cont.)

K

January
S	M	T	W	T	F	S
					1	2
3	4	5	6	7	8	9
10	11	12	13	14	15	16
17	18	19	20	21	22	23
24	25	26	27	28	29	30
31						

February
S	M	T	W	T	F	S
	1	2	3	4	5	6
7	8	9	10	11	12	13
14	15	16	17	18	19	20
21	22	23	24	25	26	27
28						

March
S	M	T	W	T	F	S
			1	2	3	4
5	6	7	8	9	10	11
7	8	9	10	11	12	13
14	15	16	17	18	19	20
21	22	23	24	25	26	27
28	29	30	31			

April
S	M	T	W	T	F	S
				1	2	3
4	5	6	7	8	9	10
11	12	13	14	15	16	17
18	19	20	21	22	23	24
25	26	27	28	29	30	

May
S	M	T	W	T	F	S
						1
2	3	4	5	6	7	8
9	10	11	12	13	14	15
16	17	18	19	20	21	22
23	24	25	26	27	28	29
30	31					

June
S	M	T	W	T	F	S
		1	2	3	4	5
6	7	8	9	10	11	12
13	14	15	16	17	18	19
20	21	22	23	24	25	26
27	28	29	30			

July
S	M	T	W	T	F	S
				1	2	3
4	5	6	7	8	9	10
11	12	13	14	15	16	17
18	19	20	21	22	23	24
25	26	27	28	29	30	31

August
S	M	T	W	T	F	S
1	2	3	4	5	6	7
8	9	10	11	12	13	14
15	16	17	18	19	20	21
22	23	24	25	26	27	28
29	30	31				

September
S	M	T	W	T	F	S
				1	2	3
4						
5	6	7	8	9	10	11
12	13	14	15	16	17	18
19	20	21	22	23	24	25
26	27	28	29	30		

October
S	M	T	W	T	F	S
					1	2
3	4	5	6	7	8	9
10	11	12	13	14	15	16
17	18	19	20	21	22	23
24	25	26	27	28	29	30
31						

November
S	M	T	W	T	F	S
	1	2	3	4	5	6
7	8	9	10	11	12	13
14	15	16	17	18	19	20
21	22	23	24	25	26	27
28	29	30				

December
S	M	T	W	T	F	S
				1	2	3
4						
5	6	7	8	9	10	11
12	13	14	15	16	17	18
19	20	21	22	23	24	25
26	27	28	29	30	31	

L (leap year)

January
S	M	T	W	T	F	S
					1	2
3	4	5	6	7	8	9
10	11	12	13	14	15	16
17	18	19	20	21	22	23
24	25	26	27	28	29	30
31						

February
S	M	T	W	T	F	S
	1	2	3	4	5	6
7	8	9	10	11	12	13
14	15	16	17	18	19	20
21	22	23	24	25	26	27
28	29					

March
S	M	T	W	T	F	S
				1	2	3
4	5					
6	7	8	9	10	11	12
13	14	15	16	17	18	19
20	21	22	23	24	25	26
27	28	29	30	31		

April
S	M	T	W	T	F	S
					1	2
3	4	5	6	7	8	9
10	11	12	13	14	15	16
17	18	19	20	21	22	23
24	25	26	27	28	29	30

May
S	M	T	W	T	F	S
1	2	3	4	5	6	7
8	9	10	11	12	13	14
15	16	17	18	19	20	21
22	23	24	25	26	27	28
29	30	31				

June
S	M	T	W	T	F	S
				1	2	3
4						
5	6	7	8	9	10	11
12	13	14	15	16	17	18
19	20	21	22	23	24	25
26	27	28	29	30		

July
S	M	T	W	T	F	S
					1	2
3	4	5	6	7	8	9
10	11	12	13	14	15	16
17	18	19	20	21	22	23
24	25	26	27	28	29	30
31						

August
S	M	T	W	T	F	S
	1	2	3	4	5	6
7	8	9	10	11	12	13
14	15	16	17	18	19	20
21	22	23	24	25	26	27
28	29	30	31			

September
S	M	T	W	T	F	S
					1	2
3						
4	5	6	7	8	9	10
11	12	13	14	15	16	17
18	19	20	21	22	23	24
25	26	27	28	29	30	

October
S	M	T	W	T	F	S
						1
2	3	4	5	6	7	8
9	10	11	12	13	14	15
16	17	18	19	20	21	22
23	24	25	26	27	28	29
30	31					

November
S	M	T	W	T	F	S
		1	2	3	4	5
6	7	8	9	10	11	12
13	14	15	16	17	18	19
20	21	22	23	24	25	26
27	28	29	30			

December
S	M	T	W	T	F	S
				1	2	3
4	5	6	7	8	9	10
11	12	13	14	15	16	17
18	19	20	21	22	23	24
25	26	27	28	29	30	31

PERPETUAL CALENDAR 1801–2000 (cont.)

M

January
S	M	T	W	T	F	S
						1
2	3	4	5	6	7	8
9	10	11	12	13	14	15
16	17	18	19	20	21	22
23	24	25	26	27	28	29
30	31					

February
S	M	T	W	T	F	S
		1	2	3	4	5
6	7	8	9	10	11	12
13	14	15	16	17	18	19
20	21	22	23	24	25	26
27	28					

March
S	M	T	W	T	F	S
		1	2	3	4	5
6	7	8	9	10	11	12
13	14	15	16	17	18	19
20	21	22	23	24	25	26
27	28	29	30	31		

April
S	M	T	W	T	F	S
					1	2
3	4	5	6	7	8	9
10	11	12	13	14	15	16
17	18	19	20	21	22	23
24	25	26	27	28	29	30

May
S	M	T	W	T	F	S
1	2	3	4	5	6	7
8	9	10	11	12	13	14
15	16	17	18	19	20	21
22	23	24	25	26	27	28
29	30	31				

June
S	M	T	W	T	F	S
				1	2	3	4
5	6	7	8	9	10	11
12	13	14	15	16	17	18
19	20	21	22	23	24	25
26	27	28	29	30		

July
S	M	T	W	T	F	S
					1	2
3	4	5	6	7	8	9
10	11	12	13	14	15	16
17	18	19	20	21	22	23
24	25	26	27	28	29	30
31						

August
S	M	T	W	T	F	S
1	2	3	4	5	6
7	8	9	10	11	12	13
14	15	16	17	18	19	20
21	22	23	24	25	26	27
28	29	30	31			

September
S	M	T	W	T	F	S
					1	2	3
4	5	6	7	8	9	10
11	12	13	14	15	16	17
18	19	20	21	22	23	24
25	26	27	28	29	30	

October
S	M	T	W	T	F	S
						1
2	3	4	5	6	7	8
9	10	11	12	13	14	15
16	17	18	19	20	21	22
23	24	25	26	27	28	29
30	31					

November
S	M	T	W	T	F	S
		1	2	3	4	5
6	7	8	9	10	11	12
13	14	15	16	17	18	19
20	21	22	23	24	25	26
27	28	29	30			

December
S	M	T	W	T	F	S
					1	2	3
4	5	6	7	8	9	10
11	12	13	14	15	16	17
18	19	20	21	22	23	24
25	26	27	28	29	30	31

N (leap year)

January
S	M	T	W	T	F	S
						1
2	3	4	5	6	7	8
9	10	11	12	13	14	15
16	17	18	19	20	21	22
23	24	25	26	27	28	29
30	31					

February
S	M	T	W	T	F	S
		1	2	3	4	5
6	7	8	9	10	11	12
13	14	15	16	17	18	19
20	21	22	23	24	25	26
27	28	29				

March
S	M	T	W	T	F	S
				1	2	3	4
5	6	7	8	9	10	11
12	13	14	15	16	17	18
19	20	21	22	23	24	25
26	27	28	29	30	31	

April
S	M	T	W	T	F	S
						1
2	3	4	5	6	7	8
9	10	11	12	13	14	15
16	17	18	19	20	21	22
23	24	25	26	27	28	29
30						

May
S	M	T	W	T	F	S
	1	2	3	4	5	6
7	8	9	10	11	12	13
14	15	16	17	18	19	20
21	22	23	24	25	26	27
28	29	30	31			

June
S	M	T	W	T	F	S
					1	2	3
4	5	6	7	8	9	10
11	12	13	14	15	16	17
18	19	20	21	22	23	24
25	26	27	28	29	30	

July
S	M	T	W	T	F	S
						1
2	3	4	5	6	7	8
9	10	11	12	13	14	15
16	17	18	19	20	21	22
23	24	25	26	27	28	29
30	31					

August
S	M	T	W	T	F	S
		1	2	3	4	5
6	7	8	9	10	11	12
13	14	15	16	17	18	19
20	21	22	23	24	25	26
27	28	29	30	31		

September
S	M	T	W	T	F	S
					1	2
3	4	5	6	7	8	9
10	11	12	13	14	15	16
17	18	19	20	21	22	23
24	25	26	27	28	29	30

October
S	M	T	W	T	F	S
1	2	3	4	5	6	7
8	9	10	11	12	13	14
15	16	17	18	19	20	21
22	23	24	25	26	27	28
29	30	31				

November
S	M	T	W	T	F	S
				1	2	3	4
5	6	7	8	9	10	11
12	13	14	15	16	17	18
19	20	21	22	23	24	25
26	27	28	29	30		

December
S	M	T	W	T	F	S
					1	2
3	4	5	6	7	8	9
10	11	12	13	14	15	16
17	18	19	20	21	22	23
24	25	26	27	28	29	30
31						

THE SEASONS

N Hemi-sphere	S Hemi-sphere	Duration
Spring	Autumn	From vernal/autumnal equinox (c.21 Mar) to summer/winter solstice (c.21 Jun)
Summer	Winter	From summer/winter solstice (c.21 Jun) to autumnal/spring equinox (c.23 Sept)
Autumn	Spring	From autumnal/spring equinox (c.23 Sept) to winter/summer solstice (c.21 Dec)
Winter	Summer	From winter/summer solstice (c.21 Dec) to vernal/autumnal equinox (c.21 Mar)

MONTHS: ASSOCIATIONS

In many Western countries, the months are traditionally associated with gemstones and flowers. There is considerable variation between countries. The following combinations are widely recognized in North America and the UK.

Month	Gemstone	Flower
January	Garnet	Carnation, Snowdrop
February	Amethyst	Primrose, Violet
March	Aquamarine, Bloodstone	Jonquil, Violet
April	Diamond	Daisy, Sweet Pea
May	Emerald	Hawthorn, Lily of the Valley
June	Alexandrite, Moonstone, Pearl	Honeysuckle, Rose
July	Ruby	Larkspur, Water Lily
August	Peridot, Sardonyx	Gladiolus, Poppy
September	Sapphire	Aster, Morning Glory
October	Opal, Tourmaline	Calendula, Cosmos
November	Topaz	Chrysanthemum
December	Turquoise, Zircon	Holly, Narcissus, Poinsettia

WEDDING ANNIVERSARIES

In many Western countries, different wedding anniversaries have become associated with gifts of different materials. There is some variation between countries.

1st	Cotton	10th	Tin	35th	Coral
2nd	Paper	11th	Steel	40th	Ruby
3rd	Leather	12th	Silk, Linen	45th	Sapphire
4th	Fruit, Flowers	13th	Lace	50th	Gold
5th	Wood	14th	Ivory	55th	Emerald
6th	Sugar	15th	Crystal	60th	Diamond
7th	Copper, Wool	20th	China	70th	Platinum
8th	Bronze, Pottery	25th	Silver		
9th	Pottery, Willow	30th	Pearl		

INTERNATIONAL TIME DIFFERENCES

The time zones of the world are conventionally measured from longitude 0 at Greenwich Observatory (Greenwich Mean Time, GMT).

Each 15° of longitude east of this point is one hour ahead of GMT (eg when it is 2pm in London it is 3pm or later in time zones to the east). Hours ahead of GMT are shown by a plus sign, eg +3, +4/8.

Each 15° west of this point is one hour behind GMT (eg 2pm in London would be 1pm or earlier in time zones to the west). Hours behind GMT are shown by a minus sign, eg −3, −4/8.

Some countries adopt time zones that vary from standard time. Also, during the summer, several countries adopt Daylight Saving Time (or Summer Time), which is one hour ahead of the times shown below.

Afghanistan	+4½	Egypt	+2	Lebanon	+2	Sao Tomé	0
Albania	+1	El Salvador	−6	Lesotho	+2	Saudi Arabia	+3
Algeria	0	Equatorial		Liberia	0	Senegal	0
Angola	+1	Guinea	+1	Libya	+1	Seychelles	+4
Antigua	−4	Ethiopia	+3	Liechtenstein	+1	Sierra Leone	0
Argentina	−3	Falkland Is	−3	Luxembourg	+1	Singapore	+8
Australia	+8/10	Fiji	+12	Madagascar	+3	Solomon Is	+11
Austria	+1	Finland	+2	Malawi	+2	Somalia	+3
Bahamas	−5	France	+1	Malaysia	+8	South Africa	+2
Bahrain	+3	Gabon	+1	Maldives	+5	South West	
Bangladesh	+6	Gambia, The	0	Mali	0	Africa	+2
Barbados	−4	Germany, East	+1	Malta	+1	Spain	+1
Belgium	+1	Germany, West	+1	Mauritania	0	Sri Lanka	+5½
Belize	−6	Ghana	0	Mauritius	+4	Sudan	+2
Benin	+1	Gibraltar	+1	Mexico	−6/8	Suriname	−3½
Bermuda	−4	Greece	+2	Monaco	+1	Swaziland	+2
Bolivia	−4	Greenland	−3	Morocco	0	Sweden	+1
Botswana	+2	Grenada	−4	Mozambique	+2	Switzerland	+1
Brazil	−2/5	Guatemala	−6	Nauru	+12	Syria	+2
Brunei	+8	Guinea	0	Nepal	+5½	Taiwan	+8
Bulgaria	+2	Guinea-Bissau	0	Netherlands	+1	Tanzania	+3
Burkina Faso	0	Guyana	−3	New Zealand	+12	Thailand	+7
Burma	+6½	Haiti	−5	Nicaragua	−6	Togo	0
Burundi	+2	Honduras	−6	Niger	+1	Tonga	+13
Cameroon	+1	Hong Kong	+8	Nigeria	+1	Trinidad and	
Canada	−3½/9	Hungary	+1	Norway	+1	Tobago	−4
Cape Verde	−1	Iceland	0	Oman	+4	Tunisia	+1
Central African		India	+5½	Pakistan	+5	Turkey	+3
Republic	+1	Indonesia	+7/9	Panama	−5	Tuvalu	+12
Chad	+1	Iran	+3½	Papua New		Uganda	+3
Chile	−4	Iraq	+3	Guinea	+10	United Arab	
China	+8	Ireland	0	Paraguay	−3/4	Emirates	+4
Colombia	−5	Israel	+2	Peru	−5	UK	0
Comoros	+3	Italy	+1	Philippines	+8	Uruguay	−3
Congo	+1	Ivory Coast	0	Poland	+1	USA*	−5/11
Costa Rica	−6	Jamaica	−5	Portugal	0	USSR	+3/13
Cuba	−5	Japan	+9	Qatar	+3	Vanuatu	+11
Cyprus	+2	Jordan	+2	Romania	+2	Venezuela	−4
Czechoslovakia	+1	Kampuchea	+7	Rwanda	+2	Vietnam	+7
Denmark	+1	Kenya	+3	St Christopher		Yemen	+3
Djibouti	+3	Kiribati	+12	and Nevis	−4	Yugoslavia	+1
Dominica	−4	Korea, North	+9	St Lucia	−4	Zaire	+1/2
Dominican		Korea, South	+9	St Vincent	−4	Zambia	+2
Republic	−4	Kuwait	+3	Samoa	−11	Zimbabwe	+2
Ecuador	−5	Laos	+7	San Marino	+1		

*For US State Time Zones, see pp 266–70

INTERNATIONAL TIME ZONES

World times at 12 noon GMT Some countries have adopted half-hour time zones which are indicated on the map as a combination of two coded zones. For example, it is 1730 hours in India at 1200 GMT. The standard times shown are subject to variation in certain countries where Daylight Saving/Summer Time operates for part of the year.

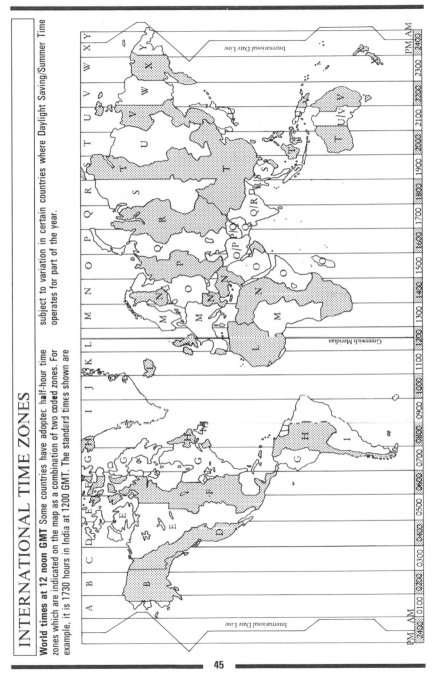

NATURAL HISTORY

CEREALS

English name	Species	Area of origin	English name	Species	Area of origin
barley	*Hordeum vulgare*	Middle East	oats	*Avena sativa*	Mediterranean basin
maize (or corn, sweet corn, Indian corn)	*Zea mays*	C America	rice rye	*Oryza sativa* *Secale cereale*	Asia Mediterranean, SW Asia
millet, common	*Panicum miliaceum*	tropics, warm temperate regions	sorghum (or Kaffir corn) wheat	*sorghum vulgare* Genus *Triticum*, 20 species	Africa, Asia Mediterranean, W Asia
millet, foxtail or Italian	*Setaria italica*	as common millet			
millet, bulrush	*Pennisetum glaucum*	as common millet			

VEGETABLES

English name	Species	Part eaten	Colour	Area of origin
artichoke, Chinese	*Stachys affinis*	tubers	white	China
artichoke, globe	*Cynara scolymus*	buds	green, purple	Mediterranean
artichoke, Jerusalem	*Helianthus tuberosus*	tuber	white	N America
asparagus	*Asparagus officinalis*	young shoots	green, white	Europe, Asia
aubergine	*Solanum melongena*	fruit	purple, white	Asia, Africa
avocado	*Persea americana*	fruit	green, purple	C America
bean sprouts	*Vigna radiata*	shoots	white, pale brown	China
beans, black-eyed	*Vigna sinensis*	seeds	white/black	India, Iran
beans, borlotti (or Boston or pinto)	*Phaseolus vulgaris*	seeds	pink/brown	America
beans, broad	*Vicia faba*	pod and seed	white	Africa, Europe

VEGETABLES (cont.)

English name	Species	Part eaten	Colour	Area of origin
beans, flageolot	*Phaseolus vulgaris*	seeds	white, pale green	America
beans, French	*Phaseolus vulgaris*	pods	green	America
beans, haricot	*Phaseolus vulgaris*	seeds	white	America
beans, kidney	*Phaseolus vulgaris*	seeds	red	America
beans, runner	*Phaseolus coccineus*	pod	green	America
beans, soya	*Glycine soja*	seeds	green	E Asia
beetroot	*Beta vulgaris*	root	white, dark red	Mediterranean
broccoli	*Brassica olearacea*	buds and leaves	green, purple	Europe
Brussels sprout	*Brassica oleracea (gemmifera)*	buds	green	N Europe
cabbage	*Brassica oleracea*	leaves	green, red, white	Europe, W. Asia
cardoon	*Cynara cardunculus*	inner stalks and flower heads	white, green	Mediterranean
carrot	*Daucus carota*	root	orange	Asia
cauliflower	*Brassica oleracea*	flower buds	white, green	Middle East
celeriac	*Apium graveolens (rapacium)*	root	white	Mediterranean
celery	*Apium graveolens*	stalks	white, green	Europe, N Africa, America
chayote (or chocho)	*Sechium edule*	fruit	white, green	America
chick-pea	*Cicer arietinum*	seed	beige, golden, dark brown	W Asia
chicory	*Chicorium intybus*	leaves	red, green	Europe, W Asia
chinese leaf	*Brassica pekinensis*	leaf stalks	white, green	E Asia, China
chives	*Allium schoenoprasum*	leaves	green, white	Europe, N America
courgette	*Cucurbita pepo*	fruit	green	S America, Africa
cucumber	*Cucumus satius*	fruit	green	S Asia
endive	*Cichorium endivia*	leaves	yellow, green	S Europe, E Indies, Africa
fennel, Florentine	*Foeniculum dulce*	leaf stalks	white and green	Europe
kale (or borecole)	*Brassica oleracea acephala*	leaves	green	Europe

VEGETABLES (cont.)

English name	Species	Part eaten	Colour	Area of origin
kohlrabi	*Brassica oleracea caulorapa*	stem	white	Europe
laver	*Porphyra leucosticta, Pumbilicalis*	leaves and stems	purple-pink	Europe
leek	*Allium porrum*	stem and leaves	green, white	Europe, N Africa
lentil	*Lens esculenta*	seed	white, green, pink, red	S Asia
lettuce	*Lactuca sativa*	leaves	green, white	Middle East
marrow	*Cucurbita pepo*	fruit	green	America
mooli	*Raphanus sativus*	roots	white	E Africa
mushroom	*Agaricus campestris*	fruiting body	brown, white	worldwide
okra	*Hibiscus esculentus*	pods and seeds	green, white	Africa
onion	*Allium cepa*	bulb	white, pink	Central Asia
parsnip	*Pastinaca sativa*	root	white, yellow	Europe
pea	*Pisum sativum*	pods and seeds	green	Asia, Europe
pepper	*Capsicum annuum*	fruit	red, green, yellow	S America
potato	*Solanum tuberasum*	tuber	white	S America
pumpkin	*Cucurbita pepo*	fruit	yellow, orange	S America
radish	*Raphanus sativus*	root	red, white	China, Japan
salsify	*Trapogon porrifolius*	roots	white	S Europe
sorrel	*Rumex acetosa*	leaves	green	Europe
spinach	*Spinacea oleracea*	leaves	green	Asia
squash, winter	*Cucurbita maxima*	fruit	green, yellow, orange	America
squash, summer	*Cucurbita pepo*	fruit	yellow, orange, green	America
swede	*Brassica napus (napobrassica)*	root	yellow, white	Europe
sweet potato	*Ipomaea batatas*	tuber	white, yellow, red to purple	C America
swiss chard	*Beta vulgaris cicla*	leaves and stems	green and white	Europe
tomato	*Lycopersicum esculentum*	fruit	red	S America
turnip	*Brassica rapa*	root	white	Middle East
watercress	*Nasturtium officinale*	leaves and stems	green	Europe, Asia
yam	Genus *Dioscorea* 60 species	tuber	white, orange	tropics

HERBS

Herbs may be used for medicinal, cosmetic or culinary purposes. Any part of those marked * may be poisonous when ingested.

English name	Species	Origin	Part of plant used
aconite* (or monkswood, winter aconite)	*Aconitum nepellus*	Europe, NW Asia	tuber
agrimony	*Agrimonia officinalis*	Europe	flowers
alecost (or costmary)	*Tanacetum balsimata*	E Mediterranean	leaves, flowers
aloe	*Aloe vera*	Africa	leaves
anise	*Pimpinella anisum*	Egypt	fruits (seed heads)
basil	*Ocimum basilicum*	Middle East	leaves, flowering shoots
borage	*Borago officinalis*	Mediterranean	leaves, flowers
celandine	*Chelidonium majus*	Europe	buds
celery	*Apium graveolens*	Europe	roots, stems, leaves
chamomile	*Chamaemelum nobile*	Europe, Asia	flowers
chicory	*Chicoium intybus*	Europe	leaves, roots
chives	*Allium schoenoprasum*	Europe, America	leaves
coriander	*Coriandrum sativum*	N Africa, W Asia	leaves, fruits
dandelion	*Taraxacum officinale*	Europe	leaves,roots
deadly nightshade*	*Atropa belladonna*	Europe, Asia	root
dill	*Anethum graveolens*	S Europe	leaves, fruits (seeds)
elderberry	*Sambucus nigra*	Europe	flowers,fruits
epazote	*Chenopodium ambrosioides*	C and S America	leaves
fennel, Florentine	*Foeniculum dulce*	Mediterranean	leaves, stems, fruits (seeds)
feverfew	*Tanacetum parthenium*	SE Europe, W Asia	leaves, flowers
foxglove*	*Digitalis purpurea*	Europe	leaves
garlic	*Allium sativum*	Asia	bulbs
gentian	*Gentiana lutea*	Europe	rhizomes, roots
ginseng	*Panax ginseng*	China	roots

HERBS (cont.)

English name	Species	Origin	Part of plant used
guaiacum	*Guaiacum officinale*	Caribbean	leaves
heartsease (or wild pansy)	*Viola tricolor*	Europe	flowers
hemlock*	*Conium maculatum*	Europe	all parts
hemp (ganja, cannabis, or marijuana)	*Cannabis sativa*	Asia	leaves, flowers
henbane	*Hyoscyamus niger*	Europe, W Asia, N Africa	leaves, fruits (seeds)
henna	*Lawsonia inermis*	Asia, Africa	leaves
horseradish	*Armoracia rusticana*	SE Europe, W Asia	roots, flowering shoots, leaves
hyssop	*Hyssopus officinalis*	S Europe	leaves, flowers
juniper	*Juniperus communis*	Mediterranean	fruits (berries), wood
lavender	*Lavandula officinalis*	Mediterranean	flowers, stems
leek	*Allium porrum*	Europe	stem, leaves
lemon	*Citrus limon*	Asia	fruits
lemon balm	*Melissa officinalis*	S Europe	leaves
lily of the valley	*Convallaria majalis*	Europe, N America	leaves, flowers
lime	*Tilia cordata*	Europe	flowers
liquorice	*Glycyrrhiza glabra*	Egypt	roots
lovage	*Levisticum officinale*	W Asia	leaves, shoots, stems, roots
mandrake	*Mandragora officina*	Himalayas, SE Europe, W Asia	roots
marjoram	*Majorana hortensis*	Africa, Mediterranean, Asia	leaves, shoots, stems
marsh mallow	*Althaea officinalis*	Europe, Asia	leaves, roots
maté	*Ilex paraguariensis*	S America	leaves
monkswood *see* aconite			
mugwort	*Artemesia vulgaris*	Europe, Asia	leaves
myrrh	*Commiphora molmol*	Arabia, Africa	resin

HERBS (cont.)

English name	Species	Origin	Part of plant used
myrtle	*Myrtus communis*	Asia, Mediterranean	leaves, flower heads, fruits (berries)
nasturtium	*Tropaelom majus*	Peru	leaves, flowers, fruits
onion	*Allium cepa*	Asia	bulbs
oregano	*Origanum vulgare*	Mediterranean	leaves, shoots, stems
parsley	*Petroselinum crispum*	Mediterranean	leaves, stems
peony	*Paeonia officinalis*	Europe, Asia, N America	roots, seeds
peppermint	*Menthaxpiperita*	Europe	leaves
poppy*, opium	*Papaver somniferum*	Asia Minor	fruits, seeds
purslane	*Portulaca oleracea*	Europe	leaves
rosemary	*Rosmarinus officinalis*	Mediterranean	leaves
rue	*Ruta graveolens*	Mediterranean	leaves, stems, flowers
saffron	*Crocus sativus*	Asia Minor	flowers
sage	*Salvia officinalis*	N Mediterranean	leaves
sorrel	*Rumex acetosa*	Europe	leaves
spearmint	*Mentha spicata*	Europe	leaves
tansy	*Tanacetum vulgare*	Asia	leaves, flowers
tarragon, French	*Artemesia dracunculus*	Asia, E Europe	leaves, stems
thyme	*Thymus serpyllum*	Mediterranean	leaves, stems, flowers
valerian	*Valeriana officinalis*	Europe, Asia	rhizomes, roots
vervain	*Verbena officinalis*	Europe, Asia, N Africa	leaves, flowers
watercress	*Nasturtium officinale*	Europe, Asia	leaves, shoots, stems
witch hazel	*Hamamelis virginiana*	N America, E. Asia	leaves, shoots, bark
wormwood	*Aretemesia absinthium*	Europe	leaves, flowering shoots
yarrow (or milfoil)	*Achillea millefolium*	Europe, W Asia	flower heads, leaves

SPICES

English name	Species	Origin	Part of plant used
allspice	*Pimenta officinalis*	America, W Indies	fruits
annatto	*Bixa orellana*	S America, W Indies	seeds
asafoetida	*Ferula assa-fetida*	W Asia	sap
bay	*Laurus nobilis*	Mediterranean, Asia Minor	leaves
black mustard	*Brassica niger*	Europe, Africa, Asia, America	seeds
caraway	*Carum carvi*	Europe, Asia	seeds
cayenne	*Capsicum frutescens*	America, Africa	fruit pods
chilli pepper	*Capiscum annuum*	America	fruit pods
cinnamon	*Cinnamomum zeylanium*	Ceylon	bark
clove	*Eugenia caryophyllata*	Moluccas	buds
cocoa	*Theobroma cacoa*	S America	seeds (beans)
coconut	*Cocus nucifera*	Polynesia	fruits
coriander	*Coriandrum sativum*	S Europe	fruits
cumin	*Cuminum cyminum*	Mediterranean	fruits (seed heads)
curry leaf	*Murraya koenigi*	India	leaves
fennel	*Foeniculum vulgare*	S Europe	fruits
fenugreek	*Trigonella foenum-graecum*	India, S Europe	seeds
horseradish	*Armoracia rusticana*	E Europe	roots
ginger	*Zingiber officinale*	SE Asia	rhizomes
mace	*Myristica fragrans*	Moluccas	seeds
paprika	*Capiscum annuum*	S America	fruit pods
pepper	*Piper nigrum*	India	seeds
sandalwood	*Santalum album*	India, Indonesia, Australia	heartwood, roots
sassafras	*Sassafras albidum*	N America	root bark
sesame	*Sesamum indicum*	tropics	seeds
soya	*Glycine max*	China	fruit (beans)
tamarind	*Tamarindus indica*	Africa	fruits
turmeric	*Curcuma longa*	SE Asia	rhizomes
vanilla	*Vanilla fragrans*	C America	fruit pods
white mustard	*Sinapis alba*	Europe, Asia	seeds

EDIBLE FRUITS (Temperate and Mediterranean)

English name	Species	Colour	Area of origin
apple	*Malus sylvestris*	green, yellow, red	temperate regions
apricot	*Prunus armeniaca*	yellow, orange	Asia
bilberry	*Vaccinium myrtillus*	blue, black	Europe, N Asia
blackberry	*Rubus ulmifolius*	purple, black	N hemisphere
blackcurrant	*Ribes nigrum*	black	Europe, Asia, Africa
blueberry	*Vaccinium vacillans*	blue, purple, black	America, Europe
cherry (sour)	*Prunus cerasus*	red	temperate regions

EDIBLE FRUITS (Temperate and Mediterranean) (cont.)

English name	Species	Colour	Area of origin
cherry (sweet)	*Prunus avium*	purple, red	temperate regions
clementine	*Citrus reticulata* (Cultured clementine)	orange	W Mediterranean
cranberry	*Oxycoccus macrocarpus*	red	N America
damson	*Prunus institia*	purple	temperate regions
date	*Phoenix dactylifera*	yellow, red, brown	Persian Gulf
fig	*Ficus carica*	white, black, purple, green	W Asia
gooseberry	*Ribes grossularia*	green, red	Europe
grape	*Vitis vinefera*	green, purple, black	Asia
grapefruit	*Citrus paradisi*	yellow	W Indies
greengage	*Prunus domestica*	green	temperate regions
kiwi fruit	*Actinidia chinensis*	brown skin, green flesh	China
kumquat	*Fortunella margarita*	orange	China
lemon	*Citrus limon*	yellow	India, S Asia
lime	*Citrus aurantifola*	green	SE Asia
loganberry	*Rubus loganobaccus*	red	America
loquat	*Eriobotrya japonica*	yellow	China, Japan
lychee	*Litchi chinensis*	reddish-brown skin, white flesh	China
mandarin (or tangerine)	*Citrus reticulata*	orange	China
medlar	*Mespilus germanica*	russet brown	SE Europe, Asia
melon	*Cucumis melo*	green, yellow	Egypt
minneola	a type of tangelo	orange	N America
mulberry	*Morus nigra*	purple, red	W Asia
nectarine	*Prunus persica*	orange, red	China
orange	*Citrus sinensis*	orange	China
peach	*Prunus persica*	yellow, red	China
pear	*Pyrus cummunis*	yellow	Middle East, E Europe
persimmon (or date-plum)	*Diospyros kaki*	yellow, orange	E Asia
physalis (or Cape gooseberry)	*Physalis peruviana*	yellow	S America
plum	*Prunus domestica*	red, yellow, purple, orange	temperate regions
pomegranate	*Punica granatum*	red, yellow	Persia
pomelo	*Citrus maxima*	yellow	Malaysia
quince	*Cydonia vulgaris*	golden	Iran
raspberry	*Rubus idaeus*	red, crimson	N hemisphere
redcurrant	*Ribes rubrum*	red	Europe, Asia, Africa
rhubarb	*Rheum rhaponticum*	red, green, pink	Asia
satsuma	*Citrus nobilis*		Japan
strawberry	*Fragaria*	red	Europe, Asia
tangelo	*Citrus paradisi* × *Citrus reticulata*	orange	N America

EDIBLE FRUITS (Temperate and Mediterranean) (cont.)

English name	Species	Colour	Area of origin
ugli	a type of tangelo	yellow	N America
water melon	Citrullus vulgaris	green, yellow	Africa
white currant	Ribes rubrum	white	W Europe

EDIBLE FRUITS (Tropical)

English name	Species	Colour	Area of origin
acerola	Malpighia glabra	yellow, red	America
avocado	Persea americana	green, purple	C America
banana	Musa sapientum	yellow	India, S Asia
breadfruit	Artocarpus incisus	greenish brown, yellow	Malaysia
carambola	Averrhoa carambola	yellow, green	S China
cherimoya	Annona cherimolia	green skin, white flesh	Peru
guava	Psidium guajava	green, yellow	S America
mango	Mangifera indica	green, yellow, orange, red, purple	S Asia
papaya	Carica papaya	green, yellow, orange	tropics
passion fruit	Passiflora edulis	purple, yellow, brown	S America
pineapple	Ananas comosus	green, yellow	S America
sapodilla plum	Achras zapota	brown	C America
soursop	Anona muricata	green	America
tamarind	Tamarindus indica	brown	Africa, S Asia

TREES (Europe and N America)

English name	Species	Deciduous/ evergreen	Continent of origin
alder, common	Alnus glutinosa	deciduous	Europe
almond	Prunus dulcis	deciduous	W Asia, N Africa
apple	Malus pumila	deciduous	Europe, W Africa
apple, crab	Malus sylvestris	deciduous	Europe, Asia
ash, common	Fraxinus exzcelsior	deciduous	Europe
aspen	Populus tremula	deciduous	Europe
bean tree, Red Indian	Catalpa bignonioides	deciduous	America, E Asia
beech, common	Fagus sylvatica	deciduous	Europe
beech, copper	Fagus purpurea	deciduous	Europe
beech, noble	Nothofagus obliqua	deciduous	S America
birch, silver	Betula pendula	deciduous	Europe, America, Asia
box	Buxus sempervirens	evergreen	Europe, N Africa
Brazil nut	Bertholletia excelsa	evergreen	S America

TREES (Europe and N America) (cont.)

English name	Species	Deciduous/ evergreen	Continent of origin
camellia, deciduous	*Stewartia pseudocamellia*	deciduous	Asia
castor-oil tree, prickly	*Kalopanax pietus*	deciduous	tropics
cedar of Lebanon	*Cedrus libani*	evergreen	Asia
cedar, smooth Tasmanian	*Athrotaxis cupressiodes*	evergreen	Australia
cedar, white	*Thuja occidentalis*	evergreen	America
cherry, morello (or sour)	*Prunus cerasus*	deciduous	Europe, Asia
cherry, wild (or gean)	*Prunus avium*	deciduous	Europe
chestnut, horse	*Aesculus hippocastanum*	deciduous	Asia, SW Europe
chestnut, sweet (or Spanish)	*Casanea sativa*	deciduous	Europe, Africa, Asia
cypress, Lawson	*Chamaecyparis lawsoniana*	evergreen	America
deodar	*Cedrus deodara*	evergreen	Asia
dogwood, common	*Cornus sanguinea*	deciduous	Europe
elm, Dutch	*Ulmus hollandica*	deciduous	Europe
elm, English	*Ulmus procera*	deciduous	Europe
elm, wych	*Ulmus glabra*	deciduous	Europe
fig	*Ficus carica*	evergreen	Asia
fir, douglas	*Pseudotsuga menziesii*	evergreen	America
fir, red	*Abies magnifica*	evergreen	America
ginkgo	*Ginkgo biloba*	deciduous	Asia
grapefruit	*Citrus paradisi*	evergreen	Asia
gum, blue	*Eucalyptus globulus*	evergreen	Australia
gum, cider	*Eucalyptus gunnii*	evergreen	Australia
gum, snow	*Eucalyptus niphophila*	evergreen	Australia
gutta-percha tree	*Eucommia ulmoides*	deciduous	China
hawthorn	*Crataegus oxyacanthoides*	deciduous	Europe
hazel, common	*Corylus avellana*	deciduous	Europe, W Asia, N Africa
hemlock, Western	*Tsuga heterophylla*	evergreen	America
holly	*Ilex aquifolium*	evergreen	Europe, N Africa, W Asia
hornbeam	*Carpinus betulus*	deciduous	Europe, Asia
Joshua-tree	*Yucca brevifolia*	evergreen	America
Judas-tree	*Cercis siliquastrum*	deciduous	S Europe, Asia
juniper, common	*Juniperus communis*	evergreen	Europe, Asia
laburnum, common	*Laburnum anagyroides*	deciduous	Europe
larch, European	*Larix decidua*	deciduous	Europe
larch, golden	*Pseudolarix amabilis*	deciduous	E Asia
leatherwood	*Eucryphia lucida*	evergreen	Australia
lemon	*Citrus limonia*	evergreen	Asia
lime	*Citrus aurantiifolia*	evergreen	Asia
lime, small-leafed	*Tilia cordata*	deciduous	Europe
locust tree	*Robinia pseudoacacia*	deciduous	America
magnolia (or white laurel)	*Magnolia virginiana*	evergreen	America
maple, field (or common)	*Acer campestre*	deciduous	Europe
maple, sugar	*Acer saccharum*	deciduous	America

TREES (Europe and N America) (cont.)

English name	Species	Deciduous/ evergreen	Continent of origin
medlar	*Mespilus germanica*	deciduous	Europe
mimosa	*Acacia dealbata*	deciduous	Australia, Europe
mockernut	*Carya tomentosa*	deciduous	America
monkey puzzle	*Araucaria araucana*	evergreen	S America
mulberry, common	*Morus nigra*	deciduous	Asia
mulberry, white	*Morus alba*	deciduous	Asia
myrtle, orange bark	*Myrtus apiculata*	evergreen	S America
nutmeg, California	*Torreya californica*	evergreen	America
oak, California live	*Quercus agrifoma*	deciduous	America
oak, cork	*Quercus suber*	evergreen	S Europe, N Africa
oak, English (or common)	*Quercus robur*	deciduous	Europe, Asia, Africa
oak, red	*Quercus borealis*	deciduous	America
olive	*Olea europea*	evergreen	S Europe
orange, sweet	*Citrus sinensis*	evergreen	Asia
Pagoda-tree	*Sophora japonica*	deciduous	China, Japan
pear	*Pyrus communis*	deciduous	Europe, W Asia
pine, Austrian	*Pinus nigra*	evergreen	Europe, Asia
pine, Corsican	*Pinus nigra Maritinia*	evergreen	Europe
pine, Monterey	*Pinus radiata*	evergreen	America
pine, Scots	*Pinus sylvestris*	evergreen	Europe
plane, London	*Platanus x hispanica*	deciduous	Europe
plane, Oriental	*Platanus orientalis*	deciduous	SE Europe, Asia
plum	*Prunus domestica*	deciduous	Europe, Asia
poplar, balsam	*Populus balsamifera*	deciduous	America, Asia
poplar, black	*Populus nigra*	deciduous	Europe, Asia
poplar, Lombardy	*Populus italica*	deciduous	Europe
poplar, white	*Populus alba*	deciduous	Europe
quince	*Cydonia oblonga*	deciduous	Asia
raoul	*Nothofagus procera*	deciduous	S America
rowan (or mountain ash)	*Sorbus aucuparia*	deciduous	Europe
sassafras, American	*Sassafras albidum*	deciduous	America
service tree, true	*Sorbus domestica*	deciduous	Europe
silver fir, common	*Abies alba*	evergreen	Europe
spruce, Norway	*Picea abies*	evergreen	Europe
spruce, sitka	*Picea sitchensis*	evergreen	America, Europe
strawberry tree	*Arbutus unedo*	evergreen	Europe
sycamore ('plane')	*Acer pseudoplatanus*	deciduous	Europe, W Asia
tamarack	*Larix laricina*	deciduous	N America
tree of heaven	*Ailanthus altissima*	deciduous	China
tulip tree	*Liriodendron tulipifera*	deciduous	America
walnut, black	*Juglans nigra*	deciduous	America
walnut, common	*Juglans regia*	deciduous	Europe, Asia
whitebeam	*Sorbus aria*	deciduous	Europe
willow, pussy, goat or sallow	*Salix caprea*	deciduous	Europe, Asia
willow, weeping	*Salix babylonica*	deciduous	Asia
willow, white	*Salix alba*	deciduous	Europe
yew, common	*Taxus baccata*	evergreen	N temperate regions

TREES (Tropical)

Name	Species	Deciduous/ evergreen	Continent of origin
African tulip tree	*Spathodea campanulata*	evergreen	Africa
almond, tropical	*Terminalia catappa*	deciduous	Asia
angel's trumpet	*Brugmansia x candida*	deciduous	S America
autograph tree	*Clusia rosea*	evergreen	Asia
avocado	*Persea americana*	evergreen	America
bamboo	*Schizostachyum glauchifolium*	deciduous	America
banana	*Musa x paradisiaca*	plant dies after fruiting	Asia
banyan	*Ficus benghalensis*	evergreen	Asia
baobob (or dead rat's tree)	*Adansonia digitata*	deciduous	Africa
beach heliotrope	*Messerschmidia argentea*	evergreen	S America
bo tree	*Ficus religiosa*	deciduous	Asia
bombax	*Bombax ceiba*	deciduous	Asia
bottle brush	*Callistemon citrinus*	evergreen	Australia
breadfruit	*Artocarpus altilis*	evergreen	Asia
brownea	*Brownea macrophylla*	evergreen	C America
calabash	*Crescentia cujete*	evergreen	America
candlenut	*Aleurites moluccana*	evergreen	Asia
cannonball	*Courouptia guianensis*	evergreen	S America
chinaberry (or bead tree)	*Melia azedarach*	deciduous	Asia
Christmas-berry	*Schinus terebinthifolius*	evergreen	America
coconut palm	*Cocus nucifera*	evergreen	Asia
coffee tree	*Coffea liberica*	evergreen	Africa
Cook pine	*Araucaria columnaris*	evergreen	America
coral tree	*Erythrina coralloides*	deciduous	C America
coral shower	*Cassia grandis*	deciduous	Asia
cotton, wild	*Cochlospermum vititolium*	deciduous	C and S America
crape myrtle	*Lagerstroemia indica*	deciduous	Asia
date palm	*Phoenix dactylifera*	evergreen	Asia and Africa
dragon tree	*Dracaena draco*	evergreen	Africa (Canary Is)
durian	*Durio zibethirius*	evergreen	Asia
ebony	*Diospyros ebenum*	evergreen	Asia
elephant's ear	*Enderolobium cyclocarpum*	deciduous	S America
flame tree	*Delonix regia*	deciduous	Africa (Madagascar)
gold tree	*Cybistax donnell-smithii*	deciduous	Asia
golden rain	*Koelreuteria paniculata*	deciduous	Asia
golden shower	*Cassia fistula*	deciduous	Asia
guava	*Psidium guajeve*	evergreen	S America
ironwood (or casuarina)	*Casuarina equisetifolia*	deciduous	Australia and Asia
jackfruit (or jack)	*Artocarpus heterophyllus*	evergreen	Asia
jacaranda	*Jacaranda mimosifolia*	deciduous	S America
kapok tree	*Ceiba pentandra*	deciduous	Old and New World tropics
koa	*Acacia koa*	evergreen	Oceania (Hawaii)
lipstick tree	*Bixa orllanna*	evergreen	America
lychee	*Litchi chinensis*	evergreen	China
macadamia nut	*Macadamia integrifolia*	evergreen	Australia
mahogany	*Swietenia mahogoni*	evergreen	S America

TREES (Tropical) (cont.)

Name	Species	Deciduous/ evergreen	Continent of origin
mango	*Mangifera idica*	evergreen	Asia
mesquite	*Prosopis pallida*	evergreen	America
monkeypod (or rain tree)	*Samanes saman*	evergreen	S America
Norfolk island pine	*Araucaria heterophylla*	evergreen	Oceania (Norfolk I)
octopus tree	*Brassaia actinophylla*	evergreen	Australia
ohi'a lehua	*Metrosideros collina*	evergreen	Oceania (Hawaii)
pandanus (or screw pine)	*Pandanus tectorius*	evergreen	Oceania
paperbark tree	*Melaleuca leucadendron*	evergreen	Australia
powderpuff	*Calliandra haematocephala*	evergreen	S America
royal palm	*Roystonea regia*	evergreen	America (Cuba)
sandalwood	*Santalum album*	deciduous	Asia
sand-box tree	*Hura crepitans*	deciduous	Americas
sausage tree	*Kigelia pinnata*	evergreen	Africa
scrambled egg tree	*Cassia glauca*	evergreen	Americas
Surinam cherry	*Eugenia uniflora*	evergreen	S America
teak tree	*Tectona grandis*	evergreen	Asia
tiger's claw	*Erythrina idica*	deciduous	Asia
yellow oleander	*Thevetia nereifolia*	evergreen	Americas (W Indies)

FUNGI

English name	Species	Colour	Edibility
base toadstool (or ugly toadstool)	*Lactarius necator*	green, brown	poisonous
beautiful clavaria	*Ramaria formosa*	yellow, ochre, red, purple	poisonous
blusher	*Amanita fubescens*	red, brown	poisonous(raw) or edible (cooked)
brain mushroom	*Gyromitra esculenta*	chestnut, dark brown	poisonous
buckler agaric	*Entoloma clypeatum*	grey, brown	edible
Caesar's mushroom	*Amanita Caesarea*	red, yellow	edible
chantarelle	*Cantharellus cibarius*	yellow, ochre	edible
clean mycena	*Mycena pura*	purple	poisonous
clouded agaric	*Lepista nebularis*	grey, brown	poisonous
common earthball	*Scleroderma aurantium*	ochre, yellow, brown	poisonous
common grisette	*Amanita vaginita*	grey, yellow	edible
common morel	*Morchella esculenta*	light brown, black	edible
common puffball	*Lycoperdon perlatum*	white, cream, brown	edible
common stinkhorn	*Phallus impudicus*	white, green	edible
death cap	*Amanita phalloides*	grey, green, yellow, brown	poisonous
deceiver, common laccaria	*Laccaria laccata*	purple, pink, orange	edible
destroying angel	*Amanita virosa*	white, brown	poisonous

FUNGI (cont.)

English name	Species	Colour	Edibility
dingy agaric	*Tricholoma portentosum*	grey, black, yellow, lilac	edible
fairy ring champignon	*Marasmius oreades*	beige, ochre, red,brown	edible
field mushroom	*Agaricus campestris*	white, brown	edible
firwood agaric	*Tricholoma auratum*	green, yellow, brown	edible
fly agaric	*Amanita muscaria*	red, orange, white	poisonous
garlic marosmius	*Marosmius scorodonius*	red, browm	edible
gypsy mushroom	*Rozites caperata*	yellow, ochre	edible
hedgehog mushroom	*Hydnum repandum*	white, beige, yellow	edible
honey fungus	*Armillariella polymyces*	honey, brown, red	poisonous (raw) or edible (cooked)
horn of plenty (or trumpet of the dead)	*Craterellus cornucopiodes*	brown, black	edible
horse mushroom	*Agaricus arvensis*	white, yellow, ochre	edible
Jew's ear fungus	*Hirneola auricula-judae*	yellow, brown	edible
larch boletus	*Suillus grevillei*	yellow	edible
lurid boletus	*Boletus luridus*	olive, brown, yellow	poisonous (raw) or edible (cooked)
naked mushroom	*Lepista nuda*	purple, brown	edible
old man of the woods	*Strobilomyces floccopus*	brown, black	edible
orange-peel fungus	*Aleuria aurantia*	orange, red	edible
oyster fungus	*Pleurotus ostreatus*	brown, black, grey, blue, purple	edible
panther cap (or false blusher)	*Amanita pantherina*	brown, ochre, grey, white	poisonous
parasol mushroom	*Macrolepiota procera*	beige, ochre, brown	edible
penny-bun boletus	*Boletus edulis*	chestnut brown	edible
perigord truffle	*Tuber melanosporum*	black	edible
Piedmont truffle	*Tuber magnatum*	white	edible
purple blewit	*Tricholomopsis rutilans*	yellow, red	edible
saffron milk cap	*Lactorius delicioses*	orange, red	poisonous (raw) or edible (cooked)
St George's mushroom	*Calocybe gambosa*	white, cream	edible
Satan's boletus	*Boletus satanus*	grey	poisonous (raw) or edible (cooked)
scarlet-stemmed boletus	*Boletus calopus*	grey, brown	poisonous
shaggy cap (or lawyer's wig)	*Coprinus comatus*	white, ochre	edible
sickener (or emetic russala)	*Russala emetica*	pink, red	poisonous
stinking russala	*Russala foetens*	ochre, brown	poisonous

FUNGI (cont.)

English name	Species	Colour	Edibility
stout agaric	*Amanita spissa*	grey, brown	edible
strong scented garlic	*Tricholoma saponaceum*	grey, green, brown	poisonous
sulphur tuft (or clustered woodlover)	*Hypholoma fasciculare*	yellow, red, brown	poisonous
summer truffle	*Tuber aestivum*	dark brown, black	poisonous
white truffle	*Choiromyces meandriformis*	cream, pale brown	edible
winter fungus (or velvet shank)	*Flammulina velutipes*	yellow, brown, ochre	edible
wood agaric	*Collybia dryophila*	yellow, brown, rust	edible
wood mushroom	*Agaricus sylvaticus*	grey, red, brown	edible
woolly milk-cap (or griping toadstool)	*Lactarius torminosus*	pink, brown	poisonous
yellow stainer	*Agaricus xanthodermus*	white, yellow, grey	poisonous
yellow-brown boletus (or slippery jack)	*Suillus luteus*	yellow, brown	edible

FLOWERS (Shrubs)

English name	Genus	Colour	Country/continent of origin
abelia	*Abelia*	white, rose-purple	Asia, China, Mexico
abutilon	*Abutilon*	lavender-blue	S America
acacia (or mimosa or wattle)	*Acacia*	yellow	Australia, tropical Africa, tropical America
almond, dwarf	*Prunus*	white, crimson, rose-pink	Asia, Europe
ampelopsis	*Ampelopsis*	green (blue-black fruit)	Far East
anthyllis	*Anthyllis*	yellow	Europe
azalea	*Rhododendron*	pink, purple, white, yellow, crimson	N hemisphere
berberis	*Berberis*	yellow, orange	Asia, America, Europe
bottle brush	*Callistemon*	red	Australia
bougainvillea	*Bougainvillea*	lilac, pink, purple, red, orange, white	S America
broom	*Sarothamnus*	yellow	Europe
buckthorn	*Rhamnus*	red, black	N hemisphere
buddleia	*Buddleia*	purple, yellow, white	China, S America
cactus	*Cactaceae*	red, purple, orange, yellow, white	America

FLOWERS (Shrubs) (cont.)

English name	Genus	Colour	Country/continent of origin
calico bush (or mountain laurel)	Kalmia	white, pink	China
camellia	Camellia	white, pink, red	Asia
caryopteris	Caryopteris	blue, violet	Asia
ceanothus	Ceanothus	pink, blue, purple	N America
ceratostigma	Ceratostigma	purple-blue	China
Chinese lantern	Physalis	orange, red	Japan
cistus	Cistus	white, pink	Europe
clematis	Clematis	white, purple, violet, blue, pink, yellow	N temperate regions
clerodendron	Clerodendron	white, purple-red	China
colquhounia	Colquhounia	scarlet, yellow	Himalayas
cornelian cherry	Cornus	yellow	Europe
coronilla	Coronilla	yellow	S Europe
corylopsis	Corylopsis	yellow	China, Japan
cotoneaster	Cotoneaster	white (red fruit)	Asia
currant, flowering	Ribes	red, white, pink	N America
Desfontainia	Desfontainia	scarlet-gold	S America
deutzia	Deutzia	white, pink	Asia
diplera	Diplera	pale pink	China
dogwood	Cornus	white	Europe, SW Asia
embothrium	Embothrium	scarlet	S America
escallonia	Escallonia	white, pink	S America
euchryphia	Euchryphia	white	Chile, Australasia
euryops	Euryops	yellow	S Africa
fakiana	Fakiana	white, mauve	S America
firethorn	Pyracantha	white (red, orange, yellow fruits)	China
forsythia	Forsythia	yellow	China
frangipani	Plumeria	white, pink, yellow	tropical America
fuchsia	Fuchsia	red, pink, white	C and S America, New Zealand
gardenia	Gardenia	white	tropics
garland flower	Daphne	pink, crimson, white, purple	Europe, Asia
garrya	Garrya	green	California and Oregon
gorse, furze, whin	Ulex	yellow	Europe, Britain
hawthorn	Crataegus	white (orange-red berries)	N America, Europe, N Africa
heath, winter-flowering	Erica	white, pink, red	Africa, Europe
heather	Calluna	pink, purple, white	Europe, W Asia
hebe	Hebe	blue-white	New Zealand
helychrysum	Helychrysum	yellow	Australia, S Africa

FLOWERS (Shrubs) (cont.)

English name	Genus	Colour	Country/continent of origin
hibiscus	*Hibiscus*	pink, mauve, purple, white, red	China, India
honeysuckle	*Lonicera*	white, yellow, pink, red	temperate regions
hydrangea	*Hydrangea*	white, pink, blue	Asia, America
hyssop	*Hyssopus*	bluish-purple	S Europe, W Asia
indigofera	*Indigofera*	rose-purple	Himalayas
ipomoea (or morning glory)	*Ipomoea*	white, red, blue	tropical America
japonica	*Chaenomeles*	white, pink, orange, red, yellow	N Asia
jasmine	*Jasminum*	white, yellow, red	Asia
Jerusalem sage	*Phlomis*	yellow	Europe
kerria	*Kerria*	yellow	China
kolkwitzia	*Kolk witzia*	pink	China
laburnum	*Laburnum*	yellow	Europe, Asia
lavender	*Lavandula*	purple	Europe
leptospermum	*Leptospermum*	red, white	Australasia
leycerteria	*Leycerteria*	claret	Himalayan
lezpedeza	*Lezpedeza*	rose-purple	China, Japan
lilac (or syringa)	*Syringa*	purple, pink, white	Balkans
lion's tail	*Leonotis*	red	S Africa
magnolia	*Magnolia*	yellow, white, rose, purple	China, Japan
mahonia	*Mahonia*	yellow	Japan
malus	*Malus*	white, pink, red	N America, Asia
menziesa	*Menziesa*	wine-red	Japan
mimosa *see* acacia			
mimulus	*Mimulus*	cream, orange, red	N America
mock orange	*Philadelphus*	white	Europe, Asia, N America
moltkia	*Moltkia*	violet-blue	Greece
morning glory *see* ipomoea			
mother-of-pearl	*Symphoricarpus*	pink, white, red fruit	N America
mountain ash *see* rowan			
myrtle	*Myrtus*	pink, white	Europe
oleander	*Nerium oleander*	white, pink, purple, red	Mediterranean
olearia	*Olearia*	white, yellow	New Zealand
oleaster	*Elaeagnus*	yellow	Europe, Asia, N America
osmanthus	*Osmanthus delavayi*	white	China
pearl bush	*Exochorda*	white	China

FLOWERS (Shrubs) (cont.)

English name	Genus	Colour	Country/continent of origin
peony	*Paeonia*	pink, red, white, yellow	Europe, Asia, N America
pieris	*Pieris*	white	China
poinsettia	*Euphorbia*	scarlet	America (Mexico)
potentilla	*Potentilla*	yellow, red, orange	Asia
rhododendron	*Rhododendron*	red, purple, pink, white	S Asia
rhus	*Rhus*	foliage grey, purple, red	Europe, N America
ribbon woods	*Hoheria*	white	New Zealand
robinia	*Robinia*	rose-pink	N America
rock rose (or sun rose)	*Helianthemum*	white, yellow, pink, orange, red	Europe
rose	*Rosa*	pink, red, white, cream, yellow	N. temperate regions
rosemary	*Rosmarinus*	violet	Europe, Asia
rowan (or mountain ash)	*Sorbus*	white (red, yellow berries)	Europe, Asia
sage, common	*Salvia*	green, white, yellow, reddish purple	S Europe
St John's wort	*Hypericum*	yellow	Europe, Asia
sea buckthorn	*Hippophae rhamnoides*	silver, orange	SW Europe
senecio	*Senecio*	yellow	New Zealand
skimmia	*Skimmia*	white	Japan, China
snowberry	*Symphoricarpos*	pink, white	N America
spiraea	*Spiraea*	white, pink, crimson	China, Japan
stachyurus	*Stachyurus*	pale yellow	China
staphylea	*Staphylea*	rose-pink	Europe, Asia
syringa *see* lilac			
tamarix	*Tamarix*	pink, white	Europe
thyme	*Thymus*	purple, white, pink	Europe
veronica	*Veronica*	white, pink, lilac, purple	New Zealand
viburnum	*Viburnum*	white, pink	Europe, Asia, Africa
Virgina creeper	*Parthenocissus*	blue, black	N America
wattle *see* acacia			
weigela	*Weigela*	pink, red	N China
winter sweet	*Chimonanthus*	yellow	China
wisteria	*Wisteria*	mauve, white, pink	China, Japan
witch-hazel	*Hamamelis*	red, yellow	China, Japan

FLOWERS (Herbaceous)

English name	Genus	Colour	Country/continent of origin
acanthus	*Acanthus*	white, rose, purple	Europe
African violet	*Saintpaulia*	violet, white, pink	Africa
alum root	*Heuchera*	rose, pink, red	N America
alyssum	*Alyssum*	white, yellow, pink	S Europe
anchusa	*Anchusa*	blue	Asia, S Europe
anemone	*Hepatica*	white, red-pink, blue	Europe, Caucasus
asphodel	*Asphodelus*	white, yellow	S Europe
aster	*Aster*	white, blue, purple, pink	Europe, Asia, N America
astilbe	*Astilbe*	white, pink, red	Asia
aubretia	*Aubretia*	purple	SE Europe
begonia	*Begonia*	pink	S America, the Pacific
bellflower	*Campanula*	blue, white	N temperate regions
bergamot	*Monarda*	white, pink, red, purple	N America
bistort	*Polygonum*	rose-pink	Japan, Himalayas
bleeding heart	*Dicentra*	pink, white, red	China, Japan, N America
bugbane	*Cimicifuga*	white	N America, Japan
busy lizzie	*Impatiens*	crimson, pink, white	tropics
buttercup	*Ranunculus*	yellow	temperate regions
carnation	*Dianthus*	white, pink, red	temperate regions
catmint	*Nepeta*	blue, mauve	Europe, Asia
celandine, giant	*Ranunculus*	white, copper-orange	Europe
Christmas rose	*Helleborus*	white, pink	Europe
chrysanthemum	*Chrysanthemum*	yellow, white	China
cinquefoil	*Potentilla*	orange, red, yellow	Europe, Asia
columbine (or granny's bonnet)	*Aquilegia*	purple, dark blue, pink, yellow	Europe
Cupid's dart	*Catananche*	blue, white	Europe
dahlia	*Dahlia*	red, yellow, white	Mexico
daisy	*Bellis perennis*	white, yellow, pink	Europe
delphinium	*Delphinium*	white, mauve, pink, blue	Europe, N America
echinacea	*Echinacea*	rose-red, purple	N America
edelweiss	*Leontopodium alpinum*	yellow, white	Europe, Asia
evening primrose	*Oenothera*	yellow	N America
everlasting flower (or immortelle)	*Helichrysum bracteatum*	yellow	Australia

FLOWERS (Herbaceous) (cont.)

English name	Genus	Colour	Country/continent of origin
everlasting flower, pearly	*Anaphalis*	white	N America, Himalayas
fleabane	*Erigeron*	white, pink, blue, violet	Australia
forget-me-not	*Myosotis*	blue	Europe
foxglove	*Digitalis*	white, yellow, pink, red	Europe, Asia
fraxinella	*Dictamnus*	white, mauve	Europe, Asia
gentian	*Gentiana*	blue, yellow, white, red	temperate regions
geranium	*Pelargonium*	scarlet, pink, white	temperate regions, subtropics
geum	*Geum*	orange, red, yellow	S Europe, N America
goat's beard	*Aruncus*	white	N Europe
golden rod	*Solidago*	yellow	Europe
granny's bonnet *see* columbine			
gypsophila	*Gypsophila*	white, pink	Europe, Asia
Hattie's pincushion (or the melancholy gentleman)	*Astrantia*	white, pink	Europe
heliopsis	*Heliopsis*	orange-yellow	N America
helleborus	*Helleborus*	plum-purple, white	Asia, Greece
herb Christopher	*Actaea*	white	N America
hollyhock	*Althaea*	white, yellow, pink, red, maroon	Europe, China
horta	*Horta*	violet, white	China, Japan
immortelle *see* everlasting flower			
kaffir lily	*Schizostylis*	red, pink	S Africa
kirengeshoma	*Kirengeshoma*	yellow	Japan
liatris	*Liatris*	heather-purple	N America
lobelia	*Lobelia*	white, red, blue, purple	Africa, N America, Australia
loosestrife	*Lysimachia*	rose-pink, purple	Europe
lotus	*Lotus*	yellow, pink, white	Asia, America
lupin	*Lupinus*	blue, yellow, pink, red	N America
marigold, African, French	*Tagetes*	yellow, orange	America (Mexico)
marigold, pot	*Calendula*	orange, apricot, cream	unknown
meadow rue	*Thalictrum*	yellow-white	Europe, Asia
mullein	*Verbascum*	yellow, white, pink, purple	Europe, Asia
nasturtium	*Tropaeolum*	yellow, red, orange	S America, Mexico

FLOWERS (Herbaceous) (cont.)

English name	Genus	Colour	Country/continent of origin
orchid	*Orchidaea*	red, purple, white violet, green, brown, yellow, pink	tropics
ox-eye daisy	*Buphthalmum*	yellow	Europe
pansy	*Viola tricolor*	white, yellow	temperate regions
peony	*Paeonia*	white, yellow, pink, red	Asia, Europe
Peruvian lily	*Alstroemeria*	cream, pink, yellow, orange, red	S America
petunia	*Petunia*	blue, violet, purple, white, pink	S America
phlox	*Phlox*	blue, white, purple, red	America
poppy	*Papaver*	red, orange, white, yellow, lilac	N temperate regions
primrose	*Primula*	yellow	N temperate regions
primula	*Primula*	white, pink yellow, blue, purple	N. temperate regions
red-hot poker	*Kniphofia*	white, yellow, orange, red	S Africa
salvia	*Salvia*	red, yellow, blue	S America, Europe, Asia
sea holly	*Eryngium*	blue, green-grey, white	Europe, S America
sidalcea	*Sidalcea*	lilac, pink, rose	N America
snapdragon	*Antirrhinum*	white, yellow, pink, red, maroon	Europe, Asia, S America
speedwell	*Veronica teucrium*	blue, white	Europe, Asia
spiderwort	*Tradescantia*	white, blue, pink, red, purple	N America
stokeria	*Stokeria*	white, blue, purple	N America
sunflower	*Helianthus*	yellow	N America
sweet pea	*Lathyrus*	purple, pink, white, red	Mediterranean
sweet william	*Dianthus*	white, pink, red, purple	S Europe
thistle, globe	*Echinops*	blue, white-grey	Europe, Asia
thistle, Scotch (or cotton)	*Onopordum*	purple	Europe
violet	*Viola*	mauve, blue	N temperate regions
water chestnut	*Trapa natans*	white, lilac	Asia
water lily	*Nymphaea*	white, blue, red, yellow	worldwide
wolf's bane	*Aconitum*	blue, white, rose, yellow	Europe, Asia
yarrow	*Achillea*	white, cream	Europe, W Asia

FLOWERS (Bulbs, corms, rhizomes and tubers)

English name	Genus	Colour	Country/continent of origin
acidanthera	*Acidanthera*	white	NE Africa
African lily (or lily-of-the-Nile)	*Agapanthus*	white, purple	S Africa
agapanthus	*Agapanthus*	blue, white	S Africa
allium	*Allium*	blue, lilac, white, rose	Asia, Europe
amaryllis (or belladonna lily)	*Amaryllis*	rose-pink	S Africa, tropical America
anemone	*Anemone*	white, lilac, blue	Mediterranean, Asia, Europe
belladonna lily *see* amaryllis			
bluebell	*Endymion nonscriptus*	blue	Europe
camassia	*Camassia*	white, cream, blue, purple	N America
chionodoxa (or glory of the snow)	*Chionodoxa*	blue, white, pink	Greece, Turkey
crinum	*Crinum*	rose-pink, white	S Africa
crocosmia	*Crocosmia*	orange	S Africa
crocus	*Crocus*	purple, rose, yellow, pink, orange	Mediterranean, Asia, Africa
crown imperial	*Fritillaria*	orange	N India
curtonus	*Curtonus*	orange	S Africa
cyclamen	*Cyclamen*	white, pink, red	Asia, Mediterranean
daffodil (or narcissus)	*Narcissus*	white, yellow, orange	Mediterranean, Europe
dog's tooth violet *see* erythronium			
erythronium (or dog's tooth violet	*Erythronium*	purple, pink, white, yellow	Europe, Asia
fritillaria	*Fritillaria*	red, yellow	Europe, Asia, N America
galtonia	*Galtonia*	white	S Africa
gladiolus	*Gladiolus*	purple, yellow	Europe, Asia
glory of the snow *see* chionodoxa			
harebell	*Campanula rotundifolium*	blue	N temperate regions
hippeastrum	*Hippeastrum*	pink, white, red	tropical America
hyacinth	*Hyacinthus orientalis*	blue, white, red	S Europe, Asia
hyacinth, grape	*Muscari*	blue	Europe, Mediterranean
hyacinth, wild	*Scilla*	blue, purple, pink, white	Asia, S Europe
iris	*Iris*	purple, white, yellow	N temperate regions
lthuriel's spear	*Brodiaea*	white, pink, blue	N America
lapeyrousia	*Lapeyrousia*	red	S Africa

FLOWERS (Bulbs, corms, rhizomes and tubers) (cont.)

English name	Genus	Colour	Country/continent of origin
lily	*Lilium*	white, pink, crimson, yellow, orange, red	China, Europe, America
lily-of-the-Nile *see* African lily			
lily-of-the-valley	*Convallaria majalis*	white	Europe, Asia, America
naked ladies	*Colchicum*	white, pink, purple	Asia, Europe
nerine	*Nerine*	pink, salmon	S Africa
ornithogalum	*Ornithogalum*	white, yellow	S Africa
peacock (or tiger flower)	*Tigridia*	white, orange, red, yellow	Asia
rouge, giant	*Tigridia*	white, yellow, red, lilac	Mexico
snake's head	*Fritillaria*	purple, white	Europe
snowdrop	*Galanthus*	white	Europe
snowflake	*Leucojum*	white, green	S Europe
solfaterre	*Montbretia*	orange, red	S Africa
Solomon's seal	*Polygonatum*	white	Europe, Asia
squill	*Scilla*	blue, purple	Europe, Asia, S Africa
sternbergia	*Sternbergia*	yellow	Europe
striped squill	*Puschkinia*	bluish-white	Asia
tiger flower *see* peacock			
tiger lily	*Lilium*	orange	Asia
tulip	*Tulipa*	orange, red, pink, white, crimson, lilac	Europe, Asia
wand flower	*Dierama*	white, pink, mauve, purple	S Africa
winter aconite	*Eranthis*	yellow	Greece, Turkey

FISH

Name	Family	Size (cm¹)	Habitat	Distribution	Special features
albacore	*Scombridae*	to 130	open waters	tropical, warm temperate	tuna fish with large pectoral fins; prized food and sport fish
anchovy	*Engraulidae*	9–12	surface ocean	temperate	important food fish in S Europe, Black Sea, Peru
angler fish	*Chaunacidae*	5–8	deep ocean	tropical, temperate	large jaws; fishing lure at tip of modified dorsal ray
barracuda	*Sphyraenidae*	30–240	surface ocean	tropical, warm temperate	carnivorous; voracious; large teeth
blenny	*Blenniidae*	20–49	sea bed	temperate, tropical	devoid of scales
bonito	*Scombridae*	to 90	open sea surface water	temperate, warm	commercially important; member of tuna family; food fish; sport fish
bream	*Cyprinidae*	41–80	freshwater lakes, rivers	temperate (N Europe)	deep-bodied; food fish
brill	*Scophthalmidae*	to 70	sea bed	temperate	flat fish; eyes on left side; food fish
butterfly fish	*Chaetodontidae*	to 15	reefs	tropical	deep, compressed body; brightly coloured
carp	*Cyprinidae*	51–61	beds of freshwater lakes, rivers	temperate	important food fish; used in aquaculture
catfish	*Ictaluridae*	90–135	sea bed	temperate (N America)	females lay eggs in nest scooped out in mud; important food fish
chub	*Cyprinidae*	30–60	lakes, rivers	temperate (Europe)	popular sport fish
cod	*Gadidae*	to 120	ocean shelf	temperate, N hemisphere	common cod very important food fish
conger eel	*Congridae*	274	sea bed, deep inshore pools	temperate	rounded cylindrical body; upper jaw longer than lower
dab	*Pleuronectidae*	20–40	shallow sea bed	temperate (Europe)	flat fish; eyes on right side; food fish

FISH (cont.)

Name	Family	Size (cm¹)	Habitat	Distribution	Special features
dace	*Cyprinidae*	15–30	freshwater lakes, rivers	temperate (Europe, USSR)	sport fish
damsel fish	*Pomacentridae*	5–15	reefs, rocky shores	tropical, temperate	brightly coloured
dogfish	*Scyliorhinidae*	60–100	sea bed	temperate (Europe)	skin very rough; food fish (sold as rock salmon)
dolphin fish (dorado)	*Corypaenidae*	to 200	surface	tropical, warm temperate	predatory; prized sport fish; food fish
dory	*Zeidae*	30–60	mainly shallow ocean	temperate	deep-bodied; food fish
eagle ray	*Myliobatidae*	to 200	mainly inshore sea bed	tropical, temperate	pectoral fins form 'wings'; young born live
eel	*Anguillidae*	to 50 (male), to 100 (female)	rivers, mid-ocean	temperate	elongate cylindrical body form; adults live in rivers but spawn in sea; important food fish
electric eel	*Electrophoridae*	to 240	shallow streams	Orinoco, Amazon basins (S America)	produces powerful electric shocks to stun prey and as defence
electric or torpedo ray	*Torpenidae*	to 180	sea bed	tropical, temperate	produces strong electric shocks to stun prey
file fish	*Monacanthidae*	5–13	reefs, shallow water	tropical, warm temperate	rough skin; food fish
flounder	*Pleuronectidae*	to 51	shallow sea bed, saline estuaries, lakes	temperate (Europe)	flatfish (eyes may be on right or left side); locally important food fish
flying fish	*Exocoetidae*	25–50	surface ocean	tropical, warm temperate	enlarged pelvic and pectoral fins give ability to jump and glide above water surface
goat fish *see* red mullet					
goby	*Gobiidae*	1–27	shallow sea bed, rocky pools	tropical, temperate	pelvic fins joined to form single sucker-like fin
goldfish	*Cyprinidae*	to 30	freshwater ponds, rivers	temperate	popular ornamental fish

grenadier *see* rat-tail

Common name	Family	Size	Habitat	Region	Notes
grey mullet	*Mugilidae*	to 75	coastal sea bed; occasionally tropical freshwaters	tropical, temperate	food fish
grouper	*Serranidae*	5–370	deep sea	tropical, warm temperate	common around reefs, wrecks; prized sport and food fish
gurnard (or sea robin)	*Triglidae*	to 75	sea bed	tropical, warm temperate	bony plates on head; many produce audible sounds
hake	*Merlucciidae*	to 180	continental shelf waters	temperate	head and jaws large; food fish
halibut	*Pleuronectidae*	to 250	sea bed	temperate (Atlantic)	flat fish; eyes on right side; prized food fish
herring	*Clupeidae*	to 40	surface ocean	temperate (N Atlantic, Arctic)	important food fish
lamprey	*Petromyzonidae*	to 91	streams, river; parasitic in open sea	temperate (N Atlantic)	primitive jawless fish; mouth sucker-like; food fish
lantern fish	*Myctophidae*	2–15	deep sea, but many migrate to surface at night	tropical, temperate	body has numerous light organs
lemon sole	*Pleuronectidae*	to 66	sea bed	temperate	flat fish; specialized feeder on polychaete worms; food fish
loach	*Cobitidae*	to 15	freshwater lakes, rivers	temperate (Europe, Asia)	popular aquarium fish
mackerel	*Scombridae*	to 66	surface ocean	temperate (N Atlantic)	seasonal migrations; important food fish
manta ray	*Mobulidae*	120–900 (width)	surface ocean	tropical	fleshy 'horns' at side of head; young born live
minnow	*Cyprinidae*	to 12	fast flowing freshwater lakes, rivers	temperate (N Europe, Asia)	locally abundant
monkfish	*Squatinidae*	to 180	sea bed	temperate (N Atlantic, Mediterranean)	pectoral fins very broad, tail slender, intermediate in shape between shark and ray; food fish
moorish idol	*Zanclidae*	to 22	reefs	tropical (Indo-Pacific)	body deep, tall dorsal and anal fins; bold black/white stripes with some yellow

FISH (cont.)

Name	Family	Size (cm¹)	Habitat	Distribution	Special features
moray eel	*Muraenidae*	to 130	rocky shores	temperate, tropical	pointed snout; long, sharp teeth; aggressive
parrot fish	*Scaridae*	25–190	reefs	tropical	jaw teeth fused to form parrot-like beak for scraping algal growth from reefs, and for breaking coral
perch	*Percidae*	30–50	freshwater lakes, rivers, Baltic Sea	temperate	food fish; sport fish
pike	*Esocidae*	to 130	freshwater lakes, rivers	temperate	snout pointed; jaws large; predatory; prized by anglers
pilchard (or sardine)	*Clupeidae*	to 25	surface	temperate (N Atlantic, Mediterranean)	important food fish, often canned
pipefish	*Syngnathidae*	15–60	shallow seas	tropical, warm temperate	slender segmented body; males of some species carry eggs in brood pouch
plaice	*Pleuronectidae*	50–90	shallow sea bed	temperate (Europe)	flatfish; eyes on right side; important food fish
puffer	*Tetraodontidae*	3–25	inshore shallow seas, reefs	tropical, warm temperate	body often spiny; some organs and tissues very poisonous, but a food delicacy in Japan
rat-tail (or grenadier)	*Macrouridae*	40–110	close to deep-sea bed	temperate, tropical	large head, tapering body; some species make sounds by resonating swim bladder
ray	*Rajidae*	39–113	sea bed	temperate	skate and ray family; front part of body flattened with large pectoral fins
red mullet (or goat fish)	*Mullidae*	to 40	sea bed	tropical, temperate	food fish
remora	*Echeneidae*	12–46	open sea	tropical, warm temperate	large sucking disc on head, with which it attaches self to other fish, especially sharks

Common name	Family	Size	Habitat	Climate	Notes
roach	*Cyprinidae*	35–53	freshwater lakes, rivers	temperate (Europe, USSR)	popular sport fish
sailfish	*Istiophoridae*	to 360	open ocean surface	tropical, warm temperate	long tall dorsal fin; prized sport fish
salmon	*Salmonidae*	to 150	surface ocean; rivers	temperate	swims upriver to breed; prized sport and food fish
sandeel	*Ammodytidae*	to 20	inshore sea bed	temperate (N hemisphere)	very important food for seabirds
sardine *see* pilchard					
scorpion-fish	*Scorpaenidae*	to 50	shallow sea bed, reefs	tropical, temperate	distinctive fin and body spines; venom glands
sea bass	*Percichthyidae*	60–100	inshore waters; reefs	tropical, temperate	food fish; popular sport fish
sea robin *see* gurnard					
sea-bream	*Sparidae*	35–51	close to sea bed	tropical, temperate	food fish; sport fish
seahorse	*Syngnathidae*	to 15	surface ocean	tropical, warm temperate	snout extended to form horse-like head; swims upright
shark, basking	*Cetorhinidae*	870–1350	surface ocean	tropical, temperate	feeds on plankton; second largest living fish
shark, great white	*Isuridae*	to 330	surface ocean	tropical live	fierce; voracious; young born
shark, hammerhead	*Sphyrnidae*	360–600	mainly surface ocean	tropical, warm temperate	head flattened into hammer shape; voracious; young born live
shark, tiger	*Galeorhinidae*	360–600	surface ocean	tropical, warm temperate	vertical stripes on body; fierce
shark, whale	*Rhinocodontidae*	1020–1800	surface ocean	tropical	largest of living fishes; feeds on plankton
skate	*Rajidae*	200–285	mid-ocean, sea bed	temperate	food fish
smelt	*Osmeridae*	20–30	freshwater lakes, rivers; inshore seas	temperate	related to salmon and trout; food fish
sole	*Soleidae*	30–60	sea bed	tropical, temperate	flat fish; eyes on right side; food fish
sprat	*Clupeidae*	13–16	surface–mid-ocean	temperate	food fish (white bait when small)
squirrel fish	*Holocentridae*	12–30	reefs	tropical	brightly coloured; nocturnal

FISH (cont.)

Name	Family	Size (cm[1])	Habitat	Distribution	Special features
stickleback	*Gasterosteidae*	5–10	freshwater lake, rivers; inshore seas	temperate (N hemisphere)	male builds nest, guards eggs
stingray	*Dasyatidae*	106–140	sea bed; tropical freshwaters	tropical, temperate	tail whip-like, armed with poison spine(s)
sturgeon	*Acipenseridae*	100–500	shallow sea bed; rivers	temperate (N hemisphere)	primitive fish; eggs prized as caviar
sunfish	*Molidae*	to 400	surface–mid open ocean	tropical, warm temperate	tail fin absent; body almost circular
surgeon fish (or tang)	*Acanthuridae*	20–45	reefs	tropical, subtropical	brightly coloured; sharp spine on sides of tail can be erected for defence
swordfish	*Xiphiidae*	200–500	surface–mid open ocean	tropical, temperate	upper jaw extended to from flathead 'sword'; food fish; sport fish
tang *see* surgeon fish					
trigger fish	*Balistidae*	10–60	sea bed outside reefs	tropical	colourful; dorsal spine can be erected to wedge fish in crevice as defence; food fish, but can be poisonous
trout	*Salmonidae*	surface ocean; freshwater lakes, rivers	23–140	temperate	brown trout confined to fresh water; sea trout migratory; prized food fish
tuna, skipjack	*Scombridae*	to 100	mid-ocean	tropical, temperate fish	fast swimmer; important food
tuna, yellow fin	*Scombridae*	to 200	surface ocean	tropical, warm temperate	elongated body, long dorsal and anal fins; important food fish
turbot	*Scoph-thalamidae*	50–100	shallow sea bed	temperate (N Atlantic)	flat fish; eyes on left side of body; prized food fish
wrasse	*Labridae*	7–210	reefs, rocky coasts	tropical, warm temperate	brightly coloured

[1] To convert cm to in, multiply by 0.3937

REPTILES

Reptiles are egg-laying vertebrates of the class Reptilia, having evolved from primitive amphibians: 6547 species divided into Squamata (lizards and snakes), Chelonia (tortoises and turtles), Crocodylia (crocodiles and alligators) and Rhynocephalia (the tuatara).

Most reptiles live on the land, breathe with lungs, and have horny or plated skins. Reptiles require the rays of the sun to maintain their body temperature,

ie they are cold-blooded or ectothermic. This confines them to warm, tropical and sub-tropical regions, but does allow some species to exist in particularly hot desert environments in which mammals and birds would find it impossible to sustain life.

Extinct species of reptile include the dinosaur and pterodactyl.

Name	Family	Size (cm¹)	Distribution	Food	Special features
alligator	*Alligatoridae*	200–550	S USA, C and S America and E China	fish, birds, mammals, amphibians, reptiles	able to inflict fatalities on humans but attacks rare; only the American alligator is currently free from being an endangered species, noted for its longevity in protected environments
anguid	*Anguidae*	6–30	N and S America, Europe, Asia and NW Africa	small lizards, mice, birds' eggs, tadpoles, earthworms, spiders, scorpions, grasshoppers, moths, wasps, larvae	distinctive bony-plated scales which reach round the under-side giving the creature a rigid appearance
boa	*Boidae*	200–400	West N America, S America, Africa, Madagascar Asia, Fiji, Solomons and New Guinea	birds, mammals	famous constricting snake, includes within its family species of anaconda
chameleon	*Chamaeleontidae*	2–28	Africa outwith the Sahara, Madagascar, Middle East, S Spain, S Arabian peninsula, Sri Lanka, Crete, India and Pakistan	insects, spiders, scorpions, small birds, mammals	noted for its ability to change colour and blend into its environment

REPTILES (cont.)

Name	Family	Size (cm¹)	Distribution	Food	Special features
crocodile	Crocodylidae	150–750	pantropical and some temperate regions of Africa	vertebrates	distinguished from the alligator by the visible fourth tooth in the lower jaw; famous for its huge jaws, fierce appearance and violent hunting and ambush techniques when capturing prey; populations have been decimated by the demand for luxury leather and several species are endangered
gecko	Gekkonidae	1.5–24	N and S America, Africa, S Europe, Asia and Australia	mainly insects	noted for its vocalization and ability to climb; able to shed its tail as a defence mechanism against predators
iguana	Iguanidae	to 200	C and S America, Madagascar, Fiji and Tonga	mainly insects	terrestrial and tree-dwelling lizard; active by day, able to survive in exceptionally high temperatures
lizard, beaded	Helodermatidae	33–45	SW United States, W Mexico to Guatemala	small mammals, birds, lizards, frogs, birds, eggs insects, earthworms, carrion	possesses a mildly venomous bite
lizard, blind	Dibamidae	12–16.5	New Guinea to Indochina	insects	so-named because the eyes are concealed within the skin
lizard, Bornean earless	Lanthanotidae	to 20	Borneo	fish, earthworms, birds' eggs	lacks an external ear opening; partly aquatic and a good swimmer; capable of short, rapid movements on land
lizard, chisel-tooth	Agamidae	4–35	Africa, Asia and Australia	insects, fruit, plants, eggs	named after its distinctive teeth; family includes the flying dragonwhich is able to glide from perch to perch

common name	family	size	distribution	diet	notes
lizard, girdle-tailed	*Cordylidae*	5–27.5	Africa south of the Sahara, Madagascar	mainly insectivorous and carnivorous	terrestrial; active by day; adapted to arid environments
lizard, monitor	*Varanidae*	12–150	Africa, S Asia, Indo-Australian archipelago, Philippines, New Guinea and Australia	carrion, large snails, grasshoppers, beetles, scorpions, crocodiles' and birds' eggs, fish, lizards, snakes, birds, shrews, squirrels	consumes its prey whole in the manner of snakes; includes the Komodo dragon, the largest living lizard which has a prodigious appetite and is capable of killing pigs and small deer
lizard, night	*Xantusiidae*	3.5–12	C America	mainly insects	most species active by night, secretive by day
lizard, snake	*Pygopodidae*	6.5–31	New Guinea and Australia	mainly insects	snake-like appearance; broad but highly extensible tongue
lizard, wall and	*Lacertidae*	4–22	Europe, Africa, Asia and Indo-Australian archipelago	mainly insects, snails, worms	highly conspicuous lizard living in open and sandy environments; terrestrial, active by day
lizard, worm	*Amphisbaenidae*	15–35	subtropical regions of N and S America, Africa, Middle East, Asia and Europe	mainly insects, snails, worms	worm-like, burrowing reptile; some of the species have the rare ability to move backwards and forwards
pipesnake	*Aniliidae*	less than 100	S America, SE Asia	snakes, eels	tail has brilliantly coloured red underside; burrows in swampy regions and feeds on other snakes
python	*Pythonidae*	100–1000	tropical and subtropical Africa, SE Asia, Australia, Mexico and C America	birds, mammals	capable of killing humans, especially children, by constriction
skink	*Scincidae*	2.8–35	tropical and temperate regions	crabs, insects, seeds	family of terrestrial, tree-dwelling or burrowing species, including highly adept swimmers and those able to swim through sand
snake, dawn blind	*Anomalepidae*	11–30	C and S America	ants, termites	short tail, indistinct head, one or two teeth in the lower jaw

REPTILES (cont.)

Name	Family	Size (cm[1])	Distribution	Food	Special features
snake, front fanged	*Elapidae*	38–560	worldwide in warm regions	frogs, snakes, eels, rodents, lizards, and other vertebrates	highly venomous family with short fangs; responsible for numerous human fatalities. includes the mamba, the adder and the cobra with its famous broad, hooded head
snake, harmless	*Colubridae*	13–350	worldwide	wide variety of vertebrates	large family which includes terrestrial, burrowing, arboreal and aquatic species; called harmless because of the inability of most species to inject or produce venomous saliva
snake, shieldtail	*Uropeltidae*	20–50	S India and Sri Lanka	earthworms and insects	small burrowing snake, with tiny eyes, so-called because the tail ends abruptly and forms a rough cylindrical shield
snake, thread	*Leptotyphlopidae*	15–90	C and S America, Africa, Asia	ants and termites	small and exceptionally slender burrowing snake
snake, typical blind	*Typhlopidae*	15–90	C and S America, Africa south of the Sahara, SE Europe, S Asia, Taiwan and Australia	ants, termites, larvae	burrowing snake with tiny, concealed eyes and no teeth on lower jaw
tortoise	*Testudinidae*	10–140	S Europe, Africa, Asia, C and S America	mainly herbivorous	includes smallest species of turtle, the Speckled Cape tortoise (10cm) and one of the longest lived turtles, the spur-thighed tortoise with a possible life span of over a century
tuatara	*Sphenodontidae*	45–61	islands off New Zealand	ground insects, geckos, skinks, birds' eggs	lizard-like reptile with a third eye in the top of its head

turtle, Afro-American side-necked	*Pelomedusidae*	12–90	S America, Africa, Madagascar, Seychelles and Mauritius	herbivorous and omnivorous species	bottom-dweller that rarely requires to come to the surface
turtle, American mud and musk	*Kinosternidae*	11–27	N and S America	molluscs, insects, crustaceans, fish, plants	lives permanently or semipermanently in freshwater, glands produce distinctive and evil smelling secretion
turtle, Austro-American side-necked	*Chelidae*	14–48	S America, Australia and New Guinea	omnivorous and carnivorous species	family includes the peculiar looking matamata, the most adept of the ambush-feeders at the gape and suck technique of capturing prey
turtle, big-headed	*Platysternidae*	20	SE Asia	small invertebrates	distinctive large head which cannot be retracted; active at night; exceptionally good climbers
turtle, C American river	*Dermatemydidae*	to 65	Vera Cruz, Mexico, Honduras	fish, insects, fruit, leaves, plants	freshwater creature with well-developed shell
turtle, Mexican musk	*Staurotypidae*	to 38	Mexico to Honduras	worms, fishes, newts	freshwater creature dwelling in marshes and swamps
turtle, pig-nosed softshell	*Carettochelyidae*	55 or over	New Guinea and N Australia	crustaceans, insects, molluscs, fish, aquatic plants and fruit	specialized swimmer named for its plateless skin and fleshy, pig-like snout
turtle, pond and river	*Emydidae*	11.4–80	N and C America, S Europe, N Africa, Asia and Argentina	insects, molluscs, vertebrates, plants	family ranges from tiny bog turtle (11.4) to the largest of the river turtles, the Malaysian giant turtle; includes box turtle with possible life span of over a century, also species of terrapin
turtle, sea	*Cheloniidae*	75–213	pantropical, and some subtropical and temperate regions	sponges, jellyfish, mussels, crabs, sea urchins, fish	rapid movement through water contrasts with characteristically slow movements of turtles on land

REPTILES (cont.)

Name	Family	Size (cm[1])	Distribution	Food	Special features
turtle, snapping	*Chelydridae*	47–66	N and C America	carrion, insects, fish, turtles, molluscs, plant food	large-headed, aggressive bottom dweller; includes other turtles in its diet; ambush feeder with rapid snapping movements; alligator snapping turtle has unique worm-like projection on the tongue which fills with blood, turns red, and acts as lure to catch fish
turtle, softshell	*Trionychidae*	30–115	N America, Africa, Asia and Indo-Australian archipelago	insects, crustaceans, fish	named after its leathered, plateless skin; noted for its prominent, pointed snout
viper	*Viperidae*	25–365	N and S America, Africa, Europe and Asia	vertebrates	famous, venomous family of snakes, including the rattlesnake which vibrates its tail when disturbed, and the sidewinder with its distinctive sideways movements
whiptail and racerunner	*Teiidae*	37–45	N and S Asia	small mammals, birds, fish, frogs, tadpoles, lizards, insects, snails and plants	captured and eaten by S American Indians, the fat and flesh also being used in traditional medicines
xenosaur	*Xenosauridae*	10–15	Mexico, Guatemala and S China	insects, tadpoles, fish	terrestrial, sedentary and secretive

[1] To convert cm to in, multiply by 0.3937

BIRDS

Birds are warm-blooded, egg-laying, and, in the case of adults, feathered vertebrates of the class Aves; there are approximately 8600 species classified into 29 Orders and 181 Families. Birds are constructed for flight. The body is streamlined to reduce air resistance, the fore-limbs are modified as feathered wings, and the skeletal structure, heart and wing muscles, centre of gravity, and lung capacity are all designed for the act of flying.

Two exceptions to this are the ratites or flightless birds which have become too large to be capable of sustained flight, eg the ostrich, kiwi and emu, and the penguin which has evolved into a highly aquatic creature.

Birds have evolved from reptiles, their closest living relative being the crocodile.

Flightless birds

Name	Family	Size (cm¹)	Distribution	Food	Special features
cassowary	*Casauriidae*	150	Australia and New Guinea	fruit, plants, insects	claws capable of inflicting fatal wounds on humans
emu	*Dromaiidae*	160–130	Australia	plants, fruit, flowers, insects	highly mobile, nomadic population
kiwi	*Apterygidae*	35–55	New Zealand	earthworms, insects, seeds, berries	smallest of the Ratitae order; nocturnal
ostrich	*Struthonidae*	275	dry areas of Africa	mainly leaves, flowers, seeds of plants	fastest animal on two legs
rhea	*Rheidae*	100–150	grasslands of S America	leaves, roots, seeds, insects, small vertebrates	live in flocks
tinamou	*Tinamidae*	15–49	C and S America	seeds, fruit, insects, small animals	sustains flight over short distances

Birds of prey

Name	Family	Size (cm¹)	Distribution	Food	Special features
barn owl	*Tytonidae*	30–45	worldwide	small vertebrates	feathered legs; nests high above ground
falcon	*Falconidae*	15–60	worldwide	birds, carrion, large insects, small mammals	remarkable powers of flight and sight
buzzard	*Accipitridae*	80	worldwide except Australasia and Malaysia	small mammals	spends much time perching; kills prey on ground

81

BIRDS (cont.)

Birds of prey

Name	Family	Size (cm¹)	Distribution	Food	Special features
condor	*Cathartidae*	60–100	the Americas	carrion	Andean condor has largest wingspan of any living bird (up to 3m)
eagle, bald	*Accipitridae*	80–100	N America	fish, birds, mammals	name refers to white plumage on head and neck; national symbol of USA
eagle, golden	*Accipitridae*	80–100	N hemishpere	rabbits, hares, carrion	kills with talons; most numerous large eagle
eagle, harpy	*Accipitridae*	90	C America to Argentina	some birds, tree dwelling mammals	the world's largest eagle; black, white and grey; large feet
eagle, sea	*Accipitridae*	70–120	coastline worldwide	fish	breeds on sea cliffs
harrier	*Accipitridae*	50	worldwide	small mammals, birds	hunts by flying low in regular search pattern
kite	*Accipitridae*	52–58	worldwide	insects, snails, small vertebrates, carrion	most varied and diverse group of hawks
sparrowhawk	*Accipitridae*	to 27 (male), to 38 (female)	Eurasia, NW Africa, C and S America	small birds	long tail, small round wings
osprey	*Pandionidae*	55–58	worldwide	fish	feet specially adapted for catching fish
owl	*Strigidae*	12–73	worldwide	mainly small mammals	acute sight and hearing; swallows prey whole; nocturnal
secretary bird	*Sagittaridae*	100	Africa	rodents, reptiles, large beetles, grasshoppers	walks up to 30km/20ml per day
vulture (New World)	*Cathartidae*	60–100	the Americas	carrion, carcasses	lives in colonies; locates food mainly by sight; head often lacking long feathers
vulture (Old World)	*Accipitridae*	150–270 (wingspan)	worldwide except the Americas	carrion	no sense of smell

Songbirds

Name	Family	Size (cm¹)	Distribution	Food	Special features
accentor	*Prunellidae*	14–18	Palaearctic	insects, seeds	complex social organization and mating systems
American warbler	*Parulidae*	10–16	N and S America	insects, berries, vegetable matter	well developed and often complex songs
Australian tree-creeper	*Climacteridae*	15	Australia and New Guinea	mainly ants	forages for food on the trunks and limbs of trees
bird of paradise	*Paradisaeidae*	12.5–100	New Guinea, Moluccas and Eastern Australia	frogs, nestling birds, insects, fruit, plants	brilliantly ornate plumage; elaborate courtship displays
bowerbird	*Ptilinorhynchidae*	23–37	Australia and New Guinea	mainly fruit, vegetable matter	male builds bowers to attract female for mating
bulbul	*Pycnonotidae*	13–23	Africa Madagascar, S As a and the Philippines	fruits, berries, insects	several species renowned for powerful, beautiful singing voice
bunting	*Emberizidae*	15–20	worldwide	seeds, crustaceans, insects	large family including species of sparrow, finch, and cardinals
butcherbird	*Cracticidae*	26–58	Australia New Guinea and New Zealand	large insects, crustaceans, reptiles, small mammals, young birds	highly aggressive; sings loudly at dawn; thus has alternative name of 'bushman's clock'
chaffinch	*Fringillidae*	11–19	Europe, N and S America, Africa and Asia	seeds	strong bill; melodious singing voice
cowbird	*Icteridae*	17–54	N and S America	fruit, seeds, crustaceans, insects	forages for food using distinctive gaping movements of the bill
crow	*Corvidae*	20–66	worldwide, except New Zeeland	omnivorous	adaptable, intelligent; with complex social systems
cuckoo-shrike	*Campephagidae*	14–40	Africa S Asia.	mainly insects, caterpillars	peculiar courtship display; family includes colourful minivets
dipper	*Cinclidae*	17–20	Europe, S Asia and W regions of N and S America	water insects, molluscs, crustaceans, worms, tadpoles, small fish	strong legs and toes allow mobility to walk under water
drongo	*Dicruridae*	18–38	S Asia and Africa	insects, lizards, small birds	pugnacious
flowerpecker	*Dicaeidae*	8–20	SE Asia and Australasia	berries, nectar, insects	short tongue specially adapted for feeding on nectar

BIRDS (cont.)

Songbirds

Name	Family	Size (cm¹)	Distribution	Food	Special features
flycatcher (Old World)	*Muscicapidae*	9–27	worldwide except N and S America	insects	tropical species brightly coloured; feeds on the wing
flycatcher, silky	*Ptilogonidae*	to 14	N and S America	insects	feeds on the wing
Hawaiian honeycreeper	*Drepanididae*	10–20	Hawaiian Islands	nectar, fruit, seeds, insects	widely varying bills between species adapted to different environments
honeyeater	*Meliphagidae*	10–32	Australasia, Pacific Islands, Hawaii and S Africa	nectar, insects, fruits, berries	brush tongue adapted for nectar feeding
lark	*Alaudidae*	11–19	worldwide	seeds, flowers, leaves, insects	ground-dwelling: elaborate singing displays
leafbird	*Irenidae*	12–24	S Asia	insects, fruit	forest dwellers; ability to mimic sounds of other birds
magpie-lark	*Grallinidae*	19–50	Australasia and New Guinea	insects, tadpoles, seeds, fruit	adaptation to urban surroundings makes it amongst the best known birds in Australia
mockingbird	*Mimidae*	20–33	N and S America	invertebrates, fruit	great ability to mimic sounds
nuthatch	*Sittidae*	14–20	worldwide except S America and New Zealand	insects, invertebrates, seeds, nuts	name reflects ability of the European species to break open nuts
oriole	*Oriolidae*	18–30	Europe, Asia, Philippines, Malaysia, New Guinea, and Australia	insects, fruit	melodious singing voice
palmchat	*Dulidae*	18	Hispaniola and W Indies	berries, flowers and plants	communal nesting with individual compartments for each nesting pair
robin	*Turdinae*	13	worldwide except New Zealand	worms, snails, fruit, insects	territorial, uses song to deter intruders
shrike	*Laniidae*	15–35	Africa, N America, Asia and New Guinea	mainly insects	noted for its sharply hooked bill

sparrow	*Ploceidae*	10–20	African tropics in origin, now worldwide	seed, insects, bread, household scraps	some species renowned for having adapted to man's urban environment
starling	*Sturnidae*	16–45	Europe, Asia and Africa	fruit, insects, pollen, nectar, seeds	gregarious; nests in colonies, roosts communally
sunbird	*Nectariniidae*	8–16	Africa, SE Asia and Australasia	insects, nectar	named for its bright plumage
swallow	*Hirundinidae*	12–23	worldwide	insects	noted for strong and agile flight
thrush	*Turdinae*	12–26	worldwide, except New Zealand	worms, snails, fruit	loud and varied singing voice
tit	*Paridae*	11–14	N America, Europe, Asia and Africa	insects, seeds, vegetable matter, nuts	nests in holes, wide range of singing voice
tree-creeper	*Certhiidae*	12–15	N hemisphere and S Africa	insects, seeds	forages on trees for food
vanga shrike	*Vangidae*	12–30	Madagascar	insects, frogs, small reptiles	dwindling numbers of population; some endangered species
vireo	*Vireonidae*	10–17	N and S America	insects, fruit	distinctive thick and slightly hooked bill
wagtail	*Motacillidae*	14–17	worldwide, although rare in Australia	insects, seeds	spectacular song in flight
wattle-bird	*Callaeidae*	25–53	New Zealand	insects, fruit, invertebrates	distinctive fleshy fold of skin at base of bill
waxbill	*Estrildidae*	9–13.5	Africa, SE Asia and Australasia	mainly seeds, grain	several species drink by sucking, in the manner of pigeons and doves
waxwing	*Bombycillidae*	18	W hemisphere	fruit, berries, insects	waxlike, red tips on secondary flight feathers
white-eye	*Zosteropidae*	12	Africa, SE Asia and Australasia	insects, spiders, nectar, fruit	distinctive ring of tiny white feathers formed round the eye
wood-swallow	*Artamidae*	15–20	tropical Asia and Australasia	insects	tends to huddle together in small groups on branches of trees; elegant flyer and glider; highly agressive towards other birds
wren	*Troglodytidae*	8–15	N and S America, Europe and Asia	invertebrates	nests play ceremonial role in courtship

BIRDS (cont.)

Waterfowl

Name	Family	Size (cm¹)	Distribution	Food	Special features
duck	*Anatidae*	wide range	worldwide	vegetation	gregarious; migratory
flamingo	*Phoenicopteridae*	90–180	tropics, N America, S Europe	minute organisms	red/pink colour of plumage caused by diet
goose	*Anatidae*	wide range	N hemisphere	grass, underwater plants	migratory
grebe	*Podicipedidae*	22–60	worldwide	insects, crustaceans, fish	highly aquatic, adapted for swimming and diving under water
hammerhead	*Scopidae*	56	Africa S of the Sahara, Madagascar, and S Arabia	mainly frogs and tadpoles, also small fish, shrimps, insects	builds a remarkably elaborate nest with entrance tunnel and internal chamber
heron	*Ardeidae*	30–140	worldwide	carnivorous; aquatic prey	mainly a wading bird
ibis	*Threskiornithidae*	50–100	warmer regions of all continents	crustaceans, insects, larvae, small fish, frogs, small reptiles	family also includes species of spoonbill named for shape of bill
loon	*Gaviidae*	66–95	High latitudes of the N hemisphere, migrating to temperate zones	mainly fish	highly territorial and aggressive; loud warning calls; also known as diver
screamer	*Anhimidae*	69–90	warmer parts of S America	herbivorous	highly vocal, trumpet-like alarm calls give it its name
shoebill	*Balaenicipitidae*	120	E Africa	fish, aquatic prey	also known as the whale-headed stork because it has a large head on a short neck
stork	*Ciconiidae*	60–120	S America, Asia, Africa and Australia	fish, insects, frogs, snakes, mice, lizards	known for its long bill and long neck
swan	*Anatidae*	100–160	worldwide, freshwater, sheltered shores and estuaries	underwater plants	very long neck

Shorebirds

Name	Family	Size (cm¹)	Distribution	Food	Special features
auk	*Alcidae*	16–76	cold waters of the N Hemisphere	fish, plankton	same family as the extinct and flightless Great Auk, species include varieties of puffin and guillemot
avocet	*Recurvirostridae*	29–48	worldwide, except high latitudes	insects, larvae	particulary graceful walk, long slender legs give rise to alternative name of stilt
courser	*Glareolidae*	15–25	Africa, S Europe, Asia and Australia	insects	inhabits dry, flat savanna, grassland and the shores of large rivers
crab plover	*Dromadidae*	38	coasts of E Africa, India, Persian Gulf, Ceylon and Madagascar	crabs	single species with mainly white and black plumage gull
gull	*Laridae*	31–76	worldwide, scarce in the tropics	fish, marine invertebrates	highly gregarious with elaborate systems of communication
jacana	*Jacanidae*	17–53	tropics	insects, frogs, fish, invertebrates	ability to walk on floating vegetation gives alternative name of lily trotters
oystercatcher	*Haematopididae*	40–45	tropical and temperate coastlines, except tropical Africa and S Asia	shellfish, worms, insects	powerful bill for breaking shells; despite the name, they do not eat oysters
painted snipe	*Rostratulidae*	19–24	S America, Africa, S Asia and Australia	molluscs, earthworms; seeds	spectacular female plumage; distinctive running action with lowered head
phalarope	*Phalaropidae*	19–25	high latitudes of N hemisphere	insects, crabs, shrimps	wading bird who also regularly swims
plover	*Charadriidae*	15–40	worldwide	shellfish, insects	swift runner; strong flier
sandpiper	*Scolopacidae*	12–60	worldwide	invertebrates, insects and berries	spectacular flight patterns
seedsnipe	*Thinocoridae*	17–28	W coast of S America	seeds, leaves	named after its diet
sheathbill	*Chionididae*	35–43	sub-Antarctic and E coast of S America	plankton, algae, carcasses, offal	scavenger of a communal and quarrelsome nature

BIRDS (cont.)

Shorebirds

Name	Family	Size (cm[1])	Distribution	Food	Special features
skimmer	*Rhynchopidae*	37–51	tropics and subtropics of N and S America, Africa and S Asia	fish, shrimps	uniquely shaped bill aids capture of prey in shallow waters
skua	*Stercorariidae*	43–61	mainly high latitudes of the N hemisphere	fish, small sea birds, insects, eggs	known for chasing other seabirds until they disgorge their food
stone-curlew	*Burhinidae*	36–52	Africa, Europe, Asia, Australia and parts of S America	eggs, insects, worms, molluscs, crustaceans, small vertebrates, amphibians	leg joints give alternative name thickknee

Seabirds

Name	Family	Size (cm[1])	Distribution	Food	Special features
albatross	*Diomedidae*	70–140	S Hemisphere	fish	noted for its size and power of flight
cormorant	*Phalacrocoracidae*	50–100	worldwide	fish and crustaceans	marine equivalent of falcons, used in fishing
darter	*Anhingidae*	80–100	tropical, sub-tropical, temperate regions	fish, insects	distinctive swimming action occasions name of snake-bird
diving-petrel	*Pelecanoididae*	16–25	S Hemisphere	fish	great resemblance to the auk
frigatebird	*Fregatidae*	70–110	tropical oceans	fish, young birds	enormous wings; adept at flying; forces other birds to disgorge their food
fulmar	*Procellariidae*	to 60	N and S oceans	fish	comes to land only to breed; can eject foul-smelling vomit to deter predators
gannet	*Sulidae*	up to 90	worldwide	fish, squid	complex ritual behaviour during mating
pelican	*Pelecanidae*	140–180	tropics and subtropics	fish, crustaceans	known for its long bill
penguin	*Spheniscidae*	40–115	S Hemisphere	fish, crustaceans, squid	flightless: wings modified as flippers; feathers waterproof; highly social

Name	Family	Size (cm¹)	Distribution	Food	Special features
shearwater	Procellariidae	28–91	subantarctic and subtropical zones	fish, plankton	many species known for long migrations
storm-petrel	Hydrobatidae	12–25	high latitudes of N and S Hemispheres	fish, other marine organisms	considerable powers of migration
tropicbird	Phaethontidae	25–45	tropical seas	small fish and squid	elongated central tail feathers produce distinctive flight pattern

Arboreal birds

Name	Family	Size (cm¹)	Distribution	Food	Special features
barbet	Capitonidae	9–32	tropics, except Australasia	mainly fruits, berries, buds, insects	nests in holes made in rotten timber or sand banks
bee-eater	Meropidae	15–38	Africa, Asia and Australia	insects	colourful plumage
cuckoo	Cuculidae	15–90	worldwide	insects, especially caterpillars	some species lay eggs in the nests of other birds and rely on foster parents to feed the young
cuckoo-roller	Leptosomatidae	38–43	Madagascar and Comoro Islands	large insects, chameleons	diminishing population due to destruction of natural habitat
honeyguide	Indicatoridae	10–20	Africa and S Asia	insects, beeswax	named for peculiar habit of eating the wax of honeycombs
hoopoe	Upupidae	31	Africa, SE Asia and S Europe	mainly small insects	named after its distinctive 'hoo hoo' call
hornbill	Bucerotidae	38–126	tropics of Africa and Australasia	fruit, insects, small animals	noted for its long, heavy bill
jacamar	Galbulidae	13–30	tropical America	insects	long, slender bill; attractive, green, metallic plumage
kingfisher	Alcedinidae	10–46	worldwide	insects, shrimps, frogs, lizards, crabs, snails, worms	colourful plumage, strong bill; characteristic diving movements to catch prey
motmot	Momotidae	20–50	tropical America	insects, frogs, small reptiles, fruit	typically attractive, with distinctive long tail feathers
mousebird	Coliidae	30–35	Africa, S of the Sahara	leaves, fruit, seeds, nectar	distinguished by its crest and long tail

BIRDS (cont.)

Arboreal birds

Name	Family	Size (cm[1])	Distribution	Food	Special features
parrot	Psittacidae	10–100	mainly tropics of S Hemisphere	seeds, nuts, berries, fruit, insects	mainly sedentary; unmelodic voice, not known to mimic sounds outwith captivity
pigeon	Columbidae	17–90	worldwide, except high latitudes	seeds, flowers, fruit, berries, leaves, small snails	large family including species of dove, known for its distinctive cooing sound
puffbird	Bucconidae	14–32	tropical America	insects, lizards	named after its stout, puffy appearance
roller	Coraciidae	27–38	Africa, Europe, Asia, Australia	insects, frogs, fruit	named after its courtship display of diving from great heights in a rolling motion
sandgrouse	Pteroclididae	25–48	Africa, S Europe and S Asia	seeds, berries, insects	mainly terrestrial birds
tody	Todidae	10–12	Greater Antilles	mainly insects, seeds	captures its insect prey from underside of leaves and twigs
toucan	Ramphastidae	34–66	S America	seeds, berries, fruits, insects, small animals	known for its bright plumage and immense bill
trogon	Trogonidae	25–35	tropics, except Australasia	mainly insects, fruit	colourful, attractive plumage
turaco	Musophagidae	35–76	Africa S of the Sahara	mainly fruit	noted for its loud and resounding call
woodhoopoe	Phoeniculidae	21–43	Africa S of the Sahara	insects, fruit	long graduated tail; strongly hooked bill (some species also called scimitar bill)
woodpecker	Picidae	10–58	worldwide, except Australasia and Antarctica	insects, fruit, nuts	named after its manner of excavating wood and tree bark for food

Aerial feeders

Name	Family	Size (cm[1])	Distribution	Food	Special features
crested swift	Hemiprocnidae	17–33	SE Asia and New Guinea	insects	named after prominent crest on its head
frogmouth	Podargidae	23–53	SE Asia and Australasia	beetles, scorpions, centipedes, frogs, snails, mice, small birds, fruit	distinctively shaped bill with extremely wide gape
hummingbird	Trochilidae	6–22	N and S America	nectar, insects	the humming sound is made by the wings when hovering
nightjar	Caprimulgidae	19–29	worldwide	mainly insects	nocturnal
oilbird	Steatornithidae	53	tropical S America	fruit	the only nocturnal, fruit-eating bird
potoo	Nyctibiidae	23–51	tropical C and S America	insects	nocturnal bird, also known as 'tree-nighthawk'
owlet-nightjar	Aegothelidae	23–44	Australasia	insects, small vertebrates	perches in upright owl-like way
swift	Apodidae	10–25	worldwide	insects	lands only on near-vertical surfaces; spends most of life flying

Passerines[2]

Name	Family	Size (cm[1])	Distribution	Food	Special features
antbird	Formicariidae	8–36	parts of S America and W Indies	small insects, spiders, lizards, frogs	named after the habit some species have of following armies of ants to prey
bellbird	Cotingidae	9–45	C and S America	fruit	long, metallic sounding display call
broadbill	Eurylaimidae	13–28	tropical Africa and Asia, and the Philippines	mainly insects	noted for its colourful broad bill
false sunbird	Philepittidae	15	Madagascar	fruit	noted for the bright blue and emerald wattle which develops around the eye of the male during breeding season
flycatcher (New World)	Tyrannidae	9–27	N and S America	insects	feed on wing
gnateater	Conopophagidae	14	parts of S America	insects	long thin legs; short tail

BIRDS (cont.)

Passerines

Name	Family	Size (cm¹)	Distribution	Food	Special features
lyrebird	Menuridae	80–90	SE Australia	invertebrates	named after its extravagant tail which resembles a Greek lyre
manakin	Pipridae	9–15	C and S America	fruit, insects	highly elaborate courtship display
New Zealand wren	Xenicidae	8–10	New Zealand	insects	bird family thought to have colonized the islands in the Tertiary Period[3]
ovenbird	Furnariidae	to 25	S America	mainly insects	one species, the true ovenbird, builds substantial nests like mud-ovens
pitta	Pittidae	15–28	Africa, SE Asia and Australasia	mainly insects, spiders, worms, snails	long legs; short tail; colourful plumage
plantcutter	Phytotomidae	18–19	western S America	buds, shoots, leaves, fruit	bill is ideally adapted for feeding on fruit and plants; regarded as a horticultural and agricultural pest
scrub-bird	Atrichornithidae	16–21	E and SW Australia	insects, small lizards, frogs	small terrestrial bird; long graduated tail
tapaculo	Rhinocryptidae	8–25	S and C America	insects, larvae, spiders	distinctive moveable flap covers the nostril
tyrant flycatcher	Tyrannidae	5–14	N and S America, W Indies and Galapagos	insects, fish, fruit	many species known for spectacular aerial courtship display
woodcreeper	Dendrocolaptidae	20–37	S America and W Indies	insects, frogs, lizards	stiff tail feathers used as support in climbing trees, foraging for food

Game-birds and Cranes

Name	Family	Size (cm¹)	Distribution	Food	Special features
bustard	Otitidae	37–132	Africa, S Europe, Asia and Australia	plants, leaves, seeds, berries, insects, small reptiles and mammals, bird eggs, nestlings	characterized by its frequent pauses during walking to observe its surroundings
button quail	Turnicidae	11–19	Africa, S Asia and Australia	insects, seeds, plants	secretive; terrestrial; only three toes, hind toe absent

coot	*Rallidae*	14–51	worldwide	small animals and vegetable food	conspicuous for its loud harsh vocal strains at night
crane	*Gruidae*	80–150	worldwide, except S America and Antartica	omnivorous	characterized by its long legs
currasow	*Cracidae*	75–112	Southern N America and S America	leaves, insects, frogs	noted for agility in running along branches of trees before taking flight
finfoot	*Heliornithidae*	30–62	tropics of America, Africa, and SE Asia	mainly insects	long, slender neck; agile on land and in water
grouse	*Tetraonidae*	30–90	Northern Hemisphere	leaves, buds, berries, fruit, insects	many species threatened by hunting and use of pesticides in agriculture
guinea fowl	*Numididae*	45–60	Africa	mainly insects, bulbs	virtually unfeathered head and neck; often domesticated
hoatzin	*Opisthocomidae*	60	tropical S America	leaves, fruit and flowers of the White Mangrove, fish, crabs	musky odour; top-heavy, retarded flight; unique digestive system
kagu	*Rhynochetidae*	56	New Caledonia	earthworms	sole species, forest dwelling
limpkin	*Aramidae*	60–70	C and S America	large snails	sole species, noted for its wailing voice
mesite	*Mesoenatidae*	25–27	Madagascar	fruit, insects	highly terrestrial, sedentary; endemic to Madagascar
pheasant	*Phasianidae*	40–235	worldwide	seeds, shoots, berries, insects	elaborate courtship display
plains wanderer	*Pedionomidae*	16	SE Australia	insects, seeds, vegetable substances	male incubates the eggs and raises the young
seriema	*Cariamidae*	75–90	S America	omniverous, especially small snakes	heavily feathered head and crest
sunbittern	*Eurypygidae*	46	forest swamps of C and S America	insects, crustacea, minnows	complex markings
trumpeter	*Psophiidae*	43–53	tropical S America	berries, fruit, insects	named after its trumpeting call of warning or alarm
turkey	*Meleagrididae*	90–110	N America	fruit, seeds, vegetation, invertebrates	characterized by male's distinctive strutting displays during breeding

[1] To convert cm to in, multiply by 0.3937
[2] Any bird of the worldwide order *Passeriformes* ('perching birds'), which comprises more than half the living species of birds; landbirds.
[3] *see* GEOLOGICAL TIME SCALE p32

MAMMALS

Mammals are the group of animals to which humans belong. They are characterized by the presence of mammary glands in the female which produce milk on which the young can be nourished. They are divided into monotremes or egg-laying mammals; marsupials in which the young are born at an early stage of development and then grow outside the mother's womb, often in a pouch; placental mammals in which the young are nourished in the womb by the mother's blood and are born at a late stage of development. A crucial aspect of mammals is the fact that their hair and skin glands allow them to regulate their temperatures from within, ie they are endothermic (warm-blooded). This confers on them the ability to adapt to more varied environments than the reptiles from which they are descended.

There are over 4000 species of mammals, most of which are terrestrial, the exceptions being species of bat which have developed the ability to fly and the whale which leads an aquatic existence.

Monotremes

Name	Family/Species	Size (cm¹)	Distribution	Food	Special features
echidna, long-beaked	Species *Zaglossus bruijni*	45–90	New Guinea	earthworms	prominent beak; short spines scattered among fur
echidna, short-beaked	Species *Tachyglossidae aculeatus*	30–45	Australia, Tasmania and New Guinea	ants, termites	fur covered in protective spines; known to live up to 50 years in captivity
platypus	Family *Ornithorhynchidae*	45–60	E Australia and Tasmania	invertebrates, larvae	noted for its duck-like snout

Marsupials

Name	Family	Size (cm¹)	Distribution	Food	Special features
bandicoot	Family *Peramelidae*	15–56	Australia and New Guinea	insectivorous and omnivorous	highest reproductive rate of all marsupials
brushtail possum	Family *Phalangeridae*	34–70	Australia, New Guinea, Solomon Islands and New Zealand	leaves, fruit, bark, eggs, invertebrates	the most commonly encountered of all Australian mammals
kangaroo	Family *Macropodidae*	to 165	Australia and New Guinea	grasses, plants	most popularly known of Australian mammals, noted for its bounding motion and prominent female pouch; includes all species of wallaby

Name	Family etc	Size cm¹	Distribution	Food	Special features
koala	Family *Phascolarctidae*	78	E Australia	eucalyptus leaves	marsupial with popular reputation; intensive management has significantly revived population numbers which at one time seemed threatened with extinction
marsupial mole	Family *Notoryctidae*	13–15	Australia	insects, larvae	only Australian mammal that has specialized in burrowing
opossum	Family *Didelphidae*	7–55	C and S America	earthworms, fruit, insects, small vertebrates, crustaceans, fish, frogs, reptiles	generally known for its dreadful smell
rat kangaroo	Family *Macropodidae*	28.4–30	Australia and New Guinea	grasses, plants	rabbit-sized version of its larger namesake
wombat	Family *Vombatidae*	870–115	SE Australia and Tasmania	grasses	poor eyesight compensated by keen senses of smell and hearing

Placental mammals

Name	Family etc	Size cm¹	Distribution	Food	Special features
aardvark	Family *Orycteropodidae*	105–130	Africa S of the Sahara	ants, termites	secretive, nocturnal creature; characterized by its long, tubular snout
anteater	Family *Myrmecophagidae*	16–22	C and S America	ants and sometimes termites	noted, particulary the Giant ant-eater, for its long, elongated snout
antelope, dwarf	Tribe *Neotragini*	45–55	Africa	leaves, grass, fruit, buds	unusual among hoofed mammals in that the female is larger than the male
armadillo	Family *Dasypodidae*	12.5–100	southern N America, C and S America	vertebrates, insects, fungi, tubers, fruit, carrion	noted, particularly the Giant armadillo, for its protective suit of armour
ass	Subgenus *Asinus*	200–210	Africa and Asia	grass, leaves	renowned as man's reluctant beast of burden
baboon and mandrill	Genus *Papio*	56–80	Africa	fruit, plants, insects, small mammals	able to walk over long distances

MAMMALS (cont.)

Placental mammals

Name	Family etc	Size (cm¹)	Distribution	Food	Special features
badger	Family *Mustelidae*	50–100	Africa, Europe, Asia and N America	vertebrates, invertebrates, fruit, roots, earthworms	mainly nocturnal, European species characterized by its distinctive black and white markings
bat	Order *Chiroptera*	15–200 (wingspan)	worldwide except for the Arctic and Antarctic	insects, vertebrates, fish, fruit	the only vertebrate, outwith birds, capable of sustained flight; famous for its powers of echo location and tendency to cluster in large numbers
bear, black	Species *Ursus americanus*	1.3–1.8m	N America	omniverous	smaller and more secretive than the brown or grizzly bear, its greater ability to adapt has helped it to survive in greater numbers
beaver	Genus *Castor*	80–120	N America, Asia and Europe	plants, wood	renowned for its industry and ability to construct dams and lodges in streams and ponds
bison, American	Species *Bison bison*	to 380	N America	grazing fodder	once numbered in millions in the prairies of N America, now survives only in parks and refuges
bison, European	Species *Bison bonasus*	to 290	USSR	grazing fodder	became extinct in the wild in 1919, but has now been re-established in parts of the USSR
boar	Family *Suidae*	58–210	Europe, Africa and Asia	plants, larvae, frogs, mice, earthworms	wild pig; characteristically ugly appearance; intelligent and highly adaptable; includes species of warthog
buffalo, wild water	Species *Bubalus arnee*	240–280	SE Asia	grazing fodder	adept at moving through the muddy areas which they inhabit
bush baby	Subfamily *Galaginae*	12–32	Africa and S Asia	insects, fruit, gum	highly agile, arboreal creature

bushbuck	Species *Tragelaphus scriptus*	110–145	Africa S of the Sahara	grazing fodder	occupies habitats with dense cover; dark brown or chestnut coat with white markings
camel	Species *Camelus bactrianus*	190–230 (height of hump)	Mongolia	plants, vegetation	two humps
capybara	Family *Hydrochoeridae*	106–134	S America	grass	largest living rodent, lives in groups by the edge of water; traditionally hunted for its meat and skin
capuchin monkey	Family *Cebidae*	25–63	S America	insects, fruit, leaves, seeds, other small mammals	mainly lives in social groupings for the purposes of defence, foraging for food, and rearing young
cattle	Family *Bovidae*	180–200	worldwide	grass	agricultural animal existing in both long-horned and polled or hornless breeds
chamois	Species *Rupicapra rupicapra*	125–135	Europe and Asia	grass, leaves, lichen	has adapted to alpine and subalpine conditions and to life on snowy mountains; part of its defence mechanism in fighting is its evasive running and dodging movement
cheetah	Family *Felidae*	112–135	Africa	hoofed animals up to 40kg, such as gazelles, impala, wildebeest calves	the fastest of all land animals, reaching speeds of 96kph/60mph
chimpanzee	Genus *Pan*	70–85	W and C Africa	fruit, leaves, seeds, insects, small mammals	most sophisticated mammal in use of tools as an aid to eg feeding and fighting
chinchilla	Family *Chinchillidae*	25	S America	grazing fodder	widely hunted as food and for its valuable fur
civet	Family *Viverridae*	33–84	Africa and Asia	fruit, small mammals, birds, rodents, insects, small reptiles	cat-like carnivore; nocturnal hunter; economic source of civet oil

MAMMALS (cont.)

Placental mammals

Name	Family etc	Size (cm¹)	Distribution	Food	Special features
colugo	Genus *Cynocephalus*	33–42	SE Asia	leaves, shoots, buds, flowers	also known as flying lemur, a reference to the membrane which stretches from its neck to the tips of its fingers, toes and tail, allowing it to glide from tree to tree
coyote	Species *Canis latrans*	70–97	N America	squirrels, rabbits, mice, antelope, deer, mountain sheep	makes unique howling sound; regarded as agricultural pest for its attacks on farm animals, but also kills off agricultural vermin
coypu	Species *Myocastor coypu*	50	S America	freshwater plants	highly aquatic rodent; burrows into banks; beaver-like qualities
deer	Family *Cervidae*	41–152	N and S America, Europe, and Asia	grass, shoots, twigs, leaves, flowers, fruit	distinguished in the male by the presence of antlers most characteristically used to attack other males during the rutting period; species include red deer, reindeer, waipiti, and the moose or elk
dingo	Species *Canis dingo*	150	Australasia	rabbits, lizards, grasshoppers, wild pigs, kangaroos	history of the dingo in Australia dates back 8000 years; descendant of the wolf, lives in packs
dog	Species *Canis familiaris*	20–75	worldwide	carnivorous	first animal to be domesticated; c.400 domestic breeds
dolphin	Family *Delphinidae*	120–400	worldwide	fish, squid	renowned for grace, agility, intelligence; highly developed social organization and communication systems

dolphin, river	Family *Platanistidae*	210–260	SE Asia and S America	fish, shrimp, squid, octopus	virtually blind, but with highly sensitive system of echo location
dormouse	Family *Gliridae*	6–19	Europe, Africa, Turkey, Asia and Japan	omnivorous	halfway between mouse and squirrel both in form and behaviour
dromedary	Species *Camelus dromedarius*	190–230 height of hump	SW Asia N Africa and Australia	plants, vegetation	domesticated camel with one hump, important to man as a beast of burden, and source of wool and milk
duiker	Subfamily *Cephalophinae*	55–72	Africa S of the Sahara	leaves, fruit, shoots, buds, sees, bark, small birds, rodents	named after its habit of diving into cover when disturbed
eland	Genus *Taurotragus*	250–330	Africa	grazing fodder	elegant and highly mobile spiral horned antelope; experiments in the agricultural domestication of the common eland have taken place in Africa
elephant, African	Species *Loxodonta africana*	600–750	Africa S of the Sahara	grass, plants, leaves, twigs, flowers, fruit	largest living mammal, with distinctive trunk and large tusks and ears; drastically reduced population
elephant-shrew	Order *Macroscelidea*	10.4–29.4	Africa	invertebrates, plants, fruit, seeds	distinctive creature with beady eyes long, pointed snout and short legs
fox	Family *Canidae*	24–100	N and S America, Europe, Asia and Africa	rodents, birds, invertebrates, fruit, fish, rabbits, hares. earthworms	justified reputation for cunning, intelligence and resourcefulness
gazelle	Genus *Gazella*	122–166	Africa	leaves, grass, fruit	birth peaks adapted to coincide with abundance of feeding vegetation during the spring and early rains
gerbil	Subfamily *Gerbillinae*	6–7.5	Africa and Asia	seeds, fruits, leaves, stems, roots, bulbs, insects, snails	defence mechanisms include colour of skin closely allied to the environment for hiding purposes, wide field of vision, and the ability to hear low frequency sounds such as the beating of owls' wings; domesticated form is the Mongolian gerbil often kept as a pet

MAMMALS (cont.)

Placental mammals

Name	Family etc	Size (cm¹)	Distribution	Food	Special features
gerenuk	Genus *Litocranius*	140–160	Africa	leaves, shoots, flowers, fruit	graceful, delicate creature; rises on hind legs in order to extend its reach when feeding on the leaves of tall shrubs and bushes
gibbon	Family *Hylobatidae*	45–65	SE Asia	fruit, leaves, invertebrates	renowned for spectacular ability to move among trees using swinging movements of arms; loud and sophisticated voice
giraffe	Species *Giraffa camelopardalis*	380–470	Africa S of the Sahara	leaves, shoots, herbs, flowers, fruit, seeds	distinguished by its mottled coat and the length of its neck which allows it to feed on foliage which is out of the reach of smaller mammals
gnu	Genus *Connochaetes*	194–209	Africa	grazing fodder	characterized by massive head and mane, bearded throat, tail which reaches almost to the ground
goat, mountain	Species *Oreamnos americanus*	to 175	N America	grazing fodder	large, ponderous rock climber, adapted to living in snowy mountains of N America
goat, wild	Species *Capra aegagrus*	130–140	S Europe, Middle East and Asia	grazing fodder	subspecies includes domestic goat
gopher	Family *Geomyidae*	12–22.5	N America	plant materials	highly adapted to its burrowing and subterranean existence
gorilla	Genus *Gorilla*	150–170	C Africa	leaves and stems	largest living primate; the most intelligent of land animals (after man); unjustified reputation for ferocity, perhaps based on its size, and habit of beating its chest in a show of aggression

	Species/Genus		Distribution	Diet	Notes
grizzly or brown bear	Species *Ursus arctos*	200–280	NW America and USSR	omnivorous	noted for its size (up to half a ton); much reduced population due to hunting, loss of natural habitat
guinea pig	Genus *Cavia*	28	S America	herbs, grasses	tailless rodent; domesticated form is the *Cavia porcellus*
hamster	Subfamily *Cricetinae*	5.3–10.2	Europe, Middle East, USSR and China	mainly seeds, shoots, root vegetables	familiar western pet, but aggressive towards own species in the wild
hare	Genus *Lepus*	40–76	N and S America, Africa, Europe, Asia and Arctic	grass, herbs, plants, bark, twigs	well-developed ability to run from predators; species include jack-rabbits and the Arctic hare
hare, Patagonian	Genus *Dolichotis*	45	S America	grasses, herbs	unusual characteristic in a mammal of being strictly monogamous
hartebeest	Genus *Alcelaphus*	195–200	Africa	grass, vegetation	distinctive long face, sloping back
hedgehog	Subfamily *Erinaceinae*	10–15	Europe, Asia and Africa	earthworms, beetles, slugs, earwigs, caterpillars	ability to curl up and use prickly, spined back as protection
hippopotamus	Family *Hippopotamidae*	150–345	Africa	terrestrial vegetation	large, heavy and barrel-shaped with short stumpy legs; wallows in water
horse	Subgenus *Equus*	200–210	worldwide in domesticated form; Asia, N and S America and Australia in the wild	grass, leaves	historically useful to man as a beast of burden and means of transport, and for agricultural, military, recreational purposes
hyena	Family *Hyaeninae*	85–140	Africa and Asia	carrion, mammals, insects, small vertebrates, eggs, fruit, vegetables	scavenger and hunter, with highly developed systems of communication; family includes the aardwolf
ibex	Species *Capra ibex*	85–143	C Europe, Asia and Africa	grazing fodder	large horned creature saved from extinction in C Europe
impala	Genus *Aepyceros*	128–142	Africa	grass, leaves, flowers, fruit, seeds	attractive, graceful creature with fawn and mahogany coat; females and young gather in large herds; male has a lyre-shaped horn

MAMMALS (cont.)

Placental mammals

Name	Family etc	Size (cm¹)	Distribution	Food	Special features
jackal	Genus *Canis*	65–106	Africa, SE Europe and Asia	fruit, invertebrates, reptiles, birds, small mammals, carrion	unfair reputation as cowardly scavenger
jaguar	Species *Panthera onca*	112–185	C and S America	deer, monkeys, sloths, birds, turtles, frogs, fish and small rodents	only cat to be found in the Americas
jerboa	Family *Dipodidae*	4–26	N Africa, Turkey, Middle East and C Asia	seeds, vegetation, insects	long hind legs allow movement by hopping and jumping
lemming	Tribe *Lemmini*	10–11	N America and Eurasia	plants, bulbs, roots, mosses	Norway lemming is noted for its mass migration which sometimes results in drowning
lemur	Family *Lemuridae*	12–70	Madagascar	flowers, leaves, bamboo shoots	mainly nocturnal and arboreal
leopard	Species *Panthera pardus*	100–190	Africa and Asia	mainly small mammals, birds	opportunistic, nocturnal hunters; adept at climbing trees
lion	Species *Panthera leo*	260–330	Africa	meat of animals which weigh 50–500kg	known as the 'King of Beasts'; the most socially organized of the cat family
llama	Species *Lama glama*	230–400	S America	plants and vegetation	S American beast of burden
lynx	Species *Felis lynx*	67–110	Europe and N America	rodents, small hoofed mammals	lives in cold northern latitudes; well adapted to travelling through deep snow
macaque	Genus *Macaca*	38–70	Asia and N Africa	mainly fruit, insects, leaves, crops, small animals	heavily built and partly terrestrial genus of monkey; includes the Rhesus monkey adapted to life in the Himalayas, and the Barbary apes imported into Gibraltar in the 18th-c

marmoset	Family *Callitrichidae*	17.5–40	S America	fruit, flowers, nectar, gum, frogs, snails, lizards, spiders, insects	small, colourful, squirrel-like monkeys; includes species of tamarins
marten	Genus *Martes*	30–75	N America, Europe and Asia	mice, squirrels, rabbit, grouse, fruit, nuts	one species, the fisher, unique for its ability to penetrate the quilled defences of the porcupine
mole	Family *Talpidae*	2.4–7.5	Europe, Asia and N America	earthworms, insect larvae, slugs	almost exclusively subterranean existence
mongoose	Family *Viverridae*	24–58	Africa, S Asia and S N Europe	vertebrates, insects, fruit, snakes	some species live in social groups; often seen in the tripod position, ie standing up on hind legs and tail
mountain beaver	Family *Aplondontidae*	30–41	Pacific Coast of Canada and USA	leaves, plant materials	land-dwelling and burrowing animal; causes great damage to forest areas
mouse *see* rat					
narwhal	Species *Monodon monceros*	400–500	N USSR, N America and Greenland	shrimp, cod, flounder	distinctive single tusk in the male can reach lengths of up to 3m
okapi	Species *Okapia johnstoni*	190–200	Zaire	mainly leaves and shoots	secretive and elusive creature; strange-looking mixture of giraffe and zebra
orang-utan	Species *Pongo pygmaeus*	150	forests of N Samutra and Borneo	fruit, leaves, insects	sparse covering of long red-brown hair; adults with large naked fatty folds around face; life span of 35 years in the wild; much diminished population
otter	Subfamily *Lutrinae*	40–123	N and S America, Europe, Asia and Africa	frogs, crabs, fish, aquatic birds	only truly amphibious members of the general weasel family; greatly reduced population due to persecution, loss of natural habitat
panda, giant	Species *Ailuropoda melanoleuca*	70–80	China	bamboo	rare; poor breeder; the success rate of breeding in captivity has been extremely low
polar bear	Species *Ursus maritimus*	250–300	N polar regions	mainly seals, carcasses of large marine animals	unique for its large size, white coat and adaptation to aquatic living

MAMMALS (cont.)

Placental mammals

Name	Family etc	Size (cm¹)	Distribution	Food	Special features
porcupine (New World)	Family *Erethizontidae*	30–86	N and S America	bark, roots, shoots, leaves, berries, seeds, nuts, flowers	arboreal version of Old World porcupine; excellent climber
porcupine (Old World)	Family *Hystricidae*	37–47	Africa and Asia	roots, bulbs, fruit, berries	heavily quilled and spiny body
porpoise	Family *Phocoenidae*	120–150	N temperate zone, W Indo-Pacific, temperate and subantarctic waters of S America and Auckland Islands	fish, squid, crustaceans	large range of sounds for the purpose of echo location
puma	Species *Felis concolor*	105–196	N and S America	deer, rodents	wide ranging hunter; includes sub-species cougar
rabbit, European	Genus *Oryctolagus*	38–58	Europe, Africa, Australia, New Zealand and S America	grass, herbs, roots, plants, bark	burrowing creature; opportunistic animal in widespread environment; noted for its breeding capacity; domesticated rabbits descended from this genus
racoon	Genus *Procyon*	55	N, S and C America	frogs, fish, birds, eggs, fruit, nuts, small rodents, insects, corn	black masked face; distinctive ringed tail; reputation for mischief
rat (New World)	Subfamily *Hesperomyinae*	5–8	N and S America	seeds, grain, plants, nuts, fruit, fungi, insects, crustaceans, fish	numerous species adapted to living in all possible forms of different habitat
rat (Old World)	Subfamily *Murinae*	4.5–8.2	Europe, Asia, Africa and Australia	omnivorous	large number of species; one of the most successful mammals at adapting to any form of environment
reedbuck	Genus *Redunca*	110–176	Africa	grass, leaves, crops	graceful, elegant animals; distinctive whistling sounds, leaping movements

rhinoceros	Family *Rhinocerotidae*	250–400	Africa and tropical Asia	plant foliage	name derives from horn growing from snout; man's desire to use the horn for commercial purposes has brought the animal to the verge of extinction
seal	Family *Phocidae*	117–490	mainly polar, subpolar and temperate seas	fish, squid, crustaceans	graceful swimmer and diver; some species have been the object of controversial culling procedures
sheep, American bighorn	Species *Ovis canadensis*	168–186	N America	grazing fodder	large horns and body similar to an ibex; clings to the vicinity of cliffs
sheep, barbary	Genus *Ammotragus*	155–165	N Africa	grazing fodder	large head and horns up to 84cm in length
sheep, blue	Genus *Pseudois*	91 shoulder height	Asia	grazing fodder	blue coat; curved horns
shrew	Family *Soricidae*	3.5–4.8	Europe, Asia, Africa, N America and northern S America	insects, earthworms	generally poor eyesight compensated for by acute sense of smell and hearing
skunk	Subfamily *Mephitinae*	40–68	N and S America	insects, small mammals, eggs, fruit	evil-smelling defence mechanism; major carrier of rabies
sloth, three-toed	Family *Bradypodidae*	56–60	S America	leaves	smaller version of the two-toed sloth; slightly more active both by day and night
sloth, two-toed	Family *Megalonychidae*	58–70	S America	leaves	arboreal, nocturnal creature noted for the slowness of its movement
springbuck	Genus *Antidorcas*	96–115	S Africa	mainly grass	gregarious creature which migrates together in herds of tens of thousands
springhare	Family *Pedetidae*	36–43	S Africa	grass and soil	burrowing creature like a miniature kangaroo, moves usually by hopping; hunted by man as a source of food and for its skin

MAMMALS (cont.)

Placental mammals

Name	Family etc	Size (cm¹)	Distribution	Food	Special features
squirrel	Family *Sciuridae*	6.6–10	N and S America, Europe, Africa and Asia	nuts, seeds, plants, insects	large number of species living in a variety of environments and including arboreal, burrowing and flying creatures; species include the marmot and chipmunk, grey squirrel noted for its abllility to strip bark and damage young trees
tapir	Genus *Tapirus*	180–250	C and S America and SE Asia	grass, leaves, vegetation, buds, fruit, shoots	strange-looking, nocturnal mammal with distinctive snout; all species exist in vastly reduced numbers
tarsier	Genus *Tarsius*	11–14	islands of SE Asia	insects, lizards, bats, birds, snakes	proportionally large eyes; extra-ordinary ability to rotate neck
tiger	Species *Panthera tigris*	220–310	India, Manchuria, China and Indonesia	hoofed animals eg deer and wild pigs	solitary hunters, stalk for prey
vole	Tribe *Microtini*	10–11	N America, Europe, Asia and the Arctic	grasses, seeds, aquatic plants, insects	population fluctuates in regular patterns or cycles
walrus	Species *Odobenus rosmarus*	250–320	Arctic seas	marine molluscs and invertebrates	characterized by its thick folds of skin, twin tusks
waterbuck	Species *Kobus ellipsiprymnus*	177–235	Africa	grasses, reeds, rushes, aquatic vegetation	shaggy coat and heavy gait; gives off an oily, detectable secretion on its coat
weasel	Subfamily *Mustelinae*	15–55	Arctic, N and S America, Europe, Asia and Africa	rodents, rabbits, birds, insects, lizards, frogs	certain species have been exploited for their fur, eg mink, ermine; includes species of ferret and polecat
whale, beaked	Family *Ziphiidae*	400–1280	worldwide	mainly squid	named after its distinctive, protuberant, dolphin-like beak

	Species		Distribution	Diet	Description
whale, blue	Species *Balaenoptera musculus*	to 3000	Arctic and subtropics	krill	largest animal that has ever lived
whale, grey	Species *Eschrichtius robustus*	1190–1520	N Pacific	fish, crustaceans, ocean floor molluscs	long migration to breed, from the Arctic to the subtropics; one of the most heavily barnacled of the whale species
whale, humpback	Species *Megaptera novaeangliae*	1600	worldwide	mainly fish, krill	highly acrobatic, with wide range of sounds; migrates between Arctic and mid-Pacific
whale, killer	Species *Orcinus orca*	900–1000	worldwide in cool coastal waters	fish, squid, birds, and other marine mammals	toothed whale; dorsal fin narrow and vertical; co-operative and highly co-ordinated hunter, with triangular fins and distinctive white and black colouring, not generally a threat to man
whale, long-finned pilot	Species *Globicephala melaena*	600	temperate waters of the N Atlantic	cuttlefish, squid	best known for mysterious mass strandings on beaches
whale, sperm	Species *Physeter catodon*	to 2070	widespread in temperate and tropical waters	mainly squid	largest of the toothed whales, prodigious deep sea diver
whale, white	Species *Delphinapterus leucas*	300–500	N USSR, N America and Greenland	crustaceans, worms, molluscs	distinctive white skin; wide range of bodily, facial and vocal expression
wild cat	Species *Felis silvestris*	50–80	Europe, India and Africa	small mammals, birds	domestic cat may be descended from the African wild cat
wolf, grey	Species *Canis lupus*	100–150	N America, Europe, Asia and Middle East	moose, deer, caribou	noted for hunting in packs
wolverine	Species *Gulo gulo*	to 83	Arctic and subarctic regions	small mammals, deer, caribou, birds, plants, carrion	heavily built; long, dark coat of fur; adapted for hunting in soft, deep snow
zebra	Subgenus *Hippotigris*	215–230	Africa	grass, leaves	famous for black and white stripes

ENDANGERED SPECIES (Reptiles, birds, mammals)

Reptiles

Name	Species	Location	Cause of endangerment
alligator, China	*Alligator sinensis*	E China	exploitation for meat, leather; extermination as vermin
anole, giant or Culebra giant	*Anolis roosevelti*	Puerto Rico	loss of habitat, probably already extinct
boa, Puerto Rican or Culebra Grande	*Epicrates inornatus*	Puerto Rico; Virgin Islands	human persecution; predation by the mongoose
boa, Round Island	*Bolyeria multocarinata*	Round Island, near Mauritius	deterioration of palm forest habitat, possibly already extinct
boa, Round Island keel-scaled	*Casarea dussumieri*	Round Island, near Mauritius	deterioration of palm forest habitat
caiman, black	*Melanosuchus niger*	S America	hunting; exploitation for hides; loss of habitat to cattle ranching
caiman, broad-nosed	*Caiman latirostris*	S America	hunting for hides
caiman, Magdalena or C American	*Caiman crocodilus fuscus*	S America	exploitation for hides; animal trade; souvenir trade for stuffed skins
caiman, Paraguay or Yacare	*Caiman crocodilus yacare*	S America	hunting; export of hides
caiman, red apaporis	*Caiman crocodilus apaporiensis*	Columbia	hunting; exploitation for hides; interbreeding with spectacled caiman
caiman, spectacled	*Caiman crocodilus crocodilus*	Venezuela, the Guianas, Amazon, Columbia and Peru	animal trade, hunting for hides; souvenir trade in stuffed skins
cobra, C Asian	*Naja oxiana*	C Asia	loss of natural habitat
crocodile, African slender-snouted	*Crocodylus cataphractus*	W and C Africa	hunting; exploitation for meat, hides, eggs
crocodile, American	*Crocodylus acutus*	Florida, USA	hunting for sport; exploitation for skin; human persecution; loss of habitat
crocodile, Cuban	*Crocodylus rhombifer*	Cuba	exploitation for skins; loss of habitat; hybridization
crocodile, dwarf	*Ostealaemus tetraspis*	Africa	loss of habitat to cultivation; exploitation for hides, meat, eggs
crocodile, marsh or mugger	*Crocodylus palustris palustris*	Pakistan, India, Iran and Sri Lanka	exploitation for skins; hunting; loss of habitat, food resources
crocodile, Morelet's	*Crocodylus moreletii*	Mexico and Honduras	exploitation for hides
crocodile, Orinoco	*Crocodylus intermedius*	Venezuela; Colombia	hunting; exploitation for hides
crocodile, Siamese	*Crocodylus siamensis*	Thailand	hunting; exploitation for hides
gavial, false	*Tomistoma schlegelii*	Malay Peninsula, Sumatra; Borneo	trapping, hunting for its hide

ENDANGERED SPECIES (cont.)

Reptiles

Name	Species	Location	Cause of endangerment
gavial, Indian or gharial	*Gavialis gangeticus*	India, Pakistan; Nepal	hunting for its skin; human disturbance; loss of habitat to cultivation
gecko, Rodriguez day	*Phelsuma edwardnewtonii*	Rodriguez Islands	predation by rats, cats
iguana, Fiji banded	*Brachylophus fasciatus*	Fiji Islands and Tonga	predation by the mongoose
iguana, Anegada ground	*Cyclura pinguis*	Virgin Islands	loss of habitat; human disturbance; predation by pets, wild animals
iguana, Watling Island ground or San Salvador rock	*Cyclura rileyi rileyi*	Bahamas	hunting; poaching; zoo trade
lizard, black or Californian legless	*Anniella pulchra niger*	California, USA	loss of habitat
lizard, blunt-nosed or San Joaquin leopard	*Cryptaphytus wislizenii silus*	USA and Mexico	destruction of habitat by agriculture
lizard, Hierro giant	*Gallotia somonyi*	Hierro, Canary Islands	human disturbance; loss of habitat
lizard, St Croix ground	*Ameiva polops*	Virgin Islands	loss of habitat; predation by the mongoose
rattlesnake, New Mexico ridge-nosed	*Crotalus willardi obscurus*	Mexico and New Mexico, USA	human disturbance; loss of habitat
snake, San Fransico garter	*Thamnophis sirtalis tetrataenia*	California, USA	collecting as specimens; loss of habitat to drainage, housing developments
terrapin, river or tuntong	*Batagur baska*	Malaysia and Burma	water pollution; damage to nesting areas by commercial sand removal, tin mining, flooding, silt deposits
tortoise, Abingdon saddlebacked	*Testudo elephantopus abingdoni*	Galapagos	slaughter by whalers; other fishermen; competition for food with goat population
tortoise, Chatham Island	*Testudo elephantopus chathamensis*	Galapagos	animal trade, exploitation; predation of nests; killing of young by wild dogs
tortoise, Cowley Mountain	*Testudo elephantopus vandenburghi*	Galapagos	poaching for meat; oil, animal trade; competition for food with wild donkeys
tortoise, Duncan saddlebacked	*Testudo elephantopus ephippium*	Galapagos	animal trade, exploitation; predation of young by black rats
tortoise, Hood saddlebacked	*Testudo elephantopus hoodensis*	Galapagos	slaughter by whalers and other fishermen; human settlement; poaching; exploitation for oil; predation by, or competition with, variety of mammals

ENDANGERED SPECIES (cont.)

Reptiles

Name	Species	Location	Cause of endangerment
tortoise, Indefatigable Island	*Testudo elephantopus nigrita*	Galapagos	human settlement; exploitation for oil, meat by farmers and fishermen; animal trade; predation by pigs, cats, rats; competition for food with goats
tortoise, James Island	*Testudo elephantopus darwini*	Galapagos	animal trade, exploitation; predation of nests by wild goats; competition for food with wild goats
tortoise, North Albemarle saddlebacked	*Testudo elephantopus becki*	Galapagos	animal trade; poaching for meat, oil; predation by cats, rats
tortoise, South Albemarle	*Testudo elephantopus elephantopus*	Galapagos	persecution; poaching; predation by cats, dogs, pigs
tortoise, Tagus Cove	*Testudo elephantopuis microphyes*	Galapagos	animal trade; illegal export
tortoise, Vilamil Mountain or South West Albemarle	*Testudo elephantopus guentheri*	Galapagos	exploitation for oil; poaching; predation by pigs, dogs, cats, rats; competition for food from goats, donkeys, cattle
turtle, Atlantic Ridley	*Lepidochelys kempi*	Gulf of Mexico, USA and Europe	exploitation of turtles for eggs; leather; killing of turtles by trawlers fishing for shrimps
turtle, green	*Chelonia mydas*	warm waters	exploitation of turtle meat, hides, eggs, shells; killing of turtles in the trawling nets of fishermen; human disturbance; loss of natural habitat; international trade in turtles
turtle, hawksbill	*Eretmochelys imbricata*	Atlantic, Pacific and Indian Oceans, Gulf of Mexico and Caribbean	exploitation for tortoiseshell, skin, stuffed turtles as souvenirs
turtle, leathery, leatherback or luth	*Dermochelys coriacea*	tropics; some temperate regions	exploitation for eggs which are considered a delicacy
turtle, Pacific Ridley or olive	*Lepidochelys olivacea*	Indo-Pacific and Atlantic Oceans	exploitation for eggs, skin, oil
turtle, short-necked or swamp	*Pseudemydura umbrina*	W Australia	drainage and clearance of habitat for agriculture; disruption by wildfires; predation by foxes, wild dogs
turtle, S American red-lined	*Pseudemys ornata callirostris*	Columbia	over-collecting for food and for the pet trade
turtle, S American river or arrau	*Podocnemis expansa*	northern S America	exploitation for meat, eggs, oil; animal trade
viper, Latifi's	*Vipera latifii*	Lar Valley, Teheran	loss of habitat to hydroelectric plant

ENDANGERED SPECIES (cont.)

Birds

Name	Species	Location	Cause of endangerment
'akiapola'au	*Hemignathus wilsoni*	Hawaiian Islands	deterioration of forest habitat; disease; competition with imported birds; predation by rats
'akiola, Kauai	*Hemignathus obscurus*	Hawaiian Islands	disease; overgrazing of forest habitat by livestock; competition with imported birds; predation by rats
albatross, short-tailed	*Diomedea albatrus*	Japan	loss of habitat; exploitation for feathers; low rate of reproduction
antwren, black-hooded	*Myrmotherula erythronotos*	SE Brazil	destruction of tropical forest habitat
barbthroat, black	*Threnetes grzimeki*	SE Brazil	hummingbird threatened by destruction of forest habitat
blackbird, grey-headed	*Turdus poliocephalus poliocephalus*	Norfolk Island, SW Pacific Ocean	destruction of habitat; competition with European blackbird; predation by rats
booby, Abbot's	*Sula abbotti*	Christmas Island, Indian Ocean	destruction of nesting areas by phosphate mining; low rate of reproduction
bristlebird, western rufous	*Dasyornis broadbenti littoralis*	W Australia	clearance, burning of scrubland habitat may have already led to extinction
bullfinch, São Miguel	*Pyrrhula pyrrhula murina*	Azores	shooting to protect budding fruit trees may have already led to extinction
bustard, great Indian	*Choriotis nigriceps*	NW India and Pakistan	hunting for its meat; loss of grassland habitat to cultivation, grazing of domestic livestock
cahow	*Pterodroma cahow*	Bermuda	human persecution; disturbance, predation by rats, wild pigs; competition for nesting sights with tropical birds
capercaillie, Cantabrian	*Tetrao urogallus cantabricus*	Spain	hunting; loss of deciduous forest habitat
condor, Californian	*Gymnogyps californianus*	California	low reproductive potential; shooting, trapping, poisoning, egg-collecting; extinction appears inevitable
crane, Mississipi sandhill	*Grus canadensis pulla*	USA Gulf Coast	hunting, loss of habitat; possible genetic deterioration
crane, Siberian white	*Grus leucogeranus*	Siberia	hunting, disturbance; destruction of nests by domesticated reindeer
crane, whooping	*Grus americanus*	USA	pollution; destruction, disturbance of wetland habitat

ENDANGERED SPECIES (cont.)

Birds

Name	Species	Location	Cause of endangerment
creeper, Molokai	*Paroreomyza maculata flammea*	Hawaiian Islands	disease to which Hawaiian honeycreepers have limited immunity; destruction of rain forest habitat by grazing livestock; competition from imported birds; predation by mammals
crow, Hawaiian	*Corvus tropicus*	Hawaiian Islands	disease; loss of habitat to wild pigs, cattle, goats; predation by black rats
crow, Marianas	*Corvus kubaryi*	Marianas	reasons for decline are unrecorded
cuckoo, south-eastern rufous-vented ground	*Neomorphus geoffroyi dulcis*	SE Brazil	rare bird threatened by the felling of forest habitat
curassow, red-billed	*Crax blumenbachii*	Brazil	hunting; loss of rainforest habitat
curassow, eastern razor-billed	*Crax mitu mitu*	Brazil	seriously threatened with extinction by hunting; loss of rainforest habitat
curlew, Eskimo	*Numenius borealis*	Arctic tundra and S America	shooting; loss of prairie habitat to agriculture; climactic changes possibly altering migratory and reproductive processes
currawong, Lord Howe	*Strepera graculina crissalis*	Lord Howe Island, SW Pacific Ocean	cause of decline unknown
eagle, Madagascar sea	*Haliaeetus vociferoides*	Madagascar	hunting; human persecution
eagle, Madagascar serpent	*Eutriorchis astur*	Madagascar	clearing of forest habitat
eagle, monkey-eating	*Pithecophaga jefferyi*	Philippines	shooting; animal trade; destruction of forest habitat
eagle, southern bald	*Heliaeetus leucocephalus leucocephalus*	US and N Mexico	mortality and breeding failure due to contamination of habitat and prey by pesticides; habitat loss; disturbance
eagle, Spanish imperial	*Aquila heliaca adalberti*	Spain and Portugal	poisoning and contamination by pesticides; shooting; loss of habitat to forest clearance, overgrazing
falcon, American peregrine	*Falco peregrinus anatum*	USA, Canada and Mexico	killing; capture; contamination of birds and eggs by pesticides
falcon, Tundra peregrine	*Falco peregrinus tundrius*	Alaska, Canada and Greenland	contamination by chlorinated hydrocarbons in S American wintering grounds

ENDANGERED SPECIES (cont.)

Birds

Name	Species	Location	Cause of endangerment
fernbird, Codfish Island	*Bowdleria punctat wilsoni*	New Zealand	modification of low scrub habitat by brush-tailed possum; predation on birds and eggs by Polynesian rats
fire-eye, fringe-backed	*Pyriglena atra*	E Brazil	loss of tropical forest habitat to human settlement; industrial, agricultural development
flycatcher, Hivoa	*Pomarea mendozae mendozae*	Marquesas Islands, S Pacific Ocean	deterioration of wooded valley habitat by overgrazing of cattle, sheep, pigs, goats
flycatcher, Nukuhiva	*Pomarea mendozae nukuhivae*	Marquesas Islands, S Pacific Ocean	deterioration of wooded valley habitat by overgrazing of cattle, wild goats
flycatcher, Seychelles black paradise	*Terpsiphone corvina*	Seychelles	human disturbance; loss of lowland forest habitat
flycatcher, Tahiti	*Pomarea nigra nigra*	Tahiti	causes of decline are unknown
fody, Mauritius	*Foudia rubra*	Mauritius	destruction of montane evergreen forest habitat; competition from other species of fody; predation of nests by macaque monkeys, black rats
fody, Rodrigues	*Foudia flavicans*	Rodrigues Island, Indian Ocean	destruction of forest habitat; competition from other species of fody
gallinule, Hawaiian	*Gallinula chloropus sandvicensis*	Hawaiian Islands	draining of wetland habitat; predation by rats, cats, mongooses
grebe, Atitlan or giant pied-billed	*Podilymbus gigas*	Guatemala	competition for food, predation on grebe chicks by bass fish; loss of nesting habitat to housing development
grebe, Colombian	*Podiceps andinus*	Colombia	competition for food from trout; possible contamination by pesticides
grebe, Junin	*Podiceps taczanowskii*	Peru	pollution of lake habitat by copper mining
guan, black-fronted piping	*Aburria jacutinga*	Brazil	hunting; loss of tropical forest habitat
guan, Cauca	*Penelope perspicax*	Colombia	almost total loss of forest habitat
guan, horned	*Oreophasis derbianus*	Mexico and Guatemala	hunting; loss of forest habitat to agriculture, coffee plantations, overgrazing
guan, Trinidad piping	*Pipile pipile pipile*	Trinidad	hunting; loss of forest habitat; may already be extinct

ENDANGERED SPECIES (cont.)

Birds

Name	Species	Location	Cause of endangerment
guan, white-winged	*Penelope albipennis*	Peru	hunting; loss of forest habitat to charcoal burning
hermit, hook-billed	*Glaucis dohrnii*	SE Brazil	destruction of forest habitat
honeyeater, helmeted	*Meliphaga melanops cassidix*	Victoria, Australia	alteration of habitat; destruction of habitat by fire; competition with other species
honeyeater, Mukojima Bonin	*Apalopteron familiare familiare*	Bonin Islands, Japan	clearance of subtropical and scrub forest habitat for tourist developments
ibis, hermit	*Geronticus eremita*	Turkey and Morocco	hunting; nest disturbance; poaching for eggs; animal, zoo trade; reproductive failure due to pesticide contamination
ibis, Japanese crested	*Nipponia nippon*	Sado Island, Japan	hunting; loss of forest habitat
kagu	*Rhynochetos jubatus*	New Caledonia	trapping; animal trade; destruction of forest habitat by nickel mining; predation by dogs, cats, pigs, rats
kakapo	*Strigops habroptilus*	New Zealand	human disturbance; loss of forest habitat; competition for food; predation by rats, stoats
kestrel, Mauritius	*Falco punctatus*	Mauritius	destruction of forest habitat; hunting; predation of nests by macaque monkeys
kingfisher, Guam Micronesian	*Halycon cinnamomina cinnamomina*	Guam, Mariana Islands, W Pacific Ocean	human development; loss of forest habitat
kite, Grenada hook-billed	*Chondrohierax uncinatus mirus*	Lesser Antilles, W Indies	hunting; decrease in numbers of snails on which the kite subsists; effects of hurricanes
macaw, glaucous	*Anodorynchus glaucus*	S America	possibly already extinct
macaw, Lear's or indigo	*Anodorhynchus leari*	S America	rare bird in great demand among aviculturists who threaten its continued existence in the wild
mallard, Marianas	*Anas oustaleti*	Mariana Islands, W Pacific Ocean	hunting; draining of wetland habitat
monal, Chinese	*Lophophorus lhuysii*	W China	hunting
nukupu'u	*Hemignathus lucidus*	Fiji, Hawaiian Islands	disease; predation by rats; competition from other birds
'o'u	*Psittirostra psittacea*	Hawaiian Islands	loss of forest habitat due to overgrazing by livestock; competition with imported birds; disease; predation

ENDANGERED SPECIES (cont.)

Birds

Name	Species	Location	Cause of endangerment
owl, Anjouan scops	*Otus rutilus capnodes*	Anjouan Island, W Indian Ocean	over-collecting; destruction of evergreen forest habitat by felling, banana cultivation, cyclones
owl, Lanyu scops	*Otus elegans botelensis*	Taiwan	loss of forest habitat; human disturbance in the form of tourism
owl, Soumagne's	*Tyto soumagnei*	Madagascar	loss of humid forest habitat
oystercatcher, Canarian black	*Haematopus moquini meadewaldoi*	Canary Islands	has always been rare, may no longer be extant
oystercatcher, Chatham Island	*Haematopus chathamensis*	Chatham Islands, off New Zealand	destruction of vegetation by grazing sheep
parakeet, Chatham Island yellow-crowned or Forbe's	*Cyanoramphus auriceps forbesi*	Chatham Islands, off New Zealand	human; climatic damage to habitat
parakeet, Mauritius	*Psittacula echo*	Mauritius	loss of evergreen forest habitat; competition for nest sites; nest predation by macaque monkeys, rats
parakeet, Norfolk Island	*Cyanoramphus novaeseelandiae cookii*	Norfolk Island, SW Pacific Ocean	competition for nest sites; shooting; loss of rainforest habitat
parakeet, Paradise or beautiful	*Psephotus pulcherrimus*	S Queensland and New South Wales, Australia	drought; expansion of livestock grazing; last confirmed sighting was in 1927, but there have been more recent unconfirmed sightings
parakeet, Uvea horned	*Eunymphicus cornutus uvaeensis*	Uvea, Loyalty Islands, SW Pacific Ocean	animal trade; loss of woodland habitat
parrot, Imperial or sisserou	*Amazona imperialis*	Lesser Antilles, W Indies	hunting for meat, sport
parrot, maroon fronted	*Rhynchopsitta pachyrhyncha terrisi*	NE Mexico	logging of pine forest habitat; animal trade; shooting
parrot, Puerto Rican	*Amazona vittata*	Puerto Rico	clearance of lowland forest habitat; predation of nests by rats
parrot, red-necked or jacquot	*Amazona arausiaca*	Lesser Antilles, W Indies	hunting; competition for nesting ranges, predation of eggs and young by pearly-eyed thrashers
parrot, red-tailed	*Amazona brasiliensis*	SE Brazil	animal trade; loss of forest habitat
parrot, St Lucia	*Amazona versicolor*	St Lucia, W Indies	hunting; loss of forest habitat to agriculture
parrot, St Vincent	*Amazona guildingii*	Lesser Antilles, W Indies	animal trade; hunting

ENDANGERED SPECIES (cont.)

Birds

Name	Species	Location	Cause of endangerment
parrot, Seychelles lesser vasa	*Coracopsis nigra barklyi*	Seychelles	destruction of palm forest habitat by cutting, burning
parrot, Western ground	*Pezoporus wallicus flaviventris*	SW Australia	clearing, burning, draining of grassland and wetland habitat
partridge, Italian grey	*Perdix perdix italica*	C Italy	interbreeding with other grey partridges; contamination by agricultural herbicides, pesticides; competition for food from pheasants
petrel, black	*Procellaria parkinsoni*	New Zealand	predation on breeding adults and fledglings by cats
petrel, Chatham Island	*Pterodroma hypoleuca axillaris*	Chatham Islands off New Zealand	competition from other subspecies
petrel, dark-rumped	*Pterodroma phaeopygia phaeopygia*	Galapagos	destruction of habitat due to agriculture; predation by dogs, pigs, black rats
petrel, Hawaiian dark-rumped	*Pterodroma phaeopygia sandwichensis*	Hawaiian Islands	predation by black rats, cats, mongooses
petrel, magenta	*Pterodroma magentae*	New Zealand	predation by cats, rats; deterioration of forest habitat due to overgrazing of livestock, presence of other herbivores
pheasant, brown-eared	*Crossoptilon mantchuricum*	N China	human persecution; loss of forest habitat
pheasant, cheer	*Catreus wallichii*	India and Nepal	hunting; destruction of forest habitat
pheasant, Elliot's	*Syrmaticus ellioti*	E China	hunting; destruction of forest habitat
pigeon, Chatham Island	*Hemiphaga novaeseelandiae chathamensis*	Chatham Islands, off New Zealand	hunting; predation by cats; destruction of woodland habitat by grazing stock, winds, fire
pigeon, laurel	*Columba junoniae*	Canary Islands	hunting; loss of laurel forest habitat
pigeon, Marquesas	*Ducula galeata*	Marquesas Islands	hunting for its meat; loss of habitat to human disturbance, grazing of cattle, pigs, goats
pigeon, Palau Nicobar	*Caloenas nicobarica pelewensis*	Palau Islands, SW Pacific Ocean	hunting
pigeon, pink	*Nesoenas mayeri*	Mauritius	predation of nests by macaque monkeys, black rats; hunting; loss of forest habitat
pigeon, Puerto Rican plain	*Columba inornata wetmorei*	Puerto Rico	human persecution; plundering of nests; loss of forest habitat to housing development
pigeon, Truk Micronesian	*Ducula oceanica teraokai*	Caroline Islands, W Pacific Ocean	hunting for its meat; loss of forest habitat

ENDANGERED SPECIES (cont.)

Birds

Name	Species	Location	Cause of endangerment
plover, New Zealand shore	*Thinornis novaeseelandiae*	Chatham Islands, off New Zealand	animal trade; destruction of vegetation by grazing sheep
quail, gorgeted wood	*Odontophorus strophium*	Colombia	absence of suitable habitat; current survival is in doubt
quail, masked bobwhite	*Colinus virginianus ridgwayi*	USA and Mexico	deterioration of habitat due to drought, overgrazing by cattle
rail, barred-wing	*Rallus poecilopterus*	Fiji Islands	predation by mongooses, cats, rats
rail, light-footed clapper	*Rallus longirostris levipes*	California, USA and Mexico	loss of saltmarsh habitat
rail, Lord Howe wood	*Tricholimnas sylvestris*	Lord Howe Island, SW Pacific Ocean	damage to vegetation by wild goats, pigs; predation of eggs by rats
rhea, Puna	*Pterocnemia pennata tarapacensis*	Peru, Chile, Bolivia and Argentina	hunting for its feathers and skin; poaching its eggs
robin, Chatham Island black	*Petroica traversi*	Chatham Islands off New Zealand	destruction and deterioration of scrub forest habitat by human disturbance, climatic conditions; nesting of petrels
robin, dappled mountain	*Modulatrix orostruthus*	Mozambique and Tanzania	loss of forest habitat to agriculture
robin, Seychelles magpie	*Copsychus sechellarum*	Seychelles	predation by cats; competition for nest sites; decreased availability of food
robin, Southern Ryukyu	*Erithacus komadori subrufa*	Ryukyu Islands	destruction of forest habitat
scrub-bird, noisy	*Atrichornis clamosus*	SW Australia	clearance of eucalyptus forest habitat; drought; predation by cats
shrike, black-capped bush	*Malaconotus alius*	Tanzania	loss of canopy forest habitat due to felling
shrike, San Clemente loggerhead	*Lanius ludovicianus mearnsi*	California, USA	deterioration of brush vegetation habitat due to overgrazing by goats, sheep, pigs
silver-eye, white-breasted	*Zosterops albogularis*	Norfolk Island, SW Pacific Ocean	almost complete destruction of rainforest habitat
siskin, red	*Spinus cucullatus*	S America	trapping for the cagebird trade
sparrow, Amok song	*Melospiza melodia amaka*	Amak Island off Alaska	predation by Arctic foxes
sparrow, dusky seaside	*Ammodramus maritimus nigrescens*	Florida, USA	destruction of salt marshland habitat by fires; human development; alterations in habitat by mosquito control, waterfowl enhancement, inundation of freshwater

ENDANGERED SPECIES (cont.)

Birds

Name	Species	Location	Cause of endangerment
sparrow, San Clemente sage	*Amphispiza belli clementeae*	S California, USA	deterioration of shrubland and grassland habitat by overgrazing of wild goats, pigs
sparrowhawk, Anjouan	*Accipiter francesii pusillus*	Anjouan Island, Indian Ocean	destruction of forest habitat by human settlement, cyclones, soil erosion; banana plantations
stilt, black	*Himantopus novaesealandiae*	New Zealand	loss of breeding and feeding habitat
starling, Rothschild's	*Leucopsar rothschildi*	Bali, Indonesia	loss of forest habitat to human settlement; competition from other starlings; trapping for the cagebird trade
stork, Oriental white	*Ciconia ciconia boyciana*	Asia	shooting; contamination by mercury causing mortality or reproductive failure; loss of wetland habitat to agriculture, extinct in Europe
takahe	*Notornis mantelli*	New Zealand	competition for food from deer; predation by stoats
tanager, cherry-throated	*Nemosia rourei*	SE Brazil	unrecorded for over a century, probably already extinct
tern, Californian least	*Sterna albifrons browni*	California, USA and Mexico	destruction and deterioration of coastal beach and marshland habitat by pollution, human settlement, development
thrasher, Martinique white-breasted	*Ramphocinclus brachyurus brachyurus*	Martinique	hunting; predation by rats, mongooses
thrasher, St Lucia white-breasted	*Ramphocinclus brachyurus sanctaeluciae*	St. Lucia	loss of habitat to human development; predation by rats, mongooses
thrush, Kauai	*Phaeornis obscurus myadestina*	Hawaiian Islands	disease; loss of rainforest habitat
thrush, Molokai	*Phaeornis obscurus rutha*	Hawaiian Islands	disease; loss of rainforest habitat; deterioration of habitat caused by grazing livestock; predation by rats, cats, mongooses
thrush, St Lucia forest	*Cichlherminia lherminieri sanctaeluciae*	St Lucia, W Indies	loss of rainforest habitat
thrush, small Kauai	*Phaeornis palmeri*	Hawaiian Islands	disease; competition with other birds; loss of habitat to grazing; predation by mammals
tinamou, Pernambuco solitary	*Tinamus solitarius pernambucensis*	Brazil	hunting; loss of forest habitat

ENDANGERED SPECIES (cont.)

Birds

Name	Species	Location	Cause of endangerment
tragopan, Cabot's	*Tragopan caboti*	SE China	loss of forest habitat to agricultural cultivation
tragopan, western	*Tragopan melanocephalus*	India and Pakistan	hunting; trapping; disturbance by humans, goats; destruction of forest habitat
trembler, Martinique	*Cinclocerthia ruficauda gutturalis*	Martinique	loss of woodland habitat to sugar cane plantations; predation by rats, mongooses
turtle dove, Seychelles	*Streptopelia picturata rostrata*	Seychelles	virtually eliminated by the introduction of the Madagascar turtle dove and the resultant interbreeding
vanga, Pollen's	*Xenopirostris polleni*	Madagascar	destruction of humid forest habitat
vanga, Van Dam's	*Xenopirostris damii*	Madagascar	clearance of deciduous forest habitat
warbler, Bachman's	*Vermivora bachmanii*	USA	destruction of deciduous swampland forest habitat for timber, agriculture, sugar cane plantation; now N America's rarest songbird
warbler, Barbados yellow	*Dendroica petechia petechia*	Barbados	clearance of mangrove swampland habitat; effects of parasitism by cowbirds
warbler, Eiao Polynesian	*Acrocephalus caffer aquilonis*	Marquesas Islands	destruction of woodland habitat by grazing sheep, swine
warbler, Kirtland's	*Dendroica kirtlandii*	USA	loss of forest habitat; roduced breeding due to invasion by cowbirds who have parasitized nests
warbler, long-legged	*Trichocichla rufa*	Fiji	predation by cats, rats, mongooses
warbler, Moorea Polynesian	*Acrocephalus caffer longirostris*	Society Islands	disease
warbler, Rodrigues brush	*Bebrornis rodericana*	Rodrigues Island, Mascarenes	human disturbance; clearance of thicket habitat
warbler, Semper's	*Leucopeza semperi*	St Lucia	predation by mongooses
white-eye, Gizo	*Zosterops luteirostris luteirostris*	Solomon Islands, SW Pacific Ocean	destruction of lowland forest habitat
white-eye, Truk greater	*Rukia rukia*	Caroline Islands, W Pacific Ocean	occupies limited and unprotected range of mountain forest habitat
woodpecker, American ivory-billed	*Campephilus principalis principalis*	SE USA	bird collection; clearance of swampland habitat; human disturbance

ENDANGERED SPECIES (cont.)

Birds

Name	Species	Location	Cause of endangerment
woodpecker, Cuban ivory-billed	*Campephilus principalis bairdii*	Cuba	shooting; loss of pine forest habitat to timber trade, sugar cane plantation
woodpecker, Imperial	*Campephilus imperialis*	Mexico	shooting; loss of forest habitat due to logging
woodpecker, Okinawa	*Sapheopipo noguchii*	Ryukyu Islands	loss of woodland habitat to woodcutting, fires
woodpecker, Tristram's	*Drycopus javenssis richardsi*	C Korea	destruction of forest habitat by logging, road-building, the effects of war
woodstar, Chilean	*Eulidua yarrellii*	Chile	reasons for decline in population are unknown
wren, Guadeloupe	*Troglodytes aedon guadeloupensis*	Guadeloupe	hunting; predation by rats, cats, mongooses
wren, New Zealand bush	*Xenicus longipes*	New Zealand	predation by black rats
wren, St Lucia	*Troglodytes aedon mesoleucus*	St Lucia	predation by mongooses, rats, boa constrictors; development of scrub forest habitat will render the bird extinct

Mammals

Name	Species	Location	Cause of endangerment
anoa, lowland	*Bubalus depressicornis*	Sulawesi	hunting; destruction of habitat
anoa, mountain	*Bubalus quarlesi*	Sulawesi	hunting; destruction of habitat
antelope, giant sable	*Hippotragus niger variani*	Angola	human settlement; destruction of habitat
ass, African wild	*Equus africanus*	Somalia and Ethiopia	hunting for the medical properties of its meat and fat; poaching; human disturbance in the form of tourism; droughts; competition for pasture and water from domestic livestock
ass, Indian wild	*Equus hemionus khur*	Gujarat and Pakistan border regions	disease; loss of habitat to agriculture, land development; droughts; competition for food from domestic livestock; human disturbance
aye-aye	*Daubentonia madagascariensis*	Madagascar	primate threatened by loss of forest habitat
bandicoot, pig-footed	*Chaeropus ecaudatus*	Australia	possibly already extinct, last seen by aborigines in 1920s
bandicoot, rabbit-eared or bilby	*Macrotis lagotis*	Australia	human settlement; competition with rabbits for habitat; subject to hunting

ENDANGERED SPECIES (cont.)

Mammals

Name	Species	Location	Cause of endangerment
bat, ghost or Australian false vampire	*Macroderma gigas*	N Australia	quarrying of the caves which form their natural habitat
bat, gray	*Myotis grisescens*	SE United States	disturbance of habitat by caving, vandalism
bat, Singapore roundleaf horseshoe	*Hipposideros ridlegi*	Malaysia	logging of its lowland peat forest habitat
bear, Baluchistan	*Selenarctos thibetanus gedrosianus*	Baluchistan and Iran	human persecution; hunting because of its damage to crops and the threat posed by it to domestic stock
bear, Mexican grizzly	*Ursus horribilis nelsoni*	Mexico	may already have been exterminated by hunting, poisoning
cat, Iriomote	*Prionailurus iriomotensis*	Ryukyu Islands	loss of natural habitat to agriculture
cat, Pakistan sand	*Felis margarita scheffeli*	Pakistan	animal trade
cheetah, Asiatic	*Acinonyx jubatus venaticus*	Turkey, Iran, Afghanistan and USSR	fur trade; decline in population of its natural prey, the gazelle
civet, Malabar large spotted	*Viverra megaspila civettina*	S India	possibly already extinct due to persecution, loss of habitat to agriculture
colobus, black	*Colobus satanas*	Cameroon, Guinea, Gabon and the Congo	hunting; loss of habitat due to logging
colobus, Preuss's red	*Colobus badius preussi*	Cameroon	hunting; loss of forest area due to logging
colobus, Tana River red	*Colobus badius rufomitratus*	Kenya	human settlement; loss of forest area due to shifting cultivation
colobus, Zanzibar red	*Colobus kirkii*	Zanzibar	human disturbance
deer, Bactrian	*Cervus elaphus bactrianus*	USSR and Afghanistan	loss of habitat to land development, damming, human settlement, stock grazing
deer, Argentinian pampas	*Ozotoceros bezoarticus celer*	Argentina	hunting; disease; loss of habitat to agriculture, domestic livestock
deer, Barbary	*Cervus elaphus barbarus*	Algeria and Tunisia border regions	poaching; loss of forest habitat
deer, Cedros Island	*Odocoileus hemionus cerrosensis*	Cedros Island off California, USA	hunting; disturbance by wild dogs; destruction of habitat by fires
deer, Colombian white-tailed	*Odocoileus virginianus leucurus*	Washington and Oregon, USA	loss of habitat to agriculture

ENDANGERED SPECIES (cont.)

Mammals

Name	Species	Location	Cause of endangerment
deer, Corsican red	*Cervus elaphus corsicanus*	Sardinia	poaching; human disturbance; loss of habitat through burning, domestic livestock grazing, deforestation
deer, northern brow-antlered	*Cervus eldi eldi*	Manipur, India	hunting; loss of habitat to domestic stock grazing, cultivation, logging, burning
deer, Persian fallow	*Dama mesopotamica*	Iran	hunting; loss of forest habitat to irrigation, agriculture, grazing of domestic livestock
deer, swamp	*Cervus duvauceli*	India and Nepal	poaching, human disturbance; competition for grazing from domestic livestock
deer, Thailand brow-antlered	*Cervus eldi siamensis*	Thailand, Laos, Kampuchea and Vietnam	hunting; loss or destruction of habitat by the effects of war, agriculture, land development, shifting cultivation, forest clearance
dog, African wild	*Lycaon pictus*	Africa south of the Sahara	human hunting, persecution
dolphin, Indus	*Platanista indi*	Indus River	withdrawal of water for irrigation; illegal exploitation by fishermen
drill	*Papio leuchopaeus*	Cameroon	hunting; loss of habitat due to clearance of forest, cultivation of land
duiker, Jentink's	*Cephalophus jentinki*	Liberia; Ivory Coast	destruction of natural habitat; almost extinct
eland, Western giant	*Taurotragus derbianus derbianus*	W Africa	hunting; persecution; disease
elephant, Asian	*Elephas maximus*	Asia	severe loss of natural habitat
ferret, black-footed	*Mustela nigripes*	USA	poisoning; loss of grassland habitat
flying fox, Guam	*Pteropus tokudae*	Guam Island	hunting; loss of forest areas
flying fox, Rodrigues	*Pteropus rodricensis*	Rodrigues Island	almost total loss of natural habitat
fox, N Kit	*Vulpes velox hebes*	USA	almost extinct due to trapping, hunting, poisoning
fox, N Simien	*Simenia simensis simensis*	Ethiopia	widespread hunting on false assumption that it is a threat to sheep
fox, Simien or Abyssinian wolf	*Canis simensis*	Ethiopia	hunting; loss of habitat; decreasing availability of rodents as food
gazelle, Arabian	*Gazella gazella arabica*	Saudi Arabia, Yemen and Red Sea	hunting; deterioration of habitat

ENDANGERED SPECIES (cont.)

Mammals

Name	Species	Location	Cause of endangerment
gazelle, Cuvier's	*Gazella cuvieri*	Tunisia, Algeria and Morocco	hunting; loss of habitat to overgrazing by livestock, forest plantation
gazelle, Dorcas	*Gazella dorcas*	N Africa, Middle East and India	hunting; loss of habitat due to overgrazing by domestic livestock
gazelle, Mhorr	*Gazella dama mhorr*	Morocco	human disturbance; occupation of habitat by domestic livestock
gazelle, Rio de Oro dama	*Gazella dama lozanoi*	Sahara	hunting; drought; loss of habitat
gazelle, sand	*Gazella subgutturosa marica*	Jordan and Arabian peninsula	hunting; deterioration of habitat due to overgrazing
gazelle, slender-horned	*Gazella leptoceros*	N Africa	hunting; deterioration of habitat
gibbon, Java or silvery	*Hylobates moloch*	Indonesia	destruction of forest habitat for timber, human settlement
gibbon, pileated, crowned or capped	*Hylobates pileatus*	Asia	loss of forest habitat
gorilla, mountain	*Gorilla gorilla beringei*	Rwanda, Zaire and Uganda	human disturbance, encroachment on natural habitat
hartebeest, Swayne's	*Alcelaphus buselaphus swaynei*	Ethiopia	hunting; destruction of habitat
hartebeest, Tora	*Alcelaphus buselaphus tora*	Ethiopia, Sudan; Egypt	hunting; loss of habitat; disease
hog, pygmy	*Sus salvanius*	N India	destruction of thatchland habitat by settlement, forestry, fires; also hunted for its meat
horse, Przewalski's or takh	*Equus przewalskii*	China and Mongolia	severe competition for natural pasture; water from domestic livestock; possibly already extinct in the wild
hyena, Barbary	*Hyaena hyaena barbara*	N Africa	loss of habitat due to human settlement, agriculture
ibex, Pyrenean	*Capra pyrenaica pyrenaica*	Pyrenees	hunting; now virtually extinct
ibex, Walia	*Capra walia*	Ethiopia	destruction of habitat by agriculture, livestock
impala, black-faced	*Aepyceros melampus petersi*	Angola and SW Africa	hunting; low reproductive rate
indris	*Indri indri*	Madagascar	primate threatened by widespread destruction of forests
jerboa, Eastern marsupial	*Antechinomys laniger*	Victoria, Australia	reasons for decline are unknown

ENDANGERED SPECIES (cont.)

Mammals

Name	Species	Location	Cause of endangerment
kangaroo rat, Morro Bay	*Dipodomys heermanni morroensis*	California, USA	loss or change of natural habitat; urban development; predation by domestic cats
kouprey	*Bos sauveli*	Kampuchea, Laos and Thailand	hunting for meat, horns; effects of warfare; low reproductive rate
langur, pig-tailed	*Simias concolor*	Mentawai Islands off Sumatra	hunting for meat; loss of forest habitat
lemur, black	*Lemur macaco macaco*	Madagascar	lack of protective measures from hunting, poisoning
lemur, red-fronted	*Lemur macaco rufus*	Madagascar	hunting; loss of habitat
lemur, red-tailed sportive	*Lepilemur mustelinus ruficaudatus*	Madagascar	hunting; destruction of forest habitat
lemur, Sandford's	*Lemur macaco sanfordi*	Madagascar	intensive hunting; loss of rain forest
lemur, Sclater's	*Lemur macaco flavifrons*	Madagascar	possibly extinct due to loss of coastal forest lands
lemur, white-footed sportive	*Lepilemur mustelinus leucopus*	Madagascar	destruction of natural environment by bad land use; competition from cattle, goats
leopard, Amur	*Panthera pardus orientalis*	Siberia, Korea, USSR; China	human persecution; depletion of natural prey
leopard, Anatolian	*Panthera pardus tulliana*	W Asia	hunting, trapping, poisoning as a protection against its predation of livestock; loss of habitat to cultivation
leopard, Barbary	*Panthera pardus panthera*	N Africa	hunting for sport, for its fur; because of the threat it poses to humans, domestic livestock
leopard, Formosan clouded	*Neofelis nebulosa brachyurus*	Taiwan	hunting for its fur
leopard, Sinai	*Panthera pardus jarvisi*	Sinai	human persecution; depletion of natural prey
leopard, snow or ounce	*Panthera uncia*	C Asia	hunting for fur and because of the threat it poses to domestic livestock; loss of natural prey
leopard, S Arabian	*Panthera pardus nimr*	Arabian peninsula	persecution by shepherds protecting their flocks
lion, Asiatic	*Panthera leo persica*	Gujarat State, India	loss of natural habitat and prey
lynx, Spanish or Pardel	*Felis pardina*	Spain and Portugal	loss of habitat due to reforestation; the effects of myxomatosis on its main prey, the rabbit; incidental killing, trapping

ENDANGERED SPECIES (cont.)

Mammals

Name	Species	Location	Cause of endangerment
macaque, lion-tailed	*Macaca silenus*	S India	loss of habitat; hunting for meat; animal trade
manatee, Amazonian	*Trichechus inunguis*	Amazon River	loss of population due to hunting
mangabey, Tana River	*Cercocebus galeritus galeritus*	Kenya	primate threatened by loss of habitat due to agriculture
markhor, straight-horned	*Capra falconeri megaceros*	Pakistan; Afghanistan	hunting; loss of habitat to stock grazing
marmoset, buff-headed	*Callithrix flaviceps*	SE Brazil	destruction of natural habitat
marmot, Vancouver Island	*Marmota vancouverensis*	Vancouver Island, Canada	collection; exploitation; loss of habitat due to logging
mole, giant golden	*Chrysopalax trevelyani*	S Africa	drought; loss of habitat
monkey, C American or red-backed squirrel	*Saimiri oerstedi*	Panama and Costa Rica	animal exportation; loss of forest habitat
monkey, woolly spider	*Brachyteles arachnoides*	São Paulo state, Brazil	hunting; clearance of forest habitat for fuel, agriculture, human settlement
monkey, yellow-tailed woolly	*Lagothrix flavicauda*	Peru	hunting for its skin, meat; destruction of its habitat for human settlement
mouflon, Mediterranean	*Ovis ammon musimon*	Corsica, Sardinia; Cyprus	hunting; predation by wild dogs; hybridization
mouse, salt-marsh harvest	*Reithrodontomys raviventris*	California, USA	water pollution; loss of habitat due to urban, industrial development
muntjac, Fea's	*Muntiacus feae*	Burma and Thailand	hunting for the meat of this small deer which is highly valued
orang-utan	*Pongo pygmaeus*	Borneo and Sumatra	animal trade; felling of forests by timber industry
ocelot, Texas	*Felis pardalis albescens*	Texas and Mexico	bush clearance, hunting for fur; because it is perceived as a threat to agricultural livestock
oryx, Arabian	*Oryx leucoryx*	Oman	hunting for its meat, skin, medical uses
otter, Cameroon clawless	*Aonyx microdon*	Cameroon and Nigeria	fur trade
otter, giant	*Pteronura brasiliensis*	S America	fur trade
otter, La Plata	*Lutra platensis*	S America	hunting for its fur; water pollution affecting stocks of fish on which it depends for food

ENDANGERED SPECIES (cont.)

Mammals

Name	Species	Location	Cause of endangerment
otter, marine	*Lutra felina*	Pacific coast of S America	persecuted; shot because it is perceived as a threat to stocks of freshwater prawns
otter, southern river	*Lutra provocax*	Chile	fur trade; water pollution
panther or Florida cougar	*Felis concolor coryi*	SE USA	loss of habitat; hunting; decreased prey on which to feed
possum, Leadbetter's	*Gymnbelideus leadbeateri*	Victoria, Australia	felling of forest areas has led to loss of habitat
pronghorn, Lower Californian	*Antilocapra americana peninsularis*	California	hunting; competition for fodder from domestic livestock
pronghorn, Sonoran	*Antilocapra americana sonoriensis*	Mexico and Arizona, USA	destruction of habitat; competition for food and water from livestock; hunting
puma, Eastern or Eastern cougar	*Felis concolor cougar*	N America	loss of habitat; hunting; decreased prey on which to feed
rabbit, Ryukyu	*Pentalagus furnessi*	Ryukyu Island	loss of habitat; predation by wild dogs
rabbit, Assam or hispid hare	*Caprolagus hispidus*	N India	loss of habitat due to human settlement; cultivation; forestry; burning of thatchlands, also illegally hunted for food
rabbit, volcano	*Romerolagus diazi*	Mexico	loss of habitat; wanton destruction by shooting
rhinoceros, great Indian	*Rhinoceros unicornis*	India and Nepal	hunting; poaching for rhino horn; loss of habitat to agriculture, stock grazing
rhinoceros, Javan	*Rhinoceros sondaicus*	Java, Laos; Kampuchea	hunting for rhino horn, medical properties of rhino blood; loss of habitat to human settlement
rhinoceros, northern square-lipped	*Caratotherium simum cottoni*	Sudan, Uganda, Zaire and C Africa	hunting for the supposed aphrodisiac qualities of the rhino horn; disturbance by military operations
rhinoceros, Sumatran	*Didermocerus sumatrensis*	SE Asia	hunting for the aphrodisiac and medical qualities of the horn and other parts of the carcass which fetches high prices; loss of forest habitat to timber exploitation, human settlement
sea lion, Japanese	*Zapophus californianus japonicus*	Japanese coastal islands	human disturbance; persecution by fishermen

ENDANGERED SPECIES (cont.)

Mammals

Name	Species	Location	Cause of endangerment
seal, Caribbean monk	*Monachus tropicalis*	Caribbean	slaughtered by 18th-c seal fishermen; natural habitat now increasingly subject to human disturbance; the demands of tourism; possibly already extinct
seal, Hawaiian monk	*Monachus schauinslandi*	Hawaiian Islands	initial decline in population due to 19th-c seal fishermen; present population threatened by attacks by sharks; human disturbance of breeding grounds leading to low rates of reproduction, high rates of juvenile mortality
seal, Mediterranean monk	*Monachus monachus*	N Africa, Lebanon, Cyprus and Turkey	persecution by fishermen; human disturbance; marine pollution
serow, Sumatran	*Capricornis sumatraensis sumatraensis*	Sumatra	hunting; destruction of habitat
sifaka, Verreaux's	*Propithecus verreauxi*	Madagascar	hunting; destruction of forests
sika, Formosan	*Cervus nippon taiouanus*	Taiwan	hunting for meat, antlers; the medical properties of the carcass; loss of habitat to agriculture; probably already extinct in the wild
sika, N China	*Cervus nippon mandarinus*	China	hunting, loss of habitat; possibly already extinct in the wild
sika, Ryukyu or Kerama deer	*Cervus nippon keremae*	Ryukyu Islands	drought; low qualities of feeding vegetation; competition with goats for grazing fodder
sika, Shansi	*Cervus nippon grassianus*	China	hunting for the antler trade; clearance of forest habitat for agriculture
sika, S China	*Cervus nippon kopschi*	China	hunting for the antler trade; trapping; loss of habitat
sloth, maned	*Bradtpus torquatus*	Brazil	loss of forest habitat
solenodon, Haitian	*Solenodon paradoxus*	Dominican Republic and Haiti	land development; deforestation
squirrel, Delmarva Peninsula fox or Bryant's fox	*Sciurus niger cinereus*	Maryland, USA	loss of habitat due to logging
stag, Hangul or Kashmir	*Cervus elaphus hanglu*	India	poaching; human disturbance; deterioration of habitat caused by domestic livestock, particularly grazing sheep

ENDANGERED SPECIES (cont.)

Mammals

Name	Species	Location	Cause of endangerment
suni, Zanzibar	*Neotragus moschatus moschatus*	Zanzibar	hunting; destruction of habitat
tahr, Arabian	*Hemitragus jayakari*	Oman	hunting; competition for food from domestic goats
tamaraw	*Bubalus mindorensis*	Philippines	hunting; loss of forest habitat
tamarin, cotton-top	*Saguinus oedipus oedipus*	NW Colombia	animal trade; loss of habitat to agriculture
tamarin, golden or lion	*Leontopithecus rosalia*	Brazil	loss of forest habitat to agriculture, urban development
tamarin, golden-headed	*Leontopithecus rosalia chrysomelas*	E Brazil	loss of Atlantic rainforest
tamarin, golden-rumped	*Leontopithecus rosalia chrysopygus*	Sao Paulo area of Brazil	loss of forest habitat; possibly careless use of defoliants by farmers
tapir, Central American	*Tapirus bairdii*	C and S America	loss of rainforest habitat; hunting; human settlement
tapir, Malayan	*Tapirus indicus*	Malaysia	human disturbance; loss of forest habitat to logging, oil exploitation, human settlement, mining, agriculture
tapir, mountain	*Tapirus pinchaque*	S America	human disturbance; competition for natural habitat with livestock
tarsier, Philippine	*Tarsius syrichta*	Philippines	primate threatened by capture, exportation; destruction of forest habitat
tiger	*Panthera tigris*	Eurasia	loss of habitat and prey; hunting for sport; because of the threat posed by it to both humans and domestic livestock
tiger, Bengal or Indian	*Panthera tigris tigris*	Indian sub-continent	loss of habitat to agriculture, urban development; depletion of natural prey; hunting for skin; poisoning; current low rate of reproduction
tiger, Bali	*Panthera tigris balica*	S and SE Asia	loss of population due to hunting; possibly already extinct
tiger, Caspian	*Panthera tigris virgata*	Turkey, Iran, USSR and Afghanistan	loss of habitat to logging, cultivation; loss of natural prey; hunting
tiger, Chinese	*Panthera tigris amoyensis*	China	hunting; clearance of habitat for agricultural development
tiger, Javan	*Panthera tigris sondaica*	Java	hunting; loss of forest habitat; loss of natural prey

ENDANGERED SPECIES (cont.)

Mammals

Name	Species	Location	Cause of endangerment
tiger, Siberian	*Panthera tigris altaica*	Siberia, China and Korea	hunting; loss of habitat and natural prey
uakari, bald	*Cacajao calvus*	S America	primate threatened by hunting; animal trade
uakari, white	*Cacajao calvus calvus*	Brazil	primate threatened by human development of its habitat
wallaby, bridle nail-tailed	*Onychogalea fraenata*	Queensland, Australia	loss of natural habitat to settlement; introduction of livestock; predation from foxes
wallaby, crescent nail-tailed	*Onychogalea lunata*	C Australia	hunting; loss of natural habitat to settlement
whale, black right	*Eubalaena glacialis*	N Atlantic and N Pacific Oceans and S hemisphere	whaling
whale, blue	*Balaenoptera musculus*	Atlantic, Pacific and Indian Oceans	whaling
whale, bowhead or Greenland right	*Balaena mysticetus*	Arctic waters	whaling
whale, humpback	*Megaptera novaeangliae*	N Atlantic and N Pacific Oceans; S hemisphere	whaling
wolf, Northern Rocky Mountain	*Canis lupus irremotus*	USA	poisoning, trapping, hunting by man
wolf, red	*Canis rufus*	Texas and Louisiana, USA	loss of habitat; hunting; trapping; hybridization with coyotes
yak, wild	*Bos grunniens*	Tibet, Kashmir and W China	hunting
zebra, Grevy's	*Equus grevyi*	Kenya and Ethiopia	hunted because of its attractive, highly-prized skin

HUMAN LIFE

COMPOSITION OF SELECTED FOODS

Approximate values given are for 100g of the food named

Food	Calories[1]	Protein (g)	Carbohydrates (g)	Fat (g)	Fibre (g)
almonds	564	19	20	54	15
apples	38	trace	15	trace	2
apricots, dried	182	5	67	1	24
apricots, raw	25	1	13	trace	2
asparagus, cooked	18	2	4	trace	1
aubergine, cooked	14	1	4	trace	2
avocados	221	2	6	16	2
bacon, back, grilled	271	15	2	24	0
bacon, streaky, grilled	308	16	2	27	0
bananas	85	1	22	trace	2
beans, broad, cooked	46	4	66	1	4
beans, dried white, cooked	118	8	21	7	25
beans, green, cooked	25	2	5	trace	4
beef, minced	221	31	0	16	0
beef, rump steak, grilled	218	30	0	12	0
beetroot, cooked	43	1	7	trace	2
biscuit, chocolate digestive	506	6	64	25	4
biscuit, digestive	486	7	62	23	5
blackberries, raw	29	1	13	1	7
blackcurrants	29	2	14	trace	9
brazil nuts, raw	618	14	11	67	9
bread, white	232	10	58	2	3
bread, wholemeal	216	10	55	3	9
broccoli, cooked	26	3	5	trace	4
brussel sprouts, cooked	18	4	6	trace	3
butter, salted	740	1	trace	82	0
cabbage, cooked	11	2	trace	trace	2
cabbage, raw	25	2	5	trace	3
carrots, cooked	20	1	5	trace	3
carrots, raw	25	1	6	trace	3
cauliflower, cooked	22	2	4	trace	2
celery, raw	36	1	2	trace	2
cheese, Brie	314	19	2	23	0
cheese, Cheddar	414	25	2	32	0
cheese, cottage	96	17	2	4	0
cheese, Edam	314	30	trace	23	0
cherries, raw	70	1	17	trace	1
chick peas, dry	320	20	50	6	15
chicken, meat only, roast	142	19	0	4	0

COMPOSITION OF SELECTED FOODS (cont.)

Food	Calories[1]	Protein (g)	Carbohydrates (g)	Fat (g)	Fibre (g)
chocolate bar, plain	510	4	63	29	0
cod, cooked	94	19	0	1	0
corn (on the cob)	91	3	21	1	5
courgettes, cooked	14	1	3	trace	1
crab, cooked	129	18	1	5	0
cream, double	446	2	3	48	0
crisps	517	6	40	37	11
cucumber, raw	15	1	3	trace	trace
dates	214	2	73	1	7
egg, boiled	163	13	1	12	0
eggplant, *see* aubergine					
figs, dried	214	4	69	1	19
flour, white	350	9	80	1	4
flour, wholemeal	318	132	56	2	10
grapefruit	41	1	11	trace	trace
grapes, raw	69	1	16	1	1
haddock, cooked	96	19	0	1	0
ham, lean	168	22	0	5	0
honey	289	trace	82	0	0
jam	261	1	79	trace	1
lamb chop, boned, grilled	353	24	0	29	0
leeks, cooked	25	1	7	0	4
lentils, cooked	106	8	19	trace	4
lettuce, raw	12	1	3	trace	1
liver, cooked	254	20	6	13	0
lobster, cooked	119	20	trace	3	0
mackerel, cooked	188	25	0	11	0
margarine	730	trace	1	80	0
melon, honeydew	21	1	5	trace	1
melon, water	21	trace	5	trace	1
milk, cow's, skimmed	36	4	5	trace	0
milk, cow's, whole	65	4	5	4	0
mushrooms, raw	14	3	4	trace	2
mussels, cooked	86	17	0	1	0
nectarines	64	1	17	trace	2
oatmeal, cooked	399	2	10	1	7
oats, porridge	377	10	70	7	7
oil, vegetable	900	0	0	100	0
onions, raw	38	2	9	trace	1
orange juice	45	1	10	trace	0
oranges, peeled, raw	49	1	12	trace	2
parsnip, cooked	50	1	17	trace	4
pasta, dry	353	12	71	2	4
peaches, raw	38	1	8	trace	1
peanuts, fresh	571	26	19	48	8
pears, raw	61	1	15	trace	2
peas, fresh, cooked	54	5	4	trace	5
pepper, green, raw	14	1	5	trace	1
pepper, red, raw	20	1	7	trace	1
pineapple, raw	46	trace	14	trace	1

COMPOSITION OF SELECTED FOODS (cont.)

Food	Calories[1]	Protein (g)	Carbohydrates (g)	Fat (g)	Fibre (g)
pork chop, boned, grilled	328	28	0	24	0
potatoes, baked in skin	86	3	21	trace	2
potatoes, boiled in skin	75	2	17	trace	2
prawns, cooked	107	18	0	1	0
prunes, raw	136	1	77	trace	14
raisins	246	3	77	trace	7
raspberries, raw	25	1	14	1	7
rice, brown, cooked	129	3	26	1	1
rice, white, cooked	121	3	33	trace	1
salmon, cooked	196	20	0	13	0
spinach, cooked	23	3	4	trace	6
strawberries, raw	37	1	8	1	2
sugar	394	0	100	0	0
swede, cooked	18	1	4	trace	3
tomatoes, raw	14	1	5	trace	1
tuna, canned in brine	118	28	0	1	0
turkey, meat only, roast	140	36	0	3	0
turnip, cooked	14	1	5	trace	2
walnuts	525	15	16	64	5
yogurt, skimmed milk	50	3	5	2	0
yogurt, whole milk	62	3	5	3	0

[1] To convert calories into kilojoules multiply by 4.187

MAIN TYPES OF VITAMIN

Fat soluble vitamins

Vitamin	Chemical name	Deficiency symptoms	Source
A	retinol (carotene)	night blindness; rough skin; impaired bone growth	milk, butter, cheese, egg yolk, liver, fatty fish, dark green vegetables, yellow/red fruits and vegetables, especially carrots
D	cholecalciferol	rickets; osteomalacia	egg yolk, liver, fatty fish; made on skin in sunlight
E	tocopherols	multiple diseases produced in laboratory animals; in humans, multiple symptoms follow impaired fat absorption	vegetable oils
K	phytomenadione	haemorrhagic problems	green leafy vegetables, beef liver

MAIN TYPES OF VITAMIN (cont.)

Water soluble vitamins

Vitamin	Chemical name	Deficiency symptoms	Source
B_1	thiamin	beri-beri, Korsakov's syndrome	germ and bran of seeds, grains; yeast
B_2	riboflavin	skin disorders; failure to thrive	liver, milk, cheese, eggs, green leafy vegetables, pulses, yeast
B_6	pyridoxine	dermatitis; neurological disorders	liver, meats. fruits, cereals, leafy vegetables
	pantothenic acid	dermatitis; neurological disorders	widespread in plants and animals; destroyed in heavily-processed food
	biotin	dermatitis	liver, kidney, yeast extract; made by microorganisms in large intestine
B_{12}	cyanocobalamin	anaemia; neurological disturbance	liver, kidney, milk; none found in plants
	folic acid	anaemia	liver, green leafy vegetables, peanuts; cooking and processing can cause serious losses in food
C	ascorbic acid	scurvy	blackcurrants, citrus fruits, other fruits, green leafy vegetables, potatoes; losses occur during storage and cooking

MAIN TRACE MINERALS

Mineral	Deficiency symptoms	Source
calcium	rickets in children; osteoporosis in adults	milk, butter, cheese, sardines, green leafy vegetables, citrus fruits
chromium	adult-onset diabetes	brewer's yeast, black pepper, liver, wholemeal bread, beer
copper	anaemia; Menkes' syndrome	green vegetables, fish, oysters, liver
fluorine	tooth decay; possibly osteoporosis	flouridated drinking water, seafood, tea
iodine	goitre; cretinism in new-born children	seafood, salt-water fish, seaweed, iodized salt, table salt
iron	anaemia	liver, kidney, green leafy vegetables, egg yolk, dried fruit, potatoes, molasses
magnesium	irregular heart beat; muscular weakness; insomnia	green leafy vegetables (eaten raw), nuts, whole grains
manganese	not known in man	legumes, cereal grains, green leafy vegetables, tea

MAIN TRACE MINERALS (cont.)

Mineral	Deficiency symptoms	Source
molybdenum	not known in man	legumes, cereal grains, liver, kidney, some dark green vegetables
phosphorus	muscular weakness; bone pain; loss of appetite	meat, poultry, fish, eggs, dried beans and peas, milk products
potassium	irregular heart beat; muscular weakness; fatigue; kidney and lung failure	fresh vegetables, meat, orange juice, bananas, bran
selenium	not known in man	seafood, cereals, meat, egg yolk, garlic
sodium	impaired acid-base balance in body fluids (very rare)	table salt, other naturally occurring salts
zinc	impaired wound healing; loss of appetite; impaired sexual development	meat, whole grains, legumes, oysters, milk

E-NUMBERS

Colours

Number	Name	Source	Function
E100	Curcumin	extract of dried rhizome of turmeric (*Curcuma longa*)	orange-yellow
E101	Riboflavin	liver, kidneys, green vegetables, malted barley, eggs, milk	yellow or orange-yellow
101(a)	Riboflavin-5'-phosphate	chemical Riboflavin	yellow or orange-yellow; vitamin B2
E102	Tartrazine	synthetic, an azo[1] dye	yellow
E104	Quinoline yellow	synthetic 'coal tar' dye	dull yellow to greenish yellow
107	Yellow 2G	synthetic 'coal tar' dye and azo[1] dye	yellow
E110	Sunset Yellow FCF	synthetic 'coal tar' and azo[1] dye	yellow
E120	Cochineal	pregnant scale insects (*Dactilopius coccus*)	red
E122	Carmoisine	synthetic azo[1] dye	red
E123	Amaranth	synthetic 'coal tar' dye and azo[1] dye	purplish red
E124	Poncean 4R	synthetic 'coal tar' dye and azo[1] dye	red
E127	Erythrosine	the di Sodium salt of 2,4,5,7-tetraiodofluorescein; synthetic 'coal tar' dye	cherry pink to red

E-NUMBERS (cont.)

Colours

Number	Name	Source	Function
128	Red 2G	synthetic 'coal tar' dye and azo[1] dye	red
129	Allura red AC	artificial, an azo[1] dye	red (prohibited throughout EC)
E131	Patent blue V	synthetic 'coal tar' dye	dark bluish-violet; diagnostic agent
E132	Indigo carmine	synthetic 'coal tar' dye	blue; diagnostic agent
133	Brilliant blue FCF	synthetic 'coal tar' dye	blue, green hues when used with tartrazine
E140	Chlorophyll	green pigment in leaf cells	olive to dark green
E141	copper complexes of Chlorphyll and Chlorophyllins	from Chlorophyll by substituting the magnesium ion with copper; by processing Chlorophyll extracts and adding copper	olive green; green
E142	Green S	synthetic 'coal tar' dye	green
E150	Caramel colour	sugar	brown to black
E151	Black PN	synthetic 'coal tar' dye and azo[1] dye	black
E153	Carbon black	animal charcoal, furnace black, lampblack, activated charcoal; laboratory preparation	black
154	Brown FK	synthetic mixture of six azo[1] dyes and sodium chloride and/or sodium sulphate	brown
155	Brown HT	synthetic 'coal tar' dye and azo[1] dye	brown
E160(a)	Alpha-carotene, beta-carotene, gamma-carotene	plant pigment, (especially in carrots, green leafy vegetables, tomatoes, apricots, rosehips and oranges)	orange-yellow; becomes vitamin A in the body
E160(b)	Annatto, Bixin, Norbixin	from the pericarp (seed coat) of the tropical Annatto tree (*Bixa orellana*)	yellow to peach or red
E160(c)	Capsanthin	from the fruit pods and seeds of the Red Pepper (*Capsicum annum*)	red to orange
E160(d)	Lycopene	tomatoes	red
E160(e)	beta-apo-8'-carotenal	synthesized pigments	orange to yellowish-red
E160(f)	Ethyl ester of beta-apo-8'-carotenoic acid	synthesized pigments	orange to yellow

E-NUMBERS (cont.)

Colours

Number	Name	Source	Function
E161(a)	Xanthophylls Flavoxanthin	alpha-, beta-, and gamma-carotenes (not commercially available)	yellow
E161(b)	Xanthophylls Lutein	plant pigment related to carotene	yellow to reddish
E161(c)	Xanthophylls Cryptoxanthin	petals and berries of the Bladder Cherry or Cape Gooseberry (*Physalis*) genus; potato and tomato family (*Solanceae*); orange rind; egg yolk; butter; (not commercially available)	yellow
E161(d)	Xanthophylls Rubixanthin	plant pigment related to carotene (rosehips) (not commercially available)	yellow
E161(e)	Xanthophylls Violoxanthin	carotene, especially from yellow pansies (*viola tricolor*) (not commercially available)	yellow
E161(f)	Xanthophylls Rhodoxanthin	carotenoid pigment; (seeds of yew tree (*Taxus baccata*)) (not commercially available)	yellow
E161(g)	Xanthophylls Canthaxanthin	carotenoid pigment (some mushrooms; various crustacea; fish; flamingo feathers); also synthesized commercially	orange
E162	Beetroot red	beetroot	deep purplish-red
E163	Anthocyanins	plant cell sap (grape skin, red cabbage)	red, blue, violet
E170	Calcium carbonate	naturally occurring white mineral	alkali for deacidification of wine; firming agent; releasing agent; calcium supplements; surface food colour
E171	Titanium dioxide	from naturally occurring mineral ileminte	white; increases opacity
E172	Iron oxides, iron hydroxides	natural iron pigments	yellow, red, orange, brown, black
E173	Aluminium	naturally occurring, from bauxite	metallic surface colour
E174	Silver	naturally occurring metal	metallic surface colour
E175	Gold	naturally occurring metal	metallic surface colour
E180	Pigment Rubine	synthetic, an azo[1] dye	reddish

E-NUMBERS (cont.)

Preservatives

Number	Name	Source	Function
E200	Sorbic acid	some fruits; berries of mountain ash (*Sorbus aucuparia*); synthetically manufactured from ketene	preservative
E201	Sodium sorbate	neutralization of sorbic acid	preservative
E202	Potassium sorbate	neutralization of sorbic acid with potassium hydroxide	antifungal and antibacterial preservative
E203	Calcium sorbate	neutralization of sorbic acid	antifungal and antibacterial preservative
E210	Benzoic acid	berries, fruits, vegetables; chemical synthesis	antifungal and antibacterial preservative (in an acid medium only)
E211	Sodium benzoate	sodium salt of benzoic acid	antifungal and antibacterial preservative (in a slightly acid medium only)
E212	Potassium benzoate	potassium salt of benzoic acid	antifungal and antibacterial preservative
E213	Calcium benzoate	calcium salt of benzoic acid	antifungal and antibacterial preservative
E214	Ethyl 4-hydroxybenzoate	benzoic acid	antifungal and antibacterial preservative
E215	Ethyl 4-hydrozybenzoate, sodium salt	benzoic acid	antifungal and antibacterial preservative
E216	Propyl 4-hydroxybenzoate	benzoic acid	antimicrobial preservative
E217	Propyl 4-hydroxybenzoate, sodium salt	benzoic acid	antimicrobial preservative
E218	Methyl 4-hydroxybenzoate	synthetic	antimicrobial preservative
E219	Methyl 4-hydroxybenzoate, sodium salt	benzoic acid	preservative, active against fungi and yeasts, less active against bacteria
E220	Sulphur dioxide	natural; chemical production by combustion of sulphur or gypsum	preservative; bleaching agent; improving agent; stabilizer; antioxidant; used in beer and wine making
E221	Sodium sulphite	sodium salt of sulphurous acid	antimicrobial preservative; sterilizer; prevents discoloration
E222	Sodium hydrogen sulphite	sodium salt of sulphurous acid	preservative for alcoholic beverages
E223	Sodium metabisulphite	sodium salt of sulphurous acid (commercially manufactured)	antimicrobial preservative; antioxidant; bleaching agent

E-NUMBERS (cont.)

Preservatives

Number	Name	Source	Function
E224	Potassium metabisulphite	sodium salt of sulphurous acid (commercially manufactured)	antimicrobial preservative; antibrowning agent
E226	Calcium sulphite	calcium salt of sulphurous acid	preservative; firming agent; disinfectant
E227	Calcium hydrogen sulphite	calcium salt of sulphurous acid	preservative; firming agent; used in washing beer casks and to prevent secondary fermentation
E230	Biphenyl	synthetic, from benzene	fungistatic agent; acts against *Penicillium*
E231	2-Hydroxybiphenyl	phenyl ether or dibenzofuran	antibacterial and antifungal preservative
E232	Sodium biphenyl-2-yl oxide	synthetic	antifungal (alternative to E231)
E233	2 (Thiazol-4-yl) benzimidazole	reaction of 4-thiazolecarboxamide with O-phenylenediamine in polyphosphoric acid	fungicide; treatment of nematode worms in man
234	Nisin	produced by growth of bacterium *Streptococcus lactis*	preservative
E236	Formic acid	ants	antibacterial preservative; flavour adjunct (prohibited in UK)
E237	Sodium formate	sodium salt from formic acid	preservative (prohibited in UK)
E238	Calcium formate	calcium salt of formic acid	preservative (prohibited in UK)
E239	Hexamine	formaldehyde and ammonia	antimicrobial preservative
E249	Potassium nitrate	potassium salt of nitrous acid	meat preservative; curing agent; prevents growth of *Clostridium botulinum* (the bacterium responsible for botulism)
E250	Sodium nitrate	chemical or bacterial action on sodium nitrate	food preservative; prevents growth of *Clostridium botulinum*; salt curing agent; red meat colour
E251	Sodium nitrate	naturally occurring mineral	preservative; salt curing agent; colour fixative
E252	Potassium nitrate	naturally occurring mineral	preservative; salt curing agent; colour fixative
E260	Acetic acid	methanol and carbon monoxide; from ethanol by oxidation	antibacterial preservative; food acidity stabilizer; colour diluent; flavouring agent

E-NUMBERS (cont.)

Preservatives

Number	Name	Source	Function
E261	Potassium acetate	potassium salt of acetic acid	preservative of natural colour; neutralizing agent; acidity regulator
E262	Sodium hydrogen diacetate	'bound' compound of sodium acetate and acetic acid	antimicrobial preservative; acidity regulator; sequestrant
262	Sodium acetate	sodium salt of acetic acid	buffer
E263	Calcium acetate	calcium salt of acetic acid	antimould agent; anti rope (development of sticky yellow patches in bread) agent; sequestrant;firming agent; stabilizer; buffer
E270	Lactic acid	naturally occurring in milk, molasses, apples and other fruit, tomato juice, some seeds; produced by the heating and fermenting of carbohydrates (whey, corn-starch, potatoes or molasses)	food preservative; increases antioxidant effect of other substances; acid and flavouring
E280	Propionic acid	naturally occurring fatty acid: foods and dairy products; commercially produced from ethylene, carbon monoxide and steam or by oxidation of proprionaldehyde; natural gas; fermented wood pulp waste liquor	antifungal food preservative
E281	Sodium propionate	sodium salt of propionic acid	antimicrobial preservative
E282	Calcium propionate	naturally occurring in Swiss cheese; propionic acid	antimicrobial preservative
E283	Potassium propionate	potassium salt of propionic acid	antimould preservative (especially of 'rope' micro-organisms in bread)
E290	Carbon dioxide	natural gas; fermentation; action of acid on a carbonate	preservative; coolant; freezant (liquid form); packaging gas; aerator
296	Malic acid	green apples, pears, redcurrants, potatoes; metabolite in all living cells; chemical synthesis	acid, flavouring
297	Fumaric acid	natural organic acid in cells; Common Fumitory (*Fumaria officinalis*), edible toadstool (*Boletus scaber*) and fungus (*Fomes igniarius*); fermentation of glucose	acidifier, raising agent, antioxidant

E-NUMBERS (cont.)

Antioxidants

Number	Name	Source	Function
E300	L-Ascorbic acid	naturally occurring in many fruits and vegetables; biological synthesis, various methods	Vitamin C; antibrowning agent; flour improving agent; meat colour preservative; antioxidant
E301	Sodium L-ascorbate	sodium salt of ascorbic acid (synthetic preparation)	Vitamin C; antioxidant; colour preservative
E302	Calcium L-ascorbate	synthetic preparation	Vitamin C; antioxidant; meat colour preservative
E304	6-0-Palmitoyl-L-ascorbic acid	ascorbic acid ester	same function as Vitamin C; antioxidant; colour preservative; antibrowning agent
E306	Extracts of natural origin rich in tocopherols	soya bean oil, wheat germ, rice germ, cottonseed, maize and green leaves	Vitamin E; antioxidant
E307	Synthetic alpha-tocopherol	synthetic	Vitamin E; antioxidant
E308	Synthetic gamma-tocopherol	synthetic	Vitamin E; antioxidant
E309	Synthetic delta-tocopherol	synthetic	Vitamin E; antioxidant
E310	Propyl gallate	propyl ester of gallic acid	antioxidant in oils and fats
E311	Octyl gallate	ester of gallic acid	antioxidant
E312	Dodecyl gallate	ester of gallic acid	antioxidant
E320	Butylated hydroxyanisole	mixture of 2- and 3-tert-butyl-4-methoxyphenol	antioxidant
E321	Butylated hydroxytoluene	synthetic	antioxidant

Emulsifiers, stabilizers and others

Number	Name	Source	Function
E322	Lecithins	animal and vegetable foodstuffs (soya beans), egg yolk, leguminous seeds	emulsifier
E325	Sodium lactate	sodium salt of lactic acid	humectant; glycerol substitute; increases antioxidant effect of other substances; bodying agent
E326	Potassium lactate	potassium salt of lactic acid	increases antioxidant effect of other substances; buffer
E327	Calcium lactate	calcium salt of lactic acid	antioxidant; buffer; firming agent; fruit and vegetable colour preservative; powdered and condensed milk improver; yeast food; dough conditioner

E-NUMBERS (cont.)

Emulsifiers, stabilizers and others

Number	Name	Source	Function
E330	Citric acid	citrus juices and ripe fruits; fermentation of molasses	enhances effects of antioxidants; fruit colour preservative; retains Vitamin C; acidity stabilizer; sequestrant; flavouring; setting agent
E331(a)	Sodium dihydrogen citrate	*mono* Sodium salt of citric acid in the anhydrous or monohydrate form	enhances effects of antioxidants; acidity-controlling and carbonation-retaining buffer; emulsifying salt; sequestrant; prevents curds forming and cream clotting in aerosols
E331(b)	*di* Sodium citrate	Sodium salt of citric acid	antioxidant; enhances effects of antioxidants; buffer; emulsifying salt
E331(c)	*tri* Sodium citrate	*tri* Sodium salt of citric acid in anhydrous, dihydrate or pentahydrate form	antioxidant; buffer; emulsifying salt; sequestrant; stabilizer; used with polyphosphates and flavours to inject into chickens before freezing
E332	Potassium dihydrogen citrate	anhydrous *mono* Potassium salt of citric acid	buffer; emulsifying salt; yeast food
E332	*tri* Potassium citrate	potassium salt of citric acid	antioxidant; buffer in confectionery and artificially sweetened jellies and preserves; emulsifying salt; sequestrant
E333	*mono-, di-,* and *tri*Calcium citrate	monohydrated *mono* Calcium, trihydrated *di* Calcium and tetrahydrated *tri* Calcium salts of citric acid	buffers to neutralize acids in jams, jellies and confectionery; firming agents; emulsifying salts; sequestrants; flour improvers
E334	L-(+)-Tartaric acid	fruit acid (grapes)	antioxidant; enhances effects of antioxidants; acidity adjuster; sequestrant; food colour diluent; flavouring; acid
E335	*mono* Sodium L-(+)-tartrate and *di* Sodium L-(+)-tartrate	monohydrated monosodium salt and dihydrated disodium salt of tartaric acid	antioxidant; enhances effects of antioxidants; buffer; emulsifying salt; sequestrant

E-NUMBERS (cont.)

Emulsifiers, stabilizers and others

Number	Name	Source	Function
E336	*mono* Potassium L-(+)-tartrate	anhydrous monopotassium salt of L-(+)-tartaric acid	(cream of tartar); acid; buffer; emulsifying salt; raising agent for flour, used with sodium bicarbonate; inverting agent for sugar
E336	*di* Potassium L-(+)- tartrate	*di* Potassium salt of L-(+)-tartaric acid	antioxidant; enhances effects of antioxidants; buffer; emulsifying salt
E337	Potassium sodium L-(+)-tartrate	derivative of L-(+)-tartaric acid; commercially available in the form of potassium sodium tartrate	buffer for confectionery and preserves: emulsifying salt; stabilizer; enhances effects of antioxidants
E338	Orthophosphoric acid	from phosphate ore	enhances effects of antioxidants; acidulant; flavouring agent; acidifier in cheese and beer production; sequestrant
E339	Sodium dihydrogen orthophosphate	phosphoric acid	texture improver; speeds brine penetration; enhances effects of antioxidants; buffer; nutrient; gelling agent; stabilizer; sugar clarifying agent
E340(a)	Potassium dihydrogen orthophosphate	phosphoric acid	buffer; sequestrant; emulsifying salt; enhances effects of antioxidants
E340(b)	*di* Potassium hydrogen orthophosphate	*di* Potassium salt of phosphoric acid	buffer; emulsifying salt; enhances effects of antioxidants; yeast food; sequestrant
E340(c)	*tri* Potassium orthophosphate	*tri* Potassium salt of phosphoric acid	emulsifying salt; enhances effects of antioxidants; buffer; sequestrant
E341(a)	Calcium tetrahydrogen diorthophosphate	naturally occurring calcium phosphate; phosphoric acid	bakery improving agent; firming agent; sequestrant; yeast food; aerator-acidulant; enhances effects of antioxidants; texturizer
E341(b)	Calcium hydrogen orthophosphate	phosphoric acid	firming agent; yeast food; nutrient mineral supplement; enhances effects of antioxidants; animal feed supplement; abrasive in toothpaste; dough conditioner

E-NUMBERS (cont.)

Emulsifiers, stabilizers and others

Number	Name	Source	Function
E341(c)	*tri* Calcium *di* orthophosphate	calcium phosphate	anti-caking agent; nutrient yeast food; vegetable extract diluent; clarifying agent
350	Sodium malate	sodium salt of malic acid	buffer; seasoning agent
350	Sodium hydrogen malate	sodium salt of malic acid	buffer
351	Potassium malate	potassium salt of malic acid	buffer
352	Calcium malate	calcium salt of malic acid	buffer; firming agent; seasoning agent
352	Calcium hydrogen malate	calcium salt of malic acid	firming agent
353	Metatartaric acid	tartaric acid	sequestrant (wine)
355	Adipic acid	organic acid in living cells (beet juice); cyclohexanol oxidized with nitric acid (synthetic preparation)	
363	Succinic acid	naturally occurring in fossils, fungi and lichens; acetic acid	acid; buffer; neutralizing agent
370	1,4-Heptonolactone	hydroxycarboxylic acid	acid; sequestrant
375	Nicotinic acid	naturally occurring in yeast, liver, legumes, rice polishings and lean meats; nicotine oxidized with nitric acid	B vitamin; colour protector
380	*tri* Ammonium citrate	salt of citric acid	buffer; emulsifying salt; softening agent
381	Ammonium ferric citrate	citric acid	dietary iron supplement; raises red blood cell level
381	Ammonium ferric citrate, green	citric acid	dietary iron supplement
385	Calcium disodium ethylenediamine-NNN'N' tetra-acetate (EDTA)	synthetic preparation	chelating agent; antioxidant
E400	Alginic acid	brown seaweeds (*Laminaria, Macrocystis, Ascophyllum*)	alginate production
E401	Sodium alginate	sodium salt of alginic acid	stabilizer; suspending agent; thickening agent; gelling agent (with a source of calcium); copper fining agent in brewing

E-NUMBERS (cont.)

Emulsifiers, stabilizers and others

Number	Name	Source	Function
E402	Potassium alginate	potassium salt of alginic acid	emulsifier; stabilizer; boiled water additive; gelling agent
E403	Ammonium alginate	ammonium salt of alginic acid	emulsifier; stabilizer; colour diluent; thickener
E404	Calcium alginate	calcium salt of alginic acid	emulsifier; stabilizer; thickener; gelling agent
E405	Propane-1,2-diol alginate	propylene ester of alginic acid	emulsifier; stabilizer; thickener; solvent; foam stabilizing agent
E406	Agar	red seaweeds (*Gelidium amansii* and Gelidiaceae family)	thickener; stabilizer; gelling agent; humectant; copper fining agent in brewing
E407	Carrageenan	red seaweeds (*Chondrus crispus* and *Gigartina*)	stabilizer; thickener; suspending and gelling agent; texture modifier
E410	Locust or Carob bean gum	Locust or Carob tree (*Ceratonia siliqua*)	gelling agent; stabilizer; emulsifier; thickening agent; texture modifier
E412	Guar gum	*Cyamopsis tetragonolobus* or *C. psoraloides* (members of the pea family)	thickening agent; emulsion stabilizer; suspending agent; dietary bulking agent; helps diabetics control blood sugar levels
E413	Tragacanth	*Astragalus gummifer* (member of the pea family)	emulsifier; stabilizer; thickener; prevents crystallization of sugar; converts royal icing to a paste
E414	Gum arabic	*Acacia senegal* (member of the pea family)	retards sugar crystallization; thickener; converts royal icing to a paste; emulsifier; stabilizer; glazing agent; copper fining agent in brewing
E415	Xanthan gum	carbohydrate fermentation	stabilizer; thickener; emulsifier; 'pseudoplasticizer' to improve pouring; gelling agent (with guar gum)
416	Karaya gum	*Sterculia urens* trees	stabilizer; emulsifier; thickener; binding agent in meat products; prevents formation of ice crystals; filling agent; citrus and spice flavouring agent

E-NUMBERS (cont.)

Emulsifiers, stabilizers and others

Number	Name	Source	Function
E420	Sorbitol syrup	Mountain ash (*Sorbus aucuparia*) fruits, cherries, pears, plums, apples; seaweeds, other algae	sweetening agent; glycerol substitute; retards crystallization; masks taste of saccharin; texturizing agent; humectant; stabilizer
E421	Mannitol	coniferous trees; seaweed; Manna ash (*Fraxinus ornus*); hydrogenation of invert sugar	texturizing agent; dietary supplement; humectant; sweetener; anti-caking agent; anti-sticking agent
E422	Glycerol	naturally occurring in plant cells; sugar fermentation; propylene	solvent; humectant; sweetener; bodying agent (with gelatins and gums); plasticizer
430	Polyoxyethylene (8) stearate	stearate and ethylene oxide mixture	emulsifier; stabilizer
431	Polyoxyethylene (40) stearate	stearate and ethylene oxide mixture	emulsifier; makes bread 'feel fresh'
432	Polyoxyethylene (20) sorbitan monolaurate	sorbitol and ethylene oxide	emulsifier; stabilizer; dispersing agent
433	Polyoxyethylene (20) sorbitan mono-oleate	sorbitol and ethylene oxide	emulsifier; de-foamer; preserves moistness; prevents oil leaking from artificial whipped cream; solubility improver
434	Polyoxyethylene (20) sorbitan monopalmitate	sorbitol and ethylene oxide	emulsifier; stabilizer; dispersing agent (flavours); defoaming agent; wetting agent
435	Polyoxyethylene (20) sorbitan monostearate	sorbital and ethylene oxide	emulsifier; stabilizer; prevents leakage of oils; preserves moistness; wetting and dispersing agent; prevents greasy taste; foaming agent
436	Polyoxyethylene (20) sorbitan tristearate	sorbitol and ethylene oxide	emulsifier; prevents leakage of oils and water; preserves moistness; wetting and solution agent; defoaming agent; flavour dispersing agent
E440(a)	Pectin	ripe fruits	emulsifying and gelling agent in acid media; bodying agent; syrups; stabilizer
E440(b)	Amidated pectin	pectin treated with ammonia	emulsifier; stablizer; gelling agent; thickener

E-NUMBERS (cont.)

Emulsifiers, stabilizers and others

Number	Name	Source	Function
442	Ammonium phosphatides	synthetic preparation	stabilizer; emulsifier
E450(a)	*di* Sodium dihydrogen diphosphate	sodium salt of pyrophosphoric acid	buffer; sequestrant; emulsifier; raising agent (with sodium bicarbonate); colour improver; chelating agent
E450(a)	*tri* Sodium diphosphate	sodium salt of pyrophosphoric aid	buffer; sequestrant; emulsifier; colour improver; chelating agent
E450(a)	*tetra* Sodium diphosphate	sodium salt of pyrophosphoric acid	buffer; emulsifying salt; sequestrant; gelling agent; stabilizer; hydration aid
E450(a)	*tetra* Potassium diphosphate	potassium salt of pyrophosphoric acid	emulsifying salt; buffer; sequestrant; stabilizer
E450(b)	*penta* Sodium triphosphate	sodium salt of triphosphoric acid	emulsifying salt; texturizer; buffer; sequestrant; stabilizer; water-binding agent; protein solubilization agent
E450(b)	*penta* Potassium triphosphate	potassium salt of triphosphoric acid	emulsifying salt; texturizer; buffer; sequestrant; stabilizer
E450(c)	Sodium polyphosphates	sodium salts of polyphosphoric acids	emulsifying salts; sequestrants; stabilizers; texturizers
E450(c)	Potassium polyphosphates	potassium salts of polyphosphoric aids	emulsifying salts; stabilizers; sequestrants
E460	Microcrystalline cellulose	plant fibres	bulking agent; binder; anti-caking agent; dietary fibre; hydration aid; emulsion stabilizer; heat stabilizer; alternative ingredient; tablet binder and disintegrant; quickdrying carrier and dispersant; cellulose component; texture modifier
E460	Alpha-cellulose	plant cells	bulking aid; anti-caking agent; binder; dispersant; thickening agent; filter aid; assists isinglass finings in brewing
E461	Methylcellulose	cellulose	emulsifier; stabilizer; thickener; bulking agent; binding agent; film former; water-soluble gum substitute; useful in sugar-and gluten-free diets; fat barrier

E-NUMBERS (cont.)

Emulsifiers, stabilizers and others

Number	Name	Source	Function
E463	Hydroxypropyl-cellulose	cellulose (synthetic preparation)	stabilizer; emulsifier; thickener; suspending agent
E464	Hydroxypropyl-methylcellulose	cellulose	gelling or suspending agent; emulsifier; stabilizer and thickening agent; fat barrier
E465	Ethylmethylcellulose	cellulose	emulsifier; foam stabilizer; thickener; suspending agent
E466	Carboxymethyl-cellulose, sodium salt	cellulose	thickening agent; texture modifier; stabilizer; moisture migration controller; gelling agent; bulking agent; prevents crystal growth and syneresis (drawing together of particles in a gel); decreases fat absorption; foam stabilizer
E470	Sodium, potassium and calcium salts of fatty acids	fatty acids	emulsifiers; stabilizers; anti-caking agents
E471	Mono- and di-glycerides of fatty acids	naturally occurring product of digestion; glycerin and fatty acids	retains foaming power of egg protein in presence of fat (in cakes); emulsifier; stabilizer; thickening agent
E472(a)	Acetic acid esters of mono- and di-glycerides of fatty acids	esters of glycerol and acetic acid	emulsifiers; stabilizers; coating agents; texture modifiers; solvents; lubricants
E472(b)	Lactic acid esters of mono- and di-glycerides of fatty acids	esters of glycerol and lactic acid	emulsifiers; stabilizers
E472(c)	Citric acid esters of mono- and di-glycerides of fatty acids	esters of glycerol and citric acid	emulsifiers; stabilizers
E472(d)	Tartaric acid esters of mono- and di-glycerides of fatty acids	esters of glycerol and tartaric acid	emulsifiers; stabilizers
E472(e)	Mono- and di-acetyltartaric acid esters of mono- and di-glycerides of fatty acids	esters of glycerol and tartaric acid	emulsifiers; stabilizers

E-NUMBERS (cont.)

Emulsifiers, stabilizers and others

Number	Name	Source	Function
E473	Sucrose esters of fatty acids	esters of glycerol and sucrose	emulsifiers; stabilizers
E474	Sucroglycerides	action of sucrose on natural triglycerides (lard, tallow, palm oil, etc)	emulsifiers; stabilizers
E475	Polyglycerol esters of fatty acids	laboratory preparation	emulsifiers; stabilizers
476	Polyglycerol esters of polycondensed fatty acids of castor oil	castor oil and glycerol esters	emulsifiers; stabilizers; improves chocolate fluidity (with lecithin) for coating
E477	Propane-1,2-diol esters of fatty acids	propylene glycol	emulsifiers; stabilizers
478	Lactylated fatty acid esters of glycerol and propane-1,2-diol	esters of glycerol and lactic acid	emulsifiers; stabilizers; whipping agents; plasticizers; surface-active agents
E481	Sodium stearoyl-2 lactylate	lactic acid	emulsifier; stabilizer
E482	Calcium stearoyl-2-lactylate	lactic acid	emulsifier; stabilizer; whipping aid
E483	Stearyl tartrate	tartaric acid	emulsifier; stabilizer; flour improver
491	Sorbitan monostearate	stearic acid and sorbitol (synthetic preparation)	emulsifier; stabilizer; glazing agent
492	Sorbitan tristearate	stearic acid (synthetic preparation)	emulsifier; stabilizer
493	Sorbitan monolaurate	sorbitol and lauric acid	emulsifier; stabilizer; antifoaming agent
494	Sorbitan mono-oleate	sorbitol and oleic acid	emulsifier; stabilizer
495	Sorbitan monopalmitate	sorbitol and palmitic acid	oil-soluble emulsifier; stabilizer
500	Sodium carbonate	naturally occurring; sea or saline lake water	base; removal of testinic acid in brewing
500	Sodium hydrogen carbonate	synthetic preparation	base; aerating agent; diluent
500	Sodium sesquicarbonate	naturally occurring in saline residues; commercial preparation	base
501	Potassium carbonate and potassium hydrogen carbonate	potassium carbonate and carbon dioxide	base; alkali

E-NUMBERS (cont.)

Emulsifiers, stabilizers and others

Number	Name	Source	Function
503	Ammonium carbonate	ammonium sulphate and calcium carbonate	buffer; neutralizing agent; raising agent
503	Ammonium hydrogen carbonae	carbon dioxide passed through ammonia water	alkali; buffer; aerating agent; raising agent
504	Magnesium carbonate	naturally occurring; magnesium sulphate and sodium carbonate	alkali; anti-caking agent; acidity regulator; anti-bleaching agent
507	Hydrochloric acid	naturally occurring in the stomach; sodium chloride and sulphuric acid	acid; for consistent quality in beer
508	Potassium chloride	naturally occurring	gelling agent; salt substitute; dietary supplement
509	Calcium chloride	salt brines; by-product of Solvay process	sequestrant; firming agent; for consistent quality in beer
510	Ammonium chloride	synthetic preparation	yeast food; flavour
513	Sulphuric acid	commercial preparation by 'contact' or 'Chamber' process	acid; for consistent quality in beer
514	Sodium sulphate	naturally occurring as thenardite and mirabilite	diluent; for consistent quality in beer
515	Potassium sulphate	naturally occurring as a triple sulphate of potassium, magnesium and calcium	
516	Calcium sulphate	naturally occurring mineral	firming agent; sequestrant; nutrient; yeast food; inert excipient; for consistent quality in beer
518	Magnesium sulphate	naturally occurring in sea and mineral waters	dietary supplement; firming agent; used in beer-making
524	Sodium hydroxide	brine; sodium carbonate and lime	
525	Potassium hydroxide	potassium chloride	base; oxidizing agent (black olives)
526	Calcium hydroxide	lime	firming agent; neutralizing agent; removes testinic acid and assures consistent quality in beer making
527	Ammonium hydroxide	ammonia gas	food colouring diluent and solvent; alkali
528	Magnesium hydroxide	naturally occurring mineral (periclase); magnesite ores	alkali
529	Calcium oxide	limestone	alkali; nutrient

E-NUMBERS (cont.)

Emulsifiers, stabilizers and others

Number	Name	Source	Function
530	Magnesium oxide	naturally occurring mineral; magnesite ores	anti-caking agent; alkali
535	Sodium ferrocyanide	synthetic manufacture	anti-caking agent; crystal modifier
536	Potassium ferrocyanide	coal gas purification by-product	anti-caking agent; metals removal in wine making ('blue finings')
540	*di* Calcium diphosphate	naturally occurring mineral (monetite); synthetic preparation	neutralizing agent; dietary supplement; buffering agent; yeast food; mineral supplement (little used in UK)
541	Sodium aluminium phosphate	phosphoric acid	aerator acidulant (raising agent)
541	Sodium aluminium phosphate, basic	phosphoric acid	emulsifying salt
542	Edible bone phosphate	animal bones	anti-caking agent; mineral supplement; tablet filler
544	Calcium polyphosphates	calcium salts of polyphosphoric acids	emulsifying salts; mineral supplements; calcium source; firming agents (not used in UK)
545	Ammonium polyphosphates	ammonium salts of polyphosphoric acids	emulsifiers; emulsifying salts; sequestrants; yeast foods; stabilizers

Anti-caking agents

Number	Name	Source	Function
551	Silicon dioxide	naturally occurring mineral	suspending agent; anti-caking agent; thickener; stabilizer; assists isinglass finings in clearing beer
552	Calcium silicate	naturally occurring as wollastonite; lime and diatomaceous earth	anti-caking agent; antacid (pharmacology); glazing, polishing and release agent (sweets); dusting agent (chewing gum); coating agent (rice); suspending agent
553(a)	Magnesium silicate, synthetic and Magnesium trisilicate	magnesium oxide and silicon dioxide (synthetic compound); sodium silicate and magnesium sulphate; Magnesium trisilicate is a naturally occurring mineral (meerschaum, parasepiolite, sepiolite)	anti-caking agent; tablet excipient; antacid (pharmacology); glazing, polishing and release agent (sweets); dusting agent (chewing gum); coating agent (rice)

E-NUMBERS (cont.)

Anti-caking agents

Number	Name	Source	Function
553(b)	Talc	naturally occurring mineral	release agent; anti-caking agent; chewing gum component; filtering aid; dusting powder
554	Aluminium sodium silicate	naturally occurring mineral (analcite, natrolite); quartz; gibbsite	anti-caking agent
556	Aluminium calcium silicate	naturally occuring as scolecite and heulandite	anti-caking agent
558	Bentonite	naturally occurring clay deposit	anti-caking agent; clarifying agent; filtration aid; emulsifier; suspending agent
559	Kaolin, heavy, and Kaolin, light	naturally occurring altered mineral in granite	anti-caking agent; clarifying agent
570	Stearic acid	naturally occurring fatty acid (animal fats and vegetable oils); synthetic preparation	anti-caking agent
572	Magnesium stearate	stearic acid (synthetic preparation)	anti-caking agent; emulsifier; release agent
575	D-Glucono-1,5-lactone	glucose	acid; sequestrant; prevents formation of milkstone (magnesium, calcium phosphate deposits) and beerstone
576	Sodium gluconate	sodium salt of gluconic acid (synthetic preparation)	sequestrant; dietary supplement
577	Potassium gluconate	potassium salt of gluconic acid (synthetic preparation)	sequestrant
578	Calcium gluconate	calcium salt from gluconic acid (synthetic preparation)	buffer; firming agent; sequestrant

Flavour enhancers

Number	Name	Source	Function
620	L-Glutamic acid	naturally occurring amino acid; carbohydrate fermentation	dietary supplement flavour enhancer; salt substitute
621	*mono* Sodium glutamate	sodium salt of glutamic acid	flavour enhancer
622	Potassium hydrogen L-glutamate	synthetic preparation	flavour enhancer; salt substitute
623	Calcium dihydrogen di-L-glutamate	synthetic preparation	flavour enhancer; salt substitute

E-NUMBERS (cont.)

Flavour enhancers

Number	Name	Source	Function
627	Guanosine 5'-(*di* Sodium phosphate)	sodium salt of 5'guanylic acid (synthetic preparation)	flavour enhancer
631	Inosine 5'-(*di* Sodium phosphate)	disodium salt of inosinic acid (meat extract and dried sardines)	flavour enhancer
635	Sodium 5'-ribonucleotide	*di* Sodium guanylate and *di* sodium inosinate mixture	flavour enhancer
636	Maltol	naturally occurring (young larch tree bark, pine needles, chicory wood, tars, oils, roasted malt); streptomycin salt (chemical preparation)	flavouring agent ('freshly baked'); synthetic coffee, fruit, maple, nut and vanilla flavours
637	Ethyl maltol	maltol (chemical preparation)	sweet taste flavouring; flavour enhancer
900	Dimethyl-polysiloxane	dimethylpolysiloxane and silicon gel or silicon dioxide	water repellent; anti-foaming agent; chewing gum base; anti-caking agent; used in beer making

Glazing agents

Number	Name	Source	Function
901	Beeswax, white, and Beeswax, yellow	naturally occurring (bee honeycomb)	glazing and polishing agent; release agent; fruit and honey flavourings
903	Carnauba wax	Brazilian wax palm (*Copernica cerifera*) leaves	glazing and polishing agent (sugar confectionery); enhances hardness and lustre of other waxes; used in cosmetic materials
904	Shellac	lac insect (*Laccifer lacca*) resin	glazing agent and polish up to 0.4 per cent.
905	Mineral hydrocarbons	petroleum distillates	polishes, glazing agents, sealing agents; chewing gum ingredient; defoaming agent; coating for fresh fruit and vegetables; lubricant and binder for capsules and tablets; lubricant in food-processing equipment and meat-packing plants

E-NUMBERS (cont.)

Glazing agents

Number	Name	Source	Function
907	Refined microcrystalline wax	petroleum	chewing gum ingredient; polishing and release agent; stiffening agent; tablet coating

Improving agents

Number	Name	Source	Function
920	L-cysteine hydrochloride and L-cysteine hydrochloride monohydrate	L-cysteine, a naturally occurring amino acid (animal hair and chicken feathers)	flour improving agent; flavouring (chicken); used in shampoo
924	Potassium bromate	synthetic preparation	flour-maturing or -improving agent; used in beer making
925	Chlorine	naturally occurring gas (earth's crust, seawater)	flour bleaching; drinking water
926	Chlorine dioxide	(synthetic preparation) chlorine and sodium chloride; potassium chlorate and sulphuric acid; nitrogen dioxide passed through sodium chlorate	bleaching agent; improving agent; oxidizing agent; water purifying agent; taste and odour control of water; batericide and antiseptic
927	Azo dicarbonamide	synthetic preparation	flour-improving or maturing agent

[1] Azo dyes are derivatives of azobenzene, obtained as the reaction products of diazonum salts with tertiary amines or phenols (hydroxy-benzenes). Usually coloured yellow, red, or brown, they have acidic or basic properties.

INFECTIOUS DISEASES AND INFECTIONS

Name	Cause	Transmission	Incubation	Symptoms
AIDS (Acquired Immune Deficiency Syndrome)	Human Immuno Deficiency Virus (HIV)	sexual relations, sharing of syringes, blood tranfusion	several years	fever, lethargy, weight loss, diarrhoea, lymph node enlargement, viral and fungal infections
amoebiasis	*Entamoeba histolytica*	organism in contaminated food	up to several years	fever, diarrhoea, exhaustion, rectal bleeding
anthrax	*Bacillus antracis* bacterium	animal hair	1–3 days	small red pimple on hand or face enlarges and discharges pus

INFECTIOUS DISEASES AND INFECTIONS (cont.)

Name	Cause	Transmission	Incubation	Symptoms
appendicitis	usually *E. coli* organism	not transmitted	sudden onset	abdominal pain, which moves from left to right after a few hours, nausea
bilharziasis (schistosomiasis)	*Schistosoma haematobium,* (also called Bilharzia) *S.mansoni* or *S.japonicum*	certain snails living in calm water	varies with lifespan of parasite	fever, muscle aches, abdominal pain, headaches
bronchiolitis (babies only)	respiratory syncytical virus (RSV)	droplet infection	1–3 days	blocked or runny nose, irritability
brucellosis	*Brucella abortus* or *B.meliteusis* bacteria	cattle or goats	3–6 days	fever, drenching sweats, weight loss, muscle and joint pains, confusion and poor memory
bubonic plague	*Yersinia pestis* bacterium	fleas	3–6 days	fever, muscle aches, headaches, exhaustion, enlarged lymph glands ('buboes')
chicken pox (varicella)	varicella-zoster virus	droplet infection	14–21 days	blister-like eruptions, lethargy, headaches, sore throat
cholera	*Vibrio cholerae*	contaminated water	a few hours to 5 days	severe diarrhoea, vomiting
common cold (coryza)	Rhinoviruses	droplet infection	1–3 days	blocked or runny nose, sneezing, sore throat, runny eyes
conjunctivitis	virus, bacterium or allergy	variable	variable	if viral, watery discharge from eyes; if bacterial, sticky yellow discharge from eyes
dengue fever (break-bone fever)	B group of arboviruses	mosquito	5–6 days	fever, severe muscle cramps, enlarged lymph nodes
diptheria	*Cornybacterium diptheriae*	droplet infection	4–6 days	grey exudate across throat; swelling of throat tissues may lead to asphyxiation; toxin secreted by bacteria may seriously damage heart

INFECTIOUS DISEASES AND INFECTIONS (cont.)

Name	Cause	Transmission	Incubation	Symptoms
dysentery	*Shigella* genus of bacteria	contaminated food or water	variable, can cause death within 48 hours	diarrhoea, with or without bleeding
gastro-enteritis	bacteria, viruses and food poisoning	droplet infection or food	variable	varying from nausea to severe fever, vomiting and diarrhoea
german measles (rubella)	togavirus	droplet infection	18 days	1–2 days catarrh and sore throat, then red rash, enlargement of lymph nodes
glandular fever (infectious mononucleosis)	Epstein-Barr virus	saliva of infected person	1–6 weeks	sore throat, fever, enlargement of tonsils and lymph nodes, lethargy, depression
gonorrhorea	*Neisseria gonorrhoreae* bacterium	usually sexually transmitted	2–10 days	in men, burning sensation on urination and discharge from urethra; in women (if any), vaginal discharge
hepatitis	hepatitis A, B or C virus	contaminated food or water (type A); sexual relations, sharing syringes, transfusion (type B)	3–6 weeks (type A); up to a few weeks (type B)	often no symptoms, otherwise similar to 'flu, loss of appetite, tenderness below right ribs, jaundice
influenza	influenza A, B or C virus	droplet infection	1–3 days	fever, sweating, muscle aches
kala-azar (leishmaniasis)	parasites genus leishmania	sandfly	usually 1–2 months, can be up to 10 years	lymph gland, spleen and liver enlargement
laryngitis	same viruses that cause colds and 'flu, ie adeno and rhinoviruses	droplet infection	1–3 days	sore throat, coughing, hoarseness
lassa fever	arenavirus	urine	3 weeks	fever, sore throat, muscle aches and pains, haemorrhage into the skin

INFECTIOUS DISEASES AND INFECTIONS (cont.)

Name	Cause	Transmission	Incubation	Symptoms
Legionnaire's disease	*Legionella pneumophila* bacterium	water droplets in infected humidifiers, cooling towers; stagnant water in cisterns and shower heads	1–3 days	'flu and pneumonia-like symtoms, fever, diarrhoea, mental confusion
leprosy	*Mycobacterium leprae* bacterium	droplet infection; minimally contagious	variable	insensitive white patches on skin, nodules, thickening of and damage to nerves
malaria	*Plasmodium falciparium, P.vivax, P.ovale, P.malariae*	anopheline mosquito	several weeks for *P.falciparium*, to several months for *P.vivax*	severe swinging fever, cold sweats, shivers
Marburg (or green monkey) disease	unclassified virus	monkeys, body fluids	5–9 days	fever, diarrhoea, affects brain, kidneys and lungs
measles	paramyxovirus	droplet infection	14 days	fever, severe cold symptoms, bloody red rash
meningitis	various bacteria, viruses or fungi eg *Cryptococcus*	droplet infection	variable	severe headache, stiffness in neck muscles, dislike of the light, nausea, vomiting, confusion
mumps	paramyxovirus	droplet infection	18 days	lethargy, fever, pain at the angle of the jaw; swelling of parotid gland(s)
orchitis	bacterium or virus: if bacterial, urinary infection due to eg gonorrhea, if viral due to eg mumps	*see* cause	variable	painful red and swollen testis, fever, nausea
osteomyelitis	usually staphylococci organisms	infection spreads from eg boil or impetigo	1–10 days	abrupt onset of fever, and pain at site of infected bone (usually tibia or femur)
parotitis	bacterium or virus	common in mumps (viral), may follow severe febrile illness or abdominal operation	1–10 days	inflammation of one or both parotid glands

INFECTIOUS DISEASES AND INFECTIONS (cont.)

Name	Cause	Transmission	Incubation	Symptoms
pericarditis	bacterium or virus eg *Coxsackie B*	infection follows a chest disease or heart attack	variable	inflamed pericardium (fibrous bag which encloses the heart); tight chest pain
peritonitis	usually *E.coli* organism; sometimes chemical irritation	usually appendicitis; perforation of the gut allows escape of barrel contents into peritoneal cavity	1–10 days	severe abdominal pain, vomiting, rigidity, shock
pharyngitis	bacteria or virus	droplet infection	3–5 days	sore throat, fever, pain on swallowing, enlarged neck glands
pneumonia	*Streptococcus pneumoniae* bacterium, *Legionella pneumophila* etc	droplet infection	1–3 weeks	cough, fever, chest pain
poliomyelitis	three types of polio virus	droplet infection and hand to mouth infection from faeces	7–14 days	affects spinal cord and brain; headache, fever, neck and muscle stiffness; may result in meningitis or paralysis
proctitis	fungal infection possible	contact	variable	inflammation of the rectum and anus resulting from thrush, piles or fissures pain on defecation
psittacosis	*Chlamydis psittaci*	infected birds (parrots)	1–2 weeks	pneumonitis, fever, nausea
puerperal fever	infection within uterine cavity or vagina	follows childbirth	1–10 days	fever; often fatal in past, now rare
pylitis	bacteria	kidney infection	1–10 days	fever, rigors, loin pain, burning on passing urine
rabies	virus	bite or lick by infected animal	2–6 weeks	headache, sickness, excitability, fear of drinking water, convulsions, coma and death
river blindness (or onchocerciasis)	*Onchocerca volvulus* worm	bites of infected flies of genus *Simulium*	worms mature in 2–4 months, may live 12 years	worms inhabit skin, causing nodules and sometimes blindness
salpingitis	infection of the Fallopian tubes	usually gonorrhoea	variable	abdominal pain, fever, irregular periods, vaginal discharge

INFECTIOUS DISEASES AND INFECTIONS (cont.)

Name	Cause	Transmission	Incubation	Symptoms
scarlet fever	*haemolytic streptococcus*	droplet infection or streptococci infected milk or ice-cream	2–4 days	sudden onset; headache, sore throat, fever, vomiting, red skin rash
shingles	*Herpes zoster* virus (also causes chickenpox)	dormant virus in body becomes active following a minor infection	variable	pain, numbness, blisters
sinusitis	virus or bacteria	droplet infection; common with a cold	1–3 days	fever, sinus pain, nasal discharge
sleeping sickness (or African trypanosomiasis)	1. *Trypanosoma brucei gambieuse* or 2. *Tb rhodesieuse*	bites by infected tsetse fly	1. weeks-months, 2. 7–14 days	fever, lymph node enlargement, headache, behavioural change, drowsiness, coma, sometimes death
smallpox	variole major or minor virus	now eradicated worldwide	12 days	fever, rash followed by pustules on face and extremities
syphilis	*Treponema pallidum*	sexually transmitted: organism enters bloodstream through a mucous membrane, usually genital skin	ulcer after 2–6 weeks, skin rash after weeks or months	late syphilis damages brain, heart and main blood vessels, and unborn babies
tetanus	*Clostridium tetni*	bacteria from soil infect wounds	2 days–weeks	muscular spasms cause lockjaw and affect breathing, potentially fatal
thrush	*Candida albicans* yeast	the yeast is present on skin of most people and multiplies when resistance to infection is low; during pregnancy or when taking contraceptive pill	variable	white spots on tongue and cheeks; irritant vaginal discharge; rash in genital area or between folds of skin
tonsillitis	usually same viruses responsible for colds; some-times bacterial (streptococci)	droplet infection	1–3 days	red inflamed tonsils, sore throat

INFECTIOUS DISEASES AND INFECTIONS (cont.)

Name	Cause	Transmission	Incubation	Symptoms
trachoma	*Chlamydia trachomatis* organism	poor hygiene: organism infects eye	5 days	conjuctivitis, swelling and scarring in cornea, often leading to blindness
tuberculosis	*Myobacterium tuberculosis bacterium*	inhalation of bacterium from person with active tuberculosis pneumonia or from infected milk	up to several years	cough with bloodstained sputum, weight loss, chest pain
typhoid	*Salmonella typhi* bacillus	contaminated water or food	10–14 days	slow onset of fever, abdominal discomfort, cough, rash, constipation then diarrhoea, delirium, coma, potentially fatal
typhus	*Rickettsiae* parasites	bite by infected flea, tick, mite or louse	7–14 days	fever, rigors, headache, muscular pain, rash
urethritis	virus or bacteria	may occur with cystitis or venereal infection	variable	bloody stools, abdominal pain, burning on urination
whooping cough	*Bordetella pertussis*	droplet infection	7–14 days	severe coughing followed by 'whoop' of respiration
yellow fever	zoonosis virus	mosquitoes infected by monkeys	3–6 days	rigors, high fever, bone pains, headache, nausea, jaundice, kidney failure, coma, potentially fatal

AN A TO Z OF PHOBIAS

Technical term	Everyday term	Technical term	Everyday term	Technical term	Everyday term
acero-	sourness	entomo-	insects	nephelo-	clouds
achulo-	darkness	eoso-	dawn	noso- (patho-)	disease
acro-	heights	eremo-	solitude	ocho-	vehicles
aero-	air	erete-	pins	odonto-	teeth
agora-	open spaces	ereuthro-	blushing	oiko-	home
aichuro-	points	ergo-	work	olfacto-	smell
ailouro-	cats	geno-	sex	omata-	eyes
akoustico-	sound	geuma-	taste	oneiro-	dreams
algo-	pain	grapho-	writing	ophido-	snakes
amaka-	carriages	gymnoto-	nudity	ornitho-	birds
amatho-	dust	gyno-	women	ourano-	heaven
andro-	men	hamartio-	sin	pan- (panto-)	everything
anemo-	wind	hapto-	touch	partheno-	girls
angino-	narrowness	harpaxo-	robbers	patroio-	heredity
anthropo-	man	hedono-	pleasure	penia-	poverty
antlo-	flood	haemato-	blood	phasmo-	ghosts
apeiro-	infinity	helmintho-	worms	phobo-	fears
arachno-	spiders	hodo-	travel	photo-	light
astheno-	weakness	homichlo-	fog	pnigero-	smothering
astra-	astral	horme-	shock	poine-	punishment
ate-	ruin	hydro-	water	poly-	many things
aulo-	flute	hypegia-	responsibility	poto-	drink
Auroro-	Northern Lights	hypno-	sleep	pterono-	feathers
bacillo-	microbes	ideo-	ideas	pyro-	fire
baro-	gravity	kakorraphia-	failure	rypo-	soiling
baso-	walking	karagalo-	ridicule	Satano-	Satan
batracho-	reptiles	keno-	void	sela-	flash
belone-	needles	kineso-	motion	sidero-	stars
bronto-	thunder	klepto-	stealing	sito-	food
cheima-	cold	kopo-	fatigue	sperma- (spermato-)	germs
chiono-	snow	kristallo-	ice	stasi-	standing
chrometo-	money	lalio-	stuttering	stygio- (hade-)	hell
chrono-	duration	linono-	string	syphilo-	syphilis
chrystallo-	crystals	logo-	words	thalasso-	sea
claustra-	closed spaces	lysso- (mania)	insanity	thanato-	death
cnido-	stings	mastigo-	flogging	thasse-	sitting
cometo-	comets	mechano-	machinery	theo-	God
cromo-	colour	metallo-	metals	thermo-	heat
cyno-	dogs	meteoro-	meteors	toxi-	poison
deme-	crowds	miso-	contamination	tremo-	trembling
demono-	demons	mono-	one thing	triskaideka-	thirteen
dermato-	skin	musico-	music	zelo-	jealousy
dike-	injustice	muso-	mice	zoo-	animals
dora-	fur	nekro-	corpses	xeno-	strangers
eisoptro-	mirror	nelo-	glass		
elektro-	electricity	neo-	newness		

AN A TO Z OF PHOBIAS

Everyday term	Technical term	Everyday term	Technical term	Everyday term	Technical term
air	aero-	God	theo-	ruin	ate-
animals	zoo-	gravity	baro-	Satan	Satano-
astral	astra-	heat	thermo-	sea	thalasso-
birds	orthino-	heaven	ourano-	sex	geno-
blood	hemato-	heights	acro-	shock	horme-
blushing	ereutho-	hell	stygio- (hade-)	sin	hamartio-
carriages	amaka-	heredity	patroio-	sitting	thasso-
cats	ailouro-	home	oiko-	skin	dermato-
closed spaces	claustra-	ice	kristallo-	sleep	hypno-
clouds	nephelo-	ideas	ideo-	smell	olfacto-
cold	cheima-	infinity	apeiro-	smothering	pnigero-
colour	cromo-	injustice	dike-	snakes	ophidio-
comets	cometo-	insanity	lysso- (mania-)	snow	chiono-
contamination	miso-	insects	entomo-	soiling	rypo-
corpses	nekro-	jealousy	zelo-	solitude	eremo-
crowds	deme-	light	photo-	sound	akoustico-
crystals	chrystallo-	machinery	mechano-	sourness	acero-
darkness	achluo-	man	anthropo-	spiders	arachno-
dawn	eoso-	many things	poly-	standing	stasi-
death	thanato-	men	andro	stars	sidero-
demons	demono-	metals	metallo-	stealing	klepto-
disease	noso-, patho-	meteors	meteoro-	stings	cnido-
dogs	cyno-	mice	muso-	strangers	xeno-
dreams	oneiro-	microbes	bacilli-	string	linono-
drinks	poto-	mirrors	eisoptro-	stuttering	lalio-
duration	chrono-	money	chrometo-	syphilis	syphilo-
dust	amatho-	motion	kineso-	taste	geuma-
electricity	elektro-	music	musico-	teeth	odonto-
everything	pan- (panto-)	narrowness	angino	thirteen	triskaideka-
eyes	omata-	needles	helone-	thunder	bronto- (tonitro)
failure	kakorrphia-	newness	neo-	touch	hapto-
fatigue	kopo-	Northern Lights	Aurora-	travel	hodo-
fears	phobo-	nudity	gymnoto-	trembling	tremo-
feathers	pterono-	one thing	mono-	vehicles	ocho-
fire	pyro-	open spaces	agora-	void	keno-
flash	sela-	pain	algo-	walking	baso-
flogging	mastigo-	pins	erete-	water	hydro-
flood	antlo-	pleasure	hedono-	weakness	astheno-
flute	aulo-	points	aichuro-	wind	anemo-
fog	homichlo-	poison	toxi-	women	gyno-
food	sito-	poverty	penia-	words	logo-
fur	dora-	punishment	poine-	work	ergo-
germs	sperma- (spermato-)	reptiles	batracho-	worms	helmintho-
ghosts	phasmo-	responsibility	hypegia-	writing	grapho-
girls	partheno-	ridicule	katagalo-		
glass	nelo-	robberies	harpaxo-		

HISTORY

EXPLORATIONS AND DISCOVERIES

Date	Name	Exploration
490 BC	Hanno	Makes voyage round part of the coast of Africa
325 BC	Alexander the Great	Leads fleet along the N Indian coast and up the Persian Gulf
84 AD	Agricola	His fleet circumnavigates Britain
1003	Leif Ericsson	Voyages to N America and discovers 'Vinland' (possibly Nova Scotia)
1418	Henry the Navigator	Sends seamen who discover Madeira
1433	Henry the Navigator	Sails round Cape Bojadar
1446	Denis Fernandez	Discovers Cape Verde and the Senegal
1469	Fernao Gomes	Crosses the equator and reaches Cape Catherine
1488	Bartholomew Diaz	Sails rounds the Cape of Storms (Cape of Good Hope)
1492	Christopher Columbus	Discovers the New World
1493	Christopher Columbus	Discovers Puerto Rico, Antigua and Jamaica
1497	John Cabot	Explores the coast of Newfoundland
1497	Vasco da Gama	Voyages round the Cape of Good Hope
1498	Vasco da Gama	Explores coast of Mozambique and discovers sea route to India
1498	Christopher Columbus	Discovers Trinidad and South America
1499	Amerigo Vespucci	Discovers mouth of the River Amazon
1500	Pedro Alvarez Cabral	Discovers Brazil
1500	Diego Diaz	Discovers Madagascar
1500	Gaspar de Corte Real	Explores east coast of Greenland and Labrador
1501	Amerigo Vespucci	Explores S American coast
1502	Christopher Columbus	Explores Honduras and Panama
1513	Vasco Nunez de Balboa	Crosses the Panama Isthmus to discover the Pacific Ocean
1520	Ferdinand Magellan	Discovers the Straits of Magellan
1521	Ferdinand Magellan	Discovers the Philippines
1524	Giovanni de Verrazano	Discovers New York Bay and the Hudson River
1526	Sebastian Cabot	Explores the Rio de la Plata
1531	Diego de Ordaz	Explores the River Orinoco
1534	Jacques Cartier	Explores the Gulf of St Lawrence
1535	Jacques Cartier	Navigates the St Lawrence River
1536	Pedro de Mendoza	Founds Buenos Aires and explores Parana and Paraguay rivers
1539	Hernando de Soto	Explores Florida
1540	G L de Cardenas	Discovers the Grand Canyon
1580	Francis Drake	Completes circumnavigation of the globe
1585	John Davis	Discovers Davis Strait on expedition to Greenland
1595	Walter Raleigh	Explores the River Orinoco
1610	Henry Hudson	Discovers Hudson's Bay

EXPLORATIONS AND DISCOVERIES (cont.)

Date	Name	Exploration
1616	William Baffin	Discovers Baffin Bay during search for the N W Passage
1617	Walter Raleigh	Begins expedition to Guiana
1642	Abel Janszoon Tasman	Discovers Tasmania and New Zealand
1678	Robert Cavelier de Salle	Explores the Great Lakes of Canada
1692	Ijsbrand Iders	Explores the Gobi Desert
1736	Andreas Celsius	Undertakes expedition to Lapland
1761	C Niebuhr	Undertakes expedition to Arabia
1766	Louis de Bougainville	Voyage of discovery in Pacific, names Navigator Is.
1769	James Cook	Names Society Islands; charts coasts of New Zealand and E Australia
1770	James Cook	Lands at Botany Bay, Australia
1774	James Cook	Discoveries and rediscoveries in the Pacific; discovers and names S Georgia and the S Sandwich Is.
1772	James Bruce	Explores Abyssinia and the confluence of the Blue Nile and White Nile
1778	James Cook	Discovers Hawaiian group; surveys coast of Bering Straits
1787	Horace Saussure	Makes first ascent of Mont Blanc
1790	George Vancouver	Explores the coast of N W America
1795	Mungo Park	Explores the course of the Niger
1818	John Ross	Attempts to discover N W Passage
1819	John Barrow	Enters Barrow Straits in the N Arctic
1823	Walter Oudney	Discovers Lake Chad in C Africa
1841	David Livingstone	Discovers Lake Ngami
1845	John Franklin	Attempts to discover N W Passage
1854	Richard Burton and John Speke	Explore interior of Somaliland
1855	David Livingstone	Discovers the Victoria Falls on the Zambesi River
1858	Richard Burton and John Speke	Discover Lake Tanganyika
1875	Henry Morton Stanley	Traces the Congo to the Atlantic
1888	Fridtjof Nansen	Crosses Greenland
1893	Fridtjof Nansen	Attempts to reach North Pole
1909	Robert Edwin Peary	Reaches North Pole
1911	Roald Amundsen	Reaches South Pole
1912	Robert Falcon Scott	Reaches South Pole
1914	Ernest Shackleton	Leads expedition to the Antarctic
1953	Edmund Hillary and Norgay Tensing	Make first ascent of Mt Everest
1961	Yuri Gagarin	Becomes first man in space
1969	Neil Armstrong and Buzz Aldrin	Make first landing on the moon

'Discovers' is used to indicate the first recorded visit by a European

MONARCHS

BELGIUM

Belgium became an indpendent kingdom in 1831. A national congress elected Prince Leopold of Saxe–Coburg as king.

Regnal dates	Name
1831–65	Leopold I
1865–1909	Leopold II
1909–34	Albert
1934–51	Leopold III
1951–	Baudouin

DENMARK

Regnal dates	Name
1448–81	Christian I
1481–1513	John
1513–23	Christian II
1523–34	Frederick I
1534–59	Christian III
1559–88	Frederick II
1588–1648	Christian IV
1648–70	Frederick III
1670–99	Christian V
1699–1730	Frederick IV
1730–46	Christian VI
1746–66	Frederick V
1766–1808	Christian VII
1808–39	Frederick VI
1839–48	Christian VIII
1848–63	Frederick VII
1863–1906	Christian IX
1906–12	Frederick VIII
1912–47	Christian X
1947–72	Frederick IX
1972–	Margaret II

ENGLAND

Regnal dates	Name
West Saxon Kings	
0802–39	Egbert
0839–58	Æthelwulf
0858–60	Æthelbald
0860–5	Æthelbert
0866–71	Æthelred
0871–99	Alfred
0899–924	Edward (the Elder)
0924–39	Athelstan
0939–46	Edmund
0946–55	Edred
0955–9	Edwy
0959–75	Edgar
0975–8	Edward (the Martyr)
0978–1016	Æthelred (the Unready)
1016	Edmund (Ironside)
Danish Kings	
1016–35	Cnut (Canute)
1035–7	Harold *Regent*
1037–40	Harold I (Harefoot)
1040–2	Harthacnut
1042–66	Edward (the Confessor)
1066	Harold II
House of Normandy	
1066–87	William I (the Conqueror)
1087–1100	William II (Rufus)
1100–35	Henry I
House of Blois	
1135–54	Stephen
House of Plantagenet	
1154–89	Henry II
1189–99	Richard I (Cœur de Lion)
1199–1216	John
1216–72	Henry III
1272–1307	Edward I
1307–27	Edward II
1327–77	Edward III
1377–99	Richard II
House of Lancaster	
1399–1413	Henry IV
1413–22	Henry V
1422–61	Henry VI
House of York	
1461–70	Edward IV
House of Lancaster	
1470–1	Henry VI
House of York	
1471–83	Edward IV
1483	Edward V
1483–5	Richard III
House of Tudor	
1485–1509	Henry VII
1509–47	Henry VIII
1547–53	Edward VI
1553–8	Mary I
1558–1603	Elizabeth I

FRANCE

France became a republic in 1793 and an empire in 1804 under Napoleon Bonaparte. The monarchy was restored in 1814 and then once more dissolved in 1848.

Regnal dates	Name
987–96	Hugh Capet
996–1031	Robert II
1031–60	Henry I
1060–1108	Philip I
1108–37	Louis VI
1137–80	Louis VII
1180–1223	Philip II Augustus
1223–6	Louis VIII
1226–70	Louis IX
1270–85	Philip III
1285–1314	Philip IV
1314–16	Louis X
1316	John I
1316–22	Philip V
1322–8	Charles IV
1328–50	Philip VI
1350–64	John II
1364–80	Charles V
1380–1422	Charles VI
1422–61	Charles VII
1461–83	Louis XI
1483–98	Charles VIII
1498–1515	Louis XII
1515–47	Francis I

MONARCHS (cont.)

Regnal dates	Name
1547–59	Henry II
1559–60	Francis II
1560–74	Charles IX
1574–89	Henry III
1589–1610	Henry IV (of Navarre)
1610–43	Louis XIII
1643–1715	Louis XIV
1715–74	Louis XV
1774–92	Louis XVI
1814–24	Louis XVIII
1824–30	Charles X
1830–48	Louis-Philippe

GERMANY

Modern Germany was united under Prussia in 1871; it became a republic (1919) after World War I and the abdication of William II in 1918.

Regnal dates	Name
1871–88	William I
1888	Frederick
1888–1918	William II

GREECE

In 1832 the Greek National Assembly elected Otto of Bavaria as King of modern Greece. In 1917 Constantine I abdicated the throne in favour of his son Alexander. In 1920 a plebiscite voted for his return. In 1922 he again abdicated. In 1923 the monarchy was deposed and a republic was proclaimed in 1924. In 1935 a plebiscite restored the monarchy until in 1967 a military junta staged a coup. The monarchy was formally abolished in 1973; Greece became a republic again in 1975.

Regnal dates	Name
1832–62	Otto of Bavaria
1863–1913	George I (of Denmark)
1913–17	Constantine I
1917–20	Alexander
1920–2	Constantine I
1922–3	George I
1935–47	George I
1947–64	Paul
1964–7	Constantine II

ITALY

Modern Italy became a united kingdom in 1861; it voted by referendum to become a republic in 1946.

Regnal dates	Name
1861–78	Victor-Emanuel II
1878–1900	Humbert I
1900–46	Victor Emanuel III
1946	Humbert II

LUXEMBOURG

The Duchy of Luxembourg formally separated from the Netherlands in 1890.

Regnal dates	Name
1890–1905	Adolf of Nassau
1905–12	William
1912–19	Marie-Adelaide
1919–64	Charlotte
1964–	John

NETHERLANDS

Regnal dates	Name
1572–84	William the Silent
1584–1625	Maurice
1625–47	Frederick Henry
1647–50	William II
1672–1702	William III
1747–51	William IV
1751–95	William V
1806–10	Louis Bonaparte
1813–40	William I
1840–9	William II
1849–90	William III
1890–1948	Wilhelmina
1948–80	Juliana
1980–	Beatrix

PORTUGAL

From 1383 to 1385 the Portuguese throne was the subject of a dispute between John of Castile and John of Aviz. In 1826 Peter IV (I of Brazil) renounced his right to the Portuguese throne in order to remain in Brazil. His abdication was contingent upon his successor and daughter, Maria II marrying her uncle, Miguel. In 1828 Miguel usurped the throne on his own behalf. In 1834 Miguel was deposed and Maria II was restored to the throne. In 1910 Manuel II was deposed and Portugal became a republic.

Regnal dates	Name
1095–1112	Henry of Burgandy
1112–85	Alfonso I
1185–1211	Sancho I
1211–23	Alfonso II
1223–45	Sancho II
1245–79	Alfonso III
1279–1325	Diniz
1325–57	Alfonso IV
1357–67	Peter I
1367–83	Ferdinand
1385–1433	John I of Aviz
1433–8	Edward
1438–81	Alfonso V
1481–95	John II
1495–1521	Manuel I
1521–57	John III
1557–78	Sebastian

MONARCHS (cont.)

1578–80	Henry
1580–98	Philip I (II of Spain)
1598–1621	Philip II (III of Spain)
1621–40	Philip III (IV of Spain)
1640–56	John IV of Braganza
1656–83	Alfonso VI
1683–1706	Peter II
1706–50	John V
1750–77	Joseph
1777–1816	Maria I
1777–86	Peter III (King Consort)
1816–26	John VI
1826	Peter IV (I of Brazil)
1826–8	Maria II
1828–34	Miguel
1834–53	Maria II
1853–61	Peter V
1861–89	Luis
1889–1908	Charles
1908–10	Manuel II

SCOTLAND

Regnal dates	Name
1005–34	Malcolm II
1034–40	Duncan I
1040–57	Macbeth
1057–8	Lulach
1058–93	Malcolm III
1093–4	Donald Bane Deposed 1094 Restored 1094–7
1094	Duncan II
1097–1107	Edgar
1107–24	Alexander I
1124–53	David I
1153–65	Malcolm IV
1165–1214	William I
1214–49	Alexander II
1249–86	Alexander III
1286–90	Margaret
1290–2	(Interregnum)
1292–96	John Balliol
1296–1306	(Interregnum)
1306–29	Robert I (the Bruce)
1329–71	David II

1371–90	Robert II
1390–1406	Robert III
1406–37	James I
1437–60	James II
1460–88	James III
1488–1513	James IV
1513–42	James V
1542–67	Mary Queen of Scots
1567–1625	James VI [1]

[1] In 1603, James VI succeeded Elizabeth I to the English throne (Union of the Crowns) and united the thrones of Scotland and England.

SPAIN

Philip V abdicated in favour of Luis in 1724, but returned to the throne in the same year following Luis' death. After the French invasion of Spain in 1808 Napoleoon set up Joseph Bonaparte as king. In 1814 Ferdinand was restored to the crown. In 1868 a revolution deposed Isabella II. In 1870 Amadeus of Savoy was elected as king. In 1873 he resigned the throne and a temporary republic was formed. In 1874 Alfonso XII restored the Bourbon dynasty to the throne. In 1931 Alfonso XIII was deposed and a republican constitution was proclaimed. From 1939 Franco ruled Spain under a dictatorship until his death in 1975 and the restoration of King Juan Carlos.

Regnal dates	Name
1516–56	Charles I (Emperor Charles V)
1556–98	Philip II
1598–1621	Philip III
1621–65	Philip IV
1665–1700	Charles II
1700–24	Philip V
1724	Luis
1724–46	Philip V

1746–59	Ferdinand VI
1759–88	Charles III
1788–1808	Charles IV
1808	Ferdinand VII
1808–14	Joseph Bonaparte
1814–33	Ferdinand VII
1833–68	Isabella II
1870–3	Amadeus of Savoy
1874–85	Alfonso XII
1886–1931	Alfonso XIII
1975–	Juan Carlos

UNITED KINGDOM

Regnal dates	Name
House of Stuart	
1603–25	James I (VI of Scotland)
1625–49	Charles I
Commonwealth and Protectorate	
1649–53	*Council of State*
1653–8	Oliver Cromwell *Lord Protector*
1658–9	Richard Cromwell *Lord Protector*
House of Stuart (restored)	
1660–85	Charles II
1685–8	James II
1689–94	William III (*jointly with* Mary II)
1694–1702	William III (*alone*)
1702–14	Anne
House of Hanover	
1714–27	George I
1727–60	George II
1760–1820	George III
1820–30	George IV
1830–7	William IV
1837–1901	Victoria
House of Saxe-Coburg	
1901–10	Edward VII
House of Windsor	
1910–36	George V
1936	Edward VIII
1936–52	George VI
1952–	Elizabeth II

ANCIENT EGYPT: DYNASTIES

Date BC	Dynasty	Period
c.3100–2890	I	**Early Dynastic Period**
c.2890–2686	II	First use of stone in building
c.2686–2613	III	**Old Kingdom**
c.2613–2494	IV	The age of the great
c.2494–2345	V	pyramid builders
c.2345–2181	VI	Longest reign in history: Pepi II, 90 years
c.2181–2173	VII	**First Intermediate Period**
c.2173–2160	VIII	Social order upset; few
c.2160–2130	IX	monuments built
c.2130–2040	X	
c.2133–1991	XI	
1991–1786	XII	**Middle Kingdom**
1786–1633	XIII	Golden age of art and craftsmanship
1786–c.1603	XIV	**Second Intermediate Period**
1674–1567	XV	Country divided into principalities
c.1684–1567	XVI	
c.1660–1567	XVII	
1567–1320	XVIII	**New Kingdom**
1320–1200	XIX	Began with colonial
1200–1085	XX	expansion, ended in divided rule
1085–945	XXI	**Third Intermediate Period**
945–730	XXII	Revival of prosperity and
817?–730	XXIII	restoration of cults
720–715	XXIV	
751–668	XXV	
664–525	XXVI	**Late Period**
525–404	XXVII	Completion of Nile–
404–399	XXVIII	Red Sea canal
399–380	XXIX	
380–343	XXX	
343–332	XXXI	Alexander the Great reached Alexandria in 332 BC

ANCIENT CHINA: DYNASTIES

Regnal dates	Name
22nd–18th-c BC	Hsai Dynasty
18th–12th-c BC	Shang or Yin Dynasty
1111–770 BC	Western (Hsi) Chou Dynasty
770–256 BC	Eastern (Tung) Chou Dynasty
475–221 BC	Warring States Period
221–206 BC	Ch'in Dynasty (Unified Empire)
206 BC–220 AD	Han Dynasty
206 BC–9 AD	Western (Hsi) Han
9–23 AD	Hsin (Wang Mang, usurper)
25–220 AD	Eastern (Tung) Han
220–265 AD	Three Kingdoms (San-kuo)
265–317 AD	Western (Hsi) Chin Dynasty
317–420 AD	Eastern (Tung) Chin Dynasty
420–589 AD	Southern Dynasties
581–618 AD	Sui Dynasty (Unified China)
618–907 AD	Tang Dynasty
907–60 AD	Five Dynasties and Ten Kingdoms Period
960–1279 AD	Sung Dynasty
96–1127 AD	Northern (Pei) Sung
990–1227 AD	Western (Hsi) Sung
1115–1234 AD	Chin or Juchen Dynasty (Tartars)
1206–1368 AD	Yuan or Mongol Dynasty
1368–1644 AD	Ming Dynasty (Capital at Nanking (1368–1421), and Peking (1421–1644)
1644–1911	Ching or Manchu Dynasty (Descendents of 1912 AD Tartars)

MUGHAL EMPERORS

The 2nd Mughal emperor, Humayun lost his throne in 1540, became a fugitive, and did not regain his title until 1555.

Regnal dates	Name
1526–30	Babur
1530–56	Humayun
1556–1605	Akbar
1605–27	Jahangir
1627–58	Shah Jahan
1658–1707	Aurangzeb (Alamgir)
1707–12	Bahadur Shah I (or Shah Alam I)
1712–13	Jahandar Shah
1713–19	Farruksiyar
1719	Rafid-ud-Darajat
1719	Rafi-ud-Daulat
1719	Nekusiyar
1719	Ibrahim
1719–48	Muhammad Shah
1748–54	Ahmad Shah
1754–9	Alamgir II
1759–1806	Shah Alam II
1806–37	Akbar II
1837–57	Bahadur Shah II

JAPANESE EMPERORS

The first 14 emperors (to Chuai) are regarded as legendary, and the regnal dates for the 15th to the 28th emperor (Senka), taken from the early Japanese chronicle, 'Nihon shoki' are not considered to be authentic.

Regnal dates	Name	Regnal dates	Name	Regnal dates	Name
660–585 BC	Jimmu	724–49 AD	Shomu	1246–59	Go-Fukakusa
581–549 BC	Suizei	749–58 AD	Koken	1259–74	Kameyama
549–511 BC	Annei	758–64 AD	Junnin	1274–87	Go-Uda
510–477 BC	Itoku	764–70 AD	Shotoku	1287–98	Fushimi
475–393 BC	Kosho	770–81 AD	Konin	1298–1301	Go-Fushimi
392–291 BC	Koan	781–806 AD	Kammu	1301–8	Go-Nijo
290–215 BC	Korei	806–9 AD	Heizei	1308–18	Hanazono
214–158 BC	Kogen	809–23 AD	Saga	1318–39	Go-Daigo
158–98 BC	Kaika	823–33 AD	Junna	1339–68	Go-Murakami
97–30 BC	Sujin	833–50 AD	Nimmyo	1368–83	Chokei
29 BC–70 AD	Suinin	850–58 AD	Montoku	1383–92	Go-Kameyama
71 AD–130 AD	Keiko	858–76 AD	Seiwa	Northern Court	
131–90 AD	Selmu	876–84 AD	Yozei	1331–3	Kogon
192–200 AD	Chuai	884–87 AD	Koko	1336–48	Komyo
270–310 AD	Ojin	887–97 AD	Uda	1348–51	Suko
313–99 AD	Nintoku	897–930 AD	Daigo	1352–71	Go-Kogon
400–05 AD	Richu	930–46 AD	Suzaku	1371–82	Go-Enyu
406–10 AD	Hanzel	946–67 AD	Murakami	1382–1412	Go-Komatsu
412–53 AD	Ingyo	967–9 AD	Reizei	1412–28	Shoko
453–6 AD	Anko	969–84 AD	En'yu	1428–64	Go-Hanazono
456–79 AD	Yuryaku	984–6 AD	Kazan	1464–1500	Go-Tsuchimikado
480–4 AD	Seinei	986–1011 AD	Ichijo	1500–26	Go-Kashiwabara
485–7 AD	Kenzo	1011–16 AD	Sanjo	1526–57	Go-Nara
488–98 AD	Ninken	1016–36	Go-Ichijo	1557–86	Ogimachi
498–506 AD	Buretsu	1036–45	Go-Suzako	1586–1611	Go-Yozei
507–31 AD	Keitai	1045–68	Go-Reizei	1611–29	Go-Mizunoo
531–5 AD	Ankan	1068–72	Go-Sanyo	1629–43	Meisho
535–9 AD	Senka	1072–86	Shirakawa	1643–54	Go-Komyo
539–71 AD	Kimmei	1086–1107	Horikawa	1654–63	Go-Sai
572–85 AD	Bidatsu	1107–23	Toba	1663–87	Reigen
585–87 AD	Yomei	1123–41	Sutoku	1687–1709	Higashiyama
587–92 AD	Sushun	1141–55	Konoe	1709–35	Nakamikado
592–628 AD	Suiko	1155–8	Goshirakawa	1735–47	Sakuramachi
629–41 AD	Jomei	1158–65	Nijo	1747–62	Momozono
642–5 AD	Kogyoku	1165–8	Rokujo	1762–70	Go-Sakuramachi
645–54 AD	Kotuko	1168–80	Takakura	1770–9	Go-Momozono
655–61 AD	Saimei	1180–3	Antoku	1779–1817	Kokaku
662–71 AD	Tenji	1183–98	Go-Toba	1817–46	Ninko
671–72 AD	Kobun	1198–1210	Tsuchimikado	1846–66	Komei
673–86 AD	Temmu	1210–21	Juntoku	1867–1912	Meiji
686–97 AD	Jito	1221	Chukyo	1912–26	Taisho
697–707 AD	Mommu	1221–32	Goshirakawa	1926–89	Hirohito
707–15 AD	Gemmei	1232–42	Shijo	1989–	Akihito
715–24 AD	Gensho	1242–6	Go-Saga		

ROMAN KINGS

The founding of Rome by Romulus is a Roman literary tradition.

Regnal dates	Name
753–715 BC	Romulus
715–673 BC	Numa Pompilius
673–642 BC	Tullus Hostilius
642–616 BC	Ancus Marcius
616–578 BC	Tarquinius Priscus
578–534 BC	Servius Tullius
534–509 BC	Tarquinius Superbus

ROMAN EMPERORS

Dates overlap where there are periods of joint rule (e.g. Marcus Aurelius and Lucius Verus, and where the government of the empire divides between east and west.

Regnal dates	Name	Regnal dates	Name
27 BC–14 AD	Augustus (Caesar Augustus)	276	Florian
		276–82	Probus
14–37	Tiberius	282–3	Carus
37–41	Caligula (Gaius Caesar)	283–5	Carinus
		283–4	Numerian
41–54	Claudius	284–305	Diocletian–(East)
54–68	Nero	286–305	Maximian–(West)
68–9	Galba	305–11	Galerius–(East)
69	Otho	305–6	Constantius I
69	Vitellius	306–7	Severus–(West)
69–79	Vespasian	306–12	Maxentius–
79–81	Titus		(West)
81–96	Domitian	306–37	Constantine I
96–8	Nerva	308–24	Licinius–(East)
98–117	Trajan	337–40	Constantine II
117–38	Hadrian	337–50	Constans I
138–61	Antoninus Pius	337–61	Constantius II
161–80	Marcus Aurelius	350–1	Magnentius
161–9	Lucius Verus	360–3	Julian
176–92	Commodus	363–4	Jovian
193	Pertinax	364–75	Valentinian I–
193	Didius Julianus		(West)
193–211	Septemius Severus	364–78	Valens–(East)
198–217	Caracalla	365–6	Procopius–(East)
209–12	Geta	375–83	Gratian–(West)
217–18	Macrinus	375–92	Valentinian II–(West)
218–22	Elagabalus	379–95	Theodosius I
222–35	Alexander Severus	395–408	Arcadius–(East)
235–8	Maximin	395–423	Honorius–(West)
238	Gordian I	408–50	Theodosius II–(East)
238	Gordian II	421–3	Constantius III–(West)
238	Maximus	423–55	Valentinian III–(West)
238	Balbinus	450–7	Marcian–(East)
238–44	Gordian III	455	Petronius Maximus–
244–9	Philip		(West)
249–51	Decius	455–6	Avitus–(West)
251	Hostilian	457–74	Leo I–(East)
251–3	Gallus	457–61	Majorian–(West)
253	Aemilian	461–7	Libius Severus–(West)
253–60	Valerian	467–72	Anthemius–(West)
253–68	Gallienus	472–3	Olybrius–(West)
268–9	Claudius II (the Goth)	474–80	Julius Nepos–(West)
		474	Leo II–(East)
269–70	Quintillus	474–91	Zeno–(East)
270–5	Aurelian	475–76	Romulus Augustus–
275–6	Tacitus		(West)

HOLY ROMAN EMPERORS

Regnal dates	Name	Regnal dates	Name
800–14	Charlemagne (Charles I)	1247–56	William of Holland
814–40	Louis I (the Pious)	1250–4	Conrad IV
840–3	(Civil War)	1254–73	*Great Interregnum*
843–55	Lothair I	*Rival claimants*	
855–75	Louis II	1257–72	Richard
875–7	Charles II (the Bold)	1257–75	Alfonso (Alfonso X of Castile)
877–81	(Interregnum)		
881–7	Charles III (the Fat)	1273–91	Rudolf I
887–91	*Interregnum*	1292–8	Adolf
Rival claimants		1298–1308	Albert I
891–4	Guido of Spoleto	1308–13	Henry VII
894–8	Lambert of Spoleto	1314–26	Frederick (III)
896–9	Arnulf	1314–46	Louis IV
901–5	Louis III	1346–78	Charles IV
911–18	Conrad I	1378–1400	Wenceslas
915–24	Berengar	1400–10	Rupert
919–36	Henry I	*Rival claimants*	
936–73	Otto I (the Great)	1410	Jobst
973–83	Otto II		Wenceslas
983–1002	Otto III		Sigismund
1002–24	Henry II (the Saint)	1410–37	Sigismund
1024–39	Conrad II	1438–9	Albert II
1039–56	Henry III (the Black)	1440–93	Frederick III
1056–1106	Henry IV	1493–1519	Maximilian I
Rival claimants		1519–56	Charles V
1077–80	Rudolf	1556–64	Ferdinand I
1081–93	Hermann	1564–76	Maximilian II
1093–1101	Conrad	1576–1612	Rudolf II
1106–25	Henry V	1612–19	Matthias
1125–37	Lothair II	1619–37	Ferdinand II
1138–52	Conrad III	1637–57	Ferdinand III
1152–90	Frederick I (Barbarossa)	1658–1705	Leopold I
		1705–11	Joseph I
1190–7	Henry VI	1711–40	Charles VI
Rival claimants		1740–42	*Interregnum*
1198–1208	Philip	1742–5	Charles VII
1198–1214	Otto IV	1745–65	Francis I
1215–50	Frederick II	1765–90	Joseph II
1220–35	Henry (VII)	1790–2	Leopold II
1246–7	Henry Raspe	1792–1806	Francis II

RUSSIAN RULERS

In 1610 Vasili Shuisky was deposed as Tsar and the throne remained vacant until the election of Michael Romanov in 1613. In 1682 a condition of the succession was that the two step-brothers, Ivan V and Peter I (the Great) should jointly be proclaimed as Tsars. In 1917 the empire was overthrown and Tsar Nicholas II was forced to abdicate.

Regnal dates	Name
1283–1303	Daniel
1303–25	Yuri
1325–41	Ivan I
1341–53	Semeon
1353–59	Ivan II
1359–89	Dimitri Donskoy
1389–1425	Vasili I
1425–62	Vasili II
1462–1505	Ivan III (the Great)
1505–33	Vasili III
1533–84	Ivan IV (the Terrible)
1584–98	Feodor I
1598–1605	Boris Godunov
1605	Feodor II
1605–6	Dimitri II
1606–10	Vasili IV Shuisky
1613–45	Michael Romanov
1645–76	Alexei
1676–82	Feodor III
1682–96	Ivan V
1682–1725	Peter I (the Great)
1725–7	Catherine I
1727–30	Peter II
1730–40	Anne
1740–1	Ivan VI
1741–62	Elizabeth
1762	Peter III
1762–96	Catherine II (the Great)
1796–1801	Paul
1810–25	Alexander I
1825–55	Nicholas I
1855–81	Alexander II
1881–94	Alexander III
1894–1917	Nicholas II

POLITICAL LEADERS 1900–1991

Countries and organizations are listed alphabetically. Rulers are named chronologically since 1900 or (for new nations) since independence. For the major English-speaking nations, relevant details are also given of pre-20th-century rulers, along with a note of any political affiliation.

The list does not distinguish successive terms of office by a single ruler.

There is no universally agreed way of transliterating proper names in non-Roman alphabets; variations from the spellings given are therefore to be expected, especially in the case of Arabic rulers.

Minor variations in the titles adopted by Chiefs of State, or in the name of an administration, are not given; these occur most notably in countries under military rule.

Listings complete to June 1991.

AFGHANISTAN

Afghan Empire

Monarch

1881–1901	Abdur Rahman Khan
1901–19	Habibullah Khan
1919–29	Inayatullah Khan
1929	Habibullah Ghazi
1929–33	Nadir Shah
1933–73	Zahir Shah

Republic of Afghanistan

Prime Minister

1973–8	Mohammad Daoud Khan

Democratic Republic of Afghanistan Revolutionary Council

President

1978–9	Nur Mohammad Taraki
1979	Hafizullah Amin

Soviet Invasion
1979–86	Babrak Karmal
1986–7	Haji Mohammad Chamkani *Acting President*
1987–	Mohammad Najibullah

General Secretary

1978–86	*As President*
1986–	Mohammad Najibullah

Prime Minister

1929–46	Sardar Mohammad Hashim Khan
1946–53	Shah Mahmoud Khan Ghazi
1953–63	Mohammad Daoud

1963–5	Mohammad Yousef
1965–7	Mohammad Hashim Maiwandwal
1967–71	Nour Ahmad Etemadi
1972–3	Mohammad Mousa Shafiq
1973–9	*As President*
1979–81	Babrak Karmal
1981–8	Sultan Ali Keshtmand

Republic of Afghanistan from 1987
1988–9	Mohammad Hasan Sharq
1989–90	Sultan Ali Keshtmand
1990–	Fazl Haq Khaleqiar

ALBANIA

Monarch

1928–39	Zog I (Ahmed Zogu)
1939–44	*Italian rule*

People's Socialist Republic

President

1944–85	Enver Hoxha
1985–	Ramiz Alia

Prime Minister

1914	Turhan Pashë Përmëti
1914	Esad Toptani
1914–18	Abdullah Rushdi
1918–20	Turhan Pashë Përmëti
1920	Sulejman Deluina
1920–1	Iljaz Bej Vrioni
1921	Pandeli Evangeli
1921	Xhafer Ypi
1921–2	Omer Vrioni
1922–4	Ahmed Zogu
1924	Iljaz Bej Vrioni
1924–5	Fan Noli

POLITICAL LEADERS 1900–1991 (cont.)

Albania (cont.)

1925–8	Ahmed Zogu
1928–30	Koço Kota
1930–5	Pandeli Evangeli
1935–6	Mehdi Frashëri
1936–9	Koço Kota
1939–41	Shefqet Verlaci
1941–3	Mustafa Merlika-Kruja
1943	Eqrem Libohova
1943	Maliq Bushati
1943	Eqrem Libohova
1943	*Provisional Executive Committee* (Ibrahim Biçakçlu)
1943	*Council of Regents* (Mehdi Frashëri)
1943–4	Rexhep Mitrovica
1944	Fiori Dine
1944–54	Enver Hoxha
1954–81	Mehmed Shehu
1981–91	Adil Carcani
1991–	Fatos Nano

ALGERIA

President

1962–5	Ahmed Ben Bella
1965–78	Houari Boumédienne
1979–	Bendjedid Chadli

ANGOLA

President

1975–9	Antonio Agostinho Neto
1979–	José Eduardo dos Santos

ANTIGUA AND BARBUDA

Prime Minister

1981–	Cornwall Vere Bird

ARGENTINA

President

1898–1904	Julio Argentino Roca
1904–6	Manuel Quintana
1906–10	José Figueroa Alcorta
1910–14	Roque Sáenz Peña
1914–16	Victorino de la Plaza
1916–22	Hipólito Yrigoyen
1922–8	Marcelo T de Alvear
1928–30	Hipólito Yrigoyen
1930–2	José Félix Uriburu
1932–8	Augustin Pedro Justo
1938–40	Roberto M Ortiz
1940–3	Ramón S Castillo
1943–4	Pedro P Ramírez
1944–6	Edelmiro J Farrell
1946–55	Juan Perón
1955–8	Eduardo Lonardi
1958–62	Arturo Frondizi
1962–3	José María Guido
1963–6	Arturo Illia
1966–70	Juan Carlos Onganía
1970–1	Roberto Marcelo Levingston
1971–3	Alejandro Agustin Lanusse
1973	Héctor J Cámpora
1973–4	Juan Perón
1974–6	Martínez de Perón
1976–81	*Military Junta* (Jorge Rafaél Videla)
1981	*Military Junta* (Roberto Eduardo Viola)
1981–2	*Military Junta* (Leopoldo Galtieri)
1982–3	Reynaldo Bignone
1983–8	Raúl Alfonsín
1988–	Carlos Menem

AUSTRALIA

Chief of State: British monarch, represented by Governor General

Prime Minister

1901–3	Edmund Barton *Prot*
1903–4	Alfred Deakin *Prot*
1904	John Christian Watson *Lab*
1904–5	George Houston Reid *Free*
1905–8	Alfred Deakin *Prot*
1908–9	Andrew Fisher *Lab*
1909–10	Alfred Deakin *Fusion*
1910–13	Andrew Fisher *Lab*
1913–14	Joseph Cook *Lib*
1914–15	Andrew Fisher *Lab*
1915–17	William Morris Hughes *Nat Lab*
1917–23	William Morris Hughes *Nat*
1923–9	Stanley Melbourne Bruce *Nat*
1929–32	James Henry Scullin *Lab*
1932–9	Joseph Aloysius Lyons *Un*

POLITICAL LEADERS 1900–1991 (cont.)

1939	Earle Christmas Page *Co*
1939–41	Robert Gordon Menzies *Un*
1941	Arthur William Fadden *Co*
1941–5	John Joseph Curtin *Lab*
1945	Francis Michael Forde *Lab*
1945–9	Joseph Benedict Chifley *Lab*
1949–66	Robert Gordon Menzies *Lib*
1966–7	Harold Edward Holt *Lib*
1967–8	John McEwen *Co*
1968–71	John Grey Gorton *Lib*
1971–2	William McMahon *Lib*
1972–5	Edward Gough Whitlam *Lab*
1975–83	John Malcolm Fraser *Lib*
1983–	Robert James Lee Hawke *Lab*

Co	*Country*
Free	*Free Trade*
Lab	*Labor*
Lib	*Liberal*
Nat	*Nationalist*
Nat Lab	*National Labor*
Prot	*Protectionist*
Un	*United*

AUSTRIA

President

1918–20	Karl Sätz
1920–8	Michael Hainisch
1928–38	Wilhelm Miklas
1938–45	*German rule*
1945–50	Karl Renner
1950–7	Theodor Körner
1957–65	Adolf Schärf
1965–74	Franz Jonas
1974–86	Rudolf Kirchsläger
1986–	Kurt Waldheim

Chancellor

1918–20	Karl Renner
1920–1	Michael Mayr
1921–2	Johann Schober
1922	Walter Breisky
1922	Johann Schober
1922–4	Ignaz Seipel
1924–6	Rudolph Ramek
1926–9	Ignaz Seipel
1929–30	Ernst Streeruwitz
1930	Johann Schober
1930	Carl Vaugoin

1930–1	Otto Ender
1931–2	Karl Buresch
1932–4	Engelbert Dollfus
1934–8	Kurt von Schuschnigg
1938–45	*German rule*
1945	Karl Renner
1945–53	Leopold Figl
1953–61	Julius Raab
1961–4	Alfons Gorbach
1964–70	Josef Klaus
1970–83	Bruno Kreisky
1983–6	Fred Sinowatz
1986–	Franz Vranitzky

THE BAHAMAS

Chief of State: British monarch, represented by Governor General

Prime Minister

1973–	Lynden O Pindling

BAHRAIN

Emir

1971–	Isa Bin Salman Al-Khalifa

Prime Minister

1971–	Khalifa Bin Salman Al-Khalifa

BANGLADESH

President

1971–2	Sayed Nazrul Islam *Acting*
1972	Mujibur Rahman
1972–3	Abu Saeed Chowdhury
1974–5	Mohammadullah
1975	Mujibur Rahman
1975	Khondaker Mushtaq Ahmad
1975–7	Abu Saadat Mohammad Sayem
1977–81	Zia Ur-Rahman
1981–2	Abdus Sattar
1982–3	Abdul Fazal Mohammad Ahsanuddin Chowdhury
1983–90	Hossain Mohammad Ershad
1990–	Shehabuddin Ahmed *Acting*

POLITICAL LEADERS 1900–1991 (cont.)

Bangladesh (cont.)

Prime Minister

1971–2	Tajuddin Ahmed
1972–5	Mujibur Rahman
1975	Mohammad Monsur Ali
1975–9	*Martial Law*
1979–82	Mohammad Azizur Rahman
1982–4	*Martial Law*
1984–5	Ataur Rahman Khan
1986–88	Mizanur Rahman Chowdhury
1988–90	Kazi Zafar Ahmed
1991–	Begum Zia

BARBADOS

Prime Minister

1966–76	Errol Walton Barrow
1976–85	JMG (Tom) Adams
1985–6	H Bernard St John
1986–7	Errol Walton Barrow
1987–	L Erskine Sandiford

BELGIUM

Monarch

1865–1909	Leopold II
1909–34	Albert I
1934–50	Leopold III
1950–	Baudoin I

Prime Minister

1899–1907	Paul de Smet de Nayer
1907–8	Jules de Trooz
1908–11	Frans Schollaert
1911–18	Charles de Broqueville
1918	Gerhard Cooreman
1918–20	Léon Delacroix
1920–1	Henri Carton de Wiart
1921–5	Georges Theunis
1925	Alois van de Vyvere
1925–6	Prosper Poullet
1926–31	Henri Jaspar
1931–2	Jules Renkin
1932–4	Charles de Broqueville
1934–5	Georges Theunis
1935–7	Paul van Zeeland
1937–8	Paul Émile Janson
1938–9	Paul Henri Spaak

1939–45	Hubert Pierlot
1945–6	Achille van Acker
1946	Paul Spaak
1946	Achille van Acker
1946–7	Camille Huysmans
1947–9	Paul Spaak
1949–50	Gaston Eyskens
1950	Jean Pierre Duvieusart
1950–2	Joseph Pholien
1952–4	Jean van Houtte
1954–8	Achille van Acker
1958–61	Gaston Eyskens
1961–5	Théodore Lefèvre
1965–6	Pierre Harmel
1966–8	Paul Vanden Boeynants
1968–72	Gaston Eyskens
1973–4	Edmond Leburton
1974–8	Léo Tindemans
1978	Paul Vanden Boeynants
1979–81	Wilfried Martens
1981	Marc Eyskens
1981–	Wilfried Martens

BELIZE

Chief of State: British Monarch, represented by Governor General

Prime Minister

1981–4	George Cadle Price
1985–9	Manuel Esquivel
1989–	George Cadle Price

BENIN

President

Dahomey

1960–3	Hubert Coutoucou Maga
1963–4	Christophe Soglo
1964–5	Sourou Migan Apithy
1965	Justin Tométin Ahomadegbé
1965	Tairou Congacou
1965–7	Christophe Soglo
1967–8	Alphonse Amadou Alley
1968–9	Émile Derlin Zinsou
1969–70	*Presidential Committee* (Maurice Kouandete)
1970–2	(Hubert Coutoucou Maga)
1972–5	Mathieu Kerekou

POLITICAL LEADERS 1900–1991 (cont.)

People's Republic of Benin
1975–91 Mathieu (*from 1980* Ahmed) Kerekou

Republic of Benin
1991–   Nicéphore Soglo

Prime Minister

1958–9	Sourou Migan Apithy
1959–60	Hubert Coutoucou Maga
1960–4	*As President*
1964–5	Justin Tométin Ahomadegbé
1965–7	*As President*
1967–8	Maurice Kouandete
1968–90	*As President*

Republic of Benin
1990–   Nicéphore Soglo

BHUTAN

Monarch (Druk Gyalpo)

1907–26	Uggyen Wangchuk
1926–52	Jigme Wangchuk
1952–72	Jigme Dorji Wangchuk
1972–	Jigme Singye Wangchuk

BOLIVIA

President

1899–1904	José Manual Pando
1904–9	Ismael Montes
1909–13	Heliodoro Villazón
1913–17	Ismael Montes
1917–20	José N Gutiérrez Guerra
1920–5	Bautista Saavedra
1925–6	José Cabina Villanueva
1926–30	Hernando Siles
1930	Roberto Hinojusa
	President of Revolutionaries
1930–1	Carlos Blanco Galindo
1931–4	Daniel Salamanca
1934–6	José Luis Tejado Sorzano
1936–7	David Toro
1937–9	Germán Busch
1939	Carlos Quintanilla
1940–3	Enrique Peñaranda y del Castillo
1943–6	Gualberto Villaroel
1946	Nestor Guillen
1946–7	Tomas Monje Gutiérrez
1947–9	Enrique Hertzog

1949	Mamerto Urriolagoitía
1951–2	Hugo Ballivián
1952	Hernán Siles Suazo
1952–6	Victor Paz Estenssoro
1956–60	Hernán Siles Suazo
1960–4	Victor Paz Estenssoro
1964–5	René Barrientos Ortuño
1965–6	René Barrientos Ortuño *and* Alfredo Ovando Candía
1966	Alfredo Ovando Candía
1966–9	René Barrientos Ortuño
1969	Luis Adolfo Siles Salinas
1969–70	Alfredo Ovando Candía
1970	Rogelio Mirando
1970–1	Juan José Torres Gonzales
1971–8	Hugo Banzer Suárez
1978	Juan Pereda Asbún
1978–9	*Military Junta* (David Padilla Arericiba)
1979	Walter Guevara Arze
1979–80	Lydia Gueiler Tejada
1980–1	*Military Junta* (Luis García Meza)
1981–2	*Military Junta* (Celso Torrelio Villa)
1982	Guido Vildoso Calderón
1982–5	Hernán Siles Suazo
1985–9	Victor Paz Estenssoro
1989–	Jaime Paz Zamora

BOTSWANA

President

1966–80	Seretse Khama
1980–	Quett Masire

BRAZIL

President

1898–1902	Manuel Ferraz de Campos Sales
1902–6	Francisco de Paula Rodrigues Alves
1906–9	Alfonso Pena
1909–10	Nilo Peçanha
1910–14	Hermes Rodrigues da Fonseca
1914–18	Venceslau Brás Pereira Gomes
1918–19	Francisco de Paula Rodrigues Alves
1919–22	Epitácio Pessoa
1922–6	Artur da Silva Bernardes

POLITICAL LEADERS 1900–1991 (cont.)

Brazil (cont.)

1926–30	Washington Luís Pereira de Sousa
1930–45	Getúlio Dorneles Vargas
1945–51	Eurico Gaspar Dutra
1951–4	Getúlio Dorneles Vargas
1954–5	João Café Filho
1955	Carlos Coimbra da Luz
1955–6	Nereu de Oliveira Ramos
1956–61	Juscelino Kubitschek de Oliveira
1961	Jânio da Silva Quadros
1961–3	João Belchior Marques Goulart
1963	Pascoal Ranieri Mazilli
1963–4	João Belchior Marques Goulart
1964	Pascoal Ranieri Mazilli
1964–7	Humberto de Alencar Castelo Branco
1967–9	Artur da Costa e Silva
1969–74	Emílio Garrastazu Médici
1974–9	Ernesto Geisel
1979–85	João Baptista de Oliveira Figueiredo
1985–90	José Sarney
1990–	Fernando Collor de Mello

BRUNEI

Monarch (Sultan)

1967–	Muda Hassanal Bolkiah Muizzadin Waddaulah

BULGARIA

Monarch

1887–1908	Ferdinand *Prince*
1908–18	Ferdinand I
1918–43	Boris III
1943–6	Simeon II

President

1946–7	Vasil Kolarov
1947–50	Mincho Naichev
1950–8	Georgi Damianov
1958–64	Dimitro Ganev
1964–71	Georgi Traikov
1971–89	Todor Zhivkov
1989–90	Petar Mladenov
1990–	Zhelyu Zhelev

Premier

1946–9	Georgi Dimitrov
1949–50	Vasil Kolarov
1950–6	Vulko Chervenkov
1956–62	Anton Yugov
1962–71	Todor Zhivkov
1971–81	Stanko Todorov
1981–86	Grisha Filipov
1986–90	Georgy Atanasov
1990	Andrei Lukanov
1990–	Dimitur Popov

First Secretary

1946–53	Vulko Chervenkov
1953–89	Todor Zhivkov
1989–90	Petar Mladenov
1990–	Alexander Lilov

BURKINA FASO

President

Upper Volta

1960–6	Maurice Yaméogo
1966–80	Sangoulé Lamizana
1980	Saye Zerbo

People's Salvation Council

1982–3	Jean-Baptiste Ouedraugo *Chairman*

National Revolutionary Council

1983–4	Thomas Sankara *Chairman*

Burkina Faso

1984–7	Thomas Sankara *Chairman*
1987–	Blaise Compaoré

BURMA (Union of Myanma)

President

1948–52	Sao Shwe Thaik
1952–7	Agga Maha Thiri Thudhamma Ba U
1957–62	U Wing Maung
1962	Sama Duwa Sinwa Nawng

Revolutionary Council

1962–74 Ne Win

POLITICAL LEADERS 1900–1991 (cont.)

State Council

1974–81	Ne Win
1981–8	U San Yu
1988	U Sein Lwin
1988	Maung Maung
1988–	Saw Maung

Prime Minister

1947–56	Thakin Nu
1956–7	U Ba Swe
1957–8	U Nu
1958–60	Ne Win
1960–2	U Nu
1962–74	Ne Win
1974–7	U Sein Win
1977–8	U Maung Maung Ka
1988	U Tun Tin
1988–	Saw Maung

BURUNDI

Monarch

1962–6	Mwambutsa IV
1966	Ntare V

President

1966–77	Michel Micombero
1977–87	Jean-Baptiste Bagaza
1987–	*Military Junta* (Pierre Buyoya)

CAMBODIA (Kampuchea)

Monarch

1941–55	Norodom Sihanouk II
1955–60	Norodom Suramarit

Chief of State

1960–70	Prince Norodom Sihanouk

Khmer Republic

1970–2	Cheng Heng *Acting Chief of State*
1972–5	Lon Nol
1975–6	Prince Norodom Sihanouk
1976–81	Khieu Samphan
1981–	Heng Samrin

Government in exile

President

1970–5	Prince Norodom Sihanouk
1982–	Prince Norodom Sihanouk

Prime Minister

1945–6	Son Ngoc Thanh
1946–8	Prince Monireth
1948–9	Son Ngoc Thanh
1949–51	Prince Monipong
1951	Son Ngoc Thanh
1951–2	Huy Kanthoul
1952–3	Norodom Sihanouk II
1953	Samdech Penn Nouth
1953–4	Chan Nak
1954–5	Leng Ngeth
1955–6	Prince Norodom Sihanouk
1956	Oum Chheang Sun
1956	Prince Norodom Sihanouk
1956	Khim Tit
1956	Prince Norodom Sihanouk
1956	Sam Yun
1956–7	Prince Norodom Sihanouk
1957–8	Sim Var
1958	Ek Yi Oun
1958	Samdech Penn Nouth
	Acting Prime Minister
1958	Sim Var
1958–60	Prince Norodom Sihanouk
1960–1	Pho Proung
1961	Samdech Penn Nouth
1961–3	Prince Norodom Sihanouk
1963–6	Prince Norodom Kantol
1966–7	Lon Nol
1967–8	Prince Norodom Sihanouk
1968–9	Samdech Penn Nouth
1969–72	Lon Nol

Khmer Republic (1970)

1972	Sisovath Sivik Matak
1972	Son Ngoc Thanh
1972–3	Hang Thun Hak
1973	In Tam
1973–5	Long Boret
1975–6	Samdech Penn Nouth
1976–9	Pol Pot
1979–81	Khieu Samphan
1981–5	Chan Si
1985–	Hun Sen

POLITICAL LEADERS 1900–1991 (cont.)

Cambodia (cont.)

Government in exile
1970–3   Samdech Penn Nouth
1982–   Son Sann

CAMEROON

President
1960–82 Ahmadun Ahidjo
1982–   Paul Biya

CANADA

Chief of State: British monarch, represented by Governor General

Prime Minister

1867–73   John A MacDonald *Con*
1873–8   Alexander Mackenzie *Lib*
1878–91   John A MacDonald *Con*
1891–2   John J C Abbot *Con*
1892–4   John S D Thompson *Con*
1894–6   Mackenzie Bowell *Con*
1896   Charles Tupper *Con*
1896–1911 Wilfrid Laurier *Lib*
1911–17   Robert Borden *Con*
1917–20   Robert Borden *Con*
1920–1   Arthur Meighen *Con*
1921–6   William Lyon Mackenzie King *Lib*
1926   Arthur Meighen *Con*
1926–30   William Lyon Mackenzie King *Lib*
1930–5   Richard Bedford Bennett *Con*
1935–48   William Lyon Mackenzie King *Lib*
1948–57   Louis St Laurent *Lib*
1957–63   John George Diefenbaker *Con*
1963–8   Lester Bowles Pearson *Lib*
1968–79   Pierre Elliott Trudeau *Lib*
1979–80   Joseph Clark *Con*
1980–4   Pierre Elliott Trudeau *Lib*
1984   John Turner *Lib*
1984–   Brian Mulroney *Con*

Con Conservative
Lib Liberal

CAPE VERDE

President
1975–91 Aristides Pereira
1991–   Antonio Monteiro

Prime Minister
1975–91 Pedro Pires
1991–   Carlos Veiga

CENTRAL AFRICAN REPUBLIC

President
1960–6   David Dacko
1966–79 Jean-Bédel   Bokassa   (*from   1977,* Emperor Bokassa I)
1979–81 David Dacko
1981–   André Kolingba

CHAD

President
1960–75 François Tombalbaye
1975–9   *Supreme Military Council* (Félix Malloum)
1979   Goukouni Oueddi
1979   Mohammed Shawwa
1979–82 Goukouni Oueddi
1982–90 Hissène Habré
1990–   Idriss Déby

CHILE

President
1900–1   Federico Errázuriz Echaurren
1901   Aníbal Zañartu *Vice President*
1901–3   Germán Riesco
1903   Ramón Barros Luco *Vice President*
1903–6   Germán Riesco
1906–10   Pedro Montt
1910   Ismael Tocornal *Vice President*
1910   Elías Fernández Albano *Vice President*
1910   Emiliano Figueroa Larraín *Vice President*
1910–15   Ramón Barros Luco
1915–20   Juan Luis Sanfuentes
1920–4   Arturo Alessandri
1924–5   *Military Juntas*
1925   Arturo Alessandri
1925   Luis Barros Borgoño *Vice President*
1925–27   Emiliano Figueroa

POLITICAL LEADERS 1900-1991 (cont.)

1927-31	Carlos Ibáñez
1931	Pedro Opaso Letelier *Vice President*
1931	Juan Esteban Montero *Vice President*
1931	Manuel Trucco Franzani *Vice President*
1931-2	Juan Estaban Montero
1932	*Military Juntas*
1932	Carlos G Dávila *Provisional President*
1932	Bartolomé Blanche *Provisional President*
1932	Abraham Oyanedel *Vice President*
1932-8	Arturo Alessandri Palma
1938-41	Pedro Aguirre Cerda
1941-2	Jerónimo Méndez Arancibia *Vice President*
1942-6	Juan Antonio Ríos Morales
1946-52	Gabriel González Videla
1952-8	Carlos Ibáñez del Campo
1958-64	Jorge Alessandri Rodríguez
1964-70	Eduardo Frei Montalva
1970-3	Salvador Allende Gossens
1973-90	Augusto Pinochet Ugarte
1990-	Patricio Aylwin Azócar

CHINA

Emperor

1875-1908	Kuang-hsü
1908-12	Hsüan-T'ung

President

1912	Sun Yat-sen
1912-16	Yüan Shih-k'ai
1916-17	Li Yuan-hung
1917-18	Feng Kuo-chang
1918-22	Hsü Shih-ch'ang
1921-5	Sun Yat-sen *Canton Administration*
1922-3	Li Yuan-hung
1923-4	Ts'ao K'un
1924-6	Tuan Ch'i-jui
1926-7	*Civil Disorder*
1927-8	Chang Tso-lin
1928-31	Chiang Kai-shek
1931-2	Ch'eng Ming-hsu *Acting President*
1932-43	Lin Sen
1940-4	Wang Ching-wei *in Japanese-occupied territory*
1943-9	Chiang Kai-shek

1945-9	*Civil War*
1949	Li Tsung-jen

People's Republic of China

1949-59	Mao Zedong (Mao Tse-tung)
1959-68	Liu Shaoqi
1968-75	Dong Biwu
1975-6	Zhu De
1976-8	Sung Qingling
1978-83	Ye Jianying
1983-8	Li Xiannian (Li Hsien-nien)
1988-	Yang Shangkun

Prime Minister

1901-3	Jung-lu
1903-11	Prince Ch'ing
1912	Lu Cheng-hsiang
1912-13	Chao Ping-chiin
1913-14	Sun Pao'chi
1914-16	*no Prime Minister*
1916-17	Chang-hsün
1917	Tuan Ch'i-jui
1918-19	Ch'ien Neng-hsün
1919	Kung Hsin-chan
1919-20	Chin Yün-p'eng
1920	Sa Chen-ping
1920-1	Chin Yün-p'eng
1921-2	Liang Shihi
1922	Yen Hui-ching
1922	Chow Tzu-ch'i
1922	Yen Hui-ching
1922	Wang Ch'ung-hui
1922-3	Wang Ta-hsieh
1923	Chang Shao-ts'êng
1923-4	Kao Ling-wei
1924	Jun Pao-ch'i
1924	Ku Wei-chiin
1924	Yen Hui-ch'ing
1924-5	Huang Fu
1925	Tuan Ch'i-jui
1925-6	Hsu Shih-ying
1926	Chia Teh-yao
1926	Hu Wei-te
1926	Yen Hui-ch'ing
1926	Tu Hsi-kuei
1926-7	Ku Wei-chün
1927	*Civil Disorder*
1927	*Executive Council*
1927-9	P'an Fu
1928-30	T'an Yen-kai
1930	Sung Tzu-wen *Acting Prime Minister*

POLITICAL LEADERS 1900–1991 (cont.)

China (cont.)

1930	Wang Ching-wei
1930–1	Chiang Kai-shek
1931–2	Sun Fo
1932–5	Wang Ching-wei
1935–7	Chiang Kai-shek
1937–8	Wang Ch'ung-hui *Acting Prime Minister*
1938–9	K'ung Hsiang-hsi
1939–44	Chiang Kai-shek
1944–7	Sung Tzu-wen
1945–9	*Civil War*
1947–8	Chang Ch'ün
1948	Wong Wen-hao
1948–9	Sun Fo
1949	Ho Ying-ch'in
1949	Yen Hsi-shan
1949–76	Zhou Enlai (Chou En-lai)
1976–80	Hua Guofeng
1980–7	Zhao Ziyang (Chao Tzu-yang)
1987–	Li Peng

Communist Party

Chairman

1935–76	Mao Zedong (Mao Tse-tung)
1976–81	Hua Guofeng
1981–2	Hu Yaobang

General Secretary

1982–7	Hu Yaobang
1987–9	Zhao Ziyang (Chao Tzu-yang)
1989–	Jiang Zemin

COLOMBIA

President

1900–4	José Manuel Marroquín *Vice President*
1904–9	Rafael Reyes
1909–10	Ramón González Valencia
1910–14	Carlos E Restrepo
1914–18	José Vicente Concha
1918–21	Marco Fidel Suárez
1921–2	Jorge Holguín *President Designate*
1922–6	Pedro Nel Ospina
1926–30	Miguel Abadía Méndez
1930–4	Enrique Olaya Herrera
1934–8	Alfonso López
1938–42	Eduardo Santos
1942	Alfonso López

1945–6	Alberto Lleras Camargo *President Designate*
1946–50	Mariano Ospina Pérez
1950–3	Laureano Gómez
1953–7	Gustavo Rojas Pinilla
1957	*Military Junta*
1958–62	Alberto Lleras Camargo
1962–6	Guillermo León Valencia
1966–70	Carlos Lleras Restrepo
1970–4	Misael Pastrana Borrero
1974–8	Alfonso López Michelsen
1978–82	Julio César Turbay Ayala
1982–6	Belisario Betancur
1986–90	Virgilio Barco Vargas
1990–	César Gaviria Trujillo

COMMONWEALTH

Secretary General

1965–75	Arnold Smith
1975–90	Shridath S Ramphal
1990–	Emeka Anyaoku

COMOROS

President

1976–78	Ali Soilih
1978–89	Ahmed Abdallah Abderemane
1989–	Said Mohammed Djohar

CONGO

President

1960–3	Abbé Fulbert Youlou
1963–8	Alphonse Massemba-Debat
1968	Marien Ngouabi
1968	Alphonse Massemba-Debat
1968–9	Alfred Raoul
1969–77	Marien Ngouabi
1977–9	Joachim Yhomby Opango
1979–	Denis Sassou-Nguesso

COSTA RICA

President

1894–1902	Rafael Yglesias y Castro

POLITICAL LEADERS 1900–1991 (cont.)

1902–6	Ascención Esquivel Ibarra
1906–10	Cleto González Víquez
1910–12	Ricardo Jiménez Oreamuno
1912–14	Cleto González Víquez
1914–17	Alfredo González Flores
1917–19	Federico Tinoco Granados
1919	Julio Acosta García
1919–20	Juan Bautista Quiros
1920–4	Julio Acosta García
1924–8	Ricardo Jiménez Oreamuno
1928–32	Cleto González Víquez
1932–6	Ricardo Jiménez Oreamuno
1936–40	León Cortés Castro
1940–4	Rafael Ángel Calderón Guardia
1944–8	Teodoro Picado Michalski
1948	Santos Léon Herrera
1948–9	*Civil Junta* (José Figueres Ferrer)
1949–52	Otilio Ulate Blanco
1952–3	Alberto Oreamuno Flores
1953–8	José Figueres Ferrer
1958–62	Mario Echandi Jiménez
1962–6	Francisco José Orlich Bolmarcich
1966–70	José Joaquín Trejos Fernández
1970–4	José Figueres Ferrer
1974–8	Daniel Oduber Quirós
1978–82	Rodrigo Carazo Odio
1982–6	Luis Alberto Monge Álvarez
1986–90	Oscar Arias Sánchez
1990–	Rafael Angel Calderón

CÔTE D'IVOIRE

President

1960–	Félix Houphouët-Boigny

CUBA

President

1902–6	Tomas Estrada Palma
1906–9	*US rule*
1909–13	José Miguel Gómez
1913–21	Mario García Menocal
1921–5	Alfredo Zayas y Alfonso
1925–33	Gerardo Machado y Morales
1933	Carlos Manuel de Céspedes
1933–4	Ramón Grau San Martín
1934–5	Carlos Mendieta
1935–6	José A Barnet y Vinagres

1936	Miguel Mariano Gómez y Arias
1936–40	Federico Laredo Bru
1940–4	Fulgencio Batista
1944–8	Ramón Grau San Martín
1948–52	Carlos Prío Socarrás
1952–9	Fulgencio Batista
1959	Manuel Urrutia
1959–76	Osvaldo Dorticós Torrado
1959–76	Fidel Castro Ruz *Prime Minister and First Secretary*
1976–	Fidel Castro Ruz *President*

CYPRUS

President

1960–77	Archbishop Makarios
1977–88	Spyros Kyprianou
1988–	Georgios Vassiliou

CZECHOSLOVAKIA

President

1918–35	Tomáš Garrigue Masaryk
1935–8	Edvard Beneš
1938–9	Emil Hácha

Occupation

1938–45	Edvard Beneš *Provisional President*
1939–45	Emil Hácha *State President*
1939–45	Jozef Tiso *Slovak Republic President*

Post-war

1945–8	Edvard Beneš
1948–53	Klement Gottwald
1953–7	Antonín Zápotocký
1957–68	Antonín Novotný
1968–75	Ludvík Svoboda
1975–89	Gustáv Husák
1989–	Vaclav Havel

Prime Minister

1918–19	Karel Kramář
1919–20	Vlastimil Tusar
1920–1	Jan Černý
1921–2	Edvard Beneš
1922–6	Antonin Švehla
1926	Jan Černý
1926–9	Antonin Švehla

POLITICAL LEADERS 1900–1991 (cont.)

Czechoslovakia (cont.)

1929–32	František Udržal
1932–5	Jan Malypetr
1935–8	Milan Hodža
1938	Jan Syrový
1938–9	Rudolf Beran
1940–5	Jan Šrámek *in exile*
1945–6	Zdeněk Fierlinger
1946–8	Klement Gottwald
1948–53	Antonin Zápotocký
1953–63	Viliam Široký
1963–8	Josef Lenárt
1968–70	Oldřich Černik
1970–88	Lubomír Štrougal
1988–9	Ladislav Adamec
1989–	Marian Calfa

First Secretary

1948–52	Rudolf Slánsky
1953–68	Antonín Novotný
1968–9	Alexander Dubček
1969–87	Gustáv Husák
1987–9	Mílos Jakes
1989	Karel Urbanek
1989–	Ladislav Adamec

DENMARK

Monarch

1863–1906	Christian IX
1906–12	Frederik VIII
1912–47	Christian X
1947–72	Frederik IX
1972–	Margrethe II

Prime Minister

1900–1	H Sehested
1901–5	J H Deuntzer
1905–8	J C Christensen
1908–9	N Neergaard
1909	L Holstein-Ledreborg
1909–10	C Th Zahle
1910–13	Klaus Berntsen
1913–20	C Th Zahle
1920	Otto Liebe
1920	M P Friis
1920–4	N Neergaard
1924–6	Thorvald Stauning
1926–9	Th Madsen-Mygdal

1929–42	Thorvald Stauning
1942	Wilhelm Buhl
1942–3	Erik Scavenius
1943–5	*No government*
1945	Wilhelm Buhl
1945–7	Knud Kristensen
1947–50	Hans Hedtoft
1950–3	Erik Eriksen
1953–5	Hans Hedtoft
1955–60	Hans Christian Hansen
1960–2	Viggo Kampmann
1962–8	Jens Otto Krag
1968–71	Hilmar Baunsgaard
1971–2	Jens Otto Krag
1972–3	Anker Jorgensen
1973–5	Poul Hartling
1975–82	Anker Jorgensen
1982–	Poul Schlüter

DJIBOUTI

President

1977–	Hassan Gouled Aptidon

Prime Minister

1977–8	Abdallah Mohammed Kamil
1978–	Barkat Gourad Hamadou

DOMINICA

President

1978–9	Louis Cods-Lartigue *Interim President*
1977	Frederick E Degazon
1979–80	Lenner Armour *Acting President*
1980–4	Aurelius Marie
1984–	Clarence Augustus Seignoret

Prime Minister

1978–9	Patrick Roland John
1979–80	Oliver Seraphine
1980–	Mary Eugenia Charles

DOMINICAN REPUBLIC

President

1899–1902	Juan Isidro Jiménez
1902–3	Horacio Vásquez

POLITICAL LEADERS 1900–1991 (cont.)

1903	Alejandro Wos y Gil
1903–4	Juan Isidro Jiménez
1904–6	Carlos Morales
1906–11	Ramon Cáceres
1911–12	Eladio Victoria
1912–13	Adolfo Nouel y Bobadilla
1913–14	José Bordas y Valdés
1914	Ramon Báez
1914–16	Juan Isidro Jiménez
1916–22	*US occupation*
	(Francisco Henríquez y Carrajal)
1922–4	(Juan Batista Vicini Burgos)
1924–30	Horacio Vásquez
1930	Rafael Estrella Urena
1930–8	Rafael Leónidas Trujillo y Molina
1938–40	Jacinto Bienvenudo Peynado
1940–2	Manuel de Jesus Troncoso de la Concha
1942–52	Rafael Leónidas Trujillo y Molina
1952–60	Hector Bienvenido Trujillo
1960–2	Joaquín Videla Balaguer
1962	Rafael Bonnelly
1962	*Military Junta* (Huberto Bogaert)
1962–3	Rafael Bonnelly
1963	Juan Bosch Gavino
1963	*Military Junta*
	(Emilio de los Santos)
1963–5	Donald Reid Cabral
1965	*Civil War*
1965	Elias Wessin y Wessin
1965	Antonio Imbert Barreras
1965	Francisco Caamaño Deñó
1965–6	Héctor García Godoy Cáceres
1966–78	Joaquín Videla Balaguer
1978–82	Antonio Guzmán Fernández
1982–6	Salvador Jorge Blanco
1986–	Joaquín Videla Balaguer

ECUADOR

President

1895–1901	Eloy Alfaro
1901–5	Leónides Plaza Gutiérrez
1905–6	Lizardo García
1906–11	Eloy Alfaro
1911	Emilio Estrada
1911–12	Carlos Freile Zaldumbide
1912–16	Leónides Plaza Gutiérrez
1916–20	Alfredo Baquerizo Moreno
1920–4	José Luis Tamayo
1924–5	Gonzálo S de Córdova

1925–6	*Military Juntas*
1926–31	Isidro Ayora
1931	Luis A Larrea Alba
1932–3	Juan de Dios Martínez Mera
1933–4	Abelardo Montalvo
1934–5	José María Velasco Ibarra
1935	Antonio Pons
1935–7	Federico Páez
1937–8	Alberto Enriquez Gallo
1938	Manuel María Borrero
1938–9	Aurelio Mosquera Narváez
1939–40	Julio Enrique Moreno
1940–4	Carlos Alberto Arroya del Río
1944–7	José María Velasco Ibarra
1947	Carlos Mancheno
1947–8	Carlos Julio Arosemena Tola
1948–52	Galo Plaza Lasso
1952–6	José María Velasco Ibarra
1956–60	Camilo Ponce Enríquez
1960–1	José María Velasco Ibarra
1961–3	Carlos Julio Arosemena Monroy
1963–6	*Military Junta*
1966	Clemente Yerovi Indaburu
1966–8	Otto Arosemena Gómez
1968–72	José María Velasco Ibarra
1972–6	Guillermo Rodríguez Lara
1976–9	*Military Junta*
1979–81	Jaime Roldós Aguilera
1981–4	Oswaldo Hurtado Larrea
1984–8	León Febres Cordero
1988–	Rodrigo Borja Cevallos

EGYPT

Khedive

1895–1914	Abbas Helmi II

Sultan

1914–17	Hussein Kamel
1917–22	Ahmed Fouad

Kingdom of Egypt

Monarch

1922–36	Fouad I
1936–7	Farouk *Trusteeship*
1937–52	Farouk I

POLITICAL LEADERS 1900–1991 (cont.)

Republic of Egypt

President

1952–4	Mohammed Naguib
1954–70	Gamal Abdel Nasser
1970–81	Mohammed Anwar El-Sadat
1981–	Mohammed Hosni Mubarak

Prime Minister

1895–1908	Mustafa Fahmy
1908–10	Butros Ghali
1910–14	Mohammed Said
1914–19	Hussein Rushdi
1919	Mohammed Said
1919–20	Yousuf Wahba
1920–1	Mohammed Tewfiq Nazim
1921	Adli Yegen
1922	Abdel Khaliq Tharwat
1922–3	Mohammed Tewfiq Nazim
1923–4	Yehia Ibrahim
1924	Saad Zaghloul
1924–6	Ahmed Zaywan
1926–7	Adli Yegen
1927–8	Abdel Khaliq Tharwat
1928	Mustafa An-Nahass
1928–9	Mohammed Mahmoud
1929–30	Adli Yegen
1930	Mustafa An-Nahass
1930–3	Ismail Sidqi
1933–4	Abdel Fattah Yahya
1934–6	Mohammed Tewfiq Nazim
1936	Ali Maher
1936–7	Mustafa An-Nahass
1937–9	Mohammed Mahmoud
1939–40	Ali Maher
1940	Hassan Sabri
1940–2	Hussein Sirry
1942–4	Mustafa An-Nahass
1944–5	Ahmed Maher
1945–6	Mahmoud Fahmy El-Nuqrashi
1946	Ismail Sidqi
1946–8	Mahmoud Fahmy El-Nuqrashi
1948–9	Ibrahim Abdel Hadi
1949–50	Hussein Sirry
1950–2	Mustafa An-Nahass
1952	Ali Maher
1952	Najib El-Hilali
1952	Hussein Sirry
1952	Najib El-Hilali
1952	Ali Maher

Republic of Egypt

1952–4	Mohammed Najib
1954	Gamal Abdel Nasser
1954	Mohammed Najib
1954–62	Gamal Abdel Nasser
1958–61	*United Arab Republic*
1962–5	Ali Sabri
1965–6	Zakariya Mohyi Ed-Din
1966–7	Mohammed Sidqi Soliman
1967–70	Gamal Abdel Nasser
1970–2	Mahmoud Fawzi
1972–3	Aziz Sidki
1973–4	Anwar El-Sadat
1974–5	Abdel Aziz Hijazy
1975–8	Mamdouh Salem
1978–80	Mustafa Khalil
1980–1	Anwar El-Sadat
1981–2	Hosni Mubarak
1982–4	Fouad Monyi Ed-Din
1984	Kamal Hassan Ali
1985–6	Ali Lotfi
1986–	Atif Sidqi

EL SALVADOR

President

1899–1903	Tomás Regalado
1903–7	Pedro José Escalon
1907–11	Fernando Figueroa
1911–13	Manuel Enrique Araujo
1913–14	Carlos Meléndez *President Designate*
1914–15	Alfonso Quiñónez Molina *President Designate*
1915–18	Carlos Meléndez
1918–19	Alfonso Quiñónez Molina *Vice President*
1919–23	Jorge Meléndez
1923–7	Alfonso Quiñónez Molina
1927–31	Pio Romero Bosque
1931	Arturo Araujo
1931	*Military Administration*
1931–4	Maximiliano H Martinez *Vice President*
1934–5	Andrés I Menéndez *Provisional President*
1935–44	Maximiliano H Martinez
1944	Andrés I Menéndez *Vice President*
1944–5	Osmin Aguirre y Salinas *Provisional President*
1945–8	Salvador Castaneda Castro

POLITICAL LEADERS 1900-1991 (cont.)

1948-50	*Revolutionary Council*
1950-6	Oscar Osorio
1956-60	José María Lemus
1960-1	*Military Junta*
1961-2	*Civil-Military Administration*
1962	Rodolfo Eusebio Cordón *Provisional President*
1962-7	Julio Adalberto Rivera
1967-72	Fidel Sánchez Hernández
1972-7	Arturo Armando Molina
1977-9	Carlos Humberto Romero
1979-82	*Military Juntas*
1982-4	*Government of National Unanimity* (Alvaro Magaña)
1984-9	José Napoleón Duarte
1989-	Alfredo Cristiani

EQUATORIAL GUINEA

President

1968-79	Francisco Macias Nguema
1979-	Teodoro Obiang Nguema Mbasogo

ETHIOPIA

Monarch

1889-1911	Menelik II
1911-16	Lij Iyasu (Joshua)
1916-28	Zawditu
1928-74	Haile Selassie *Emperor from 1930*

Provisional Military Administrative Council

Chairman

1974-7	Teferi Benti
1977-87	Mengistu Haile Mariam

People's Democratic Republic

President

1987-91	Mengistu Haile Mariam
1991-	Tesfaye Gebre Kidan *Acting*

EUROPEAN COMMUNITY (EC) COMMISSION

President

1967-70	Jean Rey

1970-2	Franco M Malfatti
1972-3	Sicco L Mansholt
1973-7	Francois-Xavier Ortoli
1977-81	Roy Jenkins
1981-5	Gaston Thorn
1985-	Jacques Delors

FIJI

Chief of State: British monarch, represented by Governor General

Prime Minister

1970-87	Kamisese Mara
1987	Timoci Bavadra

Interim Administration

Governor General

1987	Penaia Ganilau
1987	*Military administration* (Sitiveni Rabuka)

Republic

Chairman

1987	Sitiveni Rabuka

President

1987-	Penaia Ganilau

Prime Minister

1987-	Kamisese Mara

FINLAND

President

1919-25	Kaarlo Juho Ståhlberg
1925-31	Lauri Kristian Relander
1931-7	Pehr Evind Svinhufvud
1937-40	Kyösti Kallio
1940-4	Risto Ryti
1944-6	Carl Gustaf Mannerheim
1946-56	Juho Kusti Paasikivi
1956-81	Urho Kekkonen
1982-	Mauno Koivisto

POLITICAL LEADERS 1900–1991 (cont.)

Finland (cont.)

Prime Minister

1917–18	Pehr Evind Svinhufvud
1918	Juho Kusti Pasaikivi
1918–19	Lauri Johannes Ingman
1919	Kaarlo Castrén
1919–20	Juho Vennola
1920–1	Rafael Erich
1921–2	Juho Vennola
1922	Aino Kaarlo Cajander
1922–4	Kyösti Kallio
1924	Aino Kaarlo Cajander
1924–5	Lauri Johannes Ingman
1925	Antti Agaton Tulenheimo
1925–6	Kyösti Kallio
1926–7	Väinö Tanner
1927–8	Juho Emil Sunila
1928–9	Oskari Mantere
1929–30	Kyösti Kallio
1930–1	Pehr Evind Svinhufvud
1931–2	Juho Emil Sunila
1932–6	Toivo Kivimäki
1936–7	Kyösti Kallio
1937–9	Aino Kaarlo Cajander
1939–41	Risto Ryti
1941–3	Johann Rangell
1943–4	Edwin Linkomies
1944	Andreas Hackzell
1944	Urho Jonas Castrén
1944–5	Juho Kusti Paasikivi
1946–8	Mauno Pekkala
1948–50	Karl August Fagerholm
1950–3	Urho Kekkonen
1953–4	Sakari Tuomioja
1954	Ralf Törngren
1954–6	Urho Kekkonen
1956–7	Karl August Fagerholm
1957	Väinö Johannes Sukselainen
1957–8	Rainer von Fieandt
1958	Reino Iisakki Kuuskoski
1958–9	Karl August Fagerholm
1959–61	Väinö Johannes Sukselainen
1961–2	Martti Miettunen
1962–3	Ahti Karjalainen
1963–4	Reino Ragnar Lehto
1964–6	Johannes Virolainen
1966–8	Rafael Paasio
1968–70	Mauno Koivisto
1970	Teuvo Ensio Aura
1970–1	Ahti Karjalainen
1971–2	Teuvo Ensio Aura
1972	Rafael Paasio
1972–5	Kalevi Sorsa
1975	Keijo Antero Liinamaa
1975–7	Martti Miettunen
1977–9	Kalevi Sorsa
1979–82	Mauno Koivisto
1982–87	Kalevi Sorsa
1987–91	Harri Holkeri
1991–	Esko Aho

FRANCE

President

Third Republic

1899–1906	Emile Loubet
1906–13	Armand Fallières
1913–20	Raymond Poincaré
1920	Paul Deschanel
1920–4	Alexandre Millerand
1924–31	Gaston Doumergue
1931–2	Paul Doumer
1932–40	Albert Lebrun

Fourth Republic

1947–54	Vincent Auriol
1954–8	René Coty

Fifth Republic

1958–69	Charles de Gaulle
1969–74	Georges Pompidou
1974–81	Valéry Giscard d'Estaing
1981–	François Mitterrand

Prime Minister

Third Republic

1899–1902	Pierre Waldeck-Rousseau
1902–5	Emile Combes
1905–6	Maurice Rouvier
1906	Jean Sarrien
1906–9	Georges Clemenceau
1909–11	Aristide Briand
1911	Ernest Monis
1911–12	Joseph Caillaux
1912–13	Raymond Poincaré
1913	Aristide Briand
1913	Louis Barthou
1913–14	Gaston Doumergue
1914	Alexandre Ribot
1914–15	René Viviani
1915–17	Aristide Briand

POLITICAL LEADERS 1900–1991 (cont.)

1917	Alexandre Ribot
1917	Paul Painlevé
1917–20	Georges Clemenceau
1920	Alexandre Millerand
1920–1	Georges Leygues
1921–2	Aristide Briand
1922–4	Raymond Poincaré
1924	Frédéric François-Marsal
1924–5	Edouard Herriot
1925	Paul Painlevé
1925–6	Aristide Briand
1926	Edouard Herriot
1926–9	Raymond Poincaré
1929	Aristide Briand
1929–30	André Tardieu
1930	Camille Chautemps
1930	André Tardieu
1930–1	Théodore Steeg
1931–2	Pierre Laval
1932	André Tardieu
1932	Edouard Herriot
1932–3	Joseph Paul-Boncour
1933	Edouard Daladier
1933	Albert Sarrault
1933–4	Camille Chautemps
1934	Edouard Daladier
1934	Gaston Doumergue
1934–5	Pierre-Etienne Flandin
1935	Fernand Bouisson
1935–6	Pierre Laval
1936	Albert Sarrault
1936–7	Léon Blum
1937–8	Camille Chautemps
1938	Léon Blum
1938–40	Edouard Daladier
1940	Paul Reynaud
1940	Philippe Pétain

Vichy Government

1940–4	Philippe Pétain

Provisional Government of the French Republic

1944–6	Charles de Gaulle
1946	Félix Gouin
1946	Georges Bidault

Fourth Republic

1946–7	Léon Blum
1947	Paul Ramadier
1947–8	Robert Schuman
1948	André Marie
1948	Robert Schuman
1948–9	Henri Queuille
1949–50	Georges Bidault
1950	Henri Queuille
1950–1	René Pleven
1951	Henri Queuille
1951–2	René Pleven
1952	Edgar Faure
1952–3	Antoine Pinay
1953	René Mayer
1953–4	Joseph Laniel
1954–5	Pierre Mendès-France
1955–6	Edgar Faure
1956–7	Guy Mollet
1957	Maurice Bourgès-Maunoury
1957–8	Félix Gaillard
1958	Pierre Pflimin
1958–9	Charles de Gaulle

Fifth Republic

1959–62	Michel Debré
1962–8	Georges Pompidou
1968–9	Maurice Couve de Murville
1969–72	Jacques Chaban Delmas
1972–4	Pierre Mesmer
1974–6	Jacques Chirac
1976–81	Raymond Barre
1981–4	Pierre Mauroy
1984–6	Laurent Fabius
1986–8	Jacques Chirac
1988–91	Michel Rocard
1991–	Édith Cresson

GABON

President

1960–7	Léon M'ba
1967–	Omar (Bernard-Albert, *to 1973*) Bongo

Prime Minister

1960–75	*As President*
1975–90	Léon Mébiame (Mébiane)
1991–	Casimir Oyé Mba

THE GAMBIA

President

1965–	Dawda Kairaba Jawara

POLITICAL LEADERS 1900–1991 (cont.)

GERMANY

German Democratic Republic (East Germany)
President

1949–60   Wilhelm Pieck

Chairman of the Council of State

1960–73	Walter Ernst Karl Ulbricht
1973–6	Willi Stoph
1976–89	Erich Honecker
1989	Egon Krenz
1989–90	Gregor Gysi

General Secretary as Chairman

Premier

1949–64	Otto Grotewohl
1964–73	Willi Stoph
1973–6	Horst Sindermann
1976–89	Willi Stoph
1989–90	Hans Modrow
1990	Lothar de Maizière

German Federal Republic (West Germany)
President

1949–59	Theodor Heuss
1959–69	Heinrich Lübke
1969–74	Gustav Heinemann
1974–9	Walter Scheel
1979–84	Karl Carstens
1984–90	Richard von Weizsäcker

Chancellor

1949–63	Konrad Adenauer
1963–6	Ludwig Erhard
1966–9	Kurt Georg Kiesinger
1969–74	Willy Brandt
1974–82	Helmut Schmidt
1982–90	Helmut Kohl

Germany
President

1990–   Richard von Weizsäcker

Chancellor

1990–   Helmut Kohl

GHANA

President

1960–6   Kwame Nkrumah

National Liberation Council

Chairman

1966–9	Joseph Arthur Ankrah
1969	Akwasi Amankwa Afrifa
1969–70	*Presidential Committee*

President

1970–2   Edward Akufo-Addo

Chairman

1972–8	*National Redemption Council*
	(Ignatius Kuti Acheampong)
1978–9	*Supreme Military Council*
	(Fred W Akuffo)
1979	*Armed Forces Revolutionary Council*
	(Jerry John Rawlings)

President

1979–81   Hilla Limann

Provisional National Defence Council

Chairman

1981–   Jerry John Rawlings

Prime Minister

1960–9	*As President*
1969–72	Kufi Abrefa Busia
1972–8	*As President*
1978–	*No Prime Minister*

GREECE

Monarch

1863–1913	George I
1913–17	Constantine I
1917–20	Alexander
1920–2	Constantine I

POLITICAL LEADERS 1900–1991 (cont.)

1922–3	George II
1923–4	Paul Koundouriotis *Regent*

Republic

President

1924–6	Paul Koundouriotis
1926	Theodore Pangalos
1926–9	Paul Koundouriotis
1929–35	Alexander T Zaïmis

Monarch

1935	George Kondylis *Regent*
1935–47	George II
1947–64	Paul
1964–7	Constantine II
1967–73	*Military Junta*
1973	George Papadopoulos *Regent*

Republic

President

1973	George Papadopoulos
1973–4	Phaedon Gizikis
1974–5	Michael Stasinopoulos
1975–80	Constantine Tsatsos
1980–5	Constantine Karamanlis
1985–90	Christos Sartzetakis
1990–	Constantine Karamanlis

Prime Minister

1899–1901	George Theotokis
1901–2	Alexander T Zaïmis
1902–3	Theodore Diligiannis
1903	George Theotokis
1903	Demetrius G Rallis
1903–4	George Theotokis
1904–5	Theodore Deligiannis
1905	Demetrius G Rallis
1905–9	George Theotokis
1909	Demetrius G Rallis
1909–10	Kyriakoulis P Mavromichalis
1910	Stephen N Dragoumis
1910–15	Eleftherios K Venizelos
1915	Demetrius P Gounaris
1915	Eleftherios K Venizelos
1915	Alexander T Zaïmis
1915–16	Stephen Skouloudis
1916	Alexander T Zaïmis

1916	Nicholas P Kalogeropoulos
1916–17	Spyridon Lambros
1917	Alexander T Zaïmis
1917–20	Eleftherios K Venizelos
1920–1	Demetrius G Rallis
1921	Nicholas P Kalogeropoulos
1921–2	Demetrius P Gounaris
1922	Nicholas Stratos
1922	Peter E Protopapadakis
1922	Nicholas Triandaphyllakos
1922	Sotirios Krokidas
1922	Alexander T Zaïmis
1922–3	Stylianos Gonatas
1924	Eleftherios Venizelos
1924	George Kaphandaris
1924	Alexander Papanastasiou
1924	Themistocles Sophoulis
1924–5	Andreas Michalakopoulos
1925–6	Alexander N Chatzikyriakos
1926	Theodore Pangalos
1926	Athanasius Eftaxias
1926	George Kondylis
1926–8	Alexander T Zaïmis
1928–32	Eleftherios K Venizelos
1932	Alexander Papanastasiou
1932	Eleftherios K Venizelos
1932–3	Panagiotis Tsaldaris
1933	Eleftherios K Venizelos
1933	Nicholas Plastiras
1933	Alexander Othonaos
1933–5	Panagiotis Tsaldaris
1935	George Kondylis
1935–6	Constantine Demertzis
1936–41	John Metaxas
1941	Alexander Koryzis
1941	*Chairman of Ministers* George II
1941	*German Occupation* Emmanuel Tsouderos
1941–2	George Tsolakoglou
1942–3	Constantine Logothetopoulos
1943–4	John Rallis

Government in exile

1941–4	Emmanuel Tsouderos
1944	Sophocles Venizelos
1944–5	George Papandreou

Post-war

1945	Nicholas Plastiras
1945	Peter Voulgaris
1945	Damaskinos, Archbishop of Athens

POLITICAL LEADERS 1900–1991 (cont.)

Greece (cont.)

1945	Panagiotis Kanellopoulos
1945–6	Themistocles Sophoulis
1946	Panagiotis Politzas
1946–7	Constantine Tsaldaris
1947	Demetrius Maximos
1947	Constantine Tsaldaris
1947–9	Themistocles Sophoulis
1949–50	Alexander Diomedes
1950	John Theotokis
1950	Sophocles Venizelos
1950	Nicholas Plastiras
1950–1	Sophocles Venizelos
1951	Nicholas Plastiras
1952	Demetrius Kiusopoulos
1952–5	Alexander Papagos
1955	Stephen C Stefanopoulos
1955–8	Constantine Karamanlis
1958	Constantine Georgakopoulos
1958–61	Constantine Karamanlis
1961	Constantine Dovas
1961–3	Constantine Karamanlis
1963	Panagiotis Pipinellis
1963	Stylianos Mavromichalis
1963	George Papandreou
1963–4	John Paraskevopoulos
1964–5	George Papandreou
1965	George Athanasiadis-Novas
1965	Elias Tsirimokos
1965–6	Stephen C Stefanopoulos
1966–7	John Paraskevopoulos
1967	Panagiotis Kanellopoulos
1967–74	*Military Junta*
1967	Constantine Kollias
1967–73	George Papadopoulos
1973	Spyridon Markezinis
1973–4	Adamantios Androutsopoulos
1974–80	Constantine Karamanlis
1980–1	George Rallis
1981–9	Andreas Papandreou
1989	Tzannis Tzannetakis
1989–	Xenofon Zolotas

GRENADA

Chief of State: British monarch, represented by Governor General

Prime Minister

1974–9	Eric M Gairy
1979–83	Maurice Bishop

1983–4	Nicholas Braithwaite
	Chairman of Interim Council
1984–9	Herbert A Blaize
1989–	Ben Jones

GUATEMALA

President

1898–1920	Manuel Estrada Cabrera
1920–2	Carlos Herrera y Luna
1922–6	José María Orellana
1926–30	Lázaro Chacón
1930	Baudillo Palma
1930–1	Manuel María Orellana
1931	José María Reyna Andrade
1931–44	Jorge Ubico Castañeda
1944	Federico Ponce Vaidez
1944–5	Jacobo Arbenz Guzmán
1945–51	Juan José Arévalo
1951–4	Jacobo Arbenz Guzmán
1954	*Military Junta* (Carlos Díaz)
1954	Elfego J Monzón
1954–7	Carlos Castillo Armas
1957	*Military Junta*
	(Oscar Mendoza Azurdia)
1957	Luis Arturo González López
1957–8	*Military Junta*
	(Guillermo Flores Avendaño)
1958–63	Miguel Ydígoras Fuentes
1963–6	*Military Junta*
	(Enrique Peralta Azurdia)
1966–70	Julio César Méndez Montenegro
1970–4	Carlos Araña Osorio
1974–8	Kyell Eugenio Laugerua García
1978–82	Romeo Lucas García
1982	Angel Aníbal Guevara
1982–3	Efraín Rios Montt
1983–6	Oscar Humberto Mejía Victores
1986–91	Marco Vinicio Cerezo Arévalo
1991–	Jonge Serrano Elias

GUINEA

President

1961–84	Ahmed Sékou Touré
1984–	Lansana Conté

POLITICAL LEADERS 1900–1991 (cont.)

Prime Minister

1958–72	Ahmed Sékou Touré
1972–84	Louis Lansana Beavogui
1984–5	Diarra Traore
1985–	*None*

GUINEA-BISSAU

President

1974–80	Luis de Almeida Cabral
1980–4	*Revolutionary Council*
	(João Bernardo Vieira)
1984–	João Bernardo Vieira

GUYANA

President

1970	Edward A Luckhoo
1970–80	Arthur Chung
1980–5	Linden Forbes Sampson Burnham
1985–	Hugh Desmond Hoyte

Prime Minister

1966–85	Linden Forbes Sampson Burnham
1985–	Hamilton Green

HAITI

President

1896–1902	P A Tirésias Simon Lam
1902	Boisrond Canal
1902–8	Alexis Nord
1908–11	Antoine Simon
1911–12	Michel Cincinnatus Leconte
1912–13	Tancrède Auguste
1913–14	Michael Oreste
1914	Oreste Zamor
1914–15	Joseph Davilmare Théodore
1915	Jean Velbrun-Guillaume
1915–22	Philippe Sudre Dartiguenave
1922–30	Joseph Louis Bornó
1930	Étienne Roy
1930–41	Sténio Joseph Vincent
1941–6	Élie Lescot
1946	*Military Junta* (Frank Lavaud)

1946–50	Dumarsais Estimé
1950	*Military Junta* (Frank Lavaud)
1950–6	Paul E Magloire
1956–7	François Sylvain
1957	*Military Junta*
1957	Léon Cantave
1957	Daniel Fignolé
1957	Antoine Kebreau
1957–71	François Duvalier ('Papa Doc')
1971–86	Jean-Claude Duvalier ('Baby Doc')
1986–8	Henri Namphy
1988	Leslie Manigat
1988	Henri Namphy
1988–90	Prosper Avril
1990–1	Ertha Pascal-Trouillot
1991–	Jean-Bertrand Aristide

HONDURAS

President

1900–3	Terencio Sierra
1903	Juan Angel Arias
1903–7	Manuel Bonilla Chirinos
1907–11	Miguel R Dávila
1912–15	Manuel Bonilla Chirinos
1915–20	Francisco Bertrand
1920–4	Rafael López Gutiérrez
1924–5	Vicente Tosta Carrasco
1925–8	Miguel Paz Barahona
1929–32	Vicente Mejía Clindres
1932–49	Tiburcio Carías Andino
1949–54	Juan Manuel Gálvez

Head of State

1954–6	Julio Lozano Diaz
1956–7	*Military Junta*

President

1958–63	José Ramón Villeda Morales

Head of State

1963–5	Oswaldo López Arellano

President

1965–71	Oswaldo López Arellano
1971–2	Ramón Ernesto Cruz

POLITICAL LEADERS 1900–1991 (cont.)

Honduras (cont.)

Head of State

1972–5	Oswaldo López Arellano
	Juan Alberto Melgar Castro
1978–82	Policarpo Paz García

President

1982–6	Roberto Suazo Córdova
1986–9	José Azcona Hoyo
1989–	Rafael Callejas

HUNGARY

Monarch

1900–16	Franz Josef I
1916–18	Charles IV

President

1919	Mihály Károlyi
1919	*Revolutionary Governing Council*
	(Sándor Garbai)
1920–44	Miklós Horthy *Regent*
1944–5	*Provisional National Assembly*
1946–8	Zoltán Tildy
1948–50	Árpád Szakasits
1950–2	Sándor Rónai
1952–67	István Dobi
1967–87	Pál Losonczi
1987–8	Károly Németh
1988–9	Bruno Ferenc Straub
1989–90	Matyas Szuros
1990–	Arpad Göncz

Premier

1899–1903	Kálmán Széll
1903	Károly Khuen-Héderváry
1903–5	István Tisza
1905–6	Géza Fejérváry
1906–10	Sándor Wekerle
1910–12	Károly Kuen Héderváry
1912–13	László Lukács
1913–17	István Tisza
1917	Móric Esterházy
1917–18	Sándor Wekerle
1918–19	Mihály Károlyi
1919	Dénes Berinkey
1919	*Revolutionary Governing Council*

1919	Gyula Peidl
1919	István Friedrich
1919–20	Károly Huszár
1920	Sándor Simonyi-Semadam
1920–1	Pál Teleki
1921–31	István Bethlen
1931–2	Gyula Károlyi
1932–6	Gyula Gömbös
1936–8	Kálman Darányi
1938–9	Béla Imrédy
1939–41	Pál Teleki
1941–2	László Bárdossy
1942–4	Miklós Kállay
1944	Döme Sztójay
1944	Géza Lakatos
1944	Ferenc Szálasi
1944–5	*Provisional National Assembly*
	(Béla Dálnoki Miklós)
1945–6	Zoltán Tildy
1946–7	Ferenc Nagy
1947–8	Lajos Dinnyés
1948–52	István Dobi
1952–3	Mátyás Rákosi
1953–5	Imre Nagy
1955–6	András Hegedüs
1956	Imre Nagy
1956–8	János Kádár
1958–61	Ferenc Münnich
1961–5	János Kádár
1965–7	Gyula Kállai
1967–75	Jenö Fock
1975–87	György Lázár
1987–8	Károly Grosz
1988–90	Miklás Németh
1990–	Jozsef Antall

First Secretary

1949–56	Mátyás Rákosi
1956	Ernö Gerö
1956–88	János Kádár
1988–	Károly Grosz

ICELAND

President

1944–52	Sveinn Björnsson
1952–68	Ásgeir Ásgeirsson
1968–80	Kristján Eldjárn
1980–	Vigdís Finnbogadóttir

POLITICAL LEADERS 1900–1991 (cont.)

Prime Minister

1900–1	C Goos
1901–4	P A Alberti
1904–9	Hannes Hafstein
1909–11	Björn Jónsson
1911–12	Kristján Jónsson
1912–14	Hannes Hafstein
1914–15	Sigurdur Eggerz
1915–17	Einar Arnórsson
1917–22	Jón Magnússon
1922–4	Sigurdur Eggerz
1924–6	Jón Magnússon
1926–7	Jon Þorláksson
1927–32	Tryggvi Þórhallsson
1932–4	Ásgeir Ásgeirsson
1934–42	Hermann Jónasson
1942	Ólafur Thors
1942–4	Björn Þórdarsson
1944–7	Ólafur Thors
1947–9	Stefán Jóhann Stefánsson
1949–50	Ólafur Thors
1950–3	Steingrímur Steinþórsson
1953–6	Ólafur Thors
1956 8	Hermann Jónasson
1958–9	Emil Jónsson
1959–61	Ólafur Thors
1961	Bjarni Benediktsson
1961–3	Ólafur Thors
1963–70	Bjarni Benediktsson
1970–1	Jóhann Hafstein
1971–4	Ólafur Jóhannesson
1974–8	Geir Hallgrímsson
1978–9	Ólafur Jóhannesson
1979	Benedikt Gröndal
1980–3	Gunnar Thoroddsen
1983–7	Steingrímur Hermannsson
1987–8	Thorsteinn Pálsson
1988–91	Steingrímur Hermannsson
1991–	Davíd Uddsson

INDIA

President

1950–62	Rajendra Prasad
1962–7	Sarvepalli Radhakrishnan
1967–9	Zakir Husain
1969	Varahagiri Venkatagiri *Acting President*
1969	Mohammed Hidayatullah *Acting President*

1969–74	Varahagiri Venkatagiri
1974–7	Fakhruddin Ali Ahmed
1977	B D Jatti *Acting President*
1977–82	Neelam Sanjiva Reddy
1982–7	Giani Zail Singh
1987–	Ramaswami Venkataraman

Prime Minister

1947–64	Jawaharlal Nehru
1964	Gulzari Lal Nanda *Acting Prime Minister*
1964–6	Lal Bahadur Shastri
1966	Gulzari Lal Nanda *Acting Prime Minister*
1966–77	Indira Gandhi
1977–9	Morarji Desai
1979–80	Charan Singh
1980–4	Indira Gandhi
1984–9	Rajiv Gandhi
1989–90	Vishwanath Pratap Singh
1990–1	Chandra Shekhar
1991–	P V Narasimha Rao

INDONESIA

President

1945–9	Ahmed Sukarno

Republic

1949–66	Ahmed Sukarno
1966–	T N J Suharto

Prime Minister

1945	R A A Wiranatakusumah
1945–7	Sutan Sjahrir
1947–8	Amir Sjarifuddin
1948	Mohammed Hatta
1948–9	Sjarifuddin Prawiraranegara
1949	Susanto Tirtoprodjo
1949	Mohammed Hatta
1950	Dr Halim
1950–1	Mohammed Natsir
1951–2	Sukiman Wirjosandjojo
1952–3	Dr Wilopo
1953–5	Ali Sastroamidjojo
1955–6	Burhanuddin Harahap
1956–7	Ali Sastroamidjojo
1957–9	Raden Haji Djuanda Kurtawidjaja
1959–63	Ahmed Sukarno
1963–6	S E Subandrio
1966–	*No Prime Minister*

POLITICAL LEADERS 1900–1991 (cont.)

IRAN (Persia)

Shah

1896–1907	Muzaffar Ad-Din
1907–9	Mohammed Ali
1909–25	Ahmad Mirza
1925–41	Mohammed Reza Khan
1941–79	Mohammed Reza Pahlavi

Republic

Leader of the Islamic Revolution

1979–89	Ruhollah Khomeini
1989–	Sayed Ali Khamenei

President

1980–1	Abolhassan Bani-Sadr
1981	Mohammed Ali Rajai
1981–9	Sayed Ali Khamenei
1989–	Hashemi Rafsanjani

Prime Minister

1979	Shahpur Bakhtiar
1979–80	Mehdi Bazargan
1980–1	Mohammed Ali Rajai
1981	Mohammed Javad Bahonar
1981	Mohammed Reza Mahdavi-Kani
1981–9	Mir Hossein Moussavi

IRAQ

Monarch

1921–33	Faisal I
1933–9	Ghazi I
1939–58	Faisal II
	(*Regent, 1939–53*, Abdul Illah)

Republic

Commander of the National Forces

1958–63	Abdul Karim Qassem

Head of Council of State

1958–63	Mohammed Najib Ar-Rubai

President

1963–6	Abdus Salaam Mohammed Arif
1966–8	Abdur Rahman Mohammed Arif
1968–79	Said Ahmad Hassan Al-Bakr
1979–	Saddam Hussein At-Takriti

IRELAND

Governor General

1922–7	Timothy Michael Healy
1927–32	James McNeill
1932–6	Donald Buckley

President

1938–45	Douglas Hyde
1945–59	Sean Thomas O'Kelly
1959–73	Eamon de Valera
1973–4	Erskine H Childers
1974–6	Carroll Daly
1976–90	Patrick J Hillery
1990–	Mary Robinson

Prime Minister

1919–21	Eamon de Valera
1922	Arthur Griffiths
1922–32	William Cosgrave
1932–48	Eamon de Valera
1948–51	John Aloysius Costello
1951–4	Eamon de Valera
1954–7	John Aloysius Costello
1957–9	Eamon de Valera
1959–66	Sean Lemass
1966–73	John Lynch
1973–7	Liam Cosgrave
1977–9	John Lynch
1979–82	Charles Haughey
1982–7	Garret FitzGerald
1987–	Charles Haughey

ISRAEL

President

1948–52	Chaim Weizmann
1952–63	Itzhak Ben-Zvi
1963–73	Zalman Shazar
1973–8	Ephraim Katzair

POLITICAL LEADERS 1900–1991 (cont.)

1978–83	Yitzhak Navon
1983–	Chaim Herzog

Prime Minister

1948–53	David Ben Gurion
1954–5	Moshe Sharett
1955–63	David Ben Gurion
1963–9	Levi Eshkol
1969–74	Golda Meir
1974–7	Itzhak Rabin
1977–83	Menachem Begin
1983–4	Yitzhak Shamir
1984–8	Shimon Peres
1988–	Yitzhak Shamir

ITALY

Kingdom of Italy

Monarch

1900–46	Victor Emmanuel III

Italian Republic

President

1946–8	Enrico de Nicola
1948–55	Luigi Einaudi
1955–62	Giovanni Gronchi
1962–4	Antonio Segni
1964–71	Giuseppe Saragat
1971–8	Giovanni Leone
1978–85	Alessandro Pertini
1985–	Francesco Cossiga

Kingdom of Italy

Prime Minister

1900–1	Giuseppe Saracco
1901–3	Giuseppe Zanardelli
1903–5	Giovanni Giolitti
1905–6	Alessandro Fortis
1906	Sydney Sonnino
1906–9	Giovanni Giolitti
1909–10	Sydney Sonnino
1910–11	Luigi Luzzatti
1911–14	Giovanni Giolitti
1914–16	Antonio Salandra
1916–17	Paolo Boselli
1917–19	Vittorio Emmanuele Orlando
1919–20	Francesco Saverio Nitti

1920–1	Giovanni Giolitti
1921–2	Ivanoe Bonomi
1922	Luigi Facta
1922–43	Benito Mussolini
1943–4	Pietro Badoglio
1944–5	Ivanoe Bonomi
1945	Ferrucio Parri
1945	Alcide de Gasperi

Italian Republic

1946–53	Alcide De Gasperi
1953–4	Giuseppe Pella
1954	Amintore Fanfani
1954–5	Mario Scelba
1955–7	Antonio Segni
1957–8	Adone Zoli
1958–9	Amintore Fanfani
1959–60	Antonio Segni
1960	Fernando Tambroni
1960–3	Amintore Fanfani
1963	Giovanni Leone
1963–8	Aldo Moro
1968	Giovanni Leone
1968–70	Mariano Rumor
1970–2	Emilio Colombo
1972–4	Giulio Andreotti
1974–6	Aldo Moro
1976–8	Giulio Andreotti
1979–80	Francisco Cossiga
1980–1	Arnaldo Forlani
1081 2	Giovanni Spadolini
1982–3	Amintore Fanfani
1983–7	Bettino Craxi
1987	Amintore Fanfani
1987–8	Giovanni Goria
1988–9	Ciriaco de Mita
1989–	Giulio Andreotti

JAMAICA

Chief of State: British monarch, represented by Governor General

Prime Minister

1962–7	William Alexander Bustamante
1967	Donald Burns Sangster
1967–72	Hugh Lawson Shearer
1972–80	Michael Norman Manley
1980–9	Edward Phillip George Seaga
1989–	Michael Norman Manley

POLITICAL LEADERS 1900–1991 (cont.)

JAPAN

Chief of State (Emperor)

1867–1912	Mutsuhito (Meiji)
1912–26	Yoshihito (Taishō)
1926–89	Hirohito (Shōwa)
1989–	Akihito (Heisei)

Prime Minister

1900–1	Hirobumi Itō
1901–6	Tarō Katsura
1906–8	Kimmochi Saionji
1908–11	Tarō Katsura
1911–12	Kimmochi Saionji
1912–13	Tarō Katsura
1913–14	Gonnohyōe Yamamoto
1914–16	Shigenobu Ōkuma
1916–18	Masatake Terauchi
1918–21	Takashi Hara
1921–2	Korekiyo Takahashi
1922–3	Tomosaburō Katō
1923–4	Gonnohyōe Yamamoto
1924	Keigo Kiyoura
1924–6	Takaaki Katō
1926–7	Reijirō Wakatsuki
1927–9	Giichi Tanaka
1929–31	Osachi Hamaguchi
1931	Reijirō Wakatsuki
1931–2	Tsuyoshi Inukai
1932–4	Makoto Saitō
1934–6	Keisuke Okada
1936–7	Kōki Hirota
1937	Senjūrō Hayashi
1937–9	Fumimaro Konoe
1939	Kiichirō Hiranuma
1939–40	Nobuyuki Abe
1940	Mitsumasa Yonai
1940–1	Fumimaro Konoe
1941–4	Hideki Tōjō
1944–5	Kuniaki Koiso
1945	Kantarō Suzuki
1945	Naruhiko Higashikuni
1945–6	Kijūrō Shidehara
1946–7	Shigeru Yoshida
1947–8	Tetsu Katayama
1948	Hitoshi Ashida
1948–54	Shigeru Yoshida
1954–6	Ichirō Hatoyama
1956–7	Tanzan Ishibashi
1957–60	Nobusuke Kishi
1960–4	Hayato Ikeda
1964–72	Eisaku Satō
1972–4	Kakuei Tanaka
1974–6	Takeo Miki
1976–8	Takeo Fukuda
1978–80	Masayoshi Ōhira
1980–2	Zenkō Suzuki
1982–7	Yasuhiro Nakasone
1987–9	Noboru Takeshita
1989	Sasuke Uno
1989–	Toshiki Kaifu

JORDAN

Monarch

1921–51	Abdallah Bin Hussein
1951–2	Talal I
1952–	Hussein II

Prime Minister

1921	Rashid Tali
1921	Muzhir Ar-Raslan
1921–3	Rida Ar-Riqabi
1923	Muzhir Ar-Raslan
1923–4	Hassan Khalid
1924–33	Rida Ar-Riqabi
1933–8	Ibrahim Hashim
1939–45	Taufiq Abul-Huda
1945–8	Ibrahim Hashim
1948–50	Taufiq Abul-Huda
1950	Said Al-Mufti
1950–1	Samir Ar-Rifai
1951–3	Taufiq Abul-Huda
1953–4	Fauzi Al-Mulqi
1954–5	Taufiq Abul-Huda
1955	Said Al-Mufti
1955	Hazza Al-Majali
1955–6	Ibrahim Hashim
1956	Samir Ar-Rifai
1956	Said Al-Mufti
1956	Ibrahim Hashim
1956–7	Suleiman Nabulsi
1957	Hussein Fakhri Al-Khalidi
1957–8	Ibrahim Hashim
1958	Nuri Pasha Al-Said
1958–9	Samir Ar-Rifai
1959–60	Hazza Al-Majali
1960–2	Bahjat Talhuni
1962–3	Wasfi At-Tall

POLITICAL LEADERS 1900–1991 (cont.)

1963	Samir Ar-Rifai
1963–4	Sharif Hussein Bin Nasir
1964	Bahjat Talhuni
1965–7	Wasfi At-Tall
1967	Sharif Hussein Bin Nasir
1967	Saad Jumaa
1967–9	Bahjat Talhuni
1969	Abdul Munem Rifai
1969–70	Bahjat Talhuni
1970	Abdul Munem Rifai
1970	*Military Junta* (Mohammed Daud)
1970	Mohamed Ahmed Tuqan
1970–1	Wasfi At-Tall
1971–3	Ahmad Lozi
1973–6	Zaid Rifai
1976–9	Mudar Badran
1979–80	Sherif Abdul Hamid Sharaf
1980	Kassem Rimawi
1980–4	Mudar Badran
1984–5	Ahmad Ubayat
1985–9	Zaid Ar-Rifai
1989	Sharif Zaid Ibn Shaker
1989–91	Mudar Badran
1991–	Taher al-Masri

KENYA

President

1963–78	Mzee Jomo Kenyatta
1978–	Daniel Arap Moi

KIRIBATI

President

1979–91	Ieremia T Tabai
1991–	Teatao Teannaki

DEMOCRATIC PEOPLE'S REPUBLIC OF KOREA (North Korea)

President

1948–57	Kim Doo-bong
1957–72	Choi Yong-kun
1972–	Kim Il-sung

Prime Minister

1948–76	Kim Il-sung
1976–7	Park Sung-chul
1977–84	Li Jong-ok
1984–6	Kang Song-san
1986–8	Yi Kun-mo
1988–	Yon Hyong Muk

REPUBLIC OF KOREA (South Korea)

President

1948–60	Syngman Rhee
1960	Ho Chong *Acting President*
1960	Kwak Sang-hun *Acting President*
1960	Ho Chong *Acting President*
1960–3	Yun Po-sun
1963–79	Park Chung-hee
1979–80	Choi Kyu-hah
1980	Park Choong-hoon *Acting President*
1980–8	Chun Doo-hwan
1988–	Roh Tae Woo

Prime Minister

1948–50	Lee Pom-sok
1950	Shin Song-mo *Acting Prime Minister*
1950–1	John M Chang
1951–2	Ho Chong *Acting Prime Minister*
1952	Lee Yun-yong *Acting Prime Minister*
1952	Chang Taek-sang
1952–4	Paik Too-chin
1954–6	Pyon Yong-tae
1956–60	Syngman Rhee
1960	Ho Chong
1960–1	John M Chang
1961	Chang To-yong
1961–2	Song Yo-chan
1962–3	Kim Hyun-chul
1963–4	Choe Tu-son
1964–70	Chung Il-kwon
1970–1	Paik Too-chin
1971–5	Kim Jong-pil
1975–9	Choi Kyu-hah
1979–80	Shin Hyun-hwak
1980	Park Choong-hoon *Acting Prime Minister*
1980–2	Nam Duck-woo
1982	Yoo Chang-soon
1982–3	Kim Sang-hyup

POLITICAL LEADERS 1900-1991 (cont.)

Republic of Korea (cont.)

1983–5	Chin Lee-chong
1985–8	Lho Shin-yong
1988	Lee Hyun Jae
1988–90	Kang Young Hoon
1990–1	Ro Jai Bong
1991–	Chung Won Shik

KUWAIT

Emir

Family name: Al-Sabah

1896–1915	Mubarak
1915–17	Jaber II
1917–21	Salem Al-Mubarak
1921–50	Ahmed Al-Jaber
1950–65	Abdallah Al-Salem
1965–77	Sabah Al-Salem
1978–	Jaber Al-Ahmed Al-Jaber

Prime Minister

1962–3	Abdallah Al-Salem
1963–5	Sabah Al-Salem
1965–78	Jaber Al-Ahmed Al-Jaber
1978–	Saad Al-Abdallah Al-Salem

LAOS

Monarch

1904–59	Sisavang Vong
1959–75	Savang Vatthana

Lao People's Republic

President

1975–87	Souphanouvong
1987–	Phoumi Vongrichit

Prime Minister

1951–4	Souvanna Phouma
1954–5	Katay Don Sasorith
1956–8	Souvanna Phouma
1958–9	Phoui Sahanikone
1959–60	Sunthone Patthamavong
1960	Kou Abhay
1960	Somsanith
1960	Souvana Phouma
1960	Sunthone Patthamavong
1960	Quinim Pholsena
1960–2	Boun Oum Na Champassac
1962–75	Souvanna Phouma

Lao People's Democratic Republic

1975–	Kaysone Phomvihan

LEBANON

President

1943–52	Bishara Al-Khoury
1952–8	Camille Shamoun
1958–64	Fouad Shehab
1964–70	Charle Hilo
1970–6	Suleiman Frenjieh
1976–82	Elias Sarkis
1982	Bashir Gemayel
1982–8	Amin Gemayel
1988–9	*No President*
1989	Rene Muawad
1989–	Elias Hrawi

Prime Minister

1943	Riad Solh
1943–4	Henry Pharaon
1944–5	Riad Solh
1945	Abdul Hamid Karame
1945–6	Sami Solh
1946	Saadi Munla
1946–51	Riad Solh
1951	Hussein Oweini
1951–2	Abdullah Yafi
1952	Sami Solh
1952	Nazem Accari
1952	Saeb Salam
1952	Fouad Chehab
1952–3	Khaled Chehab
1953	Saeb Salam
1953–5	Abdullah Yafi
1955	Sami Solh
1955–6	Rashid Karami
1956	Abdullah Yafi
1956–8	Sami Solh
1958–60	Rashid Karami
1960	Ahmad Daouq
1960–1	Saeb Salam
1961–4	Rashid Karami
1964–5	Hussein Oweini

POLITICAL LEADERS 1900–1991 (cont.)

1965–6	Rashid Karami
1966	Abdullah Yafi
1966–8	Rashid Karami
1968–9	Abdullah Yafi
1969–70	Rashid Karami
1970–3	Saeb Salam
1973	Amin al-Hafez
1973–4	Takieddine Solh
1974–5	Rashid Solh
1975	Noureddin Rifai
1975–6	Rashid Karami
1976–80	Selim al-Hoss
1980	Takieddine Solh
1980–4	Chafiq al-Wazan
1984–8	Rashid Karami
1988–90	Michel Aoun/Selim al-Hoss
1990–	Umar Karami

LESOTHO

Monarch

1966–90	Moshoeshoe II
1991–	Letsie III

Prime Minister

1966–86	Leabua Jonathan

Chairman of Military Council

1986–91	Justin Metsing Lekhanya
1991–	Elias Tutsoane Ramaema

LIBERIA

President

1900–4	Garretson Wilmot Gibson
1904–12	Arthur Barclay
1912–20	Daniel Edward Howard
1920–30	Charles Dunbar Burgess King
1930–43	Edwin J Barclay
1943–71	William V S Tubman
1971–80	William Richard Tolbert

People's Redemption Council

Chairman

1980–6	Samuel K Doe

President

1986–90	Samuel K Doe
1991–	Amos Sawyer

LIBYA

Monarch

1951–69	Mohammed Idris Al-Mahdi Al-Senussi

Revolutionary Command Council

Chairman

1969–77	Muammar Al-Gadhafi (Qadhafi)

General Secretariat

Secretary General

1977–9	Muammar Al-Gadhafi
1979–84	Abdul Ati Al-Ubaidi
1984–6	Mohammed Az-Zaruq Rajab
1986–	Omar Al-Muntasir

Leader of the Revolution

1969–	Muammar Al-Gadhafi

LIECHTENSTEIN

Prince

1858–1929	Johann II
1929–38	Franz von Paula
1938–89	Franz Josef II
1989–	Hans Adam II

Prime Minister

1928–45	Franz Josef Hoop
1945–62	Alexander Friek
1962–70	Gérard Batliner
1970–4	Alfred J Hilbe
1974–8	Walter Kieber
1978–	Hans Brunhart

POLITICAL LEADERS 1900–1991 (cont.)

LUXEMBOURG

Grand Dukes and Duchesses

1890–1905	Adolf
1905–12	William IV
1912–19	Marie Adelaide
1919–64	Charlotte *in exile 1940–4*
1964–	Jean

Prime Minister

1889–1915	Paul Eyschen
1915	Mathias Mongenast
1915–16	Hubert Loutsch
1916–17	Victor Thorn
1917–18	Léon Kaufmann
1918–25	Emil Reuter
1925–6	Pierre Prum
1926–37	Joseph Bech
1937–53	Pierre Dupong *in exile 1940–4*
1953–8	Joseph Bech
1958	Pierre Frieden
1959–69	Pierre Werner
1969–79	Gaston Thorn
1979–84	Pierre Werner
1984–	Jacques Santer

MADAGASCAR

President

1960–72	Philibert Tsiranana
1972–5	Gabriel Ramanantsoa
1975	Richard Ratsimandrava
1975	Gilles Andriamahazo
1975–	Didier Ratsiraka

Prime Minister

1960–75	*As President*
1975–6	Joël Rakotomala
1976–7	Justin Rakotoriaina
1977–88	Désiré Rakotoarijaona
1988–	Victor Ramahatra

MALAWI

President

1966–	Hastings Kamuzu Banda

MALAYSIA

Chief of State (Yang di-Pertuan Agong)

1957–63	Abdul Rahman
1963–5	Syed Putra Jamalullah
1965–70	Ismail Nasiruddin Shah
1970–5	Abdul Halim Muadzam Shah
1975–9	Yahya Petra Ibrahim
1979–84	Haji Ahmad Shah Al-Mustain Billah
1984–9	Mahmood Iskandar
1989–	Azlan Muhibuddin Shah

Prime Minister

Malaya

1957–63	Abdul Rahman Putra Al-Haj

Malaysia

1963–70	Abdul Rahman Putra Al-Haj
1970–6	Abdul Razak bin Hussein
1976–9	Haji Hussein bin Onn
1979–	Mahathir bin Mohamad

MALDIVES

Monarch (Sultan)

1954–68	Mohammed Farid Didi

Republic

President

1968–78	Ibrahim Nasir
1978–	Maumoon Abdul Gayoom

MALI

President

1960–8	Modibo Keita
1969–91	Moussa Traoré
1991–	Amadou Toumani Touré

Prime Minister

1986–88	Mamadou Dembelé
1988–91	*No Prime Minister*
1991–	Soumana Sacko

POLITICAL LEADERS 1900–1991 (cont.)

MALTA

President

1974–6	Anthony Mamo
1976–81	Anton Buttigieg
1982–7	Agatha Barbara
1987–9	Paul Xuereb *Acting President*
1989–	Vincent Tabore

Prime Minister

1962–71	G Borg Olivier
1971–84	Dom Mintoff
1984–7	Carmelo Mifsud Bonnici
1987–	Edward Fenech Adami

MAURITANIA

President

1961–78	Mokhtar Ould Daddah
1979	Mustapha Ould Mohammed Salek
1979–80	Mohammed Mahmoud Ould Ahmed Louly
1980–4	Mohammed Khouna Ould Haydalla
1984–	Moaouia Ould Sidi Mohammed Taya

MAURITIUS

Chief of State: British monarch, represented by Governor General

Prime Minister

| 1968–82 | Seewoosagur Ramgoolam |
| 1982– | Anerood Jugnauth |

MEXICO

President

1876–1911	Porfirio Diaz
1911	Francisco León de la Barra
1911–13	Francisco I Madero
1913–14	Victoriano Huerta
1914	Francisco Carvajal
1914	Venustiano Carranza
1914–15	Eulalio Gutiérrez *Provisional President*
1915	Roque González Garza *Provisional President*
1915	Francisco Lagos Chazaro *Provisional President*
1917–20	Venustiano Carranza
1920	Adolfo de la Huerta
1920–4	Alvaro Obregón
1924–8	Plutarco Elías Calles
1928–30	Emilio Portes Gil
1930–2	Pascual Ortíz Rubio
1932–4	Abelardo L. Rodríguez
1934–40	Lazaro Cardenas
1940–6	Manuel Avila Camacho
1946–52	Miguel Alemán
1952–8	Adolfo Ruiz Cortines
1958–64	Adolfo López Mateos
1964–70	Gustavo Díaz Ordaz
1970–6	Luis Echeverría
1976–82	José López Portillo
1982–8	Miguel de la Madrid Hurtado
1988–	Carlos Salinas de Gortari

MONACO

Head of State

1889–1922	Albert
1922–49	Louis II
1949–	Rainier III

MONGOLIA

Prime Minister

1924–8	Tserendorji
1928–32	Amor
1932–6	Gendun
1936–8	Amor
1939–52	Korloghiin Choibalsan
1952–74	Yumsjhagiin Tsedenbal
1990–	Dashiyn Byambasuren

Chairman of the Praesidium

1948–53	Gonchighlin Bumatsende
1954–72	Jamsarangiin Sambu
1972–4	Sonomyn Luvsan
1974–84	Yumsjhagiin Tsedenbal
1984–90	Jambyn Batmunkh

President

| 1990– | Punsalmaagiyn Ochirbat |

POLITICAL LEADERS 1900–1991 (cont.)

Mongolia (cont.)

Premier

1974–84	Jambyn Batmunkh
1984–90	Dumaagiyn Sodnom

MOROCCO

Monarch

1927–61	Mohammed V
1961–	Hassan II

Prime Minister

1955–8	Si Mohammed Bekkai
1958	Ahmad Balfrej
1958–60	Abdullah Ibrahim
1960–3	*As Monarch*
1963–5	Ahmad Bahnini
1965–7	*As Monarch*
1967–9	Moulay Ahmed Laraki
1969–71	Mohammed Ben Hima
1971–2	Mohammed Karim Lamrani
1972–9	Ahmed Othman
1979–83	Maati Bouabid
1983–6	Mohammed Karim Lamrani
1986–	Izz Id-Dien Laraki

MOZAMBIQUE

President

1975–86	Samora Moïses Machel
1986–	Joaquim Alberto Chissanó

NAMIBIA

President

1990–	Sam Nujoma

NAURU

President

1968–86	Hammer de Roburt
1986	Kennan Adeang
1986–9	Hammer de Roburt
1989	Kenas Aroi
1989–	Bernard Dowiyogo

NEPAL

Monarch

1881–1911	Prithvi Bir Bikram Shah
1911–50	Tribhuvan Bir Bikram Shah
1950–2	Bir Bikram
1952–5	Tribhuvan Bir Bikram Shah
1956–72	Mahendra Bir Bikram Shah
1972–	Birenda Bir Bikram Shah Deva

Prime Minister

1901–29	Chandra Sham Sher Jang Bahadur Rana
1929–31	Bhim Cham Sham Sher Jang Bahadur Rana
1931–45	Juddha Sham Sher Rana
1945–8	Padma Sham Sher Jang Bahadur Rana
1948–51	Mohan Sham Sher Jang Bahadur Rana
1951–2	Matrika Prasad Koirala
1952–3	Tribhuvan Bir Bikram Shah
1953–5	Matrika Prasad Koirala
1955–6	Mahendra Bir Bikram Shah
1956–7	Tanka Prasad Acharya
1957–9	*King also Prime Minister*
1959–60	Sri Bishawa Prasad Koirala
1960–3	*No Prime Minister*
1963–5	Tulsi Giri
1965–9	Surya Bahadur Thapa
1969–70	Kirti Nidhi Bista
1970–1	*King also Prime Minister*
1971–3	Kirti Nidhi Bista
1973–5	Nagendra Prasad Rijal
1975–7	Tulsi Giri
1977–9	Kirti Nidhi Bista
1979–83	Surya Bahadur Thapa
1983–6	Lokendra Bahadur Chand
1986–91	Marich Man Singh Shrestha
1991–	Girija Prasad Koirala

THE NETHERLANDS

Monarch

1898–1948	Wilhelmina Helena Paulina Maria
1948–80	Juliana Louise Emma Marie Wilhelmina
1980–	Béatrix Wilhelmina Armgard

POLITICAL LEADERS 1900–1991 (cont.)

Prime Minister

1897–1901	Nicholas G Pierson
1901–5	Abraham Kuyper
1905–8	Theodoor H de Meester
1908–13	Theodorus Heemskerk
1913–18	Pieter W A Cort van der Linden
1918–25	Charles J M Ruys de Beerenbrouck
1925–6	Hendrikus Colijn
1926	Dirk J de Geer
1926–33	Charles JM Ruys de Beerenbrouck
1933–9	Hendrikus Colijn
1939–40	Dirk J de Geer
1940–5	Pieter S Gerbrandy *in exile*
1945–6	Willem Schemerhorn/Willem Drees
1946–8	Louis J M Beel
1948–51	Willem Drees/Josephus R H van Schaik
1951–8	Willem Drees
1958–9	Louis J M Beel
1959–63	Jan E de Quay
1963–5	Victor G M Marijnen
1965–6	Joseph M L T Cals
1966–7	Jelle Zijlstra
1967–71	Petrus J S de Jong
1971–3	Barend W Biesheuvel
1973–7	Joop M Den Uyl
1977–82	Andreas A M van Agt
1982–	Ruud F M Lubbers

NEW ZEALAND

Chief of State: British monarch, represented by Governor General

Prime Minister

1856	Henry Sewell
1856	William Fox
1856–61	Edward William Stafford
1861–2	William Fox
1862–3	Alfred Domett
1863–4	Frederick Whitaker
1864–5	Frederick Aloysius Weld
1865–9	Edward William Stafford
1869–72	William Fox
1872	Edward William Stafford
1873	William Fox
1873–5	Julius Vogel
1875–6	Daniel Pollen
1876	Julius Vogel
1876–7	Harry Albert Atkinson

1877–9	George Grey
1879–82	John Hall
1882–3	Frederick Whitaker
1883–4	Harry Albert Atkinson
1884	Robert Stout
1884	Harry Albert Atkinson
1884–7	Robert Stout
1887–91	Harry Albert Atkinson
1891–3	John Ballance
1893–1906	Richard John Seddon *Lib*
1906	William Hall-Jones *Lib*
1906–12	Joseph George Ward *Lib/Nat*
1912	Thomas Mackenzie *Nat*
1912–25	William Ferguson Massey *Ref*
1925	Frencis Henry Dillon Bell *Ref*
1925–8	Joseph Gordon Coates *Ref*
1928–30	Joseph George Ward *Lib/Nat*
1930–5	George William Forbes *Un*
1935–40	Michael Joseph Savage *Lab*
1940–9	Peter Fraser *Lab*
1949–57	Sidney George Holland *Nat*
1957	Keith Jacka Holyoake *Nat*
1957–60	Walter Nash *Lab*
1960–72	Keith Jacka Holyoake *Nat*
1972	John Ross Marshall *Nat*
1972–4	Norman Eric Kirk *Lab*
1974–5	Wallace Edward Rowling *Lab*
1975–84	Robert David Muldoon *Nat*
1984–89	David Russell Lange *Lab*
1989–90	Geoffroy Palmer *Lab*
1990	Mike Moore *Lab*
1990–	Jim Bolger *Nat*

Lab Labour
Lib Liberal
Nat National
Ref Reform
Un United

NICARAGUA

President

1893–1909	José Santos Zelaya
1909–10	José Madriz
1910–11	José Dolores Estrada
1911	Juan José Estrada
1911–17	Adolfo Díaz
1912	Luis Mena *rival President*
1917–21	Emiliano Chamorro Vargas
1921–3	Riego Manuel Chamorro
1923–4	Martínez Bartolo

POLITICAL LEADERS 1900–1991 (cont.)

Nicaragua (cont.)

1925–6	Carlos Solórzano
1926	Emiliano Chamorro Vargas
1926–8	Adolfo Díaz
1926	Juan Bautista Sacasa *rival President*
1928–32	José Marcia Moncada
1933–6	Juan Bautista Sacasa
1936	Carlos Brenes Jarquin
1937–47	Anastasio Somoza García
1947	Leonardo Argüello
1947	Benjamin Lascayo Sacasa
1947–50	Victor Manuel Román y Reyes
1950–6	Anastasio Somoza García
1956–63	Luis Somoza Debayle
1963–6	René Schick Gutiérrez
1966–7	Lorenzo Guerrero Gutiérrez
1967–72	Anastasio Somoza Debayle
1972–4	*Triumvirate*
1974–9	Anastasio Somoza Debayle
1979–84	*Government Junta of National Reconstruction*
1984–90	Daniel Ortega Saavedra
1990–	Violeta Chamorro

NIGER

President

1960–74	Hamani Diori
1974–87	Seyni Kountché
1987–	Ali Saibou

NIGERIA

President

1960–6	Nnamdi Azikiwe

Prime Minister

1960–6	Abubakar Tafawa Balewa

Military Government

1966	J T U Aguiyi-Ironsi
1966–75	Yakuba Gowon
1975–6	Murtala R Mohamed
1976–9	Olusegun Obasanjo

President

1979–83	Alhaji Shehu Shagari

Military Government

1983–4	Mohammadu Buhari
1985–	Ibrahim B Babangida

NORWAY

Monarch

1872–1905	Oscar II *union with Sweden*
1905–57	Haakon VII
1957–91	Olav V
1991–	Harald V

Prime Minister

1898–1902	Johannes Steen
1902–3	Otto Albert Blehr
1903–5	George Francis Hagerup
1905–7	Christian Michelsen
1907–8	Jørgen Løvland
1908–10	Gunnar Knudsen
1910–12	Wollert Konow
1912–13	Jens Bratlie
1913–20	Gunnar Knudsen
1920–1	Otto Bahr Halvorsen
1921–3	Otto Albert Blehr
1923	Otto Bahr Halvorsen
1923–4	Abraham Berge
1924–6	Johan Ludwig Mowinckel
1926–8	Ivar Lykke
1928	Christopher Hornsrud
1928–31	Johan Ludwig Mowinckel
1931–2	Peder L Kolstad
1932–3	Jens Hundseid
1933–5	Johan Ludwig Mowinckel
1935–45	Johan Nygaardsvold
1945–51	Einar Gerhardsen
1951–5	Oscar Torp
1955–63	Einar Gerhardsen
1963	John Lyng
1963–5	Einar Gerhardsen
1965–71	Per Borten
1971–2	Trygve Bratteli
1972–3	Lars Korvald
1973–6	Trygve Bratteli
1976–81	Odvar Nordli
1981	Gro Harlem Brundtland
1981–6	Kåre Willoch
1986–9	Gro Harlem Brundtland
1989–	Jan P Syse

POLITICAL LEADERS 1900–1991 (cont.)

OMAN

Sultan

1888–1913	Faisal Bin Turki
1913–32	Taimur Bin Faisal
1932–70	Said Bin Taimur
1970–	Qabous Bin Said

PAKISTAN

President

1956–8	Iskander Mirza
1958–69	Mohammad Ayoub Khan
1969–71	Agha Mohammad Yahya Khan
1971–3	Zulfikar Ali Bhutto
1973–8	Fazal Elahi Chawdry
1978–88	Mohammad Zia Ul-Haq
1988–	Ghulam Ishaq Khan

Prime Minister

1947–51	Liaqat Ali Khan
1951–3	Khawaja Nazimuddin
1953–5	Mohammad Ali
1955–6	Chawdry Mohammad Ali
1956–7	Hussein Shahid Suhrawardi
1957	Ismail Chundrigar
1967–8	Malik Feroz Khan Noon
1958	Mohammad Ayoub Khan
1958–73	*No Prime Minister*
1973–7	Zulfikar Ali Bhutto
1977–85	*No Prime Minister*
1985–88	Mohammad Khan Junejo
1988	Mohammad Aslam Khan Khattak
1988–90	Benazir Bhutto
1990	Ghulam Mustafa Jatoi
1990–	Mian Nawaz Sharif

PANAMA

President

1904–8	Manuel Amador Guerrero
1908–10	José Domingo de Obaldia
1910	Federico Boyd
1910	Carlos Antonio Mendoza
1910–12	Pablo Arosemena
1912	Rodolfo Chiari
1912–16	Belisario Porras
1916–18	Ramón Maximiliano Valdés
1918	Pedro Antonio Diaz
1918	Cirilo Luis Urriola
1918–20	Belisario Porras
1920	Ernesto T Lefevre
1920–4	Belisario Porras
1924–8	Rodolfo Chiari
1928	Tomás Gabriel Duque
1928–31	Florencio Harmodio Arosemena
1931	Harmodio Arias
1931–2	Ricardo Joaquín Alfaro
1932–6	Harmodio Arias
1936–9	Juan Demóstenes Arosemena
1939	Ezequiel Fernández Jaén
1939–40	Augusto Samuel Boyd
1940–1	Arnulfo Arias Madrid
1941	Ernesto Jaén Guardia
1941	José Pezet
1941–5	Ricardo Adolfo de la Guardia
1945–8	Enrique Adolfo Jiménez Brin
1948–9	Domingo Diaz Arosemena
1949–	Daniel Chanis
1949–	Roberto Francisco Chiari
1949–51	Arnulfo Arias Madrid
1951–2	Alcibiades Arosemena
1952–5	José Antonio Remón
1955	José Ramón Guizado
1955–6	Ricardo Manuel Arias Espinosa
1956–60	Ernesto de la Guardia
1960–4	Roberto Francisco Chiari
1964–8	Marco A Robles
1968	Arnulfo Arias Madrid
1968	*Military Junta*
1968–9	Omar Torrijos Herrera
1969–78	Demetrio Basilio Lakas
1978–82	Aristides Royo
1982–4	Ricardo de la Esoriella
1984	Jorge Enrique Illueca Sibauste
1984–5	Nicolás Ardito Barletta
1985–8	Eric Arturo Delvalle
1988–9	Manuel Solís Palma
1989–	Guillermo Endara Gallimany

PAPUA NEW GUINEA

Prime Minister

1975–80	Michael T Somare
1980–2	Julius Chan
1982–5	Michael T Somare

POLITICAL LEADERS 1900–1991 (cont.)

Papua New Guinea (cont.)

| 1985–8 | Paias Wingti |
| 1988– | Rabbie Namaliu |

PARAGUAY

President

1898–1902	Emilio Azeval
1902	Hector Carvallo
1902–4	Juan Antonio Escurra
1904–5	Juan Gaona
1905–6	Cecilio Baez
1906–8	Benigno Ferreira
1908–10	Emiliano Gonzáles Navero
1910–11	Manuel Gondra
1911	Albino Jara
1911	Liberato Marcial Rojas
1912	Pedro Peña
1912	Emiliano González Navero
1912–16	Eduardo Schaerer
1916–19	Manuel Franco
1919–20	José P Montero
1920–1	Manuel Gondra
1921	Félix Paiva
1921–3	Eusebio Ayala
1923–4	Eligio Ayala
1924	Luis Alberto Riart
1924–8	Eligio Ayala
1928–31	José Particio Guggiari
1931–2	Emiliano González Navero
1932	José Particio Guggiari
1932–6	Eusebio Ayala
1936–7	Rafael Franco
1937–9	Félix Paiva
1939–40	José Félix Estigarribia
1940–8	Higino Moríñigo
1948	Juan Manuel Frutos
1948–9	Juan Natalicio González
1949	Raimundo Rolón
1949	Felipe Molas López
1949–54	Federico Chaves
1954	Tomás Romero Pareira
1954–89	Alfredo Stroessner
1989–	Andres Rodríguez

PERU

President

1899–1903	Eduardo López de Romaña
1903–4	Manuel Candamo
1904	Serapio Calderón
1904–8	José Pardo y Barreda
1908–12	Augusto B Leguía
1912–14	Guillermo Billinghurst
1914–15	Oscar R Benavides
1915–19	José Pardo y Barreda
1919–30	Augusto B Leguía
1930	Manuel Ponce
1930–1	Luis M Sánchez Cerro
1931	Leoncio Elías
1931	Gustavo A Jiménez
1931	David Samanez Ocampo
1931–3	Luis M Sánchez Cerro
1933–9	Oscar R Benavides
1939–45	Manuel Prado
1945–8	José Luis Bustamante y Rivero
1948–56	Manuel A Odría
1956–62	Manuel Prado
1962–3	*Military Junta*
1963–8	Fernando Belaúnde Terry
1968–75	*Military Junta* (Juan Velasco Alvarado)
1975–80	*Military Junta* (Francisco Morales Bermúdez)
1980–5	Fernando Belaúnde Terry
1985–90	Alan García Pérez
1990–	Alberto Keinya Fujimori

PHILIPPINES

President

Commonwealth

1935–44 Manuel L Quezon

Japanese Occupation

1943–4 José P Laurel

Commonwealth

1944–6 Sergio Osmeña

First Republic

1946–8	Manuel A Roxas
1948–53	Elpidio Quirino
1953–7	Ramon Magsaysay
1957–61	Carlos P Garcia
1961–5	Diosdado Macapagal
1965–72	Ferdinand E Marcos

Martial Law

1972–81 Ferdinand E Marcos

POLITICAL LEADERS 1900–1991 (cont.)

New Republic
1981–6 Ferdinand E Marcos
1986–   Corazon C Aquino

POLAND

Polish People's Republic

Chief of State

1945–7   Bolesław Bierut *Acting President*
1947–52 Bolesław Bierut
1952–64 Aleksander Zawadzki
1964–8   Edward Ochab
1968–70 Marian Spychalski
1970–2   Józef Cyrankiewicz
1972–85 Henryk Jabłonski
1985–90 Wojciech Jaruzelski *President 1989*
1990–   Lech Walesa

Premier

1947–52 Józef Cyrankiewicz
1952–4   Bolesław Bierut
1954–70 Józef Cyrankiewicz
1970–80 Piotr Jecoszewicz
1980   Edward Babiuch
1980–1   Józef Pinkowski
1981–5   Wojciech Jaruzelski
1985–8   Zbigniew Messner
1988–9   Mieczyslaw Rakowski
1989   Czeslaw Kiszczak
1989–90 Tadeusz Mazowiecki
1991–   Jan Krzysztof Bielecki

First Secretary

1945–8   Władysław Gomułka
1948–56 Bolesław Bierut
1956   Edward Ochab
1956–70 Władysław Gomułka
1970–80 Edward Gierek
1980–1   Stanisław Kania
1981–9   Wojciech Jaruzelski
1989–   Mieczyslaw Rakowski

PORTUGAL

President

1st Republic
1910–11 Teófilo Braga
1911–15 Manuel José de Arriaga

1915   Teófilo Braga
1915–17 Bernardino Machado
1917–18 Sidónio Pais
1918–19 João do Canto e Castro
1919–23 António José de Almeida
1923–5   Manuel Teixeira Gomes
1925–6   Bernardino Machado

New State
1926   *Military Junta*
         (José Mendes Cabeçadas)
1926   *Military Junta*
         (Manuel de Oliveira Gomes da Costa)
1926–51 António Oscar Fragoso Carmona
1951–8   Francisco Craveiro Lopes
1958–74 Américo de Deus Tomás

2nd Republic
1974   *Military Junta* (António Spínola)
1974–6   *Military Junta*
         (Francisco da Costa Gomes)

3rd Republic
1976–86 António dos Santos Ramalho Eanes
1986–   Mario Soares

Prime Minister

1932–68 António de Oliveira Salazar
1968–74 Marcelo Caetano
1974   Adelino da Palma Carlos
1974–5   Vasco Gonçalves
1975–6   José Pinheiro de Azevedo
1976–8   Mário Soares
1978   Alfredo Nobre da Costa
1978–9   Carlos Alberto de Mota Pinto
1979   Maria de Lurdes Pintasilgo
1980–1   Francisco de Sá Carneiro
1981–3   Francisco Pinto Balsemão
1983–5   Mário Soares
1985–   Aníbal Cavaço Silva

QATAR

Emir

Family name: Al-Thani
1971–2 Ahmad Bin Ali
1972–   Khalifah Bin Hamad

POLITICAL LEADERS 1900–1991 (cont.)

ROMANIA

Monarch

1881–1914	Carol I
1914–27	Ferdinand I
1927–30	Michael *Prince*
1930–40	Carol II
1940–7	Michael I

Republic

President

1947–8	Mihai Sadoveanu *Interim*
1948–52	Constantin I Parhon
1952–8	Petru Groza
1958–61	Ion Georghe Maurer
1961–5	Georghe Gheorghiu-Dej
1965–7	Chivu Stoica
1967–89	Nicolae Ceauşescu
1989–	Ion Iliescu

General Secretary

1955–65	Georghe Gheorghiu-Dej
1965–89	Nicolae Ceauşescu

Prime Minister

1900–1	Petre P Carp
1901–6	Dimitrie A Sturdza
1906–7	Gheorge Grigore Cantacuzino
1907–9	Dimitrie A Sturdza
1909	Ionel Brătianu
1909–10	Mihai Pherekyde
1910–11	Ionel Brătianu
1911–12	Petre P Carp
1912–14	Titu Maiorescu
1914–18	Ionel Brătianu
1918	Alexandru Averescu
1918	Alexandru Marghiloman
1918	Constantin Coandă
1918	Ionel Brătianu
1919	Artur Văitoianu
1919–20	Alexandru Vaida-Voevod
1920–1	Alexandru Averescu
1921–2	Take Ionescu
1922–6	Ionel Brătianu
1926–7	Alexandru Averescu
1927	Ionel Brătianu
1927–8	Vintila I C Brătianu
1928–30	Juliu Maniu

1930	Gheorghe C Mironescu
1930	Juliu Maniu
1930–1	Gheorghe C Mironescu
1931–2	Nicolae Iorga
1932	Alexandru Vaida-Voevod
1932–3	Juliu Maniu
1933	Alexandru Vaida-Voevod
1933	Ion G Duca
1933–4	Constantin Angelescu
1934–7	Gheorghe Tătărescu
1937	Octavian Goga
1937–9	Miron Cristea
1939	Armand Călinescu
1939	Gheorghe Argeşanu
1939	Constantine Argetoianu
1939–40	Gheorghe Tătărescu
1940	Ion Gigurtu
1940–4	Ion Antonescu
1944	Constantin Sănătescu
1944–5	Nicolas Rădescu
1945–52	Petru Groza
1952–5	Gheorghe Gheorghiu-Dej
1955–61	Chivu Stoica
1961–74	Ion Gheorghe Maurer
1974–80	Manea Mănescu
1980–3	Ilie Verdet
1983–9	Constantin Dăscălescu
1989–	Petre Roman

RWANDA

President

1962–73	Grégoire Kayibanda
1973–	Juvénal Habyarimana

SAINT CHRISTOPHER AND NEVIS

Chief of State: British monarch, represented by Governor General

Prime Minister

1983–	Kennedy A Simmonds

POLITICAL LEADERS 1900–1991 (cont.)

SAINT LUCIA

Chief of State: British monarch, represented by Governor General

Prime Minister

1979	John Compton
1979–81	Allan Louisy
1981–3	Winston Francis Cenac
1983–	John Compton

SAINT VINCENT AND THE GRENADINES

Chief of State: British monarch, represented by Governor General

Prime Minister

1979–84	Milton Cato
1984–	James Fitz-Allan Mitchell

SÃO TOMÉ AND PRINCIPE

President

1975–91	Manuel Pinta da Costa
1991–	Miguel Trovoada

SAUDI ARABIA

Monarch

Family name: Al-Saud

1932–53	Abdulaziz Bin Abdur-Rahman
1953–64	Saud Bin Abdulaziz
1964 75	Faisal Bin Abdulaziz
1975–82	Khalid Bin Abdulaziz
1982–	Fahd Bin Abdulaziz

SENEGAL

President

1960–80	Léopold Sédar Senghor
1981–	Abdou Diouf

SEYCHELLES

President

1976–7	James R Mancham
1977–	France-Albert René

SIERRA LEONE

President

1971	Christopher Okero Cole
1971–85	Siaka Stevens
1985–	Joseph Saidu Momoh

Prime Minister

Commonwealth

1961–4	Milton Margai
1964–7	Albert Michael Margai
1967	Siaka Stevens
1967	David Lansana
1967	Ambrose Genda
1967–8	*National Reformation Council* (Andrew Saxon-Smith)
1968	John Bangura
1968–71	Siaka Stevens

Republic

1971–5	Sorie Ibrahim Koroma
1975–8	Christian Alusine Kamara Taylor
1978–	*No Prime Minister*

SINGAPORE

President (Yang di-Pertuan Negara)

1959–70	Yusof bin Ishak
1970–81	Benjamin Henry Sheares
1981–5	Chengara Veetil Devan Nair
1985–	Wee Kim Wee

Prime Minister

1959–90	Lee Kuan Yew
1990–	Goh Chok Tong

POLITICAL LEADERS 1900–1991 (cont.)

SOLOMON ISLANDS

Chief of State: British monarch, represented by Governor General

Prime Minister

1978–82	Peter Kenilorea
1982–4	Solomon Mamaloni
1984–6	Peter Kenilorea
1986–9	Ezekiel Alebua
1989–	Solomon Mamaloni

SOMALIA

President

1961–7	Aden Abdallah Osman
1967–9	Abdirashid Ali Shermarke

Supreme Revolutionary Council
1969–80 Mohammed Siad Barre

Republic
1980–91	Mohammed Siad Barre
1991–	Ali Mahdi Mohammed

Prime Minister

1961–4	Abdirashid Ali Shermarke
1964–7	Abdirizak Haji Hussein
1967–9	Mohammed Haji Ibrahim Egal
1987–90	Mohammed Ali Samater
1990–91	Mohamed Hawadie Madar
1991–	Umar Arteh Ghalib

SOUTH AFRICA

Governor General

1910–14	Herbert, Viscount Gladstone
1914–20	Sydney, Earl Buxton
1920–4	Arthur, Duke of Connaught
1924–31	Alexander, Earl of Athlone
1931–7	George Herbert Hyde Villiers
1937–43	Patrick Duncan
1943–5	Nicolaas Jacobus de Wet
1945–51	Gideon Brand Van Zyl
1951–9	Ernest George Jansen
1959	Lucas Cornelius Steyn
1959–61	Charles Robberts Swart

Republic
President

1961–7	Charles Robberts Swart
1967	Theophilus Ebenhaezer Dönges
1967–8	Jozua François Nandé
1968–75	Jacobus Johannes Fouché
1975–8	Nicolaas Diederichs
1978–9	Balthasar Johannes Vorster
1979–84	Marais Viljoen
1984–89	Pieter Willem Botha
1989–	Frederick Willem de Klerk

Prime Minister

1910–19	Louis Botha *SAf*
1919–24	Jan Christiaan Smuts *SAf*
1924–39	James Barry Munnick Hertzog *Nat*
1939–48	Jan Christiaan Smuts *Un*
1948–54	Daniel François Malan *Nat*
1954–8	Johannes Gerardus Strijdom *Nat*
1958–66	Hendrik Frensch Verwoerd *Nat*
1966–78	Balthasar Johannes Vorster *Nat*
1978–84	Pieter Willem Botha *Nat*
1984–	*No Prime Minister*

Nat National
SAf South African Party
Un United

SPAIN

Monarch
1886–1931 Alfonso XIII

Second Republic
President

1931–6	Niceto Alcalá Zamora y Torres
1936	Diego Martínez Barrio *Acting President*

Civil War
1936–9	Manuel Azaña y Díez
1936–9	Miguel Cabanellas Ferrer

Nationalist Government
Chief of State
1936–75 Francisco Franco Bahamonde

Monarch
1975– Juan Carlos I

POLITICAL LEADERS 1900–1991 (cont.)

Prime Minister

1900–1	Marcelo de Azcárraga y Palmero
1901–2	Práxedes Mateo Sagasta
1902–3	Francisco Silvela y Le-Vielleuze
1903	Raimundo Fernández Villaverde
1903–4	Antonio Maura y Montaner
1904–5	Marcelo de Azcárraga y Palmero
1905	Raimundo Fernández Villaverde
1905	Eugenio Montero Ríos
1905–6	Segismundo Moret y Prendergast
1906	José López Domínguez
1906	Segismundo Moret y Prendergast
1906–7	Antonio Aguilar y Correa
1907–9	Antonio Maura y Montaner
1909–10	Segismundo Moret y Prendergast
1910–12	José Canalejas y Méndez
1912	Álvaro Figueroa y Torres
1912–13	Manuel García Prieto
1913–15	Eduardo Dato y Iradier
1915–17	Álvaro Figueroa y Torres
1917	Manuel García Prieto
1917	Eduardo Dato y Iradier
1917–18	Manuel García Prieto
1918	Antonio Maura y Montaner
1918	Manuel García Prieto
1918–19	Álvaro Figueroa y Torres
1919	Antonio Maura y Montaner
1919	Joaquín Sánchez de Toca
1919–20	Manuel Allendesalazar
1920–1	Eduardo Dato y Iradier
1921	Gabino Bugallal Araujo
	Acting Prime Minister
1921	Manuel Allendesalazar
1921–2	Antonio Maura y Montaner
1922	José Sánchez Guerra y Martínez
1922–3	Manuel García Prieto
1923–30	Miguel Primo de Rivera y Oraneja
1930–1	Dámaso Berenguer y Fusté
1931	Juan Bautista Aznar-Cabañas
1931	Niceto Alcalá Zamora y Torres
1931–3	Manuel Azaña y Díez
1933	Alejandro Lerroux y García
1933	Diego Martínez Barrio
1933–4	Alejandro Lerroux y García
1934	Ricardo Samper Ibáñez
1934–5	Alejandro Lerroux y García
1935	Joaquín Chapaprieta y Terragosa
1935–6	Manuel Portela Valladares
1936	Manuel Azaña y Díez
1936	Santiago Casares Quiroga
1936	Diego Martínez Barrio

1936	José Giral y Pereyra
1936–7	Francisco Largo Caballero
1937–9	Juan Negrín

Chairman of the Council of Ministers

1939–73	Francisco Franco Bahamonde

Prime Minister

1973	Torcuato Fernández Miranda y Hevía
	Acting Prime Minister
1973–6	Carlos Arias Navarro
1976–81	Adolfo Suárez
1981–2	Calvo Sotelo
1982–	Felipe González

SRI LANKA

President

1972–8	William Gopallawa
1978–89	Junius Richard Jayawardene
1989–	Ranasinghe Premadasa

Prime Minister

Ceylon

1947–52	Don Stephen Senanayake
1952–3	Dudley Shelton Senanayake
1953–6	John Kutewala
1956–9	Solomon West Ridgeway Dias Bandaranaike
1960	Dudley Shelton Senanayake
1960–5	Sirimavo Ratwatte Dias Bandaranaike
1965–70	Dudley Shelton Senanayake

Sri Lanka

1970–7	Sirimavo Bandaranaike
1977–89	Ranasinghe Premadasa
1989–	D B Wijetunge

THE SUDAN

Chief of State

1956–8	*Council of State*
1958–64	Ibrahim Abboud
1964–5	*Council of Sovereignty*
1965–9	Ismail Al-Azhari
1969–85	Jaafar Mohammed Nimeiri
	President from 1971

POLITICAL LEADERS 1900–1991 (cont.)

The Sudan (cont.)

Transitional Military Council

Chairman

1985–6	Abd Al-Rahman Siwar Al-Dahab

Supreme Council

Chairman

1986–9	Ahmad Al-Mirghani

Prime Minister

1955–6	Ismail Al-Azhari
1956–8	Abdullah Khalil
1958–64	*As President*
1964–5	Serr Al-Khatim Al-Khalifa
1965–6	Mohammed Ahmed Mahjoub
1966–7	Sadiq Al-Mahdi
1967–9	Mohammed Ahmed Mahjoub
1969	Babiker Awadalla
1969–76	*As President*
1976–7	Rashid Al-Tahir Bakr
1977–85	*As President*
1985–6	*Transitional Millitary Council* (Al-Jazuli Dafallah)
1986–9	Sadiq Al-Mahdi *Military Council, Prime Minister*
1989–	Omar Hassan Ahmed al-Bashir

SURINAME

President

1975–80	J H E Ferrier
1980–2	Henk Chin-a-Sen
1982–8	L F Ramdat-Musier *Acting President*
1988–90	Ramsewak Shankar
1990–	Johan Kraag

National Military Council

Chairman

1980–90	Desi Bouterse
1990–	Iwan Granoogst

Prime Minister

1975–80	Henk Arron
1980	Henk Chin-a-Sen
1980–2	*No Prime Minister*
1982–3	Henry Weyhorst
1983–4	Errol Alibux

1984–6	Wim Udenhout
1986–7	Pretaapnarian Radbakishun
1987–	Jules Wijdenbosch

SWAZILAND

Monarch

1967–82	Sobhuza II *Chief since 1921*
1983	Dzeliwe *Queen Regent*
1983–6	Ntombi *Queen Regent*
1986–	Mswati III

Prime Minister

1967–78	Prince Makhosini
1978–9	Prince Maphevu Dlamini
1979–83	Prince Mbandla Dlamini
1983–6	Prince Bhekimpi Dlamini
1986–9	Sotsha Dlamini
1989–	Obed Dlamini *Acting Prime Minister*

SWEDEN

Monarch

1872–1907	Oskar II
1907–50	Gustav V
1950–73	Gustav VI Adolf
1973–	Carl XVI Gustaf

Prime Minister

1900–2	Fredrik von Otter
1902–5	Erik Gustaf Boström
1905	Johan Ramstedt
1905	Christian Lundeberg
1905–6	Karl Staaf
1906–11	Arvid Lindman
1911–14	Karl Staaf
1914–17	Hjalmar Hammarskjöld
1917	Carl Swartz
1917–20	Nils Edén
1920	Hjalmar Branting
1920–1	Louis de Geer
1921	Oscar von Sydow
1921–3	Hjalmar Branting
1923–4	Ernst Trygger
1924–5	Hjalmar Branting
1925–6	Rickard Sandler

POLITICAL LEADERS 1900-1991 (cont.)

1926–8	Carl Gustaf Ekman
1928–30	Arvid Lindman
1930–2	Carl Gustaf Ekman
1932	Felix Hamrin
1932–6	Per Albin Hansson
1936	Axel Pehrsson-Branstorp
1936–46	Per Albin Hansson
1946–69	Tage Erlander
1969–76	Olof Palme
1976–8	Thorbjörn Fälldin
1978–9	Ola Ullsten
1979–82	Thorbjörn Fälldin
1982–6	Olof Palme
1986–	Ingvar Carlsson

SWITZERLAND

President

1900	Walter Hauser
1901	Ernst Brenner
1902	Joseph Zemp
1903	Adolf Deucher
1904	Robert Comtesse
1905	Marc-Emile Ruchet
1906	Ludwig Forrer
1907	Eduard Müller
1908	Ernst Brenner
1909	Adolf Deucher
1910	Robert Comtesse
1911	Marc-Emile Ruchet
1912	Ludwig Forrer
1913	Eduard Müller
1914	Arthur Hoffmann
1915	Guiseppe Motta
1916	Camille Decoppet
1917	Edmund Schulthess
1918	Felix Calonder
1919	Gustave Ador
1920	Giuseppe Motta
1921	Edmund Schulthess
1922	Robert Haab
1923	Karl Scheurer
1924	Ernest Chuard
1925	Jean-Marie Musy
1926	Heinrich Häberlin
1927	Giuseppe Motta
1928	Edmund Schulthess
1929	Robert Haab
1930	Jean-Marie Musy
1931	Heinrich Häberlin

1932	Giuseppe Motta
1933	Edmund Schulthess
1934	Marcel Pilet-Golaz
1935	Rudolf Minger
1936	Albert Meyer
1937	Giuseppe Motta
1938	Johannes Baumann
1939	Philipp Etter
1940	Marcel Pilet-Golaz
1941	Ernst Wetter
1942	Philipp Etter
1943	Enrico Celio
1944	Walter Stampfli
1945	Eduard von Steiger
1946	Karl Kobelt
1947	Philipp Etter
1948	Enrico Celio
1949	Ernst Nobs
1950	Max Petitpierre
1951	Eduard von Steiger
1952	Karl Kobelt
1953	Philipp Etter
1954	Rodolphe Rubattel
1955	Max Petitpierre
1956	Markus Feldmann
1957	Hans Streuli
1958	Thomas Holenstein
1959	Paul Chaudet
1960	Max Petitpierre
1961	Friedrich Wahlen
1962	Paul Chaudet
1963	Willy Spühler
1964	Ludwig von Moos
1965	Hans Peter Tschudi
1966	Hans Schaffner
1967	Roger Bonvin
1968	Willy Spühler
1969	Ludwig von Moos
1970	Hans Peter Tschudi
1971	Rudolf Gnägi
1972	Nello Celio
1973	Roger Bonvin
1974	Ernst Brugger
1975	Pierre Graber
1976	Rudolf Gnägi
1977	Kurt Furgler
1978	Willi Ritschard
1979	Hans Hürlimann
1980	Georges-André Chevallaz
1981	Kurt Furgler
1982	Fritz Honegger
1983	Pierre Aubert

POLITICAL LEADERS 1900–1991 (cont.)

Switzerland (cont.)

1984	Leon Schlumpf
1985	Kurt Furgler
1986	Alphons Egli
1987	Pierre Aubert
1988	Otto Stich
1989	Jean-Pascal Delamuraz
1990	Arnold Koller
1991	Flavio Cotti

SYRIA

President

1943–9	Shukri Al-Quwwatli
1949	Husni Az-Zaim
1949–51	Hashim Al-Atasi
1951–4	Adib Shishaqli
1954–5	Hashim Al-Atasi
1955–8	Shukri Al-Quwwatli
1958–61	*Part of United Arab Republic*
1961–3	Nazim Al-Qudsi
1963	Luai Al-Atassi
1963–6	Amin Al-Hafiz
1966–70	Nureddin Al-Atassi
1970–1	Ahmad Al-Khatib
1971–	Hafez Al Assad

Prime Minister

1946–8	Jamil Mardam Bey
1948–9	Khalid Al-Azm
1949	Husni Az-Zaim
1949	Muhsi Al-Barazi
1949	Hashim Al-Atassi
1949	Nazim Al-Qudsi
1949–50	Khalid Al-Azm
1950–1	Nazim Al-Qudsi
1951	Khalid Al-Azm
1951	Hassan Al-Hakim
1951	Maruf Ad-Dawalibi
1951–3	Fauzi As-Salu
1953–4	Adib Shishaqli
1954	Shewqet Shuqair
1954	Sabri Al-Asali
1954	Said Al-Ghazzi
1954–5	Faris Al-Khuri
1955	Sabri Al-Asali
1955–6	Said Al-Ghazzi
1956–8	Sabri Al-Asali
1958–61	*Part of United Arab Republic*
1961	Abd Al-Hamid As-Sarraj

1961	Mamun Kuzbari
1961	Izzat An-Nuss
1961–2	Maruf Ad-Dawalibi
1962	Bashir Azmah
1962–3	Khalid Al-Azm
1963	Salah Ad-Din Al-Bitaar
1963	Sami Al-Jundi
1963	Salah Ad-Din Al-Bitaar
1963–4	Amin Al-Hafez
1964	Salah Ad-Din Al-Bitaar
1964–5	Amin Al-Hafez
1965	Yousif Zeayen
1966	Salah Ad-Din Al-Bitaar
1966–8	Yousif Zeayen
1968–70	Nureddin Al-Atassi
	Acting Prime Minister
1970–1	Hafez Al-Assad
1971–2	Abdel Rahman Khleifawi
1972–6	Mahmoud Bin Saleh Al-Ayoubi
1976–8	Abdul Rahman Khleifawi
1978–80	Mohammed Ali Al-Halabi
1980–7	Abdel Rauof Al-Kasm
1987–	Mahmoud Zubi

TAIWAN

President

1950–75	Chiang Kai-shek
1975–8	Yen Chia-kan
1978–87	Chiang Ching-kuo
1987–	Lee Teng-hui

President of Executive Council

1950–4	Ch'eng Ch'eng
1954–8	O K Yui
1958–63	Ch'eng Ch'eng
1963–72	Yen Chia-ken
1972–8	Chiang Ching-kuo
1978–84	Sun Yun-suan
1984–9	Yu Kuo-hwa
1989–90	Lee Huan
1990–	Hau Pei-tsun

TANZANIA

Pesident

1964–85	Julius Kambarage Nyerere
1985–	Ali Hassan Mwinyi

POLITICAL LEADERS 1900–1991 (cont.)

Prime Minister

1964–72	Rashid M Kawawa *Vice President*
1972–7	Rashid M Kawawa
1977–80	Edward M Sokoine
1980–3	Cleopa D Msuya
1983–4	Edward M Sokoine
1984–5	Salim A Salim
1985–90	Joseph S Warioba
1990–	Iohn Malecela

THAILAND

Monarch

1868–1910	Chulalongkorn, Rama V
1910–25	Rama VI
1925–35	Rama VII
1935–9	Rama VIII (Ananda Mahidol)
1939–46	Nai Pridi Phanomyong *Regent*
1946	Rama IX
1946–50	Rangsit of Chainat *Regent*
1950–	Bhumibol Adulyadej

Prime Minister

1932–3	Phraya Manopakom
1933–8	Phraya Phahon Phonphahuyasena
1938–44	Luang Phibun Songgram
1945	Thawi Bunyaket
1945–6	Mom Rachawongse Seni Pramoj
1946	Nai Khuang Aphaiwong
1946	Nai Pridi Phanomyong
1946–7	Luang Thamrong Nawasawat
1947–8	Nai Khuang Aphaiwong
1948–57	Luang Phibun Songgram
1957	Sarit Thanarat
1957	Nai Pote Sarasin
1957–8	Thanom Kittikatchom
1958–63	Sarit Thanarat
1963–73	Thanom Kittikatchom
1973–5	Sanya Dharmasaki
1975–6	Mom Rachawongse Kukrit Pramoj
1976	Seni Pramoj
1976–7	Thanin Kraivichien
1977–80	Kriangsak Chammanard
1980–7	Prem Tinsulanonda
1987–91	Chatichai Choonhaven
1991–	Anand Panyarachun

TOGO

President

1960–3	Sylvanus Olympio
1963–7	Nicolas Grunitzky
1967–	Gnassingbe Eyadema

TONGA

Monarch

1893–1918	George Tupou II
1918–65	Salote Tupou III
1965–	Taufa'ahau Tupou IV

Prime Minister

1970–	Fatafehi Tu'ipelehake

TRINIDAD AND TOBAGO

President

1976–87	Ellis Emmanuel Clarke
1987–	Noor Hassanali

Premier

1956–62	Eric Williams

Prime Minister

1962–81	Eric Williams
1981–6	George Chambers
1986–	Arthur Napoleon Raymond Robinson

TUNISIA

Bey

1943–57	Muhammad VIII

President

1957–87	Habib Bourguiba
1987–	Zine Al-Abidine Bin Ali

Prime Minister

1956–7	Habib Bourguiba
1957–69	*No Prime Minister*
1969–70	Bahi Ladgham

POLITICAL LEADERS 1900–1991 (cont.)

Tunisia (cont.)

1970–80	Hadi Nouira
1980–6	Mohammed Mezali
1986–7	Rashid Sfar
1987	Zine Al-Abidine Bin Ali
1987–9	Hadi Baccouche
1989–	Hamed Karoui

TURKEY

Sultan of the Ottoman Empire

1876–1909	Abdülhamit
1909–18	Mehmet Reşat
1918–22	Mehmet Vahideddin

Turkish Republic

President

1923–38	Mustafa Kemal Atatürk
1938–50	İsmet İnönü
1950–60	Celâl Bayar
1961–6	Cemal Gürsel
1966–73	Cevdet Sunay
1973–80	Fahri S Korutürk
1982–9	Kenan Evren
1989–	Turgut Özal

TUVALU

Chief of State: British monarch, represented by Governor General

Prime Minister

1978–81	Toalipi Lauti
1981–9	Tomasi Puapua
1989–	Bikenibeu Paeniu

UGANDA

President

1962–6	Edward Muteesa II
1967–71	Apollo Milton Obote
1971–9	Idi Amin
1979	Yusuf Kironde Lule
1979–80	Godfrey Lukongwa Binaisa
1981–5	Apollo Milton Obote
1985–6	*Military Council* (Tito Okello Lutwa)
1986–	Yoweri Kaguta Museveni

Prime Minister

1962–71	Apollo Milton Obote
1971–81	*No Prime Minister*
1981–5	Eric Otema Alimadi
1985	Paulo Muwanga
1985–6	Abraham N Waliggo
1986–91	Samson B Kisekka
1991–	George Cosmas Adyebo

UNITED ARAB EMIRATES

President

1971–	Zayed Bin Sultan Al-Nahyan

Prime Minister

1971–9	Maktoum Bin Rashid Al-Maktoum
1979–	Rashid Bin Said Al-Maktoum

ABU DHABI
Tribe: Al Bu Falah *or* Al Nahyan (Bani Yas)
Family name: Al-Nahyan

Shaikh

1855–1909	Zayed
1909–12	Tahnoun
1912–22	Hamdan
1922–6	Sultan
1926–8	Saqr
1928–66	Shakhbout
1966–	Zayed

AJMAN
Tribe: Al Bu Kharayban (Naim)
Family name: Al-Nuaimi

Shaikh

1900–10	Abdel-Aziz
1910–28	Humaid
1928–81	Rashid
1981–	Humaid

DUBAI
Tribe: Al Bu Flasah (Bani Yas)
Family name: Al-Maktoum

Shaikh

1894–1906	Maktoum
1906–12	Butti
1912–58	Said

POLITICAL LEADERS 1900–1991 (cont.)

1958–90	Rashid
1990–	Maktoum

FUJAIRAH
Tribe: Sharqiyyin
Family name: Al-Sharqi

Shaikh

1952–75	Mohammed
1975–	Hamad

RAS AL-KHAIMAH
Tribe: Huwalah
Family name: Al-Qasimi

Shaikh

1921–48	Sultan
1948	Saqr

SHARJAH
Tribe: Huwalah
Family name: Al-Qasimi

Shaikh

1883–1914	Saqr
1914–24	Khaled
1924–51	Sultan
1951–65	Saqr
1965–72	Khaled
1972–87	Sultan
1987	Abdol Aziz
1987–	Sultan

UMM AL-QAIWAIN
Tribe: Al-Ali
Family name: Al-Mualla

Shaikh

1873–1904	Ahmad
1904–22	Rashid
1922–3	Abdullah
1923–9	Hamad
1929–81	Ahmad
1981–	Rashid

UNION OF SOVIET SOCIALIST REPUBLICS

President

1917	Leo Borisovich Kamenev
1917–19	Yakov Mikhailovich Sverlov

1919–46	Mikhail Ivanovich Kalinin
1946–53	Nikolai Shvernik
1953–60	Klimentiy Voroshilov
1960–4	Leonid Brezhnev
1964–5	Anastas Mikoyan
1965–77	Nikolai Podgorny
1977–82	Leonid Brezhnev
1982–3	Vasily Kuznetsov *Acting President*
1983–4	Yuri Andropov
1984	Vasily Kuznetsov *Acting President*
1984–5	Konstantin Chernenko
1985	Vasily Kuznetsov *Acting President*
1985–8	Andrei Gromyko
1988–90	Mikhail Gorbachev

Executive President

1990–91	Mikhail Gorbachev
1991	Gennady Yanayev *Acting President*
1991–	Mikhail Gorbachev

Chairman (Prime Minister)

Council of Ministers

1917	Georgy Evgenyevich Lvov
1917	Aleksandr Fyodorovich Kerensky

Council of People's Commissars

1917–24	Vladimir Ilyich Lenin
1924–30	Aleksei Ivanovich Rykov
1930–41	Vyacheslav Mikhailovich Molotov
1941–53	Josef Stalin

Council of Ministers

1953–5	Georgiy Malenkov
1955–8	Nikolai Bulganin
1958–64	Nikita Khrushchev
1964–80	Alexei Kosygin
1980–5	Nikolai Tikhonov
1985–91	Nikolai Ryzhkov
1991	Valentin Pavlov
1991–	Ivan Silayev *Acting*

General Secretary

1922–53	Josef Stalin
1953	Georgiy Malenkov
1953–64	Nikita Khrushchev
1964–82	Leonid Brezhnev
1982–4	Yuri Andropov
1984–5	Konstantin Chernenko
1985–	Mikhail Gorbachev

POLITICAL LEADERS 1900–1991 (cont.)

UNITED KINGDOM

For list of previous monarchs see p 166

Monarch

House of Hanover
1714–27	George I
1727–60	George II
1760–1820	George III
1820–30	George IV
1830–7	William IV
1837–1901	Victoria

House of Saxe-Coburg
1901–10	Edward VII

House of Windsor
1910–36	George V
1936	Edward VIII
1936–52	George VI
1952–	Elizabeth II

Prime Minister

1721–42	Robert Walpole *Whig*
1742–3	Earl of Wilmington (Spencer Compton) *Whig*
1743–54	Henry Pelham *Whig*
1754–6	Duke of Newcastle (Thomas Pelham-Holles) *Whig*
1756–7	Duke of Devonshire (William Cavendish) *Whig*
1757–62	Duke of Newcastle *Whig*
1762–3	Earl of Bute (John Stuart) *Tory*
1763–5	George Grenville *Whig*
1765–6	Marquess of Rockingham (Charles Watson Wentworth) *Whig*
1766–70	Duke of Grafton (Augustus Henry Fitzroy) *Whig*
1770–82	Lord North (Frederick North) *Tory*
1782	Marquess of Rockingham *Whig*
1782–3	Earl of Shelburne (William Petty-Fitzmaurice) *Whig*
1783	Duke of Portland (William Henry Cavendish) *Coal*
1783–1801	William Pitt *Tory*
1801–4	Henry Addington *Tory*
1804–6	William Pitt *Tory*
1806–7	Lord Grenville (William Wyndham) *Whig*
1807–9	Duke of Portland *Tory*
1809–12	Spencer Perceval *Tory*
1812–27	Earl of Liverpool (Robert Banks Jenkinson) *Tory*
1827	George Canning *Tory*
1827–8	Viscount Goderich (Frederick John Robinson) *Tory*
1828–30	Duke of Wellington (Arthur Wellesley) *Tory*
1830–4	Earl Grey (Charles Grey) *Whig*
1834	Viscount Melbourne (William Lamb) *Whig*
1834–5	Robert Peel *Con*
1835–41	Viscount Melbourne *Whig*
1841–6	Robert Peel *Con*
1846–52	Lord John Russell *Lib*
1852	Earl of Derby (Edward George Stanley) *Con*
1852–5	Lord Aberdeen (George Hamilton-Gordon) *Peelite*
1855–8	Viscount Palmerston (Henry John Temple) *Lib*
1858–9	Earl of Derby *Con*
1859–65	Viscount Palmerston *Lib*
1865–6	Lord John Russell *Lib*
1866–8	Earl of Derby *Con*
1868	Benjamin Disraeli *Con*
1868–74	William Ewart Gladstone *Lib*
1874–80	Benjamin Disraeli *Con*
1880–5	William Ewart Gladstone *Lib*
1885–6	Marquess of Salisbury (Robert Gascoyne-Cecil) *Con*
1886	William Ewart Gladstone *Lib*
1886–92	Marquess of Salisbury *Con*
1892–4	William Ewart Gladstone *Lib*
1894–5	Earl of Rosebery (Archibald Philip Primrose) *Lib*
1895–1902	Marquess of Salisbury *Con*
1902–5	Arthur James Balfour *Con*
1905–8	Henry Campbell-Bannerman *Lib*
1908–15	Herbert Henry Asquith *Lib*
1915–16	Herbert Henry Asquith *Coal*
1916–22	David Lloyd George *Coal*
1922–3	Andrew Bonar Law *Con*
1923–4	Stanley Baldwin *Con*
1924	James Ramsay MacDonald *Lab*
1924–9	Stanley Baldwin *Con*
1929–31	James Ramsay MacDonald *Lab*
1931–5	James Ramsay MacDonald *Nat*
1935–7	Stanley Baldwin *Nat*
1937–40	Arthur Neville Chamberlain *Nat*
1940–5	Winston Churchill *Coal*
1945–51	Clement Attlee *Lab*
1951–5	Winston Churchill *Con*
1955–7	Anthony Eden *Con*

POLITICAL LEADERS 1900–1991 (cont.)

1957–63	Harold Macmillan *Con*
1963–4	Alec Douglas-Home *Con*
1964–70	Harold Wilson *Lab*
1970–4	Edward Heath *Con*
1974–6	Harold Wilson *Lab*
1976–9	James Callaghan *Lab*
1979–90	Margaret Thatcher *Con*
1990–	John Major *Con*

Coal Coalition   *Lib* Liberal
Con Conservative   *Nat* Nationalist
Lab Labour

UNITED NATIONS

Secretary General

1946–53	Trygve Lie *Norway*
1953–61	Dag Hammarskjöld *Sweden*
1962–71	U Thant *Burma*
1971–81	Kurt Waldheim *Austria*
1982–	Javier Pérez de Cuéllar *Peru*

UNITED STATES OF AMERICA

President

Vice President in parentheses

1789–97	George Washington (1st)
	(John Adams)
1797–1801	John Adams (2nd) *Fed*
	(Thomas Jefferson)
1801–9	Thomas Jefferson (3rd) *Dem-Rep*
	(Aaron Burr, 1801–5)
	(George Clinton, 1805–9)
1809–17	James Madison (4th) *Dem-Rep*
	(George Clinton, 1809–12)
	no Vice President 1812–13
	(Elbridge Gerry, 1813–14)
	no Vice President 1814–17
1817–25	James Monroe (5th) *Dem-Rep*
	(Daniel D Tompkins)
1825–9	John Quincy Adams (6th) *Dem-Rep*
	(John C Calhoun)
1829–37	Andrew Jackson (7th) *Dem*
	(John C Calhoun, 1829–32)
	no Vice President 1832–3
	(Martin van Buren, 1833–7)
1837–41	Martin van Buren (8th) *Dem*
	(Richard M Johnson)
1841	William Henry Harrison (9th) *Whig*
	(John Tyler)
1841–5	John Tyler (10th) *Whig*
	no Vice President
1845–9	James Knox Polk (11th) *Dem*
	(George M Dallas)
1849–50	Zachary Taylor (12th) *Whig*
	(Millard Fillmore)
1850–3	Millard Fillmore (13th) *Whig*
	no Vice President
1853–7	Franklin Pierce (14th) *Dem*
	(William R King, 1853)
	no Vice President 1853–7
1857–61	James Buchanan (15th) *Dem*
	(John C Breckinridge)
1861–5	Abraham Lincoln (16th) *Rep*
	(Hannibal Hamlin, 1861–5)
	(Andrew Johnson, 1865)
1865–9	Andrew Johnson (17th) *Dem-Nat*
	no Vice President
1869–77	Ulysses Simpson Grant (18th) *Rep*
	(Schuyler Colfax, 1869–73)
	(Henry Wilson, 1873–5)
	no Vice President 1875–7
1877–81	Rutherford Birchard Hayes (19th) *Rep*
	(William A Wheeler)
1881	James Abram Garfield (20th) *Rep*
	(Chester A Arthur)
1881–5	Chester Alan Arthur (21st) *Rep*
	no Vice President
1885–9	Grover Cleveland (22nd) *Dem*
	(Thomas A Hendricks, 1885)
	no Vice President 1885–9
1889–93	Benjamin Harrison (23rd) *Rep*
	(Levi P Morton)
1893–7	Grover Cleveland (24th) *Dem*
	(Adlai E Stevenson)
1897–1901	William McKinley (25th) *Rep*
	(Garret A Hobart, 1897–9)
	no Vice President 1899–1901
	(Theodore Roosevelt, 1901)
1901–9	Theodore Roosevelt (26th) *Rep*
	no Vice President 1901–5
	(Charles W Fairbanks, 1905–9)
1909–13	William Howard Taft (27th) *Rep*
	(James S Sherman, 1909–12)
	no Vice President 1912–13
1913–21	Woodrow Wilson (28th) *Dem*
	(Thomas R Marshall)
1921–3	Warren Gamaliel Harding (29th) *Rep*
	(Calvin Coolidge)
1923–9	Calvin Coolidge (30th) *Rep*
	no Vice President 1923–5
	(Charles G Dawes, 1925–9)

POLITICAL LEADERS 1900–1991 (cont.)

United States of America (cont.)

1929–33	Herbert Clark Hoover (31st) *Rep* (Charles Curtis)
1933–45	Franklin Delano Roosevelt (32nd) *Dem* (John N Garner, 1933–41) (Henry A Wallace, 1941–5) (Harry S Truman, 1945)
1945–53	Harry S Truman (33rd) *Dem* *no Vice President 1945–9* (Alben W Barkley, 1949–53)
1953–61	Dwight David Eisenhower (34th) *Rep* (Richard M Nixon)
1961–3	John Fitzgerald Kennedy (35th) *Dem* (Lyndon B Johnson)
1963–9	Lyndon Baines Johnson (36th) *Dem* *no Vice President 1963–5* (Hubert H Humphrey, 1965–9)
1969–74	Richard Milhous Nixon (37th) *Rep* (Spiro T Agnew, 1969–73) *no Vice President 1973, Oct–Dec* (Gerald R Ford, 1973–4)
1974–7	Gerald Rudolph Ford (38th) *Rep* *no Vice President 1974, Aug–Dec* (Nelson A Rockefeller, 1974–7)
1977–81	Jimmy Carter (39th) *Dem* (Walter F Mondale)
1981–9	Ronald Wilson Reagan (40th) *Rep* (George H W Bush)
1989–	George Herbert Walker Bush (41st) *Rep* (J Danforth Quayle)

Dem Democrat   *Nat* National Union
Fed Federalist   *Rep* Republican

URUGUAY

President

1899–1903	Juan Lindolfo Cuestas
1903–7	José Batlle y Ordóñez
1907–11	Claudio Williman
1911–15	José Batlle y Ordóñez
1915–19	Feliciano Viera
1919–23	Baltasar Brum
1923–7	José Serrato
1927–31	Juan Capisteguy
1931–8	Gabriel Terra
1938–43	Alfredo Baldomir
1943–7	Juan José de Amézaga
1947	Tomás Berreta
1947–51	Luis Batlle Berres
1951–5	Andrés Martínez Trueba

National Government Council (1955–67)

1955–6	Luis Batlle Berres
1956–7	Alberto F Zubiría
1957–8	Alberto Lezama
1958–9	Carlos L Fischer
1959–60	Martín R Etchegoyen
1960–1	Benito Nardone
1961–2	Eduardo Víctor Haedo
1962–3	Faustino Harrison
1963–4	Daniel Fernández Crespo
1964–5	Luis Giannattasio
1965–6	Washington Beltrán
1966–7	Alberto Heber Usher
1967	Oscar Daniel Gestido
1967–72	Jorge Pacheco Areco
1972–6	Juan María Bordaberry Arocena
1976–81	Aparicio Méndez
1981–4	Gregorio Conrado Álvarez Armelino
1984–90	Julio María Sanguinetti Cairolo
1990	Luis Alberto Lacalle Herrera

VANUATU

President

1980–9	George Sokomanu (*formerly* Kalkoa)
1989–	Fred Timakata

Prime Minister

1980–	Walter Lini

VENEZUELA

President

1899–1908	Cipriano Castro
1908–36	Juan Vicente Gomez
1936–41	Eleazar Lopez Contreras
1941–5	Isaias Medina Angarita
1945–7	*Military Junta* (Romulo Betancourt)
1947–8	Romulo Gallegos
1948–50	*Military Junta* (Carlos Delgado Chalbaud)
1950–9	*Military Junta* (Marcos Perez Jimenez)
1959–64	Romulo Betancourt
1964–9	Raul Leoni
1969–74	Rafael Caldera Rodriguez

POLITICAL LEADERS 1900–1991 (cont.)

1974–9	Carlos Andres Perez
1979–84	Luis Herrera Campins
1984–9	Jaime Lusinchi
1989–	Carlos Andres Perez

VIETNAM

President

Democratic Republic of Vietnam

1945–69	Ho Chi Minh
1969–76	Ton Duc Thang

State of Vietnam

1949 55	Bao Dai

Republic of Vietnam

1955–63	Ngo Dinh Diem
1963–4	Duong Van Minh
1964	Nguyen Khanh
1964–5	Phan Khac Suu
1965–75	Nguyen Van Thieu
1975	Tran Van Huong
1975	Duong Van Minh
1975–6	*Provisional Revolutionary Government* (Huynh Tan Phat)

Socialist Republic of Vietnam

1976–80	Ton Duc Thang
1980–1	Nguyen Hun Tho *Acting President*
1981–/	Truongh Chinh
1987–	Vo Chi Cong

Prime Minister

Democratic Republic of Vietnam

1955–76	Pham Van Dong

State of Vietnam

1949–50	Nguyen Van Xuan
1950	Nguyen Phan Long
1950–2	Tran Van Huu
1952	Tran Van Huong
1952–3	Nguyen Van Tam
1953–4	Buu Loc
1954–5	Ngo Dinh Diem

Republic of Vietnam

1955–63	Ngo Dinh Diem
1963–4	Nguyen Ngoc Tho
1964	Nguyen Khan
1964–5	Tran Van Huong
1965	Phan Huy Quat
1965–7	Nguyen Cao Ky

1967–8	Nguyen Van Loc
1968–9	Tran Van Huong
1969–75	Tran Thien Khiem
1975	Nguyen Ba Can
1975–6	Vu Van Mau

Socialist Republic of Vietnam

Premier

1976–87	Pham Van Dong
1987–8	Pham Hung
1988	Vo Van Kiet *Acting Premier*
1988–	Do Muoi

General Secretary

1960–80	Le Duan
1986	Truong Chinh
1986–	Nguyen Van Linh

WESTERN SAMOA

President

1962–3	Tupua Tamesehe Mea'ole Mallietoa Tanumafili II *joint Presidents*
1963–	Malietoa Tanumafili II

Prime Minister

1962–70	Fiame Mata'afa Faumuina Mulinu'u II
1970–6	Tupua Tamasese Leulofi IV
1976–82	Tupuola Tamasese Efi
1982	Va'ai Kolone
1982	Tupuola Taisi Efi
1982–6	Tofilau Eti Alesana
1986–8	Va'ai Kolone
1988–	Tofilau Eti Alesana

YEMEN

Yemen Arab Republic (North Yemen)

Monarch (Imam)

1918–48	Yahya Mohammed Bin Mohammed
1948–62	Ahmed Bin Yahya
1962–70	Mohammed Bin Ahmed

1962 Civil War

President

1962–7	Abdullah Al-Sallal
1967–74	Abdur Rahman Al-Iriani

POLITICAL LEADERS 1900–1991 (cont.)

Yemen (cont.)

1974–7	Military Command Council (Ibrahim Al-Hamadi)
1977–8	Ahmed Bin Hussein Al-Ghashmi
1978–90	Ali Abdullah Saleh

Prime Minister

1964	Hamud Al-Jaifi
1965	Hassan Al-Amri
1965	Ahmed Mohammed Numan
1965	As President
1965–6	Hassan Al-Amri
1966–7	As President
1967	Muhsin Al-Aini
1967–9	Hassan Al-Amri
1969–70	Abd Allah Kurshumi
1970–1	Muhsin Al-Aini
1971	Abdel Salam Sabra Acting Prime Minister
1971	Ahmed Mohammed Numan
1971	Hassan Al-Amri
1971–2	Muhsin Al-Aini
1972–4	Qadi Abdullah Al-Hijri
1974	Hassan Makki
1974–5	Muhsin Al-Aini
1975	Abdel Latif Deifallah Acting Prime Minister
1975–90	Abdel-Aziz Abdel-Ghani

People's Democratic Republic of Yemen (South Yemen)

President

1967–9	Qahtan Mohammed Al-Shaabi
1969–78	Salim Ali Rubai
1978	Ali Nasir Mohammed Husani
1978–80	Abdel Fattah Ismail
1980–6	Ali Nasir Mohammed Husani
1986–90	Haidar Abu Bakr Al-Attas

Prime Minister

1969	Faisal Abd Al-Latif Al-Shaabi
1969–71	Mohammed Ali Haithem
1971–85	Ali Nasir Mohammed Husani
1985–6	Haidar Abu Bakr Al-Attas
1986–90	Yasin Said Numan

Republic of Yemen

President

1990–	Ali Abdullah Saleh

Prime Minister

1990–	Haidar Abu Bakr Al-Attas

YUGOSLAVIA

Monarch

1921–34	Aleksandar II
1934–45	Petar II in exile, 1941–

Republic

National Assembly

Chairman

1945–53	Ivan Ribar

President

1953–80	Josip Broz Tito

Collective Presidency

1980	Lazar Koliševski
1980–1	Cvijetin Mijatović
1981–2	Serghei Kraigher
1982–3	Petar Stambolić
1983–4	Mika Spiljak
1984–5	Veselin Đuranović
1985–6	Radovan Vlajković
1986–7	Sinan Hasani
1987–8	Lazar Mojsov
1988–9	Raif Dizdarević
1989–90	Janez Drnovsek
1990–1	Borisav Jovic

Prime Minister

1929–32	Pear Živkovic
1932	Vojislav Marinković
1932–4	Milan Srškić
1934	Nikola Uzunović
1934–5	Bogoljub Jevtić
1935–9	Milan Stojadinović
1939–41	Dragiša Cvetković
1941	Dušan Simović

Government in exile

1942	Slobodan Jovanović
1943	Miloš Trifunović
1943–4	Božidar Purić
1944–5	Ivan Šubašić
1945	Drago Marušić

POLITICAL LEADERS 1900–1991 (cont.)

Home government

1941–4	Milan Nedić
1943–63	Josip Broz Tito
1963–7	Petar Stambolić
1967–9	Mika Špiljak
1969–71	Mitja Ribičič
1971–7	Džemal Bijedić
1977–82	Veselin Đuranović
1982–6	Milka Planinc
1986–9	Branko Mikulić
1989–	Ante Marković

Communist Party

First Secretary

1937–52	Josip Broz Tito

League of Communists

1952–80	Josip Broz Tito

League of Communists Central Committee

President

1979–80	Stevan Doronjski *Acting President*
1980–1	Lazar Mojsov
1981–2	Dušan Dragosavac
1982–3	Mitja Ribičič
1983–4	Dragoslav Marković
1984–5	Ali Šukrija
1985–6	Vidoje Žarkovic
1986–7	Milanko Renovica
1987–8	Boško Krunić
1988–9	Stipe Suvar
1989–90	Milan Pancevski
1990–	Miomir Grbovic

ZAÏRE

President

1960–5	Joseph Kasavubu
1965–	Mobuto Sese Seko
	(*formerly* Joseph Mobutu)

Prime Minister

1960	Patrice Lumumba
1960	Joseph Ileo

1960–1	*College of Commissioners*
1961	Joseph Ileo
1961–4	Cyrille Adoula
1964–5	Moïse Tshombe
1965	Evariste Kimba
1965–6	Mulamba Nyungu wa Kadima
1966–77	*As President*
1977–80	Mpinga Kasenga
1980	Bo-Boliko Lokonga Monse Mihambu
1980–1	Nguza Karl I Bond
1981–3	Nsinga Udjuu
1983–6	Kengo wa Dondo
1986–8	*No Prime Minister*
1988	Sambura Pida Nbagui
1988–90	Kengo Wa Dondo
1990–1	Lunda Bululee
1991–	Mulumba Lukeji

ZAMBIA

President

1964–	Kenneth Kaunda

Prime Minister

1964–73	Kenneth Kaunda
1973–5	Mainza Chona
1975–7	Elijah Mudenda
1977–8	Mainza Chona
1978–81	Daniel Lisulu
1981–5	Nalumino Mundia
1985–9	Kebby Musokotwane
1989–	Malimba Masheke

ZIMBABWE

President

1980–7	Canaan Sodindo Banana
1987–	Robert Gabriel Mugabe

Prime Minister

1980–	Robert Gabriel Mugabe

POPES

Antipopes (who claimed to be pope in opposition to those canonically chosen) are given in parentheses.

until c.64	Peter	483–92	Felix III (II)	752–7	Stephen II (III)
c.64–c.76	Linus	492–6	Gelasius I	757–67	Paul I
c.76–c.90	Anacletus	496–8	Anastasius II	[767–9	Constantine II]
c.90–c.99	Clement I	498–514	Symmachus	[768	Philip]
c.99–c.105	Evaristus	[498,	Laurentius]	768–72	Stephen III (IV)
c.105–c.117	Alexander I	501–5		772–95	Hadrian I
c.117–c.127	Sixtus I	514–23	Hormisdas	795–816	Leo III
c.127–c.137	Telesphorus	523–6	John I	816–17	Stephen IV (V)
c.137–c.140	Hyginus	526–30	Felix IV (III)	817–24	Paschal I
c.140–c.154	Pius I	530–2	Boniface II	824–7	Eugenius II
c.154–c.166	Anicetus	[530	Dioscorus]	827	Valentine
c.166–c.175	Soter	533–5	John II	827–44	Gregory IV
175–89	Eleutherius	535–6	Agapetus I	[844	John]
189–98	Victor I	536–7	Silverius	844–7	Sergius II
198–217	Zephyrinus	537–55	Vigilius	847–55	Leo IV
217–22	Callistus I	556–61	Pelagius I	855–8	Benedict III
[217–c.235	Hippolytus]	561–74	John III	[855	Anastasius
222–30	Urban I	575–9	Benedict I		Bibliothecarius]
230–5	Pontian	579–90	Pelagius II	858–67	Nicholas I
235–6	Anterus	590–604	Gregory I	867–72	Hadrian II
236–50	Fabian	604–6	Sabinianus	872–82	John VIII
251–3	Cornelius	607	Boniface III	882–4	Marinus I
[251–c.258	Novatian]	608–15	Boniface IV	884–5	Hadrian III
253–4	Lucius I	615–18	Deusdedit	885–91	Stephen V (VI)
254–7	Stephen I		or Adeodatus I	891–6	Formosus
257–8	Sixtus II	619–25	Boniface V	896	Boniface VI
259–68	Dionysius	625–38	Honorius I	896–7	Stephen VI (VII)
269–74	Felix I	640	Severinus	897	Romanus
275–83	Eutychianus	640–2	John IV	897	Theodore II
283–96	Caius	642–9	Theodore I	898–900	John IX
296–304	Marcellinus	649–55	Martin I	900–3	Benedict IV
308–9	Marcellus I	654–7	Eugenius I[1]	903	Leo V
310	Eusebius	657–72	Vitalian	[903–4	Christopher]
311–314	Miltiades	672–6	Adeodatus II	904–11	Sergius III
314–35	Sylvester I	676–8	Donus	911–13	Anastasius III
336	Mark	678–81	Agatho	913–14	Lando
337–52	Julius I	682–3	Leo II	914–28	John X
352–66	Liberius	684–5	Benedict II	928	Leo VI
[355–65	Felix II]	685–6	John V	928–31	Stephen VII (VIII)
366–84	Damasus I	686–7	Cono	931–5	John XI
[366–7	Ursinus]	[687	Theodore]	936–9	Leo VII
384–99	Siricius	[687–92	Paschal]	939–42	Stephen IX
399–401	Anastasius I	687–701	Sergius I	942–6	Marinus II
402–17	Innocent I	701–5	John VI	946–55	Agapetus II
417–18	Zosimus	705–7	John VII	955–64	John XII
418–22	Boniface I	708	Sisinnius	963–5	Leo VIII
[418–19	Eulalius]	708–15	Constantine	964–6	Benedict V
422–32	Celestine I	715–31	Gregory II	965–72	John XIII
432–40	Sixtus III	731–41	Gregory III	973–4	Benedict VI
440–61	Leo I	741–52	Zacharias	[974,	Boniface VII]
461–8	Hilarus	752	Stephen II	984–5	
468–83	Simplicius		(not consecrated)	974–83	Benedict VII

POPES (cont.)

983–4	John XIV	[1168–78	Callistus III]	1484–92	Innocent VIII
985–96	John XV	[1179–80	Innocent III]	1492–1503	Alexander VI
996–9	Gregory V	1181–5	Lucius III	1503	Pius III
[997–8	John XVI]	1185–7	Urban III	1503–13	Julius II
999–1003	Sylvester II	1187	Gregory VIII	1513–21	Leo X
1003	John XVII	1187–91	Clement III	1522–3	Hadrian VI
1004–9	John XVIII	1191–8	Celestine III	1523–34	Clement VII
1009–12	Sergius IV	1198–1216	Innocent III	1534–49	Paul III
1012–24	Benedict VIII	1216–27	Honorius III	1550–5	Julius III
[1012	Gregory]	1227–41	Gregory IX	1555	Marcellus II
1024–32	John XIX	1241	Celestine IV	1555–9	Paul IV
1032–44	Benedict IX	1243–54	Innocent IV	1559–65	Pius IV
1045	Sylvester III	1254–61	Alexander IV	1566–72	Pius V
1045	Benedict IX	1261–4	Urban IV	1572–85	Gregory XIII
	(second reign)	1265–8	Clement IV	1585–90	Sixtus V
1045–6	Gregory VI	1271–6	Gregory X	1590	Urban VII
1046–7	Clement II	1276	Innocent V	1590–1	Gregory XIV
1047–8	Benedict IX	1276	Hadrian V	1591	Innocent IX
	(third reign)	1276–7	John XXI[3]	1592–1605	Clement VIII
1048	Damasus II	1277–80	Nicholas III	1605	Leo XI
1048–54	Leo IX	1281–5	Martin IV	1605–21	Paul V
1055–7	Victor II	1285–7	Honorius IV	1621–3	Gregory XV
1057–8	Stephen IX (X)	1288–92	Nicholas IV	1623–44	Urban VIII
[1058–9	Benedict X]	1294	Celestine V	1644–55	Innocent X
1059–61	Nicholas II	1294–1303	Boniface VIII	1655–67	Alexander VII
1061–73	Alexander II	1303–4	Benedict XI	1667–9	Clement IX
[1061–72	Honorius II]	1305–14	Clement V	1670–6	Clement X
1073–85	Gregory VII	1316–34	John XXII	1676–89	Innocent XI
[1080,	Clement III]	[1328–30	Nicholas V]	1689–91	Alexander VIII
1084–1100		1334–42	Benedict XII	1691–1700	Innocent XII
1086–7	Victor III	1342–52	Clement VI	1700–21	Clement XI
1088–99	Urban II	1352–62	Innocent VI	1721–4	Innocent XIII
1099–1118	Paschal II	1362–70	Urban V	1724–30	Benedict XIII
[1100–2	Theodoric]	1370–8	Gregory XI	1730–40	Clement XII
1102	Albert]	1378–89	Urban VI	1740–58	Benedict XIV
[1105–11	Sylvester IV]	[1378–94	Clement VII]	1758–69	Clement XIII
1118–19	Gelasius II	1389–1404	Boniface IX	1769–74	Clement XIV
[1118–21	Gregory VIII]	[1394–1423	Benedict XIII]	1775–99	Pius VI
1119–24	Callistus II	1404–6	Innocent VII	1800–23	Pius VII
1124–30	Honorius II	1406–15	Gregory XII	1823–9	Leo XII
[1124	Celestine II]	[1409–10	Alexander V]	1829–30	Pius VIII
1130–43	Innocent II	[1410–15	John XXIII]	1831–46	Gregory XVI
[1130–8	Anacletus II]	1417–31	Martin V	1846–78	Pius IX
[1138	Victor IV][2]	[1423–9	Clement VIII]	1878–1903	Leo XIII
1143–4	Celestine II	[1425–30	Benedict XIV]	1903–14	Pius X
1144–5	Lucius II	1431–47	Eugenius IV	1914–22	Benedict XV
1145–53	Eugenius III	[1439–49	Felix V]	1922–39	Pius XI
1153–4	Anastasius IV	1447–55	Nicholas V	1939–58	Pius XII
1154–9	Hadrian IV	1455–8	Callistus III	1958–63	John XXIII
1159–81	Alexander III	1458–64	Pius II	1963–78	Paul VI
[1159–64	Victor IV][2]	1464–71	Paul II	1978	John Paul I
[1164–8	Paschal III]	1471–84	Sixtus IV	1978–	John Paul II

[1] Elected during the banishment of Martin I   [2] Different individuals   [3] There was no John XX

MAJOR BATTLES AND WARS

Date	Event	Explanation
c.1200 BC	Trojan Wars	Greeks v. Trojans
490–479 BC	Persian Wars	Persia v. Greek city states
490 BC	Battle of Marathon	Athens defeat of Persia
460–445 BC	First Peloponnesian War	Sparta v. Athens
431–404 BC	Second Peloponnesian War	Sparta, Corinth, Persia v. Athens
334–323 BC	Conquests of Alexander the Great Battle of Issus (333 BC) Battle of Granicus (334 BC) Battle of Guagmela (331 BC)	v. Persia, Indian states
306 BC	Battle of Ipsus	'Battle of the Kings', warring 'successors' of Alexander the Great
264–241 BC	First Punic War	Rome v. Carthage
218–202 BC	Second Punic War	Rome v. Carthage
149–146 BC	Third Punic War	Destruction of Carthage
112–106 BC	Numidian War	Rome v. Juguertia, King of Numidia
73–71 BC	Revolt of Spartacus	Slaves v. Rome
58–51 BC	Gallic Wars of Caesar	Rome v. Celtic tribes of Gaul (ancient France)
55 BC	Caesar's expedition to Britain	Rome v. British tribes
48 BC	Battle of Pharsalus	Julius Caesar's defeat of Pompei.
31 BC	Battle of Actium	Octavian's defeat of Antony and Cleopatra
70 AD	Siege of Jerusalem	Rome v. Israel (destruction of the Temple)
84 AD	Battle of Mons Graupius	Rome (Agricola) v. Scottish tribes
375–454 AD	Hun raids on the Roman Empire	Attila v. tribes of Gaul and Italy
665 AD	Battle of Basra	Arabs conquered by Muslims
771–814 AD	Conquests of Charlemagne (Charles the Great)	v. Saxons, Lombards, Arabs (in Spain)
800–1016	Viking Raids	v. Britain, Normandy, Russia, Spain, Morocco, Italy
1066	Battle of Hastings and Norman Conquest of England	William (the Conquerer) v. Harold II (king of Anglo Saxons)
1089–94	El Cid's conquest of Valencia	v. the Moors
1095–1272	The Crusades	Christians v. Turks
1190–1227	Conquests of Genghis Khan	v. Naimans, Uigurs, N China, Kara-Chitai empire, Kharezm empire
1211–1227	Genghis Khan's conquest of N China and development of the Mongol empire	
1206–1405	Mongol Conquests	v. China
1208–29	Albigensian Crusade	Inquisition v. Cathars
1220	Fall of Samarkand to Genghis Khan	
1282–1302	War of the Sicilian Vespers	Sicilian rebels v. French rulers
1297–1305	Revolt of William Wallace	Scots v. English
1314	Battle of Bannockburn	Scots (under Robert Bruce) v. English

MAJOR BATTLES AND WARS (cont.)

Date	Event	Explanation
1337–1453	Hundred Years' War	England v. France
	Battle of Sluys (1340)	English defeat of French
	Battle of Crécy (1346)	English defeat of French
	Battle of Poitiers (1356)	English defeat of French
	Battle of Agincourt (1415)	English defeat of French
1360–1405	Conquests of Tamerlane (Timur)	v. Mongols, Persia, Prussia, India
1388	Battle of Otterburn (Chevy Chase)	Scots' defeat of English (under Sir Henry Percy, 'Hotspur')
1403	Battle of Shrewsbury	Glendower and Percies defeated by Henry V
1411	Battle of Harlaw	Highland v. Lowland Scots
1429	Siege of Orleans	Joan of Arc's defeat of English
1453	The Fall of Constantinople	Turkish conquest of Byzantine Empire
1455–85	Wars of the Roses	Series of civil wars in England (House of York v. House of Lancaster)
	Battle of St Albans (1455)	First battle of war: Yorkist victory:
	Battle of Bosworth Field (1485)	Lancastrian victory: death of Richard III, ancession of Henry VII
1491–2	The Siege of Granada	Spanish defeat of Moors
1494–1559	Habsburg-Valois Wars	
1513	Battle of Flodden	English defeat of Scots
1542	Battle of Solway Moss	Scots defeat of English
1546–7	War of the Schmalkaldic League	France v. German Protestant Estates
1562	Massacre at Vassy	Huguenots killed by de Guize
1562–98	French Wars of Religion	Catholics v. Huguenots
1568–1648	Dutch Wars of Independence	Successful revolt of Netherlands v. Phillip II of Spain
1571	Battle of Lepanto	Spanish and Italian defeat of Turkish navy
1572	St Bartholomew's Day Massacre	Slaughter of French Huguenots by Charles IX
1585–9	War of the Three Henries	Henry IV secures succession to French throne
1587	Sack of Cadiz by Drake	Defeat of Philip II's Spanish ships
1588	Defeat of the Spanish Armada	English defeat of Spanish navy
1592–9	Japanese invasion of Korea	
1596–1603	Tyrone's Rebellion in Ireland	Irish v. English
1605	Gunpowder Plot	Catholic conspiracy against James I and the English Parliament
1609–14	War of the Julich Succession	Protestant v. Catholic powers of Europe
1618–48	Thirty Years' War	French king v. Habsburg rulers
1620	Battle of the White Mountain (Prague)	Defeat of Bohemian Protestants
1628–31	War of the Mantuan Succession	France v. Spain
1639	First Bishops' War	Scotland v. England
1640	Second Bishops' War	Scots' defeat of English
1641–9	Great Irish Rebellion	Ireland v. England
1642–6	English Civil War	Royalist forces of Charles I v. Parliamentarians under Cromwell
1644	Battle of Marston Moor	Parliamentary defeat of Royalists
1688	The Glorious Revolution	William II and Mary II ascend English throne after flight of James II

MAJOR BATTLES AND WARS (cont.)

Date	Event	Explanation
1688–97	War of the League of Augsburg	European alliance's defeat of Louis XIV
1689	Battle of Killiecrankie	Highland Scots' defeat of government
1690	Battle of the Boyne	Defeat of James II's Catholic forces by Protestant William II
1692	The Glencoe Massacre	Slaughter of McDonalds by Campbells (anti-Jacobite forces)
1701–14	War of the Spanish Succession	Grand Alliance v. Louis XIV of France
1702–13	Queen Anne's War	Britain v. France
1704	Battle of Blenheim	Allied troops' defeat of Louis XIV
1715–16	Jacobite Rebellion	Led by Earl of Mar v. Hanoverians
1715	Battle of Sherrifmuir	Hanoverians v. Jacobites, indecisive battle
1739–43	War of Jenkin's Ear	Britain v. Spain
1740–48	War of the Austrian Succession	Prussia v. Austria
1745–6	Jacobite Rebellion	Led by Charles Edward Stuart (Bonnie Prince Charlie)
1745	Battle of Prestonpans	Jacobite defeat of Hanoverians
1746	Battle of Culloden	Jacobite Highlanders crushed by Hanoverian forces
1756–63	Seven Years' War	Austria, France, Russian, Sweden and Saxony v. Prussia, Britain and Portugal
1759	Battle of Quebec	British defeat of French
1763–6	Pontiac's War	Unsuccessful uprising of American Indians v. British colonists
1775–83	US War of Independence	American settlers v. British government forces
	Battle of Bunker Hill (1775)	First battle of war; heavy British losses
	Battle of Stillwater or Saratoga (1777)	American defeat of British
	Battle of Yorktown (1781)	American defeat of British, decisive campaign of war
1789–92	French Revolution	Popular movement overthrowing *ancien régime* to establish new constitution
1792–1802	French Revolutionary Wars	French campaigns v. various neighbouring states
1792	Battle of Valmy	French defeat of Prussians
1798	Battle of Aboukir Bay or the Nile	Napoleon's French fleet destroyed by Nelson
1800–15	Napoleonic Wars	Fought to preserve new French constitution and influence under Napoleon Bonaparte
1805	Battle of Austerlitz	French defeat of Austro-Russian army
1805	Battle of Trafalgar	English defeat of Napoleonic fleet
1808–14	Peninsular War	France v. Britain
	Battle of Corunna (1809)	British commander Sir John Moor killed by French
1812	Napoleon's retreat from Moscow	
1814–16	Gurkha War	Gurkhas v. British in India
1815	Battle of Waterloo	Napoleon defeated by Allied forces under Duke of Wellington
1821–32	Greek War of Independence	Greek rebellion v. Turkish rule

MAJOR BATTLES AND WARS (cont.)

Date	Event	Explanation
1836	Texan War of Independence, Battle of the Alamo	Americans v. Mexican rule
1838–9	Boer-Zulu War	
1839–42	First Opium War in China	British defeat of China
1843–51	Siege of Montevideo	Combined Argentine-Uruguayan army v. Montevideo with French and English support
1844–7	First Maori War	Maoris v. British settlers in New Zealand
1846–7	Mexican War	USA v. Mexico
1853–6	Crimean War	Britain v. Russia
1856	Battle of Balaclava	Unsuccessful Russian attack on British base; heavy British losses
1856–60	Second Opium War in China	British defeat of China
1857–8	Mormon Utah War	Mormons v. Federal Government of USA
1859	John Brown's raid on Harper Ferry	Abolitionist attack on Federal arsenal
1859–61	Italian War of Independence	Austria v. Italy and France
1859	Battle of Solferino	French defeat of Austria
1860–72	Second Maori War	Maoris v. British settlers in New Zealand
1861–5	American Civil War	North (Union) states v. South (Confederate)
	Battle of Shiloh (1862)	Heavy losses to both sides
	Battle of Gettysburg (1863)	Unionist defeat of Confederates
	Battles of Petersburg (1864)	Successful Unionist campaign v. Confederates
1866	Seven Weeks' War	Prussia and Italy's defeat of Austria and allies
1876	Battle of Little Bighorn (Custer's Last Stand)	Defeat of US cavalry under General Custer by Sioux and Cheyenne Indians
1879	Zulu War	Zulu defeat of British
1879–84	War of the Pacific	Chile v. Peru and Bolivia
1880–1	First Boer War	Boers' defeat of British
1885	Fall of Khartoum	Mahdli defeat of British; death of General Gordon
1890	Massacre of Wounded Knee	US defeat of Sioux Indians
1899–1901	Boxer Uprising in China	Unsuccessful anti-foreign uprising
1899–1902	Great Boer War	Boers v. British
	Battle of Ladysmith (1900)	Sieges of the British by the Boers
	Battle of Mafeking (1900)	
1911–12	Chinese Revolution	Overthrow of Manchu dynasty
1914–18	World War 1	Triple Alliance (Britain, France and Russia) v. Triple Entente (Germany, Austria-Hungary and Turkey)
	Battles of Liège, Marne, Ypres and Tannenberg (1914)	Allied v. German forces
	Dardanelles and Gallipoli Campaigns (1915)	Unsuccessful Allied operations
	Battles of Loos and Ypres (1915)	Britain v. Germany
	Battle of Jutland (1916)	British fleet v. German fleet

MAJOR BATTLES AND WARS (cont.)

Date	Event	Explanation
1914–18	World War 1 (cont.)	
	Battle of Verdun (1916)	France v. Germany
	Battle of Passchendaele (1917)	Third battle of Ypres, Britain v. Germany
	Zeebrugge Raid (1918)	Failed British blockade of German fleet
	Battles of Amiens, Antwerp and the Somme (1918)	Allied v. German forces
1916	Easter Rebellion in Dublin	Unsuccessful revolt by Irish nationalists v. British rule
1917	Russian Revolution	Overthrow of monarchy and beginning of Communism
1918	Hungarian Revolution	Communist revolt
1935–6	Italian invasion of Ethiopia	Mussolini's troops v. Ethiopia under Haile Selassie
1936–9	Spanish Civil War	Republicans v. Nationalists
1938	Battle of Ebro River	Nationalist defeat of Republicans
1939–45	World War 2	Allied forces (Britain, France, USA) v. Germany, Japan, Russia, and Italy
	Battle of Britain, Battle of Flanders, Evacuation of Dunkirk, Fall of France (1940)	Allied forces v. Germany
	Babi Yar Massacre (1941)	German slaughter of Jews
	Bombing of Pearl Harbour (1941)	Japanese attack on US naval base
	Battle of Stalingrad and Moscow (1941–2)	Russian defeat of Germany
	Battle of Tobruk (1941–2)	Allied v. German forces
	Battle of Midway Island (1942)	Allied defeat of German air force
	Battle of El Alamein (1942)	British defeat of Rommel's Afrika Corps
	Battle of Singapore (1942)	Japanese siege and occupation
	Battle of Salerno, Invasion of Sicily (1943)	Allied defeat of Germany and Italy
	Burma Campaigns (1943–5)	British-Indian forces v. Japan
	D-Day allied invasion of Normandy (1944)	Allied defeat of Germany
	Battles of Anzio, Arnhem and Monte Cassino (1944)	Allied forces v. Germany
	Battle of the Bulge in the Ardennes (1944–5)	Eventual Allied defeat of Germany
	Battle of Iwo Jima (1945)	Allied capture of Japanese air-base
	Battle of the Rhine (1945)	Allied defeat of Germany
1946–54	French War of Indochina	Vietnam v. France
1947–8	Indian Civil War	Pakistan v. India
1950–3	Korean War	Communist v. non-communist forces
1952–6	Mau-Mau uprisings in Kenya	Kikuyu revolt v. white settlers
1956	Suez War	Israel, Britain and France v. Egypt
1956–1975	Vietnam War	North Vietnam (communist) v. South Vietnam (non-communist) and US forces
1960–8	Civil War in the Congo	Military coup created first Marxist state in Africa, 1968
1961	Bay of Pigs Invasion	Cuban defeat of exiles supported by USA

MAJOR BATTLES AND WARS (cont.)

Date	Event	Explanation
1962–74	Mozambique War of Independence	Nationalist revolt against Portuguese rule
1967	Six-Day War	Israel v. Arab states
1967–70	Nigerian-Biafran War	Nigerian defeat of Biafra
1968	Soviet invasion of Czechoslovakia	Defeat of attempt at liberalization from communism
1968	Tet offensive in Vietnam	USA v. North Vietnam
1970–1	Jordanian Civil War	Jordan v. Palestinian guerillas
1970–5	Cambodian War	Cambodia, South Vietnam and USA v. North Vietnam, Viet Cong and Khmer Rouge
1971	Civil war in Pakistan	East v. West Pakistan
1971	My Lai massacre	Slaughter of Vietnamese villagers by US troops
1973	Chilean Revolution	Marxist government overthrown in military coup
1974	Turkish invasion of Cyprus	Turkey v. Greek Cypriots
1975–88	Angolan Civil War	Internal fighting after independence
1978–9	Ugandan Civil War	Ugandan exiles and Tanzanian defeat of Idi Amin Dada's regime
1978	Lebanese Civil War	Israeli invasion of S Lebanon
1979–88	Afghan Civil War and Soviet Invasion	
1979	Iranian Islamic Revolution	Republic established under Ayatollah Khomeini
1980–8	Iran-Iraq Gulf War	
1982	Falklands War	British defeat of Argentina
1982–90	Nicaraguan Civil War	Contras (supported by USA) v. socialist junta
1983	Invasion of Grenada	US troops on peace-restoring mission
1983–8	Civil War in Sri Lanka	Buddhist v. Hindu groups
1986	Civil War in Haiti	Military coup and new constitution
1990	Iraqi invasion of Kuwait	
1991	Gulf War	Defeat of Iraq by US-led allies (29 countries, including UK)
1991	Civil War in Yugoslavia	

SOCIAL STRUCTURE

MAJOR CITIES OF THE WORLD

Abidjan Ivory Coast	1 850 000 (1984)	**Baltimore** USA	751 400 (1988e)
Abu Dhabi United Arab	449 000 (1980)	**Bamako** Mali	646 163 (1987)
Emirates		**Bandung** Indonesia	1 566 700 (1983e)
Acapulco Mexico	409 335 (1980)	**Bangalore** India	2 628 593 (1981)
Accra Ghana	964 879 (1984)	**Bangkok** Thailand	5 845 152 (1989e)
Adana Turkey	777 554 (1985)	**Bangui** Central African	473 817 (1984e)
Addis Ababa Ethiopia	1 495 266 (1986e)	Republic	
Adelaide Australia	993 100 (1986)	**Banjarmasin** Indonesia	423 600 (1983e)
Aden Yemen	318 000 (1984)	**Banjul** Gambia	44 183 (1983)
Agadir Morocco	700 000 (1987e)	**Baoding** China	467 000 (1988e)
Agra India	770 000 (1981)	**Baoji** China	301 000 (1988e)
Ahmdabad India	2 515 000 (1981)	**Baotou** China	936 000 (1988e)
Ahvaz Iran	470 927 (1983)	**Barcelona** Spain	1 703 744 (1987e)
Ajmer India	375 593 (1981)	**Barcelona** Venezuela	442 677 (1989e)
Alajuela Costa Rica	147 396 (1988e)	**Bareilly** India	394 938 (1981)
Albuquerque USA	378 180 (1988e)	**Bari** Italy	358 906 (1987)
Aligarh India	320 861 (1981)	**Barnaul** USSR	602 000 (1989)
Aleppo Syria	1 308 000 (1989)	**Barquisimeto** Venezuela	764 216 (1989e)
Alexandria Egypt	2 917 327 (1986e)	**Barranquilla** Columbia	899 781 (1985)
Algiers Algeria	1 721 607 (1983e)	**Basra** Iraq	616 700 (1985e)
Allahabad India	619 628 (1981)	**Beijing (Peking)** China	5 468 000 (1988e)
Alma-Ata USSR	1 128 000 (1989)	**Beirut** Lebanon	1 500 000 (1985e)
Amagasaki Japan	500 976 (1989)	**Belem** Brazil	1 116 578 (1987e)
Amman Jordan	972 000 (1986)	**Belfast** UK	354 400 (1981)
Amritsar India	594 844 (1981)	**Belgorod** USSR	300 000 (1989)
Amsterdam Netherlands	694 680 (1989)	**Belgrade** Yugoslavia	1 470 073 (1981)
Ankara Turkey	2 235 035 (1985)	**Belo Horizonte** Brazil	2 114 429 (1987e)
Anshan China	1 172 800 (1989e)	**Bengpu** China	419 000 (1988e)
Antananarivo Madagascar	662 600 (1985e)	**Benxi** China	726 000 (1988e)
Antwerp Belgium	476 644 (1987)	**Berlin (East and West)**	3 126 072 (1987e)
Anyang China	388 800 (1989e)	Germany	
Aracaju Brazil	360 013 (1987e)	**Berne** Switzerland	135 147 (1988e)
Archangel USSR	416 000 (1989)	**Bhavnagar** India	308 642 (1981)
Arequipa Peru	634 500 (1990e)	**Bhilainagar** India	319 450 (1981)
Asahikawa Japan	363 704 (1989e)	**Bhopal** India	671 018 (1981)
Ashkhabad USSR	398 000 (1989)	**Bilbao** Spain	382 413 (1987e)
Astrakhan USSR	509 000 (1989)	**Birmingham** UK	1 024 118 (1981)
Asuncion Paraguay	607 706 (1990e)	**Bissau** Guinea-Bissau	125 000 (1985e)
Athens Greece	885 737 (1981)	**Bochum** Germany	381 200 (1986e)
Atlanta USA	445 000 (1988e)	**Bogata** Colombia	3 982 941 (1985)
Auckland New Zealand	841 700 (1988e)	**Bologna** Italy	427 240 (1987)
Austin USA	467 420 (1988e)	**Bombay (Greater)** India	8 243 405 (1981)
		Bonn Germany	291 400 (1986e)
Baghdad Iraq	3 844 608 (1987)	**Boston** USA	577 830 (1988e)
Bakhtaran Iran	560 514 (1986)	**Brasilia** Brazil	1 567 709 (1987e)
Baku USSR	1 150 000 (1989)	**Brasov** Romania	351 493 (1986e)

MAJOR CITIES OF THE WORLD (cont.)

Bratislava Czechoslovakia	424 378 (1987e)	
Brazzaville Congo	596 200 (1985)	
Bremen Germany	522 000 (1986e)	
Brisbane Australia	1 157 200 (1985e)	
Bristol UK	420 169 (1981)	
Brno Czechoslovakia	385 965 (1987e)	
Brussels Belgium	970 346 (1987)	
Bryansk USSR	452 000 (1989)	
Bucaramanga Colombia	352 326 (1985)	
Bucharest Romania	1 989 823 (1986e)	
Budapest Hungary	2 104 700 (1988)	
Buenos Aires Argentina	2 922 829 (1980)	
Buffalo USA	313 570 (1988e)	
Bulawayo Zimbabwe	413 800 (1982)	
Bursa Turkey	612 510 (1985)	
Bydgoszcz Poland	377 900 (1988e)	
Cairo Egypt	5 875 000 (1983e)	
Calcutta India	3 305 006 (1981)	
Calgary Canada	671 326 (1986)	
Cali Colombia	1 350 565 (1985)	
Calicut India	394 447 (1981)	
Callao Peru	515 200 (1985e)	
Caloocan City Philippines	467 816 (1980)	
Campinas Brazil	841 016 (1987e)	
Campo Grande Brazil	384 398 (1987e)	
Campos Brazil	366 716 (1987e)	
Canberra Australia	273 600 (1985e)	
Canton (Guangzhou) China	2 718 000 (1988e)	
Cape Town South Africa	1 911 521 (1985)	
Caracas Venezuela	3 373 059 (1989e)	
Cartagena Columbia	531 246 (1985)	
Casablanca Morocco	2 904 000 (1987e)	
Catania Italy	372 212 (1987)	
Cebu City Philippines	490 281 (1980)	
Chandigarh India	379 660 (1981)	
Changchun China	1 557 000 (1988e)	
Changsha China	1 030 000 (1988e)	
Changzhou China	485 000 (1988e)	
Charlotte USA	367 860 (1988e)	
Cheboksary USSR	420 000 (1989)	
Chelyabinsk USSR	1 143 000 (1989)	
Chengdu China	1 614 000 (1988e)	
Cherepovets USSR	310 000 (1989)	
Chiba Japan	800 620 (1988)	
Chicago USA	2 977 520 (1988e)	
Chiclayo Peru	377 702 (1985e)	
Chifeng China	316 000 (1988e)	
Chihuahua Mexico	385 603 (1980)	
Chimkent USSR	393 000 (1989)	
Chita USSR	366 000 (1989)	
Chittagong Bangladesh	1 391 877 (1981)	

Chongjin North Korea	530 000 (1986)	
Chongju South Korea	350 256 (1985)	
Chonju South Korea	426 473 (1985)	
Chongqing China	2 179 000 (1988e)	
Christchurch New Zealand	300 700 (1988e)	
Chungho Taiwan	334 663 (1986)	
Cincinnati USA	370 480 (1988e)	
Ciudad Guayana Venezuela	516 596 (1989e)	
Ciudad Juárez Mexico	544 496 (1980)	
Cleveland USA	521 370 (1988e)	
Cluj-Napoca Romania	310 017 (1986e)	
Cochabamba Bolivia	360 446 (1987e)	
Cochin India	551 567 (1981)	
Coimbatore India	704 514 (1981)	
Cologne Germany	914 300 (1986e)	
Colombo Sri Lanka	609 000 (1988e)	
Columbus USA	569 570 (1988e)	
Conakry Guinea	705 280 (1983)	
Constanta Romania	332 676 (1986e)	
Constantine Algeria	448 578 (1983e)	
Contagem Brazil	383 904 (1987e)	
Copenhagen Denmark	1 351 999 (1986)	
Cordoba Argentina	983 969 (1980)	
Coventry UK	322 573 (1981)	
Cracow Poland	743 700 (1988e)	
Cucuta Colombia	379 478 (1985)	
Culiacan Mexico	304 826 (1980)	
Curitiba Brazil	1 279 205 (1983e)	
Dakar Senegal	1 382 000 (1985e)	
Dalian China	1 619 000 (1988e)	
Dallas USA	987 360 (1988e)	
Damascus Syria	1 112 214 (1981)	
Da Nang Vietnam	370 670 (1989)	
Dandong China	491 000 (1988e)	
Daqing China	601 000 (1988e)	
Dar es Salaam Tanzania	1 100 000 (1985e)	
Datong China	740 000 (1988e)	
Davao City Philippines	610 375 (1980)	
Delhi India	4 884 234 (1981)	
Denver USA	492 200 (1988e)	
Detroit USA	1 035 920 (1988e)	
Dhaka Bangladesh	3 430 312 (1981)	
Diyarbakir Turkey	305 940 (1985)	
Dnepropetrovsk USSR	1 179 000 (1989)	
Doha Qatar	217 294 (1986)	
Donetsk USSR	1 110 000 (1989)	
Dortmund Germany	568 200 (1986e)	
Douala Cameroon	1 029 731 (1968e)	
Dresden Germany	519 523 (1987e)	
Dubai United Arab Emirates	419 104 (1985)	

MAJOR CITIES OF THE WORLD (cont.)

Dublin Republic of Ireland	920 956 (1986)	**Guadalajara** Mexico	1 906 145 (1979e)
Duisburg Germany	514 600 (1986e)	**Guarulhos** Brazil	713 582 (1987e)
Dukou China	384 000 (1988e)	**Guatemala City** Guatemala	754 243 (1981)
Duque de Caxias Brazil	664 105 (1987e)	**Guayaquil** Ecuador	1 509 108 (1986e)
Durban South Africa	982 075 (1985)	**Guilin** China	341 000 (1988e)
Durgapur India	311 798 (1981)	**Guiyang** China	938 000 (1988e)
Dushanbe USSR	595 000 (1989)	**Gujranwala** Pakistan	658 753 (1981)
Düsseldorf Germany	560 000 (1986e)	**Guntur** India	367 699 (1981)
Dzhambul USSR	307 000 (1989)	**Gwalior** India	539 015 (1981)
		Gwangju South Korea	905 896 (1985)
Edinburgh UK	420 169 (1981)		
Edmonton Canada	785 465 (1986)	**Hachioji** Japan	432 731 (1988)
El Giza Egypt	1 640 000 (1983e)	**The Hague** Netherlands	443 845 (1989)
El Mahalla el-Koubra	355 000 (1983e)	**Haiphong** Vietnam	456 049 (1989)
Egypt		**Hakodate** Japan	311 591 (1988)
El Mansoura Egypt	323 000 (1983e)	**Hamamatsu** Japan	522 299 (1988)
El Paso USA	510 970 (1988e)	**Hamburg** Germany	1 571 300 (1986e)
Eskisehir Turkey	366 765 (1985)	**Hamhumg** North Korea	670 000 (1986)
Essen Germany	615 400 (1986e)	**Handan** China	778 000 (1988e)
		Hangzhou China	1 049 000 (1988e)
Faisalabad Pakistan	1 104 209 (1981)	**Hanoi** Vietnam	1 088 862 (1989)
Faridabad India	330 864 (1981)	**Hamilton** Canada	557 029 (1986)
Feira de Santana Brazil	355 201 (1987e)	**Hanover** Germany	505 700 (1986e)
Fez Morocco	933 000 (1987e)	**Harare** Zimbabwe	656 000 (1982)
Florence Italy	421 299 (1987)	**Harbin** China	2 328 000 (1988e)
Fortaleza Brazil	1 582 414 (1987e)	**Havana** Cuba	2 036 799 (1986e)
Fort Worth USA	426 610 (1988e)	**Hefei** China	669 000 (1988e)
Frankfurt am Main	592 400 (1986e)	**Hegang** China	492 000 (1988e)
Germany		**Helsinki** Finland	490 034 (1987e)
Freetown Sierra Leone	469 776 (1985)	**Hengyang** China	446 000 (1988e)
Fujisawa Japan	336 892 (1988)	**Hermosillo** Mexico	297 175 (1980)
Fukuoka Japan	1 157 111 (1988)	**Higashiosaka** Japan	502 893 (1989)
Fukuyama Japan	363 123 (1988)	**Himeji** Japan	450 374 (1988)
Funabashi Japan	515 294 (1988)	**Hirakata** Japan	385 739 (1988)
Fushun China	1 151 000 (1988e)	**Hiroshima** Japan	1 042 629 (1988)
Fuxin China	608 000 (1988e)	**Ho Chi Minh City** Vietnam	3 169 135 (1989)
Fuzhou China	832 000 (1988e)	**Hohot** China	605 000 (1988e)
		Homs Syria	346 871 (1981)
Ganzhou China	356 000 (1988e)	**Hong Kong** Hong Kong	5 736 100 (1989e)
Gaziantep Turkey	478 635 (1985)	**Honolulu** USA	376 110 (1988e)
Gdańsk Poland	461 500 (1988e)	**Houston** USA	1 698 090 (1988e)
Genoa Italy	722 026 (1987)	**Howrah** India	744 429 (1981)
Georgetown Guyana	150 368 (1986e)	**Huaibei** China	325 000 (1988e)
Gifu Japan	407 827 (1988)	**Huainan** China	655 000 (1988e)
Glasgow UK	765 030 (1981)	**Huangshi** China	430 000 (1988e)
Goiania Brazil	923 333 (1987e)	**Hubli-Dharwar** India	527 108 (1981)
Gomel USSR	500 000 (1989)	**Hunjiang** China	458 000 (1988e)
Gorakhpur India	307 501 (1981)	**Hyderabad** India	2 187 262 (1981)
Gorky USSR	1 438 000 (1989)	**Hyderabad** Pakistan	751 529 (1981)
Gorlovka USSR	337 000 (1989)		
Gothenburg Sweden	431 840 (1989e)	**Iasi** Romania	313 060 (1986e)
Grozny USSR	401 000 (1989)	**Ibadan** Nigeria	1 232 000 (1990e)

MAJOR CITIES OF THE WORLD (cont.)

Icel Turkey	314 350 (1985)	
Ichikawa Japan	412 214 (1988)	
Inchon South Korea	1 386 911 (1985)	
Indianapolis USA	727 130 (1988e)	
Indore India	829 327 (1981)	
Irkutsk USSR	626 000 (1989)	
Isfahan Iran	1 000 000 (1986)	
Istanbul Turkey	5 475 982 (1985)	
Ivanovo USSR	481 000 (1989)	
Iwaki Japan	357 056 (1988)	
Izhevsk USSR	635 000 (1989)	
Jabalpur India	649 085 (1981)	
Jaboatoa Brazil	409 528 (1987e)	
Jacksonville USA	635 430 (1988e)	
Jaipur India	977 165 (1981)	
Jakarta Indonesia	7 347 800 (1983e)	
Jalandhar India	408 196 (1981)	
Jamshedpur India	457 061 (1981)	
Jedda Saudi Arabia	1 500 000 (1983e)	
Jerusalem Israel	428 668 (1983)	
Jiamusi China	449 000 (1988e)	
Jiaozuo China	364 000 (1988e)	
Jilin China	971 000 (1988e)	
Jinan China	1 257 000 (1988e)	
Jingdezhen China	315 000 (1988e)	
Jinzhou China	641 000 (1988e)	
Jixi China	650 000 (1988e)	
Joao Pessoa Brazil	396 197 (1987e)	
Jodhpur India	506 345 (1981)	
Johannesburg South Africa	1 609 408 (1985)	
Juiz de Fora Brazil	349 720 (1987e)	
Kabul Afghanistan	1 036 407 (1982e)	
Kaesong North Korea	310 000 (1986)	
Kagoshima Japan	527 979 (1988)	
Kaifeng China	473 000 (1988e)	
Kalinin USSR	451 000 (1989)	
Kaliningrad USSR	401 000 (1989)	
Kaluga USSR	312 000 (1989)	
Kampala Uganda	458 503 (1980)	
Kanazawa Japan	422 751 (1988)	
Kano Nigeria	580 200 (1990e)	
Kanpur India	1 486 522 (1981)	
Kansas City USA	438 950 (1988e)	
Kaohsiung Taiwan	1 342 797 (1987e)	
Karachi Pakistan	5 180 562 (1981)	
Karaganda USSR	614 000 (1989)	
Karaj Iran	526 272 (1982e)	
Karl-Marx-Stadt Germany	313 347 (1987e)	
Kathmandu Nepal	235 160 (1981)	
Katowice Poland	365 800 (1988e)	

Kaunas USSR	423 000 (1989)	
Kawaguchi Japan	418 880 (1988)	
Kawasaki Japan	1 114 173 (1988)	
Kayseri Turkey	373 937 (1985)	
Kazan USSR	1 094 000 (1989)	
Keelung Taiwan	348 541 (1987e)	
Kemerovo USSR	520 000 (1989)	
Kenitra Morocco	833 000 (1987e)	
Khabarovsk USSR	601 000 (1989)	
Kharkov USSR	1 611 000 (1989)	
Khartoum Sudan	476 218 (1983)	
Khartoum North Sudan	341 146 (1983)	
Kherson USSR	355 000 (1989)	
Khulna Bangladesh	646 359 (1981)	
Kiev USSR	2 587 000 (1989)	
Kigali Rwanda	181 600 (1983e)	
Kingston Jamaica	104 000 (1980)	
Kingston upon Hull UK	325 835 (1981)	
Kinshasa Zaire	3 562 122 (1990e)	
Kirkuk Iraq	535 000 (1977)	
Kirov USSR	441 000 (1989)	
Kishinyov USSR	665 000 (1989)	
Kitakyushu Japan	1 035 053 (1988)	
Kitchener Canada	311 195 (1986)	
Kitwe Zambia	472 255 (1988e)	
Kobe Japan	1 426 838 (1988)	
Kochi Japan	311 710 (1988)	
Kolhapur India	340 625 (1981)	
Komsomolosk USSR	315 000 (1989)	
Konya Turkey	439 181 (1985)	
Koriyama Japan	303 418 (1988)	
Kota India	358 241 (1981)	
Krasnodar USSR	620 000 (1989)	
Krasnoyarsk USSR	912 000 (1989)	
Krivoy Rog USSR	713 000 (1989)	
Kuala Lumpur Malaysia	919 610 (1980)	
Kumamoto Japan	554 904 (1988)	
Kumasi Ghana	348 880 (1984)	
Kunming China	1 144 000 (1988e)	
Kurashiki Japan	415 780 (1988)	
Kurgan USSR	356 000 (1989)	
Kursk USSR	424 000 (1989)	
Kuwait City Kuwait	44 335 (1985)	
Kuybyshev USSR	1 257 000 (1989)	
Kyoto Japan	1 419 390 (1988)	
Lagos Nigeria	1 307 000 (1990e)	
Lahore Pakistan	2 952 689 (1981)	
Lanzhou China	1 121 000 (1988e)	
La Paz Bolivia	1 013 688 (1987e)	
La Plata Argentina	564 750 (1980)	
Las Palmas Grand Canary	358 272 (1987e)	

MAJOR CITIES OF THE WORLD (cont.)

Leeds	UK	451 841 (1981)	**Mar del Plata**	Argentina	414 696 (1980)
Leicester	UK	328 835 (1981)	**Mariupal**	USSR	517 000 (1989)
Leipzig	Germany	549 229 (1987)	**Marrakesh**	Morocco	1 425 000 (1987e)
Leningrad	USSR	4 456 000 (1989)	**Marseilles**	France	878 689 (1982)
Leon	Mexico	593 002 (1980)	**Masan**	South Korea	448 746 (1985)
Leshan	China	329 000 (1988e)	**Matsudo**	Japan	439 106 (1988)
Lianyungang	China	317 000 (1988e)	**Matsuyama**	Japan	433 886 (1988)
Liaoyang	China	461 000 (1988e)	**Mecca**	Saudi Arabia	550 000 (1980)
Liaoyuan	China	328 000 (1988e)	**Medan**	Indonesia	1 805 500 (1983e)
Libreville	Gabon	352 000 (1987e)	**Medellin**	Colombia	1 468 089 (1985)
Lima	Peru	5 008 400 (1985e)	**Meerut**	India	417 395 (1981)
Lipetsk	USSR	450 000 (1989)	**Meknes**	Morocco	704 000 (1987e)
Lisbon	Portugal	807 937 (1981)	**Melbourne**	Australia	2 916 600 (1985e)
Liupanshui	China	328 000 (1988e)	**Memphis**	USA	645 190 (1988e)
Liuzhou	China	561 000 (1988e)	**Mendoza**	Argentina	605 623 (1980)
Liverpool	UK	544 861 (1981e)	**Meshed**	Iran	1 500 000 (1986)
Ljubljana	Yugoslavia	305 211 (1981)	**Mexicali**	Mexico	341 559 (1980)
Lodz	Poland	851 500 (1988e)	**Mexico City**	Mexico	8 831 079 (1980)
Lomé	Togo	366 476 (1983e)	**Miami**	USA	371 100 (1988e)
London	Canada	342 302 (1986)	**Milan**	Italy	1 478 505 (1987)
London	UK	6 677 928 (1981)	**Milwaukee**	USA	599 380 (1988e)
Londrina	Brazil	346 676 (1987e)	**Minneapolis**	USA	344 670 (1988e)
Long Beach	USA	415 040 (1988e)	**Minsk**	USSR	1 589 000 (1989)
Los Angeles	USA	3 352 710 (1988e)	**Mogadishu**	Somalia	500 000 (1981e)
Luanda	Angola	1 200 000 (1982e)	**Mogilyou**	USSR	356 000 (1989)
Lublin	Poland	339 500 (1988e)	**Mombasa**	Kenya	425 600 (1984e)
Lucknow	India	916 954 (1981)	**Monrovia**	Liberia	421 058 (1984)
Ludhiana	India	607 052 (1981)	**Monterrey**	Mexico	1 090 009 (1980)
Luoyang	China	697 000 (1988e)	**Montevideo**	Uruguay	1 246 500 (1985)
Lusaka	Zambia	870 030 (1988e)	**Montreal**	Canada	2 921 357 (1986)
Luxembourg	Luxembourg	790 000 (1989)	**Moradabad**	India	330 051 (1981)
Lyons	France	418 476 (1982)	**Moscow**	USSR	8 769 000 (1989)
			Mosul	Iraq	570 926 (1985)
Maceio	Brazil	482 195 (1987e)	**Multan**	Pakistan	722 070 (1981)
Machida	Japan	335 347 (1988)	**Mudanjiang**	China	531 000 (1988e)
Madras	India	3 276 622 (1981)	**Munich**	Germany	1 274 700 (1986e)
Madrid	Spain	3 100 507 (1987e)	**Murcia**	Spain	305 278 (1987e)
Madurai	India	820 891 (1981)	**Murmansk**	USSR	468 000 (1989)
Magnitogorsk	USSR	440 000 (1989)	**Mysore**	India	479 081 (1981)
Makassar	Indonesia	840 500 (1983e)			
Makeyevka	USSR	430 000 (1989)	**Naberezhnye Chelny**	USSR	501 000 (1989)
Makhachkala	USSR	315 000 (1989)	**Nagano**	Japan	341 074 (1988)
Malaga	Spain	566 330 (1987e)	**Nagasaki**	Japan	445 814 (1988)
Malang	Indonesia	547 100 (1983e)	**Nagoya**	Japan	2 099 564 (1988)
Managua	Nicaragua	682 111 (1985e)	**Nagpur**	India	1 219 461 (1981)
Manaus	Brazil	809 914 (1987e)	**Naha**	Japan	309 641 (1988)
Manchester	UK	448 604 (1981)	**Nairobi**	Kenya	1 103 600 (1984e)
Mandelay	Burma	532 895 (1983)	**Namangan**	USSR	308 000 (1989)
Manila	Philippines	1 630 485 (1980)	**Nanchang**	China	1 003 000 (1988e)
Maputo	Mozambique	1 006 765 (1987e)	**Nanjing**	China	1 972 000 (1988e)
Maracaibo	Venezuela	1 365 308 (1989e)	**Nanning**	China	660 000 (1988e)
Maracay	Venezuela	923 673 (1989e)	**Nantong**	China	306 000 (1988e)

MAJOR CITIES OF THE WORLD (cont.)

Naples Italy	1 200 958 (1987)	
Nara Japan	338 842 (1988)	
Nashville USA	481 400 (1988e)	
Nassau Bahamas	110 000 (1980e)	
Natal Brazil	510 106 (1987e)	
N'Djamena Chad	511 700 (1986e)	
Ndola Zambia	442 666 (1988e)	
Netzahualcoyott Mexico	1 341 230 (1980)	
Newark USA	313 800 (1988e)	
Newcastle Australia	423 300 (1985e)	
New Dehli India	273 036 (1981)	
New Orleans USA	531 700 (1988e)	
New York USA	7 352 700 (1988e)	
Niamey Niger	398 265 (1988)	
Nice France	338 486 (1982)	
Nicosia Cyprus	149 100 (1982)	
Niigata Japan	469 521 (1988)	
Nikolayev USSR	503 000 (1989)	
Ningbo China	520 000 (1988e)	
Nis Yugoslavia	643 470 (1981)	
Nishinomiya Japan	412 267 (1988)	
Niteroi Brazil	441 684 (1987e)	
Nizhny Tagil USSR	440 000 (1989)	
Nova Iguacu Brazil	1 319 491 (1987e)	
Novakchott Mauritania	350 000 (1984c)	
Novokuznetsk USSR	600 000 (1989)	
Novosibirsk USSR	1 436 000 (1989)	
Nuremberg Germany	467 000 (1986e)	
Oakland United Staes	356 860 (1988e)	
Odessa USSR	1 115 000 (1989)	
Ogbomosho Nigeria	628 000 (1990e)	
Oita Japan	392 566 (1988)	
Okayama Japan	575 837 (1988)	
Oklahoma City USA	434 380 (1988e)	
Olinda Brazil	334 686 (1987e)	
Omaha United Staes	353 170 (1988e)	
Omdurman Sudan	526 287 (1983)	
Omiya Japan	383 720 (1988)	
Omsk USSR	1 148 000 (1989)	
Oporto Portugal	327 368 (1981)	
Oran Algeria	663 504 (1983e)	
Ordzhonikidze USSR	300 000 1989)	
Orenburg USSR	547 000 (1989)	
Oryol USSR	337 000 (1989)	
Osaka Japan	2 543 520 (1988)	
Osasco Brazil	591 568 (1987e)	
Osijek Yugoslavia	867 646 (1981)	
Oslo Norway	456 124 (1989)	
Ostrava Czechoslovakia	328 373 (1987e)	
Ottawa Canada	819 263 (1986)	
Oujda Morocco	895 000 (1987e)	
Padang Indonesia	656 800 (1983e)	
Palembang Indonesia	1 205 800 (1983e)	
Palermo Italy	728 843 (1987)	
Palma Majorca	306 840 (1987e)	
Panama City Panama	595 643 (1989e)	
Panchiao Taiwan	506 220 (1987e)	
Panshan China	308 000 (1988e)	
Paris France	2 188 918 (1982)	
Patna India	813 963 (1981)	
Pavlodar USSR	331 000 (1989)	
Penza USSR	543 000 (1989)	
Perm USSR	1 091 000 (1989)	
Perth Australia	1 001 000 (1985e)	
Peshawar Pakistan	566 248 (1981)	
Philadelphia USA	1 647 000 (1988e)	
Phoenix USA	923 750 (1988e)	
Pingdingshan China	403 000 (1988e)	
Pingxiang China	404 000 (1988e)	
Pittsburg USA	375 230 (1988e)	
Plovdiv Bulgaria	342 131 (1985)	
Poltava USSR	315 000 (1989)	
Pontianak Indonesia	342 700 (1983e)	
Poona India	1 203 351 (1981)	
Port-au-Prince Haiti	738 342 (1984e)	
Port Elizabeth South Africa	651 993 (1985)	
Portland USA	418 470 (1988e)	
Port Louis Mauritius	136 323 (1985e)	
Port Moresby Papua New Guinea	145 300 (1987e)	
Porto Alegre Brazil	1 272 121 (1987e)	
Port of Spain Trinidad	59 200 (1988)	
Port Said Egypt	364 000 (1983e)	
Poznan Poland	586 500 (1988e)	
Prague Czechoslovakia	1 200 266 (1987e)	
Pretoria South Africa	822 925 (1985)	
Puebla Mexico	835 759 (1980)	
Pusan South Korea	3 514 798 (1985)	
Pyongyang North Korea	2 000 000 (1986)	
Uinhuangdao China	333 000 (1988e)	
Qiqihar China	1 018 000 (1988e)	
Quebec Canada	603 267 (1986)	
Quezan City Philippines	1 165 865 (1980)	
Quito Ecuador	1 093 278 (1986e)	
Qom Iran	424 048 (1982e)	
Rabat Morocco	1 287 000 (1987e)	
Raipur India	338 245 (1981)	
Rajkot India	445 076 (1981)	
Ranchi India	489 626 (1981)	
Rangoon Burma	2 458 712 (1983)	
Rawalpindi Pakistan	794 843 (1981)	

MAJOR CITIES OF THE WORLD (cont.)

Recife Brazil	1 287 623 (1987e)	Sarajevo Yugoslavia	448 519 (1981)
Reykjavik Iceland	87 309 (1983)	Saransk USSR	312 000 (1989)
Ribeirao Preto Brazil	383 125 (1987e)	Saratov USSR	905 000 (1989)
Riga USSR	915 000 (1989)	Seattle USA	502 200 (1988e)
Rio de Janeiro Brazil	5 603 388 (1987e)	Semarang Indonesia	1 805 500 (1983e)
Riyadh Saudi Arabia	1 308 000 (1981)	Semipalatinsk USSR	334 000 (1989)
Rome Italy	2 817 227 (1987)	Sendai Japan	865 630 (1988)
Rosario Argentina	957 301 (1982)	Seoul South Korea	655 435 (1987e)
Rostov-na-Duna USSR	1 020 000 (1989)	Shanchung Taiwan	362 171 (1987e)
Rotterdam Netherlands	576 232 (1989)	Shanghai China	7 112 000 (1988e)
		Shantou China	513 000 (1988e)
Sacramento USA	338 220 (1988e)	Shaoguan China	324 000 (1988e)
Safi Morocco	793 000 (1987e)	Sheffield UK	477 257 (1981)
Sagamihara Japan	498 995 (1988)	Shenyang China	3 412 000 (1988e)
St Catherines-Niagara	343 258 (1986)	Shihezi China	301 000 (1988e)
Canada		Shijiazhuang China	987 000 (1988e)
St Louis USA	403 700 (1988e)	Shiraz Iran	800 416 (1982e)
Sakai Japan	807 680 (1988)	Shizuoka Japan	469 782 (1988)
Salem India	361 394 (1981)	Sholapur India	514 860 (1981)
Salonika Greece	406 413 (1981)	Shoubra el-Kheima Egypt	497 000 (1983e)
Salvador Brazil	1 804 538 (1987e)	Shuangyashan China	362 000 (1988e)
Samarkand USSR	566 000 (1989)	Sialkot Pakistan	302 009 (1981)
San'a Yemen Arab Republic	277 818 (1981)	Sian (Xian) China	1 828 000 (1988e)
San Antonio USA	941 150 (1988e)	Simferopol USSR	344 000(1989)
San Cristobal Venezuela	355 895 (1989e)	Singapore Singapore	2 674 000 (1989e)
San Diego USA	1 070 310 (1988e)	Sinuiju North Korea	330 000 (1986)
San Francisco USA	731 600 (1988e)	Skopje Yugoslavia	506 547 (1981)
San Juan Puerto Rica	434 849 (1980)	Smolensk USSR	341 000 (1989)
San José USA	738 420 (1988e)	Smyrna Turkey	1 489 772 (1985)
San Luis Potosi Mexico	362 371 (1980)	Sochi USSR	337 000 (1989)
San Miguel de Tucuman	498 578 (1980)	Sofia Bulgaria	1 114 759 (1985)
Argentina		Songnam South Korea	447 692 (1985)
San Pedro Sula Honduras	429 300 (1987e)	Sorocaba Brazil	327 468 (1987e)
San Salvador El Salvador	462 652 (1985e)	Srinagar India	594 775 (1981)
Santa Cruz de la Sierra	577 803 (1987e)	Stavropol USSR	318 000 (1989)
Bolivia		Stockholm Sweden	672 187 (1989e)
Santiago Chile	4 318 305 (1985)	Stuttgart Germany	565 500 (1986e)
Santiago de Cuba Cuba	364 554 (1986e)	Suita Japan	341 590 (1988)
Santo Andre Brazil	635 129 (1987e)	Surabaya Indonesia	2 223 600 (1983e)
Santo Domingo Dominican	1 313 172 (1981)	Surakarta Indonesia	490 900 (1983e)
Republic		Surat India	776 876 (1981)
Santos Brazil	460 100 (1987e)	Suva Fiji	69 655 (1986)
São Bernardo do Campo	562 485 (1987e)	Suwon South Korea	430 752 (1985)
Brazil		Suzhou China	649 000 (1988e)
São Goncalo Brazil	728 469 (1987e)	Sverdlovsk USSR	3 391 600 (1985e)
São Joao de Meriti Brazil	457 753 (1987e)	Sydney Australia	3 430 600 (1986)
São José dos Campos	372 578 (1987e)	Szczecin Poland	409 500 (1988e)
Brazil			
São Luis Brazil	561 859 (1987e)	Tabriz Iran	852 296 (1982e)
São Paulo Brazil	10 063 110 (1987)	Taegu South Korea	2n 029 853 (1985)
Sapporo Japan	1 582 073 (1988)	Taejon South Korea	2 029 853 (1985)
Saragossa Spain	575 317 (1987e)	Taichung Taiwan	715 107 (1987e)
		Tainan Taiwan	656 927 (1987e)

MAJOR CITIES OF THE WORLD (cont.)

City	Country	Population
Taipei	Taiwan	2 637 100 (1987e)
Taiyuan	China	1 480 000 (1988e)
Takamatsu	Japan	327 538 (1988)
Takatsuki	Japan	353 940 (1988)
Tallinn	USSR	482 000 (1989)
Tambov	USSR	305 000 (1989)
Tangier	Morocco	509 000 (1987e)
Tangshan	China	980 000 (1988e)
Tanta	Egypt	344 000 (1983e)
Tashkent	USSR	2 073 000 (1989)
Tbilisi	USSR	1 260 000 (1989)
Tegucigalpa	Honduras	640 900 (1987e)
Teheran	Iran	6 022 029 (1986)
Tel Aviv	Israel	327 625 (1983)
Teresina	Brazil	473 901 (1987e)
Tetouan	Morocco	800 000 (1987e)
Thane	India	309 897 (1981)
Tianjin (Tientsin)	China	4 314 000 (1988e)
Tijuana	Mexico	429 500 (1980)
Timisoura	Romania	325 272 (1986e)
Tirana	Albania	225 700 (1987)
Tiruchirapalli	India	362 045 (1981)
Tokyo	Japan	8 155 781 (1988)
Toledo	USA	340 760 (1988e)
Tolyatti	USSR	630 000 (1989)
Tomsk	USSR	502 000 (1989)
Tonghua	China	304 000 (1988e)
Toronto	Canada	3 427 168 (1986)
Toulouse	France	354 289 (1982)
Toyama	Japan	316 061 (1988)
Toyoda	Japan	314 996 (1988)
Toyohasi	Japan	325 862 (1988)
Toyonaka	Japan	405 859 (1988)
Tripoli	Libya	591 062 (1988e)
Trivandrum	India	499 531 (1981)
Trujillo	Peru	438 709 (1985e)
Tucson	USA	385 720 (1988e)
Tula	USSR	540 000 (1989)
Tulsa	USA	368 330 (1988e)
Tunis	Tunisia	596 654 (1984)
Turin	Italy	1 025 390 (1987)
Tyumen	USSR	477 000 (1989)
Ufa	USSR	1 083 000 (1989)
Ulan Bator	Mongolia	548 400 (1989)
Ulan-Ude	USSR	353 000 (1989)
Ulsan	South Korea	551 014 (1985)
Ulyanovsk	USSR	625 000 (1989)
Urawa	Japan	391 530 (1988)
Urumqi	China	986 000 (1988e)
Ust-Kamenogorsk	USSR	324 000 (1989)
Utsunomiya	Japan	415 695 (1988)
Vadodara	India	734 473 (1981)
Valencia	Spain	732 491 (1987e)
Valencia	Venezuela	1 227 472 (1989e)
Valladolid	Spain	329 206 (1987e)
Vancouver	Canada	1 380 729 (1986)
Varanasi	India	720 755 (1981)
Vargas	Venezuela	338 312 (1989e)
Varna	Bulgaria	302 211 (1985)
Venice	Italy	327 700 (1987)
Veracruz	Mexico	284 822 (1980)
Victoria	Seychelles	23 000 (1985e)
Vienna	Austria	1 531 346 (1981)
Vientiane	Laos	377 409 (1985)
Vijaywada	India	461 772 (1981)
Vilnius	USSR	582 000 (1989)
Vina del Mar	Chile	315 947 (1985)
Vinnitsa	USSR	374 000 (1989)
Virginia Beach	USA	365 300 (1988e)
Visakhapatnam	India	584 166 (1981)
Vitebsk	USSR	350 000 (1989)
Vladimar	USSR	350 000 (1989)
Vladivostok	USSR	648 000 (1989)
Volgograd	USSR	999 000 (1989)
Voronezh	USSR	887 000 (1989)
Voroshilovgrad	USSR	497 000 (1989)
Wakayama	Japan	401 194 (1988)
Warangal	India	335 150 (1981)
Warsaw	Poland	1 651 200 (1988e)
Washington, DC, USA		617 000 (1988e)
Weifang	China	332 000 (1988e)
Wellington	New Zealand	325 200 (1988e)
Wenzhou	China	383 000 (1988e)
Windhoek	Namibia	114 500 (1988e)
Winnipeg	Canada	625 304 (1986)
Wroclaw	Poland	637 400 (1988e)
Wuhan	China	3 107 000 (1988e)
Wuhu	China	409 000 (1988e)
Wuppertal	Germany	374 200 (1986e)
Wuxi	China	752 000 (1988e)
Xiamen	China	360 000 (1988e)
Xiangfan	China	351 000 (1988e)
Xiangtan	China	411 000 (1988e)
Xiangyang	China	312 000 (1988e)
Xining	China	527 000 (1988e)
Xinxiang	China	433 000 (1988e)
Xuzhou	China	753 000 (1988e)
Yakeshi	China	355 000 (1988e)
Yangquan	China	334 000 (1988e)
Yantai	China	369 000 (1988e)

MAJOR CITIES OF THE WORLD (cont.)

Yaounde Cameroon	653 670 (1968e)	Zamboanga City	343 722 (1980)
Yaroslavl USSR	633 000 (1989)	Philippines	
Yerevan USSR	1 199 000 (1989)	Zaporozhye USSR	884 000 (1989)
Yichang (Ichang) China	353 000 (1988e)	Zarqa Jordan	392 220 (1986)
Yichun (Ichun) China	770 000 (1988e)	Zhangjiakou China	511 000 (1988e)
Yinchuan China	314 000 (1988e)	Zhengzhou China	1 065 000 (1988e)
Yingkou China	391 000 (1988e)	Zhenjiang China	339 000 (1988e)
Yogyakarta Indonesia	490 900 (1983e)	Zhuzhou China	371 000 (1988e)
Yokohama Japan	3 121 601 (1988)	Zibo China	801 000 (1988e)
Yukosuko Japan	430 656 (1988)	Zigong China	376 000 (1988e)
		Zürich Switzerland	345 159 (1988e)
Zagreb Yugoslavia	768 700 (1981)		

LARGEST CITIES: WORLD

São Paulo Brazil	10 063 110	New York USA	7 352 700
Mexico City Mexico	8 831 079	Shanghai China	7 112 000
Moscow USSR	8 769 000	London UK	6 677 928
Bombay India	8 243 405	Teheran Iran	6 022 029
Tokyo Japan	8 155 781	Cairo Egypt	5 875 000

LARGEST CITIES: EUROPE

Moscow USSR	8 769 000	Madrid Spain	3 100 507
London UK	6 677 928	Rome Italy	2 817 227
Istanbul Turkey	5 475 982	Paris France	2 188 918
Leningrad USSR	4 456 000	Budapest Hungary	2 104 700
Berlin Germany	3 126 072	Bucharest Romania	1 989 823

LARGEST CITIES: USA

New York New York	7 352 760	Detroit Michigan	1 035 920
Los Angeles California	3 352 710	San Diego California	1 070 310
Chicago Illinois	2 977 520	Dallas Texas	987 360
Houston Texas	1 698 090	San Antonio Texas	941 150
Philadelphia Pennsylvania	1 647 000	Phoenix Arizona	923 750

NATIONS OF THE WORLD

In the case of countries that do not use the Roman alphabet (such as the Arabic countries), there is variation in the spelling of names and currencies, depending on the system of transliteration used.

Where more than one language is shown within a country the status of the languages may not be equal. Some languages have a 'semi-official' status, or are used for a restricted set of purposes, such as trade or tourism.

Population census estimates are for 1989 or later.

English name	Local name	Official name (in English)	Capital (English name in parentheses)	Official language(s)	Currency	Population
Afghanistan	Afghānestān	Republic of Afghanistan	Kābul	Dari, Pushtou	1 Afghani (Af) = 100 puls	14825000
Albania	Shqipëri	People's Socialist Republic of Albania	Tiranë (Tirana)	Albanian	1 Lek (L) = 100 qintars	3197000
Algeria	Al-Jazā'ir (Arabic) Algérie (French)	Democratic and Popular Republic of Algeria	El Djazair (Algiers)	Arabic	1 Algerian Dinar (AD, DA) = 100 centimes	24946000
Andorra	Andorra	Principality of Andorra; the Valleys of Andorra	Andorra La Vella	Catalan, French	French Franc, Spanish Peseta	50000
Angola	Angola	People's Republic of Angola	Luanda	Portuguese	1 Kwanza (kw. kz) = 100 lweis	9739000
Antigua and Barbuda	Antigua and Barbuda	Antigua and Barbuda	St John's	English	1 East Caribbean Dollar (EC$) = 100 cents	78400
Argentina	Argentina	Argentine Republic	Buenos Aires	Spanish	1 Austral (Arg $, $a) = 100 centavos	32425000
Australia	Australia	Commonwealth of Australia	Canberra	English	1 Australian Dollar ($A) = 100 cents	16804000
Austria	Österreich	Republic of Austria	Vienna	German	1 Schilling (S, Sch) = 100 groschen	7603000
Bahamas	Bahamas	Commonwealth of the Bahamas	Nassau	English	1 Bahamian Dollar (BA$, B$) = 100 cents	249000
Bahrain	Al-Baḥrayn	State of Bahrain	Al-Manāmah (Manama)	Arabic	1 Bahrain Dinar (BD) = 1000 fils	488500
Bangladesh	Bangladesh	People's Republic of Bangladesh	Dhaka (Dacca)	Bengali	1 Taka (TK) = 100 poisha	114718000
Barbados	Barbados	Barbados	Bridgetown	English	1 Barbados Dollar (Bds$) = 100 cents	255000
Belgium	Belgique (French) België (Flemish)	Kingdom of Belgium	Bruxelles (Brussels)	Flemish, French, German	1 Belgian Franc (BFr) = 100 centimes	9878000

NATIONS OF THE WORLD (cont.)

English name	Local name	Official name (in English)	Capital (English name in parentheses)	Official language(s)	Currency	Population
Belize	Belize	Belize	Belmopan	English	1 Belize Dollar (Bz$) = 100 cents	185000
Benin	Bénin	Republic of Benin	Porto-Novo	French	1 CFA Franc (CFAFr) = 100 centimes	4592000
Bhutan	Druk-Yul	Kingdom of Bhutan	Thimbu/Thimphu	Dzongkha	1 Ngultrum (N, Nu) = 100 chetrum	1534000
Bolivia	Bolivia	Republic of Bolivia	La Paz/Sucre	Spanish	1 Bolivian Peso (B$) = 100 centavos	7193000
Botswana	Botswana	Republic of Botswana	Gaborone	English, seTswana	1 Pula (P, Pu) = 100 thebes	1256000
Brazil	Brasil	Federative Republic of Brazil	Brasília	Portuguese	1 Cruzado (= 1000 old Cruzeiros) (Cr$) = 100 centavos	147404000
Brunei	Brunei	State of Brunei, Abode of Peace	Bandar Seri Begawan	Malay, English	1 Brunei Dollar (Br$) = 100 cents	251000
Bulgaria	Bãlgarija	People's Republic of Bulgaria	Sofija (Sofia)	Bulgarian	1 Lev (Lv) = 100 stotinki	8987000
Burkina Faso	Burkina Faso	Burkina Faso	Ouagadougou	French	1 CFA Franc (CFAFr) = 100 centimes	8714000
Burma	Myanma	Socialist Republic of the Union of Burma	Rangoon	Burmese	1 Kyat (K) = 100 pyas	40452000
Burundi	Burundi	Republic of Burundi	Bujumbura	French, (Ki) Rundi	1 Burundi Franc (BuFr, FBu) = 100 centimes	5450000
Cambodia	Cambodia	State of Cambodia	Phnum Pénh (Phnom Penh)	Khmer	1 Riel (CRI) = 100 sen	6838000
Cameroon	Cameroun	Republic of Cameroon	Yaoundé	English, French	1 CFA Franc (CFAFr) = 100 centimes	11407000
Canada	Canada	Canada	Ottawa	English, French	1 Canadian Dollar (C$, Can$) = 100 cents	26311000
Cape Verde	Cabo Verde	Republic of Cape Verde	Praia	Portuguese	1 Escudo (CVEsc) = 100 centavos	337000
Central African Republic	République Centrafricaine	Central African Republic	Bangui	French	1 CFA Franc (CFAFr) = 100 centimes	2813000
Chad	Tchad	Republic of Chad	N'Djamena	French	1 CFA Franc (CFAFr) = 100 centimes	5538000
Chile	Chile	Republic of Chile	Santiago	Spanish	1 Chilean Peso (Ch$) = 100 centavos	12961000

Country	Local name	Official name	Capital	Language	Currency	Population
China	Zhonghua	People's Republic of China	Beijing/Peking	Chinese	1 Renminbi Yuan (RMBY, $, Y) = 10 jiao = 100 fen	1133682501 (90)
Colombia	Colombia	Republic of Colombia	Bogotá	Spanish	1 Colombian Peso (Col$) = 100 centavos	32317000
Comoros	Comores	Federal Islamic Republic of the Comoros	Moroni	French	1 Comorian Franc (CFr) = 100 centimes	448000
Congo	Congo	People's Republic of the Congo	Brazzaville	French	1 CFA Franc (CFAFr) = 100 centimes	2245000
Costa Rica	Costa Rica	Republic of Costa Rica	San José	Spanish	1 Costa Rican Colón (CR₡) = 100 centavos	2954000
Côte d'Ivoire (Ivory Coast)	Côte d'Ivoire	Republic of Côte d'Ivoire	Abidjan/ Yamoussoukro	French	1 CFA Franc (CFAFr) = 100 centimes	12135000
Cuba	Cuba	Republic of Cuba	La Habana (Havana)	Spanish	1 Cuban Peso (Cub$) = 100 centavos	10540000
Cyprus	Kipros (Greek) Kibris (Turkish)	Republic of Cyprus	Levkosia (Nicosia)	Greek, Turkish	1 Cyprus Pound (£C) = 100 cents	733000
Czechoslovakia	Československo	Czech and Slovak Federative Republic	Praha (Prague)	Czech, Slovak	1 Koruna (Kčs) = 100 haler	15636000
Denmark	Danmark	Kingdom of Denmark	København (Copenhagen)	Danish	1 Danish Krone (Dkr) = 100 øre	5135000
Djibouti	Djibouti	Republic of Djibouti	Djibouti	Arabic, French	1 Djibouti Franc (DF, DjFr) = 100 centimes	512000
Dominica	Dominica	Commonwealth of Dominica	Roseau	English	1 East Caribbean Dollar (EC$) = 100 cents	82800
Dominican Republic	República Dominicana	Dominican Republic	Santo Domingo	Spanish	1 Dominican Peso (RD$, DR$) = 100 centavos	7012000
Ecuador	Ecuador	Republic of Ecuador	Quito	Spanish	1 Sucre (Su, S/.) = 100 centavos	10490000
Egypt	Misr	Arab Republic of Egypt	Al-Qāhirah (Cairo)	Arabic	1 Egyptian Pound (E£, LE) = 100 piastres	54778000
El Salvador	El Salvador	Republic of El Salvador	San Salvador	Spanish	1 Colón (ES₡) = 100 centavos	5125000
Equatorial Guinea	Guinea Ecuatorial	Republic of Equatorial Guinea	Malabo	Spanish	1 Ekuele (E, Ek) = 100 céntimos	343000
Ethiopia	Ityopiya	Socialist Ethiopia	Adis Abeba (Addis Ababa)	Amharic	1 Ethiopian Birr (Br) = 100 cents	48898000
Fiji	Fiji	Republic of Fiji	Suva	English	1 Fiji Dollar (F$) = 100 cents	734000
Finland	Suomi (Finnish) Finland (Swedish)	Republic of Finland	Helsinki Helsingfors (Swedish)	Finnish, Swedish	1 Markka (FMk) = 100 penni	4960000
France	France	French Republic	Paris	French	1 French Franc (Fr) = 100 centimes	56107000
Gabon	Gabon	Gabonese Republic	Libreville	French	1 CFA Franc (CFAFr) = 100 centimes	1077000

NATIONS OF THE WORLD (cont.)

English name	Local name	Official name (in English)	Capital (English name in parentheses)	Official language(s)	Currency	Population
Gambia	Gambia	Republic of the Gambia	Banjul	English	1 Dalasi (D, Di) = 100 butut	835000
Germany	Bundesrepublik Deutschland	Federal Republic of Germany	Berlin	German	1 Deutsche Mark (DM) = 100 Pfennige	77744000
Ghana	Ghana	Republic of Ghana	Accra	English	1 Cedi (¢) = 100 pesewas	14566000
Greece	Ellás	Hellenic Republic	Athínai (Athens)	Greek	1 Drachma (Dr) = 100 leptae	10096000
Greenland	Grønland (Danish) Kalaallit Nunaat	Greenland	Godthåb	Danish, Greenlandic	1 Danish Krone (DKr) = 100 øre	55400
Grenada	Grenada	Grenada	St George's	English	1 East Caribbean Dollar (EC$) = 100 cents	96600
Guatemala	Guatemala	Republic of Guatemala	Guatemala City	Spanish	1 Quetzal (Q) = 100 centavos	9117000
Guinea	Guinée	Republic of Guinea	Conakry	French	1 Guinean Franc (GFr) = 100 cauris	6705000
Guinea-Bissau	Guiné-Bissau	Republic of Guinea-Bissau	Bissau	Portuguese	1 Guinea-Bissau Peso (GBP, PG) = 100 centavos	953000
Guyana	Guyana	Co-operative Republic of Guyana	Georgetown	English	1 Guyana Dollar (G$) = 100 cents	754000
Haiti	Haïti	Republic of Haiti	Port-au-Prince	French	1 Gourde (G, Gde) = 100 centimes	5520000
Holland see Netherlands, The						
Honduras	Honduras	Republic of Honduras	Tegucigalpa	Spanish	1 Lempira (L, La) = 100 centavos	5104000
Hong Kong	Hsiang Kang (Chinese) Hong Kong (English)	Hong Kong	Victoria	English, Chinese	1 Hong Kong Dollar (HK$) = 100 cents	5754000
Hungary	Magyarország	Hungarian People's Republic	Budapest	Hungarian	1 Forint (Ft) = 100 fillér	10580000
Iceland	Ísland	Republic of Iceland	Reykjavik	Icelandic	1 Króna (IKr, ISK) = 100 aurar	254000
India	Bhárat (Hindi)	Republic of India	New Delhi	Hindi, English	1 Indian Rupee (Re, Rs) = 100 paisa	833422000
Indonesia	Indonesia	Republic of Indonesia	Jakarta	Bahasa Indonesia	1 Rupiah (Rp) = 100 sen	177046000
Iran	Īrān	Islamic Republic of Iran	Tehrān (Tehran)	Farsi	1 Iranian Rial (Rls, RI) = 100 dinars	54333000
Iraq	Al-ʿIrāq	Republic of Iraq	Baghdād (Baghdad)	Arabic	1 Iraqi Dinar (ID) = 1000 fils	17215000
Ireland	Éire (Gaelic) Ireland (English)	Republic of Ireland	Baile Atha Cliath (Dublin)	Irish, English	1 Irish Pound/Punt (I£, IRE) = 100 pighne	3515000

Israel	Yisra'el (Hebrew) Isrā'īl (Arabic)	State of Israel	Yerushalayim (Jerusalem)	Hebrew, Arabic	1 Shekel (IS) = 100 agorot	4563000
Italy	Italia	Italian Republic	Roma (Rome)	Italian	1 Italian Lira (L, Lit) = 100 centesimi	57436000
Ivory Coast *see* Côte d'Ivoire						
Jamaica	Jamaica	Jamaica	Kingston	English	1 Jamaican Dollar (J$) = 100 cents	2376000
Japan	Nihon	Japan	Tōkyō (Tokyo)	Japanese	1 Yen (Y, ¥) = 100 sen	123220000
Jordan	Al'Urdunn	Hashemite Kingdom of Jordan	'Ammān (Amman)	Arabic	1 Jordan Dinar = 1000 fils	3059000
Jugoslavia *see* Yugoslavia						
Kampuchea *see* Cambodia						
Kenya	Kenya	Republic of Kenya	Nairobi	(Ki) Swahili, English	1 Kenyan shilling (KSh) = 100 cents	23883000
Kiribati	Kiribati	Republic of Kiribati	Bairiki	English	1 Australian Dollar ($A) = 100 cents	69600
Korea, North	Chosŏn Minjujuŭi In'min Konghwaguk	Democratic People's Republic of Korea	P'yŏngyang (Pyongyang)	Korean	1 Won (NKW) = 100 chon	22521000
Korea, South	Taehan-Min guk	Republic of Korea	Sŏul (Seoul)	Korean	1 Won (W) = 100 chon	43247000
Kuwait	Al-Kuwayt	State of Kuwait	Al-Kuwayt (Kuwait City)	Arabic	1 Kuwaiti Dinar (KD) = 1000 fils	2048000
Laos	Lao	Lao People's Democratic Republic	Viangchan (Vientiane)	Lao	1 Kip (Kp) = 100 at	3936000
Lebanon	Al-Lubnān	Republic of Lebanon	Bayrūt (Beirut)	Arabic	1 Lebanese Pound/Livre (LL, £L) = 100 piastres	2897000
Lesotho	Lesoto	Kingdom of Lesotho	Maseru	English, (se)Sotho	1 Loti (*plural* Maloti) (M, LSM) = 100 lisente	1715000
Liberia	Liberia	Republic of Liberia	Monrovia	English	1 Liberian Dollar (L$) = 100 cents	2508000
Libya	Libyā	Socialist People's Libyan Arab Jamahiriya	Tarābulus (Tripoli)	Arabic	1 Libyan Dinar (LD) = 1000 dirhams	4080000
Liechtenstein	Liechtenstein	Principality of Liechtenstein	Vaduz	German	1 Swiss Franc (SFr, SwF) = 100 centimes	28450
Luxembourg	Lëtzeburg (Letz.) Luxembourg (Fr.) Luxemburg (Ger.)	Grand Duchy of Luxembourg	Luxembourg	French, German, Letzeburgesch	1 Luxembourg Franc (LFr) = 100 centimes	377000
Madagascar	Madagasikara	Democratic Republic of Madagascar	Antananarivo	Malagasy, French	1 Madagascar Franc (FMG, MgFr) = 100 centimes	11602000
Malawi	Malaŵi (Chewa) Malawi (English)	Republic of Malaŵi	Lilongwe	(chi)Chewa, English	1 Kwacha (MK) = 100 tambala	8515000
Malaysia	Malaysia	Malaysia	Kuala Lumpur	Malay	1 Malaysian Dollar/Ringgit (M$) = 100 cents	17421000

NATIONS OF THE WORLD (cont.)

English name	Local name	Official name (in English)	Capital (English name in parentheses)	Official language(s)	Currency	Population
Maldives	Maldives Divehi Jumhuriya	Republic of Maldives	Male	Divehi	1 Rufiyaa (MRf, Rf) = 100 laaris	209000
Mali	Mali	Republic of Mali	Bamako	French	1 CFA Franc (CFAFr) = 100 centimes	7911000
Malta	Malta	Republic of Malta	Valletta	English, Maltese	1 Maltese Lira (LM) = 100 cents	349000
Mauritania	Mauritanie (French) Mūritāniyā (Arabic)	Islamic Republic of Mauritania	Novakchott	Arabic, French	1 Ouguiya (U, UM) = 5 khoums	1946000
Mauritius	Mauritius	Mauritius	Port Louis	English	1 Mauritian Rupee (MR, MauRe) = 100 cents	1061000
Mexico	México	United Mexican States	Ciudad de México (Mexico City)	Spanish	1 Mexican Peso (Mex$) = 100 centavos	86366000
Monaco	Monaco	Principality of Monaco	Monaco	French	1 Monaco Franc (MnFr) = 100 centimes	29100
Mongolia	Mongol Ard Uls	Mongolian People's Republic	Ulaanbaatar (Ulan Bator)	Khalka	1 Tugrik (Tug) = 100 möngö	2096000
Morocco	Al-Magrib	Kingdom of Morocco	Rabat	Arabic	1 Dirham (DH) = 100 centimes	25606000
Mozambique	Mozambique	People's Republic of Mozambique	Maputo	Portuguese	1 Metical (Mt, MZM) = 100 centavos	15293000
Namibia	Namibia	Republic of Namibia	Windhoek	Afrikaans, English	1 South African Rand (R) = 100 cents	1550000
Nauru	Naeoro (Nauruan) Nauru (English)	Republic of Nauru	Yaren District	Nauruan, English	1 Australian Dollar ($A) = 100 cents	8100
Nepal	Nepāl	Kingdom of Nepal	Kathmandu	Nepali	1 Nepalese Rupee (NRp, NRs) = 100 paise/pice	18700000
Netherlands, The	Nederland	Kingdom of the Netherlands	Amsterdam/ 's-Gravenhage (The Hague)	Dutch	1 Dutch Guilder (Gld)/Florin (f) = 100 cents	14846000
New Zealand	New Zealand	New Zealand	Wellington	English	1 New Zealand Dollar ($NZ) = 100 cents	3371000
Nicaragua	Nicaragua	Republic of Nicaragua	Managua	Spanish	1 Córdoba (C$) = 100 centavos	3503000
Niger	Niger	Republic of Niger	Niamey	French	1 CFA Franc (CFAFr) = 100 centimes	7523000
Nigeria	Nigeria	Federal Republic of Nigeria	Lagos	English	1 Naira (N, ₦) = 100 kobo	115973000

Country	Native name	Official name	Capital	Language	Currency	Population
Norway	Norge	Kingdom of Norway	Oslo	Norwegian	1 Norwegian Krone (NKr) = 100 øre	4202000
Oman	'Umān	Sultanate of Oman	Masqaṭ (Muscat)	Arabic	1 Rial Omani (RO) = 1000 baizas	1422000
Pakistan	Pākistān	Islamic Republic of Pakistan	Islāmābād (Islamabad)	Urdu, English	1 Pakistan Rupee (PRs, Rp) = 100 paisa	110407000
Panama	Panamá	Republic of Panama	Panamá (Panama City)	Spanish	1 Balboa (B, Ba) = 100 centésimos	2373000
Papua New Guinea	Papua New Guinea	Independent State of Papua New Guinea	Port Moresby	English, Tok Pisin, Hi-i Motu	1 Kina (K) = 100 toea	3592900
Paraguay	Paraguay	Republic of Paraguay	Asunción	Spanish	1 Guaraní (₲) = 100 céntimos	4157000
Peru	Perú	Republic of Peru	Lima	Spanish	1 Inti (I/.) = 100 centavos	21792000
Philippines	Filipinas	Republic of the Philippines	Manila	English, Pilipino	1 Philippine peso (PP, ₱) = 100 centavos	59906000
Poland	Polska	Polish People's Republic	Warszawa (Wa-saw)	Polish	1 Złoty (Zł) = 100 groszy	37875000
Portugal	Portugal	Republic of Portugal	Lisboa (Lisbon)	Portuguese	1 Escudo (Esc) = 100 centavos	10372000
Puerto Rico	Puerto Rico	Commonwealth of Puerto Rico	San Juan	Spanish, English	1 US Dollar (US$) = 100 cents	3308000
Qatar	Qaṭar	State of Qatar	Ad-Dawḥah (Doha)	Arabic	1 Qatar Riyal (QR) = 100 dirhams	427000
Romania	România	Romania	Bucureşti (Bucharest)	Romanian	1 Leu (plural lei) = 100 bani	23168000
Rwanda	Rwanda	Republic of Rwanda	Kigali	(Kinya) Rwanda, French	1 Rwanda Franc (RF, RWFr) = 100 centimes	6989000
Saint Christopher and Nevis	Saint Christopher/Kitts and Nevis	Federation of Saint Christopher and Nevis	Basseterre	English	1 East Caribbean Dollar (CD$) = 100 cents	44100
Saint Lucia	Saint Lucia	Saint Lucia	Castries	English	1 East Caribbean Dollar (EC$) = 100 cents	150000
Saint Vincent and the Grenadines	Saint Vincent and the Grenadines	Saint Vincent and the Grenadines	Kingstown	English	1 East Caribbean Dollar (EC$) = 100 cents	114000
San Marino	San Marino	Republic of San Marino	San Marino	Italian	1 San Marino Lira (SML) = 100 centesimi	22860
São Tomé and Principe	São Tomé e Principe	Democratic Republic of São Tomé and Principe	São Tomé	Portuguese	1 Dobra (Db) = 100 centavos	118000
Saudi Arabia	Al-'Arabīyah as Sa'ūdīyah	Kingdom of Saudi Arabia	Ar-Riyāḍ (Riyadh)	Arabic	1 Saudi Arabian Riyal (SAR. SRls) = 100 halalah	13592000
Senegal	Sénégal	Republic of Senegal	Dakar	French	1 CFA Franc (CFAFr) = 100 centimes	7400000
Seychelles	Seychelles	Republic of Seychelles	Victoria	Creole French, English, French	1 Seychelles Rupee (SR) = 100 cents	67100
Sierra Leone	Sierra Leone	Republic of Sierra Leone	Freetown	English	1 Leone (Le) = 100 cents	3957000

NATIONS OF THE WORLD (cont.)

English name	Local name	Official name (in English)	Capital (English name in parentheses)	Official language(s)	Currency	Population
Singapore	Singapore	Republic of Singapore	Singapore	Chinese, English, Malay, Tamil English	1 Singapore Dollar (S$)/Ringgit = 100 cents	2 674 000
Solomon Islands	Solomon Islands	Solomon Islands	Honiara	English	1 Solomon Islands Dollar (SI$) = 100 cents	308 000
Somalia	Somaliya	Somali Democratic Republic	Muqdisho (Mogadishu)	Arabic, Somali	1 Somali Shilling (SoSh) = 100 cents	7 339 000
South Africa	South Africa (English) Suid-Afrika (Afrikaans)	Republic of South Africa	Pretoria/Cape Town	Afrikaans, English	1 Rand (R) = 100 cents	30 224 000
Spain	España	Kingdom of Spain	Madrid	Spanish	1 Peseta (Pta, Pa) = 100 céntimos	39 159 000
Sri Lanka	Sri Lanka	Democratic Socialist Republic of Sri Lanka	Colombo	Sinhala, Tamil	1 Sri Lanka Rupee (SLR, SLRs) = 100 cents	16 855 000
Sudan	As-Sūdān	Democratic Republic of Sudan	Al-Khartūm (Khartoum)	Arabic	1 Sudanese pound (LSd, £S) = 100 piastres	27 268 000
Suriname	Suriname	Republic of Suriname	Paramaribo	Dutch	1 Suriname Guilder/Florin (SGld, F) = 100 cents	405 000
Swaziland	Swaziland	Kingdom of Swaziland	Mbabane	English, (si)Swati	1 Lilangeni plural Emalangeni (Li, E) = 100 cents	746 000
Sweden	Sverige	Kingdom of Sweden	Stockholm	Swedish	1 Swedish Krona (Skr) = 100 øre	8 459 000
Switzerland	Schweiz (German) Suisse (French) Svizzera (Italian)	Swiss Confederation	Bern (Berne)	French, German, Italian, Romansch	1 Swiss Franc (SFr, SwF) = 100 centimes	6 673 000
Syria	As-Sūrīyah	Syrian Arab Republic	Dimashq (Damascus)	Arabic	1 Syrian pound (LS, SyrE) = 100 piastres	11 719 000
Taiwan	T'aiwan	Republic of China	T'aipei (Taipei)	Chinese	1 New Taiwan Dollar (NT$) = 100 cents	20 024 000
Tanzania	Tanzania	United Republic of Tanzania	Dar es Salaam	(ki)Swahili, English	1 Tanzanian Shilling (TSh) = 100 cents	23 729 000
Thailand	Muang Thai	Kingdom of Thailand	Krung Thep (Bangkok)	Thai	1 Baht (B) = 100 satang	55 258 000
Togo	Togo	Republic of Togo	Lomé	French	1 CFA Franc (CFAFr) = 100 centimes	3 622 000
Tonga	Tonga	Kingdom of Tonga	Nuku'alofa	English, Tongan	1 Pa'anga/Tongan Dollar (T$) = 100 seniti	95 900

Country	Official name	Capital	Language(s)	Currency	Population
Trinidad and Tobago	Republic of Trinidad and Tobago	Port of Spain	English	1 Trinidad and Tobago Dollar (TT$) = 100 cents	1285000
Tunisia / Tunis (Arabic) / Tunisie (French)	Republic of Tunisia	Tunis	Arabic	1 Tunisian Dinar (TD, D) = 1000 millièmes	7916000
Turkey / Türkiye	Republic of Turkey	Ankara	Turkish	1 Turkish Lira (TL) = 100 Kurus	55541000
Tuvalu	Tuvalu	Fongafale (on Funafuti)	English	1 Tuvalu Dollar = 1 Australian Dollar = 100 cents	8900
Uganda	Republic of Uganda	Kampala	English	1 Uganda Shilling = 100 cents	16452000
USSR / Soyuz Sovyetskikh Sotsialistichskikh Respublik	Union of Soviet Socialist Republics	Moskva (Moscow)	Russian	1 Rouble (Rub) = 100 kopecks	287800000
United Arab Emirates / Ittihād al-Imārāt al-'Arabīyah	United Arab Emirates	Abū Ẓaby (Abu Dhabi)	Arabic	1 Dirham (DH) = 100 fils	1827000
United Kingdom	United Kingdom of Great Britain and Northern Ireland	London	English	1 Pound Sterling (£) = 100 new pence	57218000
United States of America	United States of America	Washington, DC	English	1 US Dollar ($, US$) = 100 cents	249231000
Uruguay	Oriental Republic of Uruguay	Montevideo	Spanish	1 Uruguayan New Peso (NUr$, UrugN$) = 100 centésimos	3017000
Vanuatu	Republic of Vanuatu	Port Vila	English, French	1 Vatu (V, VT) = 100 centimes	154000
Venezuela	Republic of Venezuela	Caracas	Spanish	1 Bolívar (B) = 100 céntimos	19246000
Viêt-nam	Socialist Republic of Vietnam	Ha-noi (Hanoi)	Vietnamese	1 Đông = 10 hao = 100 xu	66820000
Western Samoa (English) / Samoa i Sisifo (Samoan)	Independent State of Western Samoa	Apia	English, Samoan	1 Tala/Western Samoan Dollar (WS$) = 100 cents	163000
Yemen / Al-Yaman	Republic of Yemen	San 'ā'	Arabic	1 Yemeni Riyal (YR, YRI) = 100 fils; 1 Yemeni Dinar (YD) = 1000 fils	11240000
Yugoslavia / Jugoslavija	Socialist Federal Republic of Yugoslavia	Beograd (Belgrade)	Macedonian, Serbo-Croat, Slovene	1 Yugoslav Dinar (D, Din) = 100 paras	23688000
Zaïre	Republic of Zaire	Kinshasa	French	1 Zaïre (Z) = 100 makuta (sing. likuta)	33336000
Zambia	Republic of Zambia	Lusaka	English	1 Kwacha (K) = 100 ngwee	8148000
Zimbabwe	Republic of Zimbabwe	Harare	English	1 Zimbabwe Dollar (Z$) = 100 cents	9122000

NATIONAL HOLIDAYS

The first part of each listing gives the holidays that occur on fixed dates (though it should be noted that holidays often vary according to local circumstances and the day of the week on which they fall). Most dates are accompanied by an indication of the purpose of the day eg Independence = Independence Day; dates which have no gloss are either fixed dates within the Christian calendar (for which see below) or bank holidays.

The second part of the listing gives holidays that vary, usually depending on religious factors. The most common of these are given in abbreviated form (see list below).

A number in brackets such as (*Independence*) (*2*) refers to the number of days devoted to the holiday.

The listings do not include holidays that affect only certain parts of a country, half-day holidays, or Sundays.

The following abbreviations are used for variable religious feast-days:

A	Ascension Thursday
Ad	Id-ul-Adha (also found with other spellings — especially Eid-ul-Adha; various names relating to this occasion are used in different countries, such as Tabaski, Id el-Kebir, Hari Raja Haji)
Ar	Arafa
As	Ashora (found with various spellings)
C	Carnival (immediately before Christian Lent, unless specified)
CC	Corpus Christi
D	Diwali, Deepavali
EM	Easter Monday
ER	End of Ramadan (known generally as Id/Eid-ul-Fitr, but various names relating to this occasion are used in different countries, such as Karite, Hari Raja Puasa)
ES	Easter Sunday
GF	Good Friday

HS	Holy Saturday
HT	Holy Thursday
NY	New Year
PB	Prophet's Birthday (known generally as Mau-lid-al-Nabi in various forms and spellings)
R	First day of Ramadan
WM	Whit Monday

The following fixed dates are shown without gloss:

Jan 1	New Year's Day
Jan 6	Epiphany
May 1	Labour Day (often known by a different name, such as Workers' Day)
Aug 15	Assumption of Our Lady
Nov 1	All Saints' Day
Nov 2	All Souls' Day
Dec 8	Immaculate Conception
Dec 24	Christmas Eve
Dec 25	Christmas Day
Dec 26	Boxing Day/St Stephen's Day
Dec 31	New Year's Eve

Afghanistan Apr 27 (Sawr Revolution), May 1, Aug 19 (Independence); Ad(3), Ar, As, ER(3), NY (Hindu), PB, R

Albania Jan 1, 11 (Republic), May 1, Nov 28 (Independence), 29 (Liberation)

Algeria Jan 1, May 1, Jun 19 (Righting), Jul 5 (Independence), Nov 1 (Revolution); Ad, As, ER, NY (Muslim), PB

Andorra Jan 1, 6, Mar 19 (St Joseph), May 1, Jun 24 (St John), Aug 15, Sep 8 (Our Lady of Meritxell), Nov 1, 4 (St Charles), Dec 8, 25, 26; A, C, CC, EM, GF, WM

Angola Jan 1, Feb 4 (Commencement of the Armed Struggle), May 1, Sep 17 (National Hero), Nov 11 (Independence), Dec 10 (MPLA Foundation), 25 (Family)

Argentina Jan 1, May 1, 25 (National), Jun 10 (Malvinas Islands Memorial), 20 (Flag), Jul 9 (Independence), Aug 17 (Death of General San Martin), Oct 12 (Columbus), Dec 8, 25, 31; GF, HT

Australia Jan 1, Apr 25 (Anzac), Dec 25, 26 (*except South Australia*); Australia (Jan), EM, GF, HS; *additional days vary between states*

Austria Jan 1, 6, May 1, Aug 15, Oct 26 (National), Nov 1, Dec 8, 24, 25, 26; A, CC, EM, WM

NATIONAL HOLIDAYS (cont.)

Bahamas Jan 1, Jul 10 (Independence), Dec 25, 26; EM, GF, WM; Labour (Jun), Emancipation (Aug), Discovery (Oct)

Bahrain Jan 1, Dec 16 (National); Ad(3), As(2), ER(3), NY (Muslim), PB

Bangladesh Feb 21 (Shaheed), Mar 26 (Independence), May 1, Jul 1, Nov 7 (National Revolution), Dec 16 (Victory), 25, 31; Ad(3), ER(3), NY (Bengali), NY (Muslim), PB, Jumat-ul-Wida (May), Shab-e-Barat (Apr), Buddah Purnima (Apr/May), Shab-I-Qadr (May), Jumat-ul-Wida (May), Durga Puza (Oct)

Barbados Jan 1, Nov 30 (Independence), Dec 25, 26; EM, GF, WM, Kadooment (Aug), May Holiday, United Nations (Oct)

Belgium Jan 1, May 1, Jul 21 (National), Aug 15, Nov 1, 11 (Armistice), Dec 25; A, EM, WM; May, Aug, Nov Bank Holidays; Regional Holiday (Jul *in N*, Sep *in S*)

Belize Jan 1, Mar 9 (Baron Bliss), May 1, 24 (Commonwealth), Sep 10 (National), 21 (Independence), Oct 12 (Columbus), Nov 19 (Garifuna Settlement), Dec 25, 26; EM, GF, HS

Benin Jan 1, 16 (Martyrs), Apr 1 (Youth), May 1, Oct 26 (Armed Forces), Nov 30 (National), Dec 25, 31 (Feed Yourself); Ad, ER

Bhutan May 2 (Birthday of Jigme Dorji Wangchuk), Jun 2 (Coronation of Fourth Hereditary King), Jul 21 (First Sermon of Lord Buddha, Death of Jigme Dorji Wangchuk), Nov 11–13 (Birthday of HM Jigme Singye Wangchuk), Dec 17 (National)

Bolivia Jan 1, May 1, Aug 6 (Independence), Nov 1, Dec 25; C(2), CC, GF

Botswana Jan 1, 2, Sep 30 (Botswana), Dec 25, 26; A, EM, GF, HS, President's Day (Jul); Jul, Oct Public Holidays

Brazil Jan 1, Apr 21 (Independence Hero Tiradentes), May 1, Sep 7 (Independence), Oct 12, Nov 2 (Memorial), 15 (Proclamation of the Republic), Dec 25; C(2), CC, GF, HS, HT

Brunei Jan 1, Feb 23 (National), May 31 (Royal Brunei Malay Regiment), Jul 15 (Sultan's Birthday), Dec 25; Ad, ER(2), GF, NY (Chinese), NY (Muslim), PB, R, Meraj (Mar–Apr), Revelation of the Koran (May)

Bulgaria Jan 1, May 1(2), 24 (Slav Literature, Bulgarian Education and Culture), Sep 9 (National) (2), Nov 7 (October Revolution)

Burkina Faso Jan 1, 3 (1966 Revolution), May 1, Aug 4, 15, Nov 1, Dec 25; A, Ad, EM, ER, PB, WM

Burma Jan 4 (Independence), Feb 12 (Union), Mar 2 (Peasants), 27 (Resistance), Apr 1, May 1, Jul 19 (Martyrs), Oct 1, Dec 25; NY (Burmese), Thingyan (Apr)(4), End of Buddhist Lent (Oct), Full Moon days

Burundi Jan 1, May 1, Jul 1 (Independence), Aug 15, Sep 18 (Victory of Uprona), Nov 1, Dec 25; A

Cameroon Jan 1, Feb 11 (Youth), May 1, 20 (National), Aug 15, Dec 25; A, Ad, ER, GF

Canada Jan 1, Jul 1 (Canada) (*except Newfoundland*), Nov 11 (Remembrance) Dec 25, 26; EM, GF, Labour (Sep), Thanksgiving (Oct), Victoria (May); *additional days vary between states*

Cape Verde Is Jan 1, 20 (National Heroes), Mar 8 (Women), May 1, Jun 1 (Children), Sep 12 (National), Dec 24, 25; GF

Central African Republic Jan 1, Mar 29 (Death of President Boganda), May 1, Jun 1 (Mothers), Aug 13 (Independence), 15, Sep 1 (Arrival of the Military Committee for National Recovery), Nov 1, Dec 1 (Republic), 25; A, EM, WM

Chad Jan 1, May 1, 25 (Liberation of Africa), Jun 7 (Liberation), Aug 11 (Independence), Nov 1, 28 (Republic), Dec 25; Ad, EM, ER, PB

Chile Jan 1, May 1, 21 (Battle of Iquique), Jun 29 (Sts Peter and Paul), Aug 15, Sep 11 (National Liberation), 18 (Independence), 19 (Armed Forces), Oct 12 (Day of the Race), Nov 1, Dec 8, 25, 31; GF, HS

NATIONAL HOLIDAYS (cont.)

China Jan 1, May 1, Oct 1 (National) (2); Spring Festival (4) (Jan/Feb)

Colombia Jan 1, 6, May 1, Jun 29 (Saints Peter and Paul), Jul 20 (Independence), Aug 7 (National), 15, Oct 12 (Columbus), Nov 1, 15 (Independence of Cartagena), Dec 8, 25, 30, 31; A, CC, GF, HT, St Joseph (Mar), Sacred Heart (Jun)

Congo Jan 1, Mar 18 (Day of the Supreme Sacrifice), May 1, Jul 31 (Revolution), Aug 13–15 (The Three Glorious Days), Nov 1 (Day of the Dead), Dec 25 (Children), 31 (Foundation of the Party and People's Republic)

Costa Rica Jan 1, Mar 19 (St Joseph), Apr 11 (National Heroes), May 1, Jun 29 (Saints Peter and Paul), Jul 25 (Annexation of Guanacaste), Aug 2 (Our Lady of the Angels), 15 (Mothers), Sep 15 (Independence), Oct 12 (Day of the Race), Dec 8, 25; CC, GF, HS, HT

Côte d'Ivoire Jan 1, May 1, Aug 15, Nov 1, Dec 7 (Independence), 24, 25, 31; A, Ad, EM, ER, GF, WM

Cuba Jan 1 (Day of Liberation), May 1, Jul 25 (National Rebellion) (2), Oct 10 (Beginning of the Independence Wars)

Cyprus Jan 1, 6, Mar 25 (Greek Independence), May 1, Oct 28 (Greek National), 29 (Turkish National), Dec 25, 26; Ad, EM, ER, GF, HS, PB

Czechoslovakia Jan 1, 2, May 1, 9 (Anniversary of Liberation), Dec 24, 25, 26, 31; EM

Denmark Jan 1, Jun 5 (Constitution), Dec 24, 25, 26; A, EM, GF, HT, WM, General Prayer (Apr/May)

Djibouti Jan 1, May 1, Jun 27 (Independence)(2), Dec 25; Ad(2), ER(2), NY (Muslim), PB, Al-Isra Wal-Mira'age (Mar–Apr)

Dominica Jan 1, May 1, Nov 3 (Independence), 4 (Community Service), Dec 25, 26; C(2), EM, GF, WM, August Monday

Dominican Republic Jan 1, 6, 21 (Our Lady of Altagracia), 26 (Duarte), Feb 27 (Independence), May 1, Aug 16 (Restoration of the Republic), Sep 24 (Our Lady of Mercy), Dec 25; CC, GF

Ecuador Jan 1, May 1, 24 (Independence Battle), Jun 30, Jul 24 (Bolivar), Aug 10 (Independence), Oct 9 (Independence of Guayaquil), 12 (Columbus), Nov 2, 3 (Independence of Cuenca), Dec 6 (Foundation of Quito), 25, 31; C(2), GF, HT

Egypt Jan 7 (Eastern Orthodox Christmas), Apr 25 (Sinai Liberation), May 1, Jun 18 (Evacuation), Jul 1, 23 (Revolution Anniversary), Oct 6 (Armed Forces); Ad(2), Ar, ER(2), NY (Muslim), PB, Palm Sunday and Easter Sunday (Eastern Orthodox), Sham El-Nessim (Apr–May)

El Salvador Jan 1, May 1, Jun 29, 30, Sep 15 (Independence), Oct 12 (Columbus), Nov 2, 5 (First Cry of Independence), Dec 24, 25, 30, 31; GF, HT, Ash Wednesday, San Salvador(4)

England & Wales Jan 1, Dec 25, 26; EM, GF, Early May, Late May and Summer (Aug) Bank Holidays

Equatorial Guinea Jan 1, May 1, Jun 5 (President's Birthday), Aug 3 (Armed Forces), Oct 12 (Independence), Dec 10 (Human Rights), 25; CC, GF, Constitution (Aug)

Ethiopia Jan 7 (Ethiopian Christmas), 19 (Ethiopian Epiphany), Mar 2 (Victory of Adwa), Apr 6 (Patriots), May 1, Sep 12 (Revolution), 27 (Finding of the True Cross); Ad, ER, NY (Ethiopian, Sep), PB, Ethiopian Good Friday and Easter

Fiji Jan 1, Oct 12 (Fiji), Dec 25, 26; D, EM, GF, HS, PB, August Bank Holiday, Queen's Birthday (Jun), Prince Charles' Birthday (Nov)

Finland Jan 1, May 1, Oct 31 (All Saints Observance), Nov 1, Dec 6 (Independence), 24, 25, 26, 31; A, EM, GF, Midsummer Eve and Day (Jun), Twelfthtide (Jan), Whitsuntide (May–Jun)

France Jan 1, May 1, 8 (Armistice), Jul 14 (Bastille), Aug 14 (Assumption Eve), 15, Oct 31 (All Saints Eve), Nov 1, 11 (Armistice), Dec 24, 25, 31; A, EM, GF, HS, WM, Ascension Eve, Whit Holiday Eve, Law of 20 Dec 1906, Law of 23 Dec 1904

NATIONAL HOLIDAYS (cont.)

Gabon Jan 1, Mar 12 (Anniversary of Renewal), May 1, Aug 17 (Independence), Nov 1, Dec 25; Ad, EM, ER, WM

Gambia Jan 1, Feb 1 (Senegambia), 18 (Independence), May 1, Aug 15 (St Mary), Dec 25; Ad, As, ER(2), GF, PB

German Democratic Republic Jan 1, May 1, Oct 7 (Foundation of GDR), Dec 25, 26; GF, WM

German Federal Republic Jan 1, May 1, Jun 17 (National), Dec 24, 25, 26; A, EM, GF, WM, Day of Penance (Nov)

Ghana Jan 1, Mar 6 (Independence), May 1, Jun 4 (June 4 Revolution), Jul 1 (Republic), Dec 25, 26, 31 (Revolution); EM, GF, HS

Greece Jan 1, 6, Mar 25 (National), May 1, Aug 15, Oct 28 (National), Dec 25, 26; GF, EM, WM, Monday in Lent

Grenada Jan 1–2, Feb 7 (Independence), May 1, Aug 3–4 (Emancipation), Oct 25 (Thanksgiving), Dec 25, 26; CC, EM, GF, WM

Guatemala Jan 1, May 1, Jun 30 (Army Day), Jul 1, Sep 15 (Independence), Oct 12 (Day of the Race), 20 (1944 Revolution), Nov 1, Dec 24, 25, 31; GF, HS, HT

Guinea Jan 1, Apr 3 (Second Republic), May 1, Aug 15, Oct 2 (Independence), Nov 1 (Army), Dec 25; Ad, EM, ER, PB

Guinea-Bissau Jan 1, 20 (National Heroes), Feb 8 (BNG Anniversary and Monetary Reform) Mar 8 (Women), May 1, Aug 3 (Martyrs of Colonialism), Sep 12 (National), 24 (Establishment of the Republic), Nov 14 (Readjustment), Dec 25

Guyana Jan 1, Feb 23 (Republic), May 1, Aug 1 (Freedom), Dec 25, 26; Ad, D, EM, GF, PB, Phagwah (Mar), Caribbean (Jul)

Haiti Jan 1 (Independence), 2 (Ancestry), Apr 14 (Americas), May 1, Aug 15, Oct 17 (Dessalines), 24 (United Nations), Nov 1, 2, 18 (Vertières), Dec 5 (Discovery), 25; A, C, CC, GF

Honduras Jan 1, Apr 14 (Pan American), May 1, Sep 15 (Independence), Oct 3 (Francisco Morazán's Birthday), 12 (America's Discovery), 21 (Armed Forces), Dec 25, 31; GF, HT

Hungary Jan 1, Apr 4 (Liberation Day), May 1, Aug 20 (Constitution), Nov 7 (October Socialist Revolution), Dec 25, 26; EM

Iceland Jan 1, May 1, Jun 17 (Independence), Dec 25, 26; A, EM, GF, HT, WM, First Day of Summer, August Holiday Monday

India Jan 1 (*some states*), 26 (Republic), May 1 (*some states*), Jun 30, Aug 15 (Independence), Oct 2 (Mahatma Ghandi's Birthday), Dec 25, 31; NY (Parsi, Aug, *some states*)

Indonesia Jan 1, Aug 17 (Independence), Dec 25; A, Ad, ER(2), GF, NY (Icaka, Mar), NY (Muslim), PB, Ascension of the Prophet (Mar/Apr), Waisak (May)

Iran Feb 11 (Revolution), Mar 20 (Oil), 21 (Now Rooz)(4), Apr 1 (Islamic Republic), 2 (13th of Farvardin), Jun 5 (15th Khordad Uprising); Ad, As, ER, PB, Prophet's Mission (Apr), Birth of the Twelfth Imam (Apr/May), Martyrdom of Imam Ali (May), Death of Imam Jaffar Sadegh (Jun/Jul), Birth of Imam Reza (Jul), Id-E-Ghadir (Aug), Death of the Prophet and Martyrdom of Imam Hassan (Oct/Nov)

Iraq Jan 1, 6 (Army Day), Feb 8 (8th February Revolution), Mar 21 (Spring Day), May 1, Jul 14 (14th July Revolution), 17 (17th July Revolution); Ad(4), As, ER(3), NY (Muslim), PB

Ireland Jan 1, Mar 17 (St Patrick), Dec 25, 26; EM, GF, June Holiday, August Holiday, October Holiday, Christmas Holiday

NATIONAL HOLIDAYS (cont.)

Israel Jan 1, May 14 (Independence Day); NY (Jewish, Sep/Oct), Purim (Mar), First Day of Passover (Apr), Last Day of Passover (Apr), Pentecost (Jun), Fast of Av (Aug), Day of Atonement (Oct), Feast of Tabernacles (Oct)(2)

Italy Jan 1, 6, Apr 25 (Liberation), May 1, Aug 14 (Mid-August Holiday)(2), Nov 1, Dec 8, 25, 26; EM

Jamaica Jan 1, May 23 (Labour), Aug 5 (Independence), Oct 20 (National Heroes), Dec 25, 26; Ash Wednesday, EM, GF

Japan Jan 1, 2, 3, 15 (Adults), Feb 11 (National Founding), Mar 21 (Vernal Equinox), Apr 29 (Emperor's Birthday), May 3 (Constitution Memorial), 5 (Children), Sep 15 (Respect for the Aged), 23 (Autumn Equinox), Oct 10 (Health-Sports), Nov 3 (Culture), 23 (Labour Thanksgiving)

Jordan Jan 1, May 1, 25 (Independence), Jun 10 (Great Arab Revolt and Army), Aug 11 (Accession of King Hussein), Nov 14 (King Hussein's Birthday), Dec 25; Ad(4), R, ER(4), NY (Muslim), PB

Kenya Jan 1, May 1, Jun 1 (Madaraka), Oct 20 (Kenyatta), Dec 12 (Independence), 25, 26; EM, GF, ER(3)

Kiribati Jan 1, Jul 12 (Independence)(3), Dec 25, 26; GF, HS, EM, Youth (Aug)

Korea, South Jan 1–3, Mar 1 (Independence Movement), 10 (Labour), Apr 5 (Arbor), May 5 (Children), Jun 6 (Memorial), Jul 17 (Constitution), Aug 15 (Liberation), Oct 1 (Armed Forces), 3 (National Foundation), 9 (Korean Alphabet), Dec 25; NY (Chinese, Jan/Feb), Lord Buddha's Birthday (May), Moon Festival (Sep/Oct)

Kuwait Jan 1, Feb 25 (National)(3); Ad(3), ER(3), NY (Muslim), PB, Ascension of the Prophet (Mar/Apr), Standing on Mt Arafat (Aug)

Lebanon Jan 1, Feb 9 (St Maron), May 1, Aug 15, Nov 1, 22 (Independence), Dec 25; Ad(3), As, EM, GF, ER(3), NY (Muslim), PB

Lesotho Jan 1, Mar 12 (Moshoeshoe's Day), 21 (National Tree Planting), May 2 (King's Birthday), Oct 4 (Independence), Dec 25, 26; A, EM, GF, Family (Jul), National Sports (Oct)

Liberia Jan 1, Feb 11 (Armed Forces), Mar 15 (J J Roberts), Apr 12 (Redemption), May 14 (National Unification), Jul 26 (Independence), Aug 24 (National Flag), Nov 29 (President Tubman's Birthday), Dec 25; Decoration (Mar), National Fast and Prayer (Apr), Thanksgiving (Nov)

Libya Mar 2 (Declaration of Establishment of Authority of People), 8 (National), 28 (Evacuation of British troops), Jun 11 (Evacuation of US troops), Jul 23 (National), Sep 1 (National), Oct 7 (Evacuation of Italian Fascists); Ad(4), ER(3), PB

Liechtenstein Jan 1, 6, Feb 2 (Candlemas), Mar 19 (St Joseph), May 1, Aug 15, Nov 1, Dec 8, 24, 25, 26, 31; A, C, CC, EM, GF, WM

Luxembourg Jan 1, May 1, Jun 23 (National), Aug 15, Nov 1, 2, Dec 25, 26, 31; A, EM, WM, Shrove Monday

Madagascar Jan 1, Mar 29 (Memorial), May 1, Jun 26 (Independence), Aug 15, Nov 1, Dec 25, 30 (National); A, EM, GF, WM

Malawi Jan 1, Mar 3 (Martyrs), May 14 (Kamuzu), Jul 6 (Republic), Oct 17 (Mothers), Dec 22 (Tree Planting), 25, 26 EM, GF, HS

Malaysia Jan 1 (*some states*), May 1, Jun 3 (Head of State's Birthday), Aug 31 (National), Dec 25; Ad, D (*most states*), ER(2), NY (Chinese, Jan/Feb, *most states*), NY (Muslim), PB, Wesak (*most states*); *several local festivals*

Maldives Jan 1, Jul 26 (Independence)(2), Nov 11 (Republic) (2); Ad(4), ER(3), NY (Muslim), PB, R(2), Huravee (Feb), Martyrs (Apr), National (Oct/Nov)(2)

Mali Jan 1, 20 (Army), May 1, 25 (Africa), Sep 22 (National), Nov 19 (Liberation), Dec 25; Ad, ER, PB, Prophet's Baptism (Nov)

NATIONAL HOLIDAYS (cont.)

Malta Jan 1, Mar 31 (National), May 1, Aug 15, Dec 13 (Republic), 25; GF

Mauritania Jan 1, May 1, 25 (Africa), Jul 10 (Armed Forces), Nov 28 (Independence); Ad, ER, NY (Muslim), PB

Mauritius Jan 1, 2, Mar 12 (Independence), May 1, Nov 1, Dec 25; Ad, D, ER, PB, Chinese Spring Festival (Feb)

Mexico Jan 1, Feb 5 (Constitution), Mar 21 (Juárez' Birthday), May 1, 5 (Puebla Battle), Sep 1 (Presidential Report), 16 (Independence), Oct 12 (Columbus), Nov 2, 20 (Mexican Revolution), Dec 12 (Our Lady of Guadaloupe), 25, 31; HT, GF

Monaco Jan 1, 27 (St Devote), May 1, 8 (Armistice, 1945), Jul 14 (National), Aug 15, Sep 3 (Liberation), Nov 1, 11 (Armistice, 1918), 19 (Prince of Monaco), Dec 8, 25; EM, WM

Mongolia Jan 1, 2, Mar 8 (International Women), May 1, Jul 10 (People's Revolution)(3), Nov 7 (October Revolution)

Morocco Jan 1, Mar 3 (Throne), May 1, 23 (Fête Nationale), Jul 9 (Youth), Aug 14 (Oued-ed-Dahab), Nov 6 (Al-Massira Day), 18 (Independence); Ad(2), ER(2), NY (Muslim), PB

Mozambique Jan 1, Feb 3 (Heroes), Apr 7 (Mozambican Women), May 1, Jun 25 (Independence), Sep 7 (Victory), 25 (Armed Forces), Dec 25

Nauru Jan 1, 31 (Independence), May 17 (Constitution), Jul 1 (Takeover), Oct 27 (Angam), Dec 25, 26; EM, GF, Easter Tuesday

Nepal Jan 11 (King Prithvi Memorial), Feb 19 (Late King Tribhuvan Memorial and Democracy), Nov 8 (Queen's Birthday), Dec 16 (King Mahendra Memorial and Constitution), 29 (King's Birthday); NY (Sinhala/Tamil, Apr), Maha Shivarata (Feb/Mar)

Netherlands Jan 1, Apr 30 (Queen's Birthday), May 5 (Liberation), Dec 25, 26; A, EM, GF, WM

New Zealand Jan 1, 2, Feb 6 (Waitangi), Apr 25 (Anzac), Dec 25, 26; EM, GF, Queen's Birthday (Jun), Labour (Oct)

Nicaragua Jan 1, May 1, Jul 19 (Sandinista Revolution), Sep 14 (Battle of San Jacinto), 15 (Independence), Dec 8, 25; GF, HT

Niger Jan 1, Apr 15 (Assumption of Power by Supreme Military Council), May 1, Aug 3 (Independence), Dec 18 (National), 25; Ad, ER, PB

Nigeria Jan 1, May 1, Oct 1 (National), Dec 25, 26; Ad(2), EM, ER(2), GF, PB

Northern Ireland Jan 1, Mar 17 (St Patrick, *not general*), Dec 25, 26, 29; GF, EM, Early May, Late May, July Bank Holiday, Summer Bank Holiday (Aug)

Norway Jan 1, May 1, 17 (Constitution), Dec 25, 26; A, EM, GF, HT, WM

Oman Nov 18 (National)(2), Dec 31; Ad(5), ER(4), NY (Muslim), PB, Lailat al-Miraj (Mar/Apr)

Pakistan Mar 23 (Pakistan), May 1, Jul 1, Aug 14 (Independence), Sep 6 (Defence of Pakistan), 11 (Death of Quaid-e-Azam), Nov 9 (Iqbal), Dec 25 (Christmas/Birthday of Quaid-e-Azam), 31; Ad(3), As(2), ER(3), PB, R

Panama Jan 1, 9 (National Mourning), May 1, Oct 11 (Revolution), 12 (Dia de la Hispanidad), Nov 3 (Independence from Colombia), 4 (Flag), 28 (Independence from Spain), Dec 8 (Mothers), 25; C(2), GF

Papua New Guinea Jan 1, Aug 15 (National Constitution), Sep 16 (Independence), Dec 25, 26; EM, GF, HS, Queen's Birthday (Jun), Remembrance (Jul)

Paraguay Jan 1, Feb 3 (St Blás), Mar 1 (Heroes), May 1, 14 (National Flag), 15 (Independence), Jun 12 (Peace with Bolivia), Aug 15, 25 (Constitution), Sep 29 (Battle of Boqueron Day), Oct 12 (Day of the Race), Nov 1, Dec 8, 25, 31; CC, GF, HT

NATIONAL HOLIDAYS (cont.)

Peru Jan 1, May 1, Jun 29 (Sts Peter and Paul), 30, Jul 28 (Independence)(2), Aug 30 (St Rose of Lima), Oct 8 (Combat of Angamos), Nov 1, Dec 8, 25, 31; GF, HT

Philippines Jan 1, May 1, Jun 12 (Independence), Jul 4 (Philippine-American Friendship), Nov 1, 30 (National Heroes), Dec 25, 30 (Rizal), 31; GF, HT

Poland Jan 1, May 1, Jul 22 (National Liberation), Nov 1, Dec 25, 26; CC, EM

Portugal Jan 1, Apr 25 (Liberty), May 1, Jun 10 (Portugal), Aug 15, Oct 5 (Republic), Nov 1, Dec 1 (Independence Restoration), Dec 8, 24, 25; C, CC, GF

Qatar Sep 3 (Independence), Dec 31; Ad(4), ER(4)

Romania Jan 1, 2, May 1(2), Aug 23 (National)

Rwanda Jan 1, 28 (Democracy), May 1, Jul 1 (Independence), 5 (Peace), Aug 1 (Harvest), 15, Sep 25 (Referendum), Oct 26 (Armed Forces), Nov 1, Dec 25; A, EM, WM

Saint Christopher and Nevis Jan 1, Sep 19 (Independence), Dec 25, 26, 31; EM, GF, WM, Labour (May), Queen's Birthday (Jun), August Monday

Saint Lucia Jan 1, 2, Feb 22 (Independence), May 1, Dec 13 (Saint Lucia), Dec 25, 26; C, CC, EM, GF, WM, Emancipation (Aug), Thanksgiving (Oct)

Saint Vincent and the Grenadines Jan 1, 22 (Discovery), Oct 27 (Independence), Dec 25, 26; C (Jul), EM, GF, WM, Labour (May), Caricom (Jul), Emancipation (Aug)

Sao Tomé and Principe Jan 1, Feb 3 (Liberty Heroes), May 1, Jul 12 (National Independence), Sep 6 (Armed Forces), 30 (Agricultural Reform), Dec 21 (Power of the People), 25 (Family)

Saudi Arabia Sep 23 (National); Ad(7), ER(4)

Scotland Jan 1, 2, Dec 25, 26; GF, Early May, Late May, Summer Bank Holiday (Aug)

Senegal Jan 1, Feb 1 (Senegambia), Apr 4 (National), May 1, Aug 15, Nov 1, Dec 25; Ad, EM, ER, NY (Muslim), PB, WM

Seychelles Jan 1, 2, May 1, Jun 5 (Liberation), 29 (Independence), Aug 15, Nov 1, Dec 8, 25; CC, GF, HS

Sierra Leone Jan 1, Apr 19 (Republic), Dec 25, 26; Ad, EM, ER, GF, PB

Singapore Jan 1, May 1, Aug 9 (National), Dec 25; Ad, D, ER, GF, NY (Chinese, Jan/Feb)(2), Vesak

Solomon Islands Jan 1, Jul 7 (Independence), Dec 25, 26; EM, GF, HS, WM, Queen's Birthday (Jun)

Somalia Jan 1, May 1, Jun 26 (Independence), Jul 1 (Union), Oct 21 (Revolution)(2); Ad(2), ER(2), PB

South Africa Jan 1, Apr 6 (Founders), May 31 (Republic), Oct 10 (Kruger), Dec 16 (Vow), 25, 26; A, GF, Family (Mar/Apr)

Spain Jan 1, 6, Mar 19 (*most areas*), May 1, Aug 15, Oct 12 (Hispanity), Nov 1, Dec 6 (Constitution), 8, 25; CC, GF, HS, HT

Sri Lanka Jan 14 (Tamil Thai Pongal), Feb 4 (Independence), May 1, 22 (National Heroes), Jun 30, Dec 25, 31; Ad, D, ER, GF, NY (Sinhala/Tamil, Apr), PB, Maha Sivarathri (Feb/Mar), Full Moon (*monthly*)

Sudan Jan 1 (Independence), Mar 3 (Unity), Apr 6 (Revolution), Dec 25; Ad(5), ER(5), NY (Muslim), PB, Sham al-Naseem (Apr/May)

Suriname Jan 1, Feb 25 (Revolution), May 1, Jul 1 (Freedom), Nov 25 (Independence), Dec 25, 26; EM, ER, GF, Holi (Mar)

Swaziland Jan 1, Apr 25 (National Flag), Jul 22 (King's Birthday), Sep 6 (Independence), Oct 24 (United Nations), Dec 25, 26; A, EM, GF, Commonwealth (Mar)

NATIONAL HOLIDAYS (cont.)

Sweden Jan 1, 6, May 1, Nov 1 (All Saints), Dec 24, 25, 26, 31; A, EM, GF, WM, Midsummer Eve and Day (Jun)

Switzerland Jan 1, Aug 1 (National), Aug 15 (*many cantons*), Nov 1 (*many cantons*), Dec 24, 25, 26; A, CC (*many cantons*), EM, GF, WM; *several local holidays*

Syria Jan 1, Mar 8 (Revolution), Apr 17 (Evacuation) May 1, 6 (Martyrs), Jul 23 (Egyptian Revolution), Sep 1 (Libyan Unity), Oct 6 (Liberation), Dec 25; Ad(3), ER(4), ES, NY (Muslim), PB

Taiwan Jan 1, 2, 3, Mar 29 (Youth), Apr 5 (Ching Ming), Jul 1, Sep 28 (Birthday of Confucius), Oct 10 (National), 25 (Taiwan Restoration), 31 (Birthday of Chiang Kai-Shek), Nov 12 (Birthday of Dr Sun Yat Sen), Dec 25 (Constitution); NY (Chinese, Jan/Feb)(3), Dragon Boat Festival (Jun), Mid-Autumn Festival (Sep/Oct)

Tanzania Jan 1, 12 (Zanzibar Revolution), Feb 5 (Chama Cha Mapinduzi and Arusha Declaration), May 1, Jul 7 (Saba Saba Peasants), Dec 9 (Independence/Republic), 25; Ad, EM, ER(2), GF, PB

Thailand Jan 1, Apr 6 (Chakri), 13 (Songkran), May 1, 5 (Coronation), Jul 1 (Mid-Year), Aug 12 (Queen's Birthday), Oct 23 (King Chulalongkorn), Dec 5 (King's Birthday), 10 (Constitution), 31; ER, Makha Bucha (Feb), Visakha Bucha (May), Buddhist Lent (Jul)

Togo Jan 1, 13 (Liberation), 24 (Economic Liberation), Apr 24 (Victory), 27 (National), May 1, Aug 15, Nov 1, Dec 25; A, Ad, ER

Tonga Jan 1, Apr 25 (Anzac), May 5 (Birthday of Crown Prince Tupouto'a), Jun 4 (Emancipation), Jul 4 (Birthday and Coronation of King Taufa'ahau Tupou IV), Nov 4 (Constitution), Dec 4 (King Tupou I), 25, 26; EM, GF

Trinidad and Tobago Jan 1, Jun 19 (Labour), Aug 1 (Discovery), 31 (Independence), Sep 24 (Republic), Dec 25, 26; CC, EM, GF, WM

Tunisia Jan 1, 18 (Revolution), Mar 20 (Independence), Apr 9 (Martyrs), May 1, Jun 1 (Victory), 2 (Youth), Jul 25 (Republic), Aug 3 (President's Birthday), 13 (Women), Sep 3 (Sep 3 1934), Oct 15 (Evacuation); Ad(2), ER(2), NY (Muslim), PB

Turkey Jan 1, Apr 23 (National Sovereignty and Children), May 19 (Youth and Sports), Aug 30 (Victory), Oct 29 (Republic); Ad(4), ER(3)

Uganda Jan 1, Apr 1 (Liberation), May 1, Oct 9 (Independence), Dec 25, 26; EM, ER, GF, HS

UK *see* **England & Wales**; **Northern Ireland**; **Scotland**

United Arab Emirates Jan 1, Aug 6 (Accession of Ruler), Dec 2 (National)(2); Ad(3), ER(4), NY (Muslim), PB, Lailat al-Miraj (Mar/Apr)

USA Jan 1, Jan 21 (Martin Luther King's Birthday) (*not all states*), Jul 4 (Independence), Nov 11 (Veterans), Dec 25; Washington's Birthday (3rd Mon in Feb), Memorial (last Mon in May), Labor (1st Mon in Sep), Discoverers' (2nd Mon in Oct), Thanksgiving (last Thurs of Nov); *much local variation*

USSR Jan 1, Mar 8 (Women), May 1(2), 9 (Victory), Oct 7 (Constitution), Nov 7 (October Revolution)(2)

Uruguay Jan 1, Apr 19 (Landing of the 33 Orientales), May 1, 18 (Las Piedras Battle), Jun 19 (Artigas), Jul 18 (Constitution), Aug 25 (Independence), Oct 12 (Columbus), Nov 2, Dec 25; C(2), GF, HT, Monday—Wednesday of Holy Week

Vanuatu Jan 1, Mar 5 (Chiefs), May 1, Jul 30 (Independence), Aug 15, Dec 25, 26; A, EM, GF, Constitution (Oct), Unity (Nov)

Venezuela Jan 1, 6, Mar 19 (St Joseph), Apr 19 (Constitution), May 1, Jun 24 (Battle of Carabobo), 29 (Saints Peter and Paul), Jul 5 (Independence), 24 (Bolivar), Aug 15, Oct 12 (Columbus), Nov 1, Dec 8, 25; A, C(2), CC, GF, HT

Vietnam Jan 1, May 1, Sep 2 (Independence)

NATIONAL HOLIDAYS (cont.)

Western Samoa Jan 1, 2, Apr 25 (Anzac), Jun 1 (Independence) (3), Oct 12 (Lotu-o-Tamai), Dec 25, 26; EM, GF, HS

Yemen Arab Republic May 1, Sep 26 (National); Ad(5), ER(4), NY (Muslim), PB

Yemen People's Democratic Republic Jan 1, Mar 8 (Women), May 1, Jun 22 (Corrective Move), Sep 26 (Revolution, *N area*), Oct 14 (Revolution), Nov 30 (Independence); Ad(3), ER(2), NY (Muslim), PB

Yugoslavia Jan 1, 2, May 1(2), Jul 4 (Fighters), Nov 29 (Republic)(3); People's Uprising (Jul)

Zaire Jan 1, 4 (Martyrs of Independence), May 1, 20 (Mouvement Populaire de la Revolution), Jun 24 (Anniversary of Currency, Promulgation, Constitution and Day of Fishers), 30 (Independence), Aug 1 (Parents), Oct 14 (Founder/Youth), 27 (Country's Change of Name), Nov 17 (Armed Forces), 24 (New Regime), Dec 25

Zambia Jan 1, May 1, 25 (Africa Freedom), Oct 24 (Independence), Dec 25; GF, HS, Youth (Mar), Heroes (Jul), Unity (Jul), Farmers (Aug)

Zimbabwe Jan 1, Apr 18 (Independence), 19 (Defence Forces), May 1, 25 (Africa), Aug 11 (Heroes)(2), Dec 25, 26; EM, GF

WORLD POPULATION ESTIMATES

Date (AD)	Millions	Date (AD)	Millions	Date (AD)	Millions
1	200	1900	1625	1970	3700
1000	275	1920	1860	1980	4450
1250	375	1930	2070	1985	4845
1500	420	1940	2295	1990	5246
1700	615	1950	2500	2000	6100
1800	900	1960	3050	2050	11000

Estimates for 2000 and 2050 are United Nations 'medium' estimates. They should be compared with the 'low' estimates for these years of 5400 and 8500, and 'high' estimates of 7000 and 13500, respectively.

UNITED NATIONS MEMBERSHIP

Grouped according to year of entry.

1945 Argentina, Australia, Belgium, Belorussian SSR, Bolivia, Brazil, Canada, Chile, China (Taiwan) (to 1971), Colombia, Costa Rica, Cuba, Czechoslavakia, Denmark, Dominican Republic, Ecuador, Egypt, El Salvador, Ethiopia, France, Greece, Guatemala, Haiti, Honduras, India, Iran, Iraq, Lebanon, Liberia, Luxembourg, Mexico, Netherlands, New Zealand, Nicaragua, Norway, Panama, Paraguay, Peru, Philippines, Poland, Saudi Arabia, South Africa, Syria, Turkey, Ukranian SSR, USSR, UK, USA, Uruguay, Venezuala, Yugoslavia

1946 Afghanistan, Iceland, Sweden, Thailand

1947 Pakistan, Yemen

1948 Burma

1949 Israel

1950 Indonesia

1955 Albania, Austria, Bulgaria, Kampuchea, (formerly Cambodia), Sri Lanka (formerly Ceylon), Finland, Hungary, Ireland, Italy, Jordan, Laos, Libya, Nepal, Portugal, Romania, Spain

1956 Japan, Morocco, Sudan, Tunisia

1957 Ghana, Malaya (Malaysia, 1963)

1958 Guinea

1960 Benin (formerly Dahomey), Burkina Faso (formerly Upper Volta), Cameroon, Central African Republic, Chad, Congo,

UNITED NATIONS MEMBERSHIP (cont.)

1960	Ivory Coast (Côte d'Ivoire), Cyprus,	1973	Bahamas, Germany (formerly German
(cont.)	Gabon, Madagascar, Mali, Niger,		Democratic Republic and German Federal
	Nigeria, Senegal, Somalia, Togo, Zaïre		Republic)
1961	Mauritania, Mongolia, Sierra Leone,	1974	Bangladesh, Grenada, Guinea-Bissau
	Tanganyika (within Tanzania, 1964)	1975	Cape Verde, Comoros, Mozambique, Papua
1962	Algeria, Burundi, Jamaica, Rwanda,		New Guinea, Sao Tomé and Principe,
	Trinidad and Tobago, Uganda		Suriname
1963	Kenya, Kuwait, Zanzibar (within Tanzania,	1976	Angola, Seychelles, Western Samoa
	1964)	1977	Djibouti, Vietnam
1964	Malawi, Malta, Zambia, Tanzania	1978	Dominica, Solomon Islands
1965	Gambia, Maldives, Singapore	1979	St Lucia
1966	Barbados, Botswana, Guyana, Lesotho	1980	St Vincent and the Grenadines, Zimbabwe
1968	Equatorial Guinea, Mauritius, Swaziland	1981	Antigua and Barbuda, Belize, Vanuatu
1970	Fiji	1983	St Christopher and Nevis
1971	Bahrain, Bhutan, China (Peoples'	1984	Brunei
	Republic), Oman, Qatar, United Arab	1990	Namibia, Yemen (formerly N Yemen and S
	Emirates		Yemen)

UNITED NATIONS — SPECIALIZED AGENCIES

Abbreviated form	Full title	Area of concern
ILO	International Labour Organization	Social justice
FAO	Food and Agriculture	Improvement of the production and distribution of agricultural products
UNESCO	United Nations Educational, Scientific and Cultural Organization	Stimulation of popular education and the spread of culture
ICAO	International Civil Aviation Organization	Encouragement of safety measures in international flIght
IBRD	International Bank for Reconstruction and Development	Aid of development through investment
IMF	International Monetary Fund	Promotion of international monetary co-operation
UPU	Universal Postal Union	Uniting members within a single postal territory
WHO	World Health Organization	Promotion of the highest standards of health for all people
ITU	International Telecommunication Union	Allocation of frequencies and regulation of procedures
WMO	World Meteorological Organization	Standardization and utilization of meteorological observations
IFC	International Finance Corporation	Promotion of the international flow of private capital
IMCO	Inter-governmental Maritime Consultative Organization	The co-ordination of safety at sea
IDA	International Development Association	Credit on special terms to provide assistance for less developed countries
WIPO	World Intellectual Property Organization	Protection of copyright, designs, inventions etc
IFAD	International Fund for Agricultural Development	Increase of food production in developing countries by the generation of grants or loans

COMMONWEALTH MEMBERSHIP

The Commonwealth is an informal association of sovereign states.

Member countries are grouped by year of entry.

1931	Australia, Canada, New Zealand, United Kingdom
1947	India, Pakistan (left 1972, rejoined 1989)
1948	Sri Lanka
1957	China, Malaysia
1960	Nigeria
1961	Cyprus, Sierra Leone, Tanzania
1962	Jamaica, Trinidad and Tobago, Uganda
1963	Kenya, Malawi
1964	Malawi, Malta, Zambia
1965	the Gambia, Singapore
1966	Barbados, Botswana, Guyana, Lesotho
1968	Mauritius, Nauru, Swaziland
1970	Tonga, Western Samoa
1972	Bangladesh
1973	Bahamas
1974	Grenada
1975	Papua New Guinea
1976	Seychelles
1978	Dominica, Solomon Islands, Tuvalu
1979	Kiribati, St Lucia, St Vincent and the Grenadines
1980	Vanuatu, Zimbabwe
1981	Antigua and Barbuda, Belize
1982	Maldives
1983	St Christopher and Nevis
1984	Brunei

Three countries have left the Commonweath: Fiji (1987), Ireland (1949), South Africa (1961)

EUROPEAN COMMUNITY MEMBERSHIP

Member countries are listed by year of entry.

1958	Belgium		1973	Denmark
1958	France		1973	Republic of Ireland
1958	Germany (Federal Republic of)		1973	United Kingdom
1958	Italy		1981	Greece
1958	Luxembourg		1986	Portugal
1958	The Netherlands		1986	Spain

Turkey has applied for membership

EUROPEAN COMMUNITY ORGANIZATIONS

Abbreviation	Full title	Area of concern	Abbreviation	Full title	Area of concern
	European Court of Justice	Adjudication of disputes arising from application of the Treaties	EIB	European Investment Bank	Greece, Spain, Portugal Financing of capital investment projects to assist development of the Community
CAP	Common Agricultural Policy	Aiming to ensure reasonable standards of living for farmers; its policies have led to surpluses in the past	ECSC	European Coal and Steel Community	Regulation of prices and trade in these commodities
EMS	European Monetary System	Assistance of trading relations between member countries; all members of the community are in the EMS except	EURATOM	European Atomic Energy Community	Creation of technical and industrial conditions to produce nuclear energy on a large scale

COUNTIES OF ENGLAND

County	Area sq km	sq ml	Population (1991 est.)	Admin. centre
Avon*	1346	520	919800	Bristol
Bedfordshire	1235	477	514200	Bedford
Berkshire	1259	486	716500	Reading
Buckinghamshire	1883	727	619500	Aylesbury
Cambridgeshire	3409	1316	640700	Cambridge
Cheshire	2328	899	937300	Chester
Cleveland*	583	225	541100	Middlesbrough
Cornwall	3564	1376	469300	Truro
Cumbria*	6810	2629	486900	Carlisle
Derbyshire	2631	1016	914600	Matlock
Devon	6711	2591	998200	Exeter
Dorset	2654	1025	645200	Dorchester
Durham	2436	941	589800	Durham
Essex	3672	1418	1495600	Chelmsford
Gloucestershire	2643	1020	520600	Gloucester
Greater London*	1579	610	6377900	—
Greater Manchester*	1287	497	2454800	—
Hampshire	3777	1458	1511900	Winchester
Hereford and Worcester*	3926	1516	667800	Worcester
Hertfordshire	1634	631	951500	Hertford
Humberside*	3512	1356	835200	Hull

COUNTIES OF ENGLAND (cont.)

County	Area sq km	sq ml	Population (1991 est.)	Admin. centre
Isle of Wight	381	147	126600	Newport
Kent	3731	1441	1485100	Maidstone
Lancashire	3063	1183	1365100	Preston
Leicestershire	2553	986	860500	Leicester
Lincolnshire	5915	2284	573900	Lincoln
Merseyside*	652	252	1376800	Liverpool
Norfolk	5368	2073	736400	Norwich
Northamptonshire	2367	914	572900	Northampton
Northumberland	5032	1943	300600	Newcastle upon Tyne
Nottinghamshire	2164	836	980600	Nottingham
Oxfordshire	2608	1007	553800	Oxford
Shropshire	3490	1347	401600	Shrewsbury
Somerset	3451	1332	459100	Taunton
Staffordshire	2716	1049	1020300	Stafford
Suffolk	3797	1466	629900	Ipswich
Surrey	1679	648	998000	Kingston upon Thames
Sussex, East	1795	693	670600	Lewes
Sussex, West	1989	768	692800	Chichester
Tyne and Wear*	540	208	1087800	Newcastle
Warwickshire	1981	765	477000	Warwick
West Midlands*	899	347	2499300	Birmingham
Wiltshire	3481	1344	553300	Trowbridge
Yorkshire, North	8309	3208	698700	Northallerton
Yorkshire, South	1560	602	1248500	Barnsley
Yorkshire, West	2039	787	1984700	Wakefield

*New counties in 1974 were formed as follows:

Avon: parts of Somerset and Gloucestershire
Cleveland: parts of Durham and Yorkshire
Cumbria: Cumberland, Westmoreland, parts of Lancashire and Yorkshire
Greater London: London and most of Middlesex
Greater Manchester: parts of Lancashire, Cheshire and Yorkshire
Hereford and Worcester: Hereford, most of Worcestershire
Humberside: parts of Yorkshire and Lincolnshire
Merseyside: parts of Lancashire and Cheshire
West Midlands: parts of Staffordshire, Warwickshire and Worcestershire
Tyne and Wear: parts of Northumberland and Durham

REGIONS OF SCOTLAND

Region	Area sq km	sq ml	Population (1991 est.)	Admin. centre	Former counties	New districts
Borders	4672	1804	102649	Newton St Boswells	Berwick, Peebles, Roxburgh, Selkirk, part of Midlothian	Berwickshire, Ettrick & Lauderdale, Roxburgh, Tweeddale
Central	2631	1016	267964	Stirling	Clackmannan, most of Stirling, parts of Perth and W Lothian	Clackmannan, Falkirk, Stirling
Dumfries & Galloway	6370	2459	147064	Dumfries	Dumfries, Kirkcudbright, Wigtown	Annandale & Eskdale, Nithsdale, Stewartry, Wigtown
Fife	1307	505	339284	Glenrothes	Fife	Dunfermline, NE Fife, Kirkcaldy
Grampian	8704	3361	493155	Aberdeen	Aberdeen, Banff, Kincardine, most of Moray	Aberdeen, Banff & Buchan, Gordon, Kincardine & Deeside, Moray
Highland	25391	9804	209419	Inverness	Caithness, Inverness, Nairn, Ross & Cromarty, Sutherland, parts of Argyll and Moray	Badenoch & Strathspey, Caithness, Inverness, Lochaber, Nairn, Ross & Cromarty, Sutherland, Skye & Lochalsh
Lothian	1755	678	723678	Edinburgh	E Lothian, Midlothian, W Lothian	Edinburgh, E Lothian, Midlothian, W Lothian
Strathclyde	13537	5227	2218229	Glasgow	Ayre, Bute, Dunbarton, Lanark, Renfrew, most of Argyll, part of Stirling	Argyll & Bute, Bearsden & Milngavie, Clydebank, Clydesdale, Cumnock & Doon Valley, Cunninghame, Cumbernauld & Kilsyth, Dunbarton, E Kilbride, Eastwood, Glasgow, Hamilton, Inverclyde, Kilmarnock & Loudoun, Kyle & Carrick, Monklands, Motherwell, Renfrew, Strathkelvin
Tayside	7493	2893	385271	Dundee	Angus, Kinross, most of Perth	Angus, Dundee, Kinross, Perth
Orkney Is	976	377	19450	Kirkwall		
Shetland Is	1433	553	22017	Lerwick		
Western Is	2898	1119	29109	Stornoway		

COUNTIES OF WALES

County	Area sq km	sq ml	Population (1991 est.)	Admin. centre	Former counties	New districts
Clwyd	2426	937	401 900	Mold	Flint, most of Denbigh	Alyn & Deeside, Colwyn, Delyn, Glyndwr, Rhuddlan, Wrexham Maelor
Dyfed	5768	2227	341 600	Carmarthen	Camarthen, Cardigan, Pembroke	Camarthen, Ceredigion, Dinefwr, Llanelli, Preseli, South Pembrokeshire
Gwent	1376	531	432 300	Cwmbrân	Most of Monmouth, part of Brecon	Blaenau Gwent, Islwyn, Monmouth, Newport, Torfaen
Gwynedd	3869	1494	238 600	Caernarvon	Anglesey, Caernarvon, Merioneth, part of Denbigh	Aberconwy, Arfon, Dwyfor, Meirionydd, Ynys Môn (Anglesey)
Powys	5077	1960	116 500	Llandrindod Wells	Montgomery, Radnor, most of Brecon	Brecknock, Montgomery, Radnor
Mid Glamorgan	1018	393	526 500	Cardiff	Parts of Glamorgan, Brecon, and Monmouth	Cynon Valley, Merthyr Tydfil, Ogwr, Rhondda, Rhymney Valley, Taff-Ely
S Glamorgan	416	161	383 300	Cardiff	Parts of Glamorgan and Monmouth	Cardiff, Vale of Glamorgan
W Glamorgan	817	315	357 800	Swansea	Part of Glamorgan	Afan, Lliw Valley, Neath, Swansea

UK ISLANDS

Name	Area sq km	sq ml	Population (1986)	Admin. centre
Channel Is				
Alderney	8	3	2000	St Anne's
Guernsey	63	24	54380	St Peter Port
Jersey	116	45	80212	St Helier
Sark	4	2	604	
Isle of Man	572	221	64282	Douglas

DISTRICTS OF NORTHERN IRELAND

District	Area sq km	sq ml	Population (1988)	Admin. centre	Formerly part of
Antrim	563	217	48100	Antrim	Antrim
Ards	369	142	64500	Newtownards	Down
Armagh	672	259	49000	Armagh	Armagh
Ballymena	638	246	57200	Ballymena	Antrim
Ballymoney	419	162	23900	Ballymoney	Antrim
Banbridge	444	171	31900	Banbridge	Down
Belfast	140	54	296900	—	Antrim
Carrickfergus	87	34	30400	Carrickfergus	Antrim
Castlereagh	85	33	58000	Belfast	Down Antrim
Coleraine	485	187	48500	Coleraine	Antrim
Cookstown	623	240	27600	Cookstown	Tyrone
Craigavon	382	147	77700	Craigavon	Armagh, Down, Antrim,
Down	646	249	57200	Downpatrick	Down
Dungannon	779	301	43700	Dungannon	Tyrone, Armagh
Fermanagh	1876	715	50400	Enniskillen	Fermanagh
Larne	338	131	29100	Larne	Antrim
Limavady	587	227	29800	Limavady	Londonderry
Lisburn	444	171	97400	Lisburn	Antrim, Down
Londonderry	382	147	97500	—	Londonderry
Magherafelt	573	221	32900	Magherafelt	Londonderry
Moyle	495	191	15100	Ballycastle	Antrim
Newry & Mourne	895	346	88900	Newry	Down, Armagh
Newtownabbey	152	59	72900	Newtownabbey	Antrim
North Down	73	28	71900	Bangor	Down
Omagh	1129	436	44900	Omagh	Tyrone
Strabane	870	336	35600	Strabane	Tyrone

COUNTIES OF IRELAND

County	Area sq km	sq ml	Population (1986)	Admin. centre	County	Area sq km	sq ml	Population (1986)	Admin. centre
Carlow	896	346	40948	Carlow	Longford	1044	403	31491	Longford
Cavan	1891	730	53881	Cavan	Louth	821	317	91698	Dundalk
Clare	3188	1231	91343	Ennis	Mayo	5398	2084	115016	Castlebar
Cork	7459	2880	412623	Cork	Meath	2339	903	103762	Trim
Donegal	4830	1865	129428	Lifford	Monaghan	1290	498	52332	Monaghan
Dublin	922	356	1020796	Dublin	Offaly	1997	771	59806	Tullamore
Galway	5939	2293	178180	Galway	Roscommon	2463	951	54551	Roscommon
Kerry	4701	1815	123922	Tralee	Sligo	1795	693	55979	Sligo
Kildare	1694	654	116015	Naas	Tipperary	4254	1642	136504	Clonmel
Kilkenny	2062	796	73094	Kilkenny	Waterford	1839	710	91098	Waterford
Laoighis (Leix)	1720	664	53270	Portlaoise	Westmeath	1764	681	63306	Mullingar
Leitrim	1526	589	27000	Carrick	Wexford	2352	908	102456	Wexford
Limerick	2686	1037	164204	Limerick	Wicklow	2025	782	94482	Wicklow

STATES OF THE USA

Population: estimates are for 1989 (US Bureau of the Census)

Time Zones Two sets of figures indicate that different zones operate in a state. The second figure refers to Summer Time (April–October, approximately).

2 Aleutian/Hawaii Standard Time
3 Alaska Standard Time
4 Pacific Standard Time
5 Mountain Standard Time
6 Central Standard Time
7 Eastern Standard Time

Alabama (AL)
Pop 4 118 000   *Time Zone* 7/8
Nickname Camellia State, Heart of Dixie
Inhabitant Alabamian
Area 133 911 sq km/51 705 sq ml
Capital Montgomery
Bird Yellowhammer   *Fish* Tarpon
Flower Camellia   *Tree* Southern Pine
Alaska (AK)
Pop 527 000   *Time Zone* 3/4
Nickname Mainland State, The Last Frontier
Inhabitant Alaskan
Area 1 518 748 sq km/586 412 sq ml
Capital Juneau
Bird Willow Ptarmigan   *Fish* King Salmon
Flower Forget-me-not
Gemstone Jade   *Tree* Sitka Spruce
Arizona (AZ)
Pop 3 556 000   *Time Zone* 5
Nickname Apache State, Grand Canyon State
Inhabitant Arizonan
Area 295 249 sq km/114 000 sq ml
Capital Phoenix
Bird Cactus Wren   *Flower* Giant Cactus
Gemstone Turquoise   *Tree* Paloverde
Arkansas (AR)
Pop 2 406 000   *Time Zone* 6/7
Nickname Bear State, Land of Opportunity
Inhabitant Arkansan
Area 137 403 sq km/53 187 sq ml
Capital Little Rock
Bird Mockingbird   *Flower* Apple Blossom
Gemstone Diamond   *Tree* Pine
California (CA)
Pop 29 063 000   *Time Zone* 4/5
Nickname Golden State
Inhabitant Californian
Area 411 033 sq km/158 706 sq ml

Capital Sacramento
Animal California Grizzly Bear
Bird California Valley Quail
Fish South Fork Golden Trout
Flower Golden Poppy
Tree California Redwood
Colorado (CO)
Pop 3 317 000   *Time Zone* 5/6
Nickname Centennial State
Inhabitant Coloradan
Area 269 585 sq km/104 091 sq ml
Capital Denver
Animal Rocky Mountain Bighorn Sheep
Bird Lark Bunting   *Flower* Columbine
Gemstone Aquamarine   *Tree* Blue Spruce
Connecticut (CT)
Pop 3 239 000   *Time Zone* 7/8
Nickname Nutmeg State, Constitution State
Inhabitant Nutmegger
Area 12 996 sq km/5 018 sq ml
Capital Hartford
Bird American Robin   *Flower* Mountain Laurel
Gemstone Garnet   *Tree* White Oak
Delaware (DE)
Pop 673 000   *Time Zone* 7/8
Nickname Diamond State, First State
Inhabitant Delawarean
Area 5 296 sq km/2 045 sq ml
Capital Dover
Bird Blue Hen Chicken   *Flower* Peach Blossom
Tree American Holly
District of Columbia (DC)
Pop 604 000   *Time Zone* 7/8
Inhabitant Washingtonian
Area 173.5 sq km/67 sq ml
Capital Washington
Bird Woodthrush   *Flower* American Beauty Rose
Tree Scarlet Oak
Florida (FL)
Pop 12 671 000   *Time Zone* 6/7, 7/8
Nickname Everglade State, Sunshine State
Inhabitant Floridian
Area 151 934 sq km/58 664 sq ml
Capital Tallahassee
Bird Mockingbird   *Flower* Orange Blossom
Gemstone Agatized Coral   *Tree* Sabal Palm
Georgia (GA)
Pop 6 436 000   *Time Zone* 7/8
Nickname Empire State of the South,
Peach State
Inhabitant Georgian
Area 152 571 sq km/58 910 sq ml

USA STATES (cont.)

Capital Atlanta
Bird Brown Thrasher *Flower* Cherokee Rose
Tree Live Oak
Hawaii (HI)
Pop 1 112 000 *Time Zone* 2
Nickname Aloha State
Inhabitant Hawaiian
Area 16 759 sq km/6 471 sq ml
Capital Honolulu
Bird Nene *Flower* Hibiscus *Tree* Kukui
Idaho (ID)
Pop 1 014 000 *Time Zone* 4/5, 5/6
Nickname Gem State
Inhabitant Idahoan
Area 216 422 sq km/83 564 sq ml
Capital Boise
Bird Mountain Bluebird *Flower* Syringa
Gemstone Idaho Star Garnet
Tree Western White Pine
Illinois (IL)
Pop 11 658 000 *Time Zone* 6/7
Nickname Prairie State, Land of Lincoln
Inhabitant Illinoisan
Area 145 928 sq km/56 345 sq ml
Capital Springfield
Bird Cardinal *Flower* Butterfly Violet
Tree White Oak
Indiana (IN)
Pop 5 593 000 *Time Zone* 6/7, 7/8 (Daylight
Saving Time not observed everywhere)
Nickname Hoosier State
Inhabitant Hoosier
Area 93 715.5 sq km/36 185 sq ml
Capital Indianapolis
Bird Cardinal *Flower* Peony
Tree Tulip Tree
Iowa (IA)
Pop 2 840 000 *Time Zone* 6/7
Nickname Hawkeye State, Corn State
Inhabitant Iowan
Area 145 747 sq km/56 275 sq ml
Capital Des Moines
Bird Eastern Goldfinch *Flower* Wild Rose
Tree Oak
Kansas (KS)
Pop 2 513 000 *Time Zone* 5/6, 6/7
Nickname Sunflower State, Jayhawker State
Inhabitant Kansan
Area 213 089 sq km/82 277 sq ml
Capital Topeka
Animal Bison *Bird* Western Meadowlark
Flower Native Sunflower *Tree* Cottonwood

Kentucky (KY)
Pop 3 727 000 *Time Zone* 6/7, 7/8
Nickname Bluegrass State
Inhabitant Kentuckian
Area 104 658 sq km/40 410 sq ml
Capital Frankfort
Bird Cardinal *Flower* Goldenrod
Tree Kentucky Coffee Tree
Louisiana (LA)
Pop 4 382 000 *Time Zone* 6/7
Nickname Pelican State, Sugar State, Creole
State
Inhabitant Louisianian
Area 123 673 sq km/47 752 sq ml
Capital Baton Rouge
Bird Eastern Brown Pelican *Flower* Magnolia
Tree Bald Cypress
Maine (ME)
Pop 1 222 000 *Time Zone* 7/8
Nickname Pine Tree State
Inhabitant Downeaster
Area 86 153 sq km/33 265 sq ml
Capital Augusta
Bird Chickadee *Flower* White Pine Cone and
Tassel *Gemstone* Tourmaline
Tree Eastern White Pine
Maryland (MD)
Pop 4 694 000 *Time Zone* 7/8
Nickname Old Line State, Free State
Inhabitant Marylander
Area 27 090 sq km/10 460 sq ml
Capital Annapolis
Bird Baltimore Oriole *Fish* Striped Bass
Flower Black-eyed Susan *Tree* White Oak
Massachusetts (MA)
Pop 5 913 000 *Time Zone* 7/8
Nickname Bay State, Old Colony
Inhabitant Bay Stater
Area 21 455 sq km/8 284 sq ml
Capital Boston
Bird Chickadee *Flower* Mayflower
Tree American Elm
Michigan (MI)
Pop 9 273 000 *Time Zone* 6/7, 7/8
Nickname Wolverine State, Great Lake State
Inhabitant Michigander
Area 151 579 sq km/58 527 sq ml
Capital Lansing
Bird Robin *Fish* Trout
Flower Apple Blossom *Gemstone* Chlorastrolik
Tree White Pine

USA STATES (cont.)

Minnesota (MN)
Pop 4 353 000 *Time Zone* 6/7
Nickname Gopher State, North Star State
Inhabitant Minnesotan
Area 218 593 sq km/84 402 sq ml
Capital St. Paul
Bird Loon *Fish* Walleye
Flower Moccasin Flower
Gemstone Lake Superior Agate
Tree Red Pine

Mississippi (MS)
Pop 2 621 000 *Time Zone* 6/7
Nickname Magnolia State
Inhabitant Mississippian
Area 123 510 sq km/47 689 sq ml
Capital Jackson
Bird Mockingbird *Flower* Magnolia
Tree Magnolia

Missouri (MO)
Pop 5 159 000 *Time Zone* 6/7
Nickname Bullion State, Show Me State
Inhabitant Missourian
Area 180 508 sq km/69 697 sq ml
Capital Jefferson City
Bird Bluebird *Flower* Hawthorn
Tree Dogwood

Montana (MT)
Pop 806 000 *Time Zone* 5/6
Nickname Treasure State, Big Sky Country
Inhabitant Montanan
Area 380 834 sq km/147 046 sq ml
Capital Helena
Bird Western Meadowlark *Flower* Bitterroot
Gemstone Sapphire, Agate
Tree Ponderosa Pine

Nebraska (NE)
Pop 1 611 000 *Time Zone* 5/6, 6/7
Nickname Cornhusker State, Beef State
Inhabitant Nebraskan
Area 200 342 sq km/77 355 sq ml
Bird Western Meadowlark *Flower* Goldenrod
Gemstone Blue Agate *Tree* Cottonwood

Nevada (NV)
Pop 1 111 000 *Time Zone* 4/5
Nickname Silver State, Sagebrush State
Inhabitant Nevadan
Area 286 341 sq km/110 561 sq ml
Capital Carson City
Bird Mountain Bluebird *Flower* Sagebrush
Tree Single-leaf Piñon

New Hampshire (NH)
Pop 1 107 000 *Time Zone* 7/8
Nickname Granite State
Inhabitant New Hampshirite
Area 24 032 sq km/9 279 sq ml
Capital Concord
Bird Purple Finch *Flower* Purple Lilac
Tree White Birch

New Jersey (NJ)
Pop 7 736 000 *Time Zone* 7/8
Nickname Garden State
Inhabitant New Jerseyite
Area 20 167 sq km/7 787 sq ml
Capital Trenton
Bird Eastern Goldfinch *Flower* Purple Violet
Tree Red Oak

New Mexico (NM)
Pop 1 528 000 *Time Zone* 5/6
Nickname Sunshine State, Land of Enchantment
Inhabitant New Mexican
Area 314 914 sq km/121 593 sq ml
Capital Santa Fe
Animal Black Bear *Bird* Roadrunner
Fish Cutthroat Trout *Flower* Yucca
Gemstone Turquoise *Tree* Piñon

New York (NY)
Pop 17 950 000 *Time Zone* 7/8
Nickname Empire State
Inhabitant New Yorker
Area 127 185 sq km/49 108 sq ml
Capital Albany
Bird Bluebird *Flower* Rose
Gemstone Garnet *Tree* Sugar Maple

North Carolina (NC)
Pop 6 571 000 *Time Zone* 7/8
Nickname Old North State, Tar Heel State
Inhabitant North Carolinian
Area 136 407 sq km/52 699 sq ml
Capital Raleigh
Animal Grey Squirrel *Bird* Cardinal
Fish Channel Bass *Flower* Dogwood
Gemstone Emerald *Tree* Longleaf Pine

North Dakota (ND)
Pop 660 000 *Time Zone* 5/6, 6/7
Nickname Flickertail State, Sioux State
Inhabitant North Dakotan
Area 180 180 sq km/69 567 sq ml
Capital Bismarck
Bird Western Meadowlark *Fish* Northern Pike
Flower Wild Prairie Rose
Gemstone Teredo petrified wood
Tree American Elm

USA STATES (cont.)

Ohio (OH)
Pop 10 907 000 *Time Zone* 7/8
Nickname Buckeye State
Inhabitant Ohioan
Area 107 040 sq km/41 330 sq ml
Capital Columbus
Bird Cardinal *Flower* Scarlet Carnation
Tree Buckeye
Oklahoma (OK)
Pop 3 224 000 *Time Zone* 6/7
Nickname Sooner State
Inhabitant Oklahoman
Area 181 083 sq km/69 919 sq ml
Capital Oklahoma City
Bird Scissor-tailed Flycatcher
Flower Mistletoe *Tree* Redbud
Oregon (OR)
Pop 2 820 000 *Time Zone* 4/5
Nickname Sunset State, Beaver State
Inhabitant Oregonian
Area 251 409 sq km/97 073 sq ml
Capital Salem
Animal Beaver *Bird* Western Meadowlark
Fish Chinook Salmon *Flower* Oregon Grape
Gemstone Thunder Egg *Tree* Douglas Fir
Pennsylvania (PA)
Pop 12 040 000 *Time Zone* 7/8
Nickname Keystone State
Inhabitant Pennsylvanian
Area 117 343 sq km/45 308 sq ml
Capital Harrisburg
Animal Whitetail Deer *Bird* Ruffed Grouse
Flower Mountain Laurel *Tree* Hemlock
Rhode Island (RI)
Pop 998 000 *Time Zone* 7/8
Nickname Little Rhody, Plantation State
Inhabitant Rhode Islander
Area 3 139 sq km/1 212 sq ml
Capital Providence
Bird Rhode Island Red *Flower* Violet
Tree Red Maple
South Carolina (SC)
Pop 3 512 000 *Time Zone* 7/8
Nickname Palmetto State
Inhabitant South Carolinian
Area 80 579 sq km/31 113 sq ml
Capital Columbia
Animal Whitetail Deer *Bird* Carolina Wren
Fish Striped Bass *Flower* Yellow Jessamine
Tree Cabbage Palmetto
South Dakota (SD)
Pop 715 000 *Time Zone* 5/6, 6/7

Nickname Sunshine State, Coyote State
Inhabitant South Dakotan
Area 199 723 sq km/77 116 sq ml
Capital Pierre
Animal Coyote *Bird* Ring-necked Pheasant
Flower Pasque *Gemstone* Fairburn Agate
Tree Black Hills Spruce
Tennessee (TN)
Pop 4 940 000 *Time Zone* 6/7, 7/8
Nickname Volunteer State
Inhabitant Tennessean
Area 109 149 sq km/42 144 sq ml
Capital Nashville
Animal Raccoon *Bird* Mockingbird
Flower Iris *Gemstone* Pearl *Tree* Tulip Poplar
Texas (TX)
Pop 16 991 000 *Time Zone* 5/6, 6/7
Nickname Lone Star State
Inhabitant Texan
Area 691 003 sq km/266 807 sq ml
Capital Austin
Bird Mockingbird *Flower* Bluebonnet
Gemstone Topaz *Tree* Pecan
Utah (UT)
Pop 1 707 000 *Time Zone* 5/6
Nickname Mormon State, Beehive State
Inhabitant Utahn
Area 219 880 sq km/84 899 sq ml
Capital Salt Lake City
Bird Sea Gull *Flower* Sego Lily
Gemstone Topaz *Tree* Blue Spruce
Vermont (VT)
Pop 567 000 *Time Zone* 7/8
Nickname Green Mountain State
Inhabitant Vermonter
Area 24 899 sq km/9 614 sq ml
Capital Montpelier
Animal Morgan Horse *Bird* Hermit Thrush
Flower Red Clover *Tree* Sugar Maple
Virginia (VA)
Pop 6 098 000 *Time Zone* 7/8
Nickname Old Dominion State, Mother of Presidents
Inhabitant Virginian
Area 105 582 sq km/40 767 sq ml
Capital Richmond
Bird Cardinal *Flower* Dogwood
Tree Flowering Dogwood
Washington (WA)
Pop 4 761 000 *Time Zone* 4/5
Nickname Evergreen State, Chinook State
Inhabitant Washingtonian

USA STATES (cont.)

Washington (cont.)

Area 176 473 sq km/68 139 sq ml
Capital Olympia
Bird Willow Goldfinch *Fish* Steelhead Trout
Flower Western Rhododendron
Gemstone Petrified Wood
Tree Western Hemlock
West Virginia (WV)
Pop 1 857 000 *Time Zone* 7/8
Nickname Panhandle State, Mountain State
Inhabitant West Virginian
Area 62 758 sq km/24 232 sq ml
Capital Charleston
Animal Black Bear *Bird* Cardinal
Flower Big Rhododendron *Tree* Sugar Maple
Wisconsin (WI)
Pop 4 867 000 *Time Zone* 6/7

Nickname Badger State, America's Dairyland
Inhabitant Wisconsinite
Area 145 431 sq km/56 153 sq ml
Capital Madison
Animal Badger, Whitetail Deer *Bird* Robin
Fish Muskellunge *Flower* Wood Violet
Tree Sugar Maple
Wyoming (WY)
Pop 475 000 *Time Zone* 5/6
Nickname Equality State
Inhabitant Wyomingite
Area 253 315 sq km/97 809 sq ml
Capital Cheyenne
Bird Meadowlark *Flower* Indian Paintbrush
Gemstone Jade *Tree* Cottonwood

AUSTRALIAN STATES

Name	Area sq km	sq ml	State Capital
Australian Capital Territory	2 400	930	Canberra
New South Wales	801 400	309 400	Sydney
Northern Territory	1 346 200	519 800	Darwin
Queensland	1 727 200	666 900	Brisbane
South Australia	984 000	379 900	Adelaide
Tasmania	67 800	26 200	Hobart
Victoria	227 600	87 900	Melbourne
Western Australia	2 525 500	975 000	Perth

CANADIAN PROVINCES

Name	Area sq km	sq ml	Provincial Capital
Alberta	661 190	255 285	Edmonton
British Columbia	947 800	365 945	Victoria
Manitoba	649 950	250 945	Winnipeg
New Brunswick	73 440	28 355	Fredericton
Newfoundland	405 720	156 648	St John's
Northwest Territories	3 426 320	1 322 902	Yellowknife
Nova Scotia	55 490	21 424	Halifax
Ontario	1 068 580	412 578	Toronto
Prince Edward Islands	5 660	2 185	Charlottetown
Quebec	1 540 680	594 856	Quebec City
Saskatchewan	652 380	251 883	Regina
Yukon Territory	483 450	186 660	Whitehorse

RANKS OF THE ARISTOCRACY

England	France	Holy Roman Empire (Germany)	Italy	Spain
king	roi	Kaiser	re	rey
prince	prince	Herzog	duca	duque
duke	duc	Pfalzgraf	principe	principe
marquess	marquis	Markgraf	marchese	marques
earl	comte	Landgraf	conde	conde
viscount	vicomte		visconte	vizconde
baronet				

MILITARY RANKS

France

Army	Air Force	Navy
Général d'Armée	Général d'Armée Aérienne	Amiral
Général de Corps d'Armée	Général de Corps Aérien	Vice-Amiral d'Escadre
Général de Division	Général de Division Aérienne	Vice-Amiral
Général de Brigade	Général de Brigade Aérienne	Contre-Amiral
Colonel	Colonel	Capitaine de Vaisseau
Lieutenant-Colonel	Lieutenant-Colonel	Capitaine de Frégate
Commandant	Commandant	Capitaine de Corvette
Capitaine	Capitaine	Lieutenant de Vaisseau
Lieutenant	Lieutenant	Enseigne de Vaisseau de 1 ère classe
Sous-Lieutenant	Sous-Lieutenant	Enseigne de 2 ère classe

Germany

Army	Air Force	Navy
General	General	Admiral
Generalleutnant	Generalleutnant	Vizeadmiral
Generalmajor	Generalmajor	Konteradmiral
Brigadegeneral	Brigadegeneral	Flotillenadmiral
Oberst	Oberst	Kapitan zur See

Germany (continued)

Army	Air Force	Navy
Oberstleutnant	Oberstleutnant	Fregatten-kapitän
Major	Major	Korvetten-kapitän
Hauptmann	Hauptmann	Kapitän-leutnant
Oberleutnant	Leutnant	Oberleutnant zur See
Leutnant	Oberfahnrich	Leutnant zur See

United Kingdom

Army	Air Force	Navy
Field Marshal	Marshal of the Royal Air Force	Admiral of the Fleet
General	Air Chief Marshal	Admiral
Lieutenant-General	Air Marshal	Vice-Admiral
Major-General	Air Vice-Marshal	Rear-Admiral
Brigadier	Air Commodore	Commodore Admiral
Colonel	Group Captain	Captain RN
Lieutenant-Colonel	Wing Commander	Commander
Major	Squadron Leader	Lieutenant Commander
Captain	Flight Lieutenant	Lieutenant
Lieutenant	Flying Officer	Sub-Lieutenant

MILITARY RANKS (cont.)

USA

Army	Air Force	Navy
General of the Army	General of the Air Force	Fleet Admiral
General	General	Admiral
Lieutenant-General	Lieutenant-General	Vice-Admiral
Major-General	Major-General	Rear-Admiral
Brigadier-General	Brigadier-General	Commodore Admiral
Colonel	Colonel	Captain
Lieutenant-Colonel	Lieutenant-Colonel	Commander
Major	Major	Lieutenant-Commander
Captain	Captain	Lieutenant
First-Lieutenant	First-Lieutenant	Lieutenant Junior Grade

USSR

Army	Air Force	Navy
Marshal of the Soviet Union	Chief Marshal of the Air Force	Admiral of the Fleet of the Soviet Union
Army General	Marshal of the Air Force	Admiral of the Fleet
Colonel-General	Marshal of the Air Force	Admiral
Lieutenant-General	Marshal of the Air Force	Vice-Admiral
Major-General	Marshal of the Air Force	Rear-Admiral
Colonel	Marshal of the Air Force	Captain 1st class
Lieutenant-Colonel	Marshal of the Air Force	Captain 2nd class
Major	Marshal of the Air Force	Captain 3rd class
Captain	Marshal of the Air Force	Captain-Lieutenant

HONOURS: EUROPE

DENMARK

Order of Dannebrog believed to have been founded in 1219 and one of the oldest orders in existence, revived in 1671, with six main classes, Grand Commanders, Knights Grand Cross, Commanders of the First Degree, Commanders, Knights of the First Degree and Knights, and an auxiliary class known as the Badge of Honour.

Order of the Elephant founded in 1462 and revived by King Christian V in 1693, the premier order of Denmark.

FRANCE

Croix du Guerre military award established in 1915 to commemorate individuals mentioned in despatches.

Légion d'Honneur instituted by Napoleon in 1802 to reward distinguished military or civil service, and divided into five classes, Grands Croix, Grands Officiers, Commandeurs, Officiers and Chevaliers.

GERMANY

The Iron Cross established by Frederick William in 1813 as an award for gallantry in action, with various grades of award.

Order of Merit instituted by the Federal German Republic in 1951, and divided into eight classes, Grand Cross (three grades), Large Merit Cross (three grades) and Merit Cross (two grades).

ITALY

Al Merita della Republica Italiana established in 1952, with five classes of award, Grand Cross, Grand Officer, Commander, Officer and Member.

NETHERLANDS

Huisorde van Oranje established in 1905, awarded for outstanding services to the Royal House, corresponds to the Royal Victorian Order in the United Kingdom.

Militaire Willemsorde founded by King William I in 1815, the highest military decoration open to members of the forces of all ranks and to civilians for acts of bravery and devotion to duty.

HONOURS: EUROPE (cont.)

Nederlandsche Leeuw also founded by King William I in 1815, awarded to those of proven patriotism, outstanding zeal and devotion to civil duty, and to those with extraordinary ability in the arts and sciences, open to civilians, members of the military and foreigners, divided into three classes, Grand Cross, Commander and Knight, with an attached brotherhood whose members are nominated for acts of distinction, self-sacrifice and philanthropy.

Orde van Oranje Nassau established in 1892, awarded to Netherlanders and foreigners for distinguished performance to the state or society, open to civilians or members of the forces, divided into five classes, Grand Cross, Grand Officer, Knight Commander, Officer and Knight.

HONOURS: UK

CBE *see* **The Most Excellent Order of the British Empire**

The Distinguished Service Order (DSO) established in 1886, bestowed as a reward for the distinguished service in action of commissioned officers in the Navy, Army and Royal Air Force, extended in 1942 to cover officers of the Merchant Navy.

The George Cross (GC) instituted in 1940 as a reward for gallantry, and conferred upon those responsible for 'acts of the greatest heroism or of the most conspicuous courage in circumstances of extreme danger'.

The Imperial Service Order (ISO) instituted in 1902 to reward members of the Civil Service, with one class of membership, numbers limited to 1,700 in total, 1,100 belonging to the Home Civil Service, and 600 coming from the Overseas Civil Service.

MBE *see* **The Most Excellent Order of the British Empire.**

The Most Ancient and Most Noble Order of the Thistle (KT) an ancient order revived by King James II in 1687, and re-established by Queen Anne in 1703, limited to 16 knights.

The Most Distinguished Order of St Michael and St George founded in 1818 by King George III, conferred upon British subjects for services abroad or in the British Commonwealth, with the motto 'Auspicium melioris aevi' (Token of a better age), and divided into three classes, Knight Grand Cross (GCMG), Knight Commander (KCMG) and Companion (CMG)

The Most Excellent Order of the British Empire an order of knighthood, the first to be granted to both sexes equally, instituted 1917, divided into military and civil divisions in 1918, with five divisions, Knight or Dame Grand Cross (GBE), Knight or Dame Commander (KBE/DBE), Commander (CBE), Officer (OBE) and Member (MBE)

The Most Honourable Order of the Bath founded in 1399, revived by King George in 1725, originally a military order, the civil branch was established in 1847. Women became eligible in 1971. The order has three divisions: Knight or Dame Grand Cross (GCB), Knight or Dame Commander (KCB/DCB), and Companion (CB).

The Most Noble Order of the Garter (KG) instituted in 1348 by Edward III, limited to 24 knights companion only, and with the motto 'Honi soit qui mal y pense' (Shame on him who thinks evil of it).

OBE *see* **The Most Excellent Order of the British Empire**

The Order of Merit (OM) instituted in 1902, with civil and military divisions, and limited to 24 in number.

The Order of the Companions of Honour instituted in 1917 at the same time as the Most Excellent Order of the British Empire. It carries no title or precedence and consists of one class ranking immediately after the first class of the Order of the British Empire. Membership is limited to 65 in number, excluding honorary members.

The Royal Red Cross instituted by Queen Victoria in 1883, the first military order designed solely for women, and conferred upon members of the nursing services for their efforts in the field, and for others undertaking voluntary work on behalf of the sick or wounded or on behalf of the Red Cross.

The Royal Victorian Chain founded in 1902 by King Edward VII, it confers no precedence on the holder, and is largely, although not exclusively, awarded to foreign monarchs.

HONOURS: UK (cont.)

The Royal Victorian Order established by Queen Victoria in 1896, with no limit to the number of members, conferred for services to the sovereign or Royal Family, bestowed upon foreigners as well as British subjects. Women became eligible in 1936.

The Victoria Cross (VC) instituted by Queen Victoria in 1856 to reward conspicuous bravery, and the most highly coveted of British military decorations.

HONOURS: USA

The Bronze Star established in 1944, awarded to members of the forces for acts of heroism or merit and for services beyond the call of duty, but not sufficiently outstanding to merit the Silver Star or Legion of Merit.

The Congressional Medal of Honor instituted in 1861/1862, and first awarded during the American Civil War, conferred upon members of the forces showing exceptional gallantry and bravery in action.

The Distinguished Service Cross instituted in 1918, confined to the army, and awarded to those showing extraordinary heroism in circumstances which do not justify the Congressional Medal of Honour.

The Legion of Merit instituted in 1942, awarded to members of both the United States and foreign forces for distinguished service and meritorious conduct over a period of time.

The Purple Heart first instituted by George Washington in 1782 and reinstituted by Congress in 1932, awarded to those wounded in military action, and bearing the inscription 'For Military Merit'.

The Medal for Merit established by President Roosevelt in 1942 to award civilians of the United States or her allies for distinguished and meritorious service.

The Silver Star first authorised during World War I, it takes precedence over the Legion of Merit.

COMMUNICATION

LANGUAGES: NUMBER OF SPEAKERS

Language families

Estimates of the numbers of speakers in the main language families of the world in the early 1980s. The list includes Japanese and Korean, which are not clearly related to any other languages.

Main language families		Main language families	
Indo-European	2 000 000 000	Nilo-Saharan	30 000 000
Sino-Tibetan	1 040 000 000	Amerindian	25 000 000
Niger-Congo	260 000 000	(North, Central, South America)	
Afro-Asiatic	230 000 000	Uralic	23 000 000
Austronesian	200 000 000	Miao-Yao	7 000 000
Dravidian	140 000 000	Caucasian	6 000 000
Japanese	120 000 000	Indo-Pacific	3 000 000
Altaic	90 000 000	Khoisan	50 000
Austro-Asiatic	60 000 000	Australian aborigine	50 000
Korean	60 000 000	Paleosiberian	25 000
Tai	50 000 000		

Specific languages

The first column gives estimates (in millions) for mother-tongue speakers of the 20 most widely used languages. The second column gives estimates of the total population of all countries where the language has official or semi-official status; these totals are often over-estimates, as only a minority of people in countries where a second language is recognized may actually be fluent in it.

Mother-tongue speakers		Official language populations	
1 Chinese	1 000	1 English	1 400
2 English	350	2 Chinese	1 000
3 Spanish	250	3 Hindi	700
4 Hindi	200	4 Spanish	280
5 Arabic	150	5 Russian	270
6 Bengali	150	6 French	220
7 Russian	150	7 Arabic	170
8 Portuguese	135	8 Portuguese	160
9 Japanese	120	9 Malay	160
10 German	100	10 Bengali	150
11 French	70	11 Japanese	120
12 Panjabi	70	12 German	100
13 Javanese	65	13 Urdu	85
14 Bihari	65	14 Italian	60
15 Italian	60	15 Korean	60
16 Korean	60	16 Vietnamese	60
17 Telugu	55	17 Persian	55
18 Tamil	55	18 Tagalog	50
19 Marathi	50	19 Thai	50
20 Vietnamese	50	20 Turkish	50

SPEAKERS OF ENGLISH

The first column gives figures for countries where English is used as a mother-tongue or first language. (A question-mark indicates that no agreed estimates are available.) The second column gives total population figures (mainly 1990 figures) for countries where English has official or semi-official status as a medium of communication. These totals are likely to bear little correlation with the real use of English in the area.

Country	First language speakers of English	Country population	Country	First language speakers of English	Country population
Anguilla	8 000 −	8 000	Nepal	?	18 910 000 +
Antigua and			New Zealand	3 000 000	3 389 000
Barbuda	80 600 −	80 600	Nigeria	?	119 812 000 +
Australia	14 000 000	17 073 000	Pakistan	?	122 666 000 +
Bahamas	253 000	253 000	Papua New Guinea		3 671 000
Bangladesh	?	113 005 000 +	Philippines		61 480 000
Barbados	257 000 +	257 000 +	St Christopher and		
Belize	100 000 +	189 000 +	Nevis	44 100	44 100
Bermuda	59 300 +	59 300 +	St Lucia	?	151 000 +
Bhutan	?	1 442 000 +	St Vincent and the		
Botswana		1 295 000 −	Grenadines	100 000 +	115 000 +
Brunei		259 000 +	Senegambia		600 000
Cameroon		11 900 000 +	Seychelles		68 700
Canada	17 000 000 +	26 620 000 +	Sierra Leone		4 151 000
Dominica	50 000 +	82 200 −	Singapore	?	2 718 000
Fiji		740 000 +	Solomon Islands		319 000 +
Ghana		15 020 000	South Africa	2 000 000 +	30 797 000
Gibraltar		30 689 +	Sri Lanka	?	17 103 000 +
Grenada	101 000 +	101 000 +	Suriname		411 000
Guyana	700 000 +	756 000	Swaziland		770 000
Hong Kong	?	5 841 000 −	Tanzania		24 403 000
India	?	853 373 000 +	Tonga		96 000 +
Irish Republic	3 515 000	3 515 000	Trinidad and		
Jamaica	2 300 000 +	2 391 000	Tobago	1 233 000	1 233 000
Kenya		24 872 000	Tuvalu		9 100 +
Kiribati		71 100 +	Uganda		16 928 000
Lesotho		1 760 000	UK	57 000 000 +	57 384 000
Liberia		2 595 000	US	215 000 000	230 000 000 +
Malawi		8 831 000	US territories in Pacific		300 000 −
Malaysia (East)		14 300 000	Vanuatu		471 000
Malta		353 000	Western Samoa		165 000 +
Mauritius		1 080 000	Zambia		8 456 000
Montserrat	12 000	12 000	Zimbabwe	200 000 +	9 369 000
Namibia		1 302 000	Other British		
Nauru		9 000 +	territories	30 000 +	30 000 +
			TOTALS	316 015 000 +	1 587 592 000 +

FOREIGN WORDS AND PHRASES

ab initio   (Lat) 'from the beginning'.

à bon marché   (Fr) 'good market'; at a good bargain, cheap.

ab ovo   (Lat) 'from the egg'; from the beginning.

absit omen   (Lat) a superstitious formula; may there be no ill omen (as in a reference just made).

a cappella   (Ital) 'in the style of the chapel'; sung without instrumental accompaniment.

achtung   (Ger) 'Look out!, Take care!'.

acushla   (Ir) term of endearment; darling.

addendum   *plural* **addenda**   (Lat) 'that which is to be added'; supplementary material for a book.

à deux   (Fr) 'for two'; often denotes a dinner or conversation of a romantic nature.

ad hoc   (Lat) 'towards this'; for this special purpose.

ad hominem   (Lat) 'to the man'; appealing not to logic or reason but to personal preferences or feelings.

ad infinitum   (Lat) 'to infinity'; denotes endless repetition.

ad litem   (Lat) 'for the lawsuit'; used of a guardian appointed to act in court (eg because of insanity or insufficient years of the litigant).

ad nauseam   (Lat) 'to the point of sickness'; disgustingly endless or repetitive.

ad referendum   (Lat) 'for reference'; to be further considered.

ad valorem   (Lat) 'to value'; 'according to what it is worth' often used of taxes etc.

advocatus diaboli   (Lat) 'devil's advocate'; person opposing an argument in order to expose any flaws in it.

affaire   (Fr) liaison, intrigue; an incident arousing speculation and scandal.

afflatus   (Lat) 'blowing or breathing'; inspiration (often divine).

aficionado   (Span) 'amateur'; an ardent follower; a 'fan'.

a fortiori   (Lat) 'from the stronger' (argument); denotes the validity and stronger reason of a proposition.

agent provocateur   (Fr) 'provocative agent'; someone who incites others, by pretended sympathy to commit crimes.

aggiornamento   (Ital) 'modernization'; reform (often political).

aide-de-camp   (Fr) 'assistant on the field'; an officer who acts as a confidential personal assistant for an officer of higher rank.

aide-mémoire   (Fr) 'help-memory'; a reminder; memorandum-book; a written summary of a diplomatic agreement.

à la carte   (Fr) 'from the menu'; each dish individually priced.

à la mode   (Fr) 'in fashion, fashionable'; also in cooking, of meat braised and stewed with vegetables; with ice-cream (American English).

al dente   (Ital) 'to the tooth'; culinary term denoting (usually) pasta fully cooked but still firm.

al fresco   (Ital) 'fresh'; painting on fresh or moist plaster; in the fresh, cool or open air.

alma mater   (Lat) 'bountiful mother'; one's former school, college, or university; official college or university song (American English).

aloha   (Hawaiian) 'love'; a salutation, 'hello' or 'goodbye'.

alumnus *plural* **alumni**   (Lat) 'pupil' or 'foster son'; a former pupil or student.

ambiance   (Fr) surroundings, atmosphere.

amende honorable   (Fr) a public apology satisfying the honour of the injured party.

amour-propre   (Fr) 'own love, self-love'; legitimate self-esteem, sometimes exaggerated; vanity, conceit.

ancien régime   (Fr) 'old regime'; a superseded and outdated political system or ruling elite.

angst   (Ger) 'anxiety'; an unsettling feeling produced by awareness of the uncertainties and paradoxes inherent in the state of being human.

anno Domini   (Lat) 'in the year of the Lord'; used in giving dates of the Christian era, counting forward from the year of Christ's birth.

annus mirabilis   (Lat) 'year of wonders'; a remarkably successful or auspicious year.

anschluss   (Ger) 'joining together'; union, especially the political union of Germany and Austria in 1938.

ante-bellum   (Lat) 'before the war'; denotes a period before a specific war, especially the American Civil War.

ante meridiem   (Lat) 'before midday'; between midnight and noon, abbreviated to am.

à point   (Fr) 'into the right condition'; to a nicety, a culinary term.

FOREIGN WORDS AND PHRASES (cont.)

a posteriori   (Lat) 'from the later'; applied to reasoning from experience, from effect to cause.

apparatchik   (Ger) a Communist spy or agent; (humorous) any bureaucratic hack.

appellation contrôlée   (Fr) 'certified name'; used in the labelling of French wines, a guarantee of specified conditions of origin, strength, etc.

après-ski   (Fr) 'after-ski'; pertaining to the evening's amusements after skiing.

a priori   (Lat) 'from the previous'; denotes argument from the cause to the effect; deductive reasoning.

atelier   (Fr) a workshop, an artist's studio.

au contraire   (Fr) 'on the contrary'.

au fait   (Fr) 'to the point'; highly skilled; knowledgeable or familiar with something.

au fond   (Fr) 'at the bottom'; fundamentally.

au naturel   (Fr) 'in the natural state'; naked; also as a culinary term: cooked plainly, raw, or without dressing.

au pair   (Fr) 'on an equal basis'; originally an arrangement of mutual service without payment; now used of a girl (usually foreign) who performs domestic duties for board, lodging and pocket money.

auto-da-fé   (Port) 'act of the faith'; the public declaration or carrying out of a sentence imposed on heretics in Spain and Portugal by the Inquisition, eg burning at the stake.

avant-garde   (Fr) 'front guard'; applied to those in the forefront of an artistic movement.

ave atque vale   (Lat) hail and farewell.

babushka   (Russ) 'grandmother'; granny; a triangular headscarf worn under the chin.

bain-marie   (Fr) 'bath of Mary'; a water-bath; a vessel of boiling water in which another is placed for slow and gentle cooking, or for keeping foods warm.

baksheesh   (Persian) a gift or present of money, particularly in the East (India, Turkey, Egypt, etc).

bal costumé   (Fr) a fancy-dress ball.

banzai   (Jap) a Japanese battle cry, salute to the emperor, or exclamation of joy.

barrio   (Span) 'district, suburb'; a (usually poor) community of Spanish-speaking immigrants (esp American English).

batik   (Javanese) 'painted'; method of producing patterns on fabric by drawing with wax before dyeing.

beau geste   (Fr) 'beautiful gesture'; a magnanimous action.

belle époque   (Fr) 'fine period'; the time of gracious living for the well-to-do immediately preceding World War I.

bête noire   (Fr) 'black beast'; a bugbear; something one especially dislikes.

Bildungsroman   (Ger) 'educational novel'; a novel concerning its hero's early spiritual and emotional development and education.

blasé   (Fr) 'cloyed'; dulled to enjoyment.

blitzkrieg   (Ger) 'lightning war'; a sudden overwhelming attack by ground and air forces; a burst of intense activity.

bodega   (Span) a wine shop that usually sells food as well; a building for wine storage.

bona fides   (Lat) 'good faith'; genuineness.

bonne-bouche   (Fr) 'good mouth'; a delicious morsel eaten at the end of a meal.

bonsai   (Jap) art of growing miniature trees in pots; a dwarf tree grown by this method.

bonvivant   (Fr) 'good living (person)'; one who lives well, particularly enjoying good food and wine; a jovial companion.

bon voyage   (Fr) have a safe and pleasant journey.

bourgeois   (Fr) 'citizen'; a member of the middle class; a merchant; conventional, conservative.

camera obscura   (Lat) 'dark room'; a light-free chamber in which an image of outside objects is thrown upon a screen.

canard   (Fr) 'duck'; a false rumour; a second wing fitted as a horizontal stabilizer near the nose of an aircraft.

carpe diem   (Lat) 'sieze the day'; enjoy the pleasures of the present moment while they last.

carte blanche   (Fr) 'blank sheet of paper'; freedom of action.

FOREIGN WORDS AND PHRASES (cont.)

casus belli   (Lat) 'occasion of war'; whatever sparks off or justifies a war or quarrel.

cause célèbre   (Fr) a very notable or famous trial; a notorious controversy.

caveat emptor   (Lat) 'let the buyer beware'; warns the buyer to examine carefully the article he is about to purchase.

c'est la vie   (Fr) 'that's life'; denotes fatalistic resignation.

chacun à son goût   (Fr) 'each to his own taste'; implies surprise at another's choice.

chambré   (Fr) 'put into a room'; (of red wine) at room temperature.

chargé-d'affaires   (Fr) a diplomatic agent of lesser rank; an ambassador's deputy.

chef d'oeuvre   (Fr) a masterpiece, the best piece of work by a particular artist, writer, etc.

chicano   (Span) *mejicano* 'Mexican'; or an American of Mexican descent.

chutzpah   (Yiddish) effrontery, nerve to do or say outrageous things.

cinéma-vérité   (Fr) 'cinema truth'; realism in films usually sought by photographic scenes of real life.

cinquecento   (Ital) 'five hundred'; of the Italian art and literature of the 16th century Renaissance period.

circa   (Lat) 'surrounding'; of dates and numbers, approximately.

cliché   (Fr) 'stereotype printing block'; the impression made by a die in any soft metal; a hackneyed phrase or concept.

cognoscente *plural* **cognoscenti**   (Lat) 'one who knows'; one who professes critical knowledge of art, music, etc; a connoisseur.

coitus interruptus   (Lat) 'interrupted intercourse'; coitus intentionally interrupted by withdrawal before semen is ejaculated; anticlimax when something ends prematurely.

comme il faut   (Fr) 'as it is necessary'; correct; genteel.

compos mentis   (Lat) 'having control of one's mind'; sane.

contra mundum   (Lat) 'against the world'; denotes defiant perseverance despite universal criticism.

cordon bleu   (Fr) 'blue ribbon'; denotes food cooked to a very high standard; a dish made with ham and cheese and a white sauce.

coup de foudre   (Fr) 'flash of lightning'; a sudden and astonishing happening; love at first sight.

coup de grâce   (Fr) 'blow of mercy'; a finishing blow to end pain; a decisive action which ends a troubled enterprise.

coup d'état   (Fr) 'blow of state'; a violent overthrow of a government or subversive stroke of state policy.

coupé   (Fr) 'cut'; (usually) two-door motor-car with sloping roof.

crème de la crème   (Fr) 'cream of the cream'; the very best.

cuisine minceur   (Fr) 'slenderness cooking'; a style of cooking characterized by imaginative use of light, simple, low-fat ingredients.

cul-de-sac   (Fr) 'bottom of the bag'; a road closed at one end.

cum grano salis   (Lat) with a grain (pinch) of salt.

curriculum vitae   (Lat) 'course of life'; denotes a summary of someone's educational qualifications and work experience for presenting to a prospective employer.

décolleté   (Fr) 'with bared neck and shoulders'; with neck uncovered; (of dress) low cut.

de facto   (Lat) 'from the fact'; in fact, actually, irrespective of what is legally recognized.

de gustibus non est disputandum   (Lat) (often in English shortened for convenience to *de gustibus*) 'there is no disputing about tastes'; there is no sense in challenging people's preferences.

déjà vu   (Fr) 'already seen'; in any of the arts, original material; an illusion of having experienced something before; something seen so often it has become tedious.

de jure   (Lat) 'according to law'; denotes the legal or theoretical position, which may not correspond with reality.

delirium tremens   (Lat) 'trembling delirium'; psychotic condition caused by alcoholism, involving anxiety, shaking, hallucinations, etc.

deo volente   (Lat) 'God willing'; a sort of good-luck talisman.

de rigueur   (Fr) 'of strictness'; compulsory; required by strict etiquette.

derrière   (Fr) 'behind'; the buttocks.

déshabillé   (Fr) 'undressed', state of being only partially dressed, or of being casually dressed.

FOREIGN WORDS AND PHRASES (cont.)

de trop   (Fr) 'of too much'; superfluous; in the way.

deus ex machina   (Lat) 'a god from a machine'; a contrived solution to a difficulty in a plot.

distingué   (Fr) 'distinguished'; having an aristocratic or refined demeanour; striking.

dolce far niente   (Ital) 'sweet doing nothing'; denotes the pleasure of idleness.

doppelgänger   (Ger) 'double goer'; a ghostly duplicate of a living person, a wraith; someone who looks exactly like someone else.

double entendre   (Fr) 'double meaning'; ambiguity (normally with indecent connotations).

doyen   (Fr) 'dean'; most distinguished member or representative by virtue of seniority, experience, and often also excellence.

droit de seigneur   (Fr) 'the lord's right'; originally the alleged right of a feudal superior to take the virginity of a vassal's bride; any excessive claim imposed on a subordinate.

dummkopf   (Ger) 'dumb-head'; blockhead; idiot.

echt   (Ger) 'real, genuine'; denotes authenticity, typicality.

eheu fugaces   (Lat); opening of a quotation (Horace *Odes* II, XIV, 1–2) 'alas! the fleeting years slip away'; bemoans the brevity of human existence.

élan   (Fr) 'dash, rush, bound'; flair, flamboyance.

el dorado   (Span) 'the gilded man'; the golden land (or city) imagined by the Spanish conquerors of America; any place which offers the opportunity of acquiring fabulous wealth.

embarras de richesse   (Fr) 'embarrassment of wealth'; a perplexing amount of wealth or an abundance of any kind.

embonpoint   (Fr) *en bon point* 'in fine form'; well-fed, stout, plump.

emeritus   (Lat) 'having served one's time'; eg of a retired professor, honourably discharged from a public duty; holding a position on an honorary basis only.

éminence grise   (Fr) someone exerting power through their influence over a superior.

enfant terrible   (Fr) 'terrible child'; a precocious child whose sayings embarrass its parents; a person whose behaviour is indiscreet, embarrassing to his associates.

ennui   (Fr) world-weary listlessness, boredom.

en passant   (Fr) 'in passing'; by the way, incidentally; applied in chess to the taking of a pawn that has just moved two squares as if it had moved only one.

en route   (Fr) on the way, on the road; let us go.

entente   (Fr) 'understanding'; a friendly agreement between nations.

épater les bourgeois   (Fr) 'shock the middle class'; to disconcert the prim and proper; commonly used of artistic productions which defy convention.

erratum *plural* **errata**   (Lat) an error in writing or printing.

ersatz   (Ger) 'replacement, substitute'; connotes a second-rate substitute; a supplementary reserve from which waste can be made good.

et al   (Lat) *et alii* 'and other things'; used to avoid giving a complete and possibly over-lengthy list of all items eg of authors.

et tu, Brute   (Lat) 'you too, Brutus' (Caesar's alleged exclamation when he saw Brutus among his assassins); denotes surprise and dismay that a supposed friend has joined in a conspiracy against one.

eureka   (Gr) *heureka* 'I have found!'; cry of triumph at a discovery.

ex cathedra   (Lat) 'from the seat'; from the chair of office; authoratively, judicially.

ex gratia   (Lat) 'from favour'; of a payment; one that is made as a favour, without any legal obligation and without admitting legal liability.

ex officio   (Lat) 'from office, by virtue of office'; used as a reason for membership of a body.

ex parte   (Lat) 'from (one) part'; 'from (one) side'; on behalf of one side only in legal proceedings; partial, prejudiced.

fait accompli   (Fr) 'accomplished fact'; already done or settled, and therefore irreversible.

fata Morgana   (Ital) a striking kind of mirage, attributed to witchcraft.

FOREIGN WORDS AND PHRASES (cont.)

fatwa   (Arabic) 'the statement of a formal legal opinion'; a formal legal opinion delivered by an Islamic religious leader.

faute de mieux   (Fr) 'for lack of anything better'.

faux ami   (Fr) 'false friend'; a word in a foreign language that does not mean what it appears to.

faux-naïf   (Fr) 'falsely naive'; seeming or pretending to be unsophisticated, innocent, etc.

faux pas   (Fr) 'false step'; a social blunder.

femme fatale   (Fr) 'fatal woman'; an irresistibly attractive woman who brings difficulties or disasters on men; a siren.

fidus Achates   (Lat) 'the faithful Achates' (Aeneas' friend); a loyal follower.

film noir   (Fr) 'black film'; a bleak and pessimistic film.

fin de siècle   (Fr) 'end of the century'; of the end of the 19th-c in Western culture or of an era; decadent.

floruit   (Lat) 'he or she flourished'; denotes a period during which a person lived.

fons et origo   (Lat) 'the source and origin'.

force de frappe   (Fr) 'strike force'; equivalent of the 'independent nuclear deterrent'.

force majeure   (Fr) 'superior force'; an unforseeable or uncontrollable course of events, excusing one from fulfilling a contract, a legal term.

führer   (Ger) 'leader, guide'; an insulting term for anyone bossily asserting authority.

gastarbeiter   (Ger) 'guest-worker'; an immigrant worker, especially one who does menial work.

gauleiter   (Ger) 'district leader'; a chief official of a district under the Nazi régime; an overbearing wielder of petty authority.

gemütlich   (Ger) amiable, comfortable, cosy.

gestalt   (Ger) 'form, shape'; original whole or unit, more than the sum of its parts.

gesundheit   (Ger) 'health'; 'your health', said to someone who has just sneezed.

glasnost   (Russ) 'publicity'; the policy of openness and forthrightness followed by the Soviet government, initiated by Mikhail Gorbachev.

gnothi seauton   (Gr) 'know thyself'.

götterdämmerung   (Ger) 'twilight of the gods'; the downfall of any once powerful system.

goy plural **goys** or **goyim**   (Hebrew) non-Jewish, a gentile.

grand mal   (Fr) 'large illness'; a violently convulsive form of epilepsy.

grand prix   (Fr) 'great prize'; any of several international motor races; any competition of similar importance in other sports.

gran turismo   (Ital) 'great touring, touring on a grand scale'; a motor car designed for high speed touring in luxury (abbreviation GT).

gratis   (Lat) *gratiis* 'kindness, favour'; free of charge.

gravitas   (Lat) 'weight'; seriousness, weight of demeanour, avoidance of unseemly frivolity.

gringo   (Mexican-Spanish) 'foreigner'.

guru   (Hindi) a spiritual teacher; a revered instructor or mentor.

habeas corpus   (Lat) 'you should have the body'; a writ to a jailer to produce a prisoner in person, and to state the reasons for detention; maintains the right of the subject to protection from unlawful imprisonment.

haiku   (Jap) 'amusement poem'; a Japanese poem consisting of only three lines, containing respectively five, seven, and five syllables.

hajj   (Arabic) 'pilgrimage'; the Muslim pilgrimage to Mecca.

haka   (Maori) a Maori ceremonial war dance; a similar dance performed by New Zealanders eg before a rugby game.

halal   (Arabic) 'lawful'; meat from an animal killed in strict accordance with Muslim law.

haute couture   (Fr) 'higher tailoring'; fashionable, expensive dress designing and tailoring.

haut monde   (Fr) 'high world'; high society, fashionable society, composed of the aristocracy and the wealthy.

hic jacet   (Lat) 'here lies'; the first words of an epitaph; memorial inscription.

hoi polloi   (Gr) 'the many'; the rabble, the vulgar.

FOREIGN WORDS AND PHRASES (cont.)

hombre   (Span) 'man'.

honoris causa   (Lat) 'for the sake of honour'; a token of respect; used to designate honorary university degrees.

hors concours   (Fr) 'out of the competition'; not entered for a contest; unequalled.

ibidem   (Lat) 'in the same place'; used in footnotes to indicate that the same book (or chapter) has been cited previously.

id   (Lat) 'it'; the sum total of the primitive instinctive forces in an individual.

idée fixe   (Fr) 'a fixed idea'; an obsession.

idem   (Lat) 'the same'.

ikebana   (Jap) 'living flowers'; the Japanese art of flower arrangement.

in absentia   (Lat) 'in absence'; used for occasions, such as the receiving of a degree award, when the recipient would normally be present.

in camera   (Lat) 'in the room'; in a private room, in secret.

incommunucado   (Span) 'unable to communicate'; deprived of the right to communicate with others.

in extremis   (Lat) 'in the last'; at the point of death; in desperate circumstances.

in flagrante dilecto   (Lat) 'with the crime blazing'; in the very act of committing the crime.

infra dig   (Lat) 'below dignity'; below one's dignity.

in loco parentis   (Lat) 'in place of a parent'.

in shallah   (Arabic) 'if God wills'; *see* **deo volente**.

inter alia   (Lat) 'among other things'; used to show that a few examples have been chosen from many possibilities.

in vitro   (Lat) 'in glass'; in the test tube.

ipso facto   (Lat) 'by the fact itself'; thereby.

je ne sais quoi   (Fr) 'I do not know what'; an indefinable something.

jihad   'struggle'; a holy war undertaken by Muslims against unbelievers.

Jugendstil   (Ger) 'youth style'; the German term for art nouveau.

kamikaze   (Jap) 'divine wind'; Japanese pilots making a suicide attack; any reckless, potentially self-destructive, act.

kanaka   (Hawaiian) 'man'; used by Europeans (and Australians) to mean South Sea islander.

karaoke   (Jap) 'empty orchestra'; in bars, clubs, etc members of the public sing a solo to a recorded backing.

karma   (Sanskrit) 'act'; the concept that the actions in a life determine the future condition of an individual.

kibbutz   (Hebrew) A Jewish communal agricultural settlement in Israel.

kitsch   (Ger) 'rubbish'; work in any of the arts that is pretentious and inferior or in bad taste.

kvetch   (Yiddish) 'complain, whine (incessantly)'.

la dolce vita   (Ital) 'the sweet life'; the name of a film made by Frederico Fellini in 1960 showing a life of wealth, pleasure and self-indulgence.

laissez-faire   (Fr) 'let do'; a general principle of non-interference.

lebensraum   (Ger) 'life space'; room to live; used by Hitler to justify his acquisition of land for Germany.

leitmotiv   (Ger) 'leading motive'; a recurrent theme.

lèse majesté   (Fr) 'injured majesty'; offence against the sovereign power; treason.

lingua franca   (Ital) 'Frankish language'; originally a mixed Italian trading language used in the Levant, subsequently any language chosen as a means of communication among speakers of different languages.

locum tenens   (Lat) 'place holder'; a deputy or substitute, especially for a doctor or a clergyman.

macho   (Mexican/Span) 'male'; originally a positive term denoting masculinity or virility, it has come in English to describe an ostentatious virility.

magnum opus   (Lat) 'great work'; a person's greatest achievement, especially a literary work.

maharishi   (Sanskrit) a Hindu sage or spiritual leader, a guru.

FOREIGN WORDS AND PHRASES (cont.)

mañana   (Span) 'tomorrow'; an unspecified time in the future.

mea culpa   (Lat) 'through my fault'; originally part of the Latin mass; an admission of fault and an expression of repentance.

memento mori   (Lat) 'remember that you must die'; an object, such as a skull, or anything to remind one of mortality.

ménage à trois   (Fr) 'household of three'; a household comprised of a husband and wife and the lover of one of them.

mens sana in corpore sano   (Lat) 'a sound mind in a sound body' (Juvenal X, 356); the guiding rule of the 19th-c English educational system.

mirabile dictu   (Lat) 'wonderful to tell'; an expression of (sometimes ironic) amazement.

modus operandi   (Lat) 'mode of working'; the characteristic methods employed by a particular criminal.

modus vivendi   (Lat)'mode of living'; an arrangement or compromise by means of which those who differ may get on together for a time.

mot juste   (Fr) 'exact word'; the word which fits the context exactly.

multum in parvo   (Lat) 'much in little'; a large amount in a small space.

mutatis mutandis   (Lat) 'with the necessary changes made'.

négociant   (Fr) 'merchant, trader'; often used for *négociant en vins* 'wine merchant'.

ne plus ultra   (Lat) 'not more beyond'; extreme perfection.

netsuke   (Jap) a small Japanese carved ornament used to fasten small objects, eg a purse, tobacco pouch, or medicine box, to the sash of a kimono. They are now collector's pieces.

noblesse oblige   (Fr) 'nobility obliges'; rank imposes obligations.

non sequitur   (Lat) 'it does not follow'; a conclusion that does not follow logically from the premise; a remark that has no relation to what has gone before.

nostalgie de la boue   (Fr) 'hankering for mud'; a craving for a debased physical life without civilized refinements.

nota bene   (Lat) 'observe well, note well'; often abbreviated NB.

nouveau riche   (Fr) 'new rich'; one who has only lately acquired wealth (without acquiring good taste).

nouvelle cuisine   (Fr) 'new cooking'; a style of simple French cookery which aims to produce dishes that are light and healthy, utilizing fresh fruit and vegetables, and avoiding butter and cream.

nouvelle vague   (Fr) 'new wave'; a movement in the French cinema aiming at imaginative quality films.

obiter dictum   (Lat) 'something said in passing'; originally a legal term for something said by a trial judge which was incidental to the case in question.

origami   (Jap) 'paper-folding'; Japanese art of folding paper to make shapes suggesting birds, boats, etc.

O tempora! O mores!   (Lat) 'O the times! O the manners' (Cicero *In Catalinam*) a condemnation of present times, as contrasted with a past which is seen as golden.

outré   'gone to excess'; beyond what is customary or proper; eccentric.

pace   (Lat) 'peace'; by your leave (indicating polite disagreement).

panem et circenses   (Lat) 'bread and circuses, or food and the big match' (Juvenal *Satires* X, 80); amusements which divert the populace from unpleasant realities.

passim   (Lat) 'everywhere, throughout'; dispersed through a book.

per capita   (Lat) 'by heads'; per head of the population in statistical contexts.

perestroika   (Russ) 'reconstruction'; restructuring of an organization.

persona non grata   (Lat) one who is not welcome or favoured (originally a term in diplomacy).

pied à terre   (Fr) 'foot to the ground'; a flat, small house, etc kept for temporary or occasional accommodation.

plus ça change   (Fr) abbreviated form of **plus ça change, plus ça la même chose** 'The more things change, the more they stay the same'; a comment on the unchanging nature of the world.

post meridiem   (Lat) 'after midday, after noon.'

FOREIGN WORDS AND PHRASES (cont.)

post mortem   (Lat) 'after death'; an examination of a body in order to determine the cause of death; an after-the-event discussion.

poule de luxe   (Fr) 'luxurious hen'; a sexually attractive promiscuous young woman; a prostitute.

pour encourager les autres   (Fr) 'to encourage the others' (Voltaire *Candide*, on the execution of Admiral Byng); exemplary punishment.

premier cru   (Fr) 'first growth'; wine of the highest quality in a system of classification.

prêt-à-porter   (Fr) 'ready to wear'; refers to 'designer' clothes that are made in standard sizes as opposed to made-to-measure clothes.

prima donna   (Ital) 'first lady'; leading female singer in an opera; a person who is temperamental and hard to please.

prima facie   (Lat) 'at first sight'; a legal term for evidence that is assumed to be true unless disproved by other evidence.

primus inter pares   (Lat) 'first among equals.'

prix fixe   (Fr) 'fixed price'; used of a meal in a restaurant offered at a set price for a restricted choice.

pro bono publico   (Lat) 'for the public good'; something done for no fee.

quid pro quo   (Lat) 'something for something'; something given or taken as equivalent to another, often as retaliation.

quod erat demonstrandum   (Lat) 'which was to be shown'; often used in its abbreviated form **qed.**

raison d'être   (Fr) 'reason for existence'.

rara avis   (Lat) 'rare bird' (Juvenal, VI, 165); something or someone remarkable and unusual.

realpolitik   (Ger) 'politics of realism'; practical politics based on the realities and necessities of life, rather than moral or ethical ideas.

recherché   (Fr) 'sought out'; carefully chosen; particularly choice; rare or exotic.

reculer pour mieux sauter   (Fr) 'move backwards in order to jump better'; a strategic withdrawal to wait for a better opportunity.

reductio ad absurdum   (Lat) 'reduction to absurdity'; originally used in logic to mean the proof of a proposition by proving the falsity of its contradictory; the application of a principle so strictly that it is carried to absurd lengths.

répondez, s'il vous plaît   (Fr) 'reply, please'; in English mainly in its abbreviated form, **RSVP**, on invitations.

revenons à nos moutons   (Fr) 'let us return to our sheep'; let us get back to our subject.

rijsttafel   (Dutch) 'rice table'; an Indonesian rice dish served with a variety of foods.

risqué   (Fr) 'risky, hazardous'; audaciously bordering on the unseemly.

rus in urbe   (Lat) 'the country in the town' (Martial XII, 57, 21); the idea of country charm in the centre of a city.

salus populi suprema est lex   (Lat) 'let the warfare of the people be the chief law' (Cicero *De Legibus* III, 3).

samizdat   (Russ) 'self-publisher'; the secret printing and distribution of banned literature in the USSR and other Eastern European countries under Communist rule.

sanctum sanctorum   (Lat) 'holy of holies'; the innermost chamber of the temple, where the Ark of the Covenant was kept; any private room reserved for personal use.

sang froid   (Fr) 'cold flood'; self possession; coolness under stress.

savoir faire   (Fr) 'knowing what to do'; knowing what to do and how to do it in any situation.

schadenfreude   (Ger) 'hurt joy'; pleasure in others' misfortunes.

shlimazel   (Yiddish) 'bad luck'; a persistently unlucky person.

shlock   (Yiddish) 'broken or damaged goods'; inferior, shoddy.

shmaltz   (Yiddish) 'melted fat, grease'; showy sentimentality, particularly in writing, music, art, etc.'

shmuck   (Yiddish) 'penis'; a (male) stupid person.

shogun   (Jap) 'leader of the army'; ruler of feudal Japan.

FOREIGN WORDS AND PHRASES (cont.)

sic   (Lat) 'so, thus'; used in brackets within printed matter to show that the original is faithfully reproduced even if incorrect.

sic transit gloria mundi   (Lat) 'so passes away earthly glory'.

sine die   (Lat) 'without a day'; the adjournment of a meeting (often in court), indicating that no day has been fixed for its resumption; an indefinite adjournment.

sine qua non   (Lat) 'without which not'; an indispensable condition.

sotto voce   (Ital) 'below the voice'; in an undertone; aside.

status quo   (Lat) 'the state in which'; the existing condition.

sub judice   (Lat) 'under a judge'; under consideration by a judge or a court of law.

subpoena   (Lat) 'under penalty'; a writ commanding attendance in court.

sub rosa   (Lat) 'under the rose'; in secret, privately.

succès de scandale   (Fr) 'success of scandal'; the success of a book, film, etc due not to merit but to its connection with, or reference to, a scandal.

summa cum laude   (Lat) 'with the highest praise'; with great distinction; the highest class of degree award that can be gained by a US college student.

summum bonum   (Lat) 'the chief good'.

table d'hôte   (Fr) 'host's table'; a set meal at a fixed price. Compare **prix fixe**.

tabula rasa   (Lat) 'scraped table'; a cleaned tablet; a mind not yet influenced by outside impressions and experience.

tai chi   (Chin) 'great art of boxing'; a system of exercise, and self-defence in which good use of balance and co-ordination allows effort to be minimized.

tempus fugit   (Lat) 'time flies'; delay cannot be tolerated.

terra incognita   (Lat) 'unknown land'; an unknown land (so marked on early maps); an area of study about which very little is known.

touché   (Fr) 'touched'; claiming or acknowledging a hit made in fencing; claiming or acknowledging a point scored in an argument.

tour de force   (Fr) 'turning movement'; feat of strength or skill.

trompe l'oeuil   (Fr) 'deceives the eye'; an appearance of reality achieved by the use of perspective and detail in painting, architecture, etc.

tsunami   (Jap) 'wave in harbour'; a wave generated by movement of the earth's surface underwater; commonly (and erroneously) called a 'tidal wave'.

übermensch   (Ger) 'over-person'; superman.

ultra vires   (Lat) 'beyond strength, beyond powers'; beyond one's power or authority.

urbi et orbi   (Lat) 'to the city and the world'; used of the Pope's pronouncements; to everyone.

vade-mecum   (Lat) 'go with me'; a handbook, pocket companion.

vin du pays   (Fr) 'wine of the country'; a locally produced wine for everyday consumption.

vis-à-vis   (Fr) 'face to face'; one who faces or is opposite another; in relation to.

viva voce   (Lat) 'with the living voice'; in speech, orally; an oral examination, particularly at a university (commonly 'viva' alone).

volte-face   (Fr) 'turn-face'; a sudden and complete change in opinion or in views expressed.

vox populi   (Lat); 'voice of the people'; public or popular opinion.

weltschmerz   (Ger) 'world pain'; sympathy with universal misery; thoroughgoing pessimism.

wunderkind   (Ger) 'wonder-child'; a 'child prodigy'; one who shows great talent and/or achieves great success at an early (or comparatively early) age.

zeitgeist   (Ger) 'time-spirit'; the spirit of the age.

ALPHABETS

There is no agreement over the use of a single transliteration system in the case of Hebrew.
The equivalents given below are widely used; but several other possibilities can be found.

HEBREW

Letter	Name	Trans-literation
א	'aleph	'
ב	beth	b
ג	gimel	g
ד	daleth	d
ה	he	h
ו	waw	w
ז	zayin	z
ח	heth	h
ט	teth	t
י	yodh	y, j
כ ך	kaph	k
ל	lamedh	l
מ ם	mem	m
נ ן	nun	n
ס	samekh	s
ע	'ayin	'
פ ף	pe	p, f
צ ץ	saddhe	s
ק	qoph	q
ר	resh	r
ש	shin	sh, š
ש	śin	ś
ת	taw	t

GREEK

Letter	Name	Trans-literation
A α	alpha	a
B β	beta	b
Γ γ	gamma	g
Δ δ	delta	d
E ε	epsilon	e
Z ζ	zeta	z
H η	eta	e, ē
Θ θ	theta	th
I ι	iota	i
K κ	kappa	k
Λ λ	lambda	l
M μ	mu	m
N ν	nu	n
Ξ ξ	xi	x
O o	omicron	o
Π π	pi	p
P ϱ	rho	r
Σ σ,ς	sigma	s
T τ	tau	t
Y υ	upsilon	y
Φ φ	phi	ph
X χ	chi	ch, kh
Ψ ψ	psi	ps
Ω ω	omega	o, ō

NATO ALPHABET

Letter	Code name	Pronunciation
A	Alpha	AL-FAH
B	Bravo	BRAH-VOH
C	Charlie	CHAR-LEE
D	Delta	DELL-TAH
E	Echo	ECK-OH
F	Foxtrot	FOKS-TROT
G	Golf	GOLF
H	Hotel	HOH-TELL
I	India	IN-DEE-AH
J	Juliet	JEW-LEE-ETT
K	Kilo	KEY-LOH
L	Lima	LEE-MAH
M	Mike	MIKE
N	November	NO-VEM-BER
O	Oscar	OSS-CAH
P	Papa	PAH-PAH
Q	Quebec	KEY-BECK
R	Romeo	ROW-ME-OH
S	Sierra	SEE-AIR-RAH
T	Tango	TAN-GO
U	Uniform	YOU-NEE-FORM
V	Victor	VIK-TAH
W	Whiskey	WISS-KEY
X	Xray	ECKS-RAY
Y	Yankee	YANG-KEY
Z	Zulu	ZOO-LOO

MORSE & BRAILLE

Letters	Morse	Braille
A	·—	·
B	—···	:·
C	—·—·	··
D	—··	:·
E	·	··
F	··—·	:·
G	——·	::
H	····	:·
I	··	·
J	·———	·:
K	—·—	··
L	·—··	··
M	——	··
N	—·	:·
O	———	··
P	·——·	:·
Q	——·—	::
R	·—·	:·
S	···	··
T	—	::
U	··—	··
V	···—	··
W	·——	·:
X	—··—	::
Y	—·——	::
Z	——··	:·

TYPEFACES

The typefaces shown are modern versions of the main groups under which most typefaces may be classified. The dates indicating the introduction of each group are approximate.

Gothic

𝔄𝔅ℭ𝔇𝔈𝔉𝔊𝔥𝔦𝔍𝔨𝔩𝔐𝔫𝔒𝔭𝔔𝔯𝔰𝔗𝔘𝔜𝔚𝔵𝔶𝔷
abcdefghijklmnopqrstuvwxyz
15 & 7pt Old English Text (c.1450)

Sans Serif

ABCDEFGHIJKLMNOPQRSTUVWXYZ
abcdefghijklmnopqrstuvwxyz
15 & 7pt Univers (c.1816)

Venetian

ABCDEFGHIJKLMNOPQRSTUVWXYZ
abcdefghijklmnopqrstuvwxyz
15 & 7pt Centaur (c.1470)

Egyptian

ABCDEFGHIJKLMNOPQRSTUVWXYZ
abcdefghijklmnopqrstuvwxyz
12 & 7pt Rockwell (c.1830)

Old Face

ABCDEFGHIJKLMNOPQRSTUVWXYZ
abcdefghijklmnopqrstuvwxyz
15 & 7pt Caslon Old Face (c.1495)

Old Style

ABCDEFGHIJKLMNOPQRSTUVWXYZ
abcdefghijklmnopqrstuvwxyz
15 & 7pt Goudy Old Style (c.1850)

Transitional

ABCDEFGHIJKLMNOPQRSTUVWXYZ
abcdefghijklmnopqrstuvwxyz
15 & 7pt Baskerville (c.1761)

Newspaper

ABCDEFGHIJKLMNOPQRSTUVWXYZ
abcdefghijklmnopqrstuvwxyz
12pt Century Bold & Century Roman (c.1890)

Modern

ABCDEFGHIJKLMNOPQRSTUVWXYZ
abcdefghijklmnopqrstuvwxyz
15 & 7pt Bodoni (c.1765)

Contemporary

ABCDEFGHIJKLMNOPQRSTUVWXYZ
abcdefghijklmnopqrstuvwxyz
12 & 7pt Times New Roman (c.1932)

FIRST NAME MEANINGS IN THE UK AND USA

The meanings of the most popular first names in the UK and USA are given below, along with a few other well-known names.

Name	Original meaning
Aaron	high mountain (*Hebrew*)
Adam	redness (*Hebrew*)
Alan	harmony (*Celtic*)
Albert	nobly bright (*Germanic*)
Alexander	defender of men (*Greek*)
Alison	*French diminutive of* Alice; of noble kind
Amanda	fit to be loved (*Latin*)
Amy	loved (*French*)
Andrea	*female form of* Andrew
Andrew	manly (*Greek*)
Angela	messenger, angel (*Greek*)
Ann(e)	*English form of* Hannah
Anthony	*Roman family name*
April	name of the month
Arthur	?bear, stone (*Celtic*)
Barbara	strange, foreign (*Greek*)
Barry	spear, javelin (*Celtic*)

Name	Original meaning
Beatrice	bringer of joy (*Latin*)
Benjamin	son of my right hand (*Hebrew*)
Bernard	bear + brave (*Germanic*)
Beth	*pet form of* Elizabeth
Betty	*pet form of* Elizabeth
Bill/Billy	*pet form of* William
Bob	*pet form of* Robert
Brandi	*variant of* Brandy, *from the common noun*
Brandon	*place name*; broom-covered hill (*Germanic*)
Brian	?hill (?*Celtic*)
Candice	*meaning unknown*
Carl	man, husbandman (*Germanic*)
Carol(e)	*forms of* Caroline, *Italian female form of* Charles
Catherine	pure (*Greek*)

FIRST NAME MEANINGS (cont.)

Name   Original meaning

Charles   man, husbandman (*Germanic*)
Christine   *French form of* Christina *ultimately from* Christian; anointed
Christopher   carrier of Christ (*Greek*)
Claire   bright, shining (*Latin*)
Colin   *form of* Nicholas
Craig   rock (*Celtic*)
Crystal   *female use of the common noun*
Daniel   God is my judge (*Hebrew*)
Danielle   *female form of* Daniel
Darren   *Irish surname*
Darryl   *surname; uncertain origin*
David   beloved, friend (*Hebrew*)
Dawn   *female use of the common noun*
Dean   *surname*; valley *or* leader
Deborah   bee (*Hebrew*)
Dennis   of Dionysius (*Greek*), *the god of wine*
Derek   *form of* Theodoric; ruler of the people (*Germanic*)
Diane   *French form of* Diana; divine (*Latin*)
Donald   world mighty (*Gaelic*)
Donna   lady (*Latin*)
Doreen   *from* Dora, *a short form of* Dorothy; gift of God
Doris   woman from Doris (*Greek*)
Dorothy   gift of God (*Greek*)
Ebony   *female use of the common noun*
Edward   property guardian (*Germanic*)
Eileen   *Irish form of* ?Helen
Elizabeth   oath/perfection of God (*Hebrew*)
Emily   *Roman family name*
Emma   all-embracing (*Germanic*)
Eric   ruler of all (*Norse*)
Erica   *female form of* Eric
Eugenie   *French form of* Eugene; well-born (*Greek*)
Frank   *pet form of* Francis; Frenchman
Frederick   peaceful ruler (*Germanic*)
Gail   *pet form of* Abigail; father rejoices (*Hebrew*)
Gareth   gentle (*Welsh*)
Gary   *US place name*
Gavin   *Scottish form of* Gawain; hawk + white (*Welsh*)
Gemma   gem (*Italian*)
Geoffrey   ?peace (*Germanic*)
George   husbandman, farmer (*Greek*)
Graham   *Germanic place name*
Hannah   grace, favour (*Hebrew*)
Harold   army power/ruler (*Germanic*)
Harry   *pet form of* Henry; home ruler (*Germanic*)

Name   Original meaning

Hayley   *English place name*; hay-meadow
Heather   *plant name*
Helen   bright/shining one (*Greek*)
Ian   *modern Scottish form of* John
Irene   peace (*Greek*)
Jacqueline   *French female form of* Jacques (James)
James   *Latin form of* Jacob; one who takes by the heel (*Hebrew*)
Jane   *from Latin* Johanna, *female form of* John
Janet   *diminutive form of* Jane
Jason   *form of* Joshua; Jehovah is salvation (*Hebrew*)
Jeffrey   *US spelling of* Geoffrey
Jean   *French form of* Johanna, *from* John
Jennifer   fair/white + yielding/smooth (*Celtic*)
Jeremy   *English form of* Jeremiah; Jehova exalts (*Hebrew*)
Jessica   he beholds (*Hebrew*)
Joan   *contracted form of* Johanna, *from* John
Joanne   *French form of* Johanna, *from* John
John   Jehovah has been gracious (*Hebrew*)
Jonathan   Jehovah's gift (*Hebrew*)
Joseph   Jehovah adds (*Hebrew*)
Joyce   ?joyful (*?Latin*)
Julie   *French female form of Latin* Julius; descended from Jove
Karen   *Danish form of* Katarina (Catherine)
Katherine   *US spelling of* Catherine
Kathleen   *English form of Irish* Caitlin (*from* Catharine)
Kelly   *Irish surname*; warlike one
Kenneth   *English form of Gaelic*; fair one *or* fire-sprung
Kerry   *Irish place name*
Kevin   handsome at birth (*Irish*)
Kimberly   *South African place name*
Lakisha   La + ?Aisha; woman (*Arabic*)
Latoya   La + *form of* Tonya (Antonia)
Laura   bay, laurel (*Latin*)
Lauren   *diminutive of* Laura
Lee   *Germanic place name*; wood, clearing
Leslie   *Scottish place name*
Lilian   lily (*Italian*)
Linda   serpent (symbol of wisdom) (*Germanic*)
Lindsay   *Scottish place name*
Lisa   *pet form of* Elizabeth
Margaret   pearl (*Greek*)
Marjorie   *from* Marguerite, *French form of* Margaret
Mark   *English form of* Marcus, *from* Mars, *god of war*

FIRST NAME MEANINGS (cont.)

Martin   from Mars, *god of war* (*Latin*)
Mary   Greek form of Miriam (*Hebrew*); unknown meaning
Matthew   gift of the Lord (*Hebrew*)
Melissa   bee (*Greek*)
Michael   like the Lord (*Hebrew*)
Michelle   *English spelling of French* Michèle, *from* Michael
Nancy   *pet form of* Ann
Natalie   birthday of the Lord (*Latin*)
Neil   champion (*Irish*)
Nicholas   victory people (*Greek*)
Nicola   *Italian female form of* Nicholas
Nicole   *French female form of* Nicholas
Pamela   ?all honey (*Greek*)
Patricia   noble (*Latin*)
Paul   small (*Latin*)
Pauline   *French female form of* Paul
Peter   stone, rock (*Greek*)
Philip   fond of horses (*Greek*)
Rachel   ewe (*Hebrew*)
Rebecca   ?noose (*Hebrew*)
Richard   strong ruler (*Germanic*)
Robert   fame bright (*Germanic*)
Ronald   counsel + power (*Germanic*)
Ruth   ?vision of beauty (*Hebrew*)
Ryan   *Irish surname*
Sally   *pet form of* Sarah

Samantha   *female form of* Samuel; heard/name of God (*Hebrew*)
Sandra   *pet form from* Alexandra
Sarah   princess (*Hebrew*)
Scott   *surname*; from Scotland
Sharon   the plain (*Hebrew*)
Shaun   *English spelling of Irish* Sean, *from* John
Shirley   bright clearing (*Germanic*)
Simon   *form of* Simeon; listening attentively (*Hebrew*)
Stephanie   *French female form of* Stephen
Stephen   crown (*Greek*)
Stuart   steward (*Germanic*)
Susan   *short form of* Susannah; lily (*Hebrew*)
Teresa   woman of Theresia (*Greek*)
Thomas   twin (*Hebrew*)
Tiffany   manifestation of God (*Greek*)
Timothy   honouring God (*Greek*)
Trac(e)y   ?pet form of Teresa
Vera   faith (*Slavic*)
Victoria   victory (*Latin*)
Vincent   conquer (*Latin*)
Virginia   maiden (*Latin*)
Walter   ruling people (*Germanic*)
Wayne   *surname*; wagon-maker
William   will + helmet (*Germanic*)
Zoë   life (*Greek*)

FORMS OF ADDRESS

In the formulae given below, *F* stands for forename and *S* for surname.
☐ Very formal ceremonial styles for closing letters are now seldom used: 'Yours faithfully' is assumed below, unless otherwise indicated.
☐ Forms of spoken address are given only where a special style is followed.
☐ Holders of courtesy titles are addressed according to their rank, but without 'The', 'The Right Hon.' or 'The Most Hon.'.
☐ Ranks in the armed forces, and ecclesiastical and ambassadorial ranks, precede titles in the peerage, eg 'Colonel the Earl of ——' or 'The Rev the Marquess of ——'.
☐ Although the correct forms of address are given below for members of the Royal Family, it is more normal practice for letters to be addressed to their private secretary, equerry, or lady-in-waiting.
☐ More detailed information about forms of address is to be found in Debrett's *Correct Form* and Black's *Titles and Forms of Address*.

Ambassadors (foreign)

Address on envelope: 'His/Her Excellency the Ambassador of ——' or 'His/Her Excellency the —— Ambassador'. (The wife of an ambassador is not entitled to the style 'Her Excellency'.) *Begin:* 'Your Excellency'. (Within the letter, refer to 'Your Excellency' once, thereafter as 'you'.) *Close:* 'I have the honour to be, Sir/Madam (or according to rank), Your Excellency's obedient servant'. *Spoken address:* 'Your Excellency' at least once, and then 'Sir' or 'Madam' by name.

FORMS OF ADDRESS (cont.)

Archbishop (Anglican communion)
Address on envelope: 'The Most Reverend the Lord Archbishop of ——'. (The Archbishops of Canterbury and York are Privy Counsellors, and should be addressed as 'The Most Reverend and Right Hon. the Lord Archbishop of ——'.) *Begin:* 'Dear Archbishop' or 'My Lord Archbishop'. *Spoken address:* 'Your Grace'. *Begin an official speech:* 'My Lord Archbishop'.

Archbishop (Roman Catholic)
Address on envelope: 'His Grace the Archbishop of ——'. *Begin:* 'My Lord Archbishop'. *Close:* 'I remain, Your Grace, Yours faithfully' or 'Yours faithfully'. *Spoken address:* 'Your Grace'.

Archdeacon
Address on envelope: 'The Venerable the Archdeacon of ——'. *Begin:* 'Dear Archdeacon' or 'Venerable Sir'. *Spoken address:* 'Archdeacon'. *Begin an official speech:* 'Venerable Sir'.

Baron
Address on envelope: 'The Right Hon. the Lord ——'. *Begin:* 'My Lord'. *Spoken address:* 'My Lord'.

Baron's wife (Baroness)
Address on envelope: 'The Right Hon. the Lady [S——]'. *Begin:* 'Dear Madam'. *Spoken address:* 'Madam'.

Baroness (in her own right)
Address on envelope: either as for Baron's wife, or 'The Right Hon. the Baroness [S——]'. Otherwise, as for Baron's wife.

Baronet
Address on envelope: 'Sir [F—— S——], Bt'. *Begin:* 'Dear Sir'. *Spoken address:* 'Sir [F——]'.

Baronet's wife
Address on envelope: 'Lady [S——]'. If she has the title 'Lady' by courtesy, 'Lady [F—— S——]'. If she has the courtesy style 'The Hon.', this precedes 'Lady'. *Begin:* 'Dear Madam'. *Spoken address:* 'Madam'.

Bishop (Anglican communion)
Address on envelope: 'The Right Reverend the Lord Bishop of ——'. (The Bishop of London is a Privy Counsellor, so is addressed as 'The Right Rev and Right Hon. the Lord Bishop of London'. The Bishop of Meath is styled 'The Most Reverend'.) *Begin:* 'Dear Bishop' or 'My Lord'. *Spoken address:* 'Bishop'. *Begin an official speech:* 'My Lord'.

Bishop (Episcopal Church in Scotland)
Address on envelope: 'The Right Reverend [F—— S——], Bishop of ——'. Otherwise as for a bishop of the Anglican communion. The bishop who holds the position of Primus is addressed as 'The Most Reverend the Primus'. *Begin:* 'Dear Primus'. *Spoken address:* 'Primus'.

Bishop (Roman Catholic)
Address on envelope: 'His Lordship the Bishop of ——' or 'The Right Reverend [F—— S——], Bishop of ——'. In Ireland, 'The Most Reverend' is used instead of 'The Right Reverend'. If an auxiliary bishop, address as 'The Right Reverend [F—— S——], Auxiliary Bishop of ——'. *Begin:* 'My Lord' or (more rarely) 'My Lord Bishop'. *Close:* 'I remain, my Lord' or (more rarely), 'my Lord Bishop'. Yours faithfully', or simply 'Yours faithfully'. *Spoken address:* 'My Lord' or (more rarely) 'My Lord Bishop'.

Cabinet Minister *see* **Secretary of State**

Canon (Anglican communion)
Address on envelope: 'The Reverend Canon [F—— S——]'. *Begin:* 'Dear Canon' or 'Dear Canon [S——]'. *Spoken address:* 'Canon' or 'Canon [S——]'.

Canon (Roman Catholic)
Address on envelope: 'The Very Reverend Canon [F—— S——]'. *Begin:* 'Very Reverend Sir'. *Spoken address:* 'Canon [S——]'.

FORMS OF ADDRESS (cont.)

Cardinal
  Address on envelope: 'His eminence Cardinal [S——]'. If an archbishop, 'His Eminence the Cardinal Archbishop of ——'. *Begin:* 'Your Eminence' or (more rarely) 'My Lord Cardinal'. *Close:* 'I remain, Your Eminence (or 'My Lord Cardinal'), Yours faithfully'. *Spoken:* 'Your Eminence'.

Clergy (Anglican communion)
  Address on envelope: 'The Reverend [F—— S——]'. *Begin:* 'Dear Sir' or 'Dear Mr [S——]'.

Clergy (Roman Catholic)
  Address on envelope: 'The Reverend [F—— S——]'. If a member of a religious order, the initials of the order should be added after the name. *Begin:* 'Dear Reverend Father'.

Clergy (Other churches)
  Address on envelope: 'The Reverend [F—— S——]'. *Begin:* 'Dear Sir/Madam' or 'Dear Mr/Mrs etc. [S——]'.

Countess
  Address on envelope: 'The Right Hon. the Countess of ——'. *Begin:* 'Dear Madam'. *Spoken address:* 'Madam'.

Dean (Anglican)
  Address on envelope: 'The Very Reverend the Dean of ——'. *Begin:* 'Dear Dean' or 'Very Reverend Sir'. *Spoken address:* 'Dean'. *Begin an official speech:* 'Very Reverend Sir'.

Doctor
  Physicians, anaesthetists, pathologists and radiologists are addressed as 'Doctor'. Surgeons, whether they hold the degree of Doctor of Medicine or not, are known as 'Mr/Mrs'. In England and Wales, obstetricians and gynaecologists are addressed as 'Mr/Mrs', but in Scotland, Ireland and elsewhere as 'Doctor'. In addressing a letter to the holder of a doctorate, the initials DD, MD, etc. are placed after the ordinary form of address, eg 'The Rev John Smith, DD', the 'Rev Dr Smith' and 'Dr John Brown' are also used.

Dowager
  Address on envelope: On the marriage of a peer or baronet, the widow of the previous holder of the title becomes 'Dowager' and is addressed 'The Right Hon. the Dowager Countess of ——', 'The Right Hon. the Dowager Lady   ', etc. If there is already a Dowager still living, she retains this title, the later widow being addressed 'The Most Hon. [F——], Marchioness of ——', 'The Right Hon. [F——], Lady ——', etc. However, many Dowagers prefer the style which includes their Christian names to that including the title Dowager. *Begin,* etc. as for a peer's wife.

Duchess
  Address on envelope: 'Her Grace the Duchess of ——'. *Begin:* 'Dear Madam'. *Spoken address:* 'Your Grace'. (For Royal Duchess, *see* Princess.)

Duke
  Address on envelope: 'His Grace the Duke of ——'. *Begin:* 'My Lord Duke'. *Spoken address:* 'Your Grace'. (For Royal Duke, *see* Prince.)

Earl
  Address on envelope: 'The Right Hon. the Earl of ——'. *Begin:* 'My Lord'. *Spoken address:* 'My Lord'. (For Earl's wife, *see* Countess.)

Governor of a colony or **Governor-General**
  Address on envelope: 'His Excellency [ordinary designation], Governor(-General) of ——'. (The Governor-General of Canada has the rank of 'Right Honourable', which he retains for life.) The wife of a Governor-General is styled 'Her Excellency' within the country her husband administers. *Begin:* according to rank. Close: 'I have the honour to be, Sir (or 'My Lord', if a peer), Your Excellency's obedient servant'. *Spoken address:* 'Your Excellency'.

FORMS OF ADDRESS (cont.)

Judge, High Court

Address on envelope: if a man, 'The Hon. Mr Justice [S——]'; if a woman, 'The Hon. Mrs Justice [S——]'. *Begin:* 'Dear Sir/Madam'; if on judicial matters, 'My Lord/Lady'. *Spoken address:* 'Sir/Madam'; only on the bench or when dealing with judicial matters should a High Court Judge be addressed as 'My Lord/Lady' or referred to as 'Your Lordship/Ladyship'.

Judge, Circuit

Address on envelope: 'His/Her Honour Judge [S——]'. If a Knight, 'His Honour Judge Sir [F—— S——]'. *Begin:* 'Dear Sir/Madam'. *Spoken address:* 'Sir/Madam'; address as 'Your Honour' only when on the bench or dealing with judicial matters.

Justice of the Peace (England and Wales)

When on the bench, refer to and address as 'Your Worship'; otherwise according to rank. The letters 'JP' may be added after the person's name in addressing a letter, if desired.

Knight Bachelor

As Baronet, except that 'Bt' is omitted. Knight of the Bath, of St Michael and St George, etc. *Address on envelope:* 'Sir [F—— S——], with the initials 'GCB', KCB', etc. added. *Begin:* 'Dear Sir'.

Knight's wife

As Baronet's wife, or according to rank.

Lady Mayoress

Address on envelope: 'The Lady Mayoress of ——'. *Begin:* 'My Lady Mayoress'. *Spoken address:* '(My) Lady Mayoress'.

Lord Mayor

Address on envelope: The Lord Mayors of London, York, Belfast, Cardiff, Dublin and also Melbourne, Sydney, Adelaide, Perth, Brisbane and Hobart are styled 'The Right Hon. the Lord Mayor of ——'. Other Lord Mayors are styled 'The Right Worshipful the Lord Mayor of ——'. *Begin:* 'My Lord Mayor', even if the holder of the office is a woman. *Spoken address:* '(My) Lord Mayor'.

Marchioness

Address on envelope: 'The Most Hon. the Marchioness of ——'. *Begin:* 'Dear Madam'. *Spoken address:* 'Madam'.

Marquess

Address on envelope: 'The Most Hon. the Marquess of ——'. *Begin:* 'My Lord'. *Spoken address:* 'My Lord'.

Mayor

Address on envelope: 'The Worshipful the Mayor of ——'; in the case of cities and certain towns, 'The Right Worshipful'. *Begin:* 'Mr Mayor'. *Spoken address:* 'Mr Mayor'.

Mayoress

Address on envelope: 'The Mayoress of ——'. *Begin:* 'Madam Mayoress' is traditional, but some now prefer 'Madam Mayor'. *Spoken address:* 'Mayoress' (or 'Madam Mayor').

Member of Parliament

Address on envelope: Add 'MP' to the usual form of address. *Begin:* according to rank.

Monsignor

Address on envelope: 'The Reverend Monsignor [F—— S——]'. If a canon, 'The Very Reverend Monsignor (Canon) [F—— S——]'. *Begin:* 'Reverend Sir'. *Spoken address:* 'Monsignor [S——]'.

Officers in the Armed Forces

Address on envelope: The professional rank is prefixed to any other rank, eg 'Admiral the Right Hon. the Earl of ——', 'Lieut.-Col. Sir [F—— S——], KCB'. Officers below the rank of Rear-Admiral, and Marshal of the Royal Air Force, are entitled to 'RN' (or 'Royal Navy') and 'RAF' respectively after their name. Army officers of the rank of Colonel or below may follow their name with the name of their regiment or corps (which may be abbreviated). Officers in the women's services add 'WRNS', 'WRAF', 'WRAC'. *Begin:* according to social rank.

FORMS OF ADDRESS (cont.)

Officers (retired and former)
Address on envelope: Officers above the rank of Lieutenant (in the Royal Navy), Captain (in the Army) and Flight Lieutenant may continue to use and be addressed by their armed forces rank after being placed on the retired list. The word 'retired' (or in an abbreviated form) should not normally be placed after the person's name. Former officers in the women's services do not normally continue to use their ranks.

Pope
Address on envelope: 'His Holiness, the Pope'. *Begin:* 'Your Holiness' or 'Most Holy Father'. *Close:* if a Roman Catholic, 'I have the honour to be your Holiness's most devoted and obedient child' (or 'most humble child'); if not Roman Catholic, 'I have the honour to be (or 'remain') Your Holiness's obedient servant'. *Spoken address:* 'Your Holiness'.

Prime Minister
Address on envelope: according to rank. The Prime Minister is a Privy Counsellor (see separate entry) and the letter should be addressed accordingly. *Begin,* etc. according to rank.

Prince
Address on envelope: If a Duke, 'His Royal Highness the Duke of ——'; if not a Duke, 'His Royal Highness the Prince [F——]', if a child of the sovereign; otherwise 'His Royal Highness Prince [F——] of [Kent or Gloucester]'. *Begin:* 'Sir'. Refer to as 'Your Royal Highness'. *Close:* 'I have the honour to remain (or be), Sir, Your Royal Highness's most humble and obedient servant'. *Spoken address:* 'Your Royal Highness' once, thereafter 'Sir'.

Princess
Address on envelope: If a Duchess, 'Her Royal Highness the Duchess of ——'; if not a Duchess, the daughter of a sovereign is addressed as 'Her Royal Highness the Princess [F——]', followed by any title she holds by marriage. 'The' is omitted in addressing a princess who is not the daughter of a sovereign. A Princess by marriage is addressed 'HRH Princess [husband's F——] of ——'. *Begin:* 'Madam'. Refer to as 'Your Royal Highness'. *Close:* as for Prince, substituting 'Madam' for 'Sir'. *Spoken address:* 'Your Royal Highness' once, thereafter 'Ma'am'.

Privy Counsellor
Address on envelope: If a peer, 'The Right Hon. the Earl of ——, PC'; if not a peer, 'The Right Hon. [F—— S——]', without the 'PC'. *Begin,* etc. according to rank.

Professor
Address on envelope: 'Professor [F   S——]'; the styles 'Professor Lord [S——]' and 'Professor Sir [F—— S——]' are often used, but are deprecated by some people. If the professor is in holy orders, 'The Reverend Professor'. *Begin:* 'Dear Sir/Madam', or according to rank. *Spoken address:* according to rank.

Queen
Address on envelope: 'Her Majesty the Queen'. *Begin:* 'Madam, with my humble duty'. Refer to as 'Your Majesty'. *Close:* 'I have the honour to remain (or 'be'), Madam, Your Majesty's most humble and obedient servant'. *Spoken address:* 'Your Majesty' once, thereafter 'Ma'am'. *Begin an official speech:* 'May it please Your Majesty'.

Rabbi
Address on envelope: 'Rabbi [initial and S——]' or, if a doctor, 'Rabbi Doctor [initial and S——]'. *Begin:* 'Dear Sir'. *Spoken address:* 'Rabbi [S——]' or '[Doctor S——]'.

Secretary of State
Address on envelope: 'The Right Hon. [F—— S——], MP, Secretary of State for ——', or 'The Secretary of State for ——'. Otherwise according to rank.

Viscount
Address on envelope: 'The Right Hon. the Viscount ——'. *Begin:* 'My Lord'. *Spoken address:* 'My Lord'.

Viscountess
Address on envelope: 'The Right Hon. the Viscountess ——'. *Begin:* 'Dear Madam'. *Spoken address:* 'Madam'.

COMPUTER LANGUAGES (HIGH-LEVEL)

Name	Full name	Main use
Ada	—	Complex on-line real-time monitoring and control (eg military applications)
AED	Algol extended for design	Computer-aided design
ALGOL	Algorithmic Orientated Language	Concise expression of mathematical and logical processes and the control of these processes
APL	A Programming Language	Educational; mathematical problems particularly those concerned with multidimensional arrays
APT	Automatically Programmed Tools	Operate machine tools using numeric codes
BASIC	Beginners All-purpose Symbolic Instruction Code	Education, games
BCPL	B Combined Programming Language	Mathematical, scientific, systems programming
C	—	Operating systems (eg UNIX), business, scientific, games
CHILL	—	Real-time language used for programming computer-based telecommunication systems and computer-controlled telephone exchanges
COBOL	Common Business Oriented Language	Business data processing
COGO	Co-ordinate Geometry	Solving coordinate geometry problems in civil engineering
COMAL	Common algorithmic language	Education
CORAL	Computer On-line Real-time Application Language	Military applications
FORTH	—	Astronomy, robotics, control applications
FORTRAN	Formula Translation	Mathematical, engineering, scientific
GPSS	General Purpose Systems Simulation	Simulation programs
LISP	List Processing	Linguistics, Artificial Intelligence, manipulation of mathematical and arithmetic logic
LOGO	—	Education, turtle graphics
ML	Meta Language	Dynamic programming
MODULA-2	—	Parallel computations (derivative of Pascal)
OCCAM	—	Artificial Intelligence applications
Pascal	—	Education
PL/1	Programming Language 1	Educational; commercial and scientific work
PL/M	Programming Language for Microcomputers	Educational; commercial and scientific work
PROLOG	Programming in logic	Artificial intelligence, expert systems
SIMULA	Simulation language	Simulation programs
SNOBOL	String Oriented Symbolic Language	Manipulation of textual data
SQL	Structured Query Language	Database querying

NEWS AGENCIES

Press name	Full name	Date founded	Location	Press name	Full name	Date founded	Location
AAP	Australian Associated Press	1935	Sydney	BOPA	Botswana Press Agency	1981	Gaborne
AASA	Agence Arabe Syrienne d'Information	1966	Damascus	BTA	Bulgarska Telegrafitscheka Agentzia	1898	Sofia
ADN	Allgemeiner Deutscher Nachrichtendienst	1946	Berlin	CANA	Caribbean News Agency	–	Bridgetown
AE	Agence Europe	1952	Brussels	CIP	Centre d'Information de Presse	1946	Brussels
AFP	Agence France-Presse	1944	Paris	CNA	Central News Agency	1924	Taipei
AIO	Agencia Informativa Orbe de Chile	1952	Santiago Chile	CNA	Cyprus News Agency	1976	Nicosia
AIP	Agence Ivoirienne de Presse	1961	Abidjan	CNS	China News Service	1952	Beijing
ALD	Agencia Los Diarios	1910	Buenos Aires	COL-PRENSA	Colprensa	1980	Bogata
ALI	Agencia Lusa de Informacao	1987	Lisbon	CP	Canadian Press	1917	Toronto
AM	Agencia Meridional	1931	Rio de Janeiro	CTK	Ceskoslovenska Tiskova Kancelar	1918	Prague
ANA	Athenagence	1896	Athens	DPA	Deutsche Presse-Agentur	1949	Hamburg
ANP	Algemeen Nederlands Persbureau	1934	The Hague	EFE	Agencia EFE	1939	Madrid
ANSA	Agenzia Nazionale Stampa Associate	1945	Rome	ENA	Eastern News Agency	1970	Dhaka
ANTARA	Indonesian National News Agency	1937	Jakarta	EXTEL	Exchange and Telegraph Company	1872	London
AN	Agencia Nacional	1946	Brasilia	FIDES	Agenzia Internazionale Fides	1926	Vatican City
APA	Austria Presse-Agentur	1946	Vienna	GNA	Agence Guinéenne de Presse	1981	Conakry
APP	Agence Parisienne de Presse	1949	Paris	GNA	Ghana News Agency	1957	Accra
APP	Associated Press of Pakistan	1948	Islamabad	GNA	Guyana News Agency	1981	George-town
APS	Agence de Presse Senegalaise	1959	Dakar	HHA	Hurriyet Haber Ajasi	1963	Istanbul
APS	Algeria Presse Service	1962	Algiers	IC	Inforpress Centroamericana	1972	Guatemala
AP	Associated Press	1848	New York	INA	Iraqi News Agency	1959	Baghdad
ATA	Albanian Telegraphic Agency	1945	Tirana	IPS	Inter Press Service	1964	Rome
AUP	Australian United Press	1928	Melbourne	IRNA	Islamic Republic News Agency	1936	Teheran
BELGA	Agence Belga	1920	Brussels	JAM-PRESS	Jampress	1984	Kingston
BER-NAMA	Malaysia National News Agency	1967	Kuala Lumpur	JANA	Jamahiriya News Agency	–	Tripoli
				JIJI	Jiji Tsushin-Sha	1945	Tokyo

NEWS AGENCIES (cont.)

Press name	Full name	Date founded	Location
JTA	Jewish Telegraphic Agency	1919	Jerusalem
KCNA	Korean Central News Agency	1946	Pyongyang
KNA	Kenya News Agency	1963	Nairobi
KPL	Khao San Pathet Lao	1968	Vientiane
KUNA	Kuwait News Agency	1976	Kuwait City
KYODO	Kyodo Tsushin	1945	Tokyo
LAI	Logos Agencia de Informacion	1929	Madrid
MENA	Middle East News Agency	1955	Cairo
MTI	Magyar Tavariti Iroda	1880	Budapest
NAB	News Agency of Burma	1963	Rangoon
NAEWOE	Naewoe Press	1974	Seoul
NAN	News Agency of Nigeria	1978	Lagos
NA	Noticias Argentinas	1973	Buenos Aires
NOTIMEX	Noticias Mexicanas	1968	Mexico City
NOVOSTI	Agentstvo Pechati Novosti	1961	Moscow
NPS	Norsk Presse Service	1960	Oslo
NTB	Norsk Telegrambyra	1867	Oslo
NZPA	New Zealand Press Agency	1879	Wellington
OPA	Orbis Press Agency	1977	Prague
OTT-FNB	Oy Suomen Tietoimisto Notisbyran Ab	1887	Helsinki
PANA	Pan-African News Agency	1979	Dakar
PAP	Polska Agencija Prasowa	1944	Warsaw
PA	Press Association	1868	London
PETRA	Jordan News Agency	1965	Amman
PNA	Philippines News Agency	1973	Manila

Press name	Full name	Date founded	Location
PPI	Pakistan Press International	1959	Karachi
PRELA	Prensa Latina	1959	Havana
PS	Presse Services	1929	Paris
PTI	Press Trust of India	1949	Bombay
RB	Ritzaus Bureau	1866	Copenhagen
REUTERS	Reuters	1851	London
ROM-PRESS	Romanian News Agency	1949	Bucharest
SAPA	South Africa Press Association	1938	Johannesburg
SDA	Schweizerische Depeschenagentur	1894	Berne
SIP	Svensk-Internationella Pressbyran	1927	Stockholm
SLENA	Sierra Leone News Agency	1980	Freetown
SOFIA-PRES	Sofia Press Agency	1967	Sofia
SOPAC-NEWS	South Pacific News Service	1948	Wellington
SPA	Saudi Press Agency	1970	Riyadh
TANJUG	Novinska Agencija Tanjug	1943	Belgrade
TAP	Tunis Afrique Presse	1961	Tunis
TASS	Telegrafnoye Agentstvo Sovietskovo Soyuza	1925	Moscow
TT	Tidningarnes Telegrambyra	1921	Stockholm
UNI	United News of India	1961	New Dehli
UPI	United Press International	1958	New York
UPP	United Press of Pakistan	1949	Karachi
XINHUA	Xinhua	1937	Beijing
YONHAP	Yonhap (United) Press Agency	1980	Seoul
ZIANA	Zimbabwe Inter-Africa News Agency	1981	Harare

NATIONAL NEWSPAPERS: EUROPE

Name	Location	Circulation	Date founded	Name	Location	Circulation	Date founded
ABC	Madrid	247 228	1905	Nieuws			
Algemeen Dagblad	Rotterdam	410 400	1946	Il Giornale	Milan	176 912	1974
				Il Giorno	Milan	211 643	1965
Apogevmatini	Athens	130 000	1956	Il Messaggero	Rome	330 000	1878
Avriani	Athens	115 000	1980	International Herald Tribune	Paris	174 200	1887
B.T.	Copenhagen	202 570	1916				
Berliner Zeitung	Berlin	296 300	1877	Irish Independent	Dublin	174 788	1905
Berlingske Tidende	Copenhagen	128 815	1749	Irish Times	Dublin	88 739	1859
Bild am Sonntag (s)	Hamburg	2 400 000	1956	La Libre Belgique	Brussels	80 813	1884
Bild Zeitung	Hamburg	5 124 000	1952	La Dernière Heure	Brussels	92 577	1906
Correio do Manha	Lisbon	70 000	1979	La Lanterne	Brussels	132 844	1944
Corriere della Sera	Milan	468 072	1876	La Republica	Rome	486 000	1976
				La Stampa	Turin	433 366	1867
De Standaard/ Het Nieuwsblad/ De Gentenaar	Brussels	378 697	N/A	La Vanguardia	Barcelona	225 000	1881
				Le Figaro	Paris	433 496	1828
				Le Monde	Paris	362 443	1944
De Telegraaf	Amsterdam	723 800	1893	Le Parisien Libère	Paris	339 271	1944
De Volkskrant	Amsterdam	323 000	1919				
Diario de Noticias	Lisbon	58 898	1864	Le Soir	Brussels	208 883	1887
				L'Humanité	Paris	117 005	1904
Diario Popular	Lisbon	62 242	1942	L'Humanité Dimanche (s)	Paris	360 006	1946
Die Welt	Bonn	225 000	1946				
Die Zeit (weekly)	Hamburg	468 000	1946	Luxemburger Wort/ La Voix du Luxembourg	Luxembourg	83 171	1848
Ekstra Bladet	Copenhagen	229 509	1904				
El Pais	Madrid	380 000	1976	Politiken	Copenhagen	152 215	1884
El Periodico	Barcelona	150 000	1978	Suddeutsche Zeitung	Munich	378 420	1945
Ethnos	Athens	150 500	1981				
Evening Herald	Dublin	132 314	1891	Sunday Independent (s)	Dublin	222 351	1905
Evening Press	Dublin	129 695	1954				
France-Dimanche (s)	Paris	721 000	N/A	Sunday Press (s)	Dublin	266 019	1949
				Sunday World (s)	Dublin	366 806	1973
France-Soir	Paris	410 679	1944	Ta Nea	Athens	155 000	1944
Frankfurter Allgemeine Zeitung	Frankfurt	360 000	1949	Welt am Sonntag (s)	Hamburg	336 000	–
Het Laatste	Brussels	301 306	1888	Ya	Madrid	380 000	1935

(s) published on Sundays only

NATIONAL NEWSPAPERS: UK

Name	Location	Circulation	Date founded	Name	Location	Circulation	Date founded
Daily Express	London	1 570 365	1900	The People (s)	London	2 932 472	1881
Daily Mail	London	1 739 756	1896	The Sunday Post (s)	Dundee	1 432 645	1920
Daily Mirror	London	3 171 720	1903				
Daily Telegraph	London	1 105 366	1855	The Sunday Telegraph (s)	London	648 317	1961
Financial Times	London	285 854	1880				
News of the World (s)	London	5 249 291	1843	The Sunday Times (s)	London	1 272 591	1822
The Guardian	London	431 716	1821	The Sun	London	4 195 056	1964
The Independent	London	422 679	1986	The Times	London	450 626	1785
The Observer (s)	London	749 644	1791	Today	London	601 871	1986

(5) published on Sundays only

NATIONAL NEWSPAPERS: USA

Name	Location	Circulation (round figures)	Date founded	Name	Location	Circulation (round figures)	Date founded
Boston Globe	Boston	516 000	1872	New York Times	New York	1 039 000	1851
Chicago Sun-Times	Chicago	579 000	1948	Newsday	New York	681 000	1940
				Philadelphia Inquirer	Philadephia	504 000	1829
Chicago Tribune	Chicago	716 000	1847				
Detroit Free Press	Detroit	629 000	1831	San Francisco Chronicle	San Francisco	569 000	1865
Detroit News	Detroit	687 000	1873	USA Today	Washington, DC	1 339 000	1982
Los Angeles Times	Los Angeles	1 116 000	1881				
New York Daily News	New York	1 282 000	1919	Wall Street Journal	New York	1 870 000	1889
New York Post	New York	550 000	1801	Washington Post	Washington, DC	769 000	1877

SYMBOLS IN GENERAL USE

&,	ampersand (*and*)		☏	telephone number follows
&c.	et cetera		☜☞	this way
@	at; per (in costs)		✂, ✄····	cut here
×	by (measuring dimensions (3 × 4)			
£	pound		**In astronomy**	
$	dollar (also peso, escudo, etc in certain countries)		●	new moon
			☽	moon, first quarter
¢	cent (also centavo, etc in certain countries)		○	full moon
			☾	moon, last quarter
©	copyright			
®	registered		**In meteorology**	
¶	new paragraph		▲▲▲	cold front (in meteorology)
§	new section		▰▰▰	warm front
''	ditto		◥◥▾	stationary front
*	born (in genealogy)		▲▲▲▲	occluded front
†	died			
*	hypothetical or unacceptable form (in linguistics)		**In cards**	
			♥	hearts
☠	poison; danger		♦	diamonds
♂,□	male		♠	spades
♀,○	female		♣	clubs
⌘	bishop's name follows			

CLOTHES CARE SYMBOLS

⊠	Do not iron		⊠	Do not tumble dry
⊿	Can be ironed with *cool* iron (up to 110°C)		⊗	Do not dry clean
⊿	Can be ironed with *warm* iron (up to 150°C)		Ⓐ	Dry cleanable (letter indicates which solvents can be used) A. all solvents Dry cleanable
⊿	Can be ironed with *hot* iron (up to 200°C)		Ⓕ	F: white spirit and solvent 11 can be used Dry cleanable
⚕	Hand wash only		Ⓟ	P: perchloroethylene (tetrachloroethylene), white spirit, solvent 113 and solvent 11 can be used
🔲60	Can be washed in a washing machine The number shows the most effective washing temperature (in °C)		Ⓟ	Dry cleanable, if special care taken
🔲60	Reduced (medium) washing conditions		△	Chlorine bleach may be used with care
🔲60	Much reduced (minimum) washing conditions (for wool products)		⊠	Do not use chlorine bleach
⊠	Do not wash			

 Can be tumble dried (one dot within the circle means a low temperature setting; two dots for higher temperatures)

CAR INDEX MARKS: UK

AA	Bournemouth	CF	Reading	EL	Bournemouth
AB	Worcester	CG	Bournemouth	EM	Liverpool
AC	Coventry	CH	Nottingham	EN	Manchester
AD	Gloucester	CJ	Gloucester	EO	Preston
AE	Bristol	CK	Preston	EP	Swansea
AF	Truro	CL	Norwich	ER	Peterborough
AG	Hull	CM	Liverpool	ES	Dundee
AH	Norwich	CN	Newcastle upon Tyne	ET	Sheffield
AJ	Middlesbrough	CO	Exeter	EU	Bristol
AK	Sheffield	CP	Huddersfield	EV	Chelmsford
AL	Nottingham	CR	Portsmouth	EW	Peterborough
AM	Swindon	CS	Glasgow	EX	Norwich
AN	Reading	CT	Lincoln	EY	Bangor
AO	Carlisle	CU	Newcastle upon Tyne		
AP	Brighton	CV	Truro	FA	Stoke-on-Trent
AR	Chelmsford	CW	Preston	FB	Bristol
AS	Inverness	CX	Huddersfield	FC	Oxford
AT	Hull	CY	Swansea	FD	Dudley
AU	Nottingham			FE	Lincoln
AV	Peterborough	DA	Birmingham	FF	Bangor
AW	Shrewsbury	DB	Manchester	FG	Brighton
AX	Cardiff	DC	Middlesbrough	FH	Gloucester
AY	Leicester	DD	Gloucester	FJ	Exeter
		DE	Haverfordwest	FK	Dudley
BA	Manchester	DF	Gloucester	FL	Peterborough
BB	Newcastle upon Tyne	DG	Gloucester	FM	Chester
BC	Leicester	DH	Dudley	FN	Maidstone
BD	Northampton	DJ	Liverpool	FO	Gloucester
BE	Lincoln	DK	Manchester	FP	Leicester
BF	Stoke-on-Trent	DL	Portsmouth	FR	Preston
BG	Liverpool	DM	Chester	FS	Edinburgh
BH	Luton	DN	Leeds	FT	Newcastle upon Tyne
BJ	Ipswich	DO	Lincoln	FU	Lincoln
BK	Portsmouth	DP	Reading	FV	Preston
BL	Reading	DR	Exeter	FW	Lincoln
BM	Luton	DS	Glasgow	FX	Bournemouth
BN	Manchester	DT	Sheffield	FY	Liverpool
BO	Cardiff	DU	Coventry		
BP	Portsmouth	DV	Exeter	GA	Glasgow
BR	Newcastle upon Tyne	DW	Cardiff	GB	Glasgow
BS	Inverness	DX	Ipswich	GC	London SW
BT	Leeds	DY	Brighton	GD	Glasgow
BU	Manchester			GE	Glasgow
BV	Preston	EA	Dudley	GF	London SW
BW	Oxford	EB	Peterborough	GG	Glasgow
BX	Haverfordwest	EC	Preston	GH	London SW
BY	London NW	ED	Liverpool	GJ	London SW
		EE	Lincoln	GK	London SW
CA	Chester	EF	Middlesbrough	GL	Truro
CB	Manchester	EG	Peterborough	GM	Reading
CC	Bangor	EH	Stoke-on-Trent	GN	London SW
CD	Brighton	EJ	Haverfordwest	GO	London SW
CE	Peterborough	EK	Liverpool	GP	London SW

CAR INDEX MARKS: UK (cont.)

GR	Newcastle upon Tyne	JW	Birmingham	MB	Chester
GS	Luton	JX	Huddersfield	MC	London NE
GT	London SW	JY	Exeter	MD	London NE
GU	London SE			ME	London NE
GV	Ipswich	KA	Liverpool	MF	London NE
GW	London SE	KB	Liverpool	MG	London NE
GX	London SE	KC	Liverpool	MH	London NE
GY	London SE	KD	Liverpool	MJ	Luton
		KE	Maidstone	MK	London NE
HA	Dudley	KF	Liverpool	ML	London NE
HB	Cardiff	KG	Cardiff	MM	London NE
HC	Brighton	KH	Hull	MN	*(not used)*
HD	Huddersfield	KJ	Maidstone	MO	Reading
HE	Sheffield	KK	Maidstone	MP	London NE
HF	Liverpool	KL	Maidstone	MR	Swindon
HG	Preston	KM	Maidstone	MS	Edinburgh
HH	Carlisle	KN	Maidstone	MT	London NE
HJ	Chelmsford	KO	Maidstone	MU	London NE
HK	Chelmsford	KP	Maidstone	MV	London SE
HL	Sheffield	KR	Maidstone	MW	Swindon
HM	London (Central)	KS	Edinburgh	MX	London SE
HN	Middlesbrough	KT	Maidstone	MY	London SE
HO	Bournemouth	KU	Sheffield		
HP	Coventry	KV	Coventry	NA	Manchester
HR	Swindon	KW	Sheffield	NB	Manchester
HS	Glasgow	KX	Luton	NC	Manchester
HT	Bristol	KY	Sheffield	ND	Manchester
HU	Bristol			NE	Manchester
HV	London (Central)	LA	London NW	NF	Manchester
HW	Bristol	LB	London NW	NG	Norwich
HX	London (Central)	LC	London NW	NH	Northampton
HY	Bristol	LD	London NW	NJ	Brighton
		LE	London NW	NK	Luton
JA	Manchester	LF	London NW	NL	Newcastle upon Tyne
JB	Reading	LG	Chester	NM	Luton
JC	Bangor	LH	London NW	NN	Nottingham
JD	London (Central)	LJ	Bournemouth	NO	Chelmsford
JE	Peterborough	LK	London NW	NP	Worcester
JF	Leicester	LL	London NW	NR	Leicester
JG	Maidstone	LM	London NW	NS	Glasgow
JH	Reading	LN	London NW	NT	Shrewsbury
JJ	Maidstone	LO	London NW	NU	Nottingham
JK	Brighton	LP	London NW	NV	Northampton
JL	Lincoln	LR	London NW	NW	Leeds
JM	Reading	LS	Edinburgh	NX	Dudley
JN	Chelmsford	LT	London NW	NY	Cardiff
JO	Oxford	LU	London NW		
JP	Liverpool	LV	Liverpool	OA	Birmingham
JR	Newcastle upon Tyne	LW	London NW	OB	Birmingham
JS	Inverness	LX	London NW	OC	Birmingham
JT	Bournemouth	LY	London NW	OD	Exeter
JU	Leicester			OE	Birmingham
JV	Lincoln	MA	Chester	OF	Birmingham

CAR INDEX MARKS: UK (cont.)

OG	Birmingham	RM	Carlisle	TR	Portsmouth
OH	Birmingham	RN	Preston	TS	Dundee
OJ	Birmingham	RO	Luton	TT	Exeter
OK	Birmingham	RP	Northampton	TU	Chester
OL	Birmingham	RR	Nottingham	TV	Nottingham
OM	Birmingham	RS	Aberdeen	TW	Chelmsford
ON	Birmingham	RT	Ipswich	TX	Cardiff
OO	Chelmsford	RU	Bournemouth	TY	Newcastle upon Tyne
OP	Birmingham	RV	Portsmouth		
OR	Portsmouth	RW	Coventry	UA	Leeds
OS	Glasgow	RX	Reading	UB	Leeds
OT	Portsmouth	RY	Leicester	UC	London (Central)
OU	Bristol			UD	Oxford
OV	Birmingham	SA	Aberdeen	UE	Dudley
OW	Portsmouth	SB	Glasgow	UF	Brighton
OX	Birmingham	SC	Edinburgh	UG	Leeds
OY	London NW	SCY	Truro (Isles of Scilly)	UH	Cardiff
		SD	Glasgow	UJ	Shrewsbury
PA	Guildford	SE	Aberdeen	UK	Birmingham
PB	Guildford	SF	Edinburgh	UL	London (Central)
PC	Guildford	SG	Edinburgh	UM	Leeds
PD	Guildford	SH	Edinburgh	UN	Exeter
PE	Guildford	SJ	Glasgow	UO	Exeter
PF	Guildford	SK	Inverness	UP	Newcastle upon Tyne
PG	Guildford	SL	Dundee	UR	Luton
PH	Guildford	SM	Glasgow	US	Glasgow
PJ	Guildford	SN	Dundee	UT	Leicester
PK	Guildford	SO	Aberdeen	UU	London (Central)
PL	Guildford	SP	Dundee	UV	London (Central)
PM	Guildford	SR	Dundee	UW	London (Central)
PN	Brighton	SS	Aberdeen	UX	Shrewsbury
PO	Portsmouth	ST	Inverness	UY	Worcester
PP	Luton	SU	Glasgow		
PR	Bournemouth	SV	Spare	VA	Peterborough
PS	Aberdeen	SW	Glasgow	VB	Maidstone
PT	Newcastle upon Tyne	SX	Edinburgh	VC	Coventry
PU	Chelmsford	SY	*Spare*	VD	*Series withdrawn*
PV	Ipswich			VE	Peterborough
PW	Norwich	TA	Exeter	VF	Norwich
PX	Portsmouth	TB	Liverpool	VG	Norwich
PY	Middlesbrough	TC	Bristol	VH	Huddersfield
		TD	Manchester	VJ	Gloucester
RA	Nottingham	TE	Manchester	VK	Newcastle upon Tyne
RB	Nottingham	TF	Reading	VL	Lincoln
RC	Nottingham	TG	Cardiff	VM	Manchester
RD	Reading	TH	Swansea	VN	Middlesbrough
RE	Stoke-on-Trent	TJ	Liverpool	VO	Nottingham
RF	Stoke-on-Trent	TK	Exeter	VP	Birmingham
RG	Newcastle upon Tyne	TL	Lincoln	VR	Manchester
RH	Hull	TM	Luton	VS	Luton
RJ	Manchester	TN	Newcastle upon Tyne	VT	Stoke-on-Trent
RK	London NW	TO	Nottingham	VU	Manchester
RL	Truro	TP	Portsmouth		

CAR INDEX MARKS: UK (cont.)

VV	Northampton	WO	Cardiff	YH	London (Central)
VW	Chelmsford	WP	Worcester	YJ	Brighton
VX	Chelmsford	WR	Leeds	YK	London (Central)
VY	Leeds	WS	Bristol	YL	London (Central)
		WT	Leeds	YM	London (Central)
WA	Sheffield	WU	Leeds	YN	London (Central)
WB	Sheffield	WV	Brighton	YO	London (Central)
WC	Chelmsford	WW	Leeds	YP	London (Central)
WD	Dudley	WX	Leeds	YR	London (Central)
WE	Sheffield	WY	Leeds	YS	Glasgow
WF	Sheffield			YT	London (Central)
WG	Sheffield	YA	Taunton	YU	London (Central)
WH	Manchester	YB	Taunton	YV	London (Central)
WJ	Sheffield	YC	Taunton	YW	London (Central)
WK	Coventry	YD	Taunton	YX	London (Central)
WL	Oxford	YE	London (Central)	YY	London (Central)
WM	Liverpool	YF	London (Central)		
WN	Swansea	YG	Leeds		

CAR INDEX MARKS: INTERNATIONAL

A	Austria	E	Spain	IRL	Ireland*
ADN	Yemen PDR	EAK	Kenya*	IRQ	Iraq
AFG	Afghanistan	EAT	Tanzania*	IS	Iceland
AL	Albania	EAU	Uganda*	J	Japan*
AND	Andorra	EAZ	Tanzania*	JA	Jamaica*
AUS	Australia*	EC	Ecuador	K	Kampuchea
B	Belgium	ES	El Salvador	KWT	Kuwait
BD	Bangladesh*	ET	Egypt	L	Luxembourg
BDS	Barbados*	ETH	Ethiopia	LAO	Lao PDR
BG	Bulgaria	F	France	LAR	Libya
BH	Belize	FJI	Fiji*	LB	Liberia
BR	Brazil	FL	Liechtenstein	LS	Lesotho*
BRN	Bahrain	FR	Faroe Is	M	Malta*
BRU	Brunei*	GB	UK*	MA	Morocco
BS	Bahamas*	GBA	Alderney*	MAL	Malaysia*
BUR	Burma	GBG	Guernsey*	MC	Monaco
C	Cuba	GBJ	Jersey*	MEX	Mexico
CDN	Canada	GBM	Isle of Man*	MS	Mauritius*
CH	Switzerland	GBZ	Gibraltar	MW	Malawi*
CI	Côte d'Ivoire	GCA	Guatemala	N	Norway
CL	Sri Lanka*	GH	Ghana	NA	Netherlands Antilles
CO	Colombia	GR	Greece	NIC	Nicaragua
CR	Costa Rica	GUY	Guyana*	NL	Netherlands
CS	Czechoslovakia	H	Hungary	NZ	New Zealand*
CY	Cyprus*	HK	Hong Kong*	P	Portugal
D	W Germany	HKJ	Jordan	PA	Panama
DK	Denmark	I	Italy	PAK	Pakistan*
DOM	Dominican Republic	IL	Israel	PE	Peru
DY	Benin	IND	India*	PL	Poland
DZ	Algeria	IR	Iran	PNG	Papua New Guinea*

CAR INDEX MARKS: INTERNATIONAL (cont.)

PY	Paraguay	RSM	San Marino	V	Vatican City
RA	Argentina	RU	Burundi	VN	Vietnam
RB	Botswana*	RWA	Rwanda	WAG	Gambia
RC	Taiwan	S	Sweden	WAL	Sierra Leone
RCA	Central African	SD	Swaziland*	WAN	Nigeria
	Republic	SF	Finland	WD	Dominica*
RCB	Congo	SGP	Singapore*	WG	Grenada*
RCH	Chile	SME	Suriname*	WL	St Lucia*
RH	Haiti	SN	Senegal	WS	W Samoa
RI	Indonesia*	SU	USSR	WV	St Vincent and the
RIM	Mauritania	SWA	Namibia*		Grenadines*
RL	Lebanon	SY	Seychelles*	YU	Yugoslavia
RM	Madagascar	SYR	Syria	YV	Venezuela
RMM	Mali	T	Thailand*	Z	Zambia*
RN	Niger	TG	Togo	ZA	South Africa*
RO	Romania	TN	Tunisia	ZRE	Zaire
ROK	Korea, Republic of	TR	Turkey	ZW	Zimbabwe*
ROU	Uruguay	TT	Trinidad and Tobago*		
RP	Philippines	USA	USA		

*In countries so marked, the rule of the road is drive on the left; in other countries, drive on the right.

UK AIRPORTS

Alderney   Channel Islands
Baltasound   Unst, Shetlands
Belfast City
Belfast International
Benbecula   Hebrides
Biggin Hill   Kent
Blackpool   Lancashire
Bournemouth   Dorset
Bristol   Avon
Cambridge
Cardiff
Coventry   West Midlands
Dundee
Dyce   Aberdeen
East Midlands   Derbyshire
Exeter   Devon
Fair Isle   Shetlands
Gatwick   London
Glenegedale   Islay

Glasgow
Grimsetter   Orkney
Guernsey   Channel Islands
Heathrow   London
Humberside
Inverness
Jersey   Channel Islands
Kirkwall   Orkney
Leeds-Bradford
Liverpool
London City
Luton   Bedfordshire
Lydd   Kent
Manchester
Newcastle
North Bay   Barra, Hebrides
Norwich   Norfolk
Penzance   Cornwall
Plymouth (Roborough)   Devon

Prestwick   Ayrshire
Ronaldsway   Isle of Man
Saint Mary's   Scilly Isles
Sandown   Isle of Wight
Scatsa   Shetlands
Southampton   Hampshire
Southend   Essex
Stansted   London
Stornoway   Hebrides
Sumburgh   Shetlands
Swansea
Teeside   Cleveland
Tingwall   Lerwick, Shetlands
Tiree   Hebrides
Tresco   Scilly Isles
Turnhouse   Edinburgh
West Midlands   Birmingham
Westray   Orkney
Wick   Caithness

INTERNATIONAL AIRPORTS

Alborg Roedslet Norresundbyr, Denmark
Abadan International Iran
Abu Dhabi United Arab Emirates
Adana Turkey
Adelaide Australia
Agno Lugano, Switzerland
Ain el Bay Constantine, Algeria
Albany County New York, USA
Albuquerque New Mexico, USA
Alexandria Egypt
Alfonso Bonilla Aragon Cali, Columbia
Alicante Spain
Almeria Spain
Amarillo Texas, USA
Amborovy Majunga, Madagascar
Amilcar Cabral International Sal I,
  Cape Verde
Aminu International Kano, Nigeria
Anchorage Alaska, USA
Archangel USSR
Arlanda Stockholm, Sweden
Arnos Vale St Vincent
Arrecife Lanzarote, Canary Is
Arturo Marino Benitez Santiago, Chile
Asturias Spain
Ataturk Istanbul, Turkey
Auckland New Zealand
Augusto C Sandino Managua, Nicaragua
Baghdad International Iraq
Bahrain International Bahrain
Bali International/Ngurah Rai Denpasar,
  Indonesia
Balice Kracow, Poland
Bandar Seri Begawan Brunei
Baneasa Bucharest, Romania
Bangkok International Thailand
Barajas Madrid, Spain
Barcelona Spain
Basle-Mulhouse Basle, Spain
Beijing (Peking) China
Beira Mozambique
Beirut International Khaldeh, Lebanon
Belfast International UK
Belgrade Yugoslavia
Belize City International Belize
Ben Gurion Tel Aviv, Israel
Benina Benghazi, Libya
Benito Juarez Mexico City, Mexico
Berlin-Schonefeld Berlin, Germany
Berline-Tegel Berlin, Germany
Berne Switzerland
Billund Denmark

Birmingham Alabama, USA
Blackburne/Plymouth Montserrat (Leeward I)
Blagnac Toulouse, France
Bole Addis Ababa, Ethiopia
Bombay India
Borispol Kiev, USSR
Boukhalef Tangier, Morocco
Boulogne France
Bourgas Bulgaria
Bradley International Hartford, Connecticut,
  USA
Brasilia International Brazil
Bremen Germany
Brisbane Australia
Brnik Ljubljana, Yugoslavia
Bromma Stockholm, Sweden
Brussels National Belgium
Buffalo New York, USA
Bujumbura Burindi
Bulawayo Zimbabwe
Butmir Sarajevo, Yugoslavia
Cairns Queensland, Australia
Cairo International Egypt
Calabar Nigeria
Calcutta India
Calgary International Canada
Cancun Mexico
Cannon International Reno, Nevada, USA
Canton Akron, Ohio, USA
Capodichino Naples, Italy
Carrasco Montevideo, Uruguay
Carthage Tunis, Tunisia
Cebu Philippines
Chang Kai Shek Taipei, Taiwan
Changi Singapore
Charleroi (Gossilies) Belgium
Charles de Gaulle Paris, France
Charleston South Carolina, USA
Charleston West Virginia, USA
Charlotte North Carolina, USA
Chteau Bougon Nantes, France
Christchurch New Zealand
Ciampino Rome, Italy
Cologne-Bonn Cologne, Germany
Columbus Ohio, USA
Congonhas São Paulo, Brazil
Copenhagen International Kastrup, Denmark
Cork Republic of Ireland
Costa Smeralda Olbia, Sardinia
Côte d'Azure Nice, France
Cotonou Benin
Cristoforo Colombo Genoa, Italy

INTERNATIONAL AIRPORTS (cont.)

Crown Point Scarborough, Tobago
Cuscatlan Comalapa, El Salvador
D F Malan Cape Town, South Africa
Dalaman Turkey
Dallas/Fort Worth Dallas, Texas, USA
Damascus Syria
Dar-es-Salaam Tanzania
Darwin Australia
Des Moines Iowa, USA
Detroit-Wayne County Detroit, Michigan, USA
Deurne Antwerp, Belgium
Dhahran International Al Khobar, Saudi Arabia
Djibouti Djibouti
Doha Qatar
Dois de Julho International Salvador, Brazil
Domodedovo Moscow, USSR
Don Miguel Hidalgo y Castilla Guadalajara, Mexico
Dorval International Montreal, Canada
Douala Cameroon
Dresden Germany
Dubai United Arab Emirates
Dublin Republic of Ireland
Dubrovnik Yugoslavia
Dulles International Washington DC, USA
Dusseldorf Germany
Ecterdingen Stuttgart, Germany
Edmonton International Canada
Eduardo Gomes Manaus, Brazil
Eindhoven Netherlands
El Dorado Bogata, Colombia
El Paso Texas, USA
Elat Israel
Elmas Cagliari, Italy
Entebbe Uganda
Entzheim Strasbourg, France
Eppley Airfield Omaha, Nebraska, USA
Erie Pennsylvania, USA
Ernesto Cortissoz Barranquilla, Colombia
Esbjerg Denmark
Esenboga Ankara, Turkey
Faleolo Apia, Samoa
Faro Portugal
Ferihegy Budapest, Hungary
Findel Luxembourg
Fiumicino (Leonardo da Vinci) Rome, Italy
Flesland Bergen, Norway
Fontanarossa Catonia, Sicily
Fornebu Oslo, Norway
Fort de France Lamentin, Martinique
Fort Lauderdale Florida, USA
Fort Myers Florida, USA
Frankfurt am Main Germany

Freeport International Bahamas
Frejorgues Montpellier, France
Fuenterrabia San Sebastian, Spain
Fuerteventura Canary Is
Fuhlsbuttel Hamburg, Germany
G Marconi Bologna, Italy
Galileo Galilei Pisa, Italy
Gatwick UK
G'Bessia Conakry, Guinea Republic
General Abelard L Rodriguez Tijuana, Mexico
General Juan N Alvarez Acapulco, Mexico
General Manuel Marquez de Leon La Paz, Mexico
General Mariano Escobedo Monterrey, Mexico
General Mitchell Milwaukee, Wisconsin, USA
General Rafael Buelna Mazatlan, Mexico
Geneva Switzerland
Gerona/Costa Brava Gerona, Spain
Gillot St Denis de la Reunion, Indian Ocean
Golden Rock St Kitts
Goleniow Szczecin, Poland
Glasgow UK
Granada Spain
Grantley Adams International Bridgetown, Barbados
Greater Cincinnati Ohio, USA
Greater Pittsburgh Pennsylvania, USA
Guam Guam
Guararapes International Recife, Brazil
Guarulhos International São Paulo, Brazil
Halifax Canada
Halim Perdanakusama Jakarta, Indonesia
Hamilton Kindley Field Hamilton, Bermuda
Hancock Field Syracuse, New York State, USA
Hanover-Langenhagen Hanover, Germany
Hanoi Vietnam
Harare Zimbabwe
Harrisburg Pennsylvania, USA
Hartsfield Atlanta, Georgia, USA
Hassan Laayoune, Morocco
Hato Curaao, Netherlands Antilles
Hahaya International Moroni, Comoros
Hanedi Tokyo, Japan
Heathrow UK
Hellenikon Athens, Greece
Henderson Field Honiari, Solomon Is
Heraklion Crete, Greece
Hewanorra International St Lucia
Ho Chi Minh City Vietnam
Hong Kong International Hong Kong
Hongqiao Shanghai, China
Honolulu Hawaii, USA

INTERNATIONAL AIRPORTS (cont.)

Hopkins Cleveland, Ohio, USA
Houari Boumedienne International
  Dar-el-Beida, Algeria
Houston Texas, USA
Ibiza Balearics, Spain
Indianapolis Indiana, USA
Indira Ghandi International Delhi, India
Inezgane Agadir, Morocco
Islamabad Pakistan
Isle Verde San Juan, Puerto Rico
Izmir Turkey
Itazuke Fukuoka, Japan
Ivanka Bratislava, Czechoslovakia
Ivato Antananarivo, Madagascar
J F Kennedy New York, USA
Jackson Field Port Moresby, Papua
  New Guinea
Jacksonville Florida, USA
James M Cox Dayton, Ohio, USA
Jan Smuts Johannesburg, South Africa
Jomo Kenyatta Nairobi, Kenya
Jorge Chavez International Lima, Peru
Jose Marti International Havana, Cuba
Juan Santa Maria International Alajuela,
  Costa Rica
Kagoshima Japan
Kalmar Sweden
Kamazu Lilongwe, Malawi
Kansas City Missouri, USA
Kaohsiung Taiwan
Karachi Pakistan
Karpathos Karpathos, Greece
Katunayake Colombo, Sri Lanka
Keflavik Reykjavik, Iceland
Kent County Grand Rapids, Michigan, USA
Kerkyra Corfu, Greece
Key West Florida, USA
Khartoum Sudan
Khoramaksar Aden, Yemen Arab Republic
Khwaja Rawash Kabul, Afghanistan
Kigali Rwanda
Kimpo International Seoul, South Korea
King Abdul Aziz Jeddah, Saudi Arabia
King Khaled Riyadh, Saudi Arabia
Kingsford Smith Sydney, Australia
Kjevik Kristiansand, Norway
Klagenfurt Austria
Komaki Nagoya, Japan
Kos Greece
Kota Kinabulu Sabah, Malaysia
Kotoka Accra, Ghana
Kranebitten Innsbruck, Austria

Kuching Sarawak, Malaysia
Kungsangen Norrkoping, Sweden
Kuwait International Kuwait
La Aurora Guatemala City, Guatemala
La Coruna Spain
La Guardia New York, USA
La Mesa San Pedro Sula, Honduras
La Parra Jerez de la Frontera, Spain
La Paz/J F Kennedy International La Paz, Bolivia
Lahore Pakistan
Landvetter Gothenburg, Sweden
Larnaca International Cyprus
Las Americas International Santo Domingo,
  Dominican Republic
Las Palmas Gran Canaria, Canary Is
Le Raizet Point-à-Pitre, Guadeloupe
Leipzig Germany
Les Angades Oujda, Morocco
Lesquin Lille, France
Lester B Pearson International Toronto,
  Canada
Libreville Gabon
Lic Gustavo Diaz Ordaz Puerto Vallarta,
  Mexico
Lic Manuel Crecencio Rejon Merida, Mexico
Liège (Bierset) Belgium
Linate Milan, Italy
Lincoln Nebraska, USA
Lindbergh International San Diego, USA
Linz Austria
Lisbon Portugal
Little Rock Arkansas, USA
Llabanère Perpignan, France
Logan International Boston, Massachusetts,
  USA
Lomé Togo
London City UK
Long Beach California, USA
Los Angeles California, USA
Loshitsa Minsk, USSR
Louis Botha Durban, South Africa
Louisville Kentucky, USA
Lourdes/Tarbes Juillan, France
Luanda Angola
Luano Lubumashi, Zaire
Lubbock Texas, USA
Luis Munoz Marin International San Juan,
  Puerto Rico
Lungi Freetown, Sierra Leone
Luqa Malta
Lusaka Zambia
Luxor Egypt

INTERNATIONAL AIRPORTS (cont.)

Maastricht Netherlands
McCarran International Las Vegas, Nevada, USA
McCoy International Orlando, Florida, USA
Mactan International Cebu, Philippines
Mahon Menorca
Mais Gate Port au Prince, Haiti
Malaga Spain
Male' Maldives
Malpensa Milan, Italy
Managua Nicaragua
Manchester New Hampshire, USA
Manchester UK
Maputo Mozambique
Marco Polo Venice, Italy
Mariscal Sucre Quito, Ecuador
Maseru Lesotho
Matsapha Manzini, Swaziland
Maupertus Cherbourg, France
Maxglan Salzburg, Austria
Maya Maya Brazaville, Congo
Medina Saudi Arabia
Meenambakkam International Madras, India
Mehrabad International Teheran, Iran
Melita Djerba, Tunisia
Memphis Tennessee, USA
Menara Marrakech, Morocco
Merignac Bordeaux, France
Miami Florida, USA
Midway Chicago, Illinois, USA
Mingaladon,Yangon Myanmar, Malaysia
Ministro Pistarini Buenos Aires, Argentina
Minneapolis/St Paul Minneapolis, USA
Mirabel Montreal, Canada
Mogadishu Somalia
Mohamed V Casablanca, Morocco
Moi International Mombasa, Kenya
Monroe County Rochester, New York State, USA
Morelos Mexico City, Mexico
Münster/Osnabrück Germany
Murmansk USSR
Murtala Muhammed Lagos, Nigeria
Nadi International Fiji
Nagasaki Japan
Narita Tokyo, Japan
Narssarsuaq Greenland
Nashville Tennessee, USA
Nassau International Bahamas
Nauru Nauru
N'djamena Chad
N'Djili Kinshasa, Zaire

Nejrab Aleppo, Syria
Newcastle UK
New Orleans Louisiana, USA
Newark New York, USA
Niamey Niger
Ninoy Aquino International Manila, Philippinnes
Nis Yugoslavia
Norfolk International Virginia, USA
Norman Manley International Kingston, Jamaica
North Front Gibraltar
Nouadhibou Mauritania
Nouakchott Mauritania
Novo-Alexeyevka Tblisi, Georgia, USSR
Nuremberg Germany
Oakland International California, USA
Octeville Le Havrets, France
Odense Denmark
O'Hare Chicago, Illinois, USA
Okecie Warsaw, Poland
Okinawa Naha, Japan
Oran Algeria
Orebro Sweden
Orlando Florida, USA
Orly Paris, France
Osaka Japan
Osvaldo Veira Bissau, Guinea Bissau
Otopeni Bucharest, Romania
Ouagadougou Burkino Faso
Owen Roberts Grand Cayman, West Indies
Pago Pago Samoa
Palese Bari, Italy
Palma Majorca
Pamplona Spain
Panama City Panama
Paphos Cyprus
Papola Casale Brindisi, Italy
Paradisi Rhodes, Greece
Patenga Chittagong, Bangladesh
Penang Malaysia
Peninsula Monterey, California, USA
Peretola Florence, Italy
Perth Australia
Peshawar Pakistan
Peterson Field Colorado Springs, Colorado, USA
Philadelphia Pennsylvania, USA
Piarco Port of Spain, Trinidad
Pleso Zagreb, Yugoslavia
Pochentong Phnom Penh, Cambodia
Point Salines Grenada
Pointe Noire Congo

INTERNATIONAL AIRPORTS (cont.)

Polonia Medan, Indonesia
Ponta Delgado São Miguel, Azores
Port Bouet Abidjan, Ivory Coast
Port Harcourt Nigeria
Portland Maine, USA
Portland Oregon, USA
Port Sudan Sudan
Porto Pedra Rubras Oporto, Portugal
Praia Cape Verde
Prestwick UK
Princess Beatriz Aruba, Netherlands Antilles
Provence Marseille, France
Pula Yugoslavia
Pulkovo Leningard, USSR
Punta Arenas International Chile
Punta Raisi Palermo, Sicily
Queen Alia Amman Jordan
Releigh/Durham North Carolina, USA
Ras al Khaimah United Arab Emirates
Rebiechowo Gdańsk, Poland
Regina Canada
Reina Sofia Tenerife
Rejon Merida, Mexico
Richmond Virginia, USA
Riem Munich, Germany
Rio de Janeiro International Brazil
Riyadh International Saudi Arabia
Roberts International Monrovia, Liberia
Rochambau Cayenne, French Guiana
Robert Mueller Municipal Airport Austin, Texas, USA
Ronchi dei Legionari Trieste, Italy
Rotterdam Netherlands
Ruzyne Prague, Czechoslovakia
Saab Linkoping, Sweden
Saint Eufemia Lamezia Terma, Italy
Saint Louis Missouri, USA
Saint Thomas Virgin Is
Sainte Foy Quebec, Canada
Sale Rabat, Morocco
Salgado Filho International Porto Alegre, Brazil
Salt Lake City Utah, USA
San Antonio Texas, USA
San Diego California, USA
San Francisco California, USA
San Giusto Pisa, Italy
San Javier Murcia, Spain
San José California, USA
San Pablo Seville, Spain
San Salvador El Salvador
Sanaa International Yemen

Sangster International Montego Bay, Jamaica
Santa Caterina Funchal, Madeira
Santa Cruz La Palma, Canary Is
Santa Isabel Malabo, Guinea
Santander Spain
Santiago Spain
Santos Dumont Rio de Janeiro, Brazil
São Tomé São Tomé
Satolas Lyon, France
Schipol Amsterdam, Netherlands
Schwechat Vienna, Austria
Seeb Muscat, Oman
Senou Bamako, Mali
Seychelles International Mahe, Seychelles
Sfax Tunisia
Shannon Republic of Ireland
Sharjah United Arab Emirates
Sheremetyevo Moscow, USA
Silvio Pettirossi Asuncion, Paraguay
Simon Bolivar Caracas, Venezuela
Simon Bolivar Guayaquil, Ecuador
Sir Seewoosagur Ramgoolam Plaisance, Mauritius
Sir Seretse Khama Gaborone, Botswana
Skanes Monastir, Morocco
Skopje Yugoslavia
Sky Harbour Phoenix, Arizona, USA
Snilow Lwow, USSR
Sofia International Bulgaria
Sola Stavanger, Norway
Sondica Bilbao, Spain
Søndre Strømfjord Greenland
Spilve Riga, Latvia
Split Yugoslavia
Spokane Washington, USA
Stansted UK
Stapleton International Denver, Colorado, USA
Sturup Malmö, Sweden
Subang International Kuala Lumpur, Malaysia
Sunan Pyongyang, North Korea
Tacoma Seattle, USA
Tallahassee Florida, USA
Tamatve Madagascar
Tampa Florida, USA
Tegucigalpa Toncontin, Honduras
Thalerhof Graz, Austria
Theodore Francis Providence, Rhode I, USA
Thessalonika Greece
Timehri International Georgetown, Guyana
Timişoara Romania
Tirana Albania

INTERNATIONAL AIRPORTS (cont.)

Tito Menniti   Reggio Calabria, Italy
Tontouta   Noumea, New Caledonia
Townsville   Australia
Tribhuyan   Kathmandu, Nepal
Tripoli   Libya
Trivandrum   India
Truax Field   Madison, Wisconsin, USA
Tucson   Arizona, USA
Tullamarine   Melbourne, Australia
Turin   Italy
Turku   Finland
Turnhouse   Edinburgh, UK
Ulemiste   Tallinn, USSR
Unokovo   Moscow, USSR
Uplands   Ottawa, Canada
V C Bird International   Antigua
Vaasa   Finland
Vagar   Faeroe Is
Valencia   Spain
Vancouver International   Canada
Vantaa   Helsinki, Finland

Varna International   Bulgaria
Verona   Italy
Victoria   British Columbia, Canada
Vigie   St Lucia
Vigo   Spain
Vilnius   USSR
Vilo de Porto   Santa Maria, Azores
Viracopos   Sao Paulo, Brazil
Vitoria   Spain
Washington International   Baltimore, Maryland, USA
Wattay   Vientiane, Laos
Wellington   New Zealand
Wichita   Kansas, USA
Will Rogers   Oklahoma City, Oklahoma, USA
Winnipeg International   Manitoba, Canada
Yoff   Dakar, Senegal
Yundam   Banjul, Gambia
Zakynthos   Greece
Zia International   Dhaka, Bangladesh
Zürich   Switzerland

AIRLINE DESIGNATORS

Code	Airline	Country
AA	American Airlines	USA
AC	Air Canada	Canada
AF	Air France	France
AH	Air Algerie	Algeria
AI	Air India	India
AM	Aromexico	Mexico
AN	Ansett Australia	Australia
AQ	Aloha Airlines	Hawaii
AR	Aerolineas Argentinas	Argentina
AS	Alaska Airlines	USA
AT	Royal Air Maroc	Morocco
AV	Avianca	Colombia
AY	Finnair	Finland
AZ	Alitalia	Italy
BA	British Airways	UK
BB	Sansa	Costa Rica
BC	Brymon Airways	UK
BD	British Midland	UK
BG	Biman Bangladesh Airlines	Bangladesh
BH	Augusta Airways	Australia
BI	Royal Brunei Airlines	Brunei
BO	Bouraq Indonesia Airlines	Indonesia
BP	Air Botswana	Botswana
BT	Ansett NT	Australia
BU	Braathens SAFE	Norway

Code	Airline	Country
BW	BWIA International Trinidad and Tobego Airways	Trinidad
BY	Britannia Airways	UK
CA	Air China	China
CI	China Airlines	Taiwan
CM	COPA (Compania Panamena de Aviación)	Panama
CO	Continental Airlines	USA
CO	Air Micronesia	Mariana Is
CP	Canadian Airlines International	Canada
CU	Cubana	Cuba
CW	Air Marshall Islands	Marshall Is
CX	Cathay Pacific Airways	Hong Kong
CY	Cyprus Airways	Cyprus
DA	Dan-Air Services	UK
DI	Delta Air Regionalflug	Germany
DL	Delta Air Lines	USA
DO	Dominicana de Aviación	Dominican Republic
DS	Air Senegal	Senegal
DT	TAAG-Angola Airlines	Angola
DX	Danair	Denmark
DY	Alyemda-Democratic Yemen Airlines	Republic of Yemen
EI	Aer Lingus	Ireland
EK	Emirates	United Arab Emirates

AIRLINE DESIGNATORS (cont.)

Code	Airline	Country	Code	Airline	Country
ET	Ethiopian Airlines	Ethiopia	KQ	Kenya Airways	Kenya
EU	Ecuatoriana	Ecuador	KU	Kuwait Airways	Kuwait
EW	Eastwest Airlines	Australia	KV	Transkei Airways	South Africa
EX	Eagle Airways	New Zealand	LA	LAN-Chile	Chile
FF	Tower Air	USA	LC	Loganair	UK
FG	Afriana Afgan Airlines	Afghanistan	LE	Link Airlines	South Africa
FI	Icelandair	Iceland	LF	Linjeflyg	Sweden
FJ	Air Pacific	Fiji	LG	Luxair	Luxembourg
FO	Western New South		LH	Lufthansa	Germany
	Wales Airlines	Australia	LJ	Sierra National Airlines	Sierra Leone
FR	Ryanair (Dublin)	Ireland	LL	Bell-Air	New Zealand
FU	Air Littoral	France	LM	ALM (Antillean Airlines)	Netherlands
GA	Garuda Indonesia	Indonesia			Antilles
GC	Lina Congo	Congo	LN	Jamahiriya Libyan Arab Airlines	Libya
GF	Gulf Air	Bahrain	LO	LOT Polish Airlines	Poland
GH	Ghana Airways	Ghana	LR	LACSA	Costa Rica
GI	Air Guinée	Guinea	LT	LTU (Luftransport-Unternehmen	
GL	Gronlandsfly	Greenland		GMBH)	Germany
GN	Air Gabon	Gabon	LU	Theron Airways	South Africa
GR	Aurigny Air Services	Channel Is	LX	Crossair	Switzerland
GT	GB Airways	Gibraltar	LY	El Al Israel Airlines	Israel
GY	Guyana Airways Corporation	Guyana	MA	Malev	Hungary
HA	Hawaiian Airlines	USA	MD	Air Madagascar	Madagascar
HH	Somali Airlines	Somalia	ME	Middle East Airlines	Lebanon
HM	Air Seychelles	Seychelles	MH	Malaysian Airline System	Malaysia
HP	America West Airlines	USA	MK	Air Mauritius	Mauritius
HT	Air Tchad	Chad	MN	Commercial Airways	South Africa
HV	Transavia Airlines	Netherlands	MR	Air Mauritanie	Mauritania
IB	Iberia	Spain	MS	Egyptair	Egypt
IC	Indian Airlines	India	MV	Ansett WA	Australia
IE	Solomon Airlines	Solomon Is	MX	Mexicana	Mexico
IP	Airlines of Tasmania	Australia	NG	Lauda Air	Austria
IR	Iran Air	Iran	NH	All Nippon Airways	Japan
IY	Yemenia Yemen Airways	Yemen Arab	NJ	Namakwaland Ludgiens	South Africa
		Republic	NM	Mount Cook Airlines	New Zealand
JE	Manx Airlines	Isle of Man	NN	Air Martinique	Martinique
JG	Swedair	Sweden	NO	Aus-Air	Australia
JL	Japan Airlines	Japan	NR	Norontair	Canada
JM	Air Jamaica	Jamaica	NS	NFD	Germany
JP	Adria Airways	Yugoslavia	NU	Southwest Airlines	Japan
JQ	Trans Jamaica Airlines	Jamaica	NV	Northwest Territorial Airways	Canada
JS	Chosonminhang Korean		NW	Northwest Airlines	USA
	Airways	DPR Korea	NX	Nationair Canada	Canada
JU	JAT (Jugoslovenski		NZ	Air New Zealand	New Zealand
	Aerotransport)	Yugoslavia	OA	Olympic Airways	Greece
JY	Jersey European Airways	Channel Is	OG	Air Guadeloupe	French W Indies
KA	Dragonair	Hong Kong	OK	CSA (Ceskoslovenske	
KE	Korean Air	Rep. of Korea		Aerolinie)	Czechoslovakia
KH	Cook Islandair	Cook Is	OM	Air Mongol-MIAT	Mongolian P R
KL	KLM	Netherlands	ON	Air Nauru	Australia
KM	Air Malta	Malta	OO	Skywest Airlines	Australia
KP	Safair	South Africa	OR	Air Comores	Comoros

AIRLINE DESIGNATORS (cont.)

OS	Austrian Airlines	Austria	TU	Tunis Air		Tunisia
PA	Pan American World Airways	USA	TW	TWA (Trans World Airlines)		USA
PB	Air Burundi	Burundi	TX	TAN (Transportes		Honduras
PC	Fiji Air	Fiji		Aereos Nacionales)		
PK	Pakistan International Airlines	Pakistan	UA	United Airlines		USA
PL	Aeroperu	Peru	UC	Ladeco		Chile
PR	Philippine Airlines	Philippines	UK	Air UK		UK
PU	PLUNA (Primeras Lineas Uruguayas		UL	Air Lanka		Sri Lanka
	de Navegación Aerea)	Uruguay	UM	Air Zimbabwe		Zimbabwe
PX	Air Niugini	Papua New	UN	Eastern Australia Airlines		Australia
		Guinea	UP	Bahamasair		Bahamas
PY	Surinam Airways	Suriname	US	USAir		USA
PZ	LAP (Lineas Aereas		UT	UTA (Union de Transports		France
	Paraguayas)	Paraguay		Aériens)		
QC	Air Zaire	Zaire	UY	Cameroon Airlines		Cameroon
QF	Qantas Airways	Australia	VA	VIASA (Venezolana Internacional		
QL	Lesotho Airways	Lesotho		de Aviación)		Venezuela
QM	Air Malawi	Malawi	VB	Birmingham European Airways		UK
QU	Uganda Airlines	Uganda	VE	Avensa		Venezuela
QV	Lao Aviation	Lao PDR	VH	Air Burkina		Burkina Faso
QX	Horizon Air	USA	VK	Air Tungaru	Republic of Kiribati	
QZ	Zambia Airways	Zambia	VN	Hang Khong Vietnam		Vietnam
RA	Royal Nepal Airlines	Nepal	VO	Tyrolean Airways		Austria
RB	Syrian Arab Airlines	Syria	VP	Vasp		Brazil
RG	Varig	Brazil	VR	Transportes Aereos de	Cape Verde Is	
RJ	Royal Jordanian	Jordan		Cabo Verde		
RK	Air Afrique	Côte d'Ivoire	VS	Virgin Atlantic Airways		UK
RL	Aeronica	Nicaragua	VT	Air Tahiti		Tahiti
RO	Tarom	Romania	VU	Air Ivoire		Côte d'Ivoire
RR	Royal Air Force	UK	VX	ACES (Aerolineas Cent-		Colombia
RY	Air Rwanda	Rwanda		rales de Colombia)		
SA	South African Airways	South Africa	WI	Rottnest Airbus		Australia
SB	Air Caledonie International	New Caledonia	WJ	Labrador Airways		Canada
SC	Cruzeiro	Brazil	WN	Southwest Airlines		USA
SD	Sudan Airways	Sudan	WR	Friendly Islands Airways		Tonga
SH	SAHSA (Servicio Aero		WT	Nigeria Airways		Nigeria
	de Honduras)	Honduras	WX	Ansett Express		Australia
SJ	Southern Air	New Zealand	WY	Oman Aviation Services		Oman
SK	SAS (Scandinavian Airlines)	Sweden	XX	Aereonaves del Peru		Peru
SM	Aberdeen Airways	UK	YB	Trans Continental Airlines		USA
SN	Sabena World Airlines	Belgium	YK	Cyprus Turkish Airlines		Cyprus
SQ	Singapore Airlines	Singapore	YN	Air Creebec		Canada
SR	Swissair	Switzerland	YP	Aero Lloyd		Germany
SU	Aeroflot	USSR	YU	Dominair	Dominican Republic	
SV	Saudia	Saudi Arabia	YZ	Transportes Aereos Da	Guinea Bissau	
SW	Namib Air	Namibia		Guiné Bissau		
TC	Air Tanzania	Tanzania	ZA	Zas Airline of Egypt		Egypt
TG	Thai Airways International	Thailand	ZB	Monarch Airlines		UK
TK	Turkish Airlines	Turkey	ZC	Royal Swazi National		Swaziland
TM	LAM (Linhas Aereas de	Mozambique		Airways		
	Moçambique)		ZP	Virgin Air		Virgin Is
TN	Australian Airlines	Australia	ZQ	Ansett New Zealand	New Zealand	
TP	TAP Air Portugal	Portugal	ZX	Air BC		Canada
TR	Transbrasil S/A Linhas Aereas	Brazil				

AIR DISTANCES

Air distances between some major cities, given in statute miles. To convert to kilometres, multiply number given by 1.6093.

* Shortest route.

	Amsterdam	Anchorage	Beijing	Buenos Aires	Cairo	Chicago	Delhi	Hong Kong	Honolulu	Istanbul	Johannesburg	Lagos	London	Los Angeles	Mexico City	Montreal	Moscow	Nairobi	Paris	Perth	Rome	Santiago	Sydney	Tokyo
Anchorage	4475																							
Beijing	6566	4756																						
Buenos Aires	7153	8329	12000																					
Cairo	2042	6059	6685	7468																				
Chicago	4109	28	7599	5587	6135																			
Delhi	3985	8925	2368	8340	2753	8119																		
Hong Kong	5926	5063	1235	3124	5098	7827	2345																	
Honolulu	8368	2780	6778	8693	9439	4246	7883	5543																
Istanbul	1373	6024	4763	7783	764	5502	2833	5998	9547															
Johannesburg	5606	1042	10108	5725	4012	8705	6765	6728	12892	4776														
Lagos	3161	7587	8030	4832	2443	7065	5196	7541	10367	3207	2854													
London	217	4472	5054	6985	2187	3956	4169	5979	7252	1552	5640	3115												
Los Angeles	5559	2333	6349	6140	7589	1746	8717	7231	2553	6994	10443	7716	5442											
Mexico City	5724	3751	7912	4592	7730	1687	9806	8794	4116	7255	10070	7343	5703	1563										
Montreal	3422	3100	7557	5640	5431	737	7421	8664	4923	4795	8322	5595	3252	2482	2307									
Moscow	1338	4291	3604	8382	1790	5500	2698	4839	3802	1089	6280	4462	1550	6992	9061	4333								
Nairobi	4148	8714	8888	7427	2203	8177	4956	8794	11498	2967	1809	3674	4245	9688	9949	7498	3951							
Paris	261	4683	5108	6392	1995	4140	4089	5985	7463	1394	5422	2922	220	5633	5714	3434	1540	4031						
Perth	9118	8368	4987	9734	7766	11281	5013	3752	7115	7846	5564	10209	9246	9535	11098	12402	8355	7373	12587					
Rome	809	5258	5306	6931	1329	4828	3679	5773	8150	852	4802	2497	898	6340	6601	5431	1478	3349	688	8309				
Santiago	7714	7919	13622	710	8029	5323	12715	3733	8147	10109	5738	6042	8568	5594	4168	5551	10118	7547	7461	15129	7548			
Sydney	1039	8522	5689	7760	9196	9324	6495	4586	5078	9883	7601	11700	10565	7498	9061	9980	9425	8565	10150	2037	10149	13092		
Tokyo	6006*	3443	1313	13100	6362	6286	3656	1807	3331	5757	8535	9130*	6218	5451	7014	6913	4668	6996	6208*	4925	6146	9785	4640	
Washington	3854	3430	7930	6037	5859	550	7841	8385	4822	5347	8199	5472	3672	2294	1871	493	4884	7918	3843	11829	4495	5061	9792	6763

FLYING TIMES

Approximate flying times between some major cities. Timings quoted (in hours and minutes) are for 'flying time' only. In many cases in order to travel between two points chosen, it is necessary to change aircraft one or more times. Time between flights has not been included.

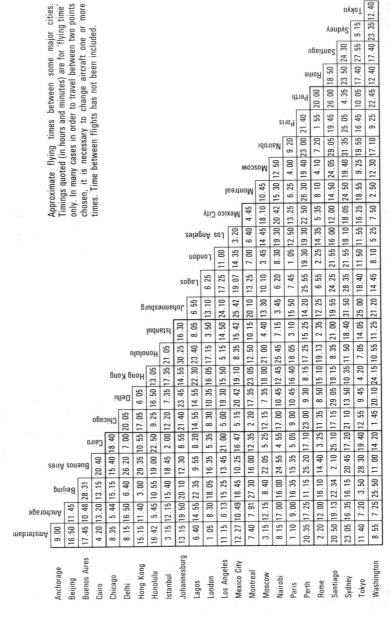

	Amsterdam	Anchorage	Beijing	Buenos Aires	Cairo	Chicago	Delhi	Hong Kong	Honolulu	Istanbul	Johannesburg	Lagos	London	Los Angeles	Mexico City	Montreal	Moscow	Nairobi	Paris	Perth	Rome	Santiago	Sydney	Tokyo
Anchorage	9.00																							
Beijing	16.50	11.45																						
Buenos Aires	17.45	10.48	28.31																					
Cairo	4.20	13.20	13.15	20.40																				
Chicago	8.35	5.44	15.15	15.40	18.40																			
Delhi	8.15	16.50	6.40	26.20	7.00	20.05																		
Hong Kong	15.15	11.40	3.00	29.35	10.55	17.05	6.05																	
Honolulu	16.42	5.45	10.55	19.00	22.50	9.25	16.50	13.05																
Istanbul	3.15	12.15	15.40	18.45	2.00	12.20	7.35	17.35	21.05															
Johannesburg	13.15	19.50	20.10	12.30	8.55	21.40	23.45	14.55	30.25	16.30														
Lagos	6.40	14.55	22.35	9.55	8.20	14.55	14.55	22.30	23.40	8.05	6.55													
London	1.05	8.30	18.05	16.35	5.35	8.30	10.35	16.05	17.15	3.50	13.10	6.25												
Los Angeles	11.15	6.13	15.25	13.45	21.00	5.00	19.30	15.50	5.15	14.50	24.10	17.25	11.00											
Mexico City	12.27	10.49	18.45	10.25	16.47	5.15	20.42	19.10	8.35	15.42	25.42	19.07	14.35	3.20										
Montreal	7.40	7.91	27.30	16.00	12.35	2.20	17.35	23.05	12.50	10.15	20.10	13.25	7.00	6.40	4.45									
Moscow	3.15	12.15	8.40	22.05	5.25	12.15	7.35	18.00	21.00	4.40	13.30	10.10	3.45	14.45	18.10	10.45								
Nairobi	8.15	17.00	16.00	24.55	4.55	17.00	10.45	12.45	25.45	7.15	3.45	6.20	8.30	19.30	20.42	15.30	12.50							
Paris	1.10	9.00	16.35	15.35	5.05	9.00	10.45	16.40	18.05	3.10	15.50	7.45	1.05	12.50	13.25	6.25	4.00	9.20						
Perth	20.35	17.25	11.15	25.20	17.10	23.00	9.30	8.15	17.25	15.25	14.20	25.55	19.30	19.30	22.50	26.30	19.40	23.00	21.40					
Rome	2.20	12.00	16.10	14.40	3.25	11.35	8.50	15.10	19.13	2.35	12.25	6.55	2.25	14.35	5.35	8.10	4.10	7.20	1.55	20.00				
Santiago	20.50	19.13	22.34	2.10	25.10	17.15	29.05	19.15	8.35	21.00	19.55	24.25	21.55	16.00	12.00	14.50	24.05	29.05	19.45	26.00	18.50			
Sydney	23.05	16.35	16.15	20.45	17.20	21.10	13.50	10.35	11.50	18.40	31.50	28.35	21.55	18.10	18.05	24.50	19.40	31.35	25.05	4.35	23.50	24.30		
Tokyo	11.40	7.20	3.50	28.30	19.40	12.55	9.45	4.20	7.05	14.05	25.00	18.40	11.50	11.55	16.25	18.55	9.25	19.55	16.45	10.05	17.40	27.55	9.15	
Washington	8.55	7.25	25.50	11.00	14.20	1.45	20.10	24.15	10.55	11.25	21.20	14.45	8.10	5.25	7.50	2.50	12.30	17.10	9.25	22.45	12.40	17.40	23.35	12.40

DEEPWATER PORTS OF THE WORLD

Aalborg Denmark
Aarhus Denmark
Abadan Iran
Aberdeen UK
Abidjan Ivory Coast
Abu Dhabi United Arab
Emirates
Acajutla El Salvador
Acapulco Mexico
Adelaide Australia
Aden South Yemen
Agadir Morocco
Ajaccio Corsica
Alcudia Majorca
Alexandria Egypt
Algeciras Spain
Algiers Algeria
Alicante Spain
Almeria Spain
Amsterdam Netherlands
Anchorage USA
Ancona Italy
Annaba Algeria
Antofagasta Chile
Antwerp Belgium
Apia Samoa
Aqaba Jordan
Archangel USSR
Arica Chile
Ashdod Israel
Asuncion Paraguay
Auckland New Zealand
Aveiro Portugal
Aviles Spain

Bahia Blanca Argentina
Balboa Panama
Baltimore USA
Bandar Abbas Iran
Bangkok Thailand
Banjul Gambia
Barcelona Spain
Bari Italy
Barranquilla Colombia
Basrah Iraq
Beira Mozambique
Beirut Lebanon
Belem Brazil
Belfast UK
Belize City Belize
Benghazi Libya
Bergen Norway
Bilbao Spain

Bissau Guinea-Bissau
Bizerta Tunisia
Bombay India
Bordeaux France
Boston USA
Boulogne France
Bourgas Bulgaria
Brazzaville Congo
Bremen Germany
Brest France
Bridgetown Barbados
Brindisi Italy
Brisbane Australia
Bristol UK
Buena Ventura Colombia
Buenos Aires Argentina
Buffalo USA
Busan South Korea

Cabinda Angola
Cadiz Spain
Caen France
Cagliari Sardinia
Calabar Nigeria
Calais France
Calcutta India
Caldera Costa Rica
Calicut India
Callao Peru
Cape Town South Africa
Cardiff UK
Cartagena Colombia
Cartagena Spain
Casablanca Morocco
Catania Sicily
Cayenne French Guiana
Cebu Philippines
Charleston USA
Cherbourg France
Chiba Japan
Chicago USA
Chittagong Bangladesh
Cienfuegos Cuba
Cleveland USA
Coatzacoalcos Mexico
Cochin India
Cologne Germany
Colombo Sri Lanka
Conakry Guinea
Constanta Romania
Copenhagen Denmark
Corinto Nicaragua
Cork Republic of Ireland

Corunna Spain
Cotonou Benin
Dakar Senegal
Dalian China
Dammam Saudi Arabia
Dampier Australia
Dar es Salaam Tanzania
Darwin Australia
Davao Philippines
Detroit USA
Dieppe France
Djibouti Djibouti
Doha Qatar
Dordrecht Netherlands
Douala Cameroon
Douglas Isle of Man
Dover UK
Dubai United Arab Emirates
Dublin Republic of Ireland
Dubrovnik Yugoslavia
Duisburg Germany
Duluth USA
Dundee UK
Dunedin New Zealand
Dunkirk France
Durban South Africa
Durres Albania

East London South Africa
Eilat Israel
Emden Germany
Esbjerg Denmark

Famagusta Cyprus
Faro Portugal
Felixstowe UK
Flensburg Germany
Flushing Netherlands
Folkestone UK
Fortaleza Brazil
Fort-de-France Martinique
Frankfurt Germany
Fredericia Denmark
Frederikshavn Denmark
Fredrikstad Norway
Freeport Bahamas
Freeport USA
Freetown Sierra Leone
Fremantle Australia
Funchal Madeira

Galveston USA
Galway Republic of Ireland
Gateshead UK

DEEPWATER PORTS OF THE WORLD (cont.)

Gavle   Sweden
Gdansk   Poland
Gdynia   Poland
Geelong   Australia
Genoa   Italy
Georgetown   Cayman Is
Georgetown   Guyana
Ghent   Belgium
Gibraltar   Gibraltar
Gijon   Spain
Glasgow   UK
Godthaab   Greenland
Goole   UK
Gothenburg   Sweden
Grangemouth   UK
Gravesend   UK
Great Yarmouth   UK
Greenock   UK
Grimsby   UK
Guayaquil   Ecuador

Haifa   Israel
Hakodate   Japan
Halifax   Canada
Halmstad   Sweden
Hamburg   Germany
Hamilton   Bermuda
Hamilton   Canada
Harstad   Norway
Hartlepool   UK
Harwich   UK
Havana   Cuba
Hay Point   Australia
Helsingborg   Sweden
Helsinki   Finland
Hiroshima   Japan
Hobart   Australia
Ho Chi Minh City   Vietnam
Hodeida   Yemen Arab
Republic
Holyhead   UK
Hong Kong   Hong Kong
Honiari   Solomon Is
Honolulu   Hawaian Is
Houston   USA
Hull   UK

Ibiza   Ibiza
Inchon   South Korea
Iskenderun   Turkey
Istanbul   Turkey
Izmir   Turkey

Jacksonville   USA

Jakarta   Indonesia
Jarrow   UK
Jeddah   Saudi Arabia

Kagoshima   Japan
Kalmar   Sweden
Kandla   India
Kaohsiung   Taiwan
Karachi   Pakistan
Kawasaki   Japan
Khulna   Bangladesh
Kiel   Germany
Kingston   Jamaica
Kirkcaldy   UK
Kitakyushu   Japan
Klaipeda   USSR
Kobe   Japan
Kompong Som   Cambodia
Koper   Yugoslavia
Kota Kinabalu   Malaysia
Kristiansand   Norway
Kuching   Malaysia
Kushiro   Japan
Kuwait   Kuwait

Lagos   Nigeria
La Guaira   Venezuela
Langesund   Norway
La Plata   Argentina
Larnaca   Cyprus
Larne   UK
Las Palmas   Grand Canary
La Spezia   Italy
Lattakia   Syria
La Union   El Salvador
Le Havre   France
Leith   UK
Leningrad   USSR
Libreville   Gabon
Liege   Belgium
Limassol   Cyprus
Limerick   Republic of Ireland
Lisbon   Portugal
Liverpool   UK
Livingstone   Guatemala
Livorno   Italy
Lobito   Angola
London   UK
Long Beach   USA
Los Angeles   USA
Lowestoft   UK
Luanda   Angola
Lubeck   Germany
Luda   China

Madras   India
Malaga   Spain
Malmo   Sweden
Manchester   UK
Manila   Philippines
Mannheim   Germany
Manzanillo   Mexico
Maputo   Mozambique
Mar del Plata   Argentina
Maracaibo   Venezuela
Mariehamn   Finland
Marsala   Sicily
Marseilles   France
Masan   South Korea
Matanzas   Cuba
Melbourne   Australia
Mersin   Turkey
Messina   Sicily
Miami   USA
Middlesborough   UK
Milwaukee   USA
Mina Qaboos   Oman
Mina Sulman   Bahrain
Mindelo   Cape Verde
Mizushima   Japan
Mobile   USA
Mogadiscio   Somalia
Mombasa   Kenya
Monrovia   Liberia
Montego Bay   Jamaica
Montevideo   Uruguay
Montreal   Canada
Mormugao   India
Moulmein   Burma
Murmansk   USSR

Nacala   Mozambique
Nagasaki   Japan
Nagoya   Japan
Nampo   North Korea
Nantes   France
Napier   New Zealand
Naples   Italy
Narvik   Norway
Nassau   Bahamas
Natal   Brazil
Nelson   New Zealand
New Amsterdam   Guyana
Newcastle   Australia
Newcastle   UK
New Haven   USA
New Mangalore   India
New Orleans   USA

DEEPWATER PORTS OF THE WORLD (cont.)

New Plymouth   New Zealand
Newport   UK
New York   USA
Nice   France
Nouakchott   Mauritania
Noumea   New Caledonia
Novorossiysk   USSR
Nukualofa   Tonga
Nyborg   Denmark

Oakland   USA
Odense   Denmark
Odessa   USSR
Oporto   Portugal
Oran   Algeria
Osaka   Japan
Oslo   Norway
Ostend   Belgium
Oulu   Finland

Pago Pago   Samoa
Palermo   Sicily
Palma   Majorca
Palm Beach   USA
Panama Canal   Panama
Papeete   Tahiti
Paradip   India
Paramaribo   Suriname
Paranagua   Brazil
Paris   France
Pasajes   Spain
Pasir Gudang   Malaysia
Penang   Malaysia
Philadelphia   USA
Phnom-Penh   Cambodia
Piraeus   Greece
Plymouth   UK
Point-a-Pitre   Guadeloupe
Pointe-Noire   Congo
Pondicherry   India
Ponta Delgada   Azores
Poole   UK
Port-au-Prince   Haiti
Port Cartier   Canada
Port Elizabeth   South Africa
Port Georgetown   Guyana
Port Gentil   Gabon
Port Harcourt   Nigeria
Port Hedland   Australia
Port Kelang   Malaysia
Port Kembla   Australia
Portland   USA
Port Limon   Costa Rica
Port Louis   Mauritius

Port Moresby   Papua New Guinea
Port of Spain   Trinidad
Port Said   Egypt
Port Sudan   Sudan
Port Talbot   UK
Port Victoria   Seychelles
Porto Alegre   Brazil
Portsmouth   UK
Prince Rupert   Canada
Providence   USA
Puerto Cortes   Honduras
Pula   Yugoslavia
Punta Arenas   Chile

Quebec   Canada

Ramsgate   UK
Rangoon   Burma
Ravenna   Italy
Recife   Brazil
Reykjavik   Iceland
Richards Bay   South Africa
Richmond   USA
Riga   USSR
Rijeka   Yugoslavia
Rio de Janeiro   Brazil
Rio Grande   Brazil
Rosaria   Argentina
Rostock   Germany
Rotterdam   Netherlands
Rouen   France

Sacramento   USA
Safi   Morocco
Saint George's   Grenada
Saint Helier   Jersey
Saint John   Canada (New Brunswick)
Saint John's   Antigua
Saint John's   Canada (Newfoundland)
Saint Malo   France
Saint Nazaire   France
Sakai   Japan
Salerno   Italy
Salina Cruz   Mexico
Salonica   Greece
Salvador   Brazil
Samsun   Turkey
San Diego   USA
San Francisco   USA
San Jose   Guatemala
San Juan   Puerto Rico

San Juan del Sur   Nicaragua
San Lorenzo   Argentina
San Pedro   Ivory Coast
San Remo   Italy
Santa Cruz de Tenerife   Tenerife
Santa Fe   Argentina
Santa Marta   Colombia
Santander   Spain
Santiago de Cuba   Cuba
Santo Domingo   Dominican Republic
Santos   Brazil
São Tomé   São Tomé
Sasebo   Japan
Sassandra   Ivory Coast
Savannah   USA
Savona   Italy
Seattle   USA
Seville   Spain
Sfax   Tunisia
Shanghai   China
Shimizu   Japan
Singapore   Singapore
Sitra   Bahrain
Sittwe   Burma
Sousse   Tunisia
Southampton   UK
Split   Yugoslavia
Stavanger   Norway
Stockholm   Sweden
Stockton   USA
Stralsund   Germany
Suez   Egypt
Sunderland   UK
Sundsvall   Sweden
Surabaya   Indonesia
Suva   Fiji
Swansea   UK
Sydney   Australia
Sydney   Canada
Syracuse   Sicily
Szczecin   Poland

Tacoma   USA
Takamatsu   Japan
Tampa   USA
Tampico   Mexico
Tanga   Tanzania
Tangier   Morocco
Taranto   Italy
Tarragona   Spain
Tauranga   New Zealand

DEEPWATER PORTS OF THE WORLD (cont.)

Three Rivers (Trois Rivières) Canada	Tripoli Libya	Vigo Spain
Thunder Bay Canada	Trondheim Norway	Visakhapatnam India
Timaru New Zealand	Tunis Tunisia	Vitoria Brazil
Tianjin China	Turku Finland	Vlaardingen Netherlands
Toamasina Madagascar	Tuticorin India	Wellington New Zealand
Tokyo Japan	Ulsan South Korea	Willemstad Netherlands
Toledo USA	Vaasa Finland	Antilles
Toronto Canada	Valencia Spain	Wilmington USA
Torshavn Faroes	Valetta Malta	Xingang China
Toulon France	Valparaiso Chile	Yokohama Japan
Townsville Australia	Vancouver Canada	
Toyama Japan	Varna Bulgaria	Zamboanga Philippines
Trebizond Turkey	Venice Italy	Zanzibar Tanzania
Trieste Italy	Velsen Netherlands	Zeebrugge Belgium
Tripoli Lebanon	Veracruz Mexico	Zhdanov USSR

INTERNATIONAL E-ROAD NETWORK ('Euroroutes')

West-East orientation   Reference roads

E10 Narvik — Kiruna — Luleå
E20 Shannon — Dublin ··· Liverpool — Hull ··· Esbjerg — Nyborg ··· Korsør-Køge — Copenhagen ···
     Malmö — Stockholm ··· Tallin — Leningrad
E30 Cork — Rosslare ··· Fishguard — London — Felixstowe ··· Hook of Holland — Utrecht — Hanover —
     Berlin — Warsaw — Smolensk — Moscow
E40 Calais — Brussels — Aachen — Cologne — Dresden — Krakow — Kiev — Rostov na Donu
E50 Brest — Paris — Metz — Nurenberg — Prague — Mukačevo
E60 Brest — Tours — Besançon — Basle — Innsbruck — Vienna — Budapest — Bucharest — Constanţa
E70 La Coruña — Bilbao — Bordeaux — Lyon — Torino — Verona — Trieste — Zagreb — Belgrade —
     Bucharest — Varna
E80 Lisbon — Coimbra — Salamanca — Pau — Toulouse — Nice — Genoa — Rome — Pescara ···
     Dubrovnik — Sofia — Istanbul — Erzincan — Iran
E90 Lisbon — Madrid — Barcelona ··· Mazara del Vallo — Messina ··· Reggio di Calabria — Brindisi ···
     Igoumenitsa — Thessaloniki — Gelibolu ··· Lapseki — Ankara — Iraq

North-South orientation   Reference roads

E05 Greenock — Birmingham — Southampton ··· Le Havre — Paris — Bordeaux — Madrid — Algeciras
E15 Inverness — Edinburgh — London — Dover ··· Calais — Paris — Lyon — Barcelona — Algeciras
E25 Hook of Holland — Luxembourg — Strasbourg — Basle — Geneva — Turin — Genoa
E35 Amsterdam — Cologne — Basle — Milan — Rome
E45 Gothenburg — Frederikshavn — Hamburg — Munich — Innsbruck — Bologna — Rome — Naples —
     Villa S Giovanni ··· Messina — Gela
E55 Kemi-Tornio — Stockholm — Helsingborg ··· Helsingør — Copenhagen — Gedser ··· Rostock —
     Berlin — Prague — Salzburg — Rimini — Brindisi ··· Igoumenitsa — Kalamata
E65 Malmö — Ystad ··· Świnoujście — Prague — Zagreb — Dubrovnik — Bitolj — Antirrion ··· Rion —
     Kalamata ··· Kissamos — Chania
E75 Karasjok — Helsinki ··· Gdańsk — Budapest — Belgrade — Athens ··· Chania — Sitia
E85 Černovcy — Bucharest — Alexandropouli
E95 Leningrad—Moscow—Yalta

MAP OF EUROPE

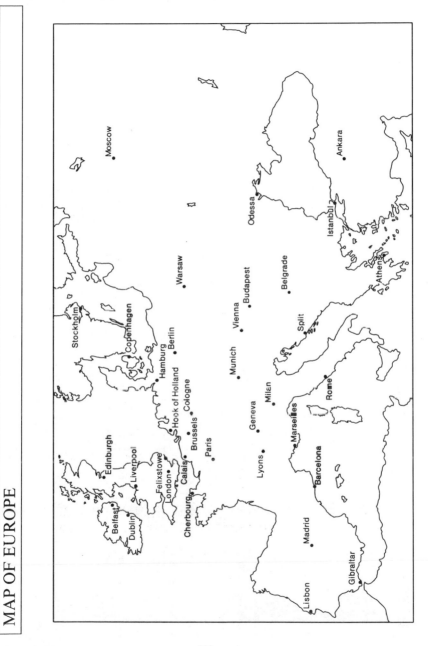

EUROPEAN ROAD DISTANCES

Road distances between some cities, given in kilometres.
To convert to statute miles, multiply number given by 0.6214

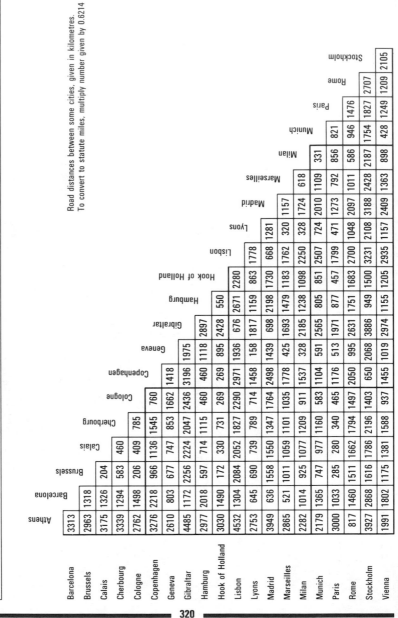

	Athens	Barcelona	Brussels	Calais	Cherbourg	Cologne	Copenhagen	Geneva	Gibraltar	Hamburg	Hook of Holland	Lisbon	Lyons	Madrid	Marseilles	Milan	Munich	Paris	Rome	Stockholm
Barcelona	3313																			
Brussels	2963	1318																		
Calais	3175	1326	204																	
Cherbourg	3339	1294	583	460																
Cologne	2762	1498	206	409	785															
Copenhagen	3276	2218	966	1136	1545	760														
Geneva	2610	803	677	747	853	1662	1418													
Gibraltar	4485	1172	2256	2224	2047	2436	3196	1975												
Hamburg	2977	2018	597	714	1115	460	460	1118	2897											
Hook of Holland	3030	1490	172	330	731	269	269	895	2428	550										
Lisbon	4532	1304	2084	2052	1827	2290	2971	1936	676	2671	2280									
Lyons	2753	645	690	739	789	714	1458	158	1817	1159	863	1778								
Madrid	3949	636	1558	1550	1347	1764	2498	1439	698	2198	1730	668	1281							
Marseilles	2865	521	1011	1059	1101	1035	1778	425	1693	1479	1183	1762	320	1157						
Milan	2282	1014	925	1077	1209	911	1537	328	2185	1238	1098	2250	328	1724	618					
Munich	2179	1365	747	977	1160	583	1104	591	2565	805	851	2507	724	2010	1109	331				
Paris	3000	1033	285	280	340	465	1176	513	1971	877	457	1799	471	1273	792	856	821			
Rome	817	1460	1511	1662	1794	1497	2050	995	2631	1751	1683	2700	1048	2097	1011	586	946	1476		
Stockholm	3927	2868	1616	1786	2196	1403	650	2068	3886	949	1500	3231	2108	3188	2428	2187	1754	1827	2707	
Vienna	1991	1802	1175	1381	1588	937	1455	1019	2974	1155	1205	2935	1157	2409	1363	898	428	1249	1209	2105

UK ROAD DISTANCES

Road distances between British centres are given in statute miles, using routes recommended by the Automobile Association based on the quickest travelling time. To convert to kilometres, multiply number given by 1.6093.

	Aberdeen	Birmingham	Bristol	Cambridge	Cardiff	Dover	Edinburgh	Exeter	Glasgow	Holyhead	Hull	Leeds	Liverpool	Manchester	Newcastle	Norwich	Nottingham	Oxford	Penzance	Plymouth	Shrewsbury	Southampton	Stranraer	York
Birmingham	430																							
Bristol	511	85																						
Cambridge	463	101	156																					
Cardiff	532	107	45	191																				
Dover	591	202	198	121	234																			
Edinburgh	130	293	373	337	395	457																		
Exeter	584	157	81	233	119	248	446																	
Glasgow	149	291	372	349	393	490	45	444																
Holyhead	457	151	232	246	209	347	325	305	319															
Hull	361	136	227	157	246	278	229	297	245	215														
Leeds	336	115	216	143	236	265	205	288	215	163	59													
Liverpool	361	98	178	195	200	295	222	250	220	104	126	72												
Manchester	354	88	167	153	188	283	218	239	214	123	97	43	34											
Newcastle	239	198	291	224	311	348	107	361	150	260	121	91	170	141										
Norwich	501	161	217	62	252	167	365	295	379	309	153	173	232	183	258									
Nottingham	402	59	151	82	170	202	268	222	281	174	92	73	107	71	156	123								
Oxford	497	63	74	82	109	148	361	152	354	218	188	171	164	153	253	144	104							
Penzance	696	272	195	346	232	362	561	112	559	419	411	401	366	355	477	407	336	265						
Plymouth	624	199	125	275	164	290	488	45	486	347	341	328	294	281	410	336	265	193	78					
Shrewsbury	412	48	128	142	110	243	276	201	272	104	164	115	64	69	216	205	85	113	315	242				
Southampton	571	128	75	133	123	155	437	114	436	296	253	235	241	227	319	192	171	67	227	155	190			
Stranraer	241	307	386	361	406	503	130	457	88	190	259	232	234	226	164	393	295	371	572	502	287	447		
York	325	128	221	153	241	274	191	291	208	190	38	24	100	71	83	185	86	185	406	340	144	252	228	
London	543	118	119	60	155	77	405	173	402	263	215	196	210	199	280	115	128	56	283	215	162	76	419	209

SCIENCE, TECHNOLOGY AND ENGINEERING

TABLE OF ELEMENTS

Atomic weights are taken from the 1983 list of the International Union of Pure and Applied Chemistry.

For radioactive elements, the mass number of the most stable isotope is given in square brackets.

Symbol	Element	Atomic No.	Weight	Symbol	Element	Atomic No.	Weight
Ac	actinium	89	[227]	Hf	hafnium	72	178.49
Ag	silver	47	107.8682	Hg	mercury	80	200.59
Al	aluminium	13	26.98154	Ho	holmium	67	164.9304
Am	americium	95	[243]	I	iodine	53	126.9045
Ar	argon	18	39.948	In	indium	49	114.82
As	arsenic	33	74.9216	Ir	iridium	77	192.22
At	astatine	85	[210]	K	potassium	19	39.0983
Au	gold	79	196.9665	Kr	krypton	36	83.80
B	boron	5	10.811	La	lanthanum	57	138.9055
Ba	barium	56	137.33	Li	lithium	3	6.941
Be	beryllium	4	9.01218	Lu	lutetium	71	174.967
Bi	bismuth	83	208.9804	Lw	lawrencium	103	[260]
Bk	berkelium	97	[247]	Md	mendelevium	101	[258]
Br	bromine	35	79.904	Mg	magnesium	12	24.305
C	carbon	6	12.011	Mn	manganese	25	54.9380
Ca	calcium	20	40.078	Mo	molybdenum	42	95.94
Cd	cadmium	48	112.41	N	nitrogen	7	14.0067
Ce	cerium	58	140.12	Na	sodium	11	22.98977
Cf	californium	98	[251]	Nb	niobium	41	92.9064
Cl	chlorine	17	35.453	Nd	neodymium	60	144.24
Cm	curium	96	[249]	Ne	neon	10	20.179
Co	cobalt	27	58.9332	Ni	nickel	28	58.69
Cr	chromium	24	51.9961	No	nobelium	102	[259]
Cs	cesium/			Np	neptunium	93	[237]
	caesium	55	132.9054	O	oxygen	8	15.9994
Cu	copper	29	63.546	Os	osmium	76	190.2
Dy	dysprosium	66	162.50	P	phosphorus	15	30.97376
Er	erbium	68	167.26	Pa	protactinium	91	[231]
Es	einsteinium	99	[252]	Pb	lead	82	207.2
Eu	europium	63	151.96	Pd	palladium	46	106.42
F	fluorine	9	18.998403	Pm	promethium	61	[145]
Fe	iron	26	55.847	Po	polonium	84	[209]
Fm	fermium	100	[257]	Pr	praseodymium	59	140.9077
Fr	francium	87	[223]	Pt	platinum	78	195.08
Ga	gallium	31	69.723	Pu	plutonium	94	[244]
Gd	gadolinium	64	157.25	Ra	radium	88	[226]
Ge	germanium	32	72.59	Rb	rubidium	37	85.4678
H	hydrogen	1	1.00794	Re	rhenium	75	186.207
He	helium	2	4.002602	Rh	rhodium	45	102.9055

Symbol	Element	Atomic No.	Weight	Symbol	Element	Atomic No.	Weight
Rn	radon	86	[222]	Tl	thallium	81	204.383
Ru	ruthenium	44	101.07	Tm	thulium	69	168.9342
S	sulphur/sulfur	16	32.066	U	uranium	92	238.0289
Sb	antimony	51	121.75	Une	unnilennium	109	[266]
Sc	scandium	21	44.95591	Unh	unnilhexium	106	[263]
Se	selenium	34	78.96	Unp	unnilpentium	105	[262]
Si	silicon	14	28.0855	Unq	unnilquadium	104	[261]
Sm	samarium	62	150.36	Uns	unnilseptium	107	[262]
Sn	tin	50	118.710	V	vanadium	23	50.9415
Sr	strontium	38	87.62	W	tungsten	74	183.85
Ta	tantalum	73	180.9479	Xe	xenon	54	131.29
Tb	terbium	65	158.9254	Y	yttrium	39	88.9059
Tc	technetium	43	[99]	Yb	ytterbium	70	173.04
Te	tellurium	52	127.60	Zn	zinc	30	65.39
Th	thorium	90	232.0381	Zr	zirconium	40	91.224
Ti	titanium	22	47.88				

PROPERTIES OF METALS

Name	Symbol	Valence no.	Atomic no.	Melting point (°C)	Name	Symbol	Valence no.	Atomic no.	Melting point (°C)
Aluminium	Al	3	13	660.37	Mercury	Hg	1 or 2	80	38.87
Antimony (stibium)	Sb	3 or 5	51	630.74	(hydrargyrum)				
Barium	Ba	2	56	725	Molybdenum	Mo	2 or 6	42	2617
Beryllium	Be	2	4	1278 ± 5	Nickel	Ni	2 or 3	28	1453
Bismuth	Bi	3 or 5	83	271.3	Osmium	Os	2 or 8	76	3045 ± 30
Cadmium	Cd	1 or 2	48	320.9	Palladium	Pd	2 or 4	46	1554
Caesium	Cs	1	55	28.40 ± 0.01	Platinum	Pt	3 or 4	78	1772
					Plutonium	Pu	-	94	641
Calcium	Ca	2	20	839 ± 2	Potassium	K	1	19	63.25
Cerium	Ce	3 or 4	58	798	(kalium)				
Chromium	Cr	2, 3, or 6	24	1857 ± 20	Rubidium	Rb	1	37	38.89
					Silver	Ag	1	47	961.93
Cobalt	Co	2 or 3	27	1495	(argentum)				
Copper (cuprum)	Cu	1 or 2	29	$1083.4 \pm .2$	Sodium (natrium)	Na	1	11	97.81 ± 0.03
Gallium	Ga	3	31	29.78	Tin	Sn	2 or 4	50	231.97
Gold (aurum)	Au	1 or 3	79	1064.43	(stannum)				
Iridium	Ir	2 or 4	77	2410	Titanium	Ti	3 or 4	22	1660 ± 10
Iron (ferrum)	Fe	2 or 3	26	1535	Tungsten	W	4 or 6	74	3410 ± 20
Lanthanum	La	3	57	918	(wolfram)				
Lead (plumbum)	Pb	2 or 4	82	327.5	Uranium	U	2 or 6	92	1132 ± 0.8
					Vanadium	V	5	23	1890 ± 10
Lithium	Li	1	3	180.5	Zinc	Zn	2	30	419.58
Magnesium	Mg	2	12	648.8 ± 0.5					
Manganese	Mn	2, 3, 4, 6, or 7	25	1244 ± 3					

PROPERTIES OF POLYMERS

Polymer	Density (kg m^{-3})	Tensile strength (MN m^{-2})	Heat capacity (Jg^{-1}K^{-1})	Resistivity (Ω cm)
Acetals	1420	65	1.46	10^{15}
Cellulose	1480–1530	80–240	1.3–1.5	10^7–10^{14}
Cellulose acetate				
Moulded	1220–1340	12–58	1.26–1.8	10^{10}–10^{14}
Sheet	1280–1320	30–52	1.26–2.1	10^{11}–10^{15}
Cellulose nitrate (celluloid)	1350–1400	50	1.3–1.7	10^{10}
Epoxy cast resins	1110–1400	26–85	1.0	10^{12}–10^{17}
Nylon-6 (Poly-E-caprolactam)	1120–1170	45–90	1.6	10^{12}–10^{15}
Nylon-66 (Polyhexa-methylene-adipamide	1130–1150	60–80	1.7	10^{14}–10^{15}
Polyacrylonitrile	1160–1180	200	-	10^{14}
Polycarbonates	1200	52–62	1.17–1.25	10^{16}
Polyethylene				
Low density	910–925	4–15	-	10^{15}–10^{18}
Medium density	926–940	8–22	-	10^{15}–10^{18}
High density	940–965	20–36	-	10^{15}–10^{18}
Polyisoprene				
Natural rubber	906–13	-	1.88	10^6
Hard rubber	1130–1180	39	1.38	10^{16}
Polypropylene	902–906	28–36	1.92	$>10^{16}$
Polystyrene	1040–1090	30–100	1.3–1.5	$>10^{16}$
Polyurethane				
Cast liquid	1100–1500	1–65	1.8	10^{11}–10^{15}
Elastomer	1110–1250	29–55	1.8	10^{11}–10^{13}
Polyvinylchloride	1300–1400	50	0.84–1.17	10^{16}
Silicone cast resin	1300	-	-	10^{14}-10^{15}

CONVERSION TABLES

To convert	To	Equation
°Farenheit	°Celsius	$-32, \times 5, \div 9$
°Farenheit	°Rankine	$+459.67$
°Farenheit	°Réaumur	$-32, \times 4, \div 9$
°Celsius	°Farenheit	$\times 9, \div 5, +32$
°Celsius	Kelvin	$+273.15$
°Celsius	°Réaumur	$\times 4, \div 5$
Kelvin	°Celsius	-273.15
°Rankine	°Farenheit	-459.67
°Réaumur	°Farenheit	$\times 9, \div 4, +32$
°Réaumur	°Celsius	$\times 5, \div 4$

Carry out operations in sequence.

OVEN TEMPERATURES

Gas Mark	Electricity		Rating
	°C	°F	
$\frac{1}{2}$	120	250	slow
1	140	275	
2	150	300	
3	170	325	
4	180	350	moderate
5	190	375	
6	200	400	hot
7	220	425	
8	230	450	very hot
9	260	500	

TEMPERATURE CONVERSION

Degrees Fahrenheit (F) → Degrees Celsius (Centigrade) (C)

°F	°C	°F	°C	°F	°C	°F	°C
1	−17.2	54	12.2	107	41.7	160	71.1
2	−16.7	55	12.8	108	42.2	161	71.7
3	−16.1	56	13.3	109	42.8	162	72.2
4	−15.5	57	13.9	110	43.3	163	72.8
5	−15.0	58	14.4	111	43.9	164	73.3
6	−14.4	59	15.0	112	44.4	165	73.9
7	−13.9	60	15.5	113	45.0	166	74.4
8	−13.3	61	16.1	114	45.5	167	75.0
9	−12.8	62	16.7	115	46.1	168	75.5
10	−12.2	63	17.2	116	46.7	169	76.1
11	−11.6	64	17.8	117	47.2	170	76.7
12	−11.1	65	18.3	118	47.8	171	77.2
13	−10.5	66	18.9	119	48.3	172	77.8
14	−10.0	67	19.4	120	48.9	173	78.3
15	−9.4	68	20.0	121	49.4	174	78.9
16	−8.9	69	20.5	122	50.0	175	79.4
17	−8.3	70	21.1	123	50.5	176	80.0
18	−7.8	71	21.7	124	51.1	177	80.5
19	−7.2	72	22.2	125	51.7	178	81.1
20	−6.7	73	22.8	126	52.2	179	81.7
21	−6.1	74	23.3	127	52.8	180	82.2
22	−5.5	75	23.9	128	53.3	181	82.8
23	−5.0	76	24.4	129	53.9	182	83.3
24	−4.4	77	25.0	130	54.4	183	83.9
25	−3.9	78	25.5	131	55.0	184	84.4
26	−3.3	79	26.1	132	55.5	185	85.0
27	−2.8	80	26.7	133	56.1	186	85.5
28	−2.2	81	27.2	134	56.7	187	86.1
29	−1.7	82	27.8	135	57.2	188	86.7
30	−1.1	83	28.3	136	57.8	189	87.2
31	−0.5	84	28.9	137	58.3	190	87.8
32	0	85	29.4	138	58.9	191	88.3
33	0.6	86	30.0	139	59.4	192	88.8
34	1.1	87	30.5	140	60.0	193	89.4
35	1.7	88	31.1	141	60.5	194	90.0
36	2.2	89	31.7	142	61.1	195	90.5
37	2.8	90	32.2	143	61.7	196	91.1
38	3.3	91	32.8	144	62.2	197	91.7
39	3.9	92	33.3	145	62.8	198	92.2
40	4.4	93	33.9	146	63.3	199	92.8
41	5.0	94	34.4	147	63.9	200	93.3
42	5.5	95	35.0	148	64.4	201	93.9
43	6.1	96	35.5	149	65.0	202	94.4
44	6.7	97	36.1	150	65.5	203	95.0
45	7.2	98	36.7	151	66.1	204	95.5
46	7.8	99	37.2	152	66.7	205	96.1
47	8.3	100	37.8	153	67.2	206	96.7
48	8.9	101	38.3	154	67.8	207	97.2
49	9.4	102	38.9	155	68.3	208	97.8
50	10.0	103	39.4	156	68.9	209	98.3
51	10.5	104	40.0	157	69.4	210	98.9
52	11.1	105	40.5	158	70.0	211	99.4
53	11.7	106	41.1	159	70.5	212	100.0

Degrees Celsius (Centigrade) (C) → Degrees Fahrenheit (F)

°C	°F	°C	°F
1	33.8	51	123.8
2	35.6	52	125.6
3	37.4	53	127.4
4	39.2	54	129.2
5	41.0	55	131.0
6	42.8	56	132.8
7	44.6	57	134.6
8	46.4	58	136.4
9	48.2	59	138.2
10	50.0	60	140.0
11	51.8	61	141.8
12	53.6	62	143.6
13	55.4	63	145.4
14	57.2	64	147.2
15	59.0	65	149.0
16	60.8	66	150.8
17	62.6	67	152.6
18	64.4	68	154.4
19	66.2	69	156.2
20	68.0	70	158.0
21	69.8	71	159.8
22	71.6	72	161.6
23	73.4	73	163.4
24	75.2	74	165.2
25	77.0	75	167.0
26	78.8	76	168.8
27	80.6	77	170.6
28	82.4	78	172.4
29	84.2	79	174.2
30	86.0	80	176.0
31	87.8	81	177.8
32	89.6	82	179.6
33	91.4	83	181.4
34	93.2	84	183.2
35	95.0	85	185.0
36	96.8	86	186.8
37	98.6	87	188.6
38	100.4	88	190.4
39	102.2	89	192.2
40	104.0	90	194.0
41	105.8	91	195.8
42	107.6	92	197.6
43	109.4	93	199.4
44	111.2	94	201.2
45	113.0	95	203.0
46	114.8	96	204.8
47	116.6	97	206.6
48	118.4	98	208.4
49	120.2	99	210.2
50	122.0	100	212.0

NUMERICAL EQUIVALENTS

Arabic	Roman	Greek	Binary numbers	Fraction	Decimal	Fraction	Decimal
1	I	α'	1	1/2	0.5000	9/11	0.8181
2	II	β'	10	1/3	0.3333	10/11	0.9090
3	III	γ'	11	2/3	0.6667	1/12	0.8333
4	IV	δ'	100	1/4	0.2500	5/12	0.4167
5	V	ε'	101	3/4	0.7500	7/12	0.5833
6	VI	ς'	110	1/5	0.2000	11/12	0.9167
7	VII	ζ'	111	2/5	0.4000	1/16	0.0625
8	VIII	η'	1000	3/5	0.6000	3/16	0.1875
9	IX	θ'	1001	4/5	0.8000	5/16	0.3125
10	X	ι'	1010	1/6	0.1667	7/16	0.4375
11	XI	$\iota\alpha'$	1011	5/6	0.8333	9/16	0.5625
12	XII	$\iota\beta'$	1100	1/7	0.1429	11/16	0.6875
13	XIII	$\iota\gamma'$	1101	2/7	0.2857	13/16	0.8125
14	XIV	$\iota\delta'$	1110	3/7	0.4286	15/16	0.9375
15	XV	$\iota\varepsilon'$	1111	4/7	0.5714	1/20	0.0500
16	XVI	$\iota\varsigma'$	10000	5/7	0.7143	3/20	0.1500
17	XVII	$\iota\zeta'$	10001	6/7	0.8571	7/20	0.3500
18	XVIII	$\iota\eta'$	10010	1/8	0.1250	9/20	0.4500
19	XIX	$\iota\theta'$	10011	3/8	0.3750	11/20	0.5500
20	XX	κ'	10100	5/8	0.6250	13/20	0.6500
30	XXX	λ'	11110	7/8	0.8750	17/20	0.8500
40	XL	μ'	101000	1/9	0.1111	19/20	0.9500
50	L	ν'	110010	2/9	0.2222	1/32	0.0312
60	LX	ξ'	111100	4/9	0.4444	3/32	0.9375
70	LXX	o'	1000110	5/9	0.5555	5/32	0.1562
80	LXXX	π'	1010000	7/9	0.7778	7/32	0.2187
90	XC	$,o'$	1011010	8/9	0.8889	9/32	0.2812
100	C	ρ'	1100100	1/10	0.1000	11/32	0.3437
200	CC	σ'	11001000	3/10	0.3000	13/32	0.4062
300	CCC	τ'	100101100	7/10	0.7000	15/32	0.4687
400	CD	υ'	110010000	9/10	0.9000	17/32	0.5312
500	D	ϕ'	111110100	1/11	0.0909	19/32	0.5937
1 000	M	$,\alpha$	1111101000	2/11	0.1818	21/32	0.6562
5 000	$\bar{V}$	$,\varepsilon$	1001110001000	3/11	0.2727	23/32	0.7187
10 000	$\bar{X}$	$,\iota$	10011100010000	4/11	0.3636	25/32	0.7812
100 000	$\bar{C}$	$,\rho$	11000011010100000	5/11	0.4545	27/32	0.8437
				6/11	0.5454	29/32	0.9062
				7/11	0.6363	31/32	0.9687
				8/11	0.7272		

NUMERICAL EQUIVALENTS (cont.)

%	Decimal	Fraction	%	Decimal	Fraction	%	Decimal	Fraction	%	Decimal	Fraction
1	0.01	1/100	15	0.15	3/20	30	0.30	3/10	45	0.45	9/20
2	0.02	1/50	16	0.16	4/25	31	0.31	31/100	46	0.46	23/50
3	0.03	3/100	$16\frac{2}{3}$	0.167	1/6	32	0.32	8/25	47	0.47	47/100
4	0.04	1/25	17	0.17	17/100	33	0.33	33/100	48	0.48	12/25
5	0.05	1/20	18	0.18	9/50	$33\frac{1}{3}$	0.333	1/3	49	0.49	49/100
6	0.06	3/50	19	0.19	19/100	34	0.34	17/50	50	0.50	1/2
7	0.07	7/100	20	0.20	1/5	35	0.35	7/20	55	0.55	11/20
8	0.08	2/25	21	0.21	21/100	36	0.36	9/25	60	0.60	3/5
$8\frac{1}{3}$	0.089	1/12	22	0.22	11/50	37	0.37	37/100	65	0.65	13/20
9	0.09	9/100	23	0.23	23/100	38	0.38	19/50	70	0.70	7/10
10	0.10	1/10	24	0.24	6/25	39	0.39	39/100	75	0.75	3/4
11	0.11	11/100	25	0.25	1/4	40	0.40	2/5	80	0.80	4/5
12	0.12	3/25	26	0.26	13/50	41	0.41	41/100	85	0.85	17/20
$12\frac{1}{2}$	0.125	1/8	27	0.27	27/100	42	0.42	21/50	90	0.90	9/10
13	0.13	13/100	28	0.28	7/25	43	0.43	43/100	95	0.95	19/20
14	0.14	7/50	29	0.29	29/100	44	0.44	11/25	100	1.00	1

MULTIPLICATION TABLE

	2	3	4	5	6	7	8	9	10	11	12	13	14	15	16	17	18	19	20	21	22	23	24	25
2	4	6	8	10	12	14	16	18	20	22	24	26	28	30	32	34	36	38	40	42	44	46	48	50
3	6	9	12	15	18	21	24	27	30	33	36	39	42	45	48	51	54	57	60	63	66	69	72	75
4	8	12	16	20	24	28	32	36	40	44	48	52	56	60	64	68	72	76	80	84	88	92	96	100
5	10	15	20	25	30	35	40	45	50	55	60	65	70	75	80	85	90	95	100	105	110	115	120	125
6	12	18	24	30	36	42	48	54	60	66	72	78	84	90	96	102	108	114	120	126	132	138	144	150
7	14	21	28	35	42	49	56	63	70	77	84	91	98	105	112	119	126	133	140	147	154	161	168	175
8	16	24	32	40	48	56	64	72	80	88	96	104	112	120	128	136	144	152	160	168	176	184	192	200
9	18	27	36	45	54	63	72	81	90	99	108	117	126	135	144	153	162	171	180	189	198	207	216	225
10	20	30	40	50	60	70	80	90	100	110	120	130	140	150	160	170	180	190	200	210	220	230	240	250
11	22	33	44	55	66	77	88	99	110	121	132	143	154	165	176	187	198	209	220	231	242	253	264	275
12	24	36	48	60	72	84	96	108	120	132	144	156	168	180	192	204	216	228	240	252	264	276	288	300
13	26	39	52	65	78	91	104	117	130	143	156	169	182	195	208	221	234	247	260	273	286	299	312	325
14	28	42	56	70	84	98	112	126	140	154	168	182	196	210	224	238	252	266	280	294	308	322	336	350
15	30	45	60	75	90	105	120	135	150	165	180	195	210	225	240	255	270	285	300	315	330	345	360	375
16	32	48	64	80	96	112	128	144	160	176	192	208	224	240	256	272	288	304	320	336	352	368	384	400
17	34	51	68	85	102	119	136	153	170	187	204	221	238	255	272	289	306	323	340	357	374	391	408	425
18	36	54	72	90	108	126	144	162	180	198	216	234	252	270	288	306	324	342	360	378	396	414	432	450
19	38	57	76	95	114	133	152	171	190	209	228	247	266	285	304	323	342	361	380	399	418	437	456	475
20	40	60	80	100	120	140	160	180	200	220	240	260	280	300	320	340	360	380	400	420	440	460	480	500
21	42	63	84	105	126	147	168	189	210	231	252	273	294	315	336	357	378	399	420	441	462	483	504	525
22	44	66	88	110	132	154	176	198	220	242	264	286	308	330	352	374	396	418	440	462	484	506	528	550
23	46	69	92	115	138	161	184	207	230	253	276	299	322	345	368	391	414	437	460	483	506	529	552	575
24	48	72	96	120	144	168	192	216	240	264	288	312	336	360	384	408	432	456	480	501	528	552	576	600
25	50	75	100	125	150	175	200	225	250	275	300	325	350	375	400	425	450	475	500	525	550	575	600	625

SQUARES AND ROOTS

No.	Square	Cube	Square root	Cube root	No.	Square	Cube	Square root	Cube root
1	1	1	1.000	1.000	13	169	2 197	3.606	2.351
2	4	8	1.414	1.260	14	196	2 744	3.742	2.410
3	9	27	1.732	1.442	15	225	3 375	3.873	2.466
4	16	64	2.000	1.587	16	256	4 096	4.000	2.520
5	25	125	2.236	1.710	17	289	4 913	4.123	2.571
6	36	216	2.449	1.817	18	324	5 832	4.243	2.621
7	49	343	2.646	1.913	19	361	6 859	4.359	2.668
8	64	512	2.828	2.000	20	400	8 000	4.472	2.714
9	81	729	3.000	2.080	25	625	15 625	5.000	2.924
10	100	1 000	3.162	2.154	30	900	27 000	5.477	3.107
11	121	1 331	3.317	2.224	40	1 600	64 000	6.325	3.420
12	144	1 728	3.464	2.289	50	2 500	125 000	7.071	3.684

COMMON MEASURES

Metric units

Length

		Imperial equiv.
	1 millimetre	0.03937 in
10 mm	1 centimetre	0.39 in
10 cm	1 decimetre	3.94 in
100 cm	1 metre	39.37 in
1 000 m	1 kilometre	0.62 mile

Area

		Imperial equiv.
	1 square millimetre	0.0016 sq in
	1 square centimetre	0.155 sq in
100 sq cm	1 square decimetre	15.5 sq in
10 000 sq cm	1 square metre	10.76 sq ft
10 000 sq m	1 hectare	2.47 acres

Volume

		Imperial equiv.
	1 cubic centimetre	0.016 cu in
1 000 cu cm	1 cubic decimetre	61.024 cu in
1 000 cu dm	1 cubic metre	35.31 cu ft
		1.308 cu yds

Liquid volume

	1 litre	1.76 pints
100 litres	1 hectolitre	22 gallons

Weight

		Imperial equiv.
	1 gram	0.035 oz
1 000 g	1 kilogram	2.2046 lb
1 000 kg	1 tonne	0.0842 ton

Imperial units

Length

		Metric equiv.
	1 inch	2.54 cm
12 in	1 foot	30.48 cm
3 ft	1 yard	0.9144 m
1760 yd	1 mile	1.6093 km

Area

		Metric equiv.
	1 square inch	6.45 sq cm
144 sq in	1 square foot	0.0929 m^2
9 sq ft	1 square yard	0.836 m^2
4840 sq yd	1 acre	0.405 ha
640 acres	1 square mile	259 ha

Volume

		Metric equiv.
	1 cubic inch	16.3871 cm^3
1728 cu in	1 cubic foot	0.028 m^3
27 cu ft	1 cubic yard	0.765 m^3

Liquid volume

	1 pint	0.57 litre
2 pints	1 quart	1.14 litres
4 quarts	1 gallon	4.55 litres

Weight

		Metric equiv.
	1 ounce	28.3495 g
16 oz	1 pound	0.4536 kg
14 lb	1 stone	6.35 kg
8 stones	1 hundredweight	50.8 kg
20 cwt	1 ton	1.016 tonnes

CONVERSION FACTORS

Imperial to metric

Length			Multiply by
inches	→	millimetres	25.4
inches	→	centimetres	2.54
feet	→	metres	0.3048
yards	→	metres	0.9144
statute miles	→	kilometres	1.6093
nautical miles	→	kilometres	1.852

Area			Multiply by
square inches	→	square centimetres	6.4516
square feet	→	square metres	0.0929
square yards	→	square metres	0.8361
acres	→	hectares	0.4047
square miles	→	square kilometres	2.5899

Volume			Multiply by
cubic inches	→	cubic centimetres	16.3871
cubic feet	→	cubic metres	0.0283
cubic yards	→	cubic metres	0.7646

Capacity			Multiply by
UK fluid ounces	→	litres	0.0284
US fluid ounces	→	litres	0.0296
UK pints	→	litres	0.5682
US pints	→	litres	0.4732
UK gallons	→	litres	4.546
US gallons	→	litres	3.7854

Weight			Multiply by
ounces (avoirdupois)	→	grams	28.3495
ounces (troy)	→	grams	31.1035
pounds	→	kilograms	0.4536
tons (long)	→	tonnes	1.016

Metric to imperial

Length			Multiply by
millimetres	→	inches	0.0394
centimetres	→	inches	0.3937
metres	→	feet	3.2808
metres	→	yards	1.0936
kilometres	→	statute miles	0.6214
kilometres	→	nautical miles	0.54

Area			Multiply by
square centimetres	→	square inches	0.155
square metres	→	square feet	10.764
square metres	→	square yards	1.196
hectares	→	acres	2.471
square kilometres	→	square miles	0.386

CONVERSION FACTORS (cont.)

Metric to imperial

Volume			Multiply by
cubic centimetres	→	cubic inches	0.061
cubic metres	→	cubic feet	35.315
cubic metres	→	cubic yards	1.308

Capacity			Multiply by
litres	→	UK fluid ounces	35.1961
litres	→	US fluid ounces	33.8150
litres	→	UK pints	1.7598
litres	→	US pints	2.1134
litres	→	UK gallons	0.2199
litres	→	US gallons	0.2642

Weight			Multiply by
grams	→	ounces (avoirdupois)	0.0353
grams	→	ounces (troy)	0.0322
kilograms	→	pounds	2.2046
tonnes	→	tons (long)	0.9842

CONVERSION TABLES: LENGTH

in	cm	in	cm	cm	in	cm	in	in	mm	mm	in
⅛	0.3	16	40.6	1	0.39	24	9.45	⅛	3.2	1	0.04
¼	0.6	17	43.2	2	0.79	25	9.84	¼	6.4	2	0.08
⅜	1	18	45.7	3	1.18	26	10.24	⅜	9.5	3	0.12
½	1.3	19	48.3	4	1.57	27	10.63	½	12.7	4	0.16
⅝	1.6	20	50.8	5	1.97	28	11.02	⅝	15.9	5	0.2
¾	1.9	21	53.3	6	2.36	29	11.42	¾	19	6	0.24
⅞	2.2	22	55.9	7	2.76	30	11.81	⅞	22.2	7	0.28
1	2.5	23	58.4	8	3.15	31	12.2	1	25.4	8	0.31
2	5.1	24	61	9	3.54	32	12.6	2	50.8	9	0.35
3	7.6	25	63.5	10	3.94	33	12.99	3	76.2	10	0.39
4	10.2	26	66	11	4.33	34	13.39	4	101.6	11	0.43
5	12.7	27	68.6	12	4.72	35	13.78	5	127	12	0.47
6	15.2	28	71.1	13	5.12	36	14.17	6	152.4	13	0.51
7	17.8	29	73.7	14	5.51	37	14.57	7	177.8	14	0.55
8	20.3	30	76.2	15	5.91	38	14.96	8	203.2	15	0.59
9	22.9	40	101.6	16	6.3	39	15.35	9	228.6	16	0.63
10	25.4	50	127	17	6.69	40	15.75	10	254	17	0.67

Exact conversions
1 in = 2.540 cm   1 cm = 0.3937 in

Exact conversions
1 in = 25.40 mm   1 mm = 0.0394 in

CONVERSION TABLES: LENGTH (cont.)

ft	m	m	ft	yd	m	m	yd	ml*	km	km	ml*
1	0.3	1	3.3	1	0.9	1	1.1	1	1.6	1	0.6
2	0.6	2	6.6	2	1.8	2	2.2	2	3.2	2	1.2
3	0.9	3	9.8	3	2.7	3	3.3	3	4.8	3	1.9
4	1.2	4	13.1	4	3.7	4	4.4	4	6.4	4	2.5
5	1.5	5	16.4	5	4.6	5	5.5	5	8.0	5	3.1
6	1.8	6	19.7	6	5.5	6	6.6	6	9.7	6	3.7
7	2.1	7	23.0	7	6.4	7	7.7	7	11.3	7	4.3
8	2.4	8	26.2	8	7.3	8	8.7	8	12.9	8	5.0
9	2.7	9	29.5	9	8.2	9	9.8	9	14.5	9	5.6
10	3.0	10	32.8	10	9.1	10	10.9	10	16.1	10	6.2
15	4.6	15	49.2	15	13.7	15	16.4	15	24.1	15	9.3
20	6.1	20	65.5	20	18.3	20	21.9	20	32.2	20	12.4
25	7.6	25	82.0	25	22.9	25	27.3	25	40.2	25	15.5
30	9.1	30	98.4	30	27.4	30	32.8	30	48.3	30	18.6
35	10.7	35	114.8	35	32.0	35	38.3	35	56.3	35	21.7
40	12.2	40	131.2	40	36.6	40	43.7	40	64.4	40	24.9
45	13.7	45	147.6	45	41.1	45	49.2	45	72.4	45	28.0
50	15.2	50	164.0	50	45.7	50	54.7	50	80.5	50	31.1
75	22.9	75	246.1	75	68.6	75	82.0	55	88.5	55	34.2
100	30.5	100	328.1	100	91.4	100	109.4	60	96.6	60	37.3
200	61.0	200	656.2	200	182.9	200	218.7	65	104.6	65	40.4
300	91.4	300	984.3	220	201.2	220	240.6	70	112.7	70	43.5
400	121.9	400	1312.3	300	274.3	300	328.1	75	120.7	75	46.6
500	152.4	500	1640.4	400	365.8	400	437.4	80	128.7	80	49.7
600	182.9	600	1968.5	440	402.3	440	481.2	85	136.8	85	52.8
700	213.4	700	2296.6	500	457.2	500	546.8	90	144.8	90	55.9
800	243.8	800	2624.7	600	548.6	600	656.2	95	152.9	95	59.0
900	274.3	900	2952.8	700	640.1	700	765.5	100	160.9	100	62.1
1000	304.8	1000	3280.8	800	731.5	800	874.9	200	321.9	200	124.3
1500	457.2	1500	4921.3	880	804.7	880	962.4	300	482.8	300	186.4
2000	609.6	2000	6561.7	900	823.0	900	984.2	400	643.7	400	248.5
2500	762.0	2500	8202.1	1000	914.4	1000	1093.6	500	804.7	500	310.7
3000	914.4	3000	9842.5	1500	1371.6	1500	1640.4	750	1207.0	750	466.0
3500	1066.8	3500	11482.9	2000	1828.8	2000	2187.2	1000	1609.3	1000	621.4
4000	1219.2	4000	13123.4	2500	2286.0	2500	2734.0	2500	4023.4	2500	1553.4
5000	1524.0	5000	16404.2	5000	4572.0	5000	5468.1	5000	8046.7	5000	3106.9

Exact conversions   Exact conversions   *Statute miles

1 ft = 0.3048 m   1 m = 3.2808 ft   1 yd = 0.9144 m   1 m = 1.0936 yd   Exact conversions

                                                   1 ml = 1.6093 km

                                                   1 km = 0.6214 ml

CONVERSION TABLES: AREA

sq in	sq cm	sq cm	sq in	sq ft	sq m	sq m	sq ft	acre	hectares	hectares	acre
1	6.45	1	0.16	1	0.09	1	10.8	1	0.40	1	2.5
2	12.90	2	0.31	2	0.19	2	21.5	2	0.81	2	4.9
3	19.35	3	0.47	3	0.28	3	32.3	3	1.21	3	7.4
4	25.81	4	0.62	4	0.37	4	43.1	4	1.62	4	9.9
5	32.26	5	0.78	5	0.46	5	53.8	5	2.02	5	12.4
6	38.71	6	0.93	6	0.56	6	64.6	6	2.43	6	14.8
7	45.16	7	1.09	7	0.65	7	75.3	7	2.83	7	17.3
8	51.61	8	1.24	8	0.74	8	86.1	8	3.24	8	19.8
9	58.06	9	1.40	9	0.84	9	96.9	9	3.64	9	22.2
10	64.52	10	1.55	10	0.93	10	107.6	10	4.05	10	24.7
11	70.97	11	1.71	11	1.02	11	118.4	11	4.45	11	27.2
12	77.42	12	1.86	12	1.11	12	129.2	12	4.86	12	29.7
13	83.87	13	2.02	13	1.21	13	139.9	13	5.26	13	32.1
14	90.32	14	2.17	14	1.30	14	150.7	14	5.67	14	34.6
15	96.77	15	2.33	15	1.39	15	161.5	15	6.07	15	37.1
16	103.23	16	2.48	16	1.49	16	172.2	16	6.47	16	39.5
17	109.68	17	2.64	17	1.58	17	183	17	6.88	17	42
18	116.13	18	2.79	18	1.67	18	193.8	18	7.28	18	44.5
19	122.58	19	2.95	19	1.77	19	204.5	19	7.69	19	46.9
20	129.03	20	3.10	20	1.86	20	215.3	20	8.09	20	49.4
25	161.29	25	3.88	25	2.32	25	269.1	25	10.12	25	61.8
50	322.58	50	7.75	50	4.65	50	538.2	50	20.23	50	123.6
75	483.87	75	11.63	75	6.97	75	807.3	75	30.35	75	185.3
100	645.16	100	15.50	100	9.29	100	1076.4	100	40.47	100	247.1
125	806.45	125	19.38	250	23.23	250	2691	250	101.17	250	617.8
150	967.74	150	23.25	500	46.45	500	5382	500	202.34	500	1235.5
				750	69.68	750	8072.9	750	303.51	750	1853.3
				1000	92.90	1000	10763.9	1000	404.69	1000	2471.1
								1500	607.03	1500	3706.6

Exact conversions
$1 \text{ in}^2 = 6.4516 \text{ cm}^2$ $1 \text{ cm}^2 = 0.155 \text{ in}^2$

Exact conversions
$1 \text{ ft}^2 = 0.0929 \text{ m}^2$ $1 \text{ m}^2 = 10.7639 \text{ ft}^2$

Exact conversions
1 acre = 0.4047 hectare
1 hectare = 2.471 acres

CONVERSION TABLES: AREA

sq ml*	sq km	sq km	sq ml*	sq ml*	sq km	sq km	sq ml*	sq ml*	sq km	sq km	sq ml*
1	2.6	1	0.39	18	46.6	18	6.95	300	777.0	300	115.83
2	5.2	2	0.77	19	49.2	19	7.34	400	1036.0	400	154.44
3	7.8	3	1.16	20	51.8	20	7.72	500	1295.0	500	193.05
4	10.4	4	1.54	21	54.4	21	8.11	600	1554.0	600	231.66
5	12.9	5	1.93	22	57.0	22	8.49	700	1813.0	700	270.27
6	15.5	6	2.32	23	59.6	23	8.88	800	2072.0	800	308.88
7	18.1	7	2.70	24	62.2	24	9.27	900	2331.0	900	347.49
8	20.7	8	3.09	25	64.7	25	9.65	1000	2590.0	1000	386.1
9	23.3	9	3.47	30	77.7	30	11.58	1500	3885.0	1500	579.2
10	25.9	10	3.86	40	103.6	40	15.44	2000	5180.0	2000	772.2

* Statute miles
Exact conversions
1 sq ml = 2.589999 sq km   1 sq km = 0.3861 sq ml

CONVERSION TABLES: VOLUME

cu in	cu cm	cu cm	cu in	cu ft	cu m	cu m	cu ft	cu yd	cu m	cu m	cu yd
1	16.39	1	0.61	1	0.03	1	35.3	1	0.76	1	1.31
2	32.77	2	1.22	2	0.06	2	70.6	2	1.53	2	2.62
3	49.16	3	1.83	3	0.08	3	105.9	3	2.29	3	3.92
4	65.55	4	2.44	4	0.11	4	141.3	4	3.06	4	5.23
5	81.93	5	3.05	5	0.14	5	176.6	5	3.82	5	6.54
6	93.32	6	3.66	6	0.17	6	211.9	6	4.59	6	7.85
7	114.71	7	4.27	7	0.20	7	247.2	7	5.35	7	9.16
8	131.10	8	4.88	8	0.23	8	282.5	8	6.12	8	10.46
9	147.48	9	5.49	9	0.25	9	317.8	9	6.88	9	11.77
10	163.87	10	6.10	10	0.28	10	353.1	10	7.65	10	13.08
15	245.81	15	9.15	15	0.42	15	529.7	15	11.47	15	19.62
20	327.74	20	12.20	20	0.57	20	706.3	20	15.29	20	26.16
50	819.35	50	30.50	50	1.41	50	1765.7	50	38.23	50	65.40
100	1638.71	100	61.00	100	2.83	100	3531.5	100	76.46	100	130.80

Exact conversions
$1\ in^3 = 16.3871\ cm^3$
$1\ cm^3 = 0.0610\ in^3$

Exact conversions
$1\ ft^3 = 0.0283\ m^3$
$1\ m^3 = 35.3147\ ft^3$

Exact conversions
$1\ yd^3 = 0.7646\ m^3$
$1\ m^3 = 1.3080\ yd^3$

CONVERSION TABLES: CAPACITY

Liquid measure UK fluid ounces	litres	US fluid ounces	litres	litres	UK fluid ounces	US fluid ounces
1	0.0284	1	0.0296	1	35.2	33.8
2	0.0568	2	0.0592	2	70.4	67.6
3	0.0852	3	0.0888	3	105.6	101.4
4	0.114	4	0.118	4	140.8	135.3
5	0.142	5	0.148	5	176.0	169.1
6	0.170	6	0.178	6	211.2	202.9
7	0.199	7	0.207	7	246.4	236.7
8	0.227	8	0.237	8	281.6	270.5
9	0.256	9	0.266	9	316.8	304.3
10	0.284	10	0.296	10	352.0	338.1
11	0.312	11	0.326	11	387.2	372.0
12	0.341	12	0.355	12	422.4	405.8
13	0.369	13	0.385	13	457.5	439.6
14	0.397	14	0.414	14	492.7	473.4
15	0.426	15	0.444	15	527.9	507.2
20	0.568	20	0.592	20	703.9	676.3
50	1.42	50	1.48	50	1759.8	1690.7
100	2.84	100	2.96	100	3519.6	3381.5

Exact conversions
1 fl oz = 0.0284 l   1 fl oz = 0.0296 l   1 l = 35.1961 UK fl oz
1 l = 33.8140 US fl oz

CONVERSION TABLES: CAPACITY

UK pints	litres	US pints	litres	litres	UK pints	US pints
1	0.57	1	0.47	1	1.76	2.11
2	1.14	2	0.95	2	3.52	4.23
3	1.70	3	1.42	3	5.28	6.34
4	2.27	4	1.89	4	7.04	8.45
5	2.84	5	2.37	5	8.80	10.57
6	3.41	6	2.84	6	10.56	12.68
7	3.98	7	3.31	7	12.32	14.79
8	4.55	8	3.78	8	14.08	16.91
9	5.11	9	4.26	9	15.84	19.02
10	5.68	10	4.73	10	17.60	21.13
11	6.25	11	5.20	11	19.36	23.25
12	6.82	12	5.68	12	21.12	25.36
13	7.38	13	6.15	13	22.88	27.47
14	7.95	14	6.62	14	24.64	29.59
15	8.52	15	7.10	15	26.40	31.70
20	11.36	20	9.46	20	35.20	105.67
50	28.41	50	23.66	50	87.99	211.34
100	56.82	100	47.32	100	175.98	422.68

Exact conversions
1 UK pt = 0.5682 l   1 US pt = 0.4732 l   1 l = 1.7598 UK pt, 2.1134 US pt
1 UK pt = 1.20 US pt   1 US pt = 0.83 UK pt   1 US cup = 8 fl oz

UK gallons	litres	US gallons	litres	litres	UK gallons	US gallons
1	4.55	1	3.78	1	0.22	0.26
2	9.09	2	7.57	2	0.44	0.53
3	13.64	3	11.36	3	0.66	0.79
4	18.18	4	15.14	4	0.88	1.06
5	22.73	5	18.93	5	1.10	1.32
6	27.28	6	22.71	6	1.32	1.58
7	31.82	7	26.50	7	1.54	1.85
8	36.37	8	30.28	8	1.76	2.11
9	40.91	9	34.07	9	1.98	2.38
10	45.46	10	37.85	10	2.20	2.64
11	50.01	11	41.64	11	2.42	2.91
12	54.55	12	45.42	12	2.64	3.17
13	59.10	13	49.21	13	2.86	3.43
14	63.64	14	52.99	14	3.08	3.70
15	68.19	15	56.78	15	3.30	3.96
16	72.74	16	60.57	16	3.52	4.23
17	77.28	17	64.35	17	3.74	4.49
18	81.83	18	68.14	18	3.96	4.76
19	86.37	19	71.92	19	4.18	5.02
20	90.92	20	75.71	20	4.40	5.28
25	113.65	25	94.63	25	5.50	6.60
50	227.30	50	189.27	50	11.00	13.20
75	340.96	75	283.90	75	16.50	19.81
100	454.61	100	378.54	100	22.00	26.42

Exact conversion   Exact conversion   Exact conversions
1 UK gall = 4.546 l   1 US gall = 3.7854 l   1 l = 0.220 UK gall, 0.2642 US gall

CONVERSION TABLES: CAPACITY

UK gall	US gall		UK gall	US gall		UK gall	US gall		US gall	UK gall		US gall	UK gall		US gall	UK gall
1	1.2		7	8.4		13	15.6		1	0.8		7	5.8		13	10.8
2	2.4		8	9.6		14	16.8		2	1.7		8	6.7		14	11.7
3	3.6		9	10.8		15	18		3	2.5		9	7.5		15	12.5
4	4.8		10	12		20	24		4	3.3		10	8.3		20	16.6
5	6		11	13.2		25	30		5	4.2		11	9.2		25	20.8
6	7.2		12	14.4		50	60		6	5		12	10		50	41.6

Exact conversion
1 UK gall = 1.200929 US gall

Exact conversion
1 US gall = 0.832688 UK gall

Dry capacity measures

UK bushels	cu m	litres		US bushels	cu m	litres
1	0.037	36.4		1	0.035	35.2
2	0.074	72.7		2	0.071	70.5
3	0.111	109.1		3	0.106	105.7
4	0.148	145.5		4	0.141	140.9
5	0.184	181.8		5	0.175	176.2
10	0.369	363.7		10	0.353	352.4

Exact conversions
1 UK bushel = 0.0369 m^3
1 UK bushel = 36.3677 l

Exact conversions
1 US bushel = 0.9353 m^3
1 US bushel = 35.2381 l

cu m	UK bushels	US bushels		litres	UK bushels	US bushels
1	27.5	28.4		1	0.027	0.028
2	55.0	56.7		2	0.055	0.057
3	82.5	85.1		3	0.082	0.085
4	110	113		4	0.110	0.114
5	137	142		5	0.137	0.142
10	275	284		10	0.275	0.284

Exact conversions
1 m^3 = 27.4962 UK bu
1 m^3 = 28.3776 US bu

Exact conversions
1 l = 0.0275 UK bu
1 l = 0.0284 US bu

UK pecks	litres		US pecks	litres		litres	UK pecks	US pecks
1	9.1		1	8.8		1	0.110	0.113
2	18.2		2	17.6		2	0.220	0.226
3	27.3		3	26.4		3	0.330	0.339
4	36.4		4	35.2		4	0.440	0.454
5	45.5		5	44		5	0.550	0.567
10	90.9		10	88.1		10	1.100	1.135

Exact conversion
1 UK pk = 9.0919 l

Exact conversion
1 US pk = 8.8095 l

Exact conversions
1 l = 0.1100 UK pk, 0.1135 US pk

CONVERSION TABLES: CAPACITY

Dry capacity measures (cont.)

US quarts	cu m	litres	US pints	cu m	litres
1	1101	1.1	1	551	0.55
2	2202	2.2	2	1101	1.10
3	3304	3.3	3	1652	1.65
4	4405	4.4	4	2202	2.20
5	5506	5.5	5	2753	2.75
10	11012	11	10	5506	5.51

Exact conversions
1 US qt = 1101.2209 cm^3
1 US qt = 1.1012 l

Exact conversions
1 US pt = 550.6105 cm^3
1 US pt = 0.5506 l

CONVERSION TABLES: TYRE PRESSURES

lb per sq in	kg per sq cm	lb per sq in	kg per sq cm
10	0.7	26	1.8
15	1.1	28	2
20	1.4	30	2.1
24	1.7	40	2.8

CONVERSION TABLES: WEIGHT

ounces*	grams	grams	ounces*	pounds	kilo grams	pounds	kilo grams	kilo grams	pounds	kilo grams	pounds
1	28.3	1	0.04	1	0.45	19	8.62	1	2.2	19	41.9
2	56.7	2	0.07	2	0.91	20	9.07	2	4.4	20	44.1
3	85	3	0.11	3	1.36	25	11.34	3	6.6	25	55.1
4	113.4	4	0.14	4	1.81	30	13.61	4	8.8	30	66.1
5	141.7	5	0.18	5	2.27	35	15.88	5	11	35	77.2
6	170.1	6	0.21	6	2.72	40	18.14	6	13.2	40	88.2
7	198.4	7	0.25	7	3.18	45	20.41	7	15.4	45	99.2
8	226.8	8	0.28	8	3.63	50	22.68	8	17.6	50	110.2
9	255.1	9	0.32	9	4.08	60	27.24	9	19.8	60	132.3
10	283.5	10	0.35	10	4.54	70	31.78	10	22	70	154.4
11	311.7	20	0.71	11	4.99	80	36.32	11	24.3	80	176.4
12	340.2	30	1.06	12	5.44	90	40.86	12	26.5	90	198.5
13	368.5	40	1.41	13	5.90	100	45.36	13	28.7	100	220.5
14	396.9	50	1.76	14	6.35	200	90.72	14	30.9	200	440.9
15	425.2	60	2.12	15	6.80	250	113.40	15	33.1	250	551.2
16	453.6	70	2.47	16	7.26	500	226.80	16	35.3	500	1102.3
		80	2.82	17	7.71	750	340.19	17	37.5	750	1653.5
		90	3.18	18	8.16	1000	453.59	18	39.7	1000	2204.6
		100	3.53								

*avoirdupois

Exact conversion
1 oz (avdp) = 28.3495 g

Exact conversion
1 g = 0.0353 oz (avdp)

Exact conversion
1 lb = 0.454 kg

Exact conversion
1 kg = 2.205 lb

CONVERSION TABLES: WEIGHT

Tons: long, UK 2240 lb; short, US 2000 lb

UK tons	tonnes	US tons	tonnes	UK tons	US tons	tonnes	UK tons	US tons	US tons	UK tons
1	1.02	1	0.91	1	1.12	1	0.98	1.10	1	0.89
2	2.03	2	1.81	2	2.24	2	1.97	2.20	2	1.79
3	3.05	3	2.72	3	3.36	3	2.95	3.30	3	2.68
4	4.06	4	3.63	4	4.48	4	3.94	4.40	4	3.57
5	5.08	5	4.54	5	5.6	5	4.92	5.50	5	4.46
10	10.16	10	9.07	10	11.2	10	9.84	11.02	10	8.93
15	15.24	15	13.61	15	16.8	15	14.76	16.53	15	13.39
20	20.32	20	18.14	20	22.4	20	19.68	22.05	20	17.86
50	50.80	50	45.36	50	56	50	49.21	55.11	50	44.64
75	76.20	75	68.04	75	84	75	73.82	82.67	75	66.96
100	101.61	100	90.72	100	102	100	98.42	110.23	100	89.29

Exact conversion 1 UK ton = 1.0160 tonnes

Exact conversion 1 US ton = 0.9072 tonne

Exact conversion 1 UK ton = 1.1199 US tons

Exact conversions 1 tonne = 0.9842 UK ton = 1.1023 US tons

Exact conversion 1 US ton = 0.8929 UK ton

Hundredweights: long, UK 112 lb; short, US 100 lb

UK cwt	kilo grams	US cwt	kilo grams	UK cwt	US cwt	kilo grams	UK cwt	US cwt	US cwt	UK cwt
1	50.8	1	45.4	1	1.12	1	0.0197	0.022	1	0.89
2	102	2	90.7	2	2.24	2	0.039	0.044	2	1.79
3	152	3	136	3	3.36	3	0.059	0.066	3	2.68
4	203	4	181	4	4.48	4	0.079	0.088	4	3.57
5	254	5	227	5	5.6	5	0.098	0.11	5	4.46
10	508	10	454	10	11.2	10	0.197	0.22	10	8.93
15	762	15	680	15	16.8	15	0.295	0.33	15	13.39
20	1016	20	907	20	22.4	20	0.394	1.44	20	17.86
50	2540	50	2268	50	56	50	0.985	1.10	50	44.64
75	3810	75	3402	75	84	75	1.477	1.65	75	66.96
100	5080	100	4536	100	102	100	1.970	2.20	100	89.29

Exact conversions 1 UK cwt = 50.8023 kg

Exact conversion 1 US cwt = 45.3592 kg

Exact conversion 1 UK cwt = 1.1199 US cwt

Exact conversions 1 kg = 0.0197 UK cwt = 0.0220 US cwt

Exact conversion 1 US cwt = 0.8929 UK cwt

stones	pounds	stones	pounds	stones	pounds
1	14	8	112	15	210
2	28	9	126	16	224
3	42	10	140	17	238
4	56	11	154	18	252
5	70	12	168	19	266
6	84	13	182	20	280
7	98	14	196		

stones	kilo grams	stones	kilo grams
1	6.35	6	38.10
2	12.70	7	44.45
3	19.05	8	50.80
4	25.40	9	57.15
5	31.75	10	63.50

Exact conversions 1 st = 14 lb
Exact conversions 1 lb = 0.07 st

Exact conversions 1 st = 6.350 kg
1 kg = 0.1575 st

INTERNATIONAL CLOTHING SIZES

Size equivalents are approximate, and may display some variation between manufacturers.

Women's suits/dresses

UK	USA	UK/Continent
8	6	36
10	8	38
12	10	40
14	12	42
16	14	44
18	16	46
20	18	48
22	20	50
24	22	52

Men's shirts

UK/USA	UK/Continent
12	30–31
12½	32
13	33
13½	34–35
14	36
14½	37
15	38
15½	39–40
16	41
16½	42
17	43
17½	44–45

Women's hosiery

UK/USA	UK/Continent
8	0
8½	1
9	2
9½	3
10	4
10½	5

Adults' shoes

UK	USA (ladies)	UK/Continent
4	5½	37
4½	6	38
5	6½	38
5½	7	39
6	7½	39
6½	8	40
7	8½	41
7½	8½	42
8	9½	42
8½	9½	43
9	10½	43
9½	10½	44
10	11½	44
10½	11½	45
11	12	46

Men's suits and overcoats

UK/USA	Continental
36	46
38	48
40	50
42	52
44	54
46	56

Men's socks

UK/USA	UK/Continent
9½	38–39
10	39–40
10½	40–41
11	41–42
11½	42–43

Children's shoes

UK/USA	UK/Continent
0	15
1	17
2	18
3	19
4	20
5	22
6	23
7	24
8	25
8½	26
9	27
10	28
11	29
12	30
13	32

INTERNATIONAL PATTERN SIZES

Young junior/teenage

Size	Bust cm	in	Waist cm	in	Hip cm	in	Back waist length cm	in
5/6	71	28	56	22	79	31	34.5	13½
7/8	74	29	58	23	81	32	35.5	14
9/10	78	30½	61	24	85	33½	37	14½
11/12	81	32	64	25	89	35	38	15
13/14	85	33½	66	26	93	36½	39	15⅜
15/16	89	35	69	27	97	38	40	15¾

INTERNATIONAL PATTERN SIZES (cont.)

Misses

Size	Bust cm	Bust in	Waist cm	Waist in	Hip cm	Hip in	Back waist length cm	Back waist length in
6	78	30½	58	23	83	32½	39.5	15½
8	80	31½	61	24	85	33½	40	15¾
10	83	32½	64	25	88	34½	40.5	16
12	87	34	67	26½	92	36	41.5	16¼
14	92	36	71	28	97	38	42	16½
16	97	38	76	30	102	40	42.5	16¾
18	102	40	81	32	107	42	43	17
20	107	42	87	34	112	44	44	17¼

Half-size

Size	Bust cm	Bust in	Waist cm	Waist in	Hip cm	Hip in	Back waist length cm	Back waist length in
10½	84	33	69	27	89	35	38	15
12½	89	35	74	29	94	37	39	15¼
14½	94	37	79	31	99	39	39.5	15½
16½	99	39	84	33	104	41	40	15¾
18½	104	41	89	35	109	43	40.5	15⅞
20½	109	43	96	37½	116	45½	40.5	16
22½	114	45	102	40	122	48	41	16⅛
24½	119	47	108	42½	128	50½	41.5	16¼

Women's

Size	Bust cm	Bust in	Waist cm	Waist in	Hip cm	Hip in	Back waist length cm	Back waist length in
38	107	42	89	35	112	44	44	17¼
40	112	44	94	37	117	46	44	17⅜
42	117	46	99	39	122	48	44.5	17½
44	122	48	105	41½	127	50	45	17⅝
46	127	50	112	44	132	52	45	17¾
48	132	52	118	46½	137	54	45.5	17⅞
50	137	54	124	49	142	56	46	18

INTERNATIONAL PAPER SIZES

A series	mm	in	B series	mm	in	C series	mm	in
A0	841 × 1189	33.11 × 46.81	B0	1000 × 1414	39.37 × 55.67	C0	917 × 1297	36.00 × 51.20
A1	594 × 841	23.39 × 33.1	B1	707 × 1000	27.83 × 39.37	C1	648 × 917	25.60 × 36.00
A2	420 × 594	16.54 × 23.39	B2	500 × 707	19.68 × 27.83	C2	458 × 648	18.00 × 25.60
A3	297 × 420	11.69 × 16.54	B3	353 × 500	13.90 × 19.68	C3	324 × 458	12.80 × 18.00
A4	210 × 297	8.27 × 11.69	B4	250 × 353	9.84 × 13.90	C4	229 × 324	9.00 × 12.80
A5	148 × 210	5.83 × 8.27	B5	176 × 250	6.93 × 9.84	C5	162 × 229	6.40 × 9.00
A6	105 × 148	4.13 × 5.83	B6	125 × 176	4.92 × 6.93	C6	114 × 162	4.50 × 6.40
A7	74 × 105	2.91 × 4.13	B7	88 × 125	3.46 × 4.92	C7	81 × 114	3.20 × 4.50
A8	52 × 74	2.05 × 2.91	B8	62 × 88	2.44 × 3.46	DL	110 × 220	4.33 × 8.66
A9	37 × 52	1.46 × 2.05	B9	44 × 62	1.73 × 2.44	C7/6	81 × 162	3.19 × 6.38
A10	26 × 37	1.02 × 1.46	B10	31 × 44	1.22 × 1.73			

All sizes in these series have sides in the proportion of $1 : \sqrt{2}$.
A series is used for writing paper, books and magazines. B series for posters. C series for envelopes.

ENGINEERING: BRIDGES

When a single date is given it is the date for completion of construction

Name	Location	Length m[1]	Type	Date
Akashi-Kaikyo Bridge	Honshu–Shikoku, Japan	1780	suspension	begun 1978, due for completion 1998
Ambassador	Detroit, Michigan, USA	564	suspension	1929
Annacis (renamed Alex Fraser)	Fraser River, Vancouver, Canada	465	(longest) cable stay	1986
Arthur Kill	Staten Island–New Jersey, USA	170	movable	1959
Astoria	Astoria, Oregon	376	truss	1966
Bayonne (Kill van Kull)	New Jersey–Staten Island, USA	504	arch	1932
Bendorf	R Rhine, Coblenz, Germany	1030	cement girder	1965
Benjamin Franklin	Philadelphia–Camden, USA	534	suspension	1926
Bosporus	Golden Horn, Istanbul, Turkey	1074	suspension	1973
Bosporus II	Istanbul, Turkey	1090	suspension	1986–88
Bridge of Sighs	Doge's Palace–Pozzi prison, Venice, Italy	c.5	enclosed arch	16th-c
Britannia tubular rail	Menai Strait, Wales	420	plate girder	1845–50
Brooklyn	Brooklyn–Manhattan Island, New York City, USA	486	suspension	1869–83
Chao Phraya	Bangkok, Thailand	450	(longest single-plane) cable-stay	1989
Cincinnati	Cincinnati, Ohio, USA	332	suspension	1867
Commodore Barry	Chester, Pennsylvania, USA	501	cantilever	1974
Cooper River	Charleston, S Carolina, USA	488	truss	1989
Delaware River	Chester, Pennsylvania, USA	501	cantilever	1971
Duisburg-Neuenkamp	Duisburg, Germany	350	cable braced	1970
Erskine	Glasgow, Scotland	305	cable braced	1970
Evergreen	Seattle, Washington, USA	longest span 2293	floating pontoon	1963
Firth of Forth (rail)	South Queensferry, Scotland	1658 (spans 521)	cantilever	1882–90
Firth of Forth (road)	South Queensferry, Scotland	1006	suspension	1958–64
George Washington	Hudson River, New York City, USA	1067	suspension	1927–31
Gladesville	Sydney, Australia	305	(longest) concrete arch	1964
Golden Gate	San Francisco, California, USA	1280	suspension	1937
Grand Trunk rail-road	Niagara Falls, New York, USA	suspension	1855 (survived until 1897)	
Greater New Orleans	Mississippi River, Louisiana, USA	480	cantilever	1958
Howrah (railroad)	Hooghly River, Calcutta, India	457	cantilever	1936–43
Humber Estuary	Hull–Grimsby, England	1410	(longest) suspension	1973–81

ENGINEERING: BRIDGES (cont.)

Name	Location	Length m[1]	Type	Date
Kincardine	R Forth, Scotland	822 (swing span 111)	movable	1936
Kniebrücke	Düsseldorf, Germany	320	cable braced	1969
Lake Pontchartrain Causeway	Maudeville–Jefferson, Louisiana, USA	38km	twin concrete trestle	1963
Lower Yarra	Melbourne, Australia	336	cable braced	1970
Lions Gate	Vancouver, Canada	473	suspension	1938
London	Southwark–City of London	centre span 46	concrete arch	1973
Mackinac	Michigan, USA	1158	suspension	1957
McCall's Ferry	USA	110	wooden covered	1815
Menai Strait	Menai Strait, N Wales	177	suspension	1820–26 (recon- structed 1940)
Minami Bisan-seto	Honshu–Shikoku, Japan	1723	suspension	1999
New River Gorge	Fayetteville, West Virginia, USA	518	(longest) arch	1977
Nord Sundet	Norway	223	lattice	1989
Plauen	Plauen, Germany	a span of 90	(longest) masonry arch	1903
Pont d'Avignon	R Rhône, France	c.60	arch	1177 87
Pontypridd	S Wales	43	single span arch	1750
Port Mann	Fraser River, British Columbia, Canada	366	arch	1964
Quebec (railroad)	St Lawrence, Canada	549	(largest-span) cantilever	1918
Rainbow	Canada–USA, Niagara Falls	300	steel arch	1941
Rialto	Grand Canal, Venice, Italy	25	single span arch	1588–92
Rio-Niteroi	Guanabara Bay, Brazil	centre span 300, length 14 km	box and plate girder	1972
Salazar	Tagus River, Lisbon, Portugal	1014	suspension	1966
Severn	Beachley, England	988	suspension	1961–66
Severn	Ironbridge, Shropshire, England	31	(first) cast-iron arch	1779
Sky Train Bridge (rail)	Vancouver, Canada	340	cable stay	1989
Sydney Harbour	Sydney, Australia	503	(widest) arch	1923–32
Tacoma Narrows II	Puget Sound, Washington, USA	854	suspension	1950
Tay (road)	Dundee, Scotland	2246	box girder	1966
Thatcher Ferry	Panama Canal, C America	344	arch	1962
Tower	R Thames, London	76	movable	1886–94
Transbay	San Francisco, USA	705	suspension	1933
Trois-Rivières	St Lawrence River, Quebec, Canada	336	steel arch	1962

ENGINEERING: BRIDGES (cont.)

Name	Location	Length m[1]	Type	Date
Verrazano Narrows	Brooklyn–Staten Island, New York Harbour, USA	1298	suspension	1959–64
Victoria Jubilee	St Lawrence River, Montreal, Canada	open steel	1854–59	
Wheeling	Wheeling, Virginia, USA	308	suspension	1849
Yokohama Bay (road)	Japan	855	suspension	1989
Zoo	Cologne, Germany	259	steel box girder	1966

[1] To convert m to ft, multiply by 3.2808

ENGINEERING: TUNNELS

When a single date is given it is the date for completion of construction

Name	Use	Location	Length	Date
Aki	rail	Japan	13 km	1975
Baltimore Harbour	road	Baltimore, Maryland, USA	2 km	1957
Box	rail	Wiltshire, England	3 km	1841
Cascade	rail	Washington, USA	13 km	1929
Channel	rail	Cheriton, England—Sargette, France	50 km	begun 1987, due to be opened 1993
Chesapeake Bay Bridge-Tunnel	road	USA	28 km	1964
Chesbrough	water supply	Chicago, USA	3 km	1867
Dai-shimizu	rail	Honshu, Japan	22 km	1979
Delaware Aqueduct		Catskill Mt, New York City, USA	169 km	1937–44
Detroit River	rail	Detroit, Michigan—Windsor, Ontario, USA	2 km	1910
Eupalinus	water supply	Samos	1037 m	c.525 BC
Flathead	rail	Washington, USA	13 km	1970
Fréjus	rail	Modane, France—Bardonecchia, Italy	13 km	1857–71
Fucino	drainage	Lake Fucino, Italy	6 km	41
Great Appennine	rail	Vernio, Italy	19 km	1934
Hokuriku	rail	Japan	15 km	1962
Holland	road	Hudson River, New York City—Jersey City, New Jersey, USA	3 km	1927
Hoosac	rail	Massachusetts	8 km	1876
Hyperion	sewer	Los Angeles, California, USA	8 km	1959
Kanmon	rail	Kanmon Strait, Japan	19 km	1975
Keijo	rail	Japan	11 km	1970
Kemano	hydro-power	British Columbia, Canada	430 m	1954
Kilsby Ridge	rail	London—Birmingham	2 km	1838
Languedoc	Canal du Midi	Malpas, France	157 m	c.1681
Lierasen	rail	Norway	11 km	1973

ENGINEERING: TUNNELS (cont.)

Name	Use	Location	Length	Date
London and Southwark Subway	rail	London, England	11 km	1890
Lötschberg	rail	Switzerland	15 km	1913
Mersey	road	Mersey River, Birkenhead—Liverpool, England	4 km	1934
Moffat	rail	Colorado, USA	10 km	1928
Mont Blanc	road	France—Italy	12 km	1965
Mt MacDonald	rail	Canada	15 km	1989
Orange-Fish River	irrigation	South Africa	(longest irrigation tunnel) 82 km	1975
Owingsburg Landing	canal	Pennsylvania, USA	137 m	1828
Posilipo	road	Naples—Pozzuoli, Italy	6 km	c.36 BC
Rogers Pass	rail	Calgary—Vancouver	15 km	1982–88
Rogers Pass	road	British Columbia, Canada	35 km	1989
Rokko	rail	Ōsaka—Kōbe, Japan	16 km	1972
Scheldt River	road-rail	Antwerp, Belgium	686 m	1969
Seikan	rail	Tsugaru Strait, Honshu—Hokkaido, Japan	(longest undersea rail) 54 km	1964–88
Shin-shimizu	rail	Japan	13 km	1961
Simplon I and II	rail	Brigue, Switzerland—Iselle, Italy	20 km	1906 and 1922
St Gotthard	rail	Switzerland	15 km	1882
St Gotthard	road	Göschenen, Switzerland—Airolo, Italy	(longest road) 16 km	1980
(First) Thames	pedestrian, rail after 1865	Wapping—Rotherhithe, London, England	366 m	1825–43
Tower Subway	rail	London	411 m	1869 70
Tronquoy	canal	France	1099 m	1810

To convert m to ft, multiply by 3.2808
To convert km to ml, multiply by 1.6092

ENGINEERING: MAJOR DAMS

When a single date is given, it is the date for completion of construction

Name	River; country	Height m[1]	Date	Name	River; country	Height m[1]	Date
Afsluitdijk Sea	Zuider Zee; Netherlands	20 (largest sea dam, length 32 km)	1927–32	Ataturk	Euphrates; Turkey	184	1990
				Bakun	Rajang; Malaysia	204	under construction
				Boguchany	Angara; USSR	79	1989
Aswan High	Nile; Egypt	111	1970	Bratsk	Angara; USSR	125	1961
				Chapeton	Paraná; Argentina	35	under construction

ENGINEERING: MAJOR DAMS (cont.)

Name	River; country	Height m[1]	Date	Name	River; country	Height m[1]	Date
Chicoasen	Grijalva; Mexico	263	1980	Mica	Columbia; Canada	244	1973
Grand Coulee	Columbia (Franklin D Roosevelt Lake); USA	168	1933–42	Nurek	Vakhsh; USSR	310	1980
				Poti	Paraná; Argentina	109 (length 150 km, most massive: volume 238180000 m³)	under con- struction
Grand Dixence	Dixence; Switzerland	285	1961				
Guavio	Guaviare; Colombia	245	1989				
Hoover	Colorado (Lake Mead); USA	221	1931–36				
Haipu	Parana; Paraguay/Brazil border	189	1982	Rogun	Vakhsh; USSR	335 (tallest)	1973–90
				Sayansk	Yenisey; USSR	236	1980
Inguri	Inguri; USSR	272	1980	Sera da Mesa	Tocantins; Brazil	144	under con- struction
Kariba	Zambezi (L. Kariba); Zambia/ Zimbabwe border	128	1959				
				Thames Barrier	Thames; UK	spans 520 (largest tidal barrier)	1984
Keiv	Dneiper; USSR	256 (longest dam, length 412 km)	1964				
				Vaiont	Vaiont; Italy	262	1961 (damaged by landslide 1963)
LaGrande 2A	LaGrande; Canada	168	under con- struction				
Mauvoisin	Drance de Bagnes; Switzerland	237	1957				

[1] To convert m to ft, multiply by 3.2808

ENGINEERING: TALLEST BUILDINGS

Name	Location	Height m[1]	Date of Con- struction	Name	Location	Height m[1]	Date of Con- struction
Sears Tower	Chicago, USA	443	1973–4	Chrysler Building	New York City, USA	319	1930
World Trade Centre	New York City, USA	417	1972	Library Tower	Los Angeles, USA	310	1989
Empire State Building	New York City, USA	381	1931	Texas Commercial Plaza	Houston, USA	305	1981
Bank of China	Hong Kong	368	1988–89				
Standard Oil Building	Chicago, USA	346	1971	Allied Bank Plaza	Houston, USA	302	1983
John Hancock Center	Chicago, USA	344	1967				

[1] To convert m to ft, multiply by 3.2808

INVENTIONS

Name	Date	Inventor (nationality*)
adding machine	1642	Blaise Pascal (Fr)
adhesive (rubber-based glue)	1850	anon
adhesive (epoxy resin)	1958	Certas Co.
aeroplane (steam powered)	1886	Clement Ader (Fr)
aeroplane	1903	Orville and Wilbur Wright (US)
aeroplane (swing-wing)	1954	Grumman Co. (US)
aerosol	1926	Erik Rotheim (Nor)
airship (non-rigid)	1851	Henri Giffard (Fr)
airship (rigid)	1900	Graf Ferdinand von Zeppelin (Ger)
ambulance	1792	Jean Dominique Larrey (Fr)
aspirin (synthesization)	1859	Heinrich Kolbe (Ger)
aspirin (introduction into medicine)	1899	Heinrich Dreser (Ger)
atomic bomb	1939–45	Otto Frisch (Aus), Niels Bohr (D) and Rudolf Peierls (Ger)
balloon	1783	Jacques and Joseph Montgolfier (Fr)
barbed wire (first patent)	1867	Lucien B Smith (US)
barbed wire (manufacture)	1874	Joseph Glidden (US)
barbiturates (preparation of barbituric acid)	1863	Adolf von Baeyer (Ger)
	1903	Emil Herman von Fischer and Emil von Behring (Ger)
barometer	1643	Evanglelista Torricelli (Ital)
battery (electric)	1800	Alessandro Volta (Ital)
bicycle	1839–40	Kirkpatrick MacMillan (UK)
bifocal lens	1780	Benjamin Franklin (US)
blood (artificial)	1966	Clark and Gollan (US)

Name	Date	Inventor (nationality*)
bronze (copper with tin)	c.3700 BC	Pre-dynastic Egypt
bunsen burner	1855	Robert Wilhelm Bunsen (Pruss)
burglar alarm	1858	Edwin T Holmes (US)
cable-car	1866	W Ritter (Ger) or anon (US)
calendar (modern)	525	Dionysius Exiguus (Scythian)
canning	1810	Nicolas Appert (Fr)
cannon	2nd-c BC	Archimedes (Gr)
car (three-wheeled steam tractor)	1769	Nicolas Cugnot (Fr)
car (internal combustion)	1884	Gottlieb Daimler (Ger)
car (petrol)	1886	Karl Benz (Ger)
car (air-conditioning)	1902	J Wilkinson (US)
car (disc brakes)	1902	Frederick W Lanchester (UK)
car (speedometer)	1902	Thorpe & Salter (UK)
carbon fibres	1964	Courtaulds Ltd. (UK)
carburettor	1876	Gottlieb Daimler (Ger)
carpet sweeper	1876	Melville Bissell (US)
cash register	1892	William Burroughs (US)
celluloid	1870	John W Hyatt (US)
cement (Portland)	1824	Joseph Aspdin (UK)
chocolate (solid)	1819	François-Louis Cailler (Swiss)
chocolate (solid, milk)	1875	Daniel Peter (Swiss)
chronometer	1735	John Harrison (UK)
cinema	1895	Auguste and Louis Lumière (Fr)
cinema (wide screen)	1900	Raoul Grimoin-Sanson (Fr)
clock (mechanical)	725	I-Hsing (Chinese)
clock (pendulum)	1656	Christiaan Huygens (NL)
clock (quartz)	1929	Warren Alvin Marrison (US)

INVENTIONS (cont.)

Name	Date	Inventor (nationality*)
coffee (instant)	1937	Nestlé (Swiss)
compact disc	1979	Philips (NL) and Sony (Japanese)
compass (discovery of magnetite)	1st-c	China
compass (first record of mariner's compass)	1187	Alexander Neckam (UK)
computer	1835	Charles Babbage (UK)
computer (electronic, digital)	1946	J Presper Eckert and John W Mauchly (US)
concrete	1st-c	Rome
concrete (reinforced)	1892	François Hennebique (Fr)
contact lenses	1887	Adolph E Fick (Ger)
contraceptive pill	1950	Gregor Pincus (US)
copper	c.8000 BC	Neolithic Man
copper (working mines)	3800 BC	King Snefru (Sinai)
corrugated iron	1853	Pierre Carpentier (Fr)
credit card	1950	Ralph Scheider (US)
crossword	1913	Arthur Wynne in New York World
crystal	c.1450	anon, Venice
decompression chamber	1929	Robert H Davis (UK)
dental plate	1817	Anthony A Plantson (US)
dental plate (rubber)	1854	Charles Goodyear (US)
detergents	1916	anon, Germany
diesel engine	1892	Rudolf Diesel (Ger)
dishwasher (automatic)	1889	Mrs W A Cockran (US)
drill (pneumatic)	1861	Germain Sommelier (Fr)
drill (electric, hand)	1895	Wilhelm Fein (Ger)
electric chair	1888	Harold P Brown and E A Kenneally (US)
electric flat iron	1882	Henry W Seeley (US)

Name	Date	Inventor (nationality*)
electric generator	1831	Michael Faraday (UK)
electric guitar	1931	Adolph Rickenbacker, Barth and Beauchamp (US)
electric heater	1887	W Leigh Burton (US)
electric light bulb	1879	Thomas Alva Edison (US)
electric motor (DC)	1870	Zenobe Gramme (Belg)
electric motor (AC)	1888	Nikola Tesla (US)
electric oven	1889	Bernina Hotel, Switzerland
electocardiography	1903	Willem Einthoven (NL)
electromagnet	1824	William Sturgeon (UK)
encyclopedia	c.47 BC	Marcus Terentius Varro
endoscope	1827	Pierre Segalas (Fr)
escalator	1892	Jesse W Reno (US)
explosives (nitroglycerine)	1846	Ascanio Sobrero (Ital)
expolosives (dynamite)	1866	Alfred Nobel (Swed)
extinguisher	1866	François Carlier (Fr)
facsimile machine (fax)	1907	Arthur Korn (Ger)
ferrofluids	1968	Ronald Rosensweig (US)
film (moving outlines)	1874	Jules Janssen (Fr)
	1888	Louis Le Prince (Fr)
	1891	Thomas Alva Edison (US)
film (with soundtrack)	1896	Lee De Forest (US)
food processor	1947	Kenneth Wood
forceps (obstetric)	c.1630	Peter Chamberlen
freeze-drying	1906	Arsene D'Arsonval and Georges Bordas (Fr)
galvanometer	1834	André Marie Ampère (Fr)

INVENTIONS (cont.)

Name	Date	Inventor (nationality*)
gas lighting	1792	William Murdock (UK)
gearbox (automatic)	1910	Hermann Fottinger (Ger)
glass (heat-resistant)	1884	Carl Zeiss (Ger)
glass (stained)	pre 850	Europe
glass (toughened)	1893	Leon Appert (Fr)
glass fibre	1713	Renée de Reaumur (Fr)
glass fibre (industrial)	1931	Owens Illinois Glass Co. (US)
glassware	c.2600 BC	
glider	1853	George Cayley (UK)
gramophone	1877	Thomas Alva Edison (US)
gun	245 BC	Ctesibius (Gr)
gyro-compass	1911	Elmer A Sperry (US)
heart (artificial)	1937	Vladimir P Demikhov (USSR)
heat pump	1851	William Thompson, Lord Kelvin (UK)
helicopter	1907	Louis and Jacques Breguet (Fr)
holography	1948	Denis Gabor (Hung/UK)
hovercraft	1955	Christopher Cockerell (UK)
integrated circuit (concept)	1952	Geoffrey Dummer (UK)
interferometry	1802	Thomas Young (UK)
interferometer	1856	J-C Jamin (Fr)
iron (working of)	c.1323 BC	Hittites (Anatolia)
jeans	1872	Levi-Strauss (US)
kidney (artificial)	1945	Willem Kolff (NL)
laser	1960	Theodore Maiman (US)
launderette	1934	J F Cantrell (US)
lawnmower	1902	James Edward Ransome (UK)
lift (mechanical)	1851	Elisha G Otis (US)
lightning conductor	1752	Benjamin Franklin (US)

Name	Date	Inventor (nationality*)
linoleum	1860	Frederick Walton (UK)
lithography	1796	Aloys Senefelder (Bav)
locomotive (railed)	1804	Richard Trevithick (UK)
lock	c.4000 BC	Mesopotamia
loom (power)	1785	Edmund Cartwright (UK)
loudspeaker	1900	Horace Short (UK)
machine gun	1718	James Puckle (UK)
maps	c.2250 BC	Mesopotamia
margarine	1868	Hippolyte Mergé-Mouriès (Fr)
match	1680	Robert Boyle (UK)
match (safety)	1845	Anton von Schrotter (Ger)
microchip	1958	Jack Saint Clair Kilby (US)
microphone	1876	Alexander Graham Bell (US) and Thomas Alva Edison (US)
microprocessor	1971	Marcian E Hoff (US)
microscope	1590	Zacharias Janssen (NI)
microscope (electron)	1933	Max Knoll and Ernst Ruska (Ger)
microscope (scanning tunnelling)	1982	Gerd Binnig and Heinrich Rohrer (Swiss)
microscope (atomic force)	1985	Gerd Binnig and Heinrich Rohrer (Swiss)
microwave oven	1945	Percy Le Baron Spencer (US)
missile (air-to-air)	1943	Herbert Wagner (Ger)
motorcycle	1885	Gottlieb Daimler (Ger)
neon lamp	1910	Georges Claude (Fr)
newspaper	59 BC	Julius Caesar (Roman)
non-stick pan	1954	Marc Grégoir (Fr)

INVENTIONS (cont.)

Name	Date	Inventor (nationality*)
novel (serialized)	1836	Charles Dickens, Chapman and Hall publishers (UK)
nylon	1938	Wallace H Carothers (US)
optical fibres	c.1955	Navinder S Kapany (Ind)
optical sound recording	1920	Lee De Forest (US)
pacemaker (implantable)	1956	Wilson Greatbach (US)
paint (fluorescent)	1933	Joe and Bob Switzer (US)
paint (acrylic)	1964	Reeves Ltd. (UK)
paper	AD 105	Ts'ai Lun (Chinese)
paper clip	1900	Johann Vaaler (Nor)
parachute	c.2nd-c BC	China
parachute (jump)	1797	André-Jacques Garnerin (Fr)
parachute (patent)	1802	André-Jacques Garnerin (Fr)
parchment	2nd-c BC	Eumenes II of Pergamum (reigned 197–159 BC)
parking meter	1932	Carlton C Magee (US)
pasteurization	1863	Louis Pasteur (Fr)
pen (fountain)	1884	Lewis Waterman (US)
pen (ball-point)	1938	Laszlo Biro (Hung)
pencil	1795	Nicholas Jacques Conté (Fr)
photoelectric cell	1896	Julius Elster and Hans F Geitel (Ger)
phototypesetting	1894	Eugene Porzott (Hung)
photographic lens (for camera obscura)	1812	William H Wollaston (UK)
photographic film	1889	Georges Eastman (US)
photography (on metal)	1816	Joseph Nicéphore Niepce (Fr)
photography (on paper)	1838	William Henry Fox Talbot (UK)

Name	Date	Inventor (nationality*)
photography (colour)	1861	James Clerk Maxwell (UK)
pianoforte	1720	Bartolomeo Cristofori (Ital)
plastics	1868	John W Hyatt (US)
pocket calculator	1972	Jack Saint Clair Kilby, James Van Tassell and Jerry D Merryman (US)
porcelain	c.960	China
pressure cooker	1954	Frederic Jean and Henri Lescure (Fr)
printing press (wooden)	c.1450	Johannes Gutenberg (Ger)
printing press (rotary)	1845	Richard Hoe (US)
propeller (boat, hand-operated)	1775	David Bushnell (US)
propeller (ship)	1844	Isambard Kingdom Brunel (UK)
radar (theory)	1900	Nikola Tesla (Croat)
radar (theory)	1922	Guglielmo Marconi (Ital)
radar (application)	c.1930	A Hoyt Taylor and Leo C Young (US)
radio telegraphy (discovery and production of sound waves)	1888	Heinrich Hertz (Ger)
radio (transatlantic)	1901	Guglielmo Marconi (Ital)
rails (iron)	1738	Abraham Barby (UK)
railway (underground)	1843	Charles Pearson (UK)
railway (electric)	1878	Ernst Werner von Siemens (Ger)
rayon	1883	Joseph Swan (UK)
razor (safety)	1895	King Camp Gillette (US)
razor (electric)	1928	Jacob Schick (US)
record (flat disc)	1888	Emil Berliner (Ger)
record (long-playing microgroove)	1948	Peter Goldmark (US)
refrigerator (compressed ether)	1855	James Harrison (UK)
refrigerator	1857	Ferdinand Carré

INVENTIONS (cont.)

Name	Date	Inventor (nationality*)	Name	Date	Inventor (nationality*)
(absorption)		(Fr)	soda (extraction of)	c.16th-	Egypt
revolver	1835	Samuel Colt (US)		c BC	
Richter seismographic scale	1935	Charles Francis Richter (US)	spectacles	c.1280	Alessandro della Spina, Salvino degli Armati (Ital)
rocket (missile)	1232	Mongols (China)	spinning frame	1768	Richard Arkwright
rubber (latex foam)	1929	E A Murphy, W H Chapman and John Dunlop (US)	spinning jenny	c.1764	(UK) James Hargreaves (UK)
rubber (butyl)	1937	Robert Thomas and William Sparks, Exxon (US)	spinning-mule	1779	Samuel Crompton (UK)
			stapler	1868	Charles Henry Gould (UK)
rubber (vulcanized)	1939	Charles Goodyear (US)	starter motor	1912	Charles F Kettering (US)
Rubik cube	1975	Erno Rubik (Hung)	steam engine	1698	Thomas Savery
safety-pin	1849	Walter Hunt (US)			(UK)
satellite (artificial)	1957	USSR	steam engine (condenser)	1769	James Watt (UK)
saw	c.4000 BC	Egypt	steam engine (piston)	1705	Thomas Newcomen (UK)
scanner	1973	Godfrey N Hounsfield (UK)	steel (production)	1854	Henry Bessemer (UK), William
scotch tape	1930	Richard Drew (US)			Kelly (US)
screw	3rd-c BC	Archimedes (Gr)	steel (stainless)	1913	Henry Brearley (UK)
serotherapy	1890	Emil von Behring (Ger)	stethoscope	1816	René Théophile Hyacinthe
sewing machine	1830	Barthelemy Thimonnier (Fr)			Laënnec (Fr)
ship (steam)	1775	Jacques C Perier (Fr)	stereotype	1725	William Ged (UK)
			submarine	c.1620	Cornelis Brebbel or Van Drebbel
ship (turbine)	1894	Charles Parsons (UK)			(NL)
ship (metal hull and propeller)	1844	Isambard Kingdom Brunel (UK)	sun-tan cream	1936	Eugene Schueller (Fr)
silk (reeling)	c.2640 BC	Hsi Ling Shi (Chinese)	suspension bridge	25 BC	China
			syringe (scientific)	1646	Blaise Pascal (Fr)
skin (artificial)	c.1980	John Tanner (US), Bell (US), Neveu (Fr), Ioannis Yannas (Gr), Howard Green (US) and Jacques Thivolet (Fr)	syringe (hypodermic)	c.1835	Charles Gabriel Pravaz (Fr)
			table tennis	1890	James Gibb (UK)
			tampon	1930	Earl Hass (US)
			tank	1916	Ernest Swinton (UK)
skyscraper	1882	William Le Baron Jenney (US)	telegraph (electric)	1774	Georges Louis Lesage (Swiss)
slide rule	1621	William Oughtred (UK)	telegraph (transatlantic cable)	1866	William Thompson, Lord Kelvin (UK)
soap	2500 BC	Sumer, Babylonia	telegraph code	1837	Samuel F B Morse (US)

INVENTIONS (cont.)

Name	Date	Inventor (nationality*)	Name	Date	Inventor (nationality*)
telephone (first practical)	1876	Alexander Graham Bell (US)	typewriter (electric)	1872	Thomas Edison (US)
telephone (automatic exchange)	1889	Alman B Strowger (US)	tyre (pneumatic, coach)	1845	Robert William Thomson (UK)
telescope (refractor)	1608	Hans Lippershey (NL)	tyre (pneumatic, bicycle)	1888	John Boyd Dunlop (UK)
television (mechanical)	1926	John Logie Baird (UK)	ultrasonography (obstetric)	1979	Ian Donald (UK)
television (colour)	1940	Peter Goldmark (US)	universal joint	c.140 BC	Fang Feng (Chinese)
tennis	1873	Walter G Wingfield (UK)	vacuum cleaner (steam powered)	1871	Ives W McGaffrey (US)
thermometer	3rd-c BC	Ctesibius (Gr)	vacuum cleaner (electric)	1901	Hubert Cecil Booth (UK)
thermometer (mercury)	1714	Gabriel Fahrenheit (Ger)	vending machine	1883	Percival Everitt (UK)
timeclock	1894	Daniel M Cooper (US)	ventilator	1858	Theophile Guibal (Fr)
toaster	1927	Charles Strite (US)	videophone	1927	American Telegraph & Telephone Co.
traffic lights	1868	J P Knight (UK)			
traffic lights (automatic)	1914	Alfred Benesch (US)	video recorder	1956	Ampex Co. (US)
transformer	1831	Michael Faraday (UK)	washing machine (electric)	1907	Hurley Machine Co. (US)
tranquillizers	1952	Henri Laborit (Fr)	watch	1462	Bartholomew Manfredi (Ital)
transistor	1948	John Bardeen (US), Walter Brattain (US), William Shockley (US)	watch (waterproof)	1927	Rolex (Swiss)
			wheel	c.3500 BC	Mesopotamia
travel agency	1841	Thomas Cook (UK)	windmill	c.600	Syria
			writing (pictography)	c.3000 BC	Egypt
traveller's cheques	1891	American Express Travel Agency	X-ray	1895	Wilhelm Konrad von Röntgen (Ger)
turbojet	1928	Frank Whittle (UK)	xerography	1938	Chester Carbon (US)
typewriter	1829	William Burt (US)	zip-fastener	1893	Whitcomb L Judson (US)

*Aus: Austrian	Ger: German	NL: Dutch
Belg: Belgian	Gr: Greek	Nor: Norwegian
Croat: Croatian	Hung: Hungarian	Pruss: Prussian
D: Danish	Ind: Indian	Swed: Swedish
Fr: French	Ital: Italian	

ENVIRONMENTAL DISASTERS ON LAND

Location	Event	Date	Consequence
Basle, Switzerland	Fire in Sandez factory warehouse resulted in major chemical spill.	November 1980	River Rhine rendered lifeless for 200 km/124 ml.
Beirut	Toxic waste dumped by Italian company.	July–September 1988	Italy forced to take back its poison drums.
Bhopal, India	Toxic gas leaked from a Union Carbide pesticide plant and enveloped a nearby slum area housing 200 000 people.	December 1984	Possibly 10 000 people died (officially 2352). Survivors suffer ravaged lungs and/or blindness. 100 km²/39 ml² affected by the gas.
Camelford, Cornwall	20 tonnes of aluminium sulphate were flushed down local rivers after an accident at a water treatment works.	July 1988	60 000 fish killed. Local people suffered from vomiting, diarrhoea, blisters, mouth ulcers, rashes and memory loss.
Chernobyl, USSR	Nuclear reactor exploded, releasing a radioactive cloud over Europe.	April 1986	Fewer than 50 people were killed, but the radioactive cloud spread as far as Britain, contaminating farmland. 100 000 Soviet citizens may die of radiation-induced cancer, a further 30 000 fatalities are possible worldwide. 250 000 people evacuated from the area in five years.
Cubatao, Brazil	Uncontrolled pollution from nuclear industry.	1980s	Local population suffer serious ailments and genetic deformities. 30% of deaths are caused by pollution-related diseases and damage to respiratory systems.
Cumbria, England	Fire in Windscale plutonium production reactor burned for 24 hours and ignited 3 tonnes of uranium.	October 1957	Radioactive material spread throughout the countryside. In 1983 the British government said 39 people probably died of cancer as a result. Unofficial sources say 1000.
Decatur, Alabama, USA	Fire at Braun's ferry reactor caused by a technician checking for air leaks with a lighted candle.	March 1975	$100 million damage. Electrical controls burned out, lowering cooling water to dangerous levels.
Detroit, Michigan, USA	Malfunction in sodium cooling system at the Enrico Fermi demonstration breeder reactor.	October 1966	Partial core meltdown. Radiation was contained.
Erwin, Tennessee, USA	Highly enriched uranium released from top-secret nuclear fuel plant.	August 1979	1000 people contaminated (with up to 5 times as much radiation as would normally be received in a year).
Flixborough, England	Container of cyclohexane exploded.	1974	28 people died.

ENVIRONMENTAL DISASTERS ON LAND (cont.)

Location	Event	Date	Consequence
Goiânia, Brazil	Major radioactive contamination incident involving an abandoned radiotherapy unit containing radioactive caesium chloride salts.	September–October 1987	People evacuated; homes demolished; 249 people affected by sickness or death.
Gore, Oklahoma, USA	A cylinder of nuclear material burst after being improperly heated at Kerr-McGee plant.	January 1986	1 worker died, 100 hospitalized.
Idaho Falls, Idaho, USA	Accident at experiment reactor.	January 1961	3 workers killed. Damage contained, despite radiation levels at the plant.
Kasli, USSR	Chemical explosion in tanks containing nuclear waste.	1957	Radioactive material spread. Major evacuation of area.
Kuwait	Iraqi forces set alight 600 oil wells.	February 1991	Air pollution consisted of clouds of soot and oil particles which obscured the sun and fell as 'black rain'. Threat that it would turn into sulphur dioxide and fall as acid rain. Incidence of fatal bronchitis expected to increase. Possible serious contamination of agricultural land and water supplies particularly in Iraq's Tigris and Euphrates valleys.
Love Canal, near Niagara Falls, New York, USA	Dumping of drums containing hazardous waste at Love Canal, which by the 1970s were leaking toxic chemicals.	1940s to 1952	More than 240 families evacuated, countryside contaminated.
Lucens Vad, Switzerland	Coolant malfunction in an experimental underground reactor.	January 1969	Large amount of radiation released into cavern, which was then sealed.
Minimata Bay, Japan	Dumping of chemicals, including methyl mercury.	1953	Minimata disease, characterized by cerebral palsy, had killed more than 300 people by 1983. Thousands more suffered genetic abnormalities, brain disease and nervous disorders.
Monongahela River, Pennsylvania, USA	Storage tank ruptured and spilled 3 800 000 gallons of diesel oil into the Monongahela river.	January 1988	Water supply to 23 000 residents of Pittsburgh cut off. Oil slick spread into W Virginia, growing to 77 km/48 ml, and reached Steubenville, Ohio.
Monticello, Minnesota, USA	Water-storage space at Northern States Power Company's reactor overflowed.	November 1971	50 000 gallons of radioactive waste water dumped in Mississippi River. St Paul water system contaminated.

ENVIRONMENTAL DISASTERS ON LAND (cont.)

Location	Event	Date	Consequence
Rochester, New York, USA	Steam-generator pipe broke at the Rochester Gas & Electric Company's plant.	January 1982	Small amounts of radioactive steam escaped.
Seveso, N Italy	Leak of toxic TCDD gas containing the poison dioxin.	July 1976	Local population still suffering; in worst contaminated area, topsoil had to be removed and buried in a giant plastic-coated pit.
Tennessee, USA	100 000 gallons of radioactive coolant leaked into the containment building of the TVA's Sequoyah 1 plant.	February 1981	8 workers contaminated.
Three Mile Island, Harrisburg, Pennsylvania, USA	Water pump broke down releasing radioactive steam.	March 1979	Pollution by radioactive gases. Some authorities claimed regional cancer, child deformity. Massive clean-up operation resulted in 150 tonnes of radioactive rubble and 250 000 gallons of radioactive water.
Tsuruga, Japan	Accident during repairs of a nuclear plant.	April 1981	100 workers exposed to radioactive material.

OIL SPILLS AT SEA

Name	Location	Date	Consequence
AmocoCadiz, Cyprus-registered tanker, grounded and spilled 65 562 000 gallons	near Portshall, France	March 1978	marine pollution, 160 km/99 ml of French coast polluted
Aragon spilled 7 350 000 gallons	—	1989	marine pollution
Atlantic Empress and *Aegean Captain*; collision between tankers caused spillage of 88 200 000 gallons	off Trinidad and Tabago	July 1979	marine pollution
Burmah Agate collided and spilled 10 700 000 gallons	Galveston Bay, Texas	November 1979	marine pollution

OIL SPILLS AT SEA (cont.)

Name	Location	Date	Consequence
Castillo de Beliver tanker; fire caused spillage of 73 500 000 gallons	off Cape Town, South Africa	August 1983	marine pollution
Ekofisk oil field; blow-out caused spillage of 8 200 000 gallons	North Sea	April 1977	marine pollution
Exxon Valdez, US tanker, grounded on Bligh Reef and spilled 10 080 000 gallons	Prince William Sound, Alaska	March 1989	1770 km/1162 ml of Alaskan coastline polluted. More than 3600 sq km/1390 sq ml of water fouled. Thousands of animals killed.
Gulf; Iraq pumped oil at a rate of 4 200 000 gallons a day into the sea	10 ml off coast near Kuwait City	January-February 1991	Threat to desalination plants and therefore to water supply. Devastating effect on all areas of marine environment.
Ixtoc oil well; blow-out caused spillage of 176 400 000 gallons	Gulf of Mexico	June 1979	marine pollution
Hawaiian Patrol; fire caused spillage of 29 106 000 gallons	N Pacific	February 1977	marine pollution
Keo; hull failure caused spillage of 88 200 000 gallons	off Massachusetts, USA	November 1969	marine pollution
Khark 5, Iranian supertanker, spilled 19 000 000 gallons of light crude oil after an explosion in its hull	700 km/435 ml N of the Canary Is, Atlantic Ocean	December 1989	370 km/230 ml oil slick almost reached Morocco. About 40% evaporated and much sank to ocean floor, endangering fish and oysters.
Kirki, Greek tanker, broke up and spilled 5 880 000 gallons of light crude oil	off Cervantes, W Australia	July 1991	pollution of conservation zones and lobster fishery

OIL SPILLS AT SEA (cont.)

Name	Location	Date	Consequence
Nowruz oil field; blow-out caused spillage of about 176 400 000 gallons	Persian Gulf	February 1983	marine pollution
Othello collided and spilled 17 640 000– 29 400 000 gallons	Tralhavet Bay, Sweden	—	marine pollution
Sea Star collided and spilled 33 810 000 gallons	Gulf of Oman	December 1972	marine pollution
Sewaren storage tank rupture caused spillage of 8 400 000 gallons	New Jersey	November 1969	marine pollution
Torrey Canyon grounded and spilled 34 986 000 gallons	off Lands's End, England	March 1967	marine pollution
Urquiola grounded and spilled 29 400 000 gallons	La Coruna, Spain	May 1976	marine pollution
World Glory; hull failure caused spillage of 13 524 000 gallons	off South Africa	June 1960	marine pollution

ARTS AND CULTURE

WRITERS

Selected works are listed

Adams, Douglas (Noel) (1952–) English novelist, short-story writer; *The Hitch Hiker's Guide to the Galaxy* (1979), *Dirk Gently's Holistic Detective Agency* (1987).

Adams, Richard (George) (1920–) English novelist, short-story writer, born Newbury, Berkshire; *Watership Down* (1972), *Shardik* (1974), *The Girl in a Swing* (1980).

Amis, Kingsley (William) (1922–) English novelist, poet, born London; *Lucky Jim* (1954), *That Uncertain Feeling* (1955), *Jake's Thing* (1978).

Amis, Martin (Louis) (1949–) English novelist, short-story writer; *The Rachel Papers* (1973), *Money* (1984).

Apuleius, Lucius (c.123 – after 161) Roman writer, born Madaura, Numidia, Africa; *Golden Ass* (the only Roman novel to survive complete), *Apologia*.

Archer, Jeffrey Howard (1940–) English novelist, short-story writer, born Somerset; *Not a Penny More, Not a Penny Less* (1975), *Kane and Abel* (1979), *First Among Equals* (1984), *A Twist in the Tale* (1989).

Asimov, Isaac (1920–) American novelist, short-story writer, born Petrovichi, USSR; *I Robot* (1950), *Foundation* (1951), *The Disappearing Man and other stories* (1985).

Atwood, Margaret (Eleanor) (1939–) Canadian novelist, poet, short-story writer, born Ottowa; *Bluebeards' Egg* (1983), *The Handmaid's Tale* (1986).

Austen, Jane (1775–1817) English novelist, born Steventon, Hampshire; *Sense and Sensibility* (1811), *Pride and Prejudice* (1813), *Mansfield Park* (1814), *Emma* (1816), *Persuasion* (1818).

Bainbridge, Beryl (1934–) English novelist, born Liverpool; *The Dressmaker* (1973), *Injury Time* (1977).

Ballantyne, R(obert) M(ichael) (1825–94) Scottish novelist, born Edinburgh; *The Coral Island* (1857), *The Gorilla Hunters* (1862).

Ballard, J(ames) G(raham) (1930–) English novelist, born Shanghai, China; *The Drowned World* (1962), *The Terminal Beach* (1964), *Empire of the Sun* (1984).

Balzac, Honoré de (1799–1850) French novelist, born Tours; *Comédie humaine* (1827–47).

Banks, Iain (1954–) Scottish novelist; *The Wasp Factory* (1984), *The Bridge* (1986).

Barnes, Julian (1946–) English novelist, born Leicester; *Flaubert's Parrot* (1984), *Staring at the Sun* (1986), *A History of the World in 10½ Chapters* (1989).

Bates, H(erbert) E(rnest) (1905–74) English novelist and short-story writer, born Rushden, Northamptonshire; *Fair Stood the Wind for France* (1944), *The Jacaranda Tree* (1949), *Love for Lydia* (1952), *The Darling Buds of May* (1958).

Beerbohm, Sir (Henry) Max(imilian) (1872–1986) English novelist, born London; *Zuleika Dobson* (1912).

Behn, Aphra (1640–89) English novelist, playwright, born Wye, Kent; *The Rover* (play) (1678), *Oroonoko* (1688).

Bellow, Saul (1915–) Canadian novelist, born Lachine, Quebec; *Henderson the Rain King* (1959), *Herzog* (1964), *Humboldt's Gift* (1974); Nobel Prize for Literature 1976.

Bennett, (Enoch) Arnold (1867–1931) English novelist, born Hanley, Staffordshire; *Anna of the Five Towns* (1902), *The Old Wives' Tale* (1908), *Clayhanger* series (1910–18).

Binchy, Maeve (1940–) Irish novelist, short-story writer; *Light a Penny Candle* (1982), *Echoes* (1985).

Blackmore, R(ichard) D(odderidge) (1825–1900) English novelist, born Longworth, Berkshire; *Lorna Doone* (1869).

Bleasdale, Alan (1946–) English novelist, playwright, born Liverpool; *Scully* (1975), *Boys from the Blackstuff* (1983).

Böll, Heinrich (1917–) German novelist, born Cologne; *And Never Said a Solitary Word* (1953), *The Unguarded House* (1954), *The Bread of Our Early Years* (1955); Nobel Prize for Literature 1972.

Borges, Jorge Luis (1899–1986) Argentinian poet, short-story writer, born Buenos Aires; *Labyrinths* (1953), *Ficciones* (1945), *El Aleph* (1949).

Bowen, Elizabeth (Dorothea Cole) (1899–1973)

WRITERS (cont.)

Anglo-Irish novelist, short-story writer, born Dublin; *The Death of the Heart* (1938), *The Heat of the Day* (1949).

Bowles, Paul (Frederick) (1910–) American novelist, short-story writer, born New York City; *The Sheltering Sky* (1949), *Pages from Cold Point and other stories* (1968).

Bradbury, Malcolm (Stanley) (1932–) English novelist, born Sheffield; *Eating People is Wrong* (1959), *The History Man* (1975).

Bradbury, Ray(mond) (Douglas) (1920–) American novelist, short-story writer, born Waukegan, Illinois; *The Martian Chronicles* (1950), *Fahrenheit 451* (1954), *Something Wicked this Way Comes* (1962).

Bradford, Barbara Taylor (1933–) English novelist; *A Woman of Substance* (1979), *Hold the Dream* (1985).

Bragg, Melvin (1939–) English novelist, playwright, short-story writer; *The Hired Man* (1969).

Braine, John (Gerard) (1922–86) English novelist, born Bradford; *Room at the Top* (1957).

Bromfield, Louis (1896–1956) American novelist, short-story writer, born Mansfield, Ohio; *Early Autumn* (1926), *Until the Day Break* (1942).

Brontë, Anne (1820–49) English novelist, poet, born Thornton, Yorkshire; *Agnus Grey* (1847), *The Tenant of Wildfell Hall* (1848).

Brontë, Charlotte (1816–55) English novelist, poet, born Thornton, Yorkshire; *Jane Eyre* (1847), *Shirley* (1849), *Villette* (1853).

Brontë, Emily (1818–1848) English novelist, poet, born Thornton, Yorkshire; *Wuthering Heights* (1847).

Brookner, Anita (1938–) English novelist, born London; *Hotel du Lac* (1984), *Family and Friends* (1985).

Brown, George Douglas (1869–1902) Scottish novelist, born Ochiltree, Ayrshire; *House with the Green Shutters* (1901).

Brown, George MacKay (1921–) Scottish novelist, poet, short-story writer, playwright, born Orkney; *Greenvoe* (1972).

Buck, Pearl (née **Sydenstricker**) (1892–1973) American novelist, born Hillsboro, W Virginia; *The Good Earth* (1913), *Pavilion of Women* (1946); Nobel Prize for Literature 1938.

Bulgakov, Mikhail (Afanasievich) (1891–1940) Russian novelist, short-story writer, born Kiev; *Diavoliada* (1925), *The Master and Margarita* (1967).

Bunyan, John (1628–88) English novelist, born Elstow, near Bedford; *Pilgrim's Progress* (1678).

Burgess, Anthony (pseudonym of **John Anthony Burgess Wilson**) (1917–) English novelist, born Manchester; *A Clockwork Orange* (1962), *The Malayan Trilogy* (1972), *Earthly Powers* (1980), *Kingdom of the Wicked* (1985), *Any Old Iron* (1989).

Burney, Fanny (Frances, Mme d'Arblay) (1752–1840) English novelist, born King's Lynn; *Evelina* (1778), *Cecilia* (1782).

Burroughs, Edgar Rice (1875–1950) American novelist, born Chicago; *Tarzan of the Apes* (1914), *The Land that Time Forgot* (1924).

Burroughs, William S(eward) (1914–) American novelist, born St Louis, Missouri; *The Naked Lunch* (1959), *The Soft Machine* (1961), *The Wild Boys* (1971), *Exterminator!* (1974).

Byatt, A(ntonia) S(usan) (1936–) English novelist, born Sheffield; *The Shadow of a Sun* (1964), *The Virgin in the Garden* (1978), *Possession* (1989), Booker Prize.

Calvino, Italo (1923–) Italian novelist, short-story writer, born Santiago de Las Vegas, Cuba; *Invisible Cities* (1972), *The Castle of Crossed Destinies* (1969), *If on a Winter's Night a Traveller* (1979).

Camus, Albert (1913–60) French novelist, playwright, born Mondovi, Algeria; *The Outsider* (1942), *The Plague* (1948), *The Fall* (1957); Nobel Prize for Literature 1957.

Canetti, Elias (1906–) Bulgarian novelist, born Russe, Bulgaria; *Auto da Fé* (1935, trans 1946), *Crowds and Power* (1960, trans 1962); Nobel Prize for Literature 1981.

Capote, Truman (1924–84) American playwright, novelist, short-story writer, born New Orleans; *Other Voices, Other Rooms* (1948), *Breakfast at Tiffany's* (1958).

Carey, Peter (1943–) Australian novelist, short-story writer, born Bacchus Marsh, Victoria; *Bliss* (1981), *Illywhacker* (1985), *Oscar and Lucinda* (1989), Booker Prize.

Carter, Angela (1940–) English novelist, poet, playwright, born London; *The Magic Toyshop* (1967), *The Infernal Desire Machines of Dr Hoffman* (1972), *Nights of the Circus* (1984).

Cartland, (Mary) Barbara (Hamilton) (1901–) English novelist, born Birmingham; prolific writer, over 400 titles, eg *The*

WRITERS (cont.)

Husband Hunters (1976), *Wings on My Heart* (1954), *The Castle Made for Love* (1985).

Cather, Willa (Silbert) (1876–1947) American novelist, poet, born near Winchester, Virginia; *O Pioneers!* (1913), *My Antonia* (1918), *One of Ours* (1922), *The Professor's House* (1925), *My Mortal Enemy* (1926), *Death Comes for the Archbishop* (1927), *Sapphira and the Slave Girl* (1940).

Cervantes Saaverda, Miguel de (1547–1616) Spanish novelist and poet, born Alcala de Henares; *La Galatea* (1585), *Don Quixote* (1605–15).

Chandler, Raymond (1888–1959) American novelist, born Chicago; *The Big Sleep* (1939), *Farewell, My Lovely* (1940), *The High Window* (1942), *The Lady in the Lake* (1943), *The Long Goodbye* (1953).

Chesterton, G(ilbert) K(eith) (1874–1936) English novelist, poet, born London; *The Napoleon of Notting Hill* (1904), *The Innocence of Father Brown* (1911).

Christie, Dame Agatha (Mary Clarissa) (1890–1976) English novelist, born Torquay, Devon; *Murder on the Orient Express* (1934), *Death on the Nile* (1937), *Ten Little Niggers* (1939), *Curtain* (1975).

Colette, Sidonie Gabrielle (1873–1954) French novelist, born Saint-Sauveur-en-Puisaye, Burgundy; *Claudine à l'école* (1900), *Chéri* (1920), *La Fin de Chéri* (1926), *Gigi* (1943).

Collins, (William) Wilkie (1824–89) English novelist, born London; *The Woman in White* (1860), *No Name* (1862), *Armadale* (1866), *The Moonstone* (1868).

Compton–Burnett, Dame Ivy (1884–1969) English novelist, born Pinner, Middlesex; *A House and its Head* (1935), *A Family and a Fortune* (1939), *Manservant and Maidservant* (1947).

Conrad, Joseph (originally **Jozef Teodor Konrad Nalecz Korzeniowski**) (1857–1924), Polish/British novelist, short-story writer, born Berdichev, Ukraine; *Lord Jim* (1900), *Heart of Darkness* (1902), *Nostromo* (1904), *The Secret Agent* (1907), *Chance* (1914).

Cookson, Catherine Ann (1906–) English novelist, born Tyne Dock, County Durham; prolific author, over 40 titles; *Tilly Trotter* (1956), *The Glass Virgin* (1969).

Cooper, Jilly (1937–) English novelist; *Men and Supermen* (1972), *Class* (1979), *Riders* (1985), *Rivals* (1988), *Polo* (1990).

Davies, (William) Robertson (1913–) Canadian novelist, short-story writer, playwright, born Thamesville, Ontario; *The Rebel Angels* (1981), *'The Deptford Trilogy'* (1970–75), *What's Bred in the Bone* (1985).

de Beauvoir, Simone (1908–86) French novelist, born Paris; *The Second Sex* (1949, trans 1953), *Les Mandarins* (1954), *Memoirs of a Dutiful Daughter* (1959).

de Quincey, Thomas (1785–1859) English novelist, born Manchester; *Confessions of an English Opium Eater* (1822).

Defoe, Daniel (1660–1731) English novelist, born Stoke Newington, London; *Robinson Crusoe* (1719), *Moll Flanders* (1722), *A Journal of the Plague Year* (1722).

Delafield, E M (pseudonym of **Edmée Elizabeth Monica Dashwood**) (1890–1943) English novelist, born Llandogo, Monmouth; *The Diary of a Provincial Lady* (1931).

Dickens, Charles (1812–70) English novelist, born Landport, Portsmouth; *Oliver Twist* (1837–9), *David Copperfield* (1849–50), *Bleak House* (1852–3), *Great Expectations* (1860–1).

Dickens, Monica (1915–) English novelist, born London; *One Pair of Hands* (1939), *Spring Comes to the World's End* (1973).

Dinesen, Isak (pseudonym of **Karen Blixen**) (1885–1962) Danish novelist, born Rungsted; *Seven Gothic Tales* (1934), *Out of Africa* (1937).

Disreali, Benjamin (1804–81) English novelist, born London; *Coningsby* (1844), *Sybil* (1846), *Tancred* (1847).

Dostoevsky, Fyodor Mikhailovich (1821–81) Russian novelist, born Moscow; *Notes from Underground* (1864), *Crime and Punishment* (1866), *The Brothers Karamazov* (1880).

Doyle, Sir Arthur Conan (1859–1930) Scottish novelist, short-story writer, born Edinburgh; *The Memoirs of Sherlock Holmes* (1894), *The Hound of the Baskervilles* (1902), *The Lost World* (1912).

Drabble, Margaret (1939–) English novelist, short-story writer, born Sheffield; *The Millstone* (1965), *Jerusalem the Golden* (1967), *The Ice Age* (1977).

du Maurier, Dame Daphne (1907–89) English novelist, born London; *Rebecca* (1938), *My Cousin Rachel* (1951).

Dumas, Alexandre (père) (Alexandre Dumas Davy de la Pailleterie) (1802–70) French

WRITERS (cont.)

novelist and playwright, born Villers-Cotterets, Aisne; *The Three Musketeers* (1844–5).

Dumas, Alexandre (fils) (1824–95) French novelist, playwright, born Paris; *La Dame aux camélias* (1848).

Durrell, Gerald Malcolm (1925–90) English writer, born Jamshedpur, India; *The Overloaded Ark* (1953), *My Family and Other Animals* (1956).

Durrell, Lawrence George (1912–) English novelist, poet, born Julundur, India; *'Alexandria Quartet'* (1957–60).

Eco, Umberto (1932–) Italian novelist, born Alessandria, Piedmont; *The Name of the Rose* (1980), *Foucault's Pendulum* (1989).

Edgeworth, Maria (1767–1849) Irish novelist, born Blackbourton, Oxfordshire; *Castle Rackrent* (1800), *The Absentee* (1809).

Eliot, George (originally **Mary Ann**, later **Marian Evans**) (1819–80) English novelist, born Arbury, Warwickshire; *Adam Bede* (1858), *The Mill on the Floss* (1860), *Middlemarch* (1871–2), *Daniel Deronda* (1874–6).

Farmer, Philip José (1918–) American novelist, short-story writer; *To Your Scattered Bodies Go* (1977), *The Magic Labyrinth* (1980).

Faulkner, William Harrison (1897–1962) American novelist, born near Oxford, Mississippi; *Sartoris* (1929), *The Sound and the Fury* (1929), *Absalom, Absalom!* (1936); Nobel Prize for Literature 1949.

Fielding, Henry (1707–54) English novelist, born Sharpham Park, near Glastonbury, Somerset; *Joseph Andrews* (1742), *Tom Jones* (1749).

Fitzgerald, F(rancis) Scott (Key) (1896–1940) American novelist, short-story writer, born St Paul, Minnesota; *The Great Gatsby* (1925), *Tender is the Night* (1934).

Flaubert, Gustave (1821–80) French novelist, born Rouen; *Madame Bovary* (1857), *Salammbô* (1862).

Fleming, Ian (Lancaster (1908–64) English novelist; author of the 'James Bond' novels eg *Casino Royale* (1953), *From Russia with Love* (1957), *Dr No* (1958), *Goldfinger* (1959), *The Man with the Golden Gun* (1965).

Ford, Ford Madox (originally **Ford Hermann Hueffer**) (1873–1939) English novelist, poet, born Merton, Surrey; *The Fifth Queen* (1906), *The Good Soldier* (1915), *Parade's End* (1924–8).

Forster, E(dward) M(organ) (1879–1970) English novelist, short-story writer, born London; *A Room with a View* (1908), *Howards End* (1910), *A Passage to India* (1922–4).

Forsyth, Frederick (1938–) English novelist, short-story writer, born Ashford, Kent; *The Day of the Jackal* (1971), *The Odessa File* (1972), *The Fourth Protocol* (1984).

Fowles, John (Robert) (1926–) English novelist, born Leigh-on-Sea; *The Magus* (1965, revised 1977), *The French Lieutenant's Woman* (1969).

Frame, Janet Paterson (1924–) New Zealand novelist, short-story writer, born Dunedin; *The Lagoon: Stories* (1952), *Scented Gardens for the Blind* (1963), *Living in the Maniototo* (1979).

Fraser, Antonia (Lady Antonia Pinter) (1932–) English novelist, born London; *Mary, Queen of Scots* (1969), *Quiet as a Nun* (1977), *A Splash of Red* (1981).

Galsworthy, John (1867–1933) English novelist, playwright, born Coombe, Surrey; *The Forsyte Saga* (1906–31); Nobel Prize for Literature 1932.

García Márquez, Gabriel (1928–) Colombian novelist, born Aracataca; *A Hundred Years of Solitude* (1970), *Chronicle of a Death Foretold* (1982); Nobel Prize for Literature 1982.

Gardner, Helen (1942–) Australian novelist, born Geelong; *Monkey Gripp* (1977).

Gaskell, Mrs Elizabeth (Cleghorn) (1810–65) English novelist, born Cheyne Row, Chelsea, London; *Cranford* (1853), *North and South* (1855), *Sylvia's Lovers* (1863).

Gerhardie, William Alexander (1895–1977) English novelist, born St Petersburg, Russia; *The Polyglots* (1925), *Resurrection* (1934).

Gibbon, Lewis Grassic (pseudonym of **James Leslie Mitchell**) (1901–35) Scottish novelist, born near Auchterless, Aberdeenshire; *Sunset Song* (1932), *Cloud Howe* (1933), *Grey Granite* (1934).

Gibbons, Stella (Dorothea) (1902–89) English novelist, born London; *Cold Comfort Farm* (1933).

Gide, André (Paul Guillaume) (1860–1951) French novelist, born Paris; *The Immoralist* (1902), *The Vatican Cellars* (1914).

Gissing, George Robert (1857–1903) English novelist, short-story writer, born Wakefield, Yorkshire; *New Grub Street* (1891), *The Private Papers of Henry Ryecroft* (1902).

Glasgow, Ellen (1873–1945) American novelist, born Richmond, Virginia; *Barren Ground* (1925), *The Sheltered Life* (1932), *In This Our Life* (1941).

WRITERS (cont.)

Godwin, William (1756–1836) English novelist, born Wisbech; *Caleb Williams* (1794), *Mandeville* (1817).

Goethe, Johann Wolfgang von (1749–1832) German novelist, poet, born Frankfurt-am-Main; *The Sorrows of Young Werther* (1774).

Gogol, Nikolai Vasilievich (1809–52) Russian novelist, short-story writer, playwright, born Sorochinstsi, Poltava; *The Overcoat* (1835), *Diary of a Madman* (1835), *Dead Souls* (1842), *The Odd Women* (1893).

Golding, (Sir) William (Gerald) (1911–) English novelist, born St Columb Minor, Cornwall; *The Lord of the Flies* (1954), *The Inheritors* (1955), *Pincher Martin* (1956), *The Spire* (1964), *Darkness Visible* (1979), *Rites of Passage* (1980), *The Paper Men* (1984), *Close Quarter* (1987), *Fire Down Below* (1989); Nobel Prize for Literature 1983.

Goldsmith, Oliver (1728–74) Anglo-Irish playwright, novelist, poet, born Pallasmore, County Longford; *The Vicar of Wakefield* (1764).

Gordimer, Nadine (1923–) South African novelist, short-story writer, born Springs, Transvaal; *Occasion for Loving* (1963), *A Guest of Honour* (1970), *The Conservationist* (1974), *A Sport of Nature* (1987).

Gorky, Maxim (pseudonym of **Aleksei Maksimovich Peshkov**) (1868–1936) Russian novelist, short-story writer, born Nizhni Novgorod (New Gorky); *The Mother* (1906–7), *Childhood* (1913), *The Life of Klim Samgin (1925–36).*

Gosse, Sir Edmund William (1849–1928) English novelist, poet, born London; *Father and Son* (1907).

Gould, Nathaniel (1857–1919) English novelist, born Manchester; *The Double Event* (1891), *Town and Bush* (1896).

Grass, Günter (Wilhelm) (1927–) German novelist, born Danzig; *The Tin Drum* (1959), *The Meeting at Telgte* (1979).

Graves, Robert von Ranke (1895–1985) English novelist, poet, born London; *I Claudius* (1934), *Claudius the God* (1934).

Gray, Alasdair (1934–) Scottish novelist, short-story writer, poet; *Lanark* (1981), *Unlikely Stories, Mostly* (1983), *1982 Janine* (1984).

Greene, (Henry) Graham (1904–91) English novelist, playwright, born Berkhamstead, Hertfordshire; *Brighton Rock* (1938), *The Power and the Glory* (1940), *The Third Man* (1950), *The Honorary Consul* (1973).

Hardy, Thomas (1840–1928) English novelist, poet, born Higher Bockhampton, Dorset; *Far from the Madding Crowd* (1874), *The Mayor of Casterbridge* (1886), *Tess of the D'Urbervilles* (1891), *Jude the Obscure* (1895).

Hartley, L(eslie) P(oles) (1895–1972) English novelist, short-story writer, born near Peterborough; *The Shrimp and the Anemone* (1944), *The Go-Between* (1953), *The Hireling* (1957).

Hawthorne, Nathaniel (1804–64) American novelist, short-story writer, born Salem, Massachusetts; *The Scarlet Letter* (1850), *The House of the Seven Gables* (1851).

Heinlein, Robert A(nson) (1907–88) American novelist; *Stranger in a Strange Land* (1962), *The Moon is a Harsh Mistress* (1967).

Heller, Joseph (1923–) American novelist, born Brooklyn, New York; *Catch-22* (1961), *Something Happened* (1974).

Hemingway, Ernest (Millar) (1899–1961) American novelist, short-story writer, born Oak Park (Chicago), Illinois; *A Farewell to Arms* (1929), *For Whom the Bell Tolls* (1940), *The Old Man and the Sea* (1952); Nobel Prize for Literature 1954.

Hesse, Herman (1877–1962) German novelist, born Calw in Württemberg; *Siddshartha* (1922), *Steppenwolf* (1927), *The Glass Bead Game* (1943); Nobel Prize for Literature 1946.

Heyer, Georgette (1902–74) English novelist, born London; 56 novels eg *The Black Moth* (1929), *Footsteps in the Dark* (1932), *Regency Buck* (1935), *The Corinthian* (1940), *Friday's Child* (1944), *The Grand Sophy* (1950), *Bath Tangle* (1955), *Venetia* (1958), *The Nonesuch* (1962), *Frederica* (1965).

Hilton, James (1900–54) English novelist, born Leigh, Lancashire; *Lost Horizon* (1933), *Goodbye Mr Chips* (1934).

Hogg, James (the **'Ettrick Shepherd'**) (1770–1835) Scottish novelist, poet, born Ettrick, Selkirkshire; *Confessions of a Justified Sinner* (1824).

Holt, Victoria (pseudonym of **Eleanor Alice Burford Hibbert**) (1906–) English novelist, prolific output, also writes as Philippa Carr, Jean Plaidy; *Catherine de 'Medici* (1969 – as JP), *Will You Love Me in September* (1981 – as PC), *The Captive* (1989 – as VH).

Hughes, Thomas (1822–96) English novelist, born Uffington, Berkshire; *Tom Brown's Schooldays* (1857).

WRITERS (cont.)

Hurston, Zora Neale (1903–60) American novelist, born Eatonville, Florida; *Their Eyes Were Watching God* (1937), *Moses Man of the Mountain* (1939).

Huxley, Aldous (Leonard) (1894–1963) English novelist, born Godalming, Surrey; *Brave New World* (1932), *Eyeless in Gaza* (1936), *Island* (1962).

Inchbald, Elizabeth (1753–1821) English novelist, playwright, born Stanningford, Suffolk; *A Simple Story* (1791), *Nature and Art* (1796).

Irving, John (1942–) American novelist, short-story writer; *The World According to Garp* (1978), *The Hotel New Hampshire* (1981), *A Prayer for Owen Meany* (1989).

Isherwood, Christopher (William Bradshaw) (1904–) English/American novelist, born Disley, Cheshire; *Mr Norris Changes Trains* (1935), *Goodbye to Berlin* (1939), *Down there on a Visit* (1962)

Ishiguro, Kazuo (1954–) British novelist, short-story writer, born Japan; *The Remains of the Day* (1989).

James, Henry (1843–1916) American novelist, born New York; *Portrait of a Lady* (1881), *The Bostonians* (1886), *The Awkward Age* (1899), *The Ambassadors* (1903), *The Turn of the Screw* (1898).

James, P(hyliss) D(orothy) (1920–) English novelist, born Oxford; *Cover Her Face* (1966), *Taste for Death* (1986).

Jhabvala, Ruth Prawer (1927–) British/Polish novelist, born Cologne, Germany; *Heat and Dust* (1975), *In Search of Love and Beauty* (1983).

Joyce, James (Augustine Aloysius) (1882–1941) Irish novelist, poet, born Dublin; *Dubliners* (1914), *A Portrait of the Artist as a Young Man* (1914–15), *Ulysses* (1922), *Finnegan's Wake* (1939).

Kafka, Franz (1883–1924) Austrian novelist, short-story writer, born Prague; *The Metamorphosis* (1916), *The Trial* (1925), *The Castle* (1926), *America* (1927).

Kazantzakis, Nikos (1883–1957) Greek novelist, poet, playwright, born Heraklion, Crete; *Zorba the Greek* (1946).

Keane, Molly (1904–) Anglo-Irish novelist, born County Kildare, Ireland; *Devoted Ladies* (1934), *Good Behaviour* (1981), *Time After Time* (1983).

Keneally, Thomas (Michael) (1935–) Australian novelist, short-story writer, playwright, born Sydney; *Bring Larks and Heroes* (1967), *Three Cheers for a Paraclete* (1968), *The Survivor* (1969), *Schindler's Ark* (1982).

Kerouac, Jack (Jean-Louis) (1922–69) American novelist, born Lowell, Massachusetts; *On the Road* (1957), *The Dharma Brums* (1958).

Kesey, Ken (Elton) (1935–) American novelist, short-story writer, born La Junta, Colorado; *One Flew Over the Cuckoo's Nest* (1962).

King, Stephen (Edwin) (1947–) American novelist, short-story writer; *Carrie* (1974), *The Shining* (1977), *Christine* (1983).

Kingsley, Charles (1819–75) English novelist, born Holne vicarage, Dartmoor; *Westward Ho!* (1855), *The Water-Babies* (1863), *Hereward the Wake* (1866).

Kipling, Rudyard (1865–1936) English novelist, poet, short-story writer, born Bombay, India; *Barrack–room Ballads* (1892), *The Jungle Book* (1894), *Kim* (1901), *Just So Stories* (1902); Nobel Prize for Literature 1907.

Kundera, Milan (1929–) French/Czech novelist, born Brno; *Life is Elsewhere* (1973), *The Farewell Party* (1976), *The Unbearable Lightness of Being* (1984).

La Fayette, Marie Madeleine Pioche de Lavergne, Comtesse de (1634–93) French novelist, born Paris; *Zaide* (1670), *La Princesse de Clèves* (1678).

Lawrence, D(avid) H(erbert) (1885–1930) English novelist, poet, short-story writer, born Eastwood, Nottinghamshire; *Sons and Lovers* (1913), *The Rainbow* (1915), *Women in Love* (1920), *Lady Chatterley's Lover* (1928).

Le Carré, John (pseudonym of **David John Moore Cornwell**) (1931–) English novelist, born Poole, Dorset; *Tinker, Tailor, Soldier, Spy* (1974), *Smiley's People* (1980), *The Little Drummer Girl* (1983).

Le Fanu, (Joseph) Sheridan (1814–73) Irish novelist, short-story writer, born Dublin; *Uncle Silas* (1864), *In a Glass Darkly* (1872).

Lee, (Nelle) Harper (1926–) American novelist, born Monroeville, Alabama; *To Kill a Mockingbird* (1960).

Lee, Laurie (1914–) English novelist, poet, born Slad, Gloucestershire; *Cider with Rosie* (1959), *As I Walked Out One Midsummer Morning* (1969).

WRITERS (cont.)

Lehmann, Rosamond (Nina) (1903–90) English novelist, born London; *Dusty Answer* (1927), *Invitation to the Waltz* (1932), *The Ballad and the Source* (1944).

Lessing, Doris (1919–) British novelist, short-story writer, born Kermanshah, Iran; *The Grass is Singing* (1950), *The Golden Notebook* (1952), *Canopus in Argus Archives* (1979–83).

Levi, Primo (1919–87) Italian novelist, born Turin; *If this is a Man* (1947), *The Periodic Table* (1984).

Lewis, (Harry) Sinclair (1885–1951) American novelist, born Sauk Center, Minnesota; *Main Street* (1920), *Babbitt* (1922), *Martin Arrowsmith* (1925), *Elmer Gantry* (1927); Nobel Prize for Literature 1930.

Lodge, David (1935–) English novelist, born London; *The British Museum is Falling Down* (1965), *Changing Places* (1975), *Small World* (1984).

London, Jack (John) Griffith (1876–1916); American novelist, born San Francisco; *Call of the Wild* (1903), *White Fang* (1907), *Martin Eden* (1909).

Macaulay, Dame (Emilie) Rose (1881–1958) English novelist, born Rugby, Warwickshire; *Dangerous Ages* (1921), *The World, My Wilderness* (1950), *The Tower of Trebizond* (1956).

MacDonald, George (1824–1905) Scottish novelist, born Huntly, Aberdeenshire; *Robert Falconer* (1868), *The Princess and the Goblin* (1872), *Lilith* (1895).

MacInnes, Colin (1914–76) English novelist, born London; *City of Spades* (1957), *Absolute Beginners* (1957).

MacKenzie, Sir (Edward Morgan) Compton (1883–1972) English novelist, born West Hartlepool; *Whisky Galore* (1942).

MacKenzie, Henry (1745–1831) Scottish novelist, born Edinburgh; *The Man of Feeling* (1771)

MacLean, Alistair (1922–87) Scottish novelist, born Glasgow; *The Guns of Navarone* (1957), *Where Eagles Dare* (1967).

Mailer, Norman (1923–) American novelist, born Long Branch, New Jersey; *The Naked and the Dead* (1949), *An American Dream* (1965).

Malamud, Bernard (1914–86) American novelist, born Brooklyn; *The Fixer* (1966), *The Tenants* (1971).

Mann, Thomas (1875–1955) German novelist, born Lubeck; *Death in Venice* (1912), *The Magic Mountain* (1924).

Manning, Olivia (1908–80) English novelist, short-story writer, born Portsmouth; *The Balkan Trilogy* (1960–5), *The Levant Trilogy* (1977–80).

Mansfield, Katherine (pseudonym of **Katherine Mansfield Beauchamp**) (1888–1923) New Zealand short-story writer, born Wellington; *Prelude* (1918), *Bliss, and other stories* (1920), *The Garden Party, and other stories* (1922).

Marsh, Ngaio (1899–1982) New Zealand novelist, born Christchurch; *Death in a White Tie* (1958), *A Grave Mistake* (1978).

Maugham, (William) Somerset (1874–1965) English novelist, born Paris; *Of Human Bondage* (1915), *The Moon and Sixpence* (1919), *The Razor's Edge* (1945).

Maupassant, Guy de (1850–93) French short-story writer, novelist, born Miromesnil; *Claire de Lune* (1884), *Bel Ami* (1885).

Mauriac, François (1885–1970) French novelist, born Bordeaux; *Le Baiser au Lépreux* (1922); Nobel Prize for Literature 1952.

Melville, Herman (1819–91) American novelist, poet, born New York; *Moby Dick* (1851).

Meredith, George (1828–1909) English novelist, poet, born Portsmouth; *The Egoist* (1879), *Diana of the Crossways* (1885).

Miller, Henry Valentine (1891–1980) American novelist, born New York; *Tropic of Cancer* (1934), *Tropic of Capricorn* (1938), *The Rosy Crucifixion Trilogy* (1949–60).

Mishima, Yukio (Kimitake Hiraoka) (1925–70) Japanese novelist, born Tokyo; *Confessions of a Mask* (1960), *The Temple of the Golden Pavilion* (1959), *The Sea of Fertility* (1969–71).

Mitchell, Margaret (1900–49) American novelist, born Atlanta, Georgia; *Gone with the Wind* (1936).

Mitchison, Naomi (1897–) Scottish novelist, poet, playwright, born Edinburgh; *The Corn King and the Spring Queen (1931)*, *The Big House* (1950).

Mitford, Nancy (1904–73) English novelist, born London; *Love in a Cold Climate* (1949), *Don't Tell Alfred* (1960).

Mo, Timothy (1950–) born Hong Kong; *The Monkey King* (1978), *Sour Sweet* (1982), *An Insular Possession* (1986).

Monsarrat, Nicholas (John Turney) (1910–79) English novelist, born Liverpool; *The Cruel Sea* (1951), *The Story of Esther Costello* (1953).

Moorcock, Michael (1939–) English novelist,

WRITERS (cont.)

short-story writer, born London; *Gloriana* (1978), *Byzantium Endures* (1983), *The City in the Autumn Stars* (1986).

Morrison, Toni (1931–) American novelist, born Ohio; *The Bluest Eye* (1970), *Song of Solomon* (1977), *Tar Baby* (1981).

Mortimer, John (Clifford) (1923–) English novelist, short-story writer, playwright, born London; *A Cat Among the Pigeons* (1964), *Rumpole of the Bailey* (1978), *Paradise Postponed* (1985).

Murdoch, Iris (1919–) Irish novelist, born Dublin; *The Bell* (1958), *The Sea, The Sea* (1978), *The Philosopher's Pupil* (1983).

Nabokov, Vladimir Vladimirovich (1899–1977) Russian/US novelist, poet, born St Petersburg; *Lolita* (1958), *Look at the Harlequins!* (1974)

Naipaul, V(idiadhar) S(urajprasad) (1932–) Trinidadian novelist, born Trinidad; *A House for Mr Biswas* (1961), *In a Free State* (1971), *A Bend in the River* (1979).

Narayan, R(asipurum) K(rishnaswami) (1906–) Indian novelist, born Madras; *Swami and Friends* (1935), *The Painter of Signs* (1977).

Oates, Joyce Carol (1938–) American novelist, short-story writer, born Millersport, New York; *A Garden of Earthly Delights* (1967), *Them* (1969), *Wonderland* (1971).

O'Brien, Edna (1932) Irish novelist, short-story writer, born Tuamgraney, County Clare; *The Country Girls* (1960), *August is a Wicked Month* (1964), *A Pagan Place* (1971).

O'Flaherty, Liam (1897–1984) Irish novelist, short-story writer, born Inishmore, Aran Islands; *The Informer* (1926), *Two Lovely Beasts* (1948).

O'Hara, John (Henry) (1905–70) American novelist, short-story writer, born Pottsville, Pennsylvania; *Spring Sowing* (1924), *Appointment in Samarra* (1934), *The Doctor's Son* (1935), *Butterfield 8* (1935), *Paul Joey* (1940).

Oliphant, Margaret (1828–97) Scottish novelist, born Wallyford, Midlothian; *The Athelings* (1857), *Salem Chapel* (1863).

Orwell, George (pseudonym of **Eric Arthur Blair**) (1903–50) English novelist, born Bengal; *Down and Out in Paris and London* (1933), *The Road to Wigan Pier* (1937), *Animal Farm* (1945), *Nineteen Eighty-Four* (1949).

Ouida (pseudonym of **Marie-Louise de la Ramée**) (1839–1908) English novelist, born Bury St Edmunds; *Held in Bondage* (1865), *Under Two Flags* (1867), *Folle-Farine* (1871).

Pasternak, Boris (Leonidovich) (1890–1960) Russian novelist, born Moscow; *Doctor Zhivago* (1957); Nobel Prize for Literature 1958.

Paton, Allan (Stewart) (1903–88) South African novelist, short-story writer, born Pietermaritzburg, Natal; *Cry, the Beloved Country* (1948).

Peacock, Thomas Love (1785–1866) English novelist, poet, born Weymouth; *Melincourt* (1817), *Nightmare Abbey* (1818).

Peake, Mervyn (Laurence) (1911–68) English novelist, poet, born Kuling, China; *Titus Groan* (1946), *Gormenghast* (1950), *Titus Alone* (1959).

Plaidy, Jean *see* **Holt, Victoria**

Poe, Edgar Allan (1809–49) American short-story writer, poet, born Boston; *Tales of the Grotesque and Arabesque* (eg 'The Fall of the House of Usher') (1840), *The Pit and the Pendulum* (1843).

Porter, Harold (Hal) (1911–84) Australian novelist, playwright, poet, short-story writer, born Melbourne; *A Handful of Pennies* (1958), *The Right Thing* (1971).

Porter, Katherine Anne (Maria Veronica Callista Russell) (1890–1980) American novelist, short-story writer, born Indian Creek, Texas; *Pale Horse, Pale Rider* (1939), *Ship of Fools* (1962).

Powell, Anthony (Dymoke) (1905–) English novelist, born London; *A Dance to the Music of Time* (1951–75), *The Fisher King* (1986).

Powys, John Cowper (1872–1963) English novelist, born Shirley, Derbyshire; *Wolf Solent* (1929), *Owen Glendower* (1940).

Priestley, J(ohn) B(oynton) (1894–1984) English novelist, playwright, born Bradford; *The Good Companions* (1929), *Angel Pavement* (1930).

Proust, Marcel (1871 1922) French novelist, born Paris; *Remembrance of Things Past* (1913–27).

Puzo, Mario (1920–) American novelist, born New York City; *The Godfather* (1969).

Pynchon, Thomas (1937–) American novelist, born Long Island; *V* (1963), *Gravity's Rainbow* (1973).

Queen, Ellery (pseudonym of **Patrick Dannay** (1905–82) and his cousin **Manfred B Lee** (1905–71)) American novelists and short-story writers, both born Brooklyn, New York; *The*

WRITERS (cont.)

French Powder Mystery (1930), *The Tragedy of X* (1940), *The Glass Village* (1954).

Radcliffe, Ann (1764–1823) English novelist, born London; *The Mysteries of Udolpho* (1794), *The Italian* (1797).

Reid Banks, Lynne (1929–) English novelist, born London; *The L-Shaped Room* (1960), *Defy the Wilderness* (1981).

Remarque, Erich Maria (1898–1970) German novelist, born Osnabrück; *All Quiet on the Western Front* (1929), *The Road Back* (1931), *The Black Obelisk* (1957).

Renault, Mary (pseudonym of **Eileen Mary Challans**) (1905–83) English novelist, born London; *The King Must Die* (1958), *Fire from Heaven* (1969), *The Persian Boy* (1972), *The Praise Singer* (1978).

Rendell, Ruth (1930–) English novelist, born London; *A Judgement in Stone* (1977), *The Killing Doll* (1980), *Heartstones* (1987).

Rhys, Jean (pseudonym of **Ella Gwendolyn Rees Williams**) (1894–1979) British novelist, short-story writer, born Dominica, West Indies; *After Leaving Mackenzie* (1930), *Wide Sargasso Sea* (1966), *Tigers are Better Looking* (1968).

Richardson, Harry Handel (pseudonym of **Ethel Florence Lindesay Richardson**) (1870–1946) Australian novelist, born Melbourne; *The Getting of Wisdom* (1910), *Ultima Thule* (1929).

Richardson, Samuel (1689–1761) English novelist, born Derby; *Pamela* (1740), *Clarissa* (1747–8), *Sir Charles Grandison* (1753–4).

Rolfe, Frederick William (Baron Corvo) (1860–1913) English novelist, born London; *Hadrian the Seventh* (1904), *The Desire and Pursuit of the Whole* (1934).

Roth, Henry (1906–) American novelist, short-story writer, born Tysmenica, Austria-Hungary; *Call It Sleep* (1934).

Roth, Philip Milton (1933–) American novelist, short-story writer, born Newark, New Jersey; *Portnoy's Complaint* (1969), *The Great American Novel* (1973), *My Life as a Man* (1974).

Rushdie, Salman (1947–) British novelist, short-story writer, born Bombay; *Midnight's Children* (1981), *Shame* (1983), *The Satanic Verses* (1988).

Sackville-West, Vita (Victoria May) (1892–1962) English poet, novelist, short-story writer, born Knole, Kent; *The Edwardians* (1930), *All Passion Spent* (1931).

Sade, Donatien Alphonse François, Comte de, (known as **Marquis**) (1740–1814) French novelist, born Paris; *Les 120 Journées de Sodome* (1784), *Justine* (1791), *Le Philosophie dans le boudoir* (1793), *Juliette* (1798), *Les Crimes de l'amour* (1800).

Saki (pseudonym of **Hector Hugh Munro**) (1870–1916) British novelist, short-story writer, born Akyab, Burma; *The Chronicles of Clovis* (1912), *The Unbearable Bassington* (1912).

Salinger, J(erome) D(avid) (1919–) American novelist, born New York; *The Catcher in the Rye* (1951), *Franny and Zooey* (1961).

Sand, George (pseudonym of **Amandine Aurore Lucille Dupin**) (1804–76) French novelist, born Paris; *Lélia* (1833), *La Petite Fadette* (1849).

Saroyan, William (1908–81) American novelist, playwright, short-story writer, born Fresno, California; *The Daring Young Man on the Flying Trapeze* (1934), *My Name is Aram* (1940), *The Human Comedy* (1942).

Sartre, Jean-Paul (1905–80) French novelist, playwright, born Paris; *Nausea* (1949), *The Roads to Freedom* (1945–7); Nobel Prize for Literature 1964.

Sayers, Dorothy L (1893–1957) English novelist, short-story writer, born Oxford; *Lord Peter Views the Body* (1928), *Gaudy Night* (1935).

Schreiner, Olive (1855–1920) South African novelist, born Wittebergen Mission Station, Cape of Good Hope; *The Story of an African Farm* (1883), *Trooper Peter Halkett of Mashonaland* (1897).

Scott, Sir Walter (1771–1832) Scottish novelist, poet, born Edinburgh; *Waverley* (1814), *The Heart of Midlothian* (1818), *The Bride of Lammermoor* (1819), *Ivanhoe* (1820).

Shelley, Mary (Wollstonecraft) (1797–1851) English novelist, born London; *Frankenstein* (1816), *The Last Man* (1826), *Perkin Warbeck* (1830).

Sholokhov, Mikhail Alexandrovich (1905–84) Russian novelist, born near Veshenskayal; *And Quiet Flows the Don* (1928–40), *The Upturned Soil* (1940); Nobel Prize for Literature 1965.

Shute, Nevil (pseudonym of **Nevil Shute Norway**) (1899–1960) English/Australian novelist, born Ealing; *The Pied Piper* (1942), *A Town Like Alice* (1950), *On the Beach* (1957).

Sillitoe, Alan (1928–) English novelist, poet, short-story writer, born Nottingham; *Saturday Night and Sunday Morning* (1958), *The Loneliness of the Long Distance Runner* (1959).

WRITERS (cont.)

Singer, Isaac Bashevis (1904–91) American novelist, playwright, born Radzymin, Poland; *The Family Moskat* (1950), *The Satan in Goray* (1955); Nobel Prize for Literature 1978.

Smollett, Tobias George (1721–71) Scottish novelist, born Dalquharn, Dunbartonshire; *The Adventures of Peregrine Pickle* (1751), *The Expedition of Humphrey Clinker* (1771).

Snow, C(harles) P(ercy) (1905–80) English novelist, born Leicester; *Strangers and Brothers* (1940–70).

Solzhenitsyn, Alexander Isayevich (1918–) Russian novelist, born Kislovodsk, Caucasus; *One Day in the Life of Ivan Denisovich* (1962), *Cancer Ward* (1968),*The First Circle* (1969).

Spark, Muriel (1918–) Scottish novelist, short-story writer, poet, born Edinburgh; *The Ballad of Peckham Rye* (1960), *The Prime of Miss Jean Brodie* (1962), *The Girls of Slender Means* (1963).

Spring, Howard (1889–1965) Welsh novelist, born Cardiff; *Oh Absalom* (1938).

Stein, Gertrude (1874–1946) American novelist, short-story writer, born Allegheny, Pennsylvania; *Three Lives* (1909), *Tender Buttons* (1914).

Steinbeck, John Ernest (1902–68) American novelist born Salinas, California; *Of Mice and Men* (1937), *The Grapes of Wrath* (1939), *Cannery Row* (1945), *East of Eden* (1952); Nobel Prize for Literature 1962.

Stendhal (pseudonym of **Henri Marie Beyle**) (1788–1842) French novelist, born Grenoble; *Le Rouge et le noir* (1830), *La Chartreuse de Parme* (1839).

Sterne, Lawrence (1713–68) Irish novelist, born Clonmel, Tipperary; *Tristram Shandy* (1760–7), *A Sentimental Journey* (1768).

Stevenson, Robert Louis (Balfour) (1850–94) Scottish novelist, short-story writer, poet, born Edinburgh; *Travels with a Donkey* (1879), *Treasure Island* (1883), *Kidnapped* (1886), *The Strange Case of Dr Jekyll and Mr Hyde* (1886).

Stewart, Mary (1916–) English novelist, born Sunderland; *This Rough Magic* (1964), *The Last Enchantment* (1979).

Stoker, Bram (Abraham) (1847–1912) Irish novelist, short-story writer, born Dublin; *Dracula* (1897).

Stowe, Harriet (Elizabeth) Beecher (1811–96) American novelist, born Litchfield, Connecticut; *Uncle Tom's Cabin* (1852).

Suskind, Patrick (1949–) German novelist; *Perfume, the story of a murderer* (1985).

Swift, Jonathan (1667–1754) Irish novelist, poet, born Dublin; *A Tale of a Tub* (1704), *Gulliver's Travels* (1726).

Tennant, Emma (1937–) English novelist, born London; *Hotel de Dream* (1978), *Alice Fell* (1980).

Thackeray, William Makepeace (1811–63) English novelist, born Calcutta; *Vanity Fair* (1847–8), *Pendennis* (1848–50).

Theroux, Paul (Edward) (1941–) American novelist, short-story writer, born Medford, Massachusetts; *The Mosquito Coast* (1981), *Doctor Slaughter* (1984), *My Secret History* (1989).

Thiong'o, Ngugi Wa (1938–) Kenyan novelist, born Limura; *The River Between* (1963), *A Grain of Wheat* (1967).

Tolkein, J(ohn) R(onald) R(euel) (1892–1973) English novelist, born Bloemfontein, South Africa; *The Hobbit* (1937), *The Lord of the Rings* (1954–5).

Tolstoy, Count Leo Nikolayevich (1828–1910) Russian novelist, born Yasnaya Polyana, Central Russia; *War and Peace* (1863–9), *Anna Karenina* (1873–7), *Resurrection* (1899).

Tranter, Nigel Godwin (1909–) Scottish novelist, born Glasgow; *The Steps to the Empty Throne* (1969), *The Path of the Hero King* (1970), *The Price of the King's Peace* (1971).

Trollope, Anthony (1815–82) English novelist, born London; *Barchester Towers* (1857), *Can You Forgive Her?* (1864), *The Way We Live Now* (1875).

Turgenev, Ivan Sergeevich (1818–83) Russian novelist, born province of Orel; *Sportsman's Sketches* (1952), *Fathers and Children* (1862).

Twain, Mark (pseudonym of **Samuel Langhorne Clemens**) (1835–1910) American novelist, born Florida, Missouri; *The Celebrated Jumping Frog of Calaveras County* (1865), *The Adventures of Tom Sawyer* (1876), *The Prince and the Pauper* (1882), *The Adventures of Huckleberry Finn* (1884), *A Connecticut Yankee in King Arthur's Court* (1889).

Updike, John (Hoyer) (1932–) American novelist, short-story writer, born Shillington, Pennsylvania; *Rabbit, Run* (1960), *Pigeon Feathers and other stories* (1962).

Van der Post, Sir Laurence (Jan) (1906–) South African novelist, playwright, born

WRITERS (cont.)

Philippolis; *Flamingo Feather* (1955), *Journey into Russia* (1964), *A Far-Off Place* (1974).

Vargas, Llosa Mario (1936–) Peruvian novelist; *The Time of the Hero* (1963), *Aunt Julia and the Scriptwriter* (1977), *The War at the End of the World* (1982), *The Green House* (1986).

Verne, Jules (1828–1905) French novelist, born Nantes; *Voyage to the Centre of the Earth* (1864), *Twenty Thousand Leagues under the Sea* (1870).

Vidal, Gore (Eugene Luther Vidal, Jr) (1925–) American novelist, short-story writer, playwright, born West Point, New York; *The Season of Comfort* (1949), *Myra Breckenridge* (1968), *Kalki* (1978).

Voltaire, François-Marie Arouet de (1694–1778) French novelist, poet, born Paris; *Zadig* (1747), *Candide* (1759).

Vonnegut, Kurt (1922–) American novelist, short-story writer, born Indianapolis, Indiana; *Cat's Cradle* (1963), *Slaughterhouse-Five* (1969).

Walker, Alice (1944–) American novelist, short-story writer, born Eatonville, Georgia; *The Third Life of Grange Copeland* (1970), *In Love and Trouble* (1973), *The Color Purple* (1983).

Warren, Robert Penn (1905–89) American novelist, poet, born Guthrie, Kentucky; *Night Rider* (1939), *All the King's Men* (1943).

Waugh, Evelyn (Arthur St John) (1903–66) English novelist, born Hampstead; *Decline and Fall* (1928), *A Handful of Dust* (1934), *Brideshead Revisited* (1945).

Weldon, Fay (1933–) English novelist, born Alvechurch, Worcestershire; *Down Among the Women* (1971), *Female Friends* (1975), *Life and Loves of a She-Devil* (1983).

Wells, H(erbert) G(eorge) (1866–1946) English novelist, born Bromley, Kent; *The Time Machine* (1895), *The War of the Worlds* (1898), *The History of Mr Polly* (1910).

Welty, Eudora (1909–) American novelist, short-story writer, born Jackson, Mississippi; *The Golden Apples* (1949), *The Optimist's Daughter* (1972).

West, Dame Rebecca (adopted name of **Cecily Isabel Fairfield**) (1892–1983) Irish novelist, born County Kerry, Ireland; *The Harsh Voice* (1935), *The Mountain Overflows* (1957).

Wharton, Edith (Newbold) (1862–1937) American novelist, short-story writer, born New York; *The House of Mirth* (1905), *Ethan Frome* (1911), *The Age of Innocence* (1920).

White, Antonia (pseudonym of **Eirene Adeline Botting**) (1899–1980) English novelist, born London; *Frost in May* (1983), *Beyond the Glass* (1954).

White, Patrick Victor Martindale (1912–) Australian novelist, playwright, short-story writer, born London; *Voss* (1957), *The Vivisector* (1970), *A Fringe of Leaves* (1976); Nobel Prize for Literature 1973.

White, T(erence) H(anbury) (1906–64) English novelist, poet, born Bombay; *Darkness at Pemberley* (1932), *The Once and Future King* (1958).

Wilde, Oscar (1854–1900) Irish novelist, short-story writer, playwright, poet, born Dublin; *The Happy Prince and Other Tales* (1888), *The Picture of Dorian Gray* (1890), *The Importance of Being Earnest* (play) (1895).

Wilder, Thornton Niven (1897–1976) American novelist, playwright, born Madison, Wisconsin; *The Bridge of San Luis Rey* (1927) *The Woman of Andros* (1930), *Heaven's My Destination* (1935).

Wilding, Michael (1942–) Australian novelist, short-story writer, born Worcester, England; *Living Together* (1974), *The West Midland Underground* (1975), *Pacific Highway* (1982).

Wodehouse, Sir P(elham) G(renville) (1881–1975) English novelist, short-story writer, born Guildford; *The Inimitable Jeeves* (1923), *Carry on, Jeeves* (1925).

Wolfe, Gene (1931–) American novelist, short-story writer; *The Shadow of the Torturer* (1980), *The Citadel of the Autarch* (1980).

Wolfe, Thomas Clayton (1900–38) American novelist, born Asheville, North Carolina; *Look Homeward, Angel* (1929), *Of Time and the River* (1935), *From Death to Morning* (1935).

Wolfe, Tom (Thomas Kennerley) (1931–) American novelist, born Richmond, Virginia; *The Electric Kool-Aid Acid Test* (1968), *The Right Stuff, The Bonfire of the Vanities* (1988).

Wright, Richard Nathaniel (1908–60) American novelist, short-story writer, born Mississippi; *Native Son* (1940), *Eight Men* (1961).

Yourcenar, Marguerite (pseudonym of **Marguerite de Crayencour**) (1903–87) French novelist, poet, born Brussels; *Memoirs of Hadrian* (1941).

Zamyatin, Evgeny Ivanovich (1884–1937) Russian novelist, short-story writer, born Lebedyan; *We* (1921), *The Dragon: Fifteen Stories* (1966).

Zola, Émile (1840–1902) French novelist, born Paris; *Thérèse Raquin* (1867), *Les Rougon-Macquart* (1871–93).

LITERARY PRIZES

Booker Prize (UK)
1970 Bernice Rubens *The Elected Member*
1971 V S Naipaul *In a Free State*
1972 John Berger *G*
1973 J G Farrell *The Siege of Krishnapur*
1974 Nadine Gordiner *The Conservationist*;
Stanley Middleton *Holiday*
1975 Ruth Prawer Jhabvala *Heat and Dust*
1976 David Storey *Saville*
1977 Paul Scott *Staying On*
1978 Iris Murdoch *The Sea, The Sea*
1979 Penelope Fitzgerald *Offshore*
1980 William Golding *Rites of Passage*
1981 Salman Rushdie *Midnight's Children*
1982 Thomas Keneally *Schindler's Ark*
1983 J M Coetzee *Life and Times of Michael K*
1984 Anita Brookner *Hotel du Lac*
1985 Keri Hulme *The Bone People*
1986 Kingsley Amis *The Old Devils*
1987 Penelope Lively *Moon Tiger*
1988 Peter Carey *Oscar and Lucinda*
1989 Kazuo Ishiguro *The Remains of the Day*
1990 A S Byatt *Possession*

Prix Goncourt (France)
1970 Michel Tournier *Le Roi des aulnes*
1971 Jacques Laurent *Les Bêtises*
1972 Jean Carrière *L'Epervier de Maheux*
1973 Jacques Chessex *L'Ogre*
1974 Pascal Lainé *La Dentellière*
1975 Emile Ajar *La Vie devant soi*
1976 Patrick Grainville *Les Flamboyants*
1977 Didier Decoin *John I'Enfer*
1978 Patrick Modiano *Rue des boutiques
obscures*
1979 Antonine Maillet *Pelagie-la-Charrette*

1980 Yves Navarre *Le Jardin d'acclimation*
1981 Lucien Bodard *Anne Marie*
1982 Dominique Fernandez *Dans la Main de
l'ange*
1983 Frederick Tristan *Les Égares*
1984 Marguerite Duras *L'Amant*
1985 Yann Queffelec *Les Noces barbares*
1986 Michel Host *Valet de Nuit*
1987 Tahar ben Jalloun *La Nuit sacrée*
1988 Erik Orsenna *L'Exposition coloniale*
1989 Jean Vautrin *Un Grand Pas Vers le Bon
Dieu*
1990 Jean Rouaud *Les Champs d'Honneur*

Pulitzer Prize in Letters (USA)
1970 Jean Stafford *Collected Stories*
1972 Wallace Stegner *Angle of Repose*
1973 Eudora Welty *The Optimist's Daughter*
1975 Michael Shaara *The Killer Angels*
1976 Saul Bellow *Humboldt's Gift*
1978 James Alan McPherson *Elbow Room*
1979 John Cheever *The Stories of John Cheever*
1980 Norman Mailer *The Executioner's Song*
1981 John Kennedy Toole *A Confederacy of
Dunces*
1982 John Updike *Rabbit is Rich*
1983 Alice Walker *The Color Purple*
1984 William Kennedy *Ironweed*
1985 Alison Lurie *Foreign Affairs*
1986 Larry McMurtry *Lonesome Dove*
1987 Peter Taylor *A Summons to Memphis*
1988 Toni Morrison *Beloved*
1989 Anne Tyler *Breathing Lessons*
1990 Oscar Hijuelos *The Mambo Kings Play
Songs of Love*

POETS LAUREATE

1617 Ben Jonson*	1718 Laurence Eusden	1843 William Wordsworth
1638 Sir William Davenant*	1730 Colley Cibber	1850 Alfred, Lord Tennyson
1668 John Dryden	1757 William Whitehead	1896 Alfred Austin
1689 Thomas Shadwell	1785 Thomas Warton	1913 Robert Bridges
1692 Nahum Tate	1790 Henry Pye	1930 John Masefield
1715 Nicholas Rowe	1813 Robert Southey	1968 Cecil Day Lewis
		1972 Sir John Betjeman
*The post was not officially established until 1668.		1984 Ted Hughes

NOBEL PRIZES 1970–90

Year	Peace	Literature	Economic Science	Chemistry	Physics	Physiology/Medicine	Year
1970	Norman E Borlaug	Alexandr Solzhenitsyn	Paul A Samuelson	Luis Federico Leloir	Louis Eugène Néel Hannes Olof Alvén	Julius Axelrod Bernard Katz Ulf von Euler	1970
1971	Willy Brandt	Pablo Neruda	Simon Kuznets	Gerhard Herzberg	Dennis Gabor	Earl W Sutherland	1971
1972	*none*	Heinrich Böll	John R Hicks Kenneth J Arrow	Stanford Moore William H Stein Christian B Anfinsen	John Bardeen Leon N Cooper John R Schrieffer	Gerald M Edelman Rodney R Porter	1972
1973	Henry A Kissinger Le Duc Tho (*declined*)	Patrick White	Wassily Leontief	Ernst Otto Fischer Geoffrey Wilkinson	Leo Esaki Ivar Giaever Brian D Josephson	Konrad Lorenz Nikolaas Tinbergen Karl von Frisch	1973
1974	Sean MacBride Sato Eisaku	Eyvind Johnson Harry Martinson	Gunnar Myrdal Friedrich A von Hayek	Paul J Flory	Martin Ryle Antony Hewish	Albert Claude George Emil Palade Christian de Duve	1974
1975	Andrei D Sakharov	Eugenio Montale	Leonid V Kantorovich Tjalling C Koopmans	John W Cornforth Vladimir Prelog	Aage N Bohr Ben R Mottelson L James Rainwater	David Baltimore Renato Dulbecco Howard M Temin	1975
1976	Mairead Corrigan Betty Williams	Saul Bellow	Milton Friedman	William N Lipscomb	Burton Richter Samuel Chao Chung Ting	Baruch S Blumberg Daniel C Gajdusek	1976
1977	Amnesty International	Vicente Aleixandre	James E Meade Bertil Ohlin	Ilya Prigogine	Philip W Anderson Nevill F Mott John H van Vleck	Rosalyn S Yalow Roger C L Guillemin Andrew V Schally	1977
1978	Menachem Begin Anwar al-Sadat	Isaac B Singer	Herbert A Simon	Peter Mitchell	Pjotr L Kapitza Arno A Penzias Robert W Wilson	Werner Arber Daniel Nathans Hamilton O Smith	1978
1979	Mother Teresa	Odysseus Elytis	Arthur Lewis Theodore W Schultz	Herbert C Brown George Wittig	Steven Weinberg Sheldon L Glashow Abdus Salam	Allan M Cormack Godfrey N Hounsfield	1979
1980	Adolfo Pérez Esquivel	Czeslaw Milosz	Lawrence R Klein	Paul Berg Walter Gilbert Frederick Sanger	James W Cronin Val L Fitch	Baruj Benacerraf George D Snell Jean Dausset	1980

Year	Peace	Literature	Economics	Chemistry	Physics	Medicine
1981	Office of the UN High Commissioner for Refugees	Elias Canetti	James Tobin	Kenichi Fukui Roald Hoffman	Nicolaas Bloembergen Arthur L Schawlow Kai M Siegbahn	Roger W Sperry David H Hubel Torsten N Wiesel
1982	Alfonso Garcia Robles Alva Myrdal	Gabriel García Márquez	George J Stigler	Aaron Klug	Kenneth G Wilson	Sune K Bergström Bengt I Samuelsson John R Vane
1983	Lech Walesa	William Golding	Gerard Debreu	Henry Taube	Subrahmanyan Chandrasekhar William A Fowler	Barbara McClintock
1984	Desmond Tutu	Jaroslav Seifert	Richard Stone	Robert B Merrifield	Carlo Rubbia Simon van der Meer	Niels K Jerne Georges J F Köhler César Milstein
1985	International Physicians for the Prevention of Nuclear War	Claude Simon	Franco Modigliani	Herbert Hauptman Jerome Karle	Klaus von Klitzing	Joseph L Goldstein Michael S Brown
1986	Elie Wiesel	Wole Soyinka	James M Buchanan	Dudley R Herschbach Yuan Tseh Lee John C Polanyi	Gerd Binnig Heinrich Rohrer Ernst Ruska	Stanley Cohen Rita Levi-Montalcini
1987	Oscar Arias Sánchez	Joseph Brodsky	Robert M Solow	Charles Pedersen Donald Cram Jean-Marie Lehn	George Bednorz Alex Müller	Susumu Tonegawa
1988	UN Peacekeeping Forces	Naguib Mahfouz	Maurice Allais	Johann Deisenhofer Robert Huber Hartmut Michel	Leon Lederman Melvin Schwartz Jack Steinberger	James Black Gertrude Elion George Hitchings
1989	Tenzin Ciyatso (Dalai Lama)	Camilo José Cela	Trygve Haavelmo	Sydney Altman Thomas Cech	Hans Dehmelt Wolfgang Paul Norman Ramsay	J Michael Bishop Harold E Varmus
1990	Mikhail Gorbachev	Octavio Paz	Harry M Markovitz Merton Miller William Sharpe	Elias James Corey	Jerome Friedman Henry Kendall Richard Taylor	Joseph E Murray E Donnall Thomas

POETS

Selected volumes of poetry are listed

Abse, Dannie (Daniel) (1923–) Welsh, born Cardiff; *After Every Green Thing* (1948), *Tenants of the House* (1957).

Adcock, (Kareen) Fleur (1934–) New Zealander, born Papakura; *The Eye of the Hurricane* (1964), *The Incident Book* (1986).

Aiken, Conrad (Potter) (1889–1973) American, born Georgia; *Earth Triumphant (1914), Preludes for Memnon* (1931).

Akhamatova, Anna (pseudonym of **Anna Andreevna Gorenko**) (1889–1966) Russian, born Odessa; *Evening* (1912), *Poem without a Hero* (1940–62), *Requiem* (1963).

Angelou, Maya (pseudonym of **Marguerite Annie Johnson**) (1928–) American, born St Louis, Missouri; *And Still I Rise* (1978), *I Shall Not Be Moved* (1990).

Apollinaire, Guillame (1880–1918) French, born Rome; *Alcools* (1913), *Calligrammes* (1918).

Aristo, Ludovico (1474–1535) Italian, born Reggio; *Furioso* (1532).

Auden, W(ystan) H(ugh) (1907–73) British, naturalized American citizen, born York; *Another Time* (1940), *The Sea and the Mirror* (1944), *The Age of Anxiety* (1947).

Baudelaire, Charles (Pierre) (1821–67) French, born Paris; *Les Fleurs du mal* (1857).

Beer, Patricia (1924–) English, born Exmouth, Devon; *The Loss of the Magyar (1959), The Lie of the Land* (1983).

Belloc, (Joseph) Hillaire (Pierre) (1870–1953) British, born St Cloud, France; *Cautionary Tales* (1907), *Sonnets and Verse* (1923).

Berryman, John (1914–72) American, born McAlester, Oklahoma; *Homage to Mistress Bradsheet* (1966), *Dream Songs* (1969).

Betjeman, John (1906–84) English, born Highgate; *Mount Zion* (1931), *New Bats in Old Belfries* (1945), *A Nip in the Air* (1972).

Bishop, Elizabeth (1911–79) American, born Worcester, Massachusetts; *North and South* (1946), *Geography III* (1978).

Blake, William (1757–1827) English, born London; *The Marriage of Heaven and Hell* (1793), *The Vision of the Daughter of Albion* (1793), *Songs of Innocence and Experience* (1794), *Vala*, or *The Four Zoas* (1800), *Milton* (1810).

Blunden, Edmund (Charles) (1896–1974) English, born Yalding, Kent; *The Waggoner and Other Poems* (1920), *Undertones of War* (1928).

Brooke, Rupert (Chawner) (1887–1915) English, born Rugby; *Poems* (1911), *1914 and Other Poems* (1915), *New Numbers* (1915).

Brooks, Gwendolyn (1917–) American, born Topeka, Kansas; *A Street in Bronzeville* (1945), *Annie Allen* (1949), *In The Mecca* (1968).

Browning, Elizabeth Barrett (1806–61) English, born Coxhoe Hall, near Durham; *Sonnets from the Portuguese* (1850), *Aurora Leigh* (1855).

Browning, Robert (1812–89) English, born Camberwell; *Bells and Pomegranates, Dramatic Lyrics, Men and Women* (1855), *The Ring and the Book* (1868–9).

Burns, Robert (1759–96) Scottish, born Alloway, Ayr; *Poems Chiefly in the Scottish Dialect* (1786), *Tam O'Shanter* (1790).

Byron, George Gordon (1788–1824) English, born London; *Hours of Idleness* (1807), *Childe Harolde* (1817), *Don Juan* (1819–24).

Catallus, Gaius Valerius (c.84–c.54 BC) Roman, born Verona; lyric poet, over one hundred poems survive.

Causley, Charles (1917–) English, born Lanceston, Cornwall; *Union St* (1957), *Johnny Alleluia* (1961), *Underneath the Water* (1968).

Chaucer, Geoffrey (c.1343–1400) English, born London; *Book of the Duchess* (1370), *Troilus and Cressida* (c.1385), *The Canterbury Tales* (1387–1400).

Clampitt, Amy (1920–) American, born Iowa; *The Kingfisher* (1983), *Archaic Figure* (1987).

Clare, John (1793–1864) English, born Helpstone, Northamptonshire.

Coleridge, Samuel Taylor (1722–1834) English, born Otterly St Mary, Devonshire; *Poems on Various Subjects* (1796), *'Kubla Khan'* (1797), *'The Rime of the Ancient Mariner'* (1798), *Christabel and Other Poems* (1816), *Sybylline Leaves* (1817).

Cowper, William (1731–1800) English, born Great Berkhampstead, Hertfordshire; *The Task* (1785).

Crabbe, George (1754–1823) English, born Aldeburgh, Suffolk; *The Village* (1783).

cummings, e(dward) e(stlin) (1894–1962) American, born Cambridge, Massachusetts; *Tulips and Chimneys* (1923), *XLI Poems* (1925), *is 5* (1926).

POETS (cont.)

Dante, Alighieri (1265–1321) Italian, born Florence; *Vita nuova* (1294), *Divine Comedy* (1321).

Day Lewis, Cecil (1904–72) Irish, born Ballintogher, Sligo; *Overtures to Death* (1938), *The Aeneid of Virgil* (1952).

de la Mare, Walter (1873–1956) English, born Charleston, Kent; *The Listeners* (1912), *The Burning Glass and Other Poems* (1945).

Dickinson, Emily (Elizabeth) (1830–86) American, born Amherst, Massachusetts; only 7 poems published in her lifetime; posthumous publications, eg *Poems* (1890).

Donne, John (?1572–1631) English, born London; *Satires & Elegies* (1590s), *Holy Sonnets* (1610–11), *Songs and Sonnets* (most verse published posthumously).

Doolittle, Hilda (known as **H D**) (1886–1961) American, born Bethlehem, Pennsylvania; *Sea Garden* (1916), *The Walls Do Not Fall* (1944), *Helen in Egypt* (1961).

Dryden, John (1631–1700) English, born Aldwinckle All Saints, Northamptonshire; *'Astrea Redux'* (1660), *'Absalom and Achitophel'* (1681), *'MacFlecknoe'* (1684).

Dunbar, William (c.1460–c.1520) Scottish, birthplace probably E Lothian; *'The Thrissill and the Rois'* (1503), *'Lament for the Makaris'* (c.1507)

Dunn, Douglas (Eaglesham) (1942–) Scottish, born Inchinnann; *Elegies* (1985), *Love or Nothing* (1974).

Dutton, Geoffrey (Piers Henry) (1922–) Australian, born Anlaby; *Antipedes in Shoes* (1955), *Poems Soft and Loud* (1968).

Eliot, T(homas), S(tearns) (1888–1965) American (British citizen 1927), born St Louis, Missouri; *Prufrock and Other Observations* (1917), *The Waste Land* (1922), *Ash Wednesday* (1930), *Four Quartets* (1944).

Éluard, Paul (pseudonym of **Eugène Grindal**) (1895–1952) French, born Saint-Denis; *La Vie immédiate* (1934), *Poésie et vérité* (1942).

Emerson, Ralph Waldo (1803–84) American, born Boston; poems published posthumously in *Complete Works* (1903–4).

Empson, Sir William (1906–84) English, born Yokefleet, E Yorkshire; *Poems* (1935), *The Gathering Storm* (1940).

Fitzgerald, Edward (1809–83) English, born near Woodbridge, Suffolk; translater of *The Rubaiyat of Omar Khayyam* (1859).

Fitzgerald, Robert (David) (1902–) Australian, born Hunters Hill, New South Wales; *To Meet the Sun* (1929), *The Wind at Your Door* (1959), *Product* (1974).

Frost, Robert (Lee) (1874–1963) American, born San Francisco; *North of Boston* (1914), *Mountain Interval* (1916), *New Hampshire* (1923), *In the Clearing* (1962).

Ginsberg, Allen (1926–) American, born Newark, New Jersey; *Howl and Other Poems* (1956), *Empty Mirror* (1961), *The Fall of America* (1973).

Graves, Robert (van Ranke) (1895–1985) English, born London; *Fairies and Fusiliers* (1917).

Gunn, Thom(son William) (1929–) English, born Gravesend, Kent; *The Sense of Movement* (1957), *Touch* (1967), *Jack Straw's Castle* (1976).

Heaney, Seamus (Justin) (1939–) Irish, born Castledawson, County Derry; *Death of a Naturalist* (1966), *Door into the Dark* (1969), *Field Work* (1979).

Henri, Adrian (Maurice) (1932–) English, born Birkenhead; *Tonight at Noon* (1968), *City* (1969), *From the Loveless Motel* (1980).

Henryson, Robert (c.1430–1506) Scottish, birthplace unknown; *Testament of Cresseid, Morall Fabels of Esope the Phrygian.*

Herbert, George (1593–1633) English, born Montgomery, *The Temple* (1633).

Herrick, Robert (1591–1674) English, born London; *Hesperides* (1648).

Hill, Geoffrey (1932–) English, born Bromsgrove, Worcestershire; *King Log* (1968), *Mercian Hymns* (1971).

Hodgson, Ralph (Edwin) (1871–1962) English, born Yorkshire; *Poems* (1917), *The Skylark and Other Poems* (1958).

Homer (10th–8th-c BC) Greek, birthplace and existence disputed; he is credited with the writing or writing down of *The Iliad* and *The Odyssey.*

Hopkins, Gerard Manley (1844–89) English, born Stratford, London; *'The Wreck of the Deutschland'* (1876), posthumously published *Poems* (1918).

Horace, Quintus Horatius Flaccus (65–8 BC) Roman, born Venusia, Apulia; *Epodes* (30 BC), *Odes* (23–13 BC).

Housman, A(lfred) E(dward) (1859–1936) English, born Flockbury, Worcestershire; *A Shropshire Lad* (1896), *Last Poems* (1922).

POETS (cont.)

Hughes, Ted (1930–) English, born Mytholm-royd, Yorkshire; *The Hawk in the Rain* (1957), *Lupereal* (1960), *Wodwo* (1967), *Crow* (1970), *Care Birds* (1975), *Season Songs* (1976), *Gaudete* (1977), *Moortown* (1979).

Jennings, Elizabeth (Joan) (1926–) English, born Boston, Lincolnshire; *Poems* (1953), *The Animals' Arrival* (1969), *The Mind Has Mountains* (1966).

Johnson, Samuel (1709–84) English, born Lichfield, Staffordshire; *The Vanity of Human Wishes* (1749).

Kavanagh, Patrick (1905–67) Irish, born Inniskeen; *Ploughman and Other Poems* (1936), *The Great Hunger* (1942).

Keats, John (1795–1821) English, born London; *Endymion* (1818), *Lamia and Other Poems* (1820).

Keyes, Sidney (Arthur Kilworth) (1922–43) English, born Dartford, Kent; *The Iron Laurel* (1942), *The Cruel Solstice* (1943).

La Fontaine, Jean de (1621–95) French, born Château-Thierry, Champagne; *Contes et nouvelles en vers* (1665), *Fables choisies mises en vers* (1668).

Langland, William (c.1332–c.1400) English, birthplace uncertain, possibly Ledbury, Herefordshire; *Piers Plowman* (1362–99).

Larkin, Philip (Arthur) (1922–85) English, born Coventry; *The North Ship* (1945), *The Whitsun Weddings* (1964), *High Windows* (1974).

Longfellow, Henry (Wadsworth) (1807–82) American, born Portland, Maine; *Voices of the Night* (1839), *Ballads and Other Poems* (1842), *Hiawatha* (1855), *'Divina Comedia'* (1872).

Lowell, Amy (Laurence) (1874–1925) American, born Brookline, Massachusetts; *A Dome of Many-Colored Glass* (1912), *Legends* (1921).

Lowell, Robert (Traill Spence, Jr) (1917–77) American, born Boston, Massachusetts; *Lord Weary's Castle* (1946), *Life Studies* (1959), *Prometheus Bound* (1967).

Macauley, Thomas (Babington) (1800–59) English, born Rothey Temple, Leicestershire; *The Lays of Ancient Rome* (1842).

MacCaig, Norman (Alexander) (1910–) Scottish, born Edinburgh; *Far Cry* (1943), *Riding Lights* (1955), *A Round of Applause* (1962), *A Man in My Position* (1969), *Voice-Over* (1988).

MacDiarmid, Hugh (pseudonym of **Christopher Murray Grieve**) (1892–1978) Scottish, born Langholm, Dumfriesshire; *A Drunk Man Looks at the Thistle* (1926).

McGough, Roger (1937–) English, educated Liverpool; *Waving at Trains* (1982), *The Mersey Sound: Penguin Modern Poets 10* (with Adrian Henri and Brian Patten) (1967), *An Imaginary Menagerie* (1988).

MacLean, Sorley (originally **Somhairle Macgill-Eain**) (1911–) Scottish, born Isle of Raasay; *Reothairt is Contraigh* (Spring Tide and Neap Tide) (1977).

MacNeice, (Frederick) Louis (1907–63) Irish, born Belfast; *Blind Fireworks*(1929), *Solstices* (1961).

Mallarmé, Stéphane (1842–98) French, born Paris; *L'Après-midi d'un faune* (1876), *Poésies* (1899).

Marvell, Andrew (1621–78) English, born Winestead, near Hull; *Miscellaneous Poems by Andrew Marvell, Esq.* (1681).

Masefield, John (Edward) (1878–1967) English, born Ledbury, Herefordshire; *Salt-Water Ballads* (1902).

Millay, Edna St Vincent (1892–1950) American, born Rockland, Maine; *A Few Figs from Thistles* (1920), *The Ballad of Harp-Weaver* (1922).

Milton, John (1608–74) English, born London; *Lycidas* (1637), *Paradise Lost* (1667, 74), *Samson Agonistes* (1667).

Moore, Marianne (Craig) (1887–1972) American, born Kirkwood, Missouri; *The Pangolin and Other Verse* (1936).

Muir, Edwin (1887–1959) Scottish, born Deerness, Orkney; *First Poems* (1925), *Chorus of the Newly Dead* (1926), *Variations on a Time Theme* (1934), *The Labyrinth* (1949), *New Poems* (1949–51).

Nash, (Frederick) Ogden (1902–71) American, born New York; *Free Wheeling* (1931).

O'Hara, Frank (Francis Russell) (1926–66) American, born Baltimore, Maryland; *A City Winter and Other Poems* (1952), *Lunch Poems* (1964).

Ovid (Publius Ovidius Naso) (43 BC – c.17 AD) Roman, born Sulmo; *Amores* (c.16 BC), *Metamorphoses, Ars Amatoria*.

Owen, Wilfred (Edward Salter) (1893–1918) English, born Oswestry, Shropshire; most poems

POETS (cont.)

published posthumously, 1920 by Siegfried Sassoon.

Paz, Octavio (1914–) Mexican, born Mexico City; *Liberty on Parole, Salamander, Collected Poems* (1988).

Petrarch, (Francesco Petrarca) (1304–74) Italian, born Arezzo; *Canzoniere.*

Plath, Sylvia (1932–63) American, born Boston, Massachusetts; *The Colossus and Other Poems* (1960), *Ariel* (1965), *Crossing the Water* (1971), *Winter Trees* (1972).

Porter, Peter (Neville Frederick) (1929–) Australian, born Brisbane; *Poems, Ancient and Modern* (1964), *English Subtitles* (1981).

Pound, Ezra (Weston Loomir) (1885–1972) American, born Haile, Idaho; *The Cantos* (1917, 48, 59).

Pushkin, Alexandr (Sergeevich) (1799–1837) Russian, born Moscow; *Eugene Onegin* (1828), *Ruslam and Lyudmilla* (1820).

Raine, Kathleen (Jessie) (1908–) English, born London; *Stone and Flower* (1943).

Rich, Adrienne (Cecile) (1929–) American, born Baltimore, Maryland; *The Diamond Cutters and Other Poems* (1955), *Snapshots of a Daughter-in-Law* (1963).

Riding, Laura (originally **Laura Reichenthal**) (1901–91) American, born New York; *The Close Chaplet* (1926).

Rilke, Rainer Maria (1875–1926) Austrian, born Prague; *Die Sonnettean Orpheus* (1923).

Rimbaud, (Jean Nicholas) Arthur (1854–91) French, born Charleville, Ardennes; *Les Illuminations* (1886).

Rochester, John Wilmot, Earl of (1647–80) English, born Ditchley, Oxfordshire; *A Satyre against Mankind* (1675).

Roethke, Theodore Huebner (1908–63) American, born Saginaw, Michigan; *Open House* (1941), *The Lost Son and Other Poems* (1948).

Rosenberg, Isaac (1890–1918) English, born Bristol; *Night and Day* (1912), *Youth* (1915), *Poems* (1922).

Saint-Jean Perse (pseudonym of **Marie René Auguste Alexis Saint-Léger Léger**) (1887–1975) French, born St Léger des Feuilles; *Anabase* (1924), *Exil* (1942), *Chroniques* (1960); Nobel Prize for Literature 1960.

Sassoon, Siegfried (Lorraine) (1886–1967) English, born Kent; *Counter-Attack and Other Poems* (1917), *The Road to Ruin* (1933).

Schwarz, Delmore (1913–66) American, born New York; *In Dreams Begin Responsibilities* (1938), *Vaudeville for a Princess and Other Poems* (1950).

Shelley, Percy Bysshe (1792–1822) English, born Field Place, Horesham, Sussex; *'Love's Philosophy'*, *'Alastor'* (1816), *'The Revolt of Islam'* (1818), *'Julian and Maddalo'* (1818), *'The Triumph of Life'* (1822).

Sidney, Sir Philip (1554–86) English, born Penshurst, Kent; *Arcadia* (1580), *Astrophel and Stella* (1591).

Sitwell, Dame Edith (Louisa) (1887–1964) English, born Scarborough; *Facade* (1922), *Colonel Fantock* (1926).

Smart, Christopher (1722–71) English, born Shipborne, Kent; *Jubilate Agno* (first published 1939).

Smith, Stevie (pseudonym of **Florence Margaret Smith**) (1902–71) English, born Hull; *Not Waving but Drowning : Poems* (1957).

Spender, Stephen (Harold) (1909–) English, born London; *Poems* (1933).

Spenser, Edmund (1552–99) English, born London; *The Shepheardes Calender* (1579), *The Faerie Queene* (1590, 96).

Stevens, Wallace (1879–1955) American, born Reading, Pennsylvania; *Harmonium* (1923), *Transport to Summer* (1947).

Tennyson, Alfred, Lord (1809–92) English, born Somersby Rectory, Lincolnshire; *Poems* (1832) (eg 'The Lotos-Eaters' and 'The Lady of Shalott'), *The Princess* (1847), *In Memoriam* (1850), *Idylls of the King* (1859), *Maud* (1885).

Thomas, Dylan (Marlais) (1914–53) Welsh, born Swansea; *Twenty-five Poems* (1936), *Deaths and Entrances* (1946), *In Country Sleep and Other Poems* (1952).

Thomas, (Philip) Edward (1878–1917) English, born London; *Six poems* (1916), *Last Poems* (1918).

Thomas, R(onald) S(tuart) (1913–) Welsh, born Cardiff; *The Stones of the Field* (1946), *Song at the Year's Turning* (1955).

Thomson, James (1700–48) Scottish, born Ednam, Roxburghshire; *The Seasons* (1730), *The Castle of Indolence* (1748).

Verlaine, Paul (1844–96) French, born Metz; *Fêtes galantes* (1869), *Sagesse* (1881).

POETS (cont.)

Virgil, Publius Vergilius Maro (70–19 BC) Roman, born near Mantua; *Eclogues* (37 BC), *Georgics* (29 BC), *The Aeneid* (19 BC).

Webb, Francis Charles (1925–73) Australian, born Adelaide; *A Drum for Ben Boyd* (1948), *The Ghost of the Cock* (1964).

Whitman, Walt (1819–92) American, born West Hills, Long Island, New York; *Leaves of Grass* (1855–89).

Wordsworth, William (1770–1850) English, born Cockermouth; *Lyrical Ballads* (with S T Coleridge, 1798), *The Prelude* (1799, 1805, 1850), *The Excursion* (1814).

Wright, Judith (1915–) Australian, born Armidale, New South Wales; *The Moving Image* (1946), *The Two Fires* (1955), *Birds* (1962).

Wyatt, Thomas (1503–42) English, born Allington Castle, Kent; poems first published in *Tottel's Miscellany* (1557).

Yeats, W(illiam) B(utler) (1865–1939) Irish, born Sandymount, County Dublin; *The Wanderings of Oisin and Other Poems* (1889), *The Wind Among the Reeds* (1894), *The Wild Swans at Coole* (1917), *Michael Robartes and the Dancer* (1921), *The Winding Stair and Other Poems* (1933); Nobel Prize for Literature 1923.

PLAYWRIGHTS

Selected plays are listed

Aeschylus (c.525–c.456 BC), Athenian; *The Oresteia trilogy (Agamemnon, Choephoroe, Eumenides)* (458 BC), *Prometheus Bound, Seven Against Thebes.*

Albee, Edward Franklin (1928–) American, born Washington DC; *The American Dream* (1961), *Who's Afraid of Virginia Woolf?* (1962).

Amos, Robert (1920–) Australian, born Austria; *When the Gravediggers Come* (1961).

Anouilh, Jean (1910–87) French, born Bordeaux; *Antigone* (1944), *Médée* (1946), *L'Alouette* (1953), *Beckett; or, the Honour of God* (1960).

Aristophanes (c.448–380 BC), Athenian; *The Acharnians* (425), *The Knights, The Clouds, The Wasps, The Birds* (414), *Lysistrata* (411), *The Frogs* (405).

Ayckbourn, Alan (1939–) English, born London; *Absurd Person Singular* (1973), *Absent Friends* (1975), *Joking Apart* (1979).

Beaumont, Sir Francis (1584–1616) English, born Grace-Dieu, Leicestershire, and **John Fletcher**; *Philaster* (1609), *The Maid's Tragedy* (1610).

Beckett, Samuel (Barclay) (1906–89) Irish, born Foxrock, near Dublin; *Waiting for Godot* (1955), *Endgame* (1958), *Krapp's Last Tape* (1958), *Happy Days* (1961), *Not I* (1973); Nobel Prize for Literature 1969.

Beynon, Richard (1925–) Australian, born Carlton, Melbourne; *The Shifting Heart* (1956), *Time and Mr Strachan* (1958).

Bond, (Thomas) Edward (1934–) English, born North London; *Early Morning* (1969), *Lear* (1971), *Summer* (1982).

Brecht, (Eugen) Berthold (Friedrich) (1898–1956) German, born Augsburg; *Galileo* (1938–9), *Mutter Courage und ihre Kinder* (Mother Courage and her Children) (1941), *Der Gute Mensch von Setzuan* (The Good Woman of Setzuan) (1943), *Der Kaukasische Kreidekreis* (The Caucasian Chalk Circle) (1949).

Brieux, Eugène (1858–1932) French, born Paris; *Les Trois Filles de M Dupont* (1897), *The Red Robe* (1900).

Chapman, George (c.1559–1634) English, born near Hitchin, Hertfordshire; *Bussy D'Ambois* (1607).

Chekhov, Anton Pavlovich (1860–1904) Russian, born Taganrog; *The Seagull* (1895), *Uncle Vanya* (1900), *Three Sisters* (1901), *The Cherry Orchard* (1904).

Congreve, William (1670–1729) English, born Bardsey, near Leeds; *Love for Love* (1695), *The Way of the World* (1700).

Corneille, Pierre (1606–84) French, born Rouen; *Le Cid* (1636), *Horace* (1639), *Polyeucte* (1640).

Coward, Noël (1899–1973) English, born Teddington, Middlesex; *Hay Fever* (1925), *Private Lives* (1933), *Blithe Spirit* (1941).

Dekker, Thomas (c.1570–1632) English, born London; *The Whore of Babylon* (1606).

Dryden, John (1631–1700) English, born

PLAYWRIGHTS (cont.)

Aldwinkle; *The Indian Queen* (1664), *Marriage à la Mode* (1672), *All for Love* (1678), *Amphitryon* (1690).

Eliot, T(homas) S(tearns) (1888–1965) American naturalized British, born St Louis, Missouri; *Murder in the Cathedral* (1935), *The Family Reunion* (1939), *The Cocktail Party* (1950).

Esson, Thomas Louis Buvelot Australian, born Edinburgh; *The Drovers* (1920), *Andeganora* (1937).

Euripides (c.480–406 BC) Athenian; *Medea* (431), *Electra* (413), *The Bacchae* (407).

Fletcher, John (1579–1625) English, born Rye, Sussex; *The Faithful Shepherdess* (1610), *A Wife for a Month* (1624).

Fo, Dario (1926–) Italian, born Lombardy; *Accidental Death of an Anarchist* (1970), *Can't Pay! Won't Pay!* (1978).

Ford, John (1586–c.1640) English, born Devonshire; *'Tis Pity She's a Whore* (1633), *Perkin Warbeck* (1634).

Galsworthy, John (1867–1933) English, born Coombe, Surrey; *Strife* (1909), *Justice* (1910); Nobel Prize for Literature 1932.

Genet, Jean (1910–86) French, born Paris; *The Maids* (1948), *The Balcony* (1956).

Giraudoux, Jean (1882–1944) French, born Bellac; *Judith* (1931), *Ondine* (1939).

Goethe, Johann Wolfgang von (1749–1832) German, born Frankfurt am Main; *Faust* (1808, 1832).

Gogol, Nikolai (Vasilevich) (1809–52) Russian, born Ukraine; *The Inspector General* (1836).

Goldsmith, Oliver (1728–74) Irish, born Pallas, County Longford; *She Stoops to Conquer* (1773).

Gray, Oriel (1921–) Australian, born Sydney; *The Torrents* (1955), *Burst of Summer* (1960).

Greene, Robert (1558–92) English, born Norwich; *Orlando Furioso* (1594), *James the Fourth* (1598).

Hauptmann, Gerhart (1862–1946) German, born Obersalzbrunn, Silesia; *Before Sunrise* (1889), *The Weavers* (1892); Nobel Prize for Literature 1912.

Hayes, Alfred (1911–85) American, born England; *The Girl on the Via Flaminia* (1954).

Hebbel (Christian) Friedrich (1813–63) German, born Wesselburen, Dithmarschen; *Judith* (1841), *Maria Magdalena* (1844).

Hewett, Dorothy (1923–) Australian, born Wickepin, West Australia; *The Chapel Perilous* (1972), *This Old Man Comes Rolling Home* (1976).

Heywood, Thomas (c.1574–1641) English, born Lincolnshire; *A Woman Killed with Kindness* (1603), *The Fair Maid of the West* (1631), *The English Traveller* (1633).

Hibberd, Jack (1940–) Australian, born Warracknabeal, Victoria; *Dimboola* (1969), *White with Wire Wheels* (1970), *A Stretch of the Imagination* (1973).

Howard, Sidney (Coe) (1891–1939) American, born Oakland, California; *They Knew What They Wanted* (1924), *The Silver Cord* (1926).

Ibsen, Henrik (1828–1906) Norwegian, born Skien; *Peer Gynt* (1867), *A Doll's House* (1879), *The Pillars of Society* (1880), *The Wild Duck* (1884), *Hedda Gabler* (1890), *The Master Builder* (1892).

Inge, William (1913–73) American, born Kansas; *Picnic* (1953), *Where's Daddy?* (1966).

Ionesco, Eugène (1912–) French, born Romania; *The Bald Prima Donna* (1948), *The Picture* (1958), *Le Rhinocéros* (1960).

Jonson, Ben(jamin) (c.1572–1637) English, born Westminster; *Every man in his Humour* (1598), *Sejanus* (1603), *Volpone* (1606), *The Alchemist* (1610), *Bartholomew Fair* (1614).

Kaiser, Georg (1878–1945) German, born Magdeburg; *The Burghers of Calais* (1914), *Gas* (1920).

Kyd, Thomas (1558–94) English, born London; *The Spanish Tragedy* (1587).

Lawler, Ray(mond Evenor) (1922–) Australian, born Footscrag; *The Summer of the Seventeenth Doll* (1955), *The Man Who Shot the Albatross* (1970).

Lorca, Federigo Garcia (1899–1936) Spanish, born Fuente Vaqueros; *Blood Wedding* (1933), *The House of Bernard Alba* (1945).

Maeterlink, Maurice (1862–1949) Belgian, born Gand; *La Princesse Maleine* (1889), *Pelleas et Melisande* (1892), *The Blue Bird* (1909).

Mamet, David Alan (1947–) American, born Chicago; *Sexual Perversity in Chicago* (1974), *Duck Variations* (1974), *American Buffalo* (1975), *Edmond* (1982).

PLAYWRIGHTS (cont.)

Marlowe, Christopher (1564–1593) English, born Canterbury; *Tamburlaine the Great* (in two parts, 1587), *Dr Faustus* (1588), *The Jew of Malta* (c.1589), *Edward II* (1592).

Marston, John (1576–1634) English, born Wardington, Oxfordshire; *Antonio's Revenge* (1602), *The Malcontent* (1604).

Miller, Arthur (1915–) American, born New York; *All My Sons* (1947), *Death of a Salesman* (1949), *The Crucible* (1952), *A View from the Bridge* (1955), *The Misfits* (1961), *After the Fall* (1964).

Molière (pseudonym of **Jean-Baptiste Poquelin**) (1622–73) French, born Paris; *Le Bourgeois Gentilhomme* (The Bourgeois Gentleman) (1660), *Tartuffe* (1664), *Le Misanthrope* (The Misanthropist) (1666), *Le Malade Imaginaire* (The Hypocondriac) (1673).

Oakley, Barry (1931–) Australian, born Melbourne; *The Feet of Daniel Mannix* (1975), *Bedfellows* (1975).

O'Casey, Sean (originally **John Casey**) (1880–1964) Irish, born Dublin; *Juno and the Paycock* (1924), *The Plough and the Stars* (1926).

O'Neill, Eugene (1888–1953) American, born New York; *Beyond the Horizon* (1920), *Desire under the Elms* (1924), *Mourning Becomes Electra* (1931), *Long Day's Journey into Night* (1941), *The Iceman Cometh* (1946); Nobel Prize for Literature 1936.

Orton, Joe (1933–67) English, born Leicester; *Entertaining Mr Sloane* (1964), *Loot* (1965), *What the Butler Saw* (1969).

Osborne, John (James) (1929–) Welsh, born Fulham, London; *Look Back in Anger* (1956), *The Entertainer* (1957), *Inadmissible Evidence* (1964).

Otway, Thomas (1652–1685) English, born Milland, Sussex; *Don Carlos* (1676), *The Orphan* (1680), *Venice Preserv'd* (1682).

Patrick, John (1905–) American, born Louisville, Kentucky; *The Teahouse of the August Moon* (1953).

Pinter, Harold (1930–) English, born East London; *The Birthday Party* (1958), *The Caretaker* (1960), *The Homecoming* (1965).

Pirandello, Luigi (1867–1936) Italian, born near Agrigento, Sicily; *Six Characters in Search of an Author* (1921), *Henry IV* (1922); Nobel Prize for Literature 1934.

Plautus, Titus Maccius (c.254–184 BC) Roman; *Menachmi, Miles Gloriosus.*

Porter, Hal (1911–84) Australian, born Melbourne; *The Tower* (1963), *The Professor* (1966), *Eden House* (1969).

Racine, Jean (1639–99) French, born near Soissons; *Andromaque* (1667), *Phèdre* (1677), *Bajazet* (1672), *Esther* (1689).

Romeril, John (1945–) Australian, born Melbourne; *Chicago, Chicago* (1970), *I Don't Know Who to Feel Sorry For* (1973).

Sackville, Thomas (1553–1608) English, born Buckhurst, Sussex; *Gorboduc* (1592).

Sartre, Jean-Paul (1905–80) French, born Paris; *The Flies* (1943), *Huis Clos* (1945), *The Condemned of Altona* (1961).

Schiller, Johann Christoph Friedrich von (1759–1805) German, born Marbach; *The Robbers* (1781), *Wallenstein* (1799), *Maria Stuart* (1800).

Seneca, Lucius Annaeus (c.4 BC–AD 65) Roman, born Corduba; *Hercules, Medea, Thyestes.*

Seymour, Alan (1927–) Australian, born Perth; *The One Day of the Year* (1962), *Swamp Creatures* (1958), *Danny Johnson* (1960).

Shakespeare, William *see* PLAYS OF SHAKESPEARE

Shaffer, Peter (Levin) (1926–) English, born Liverpool; *The Royal Hunt of the Sun* (1964), *Equus* (1973), *Amadeus* (1979).

Shaw, George Bernard (1856–1950) Irish, born Dublin; *Arms and the Man* (1894), *Man and Superman* (1903), *Pygmalion* (1913), *Saint Joan* (1924); Nobel Prize for Literature 1925.

Shepard, Sam (Samuel Shepard Rogers) (1943–) American, born Illinois; *La Turista* (1967), *The Tooth of Crime* (1972), *Buried Child* (1978), *True West* (1979), *Fool for Love* (1983).

Sheridan, Richard Brinsley (1751–1816) Irish, born Dublin; *The Rivals* (1775), *The School for Scandal* (1777), *The Critic* (1779).

Sherwood, Robert (Emmet) (1896–1955) American, born New York; *Idiot's Delight* (1936), *Abe Lincoln in Illinois* (1938), *There Shall Be No Night* (1940).

Sophocles (496–406 BC) Athenian, born Colonus; *Antigone, Oedipus Rex, Oedipus at Colonus.*

Soyinka, Wole (Akinwande Olnwole Soyinka) (1934–) Nigerian, born Abeokata,

PLAYWRIGHTS (cont.)

West Nigeria; *The Swamp Dwellers* (1958), *The Bacchae of Euripides* (1973).

Stoppard, Tom (1937–) English, born Czechoslovakia; *Rosencrantz and Guildenstern are Dead* (1966), *The Real Inspector Hound* (1968), *Travesties* (1974).

Strindberg, (Johan) August (1849–1912) Swedish, born Stockholm; *Miss Julie* (1888), *Master Olof* (1877), *The Dance of Death* (1901).

Synge, (Edmund) J(ohn) M(illington) (1871–1909) Irish, born near Dublin; *The Well of Saints* (1905), *The Playboy of the Western World* (1907).

Webster, John (c.1578–c.1632) English, born London; *The White Devil* (1612), *The Duchess of Malfi* (1614).

Wilde, Oscar (Fingal O'Flahertie Wills) (1854–1906) Irish, born Dublin; *Lady Windermere's Fan* (1892), *The Importance of Being Earnest* (1895), *Salomé* (1896).

Wilder, Thornton (Niven) (1897–1975) American, born Wisconsin; *Our Town* (1938), *The Merchant of Yonkers* (1938), *The Skin of Our Teeth* (1942), *The Matchmaker* (1954, later a musical *Hello, Dolly!*, 1964).

Williams, Tennessee (originally **Thomas Lanier Williams**) (1911–83) American, born Mississippi; *The Glass Menagerie* (1944), *A Streetcar Named Desire* (1947), *Cat on a Hot Tin Roof* (1955), *Sweet Bird of Youth* (1959).

Williamson, David Keith (1942–) Australian, born Melbourne; *The Removalists* (1971), *Don's Party* (1971).

Wycherely, William (1641–1715) English, born Clive, near Shrewsbury; *The Gentleman Dancing–Master* (1672), *The Country Wife* (1675), *The Plain–Dealer* (1676).

PLAYS OF SHAKESPEARE

William Shakespeare (1564-1616), English playwright and poet, born Stratford-upon-Avon.

Title	Date	Category	Title	Date	Category
The Two Gentleman of Verona	1590-1	comedy	Julius Caeser	1599	Roman
Henry VI Part One	1592	history	As You Like It	1599-1000	comedy
Henry VI Part Two	1592	history	Hamlet, Prince of Denmark	1600-1	tragedy
Henry VI Part Three	1592	history			
Titus Adronicus	1592	tragedy	Twelfth Night, or What You Will	1601	comedy
Richard III	1592-3	history			
The Taming of the Shrew	1593	comedy	Troilus and Cressida	1602	tragedy
The Comedy of Errors	1594	comedy	Measure for Measure	1603	dark comedy
Love's Labour's Lost	1594-5	comedy	Othello	1603-4	tragedy
Richard II	1595	history	All's Well That Ends Well	1604-5	dark comedy
Romeo and Juliet	1595	tragedy	Timon of Athens	1605	romantic drama
A Midsummer Night's Dream	1595	comedy			
King John	1596	history	The Tragedy of King Lear	1605-6	tragedy
The Merchant of Venice	1596-7	comedy	Macbeth	1606	tragedy
Henry IV Part One	1596-7	history	Antony and Cleopatra	1606	tragedy
The Merry Wives of Windsor	1597-8	comedy	Pericles	1607	romance
			Coriolanus	1608	Roman
Henry IV Part Two	1597-8	history	The Winter's Tale	1609	romance
Much Ado About Nothing	1598	dark comedy	Cymbeline	1610	comedy
			The Tempest	1611	comedy
Henry V	1598-9	history	Henry VIII	1613	history

FILM AND TV ACTORS

Selected films and television productions are listed.
Original and full names are given in brackets.

Adjani, Isabelle (1955–   ) French born Paris; *The Story of Adele H* (1975), *Nosferatu* (1978), *Possession* (1980), *Quartet* (1981), *One Deadly Summer* (1983), *Subway* (1985), *Ishtar* (1987), *Camille Claudel* (1988).

Agutter, Jenny (1952–   ) British born Taunton; *The Railway Children* (1970), *Walkabout* (1970), *Logan's Run* (1976), *The Eagle has Landed* (1977), *Equus* (1977), *The Man in the Iron Mask* (1977), *An American Werewolf in London* (1981), *Silas Marner* (TV 1985), *Child's Play 2* (1990).

Aimée, Anouk (Françoise Sorya) (1934–   ) French born Paris; *Les Amants de Verone* (1949), *La Dolce Vita* (1960), *Lola* (1961), *Un Homme et un Femme* (1966), *Justine* (1969).

Albert, Eddie (Eddie Albert Heimberger) (1908–   ) American born Rock Island, Illinois; *Brother Rat* (1938), *Four Wives* (1939), *Smash Up* (1947), *Carrie* (1952), *Leave it to Larry* (TV 1952), *Roman Holiday* (1953), *Oklahoma!* (1955), *I'll Cry Tomorrow* (1955), *Attack!* (1956), *The Teahouse of the August Moon* (1956), *The Roots of Heaven* (1958), *Orders to Kill* (1958), *The Miracle of the White Stallions* (1962), *Green Acres* (TV 1965-70), *The Longest Yard* (1974), *Escape to Witch Mountain* (1975), *Switch* (TV 1975-6), *Yes, Giorgio* (1982), *Dreamscape* (1984).

Alda, Alan (1936–   ) American born New York City; *Paper Lion* (1968), *Catch 22* (1970), *M*A*S*H* (TV 1972-83), *California Suite* (1978), *Same Time Next Year* (1978), *The Four Seasons* (1981), *Sweet Liberty* (1986), *A New Life* (1988), *Crimes and Misdemeanors* (1990), *Betsy's Wedding* (1990).

Allen, Woody (Allen Stewart Konigsberg) (1935–   ) American born Brooklyn, New York; *What's New Pussycat* (1965), *Casino Royale* (1967), *Bananas* (1971), *Play it Again Sam* (1972), *Sleeper* (1973), *Annie Hall* (1977), *Manhattan* (1979), *Stardust Memories* (1980), *Hannah and Her Sisters* (1986), *New York Stories* (1989), *Crimes and Misdemeanors* (1990), *Scenes from a Mall* (1991).

Alley, Kirstie (1955–   ) American born Wichita, Kansas; *Star Trek II: The Wrath of Khan* (1982), *Blind Date* (1983), *Champions* (1983), *Runaway* (1984), *North and South* (TV 1986), *Summer School* (1987), *Cheers* (TV 1987–   ), *Shoot to Kill* (1988), *Look Who's Talking* (1989), *Madhouse* (1990), *Loverboy* (1990), *Sibling Rivalry* (1990), *Look Who's Talking Too* (1991).

Allyson, June (Ella Geisman) (1917–   ) American born Westchester, New York; *Two Girls and a Sailor* (1944), *Music for Millions* (1944), *Little Women* (1949), *The Glen Miller Story* (1954), *The Shrike* (1955), *The June Allyson Show* (TV 1959-61).

Ameche, Don (Dominic Felix Amici) (1908–   ) American born Kenosha, Wisconsin; *Ramona* (1936), *In Old Chicago* (1938), *The Three Musketeers* (1939), *Midnight* (1939), *The Story of Alexander Graham Bell* (1939), *Swanee River* (1939), *Four Sons* (1940), *Down Argentine Way* (1940), *That Night in Rio* (1941), *Heaven Can Wait* (1943), *Happy Land* (1943), *Trading Places* (1983), *Cocoon* (1985), *Bigfoot and the Hendersons* (1987), *Coming to America* (1988), *Things Change* (1988), *Cocoon: The Return* (1988).

Anderson, Dame Judith (Frances Margaret Anderson) (1898–   ) Australian born Adelaide, also stage, *Rebecca* (1940), *The Ten Commandments* (1956), *Cat on a Hot Tin Roof* (1958), *A Man Called Horse* (1970), *Star Trek III: The Search for Spock* (1984), *Santa Barbara* (TV 1984–   ).

Andress, Ursula (1936–   ) Swiss born Berne; *Dr No* (1963), *She* (1965), *What's New Pussycat?* (1965), *Casino Royale* (1967), *The Clash of the Titans* (1981).

Andrews, Anthony (1948–   ) British born London; *Danger UXB* (TV 1978), *Brideshead Revisited* (TV 1981), *The Scarlet Pimpernel* (TV 1982), *Under the Volcano* (1984), *The Lighthorsemen* (1987).

Andrews, Julie (Julia Elizabeth Wells) (1935–   ) British born Walton-on-Thames, Surrey; *Mary Poppins* (1964), *The Americanization of Emily* (1964), *The Sound of Music* (1965), *Torn Curtain* (1966), *Thoroughly Modern Millie* (1967), *Star!* (1968), *S.O.B.* (1981), *Victor/Victoria* (1982).

Ann-Margret (Ann-Margret Olsson) (1941–   ) Swedish/American born Valsobyn, Jamtland, Sweden; *State Fair* (1962), *Bye Bye Birdie* (1962), *The Cincinnati Kid* (1965), *Carnal Knowledge* (1971), *52 Pick-Up* (1986), *A New Life* (1988).

FILM AND TV ACTORS (cont.)

Arquette, Rosanna (1959–) American born New York City; *Shirley* (1979 TV), *S.O.B.* (1981), *Johnny Belinda* (TV 1982), *The Executioner's Song* (TV 1982), *Desperately Seeking Susan* (1983), *Silverado* (1985), *After Hours* (1985), *Nobody's Fool* (1985), *Eight Million Ways to Die* (1987), *The Big Blue* (1988), *New York Stories* (1989), *The Black Rainbow* (1990).

Ashcroft, Dame Peggy (1907–) British born Croyden; also stage; *The Thirty-nine Steps* (1935), *Quiet Wedding* (1940), *Edward and Mrs Simpson* (TV 1978), *A Passage to India* (1984), *The Jewel in the Crown* (TV 1984), *Madame Sousatzka* (1988), *She's Been Away* (TV 1990).

Astaire, Fred (Frederick Austerlitz) (1899-1987) American born Omaha, Nebraska; *Flying Down to Rio* (1933), *The Gay Divorcee* (1934), *Top Hat* (1935), *Funny Face* (1957), *It Takes a Thief* (TV 1965-9), *Finian's Rainbow* (1968).

Astor, Mary (Lucille Langhanke) (1906-87) American born Quincy, Illinois; *Beau Brummell* (1924), *Don Juan* (1926), *Dodsworth* (1936), *The Prisoner of Zenda* (1937), *The Great Lie* (1941), *The Maltese Falcon* (1941), *The Palm Beach Story* (1942), *Meet Me in St Louis* (1944), *Act of Violence* (1948), *Little Women* (1949), *Return to Peyton Place* (1961).

Atkinson, Rowan (1955–) British; *The Black Adder* (TV 1984), *Blackadder II* (TV 1985), *Blackadder III* (TV 1986), *Blackadder Goes Forth* (TV 1989), *The Tall Guy* (1989), *The Witches* (1990).

Attenborough, Sir Richard (1923–) British born Cambridge; *In Which We Serve* (1942), *The Man Within* (1942), *Brighton Rock* (1947), *The Guinea Pig* (1949), *The Great Escape* (1963).

Aykroyd, Dan (1952–) Canadian born Ottowa, Ontario; *1949* (1979), *The Blues Brothers* (1980), *Neighbours* (1981), *Twilight Zone* (1983), *Ghostbusters* (1984), *Spies Like Us* (1986), *Dragnet* (1987), *The Couch Trip* (1988), *The Great Outdoors* (1988), *Caddyshack II* (1988), *Ghostbusters II* (1989), *My Stepmother is an Alien* (1989), *Driving Miss Daisy* (1989), *Loose Cannons* (1990).

Bacall, Lauren (Betty Joan Perske) (1924–) American born New York City; *To Have and Have Not* (1944), *The Big Sleep* (1946), *How to Marry a Millionaire* (1953), *The Fan* (1981), *Mr. North* (1988).

Bacon, Kevin (1958–) American born Philadelphia, Pennsylvania; *Animal House* (1978), *Friday the 13th* (1980), *Diner* (1982), *Footloose* (1984), *She's Having a Baby* (1988), *Tremors* (1989), *Flatliners* (1990), *The Big Picture* (1990).

Baker, Joe Don (1936–) American born Groesbeck, Texas; *Cool Hand Luke* (1967), *Mongo's Back in Town* (TV 1971), *Charley Varrick* (1972), *Walking Tall* (1972), *Mitchell* (1974), *The Natural* (1984), *Fletch* (1984), *Getting Even* (1985), *The Living Daylights* (1987).

Baker, Tom (1935–) British; *Nicholas and Alexandra* (1971), *Doctor Who* (TV 1975-81), *The Life and Loves of a She-Devil* (TV 1987), *The Chronicles of Narnia* (TV 1990).

Baldwin, Alec (1958–) American born Massapequa, New York; *Sweet Revenge* (TV 1984), *She's Having a Baby* (1988), *Beetlejuice* (1988), *Working Girl* (1988), *Married to the Mob* (1988), *The Hunt for Red October* (1989), *Miami Blues* (1990), *The Marrying Man* (1990), *Alice* (1991).

Ball, Lucille (1910-1989) American born Celaron, New York; *Top Hat* (1935), *Stage Door* (1937), *The Affairs of Annabel* (1938), *Five Came Back* (1939), *The Big Street* (1942), *Du Barry was a Lady* (1943), *Without Love* (1945), *Ziegfeld Follies* (1946), *Easy to Wed* (1946), *Her Husband's Affairs* (1947), *Fancy Pants* (1950), *I Love Lucy* (TV 1951-5), *The Long Long Trailer* (1954), *The Facts of Life* (1956), *The Lucy Show* (TV 1962-8), *Yours Mine and Ours* (1968), *Here's Lucy* (TV 1968-73), *Life with Lucy* (TV 1976).

Bancroft, Anne (Anna Maria Italiano) (1931–) American born Bronx, New York; *The Miracle Worker* (1962), *The Graduate* (1968), *Silent Movie* (1976), *The Elephant Man* (1980), *84 Charing Cross Road* (1986), *Torch Song Trilogy* (1988), *Bert Rigby, You're a Fool* (1989).

Bankhead, Tallulah (1902-68) American born Huntsville, Texas; *Tarnished Lady* (1931), *A Royal Scandal* (1945).

Bardot, Brigitte (Camille Javal) (1934–) French born Paris; *And God Created Woman* (1956), *En Cas de Malheur* (1958), *Viva Maria!* (1961).

Barkin, Ellen (1959–) American born Bronx, New York; *Diner* (1982), *The Adventures of Buckeroo Banzai* (1984), *The Big Easy* (1986), *Siesta* (1987), *Sea of Love* (1990), *Johnny Handsome* (1990), *Switch* (1991).

FILM AND TV ACTORS (cont.)

Barrymore, Ethel (Edith Blythe) (1879-1959) American born Philadelphia, Pennsylvania; *Rasputin and the Empress* (1932), *None but the Lonely Heart* (1944), *The Farmer's Daughter* (1947), *Young at Heart* (1954).

Barrymore, John (John Blythe) (1882-1942) American born Philadelphia, Pennsylvania; *Dr Jekyll and Mr Hyde* (1920), *Show of Shows* (1929), *Rasputin and the Empress* (1932), *Dinner at 8* (1933), *Midnight* (1939), *The Great Profile* (1940).

Barrymore, Lionel (Lionel Blythe) (1878-1954) American born Philadelphia, Pennsylvania; *Peter Ibbetson* (1917), *The Copperhead* (1918), *The Bells* (1926), *Sadie Thompson* (1928), *A Free Soul* (1931), *The Man I Killed* (1932), *Arsène Lupin* (1932), *Rasputin and the Empress* (1932), *Dinner at 8* (1933), *Grand Hotel* (1932), *David Copperfield* (1934), *Captains Courageous* (1937), *A Family Affair* (1937), *Young Dr Kildare* (1938), *Calling Dr Gillespie* (1942), *On Borrowed Time* (1939), *Three Wise Fools* (1946), *It's a Wonderful Life* (1946), *Duel in the Sun* (1946), *Key Largo* (1948).

Basinger, Kim (1953–   ) American born Athens, Georgia; *From Here to Eternity* (TV 1980), *Hard Country* (1981), *Never Say Never Again* (1983), *The Natural* (1984), *$9\frac{1}{2}$ Weeks* (1985), *No Mercy* (1986), *Blind Date* (1987), *Nadine* (1987), *Batman* (1989), *My Stepmother is an Alien* (1989), *The Marrying Man* (1990).

Bates, Alan (1934–   ) British born Allestree, Derbyshire; *A Kind of Loving* (1962), *Whistle Down the Wind* (1962), *Zorba the Greek* (1965), *Far from the Madding Crowd* (1967), *Women in Love* (1969), *The Rose* (1979), *A Prayer for the Dying* (1987), *We Think the World of You* (1988), *Hamlet* (1990).

Beatty, Ned (1937–   ) American born Louisville, Kentucky; *Deliverance* (1972), *Nashville* (1975), *Network* (1976), *All the Presidents' Men* (1976), *Exorcist II: The Heretic* (1977), *Superman* (1978), *Friendly Fire* (TV 1979), *Incredible Shrinking Woman* (1981), *Superman II* (1981), *The Toy* (1983), *Hopscotch* (1983), *Stoker Ace* (1983), *Restless Natives* (1986), *The Big Easy* (1987), *The Fourth Protocol* (1987), *Switching Channels* (1988), *The Unholy* (1988), *Midnight Crossing* (1988), *After the Rain* (1988), *Purple People Eater* (1988).

Beatty, Warren (Henry Warren Beaty) (1937–   ) American born Richmond, Virginia; *Splendour in the Grass* (1961), *The Roman Spring of Mrs Stone* (1961), *All Fall Down* (1962), *Bonnie and Clyde* (1967), *The Parallax View* (1974), *Shampoo* (1975), *Heaven Can Wait* (1978), *Reds* (1981), *Ishtar* (1987), *Dick Tracy* (1990), *Bugsy* (1991).

Bedelia, Bonnie (1952–   ) American born New York City; *They Shoot Horses Don't They* (1970), *Love and Other Strangers* (1970), *Heart Like a Wheel* (1983), *The Prince of Pennsylvania* (1988), *Die Hard* (1988), *Die Hard II: Die Harder* (1990), *Presumed Innocent* (1990).

Belmondo, Jean-Paul (1933–   ) French born Neuilly-sur-Seine, Paris; *A Bout de Souffle* (1959), *Moderato Cantabile* (1960), *Un Singe en Hiver* (1962), *That Man from Rio* (1964).

Belushi, James (1954–   ) American born Chicago; *Trading Places* (1983), *Salvador* (1986), *About Last Night* (1987), *Red Heat* (1988), *Only the Lonely* (1991), *Curly Sue* (1991).

Belushi, John (1949-82) American born Chicago; *Animal House* (1978), *1941* (1979), *The Blues Brothers* (1981), *Neighbors* (1981).

Bennett, Jill (1931-90) British born Penang, Malaysia; also stage; *Inadmissable Evidence* (1968), *For Your Eyes Only* (1981).

Bergman, Ingrid (1915-82) Swedish born Stockholm; *Intermezzo* (1939), *Dr Jekyll and Mr Hyde* (1941), *Casablanca* (1943), *For Whom the Bell Tolls* (1943), *Gaslight* (1943), *Spellbound* (1945), *Anastasia* (1946), *Notorious* (1946); *Stromboli* (1950), *Indiscreet* (1958), *Cactus Flower* (1969), *Murder on the Orient Express* (1974), *Autumn Sonata* (1978).

Berkoff, Stephen (1937–   ) British born London; *Octopussy* (1983), *Beverly Hills Cop* (1984), *Rambo* (1985), *War and Remembrance* (TV 1989).

Bernhardt, Sarah (1844-1923) (Henriette Rosine Bernhardt) French born Paris; stage, plus a few films; *Queen Elizabeth* (1912).

Bisset, Jacqueline (1944–   ) British born Weybridge, Surrey; *Cul-de-Sac* (1966), *Casino Royale* (1967), *Bullitt* (1968), *The Grasshopper* (1970), *Murder on the Orient Express* (1974), *The Deep* (1977), *Rich and Famous* (1981), *Class* (1983), *Under the Volcano* (1984), *High Season* (1987), *Scenes from the Class Struggle in Beverly Hills* (1989), *Wild Orchid* (1990).

FILM AND TV ACTORS (cont.)

Bloom, Claire (1931–) British born London; *Look Back in Anger* (1959), *The Haunting* (1963), *The Spy who Came in from the Cold* (1966).

Bogarde, Dirk (Derek Niven Van Den Bogaerde) (1921–) Dutch/British born Hampstead; *A Tale of Two Cities* (1958), *Victim* (1961), *The Servant* (1963), *Death in Venice* (1973), *Providence* (1977), *These Foolish Things* (1990).

Bogart, Humphrey (De Forest) (1899-1957) American born New York City; *Broadway's Like That* (1930), *The Petrified Forest* (1936), *High Sierra* (1941), *The Maltese Falcon* (1941), *Casablanca* (1942), *To Have and Have Not* (1944), *The Big Sleep* (1946), *The Treasure of the Sierra Madre* (1947), *The African Queen* (1952), *The Barefoot Contessa* (1954), *The Caine Mutiny* (1954).

Bonham-Carter, Helena (1966–) British born London; *Oxford Blues* (1984), *Lady Jane* (1985), *A Room with a View* (1985), *Hamlet* (1990), *Where Angels Fear to Tread* (1991).

Borgnine, Ernest (Ermes Borgnino) (1918–) American born Hamden, Connecticut; *From Here to Eternity* (1953), *Bad Day at Black Rock* (1954), *Marty* (1955), *The Catered Affair* (1956), *The Best Things in Life Are Free* (1956), *The Vikings* (1958), *Pay or Die* (1960), *McHale's Navy* (TV 1962-5), *The Dirty Dozen* (1967), *Ice Station Zebra* (1968), *The Wild Bunch* (1969), *The Poseidon Adventure* (1972), *Convoy* (1978), *The Black Hole* (1979), *Escape from New York* (1981), *Deadly Blessing* (1981), *Codename Wildgeese* (1984), *Airwolf* (TV 1984-6), *The Dirty Dozen – The Next Mission* (TV 1985).

Bow, Clara (1905-65) American born Brooklyn, New York; *Mantrap* (1926), *It* (1927), *Wings* (1927).

Bowie, David (David Robert Jones) (1947–) British born Brixton, South London; *The Man Who Fell to Earth* (1976), *Cat People* (1982), *The Hunger* (1983), *Merry Christmas Mr Lawrence* (1983), *Into the Night* (1985), *Labyrinth* (1986), *The Last Temptation of Christ* (1988).

Braga, Sonia (1951–) Brazilian born Maringa; *Kiss of the Spider Woman* (1985), *Moon over Parador* (1988), *The Milagro Beanfield War* (1988), *The Rookie* (1990).

Branagh, Kenneth (1960–) British; also stage; *High Season* (1987), *A Month in the Country* (1988), *Henry V* (1989), *Dead Again* (1991).

Brando, Marlon (1924–) American born Omaha, Nebraska; *A Streetcar Named Desire* (1951), *Viva Zapata* (1952), *Julius Caesar* (1953), *The Wild One* (1954), *On the Waterfront* (1954), *Guys and Dolls* (1955), *The Teahouse of the August Moon* (1956), *The Young Lions* (1958), *One-Eyed Jacks* (1961), *Mutiny on the Bounty* (1962), *The Chase* (1966), *The Godfather* (1972), *Last Tango in Paris* (1972), *Superman* (1978), *Apocalypse Now* (1979), *A Dry White Season* (1988), *The Freshman* (1990).

Bridges, Jeff (1949–) American born Los Angeles; *The Last Picture Show* (1971), *Hearts of the West* (1975), *Stay Hungry* (1976), *King Kong* (1976), *Somebody Killed Her Husband* (1978), *Winter Kills* (1979), *Tron* (1982), *Against All Odds* (1983), *Starman* (1984), *The Jagged Edge* (1985), *8 Million Ways to Die* (1985), *The Morning After* (1986), *Nadine* (1987), *Tucker: The Man and His Dream* (1987), *The Fabulous Baker Boys* (1989), *Texasville* (1990).

Bridges, Lloyd (1913–) American born San Leandro, California; *Home of the Brave* (1949), *Try and Get Me* (1951), *The Rainmaker* (1956), *Sea Hunt* (TV 1957-60), *The Goddess* (1958), *The Love War* (TV 1970), *Roots* (TV 1977).

Broderick, Matthew (1963–) American born New York City; *War Games* (1983), *Ladyhawke* (1984), *Ferris Bueller's Day Off* (1986), *Biloxi Blues* (1988), *Torch Song Trilogy* (1988), *Family Business* (1989), *Glory* (1989), *The Freshman* (1990).

Bronson, Charles (Charles Buchinski) (1920–) American born Ehrenfield, Pennsylvania; *Drumbeat* (1954), *Vera Cruz* (1954), *The Magnificent Seven* (1960), *This Property is Condemned* (1966), *The Dirty Dozen* (1967), *Chato's Land* (1972), *The Mechanic* (1972), *The Valachi Papers* (1972), *Death Wish* (1974), *Hard Times* (1975), *Telefon* (1977), *Death Wish II* (1982), *Death Wish III* (1985), *Death Wish IV* (1987), *Murphy's Law* (1987). *Messenger of Death* (1988).

Brooks, Mel (Melvin Kaminski) (1926–) American born New York City; *The Twelve Chairs* (1969), *Blazing Saddles* (1974), *Silent Movie* (1976), *High Anxiety* (1978), *History of the World Part One* (1981), *Spaceballs* (1987).

FILM AND TV ACTORS (cont.)

Brown, Bryan (1947–) Australian born Panania; *A Town Like Alice* (TV 1981), *The Thorn Birds* (TV 1983), *Eureka Stockade* (TV 1985), *F/X: Murder by Illusion* (1985), *Rebel* (1985), *Taipan* (1985), *The Shiralee* (TV 1987), *Cocktail* (1988), *Gorillas in the Mist* (1988).

Brynner, Yul (1915-85) Swiss/Russian, naturalized American born Sakhalin, Siberia; *The King and I* (1956), *The Brothers Karamazov* (1958), *The Magnificent Seven* (1960), *Return of the Seven* (1966).

Burton, Richard (Richard Jenkins) (1925-84) British born Pontrhydfen, S Wales; *My Cousin Rachel* (1952), *Alexander the Great* (1956), *Look Back in Anger* (1959), *Cleopatra* (1962), *The Night of the Iguana* (1964), *The Spy Who Came in from the Cold* (1965), *Who's Afraid of Virginia Woolf?* (1966), *The Taming of the Shrew* (1967), *Where Eagles Dare* (1969), *Equus* (1977), *Exorcist II: The Heretic* (1977), *Absolution* (1979), *1984* (1984).

Caan, James (1939–) American born Bronx, New York; *Brian's Song* (TV 1971), *The Godfather* (1972), *(part II–1974)*, *Rollerball* (1975), *A Bridge Too Far* (1977), *Alien Nation* (1989), *Dick Tracy* (1990).

Cage, Nicolas (Nicholas Coppola) (1964–) American born Long Beach, California; *Fast Times at Ridgemont High* (1982), *Rumblefish* (1983), *Racing with the Moon* (1984), *The Cotton Club* (1984), *Birdy* (1985), *Peggy Sue Got Married* (1986), *Raising Arizona* (1987), *Moonstruck* (1987), *Vampire's Kiss* (1988), *Wild At Heart* (1990), *Wings of the Apache* (1990).

Cagney, James (Francis Jr) (1899-1986) American born New York City; *Public Enemy* (1931), *Lady Killer* (1933), *A Midsummer Night's Dream* (1935), *The Roaring Twenties* (1939), *Yankee Doodle Dandy* (1942), *White Heat* (1949), *Love Me or Leave Me* (1955), *Mister Roberts* (1955), *One, Two, or Three* (1961), *Ragtime* (1981).

Caine, Michael (Maurice Micklewhite) (1933–) British born London; *Zulu* (1963), *The Ipcress File* (1965), *Alfie* (1966), *The Italian Job* (1969), *Sleuth* (1972), *The Man Who Would Be King* (1975), *The Eagle Has Landed* (1976), *California Suite* (1978), *Beyond the Poseidon Adventure* (1979), *Dressed to Kill* (1980), *Death Trap* (1983), *Educating Rita* (1983), *Hannah and Her Sisters* (1986), *The Whistle Blower* (1987), *Without a Clue* (1988), *Bullseye* (1990), *Shock to the System* (1990).

Cardinale, Claudia (1939–) Italian born Tunis, Tunisia; *The Pink Panther* (1963), *Once Upon a Time in the West* (1969), *Escape to Athena* (1979), *Fitzcarraldo* (1982).

Caron, Leslie (Claire Margaret) (1931–) French born Boulogne-Billancourt, near Paris; *An American in Paris* (1951), *Lili* (1953), *The Glass Slipper* (1954), *Daddy Long Legs* (1955), *Gigi* (1958), *Fanny* (1961), *The L-Shaped Room* (1962), *Father Goose* (1964), *QB VII* (TV 1974).

Carradine, David (John Arthur Carradine) (1936–) American born Hollywood, California; *Shane* (TV 1966), *Kung Fu* (1972-4), *Death Race 2000* (1975), *Bound for Glory* (1976), *North and South* (TV 1986), *Crime Zone* (1988), *The Misfit Brigade* (1988), *Bird on a Wire* (1990).

Carradine, John (Richmond Reed Carradine) (1906-88) American born New York City; *Five Came Back* (1939), *Stagecoach* (1939), *The Grapes of Wrath* (1940), *Bluebeard* (1944), *House of Frankenstein* (1945), *The Man Who Shot Liberty Valance* (1962), *Peggy Sue Got Married* (1986).

Carradine, Keith (Ian) (1950–) American born San Mateo, California; *Thieves Like Us* (1973), *Nashville* (1975), *The Longriders* (1980), *Southern Comfort* (1981), *Blackout* (1985), *Murder Ordained* (TV 1987), *The Moderns* (1988).

Carrera, Barbara (1945–) Nicaraguan/American born Managua, Nicaragua; *The Master Gunfighter* (1975), *Embryo* (1976), *The Island of Dr. Moreau* (1977), *Condorman* (1981), *Never Say Never Again* (1983), *Codename: Wildgeese II* (1984), *Dallas* (TV 1984-5), *Loverboy* (1990).

Cassavetes, John (1929-89) American born New York City; *Johnny Staccato* (TV 1959), *The Dirty Dozen* (1967), *Rosemary's Baby* (1969), *Minnie and Moskovitz* (1979), *The Fury* (1978), *Whose Life is it Anyway?* (1981), *Tempest* (1983).

Chamberlain, Richard (1935–) American born Beverly Hills, California; *Dr Kildare* (TV 1961-6), *The Music Lovers* (1970), *Lady Caroline Lamb* (1972), *The Slipper and the Rose* (1976), *The Man in the Iron Mask* (1977), *The Last Wave* (1978), *Shogun* (TV 1980), *The Thorn Birds* (TV 1983), *Island Son* (TV 1989–).

FILM AND TV ACTORS (cont.)

Chaplin, Sir Charles (Spencer) (1889-1977) British born London; *The Champion* (1915), *The Tramp* (1915), *Easy Street* (1917), *A Dog's Life* (1918), *Shoulder Arms* (1918), *The Kid* (1920), *The Idle Class* (1921), *The Gold Rush* (1924), *City Lights* (1931), *Modern Times* (1936), *The Great Dictator* (1940), *Limelight* (1952), *A King in New York* (1957).

Chaplin, Geraldine (1944–) American born Santa Monica, California; *Doctor Zhivago* (1965), *The Three Musketeers* (1974), *Nashville* (1975), *Hidden Talent* (1984), *White Mischief* (1987), *The Moderns* (1988), *Mama Turns 100* (1988).

Charisse, Cyd (Tula Ellice Funklea) (1922–) American born Amarillo, Texas; *Ziegfeld Follies* (1945), *The Unfinished Dance* (1947), *Singin' in the Rain* (1952), *The Band Wagon* (1953), *Brigadoon* (1954), *It's Always Fair Weather* (1955), *Invitation to the Dance* (1957), *Two Weeks in Another Town* (1962).

Chase, Chevy (Cornelius Crane Chase) (1943–) American born New York City; *Foul Play* (1978), *Caddyshack* (1980), *Seems Like Old Times* (1980), *Vacation* (1983), *European Vacation* (1984), *Fletch* (1985), *Spies Like Us* (1985), *The Three Amigos* (1986), *The Couch Trip* (1988), *Caddy Shack II* (1988), *Funny Farm* (1988), *Fletch Lives* (1988), *Christmas Vacation* (1989).

Cher (Cher Bono, formerly Cherilyn Sarkisian) (1946–) American born El Centro, California; *Silkwood* (1983), *Mask* (1985), *Moonstruck* (1987), *Suspect* (1987), *The Witches of Eastwick* (1987), *Mermaids* (1990).

Chevalier, Maurice (1888-1972) French born Paris; *The Innocents of Paris* (1929), *One Hour with You* (1932), *Love Me Tonight* (1932), *The Love Parade* (1932), *Gigi* (1958).

Christie, Julie (1941–) British born Chukua, Assam, India; *The Fast Lady* (1963), *Billy Liar* (1963), *Doctor Zhivago* (1965), *Darling* (1965), *Farenheit 451* (1966), *Far from the Madding Crowd* (1967), *The Go-Between* (1971), *Don't Look Now* (1974), *Shampoo* (1975), *Heaven Can Wait* (1978), *Heat and Dust* (1982), *Power* (1985), *The Gold Diggers* (1988).

Cleese, John (Marwood) (1939–) British born Weston-super-Mare; *The Frost Report* (TV 1966), *At Last the 1948 Show* (TV 1967), *Monty Python's Flying Circus* (TV 1969-74), *Monty Python and the Holy Grail* (1974), *Fawlty Towers* (TV 1975 & 1979), *The Life of Brian* (1979), *Time Bandits* (1982), *The Meaning of Life* (1983), *Clockwise* (1985), *A Fish Called Wanda* (1988), *Erik the Viking* (1989).

Clift, (Edward) Montgomery (1920-66) American born Omaha, Nebraska; *Red River* (1946), *The Search* (1948), *A Place in the Sun* (1951), *From Here to Eternity* (1953), *Freud* (1962), *Suddenly Last Summer* (1968).

Close, Glenn (1947–) American born Greenwich, Connecticut; *The World According to Garp* (1982), *The Big Chill* (1984), *The Natural* (1984), *Something About Amelia* (TV 1984), *Jagged Edge* (1985), *Fatal Attraction* (1987), *Dangerous Liaisons* (1988), *Reversal of Fortune* (1990), *Hamlet* (1991), *Meeting Venus* (1991).

Cobb, Lee J. (Lee Jacoby) (1911-76) American born New York City; *Golden Boy* (1939), *The Moon is Down* (1943), *Anna and the King of Siam* (1946), *The Dark Past* (1948), *On the Waterfront* (1954), *The Man in the Grey Flannel Suit* (1956), *Twelve Angry Men* (1957), *The Brothers Karamazov* (1958), *The Virginian* (TV 1962-6), *Come Blow Your Horn* (1963), *Death of a Salesman* (TV 1966), *Coogan's Bluff* (1968), *They Came to Rob Las Vegas* (1968), *The Young Lawyers* (TV 1970-1), *The Exorcist* (1973).

Coburn, James (1928–) American born Laurel, Nebraska; *The Magnificent Seven* (1960), *The Great Escape* (1963), *Charade* (1963), *Our Man Flint* (1966), *In Like Flint* (1966), *A Fistful of Dynamite* (1971), *California Suite* (1978), *Loving Couples* (1980), *Young Guns II* (1990).

Coleman, Dabney (1932–) American born Austin, Texas; *This Property is Condemned* (1966), *That Girl* (TV 1966-70), *Nine to Five* (1980), *On Golden Pond* (1981), *Tootsie* (1982), *War Games* (1983), *Buffalo Bill* (TV 1983), *The Man With One Red Shoe* (1985), *Dragnet* (1987), *Where the Heart Is* (1990).

Collins, Joan (Henrietta) (1933–) British born London; *Lady Godiva Rides Again* (1951), *The Virgin Queen* (1955), *The Bitch* (1979), *Dynasty* (TV 1981- 9).

FILM AND TV ACTORS (cont.)

Connery, Sean (Thomas Connery) (1930–) British born Edinburgh; *Dr. No* (1963), *Marnie* (1964), *From Russia With Love* (1964), *Goldfinger* (1965), *The Hill* (1965), *Thunderball* (1965), *A Fine Madness* (1966), *You Only Live Twice* (1967), *The Molly Maguires* (1969), *The Anderson Tapes* (1970), *Diamonds are Forever* (1971), *The Offence* (1972), *Zardoz* (1973), *Murder on the Orient Express* (1974), *The Man Who Would Be King* (1975), *Robin and Marian* (1976), *Meteor* (1979), *Outland* (1981), *Time Bandits* (1981), *Never Say Never Again* (1983), *Highlander* (1985), *The Name of the Rose* (1986), *The Untouchables* (1987), *The Presidio* (1988), *Indiana Jones and the Last Crusade* (1989), *Family Business* (1989), *The Hunt for Red October* (1990), *The Russia House* (1990).

Conti, Tom (1941–) British born Paisley; *Merry Christmas Mr Lawrence* (1983), *Reuben Reuben* (1983), *Saving Grace* (1984), *Miracles* (1985), *Heavenly Pursuits* (1985), *Shirley Valentine* (1989).

Cooper, Gary (Frank J. Cooper) (1901-61) American born Helena, Montana; *The Winning of Barbara Worth* (1926), *Lilac Time* (1928), *The Virginian* (1929), *A Farewell to Arms* (1932), *City Streets* (1932), *The Lives of a Bengal Lancer* (1935), *Sergeant York* (1941), *For Whom the Bell Tolls* (1943), *The Fountainhead* (1949), *High Noon* (1952), *Friendly Persuasion* (1956).

Costner, Kevin (1955–) American born Los Angeles; *Night Shift* (1982), *American Flyers* (1984), *Silverado* (1985), *The Untouchables* (1987), *No Way Out* (1987), *Bull Durham* (1988), *Field of Dreams* (1989), *Revenge* (1990), *Dancing With Wolves* (1990), *Prince of Thieves* (1991).

Cotten, Joseph (1905–) American born Petersburg, Virginia; *Citizen Kane* (1941), *The Magnificent Ambersons* (1942), *Journey into Fear* (1942), *Shadow of a Doubt* (1943), *I'll Be Seeing You* (1945), *Portrait of Jennie* (1948), *The Third Man* (1949), *Niagara* (1952), *Tora! Tora! Tora!* (1971).

Courtenay, Tom (1937–) British born Hull; also stage; *The Loneliness of the Long Distance Runner* (1962), *Billy Liar* (1963), *Doctor Zhivago* (1965), *The Dresser* (1983), *Let Him Have It* (1991).

Crawford, Joan (Lucille Le Sueur) (1906-77) American born San Antonio, Texas; *Our Dancing Daughters* (1928), *Our Blushing Brides* (1933), *Dancing Lady* (1933), *The Women* (1939), *Mildred Pierce* (1945), *Possessed* (1947), *Whatever Happened to Baby Jane?* (1962), *Trog* (1970).

Crenna, Richard (1926–) American born Los Angeles; *Pride of St. Louis* (1952), *Star!* (1968), *Body Heat* (1981), *Death Ship* (1981), *First Blood* (1982), *Breakheart Pass* (1983), *Table for Five* (1983), *The Flamingo Kid* (1984), *The Rape of Richard Beck* (TV 1985), *Summer Rental* (1985), *Rambo* (1986), *Rambo III* (1988), *Leviathan* (1989).

Crosby, Bing (Harry Lillis Crosby) (1904-77) American born Tacoma, Washington; *King of Jazz* (1930), *Mississippi* (1935), *Anything Goes* (1936), *Road to Singapore* (1940), *Road to Zanzibar* (1941), *Holiday Inn* (1942), *Road to Morrocco* (1942), *Going My Way* (1944), *The Bells of St Mary's* (1945), *Blue Skies* (1946), *A Connecticut Yankee in King Arthur's Court* (1949), *White Christmas* (1954), *The Country Girl* (1954), *High Society* (1956), *Road to Hong Kong* (1962).

Cruise, Tom (Tom Cruise Mapother IV) (1962–) American born Syracuse, New York; *Taps* (1981), *Endless Love* (1981), *The Outsiders* (1983), *Legend* (1984), *Risky Business* (1984), *Top Gun* (1985), *The Color of Money* (1986), *Cocktail* (1988), *Rain Man* (1988), *Born on the Fourth of July* (1989), *Days of Thunder* (1990).

Crystal, Billy (1947–) American born Long Beach, New York; *This Is Spinal Tap* (1983), *Throw Momma from the Train* (1987), *The Princess Bride* (1988), *When Harry Met Sally ...* (1989), *City Slickers* (1991).

Culp, Robert (1930–) American born Oakland, California; *I Spy* (TV 1965-7), *Bob and Carol and Ted and Alice* (1969), *The Greatest American Hero* (TV 1981-2), *The Gladiator* (TV 1986).

Curtis, Jamie Lee (1958–) American born Los Angeles; *Operation Petticoat* (TV 1978), *Halloween* (1979), *The Fog* (1980), *Halloween II* (1981), *Love Letters* (1983), *Trading Places* (1983), *Perfect* (1985), *A Fish Called Wanda* (1988), *Dominick and Eugene* (1988), *Blue Steel* (1990).

Curtis, Tony (Bernard Schwarz) (1925–) American born New York City; *Houdini* (1953), *Trapeze* (1956), *The Vikings* (1958), *Some Like it Hot* (1959), *Spartacus* (1960), *The Boston Strangler* (1968).

Cusack, Cyril James (1910–) Irish born Durban, S Africa; *Odd Man Out* (1947), *The Blue Lagoon* (1949), *Jacqueline* (1965), *The Spy Who Came in From the Cold* (1965), *Fahrenheit 451* (1966), *Day of the Jackal* (1973), *1984* (1984), *Little Dorrit* (1987), *My Left Foot* (1989), *The Fool* (1990).

FILM AND TV ACTORS (cont.)

Cusack, Sinead (1948–) Irish; *David Copperfield* (1969), *Tam Ling* (1971), *Rocket Gibraltar* (1988).

Cushing, Peter (1913–) British born Kenley, Surrey; *The Man in the Iron Mask* (1939), *Hamlet* (1947), *1984* (TV 1955), *The Curse of Frankenstein* (1957), *Dracula* (1958), *The Mummy* (1959), *The Hound of the Baskervilles* (1959), *Cash on Demand* (1963), *Dr Who and the Daleks* (1965), *Dalek's Invasion of Earth* (1966), *Sherlock Homes* (TV 1968), *Tales from the Crypt* (1972), *Horror Express* (1972), *Star Wars* (1977), *Biggles* (1988).

Dalton, Timothy (1946–) British born Wales; *The Lion in Winter* (1968), *Wuthering Heights* (1970), *Mary Queen of Scots* (1971), *Agatha* (1979), *Flash Gordon* (1980), *Centenniel* (TV 1981-2), *The Living Daylights* (1987), *License to Kill* (1989).

Dance, Charles (1946–) British born Rednal, Worcestershire; *For Your Eyes Only* (1981), *The Jewel in the Crown* (TV 1984), *The Golden Child* (1985), *Plenty* (1985), *Good Morning Babylon* (1987), *White Mischief* (1987), *Pascali's Island* (1988), *Phantom of the Opera* (TV 1990).

D'Angelo, Beverly (1953–) American born Columbus, Ohio; *First Love* (1977), *Every Which Way But Loose* (1978), *Hair* (1979), *Coal Miner's Daughter* (1980), *Paternity* (1981), *Honky Tonk Freeway* (1981), *Vacation* (1984), *European Vacation* (1985), *Aria* (1987), *High Spirits* (1988), *Christmas Vacation* (1989).

Daniels, William (1927–) American born Brooklyn, New York; *Captain Nice* (TV 1966), *The Graduate* (1967), *1776* (1972), *The Parallax View* (1974), *The Blue Lagoon* (1981), *Reds* (1981), *St Elsewhere* (TV 1982-9), *Blind Date* (1987).

Danson, Ted (1947–) American born Flagstaff, Arizona; *The Onion Field* (1979), *Body Heat* (1981), *Cheers* (1981–), *Creepshow* (1982), *Something About Amelia* (TV 1984), *Three Men and a Baby* (1988), *Cousins* (1989), *Dad* (1990), *Three Men and a Little Lady* (1990).

Davenport, Nigel (1928–) British born Fambridge; *A Man for All Seasons* (1966), *The Virgin Soldiers* (1969), *Living Free* (1972), *The Island of Dr Moreau* (1977).

Davis, Bette (Ruth Elizabeth Davis) (1908-89) American born Lowell, Massachusetts; *Bad Sister* (1931), *Dangerous* (1935), *Jezebel* (1938), *All About Eve* (1950), *Whatever Happened to Baby Jane?* (1962), *The Great Lie* (1941), *Strangers* (TV 1979), *The Whales of August* (1987).

Davis, Judy (1956–) Australian born Perth; *My Brilliant Career* (1979), *Who Dares Wins* (1982), *A Passage to India* (1987), *High Tide* (1987).

Day, Doris (Doris von Kappelhoff) (1924–) American born Cincinnati, Ohio; *Romance on the High Seas* (1948), *Storm Warning* (1960), *Calamity Jane* (1953), *Young at Heart* (1954), *Love Me or Leave Me* (1955), *The Pajama Game* (1957), *Pillow Talk* (1959), *That Touch of Mink* (1962), *With Six You Get Egg Roll* (1968), *The Doris Day Show* (TV 1968-73).

Day-Lewis, Daniel (1958–) Irish born London; *Gandhi* (1983), *My Beautiful Laundrette* (1985), *Room with a View* (1985), *The Unbearable Lightness of Being* (1988), *Stars and Bars* (1988), *Nanou* (1988), *My Left Foot* (1989).

De Havilland, Olivia (1916–) British born Tokyo, Japan; *Midsummer Night's Dream* (1935), *The Adventures of Robin Hood* (1938), *Gone with the Wind* (1939), *The Dark Mirror* (1946), *To Each his Own* (1946), *The Heiress* (1949).

De Luise, Dom (1933–) American born Brooklyn, New York; *The Twelve Chairs* (1969), *The Cannonball Run* (1980), *Going Bananas* (1988).

De Niro, Robert (1943–) American born New York City; *Bang the Drum Slowly* (1973), *Mean Streets* (1973), *The Godfather, Part II* (1974), *1900* (1976), *Taxi Driver* (1976), *The Deer Hunter* (1978), *Raging Bull* (1980), *King of Comedy* (1982), *Brazil* (1985), *Angel Heart* (1987), *The Untouchables* (1987), *Midnight Run* (1988), *Jacknife* (1989), *Stanley & Iris* (1989), *We're No Angels* (1990), *GoodFellas* (1990), *Awakenings* (1990), *Backdraft* (1991).

De Vito, Danny (1944–) American born Neptune, New Jersey; *One Flew Over the Cuckoo's Nest* (1975), *Taxi* (TV 1978-82), *Romancing the Stone* (1983), *Terms of Endearment* (1984), *The Jewel of the Nile* (1985), *Ruthless People* (1986), *Tin Men* (1987), *Throw Momma from the Train* (1987), *War of the Roses* (1989).

FILM AND TV ACTORS (cont.)

Dean, James (Byron) (1931-55) American born Fairmount, Indiana; *East of Eden* (1955), *Rebel without a Cause* (1955), *Giant* (1956).

Delon, Alain (1935–) French born Paris; *Rocco and his Brothers* (1960), *The Leopard* (1962), *Swann in Love* (1984).

Dench, Dame Judi (Judith Olivia Dench) (1934–) British born York; also stage; *The Third Secret* (1964), *Four in the Morning* (1966), *A Fine Romance* (TV 1981-4), *A Room With a View* (1985), *84 Charing Cross Road* (1987), *A Handful of Dust* (1988), *Henry V* (1989) *Behaving Badly* (TV 1989).

Deneuve, Catherine (Catherine Dorleac) (1943–) French born Paris; *Les Parapluies de Cherbourg* (1964), *Repulsion* (1965), *Belle de Jour* (1967), *Tristana* (1970), *The Hunger* (1983).

Depardieu, Gérard (1948–) French born Châteauroux; *1900* (1976), *Get Out Your Handkerchiefs* (1977), *Loulou* (1980), *The Last Metro* (1980), *The Return of Martin Guerre* (1981), *Danton* (1982), *The Moon in the Gutter* (1983), *Police* (1985), *Jean de Florette* (1986), *Streets of Departure* (1986), *Under the Sun of Satan* (1987), *The Woman Next Door* (1987), *Cyrano de Bergerac* (1990), *Green Card* (1991).

Derek, Bo (Mary Cathleen Collins) (1956–) American born Long Beach, California; *Orca* (1977), *'10'* (1979), *Tarzan, the Ape Man* (1981), *Bolero* (1984), *Ghosts Can't Do It* (1990).

Dern, Bruce (MacLeish) (1936–) American born Chicago; *Marnie* (1964), *They Shoot Horses Don't They?* (1969), *Silent Running* (1972), *The Great Gatsby* (1974), *Family Plot* (1975), *Smile* (1975), *Coming Home* (1978), *The Driver* (1978), *Tattoo* (1981), *Middle Age Crazy* (1981), *That Championship Season* (1982), *Big Town* (1987), *1969* (1988), *World Gone Wild* (1988), *The 'Burbs* (1989), *After Dark My Sweet* (1990).

Dern, Laura (Elizabeth) (1966–) American born California; *Mask* (1985), *Smooth Talk* (1986), *Blue Velvet* (1986), *Wild at Heart* (1990).

Dickinson, Angie (Angeline Brown) (1932–) American born Kulm, North Detroit; *Rio Bravo* (1951), *Big Bad Mama* (1974), *Police Woman* (TV 1975-8), *Dressed to Kill* (1980).

Dietrich, Marlene (Maria Magdalena von Losch) (1901–) German/American born Berlin; *The Blue Angel* (1930), *Morocco* (1930), *Blond Venus* (1932), *Shanghai Express* (1932), *The Scarlet Empress* (1934), *The Devil is a Woman* (1935), *Desire* (1936), *Destry Rides Again* (1939), *A Foreign Affair* (1948), *Rancho Notorious* (1952), *Judgement at Nuremberg* (1961).

Donohoe, Amanda British; *Castaway* (1987), *The Lair of the White Worm* (1988), *L.A. Law* (TV 1989–), *The Rainbow* (1989), *Paper Mask* (1990).

Dors, Diana (Diana Fluck) (1931-84) British born Swindon, Wiltshire; *Oliver Twist* (1948), *Yield to the Night* (1956), *Deep End* (1970), *There's a Girl in My Soup* (1970), *The Amazing Mr Blunden* (1972), *Theatre of Blood* (1973), *Steaming* (1984).

Douglas, Kirk (Issur Danielovitch Demsky) (1916–) American born Amsterdam, New York; *The Strange Love of Martha Ivers* (1946), *Lust for Life* (1956), *Gunfight at the OK Corral* (1957), *Paths of Glory* (1957), *The Vikings* (1958), *Spartacus* (1960), *The Man from Snowy River* (1982).

Douglas, Michael (1944–) American born New Brunswick, New Jersey; *The Streets of San Francisco* (TV 1972-5), *Coma* (1978), *The China Syndrome* (1980), *The Star Chamber* (1983), *Romancing the Stone* (1984), *Jewel of the Nile* (1985), *Fatal Attraction* (1987), *Wall Street* (1987), *Black Rain* (1989), *War of the Roses* (1989).

Dreyfuss, Richard (1947–) American born Brooklyn, New York; *American Graffiti* (1973), *The Apprenticeship of Duddy Kravitz* (1974), *Jaws* (1975), *Close Encounters of the Third Kind* (1977), *The Goodbye Girl* (1977), *Whose Life is it Anyway?* (1981), *Down and Out in Beverly Hills* (1986), *Stakeout* (1987), *Tin Men* (1987), *Moon over Parador* (1988), *Always* (1989), *The Proud and the Free* (1991), *What About Bob?* (1991).

Dunaway, (Dorothy) Faye (1941–) American born Bascom, Florida; *Bonnie and Clyde* (1967), *Little Big Man* (1970), *The Getaway* (1972), *Chinatown* (1974), *The Towering Inferno* (1974), *Network* (1976), *The Eyes of Laura Mars* (1978), *The Champ* (1979), *Mommie Dearest* (1981), *Barfly* (1987), *Midnight Crossing* (1988), *Burning Secret* (1988), *The Handmaid's Tale* (1990).

FILM AND TV ACTORS (cont.)

Durbin, Deanna (Edna Mae Durbin) (1921–) Canadian born Winnipeg, Manitoba; *Three Smart Girls* (1936), *One Hundred Men and a Girl* (1937), *Mad About Music* (1938), *That Certain Age* (1938), *Three Smart Girls Grow Up* (1939), *It Started With Eve* (1941), *Christmas Holiday* (1944), *Lady on a Train* (1945).

Duvall, Robert (1930–) American born San Diego, California; *To Kill a Mockingbird* (1963), *The Godfather* (1972), *(part II* – 1974), *Ike* (TV 1979), *Apocalypse Now* (1979), *The Great Santini* (1980), *Tender Mercies* (1983), *The Natural* (1984), *Colors* (1988).

Duvall, Shelley (1949–) American born Houston, Texas; *Thieves Like Us* (1974), *Annie Hall* (1977), *The Shining* (1980), *Popeye* (1980), *Time Bandits* (1981), *Roxanne* (1987).

Eastwood, Clint (1930–) American born San Francisco, California; *Rawhide* (TV 1958-65), *A Fistful of Dollars* (1964), *For a Few Dollars More* (1965), *The Good, The Bad, and the Ugly* (1966), *Paint Your Wagon* (1969), *Coogan's Bluff* (1968), *Where Eagles Dare* (1969), *Play Misty for Me* (1971), *Dirty Harry* (1972), *High Plains Drifter* (1973), *Magnum Force* (1973), *The Enforcer* (1976), *The Outlaw Josey Wales* (1976), *Every Which Way But Loose* (1978), *Escape from Alcatraz* (1979), *Any Which Way You Can* (1980), *Firefox* (1982), *Honky Tonk Man* (1982), *Sudden Impact* (1983), *Tightrope* (1984), *Heartbreak Ridge* (1986), *Pink Cadillac* (1989), *The Dead Pool* (1989), *White Man Black Heart* (1990), *The Rookie* (1990).

Eden, Barbara (Barbara Huffman) (1934–) American born Tucson, Arizona; *Voyage to the Bottom of the Sea* (1961), *I Dream of Jeannie* (TV 1965-70), *Harper Valley PTA* (1978), *Harper Valley PTA* (TV 1981).

Ekland, Britt (Britt-Marie Ekland) (1942–) Swedish born Stockholm; *The Man with the Golden Gun* (1974), *Casanova* (1977), *Scandal* (1989).

Elliott, Denholm (1922–) British born London; *Nothing but the Best* (1964), *Here We Go Round the Mulberry Bush* (1967), *A Bridge too Far* (1977), *Raiders of the Lost Ark* (1981), *Brimstone and Treacle* (1982), *Trading Places* (1983), *The Razor's Edge* (1984), *A Private Function* (1984), *A Room with a View* (1985), *Defence of the Realm* (1985), *Maurice* (1987), *Indiana Jones and the Last Crusade* (1989).

Estevez, Emilio (1962–) American born New York City; *The Outsiders* (1983), *Repo Man* (1984), *Breakfast Club* (1984), *St Elmo's Fire* (1985), *Stakeout* (1987), *Young Guns* (1988), *Young Guns 2* (1990).

Evans, Dame Edith (1888-1976) British born London; also stage; *The Queen of Spades* (1948), *The Importance of Being Earnest* (1951).

Fairbanks, Douglas Sr (Douglas Elton Ullman) (1883-1939) American born Denver, Colorado; *The Mark of Zorro* (1920), *The Three Musketeers* (1921), *Robin Hood* (1922), *The Thief of Baghdad* (1924), *The Black Pirate* (1926).

Fairbanks, Douglas Jnr (1907–) American born New York City; *Catherine the Great* (1934), *The Prisoner of Zenda* (1937), *Sinbad the Sailor* (1947).

Falk, Peter (1927–) American born New York City; *It's a Mad Mad Mad Mad World* (1963), *The Great Race* (1965), *Columbo* (TV 1971-8), *The Princess Bride* (1987), *Cookie* (1988), *Vibes* (1988), *Wings of Desire* (1988).

Farrow, Mia (Maria Farrow) (1945–) American born Los Angeles; *Peyton Place* (TV 1964-7), *Rosemary's Baby* (1968), *Blind Terror* (1971), *The Great Gatsby* (1973), *Death on the Nile* (1978), *A Wedding* (1978), *A Midsummer Night's Sex Comedy* (1982), *The Purple Rose of Cairo* (1985), *Hannah and Her Sisters* (1986), *Another Woman* (1988), *New York Stories* (1989), *Alice* (1991).

Field, Sally (1946–) American born Pasadena, California; *Gidget* (TV 1965), *The Flying Nun* (TV 1967-9), *Sybil* (TV 1976), *Stay Hungry* (1976), *Heroes* (1977), *Smokey and the Bandit* (1977), *Hooper* (1978), *Norma Rae* (1979), *Beyond the Poseidon Adventure* (1979), *Smokey and the Bandit II* (1980), *Absence of Malice* (1981), *Places in the Heart* (1984), *Punchline* (1988), *Steel Magnolias* (1990).

Fields, W C (William Claude Dunkenfield) (1879-1946) American born Philadelphia, Pennsylvania; *Pool Sharks* (1915), *International House* (1933), *It's a Gift* (1934), *The Old Fashioned Way* (1934), *David Copperfield* (1935), *My Little Chickadee* (1940), *The Bank Dick* (1940), *Never Give a Sucker an Even Break* (1941).

Finch, Peter (William Mitchell) (1916-77) British born London; *The Shiralee* (1957), *The Nun's Story* (1959), *No Love for Johnnie* (1961), *Far from the Madding Crowd* (1967), *Sunday Bloody Sunday* (1971), *Network* (1976).

FILM AND TV ACTORS (cont.)

Finney, Albert (1936–) British born Salford, Lancashire; *The Entertainer* (1960), *Saturday Night and Sunday Morning* (1960), *Tom Jones* (1963), *Charlie Bubbles* (1968), *Murder on the Orient Express* (1974), *Shoot the Moon* (1981), *Annie* (1982), *The Dresser* (1983), *Under the Volcano* (1984), *The Green Man* (TV 1990), *Miller's Crossing* (1990).

Fisher, Carrie (1956–) American born Beverly Hills, California; *Shampoo* (1975), *Star Wars* (1977), *The Blues Brothers* (1980), *The Empire Strikes Back* (1980), *Under the Rainbow* (1981), *Return of the Jedi* (1983), *The Man With One Red Shoe* (1985), *Hannah and Her Sisters* (1986), *The 'Burbs* (1989), *When Harry Met Sally ...* (1989), *Loverboy* (1990), *Sibling Rivalry* (1990).

Flynn, Errol (1909-59) Australian/American born Hobart, Tasmania; *In the Wake of the Bounty* (1933), *Captain Blood* (1935), *The Charge of the Light Brigade* (1936), *The Adventures of Robin Hood* (1938), *The Sea Hawk* (1940), *The Sun Also Rises* (1957).

Fonda, Henry (James) (1905-82) American born Grand Island, Nebraska; *The Moon's Our Home* (1936), *A Farmer Takes a Wife* (1938), *Young Mr Lincoln* (1939), *The Grapes of Wrath* (1940), *The Lady Eve* (1941), *The Oxbow Incident* (1943), *My Darling Clementine* (1946), *Twelve Angry Men* (1957), *Stage Struck* (1957), *Fail Safe* (1964), *The Boston Strangler* (1968), *On Golden Pond* (1981).

Fonda, Jane (Seymour) (1937–) American born New York City; *Walk on the Wild Side* (1961), *Barbarella* (1968), *They Shoot Horses Don't They?* (1969), *Klute* (1971), *Julia* (1977), *Coming Home* (1978), *The Electric Horseman* (1979), *The China Syndrome* (1980), *Nine to Five* (1981), *On Golden Pond* (1981), *The Dollmaker* (TV 1983), *The Morning After* (1986), *Old Gringo* (1989), *Stanley & Iris* (1989).

Fonda, Peter (1939–) American born New York City; *Easy Rider* (1969), *Futureworld* (1976), *Cannonball Run* (1981), *Mercenary Fighters* (1988).

Fontaine, Joan (Joan de Havilland) (1917–) British born Tokyo, Japan; *Rebecca* (1940), *Suspicion* (1941), *Jane Eyre* (1943), *Frenchman's Creek* (1944), *From This Day Forward* (1946), *Letter from an Unknown Woman* (1948), *Born to Be Bad* (1950).

Ford, Harrison (1942–) American born Chicago; *Dead Heat on a Merry-Go-Round* (1966), *American Graffiti* (1974), *Star Wars* (1977), *Heroes* (1977), *Force 10 from Navarone* (1978), *The Frisco Kid* (1979), *Hanover Street* (1979), *Apocalypse Now* (1979), *The Empire Strikes Back* (1980), *Raiders of the Lost Ark* (1981), *Blade Runner* (1982), *Return of the Jedi* (1983), *Indiana Jones and the Temple of Doom* (1984), *Witness* (1985), *Mosquito Coast* (1986), *Frantic* (1988), *Working Girl* (1988), *Indiana Jones and the Last Crusade* (1989), *Presumed Innocent* (1990), *Regarding Henry* (1991).

Foster, Jodie (Ariane Munker) (1962–) American born Bronx, New York; *Bob and Carol and Ted and Alice* (TV 1973), *Paper Moon* (TV 1974), *Alice Doesn't Live Here Anymore* (1974), *Bugsy Malone* (1976), *Taxi Driver* (1976), *The Little Girl Who Lives Down the Lane* (1976), *Candleshoe* (1977), *Freaky Friday* (1977), *Siesta* (1987), *Accused* (1988), *5 Corners* (1988), *Stealing Home* (1988), *Catchfire* (1990), *The Silence of the Lambs* (1991).

Fox, James (1939–) British born London; *The Magnet* (1950), *The Loneliness of the Long Distance Runner* (1963), *Those Magnificent Men in Their Flying Machines* (1965), *Thoroughly Modern Millie* (1967), *Performance* (1970), *A Passage to India* (1984), *Greystoke* (1984), *The Whistle Blower* (1987), *High Season* (1987), *She's Been Away* (TV 1990).

Fox, Michael J (1961–) Canadian born Edmonton, Alberta; *Letters from Frank* (TV 1979), *Family Ties* (TV 1983–), *Poison Ivy* (TV 1985), *Back to the Future* (1985), *Teenwolf* (1985), *The Secret of My Success* (1987), *Bright Lights, Big City* (1988), *Casualties of War* (1989), *Back to the Future II* (1989), *Back to the Future III* (1990).

Gable, (William) Clark (1901-60) American born Cadiz, Ohio; *Red Dust* (1932), *It Happened One Night* (1934), *Mutiny on the Bounty* (1935), *San Francisco* (1936), *Gone with the Wind* (1939), *The Hucksters* (1947), *Mogambo* (1953), *Never Let Me Go* (1953), *Teacher's Pet* (1958), *The Misfits* (1961).

Gabor, Zsa Zsa (Sari Gabor) (1918–) Hungarian born Budapest; *Lovely to Look at* (1952), *Moulin Rouge* (1952), *Lili* (1953), *Public Enemy Number One* (1954), *Queen of Outer Space* (1959), *Up the Front* (1972).

Gambon, Michael (1940–) Irish born Dublin; *Turtle Diary* (1985), *The Singing Detective* (TV 1986), *Paris by Night* (1989), *The Cook, the Thief, His Wife and her Lover* (1989).

FILM AND TV ACTORS (cont.)

Garbo, Greta (Greta Lovisa Gustafsson) (1905-90) Swedish/American born Stockholm; *Flesh and the Devil* (1927), *Anna Christie* (1930), *Grand Hotel* (1932), *Queen Christina* (1933), *Anna Karenina* (1935), *Camille* (1936), *Ninotchka* (1939).

Gardner, Ava (Lucy Johnson) (1922-90) American born Smithfield, North Carolina; *The Killers* (1946), *The Hucksters* (1947), *Show Boat* (1951), *Pandora and the Flying Dutchman* (1951), *The Snows of Kilimanjaro* (1952), *Magambo* (1953), *The Barefoot Contessa* (1954), *The Sun Also Rises* (1957), *The Night of the Iguana* (1964).

Garland, Judy (Frances Gumma) (1922-69) American born Grand Rapids, Minnesota; *The Wizard of Oz* (1939), *Babes in Arms* (1939), *For Me and My Gal* (1942), *Meet Me in St Louis* (1944), *Ziegfeld Follies* (1945), *The Clock* (1945), *Easter Parade* (1948), *Summer Stock* (1950), *A Star is Born* (1954).

Garner, James (James Scott Baumgarner) (1928–   ) American born Norman, Oklahoma; *Maverick* (TV 1957-62), *The Great Escape* (1963), *The Americanization of Emily* (1964), *The Skin Game* (1971), *Rockford Files* (TV 1974-80), *The Fan* (1980), *Victor/Victoria* (1982).

Garr, Teri (1949–   ) American born Lakewood, Ohio; *Young Frankenstein* (1974), *Oh God* (1977), *Close Encounters of the Third Kind* (1977), *The Black Stallion* (1978), *Honky Tonk Freeway* (1981), *One from the Heart* (1982), *Tootsie* (1982), *The Sting II* (1982), *The Black Stallion Returns* (1983), *Mr Mom* (1983), *First Born* (1984), *After Hours* (1985), *Full Moon in Blue Water* (1988).

Gazzara, Ben (Biago Gazzara) (1930–   ) American born New York City; *Anatomy of Murder* (1959), *Arrest and Trial* (TV 1963), *Run for Your Life* (TV 1965-7), *QB VII* (TV 1974), *Voyage of the Damned* (1976).

Gere, Richard (1949–   ) American born Philadelphia, Pennsylvania; *Yanks* (1979), *American Gigolo* (1980), *An Officer and a Gentleman* (1982), *Breathless* (1983), *The Cotton Club* (1984), *No Mercy* (1986), *Miles from Home* (1988), *Internal Affairs* (1990), *Pretty Woman* (1990), *Final Analysis* (1991).

Gibson, Mel (1956–   ) American/Australian born Peekskill, New York; *Tim* (1979), *Mad Max* (1979), *Gallipoli* (1981), *Mad Max 2: The Road Warrior* (1982), *The Year of Living Dangerously* (1982), *Mad Max Beyond Thunderdome* (1985), *Lethal Weapon* (1987), *Tequila Sunrise* (1988), *Lethal Weapon 2* (1989), *Bird on a Wire* (1990), *Air America* (1990), *Hamlet* (1991).

Gielgud, Sir John (Arthur) (1904–   ) British born London; also stage; *Julius Caesar* (1953), *The Charge of the Light Brigade* (1968), *Oh What a Lovely War* (1969), *Murder on the Orient Express* (1974), *Providence* (1977), *Brideshead Revisited* (TV 1981), *Arthur* (1981), *Gandhi* (1982), *The Whistle Blower* (1987), *Arthur 2: On the Rocks* (1988), *Loser Takes All* (1989), *Prospero's Books* (1991).

Gish, Lillian (Diana) (Lillian de Guiche) (1896–   ) American born Springfield, Ohio; *An Unseen Enemy* (1912), *Birth of a Nation* (1914), *Intolerance* (1916), *Broken Blossoms* (1919), *Way Down East* (1920), *Duel in the Sun* (1946), *Night of the Hunter* (1955), *The Whales of August* (1987).

Glover, Danny (1947–   ) American born San Francisco, California; *Silverado* (1985), *Witness* (1985), *Lethal Weapon* (1987), *Bat 21* (1988), *Lethal Weapon 2* (1989), *Predator 2* (1990).

Goldberg, Whoopi (Caryn Johnson) (1949–   ) American born Manhattan, New York; *The Color Purple* (1985), *Burglar* (1985), *Jumping Jack Flash* (1986), *Clara's Heart* (1988), *The Telephone* (1988), *Ghost* (1990).

Goldblum, Jeff (1952–   ) American born Pittsburgh, Pennsylvania; *California Split* (1974), *Death Wish* (1974), *Nashville* (1975), *Invasion of the Body Snatchers* (1978), *Escape from Athena* (1979), *The Right Stuff* (1983), *The Big Chill* (1983), *Into the Night* (1985), *Silverado* (1985), *The Fly* (1985), *Life Story* (TV 1987), *Vibes* (1988), *The Tall Guy* (1989), *Earth Girls Are Easy* (1989), *Mister Frost* (1990).

Goodman, John (1953–   ) American born St Louis, Missouri; *True Stories* (1986), *The Big Easy* (1987), *Rosanne* (TV 1988–   ), *Punchline* (1988), *Sea of Love* (1990), *Always* (1990), *Stella* (1990), *Arachnophobia* (1990).

Gossett, Louis Jr (1936–   ) American born Brooklyn, New York; *Travels with My Aunt* (1972), *Roots* (TV 1977), *The Lazarus Syndrome* (TV 1979), *An Officer and a Gentleman* (1982), *The Powers of Matthew Starr* (TV 1982), *Jaws 3D* (1983), *Iron Eagle* (1985), *Iron Eagle II* (1988), *Cover Up* (1991).

FILM AND TV ACTORS (cont.)

Granger, Stewart (James Lablanche Stewart) (1913–) British born London; *The Man in Grey* (1943), *Waterloo Road* (1944), *Love Story* (1944), *Caesar and Cleopatra* (1945), *Captain Boycott* (1947), *King Solomon's Mines* (1950), *Scaramouch* (1952), *The Prisoner of Zenda* (1952), *Beau Brummell* (1954), *The Wild Geese* (1977).

Grant, Cary (Archibald Alexander Leach) (1904-86) British born Bristol; *This is the Night* (1932), *She Done Him Wrong* (1933), *The Awful Truth* (1937), *Bringing Up Baby* (1938), *His Girl Friday* (1940), *Arsenic and Old Lace* (1944), *Notorious* (1946), *To Catch a Thief* (1953), *North by Northwest* (1959).

Grant, Lee (Lyova Rosenthal) (1930–) American born New York City; *Detective Story* (1951), *The Landlord* (1970), *Shampoo* (1975), *The Voyage of the Damned* (1976), *Damien: Omen II* (1978), *Big Town* (1987).

Grenfell, Joyce (Joyce Phipps) (1910-75) British born London; also stage; *The Happiest Days of Your Life* (1949), *Laughter in Paradise* (1951), *The Bells of St Trinians* (1954).

Greenwood, Joan (1921-87) British born Chelsea; *Whisky Galore* (1949), *Kind Hearts and Coronets* (1949), *The Man in the White Suit* (1951), *The Importance of Being Earnest* (1952), *Tom Jones* (1963), *Little Dorrit* (1987).

Griffith, Melanie (1957–) American born New York City; *Something Wild* (1987), *Cherry 2000* (1988), *Working Girl* (1988), *Stormy Monday* (1988), *Pacific Heights* (1990), *Bonfire of the Vanities* (1991).

Guinness, Sir Alec (1914–) British born London; also stage; *Oliver Twist* (1948), *Kind Hearts and Coronets* (1949), *The Mudlark* (1950), *The Lavander Hill Mob* (1951), *The Man in the White Suit* (1951), *The Card* (1952), *Father Brown* (1954), *The Ladykillers* (1955), *The Bridge on the River Kwai* (1957), *The Horse's Mouth* (1958), *Our Man in Havana* (1960), *Tunes of Glory* (1962), *Lawrence of Arabia* (1962), *Doctor Zhivago* (1966), *Star Wars* (1977), *Tinker Tailor Soldier Spy* (TV 1979), *Smiley's People* (TV 1981), *Return of the Jedi* (1983), *A Passage to India* (1984), *Little Dorrit* (1987), *A Handful of Dust* (1988).

Guttenberg, Steve (1958–) American born Massapequa, New York; *Diner* (1981), *Police Academy* (1984), *Police Academy II* (1985), *Cocoon* (1985), *Short Circuit* (1986), *The Bedroom Window* (1986), *Three Men and a Baby* (1988), *High Spirits* (1988), *Cocoon: The Return* (1988), *Three Men and a Little Lady* (1990).

Gwynne, Fred (1926–) American born New York City; *Car 54 Where are You?* (TV 1961-2), *The Munsters* (TV 1964-5); *On the Waterfront* (1954), *Munster Go Home* (1966), *The Cotton Club* (1984), *Fatal Attraction* (1987), *Kane and Abel* (TV 1988), *Pet Sematary* (1989).

Hackman, Gene (1931–) American born San Bernardino, California; *Bonnie and Clyde* (1967), *I Never Sang for my Father* (1969), *French Connection* (1971), *The Poseidon Adventure* (1972), *Young Frankenstein* (1974), *French Connection II* (1975), *A Bridge Too Far* (1977), *Superman* (1978), *Superman II* (1981), *Target* (1985), *Superman IV* (1987), *Another Woman* (1988), *Bat 21* (1988), *Full Moon in Blue Water* (1988), *Split Decisions* (1988), *Missisippi Burning* (1989), *Loose Cannons* (1990), *Postcards from the Edge* (1990), *Narrow Margin* (1990), *The Package* (1990), *Class Action* (1991).

Hagman, Larry (Larry Hageman) (1931–) American born Weatherford, Texas; *Ensign Pulver* (1964), *I Dream of Jeannie* (TV 1965-70), *The Eagles Has Landed* (1976), *Superman* (1978), *Dallas* (TV 1978-90).

Hamill, Mark (1952–) American born Oakland, California; *Star Wars* (1977), *The Big Red One* (1979), *The Empire Strikes Back* (1980), *The Night the Lights Went out in Georgia* (1981), *Return of the Jedi* (1983), *Slipstream* (1988).

Hamilton, George (1939–) American born Memphis, Tennessee; *Home from the Hill* (1960), *All the Fine Young Cannibals* (1960), *Act One* (1963), *Roots* (TV 1977), *Love at First Bite* (1979), *Zorro the Gay Blade* (1981), *Dynasty* (TV 1985), *Spies* (TV 1986).

Hanks, Tom (1957–) American born Oakland, California; *Bachelor Party* (1983), *Splash!* (1984), *The Man With One Red Shoe* (1985), *Dragnet* (1987), *Big* (1988), *Punchline* (1988), *The 'Burbs* (1989), *Turner and Hooch* (1990), *Joe Versus the Volcano* (1990), *Bonfire of the Vanities* (1991).

Hannah, Daryl (1960–) American born Chicago; *Blade Runner* (1982), *Splash!* (1984), *Clan of the Cave Bear* (1986), *Legal Eagles* (1986), *Roxanne* (1987), *Wall Street* (1987), *High Spirits* (1988), *Steel Magnolias* (1989), *Crazy People* (1990), *At Play in the Fields of the Lord* (1991).

FILM AND TV ACTORS (cont.)

Hardy, Oliver (Norvell Hardy Junior) (1892-1957) American born near Atlanta, Georgia; many Laurel and Hardy films including *Putting Pants on Philip* (1927), *The Battle of the Century* (1927), *Two Tars* (1928), *The Perfect Day* (1929), *Laughing Gravy* (1931), *The Music Box* (1932), *Babes in Toyland* (1934), *Bonnie Scotland* (1935), *Way Out West* (1937), *The Flying Deuces* (1939), *Atoll K* (1950).

Harlow, Jean (Harlean Carpentier) (1911-37) American born Kansas City, Missouri; *Red Dust* (1932), *Hell's Angels* (1930), *Platinum Blonde* (1931), *Red-Headed Woman* (1932), *Bombshell* (1933), *Dinner at 8* (1933), *Libelled Lady* (1936).

Harris, Richard (1930–) Irish born County Limerick; *The Guns of Navarone* (1961), *Mutiny on the Bounty* (1962), *This Sporting Life* (1963), *Camelot* (1967), *A Man Called Horse* (1969), *Cromwell* (1970), *The Cassandra Crossing* (1977), *Orca–Killer Whale* (1977), *The Wild Geese* (1978), *Tarzan the Ape Man* (1981), *The Field* (1990).

Harrison, Sir Rex (Reginald Carey Harrison) (1908-90) British born Huyton, Lancashire; *Major Barbara* (1940), *Blithe Spirit* (1945), *Anna and the King of Siam* (1946), *The Ghost and Mrs Muir* (1947), *The Reluctant Debutante* (1958), *The Constant Husband* (1955), *Cleopatra* (1962), *My Fair Lady* (1964), *Dr Doolittle* (1967).

Hauer, Rutger (1944–) Dutch born Amsterdam; *Nighthawks* (1981), *Blade Runner* (1982), *Eureka* (1983), *The Hitcher* (1985), *Flesh and Blood* (1985), *Escape from Sobibor, Wanted Dead or Alive* (1986), *The Legend of the Holy Drinker* (1989), *Blind Fury* (1990).

Hawn, Goldie (Jeanne) (1945–) American born Washington D.C.; *Laugh In* (TV 1968–73); *Cactus Flower* (1969), *There's a Girl in My Soup* (1970), *Butterflies are Free* (1971), *Sugarland Express* (1974), *Shampoo* (1975), *Foul Play* (1978), *Seems Like Old Times* (1980), *Private Benjamin* (1980), *Best Friends* (1982), *Swing Shift* (1984), *Bird on a Wire* (1990), *CrissCross* (1991).

Hay, Will (1889-1949) British born Stockton-on-Tees; *Good Morning Boys* (1937), *Old Bones of the River* (1938), *Oh Mr Porter* (1938), *Ask a Policeman* (1939), *The Ghost of St Michaels* (1941), *My Learned Friend* (1944).

Hayworth, Rita (Margarita Carmen Cansino) (1918-87) American born New York City; *Only Angels Have Wings* (1939), *The Lady in Question* (1940), *The Strawberry Blonde* (1940), *Blood and Sand* (1941), *You'll Never Get Rich* (1941), *Cover Girl* (1944), *Gilda* (1946), *The Lady from Shanghai* (1948), *Separate Tables* (1958).

Hepburn, Audrey (Audrey Hepburn-Ruston) (1929–) British/Dutch born Brussels, Belgium; *Roman Holiday* (1953), *War and Peace* (1956), *Funny Face* (1957), *The Nun's Story* (1959), *Breakfast at Tiffany's* (1961), *My Fair Lady* (1964), *How to Steal a Million* (1966), *Wait Until Dark* (1967), *Robin and Marian* (1976), *Always* (1990).

Hepburn, Katharine (1907–) American born Hartford, Connecticut; *A Bill of Divorcement* (1932), *Morning Glory* (1933), *Stage Door* (1937), *Bringing Up Baby* (1938), *Holiday* (1938), *The Philadelphia Story* (1940), *Woman of the Year* (1942), *Adam's Rib* (1949), *The African Queen* (1951), *Long Day's Journey into Night* (1962), *Guess Who's Coming to Dinner?* (1967), *Suddenly Last Summer* (1968), *The Lion in Winter* (1968), *The Glass Menagerie* (TV 1973), *Rooster Cockburn* (1975), *On Golden Pond* (1981).

Hershey, Barbara (formerly Barbara Seagull, originally Herzstein) (1948–) American born Hollywood, California; *Last Summer* (1968), *Diamonds* (1975), *The Flood* (TV 1976), *The Stunt Man* (1978), *Angel on My Shoulder* (TV 1980), *The Entity* (1983), *The Right Stuff* (1983), *The Natural* (1984), *Passion Flower* (TV 1985), *Hannah and Her Sisters* (1986), *Tin Men* (1987), *A World Apart* (1988), *The Last Temptation of Christ* (1988), *Beaches* (1988).

Heston, Charlton (John Charlton Carter) (1922–) American born Evanston, Illinois; *Arrowhead* (1953), *The Ten Commandments* (1956), *Touch of Evil* (1958), *Ben Hur* (1959), *El Cid* (1961), *The Greatest Story Ever Told* (1965), *The War Lord* (1965), *Khartoum* (1966), *Planet of the Apes* (1968), *Will Penny* (1968), *Earthquake* (1973).

Hiller, Wendy (1912–) British born Bramhall, Cheshire; also stage; *Major Barbara* (1940), *I Know Where I'm Going* (1945), *Separate Tables* (1958), *Sons and Lovers* (1960), *A Man for All Seasons* (1966), *Murder on the Orient Express* (1974), *Voyage of the Damned* (1976), *The Elephant Man* (1980), *The Lonely Passion of Judith Hearne* (1987).

FILM AND TV ACTORS (cont.)

Hoffman, Dustin (1937–) American born Los Angeles; *The Graduate* (1967), *Midnight Cowboy* (1969), *Little Big Man* (1970), *Papillon* (1973), *Lenny* (1974), *All the President's Men* (1976), *Kramer Vs Kramer* (1979), *Tootsie* (1982), *Death of a Salesman* (TV 1984), *Rain Man* (1989), *Dick Tracy* (1990).

Hogan, Paul (1939–) Australian born New South Wales; *Crocodile Dundee* (1986), *Crocodile Dundee II* (1988), *Almost an Angel* (1990).

Holden, William (William Franklin Beedle Jr) (1918-82) American born O'Fallon, Illinois; *Golden Boy* (1939), *Rachel and the Stranger* (1948), *Sunset Boulevard* (1950), *Born Yesterday* (1950), *Stalag 17* (1953), *Love is a Many-Splendored Thing* (1955), *Picnic* (1955), *The Bridge on the River Kwai* (1957), *Casino Royale* (1967), *The Wild Bunch* (1969), *The Towering Inferno* (1974), *Network* (1976), *Damien: Omen II* (1978), *Escape to Athena* (1979), *The Earthling* (1980), *S.O.B.* (1981), *When Time Ran Out* (1981).

Hope, Bob (Leslie Townes Hope) (1903–) British/American born Eltham; *Thanks for the Memory* (1938), *The Cat and the Canary* (1939), *Road to Singapore* (1940), *The Ghost Breakers* (1940), *Road to Zanzibar* (1941), *My Favorite Blonde* (1942), *Road to Morocco* (1942), *The Paleface* (1948), *Fancy Pants* (1950), *The Facts of Life* (1960), *Road to Hong Kong* (1961), *How to Commit Marriage* (1969).

Hopkins, Anthony (1941–) British born Port Talbot, Wales; *The Lion in Winter* (1968), *When Eight Bells Toll* (1971), *War and Peace* (TV 1972), *The Lindbergh Kidnapping Case* (TV 1976), *Magic* (1978), *The Elephant Man* (1980), *The Bunker* (TV 1981), *The Bounty* (1983), *84 Charing Cross Road* (1986), *Desperate Hours* (1991), *The Silence of the Lambs* (1991).

Hopper, Dennis (1936–) American born Dodge City, Kansas; *Rebel Without a Cause* (1955), *Giant* (1956), *Cool Hand Luke* (1967), *Easy Rider* (1969), *Apocalypse Now* (1979), *Blue Velvet* (1986), *River's Edge* (1986), *Blood Red* (1990), *Catchfire* (1990), *Paris Trout* (1991).

Hordern, Sir Michael (1911–) British born Berkhampsted; also stage; *The Constant Husband* (1955), *The Spanish Gardener* (1956), *Dr Syn – Alias the Scarecrow* (1963), *A Funny Thing Happened on the Way to the Forum* (1966), *The Bed-Sitting Room* (1969), *The Slipper and the Rose* (1976), *The Missionary* (1982), *Paradise Postponed* (TV 1986), *The Fool* (1990).

Hoskins, Bob (Robert William) (1942–) British born Bury St Edmunds, Suffolk; *Pennies from Heaven* (TV 1978), *The Long Good Friday* (1980), *Pink Floyd: The Wall* (1982), *The Honorary Consul* (1983), *The Cotton Club* (1984), *Brazil* (1985), *Sweet Liberty* (1985), *Mona Lisa* (1986), *A Prayer for the Dying* (1987), *Who Framed Roger Rabbit* (1988), *Mermaids* (1990).

Howard, Leslie (Leslie Howard Stainer) (1890-1943) British born London; *Of Human Bondage* (1934), *The Scarlet Pimpernel* (1935), *Pygmalion* (1938), *Gone with the Wind* (1939).

Howard, Trevor (Wallace) (1916-88) British born Cliftonville, Kent; *The Way Ahead* (1944), *Brief Encounter* (1946), *Green for Danger* (1946), *The Third Man* (1949), *The Heart of the Matter* (1953), *The Key* (1958), *Sons and Lovers* (1960), *Mutiny on the Bounty* (1962), *The Charge of the Light Brigade* (1968), *Ryan's Daughter* (1970), *The Night Visitor* (1971), *Catholics* (TV 1973), *Conduct Unbecoming* (1975), *Meteor* (1979), *Staying On* (TV 1980), *Gandhi* (1982), *White Mischief* (1987), *The Unholy* (1988).

Hudson, Rock (Roy Scherer Jr) (1925-85) American born Winnetka, Illinois; *Magnificent Obsession* (1954), *Giant* (1956), *Written on the Wind* (1956), *The Tarnished Angel* (1957), *Pillow Talk* (1959), *Send Me No Flowers* (1964), *Seconds* (1966), *Darling Lili* (1969), *McMillan and Wife* (TV 1971-5), *McMillan* (TV 1976), *Embryo* (1976), *The Martian Chronicles* (TV 1980), *Dynasty* (TV 1985).

Hulce, Tom (1953–) American born Plymouth, Michigan; *September 30, 1955* (1977), *Animal House* (1978), *Amadeus* (1984), *Dominick and Eugene* (1988), *Parenthood* (1989).

Hunt, Linda (1945–) American born Morristown, New Jersey; *The Year of Living Dangerously* (1983), *The Bostonians* (1984), *Silverado* (1985), *Dune* (1985), *Waiting for the Moon* (1987), *She Devil* (1989).

Hurt, John (1940–) British born Chesterfield, Derbyshire; also stage; *A Man for All Seasons* (1966), *10 Rillington Place* (1971), *The Naked Civil Servant* (TV 1975), *Midnight Express* (1978), *Alien* (1979), *The Elephant Man* (1980), *History of the World Part One* (1981), *Champions* (1983), *1984* (1984), *Spaceballs* (1987), *Aria* (1987), *White Mischief* (1987), *Scandal* (1989), *Frankenstein Unbound* (1990).

FILM AND TV ACTORS (cont.)

Hurt, William (1950–   ) American born Washington D.C.; *Altered States* (1981), *The Janitor* (1981), *Body Heat* (1981), *The Big Chill* (1983), *Gorky Park* (1983), *Kiss of the Spider Woman* (1985), *Children of a Lesser God* (1986), *Broadcast News* (1987), *A Time of Destiny* (1988), *The Accidental Tourist* (1989), *Love You to Death* (1990), *Alice* (1991).

Hussey, Olivia (1951–   ) British born Buenos Aires, Argentina; *Romeo and Juliet* (1968), *Lost Horizon* (1973), *Jesus of Nazareth* (TV 1977), *Death on the Nile* (1978), *The Man With Bogart's Face* (1980).

Huston, Anjelica (1952–   ) Irish/American born Ireland; *The Last Tycoon* (1976), *Frances* (1982), *This is Spinal Tap* (1983), *Prizzi's Honor* (1985), *The Dead* (1987), *Gardens of Stone* (1987), *A Handful of Dust* (1988), *Mr. North* (1988), *The Witches* (1990), *The Grifters* (1990), *The Addams Family* (1991).

Hutton, Timothy (1960–   ) American born Malibu, California; *Ordinary People* (1980), *Taps* (1981), *Daniel* (1983), *The Falcon and the Snowman* (1985), *Made in Heaven* (1987).

Hyde-White, Wilfrid (1903–91) British born Gloucester; *The Third Man* (1949), *My Fair Lady* (1964), *The Associates* (TV 1979), *Buck Rogers* (TV 1980-2), *Oh God Book Two* (1980), *The Fog* (1982).

Irons, Jeremy (1948–   ) British born Cowes; *The French Lieutenant's Woman* (1981), *Brideshead Revisited* (TV 1981), *Swann in Love* (1984), *The Mission* (1985), *Dead Ringers* (1988), *Reversal of Fortune* (1990).

Jackson, Glenda (1936–   ) British born Liverpool; also stage; *Women in Love* (1969), *Sunday Bloody Sunday* (1971), *Mary Queen of Scots* (1971), *Elizabeth R* (TV 1971), *A Touch of Class* (1972), *Hedda* (1975), *Stevie* (1978), *The Patricia Neal Story* (TV 1981), *Turtle Diary* (1985), *Business as Usual* (1987), *Salome's Last Dance* (1988), *The Rainbow* (1989), *Doombeach* (1989).

Jackson, Gordon (1923-89) British born Glasgow; *Whisky Galore* (1948), *Tunes of Glory* (1960), *The Great Escape* (1982), *The Ipcress File* (1965), *The Prime of Miss Jean Brodie* (1969), *Upstairs Downstairs* (1970-5), *Kidnapped* (1972), *The Medusa Touch* (1977), *The Professionals* (1977-81), *A Town Like Alice* (TV 1980), *The Shooting Party* (1984), *The Whistle Blower* (1987), *Beyond Therapy* (1987).

Jacobi, Derek (1938–   ) British born Leytonstone, London; also stage; *The Odessa File* (1964), *I Claudius* (TV 1976), *Burgess and MacLean* (TV 1977), *Mr Pye* (TV 1986), *Little Dorrit* (1987), *The Fool* (1990).

Jones, James Earl (1931–   ) American born Tate County, Missouri; *The Great White Hope* (1970), *Jesus of Nazareth* (TV 1977), *Exorcist II: The Heretic* (1977), *Roots II* (TV 1979), *Conan the Barbarian* (1982), *Beastmaster* (1982), *Coming to America* (1988), *Field of Dreams* (1988), *Three Fugitives* (1988), *The Hunt for Red October* (1989), *Best of the Best* (1990).

Jones, Jennifer (Phyllis Isley) (1919–   ) American born Tulsa, Oklahoma; *The Song of Bernadette* (1943), *Duel in the Sun* (1976), *Portrait of Jennie* (1948), *Carrie* (1951), *Love is a Many-Splendored Thing* (1955), *A Farewell to Arms* (1958), *Tender is the Night* (1961), *Towering Inferno* (1974).

Julia, Raul (1940–   ) Puerto Rican born San Juan, Puerto Rico; *The Eyes of Laura Mars* (1978), *One From the Heart* (1982), *Tempest* (1982), *Kiss of the Spider Woman* (1985), *The Morning After* (1986), *Moon over Parador* (1988), *The Penitent* (1988), *Tequila Sunrise* (1989), *Romero* (1990), *Presumed Innocent* (1990), *The Rookie* (1990), *Frankenstein Unbound* (1990).

Karloff, Boris (William Henry Pratt) (1887-1969) British/American born London; *Frankenstein* (1931), *The Mask of Fu Manchu* (1931), *The Lost Patrol* (1934), *The Raven* (1935), *The Bride of Frankenstein* (1935), *The Body Snatcher* (1945).

Kaye, Danny (David Daniel Kominski) (1913-87) American born New York City; *Up in Arms* (1944), *The Secret Life of Walter Mitty* (1947), *Hans Christian Anderson* (1952), *White Christmas* (1954), *The Court Jester* (1956), *The Five Pennies* (1959), *Skokie* (TV 1981).

Keaton, Buster (Joseph Francis Keaton) (1895-1966) American born Pickway; *Our Hospitality* (1923), *The Navigator* (1924), *The General* (1927), *San Diego I Love You* (1944), *Sunset Boulevard* (1950), *Limelight* (1952), *It's a Mad, Mad, Mad, Mad World* (1963).

Keaton, Diane (Diane Hall) (1946–   ) American born Los Angeles, California; *The Godfather* (1972), (*part II*–1974), *Sleeper* (1973), *Annie Hall* (1977), *Manhattan* (1979), *Reds* (1981), *Shoot the Moon* (1982), *Mrs Soffel* (1984), *Baby Boom* (1987), *The Good Mother* (1988), *The Godfather Part III* (1990), *Success* (1991).

FILM AND TV ACTORS (cont.)

Kelly, Gene (Eugene Curran Kelly) (1912–   ) American born Pittsburgh, Pennsylvania; *For Me and My Girl* (1942), *Cover Girl* (1944), *Anchors Aweigh* (1945), *Ziegfeld Follies* (1946), *The Pirate* (1948), *The Three Musketeers* (1948), *Take Me Out to the Ball Game* (1949), *On the Town* (1949), *Summer Stock* (1950), *An American in Paris* (1951), *Singin' in the Rain* (1952), *Brigadoon* (1954), *Invitation to Dance* (1956), *Les Girls* (1957), *Marjorie Morningstar* (1958), *Inherit the Word* (1960), *Sins* (TV 1987).

Kelly, Grace (Patricia) (1928-82) American born Philadelphia, Pennsylvania; *High Noon* (1952), *Mogambo* (1953), *Dial M for Murder* (1954), *Rear Window* (1954), *The Country Girl* (1954), *To Catch a Thief* (1955), *High Society* (1956).

Kennedy, George (1925–   ) American born New York City; *Charade* (1963), *The Flight of the Phoenix* (1967), *The Dirty Dozen* (1967), *Cool Hand Luke* (1967), *Sarge* (TV 1971), *Thunderbolt and Lightfoot* (1974), *Earthquake* (1974), *The Blue Knight* (TV 1975-6), *The Eiger Sanction* (1977), *Death on the Nile* (1979), *Bolero* (1984), *Delta Force* (1985), *Creepshow 2* (1987), *Dallas* (TV 1988–91).

Kensit, Patsy (1968–   ) British; *The Great Gatsby* (1973), *Hanover Street* (1979), *Absolute Beginners* (1986), *Lethal Weapon 2* (1989), *Chicago Joe and the Showgirl* (1990), *Twenty-one* (1991).

Kerr, Deborah (Deborah Jane Kerr-Trimmer) (1921–   ) British born Helensburgh, Scotland; *Major Barbara* (1940), *Love on the Dole* (1941), *The Life and Death of Colonel Blimp* (1943), *Perfect Strangers* (1945), *I See a Dark Stranger* (1945), *Black Narcissus* (1947), *From Here to Eternity* (1953), *The King and I* (1956), *Tea and Sympathy* (1956), *An Affair to Remember* (1957), *Separate Tables* (1958), *The Sundowners* (1960), *The Innocents* (1961), *The Night of the Iguana* (1964), *Casino Royale* (1967), *Prudence and the Pill* (1968), *The Assam Garden* (1985).

Kingsley, Ben (Krishna Banji) (1943–   ) Anglo-Indian born Snaiton, Yorkshire; *Gandhi* (1982), *Betrayal* (1982), *Turtle Diary* (1985), *Testimony* (1987), *Pascali's Island* (1988), *Without a Clue* (1988).

Kinski, Nastassja (Nastassja Nakszynski) (1960–   ) German born Berlin; *Tess* (1979), *Cat People* (1982), *One from the Heart* (1982), *Paris, Texas* (1984).

Kline, Kevin (1947–   ) American born St Louis, Missouri; *Sophie's Choice* (1983), *The Big Chill* (1983). *Silverado* (1985), *Cry Freedom* (1987), *A Fish Called Wanda* (1988), *January Man* (1989), *Love You to Death* (1990), *Soap Dish* (1991).

Ladd, Alan (1913–64) American born Hot Springs, Arkansas; *This Gun for Hire* (1942), *The Glass Key* (1942), *The Blue Dahlia* (1946), *The Great Gatsby* (1949), *Shane* (1953), *The Carpetbaggers* (1964).

Lamarr, Hedy (Hedwig Kiesler) (1913–   ) Austrian born Vienna; *Algiers* (1938), *White Cargo* (1942), *Samson and Delilah* (1949).

Lambert, Christophe (1957–   ) French born New York City; *Greystoke* (1984), *Subway* (1985), *Highlander* (1985), *The Sicilian* (1987), *Why Me?* (1990).

Lamour, Dorothy (Dorothy Kaumeyer) (1914–   ) American born New Orleans, Louisiana; *The Jungle Princess* (1936), *The Hurricane* (1937), *Road to Singapore* (1940), *Road to Zanzibar* (1941) etc, *Manhandled* (1948), *Creepshow 2* (1987).

Lancaster, Burt (Stephen Burton) (1913–   ) American born New York City; *The Killers* (1946), *Brute Force* (1947), *The Flame and the Arrow* (1950), *Come Back Little Sheba* (1953), *From Here to Eternity* (1953), *Vera Cruz* (1954), *Gunfight at the OK Corral* (1957), *Elmer Gantry* (1960), *Birdman of Alcatraz* (1962), *The Professionals* (1966), *The Swimmer* (1967), *1900* (1976), *Atlantic City* (1980), *Local Hero* (1983), *Rocket Gibraltar* (1988), *Field of Dreams* (1988).

Lange, Hope (1933–   ) American born Redding Ridge, Connecticut; *Bus Stop* (1956), *Peyton Place* (1957), *Death Wish* (1974), *Nightmare on Elm Street II* (1985), *Blue Velvet* (1986).

Lange, Jessica (1949–   ) American born Cloquet, Minnesota; *King Kong* (1976), *All That Jazz* (1979), *The Postman Always Rings Twice* (1981), *Tootsie* (1982), *Frances* (1982), *Country* (1984), *Sweet Dreams* (1985), *Crimes of the Heart* (1986), *Far North* (1988), *Music Box* (1989), *Men Don't Leave* (1990), *Blue Sky* (1991).

FILM AND TV ACTORS (cont.)

Lansbury, Angela (Brigid) (1925–) American born London; *National Velvet* (1944), *Gaslight* (1944), *The Picture of Dorian Gray* (1945), *The Private Affairs of Bel Ami* (1947), *The Three Musketeers* (1948), *The Reluctant Debutante* (1958), *The Long Hot Summer* (1958), *The Dark at the Top of the Stairs* (1960), *The Manchurian Candidate* (1962), *The Greatest Story Ever Told* (1965), *Bedknobs and Broomsticks* (1971), *Death on the Nile* (1978), *The Lady Vanishes* (1979), *Lace* (TV 1984), *Company of Wolves* (1984), *Murder She Wrote* (TV 1984–).

Laurel, Stan (Arthur Stanley Jefferson) (1890–) British/American born Ulverston, Lancashire; *Nuts in May* (1917), *Monsieur Don't Care* (1925); for films with Hardy *see* **Hardy, Oliver.**

Laurie, Piper (Rosetta Jacobs) (1932–) American born Detroit, Michigan; *The Hustler* (1961), *Carrie* (1976), *Tim* (1979), *Mae West* (TV 1982), *The Thorn Birds* (TV 1983), *Tender is the Night* (TV 1985), *Return to Oz* (1985), *Children of a Lesser God* (1986), *Tiger Warsaw* (1988), *Twin Peaks* (TV 1991–).

Lee, Christopher (1922–) British born London; *The Curse of Frankenstein* (1956), *Dracula* (1958), *The Man Who Could Cheat Death* (1959), *The Mummy* (1959), *The Face of Fu Manchu* (1965), *Rasputin the Mad Monk* (1965), *Horror Express* (1972), *The Three Musketeers* (1973), *The Man With the Golden Gun* (1974), *Return from Witch Mountain* (1976), *Howling II* (1985), *The Land of Faraway* (1988).

Leigh, Janet (Jeanette Helen Morrison) (1927–) American born Merced, California; *Little Women* (1949), *The Forsyte Woman* (1949), *Houdini* (1953), *My Sister Eileen* (1955), *The Vikings* (1958), *Psycho* (1960), *The Manchurian Candidate* (1962), *The Fog* (1980).

Leigh, Vivien (Vivien Hartley) (1913-67) British born Darjeeling, India; *Dark Journey* (1937), *A Yank at Oxford* (1938), *Gone with the Wind* (1939), *Lady Hamilton* (1941), *Caesar and Cleopatra* (1945), *Anna Karenina* (1948), *A Streetcar Named Desire* (1951), *The Roman Spring of Mrs Stone* (1961), *Ship of Fools* (1965).

Lemmon, Jack (John Uhler Lemmon III) (1925–) American born Boston, Massachusetts; *It Should Happen to You* (1953), *Mister Roberts* (1955), *Some Like It Hot* (1959), *The Apartment* (1960), *Irma La Douce* (1963), *The Great Race* (1965), *The Odd Couple* (1968), *The Prisoner of Second Avenue* (1975), *The China Syndrome* (1979), *Missing* (1982), *Dad* (1990).

Lewis, Jerry (Joseph Levitch) (1926–) American born Newark, New Jersey; *My Friend Irma* (1949), *The Bellboy* (1960), *Cinderfella* (1960), *The Nutty Professor* (1963), *It's a Mad, Mad, Mad, Mad World* (1963), *The Family Jewels* (1965), *King of Comedy* (1983), *Smorgasbord* (1983), *Cookie* (1988).

Lithgow, John (1945–) American born Rochester, New York; *Blow Out* (1973), *High Anxiety, The World According to Garp* (1982), *The Twighlight Zone* (1983), *Terms of Endearment* (1983), *The Day After* (TV 1983), *2010* (1984), *Footloose* (1984), *Distant Thunder* (1988), *Memphis Belle* (1990).

Lloyd, Christopher (1938–) American born Stamford, Connecticut; *Star Trek III: The Search for Spock* (1984), *Back to the Future* (1985), *Who Framed Roger Rabbit* (1988), *Track 29* (1988), *Eight Men Out* (1988), *Back to the Future II* (1989), *Back to the Future III* (1990), *Why Me?* (1990).

Lloyd, Emily (1970–) British born London; *Wish You Were Here* (1987), *Cookie* (1988), *In Country* (1989), *Chicago Joe and the Showgirl* (1989).

Lloyd, Harold (Clayton) (1893-1971) American born Burchard, Nebraska; *High and Dizzy* (1920), *Grandma's Boy* (1922), *Safety Last* (1923), *Why Worry?* (1923), *The Freshman* (1925), *The Kid Brother* (1927), *Feet First* (1930), *Movie Crazy* (1932).

Lockwood, Margaret (Margaret Day) (1916-90) British born Karachi, India; *Lorna Doon* (1934), *The Beloved Vagabond* (1936), *The Lady Vanishes* (1938), *Night Train to Munich* (1940), *The Man in Grey* (1943), *The Wicked Lady* (1945), *Cast a Dark Shadow* (1947), *The Slipper and the Rose* (1976).

Lollobrigida, Gina (1927–) Italian born Subiaco; *Belles de Nuit* (1952), *Bread, Love and Dreams* (1953), *Trapeze* (1956), *Woman of Straw* (1964), *Falcon Crest* (TV 1984).

Lom, Herbert (Herbert Charles Angelo Kuchacevich ze Schluderpacheru) (1917–) Czechoslovakian born Prague; *The Seventh Veil* (1946), *Duel Alibi* (1947), *State Secret* (1950), *The Ladykillers* (1950), *El Cid* (1961), *Phantom of the Opera* (1962), *A Shot in the Dark* (1964), *Murders in the Rue Morgue* (1972), *The Return of the Pink Panther* (1974), *The Pink Panther Strikes Again* (1977), *Revenge of the Pink Panther* (1978), *The Lady Vanishes* (1979), *Hopscotch* (1980), *The Dead Zone* (1983), *Whoops Apocalypse* (1986), *Going Bananas* (1988).

FILM AND TV ACTORS (cont.)

Loren, Sophia (Sofia Scicolone) (1934–   ) Italian born Rome; *Woman of the River* (1955), *Boy on a Dolphin* (1957), *The Key* (1958), *El Cid* (1961), *Two Women* (1961), *The Millionairess* (1961), *Marriage Italian Style* (1964), *Cinderella Italian Style* (1967), *A Special Day* (1977).

Lorre, Peter (Laszlo Lowenstein) (1904-64) Hungarian born Rosenberg; *M* (1931), *Mad Love* (1935), *Crime and Punishment* (1935), *The Maltese Falcon* (1941), *Casablanca* (1942), *The Mask of Dimitrios* (1944), *Arsenic and Old Lace* (1944), *The Beast With Five Fingers* (1946), *My Favourite Brunette* (1947), *20,000 Leagues Under the Sea* (1954), *The Raven* (1963).

Lowe, Rob (1964–   ) American born Charlottesville, Virginia; *Class* (1983), *Oxford Blues* (1984), *St Elmo's Fire* (1985), *Youngblood* (1985), *About Last Night* (1987), *Illegally Yours* (1987), *Masquerade* (1988), *Bad Influence* (1990).

Lugosi, Bela (Bela Ferenc Denzso Blasko) (1882-1956) Hungarian/American born Lugos (now Romania); *Dracula* (1930), *The Murders in the Rue Morgue* (1931), *White Zombie* (1932), *International House* (1933), *The Black Cat* (1934), *Son of Frankenstein* (1939), *Abbott and Costello Meet Frankenstein* (1948), *Plan 9 from Outer Space* (1956).

Lumley, Joanna (1946–   ) British born Kashmir; *On Her Majesty's Secret Service* (1969), *General Hospital* (TV 1974-5), *The New Avengers* (TV 1976-7), *Sapphire and Steel* (TV 1979), *Trail of the Pink Panther* (1982), *Curse of the Pink Panther* (1983), *Shirley Valentine* (1989).

McCallum, David (1933–   ) British born Glasgow; *Violent Playground* (1958), *The Great Escape* (1963), *The Man From UNCLE* (TV 1964-7), *The Greatest Story Ever Told* (1965), *Colditz* (TV 1972), The Invisible Man (TV 1975), Sapphire and Steel (TV 1979), *The Watcher in the Woods* (1980), *Return of the Man from UNCLE* (TV 1983), *Mother Love* (1989).

McCarthy, Andrew (1963–   ) American born New York City; *Class* (1983), *Pretty in Pink* (1986), *Mannequin* (1987), *Less Than Zero* (1987), *Fresh Horses* (1988), *Kansas* (1988).

McCarthy, Kevin (1914–   ) American born Seattle, Washington; *Death of a Salesman* (1952), *Invasion of the Body Snatchers* (1956), *The Misfits* (1961), *The Prize* (1963), *Invasion of the Body Snatchers* (1978), *Piranha* (1978), *The Howling* (1981), *S.O.B.* (1981), *Private Benjamin* (1982), *My Tutor* (1983), *Twilight Zone* (1983), *Innerspace* (1987); *Flamingo Road* (1980-1).

McDowall, Roddy (1928–   ) British born London; *How Green Was My Valley* (1941), *Planet of the Apes* (1967), *Escape from the Planet of the Apes* (1971) etc, *The Poseidon Adventure* (1972), *Embryo* (1977), *Fright Night, Don' Time on Planet Earth* (1988).

McKern, Leo (Reginald) (1920–   ) Australian born Sydney; *Time without Pity* (1957), *The Mouse That Roared* (1959), *A Jolly Bad Fellow* (1964), *A Man for All Seasons* (1966), *Ryan's Daughter* (1971), *The Omen* (1976), *Candleshoe* (1977), *Rumpole of the Bailey* (TV 1978-80), *The Blue Lagoon* (1980), *The French Lieutenant's Woman* (1981), *Ladyhawke* (1984), *Monsignor Quixote* (TV 1986), *Travelling North* (1986).

MacLaine, Shirley (Shirley Beaty) (1934–   ) American born Richmond, Virginia; *The Trouble with Harry* (1955), *Ask any Girl* (1959), *The Apartment* (1959), *Irma La Douce* (1963), *Sweet Charity* (1968), *Terms of Endearment* (1983), *Madame Sousatzka* (1988), *Postcards from the Edge* (1990).

McQueen, Steve (Terence Steven McQueen) (1930-80) American born Slater, Missouri; *Wanted Dead or Alive* (TV 1958), *The Blob* (1958), *The Magnificent Seven* (1960), *The Great Escape* (1962), *Love with the Proper Stanger* (1963), *The Cincinnatti Kid* (1965), *Bullitt* (1968), *Le Mans* (1971), *Getaway* (1972), *Papillon* (1973), *Towering Inferno* (1974), *An Enemy of the People* (1977).

Madonna (Madonna Louse Veronica Ciccone) (1958–   ) American born Bay City, Michigan; *Desparately Seeking Susan* (1985), *Shanghai Suprise* (1986), *Dick Tracy* (1990).

Malkovich, John (1953–   ) American born Christopher, Illinois; *The Killing Fields* (1984), *Places in the Heart* (1984), *Empire of the Sun* (1987), *Miles from Home* (1988), *Dangerous Liaisons* (1988), *Crazy People* (1990), *The Sheltering Sky* (1990).

Mansfield, Jayne (Vera Jayne Palmer) (1933-67) American born Bryn Mawr, Pennsylvania; *The Girl Can't Help It* (1957), *The Sheriff of Fractured Jaw* (1959), *Too Hot to Handle* (1960), *The Challenge* (1960), *Promises! Promises!* (1965).

FILM AND TV ACTORS (cont.)

Martin, Steve (1945–   ) American born Waco, Texas; *Sgt. Peppers Lonely Hearts Club Band* (1978), *The Jerk* (1978), *Muppet Movie* (1979), *Pennies from Heaven* (1981), *Dead Men Don't Wear Plaid* (1982), *The Man With Two Brains* (1983), *The Lonely Guy* (1984), *All of Me* (1984), *The Three Amigos* (1986), *The Little Shop of Horrors* (1986), *Planes, Trains, and Automobiles* (1987), *Roxanne* (1987), *Dirty, Rotten Scoundrels* (1989), *Parenthood* (1989), *My Blue Heaven* (1990), *L.A. Story* (1991).

Marvin, Lee (1924-87) American born New York City; *The Wild One* (1954), *Attack* (1957), *The Killers* (1964), *Cat Ballou* (1965), *The Dirty Dozen* (1967), *Paint Your Wagon* (1969), *Gorky Park* (1983), *Dirty Dozen 2: The Next Mission* (TV 1985).

Mason, James (1909-84) British born Huddersfield; *I Met a Murder* (1939), *The Night Has Eyes* (1942), *The Man in Grey* (1943), *Fanny by Gaslight* (1944), *The Seventh Veil* (1945), *The Wicked Lady* (1946), *Odd Man Out* (1946), *Pandora and the Flying Dutchman* (1951), *The Desert Fox* (1951), *Five Fingers* (1952), *The Prisoner of Zenda* (1952), *Julius Caesar* (1953), *20,000 Leagues Under the Sea* (1954), *A Star is Born* (1954), *Journey to the Center of the Earth* (1959), *Lolita* (1962), *The Pumpkin Eater* (1964), *Georgy Girl* (1966), *The Blue Max* (1966), *The Deadly Affair* (1967), *Voyage of the Damned* (1976), *Heaven Can Wait* (1978), *The Boys from Brazil* (1978), *Murder by Decree* (1979), *Evil Under the Sun* (1982), *The Verdict* (1982), *Yellowbeard* (1983), *The Shooting Party* (1984).

Massey, Anna (Raymond) (1937–   ) British born London; also stage; *Burning Lake is Missing* (1965), *A Doll's House* (1973), *Rebecca* (TV 1979), *The Chain* (1985).

Massey, Raymond (1896-1983) American born Toronto; *The Old Dark House* (1932), *The Scarlet Pimpernel* (1934), *Things to Come* (1936), *The Prisoner of Zenda* (1937), *Abe Lincoln in Illinois* (1940), *Arsenic and Old Lace* (1944), *The Fountainhead* (1949), *East of Eden* (1955), *I Spy* (TV 1955), *Dr Kildare* (TV 1961-6).

Mastroianni, Marcello (1924–   ) Italian born Fontana Liri, near Frosinone; *I Miserabili* (1947), *White Nights* (1957), *La Dolce Vita* (1959), *Yesterday, Today and Tomorrow* (1963), *Divorce Italian Style* (1962), *8½* (1963), *Casanova* (1970), *Diamonds for Breakfast* (1968), *Ginger and Fred* (1985), *Black Eyes* (1987), *The Two Lives of Mattia Pascal* (1988), *Traffic Jam* (1988).

Matthau, Walter (1920–   ) American born New York City; *A Face in the Crowd* (1957), *King Creole* (1958), *Charade* (1963), *Mirage* (1965), *The Fortune Cookie* (1966), *A Guide to the Married Man* (1967), *The Odd Couple* (1968), *Hello Dolly* (1969), *Cactus Flower* (1969), *Kotch* (1971), *Earthquake* (1974), *The Taking of Pelham One Two Three* (1974), *Hopscotch* (1980), *Pirates* (1986), *The Couch Trip* (1988).

Mature, Victor (1915–   ) American born Louisville, Kentucky; *One Million BC* (1940), *My Darling Clementine* (1946), *Kiss of Death* (1947), *Samson and Delilah* (1949), *The Robe* (1953), *The Egyptian* (1954), *Safari* (1956), *The Long Haul* (1957), *After the Fox* (1966).

Maura, Carmen (1945–   ) Spanish born Madrid; *Dark Habits* (1983), *What Have I Done to Deserve This?* (1984), *Law of Desire* (1987), *Women on the Verge of a Nervous Breakdown* (1988), *Baton Rouge* (1988).

Mercouri, Melina (1915–   ) Greek born Athens; *Stella* (1954), *Never on Sunday* (1960), *Topkapi* (1964).

Midler, Bette (1945–   ) American born Honolulu, Hawaii; *The Rose* (1979), *Down and Out in Beverly Hills* (1986), *Ruthless People* (1986), *Outrageous Fortune* (1987), *Beaches* (1988), *Big Business* (1988), *Stella* (1989), *Scenes from a Mall* (1991).

Mills, Hayley (1946–   ) British born London; *Tiger Bay* (1959), *Pollyanna* (1960), *The Parent Trap* (1961), *Whistle Down the Wind* (1961), *The Moonspinners* (1965), *Forbush and the Penguins* (1971), *Parent Trap II* (TV 1986).

Mills, Sir John (Lewis Ernest Watts) (1908–   ) British born Felixstowe, Suffolk; *Those Were the Days* (1934), *Cottage to Let* (1941), *In Which We Serve* (1942), *Waterloo Road* (1944), *The Way to the Stars* (1945), *Great Expectations* (1946), *The October Man* (1947), *Scott of the Antartic* (1948), *The History of Mr Polly* (1949), *The Rocking Horse Winner* (1950), *The Colditz Story* (1954), *Hobson's Choice* (1954), *Town on Trial* (1957), *Tiger Bay* (1959), *Swiss Family Robinson* (1959), *Tunes of Glory* (1960), *Ryan's Daughter* (1970), *Lady Caroline Lamb* (1972), *The Big Sleep* (1978), *The 39 Steps* (1978), *Quatermass* (TV 1979), *Young at Heart* (TV 1980-1), *Gandhi* (1982), *Sahara* (1983), *Who's That Girl?* (1987).

Minnelli, Liza (1946–   ) American born Los Angeles; *Cabaret* (1972), *New York New York* (1977), *Arthur* (1981), *Arthur 2: On the Rocks* (1988), *Rent-a-Cop* (1988), *Stepping Out* (1991).

FILM AND TV ACTORS (cont.)

Mirren, Helen (1945–) British born London; also stage; *Miss Julie* (1973), *Excalibur* (1981), *Cal* (1984), *2010* (1985), *Heavenly Pursuits* (1985), *White Nights* (1986), *Mosquito Coast* (1986), *Pascali's Island* (1988), *The Cook, The Thief, His Wife and Her Lover* (1989), *The Comfort of Strangers* (1990), *Where Angels Fear To Tread* (1991).

Mitchum, Robert (1917–) American born Bridgeport, Connecticut; *The Story of G.I. Joe* (1945), *Pursued* (1947), *Crossfire* (1947), *Out of the Past* (1947), *The Big Steal* (1949), *Night of the Hunter* (1955), *Home from the Hill* (1960), *The Sundowners* (1960), *The List of Adrian Messanger* (1963), *Ryan's Daughter* (1971), *Farewell My Lovely* (1975), *The Big Sleep* (1978), *The Winds of War* (TV 1983), *War and Remembrance* (TV 1987), *Mr. North* (1988), *Scrooged* (1988).

Modine, Matthew (1959–) American born Utah; *Private School* (1983), *Birdy* (1984), *Mrs Soffel* (1984), *Vision Quest* (1985), *Full Metal Jacket* (1988), *Streamers* (1983), *Married to the Mob* (1989), *Memphis Belle* (1990), *Pacific Heights* (1990).

Montand, Yves (Ivo Levi) (1921–) French born Monsumagno, Italy; *The Wages of Fear* (1953), *Let's Make Love* (1962), *Jean de Florette* (1986), *Manon des Sources* (1986).

Moore, Demi (Demi Guines) (1962–) American born Roswell, New Mexico; *St Elmo's Fire* (1986), *About Last Night* (1987), *The Seventh Sign* (1988), *We're No Angels* (1990), *Ghost* (1990), *The Butcher's Wife* (1991).

Moore, Dudley (1935–) British born Dagenham, Essex; *Bedazzled* (1967), *Foul Play* (1978), *'10'* (1979), *Arthur* (1981), *Lovesick* (1983), *Unfaithfully Yours* (1983), *Micki and Maude* (1984), *Best Defense* (1985), *Santa Claus* (1985), *Arthur 2: On the Rocks* (1988), *Like Father, Like Son* (1989), *Crazy People* (1990).

Moore, Roger (George) (1927–) British born London; *Ivanhoe* (TV 1957), *The Saint* (TV 1963-8), *The Persuaders* (TV 1971-2), *Live and Let Die* (1973), *The Man With the Golden Gun* (1974), *Shout at the Devil* (1976), *The Spy Who Loved Me* (1977), *The Wild Geese* (1978), *Escape to Athena* (1979), *Moonraker* (1979), *For Your Eyes Only* (1981), *The Cannonball Run* (1981), *Octopussy* (1983), *A View to a Kill* (1985).

Moorehead, Agnes (1906-74) American born Chinton, Massachusetts; *Citizen Kane* (1941), *The Magnificent Ambersons* (1942), *Jane Eyre* (1943), *The Lost Moment* (1947), *The Woman in White* (1948), *Johnny Belinda* (1948), *Summer Holiday* (1948), *The Bat* (1959), *How the West was Won* (1963), *Bewitched* (TV 1964-71).

Morgan, Frank (Francis Phillip Wupperman) (1890-1949) American born New York City; *Hallelujah I'm a Bum* (1933), *Bombshell* (1933), *The Affairs of Cellini* (1934), *The Great Ziegfeld* (1936), *Trouble for Two* (1936), *Piccadilly Jim* (1936), *Dimples* (1936), *The Last of Mr Cheyney* (1937), *The Wizard of Oz* (1939), *Boom Town* (1940), *The Vanishing Virginian* (1942), *Tortilla Flat* (1942), *The Human Comedy* (1943), *The Three Musketeers* (1948).

Morgan, Harry (Harry Bratsburg) (1915–) American born Detroit, Michigan; *High Noon* (1952), *December Bride* (TV 1954-8), *The Teahouse of the August Moon* (1956), *Dragnet* (TV 1969), *M*A*S*H* (TV 1976-83), *Aftermash* (TV 1983), *Dragnet* (TV 1987).

Murphy, Eddie (1961–) American born Brooklyn, New York; *48 Hours* (1982), *Trading Places* (1983), *Beverly Hills Cop* (1985), *The Golden Child* (1986), *Beverly Hills Cop II* (1987), *Coming to America* (1988), *Harlem Nights* (1989), *Another 48 Hours* (1990).

Murray, Bill (1950–) American born Evanston, Illinois; *Meatballs* (1977), *Caddyshack* (1980), *Stripes* (1981), *Tootsie* (1982), *Ghostbusters* (1984), *Razor's Edge* (1984), *Little Shop of Horrors* (1986), *Scrooged* (1988), *Ghostbusters II* (1989), *What About Bob?* (1991).

Neal, Patricia (1926–) American born Packard, Kentucky; *The Fountainhead* (1949), *The Hasty Heart* (1950), *Diplomatic Courier* (1952), *Breakfast at Tiffany's* (1961), *Hud* (1963), *A Face in the Crowd* (1957), *All Quiet on the Western Front* (TV 1980).

Neeson, Liam (1952–) British born Ballymena, Northern Ireland; *Excalibur* (1981), *Suspect* (1987), *Satisfaction* (1988), *High Spirits* (1988), *The Good Mother* (1988), *The Dead Pool* (1988), *The Big Man* (1990), *Dark Man* (1990).

FILM AND TV ACTORS (cont.)

Neill, Sam (1948–) New Zealander; *The Final Conflict* (1982), *Reilly Ace of Spies* (TV 1983), *Robbery Under Arms* (TV 1985), *Plenty* (1985), *Kane and Abel* (TV 1988), *A Cry in the Dark* (1988), Evil Angels (1988), *The Hunt for Red October* (1990).

Newman, Paul (1925–) American born Cleveland, Ohio; *Somebody Up There Likes Me* (1956), *The Long Hot Summer* (1958), *The Hustler* (1961), *Hud* (1963), *The Prize* (1963), *Torn Curtain* (1966), *Cool Hand Luke* (1967), *Butch Cassidy and the Sundance Kid* (1969), *Judge Roy Bean* (1972), *The Sting* (1973), *Absence of Malice* (1981), *The Verdict* (1982), *The Color of Money* (1986), *Blaze* (1990), *Mr & Mrs Bridge* (1990).

Nicholson, Jack (1937–) American born Neptune, New Jersey; *The Little Shop of Horrors* (1960), *Easy Rider* (1969), *Five Easy Pieces* (1970), *Carnal Knowledge* (1971), *The Last Detail* (1974), *Chinatown* (1974), *One Flew Over the Cuckoo's Nest* (1975), *Tommy* (1975), *The Shining* (1980), *The Postman Always Rings Twice* (1981), *Reds* (1981), *Terms of Endearment* (1983), *Prizzi's Honour* (1985), *Broadcast News* (1987), *Ironweed* (1987), *The Witches of Eastwick* (1987), *Batman* (1989), *The Two Jakes* (1991), *The Death of Napoleon* (1991).

Nielsen, Leslie (1926–) Canadian born Regina, Saskatchewan; *Forbidden Planet* (1956), *Incident in San Francisco* (TV 1970), *The Poseidon Adventure* (1972), *Airplane* (1980), *Prom Night* (1980), *Police Squad* (TV 1982), *Soul Man* (TV 1986), *The Patriot* (TV 1987), *Fatal Confession* (TV 1987), *The Naked Gun* (1988), *Repossessed* (1990), *Naked Gun 2½: the Smell of Fear* (1991).

Nimoy, Leonard (1931–) American born Boston, Massachusetts; *Star Trek* (TV 1966-8), *Mission Impossible* (TV 1970-2), *Invasion of the Body Snatchers* (1978), *Star Trek The Motion Picture* (1979), *Star Trek 2: The Wrath of Khan* (1982), *Star Trek 3: The Search for Spock* (1984), *Star Trek 4: The Voyage Home* (1986), *Star Trek V: The Final Frontier* (1989).

Niven, David (James David Graham Niven) (1910-83) British born London; *Thank You Jeeves* (1936), *The Prisoner of Zenda* (1937), *Wuthering Heights* (1939), *Bachelor Mother* (1939), *Raffles* (1940), *The Way Ahead* (1944), *A Matter of Life and Death* (1946), *Carrington V.C.* (1955), *Around the World in Eighty Days* (1956), *Separate Tables* (1958), *The Guns of Navarone* (1961), *The Pink Panter* (1964), *Casino Royale* (1967), *Candleshoe* (1977), *Death on the Nile* (1978), *Escape to Athena* (1979), *Trail of the Pink Panther* (1982), *Curse of the Pink Panther* (1982).

Nolte, Nick (1940–) American born Omaha, Nebraska; *Rich Man Poor Man* (TV 1976), *Cannery Row* (1982), *48 Hours* (1982), *Down and Out in Beverly Hills* (1986), *Weeds* (1987), *New York Stories* (1989), *Three Fugitives* (1989), *Another 48 Hours* (1990).

Oberon, Merle (Estelle Merle O'Brien Thompson) (1911-79) British/Indian born Bombay, India; *The Dark Angel* (1935), *The Scarlet Pimpernel* (1935), *The Divorce of Lady X* (1938), *Wuthering Heights* (1939), *That Uncertain Feeling* (1941), *Forever and a Day* (1943), *A Song to Remember* (1943), *The Oscar* (1966), *Hotel* (1967), *Interval* (1973).

Olivier, Sir Laurence (Kerr) (1907-89) British born Dorking; also stage; *The Divorce of Lady X* (1938), *Wuthering Heights* (1939), *Rebecca* (1940), *Pride and Prejudice* (1940), *Henry V* (1944), *Hamlet* (1948), *Richard III* (1956), *The Prince and the Showgirl* (1958), *The Devil's Disciple* (1959), *The Entertainer* (1960), *Sleuth* (1972), *Marathon Man* (1976), *A Bridge Too Far* (1977), *Brideshead Revisited* (TV 1981), *A Voyage Round My Father* (TV 1982).

O'Neal, Ryan (Patrick Ryan O'Neal) (1941–) American born Los Angeles; *Peyton Place* (TV 1964-8), *Love Story* (1970), *What's Up, Doc?* (1972), *Paper Moon* (1973), *Nickelodeon* (1976), *A Bridge Too Far* (1977), *Green Ice* (1980).

O'Neal, Tatum (1963–) American born Los Angeles; *Paper Moon* (1973), *Nickelodeon* (1976), *International Velvet* (1978), *Little Darlings* (1980).

O'Sullivan, Maureen (1911–) Irish born Boyle; *Tarzan the Ape Man* (1932), *Tarzan and His Mate* (1934) etc, *The Barretts of Wimpole Street* (1934), *Pride and Prejudice* (1940), *Never Too Late* (1965), *Hannah and Her Sisters* (1986), *Peggy Sue Got Married* (1986).

O'Toole, Peter (Seamus) (1932–) Irish born Kerry, Connemara; *Lawrence of Arabia* (1962), *How to Steal a Million* (1966), *The Lion in Winter* (1968), *Goodbye Mr Chips* (1969), *The Ruling Class* (1972), *The Stunt Man* (1980), *My Favourite Year* (1982), *The Last Emperor* (1987), *High Spirits* (1988).

FILM AND TV ACTORS (cont.)

Pacino, Al (Alfredo Pacino) (1940–) American born New York City; *The Godfather* (1972), (*part II* – 1974, *part III* – 1990), *Dog Day Afternoon* (1975), *Scarface* (1983), *Revolution* (1984), *Sea of Love* (1990), *Dick Tracy* (1990), *Frankie and Johnny in the Claire De Lune* (1991).

Page, Geraldine (1924–) American born Kirksville, Missouri; *Summer and Smoke* (1961), *Sweet Bird of Youth* (1962), *Dear Heart* (1965), *The Happiest Millionaire* (1966), *Interiors* (1978), *Harry's War* (1980), *Honky Tonk Freeway* (1981), *The Pope of Greenwich Village* (1984), *The Trip to Bountiful* (1985).

Palance, Jack (Walter Palanuik) (1920–) American born Lattimer, Pennsylvania; *Panic in the Streets* (1950), *Shane* (1953), *The Big Knife* (1953), *Arrowhead* (1953), *They Came to Rob Las Vegas* (1968), *Oklahoma Crude* (1973), *Hawk the Slayer* (1980), *Believe It or Not* (TV 1982–), *Gor* (1988), *Bagdad Cafe* (1988), *Batman* (1988).

Palin, Michael (1943–) British born Sheffield; *Monty Python's Flying Circus* (TV 1969-74), *And Now for Something Different* (1970), *Monty Python and the Holy Grail* (1974), *Three Men in a Boat* (TV 1975), *Jabberwocky* (1976), *Ripping Yarns* (TV 1976-80), *The Life of Brian* (1978), *Time Bandits* (1980), *The Meaning of Life* (1982), *The Missionary* (1982), *A Private Function* (1984), *Brazil* (1985), *A Fish Called Wanda* (1988), *Around the World in 80 Days* (TV 1990), *American Friends* (1990).

Peck, Gregory (Eldred) (1916–) American born La Jolla, California; *The Keys to the Kingdom* (1944), *Spellbound* (1945), *Duel in the Sun* (1946), *Gentleman's Agreement* (1947), *The Macomber Affair* (1947), *The Paradine Case* (1947), *Twelve O'Clock High* (1949), *The Gunfighter* (1950), *Captain Horatio Hornblower* (1951), *The Million Pound Note* (1954), *The Purple Plain* (1955), *The Man in the Grey Flannel Suit* (1956), *The Big Country* (1958), *The Guns of Navarone* (1961), *To Kill a Mockingbird* (1963), *The Omen* (1976), *Old Gringo* (1989).

Penn, Sean (1960–) American born Burbank, California; *Taps* (1981), *Fast Times At Ridgemont High* (1982), *Racing with the Moon* (1984), *The Falcon and the Snowman* (1985), *At Close Range* (1986), *Shanghai Surprise* (1986), *Colors* (1988), *Judgement in Berlin* (1988), *Casualties of War* (1989), *We're No Angels* (1990).

Perkins, Anthony (1932–) American born New York City; *The Actress* (1953), *Desire Under the Elms* (1957), *Fear Strikes Out* (1957), *This Angry Age* (1958), *Psycho* (1960), *Five Miles to Midnight* (1962), *Murder on the Orient Express* (1974), *For the Term of His Natural Life* (TV 1982), *Psycho II* (1983), *Crimes of Passion* (1985), *Psycho III* (1986), *Destroyer* (1988).

Pertwee, Jon (1919–) British born London; *Carry on Cleo* (1964), *Doctor Who* (TV 1970-4), *One of Our Dinasours is Missing* (1975), *Worzel Gummidge* (TV 1979 & 1989), *The Boys in Blue* (1983).

Pfeiffer, Michelle (1957–) American born Santa Ana, California; *Grease 2* (1982), *Scarface* (1983), *Sweet Liberty* (1982), *Into the Night* (1985), *Witches of Eastwick* (1987), *Dangerous Liaisons* (1988), *Tequila Sunrise* (1988), *Married to the Mob* (1989), *The Fabulous Baker Boys* (1989), *The Russia House* (1990), *Frankie and Johnny in the Claire De Lune* (1991).

Phoenix, River (1970–) American born Madras, Oregon; *Explorers* (1985), *Mosquito Coast* (1986), *Running on Empty* (1988), *Jimmy Reardon* (1988), *Little Nikita* (1988), *Indiana Jones and the Last Crusade* (1989), *Love You to Death* (1990).

Pickford, Mary (Gladys Mary Smith) (1893-1979) Canadian born Toronto, Ontario; *The Violin Maker of Cremona* (1909), *Rebecca of Sunnybrook Farm* (1917), *Poor Little Rich Girl* (1917), *Pollyanna* (1919), *Little Lord Fauntleroy* (1921), *Tess of the Storm Country* (1922), *The Taming of the Shrew* (1929), *Coquette* (1929), *Secrets* (1933).

Pickup, Ronald (Alfred) (1940–) British born Chester; *Day of the Jackal* (1973), *The 39 Steps* (1978), *Nijinski* (1980), *Never Say Never Again* (1983), *Fortunes of War* (TV 1987), *Testimony* (1987).

Pleasence, Donald (1919–) British born Worksop; *Robin Hood* (TV 1955-7), *Battle of the Sexes* (1959), *Dr Crippen* (1962), *The Great Escape* (1963), *The Caretaker* (1964), *Cul-de-Sac* (1966), *Fantastic Voyage* (1966), *You Only Live Twice* (1967), *Escape to Witch Mountain* (1975), *The Eagle Has Landed* (1977), *Oh! God* (1977), *Telefon* (1977), *Halloween* (1978), *Sgt. Peppers Lonely Hearts Club Band* (1979), *Escape from New York* (1981), *Halloween 4* (1988), *Hanna's War* (1988), *Ground Zero* (1988).

FILM AND TV ACTORS (cont.)

Plowright, Joan (1929–) British born Scunthorpe, Brigg, Lincolnshire; also stage; *The Entertainer* (1960), *Drowning by Numbers* (1988), *Love You to Death* (1990).

Plummer, Christopher (1927–) Canadian born Toronto, Ontario; *The Fall of the Roman Empire* (1964), *The Sound of Music* (1965), *Waterloo* (1970), *The Man Who Would Be King* (1975), *The Return of the Pink Panther* (1975), *International Velvet* (1978), *Hanover Street* (1979), *Somewhere in Time* (1980), *The Janitor* (1981), *Dreamscape* (1984), *Where the Heart Is* (1990).

Poitier, Sidney (1924–) American born Miami, Florida; *No Way Out* (1950), *Cry, the Beloved Country* (1952), *The Blackboard Jungle* (1955), *The Defiant Ones* (1958), *Porgy and Bess* (1959), *Lilies of the Field* (1963), *To Sir with Love* (1967), *In the Heat of the Night* (1967), *Guess Who's Coming to Dinner* (1967), *Little Nikita* (1988), *Shoot to Kill* (1988).

Powers, Stefanie (Stefania Federkiewicz) (1942–) American born Hollywood, California; *Experiment in Terror* (1962), *Fanatic* (1964), *Stagecoach* (1966), *The Girl from UNCLE* (1966), *Herbie Rides Again (1973)*, *Escape to Athena* (1979), *Hart to Hart* (1979-83), *Family Secrets* (TV 1984) .

Price, Vincent (1911–) American born St Louis, Missouri; *Tower of London* (1940), *Dragonwyck* (1946), *His Kind of Woman* (1941), *House of Wax* (1953), *The Story of Mankind* (1957), *The Fly* (1958), *The Fall of the House of Usher* (1961), *The Raven* (1963), *The Tomb of Ligeia* (1964), *City Under the Sea* (1965), *House of a Thousand Dolls* (1967), *The House of Long Shadows* (1983), *The Whales of August* (1987), *Dead Heat* (1988), *Edward Scissorhands* (1991).

Quaid, Dennis (1954–) American born Houston, Texas; *Breaking Away* (1978), *Caveman* (1980), *The Night the Lights Went Out in Georgia* (1980), *Bill* (TV 1981), *All Night Long* (1981), *Johnny Belinda* (TV 1982), *The Right Stuff* (1983), *Jaws 3D* (1983), *Dreamscape* (1984), *Big Easy* (1986), *Innerspace* (1987), *Suspect* (1987), *D.O.A.* (1988), *Great Balls of Fire* (1989), *Come See the Paradise* (1990), *Postcards from the Edge* (1990).

Quayle, Sir Anthony (1913-89) British born Ainsdale, Lancashire; *Ice Cold in Alex* (1958), *The Guns of Navarone* (1961), *Lawrence of Arabia* (1962).

Quick, Diana (1946–) British born Kent; *Nicholas and Alexandra* (1971), *The Big Sleep* (1981), *Brideshead Revisited* (TV 1981), *Ordeal by Innocence* (1985), *Wilt* (1989).

Quinn, Anthony Rudolph Oaxaca (1915–) Irish/American born Chihuahua, Mexico; *Viva Zapata* (1952), *La Strada* (1954), *Lust for Life* (1956), *The Guns of Navarone* (1961), *Zorba the Greek* (1964), *The Shoes of the Fisherman* (1968), *Revenge* (1989), *Ghosts Can't Do It* (1990).

Rampling, Charlotte (1946–) British born Sturmer; *Georgy Girl* (1966), *The Damned* (1969), *Zardoz* (1973), *Orca* (1977), *Stardust Memories* (1980), *The Verdict* (1982), *Max mon Amour* (1986), *Angel Heart* (1987), *Paris by Night* (1988), *D.O.A.* (1988).

Rathbone, (Philip St John) Basil (1892-1967) British born Johannesburg, South Africa; *David Copperfield* (1935), *Anna Karenina* (1935), *Captain Blood* (1935), *Romeo and Juliet* (1936), *The Adventures of Robin Hood* (1938), *The Hound of the Baskervilles* (1939), *The Adventures of Sherlock Holmes* (1939) etc, *Spider Woman* (1944), *Heartbeat* (1946), *The Court Jester* (1956).

Reagan, Ronald (Wilson) (1911–) American born Tampico, Illinois; *King's Row* (1941), *Desperate Journey* (1942), *The Hasty Heart* (1949), *Bedtime for Bonzo* (1951), *The Killer* (1964).

Redford, (Charles) Robert (1937–) American born Santa Monica, California; *Barefoot in the Park* (1967), *Butch Cassidy and the Sundance Kid* (1969), *The Candidate* (1972), *The Great Gatsby* (1973), *The Sting* (1973), *The Way We Were* (1973), *All the President's Men* (1976), *The Electric Horseman* (1979), *The Natural* (1984), *Out of Africa* (1985), *Legal Eagles* (1986), *Havana* (1990).

Redgrave, Lynn (1943–) British born London; *Tom Jones* (1963), *Georgy Girl* (1966), *Girl With Green Eyes* (1964), *Everything You Always Wanted to Know About Sex* (1972), *The Happy Hooker* (1976), *House Calls* (TV 1980-1).

Redgrave, Sir Michael (Scudamore) (1908-85) British born Bristol; also stage; *The Lady Vanishes* (1938), *The Way to the Stars* (1945), *The Browning Version* (1951), *The Importance of Being Earnest* (1952), *The Dam Busters* (1955), *The Quiet American* (1958), *The Innocents* (1961), *Nicholas and Alexandra* (1971).

FILM AND TV ACTORS (cont.)

Redgrave, Vanessa (1937–   ) British born London; also stage; *Morgan!* (1965), *Blow-Up* (1966), *Camelot* (1967), *Mary, Queen of Scots* (1971), *Julia* (1977), *Playing for Time* (TV 1980), *The Bostonians* (1984), *Consuming Passions* (1988).

Reed, Oliver (Robert Oliver Reed) (1938–   ) British born Wimbledon, London; *The Damned* (1962), *The System* (1964), *The Jokers* (1966), *Women in Love* (1969), *The Brood* (1980), *Condorman* (1981), *Castaway* (1987), *Gor* (1988), *Return of the Musketeers* (1989).

Reeve, Christopher (1952–   ) American born New York City; *Superman* (1978), (*part II* – 1980, *III* – 1983, *IV* – 1987), *Somewhere in Time* (1980), *Monsignor* (1982), *Death Trap* (1982), *The Bostonians* (1984), *Switching Channels* (1988).

Reeves, Keanu (1965–   ) American; *River's Edge* (1986), *Prince of Pennsylvania* (1988), *The Night Before* (1988), *Dangerous Liaisons* (1988), *Permanent Record* (1988), *Bill and Ted's Excellent Adventures* (1989), *Parenthood* (1989), *Love You to Death* (1990), *Bill and Ted's Bogus Journey* (1991).

Remick, Lee (1935–91) American born Quincy, Massachusetts; *Anatomy of a Murder* (1959), *Experiment in Terror* (1962), *Days of Wine and Roses* (1963), *No Way to Treat a Lady* (1968), *Jennie* (TV 1975), *The Omen* (1976), *The Medusa Touch* (1977), *Mistral's Daughter* (TV 1984).

Reynolds, Burt (1935–   ) American born Waycross, Georgia; *Gunsmoke* (TV 1965-7), *Hunters Are for Killing* (TV 1970), *Deliverance* (1972), *Nickelodeon* (1976), *Smokey and the Bandit* (1977), *Hooper* (1978), *Starting Over* (1979), *Smokey and the Bandit II* (1980), *The Cannonball Run* (1981), *Sharkey's Machine* (1981), *The Best Little Whorehouse in Texas* (1982), *Stroker Ace* (1983), *The Man Who Loved Women* (1983), *City Heat* (1984), *Rent-a-Cop* (1988), *Switching Channels* (1988), *Breaking In* (1989), *Evening Shade* (TV 1991–   ).

Richardson, Miranda (1958–   ) British born Liverpool; *Dance with a Stranger* (1984), *The Innocent* (1985), *Blackadder II* (TV 1986), *Empire of the Sun* (1987), *A Month in the Country* (1988), *Die Kinder* (TV 1990).

Richardson, Sir Ralph (1902-83) British born Cheltenham; also stage; *Bulldog Jack* (1935), *Q Planes* (1939), *The Four Feathers* (1939), *Anna Karenina* (1948), *The Fallen Idol* (1948), *The Heiress* (1949), *Richard III* (1956), *Oscar Wilde* (1960), *Long Day's Journey into Night* (1962), *Dr Zhivago* (1966), *The Wrong Box* (1967), *A Doll's House* (1973), *The Man in the Iron Mask* (1977), *Time Bandits* (1980), *Dragonslayer* (1981), *Greystoke* (1984).

Rigg, Diana (1938–   ) British born Doncaster, Yorkshire; *The Avengers* (TV 1965-7), *On Her Majesty's Secret Service* (1969), *Theatre of Blood* (1973), *Evil Under the Sun* (1981), *Mother Love* (TV 1989).

Ringwald, Molly (1968–   ) American born Rosewood, California; *The Facts of Live* (TV), *The Tempest* (1982), *Space Hunter 3D: Adventures in the Forbidden Zone* (1983), *Packin' It In* (TV 1983), *Sixteen Candles* (1984), *The Breakfast Club* (1985), *Pretty in Pink* (1986), *Maybe Baby* (1987), *The Pick-up Artist* (1987), *Fresh Horses* (1988), *For Keeps?* (1988), *Loser Takes All* (1989), *Betsy's Wedding* (1990).

Robards, Jason (Jnr) (1922–   ) American born Chicago, Illinois; *Tender is the Night* (1961), *Long Day's Journey into Night* (1962), *The Hour of the Gun* (1967), *Once Upon a Time in the West* (1969), *Tora! Tora! Tora!* (1970), *All the President's Men* (1976), *Julia* (1977), *Melvin and Howard* (1980), *The Legend of the Lone Ranger* (1981), *The Day After* (TV 1983), *Sakharov* (TV 1984), *The Long Hot Summer* (TV 1985), *Bright Lights, Big City* (1988), *The Good Mother* (1988), *Parenthood* (1989), *Reunion* (1989).

Roberts, Julia (1967–   ) American born Smyrna, Georgia; *Satisfaction* (1988), *Mystic Pizza* (1988), *Steel Magnolias* (1989), *Pretty Woman* (1990), *Flatliners* (1990), *Sleeping with the Enemy* (1991).

Robertson, Cliff (Clifford Parker Robertson III) (1925–   ) American born La Jolla, California; *Picnic* (1955), *The Girl Most Likely* (1957), *PT 109* (1963), *The Best Man* (1964), *The Honey Pot* (1967), *Charly* (1968), *Washington Behind Closed Doors* (TV 1977), *Class* (1983), *Brainstorm* (1983).

Robinson, Edward G (Emanuel Goldenberg) (1893-1973) American born Bucharest, Romania; *Little Caesar* (1930), *Five Star Final* (1931), *The Whole Town's Talking* (1935), *The Last Gangster* (1937), *A Slight Case of Murder* (1938), *The Amazing Dr Clitterhouse* (1938), *Dr Ehrlich's Magic Bullet* (1940), *Brother Orchid* (1940), *The Sea Wolf* (1941), *Double Indemnity* (1944), *The Woman in the Window* (1944), *Scarlet Street* (1945), *All My Sons* (1948), *Key Largo* (1948), *House of Strangers* (1949), *Two Weeks in Another Town* (1962), *The Cincinnati Kid* (1965), *Soylent Green* (1973).

FILM AND TV ACTORS (cont.)

Rogers, Ginger (Virginia Katherine McMath) (1911–) American born Independence, Missouri; *Young Man of Manhattan* (1930), *42nd Street* (1933), *Flying Down to Rio* (1933), *The Gay Divorcee* (1934), *Top Hat* (1935), *Follow the Fleet* (1936), *Stage Door* (1937), *Bachelor Mother* (1939), *Kitty Foyle* (1940), *Roxie Hart* (1942), *Lady in the Dark* (1944).

Rogers, Will (William Penn Adair) (1879-1935) American born Colagah, Indian Territory (now Oklahoma); *Jubilo* (1919), *State Fair* (1933), *Judge Priest* (1934), *David Harum* (1934), *Handy Andy* (1934), *Life Begins at Forty* (1935), *Steamboat round the Bend* (1935).

Rooney, Mickey (Joe Yule Jr) (1920–) American born Brooklyn, New York; *A Midsummer Night's Dream* (1935), *Ah Wilderness* (1935), *A Family Affair* (1937), *Judge Hardy's Children* (1938), *Boys' Town* (1938), *Babes in Arms* (1939), *The Human Comedy* (1943), *National Velvet* (1944), *Summer Holiday* (1948), *The Bold and the Brave* (1956), *Breakfast at Tiffany's* (1961), *It's a Mad, Mad, Mad, Mad World* (1963), *Leave 'Em Laughing* (TV 1980), *Bill* (TV 1981), *Erik the Viking* (1989), *Home for Christmas* (TV 1990).

Rossellini, Isabella (1952–) Italian born Rome; *White Nights* (1985), *Blue Velvet* (1986), *Siesta* (1987), *Zelly and Me* (1988), *Cousins* (1989), *Wild at Heart* (1990).

Rourke, Mickey (1956–) American born Schenectady, New York; *Body Heat* (1981), *Rumble Fish* (1983), *$9\frac{1}{2}$ Weeks* (1985), *The Year of the Dragon* (1985), *Angel Heart* (1987), *A Prayer for the Dying* (1987), *Johnny Handsome* (1990), *Wild Orchid* (1990), *Harley Davidson and the Marlboro Man* (1991), *Desparate Hours* (1991).

Russell, Jane (1921–) American born Bemidji, Minnesota; *The Outlaw* (1943), *The Paleface* (1948), *Gentleman Prefer Blondes* (1953).

Russell, Kurt (1951–) American born Springfield, Massachusetts; *The Quest* (TV 1976), *Elvis* (TV 1979), *Escape from New York* (1981), *The Thing* (1982), *Silkwood* (1983), *Swing Shift* (1984), *Big Trouble in Little China* (1986), *Tequila Sunrise* (1988), *Tango and Cash* (1990), *Backdraft* (1991).

Rutherford, Dame Margaret (1892-1972) British born London; also stage; *Blithe Spirit* (1945), *The Happiest Days of Your Life* (1950), *The Importance of Being Earnest* (1952), *The Smallest Show on Earth* (1957), *Murder She Said* (1961), *The V.I.P.s* (1963), *Murder Most Foul* (1964), *Murder Ahoy* (1964).

Ryan, Meg (1962–) American born Fairfield, Connecticut; *Rich and Famous* (1981), *Top Gun* (1985), *Innerspace* (1987), *D.O.A.* (1988), *Promised Land* (1988), *The Presidio* (1988), *When Harry Met Sally ...* (1989), *Joe Versus the Volcano* (1990), *The Doors* (1991).

Ryan, Robert (1909-73) American born Chicago; *Gangway for Tomorrow* (1943), *Crossfire* (1947), *The Set-Up* (1949), *Clash by Night* (1952), *God's Little Acre* (1958), *Odds Against Tomorrow* (1959), *Billy Budd* (1962), *The Dirty Dozen* (1967), *The Wild Bunch* (1969).

Ryder, Winona (1971–) American born Winona, Michigan; *Beetlejuice* (1988), *1969* (1988), *Heathers* (1989), *Great Balls of Fire* (1989), *Mermaids* (1990).

Sabu (Sabu Dastagir) (1924-63) Indian born Karapur, Mysore, India; *Elephant Boy* (1937), *The Thief of Baghdad* (1940), *The Jungle Book* (1942), *The End of the River* (1947), *Black Narcissus* (1947).

Saint, Eva Marie (1924–) American born Newark, New Jersey; *On the Waterfront* (1954), *A Hatful of Rain* (1957), *North by Northwest* (1959), *Loving* (1970), *The Best Little Girl in the World* (TV 1982), *Fatal Vision* (TV 1984), *The Last Days of Patton* (TV 1986), *Moonlighting* (TV 1987).

Sanders, George (1906-73) British born St Petersburg, Russia; *Lancer Spy* (1937), *Rebecca* (1940), *The Saint* (1940-2), *The Moon and Sixpence* (1942), *The Picture of Dorian Gray* (1944), *Scandal in Paris* (1946), *The Ghost and Mrs Muir* (1947), *Forever Amber* (1947), *The Private Affairs of Bel Ami* (1947), *Lady Windermere's Fan* (1949), *All About Eve* (1950), *Village of the Damned* (1960), *A Shot in the Dark* (1964).

Sarandon, Susan (Susan Abigail Tomalin) (1946–) American born New York City; *The Front Page* (1974), *Dragonfly* (1977), *Atlantic City* (1981), *Tempest* (1982), *The Hunger* (1983), *The Witches of Eastwick* (1987), *Bull Durham* (1988), *A Dry White Season* (1989), *White Palace* (1991), *Thelma and Louise* (1991).

Savalas, Telly (Aristotle Savalas) (1925–) Greek/American born Garden City, New York; *Birdman of Alcatraz* (1982), *The Battle of the Bulge* (1985), *The Dirty Dozen* (1967), *On Her Majesty's Secret Service* (1969), *Horror Express* (1972), *Visions of Death* (1972), *Kojak* (TV 1973-7), *Escape to Athena* (1979), *Kojak* (TV 1989–).

FILM AND TV ACTORS (cont.)

Scheider, Roy (1932–   ) American born Orange, New Jersey; *Paper Lion* (1968), *French Connection* (1971), *Jaws* (1975), *Jaws 2* (1978), *All That Jazz* (1979), *Blue Thunder* (1982), *Still of the Night* (1982), *2010* (1984), *52 Pick Up* (1986), *Night Game* (1989).

Schwarzenegger, Arnold (1947–   ) American born Braz, Austria; *Stay Hungry* (1976), *Pumping Iron* (1977), *Conan the Barbarian* (1982), *Conan the Destroyer* (1984), *The Terminator* (1984), *Red Sonja* (1985), *Commando* (1985), *Raw Deal* (1986), *Predator* (1987), *The Running Man* (1987), *Red Heat* (1989), *Total Recall* (1990), *Kindergarten Cop* (1990), *T2 – Terminator 2: Judgement Day* (1991).

Scofield, (David) Paul (1922–   ) British born Hurstpierpoint, Sussex; also stage; *That Lady* (1955), *A Man for All Seasons* (1966).

Scott, George C (1927–   ) American born Wise, Virginia; *Anatomy of a Murder* (1959), *The Hustler* (1962), *The List of Adrian Messenger* (1963), *Dr Strangelove* (1963), *Patton* (1970), *The Hospital* (1972), *Fear on Trial* (TV 1976), *The Changeling* (1980), *Taps* (1981), *Oliver Twist* (1982), *Firestarter* (1984), *A Christmas Carol* (TV 1984), *The Last Days of Patton* (TV 1986), *The Exorcist III* (1990).

Segal, George (1934–   ) American born New York City; *King Rat* (1965), *Who's Afraid of Virginia Woolf?* (1966), *The Owl and the Pussycat* (1970), *The Last Married Couple in America* (1980), *Look Who's Talking* (1989).

Selleck, Tom (1945–   ) American born Detroit, Michigan; *Coma* (1977), *Magnum* (TV 1981-9), *High Road to China* (1983), *Lassiter* (1984), *Runaway* (1984), *Three Men and a Baby* (1988), *Three Men and a Little Lady* (1990), *Tokyo Diamond* (1991).

Sellers, Peter (1925-80) British born Southsea; *The Smallest Show on Earth* (1957), *The Ladykillers* (1959), *I'm Alright Jack* (1959), *Only Two Can Play* (1962), *Lolita* (1962), *Dr Strangelove* (1963), *The Pink Panther* (1963), *A Shot in the Dark* (1964), *Return of the Pink Panther* (1975), *The Pink Panther Strikes Again* (1976), *Revenge of the Pink Panther* (1978), *Being There* (1979).

Seymour, Jane (Joyce Frankenberg) (1951–   ) British born Hillingdon, Middlesex; *Live and Let Die* (1972), *Battle Star Galactica* (TV 1978), *East of Eden* (TV 1981), *Somewhere in Time* (1980), *The Scarlet Pimpernel* (TV 1982), *War and Remembrance* (TV 1987-9), *Matters of the Heart* (1991), *Angel of Death* (1991).

Sharif, Omar (Michael Shalhouz) (1932–   ) Egyptian born Alexandria; *Lawrence of Arabia* (1962), *Doctor Zhivago* (1965), *Green Ice* (1980).

Shatner, William (1931–   ) Canadian born Montreal, Quebec; *Star Trek* (TV 1966-8), *Horror at 37,000 Feet* (TV 1974), *Big Bad Mama* (1974), *Star Trek: The Motion Picture* (1979), *The Kidnapping of the President* (1980), *Star Trek 2: The Wrath of Khan* (1982), *T. J. Hooker* (TV 1982-6), *Star Trek 3: The Search for Spock* (1984), *Star Trek 4: The Voyage Home* (1987), *Star Trek V: The Final Frontier* (1989).

Shearer, Moira (Moira King) (1926–   ) British born Dunfermline, Fife; *The Red Shoes* (1948), *Tales of Hoffman* (1950), *The Man Who Loved Redheads* (1954), *Peeping Tom* (1959), *Black Tights* (1961).

Sheedy, Ally (1962–   ) American born New York City; *Wargames* (1983), *The Breakfast Club* (1985), *St. Elmo's Fire* (1986), *Short Circuit* (1986), *Heart of Dixie* (1990), *Betsy's Wedding* (1990).

Sheen, Charlie (Carlos Irwin Estevez) (1965–   ) American born Santa Monica, California; *Ferris Bueller's Day Off* (1986), *Wall Street* (1987), *Platoon* (1987), *Eight Men Out* (1988), *Major League* (1989), *The Rookie* (1990), *Catchfire* (1990), *Navy Seals* (1991).

Sheen, Martin (Ramon Estevez) (1940–   ) American born Dayton, Ohio; *Catch 22* (1970), *Badlands* (1973), *The Execution of Private Slovik* (TV 1974), *The Little Girl Who Lives Down the Lane* (1976), *Apocalypse Now* (1979), *Gandhi* (1982), *That Championship Season* (1982), *The Dead Zone* (1983), *Firestarter* (1984), *Wall Street* (1987), *Siesta* (1987), *Da* (1988), *Judgement in Berlin* (1988), *Stockade* (1990).

Shepard, Sam (Samuel Shepard Rogers) (1943–   ) American born Fort Sheridan, Illinois; *Frances* (1982), *The Right Stuff* (1983), *Country* (1984), *Crimes of the Heart* (1986), *Baby Boom* (1987).

Shepherd, Cybill (1950–   ) American born Memphis, Tennesee; *The Last Picture Show* (1971), *Taxi Driver* (1976), *The Lady Vanishes* (1979), *The Long Hot Summer* (TV 1985), *Moonlighting* (TV 1985-9), *Texasville* (1990), *Alice* (1991).

Shields, Brooke (1965–   ) American born New York City; *The Blue Lagoon* (1980), *Endless Love* (1981), *Sahara* (1982).

FILM AND TV ACTORS (cont.)

Signoret, Simone (Simon-Henriette Charlotte Kaminker) (1921-85) French born Wiesbaden, Germany; *La Ronde* (1950), *Casque d'Or* (1952), *Les Diaboliques* (1952), *Room at the Top* (1959), *Ship of Fools* (1965), *Le Chat* (1971), *Madame Rosa* (1973).

Sim, Alastair (1900-76) British born Edinburgh; *Inspector Hornleigh* (1939), *Green for Danger* (1946), *The Happiest Days of Your Life* (1950), *Scrooge* (1951), *Laughter in Paradise* (1951), *The Bells of St Trinians* (1954).

Simmons, Jean (1929–) British born London; *Great Expectations* (1946), *Black Narcissus* (1946), *Hamlet* (1948), *The Blue Lagoon* (1948), *The Big Country* (1958), *Elmer Gantry* (1960), *Spartacus* (1960), *The Grass is Greener* (1961), *The Thorn Birds* (TV 1982), *Going Undercover* (1988), *Great Expectations* (TV 1991).

Sinatra, Frank (Francis Albert Sinatra) (1915–) American born Hoboken, New Jersey; *Anchors Aweigh* (1945), *On the Town* (1949), *From Here to Eternity* (1953), *The Man With the Golden Gun* (1955), *Pal Joey* (1957), *The Manchurian Candidate* (1962), *The Detective* (1963).

Sinden, Donald (1923–) British born Plymouth, England; *Doctor in the House* (1954), *The National Health* (1973), *The Day of the Jackal* (1973), *The Island at the Top of the World* (1973), *Two's Company* (TV 1977-80), *Never the Twain* (TV 1983–).

Slater, Christian (1969–) American born New York City; *The Name of the Rose* (1986), *Tucker: The Man and His Dream* (1988), *Heathers* (1989), *Young Guns II* (1990), *Pump Up the Volume* (1990), *Prince of Thieves* (1991).

Smith, Sir C. Aubrey (Charles Aubrey Smith) (1863-1948) British born London; *Love Me Tonight* (1932), *Morning Glory* (1933), *Lives of a Bengal Lancer* (1935), *The Prisoner of Zenda* (1937), *The Four Feathers* (1939), *Rebecca* (1940), *And Then There Were None* (1945), *An Ideal Husband* (1947), *Little Women* (1949).

Smith, Maggie (1934–) British born Ilford, Essex; also stage; *The V.I.P.s* (1963), *The Pumpkin Eater* (1964), *The Prime of Miss Jean Brodie* (1969), *Travels with My Aunt* (1972), *California Suite* (1978), *A Private Function* (1984), *A Room With a View* (1985), *The Lonely Passion of Judith Hearne* (1987).

Spacek, Sissy (Mary Elizabeth Spacek) (1949–) American born Quitman, Texas; *Badlands* (1973), *Carrie* (1976), *Coal Miner's Daughter* (1980), *Missing* (1982), *The River* (1984), *Crimes of the Heart* (1986).

Spader, James American; *Pretty in Pink* (1986), *Mannequin* (1987), *Less Than Zero* (1987), *Baby Boom* (1987), *Jack's Back* (1988), *Sex, Lies and Videotape* (1989), *The Rachel Papers* (1989), *Bad Influence* (1990), *White Palace* (1991).

Stallone, Sylvester (1946–) American born New York City; *The Lords of Flatbush* (1973), *Rocky* (1976), *(part II–1979, III – 1982, IV – 1985, V – 1990)*, *Paradise Alley* (1978), *Victory* (1981), *Nighthawks* (1981), *First Blood* (1981), *Rambo* (1985), *Over the Top* (1987), *Rambo III* (1988), *Lock Up* (1989), *Tango and Cash* (1990), *Oscar* (1991).

Stamp, Terence (1939–) British born Stepney; *The Collector* (1965), *Far from the Madding Crowd* (1967), *Superman* (1978), *Superman II* (1981), *Company of Wolves* (1985), *Legal Eagles* (1986), *Wall Street* (1987), *The Sicilian* (1988), *Alien Nation* (1988).

Stanton, Harry Dean (1926–) American born Kentucky; *How the West Was Won* (1962), *Cool Hand Luke* (1967), *The Godfather (Part II–1974)*, *Alien* (1979), *The Rose* (1979), *Private Benjamin* (1980), *Young Doctors in Love* (1982), *Christine* (1983), *Repo Man* (1984), *Paris, Texas* (1984), *Pretty in Pink* (1986), *Mr. North* (1988), *Stars and Bars* (1988).

Stanwyck, Barbara (Ruby Shaw) (1907-90) American born Brooklyn, New York; *Broadway Nights* (1927), *Miracle Woman* (1931), *Night Nurse* (1931), *The Bitter Tea of General Yen* (1933), *Baby Face* (1933), *Annie Oakley* (1935), *Stella Dallas* (1937), *Union Pacific* (1939), *The Lady Eve* (1941), *Meet John Doe* (1941), *Ball of Fire* (1941), *Double Indemnity* (1944), *The Strange Love of Martha Ivers* (1946), *Sorry Wrong Number* (1948), *The Furies* (1950), *Executive Suite* (1954), *Walk on the Wild Side* (1962), *The Big Valley* (TV 1965-9), *The Thorn Birds* (TV 1983).

FILM AND TV ACTORS (cont.)

Steiger, Rod (Rodney Stephen Steiger) (1925–) American born Westhampton, New York; *On the Waterfront* (1954), *Oklahoma!* (1955), *The Court Martial of Billy Mitchell* (1955), *The Harder They Fall* (1956), *Al Capone* (1958), *The Pawnbroker* (1964), *Doctor Zhivago* (1965), *In the Heat of the Night* (1967), *A Fistful of Dynamite* (1971), *The Amityville Horror* (1979), *Hollywood Wives* (TV 1984), *American Gothic* (1988), *The January Man* (1988).

Stewart, James (Maitland) (1908–) American born Indiana, Pennsylvania; *Seventh Heaven* (1937), *You Can't Take It With You* (1938), *Mr Smith Goes to Washington* (1939), *Destry Rides Again* (1939), *The Shop around the Corner* (1940), *The Philadelphia Story* (1940), *It's a Wonderful Life* (1946), *Harvey* (1950), *Broken Arrow* (1950), *The Glen Miller Story* (1953), *Rear Window* (1954), *The Man from Laramie* (1955), *Vertigo* (1958), *Anatomy of a Murder* (1959), *Mr Hobbs Takes a Vacation* (1962), *Shenandoah* (1965), *North and South II* (TV 1986).

Stockwell, Dean (1935–) American born Hollywood, California; *The Green Years* (1946), *The Boy with Green Hair* (1948), *Kim* (1950), *Compulsion* (1959), *Sons and Lovers* (1959), *McCloud: Twas the Fight Before Christmas* (TV 1977), *Paris, Texas* (1984), *Dune* (1984), *The Legend of Billie Jean* (1985), *Blue Velvet* (1986), *Gardens of Stone* (1987), *Tucker: The Man and His Dream* (1988), *The Blue Iguana* (1988), *Married to the Mob* (1988), *Quantum Leap* (TV 1989–).

Streep, Meryl (Mary Louise Streep) (1949–) American born Summit, New Jersey; *Julia* (1977), *The Deer Hunter* (1978), *Kramer Vs Kramer* (1979), *Manhattan* (1979), *The French Lieutenant's Woman* (1981), *Sophie's Choice* (1982), *Still of the Night* (1982), *Silkwood* (1983), *Plenty* (1985), *Out of Africa* (1986), *Ironweed* (1987), *A Cry in the Dark* (1988), *Evil Angels* (1988), *She-Devil* (1989), *Postcards from the Edge* (1990).

Streisand, Barbra (Joan) (1942–) American born Brooklyn, New York; *Funny Girl* (1968), *Hello Dolly* (1969), *On a Clear Day You Can See Forever* (1970), *Whats Up, Doc?* (1972), *The Way We Were* (1973), *A Star is Born* (1976), *Yentl* (1983).

Sutherland, Donald (1934–) Canadian born St John, New Brunswick; *The Dirty Dozen* (1967), *M*A*S*H* (1970), *Klute* (1971), *Casanova* (1976), *1900* (1976), *The Eagle Has Landed* (1977), *Animal House* (1978), *Invasion of the Body Snatchers* (1978), *Ordinary People* (1980), *Apprentice to Murder* (1988), *Lock Up* (1989), *A Dry White Season* (1989), *Backdraft* (1991).

Sutherland, Kiefer (1967–) American born Los Angeles; *Bright Lights, Big City* (1985), *Stand By Me* (1987), *The Lost Boys* (1987), *The Killing Time* (1987), *1969* (1988), *Promised Land* (1988), *Young Guns* (1988), *Renegades* (1989), *Chicago Joe and the Showgirl* (1989), *Flatliners* (1990), *Young Guns 2* (1990), *Article 99* (1991).

Suzman, Janet (1939–) S African born Johannesburg; also stage; *Nicholas and Alexandra* (1972), *Voyage of the Damned* (1976), *The Draughtsman's Contract* (1982), *Mountbatten* (TV 1985), *A Dry White Season* (1989), *Nuns on the Run* (1990).

Swanson, Gloria (Gloria May Josephine Svensson) (1897-1983) American born Chicago; *Male and Female* (1919), *The Affairs of Anatol* (1921), *Manhandled* (1924), *Sadie Thompson* (1928), *Queen Kelly* (1928), *The Trespasser* (1929), *Sunset Boulevard* (1950).

Swayze, Patrick (1954–) American born Houston, Texas; *The Outsiders* (1983), *Red Dawn* (1984), *Young Blood* (1985), *North and South* (TV 1986), *North and South II* (TV 1986), *Dirty Dancing* (1987), *Tiger Warsaw* (1988), *Road House* (1989), *Next of Kin* (1989), *Ghost* (1990).

Tandy, Jessica (1909–) British born London; *Dragonwyck* (1946), *The Birds* (1963), *Honky Tonk Freeway* (1981), *The World According to Garp* (1982), *Still of the Night* (1982), *The Bostonians* (1984), *Cocoon* (1985), *The House on Carroll Street* (1988), *Cocoon: The Return* (1988), *Driving Miss Daisy* (1989).

Taylor, Elizabeth (Rosemond) (1932–) British born London; *National Velvet* (1944), *Little Women* (1949), *The Father of the Bride* (1950), *A Place in the Sun* (1951), *Giant* (1956), *Raintree Country* (1957), *Cat on a Hot Tin Roof* (1958), *Butterfield 8* (1960), *Cleopatra* (1962), *Who's Afraid of Virginia Woolf?* (1966), *Reflections in a Golden Eye* (1967), *The Taming of the Shrew* (1967), *Suddenly Last Summer* (1968), *A Little Night Music* (1977), *The Mirror Crack'd* (1981), *Malice in Wonderland* (TV 1985), *Poker Alice* (TV 1986).

FILM AND TV ACTORS (cont.)

Taylor, Robert (Spangler Arlington Brugh) (1911-69) American born Filley, Nebraska; *Magnificent Obsession* (1935), *Camille* (1936), *Three Comrades* (1938), *Yank at Oxford* (1938), *Waterloo Bridge* (1940), *Bataan* (1943), *Song of Russia* (1943), *Quo Vadis* (1951), *Ivanhoe* (1952), *Knights of the Round Table* (1953), *Party Girl* (1958), *The Detectives* (TV 1959-61), *The Miracle of the White Stallions* (1962).

Temple, Shirley (1927–   ) American born Santa Monica, California; *Little Miss Marker* (1934), *Curly Top* (1935), *Dimples* (1936), *Heidi* (1937), *The Little Princess* (1939).

Terry-Thomas (Thomas Terry Hoar Stevens) (1911-90) British born Finchley, London; *Private's Progress* (1956), *Carleton Browne of the FO* (1958), *The Naked Truth* (1958), *I'm All Right, Jack* (1959), *It's a Mad, Mad, Mad, Mad World* (1963), *How to Murder Your Wife* (1965), *Those Magnificent Men in Their Flying Machines* (1965), *Don't Look Now* (1968).

Tierney, Gene (Eliza) (1920–   ) American born Brooklyn, New York; *The Return of Frank James* (1940), *Tobacco Road* (1941), *Belle Star* (1941), *Heaven Can Wait* (1943), *Laura* (1944), *Leave Her to Heaven* (1945), *The Ghost and Mrs. Muir* (1947), *Whirlpool* (1949), *Toys in the Attic* (1963), *The Pleasure Seekers* (1964).

Tomlin, Lily (1939–   ) American born Detroit, Michigan; *Nine to Five* (1980), *The Incredible Shrinking Woman* (1981), *Lily Tomlin, All of Me* (1984), *Big Business* (1988).

Tracy, Spencer (1900-67) American born Milwaukee, Wisconsin; *Twenty Thousand Years in Sing Sing* (1932), *The Power and the Glory* (1933), *A Man's Castle* (1933), *Fury* (1936), *San Francisco* (1936), *Libeled Lady* (1936), *Captains Courageous* (1937), *Boy's Town* (1938), *Stanley and Livingstone* (1939), *Northwest Passage* (1939), *Edison the Man* (1940), *Dr Jekyll and Mr Hyde* (1941), *Woman of the Year* (1942), *The Seventh Cross* (1944), *State of the Union* (1948), *Adam's Rib* (1949), *Father of the Bride* (1950), *Bad Day at Black Rock* (1955), *The Last Hurrah* (1958), *Inherit the Wind* (1960), *Judgment at Nuremberg* (1961), *It's a Mad, Mad, Mad, Mad World* (1963), *Guess Who's Coming to Dinner* (1967).

Travolta, John (1954   ) American born Englewood, New Jersey; *Welcome Back Kotter* (TV 1975-78), *Carrie* (1976), *Saturday Night Fever* (1977), *Grease* (1978), *Blow Out* (1981), *Staying Alive* (1983), *Two of a Kind* (1984), *Perfect* (1985), *Look Who's Talking* (1989), *Look Who's Talking Too* (1991), *Chains of Gold* (1991).

Turner, Kathleen (1954–   ) American born Springfield, Missouri; *The Doctors* (TV 1977-8), *Body Heat* (1981), *The Man With Two Brains* (1983), *Romancing the Stone* (1984), *Crimes of Passion* (1984), *Jewel of the Nile* (1985), *Prizzi's Honour* (1985), *Peggy Sue Got Married* (1986), *Switching Channels* (1988), *Julia and Julia* (1988), *The Accidental Tourist* (1988), *War of the Roses* (1989), *Warshawski* (1991).

Turner, Lana (Julia Jean Mildred Frances Turner) (1921–   ) American born Wallace, Indiana; *Dr Jekyll and Mr Hyde* (1940), *Somewhere I'll Find You* (1942), *The Three Musketeers* (1948), *Peyton Place* (1957).

Tushingham, Rita (1940–   ) British born Liverpool; *A Taste of Honey* (1961), *Girl with Green Eyes* (1964), *The Knack* (1965), *Dr Zhivago* (1965), *Judgment in Stone* (1986).

Ustinov, Peter Alexander (1921–   ) British born London; *Private Angelo* (1949), *Hotel Sahara* (1951), *Quo Vadis* (1951), *Beau Brummell* (1954), *The Sundowners* (1960), *Spartacus* (1960), *Romanoff and Juliet* (1961), *Topkapi* (1964), *Logan's Run* (1976), *Death on the Nile* (1978), *Evil Under the Sun* (1982), *Appointment With Death* (1988).

Valentino, Rudolph (Rodolpho Alphonso Guglielmi di Valentina d'Antonguolla) (1895-1926) Italian/US born Castellaneta; *The Four Horsemen of the Apocalypse* (1921), *The Sheikh* (1921), *Blood and Sand* (1922), *The Young Rajah* (1922), *Monsieur Beaucaire* (1924), *The Eagle* (1925), *The Son of the Sheikh* (1926).

Van Cleef, Lee (1925-89) American born Somerville, New Jersey; *High Noon* (1952), *For a Few Dollars More* (1967), *The Good, the Bad, and the Ugly* (1967), *Return of Sabata* (1971), *The Magnificent Seven Ride* (1972), *Escape from New York* (1981), *Code name: Wildgeese II* (1986).

Van Dyke, Dick (1925–   ) American born West Plains, Missouri; *The Dick Van Dyke Show* (TV 1961-6), *Mary Poppins* (1964), *Chitty Chitty Bang Bang* (1968), *The Cosmic* (1969), *Dropout Father* (TV 1982).

FILM AND TV ACTORS (cont.)

Vincent, Jan-Michael (1944–) American born Denver, Colorado; *The Mechanic* (1972), *The World's Greatest Athlete* (1973), *Bite the Bullet* (1974), *Hooper* (1978), *Hard Country* (1981), *Airwolf* (TV 1982-6),*The Winds of War* (TV 1983).

Von Sydow, Max (Carl Adolf) (1929–) Swedish born Lund; *The Seventh Seal* (1956), *The Face* (1959), *The Greatest Story Ever Told* (1965), *Hawaii* (1966), *Through a Glass Darkly* (1966), *Hour of the Wolf* (1967), *The Shame* (1968), *The Emigrants* (1972), *The Exorcist* (1973), *Exorcist II: The Heretic* (1977), *Flash Gordon* (1980), *Never Say Never Again* (1983), *Hannah and Her Sisters* (1986), *Pelle, the Conquerer* (1988), *Awakenings* (1990).

Wagner, Robert (John Jr) (1930–) American born Detroit, Michigan; *The Silver Whip* (1953), *Prince Valiant* (1954), *A Kiss Before Dying* (1956), *The True Story of Jesse James* (1957), *All the Fine Young Cannibals* (1959), *The Condemned of Altona* (1963), *The Pink Panther* (1963), *It Takes a Thief* (TV 1965-9), *Colditz* (TV 1972-3), *The Towering Inferno* (1974), *Switch* (TV 1975-7), *Hart to Hart* (TV 1979-84).

Walken, Christopher (1943–) American born Astoria, New York; *The Anderson Tapes* (1970), *Annie Hall* (1977), *The Deer Hunter* (1978), *The Dogs of War* (1981), *Pennies from Heaven* (1981), *The Dead Zone* (1983), *Brainstorm* (1983), *A View to a Kill* (1984), *At Close Range* (1986), *The Milagro Beanfield War* (1987), *Biloxi Blues* (1988), *Puss in Boots* (1988), *The Comfort of Strangers* (1990).

Walters, Julie (1950–) British born Birmingham; *Educating Rita* (1983), *She'll Be Wearing Pink Pajamas* (1984), *Car Trouble* (1986), *Prick Up Your Ears* (1987), *Personal Services* (1987), *Buster* (1987), *Killing Dad* (1989).

Wanamaker, Sam (1919–) American born Chicago; *Those Magnificent Men in Their Flying Machines* (1965), *The Spy Who Came in from the Cold* (1965), *Voyage of the Damned* (1976), *Death on the Nile* (1978), *Private Benjamin* (1980), *Raw Deal* (1986), *Superman IV* (1986), *Baby Boom* (1987).

Ward, Rachel (1957–) British born London; *Sharky's Machine* (1981), *Dead Men Don't Wear Plaid* (1982), *The Thorn Birds* (TV 1983), *The Good Wife* (1986), *Hotel Colonial* (1987), *How to Get Ahead in Advertising* (1989), *After Dark My Sweet* (1990).

Warner, David (1941–) British born Manchester; *Morgan* (1966), *The Bofors Gun* (1968), *The Engagement* (1970), *The French Lieutenant's Woman* (1971), *The Omen* (1976), *Holocaust* (TV 1978), *The 39 Steps* (1978), *Time Bandits* (1981), *Tron* (1982), *The Man with Two Brains* (1983), *Company of Wolves* (1984), *Mr. North* (1988), *Hanna's War* (1988), *The Secret Life of Ian Fleming* (1990).

Washington, Denzel (1954–) American born Mt. Vernon, New York; *St Elsewhere* (1982-9), *Cry Freedom* (1987), *Queen and Country* (1988), *Glory* (1989), *Mo' Better Blues* (1990), *Ricochet* (1991).

Waterman, Dennis (1948–) British born London; *Up the Junction* (1967), *The Sweeney* (TV 1974-8), *The Sweeney* (1977), *Minder* (TV 1979-86), *The Life and Loves of a She-Devil* (TV 1986).

Wayne, John (Marion Michael Morrison) (1907-79) American born Winterset, Iowa; *The Big Trail* (1930), *Stagecoach* (1939), *The Long Voyage Home* (1940), *Red River* (1948), *She Wore a Yellow Ribbon* (1949), *Sands of Iwo Jima* (1949), *The Quiet Man* (1952), *The High and the Mighty* (1954), *The Searchers* (1956), *Rio Bravo* (1959), *The Alamo* (1960), *True Grit* (1969), *The Shootist* (1976).

Weaver, Sigourney (Susan Weaver) (1949–) American born New York City; *Alien* (1979), *The Janitor* (1981), *The Year of Living Dangerously* (1982), *Ghostbusters* (1984), *Aliens* (1986), *Gorillas in the Mist* (1988), *Working Girl* (1988), *Ghostbusters II* (1989).

Welch, Raquel (Raquel Tejada) (1940–) American born Chicago; *Fantastic Voyage* (1966), *One Million Years B.C.* (1967), *Myra Breckenridge* (1970), *The Three Musketeers* (1974), *The Four Musketeers* (1975).

Welles, Orson (1915-85) American born Kenosha, Wisconsin; *Citizen Kane* (1941), *Journey into Fear* (1942), *The Stranger* (1945), *The Lady from Shanghai* (1947), *The Third Man* (1949), *The Trial* (1962), *Touch of Evil* (1965), *A Man For All Seasons* (1966), *Casino Royale* (1967), *Voyage of the Damned* (1976), *History of the World Part One* (1981).

West, Mae (1892-1980) American born Brooklyn, New York; *She Done Him Wrong* (1933), *I'm No Angel* (1933), *My Little Chickadee* (1939), *Myra Breckinridge* (1970).

FILM AND TV ACTORS (cont.)

Widmark, Richard (1914–) American born Sunrise, Minnesota; *Kiss of Death* (1947), *Night and the City* (1950), *How the West Was Won* (1963), *The Bedford Incident* (1965), *Madigan* (1968), *Madigan* (TV 1972), *Murder on the Orient Express* (1974), *Who Dares Wins* (1982), *Hanky Panky* (1982), *Against all Odds* (1983).

Wilder, Gene (Jerome Silberman) (1935–) American born Milwaukee, Wisconsin; *Bonnie and Clyde* (1967), *The Producers* (1967), *Willy Wonka and the Chocolate Factory* (1971), *Blazing Saddles* (1974), *Young Frankenstein* (1974), *The Frisco Kid* (1979), *Stir Crazy* (1982), *Hanky Panky* (1982), *The Woman in Red* (1984), *Haunted Honeymoon* (1986), *See No Evil Hear No Evil* (1989), *Funny About Love* (1991).

Williams, Kenneth (1926-88) British born London; *Carry on Sergeant* (1958), *Carry on Dick* (1974) etc, *Follow that Camel* (1968).

Williams, Robin (1952–) American born Chicago; *Mork and Mindy* (TV 1978-82), *Popeye* (1980), *The World According to Garp* (1982), *Good Morning Vietnam* (1987), *Dead Poets' Society* (1989), *Cadillac Man* (1990), *Awakenings* (1990).

Williams, Treat (Richard Williams) (1951–) American born Rowayton, Connecticut; *The Eagle Has Landed* (1977), *Hair* (1977), *1941* (1979), *Once Upon a Time in America* (1984), *Dempsey* (TV 1985), *Smooth Talk* (1985), *A Street Car Named Desire* (1986), *The Men's Club* (1986), *Dead Heat* (1988), *Heart of Dixie* (1990).

Williamson, Nicol (1938–) British born Hamilton, Scotland; *Inadmissable Evidence* (1967), *The Bofors Gun* (1968), *The Reckoning* (1969), *Excalibur* (1981), *Sakharov* (TV 1985), *Return to Oz* (1985), *Black Widow* (1986), *The Exorcist III* (1990).

Willis, Bruce (1955–) American born Penns Grove, New Jersey; *Moonlighting* (TV 1985 9), *Blind Date* (1987), *Die Hard* (1988), *Sunset* (1988), *In Country* (1989), *Die Hard 2: Die Harder* (1990), *Bonfire of the Vanities* (1991), *Hudson Hawk* (1991), *Billy Bathgate* (1991).

Winger, Debra (1955–) American born Columbus, Ohio; *Urban Cowboy* (1980), *Cannery Row* (1981), *An Officer and a Gentleman* (1982), *Terms of Endearment* (1983), *Legal Eagles* (1985), *Black Widow* (1987), *Made in Heaven* (1987), *Betrayed* (1988), *The Sheltering Sky* (1990).

Winters, Shelley (Shirley Schrift) (1922–) American born St. Louis, Missouri; *A Double Life* (1948), *The Big Knife* (1955), *The Night of the Hunter* (1955), *The Diary of Anne Frank* (1959), *Lolita* (1962), *A Patch of Blue* (1965), *Alfie* (1966), *The Poseidon Adventure* (1972), *S.O.B.* (1981), *Purple People Eater* (1988).

Wisdom, Norman (1918–) British born London; *Trouble in Store* (1955), *Man of the Moment* (1955), *Just My Luck* (1958), *There was a Crooked Man* (1960), *On the Beat* (1962), *A Stitch in Time* (1963), *Sandwich Man* (1900), *The Night They Raided Minsky's* (1968), *What's Good for the Goose* (1969).

Wood, Natalie (Natasha Gurdin) (1938-81) American born San Francisco, California; *Miracle on 34th Street* (1947), *The Ghost and Mrs. Muir* (1947), *Rebel Without a Cause* (1955), *The Searchers* (1956), *Marjorie Morningstar* (1958), *All The Fine Young Cannibals* (1959), *Splendour in the Grass* (1961), *Westside Story* (1961), *Love with the Proper Stranger* (1964), *The Great Race* (1965), *This Property is Condemned* (1966), *Bob and Carol and Ted and Alice* (1969), *From Here to Eternity* (TV 1979), *Meteor* (1979), *Brainstorm* (1983).

York, Michael (1942–) British born Fulmer; *Accident* (1967), *Romeo and Juliet* (1968), *Cabaret* (1972), *Lost Horizon* (1973), *The Three Musketeers* (1973), *The Four Musketeers* (1974), *Jesus of Nazareth* (TV 1977), *The Island of Dr Moreau* (1977), *The White Lions* (1980), *Space* (TV 1985), *The Far Country* (TV 1986), *Sword of Gideon* (TV 1986), *Return of the Musketeers* (1989).

DIRECTORS

Aldrich, Robert (1918–83) American, born Cranston, Rhode Island; *Apache* (1954), *Vera Cruz* (1954), *Kiss Me Deadly* (1955), *Attack!* (1957), *What Ever Happened to Baby Jane?* (1962), *The Dirty Dozen* (1967).

Allen, Woody (Allen Stewart Konigsberg) (1935–) American, born Brooklyn, New York; *What's Up Tiger Lily* (1966), *Bananas* (1971), *Everything You Wanted to Know About Sex, But Were Afraid to Ask* (1972), *Play it Again, Sam* (1972), *Sleeper* (1973), *Love and Death* (1975), *Annie Hall* (1977), *Interiors* (1978), *Manhattan* (1979), *Stardust Memories* (1980), *A Midsummer Night's Sex Comedy* (1982), *Broadway Danny Rose* (1984), *The Purple Rose of Cairo* (1985), *Hannah and Her Sisters* (1986), *Radio Days* (1987), *Crimes and Misdemeanors* (1990), *Alice* (1991).

Almódovar, Pedro (1951–) Spanish, born Calzada de Calatrava; *Dark Habits* (1983), *Law of Desire* (1987), *Women on the Verge of a Nervous Breakdown* (1988), *Tie Me Up! Tie Me Down!* (1990).

Altman, Robert (1925–) American, born Kansas City, Missouri; *The James Dean Story* (1957), *M*A*S*H* (1970), *McCabe and Mrs Miller* (1971), *The Long Goodbye* (1973), *Nashville* (1975), *A Wedding* (1978), *Popeye* (1980), *Come Back to the 5 & Dime Jimmy Dean Jimmy Dean* (1982), *Streamers* (1983), *Fool for Love* (1985), *Aria* (1987), *Vincent and Theo* (1990).

Asquith, Anthony (1902–68) British, born London; *Shooting Stars* (1928), *Underground* (1930), *Pygmalion* (1937), *French without Tears* (1939), *Quiet Wedding* (1940), *The Demi-Paradise* (1943), *Fanny by Gaslight* (1944), *The Way to the Stars* (1945), *The Browning Version* (1950), *The Importance of Being Earnest* (1952), *Orders to Kill* (1958), *The VIPs* (1963).

Attenborough, Sir Richard Samuel (1923–) British, born Cambridge; *Oh! What a Lovely War* (1968), *A Bridge Too Far* (1977), *Gandhi* (1982), *A Chorus Line* (1985), *Cry Freedom* (1987).

Badham, John (1939–) American, born Luton, England; *The Law* (TV 1974), *Saturday Night Fever* (1977), *Whose Life is it Anyway?* (1981), *Blue Thunder* (1982), *War Games* (1983), *American, Flyers* (1984), *Short Circuit* (1986), *Stakeout* (1987), *Bird on a Wire* (1989).

Beatty, Warren (Henry Warren Beaty) (1937–) American, born Richmond, Virginia; *Heaven Can Wait* (1978), *Reds* (1981), *Dick Tracy* (1990).

Bergman, (Ernst) Ingmar (1918–) Swedish, born Uppsala; *Crisis* (1945), *Prison* (1948), *Sawdust and Tinsel* (1953), *The Face* (1955), *Smiles of a Summer Night* (1955), *The Seventh Seal* (1957), *Wild Strawberries* (1957), *The Virgin Spring* (1959), *Through a Glass Darkly* (1961), *The Silence* (1963), *Shame* (1968), *Cries and Whispers* (1972), *The Magic Flute* (1974), *Autumn Sonata* (1978), *Fanny and Alexander* (1983).

Bertolucci, Bernardo (1940–) Italian, born Parma; *Love and Anger* (1969), *The Conformist* (1970), *Last Tango in Paris* (1972), *1900* (1976), *The Last Emperor* (1987), *The Sheltering Sky* (1990).

Besson, Luc (1959–) French, born Paris; *The Last Battle* (1983), *Subway* (1985), *The Big Blue* (1988), *Nikita* (1990).

Bogdanovich, Peter (1939–) American, born Kingston, New York; *Targets* (1967), *The Last Picture Show* (1971), *Paper Moon* (1973), *What's Up, Doc?* (1972), *Nickelodeon* (1976), *Mask* (1985), *Illegally Yours* (1987), *Texasville* (1990).

Boorman, John (1933–) English, born Epsom, Surrey; *Point Blank* (1967), *Hell in the Pacific* (1969), *Deliverance* (1972), *Zardoz* (1974), *Exorcist II: The Heretic* (1977), *Excalibur* (1981), *The Emerald Forest* (1984), *Hope and Glory* (1987).

Brook, Sir Peter (Stephen Paul) (1925–) British, born London; theatre, opera, and film director; *Lord of the Flies* (1963), *King Lear* (1971), *Carmen* (1983).

Brooks, Mel (Melvin Kaminski) (1926–) American, born Brooklynm, New York; *The Producers* (1966), *Blazing Saddles* (1974), *Young Frankenstein* (1974), *High Anxiety* (1977), *History of the World, Part 1* (1981), *Space Balls* (1987)

Buñuel, Luis (1900–83) Spanish, born Calanda; *Un Chien Andalou* (with Salvador Dali) (1928), *L'Age d'Or* (1930), *Los Olvidados* (1950), *Robinson Crusoe* (1952), *El* (1953), *Nazarin* (1958), *Viridiana* (1961), *The Exterminating Angel* (1962), *Belle de Jour* (1967), *The Discreet Charm of the Bourgeoisie* (1972), *The Phantom of the Liberty* (1974), *That Obscure Object of Desire* (1977).

Capra, Frank (1897–91) Italian/American, born Bisacquino, Sicily; *Platinum Blonde* (1932), *American Madness* (1932), *Lady for a Day* (1933),

DIRECTORS (cont.)

It Happened One Night (1934), *Mr Deeds Goes to Town* (1936), *Lost Horizon* (1937), *You Can't Take It With You* (1938), *Mr Smith Goes to Washington* (1939), *Meet John Doe* (1941), *Arsenic and Old Lace* (1944), *It's a Wonderful Life* (1946).

Carpenter, John (1948–) American, born Carthage, New York; *Dark Star* (1974), *Assault on Precinct 13* (1976), *Halloween* (1978), *Elvis – the Movie* (TV 1979), *The Fog* (1979), *Escape from New York* (1981), *The Thing* (1982), *Christine* (1983), *Starman* (1984), *Big Trouble in Little China* (1986), *Prince of Darkness* (1987).

Clair, René (originally **René Lucien Chomette**) (1898–1981) French, born Paris; *An Italian Straw Hat* (1927), *Sous Les Toits de Paris* (1929), *Le Million* (1931), *A Nous la liberté* (1931), *I Married a Witch* (1942), *It Happened Tomorrow* (1944), *And Then There Were None* (1945), *Les Belles de Nuit* (1952), *Porte des Lila* (1956), *Tout l'or du Monde* (1961).

Cocteau, Jean (1889–1963) French, born Maisons-Lafitte; *Le Sang d'un pòete* (1930), *La Belle et La Bête* (1946), *Orphée* (1950), *Le Testament d'Orphée* (1959).

Coppola, Francis Ford (1939–) American, born Detroit, Michigan; *The Godfather* (1972), (*Part II* – 1974), (*Part III* – 1991), *Apocalypse Now* (1979), *One from the Heart* (1982), *The Outsiders* (1983), *Rumble Fish* (1983), *The Cotton Club* (1984), *Peggy Sue Got Married* (1987), *Gardens of Stone* (1987), *Tucker: The Man and His Dream* (1988).

Corman, Roger (1926–) American, born Detroit, Michigan; *Not of this Earth* (1957), *Bucket of Blood* (1960), *Fall of the House of Usher* (1960), *Little Shop of Horrors* (1960), *The Intruder* (1961), *The Raven* (1963), *X–The Man with X-ray Eyes* (1963), *The Masque of the Red Death* (1964), *The Tomb of Ligeia* (1965), *Frankenstein Unbound* (1990).

Costner, Kevin (1955–) American, born Los Angeles; *Dances with Wolves* (1990).

Cronenberg, David (1943–) Canadian, born Toronto; *Shivers* (1976), *Rabid* (1977), *The Brood* (1978), *Scanners* (1980), *Videodrome* (1982), *The Dead Zone* (1983), *The Fly* (1985), *Dead Ringers* (1988).

Curtiz, Michael (Mihály Kertész) (1888–1962) American/Hungarian, born Budapest, Hungary; *Noah's Ark* (1929), *Mammy* (1930), *Doctor X* (1932), *The Mystery of the Wax Museum* (1933),

British Agent (1934), *Black Fury* (1935), *Captain Blood* (1935), *Charge of the Light Brigade* (1936), *The Adventures of Robin Hood* (1938), *Angels with Dirty Faces* (1938), *The Sea Hawk* (1940), *The Sea Wolf* (1941), *Yankee Doodle Dandy* (1942), *Casablanca* (1943), *Mildred Pierce* (1945), *White Christmas* (1954), *We're No Angels* (1955), *King Creole* (1958).

Dante, Joe (1946–) American, born Morristown, New Jersey; *Piranha* (1978), *The Howling*, *Gremlins* (1984), *Explorers* (1985), *Innerspace* (1987), *The 'Burbs* (1989), *Amazon Women on the Moon*, *Gremlins 2: The New Batch* (1990).

de Mille, Cecil B(lount) (1881–1959) American, born Ashfield, Massachusetts; *Male and Female* (1919), *King of Kings* (1927), *The Ten Commandments* (1923 & 1956), *The Greatest Show on Earth* (1952).

de Palma, Brian (1940–) American, born Newark, New Jersey; *Greetings* (1968), *Carrie* (1976), *The Fury* (1978), *Dressed to Kill* (1980), *Blow Out* (1981), *Scarface* (1983), *Body Double* (1984), *The Untouchables* (1987), *Casualties of War* (1989).

Demme, Jonathan (1944–) American, born Long Island, New York; *Citizen Band* (1977), *Swing Shift* (1984), *Something Wild* (1987), *Swimming to Cambodia* (1987), *Married to the Mob* (1988), *The Silence of the Lambs* (1991).

Donner, Richard (c.1939–) American; *The Omen* (1976), *Superman* (1978), *Inside Moves* (1980), *The Final Conflict* (1981), *The Toy* (1982), *Ladyhawke* (1984), *The Goonies* (1985), *Lethal Weapon* (1987), *Scrooged* (1988), *Lethal Weapon 2* (1989).

Eisenstein, Sergei Mikhailovich (1898–1948) Soviet, born Riga; *Stride* (1924), *Battleship Potemkin* (1925), *Alexander Nevsky* (1938), *Ten Days That Shook The World* (1928), *The Magic Seed* (1941), *Ivan the Terrible* (1942–6).

Fassbinder, Rainer Werner (1946–82) German, born Bad Wörishofen; *Warnung von einer heiligen Nutte* (1971), *Satan's Brew* (1976).

Fellini, Federico (1920–) Italian, born Rimini; *I Vitelloni* (1953), *La Strada* (1954), *La Dolce Vita* (1960), *8½* (1963), *Satyricon* (1969), *Fellini's Rome* (1972), *Casanova* (1976), *Orchestra Rehearsal* (1979), *City of Women* (1981), *The Ship Sails On* (1983), *Ginger and Fred* (1986).

DIRECTORS (cont.)

Fleming, Victor (1883–1949) American, born Pasadena, California; *Mantrap* (1926), *The Virginian* (1929), *The Wet Parade* (1932), *Red Dust* (1932), *Treasure Island* (1934), *Test Pilot* (1938), *Gone with the Wind* (1939), *The Wizard of Oz* (1939), *Dr Jekyll and Mr Hyde* (1941), *A Guy Named Joe* (1943).

Friedkin, William (1939–) American, born Chicago; *The French Connection* (1971), *The Exorcist* (1973), *The Guardian* (1990).

Gilliam, Terry (1940–) American, born Minneapolis, Minnesota; *Jabberwocky* (1976), *Time Bandits* (1981), *Brazil* (1985), *The Adventures of Baron Munchausen* (1988).

Godard, Jean-Luc (1930–) French, born Paris; *A Bout de Souffle* (1960), *Alphaville* (1965), *Le Plus Vieux Métier du Monde* (1967).

Griffith, D(avid) W(ark) (1875–1948) American, born La Grange, Kentucky; *Judith of Bethulia* (1913), *The Birth of a Nation* (1915), *Intolerance* (1916), *Hearts of the World* (1918), *Broken Blossoms* (1919), *Orphans of the Storm* (1922).

Hall, Sir Peter (Reginald Frederick) (1930–) British, born Bury St Edmunds, Suffolk; theatre and film director; *Work is a Four Letter Word* (1968), *Perfect Friday* (1971), *Akenfield* (1974).

Hawks, Howard Winchester (1896–1977) American, born Goshen, Indiana; *The Dawn Patrol* (1930), *Scarface* (1932), *Twentieth Century* (1934), *Barbary Coast* (1935), *Bringing Up Baby* (1938), *His Girl Friday* (1940), *To Have and Have Not* (1944), *The Big Sleep* (1946), *Red River* (1948), *Gentleman Prefer Blondes* (1953), *Rio Bravo* (1959).

Hill, George Roy (1922–) American, born Minneapolis, Minnesota; *The World of Henry Orient* (1964), *Thoroughly Modern Millie* (1967), *Butch Cassidy and the Sundance Kid* (1969), *Slaughterhouse 5* (1972), *The Sting* (1973), *The World According to Garp* (1982).

Hitchcock, Sir Alfred Joseph (1899–1980) British, born Leytonstone, London; *The Lodger* (1926), *Blackmail* (1929), *Murder* (1930), *The Thirty-Nine Steps* (1935), *The Lady Vanishes* (1938), *Rebecca* (1940), *Lifeboat* (1944), *Spellbound* (1945), *Notorious* (1946), *The Paradine Case* (1947), *Strangers on a Train* (1951), *Dial M for Murder* (1954), *Rear Window* (1954), *To Catch a Thief* (1955), *Vertigo* (1958), *North by Northwest* (1959), *Psycho* (1960), *The Birds* (1963), *Marnie* (1964), *Frenzy* (1972); *Alfred Hitchcock Presents* (TV 1955–61).

Huston, John Marcellus (1906–87) Irish/American, born Nevada, Missouri; *Murders in the Rue Morgue* (1932), *Juarez* (1939), *High Sierra* (1941), *The Maltese Falcon* (1941), *Key Largo* (1948), *The Treasure of the Sierra Madre* (1948), *The Asphalt Jungle* (1950), *The African Queen* (1951), *Moulin Rouge* (1952), *The Misfits* (1960), *Freud* (1962), *Night of the Iguana* (1964), *Casino Royale* (1967), *Fat City* (1972), *The Man Who Would Be King* (1975), *Annie* (1982), *Prizzi's Honour* (1985), *The Dead* (1987).

Ivory, James Francis (1928–) American, born Berkeley, California; *Shakespeare Wallah* (1965), *Heat and Dust* (1982), *The Bostonians* (1984), *A Room with a View* (1985), *Maurice* (1987), *Mr and Mrs Bridge* (1990).

Jarman, (Michael) Derek (1942–) British, born Northwood, Middlesex; *Sebastiane* (1976), *Jubilee* (1977), *The Tempest* (1979), *Caravaggio* (1985), *The Last of England* (1987), *The Garden* (1990).

Kasdan, Lawrence (1949–) American, born Miami Beach, Florida; *Body Heat* (1981), *The Big Chill* (1983), *Silverado* (1985), *The Accidental Tourist* (1989), *Love You to Death* (1990).

Kaufman, Philip (1936–) American, born Chicago, Illinois; *Invasion of the Body Snatchers* (1978), *The Wanderers* (1979), *The Right Stuff* (1983), *The Unbearable Lightness of Being* (1988), *Henry and June* (1990).

Kazan, Elia (originally **Elia Kazanjoglou**) (1909–) American, born Istanbul, Turkey; *Boomerang* (1947), *Gentleman's Agreement* (1947), *Pink* (1949), *A Streetcar Named Desire* (1951), *Viva Zapata* (1952), *On the Waterfront* (1954), *East of Eden* (1955), *Baby Doll* (1956), *A Face in the Crowd* (1957), *Splendour in the Grass* (1962), *America, America* (1963), *The Arrangement* (1969), *The Visitors* (1972), *The Last Tycoon* (1976).

Kubrick, Stanley (1928–) American, born The Bronx, New York; *The Killing* (1956), *Paths of Glory* (1957), *Spartacus* (1960/91), *Lolita* (1962), *Dr Strangelove* (1964), *2001: A Space Odyssey* (1968), *A Clockwork Orange* (1971), *Barry Lyndon* (1975), *The Shining* (1980), *Full Metal Jacket* (1987).

DIRECTORS (cont.)

Kurosawa, Akira (1910–) Japanese, born Tokyo; *Rashomon* (1950), *The Idiot* (1951), *Living* (1952), *Seven Samurai* (1954), *Throne of Blood* (1957), *The Lower Depths* (1957), *The Idden Fortress* (1958), *Dersu Uzala* (1975), *The Shadow Warrior* (1981), *Ran* (1985), *Dreams* (1990), *Rhapsody in August* (1991).

Landis, John (1950–) American, born Chicago, Illinois; *Schlock* (1971), *Kentucky Fried Movie* (1977), *Animal House* (1978), *The Blues Brothers* (1980), *An American Werewolf in London* (1981), *Twilight Zone* (1983), *Trading Places* (1983), *Into the Night* (1985), *Spies Like Us* (1985), *The Three Amigos* (1986), *Coming to America* (1988).

Lang, Fritz (1890–1976) German, born Vienna; *Destiny* (1921), *Dr Mabuse the Gambler* (1922), *Siegfried* (1923), *Metropolis* (1926), *Spies* (1927), *M* (1931), *The Testament of Dr Mabuse* (1932), *You Only Live Once* (1937), *The Return of Frank James* (1940), *The Woman in the Window* (1944), *The Big Heat* (1953), *Beyond a Reasonable Doubt* (1956), *While the City Sleeps* (1955).

Lean, Sir David (1908–91) English, born Croydon; *Pygmalion* (1938), *In Which We Serve* (1942), *Blithe Spirit* (1945), *Brief Encounter* (1946), *Great Expectations* (1946), *The Sound Barrier* (1952), *Hobson's Choice* (1954), *Summer Madness* (1955), *Bridge on the River Kwai* (1957), *Lawrence of Arabia* (1962), *Doctor Zhivago* (1965), *Ryan's Daughter* (1970), *A Passage to India* (1984).

Levinson, Barry (1942–) American, born Baltimore, Maryland; *Diner* (1982), *The Natural* (1984), *The Young Sherlock Holmes* (1985), *Tin Men* (1987), *Good Morning Vietnam* (1987), *Rain Man* (1988), *Avalon* (1990), *Bugsy* (1991).

Lucas, George (1944–) American, born Modesto, California; *THX-1138* (1971), *American Graffiti* (1973), *Star Wars* (1977).

Lynch, David K (1946–) American, born Missoula, Montana; *Eraserhead* (1976), *The Elephant Man* (1980), *Dune* (1984), *Blue Velvet* (1986), *Wild at Heart* (1990); *Twin Peaks* (TV 1990–1).

McBride, Jim (1941–) American; *Breathless* (1983), *The Big Easy* (1986), *Great Balls of Fire* (1989).

Mankiewicz, Joseph Leo (1909–) American, born Wilkes-Barre, Pennsylvania; *All About Eve* (1950), *The Barefoot Contessa* (1954), *Guys and Dolls* (1954), *Suddenly Last Summer* (1959), *Sleuth* (1972).

Miller, George (1945–) Australian, born Brisbane; *Mad Max* (1979), *Mad Max 2: The Road Warrior* (1982), *Mad Max Beyond Thunderdome* (1985), *Witches of Eastwick* (1987).

Miller, Jonathan Wolfe (1934–) British, born London; theatre and opera director; *The Magic Flute* (1986), *The Tempest* (1988).

Minnelli, Vincente (1913–86) American, born Chicago; *Ziegfeld Follies* (1946), *An American in Paris* (1951), *Lust for Life* (1956), *Gigi* (1958).

Nunn, Trevor Robert (1940–) British, born Ipswich; theatre, opera, and film director; *Cats* (1981), *Starlight Express* (1984), *Aspects of Love* (1989).

Olivier, Sir Laurence Kerr (1907–89) English, born Dorking, Surrey; *Henry V* (1944), *Hamlet* (1948), *Richard III* (1956), *The Prince and The Showgirl* (1958), *The Entertainer* (1960).

Parker, Alan (1944–) British, born London; *Bugsy Malone* (1976), *Midnight Express* (1978), *Fame* (1980), *Shoot the Moon* (1981), *Pink Floyd: The Wall* (1982), *Birdy* (1985), *Angel Heart* (1987), *Mississippi Burning* (1988), *Come See the Paradise* (1990), *The Commitments* (1991).

Pasolini, Pier Paolo (1922–75) Italian, born Bologna; *Accatone!* (1961), *The Gospel According to St Matthew* (1964), *Oedipus Rex* (1967), *Medea* (1970).

Polanski, Roman (1933–) Polish, born Paris; *Knife in the Water* (1962), *Repulsion* (1965), *Cul-de-Sac* (1966), *Rosemary's Baby* (1968), *Macbeth* (1971), *Chinatown* (1974), *Tess* (1979), *Pirates* (1985), *Frantic* (1988).

Pollack, Sydney (1934–) American, born South Bend, Indiana; *They Shoot Horses Don't They?* (1969), *The Electric Horseman* (1979), *Absence of Malice* (1981), *Tootsie* (1982), *Out of Africa* (1985), *Havana* (1990).

Powell, Michael Latham (1905–90) British, born Bekesbourne, near Canterbury; with **Emeric Pressburger** (1902–88) Hungarian/British, born Miskolc, Hungary; *The Spy in Black* (1939), *The Thief of Baghdad* (1940), *The Life and Death of Colonel Blimp* (1943), *Black Narcissus* (1946), *The Red Shoes* (1948), *A Matter of Life and Death* (1946); *Peeping Tom* (1959).

Redford, (Charles) Robert (1937–) American, born Santa Monica, California; *Ordinary People*

DIRECTORS (cont.)

(1980), *The Milagro Beanfield War* (1987), *A River Runs Through It (1991)*.

Reed, Sir Carol (1906–76) British, born London; *The Young Mr Pitt* (1942), *The Way Ahead* (1944), *The Fallen Idol* (1948), *The Third Man* (1949), *Outcasts of the Islands* (1952), *The Man Between* (1953), *Our Man in Havana* (1959), *Oliver!* (1968).

Reiner, Carl (1922–) American, born The Bronx, New York; *Oh God* (1977), *The Jerk* (1979), *Dead Men Don't Wear Plaid* (1982), *The Man with Two Brains* (1983), *Summer School* (1987).

Reiner, Rob (1945–) American, born The Bronx, New York; *This is Spinal Tap, Stand by Me* (1987), *The Princess Bride* (1988), *When Harry Met Sally ...* (1989), *Misery* (1990).

Renoir, Jean (1894–1979) French, born Paris; *Une Partie de Campagne* (1936), *La Règle du Jeu* (1939), *The Southerner* (1945).

Roeg, Nicolas Jack (1928–) British, born London; *Performance* (1970), *Walkabout* (1971), *Don't Look Now* (1973), *The Man Who Fell to Earth* (1976), *Bad Timing* (1979), *Eureka* (1983), *Insignificance* (1985), *Castaway* (1986), *Black Widow* (1988), *Track 29* (1988), *The Witches* (1990).

Rossellini, Roberto (1906–77) Italian, born Rome; *The White Ship* (1940), *Rome, Open City* (1945), *Paisan* (1946), *Germany, Year Zero* (1947), *Stromboli* (1950), *Voyage to Italy* (1953), *General Della Rovera* (1959).

Russell, Ken(Henry Kenneth Alfred Russell) (1927–) British, born Southampton; *Women in Love* (1969), *The Music Lovers* (1970), *The Devils* (1971), *Crimes of Passion* (1984), *Gothic* (1987), *Lair of the White Worm* (1989), *The Rainbow* (1989), *Whore* (1991).

Schlesinger, John Richard (1926–) British, born London; *A Kind of Loving* (1962), *Billy Liar!* (1963), *Midnight Cowboy* (1969), *Sunday, Bloody Sunday* (1971), *Marathon Man* (1976), *Honky Tonk Freeway* (1981), *An Englishman Abroad* (TV 1982), *Madame Sousatzka* (1988), *Pacific Heights* (1990).

Scorsese, Martin (1942–) American, born Queens, New York; *Boxcar Bertha* (1972), *Mean Streets* (1973), *Alice Doesn't Live Here Any More* (1974), *Taxi Driver* (1976), *Raging Bull* (1980), *King of Comedy* (1982), *After Hours* (1985), *The Mission* (1986), *The Color of Money* (1986), *The Last Temptation of Christ* (1988), *GoodFellas* (1990), *Cape Fear* (1991).

Scott, Ridley (1937–) British, born South Shields; *Alien* (1979), *Blade Runner* (1982), *No Way Out* (1989), *Thelma & Louise* (1991).

Siegel, Don (1912–91) American, born Chicago; *Riot in Cell Block 11* (1954), *Invasion of the Body Snatchers* (1956), *Baby Face Nelson* (1957), *Coogan's Bluff* (1968), *Two Mules for Sister Sara* (1969), *Dirty Harry* (1971), *Charley Varrick* (1973), *The Shootist* (1976), *Telefon* (1977), *Escape from Alcatraz* (1979).

Spielberg, Steven (1947–) American, born Cincinnati, Ohio; *Duel* (TV 1972), *Sugarland Express* (1973), *Jaws* (1975), *1941* (1979), *Close Encounters of the Third Kind* (1977), *Raiders of the Lost Ark* (1981), *ET* (1982), *Twilight Zone* (1983), *The Color Purple* (1985), *Indiana Jones and the Temple of Doom* (1984), *Empire of the Sun* (1987), *Indiana Jones and the Last Crusade* (1989).

Stevenson, Robert (1905–86) British, born Buxton, Derbyshire; *King Solomon's Mines* (1937), *Mary Poppins* (1964), *The Love Bug* (1968), *Bedknobs and Broomsticks* (1971).

Stone, Oliver (1946–) American, born New York City; *Platoon* (1987), *Wall Street* (1987), *Born on the Fourth of July* (1989), *The Doors* (1991).

Tati, Jacques (Jacques Tatischeff) (1908–82) French, born Le Pecq; *Jour de fête* (1947), *Monsieur Hulot's Holiday* (1952), *Mon Oncle* (1958), *Playtime* (1968), *Traffic* (1981).

Truffaut, Francois (1932–84) French, born Paris; *Jules et Jim* (1961), *The Bride Wore Black* (1967), *Baisers volés* (1968), *L'Enfant Sauvage* (1969), *Day for Night* (1973), *The Last Metro* (1980).

Visconti, Count Luchino (Luchino Visconti di Modrone) (1906–76) Italian, born Milan; *The Leopard* (1963), *Ossessione* (1942), *The Damned* (1969), *Death in Venice* (1971).

Weir, Peter (1944–) Australian born Sydney; *The Cars that Ate Paris* (1974), *Picnic at Hanging Rock* (1975), *The Last Wave* (1977), *Gallipoli* (1981), *The Year of Living Dangerously* (1982), *Witness* (1985), *Mosquito Coast* (1986), *Dead Poet's Society* (1989), *Green Card* (1990).

Welles, (George) Orson (1915–85) American, born Kenosha, Wisconsin; *Citizen Kane* (1941), *The Magnificent Ambersons* (1942), *Jane Eyre* (1943), *Macbeth* (1948), *Othello* (1951), *Touch of*

DIRECTORS (cont.)

Evil (1958), *The Trial* (1962), *Chimes at Midnight* (1966).

Wise, Robert (1914–) American, born Winchester, Indiana; *The Body Snatcher* (1945), *The Day the Earth Stood Still* (1951), *West Side Story* (1961), *The Sound of Music* (1965), *Star Trek The Motion Picture* (1979).

Zeffirelli, Franco (1922–) Italian, born Florence; *The Taming of the Shrew* (1966), *Romeo and Juliet* (1968), *Brother Sun, Sister Moon* (1973), *Jesus of Nazareth* (TV 1977), *The*

Champ (1979), *Endless Love* (1981), *La Traviata* (1982), *Otello* (1986), *Hamlet* (1991).

Zemeckis, Robert (1951–) American, born Chicago; *I Wanna Hold Your Hand* (1978), *Romancing The Stone* (1984), *Back to the Future* (1985), *Who Framed Roger Rabbit?* (1988), *Back to the Future II* (1989), *Back to the Future III* (1990).

Zinneman, Fred (1907–) American/Austrian, born Vienna, Austria; *High Noon* (1952), *From Here to Eternity* (1953), *A Man for All Seasons* (1966), *Five Days One Summer* (1982).

MOTION PICTURE ACADEMY AWARDS

	Best film	Best actor	Best actress
1970	*Patton* (Franklin J Schaffner)	George C Scott *Patton*	Glenda Jackson *Women in Love*
1971	*The French Connection* (William Friedkin)	Gene Hackman *The French Connection*	Jane Fonda *Klute*
1972	*The Godfather* (Francis Ford Coppola)	Marlon Brando *The Godfather*	Liza Minnelli *Cabaret*
1973	*The Sting* (George Roy Hill)	Jack Lemmon *Save the Tiger*	Glenda Jackson *A Touch of Class*
1974	*The Godfather Part II* (Francis Ford Coppola)	Art Carney *Harry and Tonto*	Ellen Burstyn *Alice Doesn't Live Here Anymore*
1975	*One Flew Over the Cuckoo's Nest* (Milos Forman)	Jack Nicholson *One Flew Over the Cuckoo's Nest*	Louise Fletcher *One Flew Over the Cuckoo's Nest*
1976	*Rocky* (John G Avildsen)	Peter Finch *Network*	Faye Dunaway *Network*
1977	*Annie Hall* (Woody Allen)	Richard Dreyfuss *The Goodbye Girl*	Diane Keaton *Annie Hall*
1978	*The Deer Hunter* (Michael Cimino)	Jon Voight *Coming Home*	Jane Fonda *Coming Home*
1979	*Kramer vs Kramer* (Robert Beaton)	Dustin Hoffman *Kramer vs Kramer*	Sally Field *Norma Rae*
1980	*Ordinary People* (Robert Redford)	Robert de Niro *Raging Bull*	Sissy Spacek *Coal Miner's Daughter*
1981	*Chariots of Fire* (Hugh Hudson)	Henry Fonda *On Golden Pond*	Katharine Hepburn *On Golden Pond*
1982	*Gandhi* (Richard Attenborough)	Ben Kingsley *Ghandi*	Meryl Streep *Sophie's Choice*
1983	*Terms of Endearment* (James L Brooks)	Robert Duval *Tender Mercies*	Shirley MacLaine *Terms of Endearment*
1984	*Amadeus* (Milos Forman)	F Murray Abraham *Amadeus*	Sally Field *Places in the Heart*
1985	*Out of Africa* (Sydney Pollack)	William Hurt *Kiss of the Spider Woman*	Geraldine Page *The Trip to Bountiful*

MOTION PICTURE ACADEMY AWARDS (cont.)

	Best film	Best actor	Best actress
1986	*Platoon*	Paul Newman	Marlee Matlin
	(Oliver Stone)	*The Color of Money*	*Children of a Lesser God*
1987	*The Last Emperor*	Michael Douglas	Cher
	(Bernardo Bertolucci)	*Wall Street*	*Moonstruck*
1988	*Rain Man*	Dustin Hoffman	Jody Foster
	(Barry Levinson)	*Rain Man*	*The Accused*
1989	*Driving Miss Daisy*	Daniel Day-Lewis	Jessica Tandy
	(Bruce Beresford)	*My Left Foot*	*Driving Miss Daisy*
1990	*Dances with Wolves*	Jeremy Irons	Kathy Bates
	(Kevin Costner)	*Reversal of Fortune*	*Misery*

COMPOSERS

Bach, Johann Sebastian   (1685–1750) German, born Eisenach; prolific composer, works include over 190 cantatas and oratorios, concertos, chamber music, keyboard music, and orchestral works (eg *Toccata and Fugue in D minor, The Well-tempered Clavier, Six Brandenburg Concertos, St Matthew Passion, Mass in B minor, Goldberg Variations, The Musical Offering, The Art Of Fugue*).

Bartók, Béla   (1881–1945) Hungarian, born Nagyszentmiklós; six string quartets, *Sonata for 2 pianos and percussion*, concertos (for piano, violin, viola, and notably the *Concerto for Orchestra*), opera, (*Duke Bluebeard's Castle*), two ballets (*The Wooden Prince, The Miraculous Mandarin*), songs, choruses, folksong arrangements.

Beethoven, Ludwig van   (1770–1827) German, born Bonn; works include thirty-three piano sonatas (eg the 'Pathetique', 'Moonlight', *Waldstein, Appassionata*), nine symphonies (eg *Eroica*, 'Pastoral', *Choral* Symphony (no. 9)), string quartets, concertos, *Lebewohl* and the opera *Fidelio*.

Berlioz, (Louis) Hector   (1803–69) French, born Côte St André, near Grenoble; works include the overture *Le carnival romain*, the cantata (*La Damnation de Faust*), symphonies (eg *Symphonie Fantastique, Romeo et Juliette*) and operas (eg *Béatrice et Bénédict, Les Toyens*).

Bernstein, Leonard   (1918–90) American, born Laurence, Massachusetts; works include ballets (*Jeremiah, The Age of Anxiety, Kaddish*), symphonies (eg *Fancy Free, The Dybbuk*), and musicals, (eg *Candide, West Side Story, On The Town, Songfest, Halil*).

Brahms, Johannes   (1833–97) German, born Hamburg; works include songs, four symphonies, two piano concertos, choral work (eg *German Requiem*), orchestral work (eg *Variations on a Theme of Haydn*), programme work (eg *Tragic overture*), also the *Academic Festival Overture* and *Hungarian Dances*.

Bruckner, Anton   (1824–96) Austrian, born Ansfelden; works include nine symphonies, a string quartet, choral-orchestral Masses and other church music (eg *Te Deum*).

Chopin, Frédéric François   (1810–49) Polish, born Zelazowa Wola, near Warsaw; wrote almost exclusively for piano – nocturnes, polonaises, mazurkas, preludes, concertos, and a funeral march.

Copland, Aaron   (1900–90) American, born Brooklyn, New York; ballets (eg *Billy The Kid, Appalachian Spring*), film scores (eg *Our Town, The Hucis*), symphonies (eg *Symphonie Ode, Connotations, Clarinet Concerto*).

Debussy, Claude Achille   (1862–1918) French, born St Germaine-en-Laye, near Paris; songs (eg the cantata *L'Enfant prodigue*, opera (*Pelléas et Mélisande*), orchestral works (eg *Prélude à l'après-midi d'un faune, La Mer*), chamber and piano music (eg *Feux d'artifice, La Cathédrale engloutie*).

Delius, Frederick   (1862–1934) English (of German Scandinavian descent), born Bradford; works include songs (eg *A Song of Summer, Idyll, Songs of Farewell*, concertos, operas (eg *Koanga, A Village Romeo and Juliette*), chamber music and orchestral variations (eg *Appalachia, Sea Drift, A Mass of Life*).

COMPOSERS (cont.)

Dvořák, Antonin (1841–1904) Czech, born near Prague; works include songs, concertos, choral (eg *Hymnus*) and chamber music, symphonies (notably 'From the New World'), operas (eg *Rusalka* (The Water Nymph), *Armida, Slavonic Dances*).

Elgar, Sir Edward (William) (1857–1934) English, born Broadheath, near Worcester; works include chamber music, two symphonies, oratorios (eg *The Dream of Gerontius, The Apostles, The Kingdom*), and the orchestral work *Enigma Variations*.

Fauré, Gabriel Urbain (1845–1924) French, born Pamiers; works include songs (eg *Après un rêve*), chamber music, choral music (eg the *Requiem*), operas and orchestral music (eg *Marques et bergamasques*).

Franck, César Auguste (1822–90) naturalized French, born Liège, Belgium; works include tone-poems, (eg *Les Béatitudes*), sonatas for violin and piano, symphony in D minor and *Variations symphoniques* for piano and orchestra.

Gershwin, George (1898–1937) American, born Brooklyn, New York; Broadway musicals (eg *Lady Be Good, Of Thee I Sing*), symphonies, songs (notably 'I Got Rhythm', 'The Man I Love'), operas (eg *Porgy and Bess*), and concert works (eg *Rhapsody in Blue, Concerto in F, An American in Paris*).

Grainger, Percy Aldridge (1882–1961) Australian, born Melbourne; works include songs, piano and chamber music (eg *Molly on the Shore, Mock Morris, Shepherds Hey*).

Grieg, Edvard Hagerup (1843–1907) Norwegian, born Bergen; works include songs, a piano concerto, orchestral suites, violin sonatas, choral music and incidental music for *Peer Gynt* and *Sigurd Jorsalfar*.

Handel, George Friederic (1685–1759) naturalized English, born Halle, Saxony; prolific output including over 27 operas (eg *Almira, Rinaldo, Beggar's Opera*), 20 oratorios (eg *The Messiah, Saul, Israel in Egypt, Samson, Jephthah*), orchestral suites (eg the *Water Music* and *Music for the Royal Fireworks*), organ concertos and chamber music.

Haydn, (Franz) Joseph (1732–1809) Austrian, born Rohrau, Lower Austria; prolific output including 104 symphonies (eg the 'Salomon' or 'London' Symphonies), string quartets and oratorios (notably *The Creation, The Seasons*).

Holst, Gustav Theodore (originally von Holst) (1874–1934) English of Swedish origin, born Cheltenham; works include choral and ballet music, operas (eg *The Perfect Fool, At the Boar's Head*), orchestral suites (eg *The Planets, St Paul's Suite for Strings*), choral music (eg *The Hymn of Jesus, Ode to Death*), and *Concerto for Two Violins*.

Ireland, John Nicholson (1879–1962) English, born Bowden, Cheshire; works include sonatas (eg Violin Sonata in A), piano music, songs (eg 'Sea Fever'), the rhapsody *Mai dun* and orchestral works (eg *The Forgotten Rite, These Things Shall Be*).

Janácek Leos (1854–1928) Czech, born Hukvaldy, Moravia; works include chamber, orchestral and choral music (eg the song cycle *The Diary of One Who Has Vanished*), operas (eg *Janufa, The Cunning Little Vixen, The Excursions of Mr Brouček, From the House of the Dead*), two string quartets and a mass.

Liszt, France (1811–1886) Hungarian, born Raiding; 400 original compositions including symphonic poems, piano music and masses (eg *The Legend of St Elizabeth, Christus*).

Mahler, Gustav (1860–1911) Austrian, born Kalist, Bohemia; works include ten symphonies, songs, the cantata *Das klagende Lied*, and the song-symphony *Das lied von der Erde* (The Song of the Earth).

Mendelssohn, (Jacob Ludwig) Felix (1809–47) German, born Hamburg; prolific output, including concerto overtures (eg *Fingal's Cave, Midsummer Night's Dream, Hebrides, Scotch Symphony*), symphonies (Symphony in C minor), quartets (B minor Quartet), operas (eg *Camacho's Wedding*), and oratorios (eg *Elijah*).

Monteverdi, Claudio (Giovanni Antonio) (1567–1643) Italian, born Cremona; works include masses (eg *Mass* and *Vespers* of the Virgin), cantatas and operas (eg *Orfeo, Il Ritorno d'Ulisse, L'Incoronazione di Poppea* (The Coronation of Poppea)).

Mozart, (Johann Chrysostom) Wolfgang Amadeus (1756–91) Austrian, born Salzburg; 600 compositions including symphonies (eg 'Jupiter', *Linz, Prague*), concertos, string quartets, sonatas, operas (eg *Marriage of Figaro, Don Giovanni, Cosi fan tutte*) and the Singspiels *The Abduction from the Seraglio, Die Zauberflöte*.

COMPOSERS (cont.)

Mussorgsky, Modeste   (1839–81) Russian, born Karevo, government of Pskov; works include operas (eg *Boris Godunov*), song cycles and instrumental works (eg *Pictures from an Exhibition, Night on the Bare Mountain*).

Nielsen, Carl August   (1865–1931) Danish, born Furen; works include operas (eg *Saul and David, Masquerade*), symphonies (eg 'The Four Temperaments'), string quartets, choral and piano music.

Palestrina, Giovanni Pierluigi da   (c.1525–1594) Italian, born Palestrina, near Rome; works include chamber music and the organ work *Commotion*, masses, choral music (eg *Song of Songs*), madrigals.

Prokofiev, Sergei   (1891–1953) Russian, born Sontsovka in the Ukraine; works include 11 operas (eg *The Gambler, The Love for the Three Oranges, The Fiery Angels, Semyon Kotko, Betrothal in a Monastery, War and Peace, The Story of a Real Man*), ballets (eg *Romeo and Juliet, Cinderella*), concertos, sonatas, cantatas (eg *We are Seven, Hail to Stalin*), film scores (eg *Alexander Nevsky*), and the 'children's piece' *Peter and the Wolf*.

Puccini, Giacomo (Antonio Domenico Michele Secondo Maria)   (1858–1924) Italian, born Lucca; 12 operas, eg *Manon Lescaut, La Bohème, Tosca, Madama Butterfly, Turandot*.

Purcell, Henry   (1659–95) English, born London; works include songs (eg 'Nymphs and Shepherds', 'Arise, ye Subterranean Winds'), sonatas, string fantasies, church music and opera (eg *Dido and Aeneas*).

Rachmaninov, Sergei Vasilyevich   (1873–1943) Russian, born Nizhi-Novgorod; works include operas, three symphonies, four piano concertos (eg *Prelude in C Sharp Minor*), the tone-poem *The Isle of the Dead*, and *Rhapsody on a Theme of Paganini* for piano and orchestra.

Ravel, Maurice   (1875–1937) French, born Ciboure, in the Basque country; works include piano compositions (eg *Sonatina, Miroirs, Ma Mère L'Oye, Gaspard de la nuit*), string quartets, operas (eg *L'Heure espagnol, L'Enfant et les sortilèges*), ballets (eg *Daphnis and Chloë*), the 'choreographic poem' *La Valse* and the miniature ballet *Boléro*.

Rimsky-Korsakov, Nikolai Andreievich   (1844–1908) Russian, born Tikhvin, Novgorod; works include orchestral music (eg the symphonic suite *Sheherazade, Capriccio Espagnol, Easter Festival*) and 15 operas (eg *Sadko, The Snow Maiden, The Tsar Sultan, The Invisible City of Kitesh, The Goldern Cockerel*).

Saint-Saëns, (Charles) Camille   (1835–1921) French, born Paris; works include four symphonic poems (eg *Danse macabre*), piano (*Le Rouet d'Omphale, Phaëton, La Jeunesse d'Hercule*), violin and cello concertos, symphonies, the opera *Samson et Dalila*, church music (eg *Messe solennelle*), and *Carnival des animaux* for two pianos and orchestra.

Schönberg, Arnold   (1874–1951) naturalized American, born Vienna; works include chamber music (eg *Chamber Symphony*), concertos (eg *Piano Concerto*), and symphonic poems (eg *Pelleas und Melisande*), the choral-orchestral *Gurrelieder*, string quartets, the oratorio *Die Jacobsiter*, and opera (*Von Heute auf Morgen, Moses und Aaron*).

Schubert, Franz Peter   (1797–1828) Austrian, born Vienna; prolific output, works include symphonies, piano sonatas, string quartets and songs (eg *Gretchen am Spinnrade, Erlkönig, Die schösne Müllerin, Winterreise, Who is Sylvia?, Hark, Hark the Lark, Schwanengesang* ('Swan-song')).

Schumann, Robert Alexander   (1810–56) German, born Zwickau, Saxony; works include piano music (eg *Fantasiestücke*), songs (eg The Fool's Song in *Twelfth Night*, the Chamisso songs *Frauenliebe und Leben* or 'Woman's Love and Life'), chamber music, and four symphonies (eg the *Rhenish*).

Shostakovich, Dmitri   (1906–75) Russian, born St Petersburg; works include 15 symphonies, operas (eg *The Nose, A Lady Macbeth of Mtensk*), concertos, string quartets and film music.

Sibelius, Jean   (1865–1957) Finnish, born Tavastehus; works include symphonic poems (eg *Swan of Tuonela, En Saga*), songs, a violin concerto, and seven symphonies.

Strauss, Johann (the Younger)   (1825–99) Austrian, born Vienna; works include over 400 waltzes (eg *The Blue Danube, Wine, Women, and Song, Perpetuum Mobile, Artist's Life, Tales from the Vienna Woods, Voices from Spring, The Emperor*), and operettas (eg *Die Fledermus, A Night in Venice*).

Strauss, Richard   (1864–1949) German, born Munich; works include symphonic poems (eg *Don Juan, Till*

COMPOSERS (cont.)

Eulenspiegel, *Also Sprach Zarathustra, Tod und Verklärung ('Death and Transfiguration'), Don Quixote, Ein Heldenleben*) and operas (eg *Der Rosenkavalier, Ariadne auf Naxos, Capriccio*).

Stravinsky, Igor (1882–1971) Russian, born Oranienbaum, near St Petersburg (naturalized French, then American); works include operas (eg *The Rake's Progress*), oratorios (eg *Oedipus Rex, Symphony of Psalms*), concertos, ballets (eg *The Firebird, The Rite of Spring, Petrushka, Pulcinella, Apollo Musogetes, The Card Game, Orpheus, Agon*), and a musical play *Elegy for J.F.K* for voice and clarinets.

Tchaikovsky, Piotr Ilyich (1840–93) Russian, born Kamsko-Votinsk; works include ten operas (eg *Eugene Onegin, The Queen of Spades*), a violin concerto, six symphonies, two piano concertos, three ballets (*The Nutcracker, Swan Lake, The Sleeping Beauty*) and tone-poems (eg *Romeo and Juliet, Italian Capriccio*).

Telemann, George Philipp (1681–1767) German, born Magdeburg; prolific composer, works include 600 overtures, 40 operas, 200 concertos, sonatas, suites, and overtures (eg *Der Tag de Gerichts, Die Tageszeiten*).

Tippett, Sir Michael Kemp (1905–) English, born London; works include operas (eg *The Midsummer Marriage, King Priam, The Knot Garden, The Ice Break*), concertos, symphonies, cantatas and oratorios (eg *A Child of our Time, The Vision of St Augustine*).

Vaughan Williams, Ralph (1872–1958) English, born Down Ampney, Gloucestershire; works include songs, symphonies (eg *London Symphony, Pastoral Symphony*), choral-orchestral works (eg *Sea Symphony, Magnificat*), operas (eg *Hugh the Drover, The Pilgrim's Progress*), a ballet *Job*, and film music (eg for *Scott of the Antartic*).

Verdi, Giuseppe (1813–1901) Italian, born le Roncole, near Busseto; church music (eg *Requiem*), operas (eg *Oberto, Nabucco, Rigoletto, Il Trovatore, La Traviata, Un Ballo in Maschera, La Forza del Destino, Aïda, Otello, Falstaff*).

Vivaldi, Antonio (1678–1741) Italian, born Venice; prolific output, works include over 400 concertos (eg *L'Estro Armonico, The Four Seasons*), 40 operas and an oratorio, *Juditha triumphans*.

Wagner, (Wilhelm) Richard (1813–83) German, born Leipzig; operas include *Lohengin, Rienzi*, the *Ring* cycle (*Das Rheingold, Die Walküre, Siegfried, Götterdämmerung*), *Die Meistersinger, Tristan und Isolde, Parsifal*.

Walton, Sir William Turner (1902–83) English, born Oldham; works include concertos, operas (*Troilus and Cressida, The Bear*), a cantata (*Belshazzar's Feast*), ballet music for *The Wise Virgins*, a song-cycle (*Anon in Love*) and film music.

SONGWRITERS

A selection of songs is listed.

Arlen, Harold (Hyman Arluck) (1905–86) American, born Buffalo, New York; over 500 songs, including 'Between the Devil and the Deep Blue Sea', 'Stormy Weather', 'Get Happy' (lyrics by Ted Koehler), *A Star is Born* (1953) ('The Man that Got Away') (lyrics by Ira Gershwin); *The Wizard of Oz* (1939) ('Over the Rainbow') (lyrics by E Y Harburg, 1896–1981).

Berlin, Irving (originally **Israel Baline**) (1888–1989) American, born Temus, Siberia; composer; *Annie Get Your Gun* (1946), *Call Me Madam* (1950); over 900 songs, including 'There's No Business Like Show Business', 'White Christmas', 'God Bless America', 'Oh, How I Hate to Get Up in the Morning'.

Bernstein, Leonard (1918–90) American composer of opera, symphonies, songs, born Laurence, Massachusetts; *West Side Story* (1958) (lyrics by Stephen Sondheim); songs include 'You Got Me', 'New York, New York'.

Britten, Baron (Edward) Benjamin, of Aldeburgh (1913–76) English, born Lowestoft; composer of choral symphonic works, opera, song cycles eg *Our Hunting Fathers, On This Island* (text by WH Auden).

SONGWRITERS (cont.)

Brown, Nacio Herb (1896–1954) American, born Deming, New Mexico; composer; *Broadway Melody* (lyrics by Arthur Field, 1894–1973); *Singin' in the Rain* (1952); songs include 'You were Meant for Me'.

Cahn, Sammy (Samuel) (1913–) American lyricist, born New York; 'I've Heard That Song Before', 'I'll Walk Alone', 'It's Magic' (with Jule Styne); 'All the Way', 'High Hopes' (with Jimmy van Heusen).

Cohan, George M(ichael) (1878–1942) American composer, lyricist, born Providence, Rhode Island; *Little Johnny Jones* (1904) ('Give My Regards to Broadway'); 'The Talk of the Town' (1907).

Coward, Sir Noël Pierce (1899–1973) English composer, lyricist, playwright, born Teddington; *Words and Music* (revue) (1932) ('Mad Dogs and Englishmen', 'Someday I'll Find You').

Dylan, Bob (Robert Allen Zimmermann) (1941–) American songwriter, musician, born Duluth, Minnesota; 'Blowin' in the Wind', 'With God on Our Side', 'The Times They are A–Changing', 'It's Alright Ma, I'm Only Bleeding', 'Mr Tambourine Man', 'Subterranean Homesick Blues', 'Like a Rolling Stone', 'Leopard-Skin Pill-Box Hat', 'Knockin' on Heaven's Door'.

Ellington, (Edward Kennedy) 'Duke' (1899–1974) American pianist, composer, bandleader, born Washington DC; 2000 works, including songs, instrumentals, film music: 'It Don't Mean a Thing if it Ain't Got That Swing' (lyrics Irving Mills), 'Best Wishes' (lyrics Ted Koehler), 'Creole Love Call' (vocal, no lyrics).

Fields, Dorothy (1905–74) American lyricist, born Allenhurst, New Jersey; 'I Can't Give You Anything But Love' (with Jimmy McHugh, from *Blackbirds* (1928)), 'On the Sunny Side of the Street (with Jimmy McHugh), 'Exactly Like You', 'Lovely to Look At' and 'The Way You Look Tonight' (with Jerome Kern); *Stars in Your Eyes* (1939) (with Arthur Schwartz); *Sweet Charity* (1966) ('Big Spender') (with Cy Coleman).

Gershwin, George (originally **Jacob Gershvin**) (1898–1937) American composer, born Brooklyn, New York, and **Ira Gershwin** (originally **Israel Gershvin**) (1896–1983) American lyricist, born New York; *Lady, Be Good!* ('The Man I Love', 'How Long Has This Been Going On?'), *Girl Crazy, Porgy and Bess* ('Summertime') (lyrics by Ira Gershwin and Du Bose Heyward); songs include 'You Can't Take That Away from Me', 'Nice Work if You Can Get It', 'Love Walked in', 'They All Laughed'.

Gilbert, Sir William Schwenck (1836–1911) English librettist, born London, and **Sir Arthur Sullivan Seymour** (1842–1900) English composer, born London; operettas and songs include *H.M.S. Pinafore* (1878), *The Mikado* (1885), *The Gondoliers* (1889).

Herman, Jerry (1932–) American composer, lyricist, born New York; *Hello Dolly!* (1964), *Mame* (1966).

Kern, Jerome (David) (1885–1945) American composer, born New York; 'The Way You Look Tonight' (lyrics Dorothy Fields), 'Ol' Man River', 'They Didn't Believe Me' (lyrics Herbert Reynold); *Show Boat* (1927) (lyrics Oscar Hammerstein II (1895–1960) American lyricist, born New York).

Lennon, John (Winston) (1940–80) English songwriter, musician, born Liverpool, and **(James) Paul McCartney** (1942–) English songwriter, musician, born Liverpool; 'Please Please Me', 'Yesterday', 'All You Need is Love', 'Strawberry Fields', 'I Want to Hold Your Hand', 'Michelle', 'Eleanor Rigby', 'Ticket to Ride', 'Dear Prudence', 'Help!'.

Livingston, Jay (1915–) American composer, lyricist, born McDonald, Pennsylvania; and **Ray Evans** (1915–) American lyricist, born Salamanca, New York; 'The Cat and the Canary', 'Mona Lisa', 'Whatever Will Be, Will Be (Que Sera Sera)', 'Dear Heart'.

Lloyd Webber, Andrew (1948–) English composer, born London, with **Tim Rice** (1944–) English lyricist, born Amersham, Buckinghamshire: *Joseph and the Amazing Technicolor Dreamcoat* (1968) ('Any Dream Will Do'); *Jesus Christ Superstar* (1970) ('Jesus Christ Superstar', 'I Don't Know How to Love Him'), *Evita* (1978) ('Don't Cry for Me, Argentina'); *Cats* (1981) (libretto TS Eliot), *Phantom of the Opera* (1986), *Les Miserables, Miss Saigon*.

Loesser, Frank (Henry) (1910–69) American composer, lyricist, born New York; *Guys and Dolls* (1950) ('I've never Been in Love Before', 'Luck Be a Lady'); *The Perils of Pauline* (1947) (words and music); lyrics for 'The Boys in the Back Room' (music by Frederick Hollander); lyrics for 'The Lady's in Love With You' and 'Some Like it Hot', from the film *Some Like it Hot* (1959).

McHugh, Jimmy (James Frances McHugh) (1896–1969) American composer, born Boston, Massachusetts; with Dorothy Fields, as above; 'I'm Shooting High' (with Ted Koehler), 'Exactly Like You' (with Al Dubin).

SONGWRITERS (cont.)

Mancini, Henry (1924–) American composer of songs and film music, born Cleveland, Ohio; over 80 films eg *Breakfast at Tiffany's* (1961); songs include 'Moon River' (lyrics Johnny Mercer), 'Days of Wine and Roses', 'Charade'.

Mercer, Johnny H (1909–76) American lyricist, born Savannah, Georgia; 1500 songs for over 70 films and 7 Broadway musicals; songs with Mancini, as above; 'Blues in the Night' (music by Harold Arlen), 'That Old Black Magic' (music by Harold Arlen), 'Jeepers Creepers' (music by Henry Warren); lyrics for *Seven Brides for Seven Brothers*.

Porter, Cole (1891–1964) American composer, lyricist, born Peru, Indiana; *Gay Divorcee* (1932), *Anything Goes* (1934), *Du Barry Was a Lady* ('Well, Did You Evah!') (1939), *Kiss Me Kate* (1948) ('So in Love'); songs include 'I'm in Love Again', 'Let's Do It, Let's Fall in Love', 'Just one of Those Things'.

Rodgers, Richard (1902–79) American composer, born Long Island, New York; with **Lorenz Hart** (1895–1943) American lyricist, born New York: *The Girl Friend* (1926), *Babes in Arms* (1937), 'Manhattan'; with **Oscar Hammerstein II** (1895–1960) American lyricist, born New York: *Oklahoma!* (1943) ('Oh, What a Beautiful Morning'), *South Pacific* (1949), *The King and I* (1959) ('Shall We Dance?'), *The Sound of Music* (1959) ('Do–Re–Mi', 'Edelweiss').

Romberg, Sigmund (1887–1951) American composer, born Nagykanizsa, Hungary; *The Desert Song* (1926), *The New Moon* (1928) ('Lover Come Back to Me'), *The Student Prince* (1924), *Girl of the Golden West* (film, 1938).

Schubert, Franz (Peter) (1797–1828) Austrian composer, born Vienna; works include 145 songs, texts by Schiller and Goethe, among others.

Schumann, Robert (Alexander) (1810–56) German composer, born Zwickau; songs to texts by Heine, among others, 1840.

Simon, Paul (1942–) American songwriter, musician, born Newark, New Jersey; 'I am a Rock', 'Bridge over Troubled Water', 'Mrs Robinson', 'Cecilia', 'Keep the Customer Satisfied', 'Homeward Bound', 'The Boxer', 'The Sound of Silence'.

Sondheim, Stephen (Joshua) (1930–) American composer, lyricist, born New York; lyrics for Bernstein's *West Side Story* (1958), *A Funny Thing Happened on the Way to the Forum* (1962), *A Little Night Music* (1973) ('Send in the Clowns') (lyrics and music).

Stynge, Jule (1905–) American composer, born London; 'There Goes that Song Again', 'I'll Walk Alone', 'It's Magic' (with Sammy Cahn)'; *Gentlemen Prefer Blondes* (1949) ('Diamonds are a Girl's Best Friend') with Leo Robin.

Warren, Harry (1893–1981) American composer of songs, film scores, born Brooklyn, New York; 'You're My Everything', 'We're in the Money', 'Chattanooga Choo–Choo', 'Jeepers Creepers' (with Mercer); with **Al Dubin** (1891–1945) American lyricist, born Zurich, Switzerland: *42nd Street* (1932), 'The Boulevard of Broken Dreams', 'I Only Have Eyes for You'.

Weill, Kurt (1900–50) German composer, born Dessau; songs, opera, with **Bertolt Eugene Friedrich Brecht** (1898–1956) German lyricist, playwright, born Augsburg: *Threepenny Opera* (1928) ('Mack the Knife'); *Lady in the Dark* (1941) (lyrics Ira Gershwin), *Street Scene* (1947) (lyrics Langston Hughes), *Lost in the Stars* (1949) (lyrics Maxwell Anderson).

OPERAS AND OPERETTAS

Name	Composer	Date	Name	Composer	Date
Aida	Verdi	1871	The Beggar's Opera	Gay	1728
Ariadne auf Naxos	Richard Strauss	1916	Bluebeard's Castle	Bartók	1918
Armide et Renaud	Lully	1686	La Bohème	Puccini	1896
The Barber of Seville	Rossini	1816	Boris Godunov	Mussorgsky	1874
The Bartered Bride	Smetana	1866	Carmen	Bizet	1875

OPERAS AND OPERETTAS (cont.)

Name	Composer	Date	Name	Composer	Date
Cavalleria Rusticana	Mascagni	1890	Der Meistersinger von Nürenberg	Wagner	1868
Cosi Fan Tutte	Mozart	1790			
The Cunning Little Vixen	Janáček	1924	The Midsummer Marriage	Tippett	1955
Dido and Aeneas	Purcell	1689	The Mikado	Gilbert and Sullivan	1885
Don Giovanni	Mozart	1787			
Einstein on the Beach	Philip Glass	1976	Nabucco	Verdi	1842
Eugene Onegin	Tchaikovsky	1879	Orpheus in the Underworld	Offenbach	1858
Falstaff	Verdi	1893			
Die Fledermaus	Johann Strauss	1874	Otello	Verdi	1887
Fidelio	Beethoven	1814	Pagliacci	Leoncavallo	1892
The Flying Dutchman	Wagner	1843	Parsifal	Wagner	1882
The Gondoliers	Gilbert and Sullivan	1889	The Pearl Fishers	Bizet	1863
			Peter Grimes	Britten	1945
			Porgy and Bess	Gershwin	1935
Hansel and Gretel	Humperdinck	1893			
H.M.S. Pinafore	Gilbert and Sullivan	1878	The Rake's Progress	Stravinsky	1951
			Rigoletto	Verdi	1851
Idomeneo	Mozart	1781	The Ring	Wagner	1876
L'Incoronazione di Poppea	Monteverdi	1642	Der Rosenkavalier	Richard Strauss	1911
			Salome	Richard Strauss	1911
Jenufa	Janáček	1904	The Tales of Hoffman	Offenbach	1881
Lady Macbeth of Mtsensk	Shostakovich	1934	Tannhäuser	Wagner	1845
			The Threepenny Opera	Weill	1928
Lohengrin	Wagner	1850			
The Love for the Three Oranges	Prokofiev	1920	Tosca	Puccini	1900
			La Traviata	Verdi	1853
Lucia di Lammermoor	Donizetti	1835	Tristan und Isolde	Wagner	1865
Madama Butterfly	Puccini	1904	Il Trovatore	Verdi	1853
The Magic Flute	Mozart	1791	Turandot	Puccini	1926
Manon Lescaut	Puccini	1893	The Turn of the Screw	Britten	1954
The Marriage of Figaro	Mozart	1786			
			Wozzeck	Berg	1925

OPERA SINGERS

Allen, Thomas (1944–) English baritone, born Seaham.

Anderson, Marian (1902–) American contralto, born South Philadelphia.

Angeles, Victoria de Los (originally **Victora Gómez Cima**) (1923–) Spanish soprano, born Barcelona.

Austral, Florence (originally **Florence Wilson**) (1892–1968) Australian soprano, born Richmond, West Melbourne.

Bailey, Norman (Stanley) (1933–) English baritone, born Birmingham.

Baker, Dame Janet (Abbott) (1933–) English mezzo-soprano, born Hatfield, Yorkshire.

Barstow, Josephine (Clare) (1940–) English soprano, born Sheffield.

Battistini, Mattia (1856–1928) Italian baritone, born Rome.

Berganza, Teresa (1935–) Spanish mezzo-soprano, born Madrid.

Bonci, Alessandro (1870–1940) Italian tenor, born Cesena.

Butt, Dame Clara (1872–1936) English contralto, born Southwick, Sussex.

OPERA SINGERS (cont.)

Callas, Maria (originally **Maria Anna Sofia Cecilia Kalogeropoulos**) (1923–77) American soprano of Greek parents, born New York.

Carreras, José (1946–) Spanish tenor, born Barcelona.

Caruso, Enrico (1873–1921) Italian tenor, born Naples.

Collier, Maria (1926–71) Australian soprano, born Ballarat.

Crossley, Ada (Jessica) (1874–1929) Australian mezzo-soprano, born Tarraville, Gippsland.

Davies, Arthur (1950–) Welsh tenor, born Wrexham, Wales.

Davies, Ryland (1943–) Welsh tenor, born Cwym, Ebbw Vale, Wales.

de Luca, Giuseppe (1876–1950) Italian baritone, born Rome.

De Lucia, Fernando (1860–1925) Italian tenor, born Naples.

de Reszke, Jean (originally **Jan Mieczislaw**) (1850–1925) Polish tenor, born Warsaw.

Del Monaco, Mario (1915–82) Italian tenor, born Florence.

Domingo, Placido (1941–) Spanish tenor, born Madrid.

Evans, Sir Geraint (Llewellyn) (1922) Welsh baritone, born Pontypridd, South Wales.

Farrar, Geraldine (1882–1967) American soprano, born Meltrose, Massachusetts.

Farrell, Eileen (1920–) American soprano, born Willimantic, Connecticut

Ferrier, Kathleen (1912–53) English contralto, born Higher Walton, Lancashire.

Field, Helen (1951–) Welsh soprano, born Awyd, North Wales.

Fischer-Dieskau, Dietrich (1925–) German baritone, born Zehlendorf, Berlin.

Flagstad, Kirsten (1895–1962) Norwegian soprano, born Hamar.

Forrester, Maureen (1930–) Canadian contralto, born Montreal.

Fremstad, Olive (1871–1951) American soprano, born Stockholm.

Galli-Curci, Amelita (1882–1963) Italian soprano, born Milan.

Galli-Marie, Celestine (1840 1905) French mezzo-soprano, born Paris.

Gigli, Beniamino (1890–1957) Italian tenor, born Recanati.

Harper, Heather (1930–) Irish soprano, born Belfast.

Jurinac, Sena (1921–) Yugoslav soprano, born Travnik.

Lehmann, Lilli (1848–1929) German soprano, born Würzburg.

Lehmann, Lotte (1888–1976) German soprano, born Perleberg.

Lind, Jenny ('the Swedish Nightingale') (1820–87) Swedish soprano, born Stockholm.

Ludwig, Christa (Deiber) (1928–) German mezzo-soprano, born Berlin.

Meier, Johanna (1938–) American soprano, born Chicago.

Melba, Madam Nellie (originally **Helen Mitchell**) (1861–1931) Australian soprano, born Burnle, near Richmond.

Melchior, Lauritz (1890–1973) Danish tenor, born Copenhagen.

Nilsson, Birgit (1918–) Swedish soprano, born near Karup.

Norman, Jessye (1945–) American soprano, born Augusta, Georgia.

Patti, Adelina (Adela Juana Maria) (1843–1919) Italian soprano, born Madrid.

Pavarotti, Luciano (1935–) Italian tenor, born Modena.

Pears, Sir Peter (1910–86) English tenor, born Farnham, Surrey.

Pinza, Enzio (1892–1957) Italian bass, born Rome.

Popp, Lucia (1939–) Czech soprano, born Llhorsaká.

Schumann, Elsabeth (1888–1952) German soprano, born Merseburg.

Schwarzkopf, Elizabeth (1915–) German soprano, born Jarotschin, near Poznan, Poland.

Smirnov, Dimitri (1882–1944) Russian tenor, born Moscow.

Söderström, Elisabeth (1927–) Swedish soprano, born Stockholm.

Sutherland, Joan (1926–) Australian soprano, born Sydney.

Tear, Robert (1939–) Welsh tenor, born Barry, South Wales.

Te Kanawa, Dame Kiri (1944–) New Zealand soprano, born Gisborne.

Tetrazzini, Luisa (1871–1940) Italian soprano, born Florence.

Wiener, Otto (1913–) Austrian baritone, born Vienna.

ORCHESTRAS

Name	Date founded	Location	Name	Date founded	Location
Academy of Ancient Music	1973	UK (London)	NBC Symphony Orchestra	1937-54	USA (New York)
Academy of St Martin-in-the-Fields	1959	UK (London)	National Symphony Orchestra	1931	USA (Washington DC)
Berliner Philharmonic	1882	Germany			
Boston Symphony Orchestra	1881	USA	New Orleans Philharmonic Symphony Orchestra	1936	USA
BBC Northern Symphony Orchestra	1934	UK	New York Philharmonic Orchestra	1842	USA
BBC Scottish Symphony Orchestra	1935	UK (Glasgow)	New York Symphony Orchestra	1878	USA
BBC Symphony Orchestra	1930	UK (London)	Orchestre Symphonique de Monréal	1842	Canada
BBC Welsh Symphony Orchestra	1935	UK (Cardiff)	Oslo Philharmonic	1919	Norway
Chicago Symphony Orchestra	1891	USA	Philadelphia Orchestra	1900	USA
			The Philharmonic Orchestra	1945	UK (London)
Cleveland Symphony Orchestra	1918	USA	Pittsburgh Symphony Orchestra	1926	UK
Concertgebouw Orchestra	1888	Netherlands (Amsterdam)	Royal Philharmonic Orchestra	1946	UK (London)
Detroit Symphony Orchestra	1914	USA	San Francisco Symphony Orchestra	1911	USA
English Chamber Orchestra	1948	UK (London)	Santa Cecelia Academy Orchestra	1895	Italy (Rome)
Hallé Orchestra	1858	UK (Manchester)	Scottish Chamber Orchestra	1974	UK (Edinburgh)
			Scottish National Orchestra	1890	UK (Glasgow)
Israel Philharmonic Orchestra	1936	Israel(Tel Aviv)	Seattle Symphony Orchestra	1903	USA
Leningrad Philharmonic Orchestra	1921	USSR	Staatskapelle Orchestra	1923	Germany (Dresden)
London Philharmonic Orchestra	1904	UK	Sydney Symphony Orchestra	1934	Australia
London Symphony Orchestra	1904	UK	Ulster Orchestra	1966	UK (Belfast)
Los Angeles Philharmonic Orchestra	1904	USA	Vienna Philharmonic	1842	Austria
Melbourne Symphony Orchestra	1906	Australia	Vienna Symphony Orchestra	1900	Austria
Milan La Scala Orchestra	1778	Italy			

POP AND ROCK MUSICIANS AND SINGERS

Selected singles and albums are listed

Abba Swedish group, 1970s to early 1980s; members include Bjorn Ulvaeus (1945–) singer, guitarist, born Gothenburg; Agnetha Faltskog (1950–) singer, born Jankoping; Anni-Frid Lyngstad (1945–) singer, born Narvik, Norway; Benny Andersson (1946–) singer, keyboardist, born Stockholm; *Waterloo* (1974), *Arrival* (1976), *Voulez-Vous* (1979), *Super Trouper* (1980).

AC/DC Australian heavy metal group, mid-1970s to present; members include Bon Scott (originally Ronald Belford Scott) (1946–80) vocalist, born Kirriemuir, Scotland; Brian Johnson (1947–) vocalist, born North Shields; Angus Young (1959–) guitarist, born Glasgow, Scotland; Malcolm Young (1953–) guitarist, born Glasgow, Scotland; Phil Rudd (1954–) drummer, born Melbourne, Australia; *High Voltage* (1976), *If you want blood, you've got it* (1978), *Highway to Hell* (1979), *Dirty Deeds Done Dirt Cheap* (1981), *For Those About to Rock* (1981), *Blow Up Your Video* (1988).

Aerosmith American group, 1970s to present; members include Steven Tyler (1948–) vocalist, born New York City; Joe Perry (1950–) guitarist, born Boston; Tom Hamilton (1951–) bassist, born Colorado Springs; Joey Kramer (1950–) drummer, born New York City; 'Come Together', 'Dream On', 'Angel', 'Dude Looks Like a Lady', 'Rag Doll', 'Love in an Elevator', 'Jamie's got a Gun', *Aerosmith* (1973), *Toys in the Attic* (1975), *Permanent Vacation* (1987), *Pump* (1989).

The Animals British group, 1960s; members include Eric Burdon (1941–) vocalist, born Newcastle-upon-Tyne; Alan Price (1942–) keyboardist, born Fairfield, County Durham; 'House of the Rising Sun', 'We've Gotta Get Out Of This Place', *Animals* (1964), *Ark* (1983).

Ant, Adam (originally **Stuart Leslie Goddard**) (1954–) British singer/songwriter, guitarist, born London; (with the Ants) 'Prince Charming', 'Stand and Deliver', 'Goody Two-Shoes', 'Apollo Nine', *King of the Wild Frontier* (1980), *Prince Charming* (1980); *Friend or Foe* (1982), *Vive Le Rock* (1985).

Armatrading, Joan (1950–) British singer, guitarist, born St Kitts Island, Caribbean; *Joan Armatrading* (1976), *To the Limit* (1978), *Walk Under Ladders* (1981), *The Key* (1983), *Sleight of Hand* (1986).

Asia British group, 1980s; Steve Howe (1947–) guitarist, born London; Carl Palmer (1951–) drummer, born Birmingham; John Wetton (1949–) bassist, vocalist, born Derby; Geoff Downes (1952–) keyboardist; 'Heat of the Moment', 'Only Time Will Tell', *Asia* (1982), *Alpha* (1983).

Baez, Joan (1941–) American singer, guitarist, born Staten Island, New York; 'The Night They Drove Ol' Dixie Down' (1972), *Any Day Now* (1968), *Farewell, Anjelica* (1975), *Diamonds and Rust* (1975), *Recently* (1987).

The Bangles American group, 1980s; Susannah Hoffs quitarist; Vicky Peterson guitarist; Debbie Peterson drummer; Michael Steele bassist; all singers; 'Manic Monday', 'If He knew what She Wants', 'Walk like an Egyptian', 'Eternal Flame', 'Be with You', *All over the Place* (1984), *Different Light* (1986), *Everything* (1988).

Bassey, Shirley (1937–) British singer, born Tiger Bay, Cardiff, Wales; 'Goldfinger', 'Big Spender', 'Diamonds are Forever'.

The Bay City Rollers Scottish 1970s band; members include Derek Longmuir (1955–) drummer; Alan Longmuir (1953–) bassist; Les McKeown (1955–) guitarist, vocalist; all born Edinburgh; 'Bye Bye Baby', 'Give Me a Little Love', 'Saturday Night'.

The Beach Boys American group, 1960s to present; members include Brian (1942–) bassist, Dennis (1944–83) drummer, and Carl (1946–) Wilson drummer, keyboardist; all born Hawthorne, California; Mike Love (1941–) vocalist; 'Surfin' USA', 'Help Me Rhonda', 'Barbara Ann', 'Good Vibrations', 'Fun, Fun, Fun', 'I Get Around', 'California Girls', 'Little Deuce Coupe', 'God Only Knows', 'Wouldn't It Be Nice'.

The Beatles British group, 1960s; John (Winston) Lennon (1940–80) singer/songwriter, guitarist; (James) Paul McCartney (1942–) singer/songwriter, guitarist; George Harrison (1943–) singer/songwriter, guitarist; Ringo Starr (originally Richard Starkey) (1940–) singer/songwriter, drummer; all born Liverpool; 'Love Me Do', 'She Loves You', 'From Me to You', 'I Want to Hold your Hand', 'Yesterday', 'Day Tripper', 'Paperback Writer', 'You've Got to Hide Your Love Away', 'Penny Lane', 'Strawberry Fields

POP AND ROCK MUSICIANS AND SINGERS (cont.)

Forever', 'Hey Jude', *Please Please Me* (1963), *With the Beatles* (1963), *A Hard Day's Night* (1964), *Beatles for Sale* (1964), *Help!* (1965), *Rubber Soul* (1965), *Revolver* (1966), *Sergeant Pepper's Lonely Hearts Club Band* (1967), *Magical Mystery Tour* (1967), *Yellow Submarine* (1968), *The White Album* (1968), *Abbey Road* (1969), *Let it Be* (1970).

The Bee Gees British/Australian group; members include Barry (1946–), Robin (1949–), and Maurice (1949–) Gibb; all born Isle of Man; 'Massachusetts', 'Jive Talkin'', 'How Deep is Your Love?', 'Staying Alive', 'Night Fever', *Children of the World* (1976).

Benatar, Pat (originally **Pat Andrzejewski**) (1953–) American singer/songwriter, born Brooklyn, New York; *Crimes of Passion, In the Heat of the Night, Live From Earth, Precious Time, Get Nervous* (1982), *Tropico* (1984), *Seven the Hard Way* (1986), *Wide Awake In Dreamland* (1988).

Berry, Chuck (originally **Charles Edward Anderson Berry**) (1926–) American singer/songwriter, guitarist; born St Louis, Missouri; 'Maybelline', 'Sweet Little Sixteen', 'Too Much Monkey Business', 'Rock and Roll Music', 'School Days', 'No Particular Place to Go', 'Johnny B Goode', 'Nadine', 'My Ding a Ling'.

B-52s American group, 1970s to present; members include Cindy Wilson (1957–) vocalist; Ricky Wilson (1953–85) guitarist; Keith Strickland (1953–) drummer; all born Athens, Georgia; Fred Schneider (1954–) vocalist, born Newark, Georgia; Kate Pierson (1948–) vocalist, keyboardist, born Weehawken, New Jersey; 'Rock Lobster', 'Love Shack', 'Roam', 'Deadbeat Club', *Wild Planet* (1980), *Mesopotamia* (1982), *Whammy* (1983), *Bouncing off the Satellites* (1986), *Cosmic Thing*.

Blondie American group, 1970s to 1980s; members include Deborah Harry (1945–) vocalist, born Miami, Florida (solo 'Island of Lost Souls', 'French Kissin' in the USA', 'Free to Fall', 'I want that Man', *Rockbird, Def, Dumb, and Blonde*); Chris Stein (1950–) guitarist, born Brooklyn; 'Denis', 'Heart of Glass', 'Union City Blue', 'Call Me', 'The Tide is High', *Blondie, Plastic Letters, Eat to the Beat, Parallel Lines, AutoAmerican*.

Blue Oyster Cult American group, 1970s to present; Eric Bloom vocalist; Buck Dharma (born Donald Roeser) guitarist; Alan Lanier guitarist, keyboardist; Joe Bouchard bassist, vocalist; Albert Bouchard drummer, vocalist; Rick Downey drummer; 'Don't Fear the Reaper', *Blue Oyster Cult* (1972), *Agents of Fortune* (1976), *Cultosaurus Erectus* (1980), *Fire of Unknown Origin* (1981), *Revolution by Night* (1983).

Bolan, Marc (and T Rex) (originally **Mark Feld**) (1947–77) British singer/songwriter, guitarist, born London; 'Get It On', 'Metal Guru', 'Children Of The Revolution', 'Jeepster', *Unicorn* (1970).

Booker T and the MG's American group, 1960s; Booker T Jones (1944–) vocalist, organist, born Memphis, Tennessee; Donald 'Duck' Dunn (1941–) bassist, born Memphis; Steve Cropper (1941–) guitarist, born Willow Springs, Missouri; 'To be a Lover', *Green Onions* (1962).

Boomtown Rats Irish group, mid 1970s to early 1980s; members include Bob Geldof (1954–) singer/songwriter, born Dublin (solo *Deep in the Heart of Nowhere* (1986)); 'Rat Trap', 'I Don't Like Mondays', 'Banana Republic', *Tonic for the Troops* (1978).

Bowie, David (originally **David Robert Jones**) (1947–) British singer/songwriter, guitarist, born Brixton, London; 'The Laughing Gnome', 'Space Oddity', 'Life on Mars', 'Jean Genie', 'Andy Warhol', 'Rebel, Rebel', 'Ashes to Ashes', 'Blue Jean', 'China Girl', 'Let's Dance', 'Modern Love', *The Man who Sold the World* (1970), *Hunky Dory* (1971), *The Rise and Fall of Ziggy Stardust and the Spiders from Mars* (1972), *Diamond Dogs* (1974), *Heroes* (1977), *Scary Monsters* (1980), *Let's Dance* (1983).

Brown, James (1928–) American singer/songwriter, drummer, pianist, born Barnwell, South Carolina; 'Papa's Got a Brand New Bag', 'It's a Man's Man's Man's World', 'Ain't It Funky Now', 'Sex Machine', 'Get Up offa That Thing'.

Bush, Kate (1958–) British singer/songwriter, keyboardist, born Plumstead; 'Wuthering Heights', 'The Man with the Child in His Eyes', 'Wow', 'Running Up That Hill', *Never Forever* (1980), *The Dreaming* (1982), *Hounds of Love* (1986).

The Byrds American group, 1960s to present; Roger McGuinn (1942–) guitarist, born Chicago; Chris Hillman (1942–) bassist, mandolin player, vocalist, born Los Angeles; David Crosby vocalist, guitarist;

POP AND ROCK MUSICIANS AND SINGERS (cont.)

Michael Clarke (1943–) drummer, born New York City; 'Mr Tambourine Man', 'Eight Miles High', *Mr Tambourine Man* (1965), *Turn, Turn, Turn* (1966), *Fifth Dimension* (1966).

Carnes, Kim (1945–) American singer/songwriter, born Los Angeles; 'Don't Fall In Love With A Dreamer', 'Bette Davis Eyes', 'Voyeur', *Gideon* (1980), *Mistaken Identity* (1991).

The Carpenters American group, 1970s to 1980s; members include Karen Carpenter (1950–83) vocalist, drummer; Richard Carpenter (1946–) vocalist, keyboardist; both born New Haven, Connecticut; *Close to You* (1970), *Yesterday Once More* (1974), *Voice of the Heart* (1983).

Cars American group, 1970s to present; Ric Ocasek singer/songwriter, guitarist, born Baltimore; Ben Orr (originally Benjamin Orzechowski) born Cleveland; Greg Hawkes keyboardist; 'My Best Friend's Girl', 'Just What I Needed', 'Since You're Gone', 'Shake it Up', 'Drive', 'You Might Think', *The Cars* (1978), *Candy-O* (1979), *Heartbeat City* (1984).

Cash, Johnny (1932–) American singer/songwriter, guitarist, born Kingsland, Arkansas; 'Don't Take Your Guns to Town', 'Rings of Fire', 'A Boy Named Sue', 'The Man in Black', 'A Thing Called Love'.

Charles, Ray (originally **Ray Charles Robinson**) (1930–) American singer/songwriter, pianist, born Albany, Georgia; 'I Got a Woman', 'Lonely Avenue', 'You Are My Sunshine', 'Crying Time', 'Hit the Road, Jack', *The Genius of Ray Charles* (1959).

Cheap Trick American group, 1970s to present; Rick Nielsen (1946–) guitarist; Tom Peterson (1950–) bassist; both born Rockford, Illinois; Bun E Carlos (originally Brad Carlson) drummer; Robin Zander (1952–) vocalist, born Loves Park, Illinois; 'I Want You to Want Me', 'Surrender', 'The Flame', *Heaven Tonight* (1978), *Dream Police* (1979), *One on One* (1982).

Cher (originally **Cherilyn Sarkasian La Pierre**) (1946–) American singer/songwriter, born El Centro, California; (with Sonny Bono) 'I Got You Babe', 'Just You', 'All I Ever Need Is You'; 'All I Really Want To Do', 'Gypsys, Tramps and Thieves', 'Half Breed', 'Dark Lady', 'The Shoop Shoop Song'.

Clapton, Eric (1945–) British singer/songwriter, guitarist, born Ripley, Surrey (was in 1960s groups Cream and The Yardbirds); 'Layla', 'Lay Down Sally', 'Wonderful Tonight', 'I Shot the Sheriff', 'Tulsa Time', 'Cocaine', 'I've Got a Rock 'n Roll Heart', *Derek and the Dominos* (with Duane Allman) (1970); *461 Ocean Boulevard* (1974), *Slowhand* (1977), *Just One Night* (1980), *Money and Cigarettes* (1983), *August* (1986).

The Clash British group, late 1970s to 1980s; members include Joe Strummer (originally John Mellors) (1952–) guitarist, vocalist, born Ankara, Turkey; Mick Jones (1955–) guitarist, vocalist, born London ; Paul Simonon (1956) bassist, born London; 'Topper' Headon (1956–) drummer, born Dover; 'I Fought the Law', 'Rock the Casbah', 'Should I Stay or Should I Go', *The Clash* (1977), *Cost of Living* (1979), *London Calling* (1979), *Combat Rock, Cut the Crap* (1985).

Cocker, Joe (1944–) British singer/songwriter, born Sheffield, England; 'With a Little Help from My Friends', 'You Are So Beautiful', 'Up Where We Belong' (with Jennifer Warnes), *Mad Dogs and the Englishmen* (1970), *I Can Stand a Little Rain* (1974), *Unchain My Heart* (1987).

Cohen, Leonard (1934–) Canadian singer/songwriter, guitarist, born Montreal; 'Suzanne', 'Famous Blue Raincoat', *Songs of Leonard Cohen* (1968), *Songs of Love and Hate* (1970), *Various Positions* (1984), *I'm Your Man* (1988).

Cooke, Sam (originally **Sam Cook**) (1935–64) American singer/songwriter, born Chicago, Illinois; 'You Send Me', 'A Change Is Gonna Come', 'Wonderful World' (1960), *Sam Cooke at the Copa* (1964), *Sam Cooke – The Man And His Music* (1986).

Cooper, Alice (originally **Vincent Furnier**) (1948–) American singer/songwriter, born Detroit; 'School's Out', 'Poison', 'Hey Stoopid', *Love it to Death* (1971), *School's Out* (1972).

Costello, Elvis (originally **Declan Patrick McManus**) (1955–) British singer/songwriter, guitarist, born Paddington, London; 'Watching the Detectives', '(I Don't Want To Go To) Chelsea', 'Accidents Will Happen', 'Alison', 'Shipbuilding', 'Every Day I Write the Book', 'Don't Let Me Be Misunderstood', *My Aim is True* (1977), *This Years Model* (with The Attractions) (1978), *Armed Forces* (1979), *Almost Blue* (1981), *Imperial Bedroom* (1982), *Punch the Clock* (1983), *Goodbye Cruel World* (1984), *King of America* (1986).

POP AND ROCK MUSICIANS AND SINGERS (cont.)

Cray, Robert (1953–) American singer, blues guitarist, born Columbus, Georgia; 'Phone Booth', *False Accusations* (1985), *Showdown!* (1985).

Cream British group, late 1960s; members include Eric Clapton (1945–) singer, guitarist; Jack Bruce singer, bass; Ginger Baker drummer; 'I Feel Free', 'Sunshine of Your Love', 'Strange Brew', 'Badge', 'Crossroads', *Fresh Cream* (1966), *Disraeli Gears* (1967), *Wheels on Fire* (1968), *Goodbye* (1969).

Creedance Clearwater Revival American group, late 1960s to early 1970s; members include John Cameron Fogerty (1945–?90) (solo 'Rockin' All Over the World', *Centerfield* (1985)), Tom Fogerty (1941–), both guitarists and vocalists, born Berkeley, California; Doug Clifford (1945–) drummer, born Palo Alto; Stu Cook (1945–) bassist, born Oakland; 'Susie Q', 'Proud Mary', 'Bad Moon Risin', 'Green River', 'Born on the Bayou', 'Down on the Corner', 'I Heard it through the Grapevine', 'Fortunate Son', 'Travellin' Band', 'Up, around the Bend', *Creedance Clearwater Revival* (1968), *Pendulum* (1970), *Mardi Gras* (1972).

Crosby, Bing (originally **Harry Lillis**) (1903–77) American singer, born Spokane, Washington; 'Swingin' on a Star', 'White Christmas', 'True Love' (with Grace Kelly).

Crosby, Stills, Nash and Young American group, late 1960s to present; David Crosby (originally David van Cortland) (1941–) guitarist, vocalist, born Los Angeles; Graham Nash (1942–) vocalist, born Blackpool, England; Stephen Stills, guitarist, vocalist, pianist; Neil Young guitarist, vocalist, pianist; 'Ohio', *Déjà vu* (1970), *Four Way Street* (1971), *Allies* (1983).

Culture Club British group, 1980s; members include Boy George (originally George O'Dowd) vocalist, born Eltham; Jon Moss (1957–) drummer, born London; 'Karma Chameleon', *Colour By Numbers*.

The Cure British group, mid-1970s to present; members include Robert Smith (1957–) guitarist, singer/songwriter, born Crawley, Sussex; Laurence Tolhurst drummer, keyboardist; 'Killing an Arab', 'Boys Don't Cry', 'Love Cats', 'The Caterpillar', 'Close to Me', 'Standing on the Beach', 'In Between Days', *Boy's Don't Cry* (1980), *Faith* (1981), *Pornography* (1982), *The Head on the Door* (1985), *Disintegration* (1989).

Davis, Sammy, Jr (1925–90) American singer, born New York City; 'Something's Gotta Give', 'That Old Black Magic', 'Candy Man', *Starring Sammy Davis Jr* (1955), *Just for Lovers* (1955), *The Wham of Sam* (1960).

Deep Purple British heavy metal group, late 1960s to 1980s; members include Ian Gillan (1945–) vocalist, born Hounslow; David Coverdale (1951–) vocalist, born Saltburn; Ritchie Blackmore (1945–) guitarist born Weston-super-Mare; Jon Lord (1941–) keyboardist, born Leicester; Roger Glover (1945–) bassist; Ian Paice (1948–) drummer; 'Black Night', 'Smoke on the Water', *Shades of Deep Purple* (1968), *Deep Purple* (1969), *Deep Purple In Rock* (1970), *Machine Head* (1972), *Made in Japan* (1972), *Perfect Strangers* (1984).

Def Leppard British heavy metal group, 1980s to present; members include Joe Elliott (1960–) vocalist; Rick Savage bassist; Pete Willis guitar, replaced by Phil Collen; Steve Clark (d.1991) guitarist; Rick Allen (c.1963–) drummer; 'Photograph', 'Foolin'', 'Rock of Ages', 'Animal', 'Women', 'Pour Some Sugar on Me', *On Through the Night* (1980), *High and Dry* (1981), *Pyromania* (1983), *Hysteria* (1987).

Depeche Mode British group, 1980s to present; Andy Fletcher (1961–); Martin Gore (1961–); Vince Clarke; Alan Wilder (1963–) keyboardist; *Speak and Spell* (1981), *Black Celebration* (1986), *Music for the Masses* (1987).

Devo American group, 1970s to 1980s; Jerry Casale bassist, singer/songwriter; Bob Casale and Mark Mothersbaugh keyboardists, guitarists, vocalists; Bob Mothersbaugh guitarist, vocalist; Alan Myers drummer; 'Satisfaction', 'Whip It', *Q:Are We Not Men? A:We Are Devo!* (1978), *Shout* (1984).

Diamond, Neil Leslie (1941–) American singer/songwriter, guitarist, born Coney Island, New York; 'Song Sung Blue', 'You Don't Bring Me Flowers' (with Barbra Streisand), 'Love on the Rocks', *Beautiful Noise* (1976), *The Jazz Singer* (1980), *Heartlight* (1982), *Headed for the Future* (1986).

Diddley, Bo (originally **Ellas McDaniel**) (1928–) American singer, guitarist, born McComb, Mississippi; 'Bo Diddley'/'I'm a Man', 'Road Runner', 'Do Wah Diddy Diddy', *Got My Own Bag of Tricks* (1971).

POP AND ROCK MUSICIANS AND SINGERS (cont.)

Dio, Ronnie James (originally **Ronald Padavona**)   (1949–) American heavy metal singer, born Cortland, New York; 'Hungry for Heaven', 'Rock 'n Roll Children', *Holy Diver* (1983), *The Last in Line* (1984), *Sacred Heart* (1985), *Dream Evil* (1987).

Dire Straits British group, late 1970s to present; members include Mark Knopfler (1949–) singer/songwriter, guitarist, born Glasgow (solo soundtrack *Local Hero*); David Knopfler guitarist replaced by Hal Lindes; John Illsley (1949–) bassist, born London; Pick Withers drummer; Alan Clark keyboardist; 'Romeo and Juliet', 'Tunnel of Love', 'So Far Away', 'Money for Nothing', 'Walk of Life', *Dire Straits* (1978), *Communiqué* (1979), *Making Moves, Love over Gold* (1983), *Alchemy* (1984), *Brothers in Arms* (1985), *Money for Nothing* (1988).

Domino, Fats (originally **Antoine Domino**)   (1928–) American singer, pianist, born New Orleans, Louisiana; 'Every Night About This Time', 'It's Midnight', 'Ain't That a Shame', 'Blue Monday', 'Blueberry Hill'.

Donovan (originally **Donovan Philips Leitch**)   (1946–) British singer/songwriter, guitarist, born Glasgow; 'Mellow Yellow', 'Sunshine Superman', *The Universal Soldier* (1966).

Doobie Brothers American group, 1970s; John Hartman (1950–) drummer, born Falls Church, Virginia; Tom Johnston vocalist, guitarist, born Visalia, California; Tiran Porter bassist, born San Francisco; Patrick Simmons (1950–) vocalist, guitarist, born Aberdeen, Washington; Michael Hossack (1950–) drummer, born Paterson, New York replaced by Keith Knudson (1952–) born Ames, Iowa; Jeff 'Skunk' Baxter (1948–) guitarist, born Washington DC; Michael McDonald keyboardist, vocalist, born St Louis (solo *Sweet Freedom* (1986)); 'Listen to the Music', 'Black Water', 'Fool', *What Were Once Vices Are Now Habits* (1974).

The Doors American group, late 1960s to early 1970s; members include Jim Morrison (1943–71), singer/songwriter, born Melbourne, Florida; Ray Manzarek (1939–) keyboardist, born Chicago; Robby Krieger (1946–) guitarist, born Los Angeles; John Densmore (1945–) drummer, born Los Angeles; 'Light My Fire', 'The End', 'When the Music's Over', 'L.A. Woman', 'Hello, I Love You', 'Five To One', 'Touch Me', 'Riders on the Storm', *The Doors* (1967), *Strange Days* (1967), *Waiting for the Sun* (1968), *L.A. Woman* (1970), *An American Prayer* (1978).

Duran Duran British group, 1980s to present; members include Simon Le Bon (1958–) vocalist, born Watford, Herfordshire; Nick Rhodes (originally Nicholas Bates) (1962–) keyboardist, born Birmingham; John Taylor (1960–) bassist, born Birmingham; Roger Taylor drummer; Andy Taylor guitarist; 'Planet Earth', 'Hungry Like the Wolf', 'Save a Prayer', 'Rio', 'Union of the Snake', 'Wild Boys', *Duran Duran* (1981), *Rio* (1982), *Seven and the Ragged Tiger* (1983), *Arena* (1984), *Notorious* (1986).

Dylan, Bob (originally **Robert Allan Zimmerman**)   (1941–) American singer/songwriter, guitarist, born Duluth, Minnesota; 'Blowin in the Wind', 'Mr Tambourine Man', 'Desolation Row', 'Like a Rolling Stone', 'Maggie's Farm', 'All Along the Watchtower', 'Lay Lady Lay', *The Freewheelin' Bob Dylan* (1963), *The Times They Are A-changin'* (1963), *Another Side of Bob Dylan* (1964), *Bringing It All Back Home* (1965), *Blonde on Blonde* (1966), *John Wesley Harding* (1968), *Nashville Skyline* (1969), *Blood on the Tracks* (1974), *The Basement Tapes* (1975), *Slow Train Coming* (1979), *Infidels* (1983)

The Eagles American group, 1970s; members include Glenn Frey (1948–) singer, guitarist, born Detroit, Michigan; Donn Henley (1947–) singer, drummer, born Texas (solo 'Dirty Laundry', 'Boys of Summer', *Building the Perfect Beast* (1984)); Bernie Leadon (1947–) guitarist replaced by Joe Walsh (1947–) guitarist, singer/songwriter, born Wichita, Kansas (solo *Life's Been Good*, *But Seriously Folks* (1976), *Got Any Gum?* (1987)); Randy Meisner (1946–) bassist, born Nebraska; 'Best of My Love', 'Lyin' Eyes', 'New Kid in Town', 'Heartache Tonight', *Eagles* (1972), *Desperado* (1973), *One of these Nights* (1975), *Hotel California* (1976), *The Long Run* (1979).

Earth, Wind and Fire American group, 1970s to present; Maurice White (1941–) vocalist, drummer, born Memphis, Tennessee; Verdine White (1951–) bassist; Philip Bailey (1951–) vocalist, born Denver, Colorado; Larry Dunn (1953–) keyboardist, born Colorado; Johnny Graham (1951–) guitarist, born Kentucky; Al McKay (1948–) guitarist, born Louisiana; Andre Woolfolk (1950–) reeds, born Texas;

POP AND ROCK MUSICIANS AND SINGERS (cont.)

Ralph Johnson (1951–) drummer, born California; 'Shining Star', 'Got to Get you into My Life', 'Boogie Wonderland', *Open Our Eyes* (1974), *That's The Way of the World* (1975).

Easton, Sheena (originally **Sheena Orr**) (1959–) British singer, born Bellshill, Scotland; 'Morning Train', 'For Your Eyes Only', 'Sugar Walls'.

Electric Light Orchestra British group, 1970s to 1980s; members include Jeff Lynne (1947–) guitarist, vocalist; Roy Wood (1946–); Bev Bevan (1946–) drummer; all born Birmingham; 'Roll Over Beethoven', 'Evil Woman', 'Hold On Tight', 'Mr Blue Sky', 'Last Train to London', 'Calling America', *Xanadu* (1980)

Emerson, Lake and Palmer British group, 1970s; members include Keith Emerson (1944–) keyboardist, vocalist, born Todmorton; Greg Lake (1948–) guitarist, vocalist, born Bournemouth; Carl Palmer (1941–) drummer, born Birmingham; 'I Believe in Father Christmas', 'Honky Tonk Train Blues'.

Eurythmics British group, 1980s; members include David Allan Stewart (1952–) songwriter, keyboardist, guitarist, born Sunderland, England; Annie Lennox (1954–) singer/songwriter, born Aberdeen, Scotland; 'Love is a Stranger', 'Who's that Girl', 'Here Comes the Rain Again', 'Sexcrime', 'Thorn in My Side', 'It's Alright (Baby's Coming Back)', 'Sisters are Doin' it for themselves' (with Aretha Franklin), 'When Tomorrow Comes', *Sweet Dreams are Made of This* (1982), *Touch* (1983), *1984* (1984), *Be Yourself Tonight* (1985), *Revenge* (1986), *Savage* (1987), *We Too are One* (1989).

Fairport Convention British group, mid 1960s to 1970s; members include Ashley Hutchings (1945–), Simon Nicol (1950–), Richard Thompson singer/songwriter, guitarist; Martin Lamble (1949–69) drummer; Judy Dyble (1948–) singer/songwriter replaced by Sandy Denny (1941–); Dave Swarbrick (1941–) fiddler; all born London; Ian Matthews (1946–) born Scunthorpe; 'Meet on a Ledge', 'A Sailor's Life', *Rosie* (1973), *Fairport 9*.

Ferry, Bryan (1945–) British singer, born Washington, County Durham; 'Tokyo Joe', 'The Price of Love', 'Slave to Love', 'Don't Stop the Dance'; *Let's Stick Together* (1976), *Bête Noire* (1987).

Fleetwood Mac British/American group, late 1960s to present; members include Peter Green (originally Peter Greenbaum) (1946–) singer/songwriter, guitarist, born London; Mick Fleetwood (1942–) drummer; John McVie (1945–) bassist; Christine McVie singer, keyboardist; Lindsey Buckingham (1947–) singer, guitarist, born Palo Alto, California; Stevie (Stephanie) Nicks (1948–) singer/songwriter, born Phoenix, Arizona (solo *Bella Donna* (1982), *The Wild Heart* (1983), *Rock A Little* (1985), *The Other Side of the Mirror*); 'Sara', 'Big Love', 'Little Lies', *Fleetwood Mac* (1975), *Rumours* (1977), *Mirage* (1982), *Tango in the Night* (1987).

Foreigner British/American group, late 1970s to late 1980s; members include Mick Jones (1947–) guitarist, born England; Dennis Elliott (1950–) drummer, born London; Lou Gramm (1950–) vocalist, born Rochester, New York; 'Hot Blooded', 'Urgent', 'Waiting for a Girl Like You', 'I Want to Know what Love is', 'That Was Yesterday' *Double Vision* (1978), *Records* (1982), *Agent Provocateur* (1984).

Frankie Goes to Hollywood British group, early 1980s; Holly Johnson (1960–) and Paul Rutherford (1959–) vocalists; Mark O'Toole (1964–) bassist; Peter Gill (1960–) drummer; Brian Nash (1963–) guitarist; 'Relax!', 'Two Tribes', 'The Power of Love', 'Ferry Across the Mersey', *Welcome to the Pleasure Dome* (1984).

Franklin, Aretha (1942–) American singer, born Memphis, Tennessee; 'Think', 'Respect', *I Never Loved A Man The Way I Love You* (1967), *Lady Soul* (1968), *Amazing Grace* (1972), *Everything I Feel in Me* (1974), *Almighty Fire* (1978), *Love All The Hurt Away* (1981), *Get It Right* (1983), *Aretha* (1986).

Gaye, Marvin (Pentz) (1939–84) American singer/songwriter, pianist, drummer, born Washington D C; 'Hitch Hike', 'Can I Get a Witness', 'I Heard it through the Grapevine', 'What's Goin' On', 'Sexual Healing', *What's Goin' On* (1971), *Let's Get it On* (1973), *Here My Dear* (1979), *In Our Lifetime* (1981), *Midnight Love* (1982).

Genesis British group, late 1960s to present; members include (at various times) Peter Gabriel (1950–) singer/songwriter, born Cobham, Surrey; Phil Collins (1951–) singer/songwriter, drummer, born London; Tony Banks (1950–) keyboardist; Michael Rutherford (1951–) guitarist, bassist, vocalist; all have

POP AND ROCK MUSICIANS AND SINGERS (cont.)

worked as solo artists; *Selling England by the Pound* (1973), *Nursery Cryme* (1971), *The Lamb Lies Down on Broadway* (1974).

Glitter, Gary (originally **Paul Gadd**)   (1944–   ) British singer/songwriter, born Banbury, Oxfordshire; 'I'm the Leader of the Gang (I Am)', 'I Love You Love Me Love'.

The Go-Go's   American group, 1980s; Jane Wiedlin (1958–   ) guitarist, born Oconomowoc, Wisconsin (solo 'Cool Places' (with Sparks), 'Blue Kiss', 'Rush Hour', *Fur* (1988)); Belinda Carlisle (1958–   ) singer, born Hollywood (solo *Heaven on Earth*, *Runaway Horses*); Charlotte Caffey (1953–   ) guitarist, born Santa Monica; Gina Schock (1957–   ) drummer, born Baltimore; Kathy Valentine (1959–   ) bassist, born Austin, Texas; 'Our Lips Are Sealed', 'We Got The Beat', *Beauty and the Beast* (1981), *Vacation* (1982), *Talk Show* (1984).

Grateful Dead   American group, late 1960s to present; members include Jerry Garcia (originally Jerome Garcia) (1942–   ) guitarist, born San Francisco, California; 'Dark Star', *Live Dead* (1970), *Europe* (1972), *Blues for Allah* (1975), *In the Dark* (1987), *Dylan and the Dead* (with Bob Dylan) (1988).

Guns 'n' Roses   American group, late 1980s to present; W Axl Rose singer; Slash guitarist; Matt Sorum drummer; 'Sweet Child O' Mine', 'Welcome to the Jungle', 'Night Train', 'Patience', 'You Could Be Mine' *Appetite for Destruction*, *G 'n' R Lies*.

Haley, Bill   (1925–81) American singer/songwriter, guitarist, born Highland Park, Michigan; (with The Comets) 'Crazy Man Crazy', 'Shake Rattle and Roll', 'Rock Around the Clock', 'See You Later, Alligator', 'Rudy's Rock'.

Hall & Oates   American duo, 1970s to present; Daryl Hall (originally Daryl Hohl) (1948–   ) singer, born Pottsdown, Pennsylvania; John Oates (1949–   ) singer, guitarist, born New York City; 'She's Gone', 'Sara Smile, 'Rich Girl', 'Kiss On My List', 'I Can't Go For That (No Can Do), 'Maneater', 'Out of Touch', *Abandoned Luncheonette* (1973), *Private Eyes* (1981), *Rock 'n' Soul Part I, Bigbamboom* (1985), *Live At the Apollo* (1985).

Hancock, Herbie (Herbert Jeffrey Hancock)   (1940–   ) American singer/songwriter, keyboardist, born Chicago; 'Gimme the Night', 'Rockit', *Maiden Voyage* (1965), *Blow-Up* (1966), *Sextant* (1972), *Head Hunters* (1973), *Thrust* (1974), *Future Shock* (1983), *Sound System* (1983).

Harrison, George   (1943–   ) British singer/songwriter, guitarist, born Liverpool; 'My Sweet Lord', 'All Those Years Ago', 'Got My Mind Set On You', 'When We Was Fab'; *All Things Must Pass* (1970), *Cloud Nine* (1987).

Hendrix, Jimi (originally **James Marshall Hendrix**)   (1942–70) American singer/songwriter, guitarist, born Seattle, Washington; (with the Experience) 'Voodoo Chile', 'Hey Joe', 'Purple Haze', 'The Wind Cries Mary', 'Crosstown Traffic', 'All Along the Watchtower', *Are You Experienced?* (1967), *Electric Ladyland* (1968), *Axis: Bold As Love* (1968).

Herman's Hermits   British group, 1960s; members include Peter 'Herman' Noone (1947–   ) singer, pianist, guitarist, born Manchester; Karl Green (1947–   ) guitarist, harmonica player, born Salford; Keith Hopwood (1946–   ) guitarist, born Manchester; Derek 'Lek' Leckenby (1945–   ) guitarist, born Leeds; Barry Whitmore (1946–   ) drummer, born Manchester; 'I'm Into Something Good', 'Mrs Brown, You've Got a Lovely Daughter', 'I'm Henry VIII, I Am'.

The Hollies   British group, 1960s to present; members include Allan Clarke (1942–   ) vocalist, born Salford; Graham Nash (1942–   ) guitarist, vocalist, born Blackpool replaced by Terry Sylvester (1945–   ) born Liverpool; Tony Hicks (1943–   ) guitarist, born Nelson; Eric Haydock (1943–   ) bassist, born Stockport replaced by Bernie Calvert (1943–   ) born Burnley; Bobby Elliott (1943–   ) drummer, born Burnley; 'Searchin'', 'Just One Look', 'He Ain't Heavy, He's My Brother', 'The Air That I Breathe', 'Stop In the Name of Love'.

Holly, Buddy (originally **Charles Hardin Holley**)   (1936–59) American singer/songwriter, guitarist, violinist, born Lubbock, Texas; (with the Crickets) 'That'll Be the Day', 'Oh Boy!', 'Not Fade Away', 'Peggy Sue', 'Every Day', 'Rave On', 'Peggy Sue Got Married'.

Houston, Whitney   (1963–   ) American singer, born Newark, New Jersey; 'Saving All My Love For You',

POP AND ROCK MUSICIANS AND SINGERS (cont.)

'How Will I Know', 'Greatest Love', 'I Wanna Dance With Somebody (Who Loves Me)', 'Where Do Broken Hearts Go', 'My Name is Not Sue', *Whitney Houston, Whitney* (1987).

Human League British group, late 1970s to present; members include Philip Oakey (1955–   ) singer; Susanne Sully (1963–   ) singer; Joanne Catherall (1962–   ) singer; Ian Burden (1957–   ) bassist; Jo Callis (1951–   ) guitarist; 'Don't You Want Me' (1981), '(Keep Feeling) Fascination', 'Mirror Man', 'Louise', *Dare* (1981), *Crash* (1986).

Idol, Billy (originally **William Michael Albert Broad**)   (1955–   ) British singer/songwriter, guitarist, born Stanmore, Essex; 'Dancing With Myself', 'Mony Mony', 'Hot in the City', 'White Wedding', 'Rebel Yell', 'Eyes Without a Face', 'To Be A Lover', *Billy Idol* (1982), *Rebel Yell* (1984), *Whiplash Smile* (1986), *Charmed Life* (1990).

Inxs Australian group, 1980s to present; Michael Hutchence (1960–   ) singer, born Sydney; Andrew Farriss keyboardist; Jon Farriss drummer; Tim Farriss guitarist; Kirk Pengilly guitarist, saxophonist; Garry Beer Beers drummer; 'Original Sin', 'This Time', 'Never Tear Us Apart', 'Need You Tonight', *Shabooh Shoobah* (1982), *The Swing* (1984), *Listen Like Thieves* (1985), *Kick* (1987), *X* (1990).

Iron Maiden British heavy metal group, mid 1970s to present; members include Steve Harris (1957–   ) bassist, born Leytonstone, London; Dave Murray (1958–   ) guitarist, born Clapham, London; Adrian Smith (1957–   ) guitarist, born London; Paul Di'anno (1959–   ) singer, born Chingford, Essex replaced by Bruce Dickenson (1958–   ) born Sheffield; Nicko McBain (1954–   ) drummer, born London; 'Running Free', 'Run to the Hills', *Iron Maiden* (1980), *Number of the Beast*, *Power Slave* (1984), *Live After Death* (1985), *Somewhere in Time* (1986).

Isley Brothers American group; Kelly (originally O'Kelly) (1937–86), Rudolph (1939–   ), Ronald (1941–   ) Isley; all born Cincinnati, Ohio; 'Shout', 'Twist and Shout', 'This Old Heart of Mine (Is Weak For You)', *Harvest for the World* (1976).

J Geils Band American group, late 1960s to present; members include Jerome Geils (1946–   ) guitarist, born New York City; Magic Dick (originally Richard Salwitz) (1945–   ) harmonica player, born New London, Connecticut; Danny Klein (1946–   ) bassist, born Worcester, Massachusetts; Peter Wolf (originally Peter Blankfield) (1946–   ) vocalist, born New York City; Stephen Jo Bladd (1942–   ) drummer, born Boston; Seth Justman (1951–   ) keyboardist, born Washington DC; 'Centerfold', *Bloodshot* (1973), *Love Stinks* (1980), *Freeze-Frame* (1981), *Showtime!* (1982).

Jackson, Janet (1966–   ) American singer/songwriter, born Gary, Indiana; 'When I Think Of You', *Control* (1986).

Jackson, Michael (Joe) (1958–   ) American singer/songwriter, born Gary, Indiana; 'Billy Jean', 'Beat It'; 'The Girl is Mine', 'Say Say Say' (with Paul McCartney); 'I Can't Stop Loving You' (with Siedah Garrett), *Ben* (1972), *Off the Wall* (1979), *Thriller* (1982), *Bad* (1987) (was in the Jacksons, American group, 1960s to 1970s).

The Jam British group, mid 1970s to early 1980s; members include Paul Weller (1958–   ) singer/songwriter, guitarist, born Woking, Surrey; Bruce Foxton (1955–   ) bassist, born Woking; Rick Butler (1955–   ) drummer; 'Going Underground', 'Eton Rifles', 'Town Called Malice', 'Beat Surrender', 'Dream of Children'.

Jarre, Jean-Michel (1949–   ) French keyboardist, composer, born Lyons; *Oxygène* (1977), *Equinoxe* (1978).

The Jefferson Airplane/Jefferson Starship/Starship American group, mid 1960s to present; many different members, often changing, include Grace Slick (originally Grace Wing) (1939–   ) singer/songwriter, born Chicago, Illinois; 'White Rabbit', 'We Built this City', 'Sara', 'Nothing's Gonna Stop Us Now', *Surrealistic Pillow* (1967), *Crown of Creation* (1968), *Red Octopus* (1975), *Spitfire* (1976), *Knee Deep in Hoopla* (1986), *No Protection* (1987).

Jethro Tull British group, late 1960s to present; members include Ian Anderson (1947–   ) flautist, guitarist, vocalist, saxophonist, born Edinburgh; Martin Barre (1946–   ) guitarist, born London; Glenn Cornick (1947–   ) bassist, born Barrow-in-Furness; Clive Bunker (1946–   ) drummer; 'Sweet Dream',

POP AND ROCK MUSICIANS AND SINGERS (cont.)

'Witch's Promise', *Aqaulung* (1971), *Living In The Past* (1972), *Songs From The Wood* (1977), *Crest of a Knave* (1987).

Joel, Billy (William Martin Joel)   (1949–) American singer/songwriter, pianist, born Hicksville, Long Island, New York; 'Say Goodbye to Hollywood', 'Just The Way You Are', 'My Life', 'It's Still Rock 'n Roll to Me', 'Tell Her About it', 'Uptown Girl', 'We Didn't Start the Fire', *The Stranger* (1977), *52nd Street* (1978), *Glass House* (1980), *The Nylon Curtain* (1982), *An Innocent Man* (1983), *The Bridge* (1986), *Storm Front* (1989).

John, Elton (originally **Reginald Kenneth Dwight**)   (1947–) British singer/songwriter, pianist, born Pinner, Middlesex; 'Your Song', 'Crocodile Rock', 'Don't Go Breakin' My Heart' (with Kiki Dee), 'Little Jeannie', 'Wrap Her Up', 'Nikita', 'No Sacrifice', *Tumbleweed Connection* (1970), *Don't Shoot Me, I'm Only The Piano Player* (1973), *Good Bye Yellow Brick Road* (1973), *A Single Man* (1979), *Too Low for Zero*, *Ice on Fire* (1985).

Jones, Grace   (1952–) Jamaican singer/songwriter, born Jamaica, West Indies; 'Private Life', 'Love is the Drug', 'Pull up to the Bumper', 'Slave to the Rhythm'.

Jones, Tom (originally **Thomas Jones Woodward**)   (1940–) British singer, drummer, born Pontypridd, S Wales; 'It's Not Unusual', 'What's New Pussycat?', 'Green Green Grass of Home', 'I'll Never Fall In Love Again', 'Delilah'.

Joplin, Janis   (1943–1970) American singer/songwriter, born Port Arthur, Texas; 'Piece of My Heart', *Cheap Thrills* (1968), *I Got dem ole Kozmic Blues Again Mama* (1969), Pearl (1971).

Journey   American group, 1970s to 1980s; members include Steve Perry (1949–) vocalist, born Hanford, California; Ross Valory (1950–) bassist, born San Francisco; Neal Schon (1955–) guitarist, born San Mateo, California; Steve Smith drummer; Gregg Rolie (1948–) keyboardist replaced by Jonathan Cain, born Chicago; 'Who's Crying Now', 'Open Arms', 'Faithfully', *Infinity* (1978), *Evolution* (1979), *Departure* (1980), *Captured* (1981), *Escape* (1981), *Frontiers* (1983), *Raised on Radio* (1986).

Joy Division/New Order   British group, late 1970s to mid-1980s; members include Ian Curtis (1957–80) vocalist, born Macclesfield; changed to New Order in 1981; members include Bernard Albrecht (originally Barney Sumner) (1956–) vocalist, guitarist, born Salford, Lancashire; Peter Hook (1956–) bassist; Stephen Morris (1957–) drummer; (as Joy Division) 'Transmission', 'Love Will Tear Us Apart', *Unknown Pleasures* (1979); (as New Order) 'Blue Monday', 'Shellshock', *Movement* (1981), *Low Life* (1985).

Khan, Chaka (originally **Yvette Marie Stevens**)   (1953–) American singer/songwriter, born Great Lakes, Illinois; (with Rufus) *Rags to Rufus* (1974); *Chaka* (1978), *I Feel For You* (1984).

King, B B (originally **Riley B King**)   (1925–) American guitarist, singer/songwriter, born Itta Bena, near Indianola, Mississippi; *Live at the Regal* (1965), *Confessin' the Blues* (1966), *Blues Is King* (1967), *Indianola Mississippi Seeds* (1970), *Live in Stock County Jail* (1971), *There Must Be A Better World Somewhere* (1981), *Six Silver Strings* (1985).

The Kinks   British group, 1960s to 1980s; Ray Davies (1944–) singer/songwriter, guitarist (solo 'A Quiet Life'); Dave Davies (1947–) singer, guitarist; both born Muswell Hill, London; Mike Avory (1944–) drummer, born Hampton, Middlesex; Peter Quaife (1943–) bassist, born Tavistock, Devon; 'You Really Got Me', 'All Day and All of the Night', 'Dedicated Follower of Fashion', 'Sunny Afternoon', 'Waterloo Sunset', 'Autumn Almanac', 'Lola', 'Come Dancing', 'Don't Forget to Dance', *Village Green Preservation Society* (1968), *Lola vs. Powerman & The Moneyground Pt 1* (1970), *State of Confusion* (1983).

Kiss   American group, 1970s to present; members include Paul Stanley (originally Paul Stanley Eisen) (1952–) guitarist, born New York City; Gene Simmons (originally Gene Klein) (1949–) bassist, born Haffa, Israel; Peter Criss (originally Peter Crisscoula) (1947–) drummer, born New York City; Ace (Paul) Frehley (1951–) guitarist, born New York City; 'Rock And Roll All Nite', 'Beth', 'I was Made for Lovin' You', 'Tears are Fallin'', *Dressed to Kill* (1975), *Double Platinum* (1978), *Lick It Up* (1983), *Crazy Nights* (1987).

Knight, Gladys   (1944–) American singer, band leader (The Pips – American group, late 1950s), born Atlanta, Georgia; (with The Pips) 'I Heard It Through The Grapevine', 'Help Me Make It Through The Night', 'Midnight Train To Georgia', 'On And On', *Imagination* (1973), *Visions* (1983), *Life* (1985).

POP AND ROCK MUSICIANS AND SINGERS (cont.)

Kraftwerk   German group, 1970s to present; Ralph Hutter and Florian Schneider; 'Radio Activity', 'The Model', 'Trans Europe Express', 'Computer Love', 'Tour de France', *Autobahn* (1975), *Man Machine* (1978), *Computer World* (1981).

Lauper, Cyndi   (1954–   ) American singer, born New York City; 'Time After Time', 'Girls Just Want To Have Fun', 'All Through The Night', 'She Bop', *She's So Unusual* (1983), *True Colours* (1986).

Led Zeppelin   British group, late 1960s to 1970s; members include Jimmy Page (1944–   ) guitarist, born Heston, London; Robert Plant (1948–   ) vocalist, born Bromwich, Staffordshire; John Paul Jones (originally John Baldwin) (1946–   ) bassist, born Sidcup; John Bonham (1948–80) drummer, born Redditch; *Led Zeppelin I* (1969), *Led Zeppelin II* (1970), *Led Zeppelin III* (1970), *Led Zeppelin IV* (1971), *Houses of the Holy* (1973), *Physical Graffiti* (1975), *In Through The Out Door* (1979).

Lee, Peggy (originally **Norma Delores Egstrom**)   (1920–   ) American singer, born Jamestown, North Dakota; 'Manana', 'Fever'.

Lennon, John Winston   (1940–80) British singer/songwriter, guitarist, keyboardist, born Liverpool; 'Give Peace A Chance', 'Working Class Hero', 'Jealous Guy', 'Merry Xmas (War Is Over)', 'Whatever Gets You Through The Night', *Imagine* (1971), *Rock 'n' Roll* (1975), *Double Fantasy* (1980).

Lewis, Huey (originally **Hugh Cregg**)   (1950–   ) American singer, born New York; (with The News – American group, 1980s to present); 'Do You Believe in Love', 'Heart and Soul', 'I Want A New Drug', 'The Heart Of Rock & Roll', 'Walking On A Thin Line', 'Power Of Love', 'Stuck With You', *Picture This* (1982), *Sports* (1983), *Fore* (1986).

Lewis, Jerry Lee   (1935–   ) American pianist, singer, born Ferriday, Louisiana; 'Great Balls of Fire', 'Whole Lotta Shakin' Goin' On', 'High School Confidential', 'Breathless'.

Little Richard (originally **Richard Wayne Penniman**)   (1935–   ) American singer/songwriter, pianist, born Macon, Georgia; 'Tutti Frutti', 'Long Tall Sally', 'Rip It Up', 'The Girl Can't Help It', 'Lucille', 'Jenny, Jenny', 'Good Golly, Miss Molly', 'Lawdy Miss Clawdy', *Life Time Friend* (1986).

Lulu (originally **Marie McDonald McLaughlin Lawrie**)   (1948–   ) British singer, born Glasgow; (with The Luvvers) 'Shout', 'Leave A Little Love'; 'To Sir With Love', 'Boom Bang-A-Bang', 'The Man Who Sold The World' (with David Bowie).

Lynyrd Skynyrd   American group, 1970s; members include Ronnie Van Zandt (1949–77) vocalist, born McCombe, Minnesota; 'Sweet Home Alabama', 'Freebird', 'Whiskey rock'n'roller', *Pronounced Leh-nerd Skin-nerd* (1973), *Second Helping* (1974), *Street Survivors* (1977), *Gold and Platinum* (1979).

McCartney, Paul   (1942–   ) British singer/songwriter, guitarist, born Liverpool; 'Wonderful Christmas-time', 'Coming Up', 'Ebony & Ivory' (with Stevie Wonder), 'No More Lonely Nights', *Tug of War* (1982), *Pipes of Peace* (1983).

McLean, Don   (1945–   ) singer/songwriter, born New Rochelle, New York; 'And I Love You So', 'Vincent', 'Castles in the Air', *American Pie* (1971), *Chain Lightning* (1981), *Dominion* (1983).

Madness   British group, late 1970s to 1980s; members include Graham 'Suggs' McPherson (1961–   ) vocalist, born Hastings, Sussex; Mike Barson (1958–   ) keyboardist, Lee Thompson (1957–   ) saxophonist; *Chris Foreman* (1958–   ) guitarist; Mark Bedford(1961–   ) bassist; Daniel 'Woody' Woodgate (1960–   ) drummer; Chas Smash (originally Carl Smith) (1959–   ) vocalist, trumpeter; 'House Of Fun', 'Our House', 'Baggy Trousers', 'Ghost Train', *One Step Beyond* (1979), *Complete Madness* (1982), *Mad Not Mad* (1985).

Madonna (originally **Madonna Louise Veronica Ciccone**)   (1958–   ) American singer/songwriter, born Rochester, Michigan; 'Holiday', 'Crazy For You', 'Gambler', 'Into The Groove', 'Live To Tell', 'Vogue', *Madonna* (1983), *Like a Virgin* (1984), *True Blue* (1986), *Who's that Girl?* (1987), *Like a Prayer* (1989), *The Immaculate Collection* (1990).

The Mamas and the Papas   American group, late 1960s; members include John Philips (1935–   ) singer/songwriter, guitarist, born Parris Island, South Carolina; Dennis Doherty (1941–   ) born Halifax, Nova Scotia; Michelle Phillips (originally Holly Michelle Gilliam) (1944–   ) born Long Beach, California;

POP AND ROCK MUSICIANS AND SINGERS (cont.)

Cass Elliott (originally Ellen Naomi Cohen) (1943–74) vocalist, born Baltimore, Maryland; 'California Dreamin'', 'Monday, Monday', 'Dedicated to the one I love', 'San Francisco'.

Manfred Mann British group, 1960s to 1980s; members include Manfred Mann (originally Michael Lubowitz) (1940–) keyboardist, born Johannesburg, South Africa; Paul Jones (originally Paul Pond) (1942–) vocalist, harmonica player, born Portsmouth; '5-4-3-2-1', 'Do Wah Diddy Diddy', 'If You Gotta Go, Go Now', 'The Mighty Quinn', 'Pretty Flamingo', 'Blinded By The Light'.

Manilow, Barry (originally **Barry Alan Pinkins**) (1946–) American singer/songwriter, pianist, born Brooklyn, New York; 'Mandy', 'I Write the Songs', 'Looks Like We Made It', 'Copacabana (At the Copa)', *Barry Manilow I*, *Barry Manilow II*, *Tryin' to Get the Feeling*, *This One's for You*, *Barry Manilow Live*, *Even Now*, *One Voice*.

Marillion British group, 1980s to present; members include Fish (Derek William Dick) (1958–) singer/songwriter, born Dalkeith, near Edinburgh; Steve Rothery (1959–) guitarist, born Bromton, Yorkshire; Mark Kelly (1961–) keyboardist, born Dublin; Pete Trewavas (1959–) bassist, born Middlesbrough; Ian Mosley (1953–) drummer, born Paddington, London; 'Market Square Heroes', 'Kayleigh', 'Lavender', 'Heart of Lothian', *Script For A Jester's Tear* (1983), *Fugazi* (1984), *Real to Reel* (1984), *Misplaced Childhood* (1985), *Clutching At Straws*.

Marley, Bob (originally **Robert Nesta Marley**) (1945–81) Jamaican singer/songwriter, guitarist, born Rhoden Hall, St Ann's Parish, Jamaica; (with The Wailers) 'No Woman, No Cry', 'I Shot the Sheriff', 'Exodus', 'Buffalo Soldier', *Catch a Fire* (1972), *Rastaman Vibration* (1976), *Uprising* (1980).

Mayall, John (1933–) British singer/songwriter, guitarist, harmonica player, born Macclesfield; *Bluesbreakers – John Mayall with Eric Clapton* (1965), *Crusader* (1967), *A Hard Road* (1967), *The Turning Point* (1970).

Mellencamp, John Cougar (1951–) American singer/songwriter, guitarist, born Seymour, Indiana; 'I Need A Lover', 'Hurt So Good', 'Jack and Diane', 'Crumblin' Down', 'Pink Houses', *American Fool* (1982), *Uh-Huh* (1983), *Scarecrow* (1985).

Michael, George (originally **Yorgos Kyriatou Panayiotou**) (1963–) British singer/songwriter (was in Wham! – British 1980s group), born Finchley, London; 'Careless Whisper', 'Different Corner', 'I Want Your Sex', *Faith* (1987).

Midler, Bette (1945–) American singer, born Honolulu, Hawaii; 'From A Distance', *The Divine Miss M* (1972), *The Rose* (1979), *No Frills* (1983).

Minogue, Kylie (1968–) Australian singer, born Melbourne; 'I Should Be So Lucky', *Kylie* (1987).

Mitchell, Joni (originally **Roberta Joan Anderson**) (1943–) Canadian singer/songwriter, guitarist, born McLeod, Alberta; 'Help Me', *Joni Mitchell* (1968), *Clouds* (1969), *Ladies of the Canyon* (1970), *Blue* (1971), *Dog Eat Dog* (1986), *Chalk Mark in a Rain Storm* (1988).

The Monkees American group, late 1960s; members include Mickey Dolenz (1945–) vocalist, drummer, born Los Angeles; Davy Jones (1946–) vocalist, guitarist, born Manchester, England; Peter Tork (originally Peter Torkelson) (1944–) bassist, born Washington DC; Mike Nesmith guitarist; 'I'm a Believer', 'Daydream Believer', *Pool It* (1987).

The Moody Blues British group, mid 1960s to 1970s; members include Justin Hayward guitarist; John Lodge bassist; Mike Pindar keyboardist; Graem Edge drummer; Ray Thomas flautist, saxophonist, and vocalist; 'Nights in White Satin, *Days of Future Passed* (1967).

Morrison, Van (originally **George Ivan Morrison**) (1945–) Irish singer/songwriter, guitarist, born Belfast; 'Brown Eyed Girl', *Blowin' Your Mind* (1967); (with Them – Irish group, 1960s) 'Baby Please Don't Go'.

Motley Crue American heavy metal group, late 1970s to present; Nikki Sixx bassist; Mick Mars guitarist; Vince Neil (originally Vincent Neil Wharton) vocalist; 'Smokin' In The Boys' Room', 'Without You', *Too Fast For Love* (1982), *Shout At The Devil* (1983), *Theatre Of Pain* (1983), *Girls, Girls, Girls* (1986), *Dr Feelgood* (1989).

POP AND ROCK MUSICIANS AND SINGERS (cont.)

Motörhead   British heavy metal group, late 1970s to present; members include Lemmy (originally Ian Kilminster) (1945–   ) vocalist, born Stoke-on-Trent; *Overkill* (1979), *Bomber* (1979), *Ace of Spades* (1980), *No Sleep Till Hammersmith* (1981), *Orgasmatron* (1986).

Mott The Hoople   British band, late 1960s to mid 1970s; members include Ian Hunter (1946–   ) vocalist, guitarist, born Shrewsbury; Mick Ralphs (1944–   ) guitarist, born Hereford; Overend (Peter) Watts (1947–   ) bassist, born Birmingham; Verden Allen (1944–   ) keyboardist, born Hereford; Dale 'Buffin' Griffin (1948–   ) drummer, born Ross-on-Wye; 'All The Way To Memphis', *All The Young Dudes* (1972), *Mott* (1973).

Moyet, Alison 'Alf'   (1961–   ) British singer, born Basildon; 'All Cried Out', 'That Ole Devil Called Love', 'Weak In The Presence Of Beauty', *Alf* (1984), *Chasing Rain* (1987).

Nelson, Ricky (originally **Eric Hilliard Nelson**)   (1940–85) American singer, guitarist, born Teaneck, New Jersey; 'Travelin' Man', 'Hello Mary Lou', *Garden Party* (1972).

The Neville Brothers   American group; Arthur Lanon Neville (1937–   ) keyboardist, vocalist, percussionist; Charles Neville (1938–   ) saxophonist, flautist, percussionist; Aaron Neville (1941–   ) keyboardist, vocalist; Cyril Neville (1948–   ) vocalist, percussionist; all born New Orleans, Louisiana.

Newman, Randy (originally **Randolph Newman**)   (1944–   ) American singer/songwriter, pianist, born Los Angeles; 'I Love L.A.', 'Gone Dead Train', *Sail Away* (1972), *Trouble In Paradie* (1983).

Newton-John, Olivia   (1948–   ) Australian/British singer, born Cambridge, England; 'Make A Move On Me', 'Twist Of Fate', *Grease* (1978), *Xanadu* (1980), *Physical* (1981), *Soul Kiss* (1985).

New York Dolls   American group, 1970s; Johnny Thunders (originally Johnny Genzale); Sylvain Sylvain guitarist; Arthur Kane bassist; Billy Murcia (1951–72) drummer, born London replaced by Jerry Nolan; David Johansen (1950–   ) singer, born Staten Island, New York; *New York Dolls* (1973).

Ocean, Billy   (1950–   ) British vocalist, born Trinidad; 'Love Really Hurts Without You', 'Red Light Spells Danger', 'Caribbean Queen', 'Loverboy', 'When The Going Gets Tough, The Tough Get Going', 'There'll Be Sad Songs', *Suddenly* (1984), *Love Zone* (1986).

Oldfield, Mike   (1953–   ) British multi-instrumentalist, composer, born Reading, Berkshire; 'Blue Peter', 'Moonlight Shadow', *Tubular Bells* (1973), *Hergest Ridge* (1974), *Ommadawn* (1975), *Killing Fields* (1984).

Orbison, Roy   (1936–88) American singer/songwriter, guitarist, born Vernon, Texas; 'Only the Lonely', 'Crying', 'Dream Baby', '(Oh) Pretty Woman', 'In Dreams', 'Blue Bayou'.

The Osmonds   American group, 1970s; members include Alan (1949–   ), Wayne (1951–   ), Merrill (1953–   ), Jay (1955–   ), Donny (originally Donald Clark Osmond) (1957–   ), and Marie Osmond (1959–   ); all born Ogden, Utah; Jimmy (1963–   ) born Canoga Park, California.

Palmer, Robert   (1949–   ) British singer, born W Yorkshire, England; 'Every Kinda People', 'Bad Case Of Loving You (Doctor Doctor)', 'Some Guys Have All The Luck', 'Addicted To Love', 'She Makes My Day', *Riptide* (1985).

Peter, Paul and Mary   American trio, 1960s to present; Peter Yarrow (1938–   ) guitarist and vocalist, born New York City; Paul Stookey (1937–   ) guitarist and vocalist, born Baltimore, Maryland; Mary Travers (1937–   ) vocalist, born Louisville, Kentucky; 'If I Had A Hammer', 'Blowin' In The Wind', 'Puff The Magic Dragon', 'Leavin' On A Jet Plane', *Peter, Paul & Mary* (1962), *In The Wind* (1963), *Peter, Paul & Mommy* (1969), *No Easy Walk To Freedom* (1986).

Pink Floyd   British group, late 1960s to present; members include 'Syd' (Roger Keith) Barrett (1946–   ) singer/songwriter, guitarist; Roger Waters (1944–   ) singer/songwriter; David Gilmour (1944–   ) singer/songwriter, guitarist; all born Cambridge; *The Piper at the Gates of Dawn* (1967), *A Saucerful of Secrets* (1968), Ummagumma (1969), *Meddle* (1971), *Dark Side of the Moon* (1973), *Wish you were Here* (1975), *The Wall* (1979), *The Final Cut* (1983), *A Momentary Lapse of Reason* (1987), *A Delicate Sound of Thunder* (1988).

Pitney, Gene   (1941–   ) American singer, born Hartford, Connecticutt; 'The Man Who Shot Liberty Valance', '24 Hours From Tulsa'.

POP AND ROCK MUSICIANS AND SINGERS (cont.)

The Pogues British/Irish group, 1980s to present; members include Shane MacGowan (1957–) singer, born London; Philip Chevron (originally Philip Ryan) (1957–) guitarist, born Dublin; James Fearnley (1954–) accordionist, born Manchester; Andrew Ranken (1953–) drummer, born London; Jem Finer (originally Jeremy Max Finer (1955–) banjo player, born Dublin; Spider Stacy (originally Peter Richard Stacy) (1958–) tin whistle player, born Eastbourne; 'Dirty Old Town', 'Sally Maclennane', 'A Pair of Brown Eyes', 'Irish Rover' (with the Dubliners), *Red Roses For Me* (1984), *Rum, Sodomy & The Lash* (1985).

Pointer Sisters American group, 1970s to 1980s; Ruth (1946–), Anita (1948–), Bonnie (1950–), June (1954–) Pointer; all born Oakland, California; 'Fairy Tale', 'Fire', 'Slow Hand', 'Jump (For My Love)', 'Automatic', 'Neutron Dance', *So Excited!* (1982), *Break Out* (1983), *Serious Slammin'* (1988).

Police British group, late 1970s to present; members include Sting (originally Gordon Sumner) (1951–), singer/songwriter, bassist, born Wallsend, Northumberland (solo 'Set Them Free', 'Russians', *The Dream of the Blue Turtles* (1985), *Nothing Like The Sun* (1987)); Stewart Copeland (1952–) drummer, born Alexandria, Virginia; Andy Summers (1942–) guitarist, born Lancaster; 'Can't Stand Losing You' (1978), 'Roxanne', 'Message In A Bottle', 'Walking On The Moon', 'Don't Stand So Close To Me', 'Every Little Thing She Does Is Magic', 'Every Breath You Take', *Outlandos d'Amour* (1978), *Regatta de Blanc* (1979), *Zenyatta Mondatta* (1980), *Ghost in the Machine* (1981), *Synchronicity* (1983).

Pop, Iggy (originally **James Newell Osterburg**) (1947–) American singer/songwriter, drummer, born Ypsilanti, Michigan; 'I Wanna Be Your Dog', *The Stooges* (1969), *Raw Power* (1973) (with the Stooges); 'Nightclubbing', 'The Passenger', 'Real Wild Child', 'Well Did You Evah' (with Deborah Harry), *The Idiot* (1976), *Lust for Life* (1977), *Blah Blah Blah* (1986), *Instinct* (1988).

Presley, Elvis (Aaron) (1935–77) American singer, guitarist, born East Tupelo, Mississippi; 'Mystery Train', 'Heartbreak Hotel', 'Hound Dog', 'Love Me Tender', 'Its Now or Never', 'Jailhouse Rock', 'King Creole', 'Crying in the Chapel', 'Suspicious Minds', 'In the Ghetto', 'Blue Suede Shoes', 'All Shook Up'.

The Pretenders British group, late 1970s to present; members include Chrissie Hynde (1951–) singer/songwriter, guitarist, born Akron, Ohio; 'Back on the Chain Gang', 'Brass in Pocket', *Pretenders* (1979), *Single Records* (1988).

Prince (originally **Prince Rogers Nelson**) (1958–) American singer/songwriter, guitarist, keyboardist, drummer born Minneapolis, Minnesota; 'Little Red Corvette', 'Delirious', 'When Doves Cry', 'Let's Go Crazy', 'Raspberry Beret', 'Kiss', *Prince* (1979), *Dirty Mind* (1980), *Controversy* (1981), *1999* (1982), *Purple Rain* (with the Revolution) (1984), *Around The World In A Day* (1985), *Parade* (1986), *Sign o' the Times* (1987), *Love Sexy* (1988).

Queen British group, 1970s to present; members include Freddie Mercury (originally Frederick Bulsara) (1946–) singer/songwriter, born Zanzibar; Brian May (1947–) guitarist, born Hampton, Middlesex; John Deacon (1951–) bassist, born Leicester; Roger Taylor (originally Roger Meadows-Taylor) (1949–) drummer, born Norfolk; 'Seven Seas of Rhye', 'Killer Queen', 'Bohemian Rhapsody', 'We are the Champions', 'Somebody to Love', 'Another one Bites the Dust', 'Crazy Little Thing Called Love', 'Under Pressure' (with David Bowie), 'Radio Ga-Ga', *Queen II* (1974), *Shear Heart Attack* (1974), *A Night at the Opera* (1975), *A Day at the Races* (1976), *The Game* (1980), *Hot Space* (1982), *The Works* (1984).

Quiet Riot American heavy metal group, late 1970s to present; members include Kevin DuBrow vocalist; Rhandy Rhoads guitarist replaced by Carlos Cavazo; Rudy Sarzo bassist; Frankie Banali drummer; 'Cum On Feel The Noize', 'Bang Your Head (Metal Health)', *Metal Health* (1983), *Condition Critical* (1984), *QRIII* (1986), *Wild, Young And Crazee* (1987).

The Ramones American group, late 1970s to present; members include Joey Ramone (originally Jeffrey Hyman) (1952–) vocalist, born New York; Johnny Ramone (originally John Cummings) (1952–) guitarist; Dee Dee Ramone (originally Douglas Colvin) (1952–) bassist; Tommy Ramone (originally Tom Erdelyi) (1952–) drummer, born Budapest replaced by Marky Ramone (originally Mark Bell); 'Beat The Brat', 'Now I Wanna Sniff Some Glue', 'Do You Remember Rock'n'Roll Radio?', 'Baby I Love You', *Ramones* (1976), *The Century* (1980), *Pleasant Dreams* (1981), *Too Tough To Die* (1985), *Halfway To Sanity* (1988).

POP AND ROCK MUSICIANS AND SINGERS (cont.)

Ray, Johnnie (1927–90) American singer, born Rosebud, Oregon; 'Cry'/'The Little White Cloud That Cried', 'Walkin' My Baby Back Home', 'Just Walking In The Rain', 'You Don't Owe Me A Thing', 'I'll Never Fall In Love Again', *The Big Beat* (1957).

Redding, Otis (1941–67) American singer/songwriter, born Dawson, Georgia; 'I've Been Loving You Too Long', 'Try a Little Tenderness', 'Mr Pitiful', 'Satisfaction', '(Sittin' On The) Dock of the Bay', 'Respect', *King and Queen*, *The Otis Redding Story* (1968), *The Dock of the Bay* (1987).

Reed, Lou (originally **Louis Firbank**) (1944–   ) American singer/songwriter, born Long Island, New York; 'Walk On The Wild Side', 'I Love You Suzanne', *Lou Reed* (1972), *Transformer* (1972), *Rock 'n' Roll Animal* (1974), *Coney Island Baby* (1976), *Street Hassle* (1978), *New Sensations* (1984), *New York* (1989).

Martha Reeves and The Vandellas American group, 1960s; members include Martha Reeves (1941–   ) singer; Rosalind Ashford (1943–   ) singer; Betty Kelly (1944–   ) singer; all born Detroit; 'Nowhere To Run', 'I'm Ready For Love', 'Jimmy Mack', 'Dancing In The Street'.

R.E.M. American group, 1980s to present; members include Michael Stipe (1960–   ) vocalist; Peter Buck (1956–   ) guitarist; Michael Mills (1958–   ) bassist; Bill Berry (1958–   ) drummer; 'World Leader Pretend', 'The One I Love', 'Stand', 'The End of the World', 'Superman', 'Orange Crush', 'Losing my Religion, 'Shiny Happy People', *Murmur* (1983), *Reckoning* (1984), *Life's Rich Pageant* (1986), *Number 5: Document* (1987), *Green* (1989), *Out of Time* (1991).

REO Speedwagon American group, late 1960s to present; members include Alan Gratzer (1948–   ) drummer, born Syracuse, New York; Neal Doughty (1946–   ) keyboardist, born Evanston, Illinois; Gary Richrath (1949–   ) guitarist, born Peoria, Illinois; Kevin Cronin singer; 'Keep On Lovin' You', 'Take It On The Run', 'Can't Fight This Feeling', *Hi Fidelity* (1980), *Good Trouble* (1982), *Wheels Are Turnin'* (1984), *Life As We Know It* (1987).

Richard, Cliff (originally **Harry Roger Webb**) (1940–   ) British singer/songwriter, guitarist, born Lucknow, India; over 100 hits including 'Livin' Doll', 'The Young Ones', 'Summer Holiday', 'Congratulations', *21 Today* (1961), *Rock & Roll Juvenile* (1971), *We Don't Talk Anymore* (1979), *Love Songs* (1981).

Richie, Lionel (originally **Lionel Brockman Richie Jnr.**) (1949–   ) American singer/songwriter, pianist, born Tuskegee, Alabama; 'All Night Long', 'Say You', *Can't Slow Down.*

The Righteous Brothers American duo, 1960s to 1970s; Bobby Hatfield (1940–   ) singer, born Beaver Dam, Wisconsin; Bill Medley (1940–   ) singer, born Los Angeles; 'You've Lost That Lovin' Feelin'', 'Just Once In My Life', 'Unchained Melody', 'Ebb Tide', 'Rock And Roll Heaven'.

The Rolling Stones British group, 1960s to present; members include 'Mick' (Michael Philip) Jagger (1943–   ) vocalist, harmonica-player, born Dartford, Kent (solo 'Just Another Night', 'Dancing In The Street' (with David Bowie), *She's The Boss* (1985)); Keith Richard (originally Richards) (1943–   ) guitarist, born Dartford, Kent; Bill Wyman (originally William Perks) (1936–   ) bassist, born Penge, London; Charlie Watts (1941–   ) drummer, born Neasden, London; Brian Jones (originally Lewis Brian Hopkin-Jones) (1942–69) guitarist, born Cheltenham replaced by Mick Taylor (1948–   ) born Hertfordshire replaced by Ron Wood (1947–   ) born Hillingdon, Middlesex; Ian Stewart (1938–85) keyboardist; 'It's All Over Now', 'Little Red Rooster', 'The Last Time', '(I Can't Get No) Satisfaction', 'Get Off of My Cloud', '19th Nervous Breakdown', 'Paint It Black', 'Mothers Little Helper', 'Let's Spend The Night Together', 'Jumpin' Jack Flash', 'Sympathy For The Devil', (1968), 'Honky Tonk Women', 'You Can't Always Get What You Want', 'Brown Sugar', 'Miss you', *The Rolling Stones* (1964), *Aftermath* (1966), *Beggar's Banquet* (1968), *Let it Bleed* (1969), *Get Yer Ya–Ya's Out* (1970), *Sticky Fingers* (1971), *Exile on Main Street* (1972), *Goat's Head Soup* (1973), *Some Girls* (1978), *Emotional Rescue* (1980), *Tattoo You* (1981), *Undercover* (1983), *Dirty Work* (1986), *Steel Wheels* (1989), *Flashpoint* (1990).

Ronstadt, Linda Marie (1946–   ) American singer, born Tuscon, Arizona; 'Blue Bayou', 'Somewhere Out There' (with James Ingram), *Heart Like A Wheel* (1974), *Simple Dreams* (1977), *Living In The USA* (1978), *Canciones de Mi Padre* (1988).

Ross, Diana (1944–   ) American singer, born Detroit, Michigan; with the Supremes – 1960s group: 'Ain't No Mountain High Enough', 'Baby Love', 'Stop! In the Name of Love', 'You Can't Hurry Love', 'You Keep

POP AND ROCK MUSICIANS AND SINGERS (cont.)

Me Hangin' On', 'Where Did Our Love Go', 'I'm Gonna Make You Love Me'; with Lionel Richie: 'Endless Love'; 'Upside Down', 'I'm Coming Out', 'My Old Piano', 'Chain Reaction', *Diana* (1980), *Eaten Alive* (1985).

Roxy Music British group, 1970s to early 1980s; members include Bryan Ferry (1945–) singer, born Washington, County Durham; Brian Eno (1948–) songwriter, keyboardist, born Woodbridge, Suffolk; Paul Manzanera (originally Philip Targett-Adams) (1941–) guitarist, born London; Andy Mackay (1946–) saxophonist; 'Virginia Plain', 'Do The Strand', 'Street Life', 'Love is a Drug', 'Dance Away', 'Angel Eyes', 'Jealous Guy', 'My Only Love', *Roxy Music* (1972), *Stranded* (1973), *Siren* (1975), *Manifesto* (1980), *Avalon* (1982).

Runrig Scottish group, 1970s to present; members include Iain Bayne (1960–) drummer, born St Andrews; Malcolm Jones (1959–) guitarist, born Inverness; Calum MacDonald (1953–) percussionist, songwriter, born Lochmaddy, N Uist; Rory MacDonald (1949–) bassist, songwriter, born Domoch, Sutherland; Donnie Munro (1953–) lead singer, born Uig, Skye; Peter Wishart (1962–) keyboarder, born Dunfermline, Fife.

Rush Canadian heavy metal group, 1970s to present; members include Geddy Lee (1953–) vocalist, bassist, born Willowdale; Alex Lifeson (1953–) guitarist, born Fernie, British Columbia; Neil Peart (1952–) drummer, born Hamilton; *2112* (1976), *All The World's A Stage* (1976), *Moving Pictures* (1981), *Power Windows* (1985), *Hold Your Fire* (1987).

Sade (originally **Helen Folasade Adu**) (1959–) British/Nigerian singer/songwriter, born Ibadan, Nigeria; 'Smooth Operator', 'Paradise', *Diamond Life* (1984), *Promise* (1985), *Stronger than Pride* (1988).

Santana, Carlos (1947–) Mexican guitarist, vocalist, born Autlan de Novarra, Jalisco, Mexico; (with band Santana – late 1960s to present) 'Black Magic Woman', *Santana* (1969), *Abraxas* (1970), *Amigos* (1976), *Moonflower* (1977), *Zebop!* (1981), *Freedom* (1987).

Sayer, Leo (originally **Gerard Hugh Sayer**) (1948–) British singer, born Shoreham-on-Sea, Sussex; 'The Show Must Go On', 'Long Tall Glasses (I Can Dance)', 'You Make Me Feel Like Dancing', 'When I Need You', 'More Than I Can Say', *Leo* (1984).

Bob Seger (1945–) American singer/songwriter, born Ann Arbor, Michigan; (with the Silver Bullet Band – mid 1970s to present) 'Still The Same', 'Hollywood Nights', 'Shame On The Moon', *Night Moves* (1976), *Stranger in Town* (1978), *Against The Wind* (1980), *The Distance* (1982), *Like A Rock* (1986).

Sex Pistols British punk group, 1970s; members include Johnny Rotten (originally John Lydon) (1956–) vocalist; Steve Jones (1955–) guitarist; Paul Cook (1956–) drummer; Sid Vicious (originally John Simon Ritchie) (1958–79) singer, bassist; 'Anarchy in the U.K.', 'God Save The Queen', 'Pretty Vacant', 'Holidays In The Sun', 'My Way', 'Something Else', 'C'mon Everybody', 'Silly Thing', *Never Mind the Bollocks – Here's The Sex Pistols* (1977), *Some Product* (1978), *Flogging a Dead Horse* (1979), *The Great Rock 'n' Roll Swindle* (1980).

The Shadows British group, late 1950s to present; members include Hank Marvin (originally Brian Rankin) (1941–) guitarist, born Newcastle; Bruce Welch (1941–) guitarist, born Newcastle; Jet Harris (originally Terry Harris) (1939–) bassist, born London; Tony Meehan (1943–) drummer, born London; 'Apache', 'Kon Tiki', 'Wonderful Land', 'Dance On', 'Foot Tapper', 'Don't Cry For Me Argentina', *Moonlight Shadows* (1986).

Sharkey, Feargal (1958–) Irish singer, born Londonderry, Northern Ireland; (with The Undertones – Irish band, late 1970s to early 1980s) 'Teenage Kicks', 'My Perfect Cousin', *All Wrapped Up* (1983); 'Listen To Your Father', 'A Good Heart', *Feargal Sharkey* (1985), *Wish* (1987).

Shocked, Michelle (c.1962–) singer/songwriter, born Texas; *Texas Campfire Tapes* (1987), *Short Sharp Shocked* (1988).

Simon, Carly (1945–) singer/songwriter, born New York City; 'You're So Vain', 'Nobody Does It Better', 'Coming Round Again', 'Let The River Run', *No Secrets* (1972).

POP AND ROCK MUSICIANS AND SINGERS (cont.)

Simon, Paul (1941–) American singer/songwriter, guitarist, born Newark, New Jersey; 'You Can Call Me Al', *Paul Simon* (1972), *Graceland* (1986), *Rhythm of the Nations* (1990) (was in Simon and Garfunkel, 1960s, formerly Tom and Gerry, with Art Garfunkel (1942–) singer, born Forest Hills, New York; 'The Sound of Silence', 'Mrs Robinson', 'Bridge over Troubled Water', 'The Boxer', 'Scarborough Fair', 'Homeward Bound', *Bridge over Troubled Water* (1970)).

Simone, Nina (originally **Eunice Waymon**) (1933–) American singer, born Tryon, N Carolina; *My Baby Just Cares For Me.*

Simple Minds British group, late 1970s to present; members include Jim Kerr singer, born Glasgow; Charlie Burchill guitarist; Mel Gaynor drummer; Derek Forbes bassist replaced by John Giblin; Mick McNeil keyboardist; Duncan Barnwell guitarist; 'Don't You (Forget about Me)', 'Belfast Child', *New Gold Dream* (1982), *Sparkle In The Rain* (1984), *Once upon a Time* (1985), *Live in the City of Light* (1987).

Simply Red British group, 1980s; members include Mick Hucknall singer/songwriter; Tony Bowers bassist; Chris Joyce drummer; Fritz McIntyre keyboardist; Sylvan Richardson guitarist; 'Money's Too Tight To Mention', 'Holding Back The Years', *Picture Book* (1985), *Men And Women* (1987).

Sinatra, Frank (Francis Albert) (1915–) American singer, born Hoboken, New Jersey; 'I've Got You Under My Skin', 'Strangers In The Night', 'The Lady Is A Tramp', 'Theme From New York, New York', 'My Way'.

Siouxsie and the Banshees British group, late 1970s to present; members include Siouxsie Sioux (originally Susan Janet Dallion) (1957–) singer/songwriter, born London; Steve Severin (originally Steve Bailey) (1955–) bassist, born London; Budgie (originally Peter Clarke) (1957–) drummer, born St Helens, Lancashire; 'Wheel's On Fire', *The Scream* (1979), *Tinderbox, Kaleidoscope* (1980), *Tinderbox* (1986), *Through The Looking Glass* (1987), *Peepshow* (1988).

Slade British group, late 1960s to present; Noddy Holder (originally Neville Holder) (1950–) guitarist, vocalist, born Walsall, Staffordshire; Jim Lea (1952–) bassist, vocalist, pianist, born Wolverhampton; Dave Hill (1952–) drummer, born Devon; Don Powell (1950–) drummer, born Bilston, Staffordshire; 'Coz I Love You', 'Mama Weer All Crazee Now', 'Cum On Feel The Noize', 'Skweeze Me, Pleeze Me', 'Merry Xmas Everybody', 'My Oh My', *Play It Loud* (1970), *We'll Bring The House Down* (1981), *Amazing Kamikazi Syndrome* (1983), *Rogues Gallery* (1985), *You Boyz Make Big Noize* (1987).

Smith, Patti (1946–) American singer/songwriter, born Chicago; 'Because the Night', *Horses* (1976), *Easter* (1978), *Dream Of Life* (1988).

The Smiths British group, 1980s; members include (Steven Patrick) Morrissey (1959–) singer/songwriter (solo 'Everyday Is Like Sunday', *Viva Hate* (1988)); Johnny Marr (1963–) guitarist, songwriter; both born Manchester; 'Hand In Glove', 'Bigmouth Strikes Again', 'Boy With The Thorn In His Side', 'Panic', *The Smiths* (1984), *Meat Is Murder* (1985), *Hatful of Hollow* (1985), *The Queen Is Dead* (1986), *Strangeways, Here We Come* (1987).

Spandau Ballet British group, 1980s to present; members include Tony Hadley (originally Anthony Patrick Hadley) (1959–) vocalist, born Islington; Gary Kemp (1960–) guitarist, songwriter; Martin Kemp (1961–) bassist; both born London; John Keeble (1959–) drummer; Steve Norman (1960–) guitarist; 'Gold', *True* (1983), *Parade* (1984), *Through The Barricades* (1986).

Springfield, Dusty (originally **Mary O'Brien**) (1939–) British singer, born Hampstead, London; 'I Only Want To Be With You', 'You Don't Have To Say You Love Me', *Dusty In Memphis* (1969).

Springfield, Rick (1949–) Australian singer/songwriter, guitarist, born Sydney; 'Jessie's Girl', *Working Class Dog* (1981), *Success Hasn't Spoiled Me Yet* (1982), *Living In Oz* (1983), *Tao* (1985), *Rock Of Life* (1988).

Springsteen, Bruce (Frederick Joseph) (1949–) American singer/songwriter, guitarist, born Freehold, New Jersey; 'Hungry Heart', 'Dancing In The Dark', 'Brilliant Disguise', *Greetings from Ashbury Park, NJ* (1973), *Born to Run* (1975), *Darkness on the Edge of Town* (1978), *The River* (1980), *Nebraska* (1982), *Born in the USA* (1985), *Tunnel of Love* (1987).

POP AND ROCK MUSICIANS AND SINGERS (cont.)

Squeeze British group, mid 1970s to present; members include Glen Tilbrook (1957–); Chris Difford (1954–); both guitarists, vocalists, songwriters; Jools Holland (1954–) keyboardist replaced by Paul Carrack (1951–) born Sheffield; John Bentley (1951–) bassist; Gilson Lavis (1951–) drummer; 'Goodbye Girl', 'Up The Junction', *Cool For Cats* (1979), *East Side Story* (1981), *Cosi Fan Tutti Frutti* (1985), *Babylon And On* (1987).

Status Quo British group, 1970s to present; members include Francis Rossi (1949–) guitarist, vocalist; Richard Parfitt (1948–) guitarist, vocalist; Alan Lancaster (1949–) bassist; John Coghland (1946–) drummer; all born London; 'Down, Down', 'Caroline', 'You're in the Army Now', *Piledriver* (1973), *Hello* (1973), *On The Level* (1975), *Blue For You* (1976), *Rockin' all over the World* (1978), *1982*.

Steeleye Span British group, 1970s to present; members include Tim Hart guitarist, vocalist; Maddy Prior; Martin Carthy guitarist, vocalist; Peter Knight fiddler; Rick Kemp bassist; Bob Johnson guitarist; Nigel Pegrum drummer, flautist; *All Around My Hat* (1975), *Back In Line* (1986).

Steely Dan American group, 1970s; Walter Becker (c.1950–) bassist, guitarist; Donald Fagen (c.1950–) keyboardist; 'Reelin' Back The Years', *Aja* (1977).

Steppenwolf Canadian group, late 1960s to early 1970s; members include John Kay (originally Joachim Krauledat) (1944–) guitarist, vocalist, born East Germany; Jerry Edmonton (1946–) drummer; Goldy McJohn (1945–) keyboardist; 'Born to Be Wild', 'Magic Carpet Ride', *Steppenwolf* (1968), *The Second* (1968), *Steppenwolf Live* (1970), *Hour Of The Wolf* (1975).

Stevens, Cat (originally **Steven Demitri Georgiou**) (1947–) singer/songwriter, born London; 'Lady D'Arbanville', 'Wild World', 'Peace Train', 'Morning Has Broken', *Tea For The Tillerman* (1971), *Teaser & The Firecat* (1971), *Catch Bull At Four* (1972), *Foreign* (1973), *Buddha And The Chocolate Box* (1974).

Stevens, Shakin' (originally **Michael Barratt**) (1948–) British singer, born Ely, Wales; 'This Ole House', 'Green Door', 'Oh Julie', *Lipstick Powder And Paint* (1985).

Stewart, Rod(erick David) (1945–) British singer/songwriter, guitarist, born London; *First Step* (1977) and *Long Player* (1971) (with the Faces); 'Maggie May', 'You Wear It Well', 'Sailing', 'Do Ya Think I'm Sexy?', 'I Don't Want To Talk About It', 'Passion', 'Baby Jane', 'Stay with Me', 'Young Turks', 'The Motown Song', *Every Picture Tells A Story* (1971), *Atlantic Crossing* (1975), *Blondes Have More Fun* (1978), *Tonight I'm Yours* (1981), *Body Wishes* (1983), *Every Beat Of My Heart* (1986), *Out Of Order* (1988).

The Stranglers British group, mid 1970s to present; members include Hugh Cornwell (1949–) vocalist, guitarist; Jean-Jacques Burnel, vocalist, bassist;'Peaches', 'Walk On By', 'Golden Brown', 'Always The Sun', '96 Tears', *Rattus Norvegicus* (1977), *No More Heroes* (1977), *Feline* (1983), *Aural Structure* (1984), *Dreamtime* (1986), *Ten* (1990).

Stray Cats American group, early 1980s; Brian Setzer (1960–) singer/songwriter, guitarist, born New York City; Lee Rocker (originally Lee Drucher) bassist; Slim Jim Phantom (originally James McDonell) drummer; 'Runaway Boys', 'Stray Cat Strut', 'Rock This Town', 'Sexy and 17', *Stray Cats* (1981), *Gonna Ball* (1982), *Built For Speed* (1982), *Rant'n'Rave* (1983).

Streisand, Barbra (Joan) (1942–) American singer/songwriter, born Brooklyn, New York; (with Neil Diamond) 'You Don't Bring Me Flowers'; 'Guilty', *Stoney End* (1971), *The Way We Were* (1974), *Streisand Superman* (1977), *Emotion* (1984), *One Voice* (1987); 30 gold albums.

Style Council British group, 1980s; members include Paul Weller singer, guitarist; Mick Talbot (1959–) keyboardist; 'You're The Best Thing', 'Shout To The Top', 'Walls Come Tumbling Down', *Café Blue* (1984), *My Favourite Shop* (1985), *The Cost Of Living* (1987).

Summer, Donna (originally **LaDonna Adrian Gaines**) (1948–) American singer, born Boston, Massachusetts; 'Love To Love You Baby', 'I Feel Love', 'Last Dance', 'Hot Stuff', 'Highway Runner', 'He's A Rebel', 'Forgive Me', 'Dinner With Gershwin', *Live And More* (1978), *Bad Girls* (1979), *The Wanderer* (1980), *She Works Hard For The Money* (1983), *All Systems Go* (1987).

Talking Heads American group, mid 1970s to present; members include David Byrne (1952–) singer/songwriter, guitarist, born Dumbarton, Scotland; Chris Frantz (1951–) drummer, born Fort

POP AND ROCK MUSICIANS AND SINGERS (cont.)

Campbell, Kentucky; Martina 'Tina' Weymouth (1950–) bassist, born Coronado, California; Jerry Harrison (1949–) keyboardist, born Milwaukee, Wisconsin; 'Psycho Killer', 'Burning Down the House', 'Road to Nowhere', 'And She Was', *Talking Heads* (1977), *Fear of Music* (1979), *Remain in the Light* (1980), *Speaking In Tongues* (1983), *Little Creatures* (1985), *True Stories* (1986), *Naked* (1988).

Tears For Fears   British group, 1980s; members include Curt Smith (1961–) singer, bassist; Roland Orzabol (1961–) singer, guitarist; 'Pale Shelter', 'Shout', 'Mothers Talk', 'Everybody Wants To Rule The World', 'Head Over Heels', *The Hurting* (1983), *Songs From The Big Chair* (1985).

10cc   British group, 1970s to early 1980s; members include Graham Gouldman (1946–) vocalist, bassist, keyboardist; Lol Creme (1947–) vocalist, guitarist; Kevin Godley (1945–) vocalist, drummer; all born Manchester; 'Donna', 'Rubber Bullets', 'I'm Not In Love', 'Dreadlock Holiday', *Bloody Tourists* (1983).

Thin Lizzy   Irish heavy metal group, 1970s to mid 1980s; members include Phil Lynott (1951–86) vocalist, bassist (solo 'Yellow Pearl', 'Nineteen'); Brian Downey (1951–) drummer; Eric Bell (1947–) guitarist, born Belfast; Gary Moore vocalist, guitarist; both born Dublin; Brian Robertson (1956–) guitarist, born Glasgow; Scott Gorham (1951–) guitarist, born Santa Monica, California; 'Whiskey In The Jar', 'Boys Are Back In Town', *Jailbreak* (1976), *Live And Dangerous* (1978), *Black Rose* (1979).

Thompson Twins   British group, 1980s; members include Tom Bailey (1956–) singer, bassist, born Halifax; Joe Leeway (1957–) percussionist, born London; Alannah Currie (1957–) saxophonist, born Auckland, New Zealand; 'Hold Me Now', 'Doctor, Doctor', 'Don't Mess With Doctor Dream', 'King For One Day', *Into The Gap* (1984), *Here's To Future Days* (1985), *Close To The Bone* (1987).

Toto   American group, 1980s; members include Jeff Porcaro (1954–) drummer; Steve Porcaro keyboardist; David Paich keyboardist; David Hungate bassist; Steve Lukather guitarist; Bobby Kimball (originally Robert Toteaux) vocalist; 'Rosanna', 'Africa', *Toto* (1978), *Toto IV* (1982), *The Seventh One* (1988).

Turner, Tina (originally **Annie Mae Bullock**)   (1938–) American singer/songwriter, born ?Brownsville, Tennessee; (with Ike Turner (1931–) singer, pianist, born Clarksdale, Mississipi) 'River Deep, Mountain High', 'Nutbush City Limits', *The Best of Ike and Tina Turner* (1976); solo: 'Let's Stay Together', 'What's Love Got to Do with It', 'Better Be Good To Me', 'We Don't Need Another Hero', *Private Dancer* (1984), *Break Every Rule* (1986).

Twisted Sister   American heavy metal group, 1980s to present; members include Dee Snider (1955–) vocalist; Jay Jay French guitarist; Mark 'The Animal' Mendoza bassist; J J Pero drummer; *Under The Blade* (1982), *You Can't Stop Rock'n'Roll* (1983), *Stay Hungry* (1984), *Come Out And Play* (1985), *Love Is For Suckers* (1987).

Tyler, Bonnie   (1953–) British singer, born Skewen, S Wales; 'It's A Heartache', 'Total Eclipse Of The Heart', 'Holding Out For A Hero', *Faster Than The Speed Of Night* (1983), *Sweet Dreams And Forbidden Fire* (1986).

UB40   British group, 1980s to present; members include Ali Campbell (1959–) singer, guitarist; Robin Campbell (1954–) guitarist, Jim Brown (1957–) drummer; Brian Travers (1959–) saxophonist; Earl Falconer (1959–) bassist; Norman Hassan (1958–) percussionist; Mickey Virtue (1957–) keyboardist; 'Red Red Wine', 'I Got You Babe', 'Don't Break My Heart', 'Sing Our Own Song', *Signing Off* (1982), *Labour Of Love* (1983), *Baggariddim* (1985), *Rat In The Kitchen* (1986).

Ultravox   British group, mid 1970s to 1980s; members include John Foxx (originally Dennus Leigh) singer born Chorley, Lancashire; Chris Cross (originally Chris Allen) (1952–) bassist; Warren Cann (1952–) drummer, born Canada; Billy Currie (1952–) keyboardist/violinist; Midge Ure (originally James Ure) (1953–) singer, guitarist, born Glasgow (solo 'If I Was', *The Gift* (1985)); *Vienna* (1980), *U-Vox* (1986).

U2   Irish group, 1980s to present; members include Bono (originally Paul Hewson) (1960–) vocalist, born Dublin; The Edge (originally David Evans) (1961–) guitarist, Larry Mullen (1961–) drummer; Adam Clayton (1960–) bassist; 'New Years Day', 'Pride (In The Name of Love)', 'Sunday, Bloody Sunday', 'With Or Without You', 'Desire', *War* (1983), *Live Under a Blood Red Sky* (1983), *The Unforgettable Fire* (1984), *The Joshua Tree* (1987), *Rattle and Hum* (1988).

POP AND ROCK MUSICIANS AND SINGERS (cont.)

Van Halen   American group, late 1970s to present; members include David Lee Roth (1955–) vocalist, born Bloomingdale, Indiana (solo 'California Girls', 'Yankee Rose', *Eat 'Em and Smile* (1986), *Skyscraper* (1987)); Sammy Hagar (1951–) singer/songwriter, guitarist, born Monterey, California (solo 'I've Done Everything For You', 'You're Love is Driving Me Crazy', 'Two Sides of Love', 'I Can't Drive 55', *Three Lock Box* (1983), *Voice of America* (1984)); Eddie Van Halen guitarist; Alex Van Halen drummer; both born Holland; Michael Anthony bassist; 'You Really Got Me', 'Jump', 'Panama', 'Hot For Teacher', 'Why Can't This Be Love', *Van Halen* (1978), *Van Halen II* (1979), *Women And Children First* (1980), *Fair Warning* (1981), *Diver Down* (1982), *1984* (1984), *5150* (1986), *OU812* (1988), *For Unlawful Carnal Knowledge* (1991).

Vega, Suzanne   American singer/songwriter, guitarist; 'Marlene On The Wall', 'Small Blue Thing', 'Left Of Center', 'Luka', 'Tom's Diner', *Suzanne Vega* (1985), *Solitude Standing* (1987).

The Velvet Underground   American group, late 1960s; members include John Cale (1940–) guitarist, viola player, born Garnant, Wales; Nico (originally Christa Paffgen) (d.1988) vocalist, born Cologne, Germany; Lou Reed (originally Louis Firbank) (1944–) singer/songwriter, guitarist, born Long Island, New York; *The Velvet Underground & Nico* (1967), *White Light, White Heat* (1968), *The Velvet Underground* (1969).

Vincent, Gene (Vincent Eugene Craddock)   (1935–71) American singer, born Norfolk, Virginia; (with the Blue Caps) 'Be-Bop-a-Lula', 'Pistol Packin' Mama', 'Bird Doggin''.

Vinton, Bobby   (1935–) American singer, multi-instrumentalist, born Canonsburg, Pennsylvania; 'Roses Are Red', 'Blue Velvet', 'There, I Said It Again', *Mr Lonely* (1965), *Melodies Of Love* (1974).

Waits, Tom   (1949–) American singer/songwriter, pianist, born Pamona, California; *Small Change* (1976), *Swordfishtrombone* (1983), *The Asylum Years* (1984), *Rain Dogs* (1985).

Warwick, Dionne   (also **Marie Dionne Warwicke**)   (1940–) American singer/songwriter, pianist, born East Orange, New Jersey; 'There Came You' (with The Spinners); (Dionne & Friends) 'That's What Friends Are For'; *Dionne, Heartbreaker* (1982).

Wham!   British group, 1980s; George Michael (originally Yorgos Kyriatou Panayiotou) (1963–) singer/songwriter, born Finchley, London; Andrew Ridgely (1963–) singer, guitarist, born Bushey, Hertsfordshire; 'Young Guns (Go For It)', 'Club Tropicana', 'Wake Me Up Before You Go-Go', 'Freedom', 'Last Christmas', 'I'm Your Man', 'Edge Of Heaven', *Fantastic* (1983), *Make It Big* (1984), *The Final* (1986).

White, Barry   (1944–) American, born Galveston, Texas; 'Can't Get Enough Of Your Love, Babe', *Can't Get Enough* (1974), *Right Now Barry White* (1987).

Whitesnake   British heavy metal group, late 1970s to present; members include David Coverdale singer; 'Fool For Your Loving', 'In The Heat Of The Night', 'Here I Go Again', *Love Hunter* (1979), *Ready An' Willing' (1980)*, *Saints And Sinners* (1982), *Slide It In* (1984), *White Snake* (1987).

The Who   British group, late 1960s to 1980s; members include Pete Townsend (1945–) singer/songwriter, guitarist (solo *Who Came First* (1972)); Roger Daltrey (1944–) vocalist, born London (solo *After The Fire* (1985)); John Entwistle (1944–) bassist, French horn player; Keith Moon (1947–78) drummer; all born London; 'Substitute', 'Won't Get Fooled Again', 'You Better You Bet', *My Generation* (1966), *The Who Sell Out* (1967), *Tommy* (1969), *Who's Next* (1971), *Quadrophenia* (1973), *Face Dances* (1981), *It's Hard* (1982).

Wings   British group, 1970s; members include Paul McCartney (1942–) singer/songwriter, guitarist; 'Give Ireland Back to the Irish', 'Venus and Mars', 'Live and Let Die', 'Crossroads', 'Mull Of Kintyre', *Band On The Run* (1973), *Wild Life* (1973), *Wings over America*.

Wonder, Stevie   (originally **Steveland Judkins** or **Stevland Morris**)   (1950–) American singer/songwriter, harmonica-player, keyboardist, born Saginaw, Michigan; 'Fingertips', 'Superstition', 'You Are The Sunshine Of My Life', 'Isn't She Lovely', 'Master Blaster', 'Happy Birthday', 'I Just Called to Say I Love You', 'Part-Time Lover', 'Ebony and Ivory' (with Paul McCartney), *Stevie Wonder/The 12 Year Old Genius* (1961), *Music Of My Mind* (1972), *Talking Book* (1972), *Innervisions* (1973), *Songs in the Key of Life* (1976), *Hotter than July* (1980), *In Square Circle* (1985), *Characters* (1987).

POP AND ROCK MUSICIANS AND SINGERS (cont.)

Yardbirds   British group, 1960s; members include Keith Relf (1943–76) singer, harmonica player, born Richmond, Surrey; Paul Samwell-Smith (1943–   ) bassist, born Twickenham, Middlesex; Chris Dreja (1946–   ) guitarist, born Surbiton, Surrey; Eric Clapton guitarist; Jeff Beck guitarist; Jimmy Page bassist, guitarist; 'Good Morning Little Schoogirl', 'For Your Love', 'I'm A Man', 'Happening Ten Years Time Ago'.

Yes   British group, 1970s to present; members include Jon Anderson (1944–   ) vocalist, born Lancashire; Rick Wakeman (1949–   ) keyboardist, born London; Steve Howe guitarist; Chris Squire (1948–   ) bassist, born London; 'Owner Of A Lonely Heart', *Fragile* (1972), *Close To The Edge* (1972), *90125* (1983), *Big Generator* (1987).

Young, Neil   (1945–   ) Canadian singer/songwriter, guitarist, born Toronto; 'Heart Of Gold', *After the Gold Rush* (1970), *Harvest* (1972), *Tonight's the Night* (1975), *Zuma* (1975), *Rust Never Sleeps* (1979), *Reactor* (1981), *Landing On Water* (1986), *Freedom* (1989).

Young, Paul   (1956–   ) British singer, born Luton, Bedfordshire; 'Where I Leave My Hat', 'Come Back And Stay', 'Love Of The Common People', 'Everytime You Go Away', *No Parlez* (1983), *The Secret Of Association* (1985).

Zappa, Frank Vincent (originally **Francis Vincent Zappa Jr**)   (1940–   ) American singer/songwriter, guitarist, band leader (The Mothers of Invention – American 1970s group), born Baltimore, Maryland; 'Valley Girl', *Apostrophe* (1974), *Joe's Garage* (1979), *Ship Arriving Too Late To Save A Drowning Witch* (1982), *The Perfect Stranger And Other Works* (1985).

ZZ Top   American group, 1970s to present; Billy Gibbons vocalist, guitarist; Dusty Hill vocalist, bassist; Frank Beard drummer; 'Gimme All Your Lovin'', 'Sharp Dressed Man', 'Legs', 'Sleeping Bag', *Tres Hombres* (1973), *Tejas* (1976), *Deguello* (1979), *Eliminator* (1983), *Afterburner* (1985).

BALLET DANCERS

Ashley, Merrill (Linda Michelle Merrill)   (1950–   ) American, born St Paul, Minnesota.

Barishnikov, Mikhail (Nikolaievich)   (1948–   ) Russian, born Riga.

Buchones, Fernando   (1955–   ) American, born Florida.

Danilova, Alexandra (Dionysievna)   (1904–   ) Russian/American, born Peterhof.

Dolin, Sir Anton (Sydney Francis Patrick Chippendall Healey-Kay)   (1904–83) British, born Slinfold.

Dowell, Anthony   (1943–   ) British, born London.

Duncan, Isadora   (1878–1927) American, born San Francisco.

Dunham, Katherine   (1912–   ) American, born Chicago.

Eglevsky, André   (1917–77) Russian/American, born Moscow.

Elssler, Fanny (Franziska Elssler)   (1810–1884) Austrian, born Gumpendorf.

Farrell, Suzanne   (1945–   ) American, born Cincinnati, Ohio.

Fonteyn, Dame Margot (Peggy Hookham)   (1919–91) British, born Reigate.

Fracci, Carla   (1936–   ) Italian, born Milan.

Genée, Dame Adelin (Anina Jensen)   (1878–1970) Danish, born Hinnerup.

Gilpin, John   (1830–83) British, born Southsea.

Gopal, Ram   (1920–   ) Indian, born Bangalore.

Gore, Walter   (1910–79) British, born Waterside, Scotland.

Gorsky, Alexander Alexeivich   (1871–1924) Russian, born St Petersburg.

Graham, Martha   (1894–1991) American, born Pittsburgh.

Gregory, Cynthia   (1946–   ) American, born Los Angeles.

BALLET DANCERS (cont.)

Grisi, Carlotta   (1819–99) Italian, born Visinada.

Hamilton, Gordon   (1918–59) Australian, born Sydney.

Haydée, Marcia (Marcia Haydee Salaverry Pereira de Silva)   (1939–   ) Brazilian, born Niteroi.

Helpmann, Sir Robert   (1909–86) Australian, born Mount Gambier.

Jasinski, Roman (Roman Czeslaw)   (1912–   ) Polish/American, born Warsaw.

Kain, Karen   (1951–   ) Canadian, born Hamilton, Ontario.

Karsavina, Tamara Platonovna   (1885–1978) Russian/British, born St Petersburg.

Kent, Allegra   (1938–   ) American, born Los Angeles.

Kirkland, Gelsey   (1953–   ) American, born Bethlehem, Pennsylvania.

Leclerq, Tanquil   (1929–   ) American, born Paris.

Lichine, David (David Lichenstein)   (1910–72) Russian/American, born Rostov-on-Don.

Markova, Dame Alicia (Lilian Alicia Marks)   (1910–   ) British, born London.

Martins, Peter   (1946–   ) Danish, born Copenhagen.

Mauri, Rosita   (1849–1923) Spanish, born Tarragona.

Neary, Patricia   (1942–   ) American, born Miami, Florida.

Nemchinova, Vera (Nicolayevna)   (1899–1984) Russian, born Moscow.

Nijinsky, Vaslav Fomich   (1889–1950) Russian, born Kiev.

Nureyev, Rudolf Hametovich   (1938–   ) Russian/British, born on a train between Lake Baikal and Irkutsk, Siberia.

Page, Ruth   (1905–   ) American, born Indianapolis.

Panov, Valeri (Matvevich)   (1938–   ) Russian, born Vitebsk.

Panova, Galina   (1949–   ) Russian, born Archangel.

Pavlova, Anna (Pavlovna)   (1881–1931) Russian, born St Petersburg.

Petipa, Lucien   (1815–98) French, born Marseilles.

Petipa, Marie (Mariusovna II)   (1857–1930) Russian, born St Petersburg.

Rambert, Dame Marie (Cyvia Rambam, then Miriam Ramberg)   (1888–1982) Polish/British, born Warsaw.

Riabochinska, Tatiana   (1917–   ) Russian/American, born Moscow.

Rubinstein, Ida Lvovna   (1885–1960) Russian, born St Petersburg.

Seymour, Lynn (Lynn Springbett)   (1939–   ) Canadian, born Wainwright.

Shearer, Moira (Moira King)   (1926–   ) British, born Dunfermline.

Shearer, Sybil   (1918–   ) American, born Toronto.

Sibley, Antoinette   (1939–   ) British, born Bromley.

Somes, Michael   (1917–   ) British, born Horsley.

Spessivtseva, Olga Alexandrovna   (1895–   ) Russian/American, born Rostov.

Taglioni, Marie   (1804–84) Swedish/Italian, born Stockholm.

Tallchief, Maria   (1925–   ) American, born Fairfax, Oklahoma.

Taras, John   (1919–   ) American, born New York.

Trefilova, Vera Alexandrovna   (1875–1943) Russian, born St Petersburg.

Ulanova, Galina (Sergeyevna)   (1910–   ) Russian, born St Petersburg.

Villella, Edward   (1936–   ) American, born Bayside, New York.

BALLET COMPANIES

Name	Date founded	Location	Name	Date founded	Location
American Ballet Theatre	1940	New York, USA	Royal Ballet (formerly Sadler's Wells Ballet)	1936	Covent Garden, UK
The Australian Ballet	1962	Melbourne, Australia	Royal Danish Ballet	ballets from 2nd half 16th-c	Copenhagen
Australian Dance Theatre	1965	Adelaide, Australia	Royal Swedish Ballet	1st court ballet 1638	Stockholm
Ballets des Champs Elysées	1944	Paris, France			
Ballet Joos	1933	Cambridge, UK	Royal Winnipeg Ballet	1938	Canada
Ballets de Paris	1948	France	The San Francisco Ballet (formerly the San Francisco Opera Ballet)	1933	USA
Ballet Rambert	1926	UK			
Ballet Russe de Monte Carlo	1938	Monte Carlo			
Ballets Russes of Sergei Diaghilev now Kirov Ballet	1909-29	Paris and Leningrad	School of American Ballet (now the American Ballet)	1933	New York, USA
Ballet-Théâtre Contemporain	1968	Amiens, France	Scottish Ballet (formed from part of Western Theatre Ballet)	1969	Glasgow, UK
Ballet du Xième Siècle	1960	Brussels, Belgium			
Bolshoi Ballet	1776	Moscow, USSR	Stanislavsky Ballet (Stanislavsky and Nemirovich-Danchenko Music Theatre Ballet)	1929	Moscow, USSR
Borovansky Ballet	1942	Melbourne, Australia			
Kirov Ballet	1935	Leningrad, USSR			
London Festival Ballet (originally Festival Ballet)	1949	UK	Stuttgart Ballet	court ballets from 1609	Germany
National Ballet of Canada	1951	Toronto	Western Theatre Ballet (divided 1969 to form Northern Ballet, Scottish Ballet)	1957	Bristol, UK
New York City Ballet	1948	USA			
Northern Ballet (formed from part of Western Theatre Ballet)	1969	Manchester, UK			

BALLETS

Ballet	Composer	Choreographer	First performance	Ballet	Composer	Choreographer	First performance
Anastasia	Tchaikovksy, Martinu	MacMillan	1971	Petroushka	Stravinsky	Fokine	1911
Apollo	Stravinsky	Balanchine	1928	Pineapple Poll	Sullivan, orch. Mackerras	Cranko	1951
L'Après-midi d'un faune	Debussy	Nijinsky	1912	Prince Igor	Borodin	Fokine	1909
La Bayadère	Minkus	Petipa	1877	The Prodigal Son	Prokofiev	Balanchine	1929
Les Biches	Pulenc	Nijinska	1924	The Rake's Progress	Gordon	de Valois	1935
Billy the Kid	Copland	Loring	1938	Raymonda	Glazounov	Petipa	1898
Bolero	Ravel	Bejart	1961	Les Rendezvous	Auber, arr. Lambert	Ashton	1933
La Boutique Fantasque	Rossini, arr. Respighi	Massine	1919	Requiem	Fauré	MacMillan	1976
Carmen	Bizet	Petit	1949	Rhapsody	Rachmaninov	Ashton	1980
Checkmate	Bliss	de Valois	1937	The Rite of Spring	Stravinsky	MacMillan	1962
Cinderella	Prokofiev	Ashton	1948	Rodeo	Copland	de Mille	1942
Coppélia	Delibes	St Léon	1870	Romeo and Juliet	Prokofiev	Lavrovsky	1940
Don Quixote	Minkus	Petipa	1869	Le Sacré du printemps (The Rite of Spring)	Stravinsky	Nijinsky	1913
Duo Concertant	Stravinsky	Balanchine	1972				
Façade	Walton	Ashton	1931	Schéhérazade	Rimsky-Korsakov	Fokine	1910
Fall River Legend	Gould	de Mille	1948	The Sleeping Beauty	Tchaikovsky	Petipa	1890
Fancy Free	Bernstein	Robbins	1944	Song of the Earth	Mahler	MacMillan	1965
The Firebird	Stravinsky	Fokine	1910	Spartacus	Khachaturian	Grigorovich	1968
The Four Temperaments	Hindemith	Balanchine	1946	La Spectre de la Rose	Weber	Fokine	1911
Giselle	Adam	Coralli and Perro (later revised by Petipa)	1841	Swan Lake	Tchaikovsky	Petipa and Ivanov	1895
				La Sylphide	Løvenskjold	Bournonville	1836
Las Hermanas	Martin	MacMillan	1963	Les Sylphides (Chopiniana)	Chopin, variously orchestrated	Fokine	1909
Jewels	Fauré, Stravinsky and Tchaikovsky	Balanchine	1967	Tales of Hoffman	Offenbach, arr. Lanchberg	Darrell	1973
Les Noces	Stravinsky	Nijinska	1923	The Three-Cornered Hat	de Falla	Massine	1919
The Nutcracker	Tchaikovsky	Ivanov	1892	La Ventana	Lumbye and Holm	Bournonville	1854
Ondine	Henze	Ashton	1958				
Onegin	Tchaikovsky, arr. Stolze	Cranko	1965	A Wedding Bouquet	Berners	Ashton	1937
Orpheus	Stravinsky	Balanchine	1948				
Parade	Satie	Massine	1917				

BALLET CHOREOGRAPHERS

Ashton, Sir Frederick William Mallandaine (1904–88) English, born Guayaquil, Ecuador; *Façade* (1931), *Les Rendezvous* (1933), *Cinderella* (1948), *Daphnis and Chloe* (1951), *Ondine* (1958), *The Two Pigeons* (1961), *The Dream* (1964), *Rhapsody* (1980).

Balanchine, George (Georgi Balanchivadze) (1904–83) Russian/American, born St Petersburg; *Apollo* (1928), *The Prodigal Son* (1929), *Bourrée Fantasque* (1949), *Jeu de cartes* (1937), *Agon* (1957), *The Seven Deadly Sins* (1958), *Davidsbundlertauze* (1980).

Bournonville, August (1805–79) Danish, born Copenhagen; *La Sylphide* (1836), *Napoli* (1842), *La Ventana* (1854).

Cranko, John (1927–73) South African, born Rustenburg; *Beauty and the Beast* (1949), *Pineapple Doll* (1951), *The Prince of the Pagodas* (1957), *Jeu de Cartes* (1965), *Onegin* (1965), *Taming of the Shrew* (1969), *Traces* (1973).

Darrell, Peter (1929–) British, born Richmond, Surrey; *A Wedding Present* (1962), *Beauty and the Beast* (1969), *Tales of Hoffman* (1972), *Swan Lake* (1977).

de Mille, Agnes (1909–) American, born New York City; *Three Virgins and a Devil* (1941), *Rodeo* (1942), *Fall River Legend* (1948), and for Broadway – *Oklahoma!* (1943), *Gentleman Prefer Blondes* (1949).

de Valois, Dame Ninette (Edris Stannus) (1898–) Irish, born Baltiboys, County Wicklow; *Job* (1931), *La Création du monde* (1931), *The Rake's Progress* (1935), *Checkmate* (1937), *Don Quixote* (1950).

Diaghilev, Sergei Pavlovich (1872–1929) Russian, born Selistchev barracks, province of Novgorod; producer, impressario, and founder of Ballet Russes; not a choreographer himself, he fostered the talents of Balanchine, Fokine, Nijinsky.

Fokine, Michel (Mikhail Mikhaylovich Fokine) (1880–1942) Russian/American dancer and choreographer, born St Petersburg; *Les Sylphides* (1907), *Petroushka* (1911).

Ivanov, Lev (Ivanovich) (1834–1901) Russian, born Moscow; *The Enchanted Forest* (1887), *The Nutcracker* (1892), *Swan Lake* (with Petipa, 1895).

Jooss, Kurt (1901–79) German, born Waaseralfingen; *Petrushka* (1930), *The Green Table* (1932), *Pulcinella* (1932), *The Mirror* (1935).

Lorring, Eugene (1914–) American, born Milwaukee; *Yankee Clipper* (1937), *Billy the Kid* (1938).

MacMillan, Sir Kenneth (1929–) British, born Dunfermline, Scotland; *The Rite of Spring* (1962), *Las Hermanas* (1963), *Romeo and Juliet* (1965), *Anastasia* (1971), *The Four Seasons* (1975), *Mayerling* (1978), *Isadora* (1981).

Massine, Léonide (Fedorovich) (1895–1979) Russian/American, born Moscow; *Parade* (1917), *La Boutique Fantasque* (1919), *The Three-Cornered Hat* (1919), *Bachanale* (1939).

Nijinska, Bronislova (Fominitshna) (1891–1972) Russian/Polish/American, born Minsk; *Le Renard* (1922), *Les Noces* (1923, 66), *Les Biches* (1924, 64), *La Valse* (1929), *The Snow Maiden* (1942).

Perrot, Jules (Joseph) (1810–94) French, born Lyons; *Ondine* (1843), *Les Elements* (1847), *Faust* (1848), *Markobomba* (1854).

Petipa, Marius (1818–1910) French, born Marseilles; *Pharoah's Daughter* (1862), *La Bayadère* (1877), *The Sleeping Beauty* (1890), *Cinderella* (1893), *Swan Lake* (1895), *Raymonda* (1898).

Robbins, Jerome (Jerome Rabinowitz) (1918–) American, born New York; *Fancy Free* (1944), *Interplay* (1945), *The Pied Piper* (1951), *Afternoon of a Fawn* (1953), *West Side Story* (musical, 1957), and for Broadway, eg *The King and I* (1951).

St-Léon, Arthur (1821–70) French, born Paris; *Le Violon du diable* (1849), *La Fille mal gardée* (1866), *La Source* (1866), *Coppélia* (1870).

Tudor, Antony (William Cook) (1908–87) English, born London; *Undertow* (1945), *Lady of the Camellias* (1951), *Shadowplay* (1967), *The Tiller in the Field* (1978).

ARTISTS

Selected paintings are listed

Altdorfer, Albrecht (c.1480–1538) German, born Regensburg; *Danube Landscape* (1520), *Alexander's Victory* (1529).

Andrea del Sarto (Andrea d'Agnolo di Francesco) (1486–1530) Italian, born Florence; *Miracles of S Filippo Benizzi* (1509–10), *Madonna del Saeco* (1525).

Angelico, Fra (Guido di Pietro) (c.1400–55) Italian, born Vicchio, Tuscany; *Coronation of the Virgin* (1430–5), *San Marco altarpiece* (c.1440).

Auerbach, Frank (1931–   ) German/British, born Berlin; *Mornington Crescent* (1967).

Bacon, Francis (1909–   ) British, born Dublin; *Three Figures at the Base of a Crucifixion* (1945), *Two figures with a Monkey* (1973), *Triptych Inspired by the Oresteia of Aeschylus* (1981).

Beardsley, Aubrey (Vincent) (1872–98) British, born Brighton; illustrations to Malory's *Morte d'Arthur* (1893), Wilde's *Salome* (1894).

Bell, Vanessa (1879–1961) British, born Kensington, London; *Still Life on Corner of a Mantlepiece* (1914).

Bellini, Gentile (c.1429–1507) Italian, born Venice; *Procession of the Relic of the True Cross* (1496), *Miracle at Ponte di Lorenzo* (1500).

Blackadder, Elizabeth (1931–   ) Scottish, born Falkirk; *Interior with Self-Portrait* (1972), *White Anemones* (1983), *Texas Flame* (1986).

Blake, William (1757–1827) British, born London; illustrations for his own *Songs of Innocence and Experience* (1794), *Newton* (1795), illustrations for the *Book of Job* (1826)

Böcklin, Arnold (1827–1901) Swiss, born Basel; *Pan in the Reeds* (1857), *The Island of the Dead* (1880).

Bomberg, David (1890 1957) British, born Birmingham; *In the Hold* (1913–14), *The Mud Bath* (1913–14).

Bonnard, Pierre (1867–1947) French, born Paris; *Young Woman in Lamplight* (1900), *Dining Room in the Country* (1913), *Seascape of the Mediterranean* (1941).

Bosch, Hieronymus (Jerome von Aken) (c.1460–1516) Dutch, born 's Hertogenbosch, Brabant; *The Temptation of St Anthony*, *The Garden of Earthly Delights* (work undated).

Botticelli, Sandro (Alessandro di Mariano Filipepi) (1444–1510) Italian, born Florence; *Primavera* (c.1478), *The Birth of Venus* (c.1485), *Mystic Nativity* (1500).

Braque, Georges (1882 1963) French, born Argenteuil-sur-Seine; *Still Life with Violin* (1910), *The Portuguese* (1911), *Blue Wash Basin* (1942).

Brueghel, Pieter (the Elder) (c.1525–69) Dutch, born Bruegel, near Breda; *Road to Calvary* (1564), *Massacre of the Innocents* (c.1566), *The Blind Leading the Blind* (1568), *The Peasant Wedding* (1568), *The Peasant Dance* (1568).

Burne-Jones, Sir Edward (Coley) (1833–98) British, born Birmingham; *The Beguiling of Merlin* (1874), *The Arming of Perseus* (1877), *King Cophetea and the Beggar Maid* (1880–4).

Burra, Edward (1905–76) British, born London; *Dancing Skeletons* (1934), *Soldiers* (1942), *Scene in Harlem (Simply Heavenly)* (1952).

Canaletto (Giovanni Antonio Canal) (1697–1768) Italian, born Venice; *Stone Mason's Yard* (c.1730).

Caravaggio, Michelangelo (Merisi da) (1573–1610) Italian, born Caravaggio, near Burgamo; *The Supper at Emmaus* (c.1598–1600), *Martyrdom of St Matthew* (1599–1600), *The Death of the Virgin* (1605–6).

Cézanne, Paul (1839–1906) French, born Aix-en-Provence; *The Black Marble Clock* (c.1869–70), *Maison du Pendu* (c.1873), *Bathing Women* (1900–5), *Le Jardinier* (1906).

Chagall, Marc (1887–1985) Russian/French, born Vitebsk; *The Musician* (1912–13), *Bouquet of Flying Lovers* (1947).

Chirico, Giorgio de (1888–1978) Italian, born Volos, Greece; *Portrait of Guillame Apollinaire* (1914), *The Jewish Angel* (1916), *The Return of Ulysses* (1968).

Cimabué (Cenni de Pepo) (c.1240–c.1302) Italian, born Florence; *Crucifix* (date unknown), *Saint John the Evangelist* (1302).

ARTISTS (cont.)

Claude Lorraine (le Lorrain) (Claude Gêllée) (1600–82) French, born near Nancy; *The Mill* (1631), *The Embarkation of St Ursula* (1641), *Ascanius Shooting the Stag of Silvia* (1682).

Constable, John (1776–1837) English, born East Bergholt, Suffolk; *A Country Lane* (c.1810), *The White Horse* (1819), *The Hay Wain* (1821), *Stonehenge* (1835).

Corot, Jean Baptiste Camille (1796–1875) French, born Paris; *Bridge at Narni* (1827), *Souvenir de Marcoussis* (1869), *Woman Reading in a Landscape* (1869).

Correggio (Antonio Allegri de) (c.1494–1534) Italian, born Corregio; *The Agony in the Garden* (c.1528).

Courbet, (Jean Désiré) Gustave (1819–77) French, born Ornans; *The After-Dinner at Ornans* (1848–9), *The Bathers* (1853), *The Painter's Studio* (1855), *The Stormy Sea*(1869).

Cranach, Lucas (the Elder) (1472–1553) German, born Kronach, near Bamberg; *The Crucifixion* (1503), *The Fountain of Youth* (1550).

Dali, Salvador (Felipe Jacinto) (1904–89) Spanish, born Figueras, Gerona; *The Persistence of Memory* (1931), *The Transformation of Narcissus* (1934), *Christ of St John of the Cross* (1951).

David, Jacques Louis (1748–1825) French, born Paris; *Death of Socrates* (1788), *The Death of Marat* (1793), *The Rape of the Sabines* (1799), *Madame Récamier* (1800).

Degas, Edgar (Hilaire Germain Edgar de Gas) (1834–1917) French, born Paris; *Cotton-brokers Office* (1873), *L'Absinthe* (1875–6), *Little Fourteen-year-old Dancer* (sculpture) (1881), *Dancer at the Bar* (c.1900).

Delacroix, (Ferdinand Victor Eugène (1798–1863) French, born St-Maurice-Charenton; *Dante and Vergil in Hell* (1822), *Liberty Guiding the People* (1831), *Jacob and the Angel* (1853–61).

Delvaux, Paul (1897–) Belgian, born Antheit, near Huys; *Vénus endormie* (1932), *Phases of the Moon* (1939), *In Praise of Melancholy* (1951).

Doré, (Louis Auguste) Gustave (1832–1883) French, born Strasbourg; Illustrations to Dante's *Inferno* (1861), Milton's *Paradise Lost* (1866).

Duccio di Buoninsegna (c.1260–c.1320) Italian; *Maestà (Siena Cathedral altarpiece) (1308–11)*.

Duchamp, (Henri Robert) Marcel (1887–1968) French/American, born Blainville, Normandy; *Nude descending a Staircase* (1912), *The Bride Stripped Bare by her Bachelors Even* (1915–23).

Dufy, Raoul (1877–1953) French, born Le Havre; *Posters at Trouville* (1906), illustrations to Guillame Appollinaire's *Bestiary* (1911), *Riders in the Wood* (1931).

Eardley, Joan (1921–63) British, born Warnham, Sussex; *Winter Sea IV* (1958), *Two Children* (1962).

Ernst, Max(imillian) (1891–1976) German/American/French, born Brühl, near Cologne, Germany; *Europe after the Rain* (1940–2), *The Elephant Célébes* (1921), *Moonmad* (1944) (sculpture), *The King Playing with the Queen* (1959) (sculpture).

Eyck, Jan van (c.1389–1441) Dutch, born Maaseyck, near Maastricht; *The Adoration of the Holy Lamb* (Ghent altarpiece) (1432), *Man in a Red Turban* (1433), *Arnolfni Marriage Portrait* (1434), *Madonna by the Fountain* (1439).

Fini, Léonor (1908–) Italian/Argentine, born Buenos Aires; *The End of the World* (1944).

Freud, Lucian (1922–) German/British, born Berlin; *Woman with a Daffodil* (1945), *Interior in Paddington* (1951), *Hotel Room* (1953–4).

Friedrich, Caspar David (1774–1840) German, born Pomerania; *The Cross in the Mountains* (1807-8).

Fuseli, Henri (Johann Heinrich Füssli) (1741–1825) Swiss/English, born Zurich; *The Nightmare* (1781), *Appearance of the Ghost* (1796).

Gainsborough, Thomas (1727–88) English, born Sudbury, Suffolk; *Peasant Girl Gathering Sticks* (1782), *The Watering Place* (1777).

Gauguin, (Eugène Henri) Paul (1848–1903) French, born Paris; *The Vision after the Sermon* (1888), *Still Life with Three Puppies* (1888), *The White Horse* (1898), *Women of Tahiti* (1891), *Tahitian Landscape* (1891), *Where Do We Come From? What Are We? Where Are We Going?* (1897-8), *Golden Bodies* (1901).

ARTISTS (cont.)

Géricault, Theodore (1791–1824) French, born Rouen; *Officer of Light Horse* (c.1812), *Raft of the Medusa* (1819).

Ghirlandaio, Domenico (Domenico di Tommaso Bigordi) (1449–1494) Italian, born Florence; *Virgin of Mercy* (1472), *St Jerome* (1480), *Nativity* (1485).

Giorgione (da Castelfranco), or Giorgio Barbarelli (c.1478–1511) Italian, born Castelfranco; *The Tempest* (c.1508), *Three Philosophers* (c.1508), *Portrait of a Man* (1510).

Giotto (di Bondone) (c.1266–1337) Italian, born near Florence; frescoes in *Arena Chapel*, Padua (1304–12), *Ognissanti Madonna* (1311–12).

Goes, Hugo van der (c.1440–82) Dutch, born probably Ghent; *Portinari Altarpiece* (1475), *Ghent Altarpiece* (1495).

Goya (y Lucientes), Francisco (José) de (1746–1828) Spanish, born Fuendetotos; *Family of Charles IV* (1799), *Los Desastres de la Guerra* (1810–14), *Black Paintings* (1820s).

Greco, El (Domenico Theotocopoulos) (1541–1614) Greek, born Candia, Crete; *Lady in Fur Wrap* (c.1577–8), *El Espolio* (The Disrobing of Christ) (1577–9), *The Saviour of the World* (1600), *Portrait of Brother Hortensio Felix Paravicino* (1609), *Toledo Landscape* (c.1610).

Grüneweld, Matthias (Mathis Nithardt or Gothardt) (c.1480–1528) German, born probably Würzburg; *Isenheim Altarpiece* (1515).

Hilliard, Nicholas (c.1547–1619) English, born Exeter; miniature of *Queen Elizabeth I* (1572), *Henry Wriothesley* (1594).

Hockney, David (1937–) British, born Bradford, Yorkshire; *We Two Boys Together Clinging* (1961), *The Rake's Progress* (1963), *A Bigger Splash* (1967), *Invented Man Revealing a Still Life* (1975), *Dancer* (1980).

Hogarth, William (1697–1764) English, born Smithfield, London; *Before and After* (1731), *A Rake's Progress* (1733–5).

Hokusai, Katsushika (1760–1849) Japanese, born Tokyo; *Tametomo and the Demon* (1811), *Mangwa* (1814–19), *Hundred Views of Mount Fuji* (1835).

Holbein, Hans, 'the younger' (1497–1543) German, born Augsburg; *Bonifacius Amerbach* (1519), *Solothurn Madonna* (1522), *Anne of Cleves* (1539).

Hundertwasser, Fritz (Friedrich Stowasser) (1928–) Austrian, born Vienna; *Many Transparent Heads* (1949–50), *The End of Greece* (1963), *The Court of Sulaiman* (1967).

Hunt, (William) Holman (1827–1910) English, born London; *The Hireling Shepherd* (1852), *Claudio and Isabella* (1853), *The Light of the World* (1854), *Isabella and the Pot of Basil* (1867).

Ingres, Jean Auguste Dominique (1780–1867) French, born Montauban; *Gilbert* (1805), *La Sources* (1807–59), *Bather* (1808), *Turkish Bath* (1863).

John, Augustus (Edwin) (1878–1961) British, born Tenby; *The Smiling Woman* (1908), *Portrait of a Lady in Black* (1917).

John, Gwen (1876–1939) British, born Haverfordwest, Pembrokeshire; *Girl with bare shoulders* (1909-10).

Kandinsky, Vasily (1866–1944) Russian/French, born Moscow; *Kossacks* (1910–11), *Swinging* (1925), *Two Green Points* (1935), *Sky Blue* (1940).

Kirchner, Ernst Ludwig (1880–1938) German, born Aschaffenburg; *Recumbent Blue Nude with Straw Hat* (1908–9), *The Drinker* (1915), *Die Amselfluh* (1923).

Kitaj, R(onald) B(rooks) (1932–) American, born Cleveland, Ohio; *The Orientalists*, *The Ohio Gang* (1964), *If not, not* (1975–6).

Klee, Paul (1879–1940) Swiss, born Münchenbuchsee, near Berne; *Der Vollmond* (1919), *Rosegarden* (1920), *A tiny tale of a tiny dwarf* (1925), *Fire in the Evening* (1929), *Twittering Machine.*

Klimt, Gustav (1862–1918) Austrian, born Baumgarten, near Vienna; *Music* (1895), *The Kiss* (1907–8), *Judith II* (Salome) (1909).

ARTISTS (cont.)

Kokoschka, Oskar (1886–1980) Austrian/British, born Pöchlarn; *The Dreaming Boys* (1908).

Landseer, Sir Edwin (Henry) (1803–73) English, born London; *The Old Shepherd's Chief Mourner* (1837), *The Monarch of the Glen* (1850).

La Tour, Georges (Dumesnil) de (1593–1652) French, born Vic-sur-Seille, Lorraine; *St Jerome Reading* (1620s), *The Denial of St Peter* (1650).

Léger, Fernand (1881–1955) French, born Argentan; *Contrast of Forms* (1913), *Black Profile* (1928), *The Great Parade* (1954).

Lely, Sir Peter (Pieter van der Faes) (1618–80) Dutch/British, born Soest, Westphalia; *The Windsor Beauties* (1668), *Admirals* series (1666–7).

Leonardo da Vinci (Leonardo di Ser Piero da Vince) (1452–1519) Italian, born Vinci; *The Last Supper* (1495–7), *Madonna and Child with St Anne* (begun 1503), *Mona Lisa* (1500–6), *The Virgin of the Rocks* (c.1508).

Lichtenstein, Roy (1923–   ) American, born New York City; *Whaam!* (1963), *As I Opened Fire* (1964).

Lippi, Fra Filippo, called **Lippo** (c.1406–69) Italian, born Florence; *Tarquinia Madonna*(1437), *Barbadori Altarpiece* (begun 1437).

Lochner, Stefan (c.1400–1451) German, born Meersburg am Bodenese; *The Adoration of the Magi* (c.1448), triptych in Cologne Cathedral.

Macke, August (1887–1914) German, born Meschede; *Greeting* (1912), *The Zoo* (1912), *Girls Under Trees* (1914).

Magritte, René (François Ghislain) (1898–1967) Belgian, born Lessines, Hainault; *The Menaced Assassin* (1926), *Loving Perspective* (1935), *Presence of Mind* (1960).

Manet, Édouard (1832–83) French, born Paris; *Déjeuner sur l'herbe* (1863), *A Bar at the Foliès-Bergère* (1882), *Ball at the Opera* (1893–4).

Mantegna, Andrea (1431–1506) Italian, born Vicenza; *Madonna of Victory* (altarpiece), *San Zeno Altarpiece* (1457–9), *Triumphs of Caesar* (c.1486–94).

Martin, John (1789–1854) English, born Haydon Bridge; *Joshua Commanding the Sun to Stand Still* (1816), *The Last Judgement* (1851–4).

Martini, or **Memmi, Simone (Simone di Martino)** (c.1284–1344) Italian, born Siena; *S Caterina Polyptych* (1319), *Annunciation* (1333).

Masaccio (Tomasso di Giovanni di Simone Guidi) (1401–28) Italian, born Castel San Giovanni di Val d'Arno; *polyptych* for the *Carmelite Church* in Pisa (1426), frescoes in *Sta Maria del Carmine*, Florence, (1424–7).

Masson, André (Aimé René) (1896–1987) French, born Balgny, Oise; *Massacres* (1933), *The Labyrinth* (1939).

Matisse, Henri (Emile Benoît) (1869–1954) French, born Le Cateau-Cambrésis; *La Desserte* (1908), *Notre Dame* (1914), *The Large Red Studio* (1948), *L'Escargot* (1953).

Michelangelo (Michelagniolo di Lodovico Buonarroti) (1475–1564) Italian, born Caprese, Tuscany; *The Pietà* (1497) (sculpture), *David* (1501–4) (sculpture), *Madonna* (c.1502), ceiling of the *Sistine Chapel*, Rome (1508–12), *The Last Judgement* (begun 1537).

Millais, Sir John Everett (1829–96) English, born Southampton; *Ophelia* (1851–2), *The Bridesmaid* (1851), *Tennyson* (1881), *Bubbles* (1886).

Millet, Jean-François (1814–75) French, born Grouchy; *Sower* (1850), *The Gleaners* (1857).

Mondrian, Piet (Pieter Cornelius Mondriaan) (1872–1944) Dutch, born Amersfoort; *Still Life with Gingerpot II* (1911), *Composition with red, black, blue, yellow, and grey* (1920), *Broadway Boogie-Woogie* (1942–3).

Monet, Claude (1840–1926) French, born Paris; *Impression: Sunrise* (1872), *Haystacks* (1890–1), *Rouen Cathedral* (1892–5), *Water-lilies* (1899 onwards).

ARTISTS (cont.)

Moreau, Gustave (1826–89) French, born Paris; *Oedipus and the Sphinx* (1864), *Apparition* (1876), *Jupiter and Semele* (1889–95).

Morisot, Berthe (Marie Pauline) (1841–95) French, born Bourges; *The Harbour at Cherbourg* (1874), *In the Dining Room* (1886).

Morris, William (1834–96) British, born Walthamstow; *Queen Guinevere* (1858).

Motherwell, Robert (Burns) (1915–91) American, born Aberdeen, Washington; *Gauloises* (1967), *Opens* (1968–72).

Munch, Edvard (1863–1944) Norwegian, born Löten; *The Scream* (1895), *Mother and Daughter* (c.1897), *Self-Portrait between the clock and the bed* (1940–2).

Nash, Paul (1899–1946) British, born London; *We Are Making a New World* (1918), *Menin Road* (1919).

Newman, Barnett (1905–70) American, born New York; *The Moment* (1946), *Onement I* (1948), *Vir Heroicus Sublimis* (1950–1).

Nicholson, Ben (1894–1982) British, born Denham, London; *White Relief* (1935), *November 11, 1947* (1947).

Nicholson, Winifred (1893–1981) British, born Oxford; *Honeysuckle and Sweet Peas* (1950), *The Copper and Capari* (1967), *The Gate to The Isles* (1980).

Nolde, Emil (Emil Hansen) (1867–1956) German, born Nolde; *The Missionary* (1912), *Candle Dancers* (1912).

Oliver, Isaac (c.1560–1617) French/English, born Rouen; *Self-Portrait* (c.1590), *Henry, Prince of Wales* (c.1612).

Palmer, Samuel (1805–81) English, born London; *Repose of the Holy Family* (1824), *The Magic Apple Tree* (1830), *Opening the Fold* (1880).

Parmigiano, or **Parmigianino (Girolamo Francesco Maria Mazzola)** (1503–40) Italian, born Parma; frescoes in *S Giovanni Evangelista*, Parma (c.1522), *Self-Portrait in a convex mirror* (1524), *Vision of St Jerome* (1526–7), *Madonna Altarpiece*, Bologna (c.1528–30), *The Madonna of the Long Neck* (c.1535).

Pasmore, (Edwin John) Victor (1908–) British, born Chelsham, Surrey; *The Evening Star* (1945–7), *Black Symphony – the Pistol Shot* (1977).

Peploe, S(amuel) J(ohn) (1871–1935) Scottish, born Edinburgh, one of the 'Scottish colourists'; *Boats of Royan* (1910).

Perugino (Pietro di Cristoforo Vannucci) (c.1450–1523) Italian, born Città della Pieve, Umbria; *Christ giving the Keys to Peter* (fresco in the Sistine Chapel) (c.1483).

Picabia, Francis (Marie) (1879–1953) French, born Paris; *I See Again in Memory my Dear Undine* (1913), *The Kiss* (1924).

Picasso, Pablo (Ruiz) (1881–1973) Spanish, born Malaga; *Mother and Child* (1921), *Three Dances* (1925), *Guernica* (1937), *The Charnel House* (1945), *The Artist and his Model* (1968).

Piero della Francesca (c.1420–92) Italian, born Borgo san Sepolcro; *Madonna of the Misericordia* (1445–8), *Resurrection* (c.1450).

Pissarro, Camille (Jacob) (1830–1903) French, born St Thomas, Danish W Indies; *Landscape at Chaponval* (1880), *The Boieldieu Bridge at Rouen* (1896), *Boulevard Montmartre* (1897).

Pollock, (Paul) Jackson (1912–56) American, born Cody, Wyoming; *No 14* (1948), *Guardians of the Secret* (1943).

Poussin, Nicolas (1594–1665) French, born Les Andelys, Normandy; *The Adoration of the Golden Calf* (1624), *Inspiration of the Poet* (c.1628), *Seven Sacraments* (1644–8), *Self-Portrait* (1650).

Raeburn, Sir Henry (1756–1823) Scottish, born Edinburgh; *Rev Robert Walker Skating* (1784), *Isabella McLeod, Mrs James Gregory* (c.1798).

Ramsay, Allan (1713–84) Scottish, born Edinburgh; *The Artist's Wife* (1754–5).

ARTISTS (cont.)

Raphael (Raffaello Santi, or Sanzio) (1483–1520) Italian, born Urbino; *Assumption of the Virgin* (1504), *Madonna of the Meadow* (1505–6), *Transfiguration* (1518–20).

Redon, Odilon (Betran-Jean Redon) (1840–1916) French, born Bordeaux; *Woman with outstretched arms* (c.1910–14).

Redpath, Anne (1895–1965) Scottish, born Galashiels; *Pinks* (1947).

Rembrandt (Rembrandt Harmensz van Rijn) (1606–69) Dutch, born Leiden; *Anatomy Lesson of Dr Tulp* (1632), *Blinding of Samson* (1636), *The Night Watch* (1642), *The Conspiracy of Claudius* (1661–2).

Renoir, (Jean) Pierre Auguste (1841–1919) French, born Limoges; *Woman in Blue* (1874), *Woman Reading* (1876), *The Bathers* (1887).

Reynolds, Sir Joshua (1723–92) English, born Plympton Earls, near Plymouth; *Portrait of Miss Bowles with her dog* (1775), *Master Henry Hoare* (1788).

Riley, Bridget (Louise) (1931–) British, born London; *Pink Landscapes* (1959–60), *Zig-Zag* (1961), *Fall* (1963), *Apprehend* (1970).

Rosa, Salvator (1615–73) Italian, born Arenella, near Naples; *Self-Portrait with a Skull* (1656), *Humana Fragilitas* (c.1657).

Rosetti, Dante Gabriel (1828–82) British, born London; *Beata Beatrix* (1849–50), *Ecce Ancilla Domini!* (1850), *Astarte Syriaca* (1877).

Rothko, Mark (Marcus Rothkovitch) (1903–70) Latvian/American, born Dvinsk; *The Omen of the Eagle* (1942), *Red on Maroon* (1959).

Rousseau, Henri (Julien Félix), known as **Le Douanier** (1844–1910) French, born Laval; *Monsieur et Madame Stevene* (1884), *Sleeping Gipsy* (1897), *Portrait of Joseph Brunner* (1909).

Rubens, Sir Peter Paul (1577–1640) Flemish, born Siegen, Westphalia; *Marchesa Brigida Spinola-Doria* (1606), *Hélène Fourment with two of her Children* (c.1637).

Sargent, John Singer (1856–1925) American, born Florence; *Madame X* (1884), *Lady Agnew* (1893), *Gassel* (1918).

Schiele, Egon (1890–1918) Austrian, born Tulln; *Autumn Tree* (1909), *Pregnant Woman and Death* (1911), *Edith Seated* (1917–18).

Seurat, Georges (Pierre) (1859–91) French, born Paris; *Bathers at Asniéres* (1884), *Sunday on the Island of La Grande Jatte* (1885–6), *Le Cirque* (1891).

Sickert, Walter (Richard) (1860–1942) British, born Munich; *La Hollandaise* (1905–6), *Ennui* (c.1914).

Sisley, Alfred (1839–99) French, born Paris; *Avenue of Chestnut Trees near La Celle Saint-Cloud* (1868), *Mosley Weir, Hampton Court* (1874).

Spencer, Sir Stanley (1891–1959) British, born Cookham-on-Thames, Berkshire; *The Resurrection* (1927), *The Leg of Mutton Nude* (1937).

Steen, Jan (Havicksz) (1627–79) Dutch, born Leiden; *A Woman at her Toilet* (1663), *The World upside Down* (1663).

Stubbs, George (1724–1806) English, born Liverpool; *James Stanley* (1755), *Anatomy of the Horse* (1766), *Hambletonian, Rubbing Town* (1799).

Sutherland, Graham (Vivian) (1903–80) British, born London; *Entrance to a Lane* (1939), *Crucifixion* (1946), *A Bestiary and some Correspondences* (1968).

Tanguy, Yves (1900–55) French/American, born Paris; *He did what he wanted* (1927), *The Invisibles* (1951).

Tintoretto (Jacopo Robusti) (1518–94) Italian, born probably Venice; *The Miracle of the Slave* (1548), *St George and the Dragon* (c.1558), *The Golden Calf* (c.1560).

Titian (Tiziano Veccellio) (c.1488–1576) Italian, born Pieve di Cadore; *The Assumption of the Virgin* (1516–18), *Bacchus and Ariadne* (1522–3), *Pesaro Madonna* (1519–26), *Crowning with Thorns* (c.1570).

ARTISTS (cont.)

Toulouse-Lautrec, Henri (Marie Raymond de) (1864–1901) French, born Albi; *The Jockey* (1899), *At the Moulin Rouge* (1895), *The Modiste* (1900).

Turner, Joseph Mallord William (1775–1851) English, born London; *Frosty Morning* (1813), *The Shipwreck* (1805), *Crossing the Book* (1815), *The Fighting Téméraire* (1839), *Rain, Steam and Speed* (1844).

Uccelo, Paolo (Paolo di Dono) (c.1396–1475) Italian, born Pratovecchio; *The Flood* (c.1445), *The Rout of San Romano* (1454–7).

Utamaro, Kitagawa (1753–1806) Japanese, born Edo (modern Tokyo); *Ohisa* (c.1788), *The Twelve Hours of the Green Houses* (c.1795).

Van Dyck, Sir Anthony (1599–1641) Flemish, born Antwerp; *Marchesa Elena Grimaldi* (c.1625), *The Deposition* (1634–5), *Le Roi à la chasse* (c.1638).

Van Gogh, Vincent (Willem) (1853–90) Dutch, born Groot-Zundert, near Breda; *The Potato Eaters* (1885), *Self-Portrait with Bandaged Ear* (1888), *The Harvest* (1888), *The Sunflowers* (1888), *Starry Night* (1889), *Cornfields with Flight of Birds* (1890).

Velázquez, Diego (Rodriguez de Silva y) (1599–1660) Spanish, born Seville; *The Immaculate Conception* (c.1618), *The Waterseller of Seville* (c.1620), *The Surrender of Breda* (1634–5), *Pope Innocent X* (1650), *Las Meninas* (c.1656).

Vermeer, Jan (Johannes) (1632–75) Dutch, born Delft; *The Astronomer* (1668), *Christ in the House of Mary and Martha* (date unknown), *A Lady with a Gentleman at the Virginals* (c.1665), *The Lacemaker* (date unknown).

Veronese, Paolo (Paolo Caliari) (1528–88) Italian, born Verona; *The Feast in the House of Levi* (1573), *Marriage at Cana* (1573), *Triumph of Venice* (c.1585).

Verrocchio, Andrea del (Andrea de 'Cioni) (c.1435–c.1488) Italian, born Florence; *Baptism of Christ* (c.1470), *David* (c.1475) (sculpture).

Warhol, Andy (Andrew Warhola) (1928–87) American, born McKeesport, Pennsylvania; *Marilyn* (1962), *Electric Chair* (1963).

Watteau, (Jean) Antoine (1684–1721) French, born Valenciennes; *The Pilgrimage to the Island of Cythera* (1717), *L'Enseigne de Gersaint* (1721).

Whistler, James (Abbott) McNeill (1834–1903) American, born Lowell, Massachusetts; *The Artist's Mother* (1871), *Nocturne in blue and silver: Old Battersea Bridge* (1872–5), *Falling Rocket* (1875).

Wilkie, Sir David (1785–1841) Scottish, born Cults, Fife; *The Village Politicians* (1806), *Chelsea Pensioners Reading the Waterloo Despatch* (1822).

Wood, Grant (1891–1942) American, born Iowa; *American Gothic* (1930), *Spring Turning* (1936).

Wright, Joseph ('of Derby') (1734–97) English, born Derby; *Experiment with an Air Pump* (1766), *The Alchemist in Search of the Philosopher's Stone Discovers Phosphorous* (1795).

Wyeth, Andrew (Newell) (1917–) American, born Chadds Ford, Pennsylvania; *Christina's World* (1948).

ARCHITECTS

Aalto, (Hugo) Alvar (Henrik) (1898–1976) Finnish, born Kuortane; *Convalescent Home*, Paimio, near Turku (1929–30), *Town Hall*, Saynatsab (1950–2), *Finlandia Concert Hall*, Helsinki (1971).

Adam, Robert (1728–92) Scottish, born Kirkcaldy; *Adelphi*, London (1769–71, demolished 1936), *General Register House* (begun 1774), *Charlotte Square* (1791), *Edinburgh University* (1789–94) — all Edinburgh; *Culzean Castle*, Ayrshire (1772–92).

Adam, William (1689–1748) Scottish, born Maryburgh; *Hopetoun House*, near Edinburgh (1721).

Alberti, Leone Battista (1404–72) Italian, born Genoa; facade of the *Palazzo Recellai*, Florence (1460), *San Andrea*, Mantua (1470).

ARCHITECTS (cont.)

Anthemias of Tralles (dates unknown) Greek, born Tralles, Lydia; *Hagia Sophia*, Constantinople (now Istanbul) (532–7).

Apollodorus of Damascus (dates unknown) Greek, born Syria; *Trajan's Forum*, Rome, *The Baths of Trajan*, Rome.

Barry, Sir Charles (1795–1860) English, born London; *Royal Institution of the Arts*, Manchester (1824), *Houses of Parliament*, London (opened 1852).

Borromini, Francesco (1599–1667) Italian, born Bissone, on Lake Lugano; *S Carlo alle Quattro Fontane* (1637–41), *S Ivo* (1642–61), both Rome.

Bramante, Donato (Donato di Pascuccion d'Antonio) (1444–1514) Italian, born near Urbino; *San Maria presso S Satiro*, Milan (begun 1482), *Tempietto of S Pietro*, Rome (1502).

Brunelleschi, Filippo (1377–1446) Italian, born Florence; *San Lorenzo*, Florence (begun 1418), *dome* of *Florence Cathedral* (begun 1420), *Ospedale degli Innocenti*, Florence (1419).

Gabriel, Ange-Jacques (1698–1782) French, born Paris; *Pavillon de Pompadour*, Fontainebleu (begun 1749), Paris; layout of *Place de la Concorde*, Paris (1753), *Petit Trianon*, Versailles (1761–8).

Gaudi, Antonio y Cornet (1852–1926) Spanish, born Reus, Tarragona; *Casa Vicens* (1878–80), *Sagrada Familia* (1884 onwards), *Casa Batlló* (1904–17), *Casa Milá* (1905–09) – all Barcelona.

Gibbs, James (1682–1754) Scottish, born Aberdeen; *St-Martin-in-the-Fields*, London (1722–6), *King's College Fellows' Building*, Cambridge (1724–49).

Gilbert, Cass (1859–1934) American, born Zanesville, Ohio; *Woolworth Building*, New York City, 1913.

Greenway, Francis Howard (1777–1837) British/Australian, born Bristol; *Macquarie Lighthouse*, Sydney Harbour (1818), *St James' Church*, Sydney (1824).

Gropius, Walter (1883–1969) German/American, born Berlin; *Fagus Shoe Factory*, Alfeld (1911), *The Bauhaus*, Dessau (1925) – both Germany; *Harvard University Graduate Centre* (1950), USA.

Hildebrandt, Johann Lukas von (1668–1745) Austrian, born Genoa; *Lower and Upper Belvedere*, Vienna, (1714–15, 1720–3).

Horta, Baron Victor (1861–1947) Belgian, born Ghent; *Hôtel Tassel* (1892), *Hôtle Solvay* (1895–1900) – both Brussels.

Itkinos and **Callicrates** (dates and place of birth unknown) Greek; *The Parthenon*, Athens (447/6– 438 BC).

Jacobsen, Arne (1902–71) Danish, born Copenhagen; *Town Hall of Aarhus* (with Erik Moller, 1938–42), *Town Hall of Rodovre* (1955–6), *SAS Tower*, Copenhagen (1960) – all Denmark; new *St Catherine's College*, Oxford (1959).

Jefferson, Thomas (1743–1826) American, born Shadwell, Virginia; *'Monticello'*, Albermale County (1769), *Virginia State Capitol* (1796).

Jones, Inigo (1573–1652) English, born London; *The Queen's House*, Greenwich (1616–18, 1629–35), *Banqueting House*, Whitehall, London (1619–22).

Kent, William (1685–1748) English, born Bridlington; *Holkham Hall* (begun 1734).

Le Corbusier (Charles-Edouard Jeanneret) (1887–1966) French, born La Chaux-de-Fonds, Switzerland; *Salvation Army Hostel*, Paris (begun 1929), *Chapel of Ronchamp*, near Belfort (1950–4), *Museum of Modern Art*, Tokyo (1957).

Loos, Adolf (1870–1933) Austrian, born Bruno, Moravia; *Steiner House*, Vienna (1910).

Mackintosh, Charles Rennie (1868–1928) Scottish, born Glasgow; *Glasgow School of Art* (1897–9), *Hill House*, Helensburgh (1902–3).

Mendelsohn, Eric (1887–1953) German, born Allenstein; *De La Warr Pavilion*, Bexhill, UK (1934–5), *Anglo-Palestine Bank*, Jerusalem (1938), Israel.

Michelozzo di Bartolommeo (1396–1472) Italian, born Florence; *Villa Medici*, Fiesole (1458–61), *San Marco*, Florence (begun 1437).

ARCHITECTS (cont.)

Nash, John   (1752–1835) English, born London; layout of *Regent's Park* and *Regent Street*, London (1811 onwards), *Brighton Pavilion* (1815).

Palladio, Andrea   (1508–80) Italian, born Padua; *Godi-Porto* (villa at Lonedo) (1540), *La Malcontenta* (villa near Padua) (1560), *San Giorgio Maggiore*, Venice (begun 1566).

Sansovino, Jacopo   (1486–1570) Italian, born Florence; *Library* and *Mint*, Venice.

Schinkel, Karl Friederich   (1781–1841) German, born Neurippen, Brandenburg; *Old Museum*, Berlin (1823–30), *War Memorial on the Kreuzberg* (1818).

Soufflot, Jacques Germain   (1713–80) French, born Irancy; *Hôtel Dieu*, Lyons (1741). *St Geneviève* (Panthéon), Paris (begun 1757).

Sullivan, Louis Henry   (1856–1924) American, born Boston; *Wainwright Building*, St Louis (1890), *Carson, Pirie and Scott Store*, Chicago (1899–1904).

Vanbrugh, Sir John   (1664–1726) English, born London; *Castle Howard* (1699–1726), *Blenheim Palace* (1705–20).

Wagner, Otto   (1841–1918) Austrian, born Penzing, near Vienna; stations for *Vienna Stadtbahn* (1894–7), *Post Office Savings Bank*, Vienna (1904–6).

Wren, Sir Christopher   (1632–1723) English, born East Knoyle, Wiltshire; *The Sheldonian Theatre*, Oxford (1664), *St Paul's*, London (1675–1710), *Greenwich Hospital* (1696).

Wright, Frank Lloyd   (1869–1959) American, born Richland Center, Wisconsin; *Larkin Building*, Buffalo (1904), *Robie House*, Chicago (1908), *Johnson Wax Factory*, Racine, Wisconsin (1936–9), *Guggenheim Museum*, New York (begun 1942).

SCULPTORS

Selected works are listed

Arp, Hans (Jean)   (1887–1966) French, born Strasbourg; *Eggboard* (1922), *Kore* (1958).

Barlach, Ernst   (1870–1938) German, born Wedel; *Moeller-Jarke Tomb* (1901), *Have Pity!* (1919).

Bernini, Gianlorenzo   (1598–1680) Italian, born Naples; *Neptune and Triton* (1620), *David* (1623), *Ecstasy of St Theresa* (1640s), *Fountain of the Four Rivers* (1648–51).

Bologna, Giovanni da (Jean de Boulogne)   (1529–1608) French, born Douai; *Mercury* (1564–5), *Rape of the Sabines* (1579–83).

Brancusi, Constantin   (1876–1957) Romanian/French, born Hobitza, Gorj; *The Kiss* (1909), *Torso of a Young Man* (1922).

Calder, Alexander   (1898–1976) American, born Philadelphia, Pennsylvania; *Stabiles and Mobiles* (1932), *A Universe* (1934).

Caro, Sir Anthony   (1924–   ) English, born London; *Sailing Tonight* (1971–74), *Veduggio Sound* (1973), *Ledge Piece* (1978).

Cellini, Benvenuto   (1500–71) Italian, born Florence; salt cellar of *Neptune and Ceres* (1543), *Cosimo de 'Medici* (1545–7), *Perseus with the Head of Medusa* (1564).

Donatello (Donato di Niccolo di Betti di Bardi)   (c.1386–1466) Italian, born Florence; *St Mark* (1411–12), *St George Killing the Dragon* (c.1417), *Feast of Herod* (1423–37), *David, Judith and Holofernes*, Piazza della Signoria, Florence.

Epstein, Sir Jacob   (1880–1959) American/British, born New York; *Rima* (1925), *Genesis* (1930), *Ecce Homo* (1934–5), *Christ in Majesty* (Llandaff Cathedral), *St Michael and the Devil* (on the facade of Coventry Cathedral) (1958–9), *Adam* (1939).

Frink, Elizabeth   (1930–   ) British, born Thurlow, Suffolk; *Horse Lying Down* (1975), *Running Man* (1985), *Seated Man* (1986).

SCULPTORS (cont.)

Gaudier-Brzeska, Henri (1891–1915) French, born St Jean de Braye, near Orléans; *Red stone dancer* (1913).

Ghiberti, Lorenzo (di Cione di Ser Buonaccorso) (c.1378–1455) Italian, born in or near Florence; *St John the Baptist* (1412–15), *St Matthew* (1419–22), *The Gates of Paradise* (1425–52).

Giacometti, Alberto (1901–66) Swiss, born Bogonova, near Stampa; *Head* (c.1928), *Woman with her Throat Cut* (1932).

Goldsworthy, Andy (1956–   ) British, born Cheshire; *Hazel Stick Throws* (1980), *Slate Cone* (1988), *The Wall* (1988–89).

González, Julio (1876–1942) Spanish, born Barcelona; *Angel* (1933), *Woman Combing her Hair* (1936), *Cactus People* (1930–40).

Hepworth, Dame (Jocelyn) Barbara (1903–75) British, born Wakefield, Yorkshire; *Figure of a Woman* (1929–30), *Large and Small Forms* (1945), *Single Form* (1963).

Leonardo Da Vinci (1452–1519) Italian, born Vinci, between Pisa and Florence; *St John the Baptist.*

Michelangelo (Michelangelo di Lodovico Buonarotti) (1475–1564) Italian, born Caprese, Tuscany; *Cupid* (1495), *Bacchus* (1496), *Pieta* (1497), *David* (c.1500).

Moore, Henry (Spencer) (1898–1986) British, born Castleford, Yorkshire; *Recumbent figure* (1938), *Fallen Warrior* (1956–7).

Paolozzi, Eduardo Luigi (1924–   ) Scottish, born Leith, Edinburgh; *Krokodeel* (c.1956–7), *Japanese War God* (1958), *Medea* (1964), *Piscator* (1981), *Manuscript of Monte Cassino*, Edinburgh (1991).

Pheidias (c.490–c.417 BC) Greek, born Athens; *Athena Promachos* (460–450 BC), marble sculptures of the *Parthenon* (447–432 BC).

Pisano, Andrea (c.1270–1349) Italian, born Pontedera; bronze doors of the *Baptistry* of Florence (1330–6).

Pisano, Giovanni (c.1248–c.1320) Italian, born Pisa; *Fontana Magiore*, Perugia (1278), *Duomo pulpit*, Pisa (1302–10).

Pisano, Nicola (c.1225–c.1248) Italian, birthplace unknown; *Baptistry* at Pisa (1260).

Praxiteles (5th-c BC) Greek, born probably Athens; *Hermes Carrying the Boy Dionysus* (date unknown).

Robbia, Luca della (Luca di Simone di Marco) (c.1400–1482) Italian, born Florence; *Cantoria* (1432–7).

Rodin, (François) Auguste (René) (1840–1917) French, born Paris; *The Age of Bronze* (1875–6), *The Gates of Hell* (1880–1917), *The Burghers of Calais* (1884), *The Thinker* (1904).

Schwitters, Kurt (1887–1948) German, born Hanover; *Merzbau* (1920–43).

Tinguely, Jean (1925–91) Swiss, born Fribourg; *Baluba No 3* (1959), *Métamécanique No 9* (1959), *Homage to New York* (1960), *EOSX* (1967).

SPORTS AND GAMES

OLYMPIC GAMES

First Modern Olympic Games took place in 1896, founded by Frenchman Baron de Coubertin; held every four years; women first competed in 1900; first separate Winter Games celebration in 1924.

Venues

Summer Games

1896 Athens, Greece	1932 Los Angeles, USA	1972 Munich, West Germany
1900 Paris, France	1936 Berlin, Germany	1976 Montreal, Canada
1904 St Louis, USA	1948 London, UK	1980 Moscow, USSR
1908 London, UK	1952 Helsinki, Finland	1984 Los Angeles, USA
1912 Stockholm, Sweden	1956 Melbourne, Australia	1988 Seoul, South Korea
1920 Antwerp, Belgium	1960 Rome, Italy	1992 Barcelona, Spain
1924 Paris, France	1964 Tokyo, Japan	1996 Atlanta, USA
1928 Amsterdam, Holland	1968 Mexico City, Mexico	

Winter Games

1924 Chamonix, France	1952 Oslo, Norway	1976 Innsbruck, Austria
1928 St Moritz, Switzerland	1956 Cortina, Italy	1980 Lake Placid, New York,
1932 Lake Placid, New York, USA	1960 Squaw Valley, California, USA	USA
1936 Garmisch-Partenkirchen, Germany	1964 Innsbruck, Austria	1984 Sarajevo, Yugoslavia
	1968 Grenoble, France	1988 Calgary, Canada
1948 St Moritz, Switzerland	1972 Sapporo, Japan	1992 Albertville, France

Olympic games were also held in 1906 to commemorate the 10th anniversary of the birth of the Modern Games.

The 1956 equestrian events were held at Stockholm, Sweden, due to quarantine laws in Australia.

Leading Medal Winners

Summer Games	Gold	Silver	Bronze	Total	Winter Games	Gold	Silver	Bronze	Total
1 USA	746	560	475	1781	1 USSR	79	57	59	195
2 USSR	395	323	299	1017	2 Norway	54	60	54	168
3 Great Britain	173	222	206	601	3 USA	42	47	34	123
4 West Germany*	157	207	207	571	4 East Germany	39	36	35	110
5 France	153	167	177	497	5 Finland	33	43	34	110
6 Sweden	131	139	169	439	6 Austria	28	38	32	98
7 East Germany	153	129	127	409	7 Sweden	36	25	31	92
8 Italy	147	121	124	392	8 West Germany*	26	26	23	75
9 Hungary	124	112	136	372	9 Switzerland	23	25	25	73
10 Finland	97	75	110	282	10 Canada	14	12	18	44

*Includes medals won as Germany 1896–1964.West and East Germany competed as two nations from 1968.

Summer	118	159	149	426
Winter	17	15	12	44

COMMONWEALTH GAMES

First held as the British Empire Games in 1930; take place every four years and between Olympic celebrations; became the British Empire and Commonwealth Games in 1954; the current title adopted in 1970.

Venues

1930	Hamilton, Canada
1934	London, England
1938	Sydney, Australia
1950	Auckland, New Zealand
1954	Vancouver, Canada
1958	Cardiff, Wales
1962	Perth, Australia
1966	Kingston, Jamaica
1970	Edinburgh, Scotland
1974	Christchurch, New Zealand
1978	Edmonton, Canada
1982	Brisbane, Australia
1986	Edinburgh, Scotland
1990	Auckland, New Zealand
1994	Victoria, Canada

Leading Medal Winners

	Nation	Gold	Silver	Bronze	Total
1	England	420	368	368	1156
2	Australia	397	374	382	1153
3	Canada	287	301	299	887
4	New Zealand	94	121	161	376
5	Scotland	56	74	109	239
6	South Africa	60	44	47	151
7	Wales	32	39	60	131
8	Kenya	35	24	33	92
9	India	37	36	31	104
10	Northern Ireland	15	20	34	69

CHAMPIONS 1980–1991

AEROBATICS

World Championships
First held in 1960 and every two years since then except 1974.

Recent winners (Men)

1968	Erwin Bloske (East Germany)
1970	Igor Egorov (USSR)
1972	Charlie Hillard (USA)
1976	Vikto Letsko (USSR)
1978	Ivan Tucek (Czechoslovakia)
1980	Leo Loudenslager (USA)
1982	Viktor Smolin (USSR)
1984	Petr Jirmus (Czechoslovakia)
1986	Petr Jirmus (Czechoslovakia)
1988	Henry Haigh (USA)
1990	Claude Bessière (France)

Recent winners (Women)

1968	Madelyne Delcroix (France)
1970	Svetlana Savitskaya (USSR)
1972	Mary Gaffaney (USA)
1976	Lidia Leonova (USSR)
1978	Valentina Yaikova (USSR)
1980	Betty Stewart (USA)
1982	Betty Stewart (USA)
1984	Khalide Makagonova (USSR)
1986	Liubov Nemkova (USSR)
1988	Catherine Maunoury (France)
1990	Natalya Sergeyeva (USSR)

AMERICAN FOOTBALL

Superbowl
First held in 1967; takes place each January; an end-of-season meeting between the champions of the two major US leagues, the National Football Conference (NFC) and the American Football Conference (AFC).

Recent winners

1980	Pittsburgh Steelers (AFC)
1981	Oakland Raiders (NFC)
1982	San Francisco 49ers (NFC)
1983	Washington Redskins (NFC)
1984	Los Angeles Raiders (AFC)
1985	San Francisco 49ers (NFC)
1986	Chicago Bears (NFC)
1987	New York Giants (NFC)
1988	Washington Redskins (NFC)
1989	San Francisco 49ers (NFC)
1990	San Francisco 49ers (NFC)
1991	New York Giants (NFC)

Most wins: (4), Pittsburgh Steelers 1975–6, 1979–80; (4) San Francisco 49ers 1982, 1985, 1989–90

ANGLING

World Fresh Water Championship
First held in 1957; takes place annually.

Recent winners (Individual)

1979 Gerard Heulard (France)
1980 Wolf-Rüdiger Kremkus (West Germany)
1981 David Thomas (England)
1982 Kevin Ashurst (England)
1983 Wolf-Rüdiger Kremkus (West Germany)
1984 Bobby Smithers (Ireland)
1985 David Roper (England)
1986 Lud Wever (Holland)
1987 Clive Branson (Wales)
1988 Jean-Pierre Fouquet (France)
1989 Tom Pickering (England)
1990 Bobb Nudd (England)

Recent winners (Team)

1979 France
1980 West Germany
1981 France
1982 Holland
1983 Belgium
1984 Luxembourg
1985 England
1986 Italy
1987 England
1988 England
1989 Wales
1990 France

Most wins: Individual (3), Robert Tesse (France)
1959–60, 1965. Team (12), France, 1959, 1963–4,
1966, 1968, 1972, 1974–5, 1978–9, 1981, 1990.

World Fly Fishing Championship
First held in 1981; takes place annually.

Winners (Individual)

1981 C. Wittkamp (Holland)
1982 Viktor Diez y Diez (Spain)
1983 Segismondo Fernandez (Spain)
1984 Tony Pawson (England)
1985 Leslaw Frasik (Poland)
1986 Slivoj Svoboda (Czechoslovakia)
1987 Brian Leadbetter (England)
1988 John Pawson (England)
1989 Wladyslaw Trzebuinia (Poland)
1990 Franciszek Szajnik (Poland)

Winners (Team)

1981 Holland
1982 Italy
1983 Italy
1984 Italy
1985 Poland
1986 Italy
1987 England
1988 England
1989 Poland
1990 Czechoslovakia

Most wins: Individual (no-one has won more than
one title). Team (4), Italy, as above.

ARCHERY

World Championships
First held in 1931; took place annually until 1959;
since then, every two years.

Recent winners
Individual (Men)

1969 Hardy Ward (USA)
1971 John Williams (USA)
1973 Vikto Sidoruk (USSR)
1975 Darrell Pace (USA)
1977 Richard McKinney (USA)
1979 Darrell Pace (USA)
1981 Kysti Laasonen (Finland)
1983 Richard McKinney (USA)
1985 Richard McKinney (USA)
1987 Vladimir Yesheyev (USSR)
1989 Stanislav Zabrodsky (USSR)

Recent winners
Team (Men)

1969 USA
1971 USA
1973 USA
1975 USA
1977 USA
1979 USA
1981 USA
1983 USA
1985 South Korea
1987 South Korea
1989 USSR

Most wins: Individual (4), Hans Deutgen (Sweden)
1947–50. Team (14), USA 1957–83.

Archery (cont.)

Recent winners
Individual (Women)

1969 Dorothy Lidstone (Canada)
1971 Emma Gapchenko (USSR)
1973 Linda Myers (USA)
1975 Zebiniso Rustamova (USSR)
1977 Luann Ryon (USA)
1979 Jin-Ho Kim (South Korea)
1981 Natalia Butuzova (USSR)
1983 Jin-Ho Kim (South Korea)
1985 Irina Soldatova (USSR)
1987 Ma Xiagjun (China)
1989 Soo Nyung-Kim (South Korea)

Recent winners
Team (Women)

1969 USSR
1971 Poland
1973 USSR
1975 USSR
1977 USA
1979 South Korea
1981 USSR
1983 South Korea
1985 USSR
1987 USSR
1989 South Korea

Most wins: Individual (7), Janina Kurkowska (Poland) 1931–4, 1936, 1939, 1947. Team (8), USA 1952, 1957–9, 1961, 1963, 1965, 1977.

ASSOCIATION FOOTBALL

FIFA World Cup
Association Football's premier event; first contested for the Jules Rimet Trophy in 1930; Brazil won it outright after winning for the third time in 1970; since then teams have competed for the FIFA (*Féderation Internationale de Football Association*) World Cup; held every four years.

Post-war winners

1950 Uruguay
1954 West Germany
1958 Brazil
1962 Brazil
1966 England
1970 Brazil
1974 West Germany

1978 Argentina
1982 Italy
1986 Argentina
1990 West Germany

Most wins: (3), Brazil, as above; (3) Italy, 1934, 1938, 1982. (3) West Germany, as above

European Championship
Held every four years since 1960; qualifying group matches held over the two years preceding the final.

Winners

1960 USSR
1964 Spain
1968 Italy
1972 West Germany
1976 Czechoslovakia
1980 West Germany
1984 France
1988 Holland

Most wins: (2), West Germany, as above.

South American Championship
First held in 1916, for South American national sides; discontinued in 1967, but revived eight years later; now played every two years.

Recent winners

1956 Uruguay
1957 Argentina
1959* Argentina
1959* Uruguay
1963 Bolivia
1967 Uruguay
1975 Peru
1979 Paraguay
1983 Uruguay
1987 Uruguay
1989 Brazil

*There were two tournaments in 1959.

Most wins: (13), Uruguay, 1916–17, 1920, 1923–4, 1926, 1935, 1942, 1956, 1959, 1967, 1983, 1987

European Champions Cup
The leading club competition in Europe; open to the League champions of countries affiliated to UEFA (Union of European Football Associations); commonly known as the 'European Cup'; inaugurated in the 1955–6 season; played annually.

Association Football (cont.)

Recent winners

1979 Nottingham Forest (England)
1980 Nottingham Forest (England)
1981 Liverpool (England)
1982 Aston Villa (England)
1983 SV Hamburg (West Germany)
1984 Liverpool (England)
1985 Juventus (Italy)
1986 Steaua Bucharest (Romania)
1987 FC Porto (Portugal)
1988 PSV Eindhoven (Holland)
1989 AC Milan (Italy)
1990 AC Milan (Italy)
1991 Red Star Belgrade (Yugoslavia)

Most wins: (6), Real Madrid (Spain), 1956–60, 1966.

Football Association Challenge Cup

The world's oldest club knockout competition (the 'FA cup'), held annually; first contested in the 1871–2 season; first final at the Kennington Oval on 16 March 1872; first winners were The Wanderers.

Recent winners

1979 Arsenal
1980 West Ham United
1981 Tottenham Hotspur
1982 Tottenham Hotspur
1983 Manchester United
1984 Everton
1985 Manchester United
1986 Liverpool
1987 Coventry City
1988 Wimbledon
1989 Liverpool
1990 Manchester United
1991 Tottenham Hotspur

Most wins: (8), Tottenham Hotspur, 1901, 1921, 1961–2, 1967, 1981–2, 1991.

Football League

The oldest league in the world, and regarded as the toughest; founded in 1888; consists of four divisions; the current complement of 92 teams achieved in 1950.

Recent winners

1979–80 Liverpool
1980–1   Aston Villa
1981–2   Liverpool
1982–3   Liverpool
1983–4   Liverpool
1984–5   Everton
1985–6   Liverpool
1986–7   Everton
1987–8   Liverpool
1988–9   Arsenal
1989–90 Liverpool
1990–1   Arsenal

Most wins: (18), Liverpool, 1901, 1906, 1922–3, 1947, 1964, 1966, 1973, 1976–7, 1979–80, 1982–4, 1986, 1988, 1990.

ATHLETICS

World Championships

First held in Helsinki, Finland in 1983, then in Rome, Italy in 1987; take place every four years.

Event	Winners (Men)
1983	
100 m	Carl Lewis (USA)
200 m	Calvin Smith (USA)
400 m	Bert Cameron (Jamaica)
800 m	Willi Wüllbeck (East Germany)
1500 m	Steve Cram (UK)
5000 m	Eamonn Coghlan (Ireland)
10000 m	Alberto Cova (Italy)
Marathon	Rob de Castella (Austria)
3000 m steeplechase	Patriz Ilg (West Germany)
110 m hurdles	Greg Foster (USA)
400 m hurdles	Ed Moses (USA)
20 km walk	Ernesto Canto (Mexico)
50 km walk	Ronald Weigel (East Germany)
4 × 100 m relay	USA
4 × 400 m relay	USSR
High jump	Gennadiy Avdeyenko (USSR)
Long jump	Carl Lewis (USA)
Triple jump	Zdzislaw Hoffman (Poland)
Pole vault	Sergey Bubka (USSR)
Shot	Edward Sarul (Poland)
Discus	Imrich Bugar (Czechoslovakia)
Hammer	Sergey Litvinov (USSR)

Athletics (cont.)

Javelin	Detlef Michel (East Germany)
Decathlon	Daley Thompson (UK)

1987

100 m	Ben Johnson (Canada)
200 m	Calvin Smith (USA)
400 m	Thomas Schoenlebe (East Germany)
800 m	Billy Konchellah (Kenya)
1500 m	Abdi Bile (Somalia)
5000 m	Said Aouita (Morocco)
10000 m	Paul Kipkoech (Kenya)
Marathon	Douglas Waikihuru (Kenya)
3000 m steeplechase	Francesco Panetta (Italy)
110 m hurdles	Greg Foster (USA)
400 m hurdles	Ed Moses (USA)
20 km walk	Maurizio Damilano (Italy)
50 km walk	Hartwig Gauder (East Germany)
4 × 100 m relay	USA
4 × 400 m relay	USA
High jump	Patrik Sjoeberg (Sweden)
Long jump	Carl Lewis (USA)
Triple jump	Khristo Markov (Bulgaria)
Pole vault	Sergey Bubka (USSR)
Shot	Werner Gunthoer (Switzerland)
Discus	Jurgen Schult (East Germany)
Hammer	Sergey Litvinov (USSR)
Javelin	Seppo Raty (Finland)
Decathlon	Torsten Voss (East Germany)

Event	Winners (Women)

1983

100 m	Marlies Göhr (East Germany)
200 m	Marita Koch (East Germany)
400 m	Jarmila Kratochvilova (Czechoslovakia)
800 m	Jarmila Kratochvilova (Czechoslovakia)
1500 m	Mary Decker (USA)
3000 m	Mary Decker (USA)
Marathon	Greta Waitz (Norway)

100 m hurdles	Bettina Jahn (East Germany)
400 m hurdles	Ekaterina Fesenko (USSR)
4 × 100 m relay	East Germany
4 × 400 m relay	East Germany
High jump	Tamara Bykova (USSR)
Long jump	Heike Daute (East Germany)
Shot	Helene Fibingerova (Czechoslovakia)
Discus	Martina Opitz (East Germany)
Javelin	Tiina Lillak (Finland)
Heptathlon	Tamona Neubert (East Germany)

1987

100 m	Silke Gladisch (East Germany)
200 m	Silke Gladisch (East Germany)
400 metres	Olga Bryzgina (USSR)
800 m	Sigrun Wodars (East Germany)
1500 m	Tatyana Samolenko (USSR)
3000 m	Tatyana Samolenko (USSR)
Marathon	Rosa Mota (Portugal)
100 m hurdles	Ginka Zagorcheva (Bulgaria)
400 m hurdles	Sabine Busche (East Germany)
10 km walk	Irinia Strakhova (USSR)
4 × 100 m relay	USA
4 × 400 m relay	East Germany
High jump	Stefka Kostadinova (Bulgaria)
Long jump	Jackie Joyner-Kersee (USA)
Shot	Natalya Lisovskaya (USSR)
Discus	Martina Hellman (née Opitz) (East Germany)
Javelin	Fatima Whitbread (UK)
Heptathlon	Jackie Joyner-Kersee (USA)

AUSTRALIAN RULES FOOTBALL

Victoria Football League
The top prize is the annual VFL Premiership Trophy; first contested in 1897 and won by Essendon.

Recent winners

1979	Carlton
1980	Richmond
1981	Carlton
1982	Carlton
1983	Hawthorn
1984	Essendon
1985	Essendon
1986	Hawthorn
1987	Carlton
1988	Hawthorn
1989	Hawthorn
1990	Collingwood

Most wins: (15), Carlton, 1906–8, 1914–15, 1938, 1945, 1947, 1968, 1970, 1972, 1979, 1981–2, 1987.

BADMINTON

World Championships
First held in 1977; initially took place every three years; since 1983 every two years.

Singles winners (Men)

1977	Flemming Delfs (Denmark)
1980	Rudy Hartono (Indonesia)
1983	Icuk Sugiarto (Indonesia)
1985	Han Jian (China)
1987	Yang Yang (China)
1989	Yang Yong (China)
1991	Zhao Jianhua (China)

Singles winners (Women)

1977	Lene Koppen (Denmark)
1980	Wiharjo Verawatay (Indonesia)
1983	Li Lingwei (China)
1985	Han Aiping (China)
1987	Han Aiping (China)
1989	Li Lingwei (China)
1991	Tang Jiuhong (China)

Most titles: (3), Han Aiping (2 singles as above, women's doubles 1985).

Thomas Cup
An international team event for men's teams; inaugurated 1949, now held every two years.

Recent winners

1964	Indonesia
1967	Malaysia
1970	Indonesia
1973	Indonesia
1976	Indonesia
1979	Indonesia
1982	China
1984	Indonesia
1986	China
1988	China
1990	China

Most wins: (8), Indonesia, 1958–61, 1964, 1970–9, 1984.

Uber Cup
An international event for women's teams; first held in 1957; now held every two years.

Recent winners

1963	USA
1966	Japan
1969	Japan
1972	Japan
1975	Indonesia
1978	Japan
1981	Japan
1984	China
1986	China
1988	China
1990	China

Most wins: (5), Japan, as above.

All-England Championship
Badminton's premier event prior to the inauguration of the World Championships; first held in 1899.

Recent winners
Singles (Men)

1980	Prakash Padukone (Indonesia)
1981	Liem Swie King (Indonesia)
1982	Morten Frost (Denmark)
1983	Luan Jin (China)
1984	Morten Frost (Denmark)
1985	Zhao Jianhua (China)
1986	Morten Frost (Denmark)
1987	Morten Frost (Denmark)
1988	Ib Frederikson (Denmark)
1989	Yang Yang (China)
1990	Zhao Jianhua (China)
1991	Ardi Wiranata (Indonesia)

Badminton (cont.)

Recent winners
Singles (Women)

1980 Lene Koppen (Denmark)
1981 Sun Ai Hwang (Korea)
1982 Zang Ailing (China)
1983 Zang Ailing (China)
1984 Li Lingwei (China)
1985 Han Aiping (China)
1986 Yun-Ja Kim (Korea)
1987 Kirsten Larsen (Denmark)
1988 Gu Jiaming (China)
1989 Li Lingwei (China)
1990 Susi Susanti (Indonesia)
1991 Susi Susanti (Indonesia)

Most titles: (21: 4 singles, 9 men's doubles, 8 mixed doubles), George Thomas (England) 1903–28.

BASEBALL

World Series
First held in 1903; takes place each October, the best of seven matches; professional Baseball's leading event, the end-of-season meeting between the winners of the two Major Baseball leagues in the USA, the National League (NL) and American League (AL).

Recent winners

1979 Pittsburgh Pirates (NL)
1980 Philadelphia Phillies (NL)
1981 Los Angeles Dodgers (NL)
1982 St Louis Cardinals (NL)
1983 Baltimore Orioles (AL)
1984 Detroit Tigers (AL)
1985 Kansas City Royals (AL)
1986 New York Mets (NL)
1987 Minnesota Twins (AL)
1988 Los Angeles Dodgers (NL)
1989 Oakland Athletics (AL)
1990 Cincinatti Reds (NL)

Most wins: (22), New York Yankees, 1923, 1927–8, 1932, 1936–9, 1941, 1943, 1947, 1949–53, 1956, 1958, 1961–2, 1977–8.

World Amateur Championship
Instituted in 1938; since 1974 held every two years.

Recent winners

1972 Cuba
1973 Cuba & USA (*shared*)
1974 USA

1976 Cuba
1978 Cuba
1980 Cuba
1982 South Korea
1984 Cuba
1986 Cuba
1988 Cuba
1990 Cuba

Most wins: (20), Cuba, 1939–40, 1942–43, 1950, 1952–3, 1961, 1969–73, 1976–80, 1984–86, 1988, 1990.

BASKETBALL

World Championship
First held 1950 for men, 1953 for women; takes place every four years.

Winners (Men)

1950 Argentina
1954 USA
1959 Brazil
1963 Brazil
1967 USSR
1970 Yugoslavia
1974 USSR
1978 Yugoslavia
1982 USSR
1986 USA
1990 Yugoslavia

Most wins: (3), USSR, as above, Yugoslavia, as above.

Winners (Women)

1953 USA
1957 USA
1959 USSR
1964 USSR
1967 USSR
1971 USSR
1975 USSR
1979 USA
1983 USSR
1987 USA
1991 USA

Most wins: (6), USSR, as above.

National Basketball Association Championship
First held in 1947; the major competition in professional basketball in the USA, end-of-season NBA

Basketball (cont.)

Play-off involving the champion teams from the Eastern (EC) Conference and Western Conference (WC).

Recent winners

1979 Seattle Supersonics (WC)
1980 Los Angeles Lakers (WC)
1981 Boston Celtics (EC)
1982 Los Angeles Lakers (WC)
1983 Philadelphia 76ers (EC)
1984 Boston Celtics (EC)
1985 Los Angeles Lakers (WC)
1986 Boston Celtics (EC)
1987 Los Angeles Lakers (WC)
1988 Los Angeles Lakers (WC)
1989 Detroit Pistons (EC)
1990 Detroit Pistons (EC)
1991 Chicago Bulls (EC)

Most wins: (16), Boston Celtics, 1957, 1959–66, 1968–9, 1974, 1976, 1981, 1984, 1986.

BIATHLON

World Championships

First held in 1958; take place annually; the Olympic champion is the automatic world champion in Olympic years; women's championship first held in 1984.

Recent winners
Individual (Men)

10 km (15 km since 1988)
1979 Frank Ullrich (East Germany)
1980 Frank Ullrich (East Germany)
1981 Frank Ullrich (East Germany)
1982 Eirik Kvalfoss (Norway)
1983 Eirik Kvalfoss (Norway)
1984 Eirik Kvalfoss (Norway)
1985 Frank-Peter Rötsch (East Germany)
1986 Valeriy Medvetsev (USSR)
1987 Frank-Peter Rötsch (East Germany)
1988 Frank-Peter Rötsch (East Germany)
1989 Frank Luck (East Germany)
1990 Mark Kirchner (East Germany)

20 km
1979 Klaus Siebert (East Germany)
1980 Anatoliy Alyabyev (USSR)
1981 Heikki Ikola (Finland)
1982 Frank Ullrich (East Germany)
1983 Frank Ullrich (East Germany)
1984 Peter Angerer (West Germany)
1985 Yuriy Kashkarov (USSR)

1986 Valeriy Medvetsev (USSR)
1987 Frank-Peter Rötsch (East Germany)
1988 Frank-Peter Rötsch (East Germany)
1989 Eric Kralfoss (Norway)
1990 Valeriy Medvetsev (USSR)

Most individual titles: (6), Frank Ullrich (East Germany), as above plus 1978 10 km.

Recent winners
Individual (Women)

5 km (7.5 km since 1988)
1984 Venera Chernyshova (USSR)
1985 Sanna Gronlid (Norway)
1986 Kaya Parva (USSR)
1987 Yelena Golovina (USSR)
1988 Petra Schaaf (West Germany)
1989 Anna Elvebakk (Norway)
1990 Anna Elvebakk (Norway)

10 km (15 km since 1988)
1984 Venera Chernyshova (USSR)
1985 Kaya Parva (USSR)
1986 Eva Korpela (Sweden)
1987 Sanna Gronlid (Norway)
1988 Anna Elvebakk (Norway)
1989 Petra Schaaf (West Germany)
1990 Svetlana Davydova (USSR)

3 × 5 km relay (3 × 7.5 km since 1989)
1984 USSR
1985 USSR
1986 USSR
1987 USSR
1988 USSR
1989 USSR
1990 USSR

BILLIARDS

World Professional Championship

First held in 1870, organized on a challenge basis; became a knockout event in 1909; discontinued in 1934; revived in 1951 as a challenge system; reverted to a knockout event in 1980.

Recent winners

1980 Fred Davis (England)
1981 *not held*
1982 Rex Williams (England)
1983 Rex Williams (England)
1984 Mark Wildman (England)
1985 Ray Edmonds (England)
1986 Robbie Foldvari (Australia)

Billiards (cont.)

1987 Norman Dagley (England)
1988 Norman Dagley (England)
1989 Mike Russell (England)
1990 *not held*
1991 Mike Russell (England)

Most wins: (knockout) (6), Tom Newman (England), 1921–2, 1924–7. (challenge) (8), John Roberts, Jnr (England), 1870–85.

BOBSLEIGHING AND TOBOGGANING

World Championships

First held in 1930 (four-man) and in 1931 (two-man); Olympic champions automatically become world champions.

Recent winners (Two-man)

1980 Erich Schärer/Josef Benz (Switzerland)
1981 Bernhard Germeshausen/Hans-Jürgen Gerhardt (East Germany)
1982 Erich Schärer/Josef Benz (Switzerland)
1983 Ralf Pichler/Urs Leuthold (Switzerland)
1984 Wolfgang Hoppe/Dietmar Schauerhammer (East Germany)
1985 Wolfgang Hoppe/Dietmar Schauerhammer (East Germany)
1986 Wolfgang Hoppe/Dietmar Schauerhammer (East Germany)
1987 Ralf Pichler/Celest Poltera (Switzerland)
1988 Janis Kipurs/Vladimir Kozlov (USSR)
1989 Wolfgang Hoppe/Bogdan Musiol (East Germany)
1990 Gustav Weder/Bruno Gerber (Switzerland)
1991 Rudi Lochner/Marcus Zimmermann (Germany)

Recent winners (Four-man)

1980 East Germany
1981 East Germany
1982 Switzerland
1983 Switzerland
1984 East Germany
1985 East Germany
1986 Switzerland
1987 Switzerland
1988 Switzerland
1989 Switzerland
1990 Switzerland
1991 Germany

Most wins: (Two-man) (8), Eugenio Monti (Italy) 1957–61, 1963, 1966, 1968. (Four-man) (14),

Switzerland, 1939, 1947, 1954–5, 1957, 1971, 1973, 1975, 1982–3, 1986–9.

Luge World Championships

First held in 1955; annually until 1981, then every two years; up to 1980 the Olympic champions were also world champions if the event was included in the Olympic programme.

Recent winners
Men's single-seater

1976 Detlef Günther (East Germany)
1977 Hans Rinn (East Germany)
1978 Paul Hildgartner (Italy)
1979 Detlef Günther (East Germany)
1980 Bernhard Glass (East Germany)
1981 Sergey Danilin (USSR)
1983 Miroslav Zajonc (Canada)
1985 Michael Walter (East Germany)
1987 Markus Prock (Austria)
1989 George Hack (West Germany)

Most wins: (3), Thomas Köhler (East Germany), 1962, 1964, 1967.

Recent winners
Women's single-seater

1976 Margrit Schumann (East Germany)
1977 Margrit Schumann (East Germany)
1978 Vera Sosulya (USSR)
1979 Melitta Sollmann (East Germany)
1980 Vera Sosulya (USSR)
1981 Melitta Sollman (East Germany)
1983 Steffi Martin (East Germany)
1985 Steffi Martin (East Germany)
1987 Cerstin Schmidt (East Germany)
1989 Susi Erdmann (East Germany)

Most wins: (5), Margrit Schumann (East Germany), 1973–7.

BOWLS

World Championships

Instituted for men in 1966 and for women in 1969; held every four years.

Men's Singles

1966 David Bryant (England)
1972 Malwyn Evans (Wales)
1976 Doug Watson (South Africa)
1980 David Bryant (England)

Bowls (cont.)

1984 Peter Bellis (New Zealand)
1988 David Bryant (England)

Men's Pairs

1966 Australia
1972 Hong Kong
1976 South Africa
1980 Australia
1984 USA
1988 New Zealand

Men's Triples

1966 Australia
1972 USA
1976 South Africa
1980 England
1984 Ireland
1988 New Zealand

Men's Fours

1966 New Zealand
1972 England
1976 South Africa
1980 Hong Kong
1984 England
1988 Ireland

Leonard Trophy
Team award, given to the nation with the best overall performances in the men's world championship.

Winners

1966 Australia
1972 Scotland
1976 South Africa
1980 England
1984 Scotland
1988 England

Most wins: (6), David Bryant (singles as above, plus Triples and Team 1980, 1988).

Women's Singles

1969 Gladys Doyle (Papua New Guinea)
1973 Elsie Wilke (New Zealand)
1977 Elsie Wilke (New Zealand)
1981 Norma Shaw (England)
1985 Merle Richardson (Australia)
1988* Janet Ackland (Wales)

Women's Pairs

1969 South Africa
1973 Australia

1977 Hong Kong
1981 Ireland
1985 Australia
1988* Ireland

Women's Triples

1969 South Africa
1973 New Zealand
1977 Wales
1981 Hong Kong
1985 Australia
1988* Australia

Women's Fours

1969 South Africa
1973 New Zealand
1977 Australia
1981 England
1985 Scotland
1988* Australia

Women's Team

1969 South Africa
1973 New Zealand
1977 Australia
1981 England
1985 Australia
1988* England

Most wins: (3), Merle Richardson (Fours 1977; Singles and Pairs 1985).
*The women's event was advanced to Dec 1988 (Australia)

World Indoor Championships
First held in 1979; take place annually.

Winners

1979 David Bryant (England)
1980 David Bryant (England)
1981 David Bryant (England)
1982 John Watson (Scotland)
1983 Bob Sutherland (Scotland)
1984 Jim Baker (Ireland)
1985 Terry Sullivan (Wales)
1986 Tony Allcock (England)
1987 Tony Allcock (England
1988 Hugh Duff (Scotland)
1989 Richard Corsie (Scotland)
1990 John Price (Wales)
1991 Richard Corsie (Scotland)

Most wins: (3), David Bryant (England), as above.

Waterloo Handicap
First held in 1907 and annually at Blackpool's

Bowls (cont.)

Waterloo Hotel; the premier event of Crown Green Bowling.

Recent winners

1979 Brian Duncan
1980 Vernon Lee
1981 Roy Nicholson
1982 Dennis Mercer
1983 Stan Frith
1984 Steve Ellis
1985 Tommy Johnstone
1986 Brian Duncan
1987 Brian Duncan
1988 Ingham Gregory
1989 Brian Duncan
1990 John Bancroft

Most wins: (4), Brian Duncan, as above.

BOXING

World Heavyweight Champions
The first world heavyweight champion under Queensbury Rules with gloves was James J. Corbett in 1892.

Champions since 1978	Recognizing Body
1978 Leon Spinks (USA)	UND
1978 Ken Norton (USA)	WBC
1978 Muhammad Ali (USA)	WBA
1978 Larry Holmes (USA)	WBC
1979 John Tate (USA)	WBA
1980 Mike Weaver (USA)	WBA
1982 Mike Dokes (USA)	WBA
1983 Gerry Coetzee (South Africa)	WBA
1984 Larry Holmes (USA)	IBF
1984 Tim Witherspoon (USA)	WBC
1984 Pinklon Thomas (USA)	WBC
1984 Greg Page (USA)	WBA
1985 Michael Spinks (USA)	IBF
1985 Tony Tubbs (USA)	WBA
1986 Tim Witherspoon (USA)	WBA
1986 Trevor Berbick (Canada)	WBC
1986 Mike Tyson (USA)	WBC
1986 James Smith (USA)	WBA
1987 Tony Tucker (USA)	IBF
1987 Mike Tyson (USA)	WBA/WBC
1987 Mike Tyson (USA)	UND
1989 Francesco Damiani (Italy)	WBO
1989 Mike Tyson (USA)	WBA/WBC/IBF
1990 James (Buster) Douglas (USA)	WBA/WBC/IBF
1990 Evandes Holyfield (USA)	WBA/WBC/IBF
1991 Ray Mercer (USA)	WBO

UND = Undisputed Champion
WBC = World Boxing Council
WBA = World Boxing Association
IBF = International Boxing Federation
WBO = World Boxing Organization

CANOEING

Olympic Games
The most prestigious competition in the canoeing calendar, included at every Olympic celebration since 1936; the Blue Riband event in the men's competition is the Kayak Singles over 1000 metres, and in the women's the Kayak Singles over 500 metres.

Single kayak (Men)

1936 Gregor Hradetzky (Austria)
1948 Gert Fredriksson (Sweden)
1952 Gert Fredriksson (Sweden)
1956 Gert Fredriksson (Sweden)
1960 Erik Hansen (Denmark)
1964 Rolf Peterson (Sweden)
1968 Mihaly Hesz (Hungary)
1972 Aleksandr Shaparenko (USSR)
1976 Rüdiger Helm (East Germany)
1980 Rüdiger Helm (East Germany)
1984 Alan Thompson (New Zealand)
1988 Greg Barton (USA)

Single kayak (Women)

1948 Keren Hoff (Denmark)
1952 Sylvi Saimo (Finland)
1956 Elisaveta Dementyeva (USSR)
1960 Antonina Seredina (USSR)
1964 Lyudmila Khvedosyuk (USSR)
1968 Lyudmila Pinayeva (USSR)
1972 Yulia Ryabchinskaya (USSR)
1976 Carola Zirzow (East Germany)
1980 Birgit Fischer (East Germany)
1984 Agneta Andersson (Sweden)
1988 Vania Guecheva (USSR)

Most wins: Men (3), Gert Fredriksson as above. No woman has won more than one title.

CHESS

World Champions

World Champions have been recognized since 1886. The first international tournament was held in London in 1851, and won by Adolf Anderssen (Germany), first women's champion recognized in 1927.

Post-war champions (Men)

1948–57	Mikhail Botvinnik (USSR)
1957–8	Vassiliy Smyslov (USSR)
1958–60	Mikhail Botvinnik (USSR)
1960–1	Mikhail Tal (USSR)
1961–3	Mikhail Botvinnik (USSR)
1963–9	Tigran Petrosian (USSR)
1969–72	Boris Spassky (USSR)
1972–5	Bobby Fischer (USA)
1975–85	Anatoliy Karpov (USSR)
1985–	Gary Kasparov (USSR)

Longest reigning champion: 27 years, Emanuel Lasker (Germany) 1894–1921.

Champions (Women)

1927–44	Vera Menchik-Stevenson (UK)
1950–3	Lyudmila Rudenko (USSR)
1953–6	Elizaveta Bykova (USSR)
1956–8	Olga Rubtsova (USSR)
1958–62	Elizaveta Bykova (USSR)
1962–78	Nona Gaprindashvili (USSR)
1978	Maya Chiburdanidze (USSR)

Longest reigning champion: 17 years, Vera Menchik-Stevenson (UK), as above.

CONTRACT BRIDGE

World Team Championship

The game's biggest championship; men's contest (The Bermuda Bowl) first held in 1951, and now takes place every two years; women's contest (The Venice Cup) first held in 1974, and since 1985 is concurrent with the men's event.

Recent winners (Men)

1973	Italy
1974	Italy
1975	Italy
1976	USA
1977	USA
1979	USA
1981	USA
1983	USA

1985	USA
1987	USA
1989	Brazil

Most wins: (13), Italy, 1957–9, 1961–3, 1965–7, 1969, 1973–5.

Recent winners (Women)

1974	USA
1976	USA
1978	USA
1981	UK
1983	not held
1985	UK
1987	Italy
1989	United States

Most wins: (4), USA, as above.

World Team Olympiad

First held in 1960; since then, every four years.

Winners (Men)

1960	France
1964	Italy
1968	Italy
1972	Italy
1976	Brazil
1980	France
1984	Poland
1988	USA

Winners (Women)

1960	United Arab Emirates
1964	UK
1968	Sweden
1972	Italy
1976	USA
1980	USA
1984	USA
1988	Denmark

Most wins: Men (3), Italy, as above; women (3), USA, as above.

CRICKET

World Cup

First played in England in 1975; held every four years; the 1987 competition was the first to be played outside England, in India and Pakistan.

Winners

1975	West Indies
1979	West Indies

Cricket (cont.)

1983 India
1987 Australia

County Championship
The oldest cricket competition in the world; first won by Sussex in 1827; not officially recognized until 1890, when a proper points system was introduced.

Recent winners

1979 Essex
1980 Middlesex
1981 Nottinghamshire
1982 Middlesex
1983 Essex
1984 Essex
1985 Middlesex
1986 Essex
1987 Nottinghamshire
1988 Worcestershire
1989 Worcestershire
1990 Middlesex

Most outright wins: (29), Yorkshire, 1893, 1896, 1898, 1900–2, 1905, 1908, 1912, 1919, 1922–5, 1931–3, 1935, 1937–9, 1946, 1959–60, 1962–3, 1966–8.

Refuge Assurance League
First held in 1969; known as the John Player League until 1987.

Recent winners

1979 Somerset
1980 Warwickshire
1981 Essex
1982 Sussex
1983 Yorkshire
1984 Essex
1985 Essex
1986 Hampshire
1987 Worcestershire
1988 Worcestershire
1989 Lancashire
1990 Derbyshire

Most wins: (3), Kent, 1972–3, 1976; Essex, as above; Lancashire 1969–70, 1989.

NatWest Bank Trophy
First held in 1963; known as the Gillette Cup until 1981.

Recent winners

1979 Somerset

1980 Middlesex
1981 Derbyshire
1982 Surrey
1983 Somerset
1984 Middlesex
1985 Essex
1986 Sussex
1987 Nottinghamshire
1988 Middlesex
1989 Warwickshire
1990 Lancashire

Most wins: (5), Lancashire, 1970–2, 1975, 1990.

Benson and Hedges Cup
First held in 1972.

Recent winners

1979 Essex
1980 Northamptonshire
1981 Somerset
1982 Somerset
1983 Middlesex
1984 Lancashire
1985 Leicestershire
1986 Middlesex
1987 Yorkshire
1988 Hampshire
1989 Nottinghamshire
1990 Lancashire
1991 Worcestershire

Most wins: (3), Kent, 1973, 1976, 1978; Leicestershire, 1972, 1975, 1985.

Sheffield Shield
Australia's leading domestic competition; contested inter-state since 1891–2.

Recent winners

1980 Victoria
1981 Western Australia
1982 South Australia
1983 New South Wales
1984 Western Australia
1985 New South Wales
1986 New South Wales
1987 Western Australia
1988 Western Australia
1989 Western Australia
1990 New South Wales
1991 Victoria

Most wins: 40, New South Wales, 1896–7, 1900, 1902–7, 1909, 1911–12, 1914, 1920–1, 1923, 1926, 1929, 1932–3, 1938, 1940, 1949–50, 1952, 1954–62, 1965–6, 1983, 1985–6, 1990.

CROQUET

McRobertson Shield

Croquet's leading tournament; held spasmodically since 1925; contested by teams from Great Britain, New Zealand and Australia.

Winners

1925	Great Britain
1928	Australia
1930	Australia
1935	Australia
1937	Great Britain
1950	New Zealand
1956	Great Britain
1963	Great Britain
1969	Great Britain
1974	Great Britain
1979	New Zealand
1982	Great Britain
1986	New Zealand
1990	Great Britain

Most wins: (8), Great Britain, as above.

CROSS COUNTRY RUNNING

World Championships

First international championship held in 1903, but only included runners from England, Ireland, Scotland and Wales; recognized as an official world championship from 1973; first women's race in 1967.

Recent winners
Individual (Men)

1980	Craig Virgin (USA)
1981	Craig Virgin (USA)
1982	Mohamed Kedir (Ethiopia)
1983	Bekele Debele (Ethiopia)
1984	Carlos Lopes (Portugal)
1985	Carlos Lopes (Portugal)
1986	John Ngugi (Kenya)
1987	John Ngugi (Kenya)
1988	John Ngugi (Kenya)
1989	John Ngugi (Kenya)
1990	Khalid Skah (Morocco)
1991	Khalid Skah (Morocco)

Recent winners (Team)

1980	England
1981	Ethiopia
1982	Ethiopia
1983	Ethiopia
1984	Ethiopia
1985	Ethiopia
1986	Kenya
1987	Kenya
1988	Kenya
1989	Kenya
1990	Kenya
1991	Kenya

Most wins: Individual (4), Jack Holden (England), 1933–5, 1939; Alain Mimoun (France), 1949, 1952, 1954, 1956; Gaston Roelants (Belgium), 1962, 1967, 1969, 1972. John Ngugi, as above. Team (44), England, between 1903 and 1980

Recent winners
Individual (Women)

1980	Greta Waitz (Norway)
1981	Greta Waitz (Norway)
1982	Maricica Puica (Romania)
1983	Greta Waitz (Norway)
1984	Maricica Puica (Romania)
1985	Zola Budd (England)
1986	Zola Budd (England)
1987	Annette Sergent (France)
1988	Ingrid Kristiansen (Norway)
1989	Annette Sergent (France)
1990	Lynn Jennings (USA)
1991	Lynn Jennings (USA)

Recent winners
Team (Women)

1980	USSR
1981	USSR
1982	USSR
1983	USA
1984	USA
1985	USA
1986	England
1987	USA
1988	USSR
1989	USSR
1990	USSR
1991	Ethiopia and Kenya (shared)

Most wins: Individual (5), Doris Brown (USA), 1967–71; Greta Waitz (Norway), 1978–81, 1983. Team (8), USA, 1968–9, 1975, 1979, 1983–5, 1987.

CURLING

World Championships
First men's championship held in 1959; first women's championship in 1979; takes place annually.

Recent winners (Men)

1979 Norway
1980 Canada
1981 Switzerland
1982 Canada
1983 Canada
1984 Norway
1985 Canada
1986 Canada
1987 Canada
1988 Norway
1989 Canada
1990 Canada
1991 Scotland

Recent winners (Women)

1979 Switzerland
1980 Canada
1981 Sweden
1982 Denmark
1983 Switzerland
1984 Canada
1985 Canada
1986 Canada
1987 Canada
1988 West Germany
1989 Canada
1990 Norway
1991 Norway

Most wins: Men (20), Canada, 1959–64, 1966, 1968–72, 1980, 1982–3, 1985–7, 1989–90. Women (6), Canada, as above.

CYCLING

Tour de France
World's premier cycling event; first held in 1903.

Recent winners

1979 Bernard Hinault (France)
1980 Joop Zoetemelk (Holland)
1981 Bernard Hinault (France)
1982 Bernard Hinault (France)
1983 Laurent Fignon (France)
1984 Laurent Fignon (France)
1985 Bernard Hinault (France)

1986 Greg LeMond (USA)
1987 Stephen Roche (Ireland)
1988 Pedro Delgado (Spain)
1989 Greg Le Mond (USA)
1990 Greg Le Mond (USA)
1991 Miguel Indurain (Spain)

Most wins: (5), Jacques Anquetil (France), 1957, 1961–4; Eddy Merckx (Belgium), 1969–72, 1974; Bernard Hinault (France), 1978–9, 1981–2, 1985.

World Road Race Championships
Men's race first held in 1927; first women's race in 1958; takes place annually.

Recent winners (Professional Men)

1979 Jan Raas (Holland)
1980 Bernard Hinault (France)
1981 Freddy Maertens (Belgium)
1982 Giuseppe Saroni (Italy)
1983 Greg LeMond (USA)
1984 Claude Criquielion (Belgium)
1985 Joop Zoetemelk (Holland)
1986 Moreno Argentin (Italy)
1987 Stephen Roche (Ireland)
1988 Maurizio Fondriest (Italy)
1989 Greg Le Mond (USA)
1990 Rudy Dhaenens (Belgium)

Recent winners (Women)

1979 Petra de Bruin (Holland)
1980 Beth Heiden (USA)
1981 Ute Enzenauer (West Germany)
1982 Mandy Jones (Great Britain)
1983 Marianne Berglund (Sweden)
1984 *not held*
1985 Jeannie Longo (France)
1986 Jeannie Longo (France)
1987 Jeannie Longo (France)
1988 Jeannie Longo (France)
1989 Jeannie Longo (France)
1990 Catherine Marsal (France)

Most wins: Men (3), Alfredo Binda (Italy), 1927, 1930, 1932; Rik Van Steenbergen (Belgium), 1949, 1956–7; Eddy Merckx (Belgium), 1967, 1971, 1974. Women (5), Jeannie Longo, as above.

CYCLO-CROSS

World Championships
First held in 1950 as an open event; separate professional and amateur events since 1967.

Recent winners (Professional)

1980 Roland Liboton (Belgium)
1981 Johannes Stamsnijder (Holland)
1982 Roland Liboton (Belgium)
1983 Roland Liboton (Belgium)
1984 Roland Liboton (Belgium)
1985 Klaus-Peter Thaler (West Germany)
1986 Albert Zweifel (Switzerland)
1987 Klaus-Peter Thaler (West Germany)
1988 Pascal Richard (Switzerland)
1989 Danny De Bie (Belgium)
1990 Hank Baars (Holland)
1991 Radomin Simunek (Czechoslovakia)

Recent winners (Amateur)

1980 Fritz Saladin (Switzerland)
1981 Milos Fisera (Czechoslovakia)
1982 Milos Fisera (Czechoslovakia)
1983 Radomir Simunek (Czechoslovakia)
1984 Radomir Simunek (Czechoslovakia)
1985 Mike Kluge (West Germany)
1986 Vito di Tano (Italy)
1987 Mike Kluge (West Germany)
1988 Karol Camrola (Czechoslovakia)
1989 Ondrej Glaja (Czechoslovakia)
1990 Andreas Buesser (Switzerland)
1991 Thomas Frischknecht (Switzerland)

Most wins: Professional (7), Eric de Vlaeminck (Belgium), 1966, 1968–73. Amateur (5), Robert Vermiere (Belgium), 1970–1, 1974–5, 1977.

DARTS

World Professional Championship
First held at Nottingham in 1978.

Winners

1978 Leighton Rees (Wales)
1979 John Lowe (England)
1980 Eric Bristow (England)
1981 Eric Bristow (England)
1982 Jocky Wilson (Scotland)
1983 Keith Deller (England)
1984 Eric Bristow (England)
1985 Eric Bristow (England)
1986 Eric Bristow (England)
1987 John Lowe (England)

1988 Bob Anderson (England)
1989 Jocky Wilson (Scotland)
1990 Phil Taylor (England)
1991 Denis Priestley (England)

Most wins: (5), Eric Bristow, as above.

World Cup
A team competition first held at Wembley in 1977; takes place every two years.

Winners (Team)

1977 Wales
1979 England
1981 England
1983 England
1985 England
1987 England
1989 England

Winners (Individual)

1977 Leighton Rees (Wales)
1979 Nicky Virachkul (USA)
1981 John Lowe (England)
1983 Eric Bristow (England)
1985 Eric Bristow (England)
1987 Eric Bristow (England)
1989 Eric Bristow (England)

Most wins: Team (5), England, as above. Individual (3), Eric Bristow (England), as above.

DRAUGHTS

World Championship
Held on a challenge basis; the champion since 1979 has been Dr M Tinsley (USA); he has defended the title five times.

British Open Championship
The leading championship in Britain; first held in 1926; now takes place every two years.

Recent winners

1970 I Edwards (Great Britain)
1972 G Davies (Great Britain)
1974 J McGill (Great Britain)
1976 A Huggins (Great Britain)
1978 J McGill (Great Britain)
1980 T Watson (Great Britain)
1982 T Watson (Great Britain)
1984 A Long (USA)
1986 H Delvin (Great Britain)
1988 DE Oldbury (Great Britain)
1990 T Watson (Great Britain)

EQUESTRIAN EVENTS

World Championships

Show Jumping championships first held in 1953 (for men) and 1965 (for women); since 1978 they have competed together and on equal terms; team competition introduced in 1978; Three Day Event and Dressage championships introduced in 1966; all three now held every four years. Renamed the World Equestrian Games in 1990.

Winners
Show Jumping (Men)

1953	Francisco Goyoago (Spain)
1954	Hans-Günter Winkler (West Germany)
1955	Hans-Günter Winkler (West Germany)
1956	Raimondo D'Inzeo (Italy)
1960	Raimondo D'Inzeo (Italy)
1966	Pierre d'Oriola (France)
1970	David Broome (Great Britain)
1974	Hartwig Steenken (West Germany)

Winners
Show Jumping (Women)

1965	Marion Coakes (Great Britain)
1970	Janou Lefèbvre (France)
1974	Janou Tissot (*née* Lefèbvre) (France)

Winners (Individual)

1978	Gerd Wiltfang (West Germany)
1982	Norbert Koof (West Germany)
1986	Gail Greenough (Canada)
1990	Eric Navet (France)

Winners (Team)

1978	Great Britain
1982	France
1986	USA
1990	France

Winners
Three Day Event (Individual)

1966	Carlos Moratorio (Argentina)
1970	Mary Gordon-Watson (Great Britain)
1974	Bruce Davidson (USA)
1978	Bruce Davidson (USA)
1982	Lucinda Green (Great Britain)
1986	Virginia Leng (Great Britain)
1990	Blyth Tait (New Zealand)

Winners (Team)

1966	Ireland
1970	Great Britain
1974	USA
1978	Canada

1982	Great Britain
1986	Great Britain
1990	New Zealand

Winners
Dressage (Individual)

1966	Josef Neckermann (West Germany)
1970	Yelene Petouchkova (USSR)
1974	Reiner Klimke (West Germany)
1978	Christine Stückelberger (Switzerland)
1982	Reiner Klimke (West Germany)
1986	Anne Grethe Jensen (Denmark)
1990	Nicole Uphoff (West Germany)

Winners
Dressage (Team)

1966	West Germany
1970	USSR
1974	West Germany
1978	West Germany
1982	West Germany
1986	West Germany
1990	West Germany

FENCING

World Championships

Held annually since 1921 (between 1921–35, known as European Championships); not held in Olympic years.

Recent winners
Foil (Men) Individual

1975	Christian Noel (France)
1977	Alexander Romankov (USSR)
1978	Didier Flament (France)
1979	Alexander Romankov (USSR)
1981	Vladimir Smirnov (USSR)
1982	Alexander Romankov (USSR)
1983	Alexander Romankov (USSR)
1985	Mauro Numa (Italy)
1986	Andrea Borella (Italy)
1987	Mathias Gey (West Germany)
1989	Alexandr Koch (West Germany)

Recent winners
Foil (Team)

1975	France
1977	West Germany
1978	Poland
1979	USSR
1981	USSR
1982	USSR
1983	West Germany

Fencing (cont.)

1985 Italy
1986 Italy
1987 USSR
1989 USSR

Most wins: Individual (5), Alexander Romankov (USSR), 1974, 1977, 1979, 1982–3. Team (15), USSR (between 1959–89).

Recent winners
Foil (Women) Individual

1975 Ecaterina Stahl (Romania)
1977 Valentina Sidorova (USSR)
1978 Valentina Sidorova (USSR)
1979 Cornelia Hanisch (West Germany)
1981 Cornelia Hanisch (West Germany)
1982 Naila Giliazova (USSR)
1983 Dorina Vaccaroni (Italy)
1985 Cornelia Hanisch (West Germany)
1986 Anja Fichtel (West Germany)
1987 Elisabeta Tufan (Romania)
1989 Olga Velitchko (USSR)

Recent winners
Foil (Team)

1975 USSR
1977 USSR
1978 USSR
1979 USSR
1981 USSR
1982 Italy
1983 Italy
1985 West Germany
1986 USSR
1987 Hungary
1989 West Germany

Most wins: Individual (3), Helène Mayor (Germany), 1929, 1931, 1937; Ilona Elek (Hungary, 1934–5, 1951; Ellen Müller-Preiss (Austria), 1947, 1949, 1950 (*shared*); Cornelia Hanisch, as above. Team (15), USSR (between 1956–86).

Recent winners
Epee (Individual)

1975 Alexander Pusch (West Germany)
1977 Johan Harmenberg (Sweden)
1978 Alexander Pusch (West Germany)
1979 Philippe Riboud (France)
1981 Zoltan Szekely (Hungary)
1982 Jenö Pap (Hungary)
1983 Ellmar Bormann (West Germany)
1985 Philippe Boisse (France)
1986 Philippe Riboud (France)
1987 Volker Fischer (West Germany)
1989 Manuel Pereira (Spain)

Recent winners
Epee (Team)

1975 Sweden
1977 Sweden
1978 Hungary
1979 USSR
1981 USSR
1982 France
1983 France
1985 West Germany
1986 West Germany
1987 West Germany
1989 Italy

Most wins: Individual (3), Georges Buchard (France), 1927, 1931, 1933; Alexei Nikanchikov (USSR), 1966–7, 1970. Team (11), Italy (between 1931–58); France (between 1934–89).

Recent winners
Epee (Women) (Individual)

1989 Anja Straub (Switzerland)

Recent winners
Epee (Women) (Team)

1989 Hungary

Recent winners
Sabre (Individual)

1975 Vladimir Nazlimov (USSR)
1977 Pal Gerevich (Hungary)
1978 Viktor Krovopuskov (USSR)
1979 Vladimir Nazlimov (USSR)
1981 Mariusz Wodke (Poland)
1982 Viktor Krovopuskov (USSR)
1983 Vasiliy Etropolski (Bulgaria)
1985 György Nebald (Hungary)
1986 Sergey Mindirgassov (USSR)
1987 Jean-François Lamour (France)
1989 Grigory Kirienko (USSR)

Recent winners
Sabre (Team)

1975 USSR
1977 USSR
1978 Hungary
1979 USSR
1981 Hungary
1982 Hungary
1983 USSR
1985 USSR
1986 USSR
1987 USSR
1989 USSR

Fencing (cont.)

Most wins: Individual (3), Aladar Gerevich (Hungary), 1935, 1951, 1955; Jerzy Pawlowski (Poland) 1957, 1965–6; Yakov Rylsky (USSR), 1958, 1961, 1963. Team (17), Hungary (between 1930–82).

GAELIC FOOTBALL

All-Ireland Championship

First held 1887; takes place in Dublin on the third Sunday in September each year.

Recent winners

1979 Kerry
1980 Kerry
1981 Kerry
1982 Offaly
1983 Dublin
1984 Kerry
1985 Kerry
1986 Kerry
1987 Meath
1988 Meath
1989 Cork
1990 Cork

Most wins: (30), Kerry, 1903–4, 1909, 1913–14, 1924, 1926, 1929–32, 1937, 1939–41, 1946, 1953, 1955, 1959, 1962, 1969–70, 1975, 1978–81, 1984–6.

GLIDING

World Championships

First held in 1937; current classes are Open, Standard and 15 metres; the Open class is the principal event, held every two years until 1978 and again since 1981.

Recent winners

1968 Harro Wödl (Austria)
1970 George Moffat (USA)
1972 Göran Ax (Sweden)
1974 George Moffat (USA)
1976 George Lee (Great Britain)
1978 George Lee (Great Britain)
1981 George Lee (Great Britain)
1983 Ingo Renner (Australia)
1985 Ingo Renner (Australia)
1987 Ingo Renner (Australia)
1989 Robin May (Great Britain)

Most wins: (3), George Lee, as above; Ingo Renner, as above.

GOLF

British Open

First held at Prestwick in 1860, and won by Willie Park; takes place annually; regarded as the world's leading golf tournament.

Recent winners

1979 Severiano Ballesteros (Spain)
1980 Tom Watson (USA)
1981 Bill Rogers (USA)
1982 Tom Watson (USA)
1983 Tom Watson (USA)
1984 Severiano Ballesteros (Spain)
1985 Sandy Lyle (Great Britain)
1986 Greg Norman (Australia)
1987 Nick Faldo (Great Britain)
1988 Severiano Ballesteros (Spain)
1989 Mark Calcavecchia (USA)
1990 Nick Faldo (Great Britain)
1991 Ian Baker-Finch (Australia)

Most wins: (6), Harry Vardon (Great Britain), 1896, 1898–9, 1903, 1911, 1914.

United States Open

First held at Newport, Rhode Island in 1895, and won by Horace Rawlins; takes place annually.

Recent winners

1979 Hale Irwin (USA)
1980 Jack Nicklaus (USA)
1981 David Graham (Australia)
1982 Tom Watson (USA)
1983 Larry Nelson (USA)
1984 Fuzzy Zoeller (USA)
1985 Andy North (USA)
1986 Ray Floyd (USA)
1987 Scott Simpson (USA)
1988 Curtis Strange (USA)
1989 Curtis Strange (USA)
1990 Hale Irwin (USA)
1991 Payne Stewart (USA)

Most wins: (4), Willie Anderson (USA), 1901, 1903–5; Bobby Jones (USA), 1923, 1926, 1929–30; Ben Hogan (USA), 1948, 1950–1, 1953; Jack Nicklaus (USA), 1962, 1967, 1972, 1980.

US Masters

First held in 1934; takes place at the Augusta National course in Georgia every April.

Recent winners

1980 Severiano Ballesteros (Spain)
1981 Tom Watson (USA)

Golf (cont.)

1982 Craig Stadler (USA)
1983 Severiano Ballesteros (Spain)
1984 Ben Crenshaw (USA)
1985 Bernhard Langer (West Germany)
1986 Jack Nicklaus (USA)
1987 Larry Mize (USA)
1988 Sandy Lyle (Great Britain)
1989 Nick Faldo (Great Britain)
1990 Nick Faldo (Great Britain)
1991 Ian Woosnam (Great Britain)

Most wins: (6), Jack Nicklaus (USA), 1963, 1965–6, 1972, 1975, 1986.

United States PGA Championship
The last of the season's four 'Majors'; first held in 1916, and a match-play event until 1958; takes place annually.

Recent winners

1979 David Graham (Australia)
1980 Jack Nicklaus (USA)
1981 Larry Nelson (USA)
1982 Ray Floyd (USA)
1983 Hal Sutton (USA)
1984 Lee Trevino (USA)
1985 Hubert Green (USA)
1986 Bob Tway (USA)
1987 Larry Nelson (USA)
1988 Jeff Sluman (USA)
1989 Payne Stewart (USA)
1990 Wayne Grady (Australia)
1991 John Daly (USA)

Most wins: (5), Walter Hagen (USA), 1921, 1924–7; Jack Nicklaus (USA), 1963, 1971, 1973, 1975, 1980.

Ryder Cup
The leading international team tournament; first held at Worcester, Massachusetts in 1927; takes place every two years between teams from the USA and Europe (Great Britain 1927–71; Great Britain and Ireland 1973–7).

Recent winners

1969	Drawn	16–16
1971	USA	18½–13½
1973	USA	19–13
1975	USA	21–11
1977	USA	12½–7½
1979	USA	17–11
1981	USA	18½–9½
1983	USA	14½–13½
1985	Europe	16½–11½

| 1987 | Europe | 15–13 |
| 1989 | Drawn | 14–14 |

Wins: (21), USA, 1927, 1931, 1935–7, 1947–55, 1959–67, 1971–83. (3), Great Britain, 1929, 1933, 1957. (2), Europe, 1985, 1987. (2), Drawn, 1969, 1989.

GREYHOUND RACING

Greyhound Derby
The top race of the British season, first held in 1927; run at the White City every year (except 1940) until its closure in 1985; since then all races run at Wimbledon.

Recent winners

1979 Sarah's Bunny
1980 Indian Joe
1981 Parkdown Jet
1982 Laurie's Panther
1983 I'm Slippy
1984 Whisper Wishes
1985 Pagan Swallow
1986 Tico
1987 Signal Spark
1988 Hit the Lid
1989 Lartigue Note
1990 Slippy Blue
1991 Ballinderry Ash

Most wins: (2), Mick the Miller, 1929–30; Patricia's Hope, 1972–3.

GYMNASTICS

World Championships
First held in 1903; took place every four years, 1922–78; since 1979, every two years.

Recent winners
Individual (Men)

1962 Yuriy Titov (USSR)
1966 Mikhail Voronin (USSR)
1970 Eizo Kenmotsu (Japan)
1974 Shigeru Kasamatsu (Japan)
1978 Nikolai Adrianov (USSR)
1979 Aleksandr Ditiatin (USSR)
1981 Yuri Korolev (USSR)
1983 Dmitri Belozerchev (USSR)
1985 Yuri Korolev (USSR)
1987 Dmitri Belozerchev (USSR)
1989 Igor Korobichensky (USSR)

Gymnastics (cont.)

Recent winners
Team (Men)

1962 Japan
1966 Japan
1970 Japan
1974 Japan
1978 Japan
1979 USSR
1981 USSR
1983 China
1985 USSR
1987 USSR
1989 USSR

Most wins: Individual (2), Marco Torrès (France), 1909, 1913; Peter Sumi (Yugoslavia), 1922, 1926; Yuri Korolev and Dmitri Belozerchev, as above. Team (7), Czechoslovakia, 1907, 1911, 1913, 1922, 1926, 1930, 1938.

Recent winners
Individual (Women)

1962 Larissa Latynina (USSR)
1966 Vera Caslavska (Czechoslovakia)
1970 Ludmila Tourischeva (USSR)
1974 Ludmila Tourischeva (USSR)
1978 Yelena Mukhina (USSR)
1979 Nelli Kim (USSR)
1981 Olga Bitcherova (USSR)
1983 Natalia Yurchenko (USSR)
1985 Yelena Shoushounova (USSR) and
     Oksana Omeliantchuk (USSR)
1987 Aurelia Dobre (Romania)
1989 Svetlana Boginskaya

Recent winners
Team (Women)

1962 USSR
1966 Czechoslovakia
1970 USSR
1974 USSR
1978 USSR
1979 Romania
1981 USSR
1983 USSR
1985 USSR
1987 Romania
1989 USSR

Most wins: Individual (2), Vlasta Dekanová (Czechoslovakia), 1934, 1938; Larissa Latynina (USSR), 1958, 1962, Vera Caslavska and Ludmila Tourischeva, as above. Team (9), USSR, as above plus 1954, 1958.

HANDBALL

World Championships

First men's championships held in 1938, both indoors and outdoors (latter discontinued in 1966); first women's outdoor championships in 1949, (discontinued in 1960); first women's indoor championships in 1957.

Winners Indoors (Men)

1938 Germany
1954 Sweden
1958 Sweden
1961 Romania
1964 Romania
1967 Czechoslovakia
1970 Romania
1974 Romania
1978 West Germany
1982 USSR
1986 Yugoslavia
1990 Sweden

Winners Outdoors (Men)

1938 Germany
1948 Sweden
1952 West Germany
1955 West Germany
1959 East/West Germany (*combined*)
1963 East Germany
1966 West Germany

Most wins: Indoors (4), Romania. Outdoors (4), West Germany (including 1 as combined East/West German team).

Winners Indoors (Women)

1957 Czechoslovakia
1962 Romania
1965 Hungary
1971 East Germany
1973 Yugoslavia
1975 East Germany
1979 East Germany
1982 USSR
1986 USSR
1990 USSR

Winners Outdoors (Women)

1949 Hungary
1956 Romania
1960 Romania

Most wins: Indoors (3), East Germany, USSR, as above. Outdoors (2), Romania, as above.

HANG GLIDING

World Championships
First held officially in 1976; since 1979, take place every two years.

Winners
Individual (Class 1)

1976 Christian Steinbach (Austria)
1979 Josef Guggenmose (West Germany)
1981 Pepe Lopez (Brazil)
1983 Steve Moyes (Australia)
1985 John Pendry (Great Britain)
1987 Rich Duncan (Australia)
1989 Robert Whittall (Great Britain)

Winners (Team)

1976 Austria
1979 France
1981 Great Britain
1983 Australia
1985 Great Britain
1987 Australia
1989 Great Britain

Most wins: Individual, no person has won more than one title. Team (3), Great Britain, as above.

HOCKEY

World Cup
Men's tournament first held in 1971, and every four years since 1978; women's tournament first held in 1974, and now takes place every three years.

Winners (Men)

1971 Pakistan
1973 Holland
1975 India
1978 Pakistan
1982 Pakistan
1986 Australia
1990 Holland

Most wins: (3), Pakistan, as above.

Winners (Women)

1974 Holland
1976 West Germany
1978 Holland
1981 West Germany
1983 Holland
1986 Holland
1990 Holland

Most wins: (5), Holland, as above.

Olympic Games
Regarded as hockey's leading competition; first held in 1908; included at every celebration since 1928; women's competition first held in 1980.

Post-war winners (Men)

1948 India
1952 India
1956 India
1960 Pakistan
1964 India
1968 Pakistan
1972 West Germany
1976 New Zealand
1980 India
1984 Pakistan
1988 Great Britain

Winners (Women)

1980 Zimbabwe
1984 Holland
1988 Australia

Most wins: Men (8), India, 1928, 1932, 1936, 1948, 1952, 1956, 1964, 1980. Women, no nation has won the title more than once.

HORSE RACING

The Derby
The 'Blue Riband' of the Turf; run at Epsom over 1½ miles; first run in 1780.

Recent winners

	Horse (Jockey)
1979	Troy (Willie Carson)
1980	Henbit (Willie Carson)
1981	Shergar (Walter Swinburn)
1982	Golden Fleece (Pat Eddery)
1983	Teenoso (Lester Piggott)
1984	Secreto (Christy Roche)
1985	Slip Anchor (Steve Cauthen)
1986	Shahrastani (Walter Swinburn)
1987	Reference Point (Steve Cauthen)
1988	Kahyasi (Ray Cochrane)
1989	Nashwan (Willie Carson)
1990	Quest For Fame (Pat Eddery)
1991	Generous (Alan Munro)

Most wins: Jockey (9), Lester Piggott, 1954, 1957, 1960, 1968, 1970, 1972, 1976–7, 1983.

The Oaks
Raced at Epsom over 1½ miles; for fillies only; first run in 1779.

Horse Racing (cont.)

Recent winners

Horse (Jockey)
1979 Scintillate (Pat Eddery)
1980 Bireme (Willie Carson)
1981 Blue Wind (Lester Piggott)
1982 Time Charter (Billy Newnes)
1983 Sun Princess (Willy Carson)
1984 Circus Plume (Lester Piggott)
1985 Oh So Sharp (Steve Cauthen)
1986 Midway Lady (Ray Cochrane)
1987 Unite (Walter Swinburn)
1988 Diminuendo (Steve Cauthen)
1989 Aliysa (Walter Swinburn)
1990 Salsabil (Willie Carson)
1991 Jet Ski Lady (Christy Roche)

Most wins: Jockey (9), Frank Buckle, 1797–9, 1802–3, 1805, 1817–18, 1923.

One Thousand Guineas
Run over 1 mile at Newmarket; for fillies only; first run in 1814.

Recent winners

Horse (Jockey)
1979 One in a Million (Joe Mercer)
1980 Quick as Lightning (Brian Rouse)
1981 Fairy Footsteps (Lester Piggott)
1982 On The House (John Reid)
1983 Ma Biche (Freddy Head)
1984 Pebbles (Philip Robinson)
1985 Oh So Sharp (Steve Cauthen)
1986 Midway Lady (Ray Cochrane)
1987 Miesque (Freddy Head)
1988 Ravinella (Gary Moore)
1989 Musical Bliss (Walter Swinburn)
1990 Salsabil (Willie Carson)
1991 Shadayid (Willie Carson)

Most wins: Jockey (7), George Fordham, 1859, 1861, 1865, 1868–9, 1881, 1883.

Two Thousand Guineas
Run at Newmarket over 1 mile; first run in 1809.

Recent winners

Horse (Jockey)
1979 Tap on Wood (Steve Cauthen)
1980 Known Fact (Willie Carson)
1981 To-Agori-Mou (Greville Starkey)
1982 Zino (Freddy Head)
1983 Lomond (Pat Eddery)
1984 El Gran Senor (Pat Eddery)
1985 Shadeed (Lester Piggott)

1986 Dancing Brave (Greville Starkey)
1987 Don't Forget Me (Willie Carson)
1988 Doyoun (Walter Swinburn)
1989 Nashwan (Willie Carson)
1990 Tirol (Michael Kinane)
1991 Mystiko (Michael Roberts)

Most wins: Jockey (9), Jem Robinson, 1825, 1828, 1831, 1833–6, 1847–8.

St Leger
The oldest of the five English classics; first run in 1776; raced at Doncaster annually over 1 mile 6 furlongs 127 yards.

Recent winners

Horse (Jockey)
1979 Son of Love (Alain Lequeux)
1980 Light Cavalry (Joe Mercer)
1981 Cut Above (Joe Mercer)
1982 Touching Wood (Paul Cook)
1983 Sun Princess (Willie Carson)
1984 Commanche Run (Lester Piggott)
1985 Oh So Sharp (Steve Cauthen)
1986 Moon Madness (Pat Eddery)
1987 Reference Point (Steve Cauthen)
1988 Minster Son (Willie Carson)
1989 Michelozzo (Steve Cauthen)
1990 Snurge (Richard Quinn)

Most wins: Jockey (9), Bill Scott, 1821, 1825, 1828–9, 1838–41, 1846.

Grand National
Steeplechasing's most famous race; first run at Maghull in 1836; at Aintree since 1839; war-time races at Gatwick 1916–18.

Recent winners

Horse (Jockey)
1979 Rubstic (Maurice Barnes)
1980 Ben Nevis (Mr Charles Fenwick)
1981 Aldaniti (Bob Champion)
1982 Grittar (Mr Dick Saunders)
1983 Corbiere (Ben De Haan)
1984 Hallo Dandy (Neale Doughty)
1985 Last Suspect (Hywel Davies)
1986 West Tip (Richard Dunwoody)
1987 Maori Venture (Steve Knight)
1988 Rhyme 'N' Reason (Brendan Powell)
1989 Little Polveir (Jimmy Frost)
1990 Mr Frisk (Marcus Armytage)
1991 Seagram (Nigel Hawke)
● 'Mr' denotes that the jockey is an amateur rider.

Horse Racing (cont.)

Most wins: Jockey (5), George Stevens, 1856, 1863–4, 1869–70. Horse (3), Red Rum 1973–4, 1977.

Prix de l'Arc de Triomphe
The leading end of season race in Europe; raced over 2400 metres at Longchamp; first run in 1920.

Recent winners

	Horse (Jockey)
1979	Three Troikas (Freddy Head)
1980	Detroit (Pat Eddery)
1981	Gold River (Gary Moore)
1982	Akiyda (Yves Saint-Martin)
1983	All Along (Walter Swinburn)
1984	Sagace (Yves Saint-Martin)
1985	Rainbow Quest (Pat Eddery)
1986	Dancing Brave (Pat Eddery)
1987	Trempolino (Pat Eddery)
1988	Tony Bin (John Reid)
1989	Caroll House (Michael Kinane)
1990	Suamarez (Gerard Mosse)

Most wins: Jockey (4), Jacko Doyasbère, 1942, 1944, 1950–1; Freddy Head, 1966, 1972, 1976, 1979; Yves Saint-Martin, 1970, 1974, 1982, 1984; Pat Eddery, as above. Horse (2), Ksar, 1921–2; Motrico, 1930, 1932; Corrida, 1936–7; Tantième, 1950–1; Ribot, 1955–6; Alleged 1977–8.

HURLING

All-Ireland Championship
First contested in 1887; played on the first Sunday in September each year.

Recent winners

1979	Kilkenny
1980	Galway
1981	Offaly
1982	Kilkenny
1983	Kilkenny
1984	Cork
1985	Offaly
1986	Cork
1987	Galway
1988	Galway
1989	Tipperary
1990	Cork

Most wins: (27), Cork, 1890, 1892–4, 1902–3, 1919, 1926, 1928–9, 1931, 1941–4, 1946, 1952–4, 1966, 1970, 1976–8, 1984, 1986, 1990.

ICE HOCKEY

World Championship
First held in 1930; takes place annually (except 1980); up to 1968 Olympic champions also regarded as world champions.

Recent winners

1978	USSR
1979	USSR
1981	USSR
1982	USSR
1983	USSR
1984	USSR
1985	Czechoslovakia
1986	USSR
1987	Sweden
1988	USSR
1989	USSR
1990	USSR
1991	Sweden

Most wins: (24), USSR, 1954, 1956, 1963–71, 1973–5, 1978–9, 1981–4, 1986, 1988–90.

Stanley Cup
The most sought-after trophy at club level; the end-of-season meeting between the winners of the two conferences in the National Hockey League in the USA and Canada.

Recent winners

1979	Montreal Canadiens
1980	New York Islanders
1981	New York Islanders
1982	New York Islanders
1983	New York Islanders
1984	Edmonton Oilers
1985	Edmonton Oilers
1986	Montreal Canadiens
1987	Edmonton Oilers
1988	Edmonton Oilers
1989	Calgary Flames
1990	Edmonton Oilers
1991	Pittsburgh Penguins

Most wins: (23), Montreal Canadiens, 1916, 1924, 1930–1, 1944, 1946, 1953, 1956–60, 1965–6, 1968–9, 1971, 1973, 1976–9, 1986.

ICE SKATING

World Championships
First men's championships in 1896; first women's event in 1906; pairs first contested in 1908; Ice Dance officially recognized in 1952.

Recent winners (Men)

1980 Jan Hoffman (East Germany)
1981 Scott Hamilton (USA)
1982 Scott Hamilton (USA)
1983 Scott Hamilton (USA)
1984 Scott Hamilton (USA)
1985 Alexander Fadeyev (USSR)
1986 Brian Boitano (USA)
1987 Brian Orser (Canada)
1988 Brian Boitano (USA)
1989 Kurt Browning (Canada)
1990 Kurt Browning (Canada)
1991 Kurt Browning (Canada)

Most wins: (10), Ulrich Salchow (Sweden), 1901–5, 1907–11.

Recent winners (Women)

1980 Anett Potzsch (East Germany)
1981 Denise Beillmann (Switzerland)
1982 Elaine Zayak (USA)
1983 Rosalynn Sumners (USA)
1984 Katarina Witt (East Germany)
1985 Katarina Witt (East Germany)
1986 Debbie Thomas (USA)
1987 Katarina Witt (East Germany)
1988 Katarina Witt (East Germany)
1989 Midori Ito (Japan)
1990 Jill Trenary (USA)
1991 Kristi Yamaguchi (USA)

Most wins: (10), Sonja Henie (Norway), 1927–36.

Recent winners (Pairs)

1980 Sergei Shakrai/Marina Tcherkassova (USSR)
1981 Igor Lissovsky/Irina Vorobyeva (USSR)
1982 Tassilo Thierbach/Sabine Baess (East Germany)
1983 Oleg Vasiliev/Yelena Valova (USSR)
1984 Paul Martini/Barbara Underhill (Canada)
1985 Oleg Vasiliev/Yelena Valova (USSR)
1986 Sergey Grinkov/Yekaterina Gordeeva (USSR)
1987 Sergey Grinkov/Yekaterina Gordeeva (USSR)
1988 Oleg Vasiliev/Yelena Valorva (USSR)
1989 Sergey Grinkov/Yekaterina Gordeeva (USSR)
1990 Sergey Grinkov/Yekaterina Gordeeva (USSR)
1991 Arthur Dmtriev/Natalya Mishkutienok (USSR)

Most wins: (10), Irina Rodnina (USSR), 1969–72 (with Aleksey Ulanov), 1973–8 (with Aleksander Zaitsev).

Recent winners (Ice Dance)

1980 Andras Sallay/Krisztina Regoczy (Hungary)
1981 Christopher Dean/Jayne Torvill (Great Britain)
1982 Christopher Dean/Jayne Torvill (Great Britain)
1983 Christopher Dean/Jayne Torvill (Great Britain)
1984 Christopher Dean/Jayne Torvill (Great Britain)
1985 Andrey Bukin/Natalya Bestemianova (USSR)
1986 Andrey Bukin/Natalya Bestemianova (USSR)
1987 Andrey Bukin/Natalya Bestemianova (USSR)
1988 Andrey Bukin/Natalya Bestemianova (USSR)
1989 Sergey Ponomarenko/Marina Klimova (USSR)
1990 Sergey Ponomarenko/Marina Klimova (USSR)
1991 Alexandra Zhulin/Maia Usova (USSR)

Most wins: (6), Aleksander Gorshkov and Lyudmila Pakhomova (USSR), 1970–4, 1976.

JUDO

World Championships
First held in 1956, now contested every two years; current weight categories established in 1979; women's championship instituted in 1980.

Recent winners
Open Class (Men)

1979 Sumio Endo (Japan)
1981 Yasuhiro Yamashita (Japan)
1983 Hitoshi Saito (Japan)
1985 Yoshimi Masaki (Japan)
1987 Noayo Ogawa (Japan)
1989 Noayo Ogawa (Japan)

Recent winners
Over 95 kg (Men)

1979 Yasuhiro Yamashita (Japan)
1981 Yasuhiro Yamashita (Japan)
1983 Yasuhiro Yamashita (Japan)
1985 Yung-Chul Cho (Korea)
1987 Grigori Vertichev (USSR)
1989 Noayo Ogawa (Japan)

Recent winners
Under 95 kg (Men)

1979 Tengiz Khubuluri (USSR)
1981 Tenzig Khubuluri (USSR)
1983 Valeriy Divisenko (USSR)
1985 Hitoshi Sugai (Japan)

Judo (cont.)

1987 Hitoshi Sugai (Japan)
1989 Koba Kurtanidze (Japan)

Recent winners
Under 86 kg (Men)

1979 Detlef Ultsch (East Germany)
1981 Bernard Tchoullouyan (France)
1983 Detlef Ultsch (East Germany)
1985 Peter Seisenbacher (Austria)
1987 Fabien Canu (France)
1989 Fabien Canu (France)

Recent winners
Under 78 kg (Men)

1979 Shozo Fujii (Japan)
1981 Neil Adams (Great Britain)
1983 Nobutoshi Hikage (Japan)
1985 Nobutoshi Hikage (Japan)
1987 Hirotaka Okada (Japan)
1989 Byung-ju Kim (South Korea)

Recent winners
Under 71 kg (Men)

1979 Kyoto Katsuki (Japan)
1981 Chon-Hak Park (Korea)
1983 Kidetoshi Nakanishi (Japan)
1985 Byeong-Keun Ahn (Korea)
1987 Mike Swain (USA)
1989 Toshitiko Koga (Japan)

Recent winners
Under 65 kg (Men)

1979 Nikolai Soludkhin (USSR)
1981 Katsuhiko Kashiwazaki (Japan)
1983 Nikolai Soludkhin (USSR)
1985 Yuriy Sokolov (USSR)
1987 Yosuke Yamamoto (Japan)
1989 Drago Becanovic (Yugoslavia)

Recent winners
Under 60 kg (Men)

1979 Thierry Ray (France)
1981 Yasuhiko Moriwaki (Japan)
1983 Khazret Tletseri (USSR)
1985 Shinji Hosokawa (Japan)
1987 Kim Jae-Yup (South Korea)
1989 Amiran Totikashvili (USSR)

Most titles: (4), Yashiro Yamashita (Japan), 1981 (Open), 1979, 1981, 1983 (over 95 kg); Shozo Fujii (Japan), 1971, 1973, 1975 (under 80 kg), 1979 (under 78 kg).

Recent winners
Open (Women)

1980 Ingrid Berghmans (Belgium)
1982 Ingrid Berghmans (Belgium)
1984 Ingrid Berghmans (Belgium)
1986 Ingrid Berghmans (Belgium)
1987 Fenglian Gao (China)
1989 Estela Rodriguez (Cuba)

Recent winners
Over 72 kg (Women)

1980 Margarita de Cal (Italy)
1982 Natalina Lupino (France)
1984 Maria-Teresa Motta (Italy)
1986 Fenglian Gao (China)
1987 Fenglian Gao (China)
1989 Fenglian Gao (China)

Recent winners
Under 72 kg (Women)

1980 Jocelyne Triadou (France)
1982 Barbara Classen (West Germany)
1984 Ingrid Berghmans (Belgium)
1986 Irene de Kok (Holland)
1987 Irene de Kok (Holland)
1989 Ingrid Berghmans (Belgium)

Recent winners
Under 66 kg (Women)

1980 Edith Simon (Austria)
1982 Brigitte Deydier (France)
1986 Brigitte Deydier (France)
1987 Alexandra Schreiber (West Germany)
1989 Emanuela Pieraniozzi (Italy)

Recent winners
Under 61 kg (Women)

1980 Anita Staps (Holland)
1982 Martine Rothier (France)
1984 Natasha Hernandez (Venezuela)
1986 Diane Bell (Great Britain)
1987 Diane Bell (Great Britain)
1989 Catherina Fleury (France)

Recent winners
Under 56 kg (Women)

1980 Gerda Winklbauer (Austria)
1982 Béatrice Rodriguez (France)
1984 Ann-Maria Burns (USA)
1986 Ann Hughes (Great Britain)
1987 Catherine Arnaud (France)
1989 Catherine Arnaud (France)

Judo (cont.)

Recent winners
Under 52 kg (Women)

1980 Edith Hrovat (Austria)
1982 Loretta Doyle (Great Britain)
1984 Kaori Yamaguchi (Japan)
1986 Dominique Brun (France)
1987 Sharon Rendle (Great Britain)
1989 Sharon Rendle (Great Britain)

Recent winners
Under 48 kg (Women)

1980 Jane Bridge (Great Britain)
1982 Karen Briggs (Great Britain)
1984 Karen Briggs (Great Britain)
1986 Karen Briggs (Great Britain)
1987 Z Li (China)
1989 Karen Briggs (Great Britain)

Most titles: (6), Ingrid Berghmans (Belgium), 1980, 1982, 1984, 1986 (Open), 1984, 1989 (both under 72 kg).

KARATE

World Championships
First held in Tokyo 1970; taken place every two years since 1980, when women first competed; there is a team competition plus individual competitions at Kumite (seven weight categories for men and three for women) and Kata.

Team winners

1970 Japan
1972 France
1975 Great Britain
1977 Holland
1980 Spain
1982 Great Britain
1984 Great Britain
1986 Great Britain
1988 Great Britain
1990 Great Britain

Most wins: (4), Great Britain, as above.

LACROSSE

World Championships
First held for men in 1967; for women in 1969; taken place every four years since 1974; since 1982 the women's event has been called the World Cup.

Winners (Men)

1967 USA
1974 USA
1978 Canada
1982 USA
1986 USA
1990 USA

Most wins: (5), USA, as above.

Winners (Women)

1969 Great Britain
1974 USA
1978 Canada
1982 USA
1986 Australia
1989 USA

Most wins: (3), USA, as above.

Iroquois Cup
The sport's best known trophy; contested by English club sides annually since 1890.

Recent winners

1979 Cheadle
1980 South Manchester
1981 Cheadle
1982 Sheffield University
1983 Sheffield University
1984 Cheadle
1985 Cheadle
1986 Heaton Mersey
1987 Stockport
1988 Mellor
1989 Stockport
1990 Cheadle
1991 Cheadle

Most wins: (17), Stockport, 1897–1901, 1903, 1905, 1911–13, 1923–4, 1926, 1928, 1934, 1987, 1989.

MODERN PENTATHLON

World Championships
Held annually since 1949 with the exception of Olympic years, when the Olympic champions automatically become world champions.

Recent winners (Individual)

1979 Robert Nieman (USA)
1980 Anatoliy Starostin (USSR)

Modern Pentathlon (cont.)

1981 Janusz Pyciak-Peciak (Poland)
1982 Daniele Masala (Italy)
1983 Anatoliy Starostin (USSR)
1984 Daniele Masala (Italy)
1985 Attila Mizser (Hungary)
1986 Carlo Massullo (Italy)
1987 Joel Bouzou (France)
1988 Janos Martinek (Hungary)
1989 Laszlo Fabien (Hungary)
1990 Gianluca Tiberti (Italy)

Recent winners (Team)

1979 USA
1980 USSR
1981 Poland
1982 USSR
1983 USSR
1984 Italy
1985 USSR
1986 Italy
1987 Hungary
1988 Hungary
1989 Hungary
1990 USSR

Most wins: Individual (6), Andras Balczo (Hungary), 1963, 1965–9, 1972. Team (17), USSR, 1956–9, 1961–2, 1964, 1969, 1971–4, 1980, 1982–3, 1985, 1990.

MOTOR CYCLING

World Championships

First organized in 1949; current titles for 500 cc, 250 cc, 125 cc, 80 cc and Sidecar; Formula One and Endurance world championships also held annually; the most prestigious title is the 500 cc category.

Recent winners (500 cc)

1979 Kenny Roberts (USA)
1980 Kenny Roberts (USA)
1981 Marco Lucchinelli (Italy)
1982 Franco Uncini (Italy)
1983 Freddie Spencer (USA)
1984 Eddie Lawson (USA)
1985 Freddie Spencer (USA)
1986 Eddie Lawson (USA)
1987 Wayne Gardner (Australia)
1988 Eddie Lawson (USA)
1989 Eddie Lawson (USA)
1990 Wayne Rainey (USA)

Most wins: (8), Giacomo Agostini (Italy), 1966–72, 1975.

Most world titles: (15), Giacomo Agostini, 500 cc as above, 350 cc 1968–74.

Isle of Man TT Races

The most famous of all motor cycle races; take place each June; first held 1907; principal race is the Senior TT.

Recent winners (Senior TT)

1979 Mike Hailwood (Great Britain)
1980 Graeme Crosby (New Zealand)
1981 Mick Grant (Great Britain)
1982 Norman Brown (Great Britain)
1983 Rob McElnea (Great Britain)
1984 Rob McElnea (Great Britain)
1985 Joey Dunlop (Ireland)
1986 Roger Burnett (Great Britain)
1987 Joey Dunlop (Ireland)
1988 Joey Dunlop (Ireland)
1989 Steve Hislop (Great Britain)
1990 Carl Fogarty (Great Britain)
1991 Steve Hislop (Great Britain)

Most Senior TT wins: (7), Mike Hailwood (Great Britain), 1961, 1963–7, 1979.

MOTOR RACING

World Championship

A Formula One drivers' world championship instituted in 1950; constructor's championship instituted in 1958.

Recent winners

1979	Jody Scheckter (South Africa)	*Ferrari*
1980	Alan Jones (Australia)	*Williams*
1981	Nelson Piquet (Brazil)	*Williams*
1982	Keke Rosberg (Finland)	*Ferrari*
1983	Nelson Piquet (Brazil)	*Ferrari*
1984	Niki Lauda (Austria)	*McLaren*
1985	Alain Prost (France)	*McLaren*
1986	Alain Prost (France)	*Williams*
1987	Nelson Piquet (Brazil)	*Williams*
1988	Ayrton Senna (Brazil)	*McLaren*
1989	Alain Prost (France)	*McLaren*
1990	Ayrton Senna (Brazil)	*McLaren*

Most wins: Driver (5), Juan Manuel Fangio (Argentina), 1951, 1954–7. Constructor (8), Ferrari, 1964, 1975–7, 1979, 1982–3.

Motor Racing (cont.)

Le Mans 24-Hour Race

The greatest of all endurance races; first held in 1923.

Recent winners

1979 Klaus Ludwig (West Germany)
     Bill Whittington (USA)
     Don Whittington (USA)
1980 Jean-Pierre Jaussaud (France)
     Jean Rondeau (France)
1981 Jacky Ickx (Belgium)
     Derek Bell (Great Britain)
1982 Jacky Ickx (Belgium)
     Derek Bell (Great Britain)
1983 Vern Schuppan (Austria)
     Al Holbert (USA)
     Hurley Haywood (USA)
1984 Klaus Ludwig (West Germany)
     Henri Pescarolo (France)
1985 Klaus Ludwig (West Germany)
     'John Winter'* (West Germany)
     Paolo Barilla (Italy)
1986 Hans Stück (West Germany)
     Derek Bell (Great Britain)
     Al Holbert (USA)
1987 Hans Stück (West Germany)
     Derek Bell (Great Britain)
     Al Holbert (USA)
1988 Jan Lammers (Holland)
     Johnny Dumfries (Great Britain)
     Andy Wallace (Great Britain)
1989 Jochen Mass (West Germany)
     Manuel Reuter (West Germany)
     Stanley Dickens (Sweden)
1990 John Nielsen (Denmark)
     Price Cobb (USA)
     Martin Brundle (Great Britain)
1991 Volker Weidler (Germany)
     Johnny Herbert (Great Britain)
     Bertrand Gachot (Belgium)
* pseudonym

Most wins: (6), Jacky Ickx (Belgium), 1969, 1975–7, 1981–2.

Indianapolis 500

First held in 1911; raced over the Indianapolis Raceway as part of the Memorial Day celebrations at the end of May each year.

Recent winners

1979 Rick Mears (USA)
1980 Johnny Rutherford (USA)
1981 Bobby Unser (USA)
1982 Gordon Johncock (USA)

1983 Tom Sneva (USA)
1984 Rick Mears (USA)
1985 Danny Sullivan (USA)
1986 Bobby Rahal (USA)
1987 Al Unser (USA)
1988 Rick Mears (USA)
1989 Emerson Fittipaldi (Brazil)
1990 Arie Luyendyk (Holland)
1991 Ric Mears (USA)

Most wins: (4), A J Foyt (USA), 1961, 1964, 1967, 1977; Al Unser (USA), 1970–1, 1978, 1987.

Monte Carlo Rally

The world's leading Rally; first held in 1911.

Recent winners

1980 Walter Röhrl (West Germany)
     Christian Geistdörfer (West Germany)
1981 Jean Ragnotti (France)
     Jean-Marc André (France)
1982 Walter Röhrl (West Germany)
     Christian Geistdörfer (West Germany)
1983 Walter Röhrl (West Germany)
     Christian Geistdörfer (West Germany)
1984 Walter Röhrl (West Germany)
     Christian Geistdörfer (West Germany)
1985 Ari Vatanen (Finland)
     Terry Harryman (Great Britain)
1986 Henri Toivonen (Finland)
     Sergio Cresto (Italy)
1987 Miki Biasion (Italy)
     Tiziano Siviero (Italy)
1988 Bruno Saby (France)
     Jean-François Fauchille (France)
1989 Miki Biasion (Italy)
     Tiziano Siviero (Italy)
1990 Didier Auriol (France)
     Bernard Occelli (France)
1991 Carlos Sainz (Spain)
     co-driver not known

Most wins: (4), Sandro Munari (Italy), 1972, 1975–7; Walter Röhrl/Christian Geistrdörfer (West Germany), as above.

NETBALL

World Championships

First held in 1963, then every four years.

Winners

1963 Australia
1967 New Zealand
1971 Australia

Netball (cont.)

1975 Australia
1979 Australia, New Zealand,
         Trinidad & Tobago (*shared*)
1983 Australia
1987 New Zealand

Most wins: (5), Australia, as above.

ORIENTEERING

World Championships
First held in 1966; takes place every two years (to 1978, and since 1979).

Winners Individual (Men)

1966 Age Hadler (Norway)
1968 Karl Johansson (Sweden)
1970 Stig Berge (Norway)
1972 Age Hadler (Norway)
1974 Bernt Frilen (Sweden)
1976 Egil Johansen (Norway)
1978 Egil Johansen (Norway)
1979 Oyvin Thon (Norway)
1981 Oyvin Thon (Norway)
1983 Morten Berglia (Norway)
1985 Kari Sallinen (Finland)
1987 Kent Olsson (Sweden)
1989 Peter Thoresen (Norway)

Winners Individual (Women)

1966 Ulla Lindqvist (Sweden)
1968 Ulla Lindqvist (Sweden)
1970 Ingrid Hadler (Norway)
1972 Sorolta Monspart (Finland)
1974 Mona Norgaard (Denmark)
1976 Lia Veijalainen (Finland)
1978 Anne Berit Eid (Norway)
1979 Outi Bergonstrom (Finland)
1981 Annichen Kringstad (Norway)
1983 Annichen Kringstad Svensson (Norway)
1985 Annichen Kringstad Svensson (Norway)
1987 Arja Hannus (Sweden)
1989 Marita Skogum (Sweden)

Most wins: Men (2), Age Hadler (Norway), Egil Johansen (Norway), Oyvin Thon (Norway), as above. Women (3), Annichen Kringstad (Norway), as above.

Winners Relay (Men)

1966 Sweden
1968 Sweden

1970 Norway
1972 Sweden
1974 Sweden
1976 Sweden
1978 Norway
1979 Sweden
1981 Norway
1983 Norway
1985 Norway
1987 Norway
1989 Norway

Winners Relay (Women)

1966 Sweden
1968 Norway
1970 Sweden
1972 Finland
1974 Sweden
1976 Sweden
1978 Finland
1979 Finland
1981 Sweden
1983 Sweden
1985 Sweden
1987 Norway
1989 Sweden

Most wins: Men (7), Norway, as above. Women (8), Sweden, as above.

POLO

Cowdray Park Gold Cup
First held in 1956, replacing the Champion Cup; the British Open Championship for club sides; so named because played at Cowdray Park, Sussex.

Recent winners

1979 Songhai
1980 Stowell Park
1981 Falcons
1982 Southfield
1983 Falcons
1984 Southfield
1985 Maple Leafs
1986 Tramontona
1987 Tramontona
1988 Tramontona
1989 Tramontona
1990 Tramontona
1991 Tramontona

Most wins: (6), Tramontona, 1986–91.

POWERBOAT RACING

World Championships
Instituted in 1982; held in many categories, with Formula One and Formula Two being the principal competitions; Formula One discontinued in 1986; Formula Two became known as Formula Grand Prix.

Winners
Formula One

1982 Roger Jenkins (Great Britain)
1983 Renato Molinari (Italy)
1984 Renato Molinari (Italy)
1985 Bob Spalding (Great Britain)
1986 Gene Thibodaux (USA)
Discontinued

Most wins: (2), Renato Molinari (Italy), as above.

Winners
Formula Two/Formula Grand Prix

1982 Michael Werner (West Germany)
1983 Michael Werner (West Germany)
1984 John Hill (Great Britain)
1985 John Hill (Great Britain)
1986 Jonathan Jones (Great Britain) and
     Buck Thornton (USA) (*shared*)
1987 Bill Seebold (USA)
1988 Chris Bush (USA)
1989 Jonathan Jones (Great Britain)
1990 John Hill (Great Britain)

Most wins: (2), Michael Werner (West Germany); John Hill (Great Britain), as above.

RACKETS

World Championship
Organized on a challenge basis, the first champion in 1820 was Robert Mackay (Great Britain).

Recent winners

1929–37 Charles Williams (Great Britain)
1937–47 Donald Milford (Great Britain)
1947–54 James Dear (Great Britain)
1954–72 Geoffrey Atkins (Great Britain)
1972–73 William Surtees (USA)
1973–74 Howard Angus (Great Britain)
1975–81 William Surtees (USA)
1981–84 John Prenn (Great Britain)
1984–86 William Boone (Great Britain)
1986–88 John Prenn (Great Britain)
1988–   James Male (Great Britain)

Longest reigning champion: 18 years, Geoffrey Atkins, as above.

REAL TENNIS

World Championship
Organized on a challenge basis; the first world champion was M Clerge (France) c. 1740, regarded as the first world champion of any sport.

Recent winners

1916–28 Fred Covey (Great Britain)
1928–55 Pierre Etchebaster (France)
1955–57 James Dear (Great Britain)
1957–59 Albert Johnson (Great Britain)
1959–69 Northrup Knox (USA)
1969–72 Pete Bostwick (USA)
1972–75 Jimmy Bostwick (USA)
1976–81 Howard Angus (Great Britain)
1981–87 Chris Ronaldson (Great Britain)
1987–   Wayne Davies (Australia)

Longest reigning champion: 33 years, Edmond Barre (France), 1829–62.

ROLLER SKATING

World Championships
Figure skating world championships were first organized in 1947.

Recent winners (Men Combined)

1979 Michael Butzke (East Germany)
1980 Michael Butzke (East Germany)
1981 Michael Butzke (East Germany)
1982 Michael Butzke (East Germany)
1983 Joachim Helmle (West Germany)
1984 Michele Biserni (Italy)
1985 Michele Biserni (Italy)
1986 Michele Tolomini (Italy)
1987 Kevin Carroll (USA)
1988 Sandro Guerra (Italy)
1989 Sandro Guerra (Italy)
1990 Justin Bates (USA)

Most wins: (5), Karl-Heinz Losch (West Germany), 1958–9, 1961–2, 1966.

Recent winners (Women Combined)

1979 Petre Schneider (West Germany)
1980 Petre Schneider (West Germany)
1981 Petre Schneider (West Germany)
1982 Claudia Bruppacher (West Germany)
1983 Claudia Bruppacher (West Germany)
1984 Claudia Bruppacher (West Germany)
1985 Chiara Sartori (Italy)
1986 Chiara Sartori (Italy)

Roller Skating (cont.)

1987 Chiara Sartori (Italy)
1988 Rafaela De Vinaccio (Italy)
1989 Rafaela De Vinaccio (Italy)
1990 Rafaela De Vinaccio (Italy)

Most wins: (4), Astrid Bader (West Germany), 1965–8.

Recent winners (Pairs)

1979 Ray Chapatta/Karen Mejia (USA)
1980 Paul Price/Tina Kniesley (USA)
1981 Paul Price/Tina Kniesley (USA)
1982 Paul Price/Tina Kniesley (USA)
1983 John Arishita/Tammy Jeru (USA)
1984 John Arishita/Tammy Jeru (USA)
1985 John Arishita/Tammy Jeru (USA)
1986 John Arishita/Tammy Jeru (USA)
1987 Fabio Trevisani/Monica Mezzardi (Italy)
1988 Fabio Trevisani/Monica Mezzardi (Italy)
1989 David De Motte/Nicky Armstrong (USA)
1990 Larry McGrew/Tina Jerve (USA)

Most wins: (4), Dieter Fingerle (West Germany), 1959, 1965–7; John Arishita and Tammy Jeru (USA), as above.

Recent winners (Dance)

1979 Dan Littel/Florence Arsenault (USA)
1980 Torsten Carels/Gabriele Achenback (East Germany)
1981 Mark Howard/Cindy Smith (USA)
1982 Mark Howard/Cindy Smith (USA)
1983 David Golub/Angela Famiano (USA)
1984 David Golub/Angela Famiano (USA)
1985 Martin Hauss/Andrea Steudte (West Germany)
1986 Scott Myers/Anna Danks (USA)
1987 Rob Ferendo/Lori Walsh (USA)
1988 Peter Wulf/Michela Mitzlaf (West Germany)
1989 Greg Goody/Jodee Viola (USA)
1990 Greg Goody/Jodee Viola (USA)

Most wins: (3), Jane Puracchio (USA), 1973, 1975–6; Dan Littel and Florence Arsenault (USA), 1977–9.

ROWING

World Championships

First held for men in 1962 and for women in 1974; Olympic champions assume the role of world champion in Olympic years; principal events are the single sculls.

Recent winners Single Sculls (Men)

1979 Perrti Karppinen (Finland)
1980 Perrti Karppinen (Finland)
1981 Peter-Michael Kolbe (West Germany)
1982 Rudiger Reiche (East Germany)
1983 Peter-Michael Kolbe (West Germany)
1984 Perrti Karppinen (Finland)
1985 Perrti Karppinen (Finland)
1986 Peter-Michael Kolbe (West Germany)
1987 Thomas Lange (East Germany)
1988 Thomas Lange (East Germany)
1989 Thomas Lange (East Germany)
1990 Yuri Janson (USSR)

Most wins: (4), Peter-Michael Kolbe (West Germany), 1975, 1978, 1981, 1983; Perrti Karppinen (Finland), as above.

Recent winners Sculls (Women)

1979 Sanda Toma (Romania)
1980 Sanda Toma (Romania)
1981 Sanda Toma (Romania)
1982 Irina Fetissova (USSR)
1983 Jutta Hampe (East Germany)
1984 Valeria Racila (Romania)
1985 Cornelia Linse (East Germany)
1986 Jutta Hampe (East Germany)
1987 Magdelena Georgieva (Bulgaria)
1988 Jutta Behrendt (East Germany)
1989 Elisabeta Lipa (Romania)
1990 Brigit Peter (East Germany)

Most wins: (5), Christine Hahn (*née* Scheiblich) (East Germany), 1974–8.

The Boat Race

An annual contest between the crews from the Oxford and Cambridge University rowing clubs; first contested in 1829; the current course is from Putney to Mortlake.

Recent winners

1980 Oxford
1981 Oxford
1982 Oxford
1983 Oxford
1984 Oxford
1985 Oxford
1986 Cambridge
1987 Oxford
1988 Oxford
1989 Oxford
1990 Oxford
1991 Oxford

Rowing (cont.)

Wins: 69, Cambridge; 67, Oxford; 1 dead-heat (1877).

Diamond Sculls
Highlight of Henley Royal Regatta held every July; first contested in 1884.

Recent winners

1979 Hugh Matheson (Great Britain)
1980 Riccardo Ibarra (Argentina)
1981 Chris Baillieu (Great Britain)
1982 Chris Baillieu (Great Britain)
1983 Steve Redgrave (Great Britain)
1984 Chris Baillieu (Great Britain)
1985 Steve Redgrave (Great Britain)
1986 Bjarne Eltang (Denmark)
1987 Peter-Michael Kolbe (West Germany)
1988 Hamish McGlashan (Australia)
1989 Vaclav Chalupa (Czechoslovakia)
1990 Erik Verdonk (New Zealand)
1991 Wim van Belleghem (Belgium)

Most wins: (6), Stuart Mackenzie (Great Britain), 1957–62. Guy Nickalls (Great Britain), 1881–91, 1983–4.

RUGBY LEAGUE

Challenge Cup Final
First contested in 1897 and won by Batley; first final at Wembley Stadium in 1929.

Recent winners

1979 Widnes
1980 Hull Kingston Rovers
1981 Widnes
1982 Hull
1983 Featherstone Rovers
1984 Widnes
1985 Wigan
1986 Castleford
1987 Halifax
1988 Wigan
1989 Wigan
1990 Wigan
1991 Wigan

Most wins: (12), Wigan, 1924, 1929, 1948, 1951, 1958–59, 1965, 1985, 1988–91.

Premiership Trophy
End-of-season knockout competition involving the top eight teams in the first division; first contested at the end of the 1974–5 season.

Recent winners

1979 Leeds
1980 Widnes
1981 Hull Kingston Rovers
1982 Widnes
1983 Widnes
1984 Hull Kingston Rovers
1985 St Helens
1986 Warrington
1987 Wigan
1988 Widnes
1989 Widnes
1990 Widnes
1991 Hull

Most wins: (6), Widnes, as above.

Regal Trophy
A knockout competition, first held in 1971–2. Formerly known as the John Player Special Trophy, it adopted its current style in 1989–90.

Recent winners

1980 Bradford Northern
1981 Warrington
1982 Hull
1983 Wigan
1984 Leeds
1985 Hull Kingston Rovers
1986 Wigan
1987 Wigan
1988 St Helens
1989 Wigan
1990 Wigan
1991 Warrington

Most wins: (5), Wigan, as above.

RUGBY UNION

World Cup
The first Rugby Union World Cup was staged in 1987; New Zealand were crowned the first champions after beating France in the final.

International Championship
A round robin competition involving England, Ireland, Scotland, Wales and France; first contested in 1884.

Recent winners

1980 England

Rugby Union (cont.)

1981 France
1982 Ireland
1983 France and Ireland
1984 Scotland
1985 Ireland
1986 France and Scotland
1987 France
1988 France and Wales
1989 France
1990 Scotland
1991 England

Most outright wins: (21), Wales, 1893, 1900, 1902, 1905, 1908–9, 1911, 1922, 1931, 1936, 1950, 1952, 1956, 1965–6, 1969, 1971, 1975–6, 1978–9.

County Championship
First held in 1889.

Recent winners

1980 Lancashire
1981 Northumberland
1982 Lancashire
1983 Gloucestershire
1984 Gloucestershire
1985 Middlesex
1986 Warwickshire
1987 Yorkshire
1988 Lancashire
1989 Durham
1990 Lancashire
1991 Cornwall

Most wins. (15) Gloucestershire, 1910, 1913, 1920–2, 1930–2, 1937, 1972, 1974–6, 1983–4.

Pilkington Cup
An annual knockout competition for English Club sides; first held in the 1971–2 season. Known as the John Player Special Cup until 1988.

Recent winners

1980 Leicester
1981 Leicester
1982 Gloucester and Moseley (*shared*)
1983 Bristol
1984 Bath
1985 Bath
1986 Bath
1987 Bath
1988 Harlequins
1989 Bath
1990 Bath
1991 Harlequins

Most wins: (6), Bath, as above.

Schweppes Welsh Cup
The knockout tournament for Welsh clubs; first held in 1971–2.

Recent winners

1980 Bridgend
1981 Cardiff
1982 Cardiff
1983 Pontypool
1984 Cardiff
1985 Llanelli
1986 Cardiff
1987 Cardiff
1988 Llanelli
1989 Neath
1990 Neath
1991 Llanelli

Most wins: (7), Llanelli, 1973–6, 1985, 1988, 1991.

SHOOTING

Olympic Games
The Olympic competition is the highlight of the shooting calendar; winners in all categories since 1980 are given below.

Free Pistol (Men)

1980 Aleksander Melentyev (USSR)
1984 Xu Haifeng (China)
1988 Sorin Babil (Romania)

Rapid Fire Pistol (Men)

1980 Corneliu Ion (Romania)
1984 Takeo Kamachi (Japan)
1988 Afanasi Kouzmine (USSR)

Small Bore Rifle (Three Position) (Men)

1980 Viktor Vlasov (USSR)
1984 Malcolm Cooper (Great Britain)
1988 Malcolm Cooper (Great Britain)

Running Game Target (Men)

1980 Igor Sokolov (USSR)
1984 Li Yuwei (China)
1988 Tor Heiestad (Norway)

Trap (Men)

1980 Luciano Giovanetti (Italy)
1984 Luciano Giovanetti (Italy)
1988 Dmitri Monakov (USSR)

Skeet (Men)

1980 Hans Rasmussen (Denmark)

Shooting (cont.)

1984 Matthew Dryke (USA)
1988 Axel Wegner (East Germany)

Small Bore Rifle (Prone) (Men)

1980 Karoly Varga (Hungary)
1984 Edward Etzel (USA)
1988 Miroslav Varga (Czechoslovakia)

Air Rifle (Men)

1984 Philippe Heberle (France)
1988 Goran Maksimovic (Yugoslavia)

Air Pistol (Men)

1988 Tariou Kiriakov (USSR)

Sport Pistol (Women)

1984 Linda Thom (Canada)
1988 Nino Saloukvadze (USSR)

Air Rifle (Women)

1984 Pat Spurgin (USA)
1988 Irina Chilova (USSR)

Small Bore Rifle (Women)

1984 Wu Xiaoxuan (China)
1988 Silvia Sperber (West Germany)

Air Pistol (Women)

1988 Jasna Sekuric (Yugoslavia)

SKIING

World Cup
A season-long competition first organized in 1967; champions are declared in downhill, slalom, giant slalom and super-giant slalom, as well as the overall champion; points are obtained for performances in each category.

Recent overall winners (Men)

1980 Andreas Wenzel (Liechtenstein)
1981 Phil Mahre (USA)
1982 Phil Mahre (USA)
1983 Phil Mahre (USA)
1984 Pirmin Zurbriggen (Switzerland)
1985 Marc Girardelli (Luxembourg)
1986 Marc Girardelli (Luxembourg)
1987 Pirmin Zurbriggen (Switzerland)
1988 Pirmin Zurbriggen (Switzerland)
1989 Marc Girardelli (Luxembourg)
1990 Pirmin Zurbriggen (Switzerland)
1991 Marc Girardelli (Luxembourg)

Recent overall winners (Women)

1980 Hanni Wenzel (Liechtenstein)
1981 Marie-Therese Nadig (Switzerland)
1982 Erika Hess (Switzerland)
1983 Tamara McKinney (USA)
1984 Erika Hess (Switzerland)
1985 Michela Figini (Switzerland)
1986 Maria Walliser (Switzerland)
1987 Maria Walliser (Switzerland)
1988 Michela Figini (Switzerland)
1989 Vreni Schneider (Switzerland)
1990 Petra Kronberger (Austria)
1991 Petra Kronberger (Austria)

Most wins: Men (4), Gustavo Thoeni (Italy), 1971–3, 1975. Women (6), Annemarie Moser-Pröll (Austria), 1971–5, 1979.

SNOOKER

World Professional Championship
Instituted in the 1926–7 season; a knockout competition open to professional players who are members of the World Professional Billiards and Snooker Association; played at the Crucible Theatre, Sheffield.

Recent winners

1979 Terry Griffiths (Wales)
1980 Cliff Thorburn (Canada)
1981 Steve Davis (England)
1982 Alex Higgins (Ireland)
1983 Steve Davis (England)
1984 Steve Davis (England)
1985 Dennis Taylor (Ireland)
1986 Joe Johnson (England)
1987 Steve Davis (England)
1988 Steve Davis (England)
1989 Steve Davis (England)
1990 Stephen Hendry (Scotland)
1991 John Parrott (England)

Most wins: (15), Joe Davis (England), 1927–40, 1946.

World Doubles
First played in 1982.

Winners

1982 Steve Davis (England)
     Tony Meo (England)
1983 Steve Davis (England)
     Tony Meo (England)

Snooker (cont.)

1984 Alex Higgins (Ireland)
　　　Jimmy White (England)
1985 Steve Davis (England)
　　　Tony Meo (England)
1986 Steve Davis (England)
　　　Tony Meo (England)
1987 Mike Hallett (England)
　　　Stephen Hendry (Scotland)
Discontinued

Most wins: (4), Steve Davis and Tony Meo (England), as above.

World Team Championship
Also known as the World Cup; first held in 1979.

Winners

1979 Wales
1980 Wales
1981 England
1982 Canada
1983 England
1984 *not held*
1985 Ireland
1986 Ireland 'A'
1987 Ireland 'A'
1988 England
1989 England
1990 Canada

Most wins: (4), England, as above.

World Amateur Championship
First held in 1963; originally took place every two years, but annual since 1984.

Recent winners

1974 Ray Edmonds (England)
1976 Doug Mountjoy (Wales)
1978 Cliff Wilson (Wales)
1980 Jimmy White (England)
1982 Terry Parson (Wales)
1984 O. B. Agrawal (India)
1985 Paul Mifsud (Malta)
1986 Paul Mifsud (Malta)
1987 Darren, Morgan (Wales)
1988 James Wattana (Thailand)
1989 Ken Doherty (Republic of Ireland)
1990 Stephen O'Connor (Republic of Ireland)

Most wins: (2), Gary Owen (England), 1963, 1966;
　Ray Edmonds (England), 1972, 1974; Paul Mifsud,
　as above.

SOFTBALL

World Championships
First held for women in 1965 and for men the following year; now held every four years.

Winners (Men)

1966 USA
1968 USA
1972 Canada
1976 Canada, New Zealand & USA (*shared*)
1980 USA
1984 New Zealand
1988 USA

Most wins: (5), USA, as above.

Winners (Women)

1965 Australia
1970 Japan
1974 USA
1978 USA
1982 New Zealand
1986 USA
1990 USA

Most wins: (4), USA, as above.

SPEEDWAY

World Championships
Individual championships inaugurated in 1936; team championship instituted in 1960; first official pairs world championship in 1970.

Recent winners

1979 Ivan Mauger (New Zealand)
1980 Mike Lee (England)
1901 Bruce Penhall (USA)
1982 Bruce Penhall (USA)
1983 Egon Muller (West Germany)
1984 Erik Gundersen (Denmark)
1985 Erik Gundersen (Denmark)
1986 Hans Nielsen (Denmark)
1987 Hans Nielsen (Denmark)
1988 Erik Gundersen (Denmark)
1989 Hans Nielsen (Denmark)
1990 Per Jonsson (Sweden)

Most wins: (6), Ivan Mauger (New Zealand), 1968–70, 1972, 1977, 1979.

Recent winners (Pairs)

1979 Ole Olsen/Hans Nielsen (Denmark)

Speedway (cont.)

1980 Dave Jessup/Peter Collins (England)
1981 Bruce Penhall/Bobby Schwartz (USA)
1982 Dennis Sigalos/Bobby Schwartz (USA)
1983 Kenny Carter/Peter Collins (England)
1984 Peter Collins/Chris Morton (England)
1985 Erik Gunderson/Tommy Knudsen
      (Denmark)
1986 Erik Gundersen/Hans Nielsen
      (Denmark)
1987 Erik Gundersen/Hans Nielsen
      (Denmark)
1988 Erik Gundersen/Hans Nielsen
      (Denmark)
1989 Erik Gundersen/Hans Nielsen
      (Denmark)
1990 Hans Nielsen/Jan Pedersen
      (Denmark)
1991 Hans Nielsen/Jan Pedersen/Tommy Knudsen
      (Denmark)

Most wins: (5), Erik Gundersen, Hans Nielsen, as above.

Recent winners (Team)

1979 New Zealand
1980 England
1981 Denmark
1982 USA
1983 Denmark
1984 Denmark
1985 Denmark
1986 Denmark
1987 Denmark
1988 Denmark
1989 England
1990 USA

Most wins: (9), Great Britain/England, 1968, 1971–5, 1977, 1980, 1989.

SQUASH

World Open Championship
First held in 1976; takes place annually for men, every two years for women.

Winners (Men)

1979 Geoff Hunt (Australia)
1980 Geoff Hunt (Australia)
1981 Jahangir Khan (Pakistan)
1982 Jahangir Khan (Pakistan)
1983 Jahangir Khan (Pakistan)
1984 Jahangir Khan (Pakistan)
1985 Jahangir Khan (Pakistan)
1986 Ross Norman (New Zealand)
1987 Jansher Khan (Pakistan)

1988 Jahangir Khan (Pakistan)
1989 Jansher Khan (Pakistan)
1990 Jansher Khan (Pakistan)
1991 Rodney Martin (Australia)

Most wins: (6), Jahangir Khan (Pakistan), as above.

Winners (Women)

1976 Heather McKay (Australia)
1979 Heather McKay (Australia)
1981 Rhonda Thorne (Australia)
1983 Vicky Cardwell (Australia)
1985 Sue Devoy (New Zealand)
1987 Sue Devoy (New Zealand)
1989 Martine Le Moignan (Great Britain)
1990 Sue Devoy (New Zealand)

Most wins: (2), Heather McKay (Australia), as above; Sue Devoy (New Zealand), as above.

SURFING

World Professional Championship
A season-long series of Grand Prix events; first held in 1970.

Recent winners (Men)

1979 Mark Richards (Australia)
1980 Mark Richards (Australia)
1981 Mark Richards (Australia)
1982 *Season changed to encompass 1982–3*
1983 Mark Richards (Australia)
1984 Tom Carroll (Australia)
1985 Tom Carroll (Australia)
1986 Tommy Curren (USA)
1987 Damien Hardman (Australia)
1988 Barton Lynch (Australia)
1989 Martin Potter (Great Britain)
1990 Heifara Tahutini (Tahiti)

Recent winners (Women)

1979 Margo Oberg (Hawaii)
1980 Lyne Boyer (Hawaii)
1981 Margo Oberg (Hawaii)
1982 *not held*
1983 Margo Oberg (Hawaii)
1984 Kim Mearig (USA)
1985 Frieda Zamba (USA)
1986 Frieda Zamba (USA)
1987 Wendy Botha (South Africa)
1988 Freida Zamba (USA)
1989 Wendy Botha (South Africa)
1990 Kathy Newman (Australia)

Most wins: Men (5), Mark Richards (Australia), 1975, 1979–83. Women (3), Margo Oberg (Hawaii), Freida Zamba (USA), as above.

SWIMMING AND DIVING

World Championships
First held in 1973 and again in 1975; since 1978 take place every four years; 1990 championships postponed; the complete list of 1991 champions is given below.

1986 World Champions (Men)

50 metres	Tom Jager
freestyle	(USA)
100 metres	Matt Biondi
freestyle	(USA)
200 metres	Georgio Lamberti
freestyle	(Italy)
400 metres	Joerg Hoffman
freestyle	(Germany)
1500 metres	Joerg Hoffman
freestyle	(Germany)
100 metres	Jeff Rouse
backstroke	(USA)
200 metres	Martin Lopez Zubero
backstroke	(Spain)
100 metres	Norbert Rozsa
breaststroke	(Hungary)
200 metres	Mike Barrowman
breaststroke	(USA)
100 metres	Anthony Nesty
butterfly	(Suriname)
200 metres	Melvin Stewart
butterfly	(USA)
200 metres	Tamas Darnyi
individual medley	(Hungary)
400 metres	Tamas Darnyi
Individual medley	(Hungary)
4 × 100 metres	USA
freestyle medley	
4 × 200 metres	East Germany
freestyle medley	
4 × 100 metres	USA
medley relay	
Springboard	Edwin Jongejans
diving	(Holland)
Highboard	Shuwei Sun
diving	(China)

1991 World Champions (Women)

50 metres	Yong Zhuang
freestyle	(China)
100 metres	Nicole Haislett
freestyle	(USA)
200 metres	Hayley Lewis
freestyle	(Australia)
400 metres	Janet Evans
freestyle	(USA)
800 metres	Janet Evans
freestyle	(USA)
100 metres	Kriszrina Egerszegi
backstroke	(Hungary)
200 metres	Kriszrina Egerszegi
backstroke	(Hungary)
100 metres	Linley Frame
breaststroke	(Australia)
200 metres	Elena Volkova
breaststroke	(USSR)
100 metres	Hong Qian
butterfly	(China)
200 metres	Summer Sanders
butterfly	(USA)
200 metres	Li Lin
individual medley	(China)
400 metres	Li Lin
individual medley	(China)
4 × 100 metres	USA
freestyle relay	
4 × 200 metres	Germany
freestyle relay	
4 × 100 metres	USA
medley relay	
Springboard	Min Gao
diving	(China)
Highboard	Mingxia Fu
diving	(China)
Synchronized swimming	
Solo	Sylvie Frechette
	(Canada)
Duet	USA
Team	USA

TABLE TENNIS

World Championships
First held in 1926 and every two years since 1957.

Recent winners
Swaythling Cup (Men's Team)

1969	Japan
1971	China
1973	Sweden
1975	China
1977	China
1979	Hungary
1981	China
1983	China
1985	China

Table Tennis (cont.)

1987	China
1989	Sweden
1991	Sweden

Recent winners
Corbillon Cup (Women's Team)

1969	USSR
1971	Japan
1973	South Korea
1975	China
1977	China
1979	China
1981	China
1983	China
1985	China
1987	China
1989	China
1991	United Korea

Most wins: Swaythling Cup (12), Hungary, 1926, 1928–31, 1933 (twice), 1935, 1938, 1949, 1952, 1979. Corbillon Cup (9), China, 1965, 1975, 1977, 1979, 1981, 1983, 1985, 1987, 1989.

Recent winners
Men's Singles

1969	Shigeo Ito (Japan)
1971	Stellan Bengtsson (Sweden)
1973	Hsi En-Ting (China)
1975	Istvan Jonyer (Hungary)
1977	Mitsuru Kohno (Japan)
1979	Seiji Ono (Japan)
1981	Guo Yuehua (China)
1983	Guo Yuehua (China)
1985	Jiang Jialiang (China)
1987	Jiang Jialiang (China)
1989	Jan-Ove Waldner (Sweden)
1991	Jorgen Persson (Sweden)

Most wins: (5), Viktor Barna (Hungary), 1930, 1932–5.

Recent winners
Women's singles

1969	Toshiko Kowada (Japan)
1971	Lin Hui-Ching (China)
1973	Hu Yu-Lan (China)
1975	Pak Yung-Sun (North Korea)
1977	Pak Yung-Sun (North Korea)
1979	Ge Xinai (China)
1981	Ting Ling (China)
1983	Cao Yanhua (China)
1985	Cao Yanhua (China)
1987	He Zhili (China)
1989	Qiao Hong (China)

1991	Deng Yaping (China)

Most wins: (6), Angelica Rozeanu (Romania), 1950–55.

Recent winners
Men's Doubles

1969	Hans Alser/Kjell Johansson (Sweden)
1971	Istvan Jonyer/Tiber Klampar (Hungary)
1973	Stellan Bengtsson/Kjell Johansson (Sweden)
1975	Gabor Gergely/Istvan Jonyer (Hungary)
1977	Li Zhenshi/Liang Geliang (China)
1979	Dragutin Surbek/Anton Stipancic (Yugoslavia)
1981	Cai Zhenhua/Li Zhenshi (China)
1983	Dragutin Surbek/Zoran Kalinic (Yugoslavia)
1985	Mikael Applegren/Ulf Carlsson (Sweden)
1987	Chen Longcan/Wei Quinguang (China)
1989	Jaerg Rosskopf/Stefen Fetzner (West Germany)
1991	Peter Karlsson/Tomas von Scheele (Sweden)

Most wins: (8), Viktor Barna (Hungary/England), 1929–33 (won two titles 1933), 1935, 1939.

Recent winners
Women's Doubles

1969	Svetlana Grinberg/Zoya Rudnova (USSR)
1971	Cheng Min-Chih/Lin Hui-Ching (China)
1973	Maria Alexandru (Romania)/Miho Hamada (Japan)
1975	Maria Alexandru (Romania)/ Shoko Takashima (Japan)
1977	Pak Yong Ok (North Korea)/Yang Yin (China)
1979	Zhang Li/Zhang Deying (China)
1981	Zhang Deying/Cao Yanhua (China)
1983	Shen Jianping/Dai Lili (China)
1985	Dai Lili/Geng Lijuan (China)
1987	Yang Young-Ja/Hyun Jung-Hwa (Korea)
1989	Quio Hong/Deng Yaping (China)
1991	Chen Zhie/Liu Wei (China)

Most wins: (7), Maria Mednyanszky (Hungary), 1928, 1930–5.

Table Tennis (cont.)

Recent winners
Mixed Doubles

1969 Nobuhiko Hasegawa/Yasuka Konno
     (Japan)
1971 Chang Shih-Ling/Lin Hui-Ching (China)
1973 Liang Geliang/Li Li (China)
1975 Stanislav Gomozkov/Anna Ferdman (USSR)
1977 Jacques Secretin/Claude Bergeret (France)
1979 Liang Geliang/Ge Xinai (China)
1981 Xie Saike/Huang Junqun (China)
1983 Guo Yuehua/Ni Xialian (China)
1985 Cai Zhenua/Cao Yanhua (China)
1987 Hui Jun/Geng Lijuan (China)
1989 Yoo Nam-Kyu/Hyun Jung-Hwa (South Korea)
1991 Wang Tao/Liu Wei (China)

Most wins: (6), Maria Mednyanszky (Hungary),
1927–8, 1930–1, 1933 (two titles).

TENNIS (LAWN)

Wimbledon Championships
The All-England Championships at Wimbledon are
Lawn Tennis's most prestigious championships; first
held in 1877.

Recent winners
Men's Singles

1979 Bjorn Borg (Sweden)
1980 Bjorn Borg (Sweden)
1981 John McEnroe (USA)
1982 Jimmy Connors (USA)
1983 John McEnroe (USA)
1984 John McEnroe (USA)
1985 Boris Becker (West Germany)
1986 Boris Becker (West Germany)
1987 Pat Cash (Australia)
1988 Stefan Edberg (Sweden)
1989 Boris Becker (West Germany)
1990 Stefan Edberg (Sweden)
1991 Michael Stich (Germany)

Most wins: (7), William Renshaw (Great Britain),
1881–6, 1889.

Recent winners
Women's Singles

1979 Martina Navratilova (Czechoslovakia)
1980 Evonne Goolagong-Cawley (Australia)
1981 Chris Evert-Lloyd (USA)
1982 Martina Navratilova (USA)

1983 Martina Navratilova (USA)
1984 Martina Navratilova (USA)
1985 Martina Navratilova (USA)
1986 Martina Navratilova (USA)
1987 Martina Navratilova (USA)
1988 Steffi Graf (West Germany)
1989 Steffi Graf (West Germany)
1990 Martina Navratilova (USA)
1991 Steffi Graf (Germany)

Most wins: (9), Martina Navratilova (Czechoslovaki-
a/USA), as above plus 1978.

Recent winners
Men's Doubles

1979 Peter Fleming/John McEnroe (USA)
1980 Peter McNamara/Paul McNamee (Australia)
1981 Peter Fleming/John McEnroe (USA)
1982 Peter McNamara/Paul McNamee (Australia)
1983 Peter Fleming/John McEnroe (USA)
1984 Peter Fleming/John McEnroe (USA)
1985 Heinz Gunthardt (Switzerland)/Balazs
     Taroczy (Hungary)
1986 Joakim Nystrom/Mats Wilander (Sweden)
1987 Ken Flach/Robert Seguso (USA)
1988 Ken Flach/Robert Seguso (USA)
1989 John Fitzgerald (Australia)/Anders Jarryd
     (Sweden)
1990 Rick Leach/Jim Pugh (USA)
1991 John Fitzgerald (Australia)/Anders Jarryd
     (Sweden)

Most wins: (8), Lawrence Doherty/Reg Doherty
(Great Britain), 1897–1901, 1903–5.

Recent winners
Women's Doubles

1979 Billie Jean King (USA)/Martina
     Navratilova (Czechoslovakia)
1980 Kathy Jordan/Anne Smith (USA)
1981 Martina Navratilova/Pam Shriver (USA)
1982 Martina Navratilova/Pam Shriver (USA)
1983 Martina Navratilova/Pam Shriver (USA)
1984 Martina Navratilova/Pam Shriver (USA)
1985 Kathy Jordan/Elizabeth Smylie (Aus)
1986 Martina Navratilova/Pam Shriver (USA)
1987 Claudia Kohde-Kilsch (West Germany)/
     Helena Sukova (Czechoslovakia)
1988 Steffi Graf (West Germany)/Gabriela
     Sabatini (Argentina)
1989 Jana Novotna/Helena Sukova
     (Czechoslovakia)
1990 Jana Novotna/Helena Sukova
     (Czechoslovakia)
1991 Natalya Zvereva/Larissa Savchenko (USSR)

Most wins: (12), Elizabeth Ryan (USA), 1914,
1919–23, 1925–7, 1930, 1933–4.

Tennis (Lawn) (cont.)

Recent winners
Mixed Doubles

1979 Greer Stevens/Bob Hewitt (South Africa)
1980 Tracy Austin/John Austin (USA)
1981 Betty Stove (Holland)/Frew McMillan
      (South Africa)
1982 Anne Smith (USA)/Kevin Curren
      (South Africa)
1983 Wendy Turnbull (Australia)/John Lloyd
      (Great Britain)
1984 Wendy Turnbull (Australia)/John Lloyd
      (Great Britain)
1985 Martina Navratilova (USA)
      Paul McNamee (Australia)
1986 Kathy Jordan/Ken Flach (USA)
1987 Jo Durie/Jeremy Bates (Great Britain)
1988 Sherwood Stewart/Zina Garrison (USA)
1989 Jim Pugh (USA)/Jan Novotna
      (Czechoslovakia)
1990 Rick Leach/Zina Garrison (USA)
1991 John Fitzgerald/Elizabeth Smylie
      (Australia)

Most wins: (7), Elizabeth Ryan (USA), 1919, 1921,
1923, 1927–8, 1930, 1932.

United States Open
First held in 1891 as the United States Championship; became the United States Open in 1968.

Recent winners
Men's Singles

1979 John McEnroe (USA)
1980 John McEnroe (USA)
1981 John McEnroe (USA)
1982 Jimmy Connors (USA)
1983 Jimmy Connors (USA)
1984 John McEnroe (USA)
1985 Ivan Lendl (Czechoslovakia)
1986 Ivan Lendl (Czechoslovakia)
1987 Ivan Lendl (Czechoslovakia)
1988 Mats Wilander (Sweden)
1989 Boris Becker (West Germany)
1990 Pete Sampras (USA)

Recent winners
Women's Singles

1979 Tracy Austin (USA)
1980 Chris Evert-Lloyd (USA)
1981 Tracy Austin (USA)
1982 Chris Evert-Lloyd (USA)
1983 Martina Navratilova (USA)
1984 Martina Navratilova (USA)
1985 Hana Mandlikova (Czechoslovakia)
1986 Martina Navratilova (USA)
1987 Martina Navratilova (USA)

1988 Steffi Graf (West Germany)
1989 Steffi Graf (West Germany)
1990 Gabriela Sabatini (Argentina)

Most wins: Men (7), Richard Sears (USA), 1881–7;
Bill Larned (USA), 1901–2, 1907–11; Bill Tilden
(USA), 1920–5, 1929. Women (7), Molla Mallory
(*née* Bjurstedt) (USA), 1915–16, 1918, 1920–2,
1926; Helen Wills-Moody (USA), 1923–5, 1927–9,
1931.

Davis Cup
International team competition organized on a
knockout basis; first held in 1900; contested on a
challenge basis until 1972.

Recent winners

1979 USA
1980 Czechoslovakia
1981 USA
1982 USA
1983 Australia
1984 Sweden
1985 Sweden
1986 Australia
1987 Sweden
1988 West Germany
1989 West Germany
1990 USA

Most wins: (29), USA, 1900, 1902, 1913, 1920–6,
1937–8, 1946–9, 1954, 1958, 1963, 1968–72,
1978–9, 1981–2, 1990.

TENPIN BOWLING

World Championships
First held in 1923 by the International Bowling
Association; since 1954 organized by the Fédération
Internationale des Quillieurs (FIQ); since 1963, when
women first competed, held every four years.

Recent winners
Individual (Men)

1954 Göska Algeskog (Sweden)
1955 Nils Bäckström (Sweden)
1958 Kaarlo Asukas (Finland)
1960 Tito Reynolds (Mexico)
1963 Les Zikes (USA)
1967 David Pond (Great Britain)
1971 Ed Luther (USA)
1975 Bud Staudt (USA)
1979 Ollie Ongtawco (Philippines)
1983 Armando Marino (Colombia)
1987 Rolland Patrick (France)

Tenpin Bowling (cont.)

Recent winners
Individual (Women)

1963 Helen Shablis (USA)
1967 Helen Weston (USA)
1971 Ashie Gonzales (Puerto Rico)
1975 Annedore Haefker (West Germany)
1979 Lita de la Roas (Philippines)
1983 Lena Sulkanen (Sweden)
1987 Edda Piccini (Italy)

Most wins: No one has won more than one title.

TRAMPOLINING

World Championships
First held in 1964 and annually until 1968; since then, every two years.

Recent winners
Individual (Men)

1970 Wayne Miller (USA)
1972 Paul Luxon (Great Britain)
1974 Richard Tison (France)
1976 Richard Tison (France)/Yevgeni Yanes
       (USSR) (*shared*)
1978 Yevgeni Yanes (USSR)
1980 Stewart Matthews (Great Britain)
1982 Carl Furrer (Great Britain)
1984 Lionel Pioline (France)
1986 Lionel Pioline (France)
1988 Vadim Krasnoshapka (USSR)
1990 Alexandr Moskalenko (USSR)

Most wins: (2), David Jacobs (USA), 1967–8; Wayne Miller (USA), 1966, 1970; Richard Tison (France) as above; Yevgeni Yanes (USSR) as above; Lionel Pioline (France) as above.

Recent winners
Individual (Women)

1970 Renee Ransom (USA)
1972 Alexandra Nicholson (USA)
1974 Alexandra Nicholson (USA)
1976 Svetlana Levina (USSR)
1978 Tatyana Anisimova (USSR)
1980 Ruth Keller (Switzerland)
1982 Ruth Keller (Switzerland)
1984 Sue Shotton (Great Britain)
1986 Tatyana Lushina (USSR)
1988 Khoperia Roussoudan (USSR)
1990 Elena Merkulova (USSR)

Most wins: (5), Judy Wills (USA), 1964–8.

TUG OF WAR

World Championships
Instituted in 1975, held yearly apart from 1979–84; contested at 560 kg from 1982.

Winners

	720 kg	640 kg	560 kg
1975	England	England	—
1976	England	England	—
1977	England	Wales	—
1978	England	England	—
1980	England	England	—
1982	England	Ireland	Switzerland
1984	Ireland	Ireland	England
1985	Switzerland	Switzerland	Switzerland
1986	Ireland	Ireland	England
1988	Republic of Ireland	England	England
1990	Republic of Ireland	Republic of Ireland	Switzerland
			Catchweight
			1984 England

Most titles: (16), England, as above.

VOLLEYBALL

World Championships
Inaugurated in 1949; first women's championships in 1952; now held every four years, but Olympic champions are also world champions in Olympic years.

Recent winners (Men)

1970 East Germany
1972 Japan
1974 Poland
1976 Poland
1978 USSR
1980 USSR
1982 USSR
1984 USA
1986 USA
1988 USA
1990 Italy

Recent winners (Women)

1970 USSR
1972 USSR
1974 Japan
1976 Japan
1978 Cuba
1980 USSR
1982 China

Volleyball (cont.)

1984 China
1986 China
1988 USSR

Most wins: Men (9), USSR, 1949, 1952, 1960, 1962, 1964, 1968, 1978, 1980, 1982. Women (8), USSR, 1952, 1956, 1960, 1968, 1970, 1972, 1980, 1988.

WALKING

Lugano Trophy
The principal Road Walking trophy; contested every two years by men's national teams; first held in 1961.

Recent winners

1970 East Germany
1973 East Germany
1975 USSR
1977 Mexico
1979 Mexico
1981 Italy
1983 USSR
1985 East Germany
1987 USSR
1989 USSR

Most wins: (5), East Germany, 1965, 1967, 1970, 1973, 1985.

Eschborn Cup
The women's equivalent of the Lugano Trophy; first held in 1979; takes place every two years.

Winners

1979 Great Britain
1981 USSR
1983 China
1985 China
1987 USSR
1989 USSR

Most wins: (3), USSR, as above.

WATER POLO

World Championship
First held in 1973, and every four years since 1978; included in the World Swimming Championships; first women's event in 1986.

Winners (Men)

1973 Hungary

1975 USSR
1978 Italy
1982 USSR
1986 Yugoslavia
1990 Italy

Winners (Women)

1986 Australia
1990 USSR

Most wins: Men (2), USSR, Italy, as above.

World Cup
Inaugurated in 1979 and held every two years.

Winners

1979 Hungary
1981 USSR
1983 USSR
1985 West Germany
1987 Yugoslavia
1989 Yugoslavia

Most wins: (2), USSR, Yugoslavia, as above.

WATER SKIING

World Championships
First held in 1949; take place every two years; competitions for Slalom, Tricks, Jumps, and the Overall Individual title.

Recent winners
Overall (Men)

1969 Mike Suyderhoud (USA)
1971 George Athans (Canada)
1973 George Athans (Canada)
1975 Carlos Suarez (Venezuela)
1977 Mike Hazelwood (Great Britain)
1979 Joel McClintock (Canada)
1981 Sammy Duvall (USA)
1983 Sammy Duvall (USA)
1985 Sammy Duvall (USA)
1987 Sammy Duvall (USA)
1989 Patrice Martin (France)

Most wins: (4), Sammy Duvall (USA), as above.

Recent winners
Overall (Women)

1969 Liz Allen (USA)
1971 Christy Weir (USA)
1973 Lisa St John (USA)
1975 Liz Allan-Shetter (USA)
1977 Cindy Todd (USA)

Water Skiing (cont.)

1979 Cindy Todd (USA)
1981 Karin Roberge (USA)
1983 Ana-Maria Carrasco (Venezuela)
1985 Karen Neville (Australia)
1987 Deena Brush (USA)
1989 Deena Mapple (née Brush) (USA)

Most wins: (3), Willa McGuire (*née* Worthington) (USA), 1949–50, 1955; Liz Allan-Shetter (USA), 1965 and as above.

WEIGHTLIFTING

World Championships
First held in 1898; 11 weight divisions; the most prestigious is the 110 kg-plus category (formerly known as Super Heavyweight); Olympic champions are automatically world champions in Olympic years.

Recent champions (110 kg)

1979 Sultan Rakhmanov (USSR)
1980 Sultan Rakhmanov (USSR)
1981 Anatoliy Pisarenko (USSR)
1982 Anatoliy Pisarenko (USSR)
1983 Anatoliy Pisarenko (USSR)
1984 Dean Lukin (Australia)
1985 Antonio Krastev (Bulgaria)
1986 Antonio Krastev (Bulgaria)
1987 Aleksander Kurlovich (USSR)
1988 Aleksander Kurlorich (USSR)
1989 Stefan Botev (Bulgaria)
1990 Stefan Botev (Bulgaria)

Most titles (all categories): (8), John Davies (USA), 82.5 kg 1938; 82.5 + kg 1946–50; 90 + kg 1951–2; Tommy Kono (USA), 67.5 kg 1952; 75 kg 1953, 1957–9; 82.5 kg 1954–6; Vasiliy Alexseyev (USSR), 110 + kg 1970–7.

WRESTLING

World Championships
Graeco-Roman world championships first held in 1921; first freestyle championships in 1951; each style contests 10 weight divisions, the heaviest being the 130 kg (formerly over 100 kg) category; Olympic champions become world champions in Olympic years.

Recent winners (Super-heavyweight/over 100 kg)
Freestyle

1979 Salman Khasimikov (USSR)
1980 Soslan Andiyev (USSR)
1981 Salman Khasimikov (USSR)
1982 Salman Khasimikov (USSR)
1983 Salman Khasimikov (USSR)
1984 Bruce Baumgartner (USA)
1985 David Gobedichviliy (USSR)
1986 Bruce Baumgartner (USA)
1987 Khadartsv Aslam (USSR)
1988 David Gobedzhishvilli (USSR)
1989 Ali Reiza Soleimani (Iran)
1990 David Gobedzhisvilli (USSR)

Graeco-Roman

1979 Aleksander Tomov (USSR)
1980 Aleksander Kolchinsky (USSR)
1981 Refik Memisevic (Yugoslavia)
1982 Nikolai Denev (Bulgaria)
1983 Jevgeniy Artiochin (USSR)
1984 Jeffrey Blatnick (USA)
1985 Igor Rostozotskiy (USSR)
1986 Thomas Johansson (Sweden)
1987 Igor Rostozotskiy (USSR)
1988 Alexsander Karoline (USSR)
1989 Alexsander Karoline (USSR)
1990 Alexsander Karoline (USSR)

Most titles (all weight divisions): Freestyle (10), Aleksander Medved (USSR), 90 kg 1962–4, 1966; 100 kg 1967–8, Over 100 kg 1969–72. Greco-Roman (7), Nikolai Balboshin (USSR), 100 kg 1973–4, 1976, 1978–9; Over 100 kg 1971, 1977; Valeriy Rezantsev (USSR), 90 kg 1970–6.

YACHTING

America's Cup
One of sport's famous trophies; first won by the schooner Magic in 1870; now held approximately every four years, when challengers compete in a series of races to find which of them races against the holder; all 25 winners up to 1983 were from the United States.

Post-war winners

	Winning Yacht (Skipper)
1958	Columbia (USA) (Briggs Cunningham)
1962	Weatherly (USA) (Emil Mosbacher)
1964	Constellation (USA) (Bob Bavier)

Yachting (cont.)

1967 Intrepid (USA) (Emil Mosbacher)
1970 Intrepid (USA) (Bill Ficker)
1974 Courageous (USA) (Ted Hood)
1977 Courageous (USA) (Ted Turner)
1980 Freedom (USA) (Dennis Conner)
1983 Australia II (Australia)
        (John Bertrand)
1987 Stars & Stripes (USA) (Dennis Conner)
1988 Stars & Stripes (Dennis Conner)*

*Stars and Stripes (USA) skippered by Dennis Conner won a special challenge match but on appeal the race was awarded to the New Zealand boat. However the decision was reversed by the New York Appeals court in 1989.

Most wins: (Skipper) (3), Charlie Barr (USA), 1899, 1901, 1903; Harold Vanderbilt (USA), 1930, 1934, 1937; Dennis Conner, as above.

Admiral's Cup

A two-yearly series of races in the English Channel, around Fastnet rock and at Cowes; four national teams of three boats per team; first held in 1957.

Recent winners

1969 USA
1971 Great Britain
1973 West Germany
1975 Great Britain
1977 Great Britain
1979 Australia
1981 Great Britain
1983 West Germany
1985 West Germany
1987 New Zealand
1989 Great Britain

Most wins: (9), Great Britain, 1957, 1959, 1963, 1965, 1971, 1975, 1977, 1981, 1989.

THOUGHT AND BELIEF

GREEK GODS OF MYTHOLOGY

Adonis   God of vegetation and re-birth
Aeolus   God of the winds
Alphito   Barley goddess of Argos
Aphrodite   Goddess of love and beauty
Apollo   God of prophecy, music, youth, archery and healing
Ares   God of war
Arethusa   Goddess of springs and fountains
Artemis   Goddess of fertility
Asclepius   God of healing
Athene   Goddess of prudence and wise council; protectress of Athens
Atlas   A Titan who bears up the earth
Attis   God of vegetation
Boreas   God of the north wind
Cronus   Father of Zeus
Cybele   Goddess of the earth
Demeter   Goddess of the harvest
Dionysus   God of wine and vegetation
Eos   Goddess of the dawn
Eros   God of love
Gaia   Goddess of the earth
Ganymede   God of rain
Hades   God of the underworld

Hebe   Goddess of youth
Hecate   Goddess of the moon
Helios   God of the sun
Hephaestus   God of fire
Hera   Goddess of marriage and childbirth; queen of heaven
Hermes   Messenger god
Hestia   Goddess of the hearth
Hypnos   God of sleep
Iris   Goddess of the rainbow
Morpheus   God of dreams
Nemesis   God of destiny
Nereus   God of the sea
Nike   Goddess of victory
Oceanus   God of the river Oceanus
Pan   God of male sexuality and of herds
Persephone   Goddess of the underworld and of corn
Poseidon   God of the sea
Rhea   The original mother goddess; wife of Cronus
Selene   Goddess of the moon
Thanatos   God of death
Zeus   Overlord of the Olympian gods and goddesses; god of the sky and all its properties

ROMAN GODS OF MYTHOLOGY

Apollo   God of the sun
Bacchus   God of wine and ecstasy
Bellona   Goddess of wine
Ceres   Goddess of corn
Consus   God of seed sowing
Cupid   God of love
Diana   Goddess of fertility and hunting
Egreria   Goddess of fountains and childbirth
Epona   Goddess of horses
Fauna   Goddess of fertility
Faunus   God of crops and herds
Feronia   Goddess of spring flowers
Fides   God of honesty
Flora   Goddess of fruitfulness and flowers
Fortuna   Goddess of chance and fate
Genius   Protective god of individuals, groups and the state

Janus   God of entrances, travel, the dawn
Juno   Goddess of marriage, childbirth, light
Jupiter   God of the sky and its attributes (sun, moon, thunder, rain, etc)
Lares   Gods of the house
Liber Pater   God of agricultural and human fertility
Libitina   Goddess of funeral rites
Maia   Goddess of fertility
Mars   God of war
Mercury   Messenger god; also god of merchants
Minerva   Goddess of war, craftsmen, education and the arts
Mithras   The sun god; god of regeneration
Neptune   God of the sea
Ops   Goddess of the harvest
Orcus   God of death

ROMAN GODS OF MYTHOLOGY (cont.)

Pales Goddess of flocks
Penates Gods of food and drink
Picus God of woods
Pluto God of the underworld
Pomona Goddess of fruit trees
Portunus God of husbands
Prosperina Goddess of the underworld
Rumina Goddess of nursing mothers

Saturn God of fertility and agriculture
Silvanus God of trees and forests
Venus Goddess of spring, gardens and love
Vertumnus God of fertility
Vesta Goddess of the hearth
Victoria Goddess of victory
Vulcan God of fire

NORSE GODS OF MYTHOLOGY

Aegir God of the sea
Aesir Race of warlike gods, including Odin, Thor, Tyr
Alcis Twin gods of the sky
Balder Son of Odin and favourite of the gods
Bor Father of Odin
Bragi God of poetry
Fafnir Dragon god
Fjorgynn Mother of Thor
Freyja Goddess of libido
Frey God of fertility
Frigg Goddess of fertility; wife of Odin
Gefion Goddess who received virgins after death
Heimdall Guardian of the bridge Bifrost
Hel Goddess of death; Queen of Niflheim, the land of mists
Hermod Son of Odin
Hoenir Companion to Odin and Loki
Hoder Blind god who killed Baldur
Idunn Guardian goddess of the golden apples of youth; wife of Bragi
Kvasir God of wise utterances
Logi Fire god

Loki God of mischief
Mimir God of wisdom
Nanna Goddess wife of Balder
Nehallenia Goddess of plenty
Nerthus Goddess of earth
Njord God of ships and the sea
Norns Goddesses of destiny
Odin (Woden, Wotan) Chief of the Aesir family of gods, the 'father' god; the god of battle, death, inspiration
Otr Otter god
Ran Goddess of the sea
Sif Goddess wife of Thor
Sigyn Goddess wife of Loki
Thor (Donar) God of thunder and sky; good crops
Tyr God of battle
Ull Stepson of Thor, an enchanter
Valkyries Female helpers of the gods of war
Vanir Race of benevolent gods, including Njörd, Frey, Freyja
Vidar Slayer of the wolf, Fenvir
Weland (Volundr, Weiland, Wayland) Craftsman god

EGYPTIAN GODS

Amun-Re Universal god
Anubis God of funerals
Apis God of fertility
Aten Unique god
Geb God of the earth
Hathor Goddess of love
Horus God of light
Isis Goddess of magic
Khnum Goddess of creation

Khonsou Son of Amun-Re
Maat Goddess of sterility
Nephthys Goddess of funerals
Nut God of the sky
Osiris God of vegetation
Ptah God of creation
Sekmet Goddess of might
Set God of evil
Thoth Supreme scribe

RELIGIOUS SYMBOLS

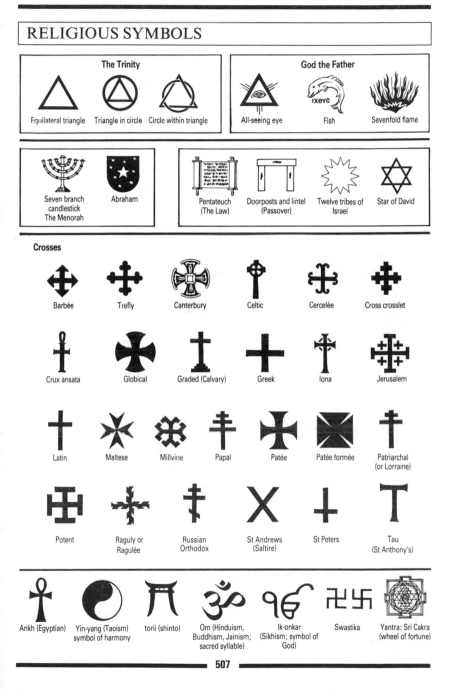

The Trinity

Equilateral triangle   Triangle in circle   Circle within triangle

God the Father

All-seeing eye   Fish   Sevenfold flame

Seven branch candlestick The Menorah   Abraham

Pentateuch (The Law)   Doorposts and lintel (Passover)   Twelve tribes of Israel   Star of David

Crosses

Barbée   Trefly   Canterbury   Celtic   Cercelée   Cross crosslet

Crux ansata   Globical   Graded (Calvary)   Greek   Iona   Jerusalem

Latin   Maltese   Millvine   Papal   Patée   Patée formée   Patriarchal (or Lorraine)

Potent   Raguly or Ragulée   Russian Orthodox   St Andrews (Saltire)   St Peters   Tau (St Anthony's)

Ankh (Egyptian)   Yin-yang (Taoism) symbol of harmony   torii (shinto)   Om (Hinduism, Buddhism, Jainism; sacred syllable)   Ik-onkar (Sikhism; symbol of God)   Swastika   Yantra: Sri Cakra (wheel of fortune)

BAHA'ISM

Founded 1863 in Persia.
Founder Mirza Husayn Ali (1817–92), known as Baha Ullah (Glory of God). He declared himself the prophet foretold by Mirza ali Mohammed (1819-50), a direct descendant of Mohammed, who proclaimed himself to be the bab ('gate' or 'door').
Sacred texts Kitab al-Aqdas, Haft Wadi, al-Kalimat al-Maknnah and the Bayan.
Beliefs Baha'ism teaches the oneness of God, the unity of all faiths, the inevitable unification of humankind, the harmony of all people, universal education, and obedience to government. It does not predict an end to this world or any intervention by God but believes there will be a change within man and society.
Organization There is virtually no organization and Baha'ism has no clergy or sacraments. Although there is little formal ritual (most assemblies are simply gatherings of the faithful), there are ceremonies for marriage, funerals and naming babies and there are shrines and temples.

BUDDHISM

Founded c. 500 BC in India.
Founder Prince Siddharta Gautama (c.563–c.483 BC) who became Buddha ('the enlightened') through meditation.
Sacred texts The Pali Canon or Tripitaka made up of the Vinaya Pitaka (Discourses of the Buddha) and the Abhidhamma Pitaka (higher subtleties of law), the Mahayana Sutras, the Milindapanha and Bardo Thodol (the Tibetan Book of the Dead).
Beliefs Buddha's teaching is summarized in the Four Noble Truths: suffering is always present in life; desire is the cause of suffering; freedom from life can be achieved by nirvana (perfect peace and bliss); the Eightfold Path leads to nirvana. Karma, by which good and evil deeds result in appropriate reward or punishment, and the cycle of rebirth can be broken by taking the Eightfold Path. All Buddhas are revered but particularly Gautama.
Organization There is a monastic system which aims to create favourable conditions for spiritual development. This involves meditation, personal discipline and spiritual exercises in the hope of liberation from self. Buddhism has proved very flexible in adapting its organization, ceremony and pattern of belief to different cultural and social conditions. There are numerous festivals and ceremonies and pilgrimage is of great spiritual value.
Divisions There are two main traditions in Buddhism. Theravada Buddhism is closest to Buddha's teaching: salvation can be attained only by the few who accept the severe discipline and effort necessary to achieve it. Mahayana Buddhism developed later and is more flexible and creative, embracing popular piety. It teaches that salvation is possible for everyone and introduced the doctrine of the bodhisattva (a personal saviour). As Buddhism spread other schools sprang up including Zen, Lamaism, Tendai, Nichiven and Soka Gakkai.

MAJOR BUDDIST FESTIVALS

Weekly Uposatha Days
Buddha's Birth Enlightenment, First Sermon and Death are observed in the different countries where Buddhism is practiced but often on different dates. In some of these countries there are additional festivals in honour of Buddha.

CHRISTIANITY

Founded 1st-c AD.

Founder Jesus Christ 'the Son of God' (c.4 BC–c.30 AD).

Sacred texts The Bible consisting of the Old and New Testaments. The New Testament written between AD 30 and 150 consists of the Gospels, the Acts of the Apostles, the Epistles, and the Apocalypse.

Beliefs A world religion, centred on the life and works of Jesus of Nazareth in Judaea; he proclaimed the most important rule of life to be love of God and love of one's neighbour. Unselfishness and compassion are central themes in Christianity. Belief in Jesus's divinity and his resurrection from the dead after his crucifixion promises victory over death. The earliest followers of Jesus were Jews who believed him to be the messiah 'Saviour' promised by the prophets in the Old Testament. Christians believe he will come again to inaugurate the 'Kingdom of God'.

Organization Jesus Christ appointed 12 men to be his disciples:

1 Peter, (brother of Andrew)
2 Andrew, (brother of Peter)
3 James, son of Zebedee (brother of John)
4 John, (brother of James)
5 Philip
6 Bartholomew
7 Thomas
8 Matthew
9 James of Alphaeus
10 Simon the Canaanite (in Matthew and Mark)
   or Simon 'the Zealot' (in Luke and the Acts)
11 Judas Iscariot

(Thaddeus in the book of Matthew and Mark is the twelfth disciple, while in Luke and the Acts the twelfth is Judas or James. Matthias succeeded to Judas's place.) Soon after the resurrection the disciples gathered for the festival of Pentecost and received special signs of the power of God, the Holy Spirit. The disciples became a defined new body, the Church. Through the witness of the Apostles and their successors, the Christian faith quickly spread and in AD 315 became the official religion of the Roman Empire. It survived the 'Dark Ages' to become the basis of civilization in the Middle Ages in Europe.

Divisions Major divisions separated as a result of differences of doctrine and practice are the Orthodox or Eastern Church, the Roman Catholic Church, acknowledging the Bishop of Rome as head, and the Protestant Churches stemming from the split with the Roman Church in the sixteenth century. All Christians recognize the authority of the Bible, read at public worship, which takes place at least every Sunday, to celebrate the resurrection of Jesus Christ. Most Churches recognize at least two sacraments (Baptism and the Eucharist, Mass, or Lord's Supper) as essential.

Major Christian Denominations

Denomination	Origins
Baptists	In radical Reformation objections to infant baptism, demands for church-state separation; John Smyth, English Separatist in 1609; Roger Williams, 1638, Providence, Rhode Island
Church of England	Henry VIII separated the English Catholic Church from Rome, 1534, for political reasons.
Lutherans	Martin Luther in Wittenberg, Germany, 1517, objected to Catholic doctrine of salvation by merit and sale of indulgences; break complete by 1519.
Methodists	John Wesley began movement, 1738, within Church of England.
Mormons	In visions of the Angel Moroni by Joseph Smith, 1827, in New York, in which he received a new revelation on golden tablets: *The Book of Mormon*.
Orthodox	Original Christian proselytizing in 1st-c; broke with Rome, 1054, after centuries of doctrinal disputes and diverging traditions.
Pentecostal	In Topeka, Kansas (1901), and Los Angeles (1906), in reaction to loss of evangelical fervour among Methodists and other denominations.

CHRISTIANITY (cont.)

Presbyterians	In Calvinist Reformation in 1500s; differed with Lutherans over sacraments, and church government. John Knox founded Scottish Presbyterian Church about 1560
Roman Catholic	Traditionally in the naming of St Peter as the 1st vicar by Jesus; historically, in early Christian proselytizing and the conversion of imperial Rome in the 4th-c.
United Church of Christ	Union of the Congregational and Christian Churches with the Evangelical and Reformed Church. An ecumenical Protestant Church, it allows for variation in organization and interpretation of doctrine but reflects its Reformed theological background.

The Ten Commandments

I	I am the Lord your God, who brought you out of the land of Egypt, out of the house of bondage. You shall have no other gods before me.
II	You shall not make for yourself a graven image. You shall not bow down to them or serve them.
III	You shall not take the name of the Lord your God in vain.
IV	Remember the sabbath day, to keep it holy.
V	Honour your father and your mother.
VI	You shall not kill.
VII	You shall not commit adultery.
VIII	You shall not steal.
IX	You shall not bear false witness against your neighbour.
X	You shall not covet.

The Ten Commandments appear in two different places in the Bible – Exodus 20:17 and Deuteronomy 5:6-21. Most Protestant, Anglican and Orthodox Christians enumerate the Commandments differently from Roman Catholics and Lutherans.

MAJOR IMMOVABLE CHRISTIAN FEASTS

For Saints' Days, *see* p 511.

Jan	1	Solemnity of Mary, Mother of God	Aug 22	Queenship of Mary
Jan	6	Epiphany	Sep 8	Birthday of the Virgin Mary
Jan	7	Christmas Day (*Eastern Orthodox*)[1]	Sep 14	Exaltation of the Holy Cross
Jan 11		Baptism of Jesus	Oct 2	Guardian Angels
Jan 25		Conversion of Apostle Paul	Nov 1	All Saints
Feb 2		Presentation of Jesus (*Candlemas Day*)	Nov 2	All Souls
Feb 22		The Chair of Peter, Apostle	Nov 9	Dedication of the Lateran Basilica
Mar 25		Annunciation of the Virgin Mary	Nov 21	Presentation of the Virgin Mary
Jun 24		Birth of John the Baptist	Dec 8	Immaculate Conception
Aug 6		Transfiguration	Dec 25	Christmas Day
Aug 15		Assumption of the Virgin Mary	Dec 28	Holy Innocents

[1] Fixed feasts in the Julian Calendar fall 13 days later than the Gregorian Calendar date.

MOVABLE CHRISTIAN FEASTS, 1990–2000

Year	Ash Wednesday	Easter	Ascension	Whit Sunday	Sundays after Trinity	Advent	Trinity Sunday	Corpus Christi
1990	28 Feb	15 Apr	24 May	3 Jun	24	2 Dec	10 Jun	14 Jun
1991	13 Feb	31 Mar	9 May	19 May	26	1 Dec	26 May	30 May
1992	4 Mar	19 Apr	28 May	7 Jun	23	29 Nov	14 Jun	18 Jun
1993	24 Feb	11 Apr	20 May	30 May	24	28 Nov	6 Jun	10 Jun
1994	16 Feb	3 Apr	12 May	22 May	25	27 Nov	29 May	2 Jun
1995	1 Mar	16 Apr	25 May	4 Jun	24	3 Dec	11 Jun	15 Jun
1996	21 Feb	7 Apr	16 May	26 May	25	1 Dec	2 Jun	6 Jun
1997	12 Feb	30 Mar	8 May	18 May	26	30 Nov	25 May	29 May
1998	25 Feb	12 Apr	21 May	31 May	24	29 Nov	7 Jun	11 Jun
1999	17 Feb	4 Apr	13 May	23 May	25	28 Nov	30 May	3 Jun
2000	8 Mar	23 Apr	1 Jun	11 Jun	23	3 Dec	18 Jun	22 Jun

Ash Wednesday, the first day of Lent, can fall at the earliest on 4 February and at the latest on 10 March.

Palm (Passion) Sunday is the Sunday before Easter; Good Friday is the Friday before Easter; Holy Saturday (often referred to as Easter Saturday) is the Saturday before Easter; Easter Saturday, in traditional usage, is the Saturday following Easter.

Easter Day can fall at the earliest on 22 March and at the latest on 25 April. Ascension Day can fall at the earliest on 30 April and at the latest on 3 June. Whit Sunday can fall at the earliest on 10 May and at the latest on 13 June. There are not less than 22 and not more than 27 Sundays after Trinity. The first Sunday of Advent is the Sunday nearest to 30 November.

SAINTS' DAYS

The official recognition of Saints, and the choice of a Saint's Day, varies greatly between different branches of Christianity, calendars and localities. Only major variations are included below, using the following abbreviations:

C Coptic   G Greek
E Eastern   W Western

January
1 Basil (E), Fulgentius, Telemachus
2 Basil and Gregory of Nazianzus (W), Macarius of Alexandria, Seraphim of Sarov
3 Geneviève
4 Angela of Foligno
5 Simeon Stylites (W)
7 Cedda, Lucian of Antioch (W), Raymond of Penyafort
8 Atticus (E), Gudule, Severinus
9 Hadrian the African
10 Agatho, Marcian
12 Ailred, Benedict Biscop
13 Hilary of Poitiers
14 Kentigern
15 Macarius of Egypt, Maurus, Paul of Thebes

16 Honoratus
17 Antony of Egypt
19 Wulfstan
20 Euthymius, Fabian, Sebastian
21 Agnes, Fructuosus, Maximus (E), Meinrad
22 Timothy (G), Vincent
23 Ildefonsus
24 Babylas (W), Francis de Sales
25 Gregory of Nazianzus (E)
26 Paula, Timothy and Titus, Xenophon (E)
27 Angela Merici
28 Ephraem Syrus (E), Paulinus of Nola, Thomas Aquinas
29 Gildas
31 John Bosco, Marcella

February
1 Bride, Pionius
3 Anskar, Blaise (W), Werburga, Simeon (E)
4 Gilbert of Sempringham, Isidore of Pelusium, Phileas
5 Agatha, Avitus
6 Dorothy, Paul Miki and companions, Vedast
8 Theodore (G), Jerome Emiliani

SAINTS' DAYS (cont.)

9 Teilo
10 Scholastica
11 Benedict of Aniane, Blaise (*E*), Caedmon, Gregory II
12 Meletius
13 Agabus (*W*), Catherine dei Ricci, Priscilla (*E*)
14 Cyril and Methodius (*W*), Valentine (*W*)
16 Flavian (*E*), Pamphilus (*E*), Valentine (*G*)
18 Bernadette (*France*), Colman, Flavian (*W*), Leo I (*E*)
20 Wulfric
21 Peter Damian
23 Polycarp
25 Ethelbert, Tarasius, Walburga
26 Alexander (*W*), Porphyrius
27 Leander
28 Oswald of York

March
1 David
2 Chad, Simplicius
3 Ailred
4 Casimir
6 Chrodegang
7 Perpetua and Felicity
8 Felix, John of God, Pontius
9 Frances of Rome, Gregory of Nyssa, Pacian
10 John Ogilvie, Macarius of Jerusalem, Simplicius
11 Constantine, Oengus, Sophronius
12 Gregory (the Great)
13 Nicephorus
14 Benedict (*E*)
15 Clement Hofbauer
17 Gertrude, Joseph of Arimathea (*W*), Patrick
18 Anselm of Lucca, Cyril of Jerusalem, Edward
19 Joseph
20 Cuthbert, John of Parma, Martin of Braga
21 Serapion of Thmuis
22 Catherine of Sweden, Nicholas of Flüe
23 Turibius de Mongrovejo
30 John Climacus

April
1 Hugh of Grenoble, Mary of Egypt (*E*), Melito
2 Francis of Paola, Mary of Egypt (*W*)
3 Richard of Chichester
4 Isidore of Seville
5 Juliana of Liège, Vincent Ferrer
7 Hegesippus, John Baptist de la Salle
8 Agabus (*E*)
10 Fulbert
11 Gemma Galgani, Guthlac, Stanislaus

12 Julius I, Zeno
13 Martin I
15 Aristarchus, Pudus (*E*), Trophimus of Ephesus
17 Agapetus (*E*), Stephen Harding
18 Mme Acarie
19 Alphege, Leo IX
21 Anastasius (*E*), Anselm, Beuno, Januarius (*E*)
22 Alexander (*C*)
23 George
24 Egbert, Fidelis of Sigmaringen, Mellitus
25 Mark, Phaebadius
27 Zita
28 Peter Chanel, Vitalis and Valeria
29 Catherine of Siena, Hugh of Cluny, Peter Martyr, Robert
30 James (the Great) (*E*), Pius V

May
1 Asaph, Joseph the Worker, Walburga
2 Athanasius
3 Phillip and James (the Less) (*W*)
4 Gotthard
5 Hilary of Arles
7 John of Beverley
8 John (*E*), Peter of Tarantaise
10 Antoninus, Comgall, John of Avila, Simon (*E*)
11 Cyril and Methodius (*E*), Mamertus
12 Epiphanius, Nereus and Achilleus, Pancras
14 Matthias (*W*)
16 Brendan, John of Nepomuk, Simon Stock
17 Robert Bellarmine, Paschal Baylon
18 John I
19 Dunstan, Ivo, Pudens (*W*), Pudentiana (*W*)
20 Bernardino of Siena
21 Helena (*E*)
22 Rita of Cascia
23 Ivo of Chartres
24 Vincent of Lérins
25 Aldhelm, Bede, Gregory VII, Mary Magdalene de Pazzi
26 Philip Neri, Quadratus
27 Augustine of Canterbury
30 Joan of Arc

June
1 Justin Martyr, Pamphilus
2 Erasmus, Marcellinus and Peter, Nicephorus (*G*), Pothinus
3 Charles Lwanga and companions, Clotilde, Kevin
4 Optatus, Petrock
5 Boniface

SAINTS' DAYS (cont.)

6   Martha (*E*), Norbert
7   Paul of Constantinople (*W*), Willibald
8   William of York
9   Columba, Cyril of Alexandria (*E*), Ephraem (*W*)
11 Barnabas, Bartholomew (*E*)
12 Leo III
13 Anthony of Padua
15 Orsisius, Vitus
17 Alban, Botulph
19 Gervasius and Protasius, Jude (*E*), Romuald
20 Alban
21 Alban of Mainz, Aloysius Gonzaga
22 John Fisher and Thomas More, Niceta, Pantaenus (*C*), Paulinus of Nola
23 Etheldreda
24 Birth of John the Baptist
25 Prosper of Aquitaine
27 Cyril of Alexandria (*W*), Ladislaus
28 Irenaeus
29 Peter and Paul
30 First Martyrs of the Church of Rome

July
1   Cosmas and Damian (*E*), Oliver Plunket
3   Anatolius, Thomas
4   Andrew of Crete (*E*), Elizabeth of Portugal, Ulrich
5   Anthony Zaccaria
6   Maria Goretti
7   Palladius, Pantaenus
8   Kilian, Aquila and Prisca (*W*)
11 Benedict (*W*), Pius I
12 John Gualbert, Veronica
13 Henry II, Mildred, Silas
14 Camillus of Lellis, Deusdedit, Nicholas of the Holy Mountain (*E*)
15 Bonaventure, Jacob of Nisibis, Swithin, Vladimir
16 Eustathius, Our Lady of Mt Carmel
17 Ennodius, Leo IV, Marcellina, Margaret (*E*), Scillitan Martyrs
18 Arnulf, Philastrius
19 Macrina, Symmachus
20 Aurelius, Margaret (*W*)
21 Lawrence of Brindisi, Praxedes
22 Mary Magdalene
23 Apollinaris, Bridget of Sweden
25 Anne and Joachim (*E*), Christopher, James (the Great) (*W*)
26 Anne and Joachim (*W*)
27 Pantaleon
28 Innocent I, Samson, Victor I
29 Lupus, Martha (*W*), Olave

30 Peter Chrysologus, Silas (*G*)
31 Giovanni Colombini, Germanus, Joseph of Arimathea (*E*), Ignatius of Loyola

August
1   Alphonsus Liguori, Ethelwold
2   Eusebius of Vercelli, Stephen I
4   Jean-Baptiste Vianney
6   Hormisdas
7   Cajetan, Sixtus II and companions
8   Dominic
9   Matthias (*G*)
10 Laurence, Oswald of Northumbria
11 Clare, Susanna
13 Maximus (*W*), Pontian and Hippolytus, Radegunde
14 Maximilian Kolbe
15 Arnulf, Tarsicius
16 Roch, Simplicianus, Stephen of Hungary
17 Hyacinth
19 John Eudes, Sebaldus
20 Bernard, Oswin, Philibert
21 Jane Frances de Chantal, Pius X
23 Rose of Lima, Sidonius Apollinaris
24 Bartholomew (*W*), Ouen
25 Joseph Calasanctius, Louis IX, Menas of Constantinople
26 Blessed Dominic of the Mother of God, Zephyrinus
27 Caesarius, Monica
28 Augustine of Hippo
29 Beheading of John the Baptist, Sabina
30 Pammachius
31 Aidan, Paulinus of Trier

September
1   Giles, Simeon Stylites (*E*)
2   John the Faster (*E*)
3   Gregory (the Great)
4   Babylas (*E*), Boniface I
5   Zacharias (*E*)
9   Peter Claver, Sergius of Antioch
10 Finnian, Nicholas of Tolentino, Pulcheria
11 Deiniol, Ethelburga, Paphnutius
13 John Chrysostom (*W*)
15 Catherine of Genoa, Our Lady of Sorrows
16 Cornelius, Cyprian of Carthage, Euphemia, Ninian
17 Robert Bellarmine, Hildegard, Lambert, Satyrus
19 Januarius (*W*), Theodore of Tarsus
20 Agapetus or Eustace (*W*)

SAINTS' DAYS (cont.)

21 Matthew (*W*)
23 Adamnan, Linus
25 Sergius of Rostov
26 Cosmas and Damian (*W*), Cyprian of Carthage, John (*E*)
27 Frumentius (*W*), Vincent de Paul
28 Exuperius, Wenceslaus
29 Michael (*Michaelmas Day*), Gabriel and Raphael
30 Jerome, Otto

October
1 Remigius, Romanos, Teresa of the Child Jesus
2 Leodegar (Leger)
3 Teresa of Lisieux, Thomas de Cantilupe
4 Ammon, Francis of Assisi, Petronius
6 Bruno, Thomas (*G*)
9 Demetrius (*W*), Denis and companions, Dionysius of Paris, James (the Less) (*E*), John Leonardi
10 Francis Borgia, Paulinus of York
11 Atticus (*E*), Bruno (*d. 965*), Nectarius
12 Wilfrid
13 Edward the Confessor
14 Callistus I, Cosmas Melodus (*E*)
15 Lucian of Antioch (*E*), Teresa of Avila
16 Gall, Hedwig, Lullus, Margaret Mary Alacoque
17 Ignatius of Antioch, Victor
18 Luke
19 John de Bréboeuf and Isaac Jogues and companions, Paul of the Cross, Peter of Alcántara
21 Hilarion, Ursula
22 Abercius
23 John of Capistrano, James
24 Anthony Claret
25 Crispin and Crispinian, Forty Martyrs of England and Wales, Gaudentius
26 Demetrius (*E*)
28 Firmilian (*E*), Simon and Jude
30 Serapion of Antioch
31 Wolfgang

November
1 All Saints, Cosmas and Damian (*E*)
2 Eustace (*E*), Victorinus
3 Hubert, Malachy, Martin de Porres, Pirminius, Winifred
4 Charles Borromeo, Vitalis and Agricola
5 Elizabeth (*W*)
6 Illtyd, Leonard, Paul of Constantinople (*E*)
7 Willibrord

8 Elizabeth (*E*), Willehad
9 Simeon Metaphrastes (*E*)
10 Justus, Leo I (*W*)
11 Martin of Tours (*W*), Menas of Egypt, Theodore of Studios
12 Josaphat, Martin of Tours (*E*), Nilus the Ascetic
13 Abbo, John Chrysostom (*E*), Nicholas I
14 Dubricius, Gregory Palamas (*E*)
15 Albert the Great, Machutus
16 Edmund of Abingdon, Eucherius, Gertrude (the Great), Margaret of Scotland, Matthew (*E*)
17 Elizabeth of Hungary, Gregory Thaumaturgus, Gregory of Tours, Hugh of Lincoln
18 Odo, Romanus
19 Mechthild, Nerses
20 Edmund the Martyr
21 Gelasius
22 Cecilia
23 Amphilochius, Clement I (*W*), Columban, Felicity, Gregory of Agrigentum
25 Clement I (*E*), Mercurius, Mesrob
26 Siricius
27 Barlam and Josaphat
28 Simeon Metaphrastes
29 Cuthbert Mayne
30 Andrew, Frumentius (*G*)

December
1 Eligius
2 Chromatius
3 Francis Xavier
4 Barbara, John Damascene, Osmund
5 Clement of Alexandria, Sabas
6 Nicholas
7 Ambrose
10 Miltiades
11 Damasus, Daniel
12 Jane Frances de Chantal, Spyridon (*E*), Vicelin
13 Lucy, Odilia
14 John of the Cross, Spyridon (*W*)
16 Eusebius
18 Frumentius (*C*)
20 Ignatius of Antioch (*G*)
21 Peter Canisius, Thomas
22 Anastasia (*E*), Chrysogonus (*E*)
23 John of Kanty
26 Stephen (*W*)
27 John (*W*), Fabiola, Stephen (*E*)
29 Thomas à Becket, Trophimus of Arles
31 Sylvester

CONFUCIANISM

Founded 6th-c BC in China.
Founder K'ung Fu-tse (Confucius) (c.551–479 BC).
Sacred texts Shih Ching, Li Ching, Chu'un Ch'iu, I Ching.
Beliefs The oldest school of Chinese thought, Confucianism did not begin as a religion. Confucius was concerned with the best way to behave and live in this world and was not concerned with the afterlife. He emerges as a great moral teacher who tried to replace the old religious observances with moral values as the basis of social and political order. He laid particular emphasis on the family as the basic unit in society and the foundation of the whole community. He believed that government was a matter of moral responsibility, not just manipulation of power.
Organization Confucianism is not an institution and has no church or clergy. However ancestor-worship and veneration of the sky have their sources in Confucian texts. Weddings and funerals follow a tradition handed down by Confucian scholars. Social life is ritualized and colour and patterns of clothes have a sacred meaning.
Divisions There are two ethical strands in Confucianism. One, associated with Confucious and Hsun Tzu (c.298–238 BC), is conventionalistic: we ought to follow the traditional codes of behaviour for their own sake. The other, associated with Mencius and medieval neo-Confucians, is intuitionistic: we ought to do as our moral natures dictate.

MAJOR CHINESE FESTIVALS

January/February	Chinese New Year
February/March	Lantern Festival
March/April	Festival of Pure Brightness
May/June	Dragon Boat Festival
July/August	Herd Boy and Weaving Maid
August	All Souls' Festival
September	Mid-Autumn Festival
September/October	Double Ninth Festival
November/December	Winter Solstice

HINDUISM

Founded c.1500 BC by Aryan invaders of India with their Vedic religion.
Sacred texts Vedas ('knowledge'), including the Upanishads which are spiritual truths and the epic poems the Ramayana and the Mahabharata. Best known of all is the Bhagavadgita, part of the Mahabharata.
Beliefs Hinduism emphasizes the right way of living (dharma) and embraces many diverse religious beliefs and practices rather than a set of doctrines. It acknowledges many gods who are seen as manifestations of an underlying reality. Devout Hindus aim to become one with the 'absolute reality' or Brahman. Only after a completely pure life will the soul be released from the cycle of rebirth. Until then the soul will be repeatedly reborn. Samsara refers to the cycle of birth and rebirth. Karma is the law by which consequences of actions within one life are carried over into the next.
Organization There is very little formal structure. Hinduism is concerned with the realization of religious values in every part of life yet there is a great emphasis on the performance of complex demanding rituals under the supervision of a Brahman priest and teacher. There are three categories of worship: temple,

HINDUISM (cont.)

domestic and congregational. The most common ceremony is prayer (puja). Many pilgrimages take place and there is an annual cycle of festivals,

Divisions As there is no concept of orthodoxy in Hinduism there are many different sects worshipping different gods. The three most important gods are Brahman, the primeval god, Vishnu, the preserver, and Shiva, both destroyer and creator of life. The three major living traditions are those devoted to Vishnu, Shiva and the goddess Shakti. Folk beliefs and practices exist together with sophisticated philsophical schools.

MAJOR HINDU FESTIVALS

S = Sukla	'waxing fortnight'.		S 1–10	'nine nights'
K = Krishna	'waning fortnight'.		Asvina	Lakshmi-puja (Homage to
Caitra	Ramanavami (Birthday of		S 15	Goddess Lakshmi)
S 9	Lord Rama)		Asvina	Diwali, Dipavali
Asadha	Rathayatra (Pilgrimage of the		K 15	('String of Lights')
S 2	Chariot at Jagannath)		Kartikka	Guru Nanak Jananti
Sravana	Jhulanayatra ('Swinging the		S 15	(Birthday of Guru Nanak)
S 11–15	Lord Krishna')		Magha	Sarasvati-puja (Homage to
Sravana	Rakshabandhana ('Tying on		K 5	Goddess Sarasvati)
S 15	lucky threads')		Magha	Maha-sivaratri (Great Night of
Bhadrapada	Janamashtami (Birthday of		K 13	Lord Shiva)
K 8	Lord Krishna)		Phalguna	Holi (Festival of Fire)
Asvina	Durga-puja (Homage to		S 14	
S 7–10	Goddess Durga) (*Bengal*)		Phalguna	Dolayatra (Swing Festival)
Asvina	Navaratri (Festival of		S 15	(*Bengal*)

ISLAM

Founded 7th-c AD.

Founder Mohammed (c.570–c.632).

Sacred texts The Koran, the word of God as revealed to Mohammed and the Hadith, a collection of the prophet's sayings.

Beliefs A monotheistic religion, God is the creator of all things and holds absolute power over man. All persons should devote themselves to lives of grateful and praise-giving obedience to God as they will be judged on the Day of Resurrection. It is acknowledged that Satan often misleads humankind but those who have obeyed God or have repented of their sins will dwell in paradise. Those sinners who are unrepentant will go to hell. Muslims accept the Old Testament and acknowledge Jesus Christ as an important prophet, but they believe the perfect word of God was revealed to Mohammed. Islam imposes five pillars of faith on its followers: belief in one God and his prophet, Mohammed; salat, formal prayer preceded by ritual cleansing five times a day, facing Mecca; saum, fasting during the month of Ramadan; Hajj, pilgrimage to Mecca at least once; zakat, a religious tax on the rich to provide for the poor.

Organization There is no organized priesthood but great respect is accorded to descendants of Mohammed and holymen, scholars and teachers such as mullahs and ayatollahs. The Shari'a is the Islamic law and applies to all aspects of life, not just religious practices.

Divisions There are two main groups within Islam. The Sunni are the majority and the more orthodox. They recognize the succession from Mohammed to Abu Bahkr, his father-in-law, and to the next three caliphs. The Shiites are followers of Ali, Mohammed's nephew and son-in-law. They believe in 12 imams, perfect teachers, who still guide the faithful from paradise. Shi'ah practice tends towards the ecstatic. There are many other subsects including the Sufis, the Ismailis and the Wahhabis.

MAJOR ISLAMIC FESTIVALS

1 Muharram	New Year's Day; starts on the day which celebrates Mohammed's departure from Mecca to Medina in AD 622.
12 Rabi I	Birthday of Mohammed (Mawlid al-Nabi) AD 572; celebrated throughout month of Rabi I.
27 Rajab	'Night of Ascent' (Laylat al-Mi'raj) of Mohammed to Heaven.
1 Ramadan	Beginning of month of fasting during daylight hours.
27 Ramadan	'Night of Power' (Laylat al-Qadr); sending down of the Koran to Mohammed.
1 Shawwal	'Feast of breaking the Fast' ('Id al-Fitr); marks the end of Ramadan.
8–13 Dhu-l-Hijja	Annual pilgrimage ceremonies at and around Mecca; month during which the great pilgrimage (Hajj) should be made.
10 Dhu-l-Hijja	Feast of the Sacrifice ('Id al-Adha).

JAINISM

Founded 6th-c BC in India.
Founder Vardhamana Mahavira (599–527 BC).
Sacred Texts Svetambara canon of scripture and Digambara texts.
Beliefs Jainism is derived from the ancient jinas ('those who overcome'). They believe that salvation consists in conquering material existence through adhering to a strict ascetic discipline, thus freeing the 'soul' from the working of karma for eternal, all-knowing bliss. Liberation requires detachment from worldly existence, an essential part of which is Ahimsa, non-injury to living beings. Jains are also strict vegetarians.
Organization Like Buddhists, the Jains are dedicated to the quest for liberation and the life of the ascetic. However rather than congregating in monastic centres, Jainist monks and nuns have developed a strong relationship with lay people. There are temple rituals resembling Hindu puja. There is also a series of lesser vows and specific religious practices that give the lay person an identifiable religious career.
Divisions There are two categories of religious and philosophical literature. The Svetambara have a canon of scripture consisting of 45 texts, including a group of 11 texts in which the sermons and dialogues of Mahavira himself are collected. The Digambara hold that the original teachings of Mahavira have been lost but that their texts preserve accurately the substance of the original message. This disagreement over scriptures has not led to fundamental doctrinal differences.

JUDAISM

Founded c.2000 BC.
Founder Abraham (c.2000–1650 BC) with whom God made a covenant and Moses (15th–13th-c BC) who gave the Israelites the law.
Sacred texts The Hebrew bible consisting of 24 books, the most important of which are the Torah or Pentateuch – the first five books. Also the Talmud made up of the Mishna, the oral law, and the Gemara, an extensive commentary.
Beliefs A monotheistic religion, the Jews believe God is the creator of the world who delivered the Israelites out of bondage in Egypt, revealed his law to them, and chose them to be a light to all humankind. However varied their communities, Jews see themselves as members of a community whose origins lie in the patriarchal period. Ritual is very important and the family is the basic unit of ritual.
Organization Originally a theocracy, the basic institution is now the synagogue, operated by the congregation and led by a rabbi of their choice. The chief rabbis in France and Britain have authority over those who accept it; in Israel the two chief rabbis have civil authority in family law. The synagogue is the

JUDAISM (cont.)

centre for community worship and study. Its main feature is the 'ark' (a cupboard) containing the hand-written scrolls of the Pentateuch. Daily life is governed by a number of practices and observances: male children are circumcised, the Sabbath is observed, and food has to be correctly prepared. The most important festival is the Passover which celebrates the liberation of the Israelites from Egypt.

Divisions Today most Jews are descendants of either the Ashkenazim or the Sephardim, each with marked cultural differences. There are also several religious branches of Judaism from ultra liberal to ultra conservative, reflecting different points of view regarding the binding character of the prohibitions and duties prescribed for Jews.

MAJOR JEWISH FESTIVALS

For Gregorian calendar equivalents, *see* p 34.

1–2	Tishri	Rosh Hashana (New Year)	10 Tevet	Asara be-Tevet (Fast of
3	Tishri	Tzom Gedaliahu (Fast of		10th Tevet)
		Gedaliah)	13 Adar	Taanit Esther (Fast of Esther)
10	Tishri	Yom Kippur (Day of Atonement)	14–15 Adar	Purim (Feast of Lots)
15–21	Tishri	Sukkoth (Feast of Tabernacles)	15–22 Nisan	Pesach (Passover)
22	Tishri	Shemini Atzeret (8th Day of	5 Iyar	Israel Independence Day
		the Solemn Assembly	6–7 Sivan	Shavuoth (Feast of Weeks)
23	Tishri	Simhat Torah (Rejoicing of the	17 Tammuz	Shiva Asar be-Tammuz
		Law)		(Fast of 17th Tammuz)
25	Kislev–	Hanukkah (Feast of Dedication)	9 Av	Tisha be-Av (Fast of 9th Av)
2–3	Tevet			

SHINTOISM

Founded 8th-c AD in Japan.

Sacred texts Kojiki and Nihon Shoki.

Beliefs Shinto 'the teaching' or 'way of the gods', came into existence independently from Buddhism which was coming to the mainland of Japan at that time. It subsequently incorporated many features of Buddhism. Founded on the nature-worship of Japanese folk religions, it is made up of many elements: animism, veneration of nature and ancestor-worship. Its gods are known as kami and there are many ceremonies appealing to these kami for benevolent treatment and protection. Great stress is laid on the harmony between humans, their kami and nature. Moral and physical purity is a basic law. Death and other pollutions are to be avoided. Shinto is primarily concerned with life and this world and the good of the group. Followers must show devotion and sincerity but aberrations can be erased by purification procedures.

Organization As a set of prehistoric agricultural ceremonies Shinto was never supported by a body of philosophical or moralistic literature. Shamans originally performed the ceremonies and tended the shrines, then gradually a particular tribe took over the ceremonies. In the 8th-c Shinto became political with the imperial family ascribed divine origins and state Shintoism was established.

Divisions In the 19th-c Shinto was divided into Shrine (jinga) Shinto and Sectarian (kyoko) Shinto. Jinga became a state cult and it remained the national religion until 1945.

MAJOR JAPANESE FESTIVALS

Public holidays in Japan are listed on p 254. In addition, the following festivals should be noted;

1–3 Jan	Oshogatsu (New Year)	7 Jul	Hoshi matsuri *or* Tanabata
3 Mar	Ohinamatsuri (Doll's *or*		(Star Festival)
	Girls' Festival)	13–31 Jul	Obon (Buddhist All Souls)
5 May	Tango no Sekku (Boys' Festival)		

SIKHISM

Founded 15th-c in India.
Founder Guru Nanak (1469–1539).
Sacred text Adi Granth.
Beliefs Nanak preached tolerance and devotion to one God before whom everyone is equal. Sikh is the Sanskrit word for disciple. Nanak's doctrine sought a fusion of Brahmanism and Islam on the grounds that both were monotheistic. God is the true Guru and his divine word has come to humanity through the ten historical gurus. The line ended in 1708 since when the Sikh community is called guru.
Organization There is no priestly caste and all Sikhs are empowered to perform rituals connected with births, marriages, and deaths. Sikhs worship in their own temples but they evolved distinct features like the langar, 'kitchen', a communal meal where people of any religion or caste could eat. Rest houses for travellers were also provided. The tenth guru instituted an initiation ceremony, the Khalsa. Initiates wear the Five Ks (uncut hair, steel bangle, comb, shorts, ceremonial sword) and a turban. Members of the Khalsa add the name singh (lion) to their name and have to lead pure lives and follow a code of discipline. Sikhs generally rise before dawn, bathe and recite the japji, a morning prayer. Hindu festivals from northern India are observed.
Divisions There are several religious orders of Sikhs based either on disputes over the succession of gurus or points of ritual and tradition. The most important current issue is the number of Khalsa Sikhs cutting off their hair and beards and relapsing into Hinduism.

TAOISM

Founded 600 BC in China.
Founder Lao-tzu (6th-c BC).
Sacred texts Chuang-tzu, Lao-tzu (Tao-te-ching).
Beliefs Taoism is Chinese for 'the school of the tao' and the 'Taoist religion'. Tao ('the way') is central in both Confucianism and Taoism. The former stresses the tao of humanity, the latter the tao of nature, harmony with which ensures appropriate conduct. Taoist religion developed later and was probably influenced by Buddhist beliefs. The doctrine emphasizes that good and evil action decide the fate of the soul. The Taoists believe that the sky, the earth and water are deities; that Lao-tzu is supreme master; that the disciple masters his body and puts evil spirits to flight with charms; that body and spirit are purified through meditation and by taking the pill of immortality to gain eternal life; and that the way is handed down from master to disciple. Religious Taoism incorporated ideas and images from philosophical Taoist texts, especially the Tao-te-ching but also the theory of Yin-yang, the quest for immortality, mental and physical discipline, interior hygiene, internal alchemy, healing and exorcism, a pantheon of gods and spirits, and ideals of theocratic states. The Immortals are meant to live in the mountains far from the tumult of the world.
Organization This is similar to Buddhism in the matter of clergy and temple. The jiao is a ceremony to purify the ground. Zhon-gyual is the only important religious festival, when the hungry dead appear to the living and Taoist priests free the souls of the dead from suffering.
Divisions Religious Taoism emerged from many sects. These sects proliferated between 618 and 1126 AD and were described collectively as Spirit Cloud Taoists. They form the majority of Taoist priests in Taiwan, where they are called 'Masters of Methods' or Red-headed Taoists. The more orthodox priests are called 'Tao Masters' or Black-headed Taoists.

SACRED TEXTS OF WORLD RELIGIONS

Religion	Texts
Baha'ism	Kitab al-Aqdas, Haft Wadi, al-Kalimat al-Maknnah, Bayan
Buddhism	Tripitaka, Mahayana Sutra, Milindapanha, Bardo Thodol
Christianity	Old Testament: Genesis, Exodus, Leviticus, Numbers, Deuteronomy, Joshua, Judges, Ruth, 1 Samuel, 2 Samuel, 1 Kings, 2 Kings, 1 Chronicles, 2 Chronicles, Ezra, Nehemiah, Esther, Job, Psalms, Proverbs, Ecclesiastes, Song of Solomon, Isaiah, Jeremiah, Lamentations, Ezekiel, Daniel, Hosea, Joel, Amos, Obadiah, Jonah, Micah, Nahum, Habakkuk, Zephaniah, Haggai, Zechariah, Malachi.
	New Testament: Matthew, Mark, Luke, John, Acts of the Apostles, Romans, 1 Corinthians, 2 Corinthians, Galatians, Ephesians, Philippians, Colossians, 1 Thessalonians, 2 Thessalonians, 1 Timothy, 2 Timothy, Titus, Philemon, Hebrews, James, 1 Peter, 2 Peter, 1 John, 2 John, 3 John, Jude, Revelation. Apocrypha: 1 Esdras, 2 Esdras, Tobit, Judith, Additions to Esther, Wisdom of Solomon, Ecclesiasticus, Epistle of Jeremiah, Baruch, Prayer of Azariah, Song of the Three Young Men, (History of) Susanna, Bel and the Dragon, Prayer of Manasses, 1 Maccabees, 2 Maccabees. (The Roman Catholic Church includes Tobit, Judith, all of Esther, Maccabbees 1 and 2, Wisdom of Solomon, Ecclesiasticus, and Baruch in its canon.)
Confucianism	Shih ching, Li ching, Shu ching, Chu'un Ch'iu, I Ching
Hinduism	Vedas (Upanishads), Ramayana, Mahabharata and the Bhagavad Gita
Islam	The Koran, the Hadith
Jainism	Svetambara canon, Digambara texts
Judaism	The Hebrew Bible:Torah (Pentateuch): Genesis, Exodus, Leviticus, Numbers, Deuteronomy. Also the books of the Prophets, Psalms, Chronicles and Proverbs. The Talmud including the Mishna and Gemara. The Zohar (Book of Splendour) is a famous Cabalistic book.
Mormons	Book of Mormon
Mandeans	Ginza, Book of John
Shintoism	Kojiki, Nohon Shoki
Sikhism	Adi Granth
Taoism	Chuang-tzu, Lao-tzu (Tao-te-ching)

SIGNS OF THE ZODIAC

Spring Signs

Aries, the Ram
21 Mar-19 Apr

Gemini, the Twins
21 May-21 Jun

Taurus, the Bull
20 Apr-20 May

Summer Signs

Cancer, the Crab
22 Jun-22 July

Leo, the Lion
23 July-22 Aug

Virgo, the Virgin
23 Aug-22 Sep

Autumn Signs

Libra, the Balance
23 Sep-23 Oct

Scorpio, the Scorpion
24 Oct-21 Nov

Sagittarius, the Archer
22 Nov-21 Dec

Winter Signs

Capricorn, the Goat
22 Dec-19 Jan

Aquarius, the
Water Bearer
20 Jan-18 Feb

Pisces, the Fishes
19 Feb-20 Mar